D1195522

Twentieth-Century Literary Criticism

Topics Volume

Guide to Gale Literary Criticism Series

For criticism on	Consult these Gale series
Authors now living or who died after December 31, 1959	*CONTEMPORARY LITERARY CRITICISM (CLC)*
Authors who died between 1900 and 1959	*TWENTIETH-CENTURY LITERARY CRITICISM (TCLC)*
Authors who died between 1800 and 1899	*NINETEENTH-CENTURY LITERATURE CRITICISM (NCLC)*
Authors who died between 1400 and 1799	*LITERATURE CRITICISM FROM 1400 TO 1800 (LC)* *SHAKESPEAREAN CRITICISM (SC)*
Authors who died before 1400	*CLASSICAL AND MEDIEVAL LITERATURE CRITICISM (CMLC)*
Black writers of the past two hundred years	*BLACK LITERATURE CRITICISM (BLC)*
Authors of books for children and young adults	*CHILDREN'S LITERATURE REVIEW (CLR)*
Dramatists	*DRAMA CRITICISM (DC)*
Hispanic writers of the late nineteenth and twentieth centuries	*HISPANIC LITERATURE CRITICISM (HLC)*
Native North American writers and orators of the eighteenth, nineteenth, and twentieth centuries	*NATIVE NORTH AMERICAN LITERATURE (NNAL)*
Poets	*POETRY CRITICISM (PC)*
Short story writers	*SHORT STORY CRITICISM (SSC)*
Major authors from the Renaissance to the present	*WORLD LITERATURE CRITICISM, 1500 TO THE PRESENT (WLC)*

ISSN 0276-8178

Volume 62

Twentieth-Century Literary Criticism

Topics Volume

Excerpts from Criticism of Various Topics in Twentieth-Century Literature, including Literary and Critical Movements, Prominent Themes and Genres, Anniversary Celebrations, and Surveys of National Literatures

Jennifer Gariepy
Editor

Pamela Willwerth Aue
Nancy Dziedzic
Thomas Ligotti
Scot Peacock
Terrie M. Rooney
Associate Editors

GALE

STAFF

Jennifer Gariepy, *Editor*

Pamela Willwerth Aue, Nancy Dziedzic, Thomas Ligotti, Scot Peacock,
Terrie M. Rooney, *Associate Editors*

Stacy A. McConnell, *Assistant Editor*

Marlene S. Hurst, *Permissions Manager*
Margaret A. Chamberlain, Maria Franklin, *Permissions Specialists*

Diane Cooper, Michele Lonoconus, Maureen Puhl, Susan Salas, Shalice Shah, Kimberly F. Smilay,
Barbara A. Wallace, *Permissions Associates*

Sarah Chesney, Edna Hedblad, Margaret McAvoy-Amato, Tyra Y. Phillips, Lori Schoenenberger,
Rita Velazquez, *Permissions Assistants*

Victoria B. Cariappa, *Research Manager*

Tamara C. Nott, Michele P. Pica, Tracie A. Richardson, Norma Sawaya, *Research Associates*

Alicia Noel Biggers, Julia C. Daniel, *Research Associates*

Mary Beth Trimper, *Production Director*
Deborah L. Milliken, *Production Assistant*

Sherrell Hobbs, *Macintosh Artist*
Randy Bassett, *Image Database Supervisor*
Robert Duncan, *Scanner Operator*
Pamela Hayes, *Photography Coordinator*

Library of Congress Catalog Card Number 76-46132
ISBN 0-8103-9307-7
ISSN 0276-8178

Printed in the United States of America
10 9 8 7 6 5 4 3 2 1

Contents

Preface   vii

Acknowledgments   xi

Preface

Since its inception more than fifteen years ago, *Twentieth-Century Literary Criticism* has been purchased and used by nearly 10,000 school, public, and college or university libraries. *TCLC* has covered more than 500 authors, representing 58 nationalities, and over 25,000 titles. No other reference source has surveyed the critical response to twentieth-century authors and literature as thoroughly as *TCLC*. In the words of one reviewer, "there is nothing comparable available." *TCLC* "is a gold mine of information—dates, pseudonyms, biographical information, and criticism from books and periodicals—which many libraries would have difficulty assembling on their own."

Scope of the Series

TCLC is designed to serve as an introduction to authors who died between 1900 and 1960 and to the most significant interpretations of these authors' works. The great poets, novelists, short story writers, playwrights, and philosophers of this period are frequently studied in high school and college literature courses. In organizing and excerpting the vast amount of critical material written on these authors, *TCLC* helps students develop valuable insight into literary history, promotes a better understanding of the texts, and sparks ideas for papers and assignments. Each entry in *TCLC* presents a comprehensive survey of an author's career or an individual work of literature and provides the user with a multiplicity of interpretations and assessments. Such variety allows students to pursue their own interests; furthermore, it fosters an awareness that literature is dynamic and responsive to many different opinions.

Every fourth volume of *TCLC* is devoted to literary topics. These topic entries widen the focus of the series from individual authors to such broader subjects as literary movements, prominent themes in twentieth-century literature, literary reaction to political and historical events, significant eras in literary history, prominent literary anniversaries, and the literatures of cultures that are often overlooked by English-speaking readers.

TCLC is designed as a companion series to Gale's *Contemporary Literary Criticism,* which reprints commentary on authors now living or who have died since 1960. Because of the different periods under consideration, there is no duplication of material between *CLC* and *TCLC*. For additional information about *CLC* and Gale's other criticism titles, users should consult the Guide to Gale Literary Criticism Series preceding the title page in this volume.

Coverage

Each volume of *TCLC* is carefully compiled to present:

- criticism of authors or literary topics, representing a variety of genres and nationalities

- both major and lesser-known writers and literary works of the period

- 8-15 authors or 3-6 topics per volume

- individual entries that survey critical response to each author's work or each topic in literary history, including early criticism to reflect initial reactions; later criticism to represent any rise or decline in reputation; and current retrospective analyses.

Organization of This Book

An author entry consists of the following elements: author heading, biographical and critical introduction, list of principal works, excerpts of criticism (each preceded by an annotation and a bibliographic citation), and a bibliography of further reading.

- The **Author Heading** consists of the name under which the author most commonly wrote, followed by birth and death dates. If an author wrote consistently under a pseudonym, the pseudonym will be listed in the author heading and the real name given in parentheses on the first line of the biographical and critical introduction. Also located at the beginning of the introduction to the author entry are any name variations under which an author wrote, including transliterated forms for authors whose languages use nonroman alphabets.

- The **Biographical and Critical Introduction** outlines the author's life and career, as well as the critical issues surrounding his or her work. References to past volumes of *TCLC* are provided at the beginning of the introduction. Additional sources of information in other biographical and critical reference series published by Gale, including *Short Story Criticism, Children's Literature Review, Contemporary Authors, Dictionary of Literary Biography,* and *Something about the Author,* are listed in a box at the end of the entry.

- Most *TCLC* entries include **Portraits** of the author. Many entries also contain reproductions of materials pertinent to an author's career, including manuscript pages, title pages, dust jackets, letters, and drawings, as well as photographs of important people, places, and events in an author's life.

- The **List of Principal Works** is chronological by date of first book publication and identifies the genre of each work. In the case of foreign authors with both foreign-language publications and English translations, the title and date of the first English-language edition are given in brackets. Unless otherwise indicated, dramas are dated by first performance, not first publication.

- Critical excerpts are prefaced by **Annotations** providing the reader with information about both the critic and the criticism that follows. Included are the critic's reputation, individual approach to literary criticism, and particular expertise in an author's works. Also noted are the relative importance of a work of criticism, the scope of the excerpt, and the growth of critical controversy or changes in critical trends regarding an author. In some cases, these annotations cross-reference excerpts by critics who discuss each other's commentary.

- A complete **Bibliographic Citation** designed to facilitate location of the original essay or book precedes each piece of criticism.

- **Criticism** is arranged chronologically in each author entry to provide a perspective on changes in critical evaluation over the years. All titles of works by the author featured in the entry are printed in boldface type to enable the user to easily locate discussion of particular works. Also for purposes of easier identification, the critic's name and the publication date of the essay are given at the beginning of each piece of criticism. Unsigned criticism is preceded by the title of the journal in which it appeared. Some of the excerpts in *TCLC* also contain translated material. Unless otherwise noted, translations in brackets are by the editors; translations in parentheses or continuous with the text are by the critic. Publication information (such as footnotes or page and line references to specific editions of works) have been deleted at the editor's discretion to provide smoother reading of the text.

- An annotated list of **Further Reading** appearing at the end of each author entry suggests secondary sources on the author. In some cases it includes essays for which the editors could not obtain reprint rights.

Cumulative Indexes

- Each volume of *TCLC* contains a cumulative **Author Index** listing all authors who have appeared in Gale's Literary Criticism Series, along with cross references to such biographical series as *Contemporary Authors* and *Dictionary of Literary Biography*. For readers' convenience, a complete list of Gale titles included appears on the first page of the author index. Useful for locating authors within the various series, this index is particularly valuable for those authors who are identified by a certain period but who, because of their death dates, are placed in another, or for those authors whose careers span two periods. For example, F. Scott Fitzgerald is found in *TCLC*, yet a writer often associated with him, Ernest Hemingway, is found in *CLC*.

- Each *TCLC* volume includes a cumulative **Nationality Index** which lists all authors who have appeared in *TCLC* volumes, arranged alphabetically under their respective nationalities, as well as Topics volume entries devoted to particular national literatures.

- Each new volume in Gale's Literary Criticism Series includes a cumulative **Topic Index,** which lists all literary topics treated in *NCLC, TCLC, LC 1400-1800,* and the *CLC* yearbook.

- Each new volume of *TCLC*, with the exception of the Topics volumes, includes a **Title Index** listing the titles of all literary works discussed in the volume. In response to numerous suggestions from librarians, Gale has also produced a **Special Paperbound Edition** of the *TCLC* title index. This annual cumulation lists all titles discussed in the series since its inception and is issued with the first volume of *TCLC* published each year. Additional copies of the index are available on request. Librarians and patrons will welcome this separate index; it saves shelf space, is easy to use, and is recyclable upon receipt of the following year's cumulation. Titles discussed in the Topics volume entries are not included the *TCLC* cumulative Title Index.

Citing *Twentieth-Century Literary Criticism*

When writing papers, students who quote directly from any volume in the Literary Criticism Series may use the following general forms to footnote reprinted criticism. The first example pertains to material drawn from periodicals, the second to material reprinted from books:

[1]William H. Slavick, "Going to School to DuBose Heyward," *The Harlem Renaissance Reexamined,* (AMS Press, 1987); excerpted and reprinted in *Twentieth-Century Literary Criticism,* Vol. 59, ed. Jennifer Gariepy (Detroit: Gale Research, 1995), pp. 94-105.

[2]George Orwell, "Reflections on Gandhi," *Partisan Review* 6 (Winter 1949), pp. 85-92; excerpted and reprinted in *Twentieth-Century Literary Criticism,* Vol. 59, ed. Jennifer Gariepy (Detroit: Gale Research, 1995), pp. 40-3.

Suggestions Are Welcome

In response to suggestions, several features have been added to *TCLC* since the series began, including annotations to excerpted criticism, a cumulative index to authors in all Gale Literary Criticism Series titles, entries devoted to criticism on a single work by a major author, more extensive illustrations, and a title index listing all literary works discussed in the series since its inception.

Readers who wish to suggest authors or topics to appear in future volumes, or who have other suggestions, are cordially invited to write the editors.

Acknowledgments

The editors wish to thank the copyright holders of the excerpted criticism included in this volume and the permissions managers of many book and magazine publishing companies for assisting us in securing reprint rights. We are also grateful to the staffs of the Detroit Public Library, the Library of Congress, the University of Detroit Mercy Library, Wayne State University Purdy/Kresge Library Complex, and the University of Michigan Libraries for making their resources available to us. Following is a list of the copyright holders who have granted us permission to reprint material in this volume of *TCLC*. Every effort has been made to trace copyright, but if omissions have been made, please let us know.

COPYRIGHTED EXCERPTS IN *TCLC*, VOLUME 62, WERE REPRINTED FROM THE FOLLOWING PERIODICALS:

Black American Literature Forum, v. 25, Fall, 1991 for "Poetry and Jazz: A Twentieth-Century Wedding" by Barry Wallenstein. Copyright © 1991 Barry Wallenstein. Reprinted by permission of the author.—*Callaloo,* v. 10, Winter, 1987. Copyright © 1987 by Charles H. Rowell. All rights reserved. Reprinted by permission of the Johns Hopkins University Press.—*The Centennial Review,* v. XVIII, Summer, 1974, for "Understanding Fathers in American Jewish Fiction" by Rita K. Gollin. © 1974 by *The Centennial Review.* Reprinted by permission of the publisher and the author.—*The Chicago Jewish Forum,* v. 23, Summer, 1965, for "Jewishness, Judaism, and the American-Jewish Novelist" by Melvin H. Bernstein. Reprinted by permission of the Literary Estate of Melvin H. Bernstein.—*Chicago Review,* v. 29, Summer, 1977. Copyright © 1977 by Chicago Review. Reprinted by permission of the publisher.—*College Literature,* v. 20, June, 1993. Copyright © 1993 by West Chester University. Reprinted by permission of the publisher.—*Commentary,* v. 8, August, 1949, for "The Stranger and the Victim: The Two Jewish Stereotypes of American Fiction" by Irving Howe. Copyright 1949, renewed 1977, by the American Jewish Committee. All rights reserved. Reprinted by permission of the publisher and the Literary Estate of Irving Howe.—*Comparative Literature,* v. XXII, Spring, 1970. © copyright 1970 by University of Oregon. Reprinted by permission of *Comparative Literature.*—*Contemporary Literature,* v. 28, Fall, 1987; v. 34, Fall, 1993. © 1987, 1993 by the Board of Regents of the University of Wisconsin System. Both reprinted by permission of The University of Wisconsin Press.—*Discourse,* v. 12, Fall-Winter, 1989-90. © 1989-90 by Neil Nehring. Reprinted by permission of Carfax Publishing Co., P. O. Box 25, Abingdon, Oxfordshire OX14 3UE, United Kingdom.—*English Literary History,* v. 56, Fall, 1989. Copyright © 1989 by The Johns Hopkins University Press. All rights reserved. Reprinted by permission of the publisher.—*The Georgia Review,* v. XLVI, Winter, 1992. Copyright, 1992, by the University of Georgia. Reprinted by permission of the publisher.—*Jahrbuch für Amerikastudien,* v. 9, 1964 for "The Assimilation of the American Jewish Writer: Abraham Cahan to Saul Bellow" by Jules Chametzky. Reprinted by permission of the author.—*Jewish Book Annual,* v. 45, 1987-1988. © 1987 by the Jewish Book Council, 15 East 26th Street, New York, NY 10010. Reprinted by permission of the publisher.—*Journal of Modern Literature,* v. III, July, 1974. © Temple University 1974. Reprinted by permission of the publisher.—*Journal of Popular Culture,* v. 26, Winter, 1992. Copyright © 1992 by Ray B. Browne. Reprinted by permission of the publisher.—*Judaism,* v. 25, Summer, 1976 for "The Holocaust in American Jewish Fiction: A Slow Awakening" by Edward Alexander. Copyright © 1976 by the American Jewish Congress. Reprinted by permission of the publisher and the author.—*MELUS,* v. 10, Spring, 1983. Copyright, MELUS, The Society for the Study of Multi-Ethnic Literature of the United States, 1983. Reprinted by permission of the publisher.—*Michigan Quarterly Review,* v. XXIII, Winter, 1984 for "The Beatles as Artists: A Meditation for December Ninth" by James A. Winn. Copyright © The University of Michigan, 1984. Reprinted by permission of the author.—*Midstream,* v. XXVIII, November, 1982. Copyright © 1982 by The Theodor Herzl Foundation, Inc. Reprinted by permission of the publisher.—*Modern Fiction Studies,* v. 25, Summer, 1979. Copyright © 1979 by Purdue Research Foundation, West Lafayette, IN 47907. All rights reserved. Reprinted by permission of The Johns Hopkins University Press.—*Modern Jewish Studies,* v. 6, 1987. Reprinted by permission of the publisher.—*Mosaic: A Journal for the Interdisciplinary Study of Literature,* v. XVI, Fall, 1983. © *Mosaic* 1983. Acknowledgment of previous publication is herewith made.—*The Music Review,* v. 47, November, 1986. Reprinted by permission of the publisher.—*New Literary History,* v. 22, Summer, 1991.

COPYRIGHTED EXCERPTS IN *TCLC,* VOLUME 62, WERE REPRINTED FROM THE FOLLOWING BOOKS:

Jewish-American Fiction

INTRODUCTION

Despite a long-standing Jewish presence in the New World, the existence of a Jewish-American literature, as such, is a relatively recent phenomenon. Its origins lie in the immigrant culture of the late nineteenth and early twentieth centuries, a period in which a massive influx of Eastern European Jews settled in America, particularly in the United States. The stigma of foreignness and the desire for cultural acceptance proved to be a prevalent theme in the writings of early Jewish-American novelists who, in works like Abraham Cahan's *The Rise of David Levinsky* (1917), detailed the struggles of Jews as they experienced acculturation and dramatized the clash between traditional Jewish ethics and American materialism. In reaction to economic misfortune and prevalent anti-Semitism, many writers in the Depression era produced proletarian novels, such as Michael Gold's *Jews without Money* (1931), as a means of social activism and protest, or toward a more introspective and personal form of the novel, the prototype of which is Henry Roth's *Call It Sleep* (1934). The years following World War II saw such writers as Bernard Malamud, Saul Bellow, and Philip Roth move to the fore of American literature, heralding a period lasting from the mid-1950s until the 1970s sometimes described as a "Jewish-American Literary Renaissance," which accompanied a growing acceptance of Jews and Jewish culture. Largely responsible for defining the Jew in modern literature, the writings of these three figures typify such Modernist themes as alienation and self-deception, and, coupled with a sensitive and at times humorous concern for the human condition, represent the transition of Jewish-American fiction from an ethnic voice to a significant force in world literature. Still, these writers, like other mainstream Jewish-American authors—among them Norman Mailer, J. D. Salinger, and Arthur Miller—chose to deemphasize their Jewishness. More recently the Modernist outlook that has been shared by many Jewish-American authors has given way to a rediscovery of Jewish tradition and conscious efforts to depict the subtleties of Jewish culture and its long religious heritage in the contemporary novel. At the forefront of this movement are such writers as Cynthia Ozick and Nobel laureate Isaac Bashevis Singer, both of whom assert the importance of the Yiddish language and culture as central to maintaining the Jewish tradition. Likewise, recent years have witnessed a growing interest in two World War II-era topics that remained neglected in Jewish-American literature: the Holocaust and the creation and continued existence of the state of Israel. Concern for both subjects has since invigorated contemporary Jewish-American fiction and gained it renewed attention from an international audience.

REPRESENTATIVE WORKS

Antin, Mary
  The Promised Land (novel) 1912
Asch, Sholem
  East River (novel) 1946
Bellow, Saul
  The Victim (novel) 1949
  The Adventures of Augie March (novel) 1953
  Seize the Day (novel) 1956
  Herzog (novel) 1964
  Mr. Sammler's Planet (novel) 1970
Broner, E. M.
  A Weave of Women (novel) 1978
Cahan, Abraham
  The Rise of David Levinsky (novel) 1917
Cohen, Arthur A.
  In the Days of Simon Stern (novel) 1973
Doctorow, E. L.
  The Book of Daniel (novel) 1971
Epstein, Leslie
  King of the Jews (novel) 1979
Epstein, Seymour
  Leah (novel) 1964
Friedman, Bruce Jay
  A Mother's Kisses (novel) 1964
Fuchs, Daniel
  Summer in Williamsburg (novel) 1934
  Homage to Blenholt (novel) 1936
Glass, Montague
  Potash and Perlmutter (novel) 1910
Gold, Michael
  Jews without Money (novel) 1930
Goldstein, Rebecca
  The Mind-Body Problem (novel) 1983
Halper, Albert
  The Chute (novel) 1937
Hecht, Ben
  A Jew in Love (novel) 1931
Heller, Joseph
  Good as Gold (novel) 1979
  God Knows (novel) 1984
Helprin, Mark
  Ellis Island, and Other Stories (short stories) 1981
Hobson, Laura
  Gentleman's Agreement (novel) 1947
Kaplan, Johanna
  O My America! (novel) 1980
Kaufmann, Myron S.
  Remember Me to God (novel) 1957
Kazin, Alfred
  A Walker in the City (novel) 1951

OVERVIEWS

Mark Shechner

SOURCE: "The Jewish Novelist in America," in *The Schocken Guide to Jewish Books: Where to Start Reading about Jewish History, Literature, Culture, and Religion,* edited by Barry W. Holtz, Schocken Books, 1992, pp. 274-302.

[*In the following essay, Shechner surveys twentieth-century Jewish-American fiction, focusing on those writers who declare their Jewish self-consciousness in their work.*]

PROLOGUE

From the start, writing by Jewish novelists in America has been a vast enterprise. Seen from afar, the house of Jewish letters may resemble a bustling sweatshop, where writers arranged by rank and by file turn out books the way garment makers used to turn out apparel for the American clothing market. If that image belies the isolation and enclosed sensibility of the writer's enterprise, it does suggest the scale of the Jewish entry into American letters along with the hothouse atmosphere in which that literary endeavor has flourished. Writing remains, as tailoring once was, a principal Jewish occupation. Plainly, a reader's guide must proceed by exclusions, by ignoring certain books that were once read by thousands and by omitting entire careers that once appeared to define the Jewish presence itself. If the reader should find scant mention of writers once as prolific and acclaimed as Edna Ferber, Sholem Asch, Ben Hecht, Jerome Weidman, Maurice Samuel, Waldo Frank, Clifford Odets, Arthur Miller, Budd Schulberg, Leon Uris, and Herman Wouk, or find Edward Lewis Wallant, Norman Mailer, and Chaim Potok given less than their due, it is not for any failure to appreciate their contributions to American writing.

We must also be prepared to turn a blind eye to such literary forms as poetry, theater, and film and restrict our survey of memoirs and autobiographies to writers who had significant careers in fiction. We must say virtually nothing of the Yiddish language and must skip over the culture and literature the immigrants brought with them and continued to produce in Yiddish decades after their arrival. Moreover, we are bound to favor a writing that declares its Jewish self-consciousness, however that may be conceived, as historical consciousness or as covenant or as folk culture, though, ironically, we need say little about Talmud, Torah, and Halakhah, which have small bearing on a literature whose well-springs were secular and even anti-religious. What follows, then, is a personal canon, a declaration of what I would cite as the enduring legacy of Jewish fiction in America.

IN THE BEGINNING

In the beginning there was Abraham Cahan, whose *The Rise of David Levinsky* (1917), though not the first Jewish novel written in America, is the earliest to have stood the test of time. It comprehended better than any other the disruptions of immigration and the ironies of acculturation. As a socialist and reformer, of both American and Jewish life, as the editor of *The Jewish Daily Forward,* as the proprietor of the "Bintel Brief" letters column to that paper, and as a peripatetic walker in the city, Cahan was uniquely positioned to write the moral history of the immigrant generation: to document its experiences, underscore its conflicts, and summarize its achievements. *The Rise of David Levinsky* is the testament of a man whose life's work was observing the culture of his people, giving it voice, and forming the institutions through which it could realize itself and gain entry into America.

As a novel about a man who starts out as a *yeshiva bokher* in Russia and ends up as a tycoon in America, *The Rise of David Levinsky* is a quintessential statement of the collision between spirit and money, Jewish values and American promises. It portrays the Jewish soul in the throes of its transformation by capitalism, opportunity, and the need to look out for number one. During and after the great immigration, this transformation became one of the chief themes of Jewish life in America. The "Bintel Brief" column of Cahan's *Jewish Daily Forward* was a compendium of life in convulsive change, as immigrants and their children set about learning how to cope with the unique American conjunction of opportunity and peril.

The Rise of David Levinsky was a typical American novel of the Progressive era. Jewish in its histories and locales, it was American in its plot, exploring themes of fortune and failure, ambition and mobility, hardship at the bottom and hardship at the top. Like a garment, it was cut from a standard pattern, borrowed in this case from William Dean Howells's 1885 novel, *The Rise of Silas Lapham.*

But *David Levinsky* had another dimension that distinguished it from the documentary and the didactic: it was an experiment in creating a modern self, whose interiority went deeper than anything Jewish writers had attempted before. The character of David Levinsky signaled the entry of the individual into Jewish-American literature. Though typical he is not generic, and he is the first in a line of Jewish heroes who become individuals by virtue of being neurotics. David Levinsky's conflicts and his instinct for defeat in love—the moral counterweight to his success in business—are forerunners of the more probing,

psychological literature that emerged some twenty years later with the stories of Delmore Schwartz and flowered after the war in the novels of Saul Bellow and Isaac Rosenfeld, Bernard Malamud, Philip Roth, Harold Brodkey, Joseph Heller, and E. L. Doctorow.

In 1917, this struggle to compose a unique self for purposes of survival was a distinctly American concept, and *The Rise of David Levinsky* was a Jewish novelty, though a novelty against the backdrop of a people discovering, *en masse,* self-reliance. As the Jews cast off their traditional habits and ways, their rituals and beliefs, it was to America that they looked for moral guidance and models of character. The great paradigm shift saw the Jews become a desanctified people and a people for whom the ceremonies of self-reliance were to be substituted for those of common purpose and common destiny. It is not surprising then that so many early books should be stories of separation and conflict: between parents and children, between tradition and exploration, between *shtetl* austerities and American horizons. Such books became blueprints of how, in a single generation, a culture founded upon "Thou Shalt Not" would find its new moral sanction in "The Pursuit of Happiness."

For more by and about Cahan, see his "Yekl: A Tale of the new York Ghetto" (1896), in *The Imported Bridegroom and Other Stories of Yiddish New York,* (1978); Ronald Sanders, *The Downtown Jews: Portraits of an Immigrant Generation* (1969); Isaac Metzker, ed., *A Bintel Brief: Sixty Years of Letters from the Lower East Side to the Jewish Daily Forward* (1971); Abraham Cahan, *The Education of Abraham Cahan* (1969), translated by Leon Stein et al. from the 1926 Yiddish autobiography *Bleter fun mein leben.*

Perhaps no novel from these years better epitomizes these struggles than Anzia Yezierska's *Bread Givers,* subtitled *A Struggle between a Father of the Old World and a Daughter of the New* (1925). Etched out on a smaller social canvas than Cahan's *The Rise of David Levinsky,* but in swifter, more jagged strokes, it was a doxology of liberation on the part of a young woman, Sara Smolinsky, for whom the shackles of life as a scholar's daughter were not to be suffered in a world where striking out and forging ahead were canonized in the national liturgy as inalienable rights. *Bread Givers* reads like a "Bintel Brief" letter in novel form. The father, a talmudic scholar cursed with four daughters, is desperate to match them with husbands who will sustain him in his old age and safeguard his privileged leisure. Sara's sisters tragically give in to their father's demands while Sara ferociously holds out for her own destiny. "Woe to a man who has females for his offspring" is the father's battle cry. "My will is as strong as yours" is Sara's retort. "I'm going to live my own life. Nobody can stop me. I'm not from the old country. I'm American!" It is not amiss to say that *Bread Givers* is the first Jewish feminist novel.

An immigrant herself, who did not arrive in America until she was sixteen, Yezierska set about with a passion to Americanize herself: to teach herself English and to express her wild yearnings in prose. It was as a factory worker, in her thirties, that she began writing the stories of im-

Abraham Cahan.

migrant life that would launch her career, which included an arid detour through Hollywood as a screenwriter and a brief, intimate relationship with the philosopher John Dewey. Like Cahan, however, Yezierska knew Americanization to be a tainted blessing. One might be liberated, but for what? To be independent, desanctified, and alone. With Sara Smolinsky, as with David Levinsky, the heart does not open toward the new life but grows rigid and prohibitive and, ironically, talmudic, as her form of self-assertion is a dedication to scholarship and study.

In life, Yezierska found the successes that her writing had thrust upon her unpalatable, as her talent dried up in Hollywood. After a brief stay there, which she describes ruefully in her autobiography *Red Ribbon on a White Horse* (1950), she returned to the claustral cityscape that had formed her gifts. Rebel against Jewish life though she might, only Hester Street and its sorrows ignited her imagination, and it was after the Hollywood fiasco that she would come back to New York and write her masterwork, *Bread Givers.* There were other books, before *Bread Givers* and after: *Hungry Hearts* (1926), the collection of stories for which Samuel Goldwyn offered $10,000; *Children of Loneliness* (1923), *Salome of the Tenements* (1923), *Arrogant Beggar* (1927), and *All I Could Never Be* (1932). All are marked by the same rawness and desire, out of which one of Yezierska's heroines declaims: "I am a Russian Je-

wess, a flame, a longing. A soul consumed with hunger for heights beyond reach. I am an ache of unvoiced dreams, the clamor of suppressed desires." Of Yezierska's novels, only *Bread Givers* is in print, though there are two anthologies of her work: *The Open Cage: An Anzia Yezierska Collection,* edited by Alice Kessler-Harris, with an afterword by Yezierska's daughter, Louise Levitas Henriksen (1979), and *How I Found America: Collected Stories of Anzia Yezierska,* introduced by Vivian Gornick (1991). There one can experience in full measure that "ache of unvoiced dreams" and "clamor of suppressed desires," which remain as stirring and unsettling as they were some sixty-five years ago.

JEWS AND THE LEFT

Any account of the evolution of Jewish writing in America must come to terms with one overwhelming fact about that history: that in the early years much of it was associated with radical ideas and left-wing movements. Throughout the first half-century of Jewish writing in America, radicalism seemed indigenous to the Jewish profile. In the 1930s especially, the Depression and fears of fascism drove many Jewish intellectuals and writers into revolutionary postures and sponsored an outpouring of "proletarian" and "popular front" novels. Since political and social agendas usually outweighed literary ones in such books, most of them have little more than historical interest today, though some, like Mike Gold's *Jews Without Money* (1930), transcend their *parti pris* through raw documentary force.

There has been no lack of efforts to explain Jewish leftism, though explanations hardly seem necessary. The greater part of the Ashkenazi Jews came to America a dispossessed people: landless, excluded, and persecuted, and discovered in America routines of labor so exploitative, when work could be found, that it is a wonder that they were not all converted to revolutionism at once. The Triangle Shirtwaist fire of 1911, in which 146 workers died, remains a symbol of the working conditions that immigrants encountered in America. There are, however, reasons why the Jews among the immigrants produced much of this literature, and not others who suffered from the same Malthusian economics: 1. Their exclusion from opportunities predisposed some toward programs that promised a world reformed to abolish Jewish isolation. 2. Yiddish-speaking Jews already constituted a de facto workers' internationale of their own and looked upon internationalist movements as instruments for initiating others into their brand of brotherhood. 3. The immigrants imported the revolutionary idealism of Russia. Marxism provided a rallying point for these insurrectionary sentiments. 4. Marxism itself was a rigorous ideology whose basic tenets existed in canonical texts, allowing the Talmudic strain in Jewish culture to express itself in political terms. The road from the Yeshiva to the barricade was paved with volumes of *Kapital.* 5. The Jewish prophetic tradition, detached from the Law, attached itself to other eschatologies that combined moral righteousness with Millenarian visions.

Mike Gold's *Jews Without Money* might well stand for the whole corpus of revolutionary testaments produced by the Jewish-radical fusion. Though it is a self-consciously "proletarian" novel, a fable of working-class life with a revolutionary moral, its staying power derives not from any formulas that Gold brought from the Communist party, for which he worked as editor of *The New Masses,* but from a searing recollection of his childhood among those whom Jacob Riis called "the other half."

Born Iztchok Granich in 1893 on New York's Lower East Side, the son of Rumanian immigrant parents, Gold changed his name to Irwin as a youth and during the Palmer raids of 1919-20 took the name of Mike Gold, an abolitionist hero who had fought in the Civil War. Everywhere around him he saw poverty and demoralization; his own father, a manufacturer of suspenders, failed in business and Gold had to leave school and go to work at the age of twelve. The experience of poverty in an environment of predatory capitalism became the source of his revolutionary ardor and grist for his literary mill.

Behind *Jews Without Money* were assumptions about literature as revolutionary action. Melodramatic though those assumptions could be—all labor was misery, all ownership exploitation—they showed Gold the way to convert the impressions of his childhood into a theater of radical initiation, bringing, in effect, Dickens together with Engels. In Gold, the theater of the grotesque merged with the documentary of conditions to form one of the most graphic literatures of disaffection America ever produced.

Jews Without Money is a contra-*Levinsky*, a look at Jewish life through the other end of the telescope. If Abraham Cahan and Anzia Yezierska depicted the immigrant experience as an ascent, however jagged, Michael Gold was intent on the fall, which was as American as the rise. *Jews Without Money* is a reminder of how immigrant society in America fell into classes and that the vast majority of the Jews did not, like David Levinsky, go into business, or like Sara Smolinsky, light out for the university. They were working people who were either self-employed at marginal levels, as pushcart vendors, or worked in whatever trades were open to them in the urban ghettos of America. For more about Gold, see *Mike Gold: A Literary Anthology,* edited by Mike Folsom (1972).

THE LANDSCAPE OF DREAMS

The great Jewish book of the 1930s was Henry Roth's *Call It Sleep* (1934), though few reviewers of the time were prepared to appreciate its power. Its emotionalism was too raw and its psychologism too radical for an age that professed to have other, more social, uses for literature. It was not until 1964, when the paperback reprint was given a front-page review in *The New York Times Book Review* by Irving Howe, that the book enjoyed anything like widespread acclaim. The ordeal of the child, David Schearl, who comes to America with his mother to encounter a father who is suspicious, estranged, and given to capricious rages, is perhaps better appreciated now than in the thirties, when its brand of literary impressionism was looked on with a certain condescension.

Call It Sleep is the story of a young boy's initiation into the mysteries of his own being: the mysteries of sex and those of religion, the mysteries of origin, and those of the world around him which appears to be ruled by ominous

and alien symbols. At the center of it is a grotesque family romance, dominated by a father whose smoldering rage ionizes the atmosphere. The novel's prologue, in which he and his mother are greeted at Ellis Island by a fearful and accusatory father, is a preview of all that is to befall David. Virtually a babe in arms, he is guilty of unnamed crimes.

Unlike anything else Jewish writers were doing in the 1930s, *Call It Sleep* was a book about symbols (basements, closets, fiery coals, rosaries), terrors, secret powers, and hidden meanings. It exposed the dark side of the psyche and read more like German Expressionist drama than anything else in Jewish-American writing. The forty pages at the end of *Call It Sleep* are the most powerful sustained writing ever done by a Jewish writer in America.

While other novelists were writing social dramas with occasional Marxist flavoring, Roth was writing a Freudian dissection of the soul in crisis. If Abraham Cahan in *The Rise of David Levinsky* invented the self for the Jewish novelist in America, it is astonishing that just seventeen years later Henry Roth, making the leap into modernism, would dismantle the self, not to restore a lost communality but to declare the vulnerability of the naked ego, alone and isolated in a strange world. The spectacular cadenza in which David hurtles through the night streets and sticks the handle of a milk ladle onto the third rail of the trolley tracks, not only brings the motifs of the book to a stunning climax but sums up a relationship to the New World that distinguishes it sharply from the Old: America is a place where loneliness can drive you insane.

FOOTNOTE TO THE THIRTIES

The pre-war literary culture was rich in writing by and about Jews, and though most of it is time-bound, a portion retains both freshness and a documentary value. Foremost among these novels are those by Daniel Fuchs, *Summer in Williamsburg* (1934), *Homage to Blenholt* (1936), *Low Company* (1937). The three novels were assembled into *The Williamsburg Trilogy* by Basic Books in 1961. Of the three, the first, a social portrait of a Williamsburg (Brooklyn) adolescence, an urban romance, and a bemused disquisition on adolescent movie-going, is the best known, though I am partial to the *Homage to Blenholt,* in which the funeral of a corrupt Commissioner of Sewers occasions a degree of civic mourning that is usually reserved for heads of state or oriental despots. In it Fuchs demonstrated a capacity for broad social satire that would later stand him in good stead as a Hollywood screenwriter. Indeed, *Low Company,* a hard-boiled novel about a gangland takeover of prostitution in Neptune, New Jersey, would be made into a film, *The Gangster,* in 1947. In all these Fuchs would demonstrate an ear for common speech, an eye for social detail, and a gift for irony. In Hollywood, where he would work continuously after 1940, Fuchs wrote or collaborated on a series of popular screenplays, including *Panic in the Streets* (1950), *Love Me or Leave Me* (1955), and *Jeanne Eagels* (1957).

Meyer Levin, regarded by some as the great neglected figure among the Jewish novelists, wrote his best book, *The Old Bunch,* in 1937. A novel about the fracturing of the Jewish community and the capriciousness of destiny in the

New World, it traces a group of poor Jewish boys out of the ghettos of the Chicago West Side into the mainstream of American life. A quintessential Chicago novel in the manner of Theodore Dreiser, James T. Farrell, and Nelson Algren, *The Old Bunch* is dense in the gritty urban detail of downtown realism and ghetto naturalism: it is a fiction inspired by stockyards and rail yards and a life in which the impossibility of romance takes on a romantic coloration of its own. In later years Levin would divide his time among fiction, journalism, and drama, and nowadays is probably best remembered for his book about the Leopold and Loeb case, *Compulsion* (1956), *The Settlers* (1972), and for the stage adaptation he did of Anne Frank's diary, which her father denied him permission to produce. This episode would eventually lead to a strange and vivid book, the autobiographical *The Obsession* (1973), Levin's bitter account of his struggles with Otto Frank and a diatribe on the politics of Jewish letters in the postwar years. See also Levin's edition of *Classic Hasidic Tales: Marvelous Tales of Rabbi Israel Baal Shem and of his Great-Grandson, Rabbi Nachman, Retold from Hebrew, Yiddish, and German Sources,* published 1932 as *The Golden Mountain.*

Fuchs and Levin both were social writers, like most of the Jewish novelists who published in the 1930s. From Mike Gold's *Jews without Money* in 1930 to Meyer Levin's *Citizens* ten years later, the social muse is in the ascendant and the song of protest is the most plangent. The plays of Clifford Odets, of which *Waiting for Lefty* (1935) and *Awake and Sing* (1935) remain the most memorable, are the dramatic counterparts of this fiction. If much of this literature seems to retain more documentary than imaginative appeal, it is nevertheless needful in reminding us how Jewish life and the Jewish spirit came of age in America, through bitter days and arid scenes.

THE ADVENT OF MODERNISM

It is common knowledge that Jewish writing through the 1930s was inspired largely by the social muse, which could construct vivid tableaux of exploitation and grief even while being imaginatively constricted and compositionally banal. In due course, however, as both social integration and success came to American Jews, Jewish writers would cast off purely social agendas and adopt psychological and spiritual ones. Parable and myth, psychological complexity and moral ambiguity, Jamesian strategy and Joycean virtuosity begin to assert their presence in the fiction written by American Jews.

Precursors could be found in the novels of Nathanael West (Nathan Weinstein), most notably *Miss Lonelyhearts* (1933) and *The Day of the Locust* (1939) (reprinted in one volume by New Directions, 1969), but West's sense of Jewish identity was marginal and it was as an American rather than as a Jew that he wrote and was read. And Roth's *Call It Sleep*, a virtual handbook of modernist clichés, was *sui generis,* a brilliant interlude that made no impact on its time and left no legacy except a certain backwash of wonder and speculation.

The Jewish writers' modernization in America—their connection to the European avant-garde—can be traced back to a slim volume of stories that appeared in 1938 under the title of its lead story, *In Dreams Begin Responsibilities, and Other Stories,* by Delmore Schwartz (1978). Schwartz's writing was more auspicious than Roth's because it had an intellectual context: *Partisan Review* magazine which, from the late 1930s on, was a rallying point for disaffected and militant writers and intellectuals. The stories in *In Dreams Begin Responsibilities* could not be characterized as "Bintel Brief" letters writ large, because Schwartz was primarily a psychological writer, the tormented stations of the soul being the keynotes of his writing. Irving Howe once called him a "comedian of alienation," which captures something of the ironic and tangential relation he bore to his time. Indeed, what would make him auspicious was that at first glance *he had no relation to his time,* preferring to establish an ongoing relation to eternity. If America was going to produce a Franz Kafka, it looked for a while as though Schwartz was the prime candidate. Certainly, the pathos of his first story, in which a young Delmore sits in a movie theater and watches in horror the scene of his as yet unmarried parents' courtship in a Coney Island restaurant, was like nothing the social muse could inspire.

Schwartz did not fulfill himself in fiction. His main impact would be in poetry, though that would prove fleeting, as insomnia, alcohol, drugs, and finally madness ground him down. He is, as most readers know, the Von Humboldt Fleisher of Saul Bellow's novel *Humboldt's Gift.* It was as a releasing agent and a guide to an alternative tradition that Schwartz affected literature. A disciple of Rimbaud and Wallace Stevens, Pound and Eliot, he claimed new horizons for others, like Saul Bellow and Isaac Rosenfeld, who would seize upon his epigrams and work them up into strategies. It was Schwartz who showed the way out of the ghettos of realism (and the realisms of the ghetto) into the more capacious worlds of symbol and allusion, parable and myth, neurosis and alienation. For more by and about Schwartz, see his selected poems, *Summer Knowledge* (1959), and the biography by James Atlas, *Delmore Schwartz: The Life of an American Poet* (1977).

SAUL BELLOW

What Schwartz inaugurated in American Jewish letters was the Europeanization of the self, and it is not too much to see Saul Bellow as the fulfillment of Schwartz's failed promise. It was in the Schwartz mode, as an underground man *à la* Dostoevski, that Bellow made his entry into American literature with *Dangling Man* (1944) and *The Victim* (1947), "post-socialist novels," whose basic strategies are neither the dissection of society nor the amelioration of its cruelties. Each is a subtle evocation of individual psychopathology, though in the context of real history. In *Dangling Man* the historical context is wartime; in *The Victim* it is the postwar malaise that would descend upon Jewish intellectuals for whom the bull market of fortune could not cauterize the wounds of war. While others celebrated, they despaired.

Probing the spirit in crisis would become the axial line of Bellow's thought, though he would take an occasional detour, as he did in his third novel, *The Adventures of Augie March* (1953), an idiosyncratic return to the sprawling

Chicago novel of Dreiser, Farrell, and Levin. But that book is now the least memorable of Bellow's performances, substituting panorama for penetration and the vast cityscape for the vivid cameo. Far more acute was *Seize the Day* (1956), in which Tommy Wilhelm, a neurotic son, finds himself in a squeeze play between two fathers, a remote and narcissistic real father and a seemingly nurturing but utterly predatory therapist-father, who places a high price tag on the love he offers—Tommy's last penny for falling lard futures.

In *Seize the Day*, all the elements of Bellow's worldview are held in perfect equipoise. It is a comedy of capitalism, in which profit and loss are blended into health and neurosis, so that Tommy Wilhelm's final wipeout in the commodities market makes him one of Sigmund Freud's "Characters Wrecked by Success." In the figure of Tamkin, guru and commodities maven, rabbi, broker, therapist, and thief, Bellow conjured up one of his greatest inventions.

Seize the Day would inaugurate the main phase of Bellow's career, which would include *Henderson the Rain King* (1959), the play *The Last Analysis* (1965), *Herzog* (1964), and *Mr. Sammler's Planet* (1970). It is possible to talk about these books, Bellow's collective chef d'oeuvre, together, since they are thematically united. They are Bellow's therapeutic novels, foregrounding issues of illness and recuperation and suggesting that to fall ill is to suffer

Saul Bellow.

from culture or history. Virtually all of Bellow's heroes are patients or convalescents: Tommy Wilhelm in *Seize the Day*, Eugene Henderson of *Henderson the Rain King*, Bummidge of *The Last Analysis*, Moses Herzog of *Herzog*, and Artur Sammler of *Mr. Sammler's Planet*. All except Sammler are neurotics who seek relief from their symptoms and throw themselves into one curative scheme or another in their febrile searches for remedy. Tommy Wilhelm submits to a therapist-shaman who betrays him; Henderson sets off for Africa and meets up with a healer-dealer who cures him; Bummidge conducts autotherapy in front of closed-circuit TV; Herzog hands himself over to women and, when that fails, tries to kill his ex-wife's lover. Only Sammler deflects the neurotic question, since, as a Holocaust survivor, he suffers from history directly, not symptomatically.

From *Humboldt's Gift* (1975) to the present, Bellow's work has turned into something of a long finale, a gathering together of impressions and memories as if, time running short, there is ever so much to say. The sprawling *Humboldt's Gift* is the most vigorous of these books, especially in those pages devoted to the failed poet and prophet, Von Humboldt Fleisher, who is Schwartz in every detail. Bellow can be a very funny writer and in *Humboldt's Gift*, the figure of Humboldt/Schwartz, whose antics grow more outrageous as his schizophrenia grows more dire, permits Bellow to release his comic impulses in a virtually uninhibited way. Humboldt's fate is black, but never too black for wisecracks.

Since *Humboldt's Gift*, Bellow has remained productive, though his recent writing has lost something of its bite. However, a blunted Bellow is worth a dozen other writers at their sharpest. His later writing includes two novels, *The Dean's December* (1982) and *More Die of Heartbreak* (1987); two novellas, *The Bellarosa Connection* (1989) and *A Theft: A Novella* (1989); a collection of stories, *Him With His Foot in His Mouth and Other Stories* (1984); and a memoir of Israel in the wake of the Six-Day War, *To Jerusalem and Back* (1976). It is all marked by the same sardonic wisdom, the same epigrammatic briskness, the same suave urbanity, the same keen perception. Bellow is the most visual of our writers. But the newcomer to Bellow who wants to catch him at his best should start with *Seize the Day* and follow it up with the difficult but dazzling *Herzog*. There may not be two better novels in all of postwar American literature.

In treating of Bellow we are compelled to mention his boyhood chum and early comrade-in-books, Isaac Rosenfeld, whose death of a heart attack in 1956, at the age of thirty-eight, was a blow to literature. Rosenfeld's promise, though troubled and erratic, was genuine. He was the only Jewish writer of his generation to write fiction in Yiddish as well as in English, and while the accumulated harvest of writing was small, the freshness and penetration of his mind is still palpable in much of it. He left behind one novel, *Passage from Home* (1948), and several collections edited posthumously by friends and admirers: *Alpha and Omega*, short stories (1966), *An Age of Enormity*, essays (1962). See especially Mark Shechner, ed., *Preserving the Hunger: An Isaac Rosenfeld Reader* (1988), a representative sampler of Rosenfeld's essays and his fiction. Rosenfeld's writing is still capable of surprising, and delighting, those who come upon it for the first time.

BERNARD MALAMUD

Bernard Malamud's Jewish patrimony was altogether different from Saul Bellow's. Whereas Bellow came on the scene as an apostle of modernism, a disciple of Dostoevski (*The Victim* was based on the plot of Dostoevski's *The Eternal Husband*), an intellectual, who would become a professor at the University of Chicago's Committee on Social Thought, and an anthropologist of the urban middle class, Malamud was something much homier and more available to the common reader: a child of Yiddish folk culture whose first principle was an abiding love for the little man, *dos klayne mentschele,* as the grandfather of Yiddish literature, Mendele Mokher Seforim, had called him.

This may not have been apparent in Malamud's first novel, *The Natural* (1952), in which a bizarre event in the history of American baseball, the shooting of Philadelphia Phillies player Eddie Waitkus by a woman he had engaged for the night, was yoked together, in metaphysical fashion, with Golden Bough fertility myths, to create the mythical figure of Roy Hobbs, pitcher, slugger, and tragic Osiris of the American cornbelt. It was a strained performance, and anyone who saw the 1983 film, with Robert Redford in the leading role, would be justified in wondering where the Jewish content was. But, given Malamud's subsequent career as a celebrant of Jewish folk myth and spiritual lore, in stories like "Angel Levine" and "Idiots First," *The Natural* may not be so alien from that world as might first be supposed, though Roy Hobbs finally is a player and not a zaddik.

Soon afterward, Malamud returned to native grounds with his two subsequent books, *The Assistant* (1957) and his first collection of stories, *The Magic Barrel* (1958). In the first, *dos klayne mentschele,* as an elderly Brooklyn grocery store owner, Morris Bober, is given homage as a hero of durability and fortitude, who tolerates a meager existence in a failing business because it is his lot to do so. For many readers, *The Assistant* remains the representative Malamud novel, for its celebration of endurance and conscience. The old grocery store, redolent of dust and neglect, the insistent weight of moral implication that leaves no act, no dialogue, no transaction free of ethical valence, the sense of moral combat between Jew, Morris Bober, and Gentile, Frank Alpine, the sustained note of lamentation—the still, sad music of daily existence—are all Malamud trademarks, and have been taken by many readers as his definitive Jewish credentials.

Yet precisely the throb of ethical pressure in *The Assistant* raises a problem that runs through Malamud's work: the Jewish content is wholly atmospheric and resistant to definition. When Morris Bober tries to define, for Frank Alpine, his Jewish identity in terms of the Law, he is hard put to specify what the Law is and ends up stuttering out a formula: "I suffer for you." When challenged on that, he adds, "I mean you suffer for me." To be sure, this elusiveness is typical of most Jewish writing in America, and

Malamud can hardly be chastened for not knowing what no other writer is in firm possession of. It is precisely this conjunction of liturgical ignorance and tonal clarity about Jewish life that defines the entire Jewish-American literary corpus.

Malamud's minimalist sensibility, his feel for Depression-era marginality, has generally found its best vehicle in his short stories, and it was with the publication of *The Magic Barrel* in 1958 that Malamud's reputation as a master was made. Some of those stories are among the most consistently anthologized of any in the postwar canon: "Angel Levine" and "The Magic Barrel" are classic modern short stories, and from a second collection, *Idiots First* (1963), "The Jewbird" and "Idiots First" have enjoyed similar ongoing appreciation. The reader who is in search of the essential Malamud should begin with the story collections: *The Magic Barrel, Idiots First, Pictures of Fidelman* (1969), and *Rembrandt's Hat* (1974), though the quintessence of Malamud is available in his personal selection of stories, *The Stories of Bernard Malamud* (1983).

The novels are more erratic performances, and though all have their moments of grace, it is generally conceded that Malamud never mastered the broader architecture of the novel. A novel that is interesting for its autobiographical reflections of Malamud's own days as a composition instructor at Oregon State University (where he was not permitted to teach literature), is *A New Life* (1961), which examines the ironies of a new world within the new world, a land so alien from Jewish experience or sensibility that one might wonder if the grocery store of *The Assistant* and the English Department of *A New Life* can possibly be on the same planet. In *The Fixer* (1966) Malamud stepped out of the personal mode to write a historical novel around the actual case of Mendel Beiliss, a Jew who was tried and acquitted on charges of ritual murder in czarist Russia at the turn of the century. Malamud's Yakov Bok, like the real Beiliss, is acquitted, but not before he is subjected to humiliating persecution and converted to revolutionism.

Malamud has never been given proper credit for his courage and his willingness to take risks. Consider the range of themes in his novels: life at the margins of existence in *The Assistant,* the ironies of liberation in the Far West in *A New Life,* the pariah's lot in czarist Russia in *The Fixer.* In 1971 he would publish *The Tenants* in which two inhabitants of an abandoned building in the South Bronx, Harry Lesser (Jewish) and Willie Spearmint (black), grow increasingly hostile to each other until, in a fit of rage, they beat each other to death. Then, in 1979, Malamud would publish what might arguably be his best novel, *Dubin's Lives,* about a Jewish writer who leaves his wife for a younger woman and discovers, like S. Levin in *A New Life* had, that liberty comes with a price tag. Finally, in *God's Grace* (1982), Malamud attempted a curious and awkward theological parable in which a paleologist named Calvin Cohn finds himself shipwrecked with a chimpanzee named Buz in a post-nuclear-holocaust world.

I don't believe we have fully come to terms with Malamud yet, surely not so long as critics continue to see him as either a placid moralist or an expert in timeless wisdom and contemporary ethics. The variety of his experiments will finally be recognized for what they are: signs of an imagination more restless, more daring, and more experimental than it is commonly thought to be. Malamud, whose voice was given to him by an ancient culture, will one day be understood to be the most modern of American writers.

PHILIP ROTH

The first thing to observe about Philip Roth's career is a certain relentlessness that bears resemblance to a military campaign. Its basic marching orders are to press forward. From *Goodbye, Columbus, and Other Stories* in 1959, Roth's literary output has seldom lost a step, and if he has experienced any of the blocks that are common to the writer's trade, they are not visible in his accumulated work, which includes eighteen novels.

To me, the early books have aged badly. Time has dealt harshly with the stories in *Goodbye, Columbus, and Other Stories* (1959) and the novels *Letting Go* (1962) and *When She Was Good* (1967), because Roth has gone so far beyond them that they now seem like voices from some far base camp of our literature. Certainly there is some clever social satire in "Goodbye, Columbus" and a few of the accompanying stories. It was Roth's verbal agility, his sense of the absurd, his quickness to skewer easy social targets, that occasioned the adulation he received as well as the blows he took from members of the Jewish community who found his irreverence toward his Jewish characters instigation enough to call him to his senses.

Because of this criticism and because of Roth's own fear of remaining merely clever, his next two novels were rather obstinately sober and fussily high-minded. *Letting Go*, in point of bulk (680 pages in the Farrar, Straus and Giroux 1982 edition), compared favorably to Bellow's *Augie March* and Levin's *The Old Bunch*. A book about the failures of love among graduate students, it is long and portentous. *When She Was Good*, a curious novel about the tragic life of a small-town girl, is today the least read and least appreciated of all of Roth's novels.

These books must be regarded as Roth's juvenilia, his investigations into his talent and his discovery that he was not fated to be the Salinger or Dreiser or Henry James of Jewish experience. Roth's own voice did not come easily, and when it came it proved to be irreverent, desperate, satirical, and unsociable. The book in which it made its debut was *Portnoy's Complaint* (1969), an exhibition so spectacular in both content and voice that it remains, twenty-two years since publication, Roth's signature book. *Portnoy's Complaint* paraded itself as a "breakthrough" novel in which psychoanalysis made its appearance as both setting and viewpoint. It was the opposite of everything the prior two books had aspired to be: raucous where they were controlled, raunchy where they were sober, irresponsible where they were dutiful. Its blend of cultural rebellion, comic mayhem, and textbook Freudianism brought Roth a mass audience and a movie contract, though not the universal approbation of literary critics or Jewish parents. The book was an exorcism, and as exorcisms will, it dealt in excess.

The Breast (1972) is a footnote. A Kafkaesque parable of an English professor who is transformed overnight into a man-sized female breast, it reads like a dream that a patient such as Alex Portnoy might have produced for his analysis. Potentially hilarious though the situation was, Roth kept the humor in check and told the story as a case history, albeit a case history narrated by the patient. Roth did not, however, jettison his comic gift in subsequent novels, he just depersonalized it and projected it outward: satirically toward President Richard Nixon, in *Our Gang* (1971), a bitter diatribe on one President Trick E. Dixon, and affectionately toward baseball in a *slapstick noir* about a team without a home field, *The Great American Novel* (1973). The former book is scattershot, while the latter book is mayhem in which the baseball evolves into a metaphor for Jewry and the wandering team becomes the diaspora. That the team comes to grief is the historical message of the parable, though along the way there is much of the madcap comedy that was, in the seventies, Roth's trademark.

But *The Breast, Our Gang,* and *The Great American Novel* were diversions from the main line of Roth's writing, the pseudo-autobiographical: autobiographical because Roth's own life has provided its basic situations, pseudo because they were so densely elaborated into "art" that no single image or event is dependably "true." In recent years, Roth would attempt to cast off his art altogether and tell his story directly, in *The Facts* (1988) and *Patrimony* (1991), though neither is an artless performance. Indeed, what often makes Roth's books so fascinating is the tension between confession and craft that keeps us wary of Roth's cat-and-mouse game with the truth, and with us.

In my estimation, *My Life as a Man* (1973) remains Roth's best novel, in part because it is abundant in social manners and in part because the counterpoint of life and art is cleverly built into the book's structure. A novel about the marital misadventures of a novelist, it contains "useful fictions," the writer's own efforts to turn his marriage into fiction, plus a long coda entitled "My True Story." The book approaches the question of truth through theme and variations, making it plain one's "true story" need be no truer than one's fictions.

If we concede the next novel, *The Professor of Desire* (1977) to be an interregnum, then Roth's next major opus is the trilogy of novels that appeared in rapid succession over a period of four years: *The Ghost Writer* (1979), *Zuckerman Unbound* (1981), *The Anatomy Lesson* (1983). We can speak of them together because Roth conceived of them as "Zuckerman variations," as one character calls them. Though there is no continuous narrative that requires us to read them in sequence, they are discrete windows on the life of the novelist Nathan Zuckerman, whose adventures at times parallel Roth's own. All are fables of martyrdom: *The Ghost Writer* a fable of the artist as a martyr to language, *Zuckerman Unbound* a fable of the artist as a martyr to his fame, *The Anatomy Lesson* a fable of the artist as a martyr to his critics.

The martyred artist in *The Ghost Writer* is Nathan Zuckerman, who has outraged his family and community with a short story which hangs family laundry out for public inspection. In his flight from censure, Zuckerman finds brief respite in the home of one E. I. Lonoff, a writer who refuses to be martyred except by sentences. In Lonoff's home, Zuckerman meets a young woman whom he fancies to be Anne Frank, and whose story of escape and flight he freely dreams up. This tinkering with Anne Frank was a gambit that most critics deemed successful, prompting some to proclaim *The Ghost Writer* Roth's most achieved piece of work. Certainly it is a daring conception in which Roth demonstrated that he could hit and sustain new notes, notes of wonder, mystery, and delicate irony.

One admires these books not for their plots or characters, though in *Zuckerman Unbound* Roth invents one Alvin Pepler, who is his most splendid grotesque, but for the delight of watching Roth do his exercises and practice his scales. If ever a writer piped at his ease, surely it is Roth in the Zuckerman trilogy. Published together as *Zuckerman Bound* in 1985, the novels were given an epilogue, *The Prague Orgy*, in which Zuckerman's trials of personal martyrdom are drowned in the greater martyrdom of a nation, Czechoslovakia. It is a report from Eastern Europe, which Roth has long been scouting, not only as a writer but as the editor of a series for Penguin Books, *Writers from the Other Europe*.

The final Zuckerman novel to date is *The Counterlife* (1986), which brings the Zuckerman variations to a furious conclusion with a Zuckerman fugue. In five episodes it counterpoints the lives of two brothers, Nathan and Henry Zuckerman, as they struggle with their heart problems (amorous and medical), their Jewish identities and faiths, and their brotherhood. As in a repertory theater, they trade lives and predicaments as snappily as actors change costumes. An elegant novel, it describes an elaborate counterpoint between the inertia of history and the agility of the imagination, demonstrating that a novel can contradict itself repeatedly and become all the more convincing. Is it any wonder that Roth's last novel to date is entitled *Deception: A Novel* (1990)? It plays not only with the question of truth and illusion in marriage and love, but also the question of what the writer is doing every time he puts words to paper.

Keeping the counterpoint alive on a larger scale are the recent autobiographical books, *The Facts* and *Patrimony*, the latter a tender story of Roth's father's last year. Indeed in *The Facts,* putatively a straightforward if miniature life story, Roth introduces the voice of a fictional Nathan Zuckerman who, as Roth's kibitzing alter ego, announces at the end that the author has got it all wrong.

After thirty-two years, Roth's career is still evolving, and still astonishing for its variety as well as for its virtuosity. Under its present marching orders, it promises books to come. About all we can predict is that each will be a surprise, since the capacity for surprise has been Roth's patrimony as an artist from day one.

POSTWAR POTPOURRI

The years following the war brought Jewish writers into American letters in unprecedented numbers, and novels by, about, and for Jews inundated the markets in a flow that has never stopped. Jews had come of age in American culture, and the children and grandchildren of butchers, grocers, fish peddlers, junk dealers, cutters, pressers, tailors, furriers, and rabbis made their way into the cultural arena by the force of their ambition and the keenness of their intellects. Given the Jewish proclivity for literacy and learning, Jews in any society will aspire to literature when granted the opportunity. The literature they have produced has not been unified in theme or form; they have followed their own paths and obeyed their own muses. From among the hundreds of novels and stories for which these writers are responsible, the best one can do is identify a handful that stand out in one's recollection.

Given the politicized nature of Jewish life everywhere, it is not surprising that some of this literature should be saturated in politics, and of the political novels that bear remembering, I would place E. L. Doctorow's *The Book of Daniel* (1971) at the head of the list. A fable of the 1950s and the wave of anti-Communism that swept America, it is a fictionalized rendering of the arrest, trial, and execution of Julius and Ethel Rosenberg, told from the vantage point of one of the children. (There is also an actual book by the Rosenberg children, Robert and Michael Meeropol, *We Are Your Sons: The Legacy of Julius and Ethel Rosenberg* [1975]). It is a novel that links the radical generations of the 1930s and the 1960s through the figure of Daniel Isaacson, whose parents are executed as spies in the 1950s, and who becomes a radical in the 1960s. What saves the book from being just a novel of protest is Doctorow's fascination with Daniel Isaacson's inner life and the psychic disturbances that afflict him as a result of his orphanage. Doctorow's novel is, I would say, the best of the novels to come out of the Jewish-Left fusion, precisely because Doctorow subordinated his political sentiment to his novelist's instincts and allowed the book to resonate beyond the case at hand.

Another political novel that is of continuing historical interest is Lionel Trilling's *The Middle of the Journey* (1947), in which one of the characters, Gifford Maxim, a blood-and-iron ideologue who has changed ideologies, was fashioned after Whittaker Chambers, whose charge of espionage in the late 1940s against State Department undersecretary Alger Hiss set off one of the most controversial political trials in recent American history. As writing, Trilling's book, a parable of the revolutionary Left in decline, is somewhat wooden, and yet it communicates something of that ideological moment in the postwar era when, to quote Yeats, the best lacked all conviction and the worst were full of passionate intensity.

I do not regard Joseph Heller's celebrated *Catch-22* (1955) as the equal of either of these two novels in either style, political savvy, or intellectual sophistication. Its antic tap dance on the tragedy of war gained a certain cachet in the 1960s, when black humor reflected the mood of an antiwar generation. However, when read apart from that context, *Catch-22* seems to be a whimsical and turgid performance. However, Heller's subsequent novel, *Something Happened* (1974), a domestic novel about the pressures and insecurities of American middle-class life, is a far better book. Its grinding rhythms and density of specification about daily life among the new suburbanites make it far more politically telling than the gallows humor of *Catch-22,* and it can be read as a fictionalized version of C.

Wright Mills's popular sociology text of the 1950s, *White Collar* (1951).

Some noteworthy pieces of shorter fiction can be added to this list. The stories in Tillie Olsen's collection, *Tell Me a Riddle* (1961) are not themselves overtly political, though they are the decay products of a Left sensibility in retreat. A novella by a little-known writer, Meyer Liben, entitled "Justice Hunger" strikes me as a subtle portrait of the depressive mental aftermath of thirties revolutionism. It can be found in *Justice Hunger, and Nine Stories* (1967). Also, Isaac Rosenfeld wrote a brilliant short story entitled "The Party" about the last days of the Trotskyist Socialist Workers Party. It has been reprinted twice, in Isaac Rosenfeld, *Alpha and Omega* (1966), and Mark Shechner, ed., *Preserving the Hunger: An Isaac Rosenfeld Reader* (1988).

It may be, however, that comic writing, pound for pound, substantially outweighs political writing by Jewish novelists since the war. Philip Roth has always had a comic edge, as have Joseph Heller, Saul Bellow, Wallace Markfield, Stanley Elkin, Bruce Jay Friedman, Mordecai Richler, Alan Lelchuk, and Max Apple. For many of them, the Yiddish theater and the Borscht-belt stage were formative cultural influences. A few representative books in which the reader may catch the flavor of this comedy would include Roth's *Portnoy's Complaint* or *The Great American Novel,* Markfield's *Titelbaum's Window* (1970), Elkin's stories in *Criers and Kibitzers, Kibitzer and Criers* (1966) or *The Rabbi of Lud* (1989), Richler's *Joshua Then and Now* (1980), and Max Apple's *The Oranging of America, and Other Stories* (1977). In all of them there is an anarchistic *schadenfreude* that seeks to overthrow every piety, every solemnity, every symbol that in our daily lives we may hold dear. So mutinous and chaotic does this comedy get that Jewish comic novelists might be regarded as revolutionaries who have chosen language as their insurrectionary medium. If they are Marxists, they belong to the Groucho school. Certainly in stable times, their brand of revolutionism has given a lot more pleasure.

Finally, there is the whole middle range of Jewish writing that has not necessarily made a great stir but which has produced over the years some fine books, and for every book I can name here there may be a half dozen others no less deserving that I have yet to read. Some belong to the tradition of the Jewish *Bildungsroman,* the book of growing up and coming of age in America. Herbert Gold's *Fathers: A Novel in the Form of a Memoir* (1966); Mordecai Richler's *St. Urbain's Horseman* (1971), E. L. Doctorow's *World's Fair* (1986), and Alan Lelchuk's *Brooklyn Boy* (1990) are representative novels on that theme. Otherwise, picking and choosing at random, I'd say, read anything by Harold Brodkey, especially the thick collection of a lifetime of story writing, *Stories in an Almost Classical Mode* (1989). Brodkey may be the slowest and most meticulous writer in America, having produced just three collections of stories in some forty years of writing. But he has a delicacy of sensibility and an exactitude of expression that few American writers can match. He is a writer to be read slowly and savored.

I would send you to Leslie Epstein's *King of the Jews*

(1979), a historical novel about the demented patriarch of the Lodz ghetto during the Shoah, "King" Rumkowsky, who played Haman toward his people and fool toward the Nazis, in an apparent effort to buy time for his ghetto and its people. He failed utterly but left behind a legend of rage and confusion, which Epstein captures with great fidelity. Read anything by Mark Helprin, but especially *A Dove of the East, and Other Stories* (1975, 1990) and *Ellis Island, and Other Stories* (1981). And don't miss Art Spiegelman's illustrated book about his father's experiences of the Shoah and life at Auschwitz, *Maus: A Survivor's Tale* (1986), in which the Jews are represented as mice, the Nazis as cats, and the Polish people as pigs. It caused much stir when it first appeared but is considered a landmark publication, now followed by *Maus II* (1991).

This is not a coherent picture of Jewish literary culture in America, which defies all attempts to see it in a unified way. Like our culture itself, our literature has all the internal schism and complexity that we look for in a rich, diverse, and open civilization, which is what Judea in our time has surely become.

LITERATURE OF ALIYAH

One might well conclude from all the foregoing that Jewish writing in America has been largely divorced from normative Judaism and from the myths, the lore, and the consciousness of collective destiny that marked Jewish life in the Old Country, until its unity was shattered in the nineteenth century by the Haskalah or Enlightenment. That is a portion of the truth: the Enlightenment has been the main patrimony of Jewish writers in America, and our literature has been one that largely shuns tradition and seeks new horizons of value and experience. "I am an American, Chicago born," boasts Augie March in the auspicious first line of Saul Bellow's novel.

The full story is more complicated. There have been two lines of sentiment in coexistence as, if you like, thesis and antithesis in a great dialectic of Jewish consciousness: the centrifugal and the centripetal, the outward bound and the inward looking, the line of Haskalah (Enlightenment) and the line of Halakhah (Law), the line of universalism and that of particularism. If the outward bound, inaugurated by Cahan, Yezierska, Gold, Fuchs, and Henry Roth, has been the dominant mode of this century, it was because the circumstances of American life have favored it and the laws of literary success have sponsored it. But the other has always been there in the shadow of its twin, biding its time and awaiting circumstances favorable to its reception. Cynthia Ozick's name has been widely associated with this literature, though she is by no means alone.

Before Ozick, Meyer Levin, who kept a foot in both camps, devoted much of his life after the war and the Holocaust agitating for an American literature of Jewish identity. As a journalist, he was with the troops who liberated concentration camps in Poland. After the war he documented, and filmed, the illegal immigration that moved Jewish refugees from Europe into Palestine and eventually broke the will of the British Mandate. See his autobiography *In Search* (1950). His novel about the days of the Yishuv in Palestine, *The Settlers* (1972), might be thought of as his effort to do for Israel what in *The Old Bunch* he had done for Chicago: write a novel of origins. Other writers devoted to Jewish consciousness during the 1920s and 1930s were Ludwig Lewisohn, whose autobiographies, *Upstream* (1927) and *Mid-Channel: An American Chronicle* (1929), are of more interest than his novels, *The Case of Mr. Crump* (1926) and *The Island Within* (1928), and Maurice Samuel, a popular journalist and champion of Jewish causes, whose books about the Zionist movement, the establishment of Israel, and the Yiddish language and literature retain their freshness long after his fiction has gone out of print. See in particular *The Gentleman and the Jew* (1952), *Harvest in the Desert* (1944), and *The World of Sholom Aleichem* (1943).

The problem with all three as writers, however, was that they were journalists and advocates first and moved all too easily from advocacy to fiction, employing the latter as an extension of the former. If, in the twentieth century, it is the literature of Jewish universalism that earns so much more cachet among American readers, it is not simply because it arouses less tension and is more easily assimilated by most Americans. It is also, in the main, just better written.

Things are changing, and there are writers devoted to the religious life and national destiny of the Jewish people who are devoted to their craft. Cynthia Ozick is surely the only disciple of Henry James to ever declare for the Jewish Covenant with God, but there are a host of others for whom Jewish identity has been central: the late Edward Lewis Wallant, the late Arthur A. Cohen, Chaim Potok, E. M. Broner, Hugh Nissenson, Anne Roiphe, Rhoda Lehrman, Jay Neugeboren, Susan Fromberg Schaeffer, Tova Reich, Steve Stern, and Rebecca Goldstein, to name but a few. For all, the devotion to Jewish identity has been crucial, and while one would be hard pressed to find a single article of belief uniting them all, their writing constitutes a testament of collective identity, prompting me to call it a literature of Aliyah, to distinguish it from the literature of the Haskalah, to which it is sharply opposed. As the term *Aliyah* suggests, this is a literature of return, since the vast bulk of it is motivated by a desire to be reconnected to Jewish existence by writers who started out as Enlightenment Jews and had to forge a connection on their own. Some of it is conversion literature, which is in itself problematic, since there is no ready-made way to return to customs and beliefs one has never had, and it is often the drama of repossessing a lost history that is enacted in these books.

A recent instance is Anne Roiphe's *Lovingkindness* (1987), in which a middle-aged Jewish mother, with a secular Left-liberal upbringing, is confronted with a daughter who discovers Orthodox Judaism in Israel, changes her name from Andrea to Sarai, and accepts an arranged marriage to a young man from Detroit who has had a similar conversion. When the young man's parents stage a kidnapping of their son to restore him to "normality," the woman is faced with a choice between her own brand of secular, open-ended Judaism and her daughter's covenanted life. Her decision to make peace with her daughter's life is not so much an endorsement of halakhic Juda-

ism as it is a statement of her own liberal principal: live and let live.

Roiphe's novel calls to mind the Judea chapter in Philip Roth's *The Counterlife,* in which Nathan Zuckerman visits his brother Henry in a fundamentalist kibbutz in Israel. Henry, having taken the name of Hanoch, has apprenticed himself to one Mordecai Lippman, a gun-toting radical settler with messianic plans for the Judea: to drive out the Arabs. Henry has made a fundamentalist conversion; Nathan remains staunch in his diaspora cosmopolitanism. The stand-off between the brothers highlights the tension in Jewish consciousness that has been sharpened of late by the reawakening of Orthodox Judaism and prophetic fundamentalism to an eminence undreamed of by the Labor-Zionist founders of Israel.

By no means, however, is the literature of Aliyah necessarily conversion literature. Much of it is an effort to draw upon Jewish myth and lore for an alternative vision of reality, and writers like Arthur A. Cohen, Steve Stern, and Ozick have found ways to reframe biblical and hasidic stories as commentaries on modern problems and events. Cohen, in *In the Days of Simon Stern* (1973), blends a Messiah legend into an American fable of social mobility, as his would-be savior of the Jews, Simon Stern, is a self-made millionaire who devotes his riches to a compound on New York's Lower East Side, a sort of Third Temple, to house the remnant of European Jews who have survived the Holocaust. The scheme goes badly, the temple is destroyed, and Simon Stern, reflecting on the cyclical nature of history, vows to rebuild it. Stern himself is not just a Jewish philanthropist, he is a *lamed vov zaddik,* one of the thirty-six hidden saints for whose sake the world continues to exist, and his fortunes are being chronicled by a blind scribe, one Nathan of Gaza, who shares a name with the prophet of the false Messiah of the seventeenth century, Sabbatai Zvi. *In the Days of Simon Stern* is an ambitious effort to bring traditional lore to bear on the Holocaust and the theological problem it raises for believing Jews: the silence of God and the tarrying of the Messiah. It is, unfortunately, a dense and difficult book, a philosophical tract strung out along a narrative frame in which there is scarcely a moment of irony or humor or a fresh line of dialogue. However, it did suggest a methodology for Jewish fiction: the mythic or midrashic technique, though its refinement would await more skilled practitioners. For more by Cohen, see especially his novel *A Hero in His Time* (1976).

More resourceful as fiction, if less ambitious as philosophy, are the stories of Steve Stern in *Lazar Malkin Enters Heaven* (1986). Stern, whose injection of visionary moments into common lives recalls the stories of Bruno Schulz, is a miniaturist whose parables of Jewish life in "The Pinch," a Jewish community in Memphis, Tennessee, bring the *shtetl* to the Mississippi and the landscape of Hasidism to the American neighborhood. In the title story, "Lazar Malkin Enters Heaven," the Angel of Death drags Lazar Malkin off into a heaven that looks exactly like a backyard only "sensitive." In "Schimmele Fly-by-Night," a young boy in conflict with his father awakens from his first spree of drinking to find himself borne aloft by birds, as if grubby pigeons might be angels. It is all quite brisk and vivacious if also rather formulaic—yoking ancient and modern to gain perspective by incongruity. But it is a formula deftly applied; here are worlds brought together with charm and brio.

The mythic technique has been exploited most fully by Cynthia Ozick, whose stories and novels since her early confrontation with modernism, *Trust: A Novel* (1983), have been excursions into "the midrashic method," narrative commentary on social situations or holy texts. Since issues of conduct and value invariably occupy Ozick, her fiction has the insistent quality of moral fable and admonition. In a famous manifesto, "Toward a New Yiddish," she argued that the only Jewish literature ever in diaspora that had any staying power was literature that was "centrally Jewish," by which she meant "whatever touches on the liturgical," ("Toward a New Yiddish," *Art & Ardor: Essays* [1985]), and it is plain that she has herself endeavored to be "centrally Jewish" and to create a fiction of liturgical significance.

Much of her best writing is in the short stories and novellas found in three collections: *The Pagan Rabbi, and Other Stories* (1971); *Bloodshed, and Three Novellas* (1976); and *Levitation* (1983). There one sees the midrashic method in incisive miniature. Sometimes the subject is Jewish life and culture itself, as in Ozick's most famous story, "Envy; or, Yiddish in America" (in *The Pagan Rabbi*) in which the rage and envy felt by a neglected and obscure Yiddish writer toward one who is world-famous in translation is a poignant reminder of one consequence of the Holocaust: the death of Yiddish and the isolation of its writers. That the envied writer, Yankel Ostrover, was plainly modeled on Isaac Bashevis Singer and that the other writer, Edelstein, was a composite of several living Yiddish writers is no small part of the notoriety the story has long enjoyed.

Another story in which the midrashic devices are more apparent is Ozick's modern golem story, "Puttermesser and Xanthippe," in *Levitation*. Drawing upon the legend of the golem created by Rabbi Loew to save the Jews of Seventeenth-century Prague, Ozick invents Puttermesser (Yiddish for butter knife), a woman and "an unmarried lawyer and civil servant of forty-six" who, out of frustrated desires and messianic longings, fashions a female golem, Xanthippe, from the dirt around her houseplants. First merely a domestic slave and then a political aide, Xanthippe goads Puttermesser into running for mayor of New York and into thinking of herself as the city's redeemer. Xanthippe, alas, quickly becomes a monster of excess, political and sexual, and must finally be destroyed. The story is a many-layered parable into which we may read a host of morals: power corrupts; "too much paradise is greed" (one of Ozick's own tag lines); keep your appetites on a short leash; pure reason is not enough in human affairs; don't hurry the Messiah. Moreover, there is a morality built into the method itself and its implicit argument that the dilemmas of humankind are unchanging and that Jewish lore and law may still cast light on basic issues of value.

Ozick's problem as a fiction writer is that she places no value upon aesthetic delight; literature for her is a moral form and "with certain rapturous exceptions, literature is

the moral life" (*Art & Ardor*). She composes homiletic texts with specifically Jewish morals, and on occasion has condemned the "iconic" as opposed to the moral weight of modern writing, even going so far as to call Wordsworth's "Tintern Abbey" Moloch. Gratefully, at times, her instinctual writer's wisdom knows when the prohibition against the aesthetic won't do, and she can write with a combination of ethical assertion and verbal attack that is virtually without parallel in American literature. However, unlike any other major writer in America, she does not define herself as an entertainer, and readers are challenged to take her on her own implacable terms. In particular, the longer fictions make demands on the reader, who is never invited to relax with them. It is said of her books, especially the intricate and overbearing *Trust,* that they reward study more than they reward reading, and while that may be harsh, it does suggest something of Ozick's exacting requirements of her readers.

Two recent novels are cases in point: *The Messiah of Stockholm* (1988) and *The Shawl* (1989). The former, a parable on literature and idolatry, features a man's search for the lost manuscript of Bruno Schulz's last book entitled *The Messiah,* which disappeared during the war after Schulz was murdered by a Nazi officer, and his manuscript, left with friends for safekeeping, was lost. It is being sought by one Lars Andemening, a deluded book reviewer living in Stockholm who dreams himself to be the son of Schulz. He is presented with something that purports to be the manuscript by book dealers who may or may not be swindling him, and in a rage he sets the manuscript afire and burns it. The novel is difficult to follow; its plot line as tangled as a bird's nest and as murky as a Swedish fog. What stays with the reader is the lesson: the cost to civilization of all the lost books, the hundreds, perhaps the thousands, that disappeared with the murder of writers. A second, subtler point, has to do with the idolatry of texts. The manuscript is an idol which does not draw Andemening toward God, toward other humans, or toward moral awareness, but only deeper into his delusion of being Schulz's son. It is an icon, a grail, which Ozick has repeatedly warned us against. The very same moral is drawn more painfully in *The Shawl,* in which a Holocaust survivor, Rosa Lublin, has invested all of her life's energy into the shawl of her daughter, who was murdered before her eyes in a concentration camp. Retired in Florida, she is a bitter recluse obsessed with the shawl, which has been left behind in New York. What she must learn is that the shawl, like Andemening's *Messiah,* is an idol that stands between her and life and that in the very act of cherishing the memory of the dead, she has denied the living: herself and those who have attempted to draw close to her.

In spite of, or possibly even because of, her moral demands upon her readers and her insistence that those demands are based in Jewish tradition, Ozick has come to symbolize those pressures in Jewish life that point the way back from the margins toward the center, even if her version of the center may be no less eccentric than anyone else's these days. For that reason, one needs to approach her through her essays, for though she frequently denies that her polemics are in any way guides to her fiction, no reader of her fiction can afford to be in the dark about the morality of reading that she has sought to sponsor in our literary culture at large. For that, see Ozick's *Art & Ardor,* cited earlier, and *Metaphor and Memory* (1989). See also the novel not discussed in this essay, *The Cannibal Galaxy* (1984).

This dialectic is far from played out, and there is reason to think that the tension out of which it springs is permanent, a given of the Jewish condition. The Jewish past is too fragmented, too various to ever be put back together into a single tradition. The schismatic is now the normal, and all the old doctrines are in disarray, the doctrines of emancipation as well as those of commitment. For the moment all we can see is that Jewish writers feel more powerfully than ever about their identities as Jews; that for them the search for the way is the way itself and that the tension between their restlessness and their commitment may not only be the root of their literary dynamism but arguably the very essence of the Jewishness they seek.

Richard Tuerk

SOURCE: "Jewish-American Literature," in *Ethnic Perspectives in American Literature: Selected Essays on the European Contribution,* edited by Robert J. DiPietro and Edward Ifkovic, The Modern Language Association of America, 1983, pp. 133-62.

[*In the following essay, Tuerk presents a historical overview of Jewish-American literature in the twentieth century.*]

In an essay entitled "The Jew as Modern American Writer" (1966), Alfred Kazin writes: "Definitely, it was now the thing to be Jewish." And in a book published in 1969, Donald L. Kaufman writes that in America, "the new look in postwar writing is Jewish." In an introduction published the next year, Charles Angoff and Meyer Levin declare: "To 'write Jewish' is in fashion." When viewed in a historical perspective, these statements are startling. As recently as 1944, Lionel Trilling proclaimed that "as the Jewish community now exists, it can give no sustenance to the American artist or intellectual who is born a Jew." But as Irving Malin and Irwin Stark point out in the introduction to *Breakthrough* (1964), "circumstances have radically changed"; a group of Jewish-American authors has "broken through" into the mainstream of American literature and become "an important, possibly even a major reformative influence in American life and letters." Yet, as Abraham Chapman observes in the introduction to his anthology, *Jewish-American Literature* (1974), until very recently in America, the Jewish author "has been viewed as an alien in the prevailing American culture unless the writing had nothing to do with Jews or anything Jewish."

Of course, all these statements oversimplify somewhat. In addition, all contain problems of definition; for example, exactly what do these writers mean when they use the word "Jew," and what does "Jewish-American" mean in the phrase "Jewish-American literature"? Although these questions may appear trivial, they are of the utmost importance to those who write about and teach Jewish-American—and, indeed, American—literature.

Before discussing Jewish-American literature, we must try to arrive at a workable definition of the word "Jew." According to Orthodox Jewish tradition, a Jew is anyone born of a Jewish mother or anyone formally converted to Judaism. Yet even this definition presents problems for the teacher of literature. Are persons who have converted away from Judaism still Jews? Large segments of the Gentile world would consider them Jews, as great numbers of converts in Europe discovered during the Hitler era. In America in the last quarter of the twentieth century, however, where total assimilation seems possible, the old saying "Once a Jew, always a Jew" no longer seems true. Instead, the word "Jew" now seems for many people to imply conscious choice. Abraham Chapman classifies as a Jew anyone of Jewish descent or any person who considers himself or herself a Jew. In his anthology of Jewish-American literature Chapman includes works by Bret Harte and Denise Levertov, the former because he had a Jewish grandfather and the latter because her father converted from Judaism and became an Anglican priest. Harte's and Levertov's ancestry would undoubtedly lead many non-Jews to call those two writers Jews. For purposes of this essay, anyone is a Jew who, as a result of either birth or conversion, whether formal or informal, *considers* himself or herself a Jew. Although, as we shall see, in connection with literature this definition probably presents as many problems as any other definition, it does give us something to work with.

Next, how do we define "Jewish-American literature"? Essentially, it is, of course, literature written by American Jews; it does not have to deal specifically with the ethnic dimension. There are many writers like J. D. Salinger whose writings rarely reflect their Jewishness. But, given the limitations of space, I have concerned myself with those works by American Jews who seem particularly or consciously concerned with their Jewishness. I recognize that even this perspective is insufficient and troublesome, for what happens to a work like *An American Dream,* by Norman Mailer? Mailer is a Jew (in a series of reviews in *Commentary,* he calls himself a "non-Jewish Jew"), and his main character, Stephen Rojack, is "half Jewish," whatever that means. Rojack's ascendance over the Irish Catholic Kennedy involves a definite ethnic dimension, but, except for mentioning that he is "descended from peddlers," Rojack's Jewishness (or lack of Jewishness) is minimally developed. Then again, even though essays have been written about, say, the Jewishness of Saul Bellow's novel *Henderson the Rain King,* the book still has no Jews in it. If we looked at Jewish-American literature as that which is in some way *consciously concerned* with the authors' Jewishness, recognizing that this is an abbreviated perspective, perhaps we can understand its success and examine the impact this extensive body of literature has made on American literary history and culture.

The works that fit into this category as we have defined it have certain tendencies in common. In their introduction to *Breakthrough,* Malin and Stark summarize these tendencies: "the American-Jewish writer has approached the divine by seeking to make his way to what is most human"; he searches "in the Old Country or New, in the image of the father or in the discoverable if unrecoverable past." Sometimes, "he violently assaults the corrupt values of his society, endeavors to mediate between the dualities which divide him from himself, recognizes suffering as the necessary condition of compassion, insists on the sanctity of life or—in the face of man's alienation from man as well as from God—reasserts . . . the centrality of love, in the reconstruction of the social order." These, then, are some of the central concerns of the authors of Jewish-American literature.

JEWS IN AMERICA

During the second half of the twentieth century, a large proportion of the major authors in American literature have been Jewish Americans, and many of their books have dealt with explicitly Jewish concerns, but this, as I have indicated, was not always so. Although Jews have been present in this nation continuously since before the Revolution, only recently have they begun to have a great impact on American literature. The first identifiable Jew in North America, Elias Legardo, came to Virginia in 1621. The first group of Jews arrived in New Amsterdam in 1654. They were fleeing from Brazil, which had just been taken over by Portugal, and the Portuguese had followed their usual practice of expelling all Jews who would not convert to Christianity. Because the Jews had fled originally from Spain and Portugal to Holland and from there had gone to parts of Brazil then under Dutch control, they naturally sought refuge in Dutch possessions. Most moved to the Dutch West Indies, but twenty-three sailed to New Amsterdam. Although Peter Stuyvesant did not want Jews settling there, the directors of the Dutch West India Company allowed them to stay. Of course, Jews have been present in New Amsterdam, later New York, ever since.

By 1776 about 2,500 Jews lived in America. Until about 1729 most of the Jews in North America were of Sephardic—that is, Spanish and Portuguese—descent. And even in 1852, when Henry Wadsworth Longfellow wrote his poem, "The Jewish Cemetery at Newport," names like Abraham Alvares and Jacob Rivera were typical of American Jews. In 1830 there were only about 6,000 Jews in America, but by 1880 the number had grown to 250,000, largely as a result of large-scale immigration of German Jews. The defeat of Napoleon, who had done much to emancipate European Jewry, and the failure of the Revolution of 1848 caused many German Jews to come to this country and establish Jewish institutions here. The largest wave of immigrants, however, came between about 1881 and 1924, the period of the great migration, when approximately 2,750,000 Jews moved from Eastern Europe to the United States. Many fled from persecution, discrimination, and pogroms. Others sought economic and political equality and opportunity as well as religious freedom. Part of the group called the "new immigrants," these Eastern European Jews are the ancestors of about ninety percent of the Jews in America today.

The passage of restrictive immigration legislation in the early 1920s started to have a profound effect in 1924, and the waves of Jewish immigrants slowed to a trickle. Nonetheless, by 1924 the center of world Jewish culture had shifted from Europe to America.

EARLY JEWISH-AMERICAN LITERATURE

No identifiable body of Jewish-American literature existed before the beginning of the twentieth century. Although several Jews wrote creative works, especially plays and poems, their writings are for the most part indistinguishable from works by non-Jews. Jewish authors before the twentieth century include Samuel B. H. Judah, Jonas B. Phillips, Isaac Harby, and Mordecai Manuel Noah. The most outstanding of these is Noah, who, although he tried to establish a Jewish state on Grand Island in the Niagara River, did not allow his plays to reflect his Jewishness. Penina Moise and Adah Isaacs Menken were nineteenth-century American Jews who wrote verse, and their verse did reflect their Jewishness. But even though Menken's verse reached a fairly large audience, she hardly achieved the distinction of Emma Lazarus, who was the only truly outstanding Jewish author before the turn of the century.

Lazarus was born in 1849. Her family traced its roots to pre-Revolutionary America. She avoided Jewish themes in her early work. But her meetings with Jewish immigrants who had fled persecution in Eastern Europe, her knowledge of the pogroms in Russia, and the publication of George Eliot's *Daniel Deronda* (1876) stirred Lazarus into asserting her Jewish identity in spite of her relatives' pleas that she not do so. As Sol Liptzin puts it, she was "shocked into dynamic activity by the suffering of Jews who had been victimized solely because of their Jewishness." Her most famous poem is, of course, "The New Colossus" (1883), which is inscribed on the pedestal of the Statue of Liberty. Allen Guttmann considers Lazarus "Too derivative to be considered a major poet," but he says that "her passionate return to an identification with her ancestors makes her a forerunner of others who responded similarly to pogroms and . . . to the catastrophic exterminations of the 1940s." Guttman hails her volume of 1882, *Songs of a Semite,* as America's "first important work of Jewish poetry."

It was, however, the new immigrants and their children who began what we today think of as Jewish-American literature. In their accounts—both fiction and nonfiction—of their lives in the Old World, their journeys to the New World, and their problems adapting to life in America are to be found the material out of which modern Jewish-American literature grew. Most of these works remain period pieces, mere curiosities for the student of American literature or American culture. Several, however, give profound insight into the problems Jews faced in trying to adjust to the new culture they found in America. Some, like Mary Antin's autobiographical volume, *The Promised Land* (1912), may be read as songs in praise of assimilation. Others, like Abraham Cahan's classic immigrant novel, *The Rise of David Levinsky* (1917), seriously question the assimilationist ethic.

In *The Promised Land,* Antin explicitly uses the biblical Exodus as the structuring metaphor for her own journey from Russia to Boston. America is her promised land, and, to her, that promise lies in assimilation. In America, she was "made over"; as an American, she experienced a "second birth." In the concluding paragraph of her book, she declares: "The endless ages have indeed throbbed through my blood, but a new rhythm dances in my veins," and she adds: "America is the youngest of the nations and inherits all that went before in history. And I am the youngest of America's children, and into my hands is given all her priceless heritage. . . . Mine is the whole majestic past, and mine is the shining future." She no longer feels that she is in exile; America is her Jerusalem. Just as she herself has, she thinks, become thoroughly assimilated into American life, she feels that all other immigrants can and should do the same.

But for many, the price of assimilation—giving up one's religion, one's language (usually Yiddish), and one's ties to one's point of origin—was too high. Many Jewish immigrants still felt themselves to be in exile even in America. And for them Antin's promised land was a place where they continued to eat the bread of affliction. One of those who seriously weighed the losses against the gains was Abraham Cahan. Born in 1860, just outside Vilna, Cahan received a secular education in Russia before he came to America in 1882, at the beginning of the waves of immigrants who were to change the face of Jewish America. He became active in union and socialist activities and helped organize the *Jewish Daily Forward,* a Yiddish-language newspaper begun in 1897; he became its editor in 1902 and held that position until his death in 1951. That he should have questioned the ethic of assimilation is ironic, for through his column, "A Bintel Brief," in the *Forward,* he hastened the Americanization and eventual assimilation of countless Jews. Even though he could hardly have been called religious, he expressed outrage at the idea of a Jewish family's having a Christmas tree, but he also assured worried Jewish parents that playing baseball would not hurt their sons. In fact, he praised this American sport because it got the children outdoors and helped keep them healthy. In "A Bintel Brief," Cahan obviously saw his role as trying to enable his fellow Jews to come to grips with the day-to-day problems that beset them in America, and for them, Americanization seemed the best answer. Nonetheless, in his more serious literary work—his fiction—Cahan made it clear that he was not so sure.

As early as 1896, when he published *Yekl: A Tale of the New York Ghetto,* Cahan questioned whether Jews gained more than they lost when they embraced the American ethic with its premium on material goods. Even this early in his career he wondered whether the Old Country ways might not have been better. In the title story of *The Imported Bridegroom and Other Stories of the New York Ghetto* (1898) Old and New World values clash directly; New World values win, but as a result, everyone is unhappy.

It is in his masterpiece, *The Rise of David Levinsky* (1917), that Cahan examines most thoroughly the effects of the desire for assimilation. Levinsky grows up in Antomir in Russia. His poor but pious mother wants nothing more than to see her son become a talmudic scholar. But when David comes home after an encounter in which some Gentile children rolling Easter eggs split his lip and tear off his cap, she runs into the street screaming that she is going to kill the boy who hurt her son. Fifteen minutes later she is carried home, mortally wounded; she dies the same eve-

ning. After continuing his talmudic studies and receiving board from various members of the community, David comes to America. Like Mary Antin, David says that his arrival in the New World was "like a second birth" in which he entered "a new world in the profoundest sense of the word." In America, Levinsky quickly loses his devotion to Judaism: he shaves off his beard, cuts his sidelocks, stops studying the Talmud, and develops a desire, never fulfilled, to study at New York's City College. Instead, like so many real-life Jewish immigrants, he goes into the garment business, first as a worker and then as a manufacturer. He becomes tremendously successful, but he is unhappy. Accordingly, he concludes his narrative by confessing:

> I don't seem to be able to get accustomed to my luxurious life. I am always more or less conscious of my good clothes, of the high quality of my office furniture, of the power I wield over the men in my pay. . . . I still have a lurking fear of restaurant waiters.

> I can never forget the days of my misery. I cannot escape from my old self. My past and my present do not comport well. David, the poor lad swinging over a Talmud volume at the Preacher's synagogue, seems to have more in common with my inner identity than David Levinsky, the well-known cloak manufacturer.

Neither wholly an American nor wholly a Jew, David ends in a kind of no-man's-land without any identity that he can understand.

Between the extremes of assimilation, as achieved by Antin and sought by Levinsky, and alienation, which involves total refusal to accommodate oneself in any way to one's new home, lies acculturation, a kind of middle ground that enables one to remain a Jew, even a "good" Jew, and still be an American. In *The Rise of David Levinsky,* the Kaplans represent this middle position. Their American-born son Ruby studies the Talmud, and when Ruby reads the Talmud in Hebrew and interprets it in Yiddish, David is reminded of himself at age eleven when he read the Talmud while his mother beamed exactly as Mrs. Kaplan beams at Ruby. Mr. Kaplan even reminds David that "One has to be a Jew," advice that David does not heed.

The drive for assimilation or even for acculturation becomes a central issue in Jewish-American literature during the twentieth century. For some Jewish authors and Jewish characters, being a Jew seems to be unpleasant; they flee in horror from their ethnic and religious identity, or they describe their fellow Jews as crass, vulgar, materialistic, and ugly. Authors who fit into this category are often labeled self-hating Jews or even anti-Semitic Jews. Such labels, however, may often be misleading, and their use by critics may be even more misleading. Among authors who have perhaps rightfully been given these labels is Montague Glass, whose *Potash and Perlmutter* (1910) humorously treats two partners in the garment industry whose lives consist of a series of shady deals and narrow escapes. Yet I doubt that readers of this book in the second half of the twentieth century find it nearly as offensive as

Jewish readers of the first half of the century found it. True, its characters are, for the most part, unpleasant, and their desire to make deals and get money plays on negative stereotypes. But a genuine friendship develops between Potash and Perlmutter, with each for the most part willing to take considerable risks for the other. Another author who at least in one phase of his career seems to deserve these labels is Ben Hecht, who in the beginning of his novel, *A Jew in Love* (1931), wrote of "Jew faces in which race leers and burns like some biological disease." But Hecht later became an outspoken Zionist and defender of the Jews.

In fact, the list of authors who have been accused of putting their "Jewish self-hate" on paper at times reads like an honor roll of Jewish-American authors: Abraham Cahan, Meyer Levin, Ludwig Lewisohn, Herbert Gold, Irving Howe, Alfred Kazin, Louis Untermeyer, Philip Roth, and even Isaac Bashevis Singer. As many critics are now recognizing and as several recognized even before 1920, whenever a Jewish writer describes Jews realistically, he or she is liable to be accused of being a Jewish anti-Semite. The usual argument runs that it would be fine to write realistic fiction in Yiddish and not allow it to be translated into English, but to write in English or to permit such works to be translated into English allows Gentiles to see them, thus making the author into an anti-Semite who wants to destroy the image of the Jew in the eyes of non-Jews. In *A Young Man in Search of Love* (1978), one of his autobiographical volumes, Singer presents a variation on this theme when he tells of his editor's saying to him:

> Why write about thieves and whores when there were so many decent Jewish men and devoted Jewish wives? If such a thing were translated into Polish and a gentile read it, he might conclude that all Jews were depraved. A Yiddish writer . . . was honor-bound to stress the good in our people, the lofty and sacred. He had to be an eloquent defender of the Jews, not their defamer.

Similar questions have been asked of Jewish authors in America by their fellow Jews who possibly see in realistic accounts of Jews with both good and bad points a threat to their own precarious position in the United States. These attacks tend to have no relation to time and space; even though they may occur sixty years apart, the charges and the responses to them tend to be the same.

The defenders of the realistic works point out that the Jewish author has just as much right as any other author to portray people in all of their complexity and that a treatment of an evil or bad Jewish character in fiction will make no one but the already committed anti-Semite think that all Jews are bad or evil. They also, at times, point out that the critics, by seeing the work as a condemnation of Judaism and Jews, are often misreading the piece of literature. Two fairly recent examples are Budd Schulberg's novel *What Makes Sammy Run?* (1941) and Philip Roth's short story "Defender of the Faith" (1959). Both stories have been condemned because they have unpleasant characters: in the former, Sammy Glick, who among other things runs from his Jewishness; in the latter, Sheldon

Grossbart, who uses his Jewishness to get special favors for himself. What the negative critics overlook is that neither Glick nor Grossbart sets the moral standards in the stories, and neither is necessarily the central character in the work. In fact, the moral standards are in each work set by the narrator: Al Manheim in Schulberg's book and Nathan Marx in Roth's story. Neither of these characters actively renounces his Judaism; in fact, Marx is reembracing it. And these two may be the central characters in these two works.

Another important aspect of early Jewish-American literature is Yiddish drama. Although Yiddish theater still exists in America, its heyday is long past. Though it served primarily to provide an escape for Jewish-American immigrants from their daily drudgery, Yiddish theater nonetheless helped introduce some to the ways and customs of America and provided to a limited extent some genuine works of art for its audiences. In spite of some American settings, however, the dramas for the most part, critics agree, lie in the tradition of European Yiddish theater rather than Jewish-American literature. In fact, one scholar asserts, "Yiddish literature in substance is *purely* Jewish" and adds, "Geographically, Yiddish literature is in two parts, Russian and American, but these two parts developed into one aim; even the plots and themes are from the old country; the aim was for Yiddish literature to stand independently and self-sustaining among the literatures of the world." This same scholar feels that when Yiddish literature became aware of "world struggles in politics, economics, problems of other religious and ethnic groups," when "an involvement with desolation in a world bereft of morality and justice, infiltrated Yiddish literature," it "became anemic." Nonetheless, the Yiddish theater in America was so popular from before the turn of the century to World War I that something about it must be included here.

Abraham Goldfaden is regarded as the father of modern Yiddish theater. Born in the Ukraine in 1840, he began his acting career in the plays given at Purim time, performances believed to be descended from the simple plays that used to dramatize the Book of Esther. He later modeled the early shows he produced on his experiences in the Purim entertainments. For a while he worked with the Broder Singers in Romania, but soon engaged his own actors and singers and formed a troupe that toured Russia and Romania.

In 1883 a Russian edict prohibited the performance of Yiddish plays, so Yiddish theater companies moved, first to countries near Russia and eventually westward, often first to London and then to the United States, where they found large Yiddish-speaking communities eager for entertainment in their native tongue. In 1887 Goldfaden was invited by some of his actors to join them in New York City, but when he got there, he found such severe competition from established producers and scriptwriters that he went back to Europe. He returned to the United States in 1903, however, and remained until his death in 1908.

In the meantime, Yiddish theater flourished in cities like Cleveland, Detroit, Chicago, Philadelphia, and especially New York. The first Yiddish production in New York was probably *The Selling of Joseph,* put on by an amateur group in the 1860s. In August 1882 the first professional performance of a Yiddish play in America probably took place. Among the actors was Boris Thomashefsky, born in the Ukraine in 1868. Even though he was young, he is supposed to have been instrumental in getting the players invited to America. Before the turn of the century Thomashefsky was running the People's Theater. He wrote original plays and adapted others like *Hamlet* (1893) and *Richard III* (1895) for the Yiddish stage. In 1912 he built the National Theater in New York, where Yiddish drama flourished until after his death in 1939.

By the early years of the twentieth century the "golden epoch" of Yiddish theater in America had begun. At first, the Yiddish shows appealed to sentimentality. The plays depended on *zingen un tantsen* (singing and dancing); used stock comedy situations, often with American settings; and allowed the actors to improvise as they saw fit. Still, several producers tried to introduce artistry into Yiddish theater. They encouraged Yiddish writers and, like Thomashefsky, translated works from other languages, usually adapting them for the Yiddish stage. The most famous play of this sort is Jacob Gordin's *Yiddish King Lear,* produced in 1892 with Jacob Adler, the matinee idol, in the leading role.

In 1918 Ukrainian-born Maurice Schwartz started in New York City the Jewish Art Theater, dedicated to producing artistically excellent dramas. The Jewish Art Theater lasted until 1950. An attempt to revive it in 1955 failed. After trying unsuccessfully to make motion pictures, Schwartz went to Israel hoping to establish a Yiddish art center, but he died in 1960, two months after opening in *Yoshe Kalb,* a play that he had earlier adapted from I. J. Singer's novel of that name.

The most important figure in the American Yiddish theater and one of the most important figures in world Yiddish theater is Jacob Gordin. Born in the Ukraine in 1853, he fled Russia for political reasons and arrived in America in 1891. Although before he came to America he had never written in Yiddish and never written a play, during about eighteen years of activity he supplied the Yiddish theater with almost eighty plays. Most were adaptations and translations in which he introduced natural Yiddish in place of Germanized dialogue and demanded that his actors stick to the scripts. Several of his plays are considered of lasting value, including *God, Man and Devil* (1900) and the previously mentioned *Yiddish King Lear.*

Other prolific playwrights include Moshe Hurwitz and Joseph Lateiner, who between them wrote about 180 mostly sentimental plays. Leon Kobrin wrote over thirty plays, including realistic dramas that try to give a faithful picture of life in America at the turn of the century.

The most outstanding works of Yiddish literature for the stage were written not in America, however, but in Eastern Europe. Sholem Asch's *God of Vengeance* was first produced in 1907, before he came to America. And the most famous and probably best Yiddish play is *The Dybbuk* by S. An-Ski, a pseudonym for Solomon Zainwill Rapoport, who died thirty days before his play was first produced, on 9 December 1920 by the Vilna Troupe. Both these plays remain powerful on the stage today, and both are available in paperback. With its emphasis on spirituality and its exorcism scene, *The Dybbuk* is especially moving.

By World War I the Jewish population of the Lower East Side of New York City was beginning to move away, and many younger Jews were unfamiliar with Yiddish. Thus, the Yiddish theaters in New York and elsewhere were losing their audiences. The theaters began to close. Even though Maurice Schwartz, as previously noted, kept his theater open until 1950, the golden epoch was past. Occasionally Yiddish plays are still produced in New York City and elsewhere, especially on university campuses, and as recently as 1968 Yiddish actors derived income from engagements at holiday resorts during the summers. But for the most part, Yiddish theater no longer functions as a living, vital force in America.

JEWISH-AMERICAN LITERATURE BETWEEN THE WARS

During the 1920s and 1930s Jewish life in America became increasingly complex as various pressures, both internal and external, were exerted on the Jewish-American community. As Sol Liptzin puts it, "Jewish life increased in complexity and difficulty even while the environmental forces of assimilation kept nibbling away at Jewish essence." And he adds that anti-Semitism, "which could formerly be dismissed as a mild irritant, began to take on virile forms as poisonous Nazi doctrines drifted across the Atlantic." Liptzin, of course, oversimplifies here. During the period before the Nazi takeover of Germany, many authors could not and did not dismiss anti-Semitism as a "mild irritant." Especially during the 1920s, many American authors responded with dismay to the anti-Semitism they found in America.

Born in Russia in 1882 and reared in the Midwest, Elias Tobenkin, a relatively minor author, questions the possibility of acculturation for Jews in an America that was, he felt, becoming increasingly anti-Semitic. Although in his first novel, *Witte Arrives* (1916), he espouses the ethic of the melting pot, in his third novel, *God of Might* (1925), he mirrors the bewilderment of a lot of American Jews who had begun to think that the doctrine of the melting pot involved not acculturation but complete assimilation, including giving up one's Jewishness altogether. In the first novel, Witte finally arrives when he decides that religious and ethnic differences are unimportant and that he will marry a Gentile of New England stock. In *God of Might,* the central character, Samuel Waterman, does marry a Gentile, only to discover that both small town America, where he lives, and big city America, in which he seeks refuge, demand either complete assimilation, including conversion, or total alienation of the Jew. In the course of his attempts to fulfill what he believes to be the American dream of individual freedom, Samuel discovers discrimination against Jews in banks, schools, universities, hotels, and apartment houses. He also becomes painfully aware of the anti-Semitism of Henry Ford and of the Ku Klux Klan.

Ludwig Lewisohn is probably the foremost chronicler of

American anti-Semitism before the 1930s. In his autobiographical volumes, *Up Stream* (1922) and *Mid-Channel* (1929), he describes his own struggles against anti-Semitism. Born in Berlin in 1882, Lewisohn came to America when he was seven years old. His family settled in South Carolina, where Lewisohn was brought up a Methodist. When he went to Columbia University to do graduate work, however, he discovered that the rest of the world did not care what he considered himself; the rest of the world considered him a Jew. Deprived of a graduate assistantship and of a job teaching English literature because he was a Jew (not until he was sixty did he get such a position, and that was at Brandeis University), Lewisohn found a job teaching German at a midwestern university. In his autobiographical volumes he describes his disillusionment with academic life, with the Midwest, and with American life in general; more important for our purposes, he describes his growing acceptance of and finally his love for his identity as a Jew.

In Jewishness Lewisohn eventually found all kinds of positive values. His final affirmation of his identity as a Jew was expressed through his espousal of Zionism; in his writing it is expressed in his novel *The Island Within* (1928), largely the story of Arthur Levy, a New York-born descendant of Jews who moved from Eastern Europe through Germany and eventually to America. Arthur and his sister Hazel experience repeated difficulties because of their lack of a firm Jewish identity, and in his profession as a psychiatrist, Arthur sees extreme examples of what Lewisohn believes can happen to Jews who lack a firm Jewish identity. After Arthur marries a Gentile and has a son, he starts to become more and more conscious of his inextricable ties to Judaism. His marriage falls apart, but he finally discovers "that Jews like himself who denied any tradition or character of their own were really trying to do a thing that was unhuman, that no one else was trying to do." For him, being a Jew and being human coincide.

Another outstanding Jewish author of fiction about Jews was Anzia Yezierska. Born in the Russian Pale in 1885, she arrived in New York when she was sixteen; she was most active as a writer during the 1920s. In her fiction she gives voice to the feelings of the women immigrants who wanted to make a place for themselves in the New World. Her first collection of stories, *Hungry Hearts* (1920), contains the basic idea that runs through her other works: no matter how bad America may be, it still has possibilities of becoming, as Mary Antin puts it, the promised land. In her novel of 1925, *Bread Givers*, Yezierska's central character, Sara Smolinsky, has to break away from her domineering father, who spends his time, he claims, studying the Talmud, who demands that his daughters act as his bread givers—that is, support him—and who arranges terrible marriages for several of them. Sara finally leaves her home, gets a college education, and becomes a teacher, a road that many of her real-life contemporaries followed. At the end of the novel, she is even able to understand and accept her father.

The outstanding works of Jewish-American fiction to appear during the 1930s were Michael Gold's *Jews without Money* (1930), Henry Roth's *Call It Sleep* (1934), and

Meyer Levin's *The Old Bunch* (1937). Many generalizations may be made about the Jewish-American literature of the Great Depression. For example, Angoff and Levin characterize the decade as one during which "writers" thought that "readers would not care to identify with Jewish fictional characters." Consequently, many Jewish "writers who had begun . . . by writing about people and backgrounds with which they were familiar soon abandoned Jewish material or falsified it." Others "tried to write honestly about the Jewish life they knew, . . . even attained critical acclaim," but "grew bitter over the lack of reader response and over publishing pressure to abandon such material." Some, most notably Henry Roth, stopped writing. Guttmann writes of "the novels of generational conflict" of the 1930s and 1940s. And Liptzin characterizes the 1930s as "the decade of the uprooted and estranged Jewish intellectuals," whom he calls "Jewish saplings that had wrested themselves loose from the cultural earth of their fathers and transplanted themselves in the rich soil of their adopted culture." Yet

> their roots were severely damaged and their healthy growth impaired. . . . Revolting against both American and Jewish realities, they took refuge in hedonism, aestheticism, communism and psychoanalytic self-dissection.

Obviously, Liptzin is far too emotional in his condemnation of the writers of the decade. And as the three works mentioned at the beginning of this paragraph attest, the 1930s did produce some outstanding Jewish-American literature.

Michael Gold was born as Irwin Granich in New York in 1893; he grew up on the Lower East Side. By 1930 he was editing the *New Masses* and trying, of course, to win people to communism. In *Jews without Money* he presents a sympathetic picture of the immigrants and their children. The novel is largely autobiographical, and the narrator is a thinly disguised version of Gold himself. Especially poignant are his recollections of his parents and their dismay with a New World that was certainly not their promised land. His father uses the by-then ubiquitous words, "A curse on Columbus! A curse on America, the thief!"—words repeated often in the Jewish-American literature of the 1920s and 1930s, usually in Yiddish. And his mother expresses her nostalgia for the forests of her youth with the words, "Ach, America, the thief, where children only see dry, dead mushrooms in grocery stores." In spite of his avowed antireligious, communist sympathies, Gold gives a touching, realistic description of the poverty-stricken Jews living on the Lower East Side during the first two decades of the twentieth century; only in the last few pages does he give vent to his communist ideas. In spite of its many flaws, which critics have examined extensively, Gold's novel remains a touching, insightful description of the lives of ghetto Jews in New York.

Call It Sleep, by Austrian-born Henry Roth, however, has been justly hailed as a masterpiece. In Roth's story of the conflicts between David Schaerl and his father, Albert, the critic Daniel Walden, for example, finds re-created "the inner pain of the second generation and its social and familial roots." And Guttmann hails the novel as the "clas-

Michael Gold.

sic study of second-generation childhood." David's attempts to come to grips with his father's violence and his mother's overpowering love lead him into a chain of deceit that culminates in his questioning aloud something his father has been questioning in silence: is he the child of Albert Schaerl or of a Gentile with whom his mother, Genya, had an affair before she met Albert? Albert explodes, and David flees to the streets in panic. In his misery, he thrusts a milk dipper into the third rail of an electrified railway. After he almost dies from the shock, he is taken home, where Albert, for the first time in the story, shows true compassion for his son. Albert is probably able to show this compassion because he has finally spoken openly to Genya of his doubts and she has reassured him that David is indeed his child. Numerous critics have recognized Roth's debts to James Joyce and Sigmund Freud, but the overall story is entirely original. The book, however, lapsed into oblivion, to be resurrected in 1960, when it was reprinted and recognized as a masterpiece.

Meyer Levin's *The Old Bunch* treats the generational conflicts of twenty boys and girls who grew up on the West Side of Chicago, Levin's native city. The novel moves from 1921 to 1934 as Levin evokes a lost era in America's history. The account of the conflict between his bobby-soxers and their boyfriends, on the one hand, and their immigrant parents with their old country ways, on the other, enables Levin to investigate sympathetically the problems of adjusting to America. Although *The Old Bunch* was, as noted earlier, attacked as an example of Jewish anti-Semitism, Levin himself became a leader in the raising of Jewish consciousness and a strong supporter of Israel, where he spent most of his last days, and his novel is now regarded as one of the monuments of Jewish-American literature.

In a later story, "After All I Did for Israel" (1951), Levin illustrates the conflicting attitudes of many older American Jews toward the Jewish state, the desire to see to it that Israel continues to exist but also the hope that one's own children will not move to Israel. The central character in the story feels that he has been betrayed by the Jewish state, for which he worked so hard to raise funds, when he discovers that his son has decided to settle there.

Other important Jewish-American works of the 1930s include Hecht's *A Jew in Love* and Jerome Weidman's *I Can Get It for You Wholesale* (1937), Daniel Fuch's Williamsburg Trilogy—*Summer in Williamsburg* (1934), *Homage to Blenholt* (1936), and *Low Company* (1937)—and Albert Halper's novel, *The Chute* (1937).

WORLD WAR II AND AFTER

The 1940s were, of course, momentous for Jewish Americans and for Jewish-American authors. The defeat of Hitler and the founding of the state of Israel caused many Jews who had not previously been concerned with their identity as Jews to reassess their situations. A revivification of Jewish consciousness occurred as Hitler's racist policies convinced many Jews that they were only deluding themselves by believing that they could escape their Jewishness through total assimilation, including conversion to Christianity. On the more positive side, the founding of Israel in 1948 brought ethnic pride to many American Jews who felt that they had in a sense survived the Nazi attempts at genocide only through an accident of birth and that European Jews had been abandoned by most of the civilized world, including Britain and the United States. Nonetheless, in helping to found Israel, that same civilized world—especially the United States—acknowledged, many American Jews felt, that Jews too had a place in the universe. This feeling of ethnic pride was, of course, reinforced by the Sinai Campaign of 1956, the Six-Day War of 1967, and the Yom Kippur War of 1973. Many American Jews felt a new sense of Jewishness, and this sense quickly manifested itself in literature. A popular manifestation was *Gentleman's Agreement* (1947) by Laura Hobson, daughter of Michael Zametkin, a Yiddish writer. In spite of its shallowness and sentimentality, Hobson's book does explore some of the problems, especially social ones, that the Jew faces in America and does denounce people who practice even less virulent forms of anti-Semitism.

During the 1940s Sholem Asch published *East River* (1946), a sentimental view of first- and second-generation American Jews in their attempts to become acculturated or assimilated. He also treated this subject in several earlier works, most notably *Uncle Moses* (1917; English trans. 1920). Asch was constantly at the center of various controversies, especially following the publication of his "Christological Trilogy"—*The Nazarene* (1939), *The Apostle* (1943), and *Mary* (1950). He wrote these three novels in an attempt to bring together Jew and Gentile; they represent Asch's desire somehow to undo the horrors of the Hitler era. But they succeeded only in creating a rift between Asch and many of his fellow American Jews, a rift so wide that the Polish-born Asch finally left America (he had become a citizen in 1920) and settled in Israel in 1956.

Probably the most important events in Jewish-American literature in the 1940s, however, were the publication of first novels by Norman Mailer and Saul Bellow. Mailer's explicit treatment of Judaism and Jewishness is limited. His own negative-positive identification of himself as a Jew (as we have seen, he calls himself "a non-Jewish Jew"), is reflected in his ambiguous attitude toward Jews in his works. In his first novel, *The Naked and the Dead* (1948), still considered his masterpiece by many critics, two Jewish characters—Privates Roth and Goldstein—figure prominently; Roth revolts against being identified as a Jew whereas Goldstein quietly accepts his Jewishness. But these two are not the central figures in this novel. Instead, it centers on Sergeant Croft, Lieutenant Hearn, and General Cummings as they lead soldiers attempting to capture a Japanese-held island in the Pacific during World War II.

In his later novels. Mailer touches on the Jewish dimension but never fully explores it. As has been noted, Rojack in *An American Dream* says that he is "half Jewish." When Rojack is asked what the other half is, he responds, "Protestant. Nothing really," a remark that certainly contains explosive implications when delivered by a "half Jew." Rojack is placing himself in a category similar to Mailer himself as a non-Jewish Jew. In *Armies of the Night* (1968), Mailer's nonfiction novel about his participation in the march on the Pentagon in 1967 in protest over the Vietnam War, Mailer asserts that "the one personality he found absolutely insupportable" within himself was that of "the nice Jewish boy from Brooklyn," a personality that in this book he nonetheless seems to find inescapable. For when he is sentenced to a prison term as a result of his activities in the march, he gives a speech in which he says that he is not a Christian, but he is "married to one," and he especially admires "her unspoken love for Jesus Christ." He concludes his speech by saying:

> it is Sunday and we are burning the body and blood of Christ in Vietnam. Yes, we are burning him there, and as we do, we destroy the foundation of this Republic, which is its love and trust in Christ.

Then, he dutifully copies into his book an article that appeared in the *Washington Post* concerning his sentencing and his speech, including the ending of the article: "Mailer is a Jew." Ultimately he is forced to come to grips with his identity as a Jew—an identity forced on him by others.

Canadian-born Saul Bellow, to be sure, does not deny that he is a Jew. And he is indeed very much a Jewish author. Even in a novel like *Henderson the Rain King* (1959), which lacks Jewish characters and explicit discussion of

Jewishness, critics find a pervasive Jewishness. But for Bellow, the Jew becomes a truly representative man, an Everyman who stands for all readers, both Jews and Gentiles. As Keith Michael Opdahl notes, "Bellow describes the Jewish experience in terms that make it representative of historical alienation and determinism." Nonetheless, Opdahl sees a true Jewishness at the heart of Bellow's vision; in his "celebration of the temporal world, his emphasis on community love, and his rejection of the formal for the spontaneous and individual" Opdahl finds elements of Hasidism. And Bellow's "love of the particular scene . . . even at the expense of larger form, conveying the sense that the particular may contain the larger mystery, may owe," Opdahl feels, "something not only to the Romantics but to the faith and the anecdotal, aphoristic literature of the Hasids."

Beginning with *Dangling Man* (1944), Bellow explores the problems of marginality faced by the Jew in America during World War II and the postwar period. A list of his works with central Jewish characters reads like a roll call of the most important works of postwar American fiction: *Dangling Man, The Victim* (1949), *The Adventures of Augie March* (1953), *Seize the Day* (1956), *Herzog* (1964), *Mr. Sammler's Planet* (1970), *Humboldt's Gift* (1975), and *The Dean's December* (1982). These works have been widely acclaimed as literary masterpieces, so much so that Bellow was awarded the Nobel Prize for Literature in 1976. His works show that Bellow is, as Guttmann rightly says, "*par excellence* the explorer of marginality, concerned with men situated somewhere between old and new, with comic and tragic characters in quest of their uncertain identities." As numerous critics have noticed, in his later works, especially from *Herzog* on, Bellow's central characters often break out of their alienation as they find their true identities.

Perhaps Bellow's explorations of marginality in part help explain his popularity and his importance for readers in the second half of the twentieth century. In explaining the willingness of post-World War II readers to accept fiction by and about Jews, Chapman writes that those readers are responding to "themes of alienation, human suffering, social criticism, the multidirectional quests for identity and meaning in a dehumanizing and irrational age." But the readers are also attracted by

> the validity of an underlying attitude to life that derives somehow from the core of the Jewish experience: learning how to live and cope with the continuous expectation of uncertainty, contradictions, the unpredictable, the unanticipated, and the unfathomable, with the realization that adversity, trouble, grief, and sorrow . . . are the normal conditions of life.

This attitude is similar to the one Max Schulz in *Radical Sophistication* (1969) finds at the center of modern Jewish-American fiction. In his excellent study, Schulz writes that the "capacity for belief in the face of 'uncertainties, mysteries, doubts' is a radical sophistication that the Jew, with a culture historically of long standing, is currently giving to a century convinced in its existential isolation of the incoherence of existence. It is as though these two critics are writing most particularly of Bellow, who exemplifies in work after work the very traits they mention.

As I indicated, the 1950s saw the Jewish author move to the center of—and possibly become the dominant force in—American literature. During this decade, in addition to Bellow and Mailer, major figures who were explicitly concerned with Jewishness and with Jews include Bernard Malamud, Philip Roth, Alfred Kazin, and even the poet Allen Ginsberg. Among popular novelists whose works had an appeal that went far beyond Jewish readers were Herman Wouk, author of *The Caine Mutiny* (1951) and *Marjorie Morningstar* (1955), and Leon Uris, author of *Exodus* (1958). Although problems of Jewish identity hardly lie at the center of *The Caine Mutiny,* they are central to the story of Marjorie Morningstar, born Morgenstern, who initially rebels against her Jewishness but eventually returns to a middle-class, suburban, conservative position and even starts to attend synagogue regularly. Uris' novel depicts the Jews and non-Jews who helped found Israel as larger-than-life heroes with few, if any, flaws. Even though *Exodus* is the most popular Zionist novel ever written in America, it can hardly be taken seriously as a literary work. Like *The Caine Mutiny* and *Marjorie Morningstar,* it too readily slips into cliché and oversimplification. Nonetheless, these three works demonstrate the kind of popular appeal Jewish authors writing about Jewish characters had in America during the 1950s.

Among the more serious authors, Bernard Malamud is outstanding. Repeatedly in his novels and short stories, he explores the role of Judaism and Jews in the modern world. In *The Assistant* (1957) he reverses the age-old theme of conversion of the Jew to Christianity and shows a Christian, Frank Alpine, who goes through a formal conversion to Judaism. Malamud uses the grocer Morris Bober to explore the meaning of Jewishness in a secular age. Morris explains to Frank that Morris is indeed a Jew:

> Nobody will tell me that I am not Jewish because I put in my mouth once in a while, when my tongue is dry, a piece ham. But they will tell me, and I will believe them, if I forget the Law. This means to do what is right, to be honest, to be good. This means to other people. Our life is hard enough. Why should we hurt somebody else? For everybody should be the best, not only for you or me. We ain't animals. This is why we need the Law. This is what a Jew believes.

Although Frank replies, "I think other religions have those ideas too," he nonetheless finds Judaism tremendously attractive.

Frank is especially concerned with what he considers Jewish suffering. When he asks Morris "why it is that the Jews suffer so damn much," Morris replies, "They suffer because they are Jews." Then Frank says, "they suffer more than they have to," and Morris responds, "If you live, you suffer. Some people suffer more, but not because they want to. But I think if a Jew don't suffer for the Law, he will suffer for nothing." Not content with generalities, Frank asks Morris why *he* suffers, and Morris replies, "I suffer for you."

The need to define a Jew runs through *The Assistant.* It surfaces at Morris' funeral, for example, when the rabbi says:

> When a Jew dies, who asks if he is a Jew? He is a Jew, we don't ask. There are many ways to be a Jew. So if somebody comes to me and says, "Rabbi, shall we call such a man Jewish who lived and worked among the gentiles and sold them pig meat, trayfe, that we don't eat it, and not once in twenty years comes inside a synagogue, is such a man a Jew, rabbi?" To him I will say, "Yes, Morris Bober was to me a true Jew because he lived in the Jewish experience, which he remembered, and with the Jewish heart." Maybe not to our formal tradition—for this I don't excuse him—but he was true to the spirit of our life—to want for others that which he wants also for himself.

Three more works by Malamud in which Jewish identity is of the utmost importance are the short stories "The Lady of the Lake" and "The Last Mohican," both collected in *The Magic Barrel* (1958), and the novel *The Fixer* (1966). In "The Lady of the Lake," Henry Levin travels to Europe after World War II. "In Paris, for no reason he was sure of, except that he was tired of the past—tired of the limitations it had imposed upon him," he decides to call himself Henry Freeman and to deny that he is Jewish. In Italy he meets and falls in love with Isabella del Dongo, who repeatedly asks him whether he is Jewish. Suspecting that she is an anti-Semite, he insists that he is not. Ironically, when he asks her to marry him, she refuses because she thinks that he is not Jewish. She reveals that she is tattooed as a result of having been sent to Buchenwald, and she replies to Henry's proposal: "I can't marry you. We are Jews. My past is meaningful to me. I treasure what I suffered for." In "The Last Mohican" Arthur Fidelman, who is also in flight from his Jewishness, is forced by Shimon Susskind to acknowledge his relation to his fellow Jews after Susskind steals Fidelman's suit and burns a chapter of a book on art that Fidelman is writing.

In *The Fixer* Yakov Bok, living in prerevolutionary Russia, intitially passes as a Gentile and denies that he is a Jew. He even goes to work for an outspoken anti-Semite. When a boy is murdered and Bok is accused, he admits that he is a Jew. The long tale of his imprisonment follows, a period during which he finds himself more and more isolated. Consistently refusing to acknowledge faith in the God of the Jews, he nonetheless finds himself labeled a Jew, and even he realizes that he cannot escape from his Jewishness. Toward the end of the novel, Bok thinks: "One thing I've learned, . . . there's no such thing as an unpolitical man, especially a Jew. . . . You can't sit still and see yourself destroyed." And he adds, "If the state acts in ways that are abhorrent to human nature, it's the lesser evil to destroy it. Death to the anti-Semites! Long live revolution! Long live liberty!" By this time Bok has become a kind of national hero for the Jews and revolutionaries, who try unsuccessfully to release him from the carriage in which he rides to trial. The carriage continues along streets lined with crowds, among whom are "Jews of the Plossky District. Some, as the carriage clattered by and they glimpsed the fixer, were openly weeping, wring-ing their hands. One thinly bearded man clawed his face. One or two waved at Yakov. Some shouted his name."

Another treatment of the return to a Jewish identity occurs in Alfred Kazin's autobiographical volume, *A Walker in the City* (1951). In this work, Kazin, an eminent critic of American literature, returns to his roots in Brownsville, roots from which, earlier in his career, he had tried hard to escape. Guttmann places Kazin's book in a larger context. "Once the mythic voyage from Antomir to New York was successfully completed," Guttmann writes, "David Levinsky was able to look back upon his youth and articulate his doubts." Similarly, "Once the children and grandchildren of the immigrant generation had moved from the urban *shtetls* of Chicago and New York to America's wider world, they too were able to indulge themselves in memories of community and in moments of regret." And he adds, "The most poignant and complex literary statement of these second thoughts is probably Alfred Kazin's memoir, *A Walker in the City.*"

A *shtetl* is a small, rural community in Eastern Europe; a large percentage of the new immigrants came to America not from ghettos in large cities but from *shtetlach* (to use the Yiddish plural). Guttmann implies that they reproduced these *shtetlach* in the big cities in America, only to escape from them again and then to return to them in memory, as Kazin does in *A Walker in the City.*

Kazin tells a tale of "making it" (to borrow Norman Podhoretz' phrase) in the New World. He leaves his Jewish neighborhood to enter the mainstream of American life, but he chooses in this book to make the mental excursion into the past, back to his roots, just as he at times makes the physical trip by subway back to Brownsville and moves "From the Subway to the Synagogue," as he entitles his first chapter.

During the 1950s at least two other writers of importance appeared, Philip Roth and Allen Ginsberg. Ginsberg is another figure who is uncomfortable with his Jewishness, even going to the point of appearing to renounce it. In a passage strongly reminiscent of Walt Whitman's "Chanting the Square Deific," Ginsberg calls himself in "Kral Majales" (1967)

> a Buddhist Jew
> who worships the Sacred Heart of Christ the
>   blue body of Krishna the straight back of
>   Ram
> the beads of Chango the Nigerian singing Shiva
>   Shiva in a manner which I have invented.

Exactly what a Buddhist Jew may be is, of course, unclear, but, like Mailer, Ginsberg at least admits here that he realizes he cannot entirely escape his Jewish identity.

In his earlier works, *Howl, and Other Poems* (1956) and especially *Kaddish and Other Poems: 1958-1960* (1961), almost in spite of himself Ginsberg acknowledges his Jewishness, especially in *Kaddish,* his largely autobiographical lament for the death of his mother. Kaddish is, of course, the Jewish prayer for the dead, and although his parents did not bring Ginsberg up in a Jewish religious context, it is interesting that he places his entire poem in that context by means of its title.

As has been noted, Philip Roth's fiction has been the center of repeated controversy about Roth's relation to his fellow Jews. He has often been accused of being anti-Semitic. In a scathing attack on Roth, Irving Howe even goes so far as to write, "I think it clear that Roth, despite his concentration on Jewish settings and his acerbity of tone, has not really been involved in this tradition [of Jewish self-criticism and satire]. For he is one of the first American-Jewish writers who finds that it yields him no sustenance, no norms or values from which to launch his attacks on middle-class complacence." Thus, Howe dismisses those critics who place Roth in the tradition of the prophets of old.

Nonetheless, Roth is a powerful force in modern American literature, and repeatedly he creates characters who are consciously aware of and concerned with their Jewishness. In "Eli the Fanatic" in *Goodbye, Columbus and Five Short Stories* (1959), for example, when confronted by the Yeshiva of Woodenton, Eli becomes intensely aware of his Jewish heritage and vows that he will pass it on to his son. And even a Jew as notorious as Alexander Portnoy, who tries to escape from his Jewish past by making love with *shikses* (Gentile women), feels himself strangely moved when he goes to Israel; his landing in "the land of Israel, where the Jewish people first came into being," causes him to be "impaled upon a memory of Sunday morning softball games in Newark." In novels like *Goodbye, Columbus* (1959), *My Life as a Man* (1974), *The Professor of Desire* (1977), and *Zuckerman Unbound* (1981), Roth explores characters involved in love-hate relationships with their own Jewishness, people who, like Portnoy, often begrudgingly admit that in their own personal histories they can find miniature versions of the history of the Jewish people. In his baseball story, *The Great American Novel* (1973), Roth parodies the whole idea of writing "the great American novel." In this book, which Roth places solidly inside American literary tradition by his use not only of baseball but also of parodies of major works of American literature and of American literary traditions, Jews and Jewishness are by no means central, so Roth's discussion of "Jewish Wheaties" and the "seventeen-year-old Jewish genius" who makes them seem out of place; the whole idea of Jewishness seems irrelevant.

During the 1960s, several writers seemed to move in slightly different directions. They returned to exploring fictional worlds that are almost exclusively Jewish, and often the Jews in those worlds are Orthodox. The foremost example is Chaim Potok, whose novels tend to center on tensions, not between Jews and non-Jews, but among various Orthodox Jews. *The Chosen* (1967) and *The Promise* (1969) treat the lives of Danny Saunders and Reuven Malter as these characters try to reconcile their traditional beliefs with modern reality. The novels are rich in description of Hasidic and non-Hasidic Orthodox life in New York City during and especially after World War II. Potok continues to treat traditional forms of Judaism in *My Name Is Asher Lev* (1972), the story of a Hasidic Jew who becomes a painter.

Other writers of the 1960s and 1970s have returned to similar themes, treating Jews, often in connection with Orthodox concerns, even though Orthodox Judaism continues to attract a smaller and smaller percentage of America's Jews. Cynthia Ozick, for example, in the title story of *The Pagan Rabbi, and Other Stories* (1971), tells the tale of Isaac Kornfeld, a brilliant Talmudist and a respected, promising young rabbi who studies pagan nature religions and becomes convinced of their validity. He deserts his wife Sheindel after falling in love with a tree nymph. When he is no longer able to have sexual relations with the nymph, he uses his *tallis* (prayer shawl) to hang himself from the nymph's tree. Hugh Nissenson, on the other hand, tends to set his stories in Israel, and in his novel *My Own Ground* (1976) he returns to the almost exclusively Jewish Lower East Side of turn-of-the-century New York. Even when his narrator, Jacob Brody, leaves New York City in the last few pages of the book, he comments almost exclusively on his relation with other Jews.

In an essay entitled "American Jewish Writing, Act II" (1976), Ruth R. Wisse examines trends in this literature during the 1970s. She concludes that:

> . . . it is Philip Roth and not Cynthia Ozick, or Hugh Nissenson, who can best afford to write about the American Jewish reality. For American Jews today in their numbers live not on Nissenson's Lower East Side or in Ozick's hasidic *shtetl* [a reference to the short story, "Bloodshed"] but in "Woodentown," the home of Eli Peck [of Roth's "Eli the Fanatic"].

Wisse writes that for those who, unlike Roth,

> . . . take Judaism seriously as a cultural alternative, and wish to weave brilliant cloth from its ancient threads, the sociological reality of the present-day American Jewish community would seem to present an almost insurmountable obstacle.

Of course, no general study of Jewish-American literature can even approach completeness without some discussion of Isaac Bashevis Singer, who even though he supervises and even helps translate his works, still writes in Yiddish and treats for the most part the now destroyed Jewish communities of his native Poland. His few stories set in America, as well as his numerous novels, stories, and autobiographical volumes written in America, testify to his growing importance in the American literary tradition. That he received the Nobel Prize for Literature in 1978 testifies to his international importance and to the vitality of the Yiddish language, even though few people now consider it their native tongue. Singer's treatment of a lost culture in such works as *The Magician of Lublin* (1960), *The Spinoza of Market Street, and Other Stories* (1961), *The Manor* (1967), and *Shosha* (1973), as well as in his three autobiographical volumes—*In My Father's Court* (1966), *A Little Boy in Search of God* (1976) and *A Young Man in Search of Love* (1978)—provides Americans living in the second half of the twentieth century with a panoramic view of the Eastern Europe from which the ancestors of most of America's Jews came. And his stories set in America, some of which are collected in *Passions* (1975) and *Old Love* (1979), show his extraordinary sensitivity to the lives of Jews, especially Jews who escaped from the Nazi terror, in the New World. Although his works really stand out-

side the mainstream of present-day Jewish-American literature, they will probably have a profound effect on Jewish-American works to come.

Notable because of its absence from this discussion is poetry by American Jews about Jewish themes. There are, of course, many Jewish-American poets besides Emma Lazarus and Allen Ginsberg who write about Jewish themes. Their works, however, are really not as consistently good as are works of Jewish-American prose writers. I agree with Harold Bloom, who, in "The Sorrows of American-Jewish Poetry" (1972), asserts that "though it causes me real grief to say this, the achievement of American-Jewish poets down to the present moment remains a modest and mixed one. There are no Bellows or Malamuds among them, though there are a few signs that this melancholy estimate some day may need to be revised upward." As promising Jewish-American poets who have produced at least some verse "of considerable distinction," Bloom mentions Allen Grossman, Alvin Feinman, Robert Mezey, and Geoffrey Hartman.

It is then in prose, especially prose fiction and autobiography, that Jewish-American authors have excelled up to now. Jewish-American literature has emerged as one of the central forces in the literature of the American nation. Although before and during World War II a Jewish-American author was often urged to change his name and write about non-Jews and non-Jewish themes, today his works about Jews and Jewishness are read repeatedly by numerous non-Jews who see themselves mirrored in the trials and tribulations of which they read. Guttmann theorizes that modern Jewish-American authors are so popular in part because "many of them are only nominally Jewish and present fictional worlds all but indistinguishable from those presented by other writers of their generation." This criticism, however, clearly cannot apply to the fictional worlds of writers like Ozick, Nissenson, and especially Potok, whose characters can exist only in a Jewish milieu and only as Jews. Yet these authors, too, enjoy widespread popularity. As we have seen, there is indeed a good deal of truth to the statements with which we began this essay, for Jewish authors and Jewish writing are indeed a predominant force, if not the dominant force, in American literature during the second half of the twentieth century.

MAJOR FIGURES

Marvin Mudrick

SOURCE: "Malamud, Bellow, and Roth," in *On Culture and Literature,* Horizon Press, 1970, pp. 200-233.

[*In the following essay, which was originally published in 1966, Mudrick considers the early works of Bernard Malamud, Saul Bellow, and Philip Roth as attempts to define the twentieth-century American Jew in fiction.*]

Malamud, Bellow, and Roth have taken upon themselves the job of inventing the contemporary fictional Jew. In contemporary America, where Jewishness has been more and more rapidly converging into the WASP matrix of neutral pristine affluence, the job is almost anachronistic, almost archeology, like setting up a wailing wall in a supermarket. It is as if a Hebrew patriarch, having outlived the wife of his youth, had married the wife of his old age and fathered three sons to say *Kaddish* for him in post-ghetto America: Bernard, traditional and belated down to the self-protective ghetto humor, a pillar of the synagogue, rather prosaic maybe but steady and reliable, his father's son; then Saul, irresistible talker, promoter, last of the big-time spenders, flashy, wilful, hypnotically charming, bottomlessly cynical and sad, home only for the high holidays when he puts on the skullcap and a pious face for services; finally Philip, nervous, vulnerable, the doomed and delicate one, least committed to the past and most troubled by the future, whom all the family fusses over and is apprehensively fond of. In post-1945 America they are not unlike Faulkner of the twenties and thirties, appropriating a subject which was already slipping out of sight at the time he began to write about it. To mention Faulkner is to propose a standard which they cannot meet, but which suggests their provincialism and their seriousness. Malamud, Bellow, and Roth are, in a dry spell for American fiction, the most intelligent and the most considerable American novelists since World War II.

What a dry spell, though! with even the better novelists redoing the slick-magazine iconographies of war, of Hollywood and New York glamor, of struggle against social injustice, of existentialism or Zen or voodoo or camp, of publicity and news; until so (probably) talented a writer as Norman Mailer can publish in *Esquire* his pop-novel *An American Dream,* which regurgitates, installment by installment, all the chic pipedreams that readers of *Esquire* customarily derive from its ads and cover articles. Against such stuff, Malamud's owlish attention to every can of beans on the shelves of a failing grocery reads like Tolstoy; Roth's Martha Reganhart is Helen of Troy; Bellow's Tommy Wilhelm, Hamlet and Faust. Still, it had better be clear that the claims for Malamud, Bellow, and Roth will have to be modest enough, and that they will exclude much or most of the work. For instance, *The Natural* is a very silly novel, a comic-book sports story tricked out with sex and a moral. Much of Bellow, especially Augie and Henderson, is an obfuscatory whirlwind of juvenile pep and philosophizing (Henderson thinks, talks, and behaves—at fifty-five!—with the shy, gawky, endearingly brainless innocence of Holden Caulfield). And *Goodbye, Columbus* is a collection of stories—knowing, ironic, salted with symbols, assembled according to the best models—by the most promising member of the advanced creative writing class at State U.

Goodbye, Columbus is a characteristic false start by a bright young man. It is also, under its machined surface, vexed by emotions it can't begin to cope with. Roth, almost a generation younger than the others, was in his middle twenties when it appeared in 1959: an acclaimed volume whose twists and gimmicks are mainly at the service of Roth's never satisfactorily explained distaste for the nearly assimilated Jew. The long title story is typical—an exposé of country-club Jews with gobs of money, whose

son is large enough to have played Big Ten basketball (though his name is Patimkin), whose daughter has the comparable temerity to play tennis, bob her nose (even though her name is not Wentworth or MacDonald but *Patimkin!*), and in the end choose her family over a penniless young Jewish librarian as lachrymose as he is uninterruptedly self-congratulatory. At a critical moment, for instance, the librarian meditates in St. Patrick's Cathedral—daring and ironic setting—on whether bed with beautiful Brenda would compensate for all the revolting, Jewish material comfort he would have to put up with (Brenda, meanwhile, is at the doctor's being fitted with a diaphragm):

> It wasn't much cooler inside the church, though the stillness and the flicker of the candles made me think it was. I took a seat at the rear and while I couldn't bring myself to kneel, I did lean forward onto the back of the bench before me, and held my hands together and closed my eyes. I wondered if I looked like a Catholic, and in my wonderment I began to make a little speech to myself. Can I call the self-conscious words I spoke prayer? At any rate, I called my audience God. God, I said, I am twenty-three years old. I want to make the best of things. Now the doctor is about to wed Brenda to me, and I am not entirely certain this is all for the best. What is it I love, Lord? Why have I chosen? Who is Brenda? The race is to the swift. Should I have stopped to think?
>
> I was getting no answers, but I went on. If we meet You at all, God, it's that we're carnal, and acquisitive, and thereby partake of you. I am carnal, and I know You approve, I just know it. But how carnal can I get? I am acquisitive. Where do I turn now in my acquisitiveness? Where do we meet? Which prize is You?
>
> It was an ingenious meditation, and suddenly I felt ashamed. I got up and walked outside, and the noise of Fifth Avenue met me with an answer:
>
> Which prize do you think, *schmuck?* Gold dinnerware, sporting-goods trees, nectarines, garbage disposals, bumpless noses, Patimkin Sink, Bonwit Teller—
>
> But, damn it, God, that *is* You!
>
> And God only laughed, that clown.

Stephen Dedalus, another sniveling prig who detested his compatriots, had better reasons.

Malamud and Bellow, each almost two decades older than Roth, grew up in the very different Jewish milieu of the Depression, an enclave of the poor and the unassimilated; and their earliest efforts to deal with it take no account of the fact that it had virtually disappeared by the time they began to write. Moreover, before they came to it, they made false starts in other directions. Bellow's first novel, *Dangling Man,* is an attempt to turn the plight of a man waiting to be drafted (during World War II) into an allegory of the rootlessness of modern life, a malicious and penetrating self-analysis by a new underground man; but

Bellow's rhetoric, even when he's being unbearably profound—

> The sense in which Goethe was right: Continued life means expectation. Death is the abolition of choice. The more choice is limited, the closer we are to death. The greatest cruelty is to curtail expectations without taking away life completely. A life term in prison is like that. So is citizenship in some countries. The best solution would be to live as if the ordinary expectations had not been removed, not from day to day, blindly. But that requires immense self-mastery.

—amounts to little more than that people get awfully tired of waiting. As for Malamud's first novel, *The Natural* is a lamentable attempt to take baseball seriously (Ring Lardner did the best that could be done, fictionally, with the game by assuming that everybody who makes a career of it is an imbecile).

It was in their second novels that both Bellow and Malamud took up the subject of the Jew in America. Bellow's title, *The Victim,* might have been Malamud's too, and proposes their emphasis and intention. *The Victim* was published in 1947, when Buchenwald was topical enough to mask the fact that anti-Semitism would not be among the political issues of the future. Bellow was still writing allegory, and it was still very literary: this time with echoes of "The Secret Sharer" and other *Doppelgänger* stories; this time drawn out well beyond the novella length of *Dangling Man* by masses of naturalistic and symbolic detail, by thriller-like accumulations of suspense and (startlingly irrelevant) complications of plot. *Dangling Man* tries to convert the topical into allegory and literature, and so does *The Victim*. But Bellow doesn't manage to sense that aspect of the topical which will outlast the day, as, say, Dostoevsky did with the newspaper murder story that launched *The Possessed*. Indeed, Bellow stakes everything on the unimpaired survival of the topical, as if newspapers were history; so that when his inquisitor-victim, Allbee, deplores the mongrelization of America—

> "Hell, yes. Well, you look like Caliban in the first place," Allbee said, more serious than not. "But that's not all I mean. You personally, you're just one out of many. Many kinds. You wouldn't be able to see that. Sometimes I feel— and I'm saying this seriously—I feel as if I were in a sort of Egyptian darkness. You know, Moses punished the Egyptians with darkness. And that's how I often think of this. When I was born, when I was a boy, everything was different. We thought it would be daylight forever. Do you know, one of my ancestors was Governor Winthrop. Governor Winthrop!" His voice vibrated fiercely; there was a repressed laugh in it. "I'm a fine one to be talking about tradition, you must be saying. But still I was born into it. And try to imagine how New York affects me. Isn't it preposterous? It's really as if the children of Caliban were running everything. You go down in the subway and Caliban gives you two nickels for your dime. You go home and he has a candy store in the street where you were born. The old breeds are out. The streets are named after them. But what are they themselves? Just remnants."

> " see how it is; you're actually an aristocrat," said Leventhal.

> "It may not strike you as it struck me," said Allbee. "But I go into the library once in a while, to look around, and last week I saw a book about Thoreau and Emerson by a man named Lipschitz . . . "

—when Allbee articulates his hatred, what at our distance in time we hear is not a threat and a prophecy, but a voice from a newspaper morgue. Bellow has failed to observe that, though the topical *contains* the threat, to reproduce the topical is not to isolate or identify the threat, which, to the confusion of newspaper-readers and apprentice novelists, insists on changing its habitat and appearance and therefore its name from one edition of the daily press to the next. Nor does Bellow regain our confidence at the end by losing his own, when he shrugs off the whole plot as a bad season through which Leventhal has safely passed. It meant more than that to the protagonist at the time, and to the author; and counted on meaning more than that to us.

Ten years later, and as much farther from Buchenwald, Malamud wrote his own version of *The Victim. The Assistant* also sees the Jew as allegorical, representative, and bedeviled, in a context—economic for Malamud, as it was political for Bellow—that recalls 1937 rather than 1957:

> He felt weightless, unmanned, the victim in a motion of whatever blew at his back; wind, worries, debts, Karp, holdupniks, ruin. He did not go, he was pushed. He had the will of a victim, no will to speak of.

> "For what I worked so hard for? Where is my youth, where did it go?"
> The years had passed without profit or pity. Who could he blame? What fate didn't do to him he had done to himself. The right thing was to make the right choice but he made the wrong. Even when it was right it was wrong. To understand why, you needed an education but he had none. All he knew was he wanted better but he had not after all these years learned how to get it. Luck was a gift. Karp had it, a few of his old friends had it, well-to-do men with grandchildren already, while his poor daughter, made in his image, faced—if not actively sought— oldmaidhood. Life was meager, the world changed for the worse. America had become too complicated. One man counted for nothing. There were too many stores, depressions, anxieties . . .

Or the view may be from outside the pale, as when the Italian assistant observes the Jewish readiness for shared misery:

> When Breitbart first came to Morris' neighborhood and dropped into the store, the grocer, seeing his fatigue, offered him a glass of tea with lemon. The peddler eased the rope off his shoulder and set his boxes on the floor. In the back he gulped the hot tea in silence, warming both hands on the glass. And though he had, besides his other troubles, the seven-year itch, which kept him awake half the night, he never com-

plained. After ten minutes he got up, thanked the grocer, fitted the rope onto his lean and itchy shoulder and left. One day he told Morris the story of his life and they both wept.

That's what they live for, Frank thought, to suffer. And the one that has got the biggest pain in the gut and can hold onto it the longest without running to the toilet is the best Jew. No wonder they got on his nerves.

One of the differences between Bellow and Malamud is in their tutelary divinities. In his first two novels Bellow is writing with a self-conscious awareness of Conrad, of Dostoevsky, of such quasi-literary metaphysical agonists as Kierkegaard and Sartre: his allegory too easily disentangles itself from plot and aims at an independent and unprovincial *Weltanschauung*. In *The Victim* Bellow is impatient with the stereotype of the Jew, he wants the Jew to be a man, and then Man; Leventhal is recognizably enough an image of the New York Jew, but his crisis is too quickly a crisis of Western civilization, or too quickly intends to be. Moreover Bellow is handicapped in his strenuous purpose by an inert and colorless style, naturalism without its possible saving doggedness of accuracy on how people pass the days of a life; nothing like, for instance, the precision and hallucinatory intimations of Conrad's best prose; nor much like Malamud either.

Malamud embraces without reservation the provincialism he has no interest in evading: his Depression Jews, their undisplaceable identity, the dreary inventory of local impedimenta that keep them where they are, and the style that may be all too faithful an analogue of their cluttered, graceless, and well-meaning lives. Malamud's great exemplar is Hardy. Like Hardy, he has a tin ear except for the dialectal speech of his locality; like Hardy, he is in no hurry to be cosmopolitan; like Hardy, he believes with the passion of perfect knowledge in what unexceptional people do. It is of course a question of likeness and not equality: Malamud resembles Hardy in subject, in method, in knowledge and conviction, in limitations, though not in size. But Bellow, aspiring to be Dostoevsky, achieves the master's occasional impression of melodramatic strain without suggesting either Dostoevsky's magnitude or any of his virtues.

Malamud, like Hardy, has the provincial bias. The allegorical intentions of *The Assistant*—like Hardy's cosmic backdrops to the events of heath and village—are momentous because Malamud really believes that life lived close to subsistence, close to the level of animal need (and therefore close to "nature," in a setting as claustrophobic as Hardy's though urban rather than rural), is the truest and most representative life, it tests the spirit and insists on the most unequivocal manifestations of fortitude, loyalty, and love. Malamud's conviction leads him to construct an allegory of expiation, prodigious labors, self-sacrifice, and what might be called—after the two millennia of the Christian ascendancy—reconversion; and his knowledge of the ordinariness out of which such extraordinary manifestations must come is so patient and unsparing that the allegory becomes simply the meaning of the events—of an event, for example, as impersonally traditional, as me-

chanical, as full of indispensable lies and omissions, as a rabbi's eulogy at the funeral of a man he never knew:

> "My dear friends, I never had the pleasure to meet this good grocery man that he now lays in his coffin. He lived in a neighborhood where I didn't come in. Still and all I talked this morning to people that knew him and I am now sorry I didn't know him also. I would enjoy to speak to such a man. I talked to the bereaved widow, who lost her dear husband. I talked to his poor beloved daughter Helen, who is now without a father to guide her. To them I talked, also to landsleit and old friends, and each and all told me the same, that Morris Bober, who passed away so untimely—he caught double pneumonia from shoveling snow in front of his place of business so people could pass by on the sidewalk—was a man who couldn't be more honest. Such a person I am sorry I didn't meet sometime in my life. If I met him somewhere, maybe when he came to visit in a Jewish neighborhood—maybe at Rosh Hashana or Pesach—I would say to him, 'God bless you, Morris Bober.' Helen, his dear daughter, remembers from when she was a small girl that her father ran two blocks in the snow to give back to a poor Italian lady a nickel that she forgot on the counter. Who runs in wintertime without hat or coat, without rubbers to protect his feet, two blocks in the snow to give back five cents that a customer forgot? Couldn't he wait till she comes in tomorrow? Not Morris Bober, let him rest in peace. He didn't want the poor woman to worry, so he ran after her in the snow. This is why the grocer had so many friends who admired him . . ."

The grocer's daughter knows better: ". . . I didn't say he had many friends who admired him. That's the rabbi's invention. People liked him, but who can admire a man passing his life in such a store? He buried himself in it; he didn't have the imagination to know what he was missing. He made himself a victim. He could, with a little more courage, have been more than he was." But the rabbi's lies are the last dignity that the corpse earned by dying; and the truths are what Frank Alpine, the hoodlum assistant, builds on with his terrible effort to transform himself into the man he robbed. Malamud's powers are not up to convincing us of the probability of Frank's ultimate decision. And the novel is more convincingly a funeral eulogy than a prospect of the future, Frank's or anybody else's. But *The Assistant* is a failure only in its terminal insistence on allegorical tidiness.

The subject of *The Assistant* is the Jew as victim and example; and it is a subject that attracts Malamud sufficiently to bring him back to it in several of his short stories: "The Mourners," for instance, "The First Seven Years," "The Death of Me," or "The Cost of Living," of which the last reads like a suicidally despondent first draft of *The Assistant*. Or the Jew is a butt, as in the farcial and sometimes very funny stories about Fidelman, the student painter in Europe, on one occasion imprisoned by an Italian thug who for the sake of an elaborate ransom scheme forces him to make a copy of the "Venus of Urbino":

What a miracle, thought Fidelman.

The golden brown-haired Venus, a woman of the real world, lay on her couch in serene beauty, her hand lightly touching her intimate mystery, the other holding red flowers, her nude body her truest accomplishment.

"I would have painted somebody in bed with her," Scarpio said.

"Shut up," said Fidelman.

Scarpio, hurt, left the gallery.

Fidelman, alone with Venus, worshipped the painting. What magnificent tones, what extraordinary flesh that can turn the body into spirit.

While Scarpio was out talking to the guard, the copyist hastily sketched the Venus, and with a Leica Angelo had borrowed from a friend for the purpose, took several new color shots.

Afterwards he approached the picture and kissed the lady's hands, thighs, and breasts, but as he was murmuring, "I love you," a guard struck him hard on the head with both fists.

Or the Jew is a genre figure in a provincial setting that emphasizes, not the imminence of ruin, but the proliferations of custom and idiosyncrasy, as when the rabbinical student consults the matchmaker in the title story of *The Magic Barrel:*

Salzman . . . placed the card down on the wooden table and began to read another:

"Lily H. high school teacher. Regular. Not a substitute. Has savings and new Dodge car. Lived in Paris one year. Father is successful dentist thirty-five years. Interested in professional man. Well Americanized family. Wonderful opportunity."

"I know her personally," said Salzman. "I wish you could see this girl. She is a doll. Also very intelligent. All day you could talk to her about books and theater and what not. She also knows current events." . . .

". . . but I'm not interested in . . . school teachers."

Salzman pulled his clasped hands to his breast. Looking at the ceiling he devoutly exclaimed, "Yiddishe kinder, what can I say to somebody that he is not interested in high school teachers? So what then you are interested?"

Leo flushed but controlled himself.

"In what else will you be interested," Salzman went on, "if you not interested in this fine girl that she speaks four languages and has personally in the bank ten thousand dollars? Also her father guarantees further twelve thousand. Also she has a new car, wonderful clothes, talks on all subjects, and she will give you a first-class home and children. How near do we come in our life to paradise?"

There are also fantasies, in a Yiddish tradition of tales of the supernatural—encounters with angels and other emissaries of God and the Devil—a tradition of which the dis-

tinguished living exponent is Isaac Bashevis Singer; but Malamud doesn't altogether avoid the temptation which the mode offers to whimsy (as in "The Jewbird" and "Angel Levine"), or to an unvalidated presumption of superearthly issues (as in "Take Pity" and the title story of *Idiots First*). The fact is that, after *The Assistant,* Malamud's interest in the Jew as fictional subject is never so intense, so apocalyptic, it becomes increasingly ironic and remote, even exploitative. The victim and example is becoming a sad sack, a vaudeville comic down to the pratfalls and rubber nightsticks, possibly a holy innocent in a world of sharpers. The ghetto is turning into a stage.

Bellow, too, after *The Victim,* seems to have lost interest in the subject; or rather to have grown impatient with its limitations. His spectacular attempts to break it up and to break away from it are, respectively, *The Adventures of Augie March* and *Henderson the Rain King.*

In *Augie,* as in *The Victim,* the protagonist is a Jew; but in all other ways Bellow seems resolved to turn inside into out and down into up. *The Victim* is a closed system, heavily plotted, in a setting as fixed as that of *The Assistant; Augie* is open, episodic, picaresque. The hero of *The Victim* is a Jew and therefore somehow a stranger and under surveillance in America; Augie March is a Jew almost fortuitously and without consequence, but from the first sentence "an American, Chicago born," who recollects the anti-Semitic brutalities inflicted upon him in his childhood only to disclaim their influence on him:

. . . I never had any special grief from it, or brooded, being by and large too larky and boisterous to take it to heart, and looked at it as needing no more special explanation than the stone-and-bat wars of the street gangs or the swarming on a fall evening of parish punks to rip up fences, screech and bawl at girls, and beat up strangers.

And, as the foregoing quotation suggests, Bellow has contrived a style for Augie's speaking voice that he hopes will convey a "larky and boisterous" quality as unlike the flat-footed somberness of *The Victim* as possible.

Not that Bellow abandons the Jews. What he does is transmogrify them into a great elbowing parade of the unsubduable robust (not at all the trampled and wailing ghetto pygmies); so that by page 20 the reader is near exhaustion from descriptions of consecutive giants and monsters:

That would be Five Properties, shambling through the cottage, Anna's immense brother, long armed and humped, his head grown off the thick band of muscle as original as a bole on his back . . .

The intention resembles Isaac Babel's in his Odessa stories. Babel's heroic desperado, Benya Krik, is not, as Babel has the narrator remark, called the King for nothing; and Babel accomplishes the *tour de force* of turning into credible giants Jews who still inhabited the Odessa ghetto. Babel is Benya's affectionate Homer, the lyrical magnifier of his fame; but Babel has a wink for the reader as well as respect for Benya's impressive deeds. Bellow's giants, though, are less agile, they are even torpid and muscle-bound, perhaps because there are so many of them that he can scarcely do more than describe them one to a page, perhaps also because he insists on stressing, not (as Babel does) the comic excess of their vitality, but their mere size.

Bellow's intention is to show the ghetto Jews as worthy progenitors of Augie the all-American boy, pure metal fresh from the melting pot; but his method is less to invent actions than to attack the reader with a calculated hubbub of assertions, data, objects, Whitmanic catalogues and lists, historical and philosophical references (Augie is bookish, a good Jewish trait), wry humor (issue of a good Jewish head), and that colloquial pitchmanship which will die trying or amalgamate all of these into a new (if you'll pardon the expression) Jerusalem, American style, a city of Olympic-size swimming pools and matching plaster monuments:

> William Einhorn was the first superior man I knew. He had a brain and many enterprises, real directing power, philosophical capacity, and if I were methodical enough to take thought before an important and practical decision and also (*N. B.*) if I were really his disciple and not what I am, I'd ask myself, "What would Caesar suffer in this case? What would Machiavelli advise or Ulysses do? What would Einhorn think?" I'm not kidding when I enter Einhorn in this eminent list. It was him that I knew, and what I understand of them in him. Unless you want to say that we're at the dwarf end of all times and mere children whose only share in grandeur is like a boy's share in fairy-tale kings, being of a different kind from times better and stronger than ours. But if we're comparing men and men, not men and children or men and demigods, which is just what would please Caesar among us teeming democrats, and if we don't have any special wish to abdicate into some different, lower form of existence out of shame for our defects before the golden faces of these and other old-time men, then I have the right to praise Einhorn and not care about smiles of derogation from those who think the race no longer has in any important degree the traits we honor in these fabulous names . . .

—which is a fancy introduction for a man who occupies little space in the book, and most of that taken up by descriptions of his not infallible bent for minor-league commercial finagling. But then, Einhorn is a fixer, a user, an operator, a man of the world who will ceremoniously, at the right hour, conduct a growing boy to his first prostitute; and Bellow is determined to see such talents as, because he conceives them to be American, primary virtues.

Bellow, through Augie, is in hot pursuit of the American experience. He wishes to glorify and praise the inveterate American obsession—Jefferson and Pound are two of its illuminati—with particulars and how to handle them, expertness, know-how: mastery of data and process, especially mechanical and impersonal process, like capturing whales and carving and boiling them up into various neat messes of merchandise; and he equally admires the parallel obsession with grand reductive abstractions, as in *Moby Dick* (the nineteenth-century American novel that aspires to be the great American novel and therefore, since Amer-

ica is the ineluctable future, the great novel of the world). Augie will know all things and how they work, will use them up like paper in a flame; though out there, always, lies a darkness still more ineluctable than America:

> However, as I felt on entering Erie, Pennsylvania, there is a darkness. It is for everyone. You don't, as perhaps some imagine, try it, one foot into it like a barbershop "September Morn." Nor are lowered into it with visitors' curiosity, as the old Eastern monarch was let down into the weeds inside a glass ball to observe the fishes. Nor are lifted straight out after an unlucky tumble, like a Napoleon from the mud of the Arcole where he had been standing up to his thoughtful nose while the Hungarian bullets broke the clay off the bank. Only some Greeks and admirers of theirs, in their liquid noon, where the friendship of beauty to human things was perfect, thought they were clearly divided from this darkness. And these Greeks too were in it. But still they are the admiration of the rest of the mud-sprung, famine-knifed, street-pounding, war-rattled, difficult, painstaking, kicked in the belly, grief and cartilage mankind, the multitude, some under a coal-sucking Vesuvius of chaos smoke, some inside a heaving Calcutta midnight, who very well know where they are.

Against this darkness, Augie's boyish charm avails him not. The best he can muster against it is a sequence of girls, some palaver about love as the infinite; most modestly and persuasively, affection for his brother, the rich businessman, whom Bellow presents with a truthful audacity that he mostly fakes for the others:

> . . . Simon worked himself into a rage at Mrs. Magnus in her brown dress. He tried to read the paper and cut her—he hadn't said a word when she came in—but finally he said, and I could see the devil in him now, "Well, you lousy old miser, I see you still buy your clothes off the janitor's wife."

> "Let her alone," said Charlotte sharply.

> But suddenly Simon threw himself across the table, spilling the cherries and overturning coffee cups. He grabbed his mother-in-law's dress at the collar, thrust in his hand, and tore the cloth down to the waist. She screamed. There were her giant soft breasts wrapped in the pink band. What a great astonishment it was, all of a sudden to see them! She panted and covered the top nudity with her hands and turned away. However, her cries were also cries of laughter. How she loved Simon! He knew it too.

> "Hide, hide!" he said, laughing.

> "You crazy fool," cried Charlotte. She ran away on her high heels to bring her mother a coat and came back laughing also. They were downright proud, I guess.

> Simon wrote out a check and gave it to Mrs. Magnus. "Here," he said, "buy yourself something and don't come here looking like the scrubwoman." He went and kissed her on the

braids, and she took his head and gave his kisses
back two for one and with tremendous humor.

It is a fine and uncharacteristic moment, in a book that
rings with the shrillness of unfulfilled ambitions.

The book is also very sad in its pretense of joy, the pretense
of a self-reforming but unregenerate misanthrope. By the
time of *Henderson the Rain King,* the pretense has become
grotesque in its frantic didacticism and lack of conviction.
Bellow is reduced to having his hero converse with Africans whose level of English is "I no know" or "I no bothah
you" or "Me Horko"; and even when the Me-Tarzan-
You-Jane dialogue is expanded for the King's quasi-
Oxonian ontological ditherings about lions, Henderson
continues to associate himself with such quaint locutions
as "strong gift of life" and "the wisdom of life," such sudden illuminations as "I don't think the struggles of desire
can ever be won," and such racy life-loving as follows: "I
am a true adorer of life, and if I can't reach as high as the
face of it, I plant my kiss somewhere lower down. Those
who understand will require no further explanation." Bellow would like Henderson to be *truly* American, purebred
old-stock Anglo-Saxon (of all things!), Paul Bunyan in an
age of bad nerves; but Henderson in the pages of the book
is half Augie, half catcher in the rye. One wonders whether Bellow has any notion of how much he is borrowing in
postures and phony wistfulness from a writer so inferior
to him as Salinger; especially at the embarrassing conclusion, when Henderson races round the plane with the
child in his arms, that Salinger child (sometimes named
Phoebe) who will redeem us all.

Between Augie and Henderson, Bellow produced his novella, *Seize the Day,* which is the real pastrami between
two thick slices of American store bread. In *Seize the Day*
Bellow comes to terms with his characteristic themes and
obsessions, at least to the extent of setting them suitably
down among the gross fleshy shocks of credible fictional
encounters; between the derivativeness of *The Victim* and
the modulated hysterias of Augie and Henderson he accomplishes, on a plateau of unharassed self-knowledge, a
style that can deal honestly with the agonies he is elsewhere content to gloss over with solemn or breezy rhetoric. The wise man, for example, is a recurrent figure in Bellow: Schlossberg in *The Victim,* Einhorn in *Augie,* Dahfu
in *Henderson*—none of whom, however, survives Bellow's
insistence on the blaring unambiguous singleness of power
and wisdom, the last golden words we must come to and
stop at. His great discovery, in *Seize the Day,* is the duplicity and chanciness of wisdom, the charlatanry of power,
the ungraspable difficulty and slipperiness of both; and his
great illustration is the connection between the poor slob,
the genuine baffled victim, Tommy Wilhelm, and the
quicksilver conman, Dr. Tamkin:

> "I want to tell you about this boy and his dad.
> It's highly absorbing. The father was a nudist.
> Everybody went naked in the house. Maybe the
> woman found men *with* clothes attractive. Her
> husband didn't believe in cutting his hair, either.
> He practiced dentistry. In his office he wore rid-
> ing pants and a pair of boots, and he wore a
> green eyeshade."

"Oh, come off it," said Wilhelm.

"This is a true case history."

Without warning, Wilhelm began to laugh. He
himself had had no premonition of his change of
humor. His face became warm and pleasant, and
he forgot his father, his anxieties; he panted
bearlike, happily, through his teeth. "This
sounds like a horse-dentist. He wouldn't have to
put on pants to treat a horse. Now what else are
you going to tell me? Did the wife play the mandolin? Does the boy join the cavalry? Oh, Tamkin, you really are a killer-diller."

"Oh, you think I'm trying to amuse you," said
Tamkin. "That's because you aren't familiar
with my outlook. I deal in facts. Facts always are
sensational. I'll say that a second time. Facts *always!* are sensational."

So they are; but Bellow has in other books impersonated
Dr. Tamkin rather than understood him, this model of the
contemporary mind, ragbag of public and private facts
and fancies lavishly scattered like farts in a windstorm, as
miscellaneous and unassemblable as amputated legs and
arms, tumbling outward toward horizons of meaninglessness:

> "Her brother. He's under my care, too. He has
> some terrible tendencies, which are to be expect-
> ed when you have an epileptic sibling. I came
> into their lives when they needed help desperate-
> ly, and took hold of them. A certain man forty
> years older than she had her in his control and
> used to give her fits by suggestion whenever she
> tried to leave him. If you only knew one per cent
> of what goes on in the city of New York. You
> see, I understand what it is when the lonely per-
> son begins to feel like an animal. When the night
> comes and he feels like howling from his window
> like a wolf. I'm taking complete care of that
> young fellow and his sister. I have to steady him
> down or he'll go from Brazil to Australia the
> next day. The way I keep him in the here-and-
> now is by teaching him Greek."

This was a complete surprise! "What, do you
know Greek?"

"A friend of mine taught me when I was in
Cairo. I studied Aristotle with him to keep from
being idle."

Wilhelm tried to take in these new claims and
examine them. Howling from the window like a
wolf when night comes sounded genuine to him.
That was something really to think about. But
the Greek! He realized that Tamkin was watching to see how he took it. More elements were
continually being added. A few days ago Tamkin had hinted that he had once been in the underworld, one of the Detroit Purple Gang. He
was once head of a mental clinic in Toledo. He
had worked with a Polish inventor on an unsink-
able ship. He was a technical consultant in the
field of television. In the life of a man of genius,
all of these things might happen. But had they
happened to Tamkin? Was he a genius? He often
said that he had attended some of the Egyptian

royal family as a psychiatrist. "But everybody is alike, common or aristocrat," he told Wilhelm. "The aristocrat knows less about life."

An Egyptian princess whom he had treated in California, for horrible disorders he had described to Wilhelm, retained him to come back to the old country with her, and there he had had many of her friends and relatives under his care. They turned over a villa on the Nile to him. "For ethical reasons, I can't tell you many of the details about them," he said—but Wilhelm had already heard all these details, and strange and shocking they were, if true. *If* true—he could not be free from doubt. For instance, the general who had to wear ladies' silk stockings and stand otherwise naked before the mirror—and all the rest. Listening to the doctor when he was so strangely factual, Wilhelm had to translate his words into his own language, and he could not translate fast enough or find terms to fit what he heard.

Wisdom may, after all, turn out to be nothing more than somebody else's cockeyed and circumstantial dreams of glory:

> "Those Egyptian big shots invested in the market, too, for the heck of it. What did they need extra money for? By association, I almost became a millionaire myself, and if I had played it smart there's no telling what might have happened. I could have been the ambassador." The American? The Egyptian ambassador? "A friend of mine tipped me off on the cotton. I made a heavy purchase of it. I didn't have that kind of money, but everybody there knew me. It never entered their minds that a person of their social circle didn't have dough. The sale was made on the phone. Then, while the cotton shipment was at sea, the price tripled. When the stuff suddenly became so valuable all hell broke loose on the world cotton market, they looked to see who was the owner of this big shipment. Me! They investigated my credit and found out I was a mere doctor, and they canceled. This was illegal. I sued them. But as I didn't have the money to fight them I sold the suit to a Wall Street lawyer for twenty thousand dollars. He fought it and was winning. They settled with him out of court for more than a million. But on the way back from Cairo, flying, there was a crash. All on board died. I have this guilt on my conscience, of being the murderer of that lawyer. Although he was a crook."

Wilhelm thought, I must be a real jerk to sit and listen to such impossible stories. I guess I am a sucker for people who talk about the deeper things of life, even the way he does.

What's more, Tamkin is a poet; and here is the second stanza of his poem, "Mechanism Vs Functionalism: Ism Vs Hism":

> *Why-forth then dost thou tarry*
> *And partake thee only of the crust*
> *And skim the earth's surface narry*
> *When all creations art thy just?*

Wilhelm's father, the ironic and self-contained Dr. Adler—all cold vanity—is an equally if less surprisingly solid character. And Wilhelm himself—at the mercy of his fears, his cannibalistic wife, his father, Dr. Tamkin, the stock market, the world—is, till the last scene, everybody's most exasperated secret image of himself, the Jew unmasked and un-Judaized, Everyman drowning in the shoreless multitudinousness of America. At the end, unluckily, Bellow thinks he has nowhere to go but up, up, up into the firmament of wishful allegory (so did Malamud at the end of *The Assistant*); and the funeral, which induces Wilhelm's presumptively clarifying tears, doesn't work. But *Seize the Day* is Bellow's triumph, and a large, distinctively American achievement.

Herzog, on the other hand, might well have been a disaster: this shapeless lament of an ill-tempered, narcissistic, misogynistic, megalomaniacal, pontificating, endlessly self-pitying middle-aged Jewish professor, lifelong patsy to wife and friends and now disgorging a lifetime of ineffectual spite at the very names of his betrayers:

> Should he have been a plain, unambitious Herzog? No. And Madeleine would never have married such a type. What she had been looking for, high and low, was precisely an ambitious Herzog. In order to trip him, bring him low, knock him sprawling and kick out his brains with a murderous bitch foot.

It is nevertheless, as this savaging of Madeleine indicates, an interesting and hectically energetic book. It has the energy and candor of a man too tired to put on customary masks, the wizard novelist's or Henderson's or Augie's: "the way you try to sound rough or reckless . . . ," says Ramona, Herzog's mistress, "like a guy from Chicago . . . It's an act. Swagger. It's not really you." Herzog may occasionally play Augie for Ramona; but for us and himself he is Augie punctured, the swagger is out of him. Only humiliation and deep loathing, and the memories that reconstitute them hourly, are his present and future:

> "Oh, balls! So now, we're going to hear how you SAVED me. Let's hear it again. What a frightened puppy I was. How I wasn't strong enough to face life. But you gave me LOVE, from your big heart, and rescued me from the priests. Yes, cured me of menstrual cramps by servicing me so good. You SAVED me. You SACRIFICED your freedom. I took you away from Daisy and your son, and your Japanese screw. Your important time and money and attention." Her wild blue glare was so intense that her eyes seemed twisted.

> "Madeleine!"

> "Oh—shit!"

> "Just think a minute."

> "Think? What do you know about thinking?"

> "Maybe I married you to improve my mind!" said Herzog. "I'm learning."

> "Well, I'll teach you, don't worry!" said the

beautiful, pregnant Madeleine between her teeth.

His love is for the irrecoverable pre-American ghetto past, out of his pain he submerges into the delusion of completeness and unattempted potencies:

> Napoleon Street, rotten, toylike, crazy and filthy, riddled, flogged with harsh weather—the bootlegger's boys reciting ancient prayers. To this Moses' heart was attached with great power. Here was a wider range of human feelings than he had ever again been able to find. The children of the race, by a never-failing miracle, opened their eyes on one strange world after another, age after age, and uttered the same prayer in each, eagerly loving what they found. What was wrong with Napoleon Street? thought Herzog. All he ever wanted was there. His mother did the wash, and mourned. His father was desperate and frightened, but obstinately fighting. His brother Shura with staring disingenuous eyes was plotting to master the world, to become a millionaire. His brother Willie struggled with asthmatic fits. Trying to breathe he gripped the table and rose on his toes like a cock about to crow. His sister Helen had long white gloves which she washed in thick suds. She wore them to her lessons at the conservatory, carrying a leather music roll. Her diploma hung in a frame. *Mlle. Hélène Herzog . . . avec distinction.* His soft prim sister who played the piano.

Back! cries poor Herzog (and Bellow seems to be crying it too), back to the racial—if not the maternal—womb. It is a sincere cry, the sentimentality of the damned, and one hesitates to laugh at it.

The novel ought to be titled *Who Killed Herzog?* or, *Placing the Blame Squarely on Anybody Else's Shoulders.* The Jewish-American writer is at last bereft of his familiar incubus: anti-Semitism is no longer there to lean one's justly suffering soul against; and Bellow relies on what he calls the "Jewish art of tears" to make the case: "Herzog wrote, *Will never understand what women want. What do they want? They eat green salad and drink human blood.*" Yet whenever the case isn't being made, and often when it is, the weary and compulsive straightforwardness of the statement makes for a kind of authenticity which Bellow nowhere else approaches except in *Seize the Day,* and which—engaging a more complex or at least a more disorderly protagonist—keeps alive and unconsummated a promise of bigger fish than Tommy Wilhelm or even Dr. Tamkin. Herzog's unmailed letters, taking up chapters in this self-indulgent novel, are hot air left over from Augie and Henderson; and Herzog's "equilibrium" at the end, which Bellow seems to regard as an Oriental calm of perfect awareness, is just brute apathy after unendurable exertions of the spirit, before the old rationalizations and remorses build up their necessary steam again. If only Bellow knew what he was seeing! But most of the time, in *Herzog,* he doesn't. Nor does he much care either; and so he makes only token efforts to get in the way of what he's seeing, which is the modern comedy of the exhausted and undefeatable ego.

Malamud's Jewish hero has no such traumas to struggle through since he doesn't begin with such a dose of hubris as Bellow's. When Malamud's Jew leaves the ghetto, he becomes not a displaced person but—as a number of the short stories have already made clear—a tourist. In Europe he has an American passport, glories in the scenery, does his best to sample the women. In Cascadia, the Northwestern locale of *A New Life,* he has the graduate school's passport to a college teaching job: his name is Levin. He is Malamud's holy innocent again, a timid, fumbling, yearning young idealist. Infants he politely picks up urinate over him, thwarted rivals steal his clothes while he is trying to make love (some day a scholarly article will be published on how many times in Malamud's fiction somebody's coitus is interrupted), his first day in class is a sensation but only because he has neglected to close his fly, automobiles are mysteries to him and turn his pleasure trip into a nightmare. Like Fidelman in love with a painted nude, he is always grateful for beauty—the beauty of the scenery for instance:

> They were driving along an almost deserted highway, in a broad farm-filled valley between distant mountain ranges laden with forests, the vast sky piled high with towering masses of golden clouds. The trees softly clustered on the river side of the road were for the most part deciduous; those crawling over the green hills to the south and west were spear-tipped fir.
>
> My God, the West, Levin thought. He imagined the pioneers in covered wagons entering this valley for the first time, and found it a moving thought. Although he had lived little in nature Levin had always loved it, and the sense of having done the right thing in leaving New York was renewed in him. He shuddered at his good fortune.

—and, of course, the beauty of women:

> "Why can't we take one of the blankets off a cow?" Levin asked. "We'll put it back later."
>
> "If you look good you'll see the cows don't sleep with blankets on them. They'd get sick if they did."
>
> Laverne spread the horse blanket on the ground, and standing on it began to undress. She was neat with her clothes, folding each thing and putting it down on a hay bale nearby. Levin placed his hat, trousers, and shoes stuffed with socks and garters, next to her things. He kept his shorts on.
>
> Watching the girl undress in the shadowy light of the lamp in the stall, Levin felt for her an irresistible desire. Ah, the miraculous beauty of women. He considered falling in love with her but gave up the idea. He embraced Laverne and they kissed passionately.
>
> "Your breasts," he murmured, "smell like hay."
>
> "I always wash well," she said.
>
> "I meant it as a compliment."

Ah, women! especially when they're not hanging around all the time to spoil that instant of beauty which is like a fading coal. While Levin is having an affair with a married woman, who has a family to get back to and a gift for quick orgasm, he experiences a bachelor's vision of the earthly paradise:

> She visited him not often but often enough. One of her "meetings" was a good enough excuse for a night out. And Gilley assisted by teaching a winter-term weekly extension course for teachers, in Marathon. Usually Pauline walked the dozen blocks to Levin's. When she had the car she parked it about two blocks from the house. Gilley was home from Marathon by eleven. She had left Levin's room at ten-thirty, short but sweet. He could read afterwards without a stray thought, a great convenience. He envisioned a new Utopia, everyone over eighteen sexually satisfied, aggression reduced, peace in the world.

If Malamud had been content to go on and on in this idyllic vein, *A New Life* might have done for Cascadia what *Typee* did for the South Seas: Come to the great state of Cascadia, admire our mountains, climb our wives. But Malamud is writing—worse luck—one of those academic novels, in which every professional type since Aristotle must be described, for the benefit of the book-club subscribers, in stupefyingly predictable detail down to the last wart, as if every college were a zoo of unheard-of beasts rather than just another enclosure for the same old fictional lapdogs, tabbies, and pet rats: the elderly stuffed prune of a chairman, the unworthy claimant, the snappish recluse, the departmental nymphomaniac, even the ghost of a departed young Turk who once threatened the whole establishment. The contest for the chairmanship fairly makes one's flesh crawl: Will evil be routed and good prevail? Will Levin get caught rifling everybody else's files? Will Levin's mistress muck up everything, as women usually do?

The trouble is that Malamud himself, through Levin, has notions about life on earth which, though more wistful and appealing than, say, Augie's, are not less extraneous to the action of the novel. Malamud really believes, when his shrewdness deserts him for the moment, that life is a contest between good and evil, or at least between readily distinguishable good and evil impulses:

> Good was as if man's spirit had produced art in life. Levin felt that the main source of conscious morality was love of life, anybody's life. Morality was a way of giving value to other lives through assuring human rights. As you valued men's lives yours received value. You earned what you sold, got what you gave. That, if not entirely true, ought to be. Our days are short, thought Levin, our bodies frail. The universe is unknown, remorseless. We have no certain understanding of Nature's intentions, nor God's if he intends. We know the meagerness, ignorance, cruelty of too many men and too many societies. We must protect the human, the good, the innocent. Those who had discovered their own moral courage or created it, must join others who are moral; these must lead, without fanaticism. Any act of good is a diminution of evil in the world.

In the context of the novel, these moony speculations are

provoked by Levin's feelings of guilt about his adulterous affair with a woman whom he understands very well:

> She had caused herself to love out of discontent, although her discontents were tolerable. Gilley was good to her; she had a better than average home, kids she loved. Maybe she was bored but she wasn't desperate; she probably could go on living with him forever. If diversion was what she had wanted, a little love on the side, she wasn't made for it, the pleasure butchered by anxiety and shame. She wasn't the type who could give "all" for love. And he doubted he could inspire such love, the limits of her passion conditioned by the man he was.

The most surprisingly effective scene in the novel is Levin's last confrontation with the husband, who confirms with sheaves of blood-curdling evidence what his wife (any wife?) is like:

> . . . She was born dissatisfied . . . you'll wake up at six A.M. to hear her already going on about her life and how it didn't pan out as she wanted it to. When you ask her what she had expected, all she can tell you is that she wanted to be a better person than she is . . . Then you will hear in long detail everything she thinks she has done wrong, or those things she tried to do and had to give up, or everything she now does and does badly. She will never once tell you what she does well, which can get pretty monotonous. After that she'll blame you for as much as she blames herself, because you married her . . . and didn't do what she calls 'bring me out,' meaning make out of her something she couldn't make out of herself though you may have broken your back trying to think up new ways to do it . . .

Moreover, according to Gilley's inexorable testimony, she's a rotten housekeeper and cook, has constipation and female ailments, is afraid of doctors, and lacks the moral capacity to be grateful for past pleasures. When Levin, notwithstanding, persists in his decision to carry her off,

> Gilley stared at him. "You expect to go on with this after what I've told you?"
>
> Levin laughed badly.

So does the reader, not only badly but incredulously, as Levin the gentle boob, deprived of job and illusions, long since deprived of love ("Was it a guilty response to experience he should have accepted as one accepts sunlight? Why must he forever insist on paying for being alive?"), drives off into the sunset with somebody else's pregnant wife and children. Maybe Jews are just born to suffer; though we had better hopes at the outset for Levin the starry-eyed scenery-buff, shy pursuer of pretty students, and happy home-wrecker. As for the novel, from an often amusing travelogue it abruptly collapses into one more allegory of self-crucifixion. But Levin is no Frank Alpine. And Malamud may have nowhere else to take his hero except on trips to each of the other forty-nine states or to Europe again; or back to the primordial ghetto.

The question is, now that the twentieth century is two-thirds finished, Whatever became of the Jew in America? In Malamud's fiction he survives as a tourist without a past; in Bellow's, barely and sourly as a displaced person, an alien tolerated and unloved, hankering after vanished patriarchal simplicities. In *Letting Go,* he is altogether absorbed into a culture he despises as much as he despises the culture from which he sprang. Whereas in *Goodbye, Columbus* Roth is unintentionally disagreeable (or, in several of the shorter stories, condescendingly sentimental) about a past that shames and exasperates him, in *Letting Go* he is intentionally and unrelentingly disagreeable about a present whose disgusts and anxieties play no favorites among the egos they feed on. After Libby's abortion, she and Paul come home to face another nightmare scene, in which the elderly Korngold, having been bilked by the equally elderly con-man, the reptilian Levy, appeals to Paul for help. Paul helps by almost strangling Levy, who eventually escapes and discharges his venom:

> But Levy was now in the doorway, slicing the air with his cane. Everyone jumped back as he made a vicious X with his weapon. "Disgusting! Killer!" he cried, slashing away. "Scraping life down sewers! I only make my way in the world, an old shit-on old man. I only want to live, but a murderer, *never!* This is your friend, Korngold," announced Levy. "This is your friend and accomplice, takes a seventeen-year-old girl and cuts her *life* out! Risks her life! Commits abortions! Commits *horrors!*" He gagged, clutched his heart, and ran from the room.

Paul, almost out of his head for fear of disgrace and prison,

> . . . sat up all night in the chair. Near four—or perhaps later, for the buses were running—he walked into the hall. He hammered twice on Levy's door.
>
> "Levy!"
>
> No answer.
>
> "Levy, do you hear me?" He kicked five distinct times on the door. He started to turn the knob but, at the last moment, decided not to. From the darkness behind the door might not Levy bring down a cane on his head?
>
> "Levy—listen to me, Levy. You never open your mouth. You never in your life say one word to anybody. Never! I'll kill you, Levy. I'll strangle you to death! Never—understand, you filthy son of a bitch! I'll kill you and leave you for the rats! You filth!"
>
> And that last word did not leave him; it hung suspended within the hollow of his being through the rest of the night, until at last it was white cold daylight.

Nor do Jews, elderly or young, have a corner on nastiness. The same day, Paul visits the young doctor who, apparently from the kindness of his heart, directed him to the abortionist:

> Had everything worked out? Wife all right? Satisfied? Fine—he did not mean to pry. Only one had to check on Smitty. He fed the osteopath patients—almost one a month—but still it was wise to keep an eye on the fellow. Every once in

a while Doctor Tom seemed to forget about slipping Dr. Esposito his few bucks. You know what I mean? Not an entirely professional group, osteopaths . . .

Most of the novel is a shuddering recoil against the horrors of human contact; for *Letting Go* is a novel about attachment, relationship, of which the intensest and most destructive instance is marriage. Paul and Libby make each other miserable in all the ways possible to husband and wife. By the end of the novel, Paul is impotent and Libby has settled into numbed and parasitic housewifery with an adopted child. Throughout the novel, Paul is helpless in practical matters, emergencies, love, anger, friendship; Libby is such a pitiable gorgon of stupid hysterical messiness that the reader can only wonder how any man could fall for her and stick with her:

> "I think I'm going to go out this afternoon," Libby said, picking at her orange.
>
> "Just dress warmly."
>
> "Don't you want to know where I'm going?"
>
> "Out. For a walk . . ." he said. "I thought you said you were going out."
>
> "If you're not interested . . ."
>
> "Libby, don't be petulant first thing in the morning."
>
> "Well, don't be angry at me for last night."
>
> "Who said anything about last night?"
>
> "That's the whole thing—you won't even bring it up. Well, I didn't behave so badly, and don't think I did."
>
> "That's over and done with. You were provoked. That's all right. That's finished."
>
> She did not then ask him who had provoked her; she's just began cloudily to accept that she had been.
>
> "Where are you going?" he asked.
>
> "When?" Now she *was* petulant, perhaps because she no longer considered it necessary to feel guilty about last night . . .

Roth's talent for dramatizing at murderous length the most squalid and irresolvable quarrels, especially between husband and wife, is exercised with bleak frequency in the novel. If it isn't Paul and Libby, it's Gabe and Libby, or Gabe and Martha. *Letting Go* intends to be almost as much about a *ménage à trois*—Paul-Libby-Gabe—as about a marriage; and in fact about four relationships that fail: Paul-Libby, Gabe-Libby, Paul-Gabe, and Gabe-Martha. The alternative to the success that eludes them is "letting go": madness, or impotence and despair. There are only two characters who do not seem created chiefly to be crammed into the gloomy design of the novel: Martha, who has enough animal vitality to enjoy herself when she can and to survive the wreckage with poise and humor; and Paul's Uncle Asher, the ancient Chorus, free outsider, who delivers the ancestral warning to his nephew before the marriage:

> " . . . Paulie, kiss the girl, caress her, stick it right up in her, but for Christ's sake do me a favor and wait a year. You're an artistic type, a serious observer of life, why kill your talent? You'll sap yourself with worry, you'll die of a hard-on in the streets. Other women will tantalize you some day and you and your conscience will wrestle till you choke . . . Listen to Uncle Schmuck, will you? Things come and go, and you have got to be a receptacle, let them pass right through. Otherwise death will be a misery for you, boy; I'd hate to see it. What are you going to grow up to be, a canner of experience? You going to stick plugs in at either end of your life? Let it flow, let it go. Wait and accept and learn to pull the hand away. *Don't clutch!* What is marriage, what is it but a pissy form of greed, a terrible, disgusting ambitiousness . . . "

Uncle Asher makes his point much later too, for a chastened Paul possibly in sight of suicide:

> " . . . what I'm in favor of is getting back in tune a little bit with nature. All this emphasis on charity and fucking. Disgusting."
>
> "But you've always had women, Asher. You told me that too, remember? A Chinese woman and so on. That's all you talked about last time we met. You made it sound as though I was leaving a harem for marriage. Let's be serious, if we're going to have discussions."
>
> "You misunderstood. Ass is no panacea. Not even the highest quality."
>
> "Then why do you pursue it?"
>
> "One, I got needs and prefer ladies to queers. Number two, I told you, I'm the child of the age. I want to understand what all the movies and billboards are about. Three, you still haven't got what I'm talking about. I'm talking about taking a nice Oriental attitude for yourself. Pre-Chiang Kai-Shek. Ungrasping. Undesperate. Tragic. Private. Proportioned. So on down the line. I only want to leave you with one thought, Paulie, because I've got to get out of here and I don't want to find you dead when I get back. Nobody owes nobody nothing. That's the slogan over the Garden of Eden. That's what's stamped on all our cells. Body cells, what makes us. There's your nature of man . . . "

Uncle Asher stands in the wings; but nobody in the action of the novel is susceptible to his philosophy of non-attachment. Indeed, the most substantial and admirable character in the novel is Martha Reganhart, who practices with spontaneous piety the doctrine of love and touch even at the price of pride, who has "a natural instinct for sharing pleasure"; the harassed, puzzled, hard-working, slovenly, man-hungry wise-cracking divorcee with two kids she worries about and a roomer to help pay the rent:

> She planted a kiss on her son's neck and he drew a purple line across the bridge of her nose.

> "Bang! Bang!" he shouted into her ear, and she left him to his drawing.
>
> "What's the matter with your nose?" Sissy asked. "You look like you've just been shat upon."
>
> "Could you control your language in my house?"
>
> "What are you coming on so salty again for?"
>
> "I don't want my children saying shat, do you mind? And put on a bathrobe. My son's earliest memory is going to be of your ass."
>
> "Now who's filthy?"
>
> "I happen to be their mother. I support them. Please, Sissy, *don't* walk around here half-naked, will you?"

The only love and passion in the novel is between Martha and Gabe, as on one occasion when Gabe is too ill for anything but pleasure:

> "Oh Gabe," she said, "my Gabe—"
>
> I left her there alone, just lips, just hands, and was consumed not in sensation, but in a limpness so total and blinding, that I was no more than a wire of consciousness stretched across a void. Martha's hair came raking up over me; she moved over my chest, my face, and I saw her now, her jaw set, her eyes demanding, and beneath my numb exterior, I was tickled by something slatternly, some slovenliness in the heavy form that pinned me down. I reached out for it, to *touch* the slovenliness—
>
> "Just lie still," I heard her say, "don't touch, just still—"
>
> She showed neither mercy then, nor tenderness, nor softness, nothing she had ever shown before; and yet, dull as I was, cut off in my tent of fever and fatigue, I felt a strange and separate pleasure. I felt cared for, labored over; I felt used . . .

The affair between Martha and Gabe develops so promisingly, in fact, that it takes all of Gabe's motiveless *Angst*, plus an outrageous trick of plot, to separate them forever and reinstate the novel's atmosphere of seamless wretchedness. For Roth is determined to keep everybody wretched, or to prove out wretchedness as the norm and pleasure as a passing aberration. He will use all his skill to show that nothing works.

The skill has protracted and damaging lapses. One of these has already been mentioned: Roth is never able to indicate why Paul marries Libby or stays married to her; or why Gabe, far more improbably, continues throughout the novel to find Libby fascinating. In general, the novel is weak on motivation: a weakness that would count little if it were not for Roth's insistence on the finicky motive-hunting by Gabe the sophisticated narrator. Gabe's "ironic" discriminations between chalk and cheese are as tedious and false as Nick Carraway's in *The Great Gatsby;* and Roth indulges him at length in his bad habit. As for Roth's own motive here, it may be that he is trying to achieve some distance from a subject too close for comfort; but he is a better novelist when he just gives up and hugs it to him unironically, letting the knifelike cross-purposes of his dialogue cut him up a bit.

Malamud and Bellow are in their fifties, each with an uneven but important *oeuvre* behind him; each, however, pretty clearly in need of new subjects now that the American Jew has disappeared into their novels. Roth is in his early thirties, a *Wunderkind,* having produced in his twenties a big novel that registers the disappearance of the American Jew not only into fiction, but into the featureless and solipsistic emotional landscapes of contemporary America. Something to have done in a first novel! Now, having put the headstone on the subject that he and Malamud and Bellow worked to death, he may be in the same fix as the others. Still it is difficult not to be hopeful about all of them, in the impasse to which their energies have rashly carried them. At least Bellow has finally given up on style; and, besides, been tempered into a wary respect for the women of America, those hard facts that Malamud and Roth also are acquainted with and astounded by.

The Jew is dead: Libby killed Paul; Pauline killed Levin; Madeleine killed Herzog. The Jew was done in by the American bitch who closed his ears against the admonitory ancestral voices. At his tomb three novelists meditate, trying to conceive an American sequel to the myth of Eden.

POSTSCRIPT 1970

Bellow's first book after *Herzog* was *Mosby's Memoirs & Other Stories,* about which I wrote that "Bellow's astonishing eclecticism looks very odd in a collection: the stories are related to one another only in the sleight-of-hand virtuosity with which each one manipulates the special style that Bellow chooses for it. Every style of Bellow's suffers from a chronic chill of pedantry and remoteness except the Herzog style, which is probably as close as we'll ever get to hearing Bellow himself. The best, if a rather slight, story is the only one in the Herzog style, 'A Father-to-Be'. . . . 'The Old System' is Augie March in a funereal mood; 'Looking for Mr. Green' is Depression naturalism, more supple than Farrell or Dos Passos; 'The Gonzaga Manuscripts' is the product of Bellow's unaccountable impulse to redo 'The Aspern Papers'; 'Leaving the Yellow House' may have compassionate intentions but it's an iceberg of a story, a demoralizing account of the nullity of a down-and-out old woman; 'Mosby's Memoirs' is in Bellow's latest brilliant, showy, dense, protective manner behind which the reader is not admitted."

Mr. Sammler's Planet, looking for a while rather like *Herzog* in late middle age, lacks the latter's electrifying hatred of its hero's enemies and so lacks everything. It is an earnest, nervous, inert jeremiad against contemporary America (materialism; the cult of revolutionary youth; Bellow's capital sinner the American woman, who this time is indicted for bad smells and alleged to be "smearing all with her female fluids"). It is a disappointing book. "I am extremely skeptical of explanations, rationalistic practices," austerely declares Mr. Sammler, Bellow's spokesman, pausing after two hundred pages of expository and rationalistic monologue, and about to wow a small rapt audience with his bookworm reasons for the world's troubles. The novel is at least unfashionable in a fashionable time, it disapproves of much; but its notions are defensive, despairing, and not very interesting ("Violence might subside, exalted ideas might recover importance"). Characteristically in Bellow's novels, his narrative keeps threatening to recede into allegory and opinion: in *Mr. Sammler's Planet* Auschwitz and the 1967 Arab-Israeli war are big ideas, pretexts for Hollywood flashbacks, but they are never events or foreshadowings of events; and the present is only the immediate pretext for the author's moral dyspepsia. Mr. Sammler is a seventy-two-year-old refugee: Bellow expects us to make every allowance for old age, foreignness, fussiness, platitude, and any other plausible defect in his protagonist. The author, however, is inexcusable, having finally condemned himself to his cosmos of Air-Wick (exalted ideas) and bad smells (reality).

I was impressed enough by *When She Was Good,* Roth's first book after *Letting Go,* to use it for the concluding exhibit in a review concerned till that point with French and American practitioners of the *nouveau roman:*

> *When She Was Good* . . . is in effect a posthumous Dreiser novel, with much family-album verisimilitude ("Edward's bronchitis had lingered nearly three weeks") and some acutely observed American domesticity. Roth continues, clumsily and anachronistically, to be gnawed—as he was in that underrated novel *Letting Go*—by the problems of sin and responsibility. Why do destructive people behave as they do? How do they persuade themselves that they are good? How does it *feel* to be bad? Roth cares about such questions, stumbling along in the burlap sack of his prose:

> This battle, too, she had fought and this battle, too, she had won, and yet it seemed that she had never in her life been miserable in the way that she was miserable now. Yes, all that she had wanted had come to be, but the illusion she had, as they drove home through the storm, was that she was never going to die—she was going to live forever in this new world she had made, and never die, and never have the chance not just to be right, but to be happy.

> Roth can even, under the stimulus of a climactic scene, revive such questions for his readers, he can hear every vibration of the terrible small voice of righteousness confronting an unworthy adversary:

> She got up and went into the bathroom. Into the mirror she said,

> "Twenty-two. I am only twenty-two."

> When she came back into the living room the radio was playing.

> "How you feeling?" he asked.

> "Fine."

> "Aren't you all right, Lucy?"

> "I'm feeling *fine*."

"Look, I didn't mean I'm going to *publish* a book even if I could."

"If you want to publish a book, Roy, publish a book!"

"Well, I won't! I was just having some fun. Jee—zuz." He picked up one of his family's old copies of *Life* and began leafing through it. He slumped into his chair, threw back his head and said, "Wow."

"What?"

"The radio. Hear that? 'It Might As Well Be Spring.' You know who that was my song with? Bev Collison. Boy. Skinny Bev. I wonder whatever happened to her."

"How would I know?"

"Who said you'd know? I was only reminded of her by the song. Well, what's wrong with that?" he asked. "Boy, this is really some Valentine's Day night!"

A little later he pulled open the sofa, and they laid out the blanket and pillows. When the lights were off and they were in bed, he said that she had been looking tired, and probably she would feel better in the morning. He said he understood.

Understood what? Feel better why?

Righteousness has its own sheer cliffs.

When She Was Good is, most of it, hopelessly old-fashioned, and it is an interesting novel. Why not? The novel, of all artifacts, remains the one least divisible from its artificer, whose idiosyncrasies and judgments may prevail over the demands of the genre itself. Roth's mind, besieged by archaic American drearinesses, is more interesting than Barthelme's or Burroughs'. Novels are too long, the novelist can't get away with gimmicks or momentary flashes; he has to disclose substance and continuity somewhere, perhaps in himself.

The most startling fact about *Portnoy's Complaint,* however, is Roth's absence from it. The feeble pun of the title is a portent: the book's organization is rudimentary; there are maybe a half-dozen amusing pages (some of the whacking-off rhetoric; several outbursts by The Monkey; Portnoy's attempt on the virtue of the tractor-sized kibbutz heroine); and the otherwise uninterrupted cornball-ethnic witlessness comes close to proving that "Philip Roth" is a clever pseudonym for this title page or all the others. "Doctor, *please,*" cries Portnoy, "I can't live any more in a world given its meaning and dimension by some vulgar nightclub clown." It's a horrid fate all right, and Roth or "Roth" ought to wipe off the greasepaint and apologize.

Malamud continues to be an honorable and conscientious writer, even in so ambitious a book as *The Fixer.* But the best part of the book is the least ambitious, the long opening section, which creates and places the promisingly irritable and disillusioned hero among the commonplaces of Jewish experience in pre-1914 Eastern Europe. When Bok

is arrested, the subject-matter abruptly changes from Yiddish to Russian: it's no disgrace that Malamud is not so competent as Dostoevsky was to prove on our nerves the whole metaphysical cycle of capture, terror, torment, endurance, and redemption; at any rate, Malamud is ambitious enough to try, and skilful enough to make the details (though never their historical resonance) convincing.

Lothar Kahn

SOURCE: "American-Jewish Literature After Bellow, Malamud, and Roth," in *Jewish Book Annual,* Vol. 45, 1987-1988, pp. 5-18.

[*In the following essay, Kahn describes writers of the American Jewish Literary Renaissance who wrote in the 1960s, 1970s, and 1980s.*]

If there was, indeed, an American-Jewish literary Renaissance it probably commenced in the mid-fifties and extended for some fifteen to twenty years into the late sixties or early seventies. Since then Jewish literature has enjoyed a diminished critical vogue and its popularity has also lessened considerably.

The Renaissance so-called is intertwined with the names of Bellow, Malamud and Philip Roth. Edward Lewis Wallant might have offered them keen competition had his life not been cut short at thirty-six. Other writers of lesser stature clearly benefited from the succès d'estime of their more illustrious brethren. Men like Herman Wouk, Irwin Shaw, Leon Uris and Jerome Weidman, previously considered literary entertainers, now received more respectful reviews in addition to appearing on the best-seller lists.

Toward the close of the Renaissance a second group of writers was published, among whom Cynthia Ozick, Hugh Nissenson, Seymour Epstein, Jerome Charyn and Chaim Potok offered the greatest promise. Before long they were joined by Johanna Kaplan, Robert Kotlowitz and Jay Neugeboren. It is to these writers that this study is devoted.

Just as Bellow, Malamud and Roth did not constitute a school with followers and disciples, so these later writers had few common denominators. They also never reached the critical heights of the pathfinders, though some individual achievements, notably by Ozick and Kaplan, could compare favorably. With the exception of the early works of Chaim Potok, the later writers rarely made the best-seller list.

Before moving on to our writers, let us review theories most often advanced for the eminence of the Jewish novel in its years of glory. Many placed the recent Holocaust background into the forefront of plausible explanations. Just enough time had elapsed since the discovery of the millions of dead to be able to view the events with perspective and tranquillity. Bellow, Malamud and Roth had gone way beyond sentimentalizing the East Side past without shedding the guilt for having made it and without achieving a satisfactory transition. They had spent the war in the safety of America, while co-religionists had suffered untold atrocities and a gruesome end. No excess of the imagination was needed for them to realize that, but for the emigration from Europe of grandparents or parents, they would have lain on the pile of the emaciated dead.

Actually not many writers chose Holocaust survivors as protagonists. There were some, to be sure, such as Bellow's Sammler, Wallant's Sol Nazerman, Meyer Levin's Eva. The bulk of writers was too fearful that they could not reconstruct events that defied the imagination, or from which artistic distance was impossible. The terror felt by many writers was more indirect, but none the less real. Malamud's *The Fixer* and Arthur Cohen's *In the Days of Simon Stern* expressed this terror through historical and theological approaches.

HOLOCAUST AWARENESS

The presence of the Holocaust was perceived by Jewish and non-Jewish readers, even when it was most indirect. The attempt to exterminate the Jew and his ability to survive had invested him with an aura of mystery, as a specialist in survival. In an age in which nuclear weapons had made survival a generalized human problem, the Jew's example was mystically endowed with some unknown quality, wisdom or attitude. How else could he have emerged tear-filled but triumphant from his martyrdom? Moreover, the media were wailing over such disintegrating forces in the general society as drunkenness, drug abuse, sexual promiscuity and somehow the Jew seemed less at risk from this triple peril. Might the Jew have something purposeful to tell on physical and spiritual survival?

There was also the presumed role of the Jew as prophet. Whether the writer used the Holocaust directly or not, his work served as a reminder of the base aspects of man's nature and his potential for evil. The Jew was almost accepted as teacher with the Christian as a willing pupil. By telling a tale, even if unconnected with the Hitler crimes, the Jewish writer unwittingly assumed the part of augur in a world grown infinitely dangerous.

Another theory advanced for the eminence of Jewish literature centered on the alleged malaise of the age, alienation. The role of the Jew was perceived historically as that of a solitary wanderer in the chaos of the world. The Jew's memories were such that they precluded uninhibited, free relationships with others. Participation in human affairs had paradoxically become more problematic at a moment when politically and socially he had become more involved than ever before. He had not forgotten his outsider status, had come to terms with his own brand of isolation and estrangement, and had developed an interest in the fate of those marginal groups who had taken over his former position. Blacks, Hispanics, Orientals were the new outsiders, still too preoccupied with their physical and economic status to be aware fully of their psychological and spiritual alienation. The Jews had seen it all and could offer lessons in all forms of alienation.

For this or other reasons, the Jewish writer who had labored for so long in the shadow of Dos Passos, Hemingway, Faulkner, Dreiser and Lewis, suddenly became interesting and fashionable. But there were even then detractors, Jewish and others, who recognized no exceptional merit in Bellow, Malamud and Roth. They attributed the Renaissance to the New York intellectual establishment that had willed its own heroes into the limelight. Others denounced the Jewish novel as just the latest fad. The American reading public would quickly weary of the Jew as it had previously of the tycoon, then the proletarian and the decadent Southerner. The Renaissance was also ascribed by some to the high number of Jewish readers, mostly educated women who then recommended the novels to husbands and others.

All theories concerning the causes, worth and success of the Jewish novel contained some truth, but none encapsuled the whole truth.

NEW HORIZONS

Given that Bellow, Malamud and Roth had surfeited the once virginal field of Jewish literature, the newer writers had the unenviable task of staking out new territory and laying claim to some originality of their own. They built, to be sure, on the work of the pathfinding trio, extended it, and then developed themes and attitudes that transcended those of the Renaissance writers.

The newer writers baked their fiction with more specifically Jewish ingredients, in which even theology and internal cultural conflicts played a role. Besides the introduction of these new concerns Holocaust survivors and Israeli problems were beckoning for attention. The Jew's connection with America was now that of a citizen secure and entrenched, no longer fearful of losing his religious innocence to a seductive materialism. The desire now was less to make it than, having made it, to make his moral influence felt in an age of affluence. A transfer was made from a once powerful commitment to Torah to an equally strong commitment to social values, the relief of racial tensions and discrimination, the war against poverty and crime, involvement in peace movements and nuclear disarmament programs.

Perhaps the most promising of the late Renaissance, early post-Renaissance writers was Cynthia Ozick, a writer who can only be described as "integrally Jewish." She has been aptly termed an uncompromising crusader against idolaters of all kinds. In the title story of *The Pagan Rabbi* (1971), the battle against paganism is literal. Ozick pits the moral discipline of religious Judaism against the nature worship and sexual libertinism of the Hellenic world. Nymphs of woods and fields and later on Christian maidens seek to seduce previously stalwart Jewish men, who were committed to the One God of Israel. Yet this God cannot be apprehended, Ozick makes it clear, through rational processes. Like I. B. Singer whose success becomes a subject of envy in one of her finest stories, she frequently invokes the supernatural. Characters levitate as a symbol of the separation of a writer from the world about her. A woman lawyer constructs a Golem that first turns New York into a Utopia, then in the manner of Golems, females included, turns against its creator and through sexual excesses leaves the city in a more chaotic state than the one from which she had rescued it. There are no limits other than good taste to the luminous, often extravagant Ozick imagination, to her inventiveness which, if not always clear or conclusive in its results, usually makes at least a fascinating speculative point.

Her war against false gods is sometimes waged through competing cultural priorities. In *Trust* (1966), her least Jewish novel, the unnamed heroine chooses between approaches to life represented by her three "fathers": the respectable WASP lawyer, the pagan, sexually profligate but exciting Nick, the ex-Marxist, state department officer and recalcitrant Jew, Enoch. Ultimately the modes of all three prove wanting. Yet at a crucial moment Enoch is seen reading Talmud. Cultural choices are again offered, inconclusively, in the much later *Cannibal Galaxy* (1986). Here the Jew Joseph Brill, who survived World War II in the dungeon of a convent consuming the library of a deceased priest, resolves to establish a school in which elements of French and Hebraic culture are to be fused into a harmonious curriculum. Ambitiously conceived within its naturally limited frame, the curriculum in practice becomes merely humdrum, as Brill himself loses enthusiasm. His teachers never understood it and mothers had their own unrelated ideas of what is good for their offspring. Other cultural choices need to be made and Ozick manages to supply a goodly share of surprises, reflecting her own ideas as to the nature of genius and its relationship to education.

ESSENTIAL JEWISHNESS

No writer on the American-Jewish scene is as integrally Jewish as Cynthia Ozick, in the sense that she blends national, cultural and religious components. If at times, more in her essays than in her fiction, she strikes many as ethnocentrically Jewish, this is at least partly due to hearing the unaccustomed voice of a wholly Jewish writer.

Ozick has crowded authentic Jewish experience into her work. Biblical references abound, the knowledge of Jewish life in other countries is live (the *Edmond Fleg* School of the *Cannibal Galaxy* is named after a deceased French-Jewish poet), and the presence of the Holocaust is felt. Enoch in *Trust* has the task after the war of tabulating the figures of the Jewish dead. Joseph Brill escaped detection only through a miracle. Though Ozick's characters feel secure in America her journalistic work more than her fiction leaves no doubt that she has not forgotten what it means to be Jewish in a largely hostile world.

In spite of her successful use of phantasy and paradox, a credible fusion of the serious with the comic, there are flaws in her work. Her fictions seem lacking in spontaneity at times, are labored and display an often obsessive seriousness about language. This leads to the impression that there are private meanings from which, consciously or otherwise, her readers are excluded.

Robert Alter has called Hugh Nissenson "the only genuinely religious writer in the whole Jewish group." Indeed, Nissenson told the late Harold Ribalow that he is truly "obsessed with religious sensibility and atheistic sensibility," and that the metaphysical Weltanschauung is of predominant interest to him. He is not greatly intrigued with social questions but all the more with the myth potential of whatever he depicts. Also, as he told Ribalow, he wants to participate in the search of finding out "just what this business of being Jewish is all about."

To find out, Nissenson has placed his characters in a variety of locales, including Israel, where most American-Jewish writers have feared to tread. Two of his stories in *Pile of Stones* (1965), his best collection, have Warsaw as their setting, symbol of the past; two others have their narratives unfold in Israel, symbol of the Now; and two others take place in America, the emblem of the Then and Now. Whatever Nissenson's location, whatever the time frame, his Jew is and remains a harried, alienated human being. What distinguishes him further is his moral earnestness and intensity and the fundamental decency and dignity he displays in a world darkened by humiliation, danger and death. In the background, addressed directly or otherwise, is the inscrutable God whom Nissenson's Jew must question, given the absurdity of the world and its inhabitants.

It is a pity that in his one novel to date, *My Own Ground* (1976), Nissenson showed limited aptitude for the longer genre. Yet for him to explore successfully his "theological obsession," he would need more than the short story or the extended story he calls here a novel. Reminiscent of Joseph Roth's *Hiob* (Job), the novel tells of the tribulations of an Orthodox Jew whose only daughter takes off with a pimp, suffers moral and physical debasement, and though she befriends a political radical after an escape, returns willingly to her pimp. In her shame, however, she kills herself. Though her father had previously refused to wash a suicide's body for burial, he now washes his daughter's. "The time has come for us, at last, to break all our holy Laws, one by one," he says. The bereft father cites the Midrash: "Israel speaks to God: When will you redeem us?" And He answers: "When you have sunk to the lowest level, at that time will I redeem you. The time has come. That level has been reached. Bring on the Messiah!" Nissenson's novel is one of salvation, a minor Jewish equivalent of the novels of grace by Mauriac, Bernanos, and perhaps Dostoyevski.

Nissenson spent some time on a Kibbutz and was in Israel at the tail end of the '67 War. In his *Notes from the Frontier* (1968) he engaged in a type of travel reportage to which only a good practitioner of fiction can do justice. He used some of his experiences in the title story of *In the Reign of Peace* (1972), a second and effective collection of stories.

POTOK'S CONTRIBUTION

Considering that Chaim Potok's novels have all been novels of culture and ideas, their success has been nothing short of phenomenal. He has eschewed the pitfalls of much fiction by rabbis, especially in Europe. He does not preach. He may instruct in that he vivifies ideas, pits one culture against another, one set of religious tenets against another, a solid religious upbringing in conflict with secular preoccupations. In the process Potok has not always succeeded in keeping his characters fully alive. At times they merely become ideas that speak and act. When his characters slide into conflict, it is rarely over jealousy, power, greed or sex. They part company over loyalty to concepts, practices, promises. Whereas Potok has been exceptionally convincing in depicting ways of life, wars of thought, even mystical and supernatural phenomena, he is far less skilled in describing scenes of daily living, or in reproducing natural dialogue. In fact, his dialogue is undifferentiated—it usually sounds the same coming from the mouths of all his characters.

In spite of these flaws, Potok has enjoyed a wide following among different levels of readers. This is all the more remarkable considering that this cultured, intelligent, scholar-novelist has written the same novel several times, with just sufficient variations to make them seem fresh and vigorous with each new work. Father-son relationships, sons attempting to break out of the prefashioned mold, the Orthodox youngster attracted to professions like psychiatry or the visual arts, the parent who must eventually let go or settle for a loving compromise, sons ashamed of the parental scientific contribution to the nuclear threat, another trying to come to grips with mystic gifts—these are the uncommon idea-character situations of a Potok novel. Yet there are powerful scenes in *The Chosen* (1967), the most truly novelistic of his novels and also in *My Name is Asher Lev* (1972), his most memorable achievements.

Some of the flaws of Potok's fiction reappear in the philosophical-cultural works of the late Arthur A. Cohen, an interpreter of Buber and a theologian of some accomplishment. Cohen's one outstanding novel has been *In the Days of Simon Stern* (1973), truly a minor masterpiece. Alas, the structure of the novel is too complex and the language too recherché so that it frightens away any but the most fascinated and stubborn of readers. Though the novel can hold its own with the best of Potok, it cannot even approximate the latter's wide popular appeal.

A blind man narrates Simon Stern's life and his determination to found his "Society for the Rescue and Resurrection of the Jews." Simon Stern, we learn, was born on the East Side and rose to be a millionaire, a whiz at real estate transactions. When he finds out at a mass meeting that Hitler was wantonly killing uncountable numbers of Jews, Stern acts out his "predetermined role of Messiah." But this Messiah can't stop the killings, only think of the redemption and reconstruction ahead. He sets about rebuilding a city block and plans an enclave there for Jewish survivors. He will bring them over to America and settle them in his compound. Stern's action is largely symbolic, as he strives for Jewish continuation through rescue and rehabilitation. Arthur Cohen's Simon Stern is less a messenger from God than an ambassador to God. "Choose, dear God, if you wish to remain our God," is the defiant challenge flung at the divinity.

The narrative becomes a chain of biblical and kabbalistic legends, theological tracts, virtual homilies. Cohen tells his story on several levels. Thus he integrates his own vision of Jewish history. In his enclave he builds a replica of the Temple which is destroyed in the end and forces Stern's Jews to disperse once more. Yet, any attempt to summarize adequately this brilliant, multi-layered work is fraught with danger.

Chaim Potok.

Cohen was less successful in other works, including his fictional attempt to define the personality and achievement of a Hannah Arendt type figure in *An Admirable Woman* (1983). Cohen never managed to reach beyond an intellectual portrait, and even here he did not fully succeed. Ultimately Cohen's reputation as a novelist must rest on his striking, imaginative, theological Holocaust novel.

SURVIVOR'S TALE

A Holocaust novel is also the most striking and moving work to date of Susan Fromberg Schaeffer. *Anya* (1974) does not dwell on the atrocities nor does it seek to transform the Holocaust into a symbol. This story of a Polish medical student, a fiercely protective mother, caught in a net of history that envelops her and forever alters the nature of her calm and orderly life, is a profoundly moving document. It is also a superb achievement considering that the author, a professor of English at Brooklyn College, had never been to Poland, and had initially become acquainted with the notion of Holocaust through the Diary of Anne Frank. Schaeffer interviewed survivors and was touched especially by the tale of one whose life approximated that of the Anya to be. Schaeffer combined her new knowledge with the imagination and sensibility of the poetess she is.

The result is the somewhat idealized vision of a survivor, a woman with the determination not to be reduced to permanent victim status nor to accept passively the loss of her child. In the end Anya was reunited with her child, outlasting the years of horror, whereas the Nazi killers did not.

The fact bears repeating that Schaeffer does not seek to impart any special wisdom on the events of the forties. There are no new insights on killer Nazis, cowardly witnesses or pious, passive or even rebellious Jews. She is content to tell one person's encounter with history intruding itself cruelly into her existence.

In American situations which surely Schaeffer knew better, she has not always fared equally well. In her first novel, *Falling* (1973), she told the story of three generations of women in one family, presumably her own. In *Love* (1981), she relates the almost unrelieved suffering of a pharmacist. The title of this unsuccessful novel is puzzling, as love is one element that eludes the hero as well as most other characters. In *The Madness of a Seduced Woman* (1983), her one work without Jewish ties, she dealt more successfully with an obsessive, thoroughly destructive love that culminated in murder. Perhaps she wrote *Mainland* two years later to show love in a different light. Here an upper class New York woman finds salvation through a constructive love.

Love and what it is and can be, elevating in some instances, corrosive and debilitating in others, has been the focus of this writer's fiction to date. Schaeffer belongs to the finest stylists that the American Jewish late and post-Renaissance has produced.

Perhaps the most accomplished novelist among the writers of vision is Johanna Kaplan, who thus far has contributed only a collection of short stories, *Other People's Lives*

(1975) and *O My America* (1980), a superb novel. A teacher of disturbed children for many years, Kaplan translated her experiences in psychology into several lively stories of New Yorkers, the complexity of whose lives manifests itself through idiosyncratic behavior, which becomes less enigmatic as Kaplan unravels their tales of frustrations and exaltation. Here and in *O My America* she is also adroit in delineating the Jewishness of her characters, which is skillfully woven into the overall makeup.

PORTRAIT OF AN INTELLECTUAL

O My America is the novel of a culture hero of the 1960's, Ezra Slavin, the public worship he receives and the private misery he inflicts. For once ideas and character are intermeshed. Irony is fused with addictive belief, vision with experience. The novel traces the revolutionary change in the Jew's status from the early decades on the East side, when his goal was getting to "Allrightniks Row" and becoming one with the chosen people, accepted Americans. By 1960 he has arrived and in the person of Ezra Slavin, has impressed his influence on the minds of American intellectuals everywhere. The novel opens with Ezra's death which leads his one legitimate daughter, Merry, to a virtual biographical reconstruction of the Great Man's life. We learn of the radically different women with whom he has entertained liaisons and each one of whom gave him children. This theorist of a new education, this visionary of a new life and man, this anti-bourgeois, virtually Jewish anti-Semite feels uncomfortable with his women, his children and his disciples. The contradictions in his makeup offer more clues to Merry than almost anything else in her attempt to make sense of her father's life. Harsh in his own criticisms of Jews, he reacts violently to others indulging in the same criticism. Oblivious to facts and figures that others have known forever, Slavin sees them as new and casts them in a new light. He demands approbation of his ideas, but cannot bear to note the low cultural level for which his own influence is partly responsible. Ezra, the Jewish Guru with a vision of America all his own, is not at all at peace with the consequences of his vision which he has implanted in the American cultural landscape.

Slavin's vision of America represents an amalgam of influences, the Jewish, the immigrant, one wife's experience in the work force, another's background in the American hinterlands. Slavin is more of a puzzle to himself than he is at the end to Merry. Her own moderate lifestyle with tolerant views of the Right and Left represents her own vision of America, distinct from her father's. Ezra's mother called him an anti-Semite, Ezra himself was both intolerant of Jewish ethnocentrism and of anti-Semitism on the part of others. Merry has a complete view. She is moved, as is the reader, when one of Ezra's sons, whom he has hardly treated generously or paternally, yet says the words of the Kaddish at the memorial service.

With the exception of his most ambitious novel, *The Stolen Jew* (1981), which amply utilizes mythic material, the prolific Jay Neugeboren has depended on his sharp eyes and keen ears to delineate how people live, think and suffer and how they identify themselves as Jews. It is in this work that Neugeboren seems most conscious that Jews have a history of their own, that this history has never ceased to intrude itself into their lives—perhaps never more than in our own time. Yet in America, by contrast, Jews have a sense of security unprecedented in the Diaspora. The frequent involvements of his heroes in baseball or basketball show, much more than the intellectual Jews of *The Stolen Jew,* that they share in the simple though no longer innocent pleasures of U.S. sports. They feel sufficiently at home so that they can assume the role of companion and guide to the new Jews, the Blacks of America, with whom a silent, real though never untroubled bond has developed. In *The Stolen Jew,* the combination of compassion and daring is applied to the rescue of a Russian Jew.

The relationship between Jews and Blacks which permeates so much of Neugeboren's fiction is not based on conscious desires for closer bonds, nor is it always founded on mutual interest. Only rarely is there awareness on the part of the Jew that the Black now occupies a role that had once been his. There is little politics in Neugeboren's work, but in *Before my Life Began* (1985), Neugeboren succeeds in creating one of the most harrowing scenes in modern literature of Southern roughnecks harrassing, threatening, nearly killing Northern Freedom Marchers of whom his Jewish hero has been a leader.

Some critics have half-seriously suggested that the author's name of "born anew" is a significant clue to an understanding of his novels. Indeed, there is often a distinct rupture in the lives of his characters and the new life appears to have little in common with the life previously lived. In *Before My Life Began* the young hero is an assistant to his mobster uncle, has committed a murder, is forced to flee, leaving his wife and child behind. He reappears, this time as a builder, with a new wife and new family, and with interests dramatically different from those of his first life. Neugeboren does not succeed fully in getting the two lives to fuse into an harmonious whole. He does succeed here, as elsewhere, in dealing successfully with the themes of survival, life, death, and the usually futile search for self.

OLD WORLD ROOTS

Like Susan Fromberg Schaeffer, Robert Kotlowitz used an unfamiliar European setting for his distinguished *Somewhere Else* (1972). This is the story of Mendel, a rabbi's son, who chooses to leave his Polish home for the London of pre-World War I. The author's research took him to the archives of YIVO, to maps of pre-war Poland, to remembering the stories his grandfather had told him of a time gone by. Kotlowitz eschews the pitfall of sentimentalizing either the past or what is probably an ancestor. In London his hero Mendel quickly turns into Moritz. He changes from cantor to cafe singer and yields willingly to the secular temptations of the city.

Kotlowitz has stayed with topics of the recent Jewish past. *The Boardwalk* (1977) centers on the late summer vacation of a Jewish adolescent in Atlantic City in those nerve-wracking days before the guns of September started booming in Poland. *Sea-Changes* (1986), his most recent entry, tells of the immigration of a teenaged German Jewish boy in the early Hitler years. He is adopted by a Baltimore

Jewish family with ways very different from his own. The young hero is neither terribly convincing nor his adjustment to a new culture either persuasive or interesting.

Jerome Charyn has failed to live up to the promise of an exceptional talent. His first novels featured predominantly Jewish milieux. In later works he shifted sometimes to Italian or Polish immigrants, but they are little more than substitutes for the Jewish immigrant background he knows so well. For one whose keen powers of observation have sometimes turned him into an effective satirist, Charyn has remained charitable and compassionate. Though aware of follies and foibles, he doesn't forget that he is dealing with human beings, however absurd, dishonest, even repellent their actions.

The very versatility of his talent has been Charyn's most formidable enemy. He has tried too desperately to be inventive and, in the process, has often let his imagination get the better of him. While this sometimes uncontrolled inventiveness exudes a certain charm and elicits many a chuckle, it can grow wearisome and at times enigmatic. It is often difficult to fathom his meanings or to comprehend his conclusions, if any. His characters have picaresque adventures that take them from New York gangsterdom to Atlantic City hotels for whores, to Wild Bill Hickok country, Louisiana swamps, and other bizarre settings. Yet it is clear that, as for most of our writers, Charyn's heart belongs to New York. There are especially frequent returns to the Bronx of the 1940's. It is doubtful that in spite of an astounding virtuosity in a prolific body of work, Charyn ever again equalled the work that first brought his name to public attention, his 1964 accomplishment in *Once Upon a Droshky.*

UNIQUE WRITER

Finally, there is the unique case of Seymour Epstein, virtually unknown among Jewish readers. Epstein may well be the finest craftsman and yet the most natural and spontaneous writer of the group, a man with exceptional narrative speed and a well-controlled imagination. But Epstein is also that unusual Jewish writer who does not deal in the main with intellectuals and who has retained a positive though not uncritical sympathy for the bourgeoisie. In many ways, Epstein dares to be what critics do not find intriguing—a conservative, a realist, a straight story teller. That he often brilliantly reflects and comments on the human condition in books that are hard to put down is at best a mitigating circumstance for symbol-hunting critics.

Epstein's protagonists are fallible, forgiving, self-demanding, generous. They are puzzled by what life has doled out to them, what burdens they have been asked to carry, and how they can rid themselves of them without losing their dignity in the process. The big city loneliness of Leah, the befuddlement of David Lang's marital and paternal relations (*The Dream Museum,* 1971) all disclose a deep compassion for suffering humanity.

His characters are often Jewish. They have a Jewish sensibility, although they have little Jewish awareness and even less knowledge. Perhaps one of his characters was speaking for Epstein when he complained that, in his formative years, he was never given the opportunity to become informed about his Jewishness, not taught, not allowed or encouraged to become interested.

With the exception of Epstein and perhaps Charyn, the newer writers dealt more directly with Jewish subjects than the great trio that made Jewish fiction fashionable and critically respectable. Some, like Cohen, Ozick, Potok and Kaplan utilized Jewish experience in a new and often effective way. They had the knowledge and the desire to search for meaning in Jewish tradition and myth. While they did not shy from sociology and certainly not psychology, they did not limit themselves to this amply explored area. In one way or another, at least some sought to deal with the mysteries of the Holocaust, the wisdom of its survivors, the miracle of Israel and the new conflicts which the Jewish State engendered. They have broadened the field of Jewish literature, while not succeeding in restoring it to the eminence it enjoyed during the so-called Renaissance.

Arlene Fish Wilner

SOURCE: "The Jewish-American Woman as Artist: Cynthia Ozick and the *Paleface* Tradition," in *College Literature,* Vol. 20, No. 2, June, 1993, pp. 119-32.

[*In the following essay, Wilner discusses the thought and writing of Cynthia Ozick in terms of the American literary tradition.*]

A few years ago, on the fiftieth anniversary of Philip Rahv's essay, "Paleface and Redskin," Sanford Pinsker considered the current relevance of the 1939 analysis that became a touchstone critique of American literature. The nature of the literary "split personality" to which Rahv drew attention has become familiar. Simply put, it is a split between the cultivated abstractions of the intellectual and the raw, experiential mode that disdains ideas. The paleface, represented most clearly by Henry James and T. S. Eliot, "continually hankers after religious norms, tending toward a refined estrangement from reality. . . . At his highest level the paleface moves in an exquisite moral atmosphere, at his lowest he is genteel, snobbish, and pedantic." Redskins, in contrast, are writers like Whitman and Twain, men whose "reactions are primarily emotional, spontaneous, and lacking in personal culture." At their best redskins express "the vitality and . . . the aspirations of the people"; at their worst they are "vulgar anti-intellectual[s], combining aggression with conformity and reverting to the crudest forms of frontier psychology." Needless to say, both redskins and palefaces are male, white, and Christian.

How may the Jewish-American writer and in particular the female Jewish-American writer be viewed with regard to this dichotomous tradition? As Pinsker points out, Rahv believed that by 1939 the redskins had triumphed, since, after all, their perspective was the native, indigenous one, generated out of a specifically American, non-European culture and psyche. Pinsker argues that what immigrant Jews brought to this culture was a brand of European intellectualism, a texture of ideas and a sense of history. This infusion of theory and ideas into the redskin (read macho, frontiersman-like, cult-of-experience) tradi-

tion creates a new tension that makes itself felt among various works by the same author and also within individual works. Irving Howe sees in Saul Bellow, for example, the achievement of a new American style, as distinct as Hemingway's or Faulkner's: "a mingling of high-flown intellectual bravado with racy-tough street Jewishness, all in a comic rhetoric that keeps turning its head back toward Yiddish even as it keeps racing away from it." In a different but analogous way this split between head and heart also characterizes Malamud's *The Fixer,* whose protagonist, tormented by forces against which he is powerless, and forced to rely solely on his mental resources, rejects the temptation of martyrdom in favor of a commitment to work actively within the historical moment, even if such activity means only stubbornly enduring, that is, insisting on survival without loss of identity. A major irony of the book is that the fixer, Jesus-like in his patient suffering, ultimately achieves a kind of heroism in refusing to forgive and finds satisfaction in a fantasy of vengeance and retribution.

It is Philip Roth, however, who has spoken most directly of the competing claims on the Jewish-American writer. Roth describes his double heritage of (on the one hand) Jake the Snake H., owner of the corner candy store in the world of Roth's Newark childhood, "a middle-aged master of invective and insult, and a repository of lascivious neighborhood gossip" and (on the other hand) Henry James, whose "linguistic tact and moral scrupulosity" ravished Roth during his graduate student days at the University of Chicago. Redskin Jake, like comedian Henny Youngman, "demythologized [Jewish] yearnings for cultural superiority—or for superiority through culture" ("On *The Great American Novel*"). For the nice, talented Jewish boy from Newark, paleface James seemed an impossible predecessor (i.e., "the paleface one could never be in a million [or, to be precise, 5,733] years"). Together, Jake and James inevitably produced—in addition to a severe case of the anxiety of influence—the hybrid "redface," Roth's characterization of himself, the writer who is comfortable in neither world and therefore "reenacts the argument [between redskin and paleface] within the body of his own work." The difficulty of defining oneself in terms of traditions antithetical to each other, each only partly one's own, accounts, says Roth, for what he considers the enormous differences among his books, "each book veering sharply away from the one before, as though the author were mortified at having written it as he did and preferred to put as much light as possible between that kind of book and himself."

To what extent is Roth's identity crisis applicable to the case of an equally introspective female writer? Since Philip Roth and Cynthia Ozick are often considered to have defined divergent paths for the Jewish-American novel, and since both have deliberated quite openly on their respective endeavors, it is instructive to compare them. Despite the vast difference between Roth's fiction and Ozick's, one is reminded that Ozick, like Roth, battened on Henry James in her youthful days and was so seduced by his "mandarin" prose that she set out in her early twenties to duplicate James' artistry, ultimately giving birth to her first and only long novel, *Trust* (now out of print). However-er, Roth's dual allegiance to redskin Jake and paleface James did not find an analogy in Ozick, whose obsession with writing as an act of idolatry (forbidden by the Second Commandment) has instead posed for her the choice between paleface and nonface. That is, for Ozick the posited contradiction has been between high art and the religious values that transcend art altogether. Roth feels compelled somehow to accommodate Jake the Snake's earthy cynicism and directness with Henry James' cultivated refinement. The virtual impossibility of doing so accounts for what Roth calls his "continuing need for self-analysis and self-justification." Ozick, in contrast, believes that (as she wrote in a sketched self-portrait where the missing facial features should have been) "ego is not interesting."

I would suggest that this denial of artistic ego marks not a conflict but rather a connection between Ozick as committed Jew and Ozick as feminist. As critics have noted, the argument that the artist attempts to compete with God as creator and that art is therefore morally dangerous pales before the fact of Ozick's perseverance as a writer of consummate creativity. Her insistence on artistic-self-effacement, then, has to do with something more than repugnance at idolatry, namely, the otherness of gender. If Roth feels himself to be at some level a cultural pariah because of his suspension between two traditions, one never entirely escapable and one never entirely attainable, Ozick must cope in addition with the feminine mystique, a myth assiduously cultivated by paleface and redskin alike. In denying ego, she is not denying only the chutzpah of the creative act, but also the cultural determinedness of having been born female. Ozick's parable-like story "Virility" crystallizes with sharp comedy her fear of being read as a "woman writer" or, worse, a "woman's writer." Indeed, it was this very fear that caused Ozick to deny any nuance of "femaleness" to the protagonist/narrator of *Trust:*

> I would have to drain my narrator of emotive value of any kind, because I was afraid to be pegged as having written a "woman's" novel. Nothing was more certain to lead to that than a point of view seemingly lodged in a woman, and no one takes a woman's novel seriously. . . . My machine-narrator was there for efficiency only, for flexibility only, for craftiness, for subtlety, but never, never, as a "woman." ("We Are the Crazy Lady")

Ozick's response to the disappointing reception of her first published novel was to remain focused on ideas while experimenting with narrative structure and point of view. She has taken risks in writing stories from the viewpoint of a male character, even when the story (*The Cannibal Galaxy,* for example) contains an obvious alter ego of herself. (Consider, in contrast, Roth's *The Counterlife,* where all four lives are clearly projections of the author.) While Ozick's writing often does reflect the struggle to integrate splintered aspects of identity, her concerns are never only with psychology or personality; rather she is driven by a commitment to what she has called "literary seriousness, which is unquestionably a branch of life seriousness" ("Metaphor and Memory").

Given the intellectual nature of her fiction, there can be no doubt that Ozick is in the paleface tradition that focus-

es on refinement of ideas and the interconnectedness of manners and morals. Indeed, she is often viewed as too intellectual—willing to sacrifice character development in favor of elaboration of an idea. Those who find fault with her stories view them as detached and abstract and thus unsuccessful in engaging the reader's emotions. Clearly this profound intellectuality and suspicion of sentiment are counter to the stereotype of women's writing, and even to much of the recent writing by feminists. The stereotype we know all too well, but Pinsker provides a powerful reminder when he cites John Crowe Ransom's claim (in "The Poet as Woman") that "A woman lives for love . . . and is indifferent to intellectuality" ("Philip Rahv's"). Pinsker counters the stereotype by assembling a list of popular female—and feminist—writers, such as Alix Kate Shulman, Erica Jong, Marge Piercy, Lisa Alther, Marilyn French, and Toni Morrison, whose works "suggest some of the range and the power of writing by and for women," adding that such writing by women proves that "it is simply no longer true that our most interesting, most radical 'redskins' are always male." One wonders, however, whether such a list has the effect of reinforcing old prejudices regarding writing by women. Would so diverse a group of male writers have been lumped together by virtue of their maleness and their "male" perspective? Moreover, the absence of Ozick, a female paleface writer whose work Pinsker has studied and regards very highly, brings to mind the fear Ozick expressed in 1977 that critics and writers who think that writing by women should also be mainly about women and for women serve only to keep women writers ghettoized:

> More and more, there are writers and artists and other masters of imagination who declare themselves freed by voluntary circumscription. "Up till now I was mistaken," they will testify; "I was trying to write like a man. Then I began to write about myself as a daughter, as a lover, as a wife, as a mother, as a woman in relation to other women; as a self. I learned to follow the contours of my emotional life. I began to write out of my femaleness." . . . Artists who insist on defining themselves as "women" artists . . . should not stumble in to the misnomer of calling voluntary circumscription "feminism." . . . Feminism means, has always meant, access to possibilities beyond self-consciousness. . . . polemical self-knowledge is restricted knowledge. . . . Self-discovery is only partial discovery. . . . Self-consciousness—narcissism, solipsism—is small nourishment for a writer. ("Literature and the Politics of Sex")

There is no room in Rahv's categories for Ozick because "Real American literature was seen then [i. e., in the 30s] as clearly a man's game" (Pinsker, "Philip Rahv's") and, despite Pinsker's appreciation of her work, no comfortable slot in his paradigm either, because important contemporary writing by women is defined by its "redskin" character. That is, in its insistence on the specifically female experience, it is the obverse of typical redskin writing by men, which reflects a macho or at least an identifiably masculine perspective (think of Steinbeck, Dos Passos, Hemingway et al.). Ozick's writing appears to defy classification because it is neither "feminine" in the old sense of decorative, delicate, and emotional nor "feminist" in the new sense of confronting and examining what many have come to view as the unique abilities of women.

The anomaly of the female Jewish-American paleface is worth considering. That is, one might well expect those on the social and cultural margin to disdain the elitism and ethnocentrism of the quintessential paleface, T. S. Eliot ("classicist in literature, royalist in politics, and Anglo-Catholic in religion") in favor of the humane universalism of Whitman ("Of every hue and caste am I, of every rank and religion" ["Song of Myself," verse 16, line 346]). However, a study of Ozick's fiction and essays reveals the nature of her attraction to Eliot and thereby illuminates her paleface characteristics. In an essay commemorating what would have been Eliot's 101st birthday, Ozick, looking in Eliot's work beyond the explicit anti-Semitism she had once tried to ignore and almost forgiving his "backward longing for the medieval hegemony of cathedral spires" ("Eliot at 101"), finds a rootedness in tradition and a respect for history that she fears is sadly lacking among contemporary writers. The "historical sense" that Eliot insists upon so emphatically in "Tradition and the Individual Talent" lends itself in a way that he would not have imagined to Ozick's sense of herself as shaping the present through witnessing the past and cultivating the heritage of her ancestors. "Everybody is born into a civilization," she has said, "and if you want to live the life that can best bring you into a sense of being a civilized person, then you have to seize it through your own culture." For Eliot, "the historical sense compels a man to write not merely with his own generation in his bones, but with a feeling that the whole of the literature of his own country has a simultaneous existence and composes a simultaneous order" ("Tradition"). Ozick shares Eliot's sense of the "presentness" of the past, feeling that she "grew up as a witness— of the Inquisition, of the pogroms, of the Crusades, of the Holocaust, all at once."

A further irony (because Ozick is hardly the sort of writer Eliot envisioned as the inheritor of the literary or cultural tradition he valued) is that the "difficult" nature of Ozick's writing—her dense and sometimes shocking imagery, her learned allusiveness, her recondite vocabulary, her complex and multi-layered narratives—provide another link with Eliot, who insisted that modern civilization demands "difficult" poetry:

> Our civilization comprehends great variety and complexity, and this variety and complexity, playing upon a refined sensibility, must produce various and complex results. The poet must become more and more comprehensive, more allusive, more indirect, in order to force, to dislocate if necessary, language into his meaning. ("The Metaphysical Poets")

It is precisely the "difficulty" of Ozick's writing that many critics have found off-putting, much as Eliot's readers were stunned by the complexity, apparent disjointedness, and allusiveness of his poems. Like Eliot, Ozick charts new territory by glossing prior texts. In "Bloodshed," the text is Roth's "Eli the Fanatic"; in "Usurpation," the text is Bernard Malamud's "The Silver Crown"; in *The Cannibal Galaxy,* it is Rabbi Akiva's parable about the destruc-

tion of the Temple (as well as an earlier published version of her story, called "The Laughter of Akiva"); in "Rosa," it is a tightly constructed parable of her own, "The Shawl," which she elaborates in midrashic fashion.

Perhaps we don't enjoy this sort of difficulty as much as we used to. Not every reader has appreciated the convoluted layers of Ozick's narratives or been willing to invest in unraveling them the sort of energy that graduate students have lavished on "The Four Quartets." Indeed, one critic peevishly confesses that he could not have provided an intelligible summary of "Usurpation" without the aid of Ozick's explanatory preface. It may be that the tough intellectual web of Ozick's texts accounts in part for what has been seen as her failure to engage the reader affectively in her narratives. And on this ground too we may draw a parallel with Eliot, whose insistence on the difference between art, on the one hand, and the expression of raw emotion, on the other, shaped several generations of critics and teachers. In addition to providing a defense against neofeminism (the ideology that promotes feminist discourse by underlining the difference between women's modes of perception and men's), Ozick's wry claim that "ego is not interesting" is a putative descendant of Eliot's declaration that "The progress of an artist is a continual self-sacrifice, a continual extinction of personality" ("Tradition").

For both writers the rejection of personality combines with the impulse to develop a sense of self in the context of history to produce themes of displacement and purposefully constructed identity. Eliot fled America to absorb the European experience; Ozick, as a witness to the past, brings the legacy of Europe to America, as do several of her protagonists, who are immigrants. Ozick's writings suggest that she, like Eliot in England, feels like something of a "resident alien" ("Eliot at 101"). Critics have taken her to task for not doing what Roth has done, that is, focused on the Jewish-American scene, whether urban northeastern intellectuals or suburbanites aspiring to assimilation. It is notable that even her best-received works, *The Cannibal Galaxy* and *The Shawl,* which are set mostly in America, involve displaced or seemingly misplaced protagonists. This is because for Ozick, much more than for Roth, there always looms a clear sense of history, a sense that, in Eliot's words, "involves a perception not only of the pastness of the past, but of its presence" ("Tradition"). To appreciate the difference between redface Roth and paleface Ozick, one need only consider the following passage from Roth's *The Ghost Writer,* a phone conversation between aspiring writer Nathan Zuckerman (Roth's alter ego) and his mother regarding a story he has written in which the main characters, who are of course Jewish, are portrayed negatively, much to the chagrin of Nathan's family. A local judge named Wapter, an old family friend, has reviewed the story and written Nathan a lengthy letter in which he compares the young writer to the Nazi propagandists. Nathan, utterly disgusted by Wapter's philistinism and self-righteousness, is implored by his mother to be courteous, humble, and modest. But he is enraged:

> "The Big Three, Mama! Streicher, Goebbels, and your son! What about the judge's humility? Where's his modesty?"

"He only meant that what happened to the
Jews—"

"In Europe—not in Newark! We are not the
wretched of Belsen! We were not the victims of
that crime!"

"But we could be—in their place we would be.
Nathan, violence is nothing new to the Jews, you
know that!"

"Ma, you want to see physical violence done to
the Jews of Newark, go to the office of the plastic
surgeon where the girls get their noses fixed.
That's where the Jewish blood flows in Essex
county, that's where the blow is delivered—with
a mallet! To their bones—and to their pride!"

Later that evening, trying to compose an explanatory letter to his father, Zuckerman tells himself that in being
misunderstood and condemned by his readers, he is in the
tradition of Joyce, Flaubert, and Thomas Wolfe. But then
he considers the specter of the Holocaust and the particularity of the Jews, "Of which [Nathan reminds himself],
only some five thousand days past, there had been millions
more." Nonetheless, what triumphs is Nathan's anger
with the ignorance and shallow hypocrisy that the wealthy
judge and his wife represent. Against his fury and his artistic ambitions the murdered millions cannot maintain their
emotional hold; nor should they, Roth seems to say. The
Holocaust is naturally a specter in Ozick's work too, but
Ozick has composed no fictional female counterpart to
what Roth called "Nathan Dedalus," his portrait of the
cultural angst of the Jewish artist as a young man. It is
surely Jake the Snake talking when Roth compares the
ovens and gas chambers of Germany and Poland to the
plastic surgeon's office in Newark. This technique works
brilliantly as satire, but instead of informing the present
with the past, it drives a wedge between them, finally justifying a cleavage that Ozick cannot and will not admit. Instead of rending the American artist from the millions of
annihilated Europeans, she offers the reader in cadenced
and imagistic but curiously detached prose the execution
of a small child named Magda in a concentration camp
within the full and helpless view of her mother. Here is the
last paragraph of "The Shawl":

> All at once Magda was swimming through the
> air. The whole of Magda traveled through lofti-
> ness. She looked like a butterfly touching a silver
> vine. And the moment Magda's feathered round
> head and her pencil legs and balloonish belly and
> zigzag arms splashed against the fence, the steel
> voices went mad in their growling, urging Rosa
> to run and run to the spot where Magda had fall-
> en from her flight against the electrified fence;
> but of course Rosa did not obey them. She only
> stood, because if she ran they would shoot, and
> if she tried to pick up the sticks of Magda's body
> they would shoot, and if she let the wolf's
> screech ascending now through the ladder of her
> skeleton break out, they would shoot; so she
> took Magda's shawl and filled her own mouth
> with it, stuffed it in and stuffed it in, until she
> was swallowing up the wolf's screech and tast-
> ing the cinnamon and almond depth of Magda's

saliva; and Rosa drank Magda's shawl until it
dried.

In the story "Rosa," which describes the declining years
of Magda's mother, an immigrant to America now retired
from her Brooklyn antique store and living in Florida,
Ozick suggests that while the atrocities of history can neither be evaded nor forgotten, they need not dehumanize
us nor lead to despair. As her gentleman friend Persky
tells her, "Sometimes a little forgetting is necessary, if you
want to get something out of life" (*The Shawl*). There are
comic moments in this story, but, consistent with Ozick's
earlier work, none of the "comic recklessness" that Roth
attributes to his "old mentor, Jake the Snake, the indecent
candy-store owner" ("On *The Great American Novel*").
Roth, much more than Ozick, writes directly out of his
own experience; as I have suggested, it is the tension between his experience and the tradition he hallows as an
artist that makes him that hybrid, the "redface." However, even if Ozick were to create fictions more obviously re-
flective of her experience, it is doubtful that she would
hear the redskin voices that call so loudly to Roth for the
simple reason—and here we have come full circle back to
gender—that Ozick did not hang out at the corner candy
store with the Bronx's version of Jake the Snake.

Feeling isolated and alienated in school by virtue of both
gender and religion, the child Cynthia turned for solace
to books and, as she has revealed in a graceful and moving
memoir, sequestered herself in her father's pharmacy and
read voraciously. Although formally educated (she wrote
her Master's thesis on Henry James), she was, like Eliot,
a prodigious autodidact. She was also remarkably ambitious, dedicating many of her early years to the task of
writing an enormous, all-encompassing Jamesian novel. It
was not until many years later that she learned, through
reading Leon Edel's biography, that the sort of novel she
had aspired to, James could write only in his advanced
years after decades of apprenticeship. Given this early—
and ultimately deeply disappointing—renunciation of Life
for Art, we can hardly be surprised that "comic recklessness" was never Ozick's forte. (In contrast, one may note,
renunciation of any kind has never seemed a defining aspect of the life or art of Philip Roth.)

It is reasonable to conjecture that Ozick's early commitment to the discipline of high art is at least partly the defensive response of an intellectual and creative woman to
the myth that the culture of Woman is "a culture of busy-
work and make-believe and distraction" ("Previsions").
Ozick reminds us that the appeal of this culture and the
power of the myth that perpetuates it should never be un-
derestimated. It is subscribed to by both men and women.
Thus, the topic of a talk Ozick once gave at the invitation
of a women's club was misprinted on the luncheon program: instead of "The Contemporary Poem," the audience was expecting to be advised on "The Contemporary
Home" ("We Are the Crazy Lady"). Ozick recounts a
more painful example of this sort of reductiveness in her
angry but comic essay, "We Are the Crazy Lady," where
she recalls how Lionel Trilling seemed unable or unwilling
to distinguish her from the only other female in his Columbia graduate class, a highly intelligent but annoyingly
argumentative woman who became known as the Crazy

Lady. One of the morals of the story is that "even among intellectual humanists, every woman has a Doppelgänger—every other woman." If we are at first puzzled that while Ozick insists relentlessly on the particularity of culture and ethnicity, she wants to deny special attributes to gender, we are reminded that, historically, power struggles in these areas have not been analogous: gender distinctions, persuasively buttressed by biological differences, have always implied a hierarchy that subordinates females; on the other hand, attempts to obliterate cultural differences seem inevitably to entail the sacrifice of the minority culture. That is, gender distinctions have traditionally served the agenda of oppression, while cultural distinctions are essential to cultural continuity.

Furthermore, a careful reading of Ozick's essays dispels even the appearance of contradiction or paradox. Actually, Ozick's insistence on her rootedness in Judaism and her refusal to recognize "woman writer" as a viable category are not inconsistent, but are rather expressions of the same moral and intellectual vision. The struggle against the culture of Woman (traditionally defined) is analogous to the struggle to keep the Covenant. Both require a willful, muscular resistance to the sin of Sloth:

> Nature offers ease: here you are, and what you need to be is only what your biology requires of you: all the rest is dream and imagination. History offers the hard life: history says, Beyond your biology lies Clarification . . . The Jew chooses against nature and in behalf of the clarifying impulse. He chooses in behalf of history. The terrible—and terrifying—difficulty is that it is truly against our natures to choose against nature.

That is, it is easier—and thus more "natural"—for the ethnic minority to be assimilated than to maintain a cultural identity and a connection with a specific past; it is easier—and thus more "natural"—to succumb to powerful gender stereotypes that define anatomy as destiny than to prove them wrong. In both instances—as a Jew and as a woman—Ozick chooses "the hard life."

It is not surprising, therefore, that she makes the same choice as an artist, rejecting the easy literary conventions—what she calls "the trodden path and the greased pole" of her Jewish-American predecessors—in favor of a new literature not yet definable:

> In literature the chief post-Enlightenment value is "originality"; but nothing is less original, by now, than, say, a Parisian or New York novelist "of Jewish extraction" to write as if he had never heard of a Jewish idea, especially if, as is likely, he never has heard of a Jewish idea. . . . By now, for writers to throw themselves entirely into the arms of post-Enlightenment culture is no alternative at all. It is a laziness. ("Bialik's Hint")

The term "laziness" is here applied to writers who, avoiding the tough confrontation with ideas, lapse into literary clichés and stereotypes, triviality and parochialism. "Laziness" recalls the effortless "slide into nature" offered both by the "culture of Woman" and by the attractions of ethnic and religious assimilation. The Jew, the woman, the artist—all are bound by the obligation constantly to exert the will, to resist what comes "naturally," and to choose instead the constant struggle toward "clarification," that is, toward the judgment and interpretation that grow from historical understanding. Although Ozick's deep concern with the artist as idolater has received a good deal of critical attention, one is thus led to conclude that what she finds most threatening to all aspects of her identity is the sin of Sloth. As Jew, as woman, and as artist, she insists upon "the reality-pain that clarification imposes." Moreover, she demands that her readers choose the "damn hard work" of resisting "naturalness and worldliness and sentiment." Like Milton's "fit audience though few," Ozick's readers must be willing to accept the challenge of her "mandarin" prose and "cerebral" fictions, to see beyond what one critic has called the "sheer force of stylistic razzledazzle." In doing so, Ozick's readers can come to appreciate the experience and the emotion—born of an enduring resistance—that make the stylistic ingenuity not only possible but both a moral and esthetic necessity.

Ultimately, Ozick's emotional ambivalence toward Eliot—her powerful sympathy with his veneration of knowledge, tradition, history, and high culture coupled with her recognition of the moral danger represented by his hegemonic views—measures both her struggle to find a place in the great tradition and the profound humanity of her interpretation of the past. While she mourns what she views as the disintegration of high art that has accompanied the decline of Eliot, she agrees with Rahv that palefaces had inevitably to lose out to redskins in America— "it may simply be [she wrote] that it is in the renunciatory grain of America to resist the hierarchical and the traditional" ("Eliot at 101"). Yet the "principles of democracy, tolerance, and individualism" inherent in the American ideal—principles that stood outside Eliot's moral vision— do not in her mind atone for all that has been lost in the postmodern quest for diversity, universality, and deconstruction. Indeed, she finds fearsome our present culture, in which history, tradition, and learnedness are devalued:

> Tradition is equated with obscurantism. The wall that divided serious high culture from the popular arts is breached; anything can count as a "text." Knowledge . . . is displaced by information, or memory without history: data. Allusiveness is cross-cultural in an informational and contemporary way (from say, beekeeping to filmmaking), rather than in the sense of connecting the present with the past. ("Eliot at 101")

However, no one familiar with Ozick's fiction will need to be reminded that this is not an echo of Allan Bloom calling for the inviolability of the canon or—even worse—the establishment of social conditions in which only the "right" sort of books will be tolerated. For Ozick, unlike Eliot, the cultural centeredness of the individual talent need not mean the exclusion or intolerance of other cultures. To the contrary, what she opposes is the dissipation or annihilation of culture whether it be by "liberals" who want to universalize particular human experience even if that means denying historical event or—to use one of her favorite metaphors—by those who would "cannibalize" others (or the Other) through gradual or violent appropriation. In Ozick's oeuvre, such cannibals run the gamut from the Nazi soldier who murders Rosa's baby daughter to the plagiaristic "poet" of "Virility" to the well-intentioned but sadly misguided pedagogue Joseph Brill of *The Cannibal Galaxy.*

Finally, the bookish, serious Ozick is neither bitter nor self-righteous. Once called to account because her characters were considered "crabby, bitter, uneasy, spiteful, full of acid observation about a discomfiting world," Ozick replied, "I am nicer in life than I am in my [fiction] writing." Her essays lend truth to this assertion, but perhaps a more revealing indication of her "niceness" is her respect and admiration for Philip Roth, to whom she dedicated her novel *The Messiah of Stockholm.* Unlike Pope's Atticus, she does not feel threatened by a "brother near the throne" ("Epistle," line 198). In the final account she shuns both conquest and assimilation. Perhaps it is this quality that most distinguishes her from her great (male) predecessors and contemporaries—regardless of the depth of their pallor.

JEWISH WRITERS AND AMERICAN LIFE

Leslie A. Fiedler

SOURCE: "Zion as Main Street" and "Jewish-Americans, Go Home!" in *Waiting for the End,* Stein and Day, 1964, pp. 65-103.

[*Fiedler is a controversial and provocative American critic. While he has also written novels and short stories, his personal philosophy and insights are thought to be most effectively expressed in his literary criticism. Fiedler often views literature as the mirror of a society's consciousness, and his most important work,* Love and Death in the American Novel *(1960), assesses American literature, and therefore American society, as an infantile flight from "adult heterosexual love." In the following essay, he examines the place of the Jew in twentieth-century American culture and literature.*]

Certainly, we live at a moment when, everywhere in the realm of prose, Jewish writers have discovered their Jewishness to be an eminently marketable commodity, their much vaunted alienation to be their passport into the heart of Gentile American culture. It is, indeed, their quite justified claim to have been *first* to occupy the Lost Desert at the center of the Great American Oasis (toward which every one now races, Coca-Cola in one hand, Martin Buber in the other), which has made certain Jewish authors into representative Americans, even in the eyes of State Department officials planning cultural interchanges. The autobiography of the urban Jew whose adolescence coincided with the Depression, and who walked the banks of some contaminated city river with tags of Lenin ringing in his head, who went forth (or managed not to) to a World War in which he could not quite believe, has come to seem part of the mystical life history of a nation.

Even in the realm of poetry, writers of Jewish origin are beginning for the first time, not only to project the most viable images of what it means to be an American, but to determine the cadences with which we glorify or deplore that condition. The very lines inscribed on the base of the Statue of Liberty are, to be sure, by Emma Lazarus, who called one collection of her poems *Songs of a Semite;* but it was not until the appearance of Delmore Schwartz and Karl Shapiro, in the years just before and after World War II, that Jewish-American poets succeeded in producing verse capable of living in libraries and the hearts of other poets, rather than on monuments and in the mouths of politicians. And only within the last decade has a poet as Jewish in his deepest memories (whatever his current allegiances) as Allen Ginsberg been able to stand at the head of a new poetic movement.

Yet the moment of triumph for the Jewish writer in the United States has come just when his awareness of himself as a Jew is reaching a vanishing point, when the gesture of rejection seems his last possible connection with his historical past; and the popular acceptance of his alienation as a satisfactory symbol for the human condition threatens to turn it into an affectation, a fashionable cliché. Indeed, the recent recognition of even the most serious Jewish-American writers seems somehow less an event in literary history than an incident in the development of middle-brow taste, part of the minor revolution which has made Harry Golden into a modern prophet and has enabled newspapers to build circulation by running serializations of the latest pseudo-books of Leon Uris. Surely, a kind of vicarious shame at the monstrosities practiced against the Jews of Germany by the Nazis has something to do with this revolution; and the establishment of the State of Israel has tended to give even the Jews in exile a less ambiguous status, while the struggle against Great Britain leading to that establishment has lent them a certain sentimental cachet, ranking them, in the minds of American Anglophobes, with the Irish and the mythical revolutionary ancestors of us all.

But it is chiefly the resurgence of "intergroup understanding," the tidal wave of toleration that has flowed into the vacuum left by the disappearance of zeal and the attenuation of faith among churchgoers, which has carried the Jews along with it. And they have benefited, too, by the canonization of support for "little people" among the pieties of yesterday's liberalism which have become the orthodoxy of today's New Deal-New Frontier conservatism. Armenians, Greeks, Chinese, Cubans, low-caste Indians, Mexican wetbacks, women without suffrage, paraplegics, teen-agers—one group after another has been dubbed with that condescending tag. But, maybe, from this point of view the ordeal of the Jew is almost over, for he no longer occupies the number-one slot among the insulted and injured. Even the *New Yorker* has recognized that the Negro is, at the moment, *up;* and it is the Baldwins rather than the Bellows who have to wrestle now with the mystery of the failure of success in America. The general *détente* in the cold war between Gentile and Jew in the United States persists, and though other sentimental fashions challenge it, it remains chic in certain middlebrow, middle-class, middle-liberal quarters to be pro-Jewish. Philo-Semitism is required—or perhaps, by now, only assumed—in the reigning literary and intellectual circles of America, just as anti-Semitism used to be required—and after a while only assumed—in the Twenties.

But the Judaization of American culture goes on at levels far beneath the literary and the intellectual. The favorite wine in Missoula, Montana, which does not have a dozen Jewish families, is Mogen David; and for years now, "Nebbishes" have stared out of the windows of the local gift shop from greeting cards, ash trays, beer mugs, and pen stands. And why not? Everyone everywhere digs Jules Feiffer and Mort Sahl, just as everyone tells "sick" jokes and sends "hate" cards to celebrate birthdays and weddings and national holidays. The "sick" joke and the "hate" card, however, represent the entry into our popular culture not only of certain formerly exclusive properties of the avant-garde (the mockery of bourgeois pieties, a touch of psychoanalysis) but also of Jewish humor at its most desperate. There is nothing entirely unprecedented here, of course; Potash and Perlmutter were best-sellers in the opening years of this century, and Charlie Chaplin's debut was almost contemporaneous with theirs. As a matter of fact, the Jew enters American culture "on the stage, laughing."

It might be possible, indeed, to make a graph showing, decade by decade, the point at which it became possible for Jews:

1) to act out travesties of themselves on the stage;

2) to act out travesties of other "comical" ethnic gropus (Chico Marx as an Italian, Al Jolson in blackface);

3) to write popular songs and patriotic sub-poetry and begin the wholesale entry into universities as students;

4) to produce comic strips and popular novels;

5) to argue cases in court and judge them from the bench, to prescribe for the common cold and analyze the neurotic;

6) to write prose fiction and anti-academic criticism;

7) to teach in the universities and help determine official taste in the arts;

8) to write serious poetry, refuse to go to college, and write on the walls, "Down with the Jews!"

Presently all of these things are possible at once, for no new gain has canceled out another, our successes expand at dazzling speed. Huckleberry Finn becomes Augie March; Daisy Miller turns, via Natalie Wood, into Marjorie Morningstar; Eddie Fisher is drafted as the symbol of clean young American love, while Danny Kaye continues to play the blue-eyed jester; and finally we enter an age of strange conversions to Judaism (Marilyn Monroe, Elizabeth Taylor, Sammy Davis, Jr.), and symbolic marriages. Eros himself turns, or seems to for a little while, Jewish, as the mythical erotic dream-girls of us all yearn for Jewish intellectuals and learn to make matzo-balls.

Even more startlingly, the literature of busy males, of politicians and executives seeking at once relaxation and the reinforcement of their fantasies, is Judaized, too. The long dominance of the Western and the detective story is challenged by that largely Jewish product, science fiction. There are a score of Jewish authors among the most widely read writers in that popular genre as compared with practically none in the two older types of institutionalized fantasy. The basic myths of science fiction reflect the urban outlook, the social consciousness, the utopian concern of the modern, secularized Jew. The traditional Jewish waiting-for-the-Messiah becomes, in lay terms, the commitment-to-the-future, which is the motive force of current science fiction. The notion of a Jewish cowboy is utterly ridiculous, of a Jewish detective, Scotland-Yard variety or tough private eye, nearly as anomalous—but to think of the scientist as a Jew is almost tautological.

> **The basic myths of science fiction reflect the urban outlook, the social consciousness, the utopian concern of the modern, secularized Jew. The traditional Jewish waiting-for-the-Messiah becomes, in lay terms, the commitment-to-the-future, which is the motive force of current science fiction.**
>
> **— *Leslie A. Fiedler***

Much science fiction, set just before or after the Great Atomic War, embodies the kind of guilty conscience peculiar to such scientist-intellectuals (typically Jewish) as Robert Oppenheimer, while the figure of Einstein presides over the New Heaven and New Earth which such literature postulates, replacing an earlier Hebrew god who is dead. Even in its particulars, the universe of science fiction is Jewish; the wise old tailor, the absurd but sympathetic *yiddishe momme,* plus a dozen other Jewish stereotypes, whiz unchanged across its space and time. Even secret Jewish jokes are made for the cognoscenti: the police on a corrupt, trans-galactic planet are called, in the exotic tongue of that only half-imaginary world, *Ganavim* (thieves). And in the Superman comic books (the lowbrow equivalent of science fiction), the same aspirations and anxieties are projected in the improbable disguise of the Secret Savior, who may look like a *goy,* but who is invented by Jews. The biceps are the biceps of Esau, but the dialogue is the dialogue of Jacob.

Even for those who read neither books nor comics, Jewish culture lies in wait—not only in the gift shop and the saloon, but in what is our only truly living museum, the real cultural storehouse of the average man: the supermarket. There—even in the remotest hamlets—beside the head-cheese, the sliced ham, the pseudo-hot-dogs composed of flour and sawdust, one finds kosher salami; beside the hardtack, Rye Krisp, and löfsa—matzos; beside the chocolate-covered ants, fried grasshoppers, and anchovy hearts—Mother's Gefilte Fish. But whatever is in the supermarket, like whatever is in *Life* (both organized on the same pseudo-catholic principle: everything glossily packaged and presented without emphasis and distinction) is in the great democratic heart of America. In that heart, at least, Jewish culture, as defined by gefilte fish and Natalie Wood, the Jewish scientist and the Nebbish, has established itself as if it meant to stay. And it is in light of this cultural fact that Jewish-American writers must assess the mounting sales of their books and the warm reviews which greet them; but the confrontation leaves the best of them amused, the second best embarrassed, and the worst atrociously pleased.

Yet this kind of success is, in a way, what the Jewish-American writer has all along desired—though for a long time he was able to depend on the realities of his situation, the exclusion from which he began, to protect him against his own lust for belonging. From the start, the Jewish-American writer has desired not only to create living images of his people in the imagination of all Americans, and to redeem them from psychic exploitation at the hands of anti-Semitic Gentile authors; but also, by creating such images and achieving such a redemption, to become himself part of the American scene, a citizen among citizens, one more author on a list which begins with Benjamin Franklin and Washington Irving. The very notion of a Jewish-American literature represents a dream of assimilation, and the process it envisages is bound to move toward a triumph (in terms of personal success) which is also a defeat (in terms of meaningful Jewish survival). If today Jewish-American writers seem engaged in writing not the high tragedy of Jewish persistence in the midst of persecution, but the comedy of Jewish dissolution in the midst of prosperity, this is because they tell the truth about a world which neither they nor their forerunners can consider themselves guiltless of desiring.

Yet at first the striving of the American-Jewish community, through its artists, to become a fact of the imagination as well as of the census seemed merely gallant and happily foredoomed. In the beginning, the Jewish author and the Jewish character, whether invented by Gentile or Jew, played only a slight and peripheral role in the literature of the United States and in the deep mind of the American people which that literature at once reflects and makes. This is in part the result of the simple sociological fact that Jews were, in the earliest years of our nation, few and insignificant and that, therefore, the mythology of the Jew, which we inherited along with the English language and the corpus of English literature, moved the popular American mind scarcely at all. What could the figures of the Wandering Jew, of Shylock and Jessica, Isaac of York and Rebecca, Riah and Fagin mean to a people whose own guilts and fears and baffled aspirations were projected onto quite different ethnic groups? Associated with the names of Shakespeare, Sir Walter Scott and Dickens, authors sometimes revered, even loved, but chiefly, alas, resented as required reading in the classroom, such figures assume the vicarious reality of classroom facts, of something learned for the first time out of books, rather than *recognized* in books as the truths of nightmare and dream.

It is those whom the white Anglo-Saxon Americans persecuted in the act of becoming Americans, even as the Europeans persecuted the Jews in the act of becoming Christians, who live in the American psyche as Shylock and the Wandering Jew live in the European one: the Indian and the Negro, who are facts of the American imagination from the moment that imagination is formed. The Anglo-Saxon immigrant could maintain only a theoretical anti-Semitism in the New World, just as he could maintain only a theoretical opposition to the aristocracy; his real struggles were elsewhere, and his attempts to project his own psychological difficulties onto the enemies of his ancestors never took root in literature. So, also, with later generations of immigrants, from other parts of Europe. The Germans, the Poles, the Czechs may have brought with them certain traditional anti-Semitic fantasies of their native lands; but at the moment that their assimilation to America moved from the social to the psychic level (and in the country of the melting pot this moment comes quite soon), they began to find their old nightmares driven out by new.

James Fenimore Cooper, greatest of American mythographers, tried to identify the evil Indian of the *Last of the Mohicans* with Shylock, and, in one of the last of his novels, portrayed the Indians as New World Jews re-enacting the crucifixion in the midst of the wilderness; but this major attempt to make transatlantic and cisatlantic attitudes of hatred and guilt reinforce each other failed. The Jew could not figure as the archetypal Other, the psychic whipping boy, in a society which was not bound to him by ancient and terrible guilts: guilts lived, as well as read about in schoolrooms or even sacred books. Exclusions from jobs and country clubs is no substitute for pogroms and massacres, and even the anti-Semitism implicit in Christianity has remained, in America, largely theoretical; an occasional schoolchild has been sent running home in tears with the cry of his classmates, "You killed our Christ!" ringing in his bewildered head; but practically nobody in the United States *has ever died from it!* And this is perhaps why in our classic literature, much concerned with precisely those conflicts from which men had indeed died, Jewish characters play such unimportant roles.

It is worth remembering that the poet who wrote and rewrote, from just past the middle of the last century to almost the beginning of ours, the four-hundred-page poem which declares itself the most broadly inclusive of all all-American poems, included no Jewish character or scene in his mythic world. There are no Jews in *Leaves of Grass;* and the single appearance of the adjective "semitic" recorded in the concordances to that work turns out to be an error. Whitman, meaning to describe the ideal American poet as "plunging his seminal muscle" into the "merits and demerits" of his country, miswrote "semitic muscle" the first time around, but changed it when some amused reader called it to his attention. White, red, and black make up his America, and even the yellow oriental makes an occasional appearance; but the Jew was represented by no color on his palette and constitutes no part of the myth he has left us. No more are there Jews included in that otherwise universally representative crew: the Manx, African, Irish, Spanish, Italian, Polynesian, and

Middle-Eastern human flotsam of the world who, under a mad Yankee skipper, sail a ship called after a defunct Indian tribe in the pages of Melville's *Moby Dick*. Nor does Huck Finn meet a single Jew, either ashore or afloat on the great river whose course he follows down the center of civilized America.

There are, to be sure, occasional Jewish characters elsewhere in Melville, and in Hawthorne, Henry James, even Longfellow; but, by and large, these are either borrowed bugaboos, male and female, or inventions of a sentimentality which kept itself pure by keeping its Jews imaginary. In Melville's long narrative poem *Clarel,* for instance, one finds the major attempt to adapt for American uses the archetypal pattern story which has most appealed to the American imagination when it has sought at all to deal with things Jewish: the myth of Shylock and Jessica, the sinister Jew deprived of his lovely daughter. But the American imagination does not permit the Gentile hero to get the Jewish girl in a blithe Shakespearean ending; on this side of the ocean, a tragic blight falls over the European myth of assimilation: the dream of rescuing the desirable elements in the Judaic tradition (maternal tenderness and exotic charm: the figure of Mary) from the unsympathetic elements (patriarchal rigor and harsh legalism: the figure of the High Priest and Father Abraham with a knife).

The trouble is that the Jewish girl is thought of not in terms of Mary, but of Lilith, and becomes one with all those dark ladies (otherwise Latin) who are paired off against the fair, Anglo-Saxon girl: the former representing all the Puritan mind most longs for, and fears, in passion; the latter standing for a passionless, sexless love. At the very beginnings of our literature, Charles Brockden Brown could permit his hero to marry a Jewish woman, but neither Melville nor Hawthorne could forget his own pale, Anglo-Saxon bride long enough to follow Brown's example. Even in our presumably post-Puritan times, the protagonist of *Two for the Seesaw* finally abandons his Gittel Mosca, Jewish embodiment of impulse and sexual generosity, to return like a good American to the Gentile wife he left behind.

But beside the nightmare of the Jew's alluring daughter flanked by the castrating father, there exists for the American imagination a dream of the "little Jew," too, enduring and forgiving under abuse—a kind of Semitic version of "Uncle Tom." Unfortunately, this is to be found nowhere in our serious writers and is, I suspect, an English importation where found, a spreading out and down of George Eliot's hortatory philo-Semitism. There appeared, at any rate, in the 1868 volume of the children's magazine called *Our Young Folks,* a poem which begins:

> We were at school together,
> The little Jew and I.
> He had black eyes, the biggest nose,
> The very smallest fist for blows,
> Yet nothing made him cry.

and which ends, after the speaker has thrust an apple under that "biggest nose" on Yom Kippur, mocking the child for his fast, and has then repented:

> Next day when school was over,
> I put my nonsense by;
> Begged the lad's pardon, stopped all strife.
> And—well, we have been friends for life,
> The little Jew and I.

A second-hand nightmare is answered by a borrowed dream.

The Jewish writer himself was engaged with these half-felt stereotypes in the latter half of the nineteenth century, and his responses seem as unreal, as far from the center of American psychic life, as those stereotypes themselves. Up to the end of the last century (and in a certain sense that century did not end for us until the conclusion of World War I), Jewish-American literature, the stories and poems written out of their own experience by those willing to call themselves Jews, or descended immediately from those so willing, remains not only theoretical but parochial. In this regard, it is like all the sub-literature which we customarily call "regional"—writing intended to represent the values and interests of a group which feels itself penalized, even threatened, by the disregard of the larger community. From one side, such writing constitutes a literature of self-congratulation and reassurance, intended to be consumed by an in-group which knows it is abused and suspects that it is hardly noticed by those who abuse it; and from another, it aims at becoming a literature of public relations, intended to "sell" that in-group to certain outsiders, who, it is assumed, will respond favorably only to "positive," i.e., innocuous or untrue, images of the excluded group.

Regional writing ceases to be sub-literary, however, not when those it portrays are made to seem respectable, but when they are presented as representative (in all their particularity) of the larger community: the nation, an alliance of nations, all of mankind. But this only begins to happen when regional writers stop being apologists and become critics, abandon falsification and sentimentality in favor of treating not the special virtues of the group from which they come, whether those virtues be real or fancied, but the weaknesses it shares with all men. Such writers seem often to their fellows, their very friends and parents, traitors—not only for the harsh things which they are led to say about those fellows, friends and parents in the pursuit of truth, but also because their desire for universality of theme and appeal leads them to begin tearing down from within the walls of a cultural ghetto, which, it turns out, has meant security as well as exclusion to the community that nurtured them.

The plight is particularly difficult for those who are not even psychically exploited, not even used to represent certain deep uncertainties and guilts in the undermind of the larger community, but only psychically ignored, which is to say, blanked out of the range of vision of that larger community. They may, indeed, congratulate themselves on their social invisibility, taking it for a result of their own firm resolve not to be assimilated to the ways of strangers. Mythically invisible men, that is, tend to confuse their essential peculiarity, to which they are resolved to cling, with the psychic walls that make them invisible and which they know they must someday breach. They are, therefore, likely to think of those who first begin to breach these walls, in quest of the freedom to become the selves of their own imagining, as apostates from their ancestral identity and the values which sustain it.

The breakthrough to such psychic freedom and to the cultural assimilation which is its concomitant requires, then, a series of revolutionary acts at a critical point in the history of a minority group; but that critical point is determined not by the revolutionary writers alone. It is no more a mere matter of a certain number of heroic individual decisions than it is of the simple growth in size and prestige and power of the mythically non-existent community. The mass immigrations of Eastern European Jews to the United States was over by 1910, and, some decades before that, a novelist who called himself Sidney Luska had attempted single-handed to transform various aspects of Jewish immigrant life in New York, which he had observed at first hand, into fictions capable of moving all Americans. Even the names of his novels, however (*As It Was Written, The Yoke of the Thorah,* etc.), are by now forgotten; for he had begun by imposing on the facts, as he knew them, a vision of the Jew as the infinitely sensitive artist and the herald of the future, compounded out of George Eliot's portrait of herself as a young Jew in *Daniel Deronda,* and the dreams of the Ethical Culturists of his time. And "Sidney Luska" was not really a Jew, only a disaffected white Anglo-Saxon Protestant who had affected what he took to be a "Jewish" beard as well as a "Jewish" name; and who, when confronted by the pettiness and weakness of actual Jews, returned to his own name, Henry Harland, and ended as an expatriate and editor of the *Yellow Book* and the author of a fashionably Catholic, anti-Semitic bestseller called *The Cardinal's Snuffbox.* It is the comic-pathetic catastrophe fitting to one hubristic enough to have attempted single-handed to give to Jews the status that only time and history could bestow.

The creation of Jewish characters able to live in the American imagination cannot be the work of Jewish writers, real or imagined, alone. As the Jewish writer goes out in search of his mythical self, he is bound to encounter the Gentile writer on a complementary quest to come to terms with him, the stranger in the Gentile's land. As collaborators or rivals, wittingly or not, Jewish author and Gentile must engage in a common enterprise if either is to succeed. The presence of talented Jewish writers concerned with Jewish life, and of a rich and complex Jewish life itself, are essential preconditions of the Jewish breakthrough into the deep psyche of Gentile America; but there is a necessary third precondition, too. At the moment of such a breakthrough, the Jew must *already* have become capable of projecting psychological meanings with which the non-Jewish community is vitally concerned, must already have come to represent in his mode of existence, symbolically at least, either a life lived and aspired to by those others— or at least (and more probably) one passionately rejected and secretly regretted by those others. But this is the job of non-Jewish writers, and for this reason we must look to such writers, rather than to the Jewish writers of the period, to understand just how the Jewish character became mythically viable during and just after World War I.

> The creation of Jewish characters able to live in the American imagination cannot be the work of Jewish writers, real or imagined, alone. As the Jewish writer goes out in search of his mythical self, he is bound to encounter the Gentile writer on a complementary quest to come to terms with him, the stranger in the Gentile's land. As collaborators or rivals, wittingly or not, Jewish author and Gentile must engage in a common enterprise if either is to succeed.
>
> *— Leslie A. Fiedler*

There were, to be sure, Jewish writers of varying degrees of talent who not only published during this period but were, in certain cases, widely read. In fiction, for instance, there were the mass entertainers: Fannie Hurst and Edna Ferber; middlebrow wits like Dorothy Parker; and even quite serious novelists like Ben Hecht (before his removal to Hollywood) and Ludwig Lewisohn (before his surrender to Zionist apologetics). The nineteenth-century "poetesses" from good Sephardic families, chief of whom was Emma Lazarus, were giving way to high school teachers with social consciences: Louis Ginsberg, James Oppenheim, Alfred Kreymborg. The minor achievements of such poets were preserved, along with the brittle verse of F.P.A. and Arthur Guiterman, the efforts of certain Village Bohemians of the Twenties (e.g., Maxwell Bodenheim), and the verses of Jewish prodigies like Nathalia Crane in the pages of Louis Untermeyer's earlier anthologies. In a time when poetry was in the process of becoming what was read in classrooms, certain Jewish journalists and educators compiled the standard classroom anthologies. Though these Jewish-American writers thus controlled American taste to some extent, they did not—in verse any more than in prose—succeed in making images of even their own lives that were capable of possessing the American mind. In any case, the writers anthologized by Untermeyer and others had little consciousness of themselves as Jews, were engaged, in fact, in assimilating themselves to general American culture by pledging allegiance to social or cultural ideals larger than their Jewishness, whether Bohemianism or socialism or humanism in its broadest sense.

No, the compelling images of Jews were made by writers who were not merely Gentiles but anti-Semites, interested in resisting this assimilationist impulse and keeping the Jews Jews. It is important to understand, however, the precise nature of their anti-Semitism. Quite different from working-class or populist, economic anti-Semitism, that "Black Socialism" of the American factory hand or poor farmer which identifies the Jews with Wall Street and international bankers, theirs was the cultural anti-Semitism of the educated bourgeois seeking status through a career in the arts; and it was, therefore, aimed not at expelling the moneychangers from the Temple, but at distinguishing the Jewish exploiters of culture from its genuine Gentile makers, at separating the pseudo-artists (naturally, Jews) from the true ones (of course, Gentiles). This cultural anti-Semitism was the inevitable result of certain provincial Gentile Americans' moving toward the big city (Theodore Dreiser, for instance, and Sherwood Anderson) and discovering that the Jews had beat them to the artists' quarters of Chicago and New Orleans and New York; and it was exacerbated when still other provincial Gentile Americans, attempting expatriation (Pound and Eliot, Hemingway and Fitzgerald, and E. E. Cummings), found Jews even on the Left Bank, in the heart of what they had always dreamed of as Heaven. What the expatriates discovered in fact when they arrived at the Paris of their dreams was most vividly sketched not in a book by any one of them, but rather in one about all of them, Wyndham Lewis's *Paleface:* "Glance into the Dôme, anyone . . . who happens to be in Paris. You would think you were in a League of Nations beset by a zionist delegation, in a movie studio, in Moscow, Broadway or even Zion itself, anywhere but in the mythical watertight America . . . "

And when, in the Thirties, Henry Miller belatedly arrived in the same city, abandoned now, as far as Americans went, to the second-rate and the shoddy, he found the same overwhelming proportion of Jews in the expatriate community and exploded with baffled rage:

> He is a Jew, Borowski, and his father was a phi-latelist. In fact, almost all Montparnasse is Jew-ish, or half-Jewish, which is worse. There's Carl and Paula, and Cronstadt and Boris, and Tania and Sylvester, and Moldorf and Lucille. All except Fillmore. Henry Jordan Oswald turned out to be a Jew also. Louis Nichols is a Jew. Even Van Norden and Chérie are Jewish. Frances Blake is a Jew, or a Jewess. Titus is a Jew. The Jews then are snowing me under. I am writing this for my friend Carl whose father is a Jew. All this is important to understand.

> Of them all the loveliest Jew is Tania, and for her sake I too would become a Jew. Why not? I al-ready speak like a Jew. And I am ugly as a Jew. Besides, who hates the Jews more than the Jew?

No wonder the German occupation forces in Paris made Miller a favorite author, finding in him not only sex but their favorite obsession with the Jew as the absolute Other. And, meanwhile, Miller's fellow German-American writer of the Thirties (one is almost tempted to say Nazi-American), Thomas Wolfe, was finding in New York City similar occasions for anti-Semitic outbursts, reacting with hatred and fear, and a lust of which he was ashamed, to the young Jewesses at New York University, forerunners of later Jewish coeds, who, a short generation later would be writing (under Jewish advisors) theses about the very anti-Semites of the decades before.

Even Jewish writers of the Thirties were more likely than not to produce hostile travesties of their own people, especially if—like Michael Gold, for instance, whose *Jews Without Money* was the first "proletarian novel" of the period—their Messiah was a Marxian rather than a Jewish one. The anti-Semitism so deeply implanted in Russian Communism during the Stalin regime was reflected in the American Communist Party, largely Jewish though it was, and in the literature which followed its line. Indeed, the presence of such anti-Semitism was taken as evidence that American Jewish Communists were emancipated from parochialism and chauvinism. In Michael Gold, at any rate, only the *yiddishe mamme,* the long-suffering maternal figure, comes off well; the Rabbi, the landlord, the pawnbroker are treated as egregious villains, and Gold's portraits of them disconcertingly resemble both those of European Jew-baiters like Julius Streicher, and native American provincials like Thomas Wolfe.

There are ironies involved here disturbing to both sides; for the anti-Semite, intending merely to excoriate the Jew, learns eventually that he has mythicized him. And the offended Jew realizes, after a while, that before the Jewish character could seem to author and reader in the United States an image of the essential American self, he had first to seem the essential American enemy. Nevertheless, it is depressing for the Jewish American to think how many of our most eminent and central writers in the decades during which we entered fully into world literature produced anti-Semitic caricatures, not from mere habit or tradition, but from conviction and passion. What a black anthology lives in his head: out of Cummings ("and pity the fool who cright/ god help me it aint no ews/ eye like the steak all ried/ but eye certainly hate the juse."); and Eliot ("And the jew squats on the window sill, the owner,/ Spawned in some estaminet of Antwerp,/ Blistered in Brussels, patched and peeled in London."), and Pound ("the yidd is a stimulant, and the goyim are cattle/ in gt/ proportion and go to saleable slaughter/ with the maximum of docility . . . "), and Hemingway ("No, listen, Jake. Brett's gone off with men. But they weren't ever Jews, and they didn't come and hang about afterward."), and Fitzgerald ("A small, flatnosed Jew raised his large head and regarded me with two fine growths of hair which luxuriated in either nostril. After a moment I discovered his tiny eyes in the half-darkness. . . . 'I see you're looking at my cuff buttons.' I hadn't been looking at them, but I did now. . . . 'Finest specimens of human molars,' he informed me."), and Michael Gold ("The landlord wore a black alpaca coat in the pawnshop, and a skull cap. He crouched on a stool behind the counter. One saw only his scaly yellow face and bulging eyes; he was like an anxious spider."), and Thomas Wolfe (" . . . Jews and Jewesses, all laughing, shouting, screaming, thick with their hot and sweaty body-smells, their strong female odors of rut and crotch and armpit and cheap perfume . . . ").

How hard it is, after Hitler, for any man of good will, Gentile or Jew, to confess that the most vivid and enduring portraits of Jews created in the period are not works of love and comprehension, but the products of malice and paranoia: Robert Cohen of Hemingway's *The Sun Also Rises* and the multiformed Jewish usurer of Ezra Pound's *Cantos,* Boris of Miller's *Tropic of Cancer* and Abe Jones of Wolfe's *Of Time and the River*—anti-*goyim* and anti-artists one and all. And yet they are not all quite the same; though Hemingway and Pound, for instance, were motivated by a similar malice, and though both moved through the salons of Paris just after World War I, learning, as it were, their anti-Semitism in the same school, their ideologies must be sharply distinguished.

For writers like Pound and Eliot, on the one hand, it is European culture, particularly of the Middle Ages and the Renaissance, which represents the essential meaning of life when it is more than just "birth, copulation and death." And to them the Jew, excluded from the culture in the days of its making, is the supreme enemy; for as merchant-tourist and usurious millionaire, he desires now to appropriate what he never made, to buy and squat in the monuments of high Christian culture, fouling them by his mere presence. He is, therefore, felt and portrayed not only as the opposite to the artist but also to the aristocrat, who, traditionally, sustained the artist in his days of greatest glory.

To writers like Hemingway, on the other hand, to the devotees of raw experience who went to Europe to fish rather than to pray (though also, of course, to make books), the Jew stands for the pseudo-artist. Along with the homosexual, he seems to them to travesty and falsify their own real role; to help create in the public eye an image, from which they find it hard to dissociate themselves, of the effete intellectual, the over-articulate, pseudo-civilized fake. For them, too, the Jew represents the opposite of the Negro, Indian, peasant, bullfighter, or any of the other versions of the noble savage with whom such writers, whether at home or abroad, sought to identify themselves. When either the cult of the primitive or a genteel tradition is in the ascendancy, the Jew is likely to be regarded as the Adversary; for he is the anti-type of Negro and Indian, a projection of the feared intelligence rather than the distrusted impulse, and "genteel" equals Gentile in the language of the psyche. Neither paleface nor redskin, neither gentleman nor genital man, to what can the Jew appeal in the American imagination, which seems to oscillate helplessly between these two poles? Is he doomed to remain merely the absolute un-American, everybody's outsider?

This seems an unanswerable question at first; but it answers itself with the passage of time, and in the very terms in which it is posed. When Americans have grown tired of the neo-gentility, the selective ancestor worship and high-churchly piety of Eliot, and when they are equally sick of the white self-hatred and the adulation of blood sports and ignorance, but especially when they are sick and tired of the oscillation between the two, they can find in the Jewish writer and the world he imagines a way out. Through their Jewish writers, Americans, after the Second World War, were able to establish a new kind of link with Europe in place of the old paleface connection—a link not with the Europe of decaying castles and the Archbishop of Canterbury, nor with that of the Provençal poets and Dante and John Donne, nor with that of the French *symbolistes* and the deadly polite *Action Française*—for these are all Christian Europes; but with the post-Christian Europe of Marx and Freud, which is to say, of secularized Judaism, as well as the Europe of surrealism and existentialism, Kafka, neo-Chasidism—a Europe which at once abhors and yearns for the vacuum left by the death of its Christian god.

And through the same intermediaries, Gentile Americans

discovered the possibility of a new kind of vulgarity unlike the old redskin variety, the when-the-ladies-are-out-of-the-room grossness of works like Mark Twain's *1601*, which depended upon naïveté and simplicity in writer and audience alike. The special Jewish vulgarity exemplified with greater or lesser skill from Ben Hecht through Michael Gold and Nathanael West to Norman Mailer and Philip Roth, is not merely sophisticated, but compatible with high complexity and even metaphysical transcendence. The Semite, someone once said (thinking primarily of the Arabs, but it will do for the Jews, too), stands in dung up to his eyes, but his brow touches the heavens. And where else is there to stand but on dung in a world buried beneath the privileged excretions of the mass media; and where else to aspire but the heavens, in a world whose dreams of earthly paradises have all come to nothing?

Moreover, the Jewish-American mind, conditioned by two thousand years of history, provides other Americans with ways of escaping the trap of vacillation between isolationism and expatriation, chauvinism and national self-hatred. Jewish-American writers are, by and large, neither expatriates nor "boosters"; and they do not create in their protagonists images of the expatriate or the "booster." More typically, they have begun to produce moderately cynical accounts of inpatriation, the flight from the quasi-European metropolis to the provincial small town. This flight they have, indeed, lived, moving in quest of more ultimate exile not out of but *into* America, moving from New York or Chicago, Boston or Baltimore, to small towns in New Mexico, Oregon, Nebraska, and Montana.

After all, if it is a *difference* from what one is born to that is desirable, there is a greater difference between New York and Athens, Georgia, than between New York and Athens, Greece, or between Chicago and Moscow, Idaho, than between Chicago and Moscow, Russia. Within the past couple of years the first fictional treatment of this new migration, a comedy involving an urban Jew in a small university community in the West, has appeared in the form of *A New Life,* the novel by Bernard Malamud. . . . But though Malamud's book begins with exile, it ends with return; for, like the expatriates of the past, the inpatriate of the present also ends by going home, returning East as inevitably as his forebears returned West.

All flights, the Jewish experience teaches, are from one exile to another; and this Americans have always known, though they have sometimes attempted to deny it. Fleeing exclusion in the Old World, the immigrant discovers loneliness in the New World; fleeing the communal loneliness of seaboard settlements, he discovers the ultimate isolation of the frontier. It is the dream of exile as freedom which has made America; but it is the experience of exile as terror that has forged the self-consciousness of Americans.

Yet it is the Jew who has best been able to recast this old American wisdom (that home itself is exile, that it is the nature of man to feel himself everywhere alienated) in terms valid for twentieth-century Americans, which is to say, for dwellers in cities. The urban American, looking about him at the anonymous agglomeration of comfort-producing machines that constitutes his home, knows that exile is what one endures, not seeks, and he is willing to believe the Jewish writer who tells him this. That the Jewish writer be his spokesman in this regard is natural enough, for he descends from those whose consciousness had already been radically altered by centuries of living in cities; and he stands at ease, therefore, in the midst of the first generation of really urban writers in the American twentieth century. Unlike those who made up the first waves of the movement in the United States, replacing the representatives of proper old Boston and old New York, he is no provincial, no small-town Lewis or Anderson or Pound come to the big city to gawk; he is the metropolitan at home, though expert in the indignities, rather than the amenities, of urban life.

Therefore the American-Jewish writer chooses, characteristically, to work in neither the traditional tragic nor the traditional comic mode; for he feels both modes to be aristocratic, that is, pre-industrial, pre-mass-culture genres, reflecting the impulse of a reigning class to glorify its own suffering and to laugh at the suffering of others postulated as inferior to them, to treat only its own suffering as really real. The Jew, however, functions in his deepest imagination (influenced, of course, by the Gentile culture to which he aspires) as his own other, his own inferior; and he must consequently laugh at himself—glorify himself, if at all, *by* laughing at himself. This is the famous Jewish humor, rooted in a humility too humble to think of its self-abasement as religious, and a modesty too modest to think of its encounter with pain as really real. But this is also the source of a third literary genre, neither tragedy nor comedy, though, like both, based on the perception of human absurdity—a genre for whose flourishing in recent American literature certain Jewish-American writers are largely responsible, though with thanks to Mark Twain as well as Sholom Aleichem.

We have similarly witnessed, over the last thirty years or so, the recasting in terms of second-generation American urban life certain American archetypal heroes and the re-rendering of their adventures in an American English affected by the rhythms of Yiddish and shot through with a brand of wit conditioned by the Jewish joke. These great figures out of our deepest imagination, whom we had thought essentially American, we now learn are—or at least can be made to seem—characteristically Jewish as well. It is not a matter of cultural kidnaping, but of the discovery of cultural resemblances. What, for instance, has happened in the middle of the twentieth century to Huckleberry Finn: loneliest of Americans; eternally and by definition uncommitted; too marginal in his existence to afford either conventional virtue or ordinary villainy; excluded, by the conditions which shape him, from marriage and the family; his ending ambiguously suspended between joy and misery; condemned to the loneliness which he desperately desires? Reimagined by Saul Bellow for the survivors of the thirties. he comes now from northwest Chicago, works for petty Jewish gangsters, reads Kafka and Marx, goes to live with Leon Trotsky, and is called Augie March. Or re-invented yet again by J. D. Salinger for a younger and more ignorant audience, he comes from the west side of New York, a world of comfortably assimi-

lated and well-heeled Jews (though his name cagily conceals his ethnic origin), plays hooky from an expensive prep school, slips unscathed through a big-city world of phonies and crooks, and is called Holden Caulfield.

Meanwhile what has happened to the most typical of all the heroes of American poetry? Conceived so deeply and specifically, expressed so passionately and intensely out of the self of the poet who first invented him, this mock-epic hero, crying the most pathetic and lovely of American boasts, "I was the man, I suffered, I was there," once seemed doomed to remain forever what he was to begin with—Walt Whitman, who was born of Quaker parents and moved through a world without Jews. But now, improbably reborn, he remembers listening beside his mother to Israel Amter, idol of the Jewish-American Communists of the Thirties, scolds America for what it has done to his Uncle Max, howls his rage at his father's world (the world of Jewish high-school-teacher-poets memorialized by Louis Untermeyer), and when he has symbolically killed it, writes a volume called *Kaddish,* title of the Hebrew prayer for the dead and tenderest of pet names by which a Jew calls his son. Walt Whitman, that is to say, becomes Allen Ginsberg.

Not only on the highbrow level of Bellow and Ginsberg, however, but on all levels of our literature, archetype and stereotype alike are captured by the Jewish imagination and refurbished for Gentile consumption. Norman Mailer and Irwin Shaw, for instance, have conspired to teach us that no platoon in the United States Army is complete without its sensitive Jew to suffer the jibes of his fellows and record their exploits, while Herman Wouk has made it clear that the valiant virgin beset by seducers, whom female Anglo-Saxondom once thought of as the pale projection of its own highest aspirations, is really a nice Jewish girl who has misguidedly changed her name. What Shaw and Wouk teach, the movies and *Time* magazine transmit to the largest audience; and who is to say them nay in a day when all rightminded men approve the fact of Israel and detest the memory of Hitler, a world in which Anne Frank, our latest secular saint, looks down from the hoardings on us all. Even the crassest segregationists sometimes combine their abuse of Negroes with praise for the Jews. "From the days of Abraham . . . " writes a certain Reverend G. T. Gillespie of Mississippi, "the Hebrews . . . became a respected people . . . and they . . . have made an invaluable contribution to the moral and spiritual progress of mankind." So the occasional anti-Semitic crank who still sends through the mail a cry of protest ("Every book that goes into print . . . is either written by, edited by, advertised by, published by—or what is common, all four—Jewish people . . . these publishers are at war with the American intelligence, as well as its. Christian morality.") seems scarcely worth our contemptuous notice.

And there is no end. Very recently, for example, there has been an attempt, in the screenplay for *The Misfits* written by Arthur Miller, to adapt the classical American Western to new times and new uses. It is not merely a matter of making the Western "adult," as certain middlebrow manipulators of the form like to boast of their efforts on television, but of turning upside down the myth embodied in such standard versions of our archetypal plot as *The Virginian* and *High Noon*. In both of these, a conflict between a man and a woman, representing, respectively, the chivalric code of the West and the pacificism of Christianity, ends with the capitulation of the woman, and the abandonment of forgiveness in favor of force. In *The Misfits,* however, the woman is no longer the pious and pretty but flat-chested schoolmarm that Gentile Americans know their actual grandmothers to have been, but the big-busted, dyed blonde, life-giving and bursting with animal vitality; she is all that the Jew dreams the *shiksa,* whom his grandmothers forbade him as a mate. In Miller's film, that archetypal blonde was played by Marilyn Monroe (at that point Miller's wife and converted to Judaism), who, under the circumstances, was bound to triumph over the male Old West: the Gentiles' Saturday-matinee dream of violence and death, personified by Clark Gable, tamer of horses and females. What remained for Gable, after so ignominious a defeat, except, aptly, to die? Only the author lived on, though his marriage, too, was doomed by the very dream out of which he made a movie in its honor.

Generation after overlapping generation, American-Jewish writers continue to appear: Bellow and Malamud, Irwin Shaw and Arthur Miller and Karl Shapiro, followed by J. D. Salinger and Norman Mailer and Grace Paley, after whom come Philip Roth and Bruce Jay Friedman and Norman Fruchter, on and on, until at last Gore Vidal, himself a white Anglo-Saxon Protestant, writes in mock horror (but with an undertone of real bitterness, too) in the pages of the *Partisan Review,* where, indeed, many of these authors first appeared: "Every year there is a short list of the O.K. writers. Today's list consists of two Jews, two Negroes and a safe floating *goy* of the old American Establishment (often Mr. Wright Morris) . . . "

But it is the whole world, not merely *our* critics, who list, year after year, the two new Jews, plus the two Negroes and the one eternally rediscovered *goy*. The English boy in the sixth form of the Manchester Grammar School digs Norman Mailer; and his opposite number in the classical *liceo* in Milan sees himself as Salinger's *giovane Holden*. At the moment that young Europeans everywhere (even, at last, in England) are becoming imaginary Americans, the American is becoming an imaginary Jew. But this is only one half of the total irony we confront; for, at the same moment, the Jew whom his Gentile fellow-citizen emulates may himself be in the process of becoming an imaginary Negro. "Do we have to become Gentile Jews before we can become White Negroes?" an impatient and reasonably hip youngster from a college audience I addressed recently asked me; and he was only half joking.

· · · · ·

In any case, the Jewish-American writer is likely to view with detached amusement (and the younger he is, the more likely this is to be the case) the fact that his Jewishness is currently taken as a patent of his Americanism, and that he is, willy-nilly, the beneficiary of a belief that in their very alienation the Jews were always mythically twentieth-century Americans—long before the twentieth century and even, perhaps, America itself had been

reached. Quite simply, he does not know in what his Jewishness—so symbolically potent—consists; he is only aware that it is on the point of disappearing. This disappearance he may celebrate or deplore when he is called on to take a stand in the symposia on the subject which have tended to become staple items in the Jewish press (we have seen them recently in *Commentary, Judaism,* and *Midstream*); and, indeed, he is free in this regard, so long as he is willing to suffer criticism and reproach, to plump for persistence or annihilation as his principles or instincts incline. But when he functions as a writer, when he pledges himself, that is to say, to describe in fictional form the kind of Jew he most probably is and the kinds of Jews he most probably knows, these *must* be, if not terminal Jews, at least penultimate ones: the fathers or grandfathers of (barring always some horrific or miraculous turn of events) America's last Jews.

Such are the inhabitants of Philip Roth's re-created suburban America: vestigial Jews who find the appearance in their midst (as recounted in "Eli the Fanatic") of a Chasidic Jew, garbed still and believing still as their ancestors were garbed and believed, quite as disturbing as Dostoevsky's Grand Inquisitor found the return of Christ; and such, too, are the inhabitants of J. D. Salinger's New York west side, those parents and friends of Holden Caulfield whose Jewishness has faded and paled until it could be proved against them in no court. But the portrait of the terminal Jew *in extremis* has recently been drawn in the title character of Bruce Jay Friedman's wicked and veracious short novel, *Stern;* a man whose Jewishness has lost all ideological content, positive or negative, and survives only as a psychological disease (strong enough to create an ulcer and motivate a breakdown), kept alive by an equally vestigial and almost equally impotent anti-Semitism.

Moreover, the Jewish writer begins to be influenced by the responsibilities he feels implicit in the recognition accorded him. Quite as the work of certain Nobel Prize winners is altered, even falsified, by the award, and they are tempted to respond imaginatively not to the world of their own making, but to another, more "real" world of whose existence the applause and the prize money reminds them, the Jewish writer's work is altered, even falsified: he has, it is borne in on him, an unsuspected *noblesse* which begins to *oblige* him. If, indeed, the particular experiences into which he happens to have been born have come to seem archetypal to Gentiles, if it is he who must "forge the conscience" of his nation in his time, he must attempt to become worthy of the role (he is likely to think) by guarding himself against the parochial and eliminating from his books all merely local and chauvinistic concerns.

Like the Negro, the homosexual, the southern author who has left the literature of protest and apology behind, he starts to feel uneasy about eternally projecting characters who are images of himself and his people: Jews, Jews, Jews, Jews! He is not, of course, in the situation of those early Jewish (or Negro or homosexual or southern writers) who wanted only to *pass,* to mingle unnoticed in the world of northern, white, Anglo-Saxon Protestants. That is to say, he wants to be not a Jewish writer who is less than Jewish, but one who is more than Jewish. And the devices open to him are many, ranging from the quite simple (and patently false) to the quite devious (and complexly true). He can, like Arthur Miller, for instance, and Paddy Chayefsky, create crypto-Jewish characters; characters who are in habit, speech, and condition of life typically Jewish-American, but who are presented as something else—general-American say, as in *Death of a Salesman,* or Italo-American, as in *Marty.* Such pseudo-universalizing represents, however, a loss of artistic faith, a failure to remember that the inhabitants of Dante's Hell or Joyce's Dublin are more universal as they are more Florentine or Irish. The works influenced by pseudo-universalizing lose authenticity and strength.

Or the Jewish writer can, like Herman Wouk in *The Caine Mutiny,* reverse the stereotypes of popular art: set in opposition a hyper-articulate intellectual, who ought to be a Jew but is disguised as a *goy,* and a hard-bitten fighting man, dedicated to the armed forces and loving authority, who ought to be a *goy* but is given a Jewish name and face. This kind of stereotype-inversion, however, merely substitutes falsification for falsification, sentimentality for sentimentality, even when, as in Leon Uris's *Exodus,* the Jewish military heroes are presented as Jews already become, or in the process of becoming, Israelis. The work of both Wouk and Uris represents, in fact, a disguised form of assimilationism, the attempt of certain Jews to be accepted by the bourgeois, Philistine Gentile community on the grounds that, though they are not Christians, they are even more bourgeois and philistine so that one is not surprised to find Uris appearing in court in the role of *all-rightnik* and enemy of literature, to cry out that Henry Miller's *Tropic of Cancer* "goes beyond every bound of morality I've ever known in my life—everything I've been taught. And I'm not ashamed to say I have morals."

On a more serious level, it is possible to create characters who are specifically half-Jewish, like Salinger's Glass family, those witnesses against the general corruption of a society who appear in story after story in the *New Yorker* and seem always on the verge of becoming the actors in a full-fledged novel, which, alas, never materializes. That the Glasses are Irish as well as Jewish is especially attractive to a public the older members of which have been conditioned by *Abie's Irish Rose* on the stage and the Cohens and the Kellys in the movies; but Salinger seems bent on making more of the popular contrast than its earlier commercial exploiters. In a similar way, I have attempted to pass beyond the Philistine uses of stereotype inversion, as practiced by Herman Wouk, reversing in my *The Second Stone* the traditional roles of accepted Gentile and excluded Jew in order to raise the disturbing question: who in this time of semi-required philo-Semitism is the *real* Jew, the truly alienated man?

It is possible, too, to experiment, as Bernard Malamud has in *A New Life,* with writing a book about Jewish experience that scarcely mentions the word Jew, presenting a character Jewish in name and background, but not identifying him as a Jew until the book's final pages, and then only indirectly. Even more daring, and finally, I think, more successful, is Malamud's attempt in *The Assistant* to

create a Jewish Gentile in Frankie Alpine: a man who moves from a position of vague hostility to the Jews, through exclusion and suffering, to the point where he is ready to accept circumcision—to become *de jure* what he is already *de facto,* one of the ultimately insulted and injured, a Jew: "One day in April Frank went to the hospital and had himself circumcised. For a couple of days he dragged himself around with a pain between his legs. The pain enraged and inspired him. After Passover he became a Jew." It is one of the oldest and (from the vantage point of 1789) one of the most unforeseen happy endings in a literature of strange happy endings; and it could only have happened in 1957, at the high point of the movement we have been examining.

This solution of Malamud's already begins to look a little old-fashioned, appearing as it does in a book which seems a belated novel of the Thirties, a last expression of the apocalyptic fears and Messianic hopes of those terrible but relatively simple times. Certainly *The Assistant* is a book which reminds us of ancestors, rather than suggesting to us progeny, like, say, certain works of Saul Bellow and Norman Mailer, a book, for all its desperation, not quite desperate enough to be in tune with the more post-apocalyptic fears and hopes of our bland but immensely complex times. Nowhere in Malamud's pages, for instance, do we find allusions either to Zen Buddhism or the psychology of Wilhelm Reich; and this is an important clue. For not only in Bellow and Mailer, but in Paul Goodman and Isaac Rosenfeld and Allen Ginsberg and Karl Shapiro, there is felt the influence of Reich, one-time brilliant exponent of Freudian insights, and later independent *magus* and healer, who taught that through full genitality man could conquer the ills of the flesh and the corruptions of society; and who died—convicted for quackery under the Pure Food and Drug Act—in jail, an ambiguous martyr. A flirtation with Zen, and especially a commitment to Reichianism, however, often indicates a discontent with simple or conventional plot resolutions and hence a deeper awareness of the contradictions in the situation of the Jewish-American writer than that possessed by Roth or Malamud or Salinger (who has played with Zen but avoided Reich), much less Uris and Wouk.

It is not enough merely to know that at the moment serious Jewish writing comes to play a central part in American life, the larger Jewish community is being assimilated to certain American values which are inimical to everything for which that serious writing stands, pledging allegiance to belongingness and banality and sociability while condemning abberration and intellectual concern and dissent. One must also be aware (as perhaps even a belated Forties writer like Philip Roth is not sufficiently aware) that the opposition to belongingness and banality and sociability has been itself kidnaped by suburbia. Anti-conformism has become a comfortable slogan of the well-to-do middle-aged with B.A. degrees, and intellectual concern itself has been transformed into academic diligence: standard equipment for teaching jobs at the colleges to which more and more young Jewish people go to sit at the feet of professors, more and more often Jewish, too; not City College any longer—but Amherst or Princeton or Vassar.

Similarly, the radicalism of the Thirties has, with the passage of time, become a polite, accepted leftism—in whose name certain well-meaning Jews, along with their Gentile opposite numbers, twice worked hopelessly to elect Adlai Stevenson President of the United States and then accepted, with a sigh, John F. Kennedy. Meanwhile the great sexual revolution of the Twenties has turned into a vaguely Freudian broadmindedness toward masturbation in the very young and casual copulation in the somewhat older; and the search for sources of cultural strength in the European avant-garde has become the frantic quest for prestige in the pursuit of the chic.

To some contemporary Jewish writers, therefore, the effort simultaneously to exploit a vestigial Jewishness (never quite understood) and to satirize the American-Jewish Establishment (pitifully easy to understand) seems itself an outworn convention, conformism once removed. Such writers are driven, in their attempt to preserve what seems to them the essential Jewish tradition of dissent, to attack the academy in which the second degree Philistinism of the sub-Freudian pseudo-left especially flourishes. Their heroes are likely to be boys running away from school, perpetually "on the road"; and revolt for them tends to be defined as high-level (involving prep school at least, and preferably the university) hooky playing. Such an attack on school and professors inevitably becomes an attack on the kind of literature and criticism which such schools and professors foster, and then an attack on literature and criticism themselves—finally an onslaught against and a rejection of intelligence: the very quality for which, in the deepest American imagination, the Jew has traditionally stood. Imagine living in an age when, with whatever reservations and ironies, an American-Jewish novelist has founded a magazine called *The Noble Savage,* and an American-Jewish poet has collected certain of his essays under the title *In Defense of Ignorance!*

Astonishingly, the literary and cultural ideals of many younger Jewish writers (and these by no means the worst among us) appear no longer to be conceived primarily in terms of the European avant-garde, but rather to be modeled after the examples of certain nativist hyper-American authors of the immediate or remote past. To be sure, no American, not even a Jew in pursuit of a Utopian Americanism, can escape European culture completely; after all, Reich himself was a European before becoming an American and shreds and scraps of existentialism play an important role in the works of the writers in question. But it is Walt Whitman who most deeply possesses the imagination of such writers, along with Henry Miller and William Carlos Williams; and from them is derived the dream of a literature native as well as unbuttoned, untidy, intuitive, and passionate. Indeed, there are some Jewish-American authors (most notably Karl Shapiro) who have tried to argue that in Judaism itself there are to be found grounds for a revolt against the academic, formalistic, and genteel, that our tradition has been all along more Whitmanian than Eliotic.

At any rate, certain Jews now stand in the forefront of the newest American revulsion from Europe and the life of the intelligence which Europe represents to the popular imagination in the United States. Under the aegis of such publishers as Grove Press, and in such magazines as *Big Table* and the *Evergreen Review,* the Jewish offspring of Twenties schoolmasters and Thirties Communists have oddly banded together with Gentile ex-athletes and junkies to make the movement called "beat," and to define for that movement a program advocating the rediscovery of America and the great audience via marijuana and jazz, more and better orgasms, and a general loosening of literary form. Some of the bright young Jews currently producing first novels and early poems are "beat" or "hip" as their parents were once Stalinists or Trotskyites, only in their larval stage; with maturity (i.e., marriage or a graduate fellowship), they are likely to shave off their beards and settle down to doctoral dissertations or new publishing ventures. And some of the older writers who have climbed on the bandwagon in search of a second youth may have been driven less by their conviction that youth is an absolute good, to be repeated as often as possible, than by a sense of flagging powers, sexual or creative; and they may not preserve their new-found allegiances past the next turn of fashion. But the new Jewish anti-intellectualism cannot be wholly explained away by an analysis of its psychogenesis; the works produced in its name will survive the allegiances behind them, and the critic must deal with them in their own terms.

In their own terms, they are marked by the abandonment of the Jewish character as a sufficient embodiment of the Jewish author's aspirations and values, and by the invention, beside him or in his place, of characters who are not merely non-Jewish, but are, in fact, hyper-*goyim,* super-Gentiles of truly mythic proportions: specifically, sexual heroes of incredible potency. Such characters represent a resolve on the part of certain Jewish writers to invent (reversing the traditional roles) mythical Gentiles with whom they can identify themselves. But even here, they were anticipated by a non-Jewish writer, Henry Miller, who enjoys the special distinction of being the first Gentile author in our literature to see himself not directly as an American, but defensively as a Gentile, the Jew's *goy*—even as certain white writers now begin to see themselves as the Negro's *o'fay.* "I sometimes ask myself," Miller writes in *Tropic of Cancer,* "how it happens that I attract nothing but crackbrained individuals, neuraesthenics, neurotics, psychopaths—and Jews especially. There must be something in a healthy Gentile that excites the Jewish mind, like when he sees sour black bread." It is perhaps because Miller has already provided them with a living imaginary Gentile that American-Jewish writers did not turn, as one might have expected, to the Negro as a model for their re-invented selves. Certainly the Negro is the Jew's archetypal opposite, representative of the impulsive life even as the Jew is the symbol of the intellectual; and the Negro is everywhere in these times at the center of our concern. Indeed, there were tentative efforts in this direction: the account, for instance, written by Bernard Wolfe along with Mezz Mezzrow, of how the latter had passed, or almost passed, by way of the world of jazz, into the deep world of the Negroes; and the manifesto, or more properly pre-manifesto, of Norman Mailer in which the life of the "hipster," the White Negro, is more sighed for than advocated.

Mailer, however, when he dreamed his mythical *goy* in the character of Sergius O'Shaughnessy (who moves through the novel *The Deer Park,* is hinted at in the story "The Man Who Studied Yoga," and reappears heroically in "The Time of Her Time") created a protagonist who seems less White Negro than Jew's Hemingway and, in this respect, improbably resembles the Eugene Henderson of Saul Bellow's *Henderson the Rain King,* though Bellow, for all his commitment to Wilhelm Reich, is not "hip" or "beat" at all. Both writers at any rate, have recently projected similar versions of the good life: passionate, genital, anti-intellectual, impulsive, though the one has lived a life of risk, daring drug-addiction, and even jail, while the other is a professor at the University of Chicago, daring only boredom and the dangers of security.

While the general American reader is still eager to identify himself with the mythical Jews of the Forties and the Fifties, alienated intellectuals like Mailer and Bellow, who began by portraying such Jews, have moved on to imagine themselves as mythical Gentiles: paleface Protestant noble savages, great muscular conquerors of women and jungles, aging athletes, who, to the parents of those writers, would still have represented the absolute Other. Where, then, has he come from, this Anglo-Saxon hero-monster, the "Golden Goy," with which certain hitherto dutiful Jewish-American boys insist on confusing themselves? Appropriately enough, out of the ambivalence stirred in the minds of these writers by the public image of Ernest Hemingway: inventor—out of anti-Semitic malice—of the first notable Jewish character in American fiction, Robert Cohen. Committed to Hemingway insofar as they are Americans of a generation that learned its speech and its life-style from his books, but cut off from him insofar as they are Jews and, therefore, to Hemingway embodiments of the fake artist, the fake lover, the fake outsider—they constructed, in irony and desperate love, portraits of the elder novelist at the moment of his artistic defeat and just before his death.

Norman Mailer's Sergius O'Shaughnessy is portrayed in "The Time of Her Time" as giving bullfight lessons in a loft in Greenwich Village: a bullfighter without real bulls, though surrounded by real enough women whom he actually possesses, in the place of imaginary conflict. It all amounts to a strange yet somehow tender travesty of the images of Eros and death and of Hemingway himself as connoisseur in both areas which run through *The Sun Also Rises* and *Death in the Afternoon.* In Bellow's *Henderson the Rain King,* the same author is evoked by a hulking giant of a protagonist whose initials are E.H., and who seeks in the heart of Africa, in an encounter with savages and wild beasts, the answers to questions he is not articulate enough to formulate; and for all its mannered irony and outright burlesque, Bellow's book, too, seems—especially now—a memoir and a tribute. But Hemingway, as we have noticed earlier, could never tell the difference between himself and Gary Cooper, who came to play on the screen so many of the roles projected by Hemingway out of his own anguish and vanity, while Gary Cooper is finally an up-dated Natty Bumppo, perhaps the last Natty

we can afford. And Natty was to begin with, of course, the American Indian in whiteface.

The Jewish writer, trying to imagine the *goy* he longs to be, or at least to contemplate, succeeds finally in re-inventing the mythical redskin out of James Fenimore Cooper, which is amusing enough. But it is not the whole story; for Henderson and O'Shaughnessy are half-breeds, and the Indian in them, which is to say, their American component, is improbably crossed with a legendary horror out of the deep Jewish past, a component rooted in the life of the *shtetl* and memories of that life: a world the first Cooper surely never made and the second never acted. There are clues to the true nature of this second component in both Bellow and Mailer, though in Bellow they are few and obscure. Nonetheless, before Henderson became fully himself, turned loose in Africa to flee dark princesses and mate chastely with African kings who tame lions and read Wilhelm Reich, he was tentatively sketched as the Kirby Allbee of Bellow's earlier novel *The Victim:* a seedy Anglo-Saxon anti-Semite, bound to Asa Leventhal, his Jewish victim (or victimizer) with a passion like that which binds the cuckold to his cuckolder. That passion is rendered in terms of an appalling physical intimacy: "Leventhal . . . was so conscious of Allbee . . . that he was able to see himself as if through a strange pair of eyes: the side of his face, the palpitation of his throat, the seams of his skin. . . . Changed in this way into his own observer, he was able to see Allbee, too . . . the weave of his coat, his raggedly overgrown neck . . . he could even evoke the odor of his hair and skin. The acuteness and intimacy of it astounded him, oppressed and intoxicated him." And its consequences are violence, a final scene in which Leventhal thrusts Allbee from his apartment, though not until they have been joined in the embrace of struggle, an even closer contact of the flesh, and a kind of consummation in horror. Allbee, Bellows makes clear, is Leventhal's beloved as well as his nightmare, just as Leventhal is Allbee's beloved as well as his nightmare; and the climax of such ambivalence is a kind of rejection scarcely distinguishable from rape. What Bellow leaves unclear, perhaps deliberately, is the order of generation of these nightmares. We suspect that Leventhal (closer to his author in origin and temperament, though by no means a self-portrait) is dreaming Allbee dreaming him, but Bellow does not tell us this.

Mailer, on the other hand, has placed the question of the genesis of the mythical *goy* at the center of his most recent work, commenting on it editorially and including it inside his fictional framework as well. Originally, he tells us, for instance, the two Sergius short stories preserved in *Advertisements for Myself* and the one Sergius novel were to be part of a larger, immensely ambitious scheme: a study of how an inadequate Jew, baffled sexually and artistically, invents, in his troubled sleep, the synthetic *Ubermensch,* Sergius O'Shaughnessy. "I woke up in the morning," Mailer writes in *Advertisements for Myself,* "with the plan for a prologue and an eight-part novel in my mind, the prologue to be the day of a small, frustrated man, a minor artist manqué. The eight novels were to be eight stages of his dream later that night, and the books would revolve around the adventures of a mythical hero, Sergius

O'Shaughnessy . . . " The "artist manqué" is not identified in these notes as a Jew, but we are not surprised to discover, reading the novella into which Mailer's "prologue" turned, that his name is Sam Slabovda, and that he is given to making statements beginning, "You see, *boychick* . . . "

Mailer's scheme has fallen apart in his hands, as his view of the world and himself has fragmented perilously; and surely one of his basic problems has been a temptation to believe that, after all, he himself is the *goy* O'Shaughnessy rather than the small Jew, Slabovda, who, in defeat and distress, has dreamed O'Shaughnessy. Hemingway had the same difficulty in keeping himself, brown-eyed poet and laureate of impotence, distinct from the *Amerikanski* heroes of his later works; yet in Hemingway no ethnic-mythic gulf separated him from his Gentile protagonists. And he was never driven, even in his moment of acutest anxiety, to imagine a mating, brutal as an evisceration, between his passive self and its more active projection. Such a mating, however, constitutes both the action and theme of Mailer's most successful piece of fiction, the short story "The Time of Her Time." At once a confession of terrifying candor and a parable of our times, "The Time of Her Time" imagines an encounter between O'Shaughnessy and a Jewish coed from N.Y.U., whom we might well take for his *anima*-figure did we not know that she represents the Jewish author, and O'Shaughnessy the *animus* of his fantasies. No wonder the "heroine" is possessed completely and at last, not as a woman may be but as a man must, through what Mailer calls "love's first hole."

Mailer opens his tale in a Negro hash-house, but cannot keep it there. Ill at ease in that theoretically preferred milieu, he returns quickly to the pseudo-Hemingwayesque Village loft and his true subject: the long struggle between his mythic, beloved hero and his equally mythic but hated heroine, called Denise. Denise seems at first glance the Temple Drake of the Sixties, as archetypal a coed for our troubled days as Temple for the Twenties. Like her prototype, she is hot for love but incapable of submission to it, and therefore incapable of an orgasm; but, unlike Temple, she is no decadent last product of Anglo-Saxon gentility—only the black-haired offspring of a hardware merchant from Brooklyn (out of, presumably, one of those sexually aggressive Jewesses who terrified and allured Thomas Wolfe in the Thirties); and she is not driven, but committed to bohemian freedom, T. S. Eliot, and Sigmund Freud, or at least to her own analyst.

The blow-by-blow description of the sexual combat between her and O'Shaughnessy threatens momentarily to turn into an allegory of the cultural plight we have been examining, but it is saved by the vigor of Mailer's language and the acuteness of his senses, especially his nose. We are not surprised to discover that it is rape, on either the literal or symbolic level, which Mailer's coed demands before she will pay any man the tribute of her orgasm; though we may not have been as prepared as is Mailer's O'Shaughnessy to understand just what sort of rape she had all along required. And why not, since Sam Slabovda (who is Mailer, who is Denise) invented him? ". . . and

then she was about to hang again," Mailer makes his protagonist say, "and I said into her ear, 'You dirty little Jew.' That whipped her over . . . " And whipped Mailer over with her; for precisely here, I think, *he* made it, too, for the first time in his life, made it artistically as his heroine made it sexually; and he has been more or less peacefully writing *midrashim* on Buber's retelling of Chasidic tales ever since.

What is finally clear in Mailer as well as in Bellow, though clearer in the former, is that the other half of Henderson-O'Shaughnessy, the non-Hemingway half, is the *pogrom-chik*, the Cossack rapist of the erotic nightmares of the great-grandmothers of living American Jews and that the great-grandchildren respond to him precisely as their archetypal female ancestor in the not-very-funny old Jewish joke, who whispers over the shoulder of her assaulter to the child indignantly screaming and attempting to tug him away, "Quiet, Rosalie, a pogrom is a pogrom." Adopted to our needs of today, however, it seems funny enough: a joke both very American and very Jewish this time around; not merely one more but perhaps the greatest, as well as the latest, Jewish-American joke. Yet there is one more: the Jew who thinks he is an American, yet feels in his deepest heart an immitigable difference from the Gentile American who thinks he is a Jew, need only go abroad to realize that, in the eyes of non-Americans, the difference does not exist at all.

"*Americans go home!*" the angry crowds cry before our embassies; and hearing them, the Jew knows not only that he is quite as American as his Gentile fellow-tourist, but also that the fellow-tourist along with him, that *all* Americans, are the Jews of the second half of the twentieth century: refused (outside of their own country, at least) any identity except the general one contained in a name which is an abusive epithet. "*Americans go home!*" the crowds roar again, while the rocks fly, the police-lines buckle; and running for cover, the Jewish-American keeps imagining that he hears behind him (as, running from the schoolyard once, he heard the cry, "You killed our Christ!") the shout, "You killed our Julius and Ethel Rosenberg!" "Your Rosenbergs?" he wants to yell back, "*your* Rosenbergs?" as once he had wanted to holler, "*Your* Christ?" And remembering the childhood indignity in the midst of adult ones, remembering when it was as difficult to be a Jew as it has become to be an American, he finds himself laughing too hard to be dismayed.

Alfred Kazin

SOURCE: "The Jew as Modern American Writer," in *The Commentary Reader: Two Decades of Articles and Stories,* edited by Normal Podkhoretz, Atheneum, 1966, pp. xv-xxv.

[*A highly respected American literary critic, Kazin is best known for his essay collections* The Inmost Leaf (1955), Contemporaries (1962), *and* On Native Grounds (1942), *a study of American prose writing since the era of William Dean Howells. In the following essay, he details the rise of the Jewish-American writer.*]

Emma Lazarus, who wrote those lines inscribed on the base of the Statue of Liberty ("Give me your tired, your poor . . . Your huddled masses, yearning to breathe free"), was the first Jew whom Ralph Waldo Emerson ever met. Emerson's daughter Ellen, an old Sunday-school teacher, noted how astonishing it was "to get at a real unconverted Jew (who had no objections to calling herself one, and talked freely about 'our Church' and 'we Jews'), and to hear how Old Testament sounds to her, and find she has been brought up to keep the Law, and the Feast of the Passover, and the day of Atonement. The interior view was more interesting than I could have imagined. She says her family are outlawed now, they no longer keep the Law, but Christian institutions don't interest her either."

Emma Lazarus had been sending Emerson her poems for years; he responded with uncertain praise, for they were excessively literary and understandably raised questions in the mind of so subtle a critic. But although she was not to become a consciously "Jewish" poet until the Russian pogroms aroused her, her being a Jew had certainly distinguished her in the literary world of Victorian America. She was that still exotic figure, that object of Christian curiosity, "the Jew"—and to descendants of the New England Puritans, straight out of their Bible.

Proust was to say that in every Jew "there is a prophet and a bounder." Emma Lazarus was still the "prophet" when she visited Concord. This was in 1876, when Jews in this country were getting known as "bounders." General Grant in a Civil War order had said "Jew" when he meant peddler, but impoverished farmers in the West now said "Jew" when they meant Wall Street financier. New England writers like James Russell Lowell and Henry Adams became obsessed with Jews and "the Jewish question" as soon as there were real Jews on the American scene. The "prophet" figure that literary New England had always known from books had become the "bounder"—and, worse, the ragged *shtetl* Jew whom Adams examined with such loathing from a Russian railway car and in New York when he heard him speaking "a weird guttural Yiddish." Henry James, returning to his native downtown streets, announced that "the denizens of the New York Ghetto, heaped as thick as the splinters on the table of a glass-blower, had each, like the fine glass particle, his or her individual share of the whole hard glitter of Israel." The Jew in New York was an instance of alienness, an object to be studied. James would have been astonished to think of a writer coming out of this milieu. And, to do him justice, not many immigrant Jews saw themselves as writers in English. Henry Adams' sometime protégé, Bernard Berenson, who had come here from Lithuania, was to find himself only as an art historian in Italy.

William Dean Howells, now a Socialist in New York, praised Abraham Cahan's *Yekl: A Tale of the New York Ghetto.* But Howells was predisposed to Russian literature, Cahan was a "Russian" realist in English, and Howells, like so many Westerners enjoying or soon to enjoy

New York's "Europeanness," was also a democratic idealist, naturally friendly to all these new peoples in New York. His friend Mark Twain said that Jews were members of the human race; "that is the worst you can say about them." But this easy Western humor was still very far from the creative equality that Jewish and non-Jewish writers were some day to feel. Mark Twain, like Maxim Gorky in Russia, protested against pogroms and was friendly to Jews; but as late as 1910, when he died, there was no significant type of the Jewish writer in this country. The older German-Jewish stock had produced many important scholars and publicists; it was to produce an original in Gertrude Stein. But the positive, creative role of the Jew as modern American, and above all as a modern American writer, was in the first years of this century being prepared not in the universities, not even in journalism, but in the vaudeville theaters, music halls, and burlesque houses where the pent-up eagerness of penniless immigrant youngsters met the raw urban scene on its own terms. It was not George Jean Nathan, Robert Nathan, or Ludwig Lewisohn any more than it was Arthur Krock, David Lawrence, Adolph Ochs, or Walter Lippmann who established the Jew in the national consciousness as a distinctly American figure; it was the Marx Brothers, Eddie Cantor, Al Jolson, Fannie Brice, George Gershwin. Jewish clowns, minstrels, song-writers helped to fit the Jew to America, and America to the Jew, with an élan that made for future creativity in literature as well as for the mass products of the "entertainment industry."

Proust, with his artist's disengagement from both "prophet" and "bounder"; Henry Adams, with his frivolous hatred of the immigrant ("five hundred thousand Jews in New York eating kosher, and saved from the drowning they deserve"), had never conceived of the Jew as a representative national entertainer. But in the naturalness and ease with which the Jewish vaudevillian put on blackface, used stereotypes, and ground out popular songs, in the avidity with which the public welcomed him, was the Jew's share in the common experience, the Jew's averageness and typicality, that were to make possible the Jew-as-writer in this country. In Western Europe, Jewish "notables" had been a handful—as odd as the occasional prime minister of Italy or Britain; in Eastern Europe, where the Jews were a mass, it was their very numbers that was so disturbing to anti-Semites in office, who even in Soviet Russia were to keep Jews down because the thought of too many Jews being allowed to exercise their talents at once could obviously be viewed as a threat to their own people. As Mikoyan was to say some years ago to a Jewish delegation, "We have our own cadres now." But in this country the very poverty and cultural rawness of the Jewish immigrant masses, the self-assertive egalitarianism of the general temper, and the naturalness with which different peoples could identify with each other in the unique halfway house that was New York (without New York it would no doubt all have been different, but without New York there would have been no immigrant epic, no America) gave individual performers the privilege of representing the popular mind. Never before had so numerous a mass of Jews been free citizens of the country in which they lived, and so close to the national life. And although many a genteel young literatus now analyzing Nathanael West and Saul Bellow shudders at his connection with Potash and Perlmutter, Eddie Cantor, and Fannie Brice, it is a fact that this "vulgar culture," proceeding merrily to the irreverent genius of the Marx Brothers (whose best movies were written by S. J. Perelman, the college chum and brother-in-law of Nathanael West), helped to found, as a natural habitat for the Jews in this country, the consciously grotesque style of parody that one finds in Perelman, West, Odets, Bellow, in many Broadway-Hollywood satirists, and even in an occasional literary critic, like Isaac Rosenfeld and Harold Rosenberg, impatient with the judicial tone that comes with the office. The Jewish writer, a late arrival in this country and admittedly of uncertain status, had to find his model in the majority culture, and although this had some depressing consequences in the mass, it was on the whole fortunate, for the sharply independent novelists, poets, and critics to come, that they were influenced more by the language of the street than by the stilted moralism that has always been a trap for the Jewish writer.

But of course the popular culture was invigorating and even liberating so long as it was one of many cultures operating simultaneously on the Jewish writer's mind. Ever since the legal emancipation of the Jews in Western Europe, there had been two principal cultures among the Jews—the orthodox, religious tradition, pursuing its own way often magnificently indifferent to the issues shaking European thought; and the newly secularistic culture of the "Jewish intellectuals," who found in the cause of "progressive humanity," in philosophic rationalism, in socialism, and cultural humanism, their sophisticated equivalent of Judaism. In Western Europe, for the most part, these two cultures no longer irritated each other. But among the Yiddish-speaking Jews of Eastern Europe, "enlightenment" did not appear until late in the 19th century; while in Western Europe the medieval ghettos were a barely tolerated memory, in Russia the Jewish Pale of Settlement, restricting most Jews to certain areas and restricting the intensity of their existence to the *shtetl* and its religious customs, remained a searing memory in the lives of immigrants and their children. The "dark" ages and the "modern" age, the ghetto and the revolutionary movement, persecution and free human development, were conjoined in the Jewish mind. The tension and ardor with which the two cultures of modern Jewry were related, in individual after individual, helps to explain the sudden flowering of painters among Russian Jews in the first years of this century, the extraordinary spiritual energy invested in the idea of socialism, the "twist" that Isaac Babel liked to give his Russian sentences, the general passion for "culture" and "cultural advancement," the revolutionary zeal with which former yeshiva boys turned political commissars spoke of the great new age of man.

Babel wrote of ex-seminarists riding away with the Red Cavalry from their "rotted" Bibles and Talmuds, Chagall's *rebbes* sprouted wings over the thatched roofs of Vitebsk and sang the joys of the flesh. The force of some immense personal transformation could be seen in the conscious energy of Trotsky's public role in the Russian Revolution. These revolutionaries, writers, scientists, painters were the "new men," the first mass secularists in the long religious history of the Jews, yet the zeal with which they engaged themselves to the "historic" task of desacralizing the European tradition often came from the profound history embedded in Judaism itself—it certainly did not come from the experience of Jews with other peoples in Eastern Europe. These "new men" had a vision of history that, as their critics were to tell them, was fanatically all of one piece, obstinately "Jewish" and "intellectual"—a vision in which some subtle purposiveness to history always managed to reassert itself in the face of repeated horrors. But what their critics could not recognize was that this obstinate quest for "meaning" was less a matter of conscious thought than a personal necessity, a requirement of survival, the historic circumstance that reasserted itself in case after case among the Jews, many of whom had good reason to believe that their lives were a triumph over every possible negation, and who, with the modesty of people for whom life itself is understandably the greatest good, found it easy to rejoice in the political and philosophical reasoning that assured them civic respect, civic peace, and the life of the mind.

"Excess of sorrow laughs," wrote Blake in *The Marriage of Heaven and Hell*. "Excess of joy weeps." For Jews in this country, who had triumphed over so much, remembered so much, were in such passionate relations with the two cultures—of religion and "modernity" that many believed in simultaneously—their conscious progress often became something legendary, a drama rooted in the existential fierceness of life lived and barely redeemed every single day. There was an intensity, a closeness to many conflicting emotions, that often seemed unaccountably excessive to other peoples. The need to explain himself to himself, to put his own house in order, was a basic drive behind many a Jewish writer. People to whom existence has often been a consciously fearful matter, who have lived at the crossroads between the cultures and on the threshold between life and death, naturally see existence as tension, issue, and drama, woven out of so many contradictions that only a work of art may appear to *hold* these conflicts, to compose them, to allow the human will some detachment. Surely never in history has a whole people had to endure such a purgation of emotions as took place at the Eichmann trial. It was this that led Harold Rosenberg to show the cruel dramatic necessity behind the trial—the need of the Jews to tell their story, to relive the unbearable, the inadmissible, the inexpressible. The Jew who has lived through the age of Hitler cannot even say, with Eliot, "After such knowledge, what forgiveness?" For he has to live with his knowledge if he is to live at all, and this "knowledge" enforces itself upon him as a fact both atrocious and dramatic, a mockery of the self-righteous Christianity that has always surrounded him, a parody of the Orthodox Judaism that has sought to justify the ways of God to man, a drama founded on the contrast between the victims and all those who remained spectators when the Jews were being slaughtered.

"Excess of sorrow laughs," wrote Blake in *The Marriage of Heaven and Hell*. "Excess of joy weeps." For Jews in this country, who had triumphed over so much, remembered so much, were in such passionate relations with the two cultures—of religion and "modernity" that many believed in simultaneously—their conscious progress often became something legendary, a drama rooted in the existential fierceness of life lived and barely redeemed every single day.

— *Alfred Kazin*

There are experiences so extreme that, after living them, one can do nothing with them *but* put them into words. There are experiences so terrible that one can finally do nothing with them but not forget them. This was already the case with many of the young Jewish writers just out of the city ghettos, who began to emerge in significant numbers only in the early 30's. Looking back on this emergence, one can see that it needed the peculiar crystallization of ancient experiences, and then the avidity with which young writers threw themselves on the American scene, to make possible that awareness of the Jew as a new force that one sees in such works of the 30's as Henry Roth's *Call It Sleep*, Michael Gold's *Jews Without Money*, Daniel Fuchs's *Summer in Williamsburg*, Albert Halper's *The Chute*, Odets' *Awake and Sing*, Meyer Levin's *The Old Bunch*, and even in West's *Miss Lonelyhearts*, whose hero is not named a Jew but who is haunted by the indiscriminate pity that was to mark the heroes of Bernard Malamud and Edward Wallant. In the 20's there had been several extraordinarily sensitive writers, notably Paul Rosenfeld and Waldo Frank, out of the older, German-Jewish stock; but on the whole, it needed the turbulent mixing of the ghetto and the depression to make possible the wild flurry of strong new novels and plays in the 30's.

Yet the social realists of the 30's were often boxed in, mentally, by the poverty and hopelessness of their upbringing and the bitterness, deprivations, and anti-Semitism of depression America. The extraordinary brevity of so many literary careers in America is a social fact that any account of the Jewish writer in America must contend with as an omen for the future. Although the aborted career is common enough in American writing and was particularly marked among writers of the 30's—many were shipwrecked by the failure of their political hopes, and many crippled as artists by the excessive effort it took to bring out their non-selling books—it is also a fact that writers from the "minorities" have a harder time getting started, and tend, as a group, to fade out more easily, than those writers from the older stocks whose literary culture was less deliberately won and is less self-conscious. A historian of the Negro novel in this country says that most Negroes who have published one book have never published another—and one might well wonder what, until the sudden fame of James Baldwin, would have induced any Negro writer in this country to keep at it except the necessity of telling his own story. Thinking of the family situation portrayed in *Call It Sleep*, one can see why, having written *that* up, to the vast indifference of the public in the 30's, the author should have felt that he was through. The real drama behind most Jewish novels and plays, even when they are topical and revolutionary in feeling, is the contrast between the hysterical tenderness of the Oedipal relation and the "world"; in the beginning there was the Jewish mother and her son, but the son grew up, he went out into the world, he became a writer. That was the beginning of his career and usually the end of the novel. Jews don't believe in original sin, but they certainly believe in the original love that they once knew in the *shtetl*, in the kitchen, in the Jewish household—and after *that* knowledge, what forgiveness? In this, at least, the sentimental author of *Jews Without Money* parallels the master of childhood in *Call It Sleep*.

What saved Jewish writing in America from its innate provincialism, what enabled it to survive the moral wreckage of the 30's, was the coming of the "intellectuals"—writers like Delmore Schwartz, Saul Bellow, Lionel Trilling, Karl Shapiro, Harold Rosenberg, Isaac Rosenfeld, Lionel Abel, Clement Greenberg, Bernard Malamud, Irving Howe, Philip Rahv, Leslie Fiedler, Robert Warshow, Paul Goodman, Norman Mailer, Philip Roth, William Phillips. It was these writers, and younger writers in their tradition, who made possible intellectual reviews like *Partisan Review* and serious, objective, unparochial magazines like *Commentary*—a magazine which has emphasized general issues and regularly included so many writers who are not Jews. *Commentary*, founded in November 1945, was hospitable to this new maturity and sophistication among Jewish writers in America; it established itself on the American scene easily, and with great naturalness, exactly in those years immediately after the war when American Jews began to publish imaginative works and intellectual studies of distinction—*Dangling Man, The Victim, The Middle of the Journey, The Liberal Imagination, Death of a Salesman, The Naked and the Dead, The World Is a Wedding, The Lonely Crowd, The Natural, The Adventures of Augie March, The Mirror and the Lamp, The Tradition of the New*.

Even a gifted writer outside this group, Salinger, contemptuous of its ideologies, was an "intellectual" writing about "intellectuals." Even a middlebrow sullenly critical of its preoccupations, Herman Wouk, did it the honor of "exposing" an intellectual in *The Caine Mutiny*. Whether they were novelists or just intellectual pundits at large, what these writers all had in common was the ascendancy of "modern literature," which has been more destructive of bourgeois standards than Marxism, was naturally international-minded, and in a culture bored with middle-class rhetoric upheld the primacy of intelligence and the freedom of the imagination. The heroes of these "intellectuals" were always Marx, Freud, Trotsky, Eliot, Joyce, Valéry; the "intellectuals" believed in the "great enlighteners," because their greatest freedom was to be enlighteners of all culture themselves, to be the instructors and illuminati of the modern spirit. Unlike so many earlier writers, who had only their hard story to tell and then departed, the Jewish "intellectuals" who emerged in the 40's found shelter under the wide wings of the "modern movement," and so showed an intellectual spirit that Jews had not always managed in the great world.

Commentary has, more than any other "Jewish" magazine known to me, been a symbol of and a home for this intellectual spirit. I remember that as the first issues began to appear at the end of that pivotal year of 1945, I was vaguely surprised that it dealt with so many general issues in so subtly critical and detached a fashion, regularly gave a forum to non-Jewish writers as well as to Jewish ones. Like many Jewish intellectuals of my time and place, brought up to revere the universalism of the Socialist ideal and of modern culture, I had equated "Jewish" magazines with a certain insularity of tone, subject matter, writers' names—with mediocrity. To be a "Jewish writer"—I knew several, and knew of many more, who indefatigably managed this by not being any particular kind of writer at all—was somehow to regress, to strike attitudes, to thwart the natural complexities of truth. There were just too many imprecisions and suppressions in the parochially satisfied "Jewish" writer. It was enough to be a Jew *and* a writer. "Jewish" magazines were not where literature could be found, and certainly not the great world. "Jewish" magazines worried over the writer's "negative" attitude toward his "jewishness," nagged you like an old immigrant uncle who did not know how much resentment lay behind his "Jewishness."

But *Commentary,* to the grief of many intellectual guardians of the "Jewish" world, marked an end to that, which is why its interest for a large intellectual public has been so significant. It has always been natural for Protestant Americans to believe, in the words of John Jay Chapman, that "the heart of the world is Jewish." But after 1945 and the unparalleled, inexpressible martyrdom of the Jewish people in Europe, it was natural for non-Jews everywhere to believe, as Jews now had more reasons than ever to believe, that Jewish survival and Jewish self-determination related to everything in the world. The particular distinction of *Commentary* among Jewish magazines has been to articulate and to support this many-sided relatedness. As one can see from the extraordinary opening section of [*The Commentary Reader*]—"The Holocaust and After"—the Jewish writer after 1945 had particular reason to feel that this most terrible of all events in Jewish history bound him more closely to every fundamental question of human nature and historic failure involved in Europe's self-destruction. As the late Solomon Bloom showed in his detached and heart-rending study of Mordechai Chaim Rumkowski, the "Dictator of the Lodz Ghetto" who sent so many of his own people to death, the Jewish historian had materials more atrocious than any in modern literature for the recognition of how squalid and self-deluded human nature could be. Yet, as this anthology goes on to show, the Jewish art critic, essayist, economist, political observer, psychoanalyst, sociologist had only to take up aspects of contemporary experience in general to show the relevance to all this experience of his native, obstinate, questing spirit as a Jew. One can cite from this brilliant anthology, virtually at random, materials so various and fascinating as George Lichtheim's "Reflections on Trotsky," Hannah Arendt's stark notes on the German scene, David Daiches' examination of the new Biblical scholarship, Leslie Farber's " 'I'm Sorry, Dear.' " And where else would the non-Jewish writer and our common American problems come together so happily as in Dwight Macdonald's "By Cozzens Possessed," James Baldwin's "Equal In Paris," Edmund Wilson's "Paul Rosenfeld: Three Phases"?

Of course the prosperity that began with the war encouraged the new Jewish writers to feel that the country was theirs. Immediately after the war, indeed, some of them embraced this newfound land, their America, with an enthusiasm made slightly hysterical by the need to cast off Marxist ideology. Yet this new liveliness could be attributed in the greatest part to the closing up of a time-lag, to the sudden eruption of writers whose time had come—and who had often been brought up in old-fashioned ways that impressed the dizzyingly complex new world upon their minds with special vividness. Jean-Paul Sartre says in *Les Mots* of the grandfather who brought him up—"Between the first Russian Revolution and the first World War, fifteen years after Mallarmé's death . . . a man of the 19th century was foisting upon his grandson ideas that had been current under Louis Philippe. . . . Ought I to complain? . . . In our bustling societies, delays sometimes give a head start." Many a Jewish writer has been brought up on his grandfather's ideas, and now engages the last third of the 20th century with special eagerness. Generally speaking, the Jewish intellectuals who since the 40's have exercised so much influence on American culture started very far back. If the young man from the provinces, as Lionel Trilling named him, typifies the encounter with the great world in 19th-century novels, it was significantly the Jewish intellectual who was now to write the key book on Matthew Arnold, the definitive biographies of Henry Adams, Henry James, James Joyce, who was to become the theoretician of action painting, the most resourceful American novelist of the postwar period, the editor of the leading cultural review, the Reichian *enfant terrible* of the universities, the novelist of orgiastic high life in Palm Springs, Las Vegas, Hollywood, and the Waldorf Towers. Often enough graduates of the old revolutionary movement, with its intellectual ardor, its internationalism, its passion for political complexities, and its taste for action, these Jewish intellectuals combined an American belief in the "tradition of the new" with their own moral tradition and their passion for the Europe of the great thinkers, their driving personal ambition with the knowledge that they were exceptions, "survivors," as Moses Elkanah Herzog said, of the age that had seen their brethren slaughtered like cattle in the abattoirs that the Nazis had made of Eastern Europe. Just as it was Southern writers, with their knowledge of defeat and their instinctive irony, who in the 40's spoke to the chastened American mind, so it is Jewish writers who now represent to many Americans the unreality of their prosperity and the anxiety of their condition. In situations of inestimable complexity, requiring the most "sophisticated" and "expert" "analysis" of the "complex factors," it was often enough Jews, born and pushed to be intellectuals, who became the connoisseurs of the new chaos, the mental elite of the power age. Never was interpretation, explanation, commentary, a vital new *midrash,* so much needed as in the period, starting with the war, when the world was so much compressed and subtilized by the new technological revolution—and never were there so many Jewish intellectuals prepared to do the explaining. The ragged old "prophet" was not much in evidence, and the Jew-as-bounder was not to be thought of, but the age of the intellectuals was in full swing.

All the writers were intellectuals now, the best writers as well as the most conformist—novelists like Saul Bellow and Norman Mailer dealt in the drama of concepts, had heroes who lived by concepts, and suffered for them. The world seemed suspended on concepts, and in the mass magazines as in the universities and publishing houses, a mass of indistinguishable sophisticates genuflected to the modern idols and talked the same textbook formulae about Joyce, James, Eliot, Faulkner, Picasso, Stravinsky. The Sunday book supplements were soon all as apocalyptic as a Jewish novelist after a divorce, and one could regularly read footnotes to the absurdity of the human condition, the death of tragedy, and the end of innocence by pseudo-serious minds who imitated Bellow, Mailer, Fiedler, Ginsberg, Goodman as humorlessly as teen-age girls copied hair styles from the magazines.

Definitely, it was now the thing to be Jewish. But in Western universities and small towns many a traditional novelist and professor of English felt out of it, and asked, with varying degrees of self-control, if there was no longer a good novel to be written about the frontier, about Main Street, about the good that was in marriage? Was it possible, these critics wondered aloud, that American life had become so deregionalized and lacking in local color that the big power units and the big cities had pre-empted the American scene, along with the supple Jewish intellectuals who were at home with them? Was it possible that Norman Mailer had become the representative American novelist?

It was entirely possible, and certainly the thought would not have astonished Mailer, just as the power of his example for other novelists did not astonish Saul Bellow. Whatever pain this ascendancy might cause to writers who felt out of it because they lived in Montana or in the wrong part of California, it was a fact that there were now Jewish novelists who, as writers, had mastered the complex resources of the modern novel, who wrote English lovingly, possessively, masterfully, for whom the language and the form, the intelligence of art, had become as natural a way of living as the Law had been to their grandfathers. Literature had indeed become their spiritual world, their essential personal salvation, in a world where all traditional markers were fast disappearing. But in the frothy turbulent "mix" of America in the 60's, with its glut, its power drives, its confusion of values, the Jewish writer found himself so much read, consulted, imitated, that he knew it would not be long before the reaction set in—and in fact the decorous plaint of the "Protestant minority" has been succeeded by crudely suggestive phrases about the "Jewish Establishment," the "O.K. writers and the Poor Goy," "The Jewish-American Push." Yet it is plainly a certain success that has been resented, not the Jew. And if the Jew has put his distinct mark on modern American writing, it is surely because, in a time when the old bourgeois certainties and humanist illusions have crumbled, the Jew is practiced in what James called "the imagination of disaster" and "does indeed see life as ferocious and sinister." The contemporary literary temper is saturnine, panicky, black in its humor but adroit in shifting the joke onto the shoulders of society. And the Jewish writer, with his natural interest in the social fact, has been particularly quick to show the lunacy and hollowness of so many present symbols of authority. Anxiety hangs like dry electricity in the atmosphere of modern American life, and the stimulus of this anxiety, with all its comic overtones, is the realized subject in the novels of Joseph Heller, Bruce Jay Friedman, Richard Stern, Jeremy Larner, the plays of Jack Gelber and Arthur Kopit. There is real madness to modern governments, modern war, modern moneymaking, advertising, science, and entertainment; this madness has been translated by many a Jewish writer into the country they live in, the time that offers them everything but hope. In a time of intoxicating prosperity, it has been natural for the Jewish writer to see how superficial society can be, how pretentious, atrocious, unstable—and comic. This, in a secular age when so many people believe in nothing but society's values, is the significance to literature of the Jewish writer's being a Jew.

Jules Chametzky

SOURCE: "The Assimilation of the American Jewish Writer: Abraham Cahan to Saul Bellow," in *Our Decentralized Literature: Cultural Mediations in Selected Jewish and Southern Writers,* The University of Massachusetts Press, 1986, pp. 46-57.

[*In the following essay, which was originally published in* Jahrbuch für Amerikastudien *in 1964, Chametzky illustrates the developments in literary control that occurred over three generations of Jewish-American writers.*]

The starting point for these observations is the appearance of two publications at the end of the 1950s. On 6 November 1959, the *Times Literary Supplement* was devoted to "The American Imagination," a sequel to *TLS*'s first special supplement on American literature five years earlier. The 1959 issue included a long article on a subject not previously mentioned: "A Vocal Group—The Jewish Part in American Letters." The year before, Mr. Leslie Fiedler delivered three important and provocative lectures surveying what he called, martially enough, "the breakthrough" of the American Jewish writer. These lectures were collected in 1959 and published as a pamphlet entitled *The Jew in the American Novel* (1959).

Two things should be said at once about both the *TLS* piece and Mr. Fiedler's articles. First, the number and quality of the writers discussed in them provide impressive evidence, by any standards, of the important part played in the American literary scene by writers of Jewish background. Second, there is the awareness that it was in the 1950s that this part became most apparent and most significant. Before this time of course there had been American writers of Jewish background, but it was only then that a difference in the quality of their contribution to American letters became apparent. What was discerned is that many serious writers turned toward the materials of Jewish life in America without an awkward self-consciousness that had led in the past to a crippling defensiveness, sentimentality, or hatred.

A persuasive explanation of the changes apparent in the writing of American Jewish writers over three generations is that by the 1950s, the Jewish situation itself had changed in America. By then the Jews had moved well beyond the stage of cultural trauma familiar to all new immigrants, or of the aggressive-defensiveness of the *arriviste* making his way in an essentially strange, if not actively hostile, society. By the 1950s a secure Americanism seems to have been won—a position, at the least, of nonmarginality. A growth in the idea of tolerance in America, following upon the frightful example of the horrors to which intolerance could lead in Nazi Germany, undoubtedly played a part (as Oscar Handlin has pointed out), as did effective Jewish "defense" and cultural organizations operating within a favorable social and political climate. Among writers and intellectuals, the process of acculturation, after several decades of immersion in American life, had taken place more quickly and firmly.

I will briefly illustrate this process of acculturation over three generations in the work of several writers. The process may be seen as a kind of assimilation into the broader stream of American letters. I use the term "assimilation" provocatively: it must be understood within a specifically American context, whose meaning will be suggested throughout this paper. Primarily, I am concerned to show what "assimilation" means to the American writer of Jewish background as *writer*—that is, through an analysis of language, what differences of tone, point-of-view, and meaning are revealed in the characteristic work of writers of three generations.

II

Let us consider some examples in the work of several Jewish writers representing these generations. The work of Abraham Cahan, Michael Gold, Clifford Odets, and Saul Bellow exemplifies three stages in an evolution toward the assurance, poise, and wealth of linguistic and emotional resources that are the precondition of important literary creation. My illustrations fall into two groups, each revealing three ways in which a common subject is treated.

The common element in the first group of three examples is the speaker's attempt to convey an emotional attitude toward his mother. Such a situation inevitably tests a writer's ability to project sentiment without sentimentality and emotion without hysteria—in short, the extent of his control of his materials and expression:

1. As I went to bed on the synagogue bench, however, instead of in my old bunk at what had been my home, the fact that my mother was dead and would never be alive again smote me with crushing violence. It was as though I had just discovered it. I shall never forget that terrible night.

2. My humble funny little East Side mother. . . . She would have stolen or killed for us. . . . Mother! Momma! I am still bound to you by the cords of birth. . . . I must remain faithful to the poor because I cannot be faithless to you.

3. Mamma surrendered powers to her that maybe she had never known she had and took her punishment in drudgery; occupied a place, I suppose, among women conquered by a superior force of love, like those women whom Zeus got the better of in animal form and who next had to take cover from his furious wife. Not that I can see my big, gentle, dilapidated, scrubbing, and lugging mother as a fugitive from such classy wrath, or our father as a marble-legged Olympian. . . . But she does have a place among such women by the deeper right of continual payment.

The first excerpt is from *The Rise of David Levinsky*, by Abraham Cahan. Published in book form in 1917, *Levinsky* is sometimes thought to be the classic, if not the greatest, novel of the Jewish immigrant experience in America. Cahan was editor for many years of the *Jewish Daily Forward*, America's most widely read Yiddish-language newspaper. Cahan came to the United States from Russia in 1882, the year the great migratory waves began, at the age of twenty-two. He was a prolific writer, almost always in Yiddish, although in the 1890s he was writing for several important English-language newspapers, and was even, for a time, the American correspondent for Russian newspapers. He died at the age of ninety-one, having been an important and influential figure in American Jewish affairs throughout his long life.

The narrator in the novel looks back upon his life from the vantage point of a successful garment manufacturer of sixty. As a boy, he was a Yeshiva student in a Russian *shtetl;* at seventeen he migrated to the United States. He develops new patterns of thought in the desperate business of making a life in America, takes pride in such achievements as the acquisition of a new language, and of business success, but is disappointed by certain emotional failures. This scheme of the book provides Cahan with a good vehicle for much realistic observation, especially of such relatively exotic matters (exotic to his contemporary American audience) as life on the old East Side of New York and the ins and outs of New York's important new garment industry. But the discrepancy Levinsky feels between his past and his present status—the two halves of his life do not "comport" well, he says—adds a poignancy and depth to the novel that transcend its purely sociological interest. What Cahan has caught and fixed—and I think unconsciously, for his intention was not consciously ironic—was a reflection of the discrepancy in the very language and mode of thought available to Levinsky—and behind him Cahan—and the experience it is meant to render and express.

> As I went to bed on the synagogue bench, however, instead of in my old bunk at what had been my home, the fact that my mother was dead and would never be alive again smote me with crush-

ing violence. It was as though I had just discovered it. I shall never forget that terrible night.

Levinsky is trying to convey a sense of tremendous loss.
What emerges, instead, is a *report* that a loss has occurred.
The emotional impact of the passage is stifled by the language; indeed, it is never really released because of the language. The passage is "correct," but lifelessly stiff ("the
fact that," "It was as though I had just . . .", literary in
the worst sense of that word ("smote me with crushing violence," "that terrible night"), above all *described,* as if
from the outside. We are *told* that he was "crushed," and
that the night was memorably "terrible"; there is no dram-
atization of these emotions. If this first passage is incapable, finally, of transmitting a fully dramatized sense of loss,
it is probably because the loss was too great and traumatizing. It was too much part of a world irrecoverably lost, yet
unassimilable, to the writer, especially in a language newly
mastered.

The next passage is from Michael Gold's *Jews without
Money,* published in 1930. It was widely read at one time
(going through eleven editions in its first year) in the original and in many translations. Gold was editor at the time
of *New Masses,* and his book strongly influenced the style
of the short-lived (1930-1935) vogue of proletarian fiction.
Gold belongs to a second generation of American Jews.
The book chronicles, more or less connectedly, in a series
of presumably autobiographical sketches, the hard life of
thousands of impoverished Jews living on the East Side of
New York during the early years of the century. The passage cited attempts to convey the nostalgic affection and
commitment to his past that is the basis of the narrator's
firm commitment to the poor. It is a step forward, we see,
from Levinsky and the sense of the irrecoverable quality
of the past and the hollow sense, therefore, of loss of both
past and future.

> My humble funny little East Side mother. . . .
> She would have stolen or killed for us. . . .
> Mother! Momma! I am still bound to you by the
> cords of birth. . . . I must remain faithful to the
> poor because I cannot be faithless to you.

The final commitment ("I must remain faithful to the
poor . . .", I submit, is less than convincing in the context, because the initial commitment sounds to our ears so
mawkish. The three adjectives, "humble," "funny," "little," are being asked to carry a large burden of emotion
and sag a little, with a dying fall, under the weight. These
lines express, too, how *far* he's come from his mother (and
past) and how separate he considers her from him, to be
able to refer to her—surely with unconscious condescension—as "humble, funny, little." This adds an element of
strain and a certain forced quality to his *assertion* (and
that is all it can be) that he'll "remain true."

And yet, there is a strong, even violent, emotion evident
in the passage, "She would have stolen and killed for us."
Levinsky would never have permitted himself this revelation in such blunt terms. There are two voices jostling for
dominance in this passage—and an inability, finally, to integrate them or to decide between them. "Mother!" and
"Momma!" side by side—two worlds—which is it to be?
If the narrator really is umbilically bound to the past, can

he really be as complacent as the bravado tone suggests?
Surely the rhetoric sounds forced and overdramatized?
That these questions can arise reveals the uncertainties,
the tensions, that exist in this second, or transitional,
phase.

And so we come to the third excerpt: from Saul Bellow's
The Adventures of Augie March, published in 1953. Bellow, one of the most distinguished contemporary novelists, may be thought of, from one point of view, as a peculiar product of the American intelligentsia—which sets
him apart at once from such familiar and hallowed names
as Steinbeck, Wolfe, Hemingway, and Faulkner. He has
long been a teacher in the universities, but more to the
point, his thought took shape in the avant-grade of literature and politics, and in the magazines of that avant-
garde. *Augie March* is Bellow's celebration of experience;
explicitly, his celebration of the American experience. His
two earlier books had been introspective, thoughtful parables influenced by, among others, Dostoevsky; *Augie
March* was different in tone and style, and was the first
book to win wide attention—it was awarded the National
Book Award in 1953.

To the subject he celebrates, his form—a sprawling, episodic, apparently picaresque novel—seems peculiarly appropriate: as if that sprawl and shapelessness is America.
But the formlessness is superficial and deceptive. The
novel has a tough center, a consistent line of development,
in the character of Augie March. His fate (which, he informs us in the opening sentence, quoting Heraclitus, is
character) is inextricably bound up with his experience,
but, paradoxically, transcends it. Augie searches through
and beyond his experience toward the essential: his own
identity, that most elusive commodity, which slips away
from his grasp in the very act of grabbing. As a novel cen-
tering on the quest for identity, it is as securely in the
American grain as are the novels about Ishmael and Huck
Finn. Augie March, fatherless, without a firm past and
code to live by, embodies an important theme running
through the fictional image of the American experience.
He is also Jewish and from Chicago, and the experiences
he has would be recognizable to other urban Jews of his
generation.

> Mamma surrendered powers to her that maybe
> she had never known she had and took her pun-
> ishment in drudgery; occupied a place, I sup-
> pose, among women conquered by a superior
> force of love, like those women whom Zeus got
> the better of in animal form and who next had
> to take cover from his furious wife. Not that I
> can see my big, gentle, dilapidated, scrubbing,
> and lugging mother as a fugitive from such
> classy wrath, or our father as a marble-legged
> Olympian. . . . But she does have a place among
> such women by the deeper right of continual
> payment.

There is authority behind Bellow's language—assurance
and precision in his thought and emotion. He is unapolo-
getic in beginning the passage with "Mamma!" He knows
who she is, and more important, who he is. No cloying
sentimentality is attached, nor any fear of overvaluation—
or nasty Oedipal overtones—when he elevates her with a

simile to the world of the Greek gods. One resource that saves the passage from pretension, mere rhetoric, or sentimentality, is Bellow's sure use of the ironic, deflating energy of the vernacular (as in the expressions, "a fugitive from such classy wrath," "a marble-legged Olympian"). Where Gold's mother was "humble" and "little," Bellow's is "big" and "gentle"—so far the same: "purr" words as Stuart Chase might say. But Bellow's soft adjectives are immediately made palatable by his use of the vigorous, visual, and certainly deflating "dilapidated" and "lugging," to complete the series. The combination of learning and observation, of high style and vernacular, by its wit and delicate irony convinces us that here is an author *in control*. The voice of this "I" is free of inhibitions, his mind free of preconceptions, it is the voice of a narrator at ease with himself. He has placed his mother accurately. Distanced and mythicized—as a consort of a god she is not to be patronized from a distance as "humble, funny, little"—she is nevertheless present and solid and humble as life. The final sentence, therefore, can convince us of the narrator's unambivalent affection for her memory.

III

The second group of selections—"The New World"—again reveals the pattern I have discussed above. The first and third are again the words of David Levinsky and Augie March, while the second is an excerpt from Clifford Odets's *Awake and Sing,* from 1935. It serves the same purpose as the excerpt from Gold's book—Odets, too, being of that radically minded generation of the early thirties. Odets is probably the best playwright produced by any American left-wing theatre of that period.

> 1. The immigrant's arrival in his new home is like a second birth to him. . . . I conjure up the gorgeousness of the spectacle as it appeared to me on that clear June morning: the magnificent verdure of Staten Island, the tender blue of sea and sky, the dignified bustle of passing craft—above all, those floating, squatting, multitudinously windowed palaces which I subsequently learned to call ferries.

> 2. JAKE: From *L'Africana* . . . a big explorer comes on a new land—"O Paradiso." From act four this piece. Caruso stands on the ship and looks on a Utopia. You hear? "Oh paradise! Oh paradise on earth! Oh blue sky, oh fragrant air—" MOE: Ask him does he see any oranges?

> 3. I drank coffee and looked out into the brilliant first morning of the year. There was a Greek church in the next street of which the onion dome stood in the snow-polished and purified blue, cross and crown together, the united powers of earth and heaven, snow in all the clefts, a snow like the sand of sugar. I passed over the church too and rested only on the great profound blue. The days have not changed, though the times have. The sailors who first saw America, that sweet sight, when the belly of the ocean brought them, didn't see more beautiful color than this.

Again, in the first example we perceive language that seems to come to the writer second hand. It is high-sounding and scrupulously literary: "I conjure up," "magnificent verdure," "tender blue," "dignified bustle"—and diction that is painfully pretentious: if Levinsky has learned to call "multitudinously [and where have we seen that word outside of *Macbeth?*] windowed palaces" "ferries," he apparently has not learned to call "verdure" trees and grass, nor a "spectacle" anything but "gorgeous."

He opens the passage by describing the immigrant's arrival as a second birth—and indeed it is and must have been—but bemused by those ferries, where is the pain and glory and wonder of birth? The older Levinsky is really caught by the contrast between what he is and has become with that other, "green" Levinsky, who thought that ferries were palaces, so that the experience of rebirth is sidetracked completely. In this passage, there is not only a failure of communication, as in the earlier Levinsky passage cited, but a failure of the narrator to fix exactly what it was he was trying to communicate.

Odets's dialogue is from *Awake and Sing,* his first and, with *Waiting for Lefty,* his best-known play. The action of the play centers on a Jewish family hammering out their lives in a Bronx apartment, whose confining quality is made even more oppressive by the bleak depression period in which they live. The first speaker, Jake, the idealistic grandfather, is a retired barber who tries to retain his dignity while forced to live off his children. He is an immigrant, who retains humanistic and socialistic ideals in an Old World, bookish way. One of his last functions, as he sees it, is to impart to an embattled grandson some of his ideals—as well as the material and spiritual means to free himself from sordid surroundings. This speech communicates well his loftiness of vision, his aspiring nature, his faith that Utopia can be seen, can be achieved, here and now, and its scene is the New Land. Moe, the second speaker, is a one-legged veteran of the First World War who makes his living as a "bookie." Moe Axelrod is the real hero of the play: American-born, he is tougher, more cynical (on the surface) than old Jake—and more in touch with the vernacular realities of American life. His "ask him does he see any oranges?" is a perfect, ironic deflation of Jake's impassioned, but self-deluded vision. In his reply is to be seen the same undercutting of the naive immigrant as in Cahan's piece, but more subtly done, and Moe's discomfort is a more honest expression of the uneasiness Gold displayed in his "Mother! Mamma!" passage. And yet Moe and Jake like each other. Jake's vision and his expression of it are, after all, felt along the bone and expressed honestly: the phrase "a big explorer comes on a new land" is unpretentiously in Jake's own language, the foreigner's English, and he lets the blue sky speak for itself.

The two views, the two voices, neither penetrate nor wholly invalidate the other, finally, but there is no synthesis—as perhaps there need not be in a dramatic situation. They merely exist, side by side—the old and the new, the past and the present, the lofty promise of America and the hard-boiled lessons learned in its streets. This excerpt dramatizes well, I think, the bifurcation of sensibility in the second, transitional generation of American Jewish writers.

And so, again, to Saul Bellow's *Augie March*. Augie has been in anguish most of the night before the scene here described. He was with a friend in the labor room of a hospital while she lost a baby and, for reasons too complicated to summarize, has had his engagement to an attractive, rich young girl broken off as a consequence. On this New Year's Day, then, we are also in the presence of a rebirth—one life has ended for Augie and another is about to begin as he looks out upon a new land.

When Bellow talks of the "profound blue," is it only my ear that detects a personal resonance in the adjective "profound," instead of the cliché I detect in Levinsky's "tender?" In any case, Augie sees a "sight," not a "spectacle." Further, when the mother ocean gives birth to the new-world traveler, it does so, Augie unself-consciously asserts, from its "belly." And surely the double comparison compounded of homely materials—not to mention the alliterative grace—of "a snow like the sand of sugar" is simply beyond the linguistic resource of Levinsky. The homely materials—the vernacular, if you will—comport well with learning ("cross and crown together, the united powers of earth and heaven") and an aspiring ideal. One frame of reference does not contradict another: both are aspects of an enlarged and confident sensibility. The "I" starts quietly and simply in this passage—over a cup of coffee—and carries us with assurance—with no sense that we are being "had"—to an affirmation that the promise of America still exists and is valid.

Our navigator here styles himself "a Columbus of the near-at-hand." Behind him, Saul Bellow, of course, is the real explorer of the new territory. For, as Fiedler has observed, with Bellow in the early 1950s, we approach the period of the Jewish writer's liberation from his material. This sounds paradoxical. What I mean, simply, is that the writer is now free to bend the materials of his experience to his independent vision. He can approach those materials without shame, uneasiness, or uncertainty. The inability to do this, in one degree or another, comes through, I believe, in the work of Cahan, Gold, and Odets. One way of seeing this is to think of Cahan as saying, in effect, "I can write English as well as the Gentiles," whereas Gold and Odets, at a later stage, seem to suggest that this doesn't matter at all—so long as the emotion is honest—and *their* struggle was to find the honest emotion. With Bellow, however, these problems seem simply to drop away. The language he uses is unquestionably his and, his present being secure, he can regard the past with a clear eye.

In the period ushered in by Saul Bellow—one of acceptance and achievement (a kind of assimilation) in the world of letters—the writer could use whatever he wished of the Jewish past or Jewish present in America. This could be done without obsessiveness or without a sense of wounds suffered from his experience as a Jew. When "Jewishness" is seen to be a factor among serious Jewish writers of the fifties, it will often be so from the vantage point of, and with the aim of accommodating it to, a secure Americanism. In the process, one senses, also, with the wide differences among such writers as Saul Bellow, Bernard Malamud, Philip Roth, Delmore Schwartz, Karl

Shapiro—to name only a few—the drive to discover, name, win back (or perhaps only not to lose) some important part of themselves.

This last impulse may not be as paradoxically related to "a secure Americanism" as it first seems. First of all, while the opportunity for this fresh exploration of self arises from a secure position, the *impulse* to do so may also have come as a reaction to a certain bland, characterless image of American society from which so many intellectuals recoiled in the gray-flannel-suited Eisenhower years. The opportunity and the impulse do work together—to the enrichment of both the specific, peculiar self and the wider society. In an article on Bellow written at the end of the fifties, J. C. Levenson sums up this development exceedingly well:

> The Negro, the Catholic, and the Jew have in the present generation joined the Southerner in discovering the advantage of being in a conscious minority; if the politicians and authors of textbooks had not been saying so for so long, one might speculate that this is one of the most viable ways to be an American.

What this means, I must make clear, is that acculturation—or assimilation as I have used the term—in an American context does not have to mean faceless conformity to a conforming society, but rather the reverse: to the discovery of the resources and human richness inherent in differences. The assimilated American writer (that is, the American writer) does not have to placate an Establishment, real or imaginary. He does not have to write like T. S. Eliot, a Southern agrarian, or a Presbyterian elder—although he is of course free to do so and will achieve an audience if he is good enough—but he is free also to write about, discover, and celebrate life seen from his own vantage point.

Alan Lelchuk

SOURCE: "The Death of the Jewish Novel," in *The New York Times Book Review,* November 25, 1984, pp. 1, 38-39.

[*In the following essay, Lelchuk argues that Jewish writers in America have moved to a new phase in which ethnicity is still apparent but secondary to artistic accomplishment.*]

Let me start with two anecdotes concerning Saul Bellow and the varieties of ethnic displeasure he has caused. In Jerusalem in the 1970's, I was sitting in the living room of Gershom Scholem, the great scholar of Jewish mysticism and one of the tribal chiefs of secular Judaism, when the discussion turned to American literature. At the mention of the name Bellow, Scholem, normally cool and relaxed, immediately grew livid, stood up and, striding back and forth, began to downgrade Bellow as a writer and to berate him personally. At the bottom of Scholem's ire, it turned out, was Bellow's remark after he had received the Nobel Prize, that he was "An American writer first, and a Jew second." How could an intelligent man who was Jewish say such a thing, Scholem charged, instead of acknowledging his Jewish identity first and foremost? To Scholem, the claim was either stupid or cowardly, the product of an assimilationist culture and/or personality, and Scholem would never forgive Bellow for it. For Scholem had not come to primitive Palestine in the early 1930's—abandoning his civilized Germany to be mocked by family and assimilationist friends—only to hear a Jewish Nobel Prize-winner de-emphasize his Jewish heritage.

The second incident took place in a somewhat duller setting, at the 1978 commencement ceremonies at Brandeis University, where I was teaching, when Bellow and Lionel Trilling were among the recipients of honorary degrees, and Bellow was the official commencement speaker. His talk, that hot Sunday, was unusual in that it bypassed a public topic in order to track his own life as a young writer. He recounted his early days in Montreal, where he studied in a Hebrew school, and then in Chicago, where he composed on a table in the kitchen while his aunt made Russian borscht and argued in Yiddish with family members. With affection and humor, Bellow recalled his student days at the University of Chicago, too, and his growing mixture of college sophistication and homespun wisdoms. Characteristically, along the way, Bellow offered rich autobiographical glimpses into the making of a novelist.

For me, a young writer about to have yet another commencement address inflicted on him, it was a wonderful surprise—an honest and detailed talk, free of the usual piety and palaver that clutter those speeches. Trilling, however, thought otherwise. Speaking with him later, I asked how he liked Bellow's talk. His face tightening, Trilling retorted, "Not at all." Why not, I wondered? "It was inappropriate. Highly inappropriate."

Inappropriate. Trilling announced it like a judge repeating the jury's verdict, "Guilty," Clearly, for Trilling, Bellow had committed a gross act of violence, a violation of the strict code of academic behavior. Poor Bellow—in his way he was being an errant patient, a wayward Jew, not quite in touch with reality. You just didn't talk about your personal life, especially not a Jewish ghetto life, at a university ceremony.

Now, what was inappropriate for Bellow in life, according to Scholem's terms of identification for a writer and Trilling's standards for a public speaker, was also not appropriate—in terms of ethnicity—for Bellow as a novelist at an earlier point in his career. It was Katherine Anne Porter who, after *The Adventures of Augie March* won the National Book Award in 1953, complained that this reward might start a dangerous trend, since the author in question was "bastardizing" the English language and lowering the standards of the American novel with his use of "foreign"—i.e., Yiddish—inflections, words, syntax. Although strains of anti-Semitism have always existed in the literary community, Porter's genteel attack found few believers, perhaps because it was already clear to most, including Edmund Wilson and Philip Rahv, that not only was Bellow a gifted talent but also an outstanding new stylist. But once again Bellow was paying the price of not behaving appropriately—this time in his fiction, not leaving off his ethnic ways and acting as if he were a well-behaved gentile writer. Naturally, this was a bit difficult, since he wasn't one, and since one of his greatest strengths

was precisely in playing out his strong ethnic suit, in language as well as landscape.

The issue here is not Bellow, though the example speaks for itself. And, of course, much has changed in literary and social history in the last few decades. But the example gives us a starting point for discussing the complex issue of a writer's ethnic origins and their (possible) uses in his work. Now, to put my foot in my mouth immediately, if anything is "appropriate" for a writer to write about, surely it is to write about what he/she knows. So that if he grew up Jewish—whether believer, skeptic, rebel or secularist—then that upbringing, that sensibility, will shape and at times constitute his fictional world. It is surprising to see how often narrow definitions of the Jewish writer are voiced or projected by critics who should know better.

Need it be said, at this late date, that the return to one's origins by itself is not enough to sustain a book's literary interest, let alone make it a work of art? I fear it does. It seems unfortunate but true that the pendulum has swung the other way and the fashion of the times has been to celebrate the "ethnic writer," trying in part to catch up with the recent shifts in American social history, in which ethnic groups have fought hard to assert themselves and gain their share of the American pie. So the culture of the past decade, both popular and literary culture, has rewarded those returns to the ethnic past that have brought back a measure of certainty, of celebration, of lament. And I don't mean the enormous success in the mass media of full-blown pageants like *Roots* or *Holocaust*, but the many works that have come along and been hailed as works of art or literary masterpieces when really they are no more than sentimental journeys to the past. This critical pattern is dangerous, for it demeans works of fiction that are deeply and obviously rooted in ethnic sources, at the same time that they move beyond to art.

Consider a work like *Call It Sleep* by Henry Roth, that small gem published in the 1930's, then buried for several decades, precisely because it appeared too ethnic. Yet it is clear to me that to name Henry Roth as an ethnic writer and leave it at that is a disservice; he is a writer, period. *Call It Sleep* is distinguished by its strong sense of character and rich play with language, as well as its resonant evocation of Brooklyn immigrant experience viewed from the perspective of a young boy. Henry Roth was not merely taking a trip down memory lane; he was creating the complex world of a childhood. Now, without the landscape of the ethnic, *Call It Sleep* would have been impossible to imagine; but in the hands of a lesser writer, it would not have been a novel to remember. It would have been a period piece.

I must cite here another recent development, not altogether pleasant. The danger of pushing primarily ethnic works as serious literature has unfortunately been extended to novels of the Holocaust as well. In recent years we have witnessed a deluge of novels that have been debasing to the actual experience. The Holocaust is In. At first, there was simply the tendency to describe the horrors and document the victims' plight; next, the tendency to universalize the particular, to turn the Jew into mankind and, recently, a new wrinkle—to show the "humanness" of the torturers. Ah, imagination!

For the best of intentions, *maybe,* the cheapest books have been manufactured. And, in the process, the very few pieces of genuine literature about the terrible experience have been passed over, forgotten. *Sophie's Choice* is far better known than *This Way for the Gas, Ladies and Gentlemen* by the tragic Pole Tadeusz Borowski. And *King of the Jews* enjoys greater renown than a much finer novel written in the early 1960's, *An Estate of Memory,* by the Polish Ilona Karmel. This long, flawed but serious novel traces and contrasts the experience of three very different women in the camps, where the author herself lived for four years, and yet, despite its high merits, it has remained obscure. In both Borowski and Karmel, the emphasis is on character, motive, detail, tone, rather than on the horrors themselves; in short, they focus on the literature to be made from the world they knew.

For Borowski and Karmel, Auschwitz, Maidanek and Treblinka were their New York playgrounds and hangouts, their Chicago streets or Pennsylvania farms. It was the turf they knew and were, literally, condemned to, and it is a measure of their courage that they stayed with it and honed their talent on that forbidding subject matter. And, for readers, the horrors are more authentic within the context of everyday routine—in a Borowski tale 3,000 Jews disappear to the crematorium between throw-ins at a camp soccer game. These novels, among a few others, not to mention the important nonfiction accounts of Lucy Dawidowicz, are dishonored by the easy and spurious novels exploiting the issue.

Now the aims of literature are, as we know, not so much to comfort or celebrate as they are to confront and disturb. Literature is a force for disturbing the complacencies of our reason, the prejudices of our emotion, the formulas of our language. In other words, it is a force for restabilization—at times revaluation—all in the interest of removing our bondage to the received wisdom of family, country, religion, whatever tyrannizes us in the helpless years of childhood and youth. It is no surprise therefore that the returns home of adults, in literature as in life, are fraught with violent ambivalences and paradoxes. For most of us, the real wars take place in the family trenches, not the battlefields, and those form the stuff for rich imaginings. To miss out on this human dilemma and concentrate on the newly discovered meaning of this or that ethnic ceremony is to sacrifice literary possibility for sentimentality.

Having said that, let me counter by adding that richness of all sorts takes place when the ethnic can be joined with the familial to provide conflict. Let me give a brief personal example of where the two—ethnic and familial—coalesced for me and how I look to make fiction from it. When I was approaching my 13th birthday, my father began to give me lessons in preparation for my bar mitzvah ceremony. My father, possessor of a fine self-taught Hebrew and no less fine singing voice, decided he would be my teacher instead of the usual hired teacher, for reasons of economics and pride. So, several times a week, we sat at the wooden table covered with oilcloth and, armed with haphtara and torah texts, went through my assigned

portions. Interestingly, many of my friends envied me, since they were forced to put up with the hired tutor, usually a middle-aged rabbi of unfailing severity.

Now it might be "appropriate," and certainly easy for me, in looking back, to write of the warmth and coziness of the scene—father and son learning together, the ancient Jewish ritual rehearsed with meticulous care and warmth, and so on. Unfortunately—or fortunately—reality proved far more complex. In fact, I was the one who secretly envied my friends their stranger-tutor, for my father, a perfect gentleman in public, changed masks when alone with me. He was unforgiving of error, impatient with my weak Hebrew and poor singing voice—an attitude that made both Hebrew and voice worse, of course—and frequently wound up chastising me with choice epithets and sharp slaps. Moreover, those occasions were opportunities for him to get back at me for siding with my mother in their long-standing marital conflict.

The result for me was an ordeal that lasted for three or four steamy months, during which the upcoming ceremony lost whatever joy or wisdom one was supposed to get from it. And when it was over and I passed through it well in the small synagogue on Strauss Street in Brooklyn—a few doors away from the barbershop where Bugsy Siegel used to assist the barber with his shaves—my father took full credit for my "success." At the reception, through my restrained smiles with friends, I swore a cold Sicilian revenge.

What was a long trial and semiweekly torture for the young boy turned into fruitful material for the adult writer; because of the heat between father and son, scenes of greater emotional power were available than any offered by a renewed celebration of the bar mitzvah experience, at the same time that the religious ceremony provided a nice backdrop of irony.

Being an American is no less easy, if taken seriously, than being a Jew, if taken playfully; and the one without the other is a thinner experience, if an easier one to comprehend. Like most native types, whether Midwest Lutherans, Boston Catholics, inner city blacks or chicanos, Brooklyn Jews know that we are richer *because of the other,* and they in turn are enriched by us. One tries fiction to understand if not actually dramatize this duality, to be genuine about one's origins while reaching out beyond, to other worlds. In my heart, I have always remained as loyal to Jackie Robinson stealing home in Ebbets Field as I have to memories of Hebrew school.

Of course, it should be remembered, there have been Jewish writers who have declared open war on their ethnic experience. In our time, Philip Roth has waged a continuing battle against various aspects of middle-class Jewish life, secular and religious, a battle that has incited the wrath of critics and rabbis. And most recently, Joseph Heller has turned to the Old Testament in an effort to give contemporary voice to ancient stories and religious pieties. But there have been earlier novelists, less known but perhaps even fiercer in their struggle for independence from the clan. A little more than 100 years ago in Warsaw, Joel Linetski wrote *The Polish Lad,* which was such an outspoken, insider's attack on the Hasidic way of life that the writer was expelled from the community, never to return.

And in the early 1900's a Russian Jew began writing stories and novellas about Jews and Jewish questions that exemplify the toughest love-hate relationship of all. In his novel *Breakdown and Bereavement* and in novellas such as *Nerves,* Josef Hayim Brenner reveals his exquisite torment over Jewish traditions, aspirations, ideals, failures. Steeped in self-conscious Dostoyevskian anguish, Brenner's antiheroes suffer the crippling fates of hearts that desire Jewish salvation and emancipation, but minds that perceive the insufficiency of ideas, land and people to achieve them.

This cosmopolitan, skeptical spirit, who lived in London before settling in Palestine in 1909, was obsessed with the Jewish experience and its many paradoxes. The "ethnic" issue itself, with debates over assimilation versus tribal attachment, Palestine versus the Diaspora, was the source of his drama, and he attacked all traditions fiercely, forever undercutting his protagonist's positions by his own lacerating ambivalence. For those of you who have never read Brenner, a provocative experience awaits you. Dead at 43, in 1921, he made his mark as a kind of Nietzschean tough guy, as passionate a critic of all things Jewish as he was a passionate Jew.

In America today, the predicament of the Jewish writer is no less uneasy because of acceptance than it was in the many years of rejection. No longer does he have to guard the Yiddish phrase, clean up the ghetto grocery, explain the bar mitzvah ritual. These formerly esoteric particulars have become a part of the literary lingo of the times. The Jewish writer, like the Holocaust, has made it. But the paradox is, America has made it too, using success to take its toll on the rebellious spirits—accepting them, celebrating them, coopting them. When the enemy, imagined and/or real, becomes one's ally, what does one do?

We have come a long way from Abraham Cahan's *The Rise of David Levinsky* (1917), that story of a Russian immigrant's rise on the fabled East Side that embarrassed the decent liberal critics as well as offended genteel professor-reviewers. Poor Levinsky, alone and lonely at the end of that interesting, raw book, dares not cross the ethnic barrier and propose to the gentile woman he loves. And indeed, since Levinsky we have witnessed various steps and stages—the trials of just such a mixed marriage in Ludwig Lewisohn's neglected tale of the Jewish professor and his upper-class wife *The Island Within,* and after that, in Bellow's *Dangling Man,* the declaration by Joseph K. of his full literary and philosophical independence from the dominating voice and code of the Hemingway man. We are no longer startled by Portnoy's desire to deflower every Mayflower shiksa as a way of getting back at Protestant America.

One response to the easing of the Jew into the majority (literary) society has been a turning backward, a return to the religious shell, the old neighborhood, or the recent nightmare of Europe, in an attempt to stem the flow of assimilation. But what about that "other" Jewish writer, who recognizes with exacting honesty that the European grand-

parents and parents have left or are just leaving us, for good, and that with them the language and manners of a whole way of life will depart?

In other words, that world of riches is on the edge of vanishing, both as fact and as potential fiction. Oh, he or she might scratch out a Yiddish word here, a ritual there, but the truth is, a species and a culture are disappearing. And there is little use in pretending otherwise, in calling for a "new Yiddish-American" lingo, in euphemizing or sentimentalizing the truth. Yes, there is American Jewish life, but that is mostly a religious affair, available to a narrow minority. For the rest of us, the loss is the truth, and we should face the matter squarely. The felt experience of the Viennese, Berlin, Warsaw, Budapest, Moscow Jew, found in the generation of immigrants and passed into the literature through their sons and grandsons, is becoming, if it is not already, a thing of the past.

Paradoxically, however, the time of this inward loss for the Jewish writer coincides with the time of his greatest gain outwardly. Once again, we are speaking of this "other Jewish writer," this skeptical, exuberant and more independent fellow shaped by the odd Enlightenment called America, not the fragile, harried European gentleman molded by the Dark Ages of Mosaic Laws and tribal codes and institutionalized anti-Semitism. This more modern Jewish artist writes under the handicap of recent American success. He is a freer man in certain respects. He has more or less rid himself of the scars and wounds of his uniquely disfigured history. Though this may violate the ideas, if not the out-and-out-prescriptions of critics such as Cynthia Ozick, I myself find it coercive, not to mention subtly exploitative, to carry around the luggage of that disfigured history and count it as some sure sign of artistic superiority, let alone merit. After all, each ethnic group has a disfigured history of its own; to rely on it alone for art is a mistaken strategy.

So if what I am saying is that the time has come for the modern Jewish writer to become just *the* writer, *a* writer, I consider this no small victory for this time, this place. He will certainly have given up something of value, but also in the process gained something. He will have given up his special claim to ancestral injury and European wound, and taken up instead his American passport—to confusion, paradox, mystery, pleasure.

I am describing here an emancipation of sorts, but not the kind imagined by the Messianic-projectors or decreed by the prophet-critics. This is a more ambiguous emancipation that leads only to native challenge, the wide-open challenge perhaps best visualized in our great crisscrossing highways, where we are led to disaster as often as to destination, to the despair of nowhere as much as to a locale of purpose. No longer bound by insulating landscape, language or experience, we mustn't pretend that we are, for that is a disingenuous paranoia in place of historical reality. The writer who grows in childhood here, endures adolescence here, matures and breaks down here, marries or divorces here, ages here, is celebrated or defeated here, well, he *is here,* whether he wills it or not; his imagination, the rich computer of his work, must start at the starting point to open his true file. If he chooses not to let it, he will be escaping his turf, his audience will remain partisan, his work marginal.

If I seem to be speaking about the end of the Jewish writer as an ethnic entity, I am not speaking of the end of things Jewish in his work. The sensibility that is skeptical and ironic, especially about its own failure and misfortune, like a Kafka; the temperament that is emotionally high-pitched and accepts itself as such without seeking refuge in cooler realms, like a Bellow; the imagination that is humorous and serious simultaneously and that perceives in one quality the beginning of its opposite, like an Italo Svevo; these I associate—as much as, or really more than, particular objects and rituals—with Jewishness. When Elizabeth Hardwick, a Southerner, explains that she came to New York to make herself over into a Jewish intellectual or John Berryman avers that he considers himself an honorary Jew, they describe the sort of ethnicity most appealing to me. The opposite of pious, chauvinist, sentimental, this version of Jewishness is defined by emotional breadth, critical inquiry, tactile curiosity. It prefers the historical to the absolute, the concrete to the abstract, the American to the European.

Let's say this, the Jewish writer should resemble others of his international troupe, writers performing in the peculiar circus of literature. At times they play the clown; at times they play the impresario; sometimes they fly high on the trapeze; sometimes they attempt to walk the tightrope. In all this, independence is the Jewish writer's play and beauty and excellence his purpose, imperfection his only premise. In other words, accomplishment is all, at last.

Ted Solotaroff

SOURCE: "Marginality Revisited," in *The Writer in the Jewish Community: An Israeli-North American Dialogue,* edited by Richard Siegel and Tamar Sofer, Fairleigh Dickinson University Press, 1993, pp. 59-66.

[*In the following essay, Solotaroff maintains that Jewish writers still occupy a marginal position in American culture, and that they could achieve renewed appeal by focusing on the subject of Israel.*]

Twenty-five years ago, when American Jewish writing was in its heyday, much of the discussion of its prominence turned upon the issues of marginality.

Not the most precise concept, marginality had the implication of standing apart, as the American Jewish writer was perceived to do with respect to both sides of the hyphen. Being an outsider in both the American and Jewish communities, he was enabled to see what more accustomed eyes would miss at a faculty meeting in Oregon or on the screen of a western or in the Jewish dietary laws. Marginality also sometimes referred to the overlap between the two cultures where the postimmigrant writer had grown up and considered himself an expert on its various phenomena, ranging from Trotskyism and Freudianism to the riffs of Benny Goodman, the humor of Lenny Bruce.

As Irving Howe suggests, marginality also conveyed the sense of a waning and an adjustment of the more extreme condition of alienation that had been bred by the Depression, Marxism, and the Holocaust as well as by the anti-Semitism and Jewish chauvinism that the writer experienced growing up in the postimmigrant community of the 1920s and 30s. The progress of assimilation has continued to erode the traces of Jewish mores and ethos. The special angle of vision has blurred, and Jewish identity as a subject with a moral edge has tended generally to decline. This development is particularly marked, as one would expect, in the writers of the present generation—the David Leavitts and Deborah Eisenbergs. On the other hand, an unprecedented development in Jewish life is creating a different kind of marginality. If Jewish leaders like Arthur Hertzberg and writers like Philip Roth are correct, and I think they are onto something very important, the new and increasingly tense margin of Jewish consciousness and conscience lies in the preoccupation with Israel. As Rabbi Hertzberg has observed, Israel is the religion of American Jewry and as Mr. Roth has shown, Israel is a rich subject. Part of its great promise for American as well as Israeli writers is its uncanny replication of the precarious, unstable, hemmed-in, contentious, revered conditions of the Diaspora that have all but disappeared in America, which in turn has become the land of Jewish freedom, security, and normality that Zionism envisioned.

On the other hand, the sense of arrival, achievement, and opportunity that the breakthrough sponsored tended to exaggerate the significance of the marginality. After all, a margin that was broad enough to harbor Robert Warshow (an elegant film critic) and Manny Farber (an intensely demotic one), Stanley Kunitz and Allen Ginsberg, Bernard Malamud and Norman Mailer, Irving Kristol and Paul Goodman was bound to be almost as broad as the mainstream it was supposedly set off from. Moreover, it was evident that for many of these writers to begin with, and for almost all of them as their careers subsequently developed, their American rather than their Jewish interests were much more evident. In the context of their careers the Jewish element was typically refracted through their shared disposition to radicalism and their recoil therefrom: it was not until the mid-1960s that such concerns as the Holocaust and the security of Israel began to compete with anti-Communism as the issue of the hour. Similarly, the working out of a literary influence—of, say, Hemingway or Eliot or Edmund Wilson—created a more evident tension in a given career than did the effort to adapt a discernible heritage of Judaism or even of *Yiddishkeit* to American letters.

Instead, then, of being camped on some fertile bicultural margin, American Jewish writing has come to look more and more like the avant-garde of acculturation. Though the writer liked to think he was manning a risky outpost, he was often destined to find the day that the letter arrived from the National Book Awards or the American Academy of Arts and Letters or the English department at Amherst that he had been all along riding an escalator. The real figures of the margin were the European intellectuals, the Hannah Arendts and Hans Morgenthaus and Erik Eriksons and Max Horkheimers et al., whose power of detachment and perception were like a new sun in our sky.

The margin that American Jewish writers actually occupied was so narrow that it is better thought of as an edge. However diverse they may have been in their points of view, they shared a common situation: they stood at an extraordinary point in Jewish history: the end of the Diaspora mentality that was taking place in America. This disjunction between themselves and all those generations behind them of *shtetl* and ghetto Jews, and of a generation or two at most of partially and insecurely emancipated ones, created a characteristic edginess of identity: a concern with who one was now that being a Jew was no longer a fate, as it had been so recently and completely in Europe, but rather was now more like a fact, and not necessarily the central one, about oneself. Instead of the burdens of the chosen people there were now the exhilarations of a choosing one. Except that the terms could become reversed, since a mind-set of centuries doesn't vanish overnight. Hence the tensions, the sharp shifts of focus, the mood swings that characterized the fiction (the writing that was most at the cutting edge of the change) as one went, say, from the coiled anxiety of *The Victim* to the expansive confidence of *Augie March* to the bitter wages of the American Dream in *Seize the Day*; or from the American pastoral of *The Natural* to the ghettoized New York of *The Assistant*; or from one story in *Goodbye, Columbus* that deals with the overbearing piety of the old urban neighborhood to another story that rebels against the vacuous secularism of the new suburban life. Nonetheless, the main issue was already becoming clear or at least pressing for expression: as the mentality of pluralism waxed and of *Galuth* (exile) waned, the American Jewish writer recognized that he was less marginally American than marginally Jewish. What then did his passage from home (the title of Isaac Rosenfeld's archetypal novel) signify? What belongings was he taking with him?

Because marginality was an elastic concept in the 1950s and 60s, and because their generational experience was fairly similar and their relations often clannish, diverse figures such as the novelist Saul Bellow, the dramatist Arthur Miller, the poet Delmore Schwartz and the critic Alfred Kazin could be brought under the canopy of American Jewish writing and used to exemplify its fresh, independent, and heightened perspectives. In general, American Jewish writers and intellectuals were seen to be hovering intently between residual feelings of disdain for WASP elitedom ("the scrimmage of appetite," as Delmore Schwartz put it, "behind the hedges of privilege") and new or revived feelings of attachment to the postwar America that was diminishing the WASP hegemony and, to some extent, absorbing it. Their experience as born-again liberals or battle-hardened democratic socialists made them particularly alive to the ideological positions, distinctions, and cultural infiltrations that lay between the extremes of McCarthyism and Stalinism in the new political arena of the cold war. (Their political consensus and role playing as former Communists prompted Harold Rosenberg to refer to them in the late 1950s as "the herd of independent minds.") Similarly, their social background made them sensitive to the emerging society—urban, mobile, pluralist, and mass—that was dislodging the traditional communal, class, regional, ethnic, and religious markers of one's place in it. If political realism, urban savvy, and cultural mobility were now the name of the game, it figured that the keen-eyed products of Jewish skepticism and aspiration would have something pioneering to say about it in books like Saul Bellow's *Adventures of Augie March*, Paul Goodman's novel *The Empire City*, Norman Mailer's *Deer Park*, and Grace Paley's *Little Disturbances of Man*, as well as David Riesman's *Lonely Crowd*, Trilling's *Liberal Imagination*, Daniel Bell's *End of Ideology*, Daniel Patrick Moynihan and Nathan Glazer's *Beyond the Melting Pot*, and Leslie Fiedler's *End to Innocence*, etc.

The other—Jewish—side of the margin that the writer-intellectuals bestrode had something of the same dynamic of healed alienation and changes of heart and mind. The accounts of the bitter strife between immigrant fathers and acculturated sons that marked the literature of the 1940s gave way to a more positive evaluation of the Jewish heritage, often by the very same writers. Similarly, the Yiddish that had been so embarrassing when they were children was now the language of Isaac Bashevis Singer and the host of gifted fiction writers and poets before him who were being translated and anthologized. Their work reinforced the view that American Jewish writing was shaped by traditions of moral concern, erudition, dialectical thinking, and vast reserves of self-irony, the one international currency, to paraphrase Isaac Rosenfeld, that the Jews actually controlled. The margin was also said to sponsor a distinctive style that spurned the fanciness and reticence of the literary cafe for the position-taking, point-making insistence of the intellectual cafeteria.

All of which made good copy in the pages of *Commentary, Midstream,* and *Partisan Review* and, as literary sociology, was more plausible than most generalizations about groups of writers. There was no question that a breakthrough of sensibility was occurring, that it was changing the cultural climate, that it was enabling Jewish writers to feel they had a place as well as positions, and that their Jewish upbringing was no longer to be discounted.

The fiction of this era was characteristically a fiction of conscience, being the main locus of the edginess, for it was much easier for a Jew to stop observing the High Holy Days than to stop observing and criticizing how he and his fellow Jews were leading their lives in an open society. The permutations of the theme are everywhere evident. Now we can see that Saul Bellow's novel *The Victim,* published in 1947, is a major document in the changing of direction and emphasis of Jewish defensiveness from the source of its representative fiction to the object of it. *The Victim,* with one decisive blow of the imagination, turns the theme of anti-Semitism inside out by focusing on the prejudices and resistances of Asa Leventhal as they come under attack from Kirby Allbee, a fallen WASP and former colleague who claims that Leventhal has heedlessly ruined his life and owes him reparation. Most of Philip Roth's stories in *Goodbye, Columbus* some ten years later are similarly devoted to an aggressive and astute exposure of the moral ghetto of Jewish ethnocentrism cemented by self-righteousness that his young protagonists are struggling to escape from.

In Bernard Malamud's stories of this period, and notably in his novel *The Assistant,* the New York of the Depression is transformed into virtually five boroughs of conscience, a hard-pressed twilight zone of good and bad faith.

On the other hand, a novel like *The Deer Park*—or a play like *Death of a Salesman* or much of J. D. Salinger's chronicle of the Glass family—is dressed in diverse American styles, as it were, but feels Jewish because of the particular resonance, in each case, of its social and moral concerns. Indeed, much of the literature of "the breakthrough" brings to mind the classic joke about the *nudge* on the Fifth Avenue bus who can't restrain herself from asking the very proper gentleman in a seat across the aisle if he is maybe Jewish. He tries to ignore her, she persists, and finally he admits he is to shut her up. "That's funny," she says. "You don't look it."

Like the brilliant outcropping of modernism among the Yiddish writers of the 1920s, the literature of the American Jewish edge was fed by the dynamics of acculturation that would soon undermine its viability. A work like Cynthia Ozick's novel *The Pagan Rabbi* or I. B. Singer's *Enemies, A Love Story* feels like it is drawing its intensity from the death pangs of the Diaspora: the moral imagination of the writer reconstituting the ethos of Jewish survivalism even as it is fading from the lives of her or his secure middle-class American readers.

Malamud's subsequent career—Bober, the righteous grocer in *The Assistant,* and Yaakov Bok, the wily victim of the blood libel in *The Fixer,* giving way to the Levins and Dubins of academic life, the Fidelmans and Lessers of the arts—provides a paradigm of sorts of the transition that has marked the careers of writers who were raised, to a greater or lesser degree, as Jews who lived in America but have spent the greater part of their adult lives as American novelists or playwrights, poets or critics who happen to be Jewish. As assimilation continues to practice its diluting and dimming ways, it seems evident that the interesting Jewish bargain or edge in American fiction will be more and more in the keeping of writers like Cynthia Ozick, the late Arthur A. Cohen, and Tova Reich, or younger ones like Nessa Rapoport, Daphne Merkin, and Allegra Goodman, who are anchored in the present-day observant Jewish community and who are drawn to the intense and growing dialogue between Judaism and modernity under the impact of feminism, the sexual revolution and the Holocaust. In other words, what remains of the former margin is likely to present itself in the tensions between spiritual and secular being, much as it does for the Christian writer. I'm referring, of course, to Judaism as a living, complex history and faith rather than as shtick, as in Joseph Heller's *God Knows.*

Meanwhile, a new and fertile and increasingly tense margin of Jewish consciousness and conscience has come into being and has only begun to be explored: that is, the relations of American Jews to Israel. Indeed, as Philip Roth has shown in the brilliant second chapter of *The Counterlife,* Israel is our counterlife.

"In the Diaspora a Jew like you lives securely," Shuki Elchanan, Mr. Roth's Israeli commentator par excellence, remarks to Zuckerman, "while we are living just the kind of imperiled Jewish existence that we came here to replace. . . . We are the excitable, ghettoized, jittery little Jews of the Diaspora, and you the Jews with all the confidence and cultivation that comes of feeling at home where you are."

That is the objective side of the situation, as Mr. Roth sees it. He views the subjective one no less incisively: Israel as the very image of the confused desires of American Jews. Again to quote Elchanan: "Reasonable people with a civilized repugnance for violence and blood, they come on tour from America, and they see the guns and they see the beards, and they take leave of their senses. The beards to remind them of saintly Jewish weakness and the guns to reassure them of heroic Hebrew force . . . and out of them flows every sentimental emotion that wish fulfillment can produce. A regular pudding of emotions. The fantasies about this place make me sick."

The rest of *The Counterlife* pales for me beside the vigor and interest of this chapter called "Judea"—as does, to my mind, the body of recent American Jewish fiction. There is an élan everywhere in the pages of Zuckerman's effort to rescue his brother from the fanatic West Bank settlers. Such is generally the case when a mature writer hits upon a genuinely new subject. This extraordinary twist of the dialectic of Jewish history whereby American has become, in large part, the fulfillment of the Zionist dream of full emancipation from the past and Israel has become, in Elchanan's words, the country where "every Jewish dilemma there ever was is encapsulated"—creates, in effect, a multivalent international subject that awaits its Henry James and Joseph Conrad.

Hugh Nissenson and Mark Helprin, two of the most gifted novelists of the middle generation, began their careers by writing about their experience in Israel. Both have developed into shapers of myth, and I'd love to see what each of them would make of the American-Israeli subject now. But the American writer doesn't have to leave home or the immediate realities to tackle this theme, so strongly does the fate of Israel affect and shape the consciousness of American Jews, so firmly is it lodged at the top of the national community's agenda. Since the Six-Day War the survival of Israel has been the paramount concern of organized Jewish life and probably the paramount source of Jewish identity. Given this pervasive and deeply entrenched mind-set, the remarkable thing about Jonathan Pollard the spy is not that he is an anomalous kook, about whom the less said the better, as Jewish officialdom would have it, but rather that he embodies the crisis of conscience that would beset almost any American Jew who came into possession of information that he or she believed to be vital to preserving Israeli lives and that was being withheld. An embarrassment to say the least to the Jewish community's public relations, Pollard is at the same time the product of its ideology, and to say that he was acting out his bizarre fantasies is to corroborate the force of the "counterlife" that Roth has begun to explore.

Other fiction writers, I believe, will follow his lead. Since the Palestinian uprising and the government's response, Israel has moved even closer as a subject; it looms now not only as the hero of our illusions but as the victim of its own; the face that shone its light upon us now bears a grimace, a scowl, a timeless shrug. To the extent that American Jews are marginal Israelis, we find ourselves connected once again to the Diaspora and to the condition of radical doubt that has produced much of its salient modern fiction, from I. L. Peretz and Isaac Babel to Kafka and Joseph Roth, from I. J. Singer's *Brothers Ashkenazi* and André Schwartz-Bart's *Last of the Just* to E. L. Doctorow's *Book of Daniel* and Cynthia Ozick's Cannibal Galaxy. We also find ourselves connected to a country with powers and problems that the Diaspora never dreamed of. A Likud government with a free hand in the West Bank and Gaza for the next four years pretty much insures that both the powers and problems will increase and that American Jews will feel even more implicated.

In the overlapping area of consciousness that Israeli and American Jewish writers share, the seeds of a new fiction are waiting to sprout.

Irving Howe

SOURCE: "Response to Ted Solotaroff: The End of Marginality in Jewish Literature," in *The Writer in the Jewish Community: An Israeli-North American Dialogue,* edited by Richard Siegel and Tamar Sofer, Fairleigh Dickinson University Press, 1993, pp. 67-71.

[*A longtime editor of the leftist magazine* Dissent *and a regular contributor to the* New Republic, *Howe is one of America's most highly respected literary critics and social historians. He has been a socialist since the 1930s, and his criticism is frequently informed by a liberal social viewpoint. In the following essay, he explains the contemporary period in Jewish-American literature as one in transition from a concentration on "Jewishness as experience" to "Jewishness as essence."*]

The notion of marginality, often under the more imposing guise of alienation, became central to the self-understanding of Jewish American writers a few decades ago. A declared alienation was, in part, a way of preserving the psycho-social stance derived from Marxist politics while simultaneously abandoning that politics. It also reflected, in part, a genuine feeling of dislocation, or more exactly, of *uncertain* location, among young writers recently emerging from the immigrant streets but starting to find a place in the American literary milieu.

Among the more prominent of these writers, there was usually a mixed feeling about marginality or alienation. Saul Bellow succeeded, for a time, in writing out of quite contrary impulses and premises, no doubt because he felt the pressures of both. A sense of alienation is powerful in his early fiction, and reaches a tragic fulfillment in his wonderful short novel *Seize the Day.* But by the time he wrote *The Adventures of Augie March* he was already repudiating styles of marginality and declaring himself an enthusiast for the openness and (to use a term favored at the time) the "craziness' of the American experience—which might account for a certain *willed* quality in his work, a *stress* upon energy when energy would be enough. Philip Roth completed the turn from marginality.

For other writers of the time, marginality figured ambiguously. If it lurks behind Bernard Malamud's *The Assistant,* in his best stories he writes as if the immigrant milieu were self-sufficient, encompassing imaginatively and sustaining morally for its ethos of affliction and endurance. And thereby marginality seems to evaporate, as a mere indulgence. Something like this might also be said for earlier writers like Henry Roth and Daniel Fuchs, both firmly planted in the immigrant space. They commanded a locale or better yet, a subject commanded them, and thereby they came into possession of a scale of values that allowed them terms of self-definition. Perhaps the most sensitive perception with regard to marginality appears in the work of Delmore Schwartz, especially in his beautiful story "America, America," where Shenandoah Fish (the very name a comic suggestion of psychic fissure) hopes, probably in vain, to dissociate himself from his own smugness as an intellectual looking down upon the older, immigrant generation.

In the experience, then, of the Jewish American writers marginality serves a number of uses:

These writers had left behind the immigrant world but its stigmata were still stamped on their souls. Nearing high culture but uneasy with its manners and maneuvers, they tried to carve out a little space for themselves, practically and imaginatively. If they were uncertain, however, as to who they were, they knew what they had been. Did not the mere fact of becoming an *American* writer signify a subtle betrayal, though why or of what was unclear. To stay with the old folks, we all felt, would mean provincialism and tedium; a refusal of gifts from Western culture. (Parenthetically, the great Yiddish poet Yaakov Gladstein once said to me, "We taught them how to read, and then they went to T. S. Eliot.") Such embarrassments, overcome after a time, reflected a transitional experience, just as Jewish American writing can itself be seen as a transitional experience.

Marginality was itself part of a tradition, inherited from the immigrant milieu. Rubbing up against an alien culture, the immigrant Jews had first to pull inward in order later to move outward, with collective identity serving as a springboard for individual dispersion. Yet in that interval the immigrant world gave its literary offspring a lovely blessing: it gave them memories, it gave them evocative place names and dubious relatives, it gave them thickness of milieu. Their marginality was thus indistinguishable, for a while, from an overpowering, and even oppressive sense of community. But that's what writers need: the pressure of inescapable situations.

The rhetoric of marginality also served as a strategy for the New York writers, identifiably Jewish yet not identifying themselves as Jews—a strategy by which they could briefly maintain what I'd call their politics after politics; by which they could band together for common ambitions; by which they could give symbolic status to an uneasiness they could not always name.

Perhaps the most important meaning, ultimately, of marginality was as a way to initiate, all but unconsciously, a link with nineteenth-century American writers like Emerson and Thoreau, Whitman and Melville. Despite a professed distaste for the Emersonian tradition, which for many years I foolishly shared, the Jewish American writers were in part reenacting some of the styles and postures of that tradition. The great nineteenth-century American writers had been inspired by a vision of human possibility that, as it faded into helplessness and despair, also became a fierce critique of America society. Most Jewish American writers consciously aligned themselves with the cultural modernism of Europe, though uneasily, since they knew about its deep strains of reaction and even anti-Semitism. Yet I think it can be said in retrospect that American Jewish writing represented a slow coming to terms with American culture, first as a curious repetition of the strategies of American regionalism, in which writers breaking out of provincial settings create themselves as adversaries of a national center that is probably not even present, and second, as a partial and rather awkward inheritor of Emersonianism, not so much of its doctrines as of its adversarial stance. For the Jewish American writers were steadily becoming Americans, Americans above all.

In a fine essay, the Southern writer Eudora Welty discusses the ways in which the physical setting of a story establishes and validates its meanings. Place is where the writer "has his roots, place is where he stands; in his experience out of which he writes it provides the base of reference, in his work the point of view." Far from being mere inert locale, place becomes an organizing principle in the work of fiction. Bellow's Chicago, Henry Roth's East Side, Daniel Fuchs's Brooklyn: to visualize these settings is to grasp theme and idea. As Welty writes: "The moment the place in which the novel (or story) is accepted as true, through it will begin to glow, in a kind of recognizable glory, the feelings and thought that inhabited the novel (or story) in the author's head and animated the whole of his work. . . . Location is the crossroads of circumstance, the proving ground of 'What happened? Who's here? Who's coming' and that is the heart's field."

The heart's field. A lovely phrase. The heart's field for many American Jewish writers will forever be grey, packed streets that they kept in memory long after the actuality was erased.

American Jewish fiction has primarily been a fiction of immigrant life, intimately known and nervously recalled. Delancey Street, Pitkin Avenue, Napoleon Street, these are inducements, props, stimulants. Place, insofar as it becomes "the heart's field," also entails a cluster of inherited styles and values, ways of life—as well as specifically literary styles yoking together mandarin refinements with gutter vividness, inherited demotic with acquired high culture. What this meant for the American Jewish writers was, above all, the advantages, and limitations also, of an inescapable subject, with abundance of memory turned into discipline of narration.

American Jewish fiction, drawing heavily upon the immigrant locale, finds its substance and its value in a Jewishness of experience. The most recent Jewish writers, perhaps as talented and probably more knowing than their elders, lack this resource; for them Jewishness appears as a problem, a sentiment, a commitment. Harold Brodkey in

one story has a character say that "being Jewish was a great truth," but what that truth consists of, and how it manifests itself in life, seems very elusive in his writing. This is not a fault, it is a condition. For we are witnessing a transition from *Jewishness as experience* to *Jewishness as essence*. Intellectually, the latter may even be preferable, since the Jewish experience of the earlier American Jewish writer was one in which much of Jewish tradition, learning, and knowledge had been lost. Those who think of, or write about, Jewishness as an essence—a religious or metaphysical content—may indeed be seeking to affirm a stronger connection with the Jewish past. But for literature, for the writing of novels and stories, the experience of the writers who came out of the immigrant milieu provided a richer setting, a more accessible dramatic substance, a more powerful and enclosing subject.

And that is why I am a little skeptical about Ted Solotaroff's prescription, if it is that, at the end of his paper: that writers turn to the relations between American Jews and Israel. For intellectual debate, political analysis, cultural essays: yes. For fiction, it all seems to me too entangled with polemic, too distant from common life. And the example of the Pollard case that he gives strikes me as better for a Graham Greene or a Joseph Conrad than for the younger Jewish American writers. I do not wish to seem dogmatic on this matter; the future may prove me wrong. But my inclination is to believe that while there remain of course many areas of American Jewish life open to scrutiny, from the suburbs to the *makhers* to the universities, they are too diverse, too lacking in dramatic concentration, too unfocused conceptually for ready fictional treatment. There is, in short,—or so I think—*a crisis of subject matter* and it is not likely to be overcome very soon.

But this crisis—which, in the barest shorthand, I designate as the transition from Jewishness as experience to Jewishness as essence—is only secondarily a literary one. It is actually becoming the crisis of nonreligious Jews themselves, who search, with varying degrees of seriousness and authenticity, for some residual—symbolic, analogical, "cultural"—fragments with which to retain a Jewish identity steadily being drained of substance. No example of this could be more poignant than some recent writings of Harold Bloom, in which he tries to establish, in a sort of inspired madness of analogy, Freud, Kafka, and Scholem as new centers of conviction for secular Jewishness: an effort he himself admits must at best be confined to an elite and that ineluctably cuts itself off from what has traditionally been source and base of Jewish existence, namely, the folk as community of shared belief.

Finally, a few words on the question: Why so much talk about American Jewish writing? In American literature it is a fairly minor phenomenon. There has not been one Jewish writer comparable to the great nineteenth- and twentieth-century gentile American novelists and poets. What we can reckon with is one major novel, *Call It Sleep,* Fuchs's fine trilogy of Jewish life in Depression Brooklyn, some of Schwartz's stories, a few novels by Bellow, etc. Impressive, but hardly warranting the hullabaloo that has occurred. I have a few speculations:

(a) It was all part of Jewish self-consciousness, Jewish self-advertisement, part of the painful struggle of a minority, non- Christian subculture, to establish itself in America. A certain amount of exaggeration was unavoidable.

(b) It was also part of the effort of the *Partisan Review* circle to consolidate its claims to literary importance. If the New Critics had Warren, Jarrell, and Lowell, then the New York critics came back with Schwartz, Bellow, and Malamud. A certain amount of exaggeration was unavoidable.

(c) The interest of the American Jewish community in American Jewish writing (it doesn't by the way extend to Israeli writing) served it in extremely important ways. This helped, or seemed to help, fill the spiritual vacuum that has become increasingly evident—*a glaring emptiness*—at the center of American Jewish life. With the fading immigrant Yiddish culture and the disinclination of most American Jews to take religion seriously, the Jewish community became dimly aware that it needed "something" other than check writing, banquets, and lobbying to justify its claims to cultural substance. Half in submission and half in resentment, it turned to the very Jewish American writers it felt to be excessively "negative." There followed a serio-comic misunderstanding which forms all too large a part of what passes for so-called Jewish American culture.

And then, even this began to slip away. It did not last. It could not.

JEWISH CHARACTERS IN AMERICAN FICTION

Leslie Fiedler

SOURCE: "The Jew in the American Novel," in *The Collected Essays of Leslie Fiedler, Vol. II,* Stein and Day, 1971, pp. 65-117.

[*In the following essay, which was originally published in 1959, Fiedler surveys the defining characters and characteristics of the Jewish-American novel as they developed up to the end of the 1930s.*]

FOREWORD

This essay is intended to be not exhaustive but representative. The few writers who are discussed at any length are those who seem to me (and my personal taste plays a role of which any reader enamored of objectivity should be warned) both most rewarding as artists and most typical as actors in the drama of Jewish cultural life in America. I have not deliberately, however, omitted as untypical any Jewish American fictionist of first excellence. I am aware of how many rather good novelists I have slighted (along with some rather bad ones whom I am glad to pass over in silence); but I will not try to list them here, thus risking further injustice to those whose names fail to come to mind.

What I hope emerges from my study is a general notion of the scope and shape of the Jewish American tradition in fiction—useful to Gentile and Jew, reader and writer alike, not merely as history but as a source of pleasure and self-knowledge. The bonus of satisfaction for the critic engaged on such a job is the privilege of saying once more how much joy and terror and truth he has found, not only in certain widely respected authors but also in such relatively neglected ones as Abraham Cahan, Daniel Fuchs and Henry Roth.

1. ZION AS EROS

The novel in which the Jewish writer attempts to make meaningful fiction of his awareness of himself as a Jew in America remains for a long time of merely parochial interest. In the first fifty years of such writing, only four novelists emerge whose work seems worth remembering; yet even of these none is mentioned in the most recent standard history of the American novel. The omission does not arise from ignorance or discrimination; it is a matter of simple justice. The fiction of Sidney Luska, Abraham Cahan, Ludwig Lewisohn, and Ben Hecht appears in retrospect not merely to fall short of final excellence, but to remain somehow irrelevant to the main lines of development of fiction in the United States.

For American Jews, their achievement has, of course, a symptomatic, an historical importance since they act as surrogates for the whole Jewish-American community in its quest for an identity, a symbolic significance on the American scene. Such early novelists begin to establish an image of the Jew capable not only of satisfying the Jews themselves, but also of representing them to their Gentile neighbors. The writing of the American-Jewish novel is essentially, then, an act of assimilation: a demonstration that there is an American Jew (whose Jewishness and Americanism enrich each other) and that he feels at home!

The striving of Jews to become in the United States not merely facts of the census but also of the imagination is only half of a double process that must be seen whole to be understood at all. As the Jewish writer goes out in search of himself, he encounters the Gentile writer on a complementary quest to come to terms with the Jew, the stranger in his land. Collaborators or rivals, whether willingly or not, Jewish fictionist and Gentile engage in a common enterprise. For a long time, indeed, it is hard for the Jewish novelist to compete with the Gentile in the creation of images of Jewishness. Ludwig Lewisohn's *The Island Within* may not be recorded in the standard history, but *The Sun Also Rises* is; for it is a subtler and truer book, and Robert Cohn, middleweight boxing champion from Princeton, is a realer Jew than any of Lewisohn's. That he is the product of anti-Semitic malice rather than love is from a literary point of view irrelevant. For better or worse, it is Hemingway's image of the Jew which survives the twenties: an overgrown boy scout and hangdog lover—an outsider still, even among outsiders, and in self-imposed exile.

It is hardly surprising that as late as 1930, Gentile writers are more effective at representing American Jews than are Jews themselves; for behind them there is a longer tradition of working with the American scene, and even a longer experience in projecting images of the American Jew than we are likely to remember. The first Jewish character in American fiction is the creation of the first professional novelist in the United States, Charles Brockden Brown. In 1799, he published *Arthur Mervyn,* the protagonist of which, after two volumes of being buffeted by a stubbornly perverse destiny, finds himself with a haven in sight. Like the typical Brown hero, he is about to redeem his fortune by marriage to a woman mature and well-to-do; and like all such heroes, he addresses her more as a mother than as a bride—though this time with an overtone of terror. "As I live, my good mamma," he says gazing into the eyes of Achsa Fielding, "those eyes of yours have told me a secret. I almost think they spoke to me. . . . I might have been deceived by a fancied voice . . . but let me die if I did not think they said you were—a *Jew.*" "At this sound," the author tells us, "her features were instantly veiled with the deepest sorrow and confusion."

Arthur Mervyn has, indeed, guessed right, and for a moment the promised Happy Ending trembles in the balance; but Jewess or not, Mrs. Fielding offers too great a hope of security to be rejected, and Mervyn marries her. So sane and bourgeois a climax infuriated Shelley, who, though an admirer of Brockden Brown, could never forgive him for allowing his hero to desert an Anglo-Saxon "peasant girl" for a rich Jewish widow. Despite so prompt an appearance in American literature, however, the Jewish character does not immediately prosper, remaining an exotic or occasional figure until our own century. When present at all in classic American fiction, the image of the Jew is likely to appear, as it had in *Arthur Mervyn,* in female form—superficially just another variant of the Dark Lady, who is otherwise Mediterranean or vaguely "Oriental" (though, indeed, the term seems sometimes a mere euphemism for Jewish) or even Negro. The Ruth of Melville's long narrative poem *Clarel* or the Miriam of Hawthorne's *The Marble Faun* are, like Brockden Brown's prototype, dark projections of sexual experience or allure, foils to the pale, Anglo-Saxon maiden. Though objects of great erotic potency, they do not ordinarily survive to their book's endings, being death-ridden as well as death-bearing, but are consigned to imprisonment or an early grave.

The American writer is attracted toward the archetypal pattern of Shylock and Jessica, the sinister Jew deprived of his lovely daughter; but he cannot treat it with the comic aplomb of Shakespeare or even the Romantic blitheness of Scott. In his work, a tragic blight falls over the Gentile myth of assimilation, the dream of rescuing the desirable elements in the Judaic tradition (maternal tenderness and exotic charm: the figure of Mary) from the unsympathetic (patriarchal rigor and harsh legalism: the figure of the High Priest and Father Abraham). Indeed, except as the threatening guardians of sloe-eyed ambiguous beauties, male Jewish characters seldom make more than peripheral appearances in earlier American fiction. There are neither American Riahs nor Fagins though one of the villains in George Lippard's *The Quaker City, or the Monks of Monk Hall* is called, unsubtly enough, Gabriel von Gelt. ("Vot you scratch your fingersh on te floor? Hey?" Gabriel is reported as saying in the earliest of literary "Jewish accents.")

This novel, an astonishing blend of home-grown socialism, violence, and genteel pornography, appeared in 1844 and won rapidly an immense number of readers, who probably did not single out the lone Jew from the crew of thugs who run a Gothic whorehouse for the off-hours amusement of Philadelphia's respectable citizens. Yet it is not unimportant that in the nightmare phantasmagoria of the populist imagination run wild—among the hunchback dwarfs, deaf and dumb Negroes, corrupt clergymen, and millionaires gloating over the bared breasts of drugged virgins—the figure of the hawknosed, conniving Jew takes his due place. Gabriel von Gelt is the ancestor of the fictional Jewish gangster, the Wolfsheim, say, of Fitzgerald's *The Great Gatsby.*

Long before the Jewish novelist existed in America, at any rate, the Jewish character had been invented, and had frozen into the anti-Jewish stereotype. Indeed, one of the problems of the practicing Jewish-American novelist arises from his need to create his protagonists not only out of the life he knows, but *against* the literature on which he, and his readers, have been nurtured. In order to become a novelist, the American Jew must learn a language (learn it not as his teachers teach it, but as he speaks it with his own stubborn tongue) more complex than a mere lexicon of American words. He must assimilate a traditional vocabulary of images and symbols, changing even as he approaches it—must use it, against the grain as it were, to create a compelling counter-image of the Jew, still somehow authentically American.

No wonder Jews are not only businessmen and workers, trade-union officials and lawyers, psychoanalysts and theater-owners but even actors, singers, musicians, composers of popular songs and makers of movies before they are writers. First the world of work and commerce, then of the professions, next that of popular culture, and only last of all, that of serious literature opens up to the American Jew. He can make the nation's songs like Irving Berlin or define its dream of the vamp like Theda Bara; he can even provide the *ersatz* of fiction like Fannie Hurst or Edna Ferber, act out for the laughs travesties of himself on the vaudeville stage with Smith and Dale or in the *Saturday Evening Post* with Montague Glass's Potash and Perlmutter. On such a level he speaks neither as a Jew becoming an American nor as an American who was a Jew; he communicates in the nonlanguage of anticulture, becomes his own stereotype. It is for this reason that the popular arts in the United States continue to this day to speak with a stage "Jewish accent." This is, however, only one more hindrance in the way of the serious Jewish writer, who must come to terms not only with Achsa Fielding and Gabriel von Gelt, but also with Sophie Tucker and Eddie Cantor.

Yet even before the triumph of the Jews in the world of mass culture, even before the perfection of the movies which sealed that victory, the Jewish-American novel had been created, the Jewish-American writer invented. The author of this achievement was, however, a *goy*—one of the most elusive and riddling figures in all American literature. He emerges in the 1880's out of those rather highminded, assimilationist circles in German-Jewish New

York, in which Ethical Culture seemed to promise a revivifying intellectual movement, at once secular and morally committed, Jewish and American. The name on the title pages of his "Jewish" books (*As It Was Written, Mrs. Peixada, The Yoke of the Thorah,* etc.) is Sidney Luska, a pseudonym obviously intended to suggest that the writer was himself Jewish; but he had apparently been born Henry Harland, a Protestant American, as discontented with his past, as uncertain of his identity as any alienated Jew. There is a certain appropriate irony in the fact that the first Jewish-American novelist was not a Jew at all, or that, more precisely, he was the creation of his own fiction, an imaginary Jew.

It is not easy to find the truth about so elusive an existence. Henry Harland was above all else an inveterate poseur, a liar who lied for his soul's sake; and the ordinary biographical sources are likely to contain whatever fabrication suited his view of himself at the moment he was asked for information. The ordinarily quite dependable *Dictionary of National Biography,* for instance, reports that Harland was born in St. Petersburg, that he was educated in Rome and studied at the University of Paris, "acquiring a knowledge of the life of the Latin Quarter"; the groundless romance of a provincial aesthete. Actually, he seems to have been born in Connecticut, to have moved early in life to New York, to have attended the Harvard Divinity School for one year—and then to have fallen under the influence of Felix Adler, who changed his whole life.

There still exists in my own mind a vestigial doubt (unsupported by any fact I have been able to discover) that Luska-Harland may, after all, have been a Jew pretending to be a Gentile pretending to be a Jew; it would be the best joke of all! More probably, however, he was a refugee from Protestantism who passed via Ethical Culture into the German-Jewish society of late nineteenth-century New York, and who tried even growing what he liked to think of as a "Jewish beard" to pass for a Jew. His books are Jewish not only in theme and point of view, but are meticulously documented with references to Jewish-American customs and to the rituals of Judaism. In one of his novels, the pursuit of verisimilitude (or exoticism!) is carried to the point of printing the name of God only as the two letter abbreviation used in Hebrew to avoid profaning the Holy Name.

Though he is now almost forgotten, Luska was in his own day a success, hailed not only by self-conscious spokesmen for Jewish culture, but greeted by William Dean Howells himself as one of the most promising younger realists. At the peak of his first fame, however, Luska committed a kind of suicide, becoming once again Henry Harland and fleeing America in one of the earliest acts of literary expatriation. He reappeared in England as the editor of *The Yellow Book,* chief journal of the *fin de siècle,* in which his own crepuscular prose (a new collection of his work was called *Grey Roses*) appeared beside the elegantly obscene decorations of Aubrey Beardsley. Harland proved to be a first-rate editor, printing, among other representatives of the advanced literature of his time, Henry James, who responded with a grateful tribute to Harland's own fiction;

but his old schizoid doubts about who he was were not allayed by his new role.

During his entire term on the magazine, he wrote letters to himself signed "The Yellow Dwarf," attacking his own editorial policy. Only he knew the identity of this constant critic and relished, as he had before, his own secret duplicity. Still restless, however, he felt impelled to move once more, this time quite out of anglosaxondom, to France, where he was converted to Catholicism and ended by writing a best-seller called *The Cardinal's Snuffbox.* This piece of pseudo-aristocratic, pious fluff, whose title reveals its appeal for the provincials Harland had left behind, earned him $75,000 in its first year and enabled him to live out his life in elegant conversation amid the elegant bricabrac of pre-World War I Europe.

In his final reincarnation, he was asked once by a reporter about Sidney Luska and answered, "I never knew a Sidney Luska . . . ," and spoke of a nightmare, dimly remembered, from which he was now awakened. There is, indeed, something sufficiently nightmarish about the whole episode, though it is from this nightmare that the Jewish novel in the United States begins. But what precisely did Henry Harland dream himself in that bad dream from which it took him so long to wake? He dreamed himself the excluded artist, poor, passionate, gifted and antibourgeois, offering to a world that rebuffed him the dowry of sensibility and insight amassed by an ancient suffering race. For Harland, such mythic Jews seemed to promise the redemption of American culture, a revitalization of American life. But where were they to be found outside of his own books?

He thought, perhaps, that he had discovered the embodiment of his ideal in Felix Adler and in his own deepest self which Adler had revealed to him; but actually Harland's Jewish heroes seem to have been derived first of all from literature. The protagonist of his first book, *As It Was Written: A Jewish Musician's Story,* seems to have been suggested by the Daniel Deronda of George Eliot, who was one of Harland's favorite writers. But that oddly sexless portrait of the female artist as a Young Jew he naturalized to the American scene endowed him with a particularly American mission. "It is the Jewish element that will leaven the whole lump . . . " he writes in his novel. "The English element alone is, so to speak, one portion of pure water; the German element one portion of *eau sucrée;* now add the Jewish—it is a dose of rich strong wine. . . . The future Americans, thanks to the Jew in them, will have passions, enthusiasms. They will paint great pictures, compose great music, write great poems, be capable of great heroism. . . . " In such praise lurks an implicit threat. What if the Jew refuses the obligation, rejects even the assimilation which is the first step demanded of him in his role of secular savior?

Harland-Luska does not at first face up to this question; but there is present in his work from the start an undertone of hostility, lurking beneath the exaggerated philo-Semitism of the surface. Though his conscious mind writes the editorials that make the avowed point of his fictions, his ambivalent unconscious is writing the plots. Ernest Neuman, the artist of *A Jewish Musician's Story,* is only one-half artist; the other half is murderer! He is a Jekyll and Hyde character not merely because the exigencies of Harland's Gothic plot demand it, but because the deeper exigencies of Harland's divided mind demanded that plot to begin with. Neuman is a schizophrenic who has murdered his wife and remains unaware of it, who is consciously horrified and baffled until an experiment in automatic writing reveals to him, and to us, his guilt. This "new man," the new Jewish-American proposed as a symbol of assimilation, of the mating of the Jewish and American psyche, ends by killing his Gentile bride and proves capable only of destruction.

In *Mrs. Peixada,* Harland does permit the mating of Gentile and Jew, though he returns to the pattern of Brockden Brown and makes his symbol of Judaism a woman. It is always easier to breach the barriers against intermarriage in the popular mind by permitting the assimilation of the forbidden group through the female rather than through the male. So in the the earliest novel, marriages of aristocrats and lower-class women were applauded, while the Lady who ran off with her groom was held up as an object of contempt; and so now in the movies, Marlon Brando is allowed a Japanese wife, but his abandoned Caucasian girl is forbidden anything more than sympathetic conversation with a Japanese male. At any rate, Mrs. Peixada represents the return of the Jessica-figure in her American form; though this time she is not only stained by sexual experience (she is a widow, of course, rather than anything less genteel), she is the murderer of her first husband. Legally, to be sure, she is innocent, having acted in self-defense against that husband, who is the monstrous projection of all the evil ever attributed by the Gentile mind to the Jew: a pawnbroker, "gaunt as a skeleton . . . a hawk's beak for a nose, a hawk's beak inverted for a chin—lips, two thin, blue, crooked lines across his face, with yellow fangs behind them. . . . "

But there is worse to come. Though Luska was able to maintain in his mind not only Shylock and Jessica, but Daniel Deronda as well—nightmare and idealization in a dreamlike truce—none of those mythic figures could survive the intrusion of real Jews. Real Jews do, however, take over in *The Yoke of the Thorah,* which is perhaps the first genuine genre study of American-Jewish life in the New World. They are no longer mere projections of Anglo-Saxon self-hatred or guilt, these German-Jewish merchants of the eighties, eating, matchmaking, talking over the market. They are coarse, vulgar, platitudinous, loud, sentimental, gregarious, not saviors at all but only human beings; and the character who represents Harland moving among them shrivels and withdraws in their presence. But he cannot help listening to them, and catches for the first time (ironically, *loses* by catching) what is to be the real material of the Jewish writer.

> "Oh my daughter," Mrs. Morgenthau returned. "She works like a horse. . . . And such a *good* girl. Only nineteen years old and earns more than a hundred dollars a month. . . . She's grand. She's an angel."
>
> "Tillie's all wool from head to foot," put in Mr. Koch, "and a yard wide."

> "Such a brilliant musician," said Elias.
>
> "Musician," echoed her mother. "Well, I should say so. You ought to hear her play when she really knuckles down to it. Why you—you'd jump, you'd get so excited. The other night she was only drumming—for fun. I tell you what you do. You come around and call on us some evening."

Where now is the "rich strong wine"? Even music, which represented for Harland the essence of Jewish genius, becomes in such scenes bait in the matrimonial trap and matrimony itself merely an adjunct of business. Such an insight into the discrepancy between the traditional mission of the Jew and his actual accommodation to the American scene might have provided Harland the cue for genuine comedy or tragedy; it became instead merely the occasion for personal disillusion. It is hard to tell whether he is more distressed because the Jews will not assimilate to his heroic, artistic ideal or because they have already assimilated to the actual values of the world around them. Their very vitality parodies the American mores they accept; and face to face with that vitality as it exists not in the imaginary artist but in the real businessman, Harland experiences only a desire to go away.

The divorce to which this desire will eventually lead him is already signalled in *The Yoke of the Thorah.* The fable is a simple one: a young Jew, talented but weak and superstitious, is bullied out of marrying a sensitive and beautiful Gentile girl by the chicanery of his uncle who is a rabbi. He marries instead the gross daughter of a family of German-Jewish merchants; and having rejected a union with the Gentile world which would have redeemed him, dies lonely and disenchanted. His final gesture is to commit suicide in the middle of Central Park; but that gesture only acknowledges the fact that inwardly he had died long since. The publication of such a book by their former champion and literary hope apparently stirred the Jews of New York to bitterness. They had taken Harland in, and he had turned on them and attacked them—quite as their own writers would do in the years to come. That his attack was rooted in a burgeoning anti-Semitism, Harland himself did not at first realize; but he arose to defend himself in public forums at Jewish synagogues and temples and even wrote a couple of other "Jewish" books, quite innocent of innuendo or offense.

He was, however, really through; he had exhausted Jewishness as a subject and as a mask and was preparing for his next removal. In England and in France, he exiles the Jews from the center of his fiction to its periphery, and his last word on the subject is a casual sneer in the book that made his fortune. The words are put into the mouth of a lovely though improbable lady with an equally improbable Italian title, his gentle heroine: "The estate fell into the hands of the Jews, as everything more or less does sooner or later; and if you can believe me—they were going to turn the castle into . . . one of those monstrous, modern hotels, for other Jews to come to." The sentence foreshadows one theme of a somewhat later and certainly much greater expatriate American, with similar yearnings for orthodoxy and "the tradition."

And the Jew squats on the window sill, the
    owner,
Spawned in some estaminet of Antwerp.

. . . On the rialto once
    The rats are underneath the piles. The Jew is
    underneath
    the lot.

The history of Henry Harland is, finally, even more ridiculous than pathetic, a success story in the end: From Rags to Riches, from Ethical Culture on the East Side to Roman Catholicism on the Riviera. Yet before his last metamorphosis, Harland had defined what was to be the obsessive theme of the American-Jewish novel through the twenties: the theme of intermarriage, with its ambiguous blending of the hope of assimilation and the threat of miscegenation. The tradition that begins with Luska-Harland descends in one line to *The Island Within* and in another to the Cohens and the Kellys and *Abie's Irish Rose.*

It is self-evident that the Jewish-American novel in its beginnings must be a problem novel, and its essential problems must be those of identity and assimilation. The very concept of such a novel involves an attempt to blend two traditions, to contribute to the eventual grafting of whatever still lives in Judaism onto an ever-developing Americanism. One cannot, however, propose to lose himself without raising the question of what the self is which may be surrendered or kept; and the Jewish-American writer who is, of course, almost necessarily non-orthodox finds a riddle in the place where he looks for an answer. *Is* there a Jewish identity which survives the abandonment of ghetto life and ghetto beliefs, which for so long defined the Jew? Or has the Jew left in Europe, along with the pain and squalor he fled, the possibility of any definition?

What is unexpected is that these problems be posed in terms of sexual symbols, that the Jewish-American novel before 1930 be erotic fiction. The approach to and retreat from the Gentile community, the proffering of himself and the shying away out of fear of acceptance or rejection, becomes in the imagination of the Jewish writer a kind of wooing, an act of timid and virginal love. It becomes associated in his thinking with his attitude toward the new sexual freedom offered him by the breakdown of ghetto life and with the erotic subject matter that takes a central place in art once religion has been replaced as the essential subject. The Jewish-American novelist begins his attempts at a moment when the triumphs of European naturalism make it possible for fiction in the United States to break through the taboos of gentility, when the antibourgeois writer, in particular, delights in portraying himself as the exponent of the instinctual life, as the lover.

There is a real pathos in the efforts of the Jewish intellectual to see himself as Don Juan, an essential vanity in his striving to embody current theories of sexual freedom. There is nothing, either in his own deepest traditions or in the stereotypes imposed on him by Western fiction, to justify such a mythicization of himself: Shylock as Don Juan, Rashi as Don Juan, Daniel Deronda as Don Juan—they are all equally improbable. Yet it is in the role of passionate lover that the American-Jewish novelist sees himself at the moment of his entry into American literature; and the community with which he seeks to unite himself he sees as the *shikse.* Don Juan and the *shikse*—it is this legend, this improbable recasting of Samson and Delilah, which underlies American-Jewish fiction up to the end of the twenties.

The erotic theme had already been proposed by Henry Harland, and it is taken up again by Abraham Cahan in *The Rise of David Levinsky,* certainly the most distinguished novel written by an American Jew before the 1930's. It is easy to forget the sense in which Cahan's book is a love story, or even more precisely a story of the failure of love; for superficially it is another up-from-the-ghetto book, its concerns chiefly social. Indeed, it appeared in 1917, the year of the Russian Revolution, when for a little while it seemed possible that the dream of Socialism might become a fact and the Jew really assimilate to the emancipated Human Race instead of to the nation in which he happened to find himself. No wonder that even the more perspicuous critics were content to talk about *David Levinsky* as a social document: a commentary on the rise of the garment industry and its impact on American life; a study of the crisis in American-Jewish society when the first wave of German immigrants were being overwhelmed by Jews from Galicia and the Russian Pale; a case history of the expense of spirit involved in changing languages and cultures; a portrayal of New World secularism which made of City College a Third Temple and of Zionism and Marxism enlightened religions for those hungry for an orthodoxy without God.

Certainly, *David Levinsky* is all these things, as it is also the account of a Jew who dissipated the promise of his life in the pursuit of wealth; it is a rich and complex book, a retrospective and loving essay on the failures of his people by a man nearly sixty when he wrote it. An anti-Semitic book, the conservative Jewish reviewers blindly called it: "Had the book been published anonymously, we might have taken it for cruel caricature of a hated race by some anti-Semite. . . ." It is to remain the typical response of the "guardians of the Jewish Community" to any work which treats with art and candor the facts of Jewish life in the United States. Both the traditions of the European naturalist novel, on which Cahan really drew, and those of the American novel, to which he aspired, prescribe for the author a "negative" attitude toward the philistine society around him; and as a Jew he found especially abhorrent the drift of his own people, the chosen remnant, toward delusive bourgeois values. The disenchantment that became anti-Semitism in the imaginary Jew, Harland, becomes in Cahan a prophetic rage which is really love, an apparent treason which is the profoundest loyalty. In this respect, he remains the model for all serious Jewish-American novelists.

His ultimate subject is, aptly enough, loneliness: the loneliness of the emancipated Jew, who has lost the shared alienation of the ghetto to become a self-declared citizen of a world which rejects even as it rewards him. The unique loneliness of the "successful" immigrant Jew, however, suggests to Cahan the common human loneliness of those who have failed at love; and in the end it is hard to tell with which loneliness his book is primarily concerned. It is with the melancholy of David Levinsky that the novel begins; he came to America, he tells us, with four cents in his pocket and has now $2,000,000, but his life is "devoid of significance." To explain his joylessness David has certain theories. It is all due, he insists, to "a streak of sadness in the blood of my race"; to be a Jew is to be sad! But he asserts, too, that it is his wealth and the devices by which he has pursued it that have cut him off from the sources of happiness: "There are cases when success is a tragedy."

Yet Cahan makes the point with some care that David is only *incidentally* a capitalist, that he is not fundamentally different from other immigrant Jews of his generation who have become trade-unionists and socialists; what is peculiar in his development has occurred almost by accident. "Had I chanced to hear a socialist speech," he says at one point, "I might have become an ardent follower of Karl Marx." Instead he read Spencer and Darwin! What, then, is *essentially* wrong with David? Cahan does not answer unequivocally, but at times at least he suggests that he is somehow sexually or affectively incapacitated; that no boy brought up in the Talmudic tradition "that to look at the finger of a woman in desire is equivalent to seeing her whole body naked" can enter into the full heritage of modernity, which includes an ideal of sexual freedom as well as the hope of a classless society. Like Peretz, he considers the vestiges of ghetto Puritanism one of the hindrances that stand between the Jew and his full humanity.

Each failure of David Levinsky at winning a woman (and the book is in effect a tally of such failures) is given a symbolic social meaning. He does not get Matilda, his first love whom he desires while still in Europe, because he is not yet sufficiently emancipated from his Talmudic training; he cannot keep Dora, the wife of a friend with whom he carries on an inconclusive affair, because he has stepped outside of the Jewish family and cannot smuggle his way back in; he cannot win Anna Tevkin, young socialist and daughter of an eminent Hebrew poet, because he has learned to sing *The Star-Spangled Banner* with tears in his eyes, because he is a "Good American."

But for all his "Americanism," he remains still in some baffling sense a Jew and is, therefore, forbidden the possibility of marrying a Gentile. His last real chance at love seems, indeed, to be offered him by a Gentile woman "of high character," who all but proposes to him; yet at the last moment he feels between them "a chasm of race." There is always something! Though he cannot abide loneliness and prowls the streets ("I dream of marrying some day. I dread to think of dying a lonely man. Sometimes I have a spell of morbid amativeness and seem to be falling in love with woman after woman. . . ."), it is no use; some deep impotence dogs him. They are not symbols only, these failed love affairs of David Levinsky; they are real failures of the flesh and spirit, failures of a Jew in love with love and money.

In Ludwig Lewisohn and Ben Hecht, the two most admired Jewish novelists of the twenties, the erotic theme is restated in exaggerated, almost hysterical tones. There is something about their work not merely brash and provocative (this they intended), but vulgar and crude; and it becomes hard to remember that they seemed once the most promising of young novelists, before one was translated into a prophet of the new Zion and the other into a maker of successful movies. "More gross talent than net accomplishment," a disgruntled critic finally said of Hecht, and the phrase will do for Lewisohn, too. They chose to begin with such different masks, the professor and the reporter, that it is difficult to see how much they had in common, how both contrived sexual melodramas to project the plight of the Jew in the Jazz Age. A pair of titles, however, Lewisohn's *Don Juan* (1923) and Hecht's *A Jew in Love* (1931), frame the period and define its chief concern.

Unlike Cahan, who preceded them, and the Proletarian novelists, who were to follow them, Lewisohn and Hecht are hostile to Marxism; and the Marxists (most of them Jewish, of course) who appear in their books are portrayed as self-deceivers, attempting to conceal their personal anguish behind an artificial fog of socialist cant. The secular Jewish prophet honored by Hecht and Lewisohn is not Marx but Freud; and the secular religion to which they respond is what they call Freudianism, though, like many intellectuals in their time, they were not quite sure where Freud ends and D. H. Lawrence begins. Psychoanalysis seemed to them primarily one more device for mocking the middle class, one more source for arguments in defense of sexual emancipation. Beyond this, their interest remained superficial. Lewisohn's novel, *The Island Within,* contains what is probably the most unconvincing psychoanalyst in literature and manages to tuck away an utterly improbable description of an analysis, somewhere between its "epical" beginning and the little sermon on mixed marriages with which it ends.

Their common devotion to Eros and to Freud as his prophet, Lewisohn and Hecht develop in quite different ways. Lewisohn sets his in a context of belated German Romanticism, from which he derives a mystique of passion somehow synthesized with internationalism, pacifism, and a Crocean commitment to art. Hecht, on the other hand, adjusts his to a provincial version of *symbolisme,* which means for him a dedication to disorder and cynicism in art and life. Celebrated in his day as a new American Huysmans, he has become for us undistinguishable from the pressroom heroes of his *Front Page,* flip hard-guys to whom whiskey is the Muse and Chicago the Earthly Paradise. Lewisohn typically identifies himself with his protagonists, harried by women and bourgeois taboos, but pledged to fight for freedom with the sole weapon of art; Hecht presumably separates himself from the scoundrels who are the heroes of his books, though he covertly sympathizes with their amoral contempt for decency and tenderness.

The leading characters of both, though presumably intellectuals, are notable not for their ideas but for their efforts, successful or baffled, to find in themselves the demonic, impulsive sources of life. In this they are the authentic products of their age, though uneasy projections of their Jewish authors. What has a Jew to do finally with the primitivism and phallic mysticism which possessed the era? Only when he revolts not merely against philistinism but against his own most authentic traditions can he espouse such a cause. It is illuminating to remember that writers like D. H. Lawrence and Sherwood Anderson, the real high priests of the erotic religion, portrayed Jews in their fiction as natural enemies of the primitive ideal, antitypes of the passionate hero: cold, cerebral, incapable of the dark surrender of the self.

It is true enough that when Lewisohn uses *Don Juan* as a book title, he does so ironically and that he somehow feels obliged to pretend (however unconvincingly) that his protagonist is not a Jew; but he is all the while *living* the role in his own much-publicized life. In the news and gossip columns as well as in the pages of his novels, Lewisohn concentrated on justifying his love life—with time off for belaboring the poor women who failed him and the divorce laws which hampered his style. The only subject to which Lewisohn responds in his fiction with real fervor, the single spring of his creative work, is his own sex life desperately projected as typical.

The Island Within, his attempt at a major novel, opens with a manifesto declaring his epic ambitions and defending them against the proponents of the novel of sensibility, just then replacing the older, objective form. His declared intent is esthetically reactionary enough, but he cannot abide even by that; before the book is half over, he has abandoned the broad-canvas portrayal of three generations of Jewish life in Poland and Germany for a more intimate evocation of modern marital difficulties, for his usual blend of self-pity and editorial. No sooner has he reached America, than he heads for the bedroom, the old battle ground on which the sensitive Jew, a psychoanalyst this time, still struggles with the *shikse* (in the teeth of public opinion and benighted law) for the possession of his own soul.

Hecht, on the other hand, goes immediately to his theme—in this case not a direct exculpation of himself but the satirizing of another, a successful Jew. When the book first appeared, it was read as a *roman à clef;* and those in the know were more than willing to let the ignorant in on the secret of who Jo Bosshere, the publisher-protagonist, *really* was. At this point, when we no longer care about such revelations, it becomes clear that the book is more than a wicked jibe at an identifiable public figure; it is a work of inspired self-hatred: a portrait of the Jewish author as his own worst (Jewish) enemy. At any rate, the hero of Hecht's novel, whose original name was Abe Nussbaum, juggles a wife, a mistress, a whore whom he really loves, the wife of a good friend, in a frenzy of erotic machiavellianism, behind which there is no real desire. He braces himself for each sexual encounter with an energy so neurotically tense that it is dissipated by a knock at the door, a chance remark, the slightest shift in affective tone. What drives him is not passion but the need to force from the world unwilling avowals of love for his absurdly horrifying Jewish face. Bosshere-Nussbaum is portrayed by Hecht as the caricature of the anti-Semite come to life: not merely the Jew, but the nightmare of the Jew (as hawk-beaked and vulpine as Mr. Peixada) as Don Juan.

Of all the women he has possessed without desire, the one to whom Bosshere most desperately clings is, of course, the single *shikse* among them: the pure blonde tantalizing

image of a world which all of his assaults and betrayals cannot make his own. Toward her he is impelled by something deeper than sadism and self-hatred, by what Hecht calls brutally "the niggerish delight of the Jew in the blonde." If he is defeated in the end, however, it is not because of the resistance of his *shikse* so much as because of his own inability to accept himself as the seducer and scoundrel. "To himself he was only this greedy, monogamous Jew full of biblical virtues. . . ." To himself he was only the child of his people, not a great lover but a martyr to women, who cries out finally in the unexpected scriptural allusion, "My God, my God, why hast Thou forsaken me," and does not know whether he is invoking Eros or the God of Abraham, Isaac, and Jacob.

This is implicitly at least a self-criticism of the Jewish intellectual that cuts much deeper than personal satire, but it is marred by an imprecision of language and an uncertainty of tone that ends in incoherence. Lewisohn is explicit, however pat and superficial, and in *The Island Within* (actually published three years before *A Jew in Love*) he gives to the erotic-assimilationist novel its final form. Arthur Levy, the protagonist of Lewisohn's novel, never abandons his vocation as a lover; he merely transfers his desire from the representative of an alien world to the symbol of his own people, thus reinforcing a battered Romantic faith in sexual passion with an equally Romantic commitment to Zionism. As he has earlier combined the advocacy of sexual freedom with a vaguely internationalist humanism, so now he combines it with a revived Judaism, adapted to the modern scientific mind.

He pretends, indeed, to find in the Jewish tradition sanctions for his view of love. Is not Jewish divorce, he asks rhetorically, easier than Christian? Were not the Jews always skeptical about the notion of marriage as a sacrament? Have Jewish women historically not represented a *tertium quid:* neither servile like the slave-women of the Anglo-Saxon world before modern times, nor hopelessly lost like the "emancipated" Gentile women of the current era? Have they not remained at the heart of the tradition the Jewish intellectual has temporarily abandoned, waiting to bestow on him when he returns the warm fulfillment he has vainly sought in strangers? We have come full circle from Cahan's view of ghetto Judaism as a castrating force.

But Lewisohn is prepared to go even further than this, from a defense of Zion as the true Eros, to an attack on the Gentile woman as the false Aphrodite. It has all been the fault of the *shikse* and of the Jewish intellectual only so far as he has become her victim. It is no longer the Gentile world which rejects the Jew in Lewisohn's fiction (that world is, indeed, eager to draw him in and suck him dry), but the Jew who rejects it—even as Arthur Levy rejects the hope of assimilation and sets out at his story's end back to Europe, back to his people's past, to investigate the plight of his fellow Jews in Rumania.

We have reached at last the reverse of Harland-Luska's theory in *The Yoke of the Thorah;* Jessica has yielded to Delilah. Not by rejecting the Gentile girl for the Jewish one but by preferring her, the sensitive Jew commits spiritual suicide. The *shikse* represents no longer the promise of fulfillment, of a blending of cultures, but only the threat of death, of the loss of identity. The reversal, however, like the original thesis, remains a little too pat, more suited for sermonizing than poetry; at any rate, in neither case did the authors make of their themes moving and memorable fictions. Yet with Lewisohn's establishment of the antistereotype in its classic form something has been accomplished, that is to say, the last possibility of the erotic-assimilationist novel has been exhausted. His novel rests like a melancholy capstone on the whole period which reaches from the eighties to the dying twenties, a monument to an unsuccessful quest by whose example later writers have profited. After *The Island Within,* the Jewish-American novelist knew at least one direction in which he could not go.

2. ZION AS ARMAGEDDON

Though there were American Jewish novelists of real distinction in the first three decades of the twentieth century, it is not until the thirties that such writers play a critical role in the total development of American literature. From that point on, they have felt themselves and have been felt by the general public as more than pioneers and interlopers, more than exotics and eccentrics. Indeed, the patterns of Jewish speech, the experiences of Jewish childhood and adolescence, the smells and tastes of the Jewish kitchen, the sounds of the Jewish synagogue have become, since 1930, staples of the American novel.

It is, of course, Jewish urban life in particular which has provided a standard décor for the novel: the life of New York, and especially of the ghettos of the East Side, Williamsburg, etc. In a certain sense, indeed, the movement of Jewish material from the periphery to the center is merely one phase of a much larger shift within the world of the American novel: that urbanization of our fiction which accompanies the urbanization of our general culture.

Our literary twenties were dominated by provincial writers like Theodore Dreiser, Sherwood Anderson, and Sinclair Lewis, even Faulkner and Hemingway, who close that period and provide a bridge into the age that succeeds it. Whatever their talent, they remained essentially country boys who had come to the big city, who had wandered under their own power into New Orleans or New York, who had been transported by the A.E.F. to Paris. Whether they stayed or returned home again did not finally matter; even when they wrote about the city, they wrote about it as seen through the eyes of one who had come late into it and had remained a stranger.

Despite an occasional sport like Myron Brinig, who writes about Montana, or MacKinlay Kantor, whose subject matter includes hound dogs, Jewish writers do not fit into such a provincial pattern, which does not, in any case, reflect the typical, the *mythical* Jewish experience in America. Their major entry into the American novel had to await its urbanization, though that entry is not, to be sure, only a function of such urbanization. It is an extension, too, of the break-up of the long-term Anglo-Saxon domination of our literature which began in the generation just before the First World War. The signal that this double

process had started was the emergence of Dreiser as the first novelist of immigrant stock to take a major position in American fiction. There is something ironic in the fact that the breach through which succeeding Jewish writers poured was opened by one not innocent of anti-Semitism; but once the way was opened for immigrants in general, it was possible for Jews to follow.

At any rate, by the end of the thirties (a recent historian of Jewish literature points out) there were some sixty American Jewish writers of fiction who could be called without shameless exaggeration "prominent." A close examination of that historian's list proves rather disheartening; for of the sixty-odd names he mentions, fewer than ten seem to me worthy of remembering; and three of these (Abe Cahan, Ludwig Lewisohn and Ben Hecht) belong, in theme and significance, to the twenties in which their major work was accomplished. The writers who remain of the original sixty are Edward Dahlberg, Leonard Ehrlich, Daniel Fuchs, Meyer Levin (recently come to life by reaching back into the Jewish Society of the twenties for an image of violence and disgust stark enough to move us) and Henry Roth. Even if one were to add to these certain others not included in the original group, say, Waldo Frank, Maurice Samuel, Isidor Schneider and Michael Gold, who are at least symptomatically important, it would make a constellation by no means inspiring; for no one of them is a figure of first importance even in the period itself.

Fuchs and Roth are writers of considerable talent, even of major talent, perhaps; but for various reasons, their achievement is limited. Roth is the author of a single novel, *Call It Sleep;* and Fuchs, though he wrote three before his retreat to Hollywood and popular fiction for ladies' magazines (and despite a recent comeback in short fiction) wrote only one book of considerable scope: *Homage to Blenholt.* There remains, of course, Nathan Wallenstein Weinstein, who preferred to call himself Nathanael West—and whose long neglect by official writers on the period is now being overbalanced by his enthusiastic rediscoverers. For a long time, scarcely anyone but Henry Popkin considered him worth touting; but now the republication of his whole works and his translation into a Broadway play have given West back a full-scale existence. There is no use being carried away, however, no use in concealing from ourselves the fact that what has been restored to us is only another tragically incomplete figure, whose slow approach to maturity ends in death. And there remains further the troublesome question: is West in any effective sense a Jew?

Though the thirties mark the mass entry of the Jewish writer into American fiction, they do not last long enough to see any major triumphs. There is no Jewish writer among the recognized reigning figures of the period: no Dos Passos, no Farrell, no Steinbeck; there is no Jewish writer who played a comparable role to the continuing major novelists of the twenties: no Fitzgerald, no Hemingway, no Faulkner. There is no Jewish author (with the possible exception of West) who can rank even with middle-generation fictionists like Robert Penn Warren, who seemed at the end of the thirties promising young men.

Even in the creation of images of the Jew, a job the Jewish writer in the United States has long been struggling to take out of the hands of the Gentiles, there is no Jewish writer who can compare in effectiveness to Thomas Wolfe. Just as Sherwood Anderson and Hemingway and Fitzgerald succeeded in making their hostile images of Jews imaginative currencies in the twenties, Wolfe succeeded in imposing on his period a series of portraits derived from his experiences at New York University: enameled Jewesses with melon breasts; crude young male students pushing him off the sidewalk; hawkbeaked Jewish elders, presumably manipulating the world of wealth and power from behind the scenes.

What, then, was the modest contribution of the Jewish writer to the fiction of the thirties, and how did this prepare for later successes going beyond anything he himself achieved? Predictably enough, a large number of American Jewish writers of the period were engaged in the production of the best-advertised (though, alas, quite infertile) art-product of the period: the Proletarian Novel. Perhaps the best way to define that subform of the novel is to remind ourselves that it is the major result of applying to the creation of literature the theory that "art is a weapon"; and that therefore it was in intent anti-art, or at least, opposed to everything which "petty-bourgeois formalism" considered art to be. Perhaps because of the contradictions inherent in such a view, it had one of the shortest lives ever lived by a literary genre. One speaks of the Proletarian Novel as a form of the thirties, but in fact it was finished by 1935 or 1936, becoming at that point merely formula writing, completely at the mercy of political shifts inside the Communist movement.

In any case, the Proletarian Novel is not, as its name suggests, merely a book about proletarians; it is alternatively about poor farmers, members of the lower middle class; and most often, in *fact* if not in theory, about intellectuals, specifically about the intellectual's attempt to identify himself with the oppressed and with the Movement which claimed to represent them. The Proletarian Novel was, then, ideological fiction dedicated to glorifying the Soviet Union and the Communist Party and to proving that the Party was the consciousness of the working class in America as well as in the rest of the world. Yet the most characteristic aspect of such novels escapes ideological definition completely, for it is a product of the age as it worked on writers beneath the level of consciousness of class or anything else. This is the *tone* of the Proletarian Novel: a note of sustained and self-satisfied hysteria bred on the one hand of Depression-years despair and on the other of the sense of being selected as brands to be snatched from the fire.

The Stalinist movement in the United States has always attracted chiefly marginal and urban groups; and if one thinks of the marginal and urban in the United States, he thinks, of course, largely of Jews. Especially in its cultural activities, in the John Reed Clubs, in the *New Masses* (and those cultural activities were of major importance in the thirties when the Communists captured few factories but many publishing houses), Jews participated in a proportion completely out of accord with their role in the total population. Indeed, the Movement was by way of being the typical strategy of the ambitious young Jew in a time of Depression for entering fully into American life. Jews who would have been dismayed by older kinds of bourgeois assimilation embraced this new method which allowed them at once to identify themselves with America and protest against certain aspects of its life.

Similarly, the intellectual, whether Jewish or not, found in the Movement an escape from the sense of alienation from American society which the twenties had brought to acute consciousness. One must realize the attractiveness of the orthodox Communist "culture" sponsored by the *New Masses* for the young man who was both an intellectual and a Jew. It is scarcely surprising that so many of them turned to the Proletarian Novel as their chosen form; even those who for aesthetic reasons found the genre unpalatable apologized for their apostasy, or tried to make up for it: like Nathanael West feeding his more orthodox contemporaries at the family hotel and boasting of having walked the picket line with James T. Farrell and Leane Zugsmith.

Still, no matter how alluring the Proletarian Novel might have been to the unproletarian Jewish writer, he could not, of course, write such a novel *as a Jew.* It was during the thirties, one remembers, that the Stalinists were officially condemning Jewish chauvinism in Palestine, and attacking Ludwig Lewisohn (who had entered his Zionist phase) as the blackest of reactionaries; and in those days, "race consciousness" was thought to be inimical to class consciousness. It is not surprising, after all, that a recent survey of the literature of the period, in a book called *The Radical Novel in America,* can point out only *one* Proletarian Novel which dealt specifically with anti-Semitism. This is a problem which must wait for the Popular Front novel and the Middlebrow Liberal Novel, which is to say, for the forties.

All of which does not mean, of course, that a Jewish writer could not *begin* with his Jewishness; and, as a matter of fact, Michael Gold's *Jews Without Money,* which appeared in 1930, was the prototype of the Proletarian Novel, going through eleven printings in its first year and setting a pattern for succeeding writers. Not quite a novel, really, or quite an autobiography, it seems more than anything a collection of vignettes of Jewish life making a moral point—a conversion tract illustrating the passage of a thinking man from Judaism to Communism. The pattern is simple enough (it is picked up and reinforced later in Isidor Schneider's *From the Kingdom of Necessity*): to make of "Jewish nationalism" and the Jewish religion the chief symbols of reaction; the pious man, the pillar of the synagogue, appears as a landlord and an owner of whorehouses; the rabbi becomes an old lecher; and the rituals of the Jews instances of hypocrisy and backwardness. The *Seder* (one thinks of what Herman Wouk will be doing fifteen years later to redeem all this!) an especial horror: "Ironical, isn't it? No people has suffered as the Jews have from the effects of nationalism and no people has held to it with such terrible intensity. . . ."

Can there be, then, in the American Jewish proletarian writer any Jewishness beyond a peculiarly Jewish self-hatred, a Jewish anti-Jewishness? To be sure, there is always available to him Jewish local color: the stumbling speech, the squalor, the joy peculiar to the Lower East Side or Brownsville; but these are by the thirties already sentimentalized clichés also available to the makers of Cohen and Kelly type movies. There is, beyond this, the constant awareness of alienation which belongs to the Jew: the sense of loneliness not as an accident but as a kind of chosenness; and in a writer like Gold the ancestral cry of "*Eli, Eli . . .*" persists. "In my ears still ring the lamentations of the lonely old Jews without money: 'I cash clothes, I cash clothes, my God, why hast thou forsaken me!' "

Not only has the concept of the choosing of all Israel in an election which seems an abandonment been transferred from the whole people to a part—to the poor alone—but in the process, what began as a mystery has become hopelessly sentimentalized. It is not for nothing that Mike Gold has been called the Al Jolson of the Communist Movement; indeed, in and through him, a cloying tradition of self-pity, which is also, alas, Jewish, and which had already possessed the American stage, moves on into literature. If the Communist Jewish writer can sing "*Eli, Eli . . .*" to his own tune, he can also sing "*A Yiddishe Mamme*" in a proletarian version. Here is Mike Gold once more: "My humble funny little East Side mother. . . . She would have stolen or killed for us. . . . Mother! Momma! I am still bound to you by the cords of birth. . . . I must remain faithful to the poor because I cannot be faithless to you."

All of this is secondary, however; the special meaning of Judaism for the radical writer of the thirties is, expectedly enough, its Messianism. "I believed," Gold writes, "the Messiah was coming, too. It was the one point in the Jewish religion I could understand clearly. We had no Santa Claus, but we had a Messiah." It is understandable, after all, that Marxism should feel at home with the Messianic ideal, since Marx seems to have envisaged himself, more often than not, as a prophetic figure: the last of the prophets promising a new heaven and a new earth. With the Russian Revolution, however, and the differentiation of Bolshevism, a new tone is apparent in Socialist messianism: a note at once apocalyptic and violent.

The old-fashioned sanity that characterizes Abraham Cahan is abandoned; and especially anything that smacks of the pacifism of the twenties is rejected in favor of an ideal of "hard Bolshevism" and class war. Two quite different sorts of feelings are involved, often confused with each other but logically quite separable: on the one hand, the desire, compounded of the self-hatred of the Jew and the self-distrust of the intellectual, that the good, clean, healthy workers of the future take over and destroy all that has come before them; on the other, an impulse to identify oneself with the future, to feel oneself for once strong and brutal and capable of crushing all that has baffled and frustrated one's dreams. "Oh workers' Revolution," Gold's protagonist cries out at the book's climax. "You brought hope to me, a lonely suicidal boy. You are the true Messiah. . . . "

Jewish American fiction in the thirties, whether specifically "proletarian" or not, is characterized by this frantic religiosity without God, this sense of the holiness of violence. Wherever one turns, there is the sense of a revelation, mystic and secular and terrible, as the only possible climax: the challenge to an unbelieved-in God to redeem Williamsburg at the end of Fuchs' first novel; the prayer to Pure Mathematics as a savior in Maurice Samuel's *Beyond Woman;* the invocation of the holy rage of John Brown in Leonard Ehrlich's *John Brown's Body;* the baffled and self-destructive attempt of Nathanael West's Miss Lonelyhearts to become Christ in a Christless world.

The Jewish novel of the twenties has as its typical theme assimilation and as its typical imagery the erotic; but the novel of the thirties is in theme and imagery, as well as politics, apocalyptic. Sex does not disappear from it completely, for the conquest of erotic taboos is a continuing concern of the contemporary novel; but its meaning and importance alike have been altered as compared with, say, *The Rise of David Levinsky* or Ben Hecht's *A Jew in Love.* From the Jew in love to the Jews without money of the thirties is a long way whose direction is indicated by Maurice Samuel's title *Beyond Woman.* Where erotic material does appear, it is likely to have the function which it assumes in Gold's book, to have become one more exhibit in the Chamber of Horrors: evidence of the evils of prostitution or the prevalence of the homosexual rape of small boys under Capitalism. More generally speaking, after Mike Gold, sex tends to be treated as just another sort of violence in a violent America.

In the 1930's, the Jewish-American novelists, like most of their Gentile fellows, become subscribers to the cult of violence, though for the Jewish writer such an allegiance has a special pathos because of the long opposition to violence in the Jewish inheritance. It is one more way of denying his fathers. And what could he do in any case? In those shabby, gray years, the dream of violence possesses the American imagination like a promise of deliverance. Politics is violent and apolitics equally so; whatever else a man accepts or denies, he does not deny terror.

Obviously, the thirties did not invent terror and violence in our fiction; as far back as our books go, there are images of horror: the torn corpse stuffed up the chimney; the skull split by a tomahawk; the whale spouting blood. Even a "funny book" like *Huckleberry Finn* has more corpses than anybody can ever remember. There are, however, two transformations in the thirties of the role and handling of violence.

The first is the *urbanization of violence;* that is to say, violence is transferred from the world of nature to the world of society, from what man must endure to what man has made. There is, of course, a special horror in considering the law of fang and claw walled in but unmitigated by the brick and glass of the city planners. Even a provincial writer like Faulkner is driven in those years to move into the city streets for images of terror adequate to the times; and *Sanctuary* remains of all his books the most appalling and Popeye, his sole urban protagonist, his most monstrous creation.

But the thirties mark the climax of an even more critical change: the ennobling of violence as "the midwife of history." Under the name of the Revolution, violence becomes not something to be fled, not the failing of otherwise admirable men, not a punishment for collective guilt—but the crown of social life. What had begun just after 1789 with the Terror and been hailed in America by the theoretically bloody Jefferson received in an age of mechanized warfare and mass production its final form. The lust for pain of Nietzsche and the hypostasizing of history by Hegel culminated in the twin horrors of Nazi and Soviet brutality; but a worse indignity had already been worked on the minds of intellectuals, conditioned in advance to accept one or the other.

In light of this, it is easy to understand that questions of ideology are secondary, that it is the pure love-fear of violence which distinguishes the novel of the thirties: a kind of passion not unlike that which moved the Germans before their final defeat, a desire for some utter cataclysm to end the dull-dragging-out of impotent suffering. Not only Communist-oriented writers produced such horror literature, but southerners like John Peale Bishop (in *Act of Darkness*) or Robert Penn Warren (in *At Heaven's Gate*); Hemingway made his obeisance to the mode in *To Have and Have Not;* and even so mild an upper-middlebrow traditionalist as James Gould Cozzens produced in *Castaway* a novella of the required shrillness.

In the official Communist version, the vision of the apocalypse is translated into that of the "Final Conflict" between worker and boss, Good and Evil; but this pat formula the better Jewish-American novelists could not quite stomach. Rather typically they temper the violence they cannot reject with humor, an ironic refusal to enter the trap completely. At the close of Daniel Fuchs' *Homage to Blenholt,* the three *shlemiels* who are his protagonists have reached the end of their illusions and are looking at each other in despair. One has come to realize that he will run a delicatessen for the rest of his life; another has come to see that the greatest event in his career will be winning three hundred dollars on a long shot.

> "Well," said Coblenz, "don't take it so hard. Cheer up. Why don't you turn to Communism?"
>
> "Communism?" cried Mrs. Balkin. "Listen to Mr. Bungalow. Communism!"
>
> "What has Communism got to do with it?" Munves sincerely wanted to know.
>
> "It's the new happy ending. You feel lousy? Fine! Have a revelation and onward to the Revolution!"

Fuchs' protagonists remain to the end victims and antiheroes, incapable of any catastrophe more tragic than the pratfall; but this is the traditional strategy of the comic writer. In a more complex way, Nathanael West and Henry Roth manage to achieve at once the antiheroic and the almost-tragic. In West, the comic butt is raised to the level of Everybody's Victim, the skeptical and unbelieved-in Christ of a faithless world; in Roth, the *shlemiel* is moved back to childhood, portrayed as the victim of circumstances he can never understand, only transcend.

West, of course, remains a humorist still; though in him humor is expressed almost entirely in terms of the grotesque, that is to say, on the borderline between jest and horror. In his novels, violence is not only subject matter; it is also technique, a way of apprehending as well as a tone and theme. Especially in the *Dream Life of Balso Snell,* one can see what West learned from the Surrealists during his stay in France: the violent conjunctions, the discords at the sensitive places where squeamishness demands harmony; the bellylaugh that shades off into hysteria.

Yet he is a peculiarly American case, too. In one of his few published critical notes he announces: "In America violence is idiomatic, in America violence is daily." And it is possible to see him as just another of our professional tough guys, one of the "boys in the backroom" (the phrase is Edmund Wilson's—the title of a little book in which he treated West along with John O'Hara). But West is, despite his own disclaimers, in a real sense, a Jew. He is racked, that is to say, by guilt in the face of violence, shocked and tormented every day in a world where violence *is* daily. In *Miss Lonelyhearts,* he creates a kind of portrait of himself as one all nerves and no skin, the fool of pity whom the quite ordinary horror of ordinary life lacerates to the point of madness. His protagonist is given the job of answering "letters from the lovelorn" on a daily newspaper and finds in this job, a "joke" to others, a revelation of human misery too acute to bear.

But this is West's analogue for the function of the writer, whom he considers obliged to regard unremittingly a suffering he is too sensitive to abide; and in no writer is there so absolute a sense of the misery of being human. He is child enough of his age to envision an apocalypse; but his apocalypse is a defeat for everyone. The protagonist of *Miss Lonelyhearts* is shot reaching out in love toward a man he has (against his will) offended; the hero-*shlemiel* of *A Cool Million: or The Dismantling of Lemuel Pitkin* goes from one absurd anti-Horatio-Alger disaster to another, and after his death becomes the hero of an American Fascist movement. But the real horror-climax of his life and the book comes when, utterly maimed, he stands on a stage between two corny comedians who wallop him with rolled up newspapers in time to their jokes until his wig comes off (he has been at one point scalped), his glass eye falls out, and his wooden leg falls away; after which they provide him with new artificial aids and begin again.

It is in *The Day of the Locust,* however, West's last book and the only novel on Hollywood not somehow trivialized by its subject, that one gets the final version of The Apocalypse according to Nathanael West. At the end of this novel, a painter, caught in a rioting mob of fans at a Hollywood premiere, dreams, as he is crushed by the rioters, his masterpiece, "The Burning of Los Angeles":

> Across the top he had drawn the burning city, a great bonfire of architectural styles. . . . Through the center . . . spilling into the middle foreground, came the mob carrying baseball bats and torches—all those poor devils who can only be stirred by the promise of miracles and then only to violence, a great United Front of screwballs and screwboxes to purify the land. No longer bored, they sang and danced joyously in the red light of the flames.

West does not seem to be finally a really achieved writer; his greatness lies like a promise just beyond his last novel and is frustrated by his early death; but he is the inventor for America of a peculiarly modern kind of book whose claims to credence are perfectly ambiguous. One does not know whether he is being presented with the outlines of a nightmare endowed with a sense of reality or the picture of a reality become indistinguishable from nightmare. For the record, it must be said that the exploiters of such ambiguity are typically Jews: Kafka for the continent, West for us.

But in what sense is West a Jew at all? There is a violent flight from Jewish self-consciousness in his work; indeed, in *Balso Snell,* there is a bitter portrait of the kind of Jewish artist who feels obliged to insist on his origins:

> "Sirrah!" the guide cried in an enormous voice, "I am a Jew! and whenever anything Jewish is mentioned, I find it necessary to say that I am a Jew. I'm a Jew! A Jew!"

Indeed, whenever a Jew is directly identified in West, he is portrayed viciously enough to satisfy the most rabid anti-Semite; although one must hasten to add that this is balanced by portraits of anti-Semites which would gratify any Jew. Finally, however, anti-Semitism and anti-anti-Semitism do not really add up to Jewishness, much less cancel each other out. West's changed name is surely a clue; he is the first American Jewish writer to wear a name which is a disguise; the exact opposite of Henry Harland, first author of an American book with a Jewish milieu, who called himself Sidney Luska and tried to pass as a compatriot of his protagonists.

West, we are told, made a point of dressing in a Brooks Brothers suit, carrying a tightly rolled umbrella and going, conspicuously, on hunting trips—which is to say, he insisted in all ways on making himself the antitype of the conventional Jewish intellectual. Yet it seems to me inconceivable that anyone but an urban, second-generation Jew in revolt against his background could have produced the novels from *Balso Snell* to *The Day of the Locust.* Certainly, the epigram of C. M. Doughty, which he himself quotes, seems applicable to Nathanael West: "The Semites are like to a man sitting in a cloaca to the eyes, and whose brows touch heaven."

Henry Roth is quite another matter. *Call It Sleep,* which appeared in 1935, and which no one will reprint despite continuing critical acclaim, is a *specifically* Jewish book, the best single book by a Jew about Jewishness written by an American, certainly through the thirties and perhaps ever. Technically, Roth owes a great deal to James Joyce; and, indeed, it is the strategy of intense concentration on fragmented detail and the device of stream-of-consciousness (both learned from *Ulysses*) which protect his novel from the usual pitfalls of the ghetto book. He reverses the fatal trend toward long-winded chronicle, which had at once inflated and dimmed the portrayal of Jewish immigrant society from Abe Cahan's lifelong study of David Levinsky to Ludwig Lewisohn's "saga" of four generations. The events of *Call It Sleep* cover two years of ghetto life, from 1911 to 1913, and are funneled through the mind of a boy who is six at the start of the book. It

is through the sensibility of this sensitive, poetic, mama-haunted, papa-hating Jewish child, full of fears and half-perceptions and misunderstandings, that the clichés of the form are redeemed to poetry.

But he serves another purpose, too, that of helping the author, apparently committed to the ends of the Movement, evade ideology completely. In the place of the Marxian class struggle, Roth sets an almost Dickensian vision of the struggle between the child and society, of the child as Pure Victim. The lonely boy and the hostile city make only the first in a series of counterpoints on which the book is based: the greenhorn and the American; a subtle and lovely Yiddish and a brutal, gray English; grossness and poetry; innocence and experience, finally Gentile and Jew. In a way, quite unexpected in the thirties, Roth plays off the values of the *Cheder* against the values of an outside world dedicated to a pagan hunger for sex and success.

The climax of the book comes when David, the young protagonist, thrusts the handle of a milk ladle down into a crack between streetcar rails and is shocked into insensibility. He has learned earlier of the power of the rails, when captured and tortured by a gang of Gentile hoods on the previous Passover, and has come somehow to identify that power with the coal of fire by which the mouth of Isaiah was cleansed. He feels the need of a similar cleansing, for young as he is, he has the sense of having played pander to his cousin Esther and a Gentile boy in order to be accepted in that boy's world. Just before he passes into complete unconsciousness, David is granted a vision—once more the apocalypse—in which all that troubles him is healed: his father's paranoiac rage and fear of cuckoldry; his mother's mute suffering and erotic fantasies; his own terrors and apostasies. Blended into his vision are the harsh cries of the street and the voice of a Socialist speaker prophesying the day on which the Red Cock will crow. For the vision, neither the eight-year-old David nor the author has a name; and as the boy falls from consciousness, he thinks: "One might as well call it sleep."

After this spectacular achievement, Roth wrote no more novels; he works now, one hears, in an insane asylum in upstate New York—and an occasional story reveals him still haunting his old material without conviction or power. It is not an untypical case in the history of American Jewish writers in the thirties. Gold and Schneider lapsed into mere pamphleteering: West and Fuchs moved off to Hollywood, where the former died; no promises were fulfilled. Looking back, one sees a series of apparent accidents and ideological cripplings, acts of cowardice and despair; and yet there is a sense that this universal failure is not merely the function of personal weakness but of a more general situation. Although all outward circumstances in the time of the Great Depression conspired to welcome the Jewish writer, the inward life of the Jewish community was not yet defined enough to sustain a major writer, or even to provide him with something substantial against which to define himself in protest.

Irving Howe

SOURCE: "The Stranger and the Victim: The Two Jewish Stereotypes of American Fiction," in *Commentary,* Vol. 8, No. 2, August, 1949, pp. 147-56.

[*In the following essay, Howe traces the portrayal of Jews in American fiction, highlighting various inadequacies and stereotypes.*]

Most novels about American Jews are afflicted with stereotyped characterizations. Seldom does the Jew appear in them as an individual; almost always he is made the representative of a group or subgroup (a "kind" of Jew: a good or a strange Jew); in the eyes of both writer and reader he is first *the* Jew and second *a* person. If conceived with hostility, he is drawn from hidden regions of the unconscious, for in America anti-Semitism is not respectable and therefore is largely repressed in public. (This perhaps explains the relative scarcity of Jewish characters in our fiction: the novelist, balking at the difficulties involved, simply suppresses his awareness of the existence of Jews.) If the object of sympathy, the Jew is put together out of the thin surfaces of conventional social-behavior patterns and idealizations. But it makes little moral or aesthetic difference which attitude the writer takes, since both deny the one right the Jew needs most: existence as a unique human being, with an individuality of his own. And in either case the central illusion of the novel—that it somehow "exists" as a refracted version of experience in which characters enjoy a spontaneous being—is destroyed. Without that illusion, a work of fiction is valueless.

To suggest reality, fictional characterization must project distinctive personalities. Even when a character is intended to represent a social type, he must first exist as an individual being. When stereotyped, a character becomes nothing more than a function of the author's perceptions, a bundle of the most obvious and superficial traits conventionally associated with a social type. Some of these traits may originally have had some relevance or reality since people in actual life often live according to conventional patterns, but at best their validity remains partial and external. And a fictional character in whose individuality we cannot believe is not likely to impress us as a valid representative of a social type. Another difficulty is that stereotypes tend to persist in fiction about Jews long after they have disappeared from reality. Thus, the Jewish father as sage and scholar reflected the existence of a certain type in Jewish life, but most actual Jewish fathers were not dreamers or prophets—and in present-day America the type has become virtually extinct. Yet the stereotype survives in current fiction.

Almost all fictional characterizations of Jews stem from two great historical myths, and most of them from an interweaving of these myths. The first, and by far the most powerful, is almost an invariable of Christian civilization: the Jew as Judas, as devil, as alien and therefore suspect. The second, less substantial myth is a result of the philo-Semitism that arose during the Enlightenment and was strengthened by the bourgeois democratic revolutions. The first myth is found in the work of Chaucer, Shakespeare, and Marlowe; the second one most classically in George Eliot's *Daniel Deronda.* It is interesting that most Jewish authors also order their novels, whether consciously or not, according to these myths. The stigmatized help perpetuate their own stigma.

Whether novels indulge in aggressive denunciation of Jews or sentimental pleading for them, they are bound together by one common assumption: that the Jews are not human like other people, somehow not subject to the same pressures of experience as other men. Whether illimitably sinister or uncannily wise, Jews appear in fiction as odd, strange, different by nature. Let us look at some of the prevalent stereotypes in which the two major myths about the Jews are expressed and interwoven.

RAGS TO RICHES

The primary fact about the life of the Jew in America is that until quite recently he was almost always an immigrant. Since the turn of the century New York City's Lower East Side has been the focal point of Jewish immigrant life, and in American fiction has been transformed from an actual place into a symbolic presence dominating all the characters created in its image. Most novels written about the Lower East Side have followed a common pattern: a conflict between Orthodox father and Americanized son in the midst of which is trapped the faithful, perplexed mother.

Inevitably these novels are full of sentimental stereotypes. In dripping prose, Samuel Ornitz's *Haunch, Paunch and Jowl* and Michael Gold's *Jews without Money* seize on every unfamiliar custom, every touch of "quaintness," to pander to the public conception of the East Side as an exotic curiosity. Their novels abound in all the expected symmetrical contrasts—the "sights and sounds"; the rabbis and prostitutes uneasily jostling each other; the bums and the intellectuals lost in common futility; the idealistic virgins and yielding servant girls equally betrayed. Here even poverty becomes a curiosity, a piece of local color to be waved before the eyes of American readers. These caricatures are all the more malicious in that their creators intend no malice.

It is remarkable that Gold's Communist hero should indulge in reminiscences essentially similar in outlook to those of Ornitz's reactionary judge. Both view the East Side, and thereby all of life, in the same masochistic-sentimental terms. And though Ornitz was attempting irony and Gold wanted a passionately direct statement, neither was capable of that balanced regard for the object which is the prerequisite of realistic fiction. Thus the nostalgia of Ornitz, Gold, and a host of others for the days of their youth is really a libel; their elegies on its vanished color conceal a rejection of its human qualities. Their apologies for the East Side have meaning only as repudiations.

One novel did view the East Side without succumbing to the prevalent stereotypes. In *The Rise of David Levinsky,* Abraham Cahan, too, takes as his theme the rise of an immigrant from East Side poverty to wealth. But in probing the failure of David Levinsky to live a meaningful life, he rejects the sentimental falsehood that wealth necessarily brings decay, and the parochial falsehood that rich Jews inevitably come to an unhappy end because they try to assimilate themselves to the Gentile world. Levinsky's life is a failure because he has had to destroy in himself the social and moral values he absorbed in his childhood.

Levinsky realizes in the end that his success has been achieved by wilfully truncating his personality. But this self-destruction is not seen as the necessary result of Americanization as such; it is only the logical outcome of his acceptance of Babbittry, which of all aspects of American life is least compatible with the roots of his personal life. Never making this idea too explicit, Cahan skillfully weaves it through the whole fabric of his novel. Often he can trap in one image the whole character of Levinsky's development: "At this time the magic word 'credit' loomed in letters of gold before me. I was aware of the fascination of check-books. . . ." Cahan gave a validity to the rags-to-riches theme that none of the sentimentalists could; he transformed the abstract idea into a dramatic conflict embodying a genuine moral dilemma. His fiction was buttressed by a Marxist outlook but not imprisoned in a dogmatic straitjacket.

Cahan's achievement was possible because he wrote from a secure base. He did not suffer from the ambiguous feelings about his relations with Jewish life and the American world that were to afflict later writers. He was in both worlds, the Jewish and the American, and since he believed strongly in their continuity and contiguity he felt no need to apologize for one to the other. His viewpoint was that of a socialist and his cultural medium was Yiddish—a combination giving rise to attitudes of irony and detachment that permitted him to observe the two worlds and their interactions with a sharply sardonic eye. (The native American, Cahan shrewdly noticed, has an "unsmiling smile." American businessmen "laugh with their teeth only.") Thus Cahan's novel, published in 1917, remains one of the best products of American naturalism.

THE GREAT ROMANCE

There is a maudlin Jewish folk tale perpetuated by old women who feel themselves neglected by their children: At the command of his wife, a man once cut out his mother's heart. While bringing the heart to his wife, he dropped it on the ground where it crumbled into many pieces. The son wailed that now he would not be able to satisfy his wife's demand for his mother's heart; but from the earth there rose a gentle voice: "Do not weep, my child, your mother's heart will mend itself so that you may bring it to your wife."

The great romance of American Jewish life is between mother and son. It can be found in almost every novel written about the Jewish family in America; the heroes of these novels may be different, but they are all born of the same mother: patient, loving, sweet, a trifle uncomprehending and humorless, everlastingly faithful—a stereotype compounded equally of filial self-deception, nostalgia, and guilt. She appears in the novels of as diverse a group of writers as Sholem Asch, Ludwig Lewisohn, Thyra Samter Winslow, Samuel Ornitz, Jerome Weidman, Budd Schulberg, and—Thomas Wolfe. She is the most celebrated contemporary heroine of the Oedipal myth, and, as the folk tale above indicates, she is herself ready to join in the celebrating.

One American Jewish writer has raised this stereotype to a genuine characterization. Genya, in Henry Roth's *Call It Sleep,* is so endlessly patient and innocent that it is evident she has been conceived as "the Jewish mother"; yet Roth has poured so much feeling and vitality into this characterization that we eventually become convinced of her independent existence.

This highly serious novel describes the relationship between the six-year-old David and his mother entirely in terms of the child's own perceptions. Roth sustains this perspective throughout the novel; never does the child's vision become confused with his own. A remarkable sympathy exists between son and mother, which puts them in league against the father, a harried man who hates David with a wrath he cannot motivate or understand. The father's preoccupation with bread-winning sours his personality and makes even more unbearable his resentment of the affection Genya lavishes on their child. Each incident of the novel complicates its web of human misunderstanding and misery; each development of its relations accentuates the innocent tyranny of maternal love.

Genya is a superb figure: gracious, loving, innocently oblivious to the self-indulgent aspects of her love for the child. The delicately ambivalent nature of the mother-child relationship, so full both of horror and innocence, is lyrically expressed when Genya fondles her child: " 'I really believe,' she continued in a scolding and bantering whisper, 'that you think of nothing. Now honest, isn't that so? Aren't you just a pair of eyes and ears? You see, you hear, you remember, but when will you know? And no kiss?' She caught him by the shoulders, kissed him. 'There! Savory, thrifty lips.' "

The child's sense of guilt becomes a dominating obsession—the guilt caused by his father's arbitrary and awesome wrath, by his discovery that his own mother is a woman like other women, and most of all by his trembling uncertainty about his own existence. In this child there rumble all the terrors of innocence and guilt, of expiation and damnation, of separation and identification that oppress adult life. His pitiful father becomes for David the symbol of exterior wrath, the surely deserved punishment for all those secret, barely divined guilts borne by the child's precocious consciousness. "Answer me, his words rang out. Answer me, but they meant, Despair! Who could answer his father? In that dread summons the judgment was already sealed. Like a cornered thing, he shrank within himself, deadened his mind because the body would not be deadened, and waited. Nothing existed any longer except his father's right hand. . . . " Who could answer his father?

In *Call It Sleep* the personal patterns of Jewish immigrant life are presented with the same validity as are its social patterns in *The Rise of David Levinsky.* Two lone books of truth and imagination in a sea of mediocrity!

THE FATHER AS PATRIARCH

If in the legend of Jewish immigrant life the mother's function is to love, then the father's is to understand. He is the repository of racial wisdom; even when he picks his nose, there is revealed in this act something of the philosopher and seer. Of course, he is not really at home in America. In Europe, the legend runs, he spent his time as a dedicated religious student who did not concern himself with the things of this world. But in America he is overwhelmed by the problem of earning a living, his personality is assaulted by the pressures of an alien and heathen world, and he suffers the pain of seeing the cleavage between himself and his Americanized children widen each day. That is the pattern, and most writers accept it.

Sholem Asch, never one to neglect a stereotype, has created the central character of *East River,* Moshe Davidowsky, in this image. Though forced to work as a grocer, Davidowsky is still the Jewish patriarch, the neighborhood dispenser of wisdom. No matter how much unhappiness his children cause him (one son is stricken with paralysis and the other marries a *shiksa*—apparently equal strokes of misfortune), he eventually forgives them. In an act of symbolic religious reconciliation, he accepts his Gentile daughter-in-law, thus adding a Christian tinge to his Judaic halo; but by the novel's end, his goodness and patience have become ludicrous. Asch combines the melodrama of a Second Avenue tear-jerker with the contrivances of American soap opera, adds a pinch of his homemade religiosity, and reaches the best-seller lists. . . .

The father in Ludwig Lewisohn's *The Island Within* is cut from the same stencil. Lewisohn's Levy, a German Jew, is more tolerant of his son's *shiksa* than is Davidowsky, but Lewisohn is a less skillful contriver than Asch, and Levy is never more than a dignified cipher, the product of his creator's tendency to apostrophize rather than delineate character. Both these writers are so obsessed with their conceptions of Jewishness that they cannot create a Jew.

A more satisfactory version of the father-as-seer is given in Albert Halper's *Sons of the Fathers.* Unlike Davidowsky and Levy, Halper's Saul Bergman has something of the ambiguity and imperfection of a human being. A Yiddish sceptic whose only certainty is life itself, with its simple processes and rhythms, he questions all worldly affairs beyond the range of his immediate experience. Believing the world to be a jungle, he hopes only to cut a little clearing for his family.

On Armistice Day in 1918, the news that his son has been killed reaches him, and while the streets are full of cheering mobs, he searches for a *minyan* to say the prayer for the dead. What the mob forgets he remembers; while the thoughtless cheer he weeps. At this point he reaches his full stature, his awareness of tragic destiny. One believes in both his existence and in the need for his existence; he is really a father.

Yet *Sons of the Fathers* is a poor novel because it is as a whole a pattern of stereotypes through whose limitations the main character has managed to erupt. In creating Bergman, Halper wrote, as it were, over his head. Nothing in the rest of the book has any genuine relationship with Bergman, and Halper's effort to exalt the private values destroyed by war collapses into the philistinism of completely un-ironic acceptance; life is good; the family exists; there is . . . oh yes, there *is* a father!

THE BOHEMIAN REJECTION

If the life of the Jew in America, at least before the 1930's, was embodied fictionally in the sentimental family stereotype, then it was inevitable that sooner or later a Jewish writer would appear to reject that stereotype violently and completely. But when that Jewish writer did appear he fell into a reactive stereotype equally one-sided and false. Though many Jewish writers had urged assimilation to American life, the first to attack Jewish group existence from a standpoint close to fashionable Bohemian anti-Semitism was Ben Hecht in *A Jew in Love.*

Hecht's Jo Boshere is a product of the 20's: shallow, flamboyant, pretentious, and, in retrospect, unspeakably silly. His is the pose of a Bohemian trying to be clever and *au courant;* Hecht's hero is neither an individual nor the representative of a type; he is simply a monster. Specializing in emotional assaults on his friends, this gutter Don Juan engages in a wearisome succession of frenetic love affairs whose pleasure consists only in sadistic chase and masochistic rejection. He is a looter of egos—the amatory parallel of the common myth about the social or economic role of the Jews.

Whatever Hecht's original intention, or Boshere's initial resemblance to the actual person from whom he was drawn, his figure turns very soon into a vehicle for Hecht's subterranean articulation of some of the more newfangled myths of anti-Semitism: "The niggerish delight of the Jew in the blonde was no part of Boshere's enthusiasm in his new conquest. . . ." "These Jews decadent, humanless, with minds sharp as banjos, offer through the mask of their perversities the last blatant sob of Jewish culture. . . . Their songs quiver with self-pity, are full of unscrupulous wailings of ancient Jewish griefs . . . pounded home with the rabbinical slobber of an atonement prayer. . . ." "Sara of the tribe of soft and oriental Jewesses whose lips need no painting, whose cheeks bloom with pale, ivoried roses, whose eyes float like black seeds in a juicy pod, had dominated the doctor's senses through six years of marriage. Pictorially they made a pretty union, the Hebraic madonna and the moonlit Talmudist. . . . Sara possessed that calm, undemeaning servility which lights the love of a true Jewess."

It is difficult in 1949 to take Hecht's ideas or prose very seriously. In light of the terrors we have become acquainted with since, the novel's bizarre vagaries seem almost comic, like the posturings of a precocious adolescent. What is interesting, however, is the possible connection between Hecht's strange novel and his later political activities on behalf of terrorists in Palestine.

THROUGH NATIVE EYES

Few non-Jewish writers have dared to express themselves freely about Jews; many of them, even if they did feel free to express their deepest attitudes, would not know what they were. So pervasive is this self-censorship that when Gentile writers do risk creating Jewish characters they usually produce idealizations that are merely the slanders turned inside out. Not that such writers are "really anti-Semitic"; such a view is much too simple and, what is more, quite untrue. I mean rather that the pull of the conventional symbol is so powerful that even when writers feel sympathy towards Jews they often express it in censored and not genuinely spontaneous perceptions.

The Gentile American novelists think of the Jew primarily as a means of setting off, of sharpening by contrast their vision of America. They see him, usually, as a stranger, an emanation of the romantic past, somehow connected with Europe and its wisdom, sophistication, and over-ripeness. The stereotype fluctuates between two traditional extremes. On the one hand, the Jew is seen as highly self-conscious and calculating, never able to "let himself go," always measuring the advantages to be gained from personal relations. On the other hand, he is seen as deeply passionate, richly steeped in his heritage, "oriental." Often these logically incompatible stereotypes are blended into a single fictional character.

In Djuna Barnes' *Nightwood,* the stereotype of the Jew as stranger is represented by Felix, a wandering Jew—he wanders from salon to salon, "searching for the correct thing to which to pay tribute." He is so calculating that he can never act on the decisions he formulates: he is paralyzed by the process of decision. The author records that on one occasion he let go of his emotions as much as he, a Jew, could. In that remark is summed up her conception of the Jew: a man forever chained to self-consciousness.

The brilliant old scientist Gottlieb of Sinclair Lewis's *Arrowsmith* is a Jewish stereotype because of what might be considered a case of mistaken identity. An extreme version of the scientist (an irascible extension of what many Americans imagine Einstein to be), he is so impersonal a being that there is no necessary reason for his being a Jew at all. Lewis seems to feel that Gottlieb must be a Jew only because he is first a scientist. For it is a common American belief that great theoretical scientists are brilliant but eccentric; that this eccentricity is somehow connected with foreignness (that is, Jewishness); and that therefore most great scientists are Jews. As a writer who, despite a superficially satirical outlook, largely accepts America on its own terms, Lewis uncritically borrowed this notion of the scientist as Jew from the common store of folk belief. His portrait of Gottlieb is therefore a stereotype of a stereotype.

When we come to Thomas Wolfe, F. Scott Fitzgerald, and Ernest Hemingway, we are dealing with writers of far greater abilities than any yet discussed. Yet they, too, viewed the Jew in much the same hackneyed way that most Americans do.

Thomas Wolfe was fascinated by Jews. No other writer so nearly expressed in their most primitive terms American folk attitudes towards "the strangers from the East." In Wolfe's lust for knowledge, he saw them as the knowing people; in his lust for experience, he saw them as the people in whom there still throbbed memories of the times of David—and precisely because they seemed most to represent the depths for which he yearned, did he most suspect them. He feared and loved them as a child fears something strange and grand and old. *Of Time and the River* is full of all this. Eugene Gant's friend, Abe Jones, has a face that is "a vast, gray acreage of painful Jewishness and invo-

luted intellectualism." Abe's spirit is "as steady as a rock, as enduring as the earth. . . . The sight of his good gray, ugly face could always evoke for Eugene the whole wrought fabric of his life in the city, the whole design of wandering and return. . . . " Abe is "dreary, tortured, melancholy, dully intellectual, and joylessly poetic, his spirit gloomily engulfed in a great cloud of Yiddish murk . . . yet a dogged, loyal and faithful friend, the salt of the earth. . . . " Jewesses are "as old as nature and as round as the earth . . . they had a curve in them . . . the strong convulsive faces . . . ripe with grief and wisdom . . . female, fertile, yolky, fruitful as earth. . . . "

Has ever a writer paid a more involuted and preposterous tribute? For Wolfe never saw individuals: where there lived a person, he saw a "race." All that was weird, fearful, strange, passionate, and *deep*—the Unknown and the Knowing, in the quest of which he spent his life—Wolfe found in the Jews. To this profoundly indigenous American they seemed the very personification of that Otherness which he always sought. For him the Jews were the forbidden fruit, and he bit into it eagerly.

F. Scott Fitzgerald, a writer with much more self-awareness than Wolfe, also saw the Jew as an alien whom he could not quite understand. But he was interested in the Jew, not because the Jew was "ripe with grief and wisdom," but because he could be used as a dramatic symbol to fix Fitzgerald's vision of America as a civilization of grace entering its decline.

In *The Great Gatsby,* the Jew Meyer Wolfsheim, a professional gambler, is used to personify the essentially impersonal forces of corruption that bring tragedy to the "simple" American, Jay Gatsby. This was the primary aspect of the myth: the Jew as a source of pollution. Near the end of his life, in the unfinished novel *The Last Tycoon,* Fitzgerald turned to the other side of the coin. Monroe Stahr, the Jewish film producer who is the hero of Fitzgerald's *The Last Tycoon,* is one of the few genuinely tragic heroes of American literature. Into him Fitzgerald poured all his yearnings for a state of human grace; all his desire for sustained and facile creativity; all his deeply pessimistic conviction that the things he so desperately wanted were doomed. Stahr, an instinctive master with no ordered comprehension of his art, seemed to Fitzgerald the most adequate symbol of the tragedy of American life: Stahr, the creator, the craftsman, the Jew, could not survive in America. In this very deepening of the myth, its nature becomes clear: if for Fitzgerald America had become barren and Stahr represented the surviving principle of the creative, that contrast was possible only because Stahr was somehow alien, a Jew whose creativity did not flow from American sources. Like Joyce he chose a Jew for his most deeply felt symbol of his sense of the human fate, as well as for a final puzzled apostrophe to human potentiality.

Of all the American writers who approached the Jew as a stranger, none succeeded in depicting him as well as did Ernest Hemingway in *The Sun Also Rises.* Hemingway saw Robert Cohn as a unity of both extremes of the Jew-as-stranger stereotype. Cohn was both more calculating and more natural, more inhibited and more passionate than his Gentile friends. Since Hemingway's perceptions were always of a palpable thing or being, he was unable to think in abstractions; and so "the Jew" became Robert Cohn, an individual creature of flesh and blood.

Cohn is not an admirable character. He is an outsider and "different," but Hemingway does not allow him the excuse of a youth "scarred by poverty." Though Cohn's external experience is the same as that of his expatriate friends, he is not at home in their world; he breaks their accepted patterns of behavior. In Hemingway's world of cripples, Robert Cohn is a special kind of cripple. His friends resent Cohn because he has opinions, because he talks instead of grunting, because he still takes the trouble to articulate his feelings. He cannot relax with them into drunkenness and restful inarticulateness. To that extent, he is the Jew who calculates and can't let himself go. But at the same time Cohn is the most viable character of the novel. He at least feels and reacts. Often enough his manners are bad, but he does retain his emotional vitality, no matter how unattractive some of its consequences may be. In a world of dried-out wrecks, he still thrashes about. As the others are cursed by some variety of imposed physical or psychological impotence, Cohn is cursed by his bar to grace: his Jewishness. Yet Cohn is a triumph of characterization: a Jew who is both a Jew and a human being. And once a Jew has been granted truly human status, he has been granted everything.

NOTHING TO LOSE BUT YOUR CHAINS

The great dividing line in American fiction about Jews was the depression era. In the novels of the 30's and 40's, the Jew was assigned new roles. He was now the young radical, the small businessman, or just the Jew for whom one felt sorry or raised placards. He became a favorite "subject" of problem novels, a "terrible lesson" to whom novelists of the slogan pointed dramatically. The older stereotypes of the Jew, in which he was conceived primarily as the stranger, were at least based on a certain curiosity about his life. But in these more recent stereotypes, which showed the Jew as a victim, he was simply abstracted into a convenient symbol toward which writers could take a stance. It was an exchange of masks—from an exotically colored one to a rigidly blank one.

The "Jewish radical," who turned up in virtually all of the now happily forgotten "Marxist" novels, was a New York boy, of course; he came from poor parents and his father was usually a garment worker; he was a CCNY graduate, very brainy and rebellious—though given to occasional lapses into petty-bourgeois moodiness (Jews, it is well known, are very moody). In the end he always managed to overcome the handicaps of his background as well as the suspicions of the workers whose strikes he invariably led.

There was just enough blurred truth in this stereotype to make it easily recognizable. In fact, it was too recognizable. Precisely because of the verisimilitude of the externals, it became the more obvious that nothing of the actual individual quality of the Jewish radicals of our time had really been described, nothing of their genuine experience

and feeling projected. Life as a radical was never so simple, so monolithic, so dull as these novels made it seem.

In all of American fiction one recalls only one somewhat convincing characterization of a Jewish radical: Ben Compton in John Dos Passos's *USA*. Without inner life, unable to talk to people because he can talk only at mass meetings, Compton ends his political career by breaking with the Communist party. Distrusted by his former comrades, weak from police beatings and jail sentences, quite without belief or orientation, Compton personifies for the Dos Passos of the early 30's his own most poignant attitude: his commitment to the necessity of rebellion and his belief in its hopelessness.

Alfred Kazin has pointed out that *USA* is an attempt to rewrite the American myth in the bitter terms of social bifurcation, of a nation split into warring classes; and its characters suffer from the fact that they are often symbolic versions of social forces rather than genuine individuals. But Dos Passos's own passionate intervention in his novel manages to some extent to overcome this weakness. The lonely rebel, the stubborn fighter doomed to defeat—this is the one thread of American belief Dos Passos still accepts, and which he identifies, in the person of Ben Compton, with the Jew. So fierce is Dos Passos's paean to rebellion and so warm his love for Ben, that for a moment we can forget that this Ben, the most rebellious of Jews, is more a generalized tribute than a genuinely realized character.

THE ARTIST AS BUSINESSMAN

At the other extreme of value and vocation, there appeared in American fiction of the late 30's the Jewish shoe-string businessman, representing all that was rotten in big-city life.

Jerome Weidman and Budd Schulberg, focussing on the Jewish "operator," offer their novels as realistic and critical approaches to metropolitan Jewish life. Many Jewish critics, however, have denounced their novels as slanders, deriving from the "self-hatred" of "alienated Jewish intellectuals." Both views are simplifications. There is much healthy critical perception in Weidman's and Schulberg's novels, but obviously there is also something more that is both disturbing and irritating. This "something more," which, I think, is felt by every perceptive reader, is not anti-Semitism. Actually, Weidman and Schulberg are as romantic about Jews as Lewisohn or Ornitz, and their caricatures of Jews arise from attitudes as sentimental as the idealizations against which they rebelled. Weidman and Schulberg continue to portray Jews as members of a specially endowed group with powers beyond the range of ordinary mortals; in a strange way, they see them as still a "chosen people."

Harry Bogen, the hero of Weidman's *I Can Get It For You Wholesale*, is a small garment manufacturer, vulgar and utterly unscrupulous. He is a recognizable facsimile of a distinct social type and at the same time a sharply demarcated individual. Bogen personifies the small Jewish entrepreneur who feels that, in order to survive, he must accept and drive to its extreme the amoral ethos of American business life. Yet he knows better, he doesn't fool himself about the meaning of his choice: "I had to laugh at these *goyim* and their politeness. They aren't born smart, like Jews. And they know it, and it scares them. So they figure out a substitute. They act like gentlemen to each other. They're polite all the time, so they can be sure one won't screw the other. . . . "

Though Bogen believes he is beating the *goyim* at their own game, he feels that he is somehow different from them. By carrying the traditional caricature of the Jewish businessman to an extreme that even the *goyim* don't anticipate, Bogen confirms his conviction of superiority: if a Jew is smart he can do anything—and Jews are smart.

Budd Schulberg's *What Makes Sammy Run?* is cut on the same pattern, but more crudely. Schulberg writes in a slick wise-guy prose—the style of those for whom Toots Shor's is the seat of American culture and "to make with" a universal verb. His Sammy Glick is so gruesome a caricature, such a horror of selfishness and misanthropy, that one questions the relevance of his existence (even if that existence is granted) to any sort of moral or social reality. He exists, if he exists at all, in moral isolation; he cannot be significantly related to either life or literature; he is drawn according to the Hollywood conception of character. And unlike Harry Bogen, he is not even sentimental about his mother.

Schulberg glibly explains Sammy's adult misanthropy in terms of an ugly, poverty-stricken childhood, thereby fusing the two major stereotypes about the Jewish businessman. But neither the too inclusive denunciation of Sammy as an adult nor the too easy explanation of his character in terms of childhood unhappiness is satisfactory; together they overload Schulberg's novel with embarrassing clichés (Sammy's mother is "sensitive with the sufferings of five thousand years. . . . ").

This odd mixture of hatred and sentimentality—quite sincerely expressed by Weidman, consciously manipulated by Schulberg—reveals less of their approach toward Jews than of their feelings about themselves. On closer examination, Harry Bogen and Sammy Glick seem to be lay figures on which are projected frustrations and conflicts rooted in quite another area of American life. More like skilled technicians than serious artists, Weidman and Schulberg have in varying ways succumbed to Broadway's commercialism, anti-intellectualism, cheap cleverness, and easy success. Yet somewhere in them, I would guess, is an awareness of their self-betrayal as writers. (Schulberg knows more than Weidman, but seems to care less.) May not the terrible viciousness of their portraits of Jewish businessmen be an index less of their "self-hatred" as Jews than of their feelings about their own status as artists? When they write with passionate hatred of their characters' deviations from what they conceive to be Jewish morality, are they not perhaps castigating themselves for their own deviations from the highest artistic morality? Through their portraits of the Jew as businessman they may thereby be expressing their contempt for the artist as businessman—which, if at all true, would be a curious use of the popular stereotypes of the Jew as both the stranger and the cunning exploiter.

THE JEW AS PLACARD

After the European catastrophe a large number of novelists discovered not so much the Jew as "the Jewish problem"; their novels are usually of great moral earnestness but slight literary interest, for their message seldom emerges from a serious imaginative structure.

A forerunner of this kind of novel is Ludwig Lewisohn's *The Island Within*. Written in a tone of oppressive earnestness that sometimes does reach a certain Biblical eloquence, it implores American Jews to return to the ways of their fathers. The story drives so inexorably to its destined goal (Lewisohn confuses his will with destiny) that the breath of life, of contingency and variety, is banished. *The Island Within* contains only one active character: Lewisohn himself, the Jeremiah thundering against assimilation.

Lewisohn bases his rejection of assimilation on the failure of his hero, Arthur Levy, to succeed in his marriage with the Gentile Elizabeth, but his account of that marriage is so obviously contrived according to antecedent ideological biases, that its failure is unavoidable and unconvincing. Nor do the characters in this book come to Jewishness at the end of an independent quest; they have it thrust upon them by the author. The result is more a tract than a novel, with the moral smothering both narrative and characterization.

A number of journalist-novelists have also written recently on the "Jewish problem." They possess neither the eloquence nor the seriousness of Lewisohn, and where his writing collapses under the weight of his moral, theirs simply dissolves into thin air for lack of any weight at all.

For Laura Hobson and Arthur Miller the "Jewish problem" is stated and solved in journalistic terms. Miss Hobson reduces the problem to a means of indicating her superior moral position (the liberal whose heart is in the right place). Written in a cuddly popular style, *Gentleman's Agreement* rests on the agonizingly superficial notion that to demonstrate the painful results of anti-Semitism is to convince people that it is evil. The novel itself is the real stereotype—the stereotype of a gesture of good will, with all the heartless indifference toward human reality that mere gestures of good will always entail.

Arthur Miller's *Focus,* another "problem novel," resembles nothing so much as a melodramatic movie scenario. The protagonist, Newman, is attacked by his Christian Front neighbors in Queens because his name "sounds Jewish" and his face "looks Jewish." Shocked into an awareness of how mean—and undiscriminating—anti-Semitism can be, Newman identifies himself in the end with the Jews. *Focus* is built on a mere trick—for if anti-Semites were intelligent instead of stupid, Newman wouldn't be hurt, he wouldn't care, and there'd be, apparently, neither a novel nor a problem. As a product of the Stalinoid mentality, *Focus* generates ideological phantoms rather than characters; it provokes pre-established and confirmed reactions rather than fresh insights or emotions; its only claim to individuality is a brutal and violent style, as hard and glossy as a GPU man's blackjack.

Ludwig Lewisohn.

Jo Sinclair's *Wasteland* substitutes psychiatry for "liberalism" or Stalinism as the solution to the "Jewish problem." For Miss Sinclair Jewishness is something to which one adjusts—like an artificial leg or the menopause. But like so many other results of the "adjustments" arranged by popular ameliorative psychiatry, Miss Sinclair's casework Jewishness is without substance, variety, color, or character. *Wasteland* is an appropriate novel with which to end a discussion about "Jewish problem" novels, for it exaggerates their faults to final absurdity by hoisting a placard completely and terrifyingly blank.

To the extent that one can discern any trend in the characterization of Jews in American novels of the last few decades, it is toward an increasingly totalitarianized vision of the Jew. While almost all of the novels discussed in the early part of this essay saw the Jew either as a sentimental souvenir or as a stranger and alien, they at least showed a certain live curiosity about him. But in novels of the 30's and 40's, the characterization of Jews has been frozen into a calculated gesture. Seldom genuinely interested in the novel as an art form, most contemporary writers who deal with Jews devote themselves to scoring points in behalf of some rather simple and obvious thesis. As a result, their portraits of "the Jew" become merely ideological figments. Beside the regimented abstractions of such writers as Hobson, Miller, and Sinclair, the characterization of Jews in the novels of the 20's seems positively full of variety and color.

It is by now extremely difficult to say just what we mean when we demand that a Jewish character in fiction be shown as an individualized human being, rather than a stereotype. When is a Jew in fiction—or in life—human, and when is he a stereotype? Cannot the creators of stereotyped Jewish characters claim that their work has verisimilitude because Jewish life is itself stereotyped? And by what norm—in the modern world!—are we to measure the human?

These questions cannot be answered in simple and unhazardous terms. The catastrophic blend of "high" and "low" cultures in our time has resulted in a debasement of the former and a weedlike growth of the latter, which make it difficult to keep sharply demarcated the authentic experience or rendering of experience from the inauthentic. That may be why those few writers who have tried, with some success, to create genuine Jewish characters—Daniel Fuchs, Michael Seide, Delmore Schwartz, Isaac Rosenfeld, Saul Bellow—have begun by deliberately sloughing off large preconceptions and rhetorical patterns. The most accomplished of these writers, Delmore Schwartz, is characterized by an insistent determination to return to the simplest facts and patterns of Jewish experience as the only means of reaching its possible larger meanings.

The mechanized characterizations of Jews in most recent novels is not, however, an isolated phenomenon; it is part of a general social tendency. For when the American novel characterizes Jews by means of stereotypes—when it in fact assumes the existence of that generic monster, "the" Jew—it drives to an extreme a tendency already present in all areas of modern life. The Jew cannot reach full human status in American literature and life because modern man cannot reach that status. When a Jew cries out, "I am *a* man," and society replies, "No, you are *the* Jew," his dilemma is but an extreme version of every other man's.

Louis Harap

SOURCE: "Jewish Anti-Semitism: The Problem of Self-Hate," in *Creative Awakening: The Jewish Presence in Twentieth-Century American Literature, 1900-1940s*, Greenwood Press, 1987, pp. 151-65.

[*In the following essay, Harap examines various indications of ethnic self-hatred in Jewish authors and literary characters.*]

For over two thousand years the Jews have been afflicted with numbers among them who wish to transfer their identity to that of their host people. Their lack of a national state before 1948 and the worldwide persistence of anti-Semitism in all its varieties, economic, political, and social, have caused them to be regarded as an alien people nearly everywhere they settled. Many have succumbed to the all-too-human tendency to avoid the ineligibilities attaching to their alien status and, as they thought, to head off anti-Semitism by religious conversion to a socially approved faith or by renouncing or concealing their Jewish origin. This tendency has become stronger since Emancipation opened these escape routes wide and equality before the law protected such changes. The problem often became acute when a Jew wished to intermarry. Before Emancipation, when ghettoization prevailed, such changes were undertaken only by the adventurous, but were beyond even the range of thought for most Jews.

The term "self-hate" has been applied to those who are born Jews but feel negatively or antagonistically toward their fellow Jews and Jewishness in general. Such a person may not be in a position to deny his Jewish origin or to separate himself from other Jews. Thus it can coexist with acceptance of one's status as a Jew as a fact of life while one entertains the notion that the world would be better off if there were no Jews. This species of Jew is the Jewish version of the anti-Semite.

The term "self-hate" is of recent coinage. There is not even a listing of the term in the Second Edition of *Webster's Dictionary* (1913), even as late as its 1945 printing. The term is probably a translation of the German *Selbsthass*, first used in Theodor Lessing's *Der Judische Selbsthass* (1930). As Clement Greenberg has pointed out, the phenomenon is "strictly speaking, more self-doubt and self-contempt than actual self-hatred" and "is better defined as 'the Jewish inferiority complex.' " But the term self-hatred has gained a certain currency with its specific meaning of Jews rejecting other Jews and oneself as a Jew as analyzed by the German émigré social psychologist Kurt Lewin in his essay, "Self-Hatred Among Jews" (1941). Lewin used the term broadly to apply to both groups and individuals. Group manifestations are the hostile feeling in Europe of German Jews for the East European; and in the United States, of the established Spanish Jews for the German immigrants of the mid-nineteenth century, and of German Jews toward the Eastern European Jews of the mass immigration. We have encountered many instances of these prejudices in the fiction we have examined.

However, Lewin has overlooked the distinction between rejection, on the one hand, by an individual Jew of *all* Jews and Jewishness, and on the other hand, of one group of Jews by another group of Jews. The first is individual renunciation of Jewish identity and ethnicity, the other social dissociation of, usually, one class of Jews by another class. In the latter case, for instance, middle-class German Jews used to look down upon immigrant East European Jews of the working class, or even Jews of this group who had only recently risen from the working class and had not yet acquired middle-class manners. But in the case of the "self-hating" Jew it is Jewishness as such which is rejected. The difference becomes clear when one recalls that middle-class German Jews usually retain close association with their fellow German Jews as fellow Jews, which is far from the self-hating rejection of Jewishness. It is well-known that German Jews in Germany wished to reduce the visibility of the *Ostjuden* just as the German Jews in the United States, during the mass immigration and later,

resented being identified with the uncouth ghetto Jews. They tried to reduce the visibility of the immigrants by settling them, if possible, in small cities or rural areas, without much success.

Middle-class, established, acculturated Jews were fearful that anti-Semitism might be generated by the presence of numerous newer Jews with their residue of ghetto mentality and language singularity. This drew them closer to one another as Jews, since they did not hate Jews as such but only disapproved and were contemptuous of the strange lower-class Jews from Eastern Europe, whom they called "kikes," an appellation they introduced. But among these middle-class Jews were also some who wished to dissociate themselves from Jews altogether. Confusion on this point is possible if Lewin's concept of "self-hatred," which includes both types of attitude, is adopted uncritically. In our discussion, therefore, *we shall use the term exclusively to refer to those who reject any identification with the ethnic group of their origin.* Especially despised by the established German Jews, and even by many assimilated Jews generally, was the audible stigma of Yiddish, the language usually used by the new immigrants, which was often regarded as an ill-sounding, vulgar "jargon." Such middle-class Jews were perhaps unaware of, or ignored, the existence of a large and growing significant literature in this "jargon," which is today indisputably recognized as a language in which a universal literature was created. The real reason for the rejection of the language was its association with the segregated life of the *shtetl* and the ghettos of American cities, which stamped Yiddish speakers as unacculturated Americans.

In terms of understanding the Jewish community, therefore, and the behavior of American Jews, the distinctions I have tried to draw here take on considerable significance. To illustrate the distinction as it is exemplified in literature, we shall first examine a novel exemplifying each type. The first is Vera Caspary's *Thicker than Water* (1935), and the second is Ben Hecht's *A Jew in Love* (1928), to be followed by a number of examples of the latter type.

The Caspary novel epitomizes the relations among the three major Jewish immigrations, the earliest Sephardic of the seventeenth century, the German of the mid-nineteenth, and the Eastern European mass immigration of the late nineteenth and early twentieth.

The Caspary novel vividly illustrates the haughty attitude of the proud Piera family toward both German and Eastern European Jewish newcomers and the "decline" of the family through its "dilution" by intermarriage with both "inferior" groups. As the pecuniary fortunes of the family go down, they are rescued and enhanced by Ashkenazi spouses. The Pieras could trace their ancestors back many centuries to rich and powerful patrons of art in Spain and Portugal, and the first Piera had come to the United States in 1660. In the 1880s the family is settled in Chicago. Rosalie Piera is about to marry one of those "newcomers to America, the aliens, and barbarian Germans, half of whom never knew their great-grandparents' given names." Never had Rosalie's mother "thought her beloved daughter could consider a suitor of German descent." Even worse, another daughter marries Julius

Smith (né Sliwoski) who conceals his Polish origin until his mother appears; she wears a *sheitel* and speaks Yiddish! The haughty Pieras regularly refer to their German and East European fellow Jews as "kikes." The author records that,

> with the exodus of Jews from Russia and Polish Russia in the two decades since a bomb had been hurled at Alexander II [1881], bitter prejudice had arisen among American Jews against their Russian co-religionists. This bitterness did not ferment so rapidly in the Middle West as in Eastern cities where the greatest number of immigrants settled. But gradually as they came to Chicago, as the section around Maxwell Street grew crowded with uncouth, unclean strangers sputtering a guttural jargon, the solid citizens felt their security threatened, their place in the community, the respect of their Gentile neighbors, their social position and their prosperity.

Just as the Sephardi condescended to the Germans, the Germans in turn looked down upon the East Europeans. In the 1920s, one of the family married the "kike" Sam Chodorov, and the younger generation realize that at least the aristocratic Sephardi are scarcely known as such any more. In this competent and rather slickly written story the moving force of the narrative is intra-Jewish class prejudice.

There is no subtlety in the Jewish self-hatred depicted in Ben Hecht's *A Jew in Love* (1928). A clearer case could hardly be found. It is doubtful if Ben Hecht was aware of this or would grant it. He seemed unconsciously anti-Semitic. He may rather have viewed his characterizations as cleverly cynical, but this was a rationalization: in reality it was self-deceptive and shallow. The description of his central character, Jo Boshere (born Abe Nussbaum), is given in terms that would be appropriate for *Der Stuermer,* and Boshere's revulsion from his Jewish appearance gives the book its central theme—"this biologic handicap he sought to overcome" by exploiting women sexually, especially non-Jewish women. He is a monster of corruption, not only with his wife and Jewish mistress, but especially with his blonde, non-Jewish lover Tillie, from whom he plots to extort obsessive love to compensate for his appearance. He heartlessly, cruelly, cynically manipulates his women to feed his egomaniacal erotic plots. The story is profoundly self-hating and anti-Semitic.

There is no subtlety in the Jewish self-hatred depicted in Ben Hecht's *A Jew in Love* (1928). A clearer case could hardly be found. It is doubtful if Ben Hecht was aware of this or would grant it. He seemed unconsciously anti-Semitic.

— *Louis Harap*

Boshere, at thirty, is a dark-skinned little Jew with vulturous and moody face. . . . The Jews now and then hatch a face which for Jewishness surpasses the caricatures of the entire anti-Semitic press. The Jew faces in which race leers and burns like some biologic disease are rather shocking to a mongrelized world. People dislike being reminded of their origins. They shudder a bit mystically at the sight of anyone who looks too much like a fish, a lizard, a chimpanzee or a Jew . . . [Boshere had] an uncomfortably Semitic face, a face stamped with the hieroglyphic curl of the Hebrew alphabet. . . . [He had] . . . the look of a Prince Charming in the midst of a pogrom.

How confused Hecht is appears from his observation, in the midst of this anti-Semitic, self-hating description, that "The Jew face is an enemy totem, an ancient target for spittle and, like a thing long hated, a sort of magic propagandist of hate." If there is any doubt of this confusion, Boshere took in Tillie "the niggerish delight of the Jew in the blonde." The mood of the radical brother of his Jewish mistress Alice Stein "struck Boshere as that of a rascally Oriental during a horse trade." Boshere's sister Esther, an ardent Zionist, had a "cowl nose, nigger eyes, red rubber lips and Spanish jaws . . . and beside her, Boshere's ugliness appeared as a species of perfection."

That a Jew should be "charming looking" in such a context is anomalous to the author. Of Dr. Julie Goldstein, writes Hecht, "[That] this charming looking man about whom hovered so engaging and brittle an air of ancient princeliness should be named Goldstein was one of those farcical accidents with which Jewish nomenclature abounds—a product of racial caste degeneration which injects its ghetto history into the names of its poets, artists, elegantes and philosophers." The precise meaning of this "racial caste degeneration" is unclear. It can only mean that the "charming" feature cannot be derived from his Jewish forebears, but only from a non-Jewish admixture, a "degeneration" because mixed with the Jewish. And Goldstein's wife Sara receives from Hecht the dubious compliment of possessing "that calm, undemeaning servility which lights the love of the true Jewess."

We have no reason to suppose that Hecht's own view of the Jew when he wrote the novel was different from that expressed by Boshere in his discussion with his sister Esther. Its tone and import are the same as the author's own description of Boshere. She has been collecting money for the Jews of Palestine, and Boshere barates her for "running around like a half-witted *yenta* raising nickels for a lot of God damn stinking Jews in Palestine." She answers, "You're ashamed to have me associated with the Jewish cause because it reflects on you. It reminds people that you're a Jew." His reply is that "I'm no more Jew than kangaroo. I'm Boshere. I have no connection with Jews . . . this Jew consciousness is because I once had it. It's the consciousness of not being a normal social human being. . . . Once in a while a Jew comes to light whose ego is stronger than his label, who has enough brains, character, genius to lift his soul out of the God damn slimy stranglehold of Jew consciousness." One has a deep suspicion that Hecht believes he is describing himself here. Sixteen years later Hecht was himself to become an extreme Zionist, awakened to his Jewishness at last by Hitlerism.

He became a leading propagandist for the right-wing terrorist Irgun Zvai Leumi and was instrumental in raising large sums for their activities. In 1944 he published *A Guide for the Bedevilled* in which he confesses to the astonishing fact—if it is a fact, which seems incredible—that "I lived forty years in my country without encountering anti-Semitism or concerning myself even remotely with its existence." This included the 1920s, it may be recalled, when anti-Semitism was overt and widespread. Although a journalist in Chicago, he was apparently unaware of Henry Ford's anti-Semitic campaign in the *Dearborn Independent* and the period of Ku Klux Klan strength, especially in the Middle West.

But in his autobiography, *A Child of the Century* (1954), there is still no evidence that he was really aware of the anti-Semitic character of *A Jew in Love.* He calls Boshere "this worthless fellow, who cost me so much trouble with Jews who do not like the word 'Jew' used in a title," thus ignoring the point of the criticism, namely, the Jew-baiting aura of the book and the character of the Jew he depicts. Yet he named this novel as one of the five books he had written for which he still cared. He had, he writes, "always considered myself un-Jewish. My un-Hebrewizing had been achieved without effort or self-consciousness. I would have said in the days before I came to New York that I was a Jew by accident, and that I had shed this accidental heritage as easily as ridding myself of some childhood nickname. . . . I met anti-Semitism only through Jews who were more open to its distress." But in New York he came "to look with pride on what was obviously

Ben Hecht.

a Jewish-dominated culture." But one looks in vain for any recognition or acknowledgment of the self-hating nature of his favored novel.

Like Hecht's Boshere, the self-hating Jew aspires to identification with the dominant ethnic majority group, and professedly adopts and projects upon the Jew the stereotypical view. This phenomenon of minimizing or trying to eradicate one's original ethnicity is not unique to the Jews. It may be found in any minority group subjected to a threat of discrimination on grounds of origin, evidence the not uncommon name changes in many groups to approximate the Anglo-Saxon. Except perhaps for short periods, the entire phenomenon was far less severe among these non-Jewish ethnic groups. No other group has had as long or as drastic a history of persecution that additionally had a strong religious component (Jews as "Christ-Killers"). Other immigrant groups were mostly Christians. True, during some periods of American history various Christian denominations, such as the Quakers in the seventeenth century or the Catholics in the nineteenth, were victimized and became targets of discrimination for their fellow Christians. But these prejudices were temporary while anti-Semitism has endured for several thousand years.

Another source of confusion is the charge of self-hate against a Jewish author who deals with "negative" features of Jewish life, as if Jews were immune from such features or could be harmed by the exposure of such features. Excessive caution may be involved in condemning such writing as inciting or abetting anti-Semitism by providing fuel for the case made against the Jews. Often a realistic portrait of Jewish life is taken as a self-hating expression. Hypersensitive, overprotective Jewish critics have in fact greeted almost every attempt to face the realities of Jewish life squarely in literature as self-hatred even before the term was invented. Indeed, many significant novels of Jewish life, beginning with Cahan's *The Rise of David Levinsky,* have been so treated. Ornitz's *Haunch, Paunch and Jowl,* Gold's *Jews Without Money,* Levin's *The Old Bunch*—all were criticized by some Jews as representing Jews in an unflattering manner and indicating self-hatred on the part of their authors or as being injurious to Jewish welfare. These critics feared that exposure of unfavorable aspects of Jewish life would lend credence to charges by anti-Semites and hence reinforce anti-Semitism. A longer perspective has shown that such criticism is mistaken, for we now look back on such fiction as providing some of the most revealing pictures of how Jews lived in their time. Their durability as social documents is symptomatic of their superiority to the common run of fiction. Our discussion of these novels earlier by no means found rejection of Jewish identity by their authors but a determination to face the negative as well as the positive realities of the life they had experienced.

The concept of self-hate can be further clarified by examining other examples perhaps less clear-cut and unambiguous than that of Ben Hecht's Boshere, a self-hate clearly shared by both character and author. There are, however, problematic and ambiguous cases like those of Jewish writers such as Nathanael West, Norman Katkov, and Jerome Weidman. There are also authors whose self-hate was usually *not* shared by their authors, authors whose purpose was explicitly to expose self-hatred, writers like Ludwig Lewisohn, Budd Schulberg, Jo Sinclair, and Myron S. Kaufmann.

Like several other notable writers of the 1930s, such as Henry Roth and Daniel Fuchs, Nathanael West had to wait several decades after his early death in an auto accident in 1940 for general recognition. His four novels sold poorly and were reissued only in the 1950s. If rejection of anti-Semitism is not as categorical as we should like from a Jewish writer such as Nathanael West, it is in part because he was an artist who identified the Jews with the commercial spirit of his father, a successful real estate agent. In part, too, it was a consequence of West's aspirations toward an aristocratic status in general American society, which is hard to reconcile with his radicalism. In fact, his attitude toward the Jew was confused and complex. When he took out a passport in 1926 on the eve of a Paris trip, he legally changed his name from his original Nathan Wallenstein Weinstein to Nathanael West in order to present a more aristocratic front there. He tended to identify Jewishness with Orthodox Jewish religion, in which he did not believe; and he also tended to hold that commercialism was specifically associated with Jewish life.

In his eagerness to minimize his Jewishness, he even denied that there was any such group as the Jews. A friend reported, "He held and underwrote his opinion with facts and figures, that the original Jewish people had wandered so far and blended so deeply into the blood of the countries they found that it was senseless to identify them as a blood strain." In other words, he had no conception of the Jews, or any other socially coherent group as having an ethnic character, even if composed of many "blood strains," as most peoples are.

Yet, to complicate matters further, West never did or would deny that he was Jewish. When he attended Brown University in the 1920s, he longed to join a fraternity, but Jews and Catholics (I assume that Black membership was "no problem" because no Blacks, or at least very few, attended college) were excluded from membership. He had good reason to resent anti-Semitism. Quoting the same friend: "He knew more about it [anti-Semitism] than any man I have ever met." At Brown he regarded himself as a "Jewish outsider" but also as "a Jew and a non-Jew at the same time." His creed was that of the literary intellectual adherent of French and English modernism. "His feeling about his minority status," concludes his biographer Jay Martin, "had long since been translated into a sense of superior status as part of the elite minority of well-dressed men, of the gentleman and the author. He had become Nathanael West."

There were some resemblances between his attitude toward Jewishness and toward radicalism. Most of his friends were Communists or left-wingers. He was himself drawn to radicalism but never became a member of the Communist party. He tended to distance himself from the ideological doctrines and, of course, the dogmatism of the Communists and was sardonically amused at the concern

for the poor evinced by the Hollywood Communists in contrast to their lavish mode of life. But he was immersed in radical activities, from his participation in the Writers and Artists Congresses to fund raising for the Spanish Loyalists. His attitude toward radicals, therefore, was ambivalent, accepting their practice but not necessarily their theory. So, also, he denied his Jewishness in theory but accepted his Jewish identity in practice. In both cases he operated on the basis of his basic conception of himself as a person detached from what he considered the follies and foibles of those with whom he shared some kind of identity.

The several aspects of West's ambivalence about the Jews are exemplified in his novels. His writings are not free from occasional stereotypical allusions to Jews. In *A Cool Million* (1934), a searing satire of American life, especially in its susceptibility to the pro-fascist demagogues of the 1930s, a fascist organization called the "National Revolutionary Party," wearing "leather shirts," advertises "Ezra Silverblatt" as "Official Tailor" to the party selling "everything for the American fascist at rock bottom prices." The novel is couched in a style parodic of the dime novel or Horatio Alger story, when the young hero is jailed for trying to rescue an innocent girl from a bawdy house. The next day, "a small man of the Jewish persuasion entered his cell. 'Have you any money?' said this member of the chosen people." He is Sam Abramovitz, obviously a predatory shyster lawyer, and when Lem rejects his service, the lawyer threatens him if he doesn't pay for this unsolicited conference. Another Jewish character is the bizarre interior decorator, Asa Goldstein, who has no personal traits except for an extraordinary power to imitate any historical style of decoration, from American colonial to any regional American style. His main assignment is to furnish the rooms of a bawdy house, each in a different American regional style, a mode of satire, one would suppose, of varieties of American nostalgia callously exploited for commercial purposes by a Jew in accordance with West's invidious conception of the Jew.

On the other hand, West also amply satirizes anti-Semitism, among other ethnic prejudices. In *Miss Lonelyhearts* (1933), the titular hero stops for gas at the "Aw-Kum-On Garage" in Connecticut telling the attendant about deer he had seen at a pond the day before. "The man said that there were still plenty of deer at the pond because no yids ever went there. He said it wasn't the hunters who drove out the deer, but the yids." In *A Cool Million,* the young hero Lem becomes associated with the ex-President "Shagpoke Whipple," who has been jailed for bank malfeasance. Shagpoke doesn't blame "the mob" for thus repaying him for his services to the nation, but rather "do I blame Wall Street and the Jewish international bankers. . . . It was Wall Street working hand in hand with the Communists that caused my downfall." Shagpoke addresses a crowd. Why are there unemployed? "Because of the Jewish international bankers and the Bolshevistic labor unions, that's why." Shagpoke informs another audience that "here in Detroit there are too many Jews, Catholics, and members of unions." In the Mississippi River town of Beulah, "all the inhabitants of Beulah who were not coloured, Jewish, or Catholic assembled under a famous tree from whose every branch a Negro had dangled at one time or another." Shagpoke is introduced to "Southerners, Protestants, Americans." They are assured he "ain't no nigger lover, he don't give a damn for Jewish culture, and he knows the fine Italian hand of the Pope when he sees it." In the riot which followed "the heads of Negroes were paraded on poles. A Jewish drummer was nailed to the door of his hotel room. The housekeeper of the local Catholic priest was raped."

West felt no personal attachments to his Jewish identity or Jewishness, and occasionally falls into conventional stereotyping, but his *A Cool Million* is a devastating satire on American gullibility to demagogic reactionism, in which anti-Semitism is a useful element.

While self-hatred is present in some degree in West, that of Norman Katkov in *Eagle at My Eyes* (1947) is patently self-torturing and guilt-ridden. The author is as much confused as his central character, Joe Goodman, who has no greater comprehension of his situation as a Jew at the end than at the beginning of the story. The writing is journalistic, more like a newspaper report of the suffering of Joe as a Jew in the toils of love for the non-Jewish Mary Simpson whom he cannot leave despite his conviction that intermarriage is not viable. Katkov was a Midwestern journalist, and the locus of his story is St. Paul. Like his creator, Joe Goodman is a reporter and the author seems to share his creation's superficial cynicism. Although his family is not religious, they generally hate *goyim* in reprisal for anti-Semitism and believe that a Jew is dead if he marries a non-Jew. But Joe is desperately in love with Mary, and after refusing to marry her for a few years, he does so at last under threat of losing her altogether. Yet he feels no different about the non-viability of intermarriage.

Joe's relationship to Jews is confused. He cannot throw off his identity, since it is part of him. Yet he hates the hostility and isolation that he believes it causes him, and the unhappiness of his marriage, and in turn hates the imputed cause of his unhappiness, his Jewishness. So far as the story shows, he has no special positive feeling for Jews, and even prefers to avoid them, especially when he is with Mary. His attitude toward Jewishness is that of a prisoner to his prison. We may conclude that this, too, is a form of self-hate, or rather, self-contempt, with the proviso that his ultimate point of view is one of tortured confusion.

Following World War II the Jewish "rogue" novel was combined with the vogue for gangsters, sex, and violence in films to produce what Meyer Levin called in a famous 1955 article, "The East Side Gangsters of the Paperbacks." Actually some of these novels were first issued in hard cover and later reprinted in millions of copies in cheap paperback. Levin was alluding to novels like Irving Shulman's *The Amboy Dukes* (1947), Leonard Bishop's *Down All Your Mean Streets* (1952), and Harold Robbins' *A Stone for Danny Fisher* (1953). "Novels of this kind," wrote Levin, "have their source in classic impulses of Jewish self-hatred," of which he cites other examples like Weidman's Harry Bogen. He was concerned about the Jewish image conveyed by these trashy novels.

> Following World War II the Jewish "rogue" novel was combined with the vogue for gangsters, sex, and violence in films to produce what Meyer Levin called in a famous 1955 article, "The East Side Gangsters of the Paperbacks."
>
> — *Louis Harap*

While the self-hating character of Jerome Weidman's Harry Bogen in *I Can Get It for You Wholesale* (1937) and its sequel, *What's in It for Me?* (1938) is obvious, the attitude of the author—at least in the first novel—is not entirely clear. The unclarity follows from the detached tone which the author, in accordance with his naturalistic method, adopts toward the villainies of his central character. It is possible to attribute Harry Bogen's self-hate to the author. Thus Meyer Levin's frequent allusions to such novels as Weidman's as in "the tradition of self-hating Jewish literature" are ambiguous. Marie Syrkin's characterization of these Weidman novels as "a morbid literary expression of Jewish self-hatred and self-contempt" and "a pathological exhibition of masochistic self-flagellation" attributes the self-hatred to the author, even if it is "unconscious," as she says. With less concern for the sociology of literature and more detachment from the motivations of the author, David Boroff designated the self-hating character as the "rogue-hero," which is at least unambiguous in attributing the self-hate strictly to the literary character. Except where the evidence is clear, as in *A Jew in Love*, it is best either to recognize ambiguity or refrain from imputing self-hate to the author.

Harry Bogen of *I Can Get It for You Wholesale* is an unmitigated scoundrel who is bent on getting rich by any means, and who succeeds, for a time, by climbing over the prostrate bodies of colleagues and partners, everybody or anything barring his way. His sentimental, obsessive resort to his mother for love and comfort, although she is under no illusions as to his villainy, throws into relief his callousness toward everyone else. Even though his business practices are criminal, he contrives that others should take the punishment, and escapes scot-free. Starting at about twenty as a shipping clerk, he devises scheme after scheme—always at others' expense—to raise himself, at one time, inciting a violent strike and manipulating it to set himself up in a lucrative business.

His self-hating nature emerges from his mother's attempt to interest him in Ruthie Rivkin, her intelligent, warm young Bronx neighbor. He does not respond to his mother's coaxing, and she finally extracts the reason from him. "She's so damn Jewish-looking. You take one look at her, you see right away she's a kike from the Bronx. For crying out loud, what do you want me to do, walk down the street and have everybody giving me the horse laugh." His mother replies, "You crazy dumbell without shame! . . . so *that's* what's eating you. . . . Haven't you got a little feeling in you? What are you, ashamed of what you are?. . . . Don't think you're so smart, Heshie. The world is smarter. . . . They have only to look at you to know." Despite the attraction he feels for Ruthie, he rejects her, and establishes a mercenary liaison with the non-Jewish actress and singer Martha Mills whom he finally lures to bed by promises of a diamond bracelet.

The novel was immensely successful and was swiftly followed by a sequel, *What's in It for Me?* (1938). At the opening, Harry Bogen is at the zenith of his power and success. He has plenty of money, is keeping his mistress Martha, whom he has come to love and whom he supplies plentifully with money, and visits his mother for comfort. By the end of the book his whole life has collapsed: Martha runs off to Europe with his partner; the police are seeking him for funds he has embezzled; he is penniless; and his mother has died. His excesses of corruption and dishonesty have caught up with him, and his life is in ruins. It is as if Weidman were stung by the criticism with which the earlier book had been greeted, especially in the Jewish community, and tried to make amends by demonstrating that heartless, dehumanized behavior is in the end simply not viable. More specifically, Weidman creates a character who challenges Bogen's inhumanity and self-hatred and tries to make clear to him why Jews are especially vulnerable.

Weidman is a popular writer with a talent for rapid, facile narrative motion swiftly borne along almost totally by lively dialogue. While his Harry Bogen is clearly a self-hating Jew whose life and conduct are execrable, the second volume of Bogen's story quite obviously is intended to clear the author of the charge of self-hate, although the condemnation of Bogen is also implicit in the first volume in his mother's judgment on him. Meyer Levin was right when, at the end of the article mentioned earlier, he wrote that "the question becomes one of literary judgment," although "Jewish writers must recognize a particular responsibility in regard to the image of the Jew" because of their special vulnerability. He disclaimed the need for using only positive Jewish characters, pointing to his own contrary practice in *The Old Bunch,* and asked rather for "penetrating" portraits, even of Jewish gangsters, that were compatible with their humanity. He urges the Jewish writer to ask himself, "Is this true in depth? Am I merely perpetuating a myth without showing that it is a myth? Am I tailoring my writing to hot sales? Am I perhaps working out some self-hating impulses, or am I truly trying to make my characters understood?" These are relevant questions, for they concern not only the sociological but also the literary aspects of the novel. In the case of the novels mentioned above, it is a question whether a finer literary talent was lacking or whether the commercial or self-hating motivations were allowed to overwhelm the literary quality.

There are novels, however, in which some readers and critics carelessly fail to distinguish the self-hatred of the central character from the attitude of the author. Budd Schulberg's *What Makes Sammy Run?* (1941) is a case in point. The author's purpose, far from sharing Sammy's self-hate, is rather to expose it. When the book first appeared, it was often criticized as fueling anti-Semitism, for it came out when Hitlerism was riding high and had supporters in the United States among many neo-fascist groups. The novel has since often been indiscriminately grouped, because of the usual confusion between author and central character, with other novels by self-hating authors.

To regard Schulberg as a self-hating author is to misread his novel. Sammy does not "run" because he is a Jew. The author seeks an answer to why Sammy runs, from his beginning as a desperately poor East Side boy, to his development as a preternaturally shrewd operator in Hollywood who rises from office boy to studio boss by utterly unscrupulous methods. The answer, given by the narrator, Al Manheim, is the last sentence in the book: it is "a blueprint of a way of life that was paying dividends in America in the first half of the twentieth century." From beginning to end the author goes out of the way explicitly to depart from the stereotype, as when he describes Sammy's "little ferret face . . . with a nose growing large, but still straight and sharp, giving the lie to the hook-nosed anti-Semitic cartoons." Unlike Sammy, there were in the world, "Jews without money, without push, without plots, without any of the characteristics which such experts on genetics as Adolf Hitler, Henry Ford and Father Coughlin try to tell us are racial traits. I have seen . . . too many Jewish nebs [nebbishes] and poets and starving tailors and everyday little guys to consider the fascist answer to what makes Sammy run."

More common than novels with self-hating authors are those whose condemnation of their self-hating characters is unequivocal. One of the earliest and strongest indictments of self-hate is Lewisohn's *The Island Within.* In my opinion the treatment of his contemporary self-hating Jews has more validity than of his central character. The novel was written in the 1920s, the decade in which the second generation was perhaps most acutely experiencing self-hatred. The young Hazel Levy responds to her father's sad, "Are you ashamed of being Chewish?"—"Yes, I am! I'm just as good as anybody else and I'm just like everybody else." Young Joey Goldmann early asserts, "Jewishness is a curse," and later, as a lawyer, "a very successful lawyer now, his office full of Jewish clients, . . . always in love with some blonde Gentile girl in order to transcend vicariously in conquest of her his Jewish feeling of inferiority." In a story like this one, the lines are clearly and explicitly drawn. In fact, the contrary of self-hatred, passionate affirmation of Jewishness is the central theme of the novel.

Even more explicit in separation of the self-hate of the character from the author is *Wasteland* (1946) by Jo Sinclair (Ruth Seid). Indeed, a central aim of the novel is to expose what the author believes is the psychopathological nature of self-hate, as Lewisohn, too, conjectured, and its exorcism by psychoanalysis. Jake Brown (born Braunowitz), a newspaper photographer, lives in the "wasteland" of hatred for his family, which originates in and exacerbates his hatred of his Jewish identity. But he does love his mother and his sister Deborah. His sister is a lesbian who is ashamed of her sexuality and is self-denigrating. She tells Jake about her past and that her recourse to a psychoanalyst has cured her of guilt for her sexuality. She persuades him to consult a psychoanalyst about his problems, his self-hate, his unhappiness, and his excessive drinking. The body of the novel is then devoted to the unraveling of Jake Brown's neurotic situation. It is a matter of accepting his identity, both familial and Jewish. As the author conveys it, Jake's problem is the obtuseness that rises in human relations out of poverty and ignorance in father and mother. Being Jewish under these circumstances only aggravates this basic problem and gives rise to his difficulties outside the family. Jake had for years been trying to find an "identity—for himself, away from these people, who were unreal and strange to him. Away from the house, he had no identity, he was not alive, he was without framework of name, without flesh of heritage, without blood of pride or love. And yet, within the house he was without identity, too." This passage states well the tensions that gave tortured ambiguity to his feelings. "Was he ashamed of being a Jew? It looked like it, didn't it! And yet, everytime he read about what was happening to Jews all over the world he wanted to smash faces, he wanted to get up and shoot faces . . . and shoot all those bastards who were doing it." He had never mentioned his being Jewish at the paper for which he worked. "All right, maybe he was ashamed of being a Jew! But that wasn't the big thing he was ashamed . . . about without having to be ashamed of being a Jew."

Passover Seders are represented as crucial events in Jake's rejection of his Jewish identity. As a young man, he is deeply shocked at the Seder by his hatred and contempt for his father, who "pretended to sit like this and tell a beautiful story. It was all a lie. If his father was a Jew, then he didn't want to be a Jew." It was the incompatibility of the beauty of the story and the falseness of the man who was relating it which set up a contradiction. Yet it was an inescapable part of him. His solution was simply to flee from his Jewish identity, a plight symbolized by his refusal to attend Seders any longer. Jake was "ashamed that he was my father, that I was a Jew. Because he was one, the whole family—we were Jews. I blamed everything on that, I guess—on the fact that we were Jews." But renunciation of Jewishness was no solution: the conflict remained. After treatment by the psychiatrist, Jake is at last ready to face his Jewishness fully, a readiness symbolized by his giving blood (during World War II), which signified to him the restoration of his identity in its several aspects. "He gave as a Jew, and as a patriot, he gave as Everyman." Giving thus, most importantly, as "a member of society, a working part of it," signified restoration of mental health. For accepted as "Everyman," he was no longer "a part of wasteland." While the literary psychiatry of the novel, like most attempts of this kind, is not convincing, the author does succeed in exposing the tensions and ambiguities underlying self-hate.

Several short stories of the 1940s focus on the problem of self-hate. Paul Goodman's "The Facts of Life" exposes parental evasion of Jewishness when their child reports her first encounter with anti-Semitism at school. Nine-year-old Marcia was never told she was Jewish by her parents of a mixed marriage. She discovers it when a school-mate calls her "just an old-time Jew," and she is bewil-

dered. She's not sure she has heard right. Did the child call her "shoe," "Jao," "Juice," or what? Her father Ronnie denies he's Jewish because he is not "racially" a Jew in appearance. The non-Jewish mother, Martha, tells Ronnie, "you Jews are not doing yourselves any favor by putting yourselves forward too much. . . . Every Jew who gets in the Supreme Court makes it so much harder for Marcia." "It's true enough," thinks Ronnie. "You're a Jew, so all right!" Says Martha, "It's nothing to be ashamed of. But why bring it up in public?"

Miriam Bruce wrote her *Linden Road* (1951) out of a personal need, as she said, "emotionally, compulsively," to explore the problem that "The American Jew is in constant danger of contracting anti-Semitism himself and dying of a sort of quiet soul-rot which so far nobody deems it worthwhile to discuss." The Westchester, well-to-do garment manufacturer's family of her heroine, Hagar (the name is not accidental) Tobias, are trying to suppress their Jewish identity in their suburban, bourgeois, philistine existence. Hagar soon discovers in her high school years that she cannot control this process, since she is no longer invited to dances of mixed sexes. The story is so completely taken up with the problem of to be or not to be a Jew that the Depression receives no mention and Hitler scarcely any, even though the first half of the story takes place in the mid-1930s. Jewish counterpoint is supplied by an aunt who is continually critical of the family's efforts to suppress their Jewishness. Hagar even blames her aunt and other conscious Jews for the discrimination she suffers. She falls in love with a self-hating German-Jewish young man, Richard. Richard goes to England on a fellowship, and Hagar leaves home in hopes of ridding herself of the Jewish incubus. Her Aunt Vicky exclaims, "My God, what's the matter with all of you? Why do you hate yourselves so much? You've turned it into a disease, being a Jew . . . there isn't any place you can hide. It'll go with you."

During World War II Hagar serves with the Red Cross in Italy; there her meeting with German-Jewish refugees modifies her attitude, and she is accepted by them. Richard has, in the meantime, served in the British army and tried to pass as a non-Jew. Hagar meets a close British army friend of Richard's, a neo-Catholic scholar, esthete, and anti-Semite, and is shocked. When she hears of a young Jewish soldier on the point of death at the hospital where no one understands Yiddish, she takes the final step in her return by volunteering to talk to him. While she is still in love with Richard, she rejects his offer of marriage at the end of the war because she refuses to deny her Jewishness. Hagar is an attractive character but a victim of her rearing. At the last she is reconciled to accepting what she is—a Jew. The writing is competent and smooth, but in the end the novel is in the manner of popular magazine fiction.

The subject returns again and again in subsequent writing because it remains an ongoing issue. In 1957 another novel, this one a great commercial success, *Remember Me to God* by Myron S. Kaufmann, is centered on the problem of self-hate. Like others, it has been criticized indiscriminately as a "self-hate" novel without noting that it is a merciless exposure of the self-hatred of its central character, Richard Amsterdam, a student at Harvard and aspirant for acceptance as a Yankee. Born and bred in Boston, Richard went to school with Yankees and believes they "don't care what my origin is," but actually judge people on an individual basis, "put aside their prejudices and accept a friend on his merits." He believes that acceptance can be permanent if a Jew conforms his "manners" to what they approve.

The case for and against Richard's conformism and assimilationism is argued in several ways through his relations with characters in the novel. His father Adam is a self-made man who has risen to a judgeship through political influence. Richard has become a close friend of the Boston WASP, Hodges, and even succeeds in getting himself elected to the exclusive Hasty Pudding Club. He falls in love with Wilma Talbot, daughter of an old Boston family. Wilma's anti-Semitic father withholds consent unless Richard converts. He agrees, and "his choice to take on the Christian faith seemed an act of total freedom." He asks the Reverend Todd to baptize and convert him. Todd easily perceives that Richard's reason for converting is social, not religious, and categorically refuses to comply. He tells Richard that he (Richard) has "rationalized a conversion" without any "reference to God," who "never enters your calculation at all." And he caps his refusal with the phrase, "I'm trying to bring people to Christ, not to Beacon Hill." Richard's fantasies now fade. It is clear that he will now abandon his fatuous ideas. This is possible because Kaufmann has rendered Richard as possessing a peculiar kind of integrity, of honesty within the bounds of his rationalizations. And when those rationalizations are exposed for what they are, that same striving for honesty, one feels at the end, will lead him to revise his outlook.

Although the novel was a best seller, it met with an erratic variety of criticism. Some critics thought the book trashy, others considered it a memorable treatment of the problem. I share the latter view, although the novel's most serious lack is that it views the problem for the most part within a narrow religious context—viewing Jewishness as primarily a religious category.

Robert Alter

SOURCE: "Sentimentalizing the Jews," in *After the Tradition: Essays on Modern Jewish Writing,* E. P. Dutton & Co., 1969, p. 35-45.

[*An American educator and critic, Alter has published highly respected studies of Stendhal, American Jewish writers, and the picaresque novel. In the following essay, which was originally published in 1965, he describes the ways in which a "sentimental literary myth of the Jew" has been promulgated in contemporary Jewish-American literature.*]

The peculiar cultural phenomenon which some choose to call an American Jewish literary renaissance is by now showing signs of having overstayed its critical welcome: one begins to suspect that too much has been made of what may not have been such a significant or valid development in the first place. There is no question that a great many writers now active in America are of Jewish descent.

This hardly justifies, however, those critics, readers, publishers, members of the organized Jewish community, and a few of the writers themselves, who all insist on the Jewish character of this literary activity in order to give weight to both its contemporary and traditional implications.

It ought to be self-evident, first of all, that a literary renaissance can take place only where there is a general cultural milieu alive enough to nourish an original, distinctive literature. A case in point is the extraordinary flowering of Hebrew poetry in Spain from the eleventh to the fourteenth centuries—a movement which has been seized on by some overly optimistic Jewish observers as an analogy for contemporary Jewish writing in this country. But a genius like Shmuel Hanagid, the poet-vizier of eleventh-century Granada, transcended his Arabic models in his contemplative personal lyrics and in his great battle poems not because of some mysterious Jewish "sensibility," but because his imagination could draw freely and variously on a living literary tradition that ran from Genesis to the Responsa. A necessary precondition for the literary renaissance created by Hanagid and his successors was a deeply rooted autonomous Jewish culture which could supply these sources of significant innovation from within the larger context of Arabic secular culture.

By contrast, the so-called renaissance of American Jewish literature has come into being out of what is, from the Jewish point of view, almost a complete cultural vacuum. Given the general state of Jewish culture in America, it is quite understandable that nearly all the American Jews who have become writers are just like other Americans, if not even more so. The typical involvement in Jewish culture consists of an acquaintance with *gefilte* fish and crass *bar mitzvahs,* a degree of familiarity with overstuffed Jewish matriarchs, and a mastery of several pungent Yiddish synonyms for the male organ. With such a cultural heritage at his command, the American Jewish writer is vaguely expected to produce imaginative work rich in Jewish moral insights, alive with Jewish fantasy, humor, and pathos, in a prose whose varied textures will reproduce the exciting differentness of "marginal" experience.

One of the stories in *Roar Lion Roar,* a first volume of fiction by Irvin Faust, includes a delightful incident that can be taken as a paradigm for the predicament of many American Jewish writers, especially the younger ones who have begun to publish recently. Myron Leberfeld, the teen-age protagonist of "Miss Dorothy Thompson's American Eaglet," has ventured forth from his native Brooklyn, impelled by wartime patriotism, to work on a Vermont farm. There he is confronted—for in such a setting, nothing less than a confrontation could be expected—by the inevitable farmer's daughter, who is, of course, a piece of quintessential America: backwoodsy, big-busted, good-natured, and irrevocably naïve. Rita Ann, a hospitable girl in any case, is thrilled by the idea of having so exotic a creature as a Jew in her own home. But she inadvertently confounds the newcomer when she turns to him with the request, "Myron, talk Jew to me." Myron, with a knowledge of "Jew" scarcely larger than Rita Ann's, rummages through his memory and finally seizes on a phrase recalled from a favorite German record of his aunt's: "Ish leeba Dick," he pronounces mysteriously.

> The effect was exhilarating. "Oh," Rita Ann moaned softly, "say that again."
>
> "Ish . . . leeba . . . Dick."
>
> "Oooh. What's it mean?"
>
> This I remembered, at least to a point. "I love you . . . Dick."

Faust, whose stories are refreshingly free of portentiousness, does not mean this encounter to symbolize anything, but the analogy to his generation of American Jewish writers is in some cases painfully close. These younger writers, appearing as they do after the successes of Bellow, Malamud, and Roth in the fifties and especially now after the spectacular popularity of *Herzog* and the remarkable revival of *Call It Sleep,* often end up playing the role of a pseudoexotic Myron opposite the American reading public's gaping Rita Ann. The one quality which seems most to distinguish Jewish writing in this country is its growing self-consciousness about its own Jewishness. Everyone is by now aware of the fact that literary Jewishness has become a distinct commercial asset, and at least Bellow and Isaac Bashevis Singer have shown that it can be an artistic resource as well. Some of the younger writers thus feel called upon to "talk Jew" in their fiction, but, unlike Myron in the story, they do not seem to realize either their own ignorance or the falseness of their position.

The one quality which seems most to distinguish Jewish writing in this country is its growing self-consciousness about its own Jewishness. Everyone is by now aware of the fact that literary Jewishness has become a distinct commercial asset.

— *Robert Alter*

One clear symptom of this general condition are the palpably ersatz touches of Jewish local color that have been appearing with increasing frequency in recent novels and stories—garbled Yiddish, misconstrued folklore, plainly impossible accounts of synagogue services and religious observances. Faust again offers a convenient model in his "Jake Bluffstein and Adolph Hitler." The story is transparently a *conte à thèse* about Jewish self-hatred and the Jew's fascination with moral qualities dramatically antithetical to his own. This schematic presentation of a complex psychological phenomenon is embarrassingly inept because Jake Bluffstein, as even his name suggests, has been imagined with no more individuality or ethnic authenticity than the stereotyped Jew of a tired anecdote. Jake Bluffstein's thought and speech are flavored, if that is really the right word, with an oddly limited set of Yiddishisms—the usual obscenities, and a few words like *shikkah* (which Faust seems to think is Yiddish for "drunk") and *tzoris* (which is construed as a singular noun). The place of worship Bluffstein frequents is an androgynous sort of affair that is sometimes described as an old-fashioned *shul* and alternately spoken of as a "temple" with an Americanized rabbi. The entire story was obviously a mistake on Faust's part—he does considerably better with other materials—but it is a mistake which illustrates the compromised position into which many American Jewish writers have worked themselves.

In more general terms, what has happened over the last decade is that a new sentimental literary myth of the Jew has gained what appears to be general acceptance in American fiction and criticism. A sentimental literary myth usually represents the failure of a culture to come to terms with some vital aspect of its own life; most often, the culture responds to its own inadequacy by projecting its secret fears, its unadmitted desires or illusory fantasies of itself onto a patently unreal image of a figure from another culture. (One has only to recall the image of the South- or East-European slinking through Victorian fiction, dark, sultry, sexually potent and attractive, an embodiment of bold and perhaps unsettling possibilities of freedom.) Such myths are sentimental because they are not live responses to any observable realities but rather sets of contrivances—stock situations, characters, and images—intended to produce certain desired emotions or predetermined states of imagination.

To understand how a sentimental myth about the Jew has been fostered in recent American literature, we have to remind ourselves that the so-called American Jewish writers are—with rare exceptions—culturally American in all important respects and only peripherally or vestigially Jewish. It seems to me that this elementary fact needs a great deal of emphasis. We are accustomed to admiring the marginal man's supposed advantage in perspectives on the disparate worlds he straddles: so many great modern writers have been outsiders, the argument runs, and this has been preeminently true of the Jews. But the fact is that the role of the Jew—and especially the intellectual Jew—as an outsider in American life has generally dwindled into an affectation or a stance of pious self-delusion.

Ironically, what most American Jewish writers are outsiders to is that very body of Jewish experience with which other Americans expect them to be completely at home. The result of this reversed situation is a reversal of the critical perspective which is an outsider's proverbial birthright. That is, the American writer of Jewish descent finds himself utilizing Jewish experience of which he is largely ignorant, and so the Jewish skeletons of his characters are fleshed with American fantasies about Jews. The result is a kind of double sentimental myth: the Jew emerges from this fiction as an imaginary creature embodying both what Americans would like to think about Jews and what American Jewish intellectuals would like to think about themselves. From the larger American point of view, the general assent to the myth of the Jew reflects a decay of belief in the traditional American literary heroes—the eternal innocent, the tough guy, the man in quest of some romantic absolute—and a turning to the supposed aliens in our midst for an alternative image of the true American.

Leslie Fiedler has for years been an ideologue of the new sentimental myth; *Back to China,* his most recent novel, because it illustrates the myth with the engaging clarity of a well-drawn comic strip, marks out most of the important guidelines that both generations of American Jewish writers seem to be using for their literary ideal of the Jew. Baro Finklestone, the hero of Fiedler's novel, is, predictably, an archetypal outsider—a Jew in Montana, an intellectual among the hicks, a square despite himself among hipsters, and so forth. Like all Jews who are allowed to be the protagonists of novels, Finklestone is an inveterate *shlemiel,* but in his very ineffectuality and muddleheadedness, he is also—Fiedler must insist—morally sensitive in a way that others are not. He is not just a well-meaning, perennially protesting liberal; he really cares about other human beings, he carries the world's guilt on his shoulders, and he is driven to a sort of self-immolation in an attempt to expiate that guilt. This last touch, incidentally, introduces the by-now-familiar motif of the Jew as Christ, which itself is a good indication of the degree to which the fantasy-image of the Jew in American fiction is American and Christian in its deepest imaginings.

Finklestone, as a moral preceptor without real disciples, also illustrates one version of the fashionable archetype with diagrammatic neatness in being a father in quixotic search of a son. (Here Leopold Bloom lurks in the background.) Since we no longer like to take our moral preceptors straight, Fiedler supplies his with elaborate camouflage. Finklestone is a compassionate and honest man—in the bed of his best friend's wife; a seeker for the truth—through the agency of mescaline. Like the heroes of many American Jewish novels, he alternates between the role of the zany and that of an updated version of the Hebrew sage, "caught between the impulse to play the clown and a resolve to act the professor." But one begins to suspect that the former role is intended mainly to make the latter more palatable. I, at any rate, become skeptical when Fiedler writes of his archetypal exiled hero that there is a "trace of something oriental about him which had made him feel always a visible stranger in the ultimate West." This sounds perilously close to Daniel Deronda, that well-meant but silly Gentile fantasy of the Jew as Mysterious Stranger, a dark, exotic figure from the East who has been through the crucible of suffering and emerged a creature of saintly gentleness, with unguessed inner stores of moral wisdom.

The general formula, in fact, for the Jew as literary hero in this new version of an old sentimental myth is Daniel Deronda with cap and bells, Daniel Deronda in the cool world or on the dissident fringes of academia, perhaps flouting conventional morality, certainly talking and acting bizarrely, but Daniel Deronda nevertheless. Whatever the particular twists, he is a man with a luminous past and a great if desperate dream for the future, his heritage of suffering and survival providing him with a unique adeptness in the ultimate science of knowing how to be.

Earl Rovit's *The Player King,* a first novel published in 1965, could serve as a textbook introduction to this whole literary image of the Jew. Rovit is a novelist with dazzling verbal gifts (in sharp contrast to all the other new writers) and with an artistic self-consciousness that is occasionally an asset but more often a serious impediment to his writing. His novel is framed by opening and concluding dialogues between the author and a Yiddish-accented alter ego. Moreover, there is an inner frame, the journal of a novelist who is presumably writing the principal story; and inserted between chapters of what one hesitantly calls the novel itself are parodies of imagined reviews of the book and a *Paris Review* interview with the author of *The Player King.* In all this literary talk, which is sometimes very bright and often quite funny, Rovit suggestively characterizes the myth in which his characters are caught up in and out of which he—"vaudevillian of the interior consciousness . . . crucified clown of the esthetic high wire"—has contrived a distinctive narrative mode.

According to Rovit, or rather one of his several personae, the two great myths of Christian literature, Christ and Faust, the Victim and the Victimizer, are dead, and their place is now taken by the myth of the Jew, at once a grotesque figure of fun and an uncanny shaman-hero:

> The Wandering Jew has taken off his cloak (the mysterious greasy black of the ghetto, the usurer's pit, the worn entrails of the peddler's pack) and he is naked revealed for the first time. There is a white scar on his side which has sealed into a pious caricature of the comic mask. . . . The feet are strangely pale and long-boned, and he rolls from heel to ball in dark reminiscence of the Mourner's Chant.

There is unresolved irony here: it is hard to know just what is meant seriously and what satirically. This very irresolution is Rovit's way of hanging onto both the grotesque mask and the sentimental image behind the mask. But the mythicized Jew, sheltering in that "mysterious greasy black of the ghetto," is clearly present both in this passage and elsewhere in the novel, for all the ingenious disguises Rovit provides him.

"Mysterious" is notoriously a dangerous word to use in a novel, even half-ironically. It is usually a sign that the novelist is in some way asking us to assume complexities of feeling which his art has not in fact been able to evoke. In this connection, there is a very funny moment in *The Player King* which inadvertently points to the core of hollowness in the fashionable mythic version of the Jew. The protagonist discovers that the zipper of his fly won't close, and, shielding himself with a copy of *Ebony,* he makes his way to the nearest tailor, who he finds has just locked up for the day. When the little old Jew refuses to open the door, the stricken hero explains that "It's worse than trouble, it's tzoris I got." This is the magic tribal password: the door swings open and the tailor, grinning, answers, "Trouble is trouble, but tzoris—dat's someding else."

But is it really? The two words, of course, were created in different historical circumstances, each was gradually molded into its own particular contours of meaning by different kinds of experience. But the pressure of collective experience that has shaped the Yiddish word is scarcely present in Rovit's book: it is the word itself which is waved like a magic wand, just as in this and other novels the name or idea of the Jew is invoked and the naked invocation is expected to conjure up all sorts of images, from epiphany to pogrom, of a unique history and a unique moral heritage.

One of the most bizarre expressions of the sentimentality of this myth is the motif of conversion or quasi-conversion that has been improbably cultivated in American Jewish fiction. The model, of course, is the circumcision of Frank Alpine at the end of Malamud's *The Assistant*. There is something instructively peculiar about that act. Circumcision, after all, is a theologically serious matter; it means sealing a covenant in the flesh between a people and its God. But the idea of being a Jew in Malamud's novel—as is generally the case in American Jewish fiction—is shorthand for a set of moral abstractions: Jewishness is equated with an ethic of hard work, integrity, acceptance of responsibility, forbearance in distress, and so forth. Since there is no necessary connection between any of these qualities and being a flesh-and-blood Jew, the symbol inflicted on Frank Alpine's flesh seems gratuitous, or, rather, obtrudes as a merely symbolic contrivance.

More often, the conversion motif appears under the guise of discipleship. One clear example is the relation between Angelo DeMarco (another wayward Italian lad) and Sammy the orderly in Edward Wallant's posthumously published novel, *The Children at the Gate*. Angelo, who doesn't believe in the genuineness of feelings and would like to think of human beings as machines, is taken by Sammy on the rounds of suffering at his hospital to be taught the lesson of redemptive love. Sammy, in keeping with the general formula, has the mannerisms of the bizarre comedian: his mouth is full of obscenities, his past is queer and sordid, and he is generally suspect at the hospital. But of course he has a real Jewish Heart, and for all his bizarreness he is a true Jew, which, as one often discovers in American Jewish fiction, means that he turns out to be a true Christ—at the end of the book Sammy, impaled on a stake outside a hospital filled with false plaster Christs, imparts through his death the redeeming agony of love and life to Angelo. *The Children at the Gate* manages to be a moving book, but it would have been more completely honest, I think, if its ethical guide had more authentic credentials for his role than a command of Yiddish slang and a ghetto childhood.

Perhaps the most ingenious variant of the conversion motif is the metamorphosis of Nick Lapucci into Lipshitz in Jerome Charyn's recently published second novel, *On the Darkening Green*. (The Italians may begin to wonder why they should be made the object of all this fictional missionary zeal. Perhaps it is simply a matter of sociological convenience, since Italian and Jewish neighborhoods have often bordered on or overlapped each other.) Nick Lapucci has from the outset some suspiciously Semitic features: he is bookish, unathletic, an outsider in a neighborhood of tough (Jewish) kids, and, of course, he is something of a *shlemiel*. So he is ripe for symbolic conversion when he takes a job as counselor-jailer at a Jewish school for delinquent and retarded boys in upstate New York.

The requisite Jewish elements of grotesqueness are generously multiplied and unusually contorted in this novel. The upstate institution is run like a concentration camp by its director, Uncle Nate, a self-deluded sadist and Jewish chauvinist, a sort of comic-gothic version of Faust's Jake Bluffstein, the Jewish Nazi. Probably the most important person for Nick on the school's staff is Rosencrantz, who works for Uncle Nate as part-time chaplain, part-time chauffeur, and full-time thorn-in-the-side. A defrocked rabbi, he is one of the stock types of the new sentimental myth of the Jew, possessing in fine balance through his heretical-clerical status all the necessary qualities of grotesqueness and moral insight. He is way outside institutional Judaism, yet significantly linked with it. He is utterly unillusioned, yet he ultimately evinces faith in the possibility of becoming human. Though a lost soul himself, he somehow manages to be a guide to others. Virtually crazy, he is nevertheless reliable in teaching his Torah of stubborn survival and of the seductive danger of hate and violence to all men, the persecuted as well as their persecutors.

Nick's eventual success in becoming part of the weird society of wayward and deranged Jewish boys means, predictably, his entrance into the sphere of significant moral experience. The rebellion in which he participates with them is the moral climax of the novel because it demonstrates that real solidarity is possible and that people can muster enough concern for their own human dignity to protest being deprived of it. Charyn handles his bizarre moral microcosm imaginatively, but his inclination to treat the novel as parable unfortunately encourages the tendencies inherent in the sentimental myth to schematize and simplify moral issues. And his enlisting a Jewish group to serve as moral paradigm reinforces the fashionable conception of the Jew as primarily a symbolic entity: to become truly human one must become True Israel, like the elect in the Book of John.

Hugh Nissenson's *A Pile of Stones*, another recent first volume of fiction, is worth mentioning because it provides such a striking contrast to all the books we have been considering. Nissenson is, as far as I can recall, the only genuinely religious writer in the whole American Jewish group. His fiction represents an attempt to follow the twisting, sometimes treacherous ways between God and man; his stories reach out for Jewish experience in Eastern Europe, in Israel, and in America, in an effort to discover what Jews do with their faith in a God who so often seems conspicuous by His absence. Where other Jewish writers haul in forefathers by their pious beards to provide scenic effect or symbolic suggestiveness, the introduction of such figures in Nissenson's work is an act of serious self-examination: can the God of the kaftaned grandfather still be the God of the buttoned-down grandson, especially with the terrible shadow of the Holocaust intervening between then and now?

This exploratory relationship to Jewishness reflects an order of imaginative integrity lacking in the writers who end up merely using Jewishness, but it is not without its own artistic difficulties. Religious fiction—witness Graham Greene—is often problematic: it is probably easier on the whole to talk precisely and persuasively about encounters with transcendence in poetry than in narrative prose. Nissenson's fiction, moreover, seems to suffer from some of the intrinsic limitations of the modern intellectual's religion-in-the-head, culled from the pages of Buber, Heschel, Herberg, Tillich, Niebuhr, and the rest. There is an odd element of abstractness in his stories; they read like neatly arranged laboratory situations for testing out a series of problems of faith and theodicy. But whatever the drawbacks of this kind of writing, one senses that it is about something real, and that there is a necessary connection between the Jewishness of its subjects and what it has to say.

Nissenson, however, is obviously a rather special case. *A Pile of Stones* offers welcome relief but hardly an indication of a change in the current trend of American Jewish fiction. It allows one to hope for more writers who will try in varying ways to observe the Jew as a real human being, but what seems immediately in prospect is a continuing parade of Jews as holy sufferers, adepts of alienation, saintly buffoons, flamboyant apostles of love—in all the twisted, grinning masks of a literary convention that keeps literature from making imaginative contact with reality.

THEMES IN JEWISH-AMERICAN FICTION

Melvin H. Bernstein

SOURCE: "Jewishness, Judaism, and the American-Jewish Novelist," in *The Chicago Jewish Forum,* Vol. 23, No. 4, Summer, 1965, pp. 275-82.

[*In the following essay, Bernstein characterizes the half-century between the publication of* The Rise of David Levinsky *and* Herzog *as a period of waiting "to rediscover in Judaistic values the definition of the worth of self, heart, mind, and society."*]

Today the Jewish writer is the subject of scrutiny in Germany, in England, and in America. On the East Coast he is studied in the Jewish-supported *Commentary;* on the West Coast he is studied in the Catholic-supported *Ramparts.* Last year the Jewish Publication Society (Philadelphia) not only issued Irving Malin and Irwin Stark's *Breakthrough,* an anthology of thirty-one American Jewish writers but also Oscar Janowsky's edited collection of essays by many hands, *The American Jew, A Reappraisal.* For the 1964-65 season the New York City 92nd Street YMHA-YWHA has advertised a ten-lecture series on American Jewish novelists by Dr. Eugene Borowitz.

To Dr. Janowsky's book professor Marie Syrkin (Brandeis) contributes an essay, "Jewish Awareness Literature," in which she writes: "One must conclude a survey of the American Jewish novel with the unhappy reflection that for many of the ablest of its sons, 'being Jewish' has become a dry well." Regrettably, prof. Syrkin had formulated her conclusion before the publication of Saul Bellow's *Herzog.* It is precisely Bellow's deep, full well meaning that controverts her statement. The development that

brings us to Bellow is a significant chapter in American life and literature.

Before Abraham Cahan published *The Rise of David Levinsky* in 1917 the Jew in America was a literary accident not an essence, as Leslie Fiedler points out in his Herzl Institute pamphlet, *The Jew in the American Novel* (1959). In nineteenth-century American literature he was potential, rarely kinetic, as in the short stories of Hawthorne, in his *The Marble Faun,* in Melville's and Longfellow's poetry, and, according to Edmund Wilson's *A Piece of My Mind,* in the curious rabbinism that made some New Englanders eccentric. The Jew crossed the Atlantic a stereotype: he was a stage Shylock and a fictional Fagan, softened somewhat by Scott's Rebecca, Eliot's Daniel Deronda, and ennobled in Browning's Rabbi ben Ezra, a puzzle in Disraeli, and a fear in Dreyfus. (Browning's philo-semitism was such that there was a minor English and American magazine controversy whether or not Browning was a Jew, perhaps a Marrano. The controversy died from anoxia of facts).

Late in the century Emma Lazarus published an idealistic American request. In "The New Colossus" she pleaded: "Give me your poor, your tired, your huddled masses." Cahan's David Levinsky was one of these, not a stereotype but a steerage passenger. He was poor, huddled, but not tired.

David Levinsky of Antomir, Russia, grows up a poor Talmud student, becomes an orphan when his mother is beaten by a pogromist, gets to America, and changes from idealist to egotist, from innocent to experienced, from Talmudist to secularist, from European to American. We watch the Americanization of Jacob Riis without that Dane's energetic altruism. Cahan the Socialist had no love for Levinsky's Social Darwinist triumph, his anti-unionism, anti-socialism, and egotistical philanthropy. In Americanizing himself, Levinsky dejudaized himself. Cahan awards him success but withholds from him happiness. The Jewish immigrant novel had been born. It was to be sub-genre.

Samuel Ornitz published anonymously in 1923 *Haunch Paunch and Jowl. An Anonymous Autobiography,* a novel masked as an autobiography, adding a dimension of personal bitterness to the fiction he chose to tell with bitterness. It is an up-from-steerage, out of the East Side, up to a judgeship and on to Riverside Drive novel. Meyer Hirsch, an only son, living with a sweated garment worker father who is dying of the immigrant's occupational disease, TB, paying scant attention to his mother who yearns for respectability, assimilating the instruction not of his Cheder teacher but of his uncle Philip whose overriding desire is to be a Russian Jewish American gentleman as good as the German Jewish American gentleman (that is, to be rich)—Meyer Hirsch uses his brains to lead his gang, haggle with the fences over the stolen goods, run cases for crooked lawyers, break strikes with goons, and compromises justice by getting a bribed appointment to the judge's bench. Judaism was no deterrent to the jungle morality of America. In a chapter headnote Ornitz quotes *The Education of Henry Adams:* "neither to him nor his brothers was religion real." And Uncle Philip could define a *rov* (rabbi) as "a scholar a thousand years behind the times." On his Bar Mitzvah day Meyer can't swallow that bunk: "I puke it right back." At the end of his life he lives among the *allrightnicks* on Riverside Drive, and the be-jeweled plump women, the fat cigar-chewing men playing pinochle, among people whose religion was "a bumptious holding forth in swell temples and synagogues." At the end of the novel he wonders whether the new generation will be made as dizzy and giddy by sudden riches as his sordid generation.

The common denominator of these two American-Jewish novels is their assimilationist complaint. Both threw out the Yahweh of Moses and Isaiah, of legalism and compassionate morality. Levinsky and Hirsch turn out to be apostates and moral cripples holding on to dead twigs of the tree of life. They are Jewish victims of American life.

And life in America was a conspiracy against the Schearl family in *Call It Sleep.* The 600-page story covers the years 1911-1913, the years six to eight, in the young life of David Schearl whose father is irascible and suspicious, whose mother is resigned, resourceful and loving, whose Aunt Bertha is the salt of the earth, whose urchin friends educate him in sex, wilyness, violence, and if one is lucky, survival. It is a moving, unforgettable novel about people who happen to be Jewish immigrants, who talk Yiddish, immigrants from Europe bringing into the Golden Land their character. It is a Jewish novel not a Judaistic novel.

Its Jewishness lies in its characters acting out their destiny in translated Yiddish, doffing their European Jewishness (phylacteries, dietary laws), little by little but trying not only to maintain the family, honorable marriage, and human dignity, but also to endure with the stiff-necked humanism that lies at the core of the Jewish contract between God and man. Its sense of peopleness makes it a fiction without ideology but with an empirical theology. Genya is like her Jewish God: a creature of wide nostrils, which translates into a metaphor for long suffering. She is the Jewish mother of fiction in the tradition of Sarah, Rebecca, Rachel, and Ruth—a good woman whose value cannot be measured in pearls or rubies, split-level houses or mink stoles. To the sophisticated, she is a category: a side of the Oedipal triangle. In terms of what Saul Bellow calls "potato love," she is Al Jolson's Mammy and George Jessel's Yiddishe Momma. To David Schearl she is love.

What we have been observing chronologically in Cahan, Ornitz and Roth is the dejudaizing of the Jew. He becomes like everyone else in America. The 1930's continued the transformation of the Jew from the villages of Sholom Aleichem, Peretz, and Babel. He became Michael Gold, Albert Halper, and Howard Fast; he became the *New Masses* man. Just as the reverberations of the German Jewish Enlightenment turned the grandson of Lessing's Nathan the Wise (Rabbi Moses Mendelssohn) into Christian Felix Bartholdy Mendelssohn, so the *Aufklarung und Wahrheit* of Hegel, Marx, Trotsky, and Lenin turned American Jewish messianists against their sectarian past, and their ideological bourgeois selves. For their lost theology and messianic Zion, they substituted their own secularized, internationalized dream of the end of days. *Das Kapital* was substituted for Talmud; the cell was the *minyan* (mini-

mum congregation); the front was the congregation; and Lenin was Rashi. Emancipation from primitive religion was a delirium.

During this time a number of Robert Cohns had gone to more colleges than Princeton, but only a few of them remained to teach. It was to be a while before the literary appreciation of the fictional Leopold Bloom, the fictional Tevya, and Zero Mostel's stage Tevya were to be translated into acceptance of human beings called Bloom and Tevya. In the meantime the Jew had to cleanse himself from pacifism by fighting in World War II in the novels of Shaw and Mailer. But he still ran like Sammy Glick; and Schulberg wrote Sammy's obituary in terms of dozens of pairs of shoes, just as Fitzgerald had written Gatsby's in dozens of shirts. Herman Wouk changed his name Ehrmann to Airman, hers from Morganstern to Morningstar. And in Arthur Miller's Willy Loman and Salinger's Holden Caulfield, and especially in the Glass family, the Jew exists as an American hybrid so many times cross-pollinated that his Jewish archetypal origins are ignored. Gentiles take them to their bosoms as one of their own; and Jews say *Kaddish* (memorial prayers) for Willy Loman and Seymour Glass—killed in America, by America.

Current Jewish-American novelists are hardly through with the self-hatred created by being outside the power structure of the Golden Land first advertised by Capt. John Smith and splendidly exploited to the detriment of their Christianity by the Bildads and Pelegs, the Carnegies and Rockefellers. (Incidentally, it's a North American phenomenon. Things are not better in Canada, according to the novel of Mordecai Richler, *The Apprenticeship of Duddy Kravitz,* 1959).

Current Jewish-American novelists are hardly through with the self-hatred created by being outside the power structure of the Golden Land first advertised by Capt. John Smith and splendidly exploited to the detriment of their Christianity by the Bildads and Pelegs, the Carnegies and Rockefellers.

— *Melvin H. Bernstein*

Consider Burt Blechman's second novel, *The War of Camp Omongo* (1963).

Out of pencil scrawlings on toilet walls (jottings less poetic than Genet's prison fantasies), out of the civil war of status-seeking Jews who in their pecking order dislike Jews poorer than themselves, out of the conniving of dishonest men in the clothing business, out of the unhappy marriage of a Jewish high school math teacher to a lecherous wife, out of the summer camp business of this teacher who runs Camp Omongo for boys complete with a para-military color war that climaxes the camping season, Blechman has written a novel trite in its satire, tired in its *ersatz* plot. This is not a tentative reading of human nature comparable with William Golding's *Lord of the Flies;* rather it is a sociological document. The value on the stake is not a Jewish value; it is an American value—success. The people in the book (Levine, Oronsky, Greenberg, Bernstein) happen to have Jewish names, that's all. America—not the Jews—is on the verge of Omongo extinction is what the book is saying. This book is a look at the other side of the Cahan-Ornitz coin. If the earlier novelists portrayed the Jewish sociology of being poor in rich America, Blechman is reporting the Jewish sociology of being affluent. In addition, the camp rabbi is a fool and is treated as one. In this respect the portrayal of the ineffectual rabbi is equivalent to the ineffectual minister in Faulkner, in Updike, in Styron, and in Heller's *Catch-22.*

One realizes how big a failure Blechman's extravagant satire is when his anger is compared with the more delirious satirical humor of Bruce Jay Friedman. Friedman's two novels, *Stern* (1962) and *A Mother's Kisses* (1964) concentrate absurdly, surrealistically in parts, on two facets of Jewishness, one more Judaistic than the other. In *Stern* the story turns on Anti-Semitism; In *A Mother's Kisses* the object is the phenomenon of the Jewish mother, the modern Rebekah, the mother who tricked Isaac into blessing Jacob not Esau. It is a bold writer who would make jests remembering the six million who died of Jewishness; it is an equally bold writer who would desecrate the *Yahrzeit* (memorial) candle lit for Momma. Yet Friedman does it.

No summary does justice to *Stern,* for the point of the book is its hallucinatory verbalization of a compound *angst.* Stern, a writer of labels in an advertising agency, buys a house and moves to the commuter's suburbs with his wife and young son. One day an arrogant Gentile in the neighborhood insults Stern's wife—calls her kike— and in the altercation she either falls or is pushed so that the hostile anti-Semite looks up her skirt under which she habitually wears nothing. Stern is told about it and his inability to deal with the ethnic insult and the accidental voyeuristic aggression against his property in his wife's sexual parts both lead him to torture himself into an ulcer. Returning from a rest home he learns that his son has been insulted again. Stern decides to face his insulter, gets beaten, and stumbles home, still afraid of the man who threatens his wife's world, his son's world, and his world.

I confess to an inability to be precise about the many things that are working in this book. In the world of Job there was discourse: "Come let us reason together." In Friedman's world reason, order, cause and effect, and certitude are gone. One possible meaning is that there is no freedom from insult in the existence of the Jew—at least, not yet, not now. But before taking this one key from the key ring of many keys for the meaning, consider these two quotations:

> [His son Donald is speaking.] "Listen, do you know where we are?"
>
> "Where?" Stern said.
>
> "In God's hand; right on his pinkie, as a matter of fact."

> "Who teaches him God things?" Stern said to his wife.
>
> "The baby-sitter. She's inside."
>
> Stern said, "She shouldn't." He wanted to go inside and tell her to discontinue the God information, but he was afraid she would come after him one night with a torch-bearing army of Gentiles and tie him in a church.

And this:

> He wanted to go out of his house and say to the man who'd kiked his wife and peered between her legs, "You've got me wrong. I'm no kike. Come and see my empty house. My bank account is lean. I drive an old car, too, and Cousy thrills me at the backcourt just as you. No synagogue has seen me in ten years. It's true my hips are wide, but I have a plan for thinness. I'm no kike."

According to this *reducto ad absurdum,* according to Friedman, a Jew is any man who is like every irreligious American around him, but for some irrational non-Jewish reason gets *angst* when he is called a kike. *Stern* is a novel of social cruelty and comic distortion suggesting the domestic nonsense of Norman Simpson's *A Resounding Tinkle* and Ionesco's *The Bald Soprano,* Salinger's short story "De Daumier—Smith's Blue Period," and the *Complete Works* of Nathanael West, with Friedman extending their satiric revulsion by his fertile scatology.

The core of Friedman's second novel, *A Mother's Kisses,* is as deceptively economical as his first. Seventeen-year old Joseph hangs around Brooklyn that summer waiting for the mail to bring him an acceptance into college. He receives rejections. His mother Meg takes over his college problem. Sinking her untiring mind (and perhaps her indefatigable body) into that of a retired Navy officer who has college entrance connections, Meg gets her son into Kansas Land Grant Agricultural College. And that isn't all. She takes him there, delivers him to class, makes friends with fraternity men who've invited Joseph to their house. Having achieved her mother's wish—to see her son in the Gentile world of Kansas Land Grant Agricultural, in a city where there are, thank God, some Jewish cab drivers.

This is Jewish Momism, bringing up Father and children, and bringing the whole world as tribute to her son by extraordinary feats of family technology and social engineering. This is the Jewish world of food, clothes (she wears Toreador pants), hennaed hair, mountain resorts, health, specialists (not doctors), conniving (ostentatious tipping averts the evil decree of anti-Semitic prejudice), imaginative cursing, and giving lip service to the posture of bowed head bent to the Wailing Wall but secretly having the strength of a Caterpillar earthmover that turns rivers from their courses. This is the Jewish mother, a Darwinian type of adaptable species fiercely overriding adversity, violently subverting the sex-survival-success myth of America to her tenacious and resilient ideal of masochistic service and sadistic mastery. She is the six days of creation in one, and for her there is never a Sabbath to her mastery, manipulating, and motherlove. *Stern* and *A Mother's Kisses* are novels not of Judaism but of Jewishness.

The bitter reassessment of Jewishness, the circling of the Judaistic living cell around which Jewishness builds its spore, is painfully, satirically, compassionately, and savagely explored in the fiction of Norman Fruchter, Bernard Malamud, and Philip Roth.

Norman Fruchter's first novel, *Coat Upon a Stick* (1962), covers the day of a nameless 68-year old man living on the East Side of New York, a shamos (sexton) in a synagogue, a father of a married son Carl who has a son David and lives in New Jersey. Ritually observant, comforted by his rabbi, befriended by his cronies, looked after by his son, the old man is locked up in his mind, haunted by retributive thoughts. In Russia he had got a girl pregnant and palmed her off on an innocent man; he had promised the man who agreed to take him to America to work for him for passage money; instead, he stole his benefactor's heirloom silver and pawned it; working in a butcher shop he made false weights, stole the over-price he charged; he had married for advancement, was never tender to his wife who died in childbirth. To this day he steals: tea and crackers from the supermarket, and a Yiddish paper, the *Forward,* from the newspaper stand.

Although the old man has violated all of the 613 Commandments of the Torah, yet he is bitter toward his son for not being ritually exacting in the education of grandson David. After an unhappy visit with his father and accompanied by David, Carl is home in New Jersey talking with Millie, his wife:

> What'd he pick on David about?

> Oh, the usual thing. Wanted to know how often David went to synagogue, whether he laid *tephillin* (phylacteries) and all. I said it wasn't fair to ask David, so then he jumped on me. Said it was my fault. Said I was bringing David up to be a goy. . . .

A few minutes later Carl asks:

> Does it ever worry you, the way we're bringing David up? You think maybe we're doing something wrong? You think he's not Jewish enough?

> Oh, Carl, he's Jewish enough, for God's sake. It's bad enough you have to go see the old man, you don't have to take him seriously.

Is he Jewish enough? What (among other things) Fruchter is asking is: what is the connection between religious ritual (one form of Jewishness, a controversial Judaistic essence) and morality? The old man is not a scheming hypocrite. Praying the counsel of perfection three times a day, yet he has sinned against man and Torah, and lives sheltered under the wings of the Temple lions who guard the Torah. Whether or not Fruchter wants to show the inability of institutionalized religion to reach precisely down to the old heart of man, unable to give him the "new heart" of self-knowledge, atonement, and moral reconstruction, I am not sure. But the Judaistic essence of the book is this: the God of Moses is in tension with the God of the prophets; Law and the spirit of the Law are at odds in the body and

spirit of man. And man—the Jewish man without intercessor—must keep peace between himself and God by keeping peace, justice, and mercy with his fellow man, and by striving against the imperfections of his compulsive flesh. Nor is it America that has corrupted the old man; he was a scoundrel in heart and mind in Europe. The novel is less Jewish than it is Judaistic. It is a morality novel not a novel of mores.

Bernard Malamud's old man, Morris Bober, in *The Assistant* (1958) is in many ways the vital opposite of Fruchter's old man. He is the normative Jew (whose ethos not his sociology is his Jewishness) living a marginally successful life, enterprisingly incompetent to get rich, doggedly persisting in giving service, credit to customers, and charity to the poor; he forgives, he forgets, he endures. He is the education of the Christian Frank Alpine, his store assistant, who enters his life as a hooligan and ends the novel as a repentant, learning service and self-denial, experiencing atonement and community and undergoing the circumcision of his heart. Circumcision has moot origins but one thing it did. It served to divide truth from error, the monotheists from the idolators. Idolatry is many things but one thing it is. It treats things as if they were people. Judaism ever repudiates this. God is not a thing. People are not things. And Frank Alpine had to learn that Morris Bober, his daughter Helen, and even Frank Alpine himself were not things. They were people, related not to an idol but to other people and to God.

Malamud's fiction (*Idiot's First, A New Life*) for all its experimentalism with sober fantasy, zany fantasy, and its locations in Rome, New York, or the West Coast, is richly veined with Jewishness. Its bigger arteries carry transplanted European Yiddish and close to Judaistic affirmative values. The Jew emerges as a folkhero, now saint now rogue, but always carrying on his tough back the heavy peddler's pack of sorrow in every land, in every time, time without end. His task is ever to wrestle with the Angel of Death and win not the whole match but at least a fall. The Chosen People must choose and wisdom says (as in the title of one of Malamud's stories), "Life is better than death." Much of Malamud's fiction explores the tragicomedy of choosing.

No such tenderness inhabits the fiction of Philip Roth. He is appalled by American life. Writing in *Commentary* (March, 1961) on the difficulties of writing American fiction, Roth observed:

> The American writer in the middle of the 20th Century has his hands full in trying to understand and, then describe, and then make *credible* much of the American reality. It stupefies, it sickens, it infuriates. . . . The actuality is continually outdoing our talents. Who could have invented Charles Van Doren, Cohn and Schine, Eisenhower in Columbia?

His disgust is less controlled than Malamud's either by taking thought, or using benign and healing humor, or expressing a poetized compassion. His anger is expressed in chiaroscuro, in desperation, and in mercilessness.

In the novella, *Goodbye, Columbus* Roth scores the Americanized Jewish life of the Newark rich, although the Columbus of the story is Columbus, Ohio. In Roth's short fiction, the beatings of a cheder rabbi drive a little boy desperate. A World War II Jewish soldier uses his Jewishness to get favors from sergeants and congressmen and tries to get his name off a shipping list. The moving of a Hasidic school to a largely-free-of-Jews-New-York-City suburb drives one Jew in Woodenton to a nervous breakdown. The troubled characters in this tedious novel, *Letting Go* (1962), are not helped by their Jewishness; indeed, they are further demoralized. Gabe Wallach, the Jamesian observer of, and participant in, this Judaeo-American debacle, is helpless to ameliorate the condition, for he is quite dejudaized himself. Libby, one of the tortured women in the novel, says, "You're a hundred percent right, religion is very important to a child. But . . . my husband and I don't believe a God damn bit of it." *Letting Go* is not an able novel, not well written, not clear. Its mood is destructive and agnostic, renouncing the possibility that Jewish balm can come out of the American-Jewish Gilead.

The mood is different in the fiction of Saul Bellow, in *Herzog.* Suffering the Ten Plagues of spiritual distress, twice-divorced Moses Elkanah Herzog, Ph.D., University of Chicago, wanders in the dark Egypt of bondage to love of flesh and ideas and through the blooming desert of self-examination. He writes unmailed letters addressed to persons in the modern world of change, and compulsively fondles the blooming, prickly cacti of memory. Doggedly he seeks the milk of love and the honey of ideas. That is the story.

The plot of *Herzog* is contained in the unmailed letters Herzog writes in this novel. It is a testing of the Jewish definition of life and living, of purpose and death in the world—nothing less. It is a novel of ancient belief tested against modernism in the person of Herzog. The total sensibility of Herzog is Judaistic. His mind is rich in Biblical allusions, many of them parodies. Herzog's God identified Himself to Moses as I AM THAT I AM. And Moses Herzog several times in the book says of himself "he was what he was." From this stems his agony: can he be what he wants himself to be? How does one in the twentieth century translate the injunction: "Thou shalt love the Lord with all thy heart, with all thy soul, with all thy might?" Does man bring on his fate by too much willing and wanting with all his might?

For the American-Jewish world of affection, self-pity, Cadillacs, and yearning for the old time Orthodox religion of *shuls* and *chazans* not cantors and temples, Herzog has compassionate understanding. But it is Herzog's Jewish mind that rejects the doctrine of the First Fall of Man, Heidegger's Second Fall of Man, the scientific assertion that no certitude can be reached in questions of value, the notion that universal space destroys human value, the Freudian assertion that the mind is merely tropistic, and the Hegelian assertion that man is the cork that bobs in the stream of determinism. As a Jew he believes that his "own actions has historic importance." As a Jew, he believes in "personal responsibility" with its corollary of personal dignity. Herzog's mind is the Jewish mind historically at home in all civilizations but rejecting the anti-

Jewish, the non-Jewish, those values that do not affirm empirical and transcendental Judaistic values.

To the Jew Herzog reality (facts) leads to spirituality, to transcendence. To the Jew Herzog, the Jew in history although outcast, despised, persecuted, killed in numbers and by the concentration camp numbers, could still pray: *"Ma tovu ohaleha Yaakov. . . .* How goodly are thy tents, O Israel." This is optimism. As a boy, Herzog had studied in cheder the story of Cain's murder of Abel and Potiphar's wife's attempted adultery with Joseph. Life (the Bible was clear about it) had in it murder and adultery. This is realism. Yet the Jew aspired; Herzog aspired.

In these details is contained the vexatious empirical transcendentalism of the Jewish ethos. Life is hard, and yet, yet one tries, one chooses. It is important, nay, it is vital to choose. Out of the million facts of our modern fact hoard choose, but make the choice for life not for death. This is the Bible: "I call heaven and earth to witness against you this day, and I have set before thee life and death, the blessing and the curse; therefore choose life, that thou mayest live, thou and thy seed." (Deut. 30:19) And this is the way Herzog muses in accents of empirical transcendentalism and Hasidic aphorism: "His duty was to live. To be sane, and to live, and to look after the kids." "To him, perpetual thought of death was a sin." "On the knees of your soul? Might as well be useful. Scrub the floor." Significantly, his memories contain not only Yiddish but fragments of Hebrew prayers with their emphasis on life. Always life. The Jews toast each other with the words: "L-chayyim" (To life). Herzog believes that he owes to the powers that created him a human life.

Herzog's epistolary dialogue with the world includes an unmailable letter to God in whom he continues to believe "though never admitting it." He feels God in the summer ambiance of his Berkshire house and addresses Him in Abraham's obedient language, *"Hineni"* (Here I am). In his Job-like exhaustion and acceptance of self with its flawed humanness, he concludes: "But I have no arguments to make about it. 'Thou movest me.' But what do you want, Herzog? But that's it—not a solitary thing. I am pretty well satisfied to be just as it is willed, and for as long as I may remain in occupancy." The Day of Atonement of his spirit has ended. His New Year begins.

Bellow's *Herzog* came some forty-seven years after Cahan's *The Rise of David Levinsky.* In the interim, except for *Call It Sleep,* American Jewish fiction is predominantly sociology, anthropology, psychiatry, and Jewish imitations of Dreiser, Farrell, Dos Passos, Algren, Cain, Schulberg, Shaw, Wouk, and Ferber (that is, Jewish writers imitating Jewish writers who were imitating the sociological realists among Christian writers; they were Jewish writers trying to get into the Establishment). The early novelists reflected naturalism and realism. Bruce Jay Friedman uses the current American mode of the comic, but is still writing parodistic, cinematic studies of the sociology of being Jewish. Herbert Tarr's *The Conversion of Chaplain Cohen* is a *kitsch* novel, which in its "Jewishness" is comparable to the "Jewishness" of, let's say, Shelley Berman in particular and Jewish vaudeville entertainers in general.

It took some fifty years for the American-Jewish novelist to make his way in the Golden Land, to resist its assimilationist pressures for cause, and to rediscover in Judaistic values the definition of the worth of self, heart, mind, and society. Because of the success of *Herzog,* today it is less rewarding to talk of Malin and Stark's academic categories of Jewish-American fictional themes—alienation, the Old Country, the sense of past, and what all. As Herzog says, "Foo on all categories." Also, Prof. Syrkin can revise her opinion, for *Herzog* with its fictional artistry, complexity, and unity, is, today, the American Jewish novel, the culmination of the immigrant novel of fifty years ago, with Jewish here meaning not sociology but values.

Leo W. Schwarz

SOURCE: "Mutations of Jewish Values in Contemporary American Fiction," in *Tradition and Change in Jewish Experience,* edited by A. Leland Jamison, Syracuse University Press, 1978, pp. 184-97.

[In the following essay, which was originally published in 1966, Schwarz contrasts the literature of alienation with literature that affirms traditional values.]

Contemporary American novelists are preoccupied with man's condition and his attempts to find meaning in it. This preoccupation has elicited opposite responses: no one is less capable than the writer of describing his times and his contemporaries; no one has this capacity in greater degree than the writer. The literary artist, it is argued, cannot be trusted as an elucidator of man's condition and fate because on the one hand he has escaped into incomprehensible imagery and symbolism, and on the other hand he sees in man only absurdity, self-deception and insignificance. No doubt something like this has happened, but it does not follow that a writer who despairs of a world in which he sees no meaning must fail to lend reality to the segment of life he has chosen to record. True as it may be that a scientific and technological society is creating a man without values, it is also true that, science and technology notwithstanding, there are men who cherish traditional values.

Of course the probing of man's situation and his search for self-significance is not the walled-in preserve of the literary artist. Critics, philosophers, sociologists, and theologians are there to testify to the contrary, but the point is that they are concerned in the main with mankind and society; that is to say, with man collectively and metaphysically. The case is different with the literary work. It deals with individual human beings in their infinite variety and complexity, their dilemmas and delusions, their frauds and failures, their fears and faiths, their degradation and ennoblement, their coarse malignancy, and lyric tenderness. The writer's province is not statistical tables or clinical experiments or subcommittee meetings or press relations. His aim is insight, not manipulation. No one is more sensitive to the self-righteous, the sanctimonious, the fraudulent, the obscene, and quicker to express them. He uses his gifts—his sense of irony and his sense of pity—to hold the mirror up to our face, to project images of human life. He

persuades us to think, wonder, feel, and, in his best creations, to confront life at its most real levels.

All this is general, but it establishes the context in which I propose to examine traditional values and the changes they have undergone in contemporary American fiction. I mean by "values" the beliefs, ideas, and lifeways which give human life and human beings significance and meaning. I shall confine myself to certain moral values which, though not peculiar to, are essential to the Jewish structure of beliefs. It may be well to point out here that in speaking of values I employ the term "moral" rather than "ethical." Ethics is concerned with the theoretical formulation of a system of values—a speculative task for philosophers and theologians. Morality has to do with commitment to standards of conduct. You can solve ethical problems in an armchair. Moral problems are resolved in life.

I

The novels of Philip Roth and Saul Bellow provide numerous illustrations of the present-day change of values. Whether the vogue of these writers is owing to their literary talent or their ideological bent, or to their appearance at a time when literature has become big business, I do not know. That they are epicures of psychopathology and sex is doubtless part of the explanation. In any case, the characters who people their novels project a view of man and society which emphasizes that the individual is alone, forsaken, and alienated by powerful impersonal forces that grind him down to anonymity and hopelessness. Coupled with a passion for introspection and a sense of disillusionment, the positive non-belief of these novelists has made for a version of American reality that negates tradition and religion. Their books present an American version of the *Luftmensch,* Americans wallowing in confusion and misery without an ideal or value to their name. Specifically, these writers are engaged in assaulting the American middle-class and middle-brow, and since American Jews are practically or potentially middle-class, and Jewish characters fill their pages, the gallery of Jews they portray seem like figures embalmed in pop art—rootless, neurotic, frozen in a scatological daymare. They see in man only absurdity, self-deception, and insignificance.

Philip Roth has given us, in his *Letting Go,* the alphabet and syntax of the alienated American, both Gentile and Jewish. All the characters in the book are trapped in lives of noisy desperation. Whether in Chicago or New York, the atmosphere in which they live is polluted to the point of suffocation. Roth shows with remarkable psychological insight how the involvement of the four principal characters with each other is a process of pushing and pulling in which each is letting go of his past and of the values associated with that past. They are like young teenagers who are torn between self-dependence and over-dependence, and haunted by excessive feelings of personal guilt. As the emotional intensity is built up to a nerve-wracking pitch, childhood values and loyalties disappear as if in a cauldron. Paul Herz says, in talking of his planned marriage to a Catholic girl, "She's a Catholic like I'm a Jew. It's not the kind of thing that'll have much to do with our lives. It hasn't to do with us. It's another ruse." The protagonist, Gabe Wallach, intelligent, rich, and well-intentioned, who is drawn capriciously into the lives of the Herzes and Martha Regenhart, avoids full involvement and is conscience-stricken because he cannot let go and become responsible for the health and security of others. In the last pages of the book, Gabe is free of his involvements: he has escaped to London, but he remains the slave of his incapacity to cope with his guilt and has nothing to cling to. He has no values and hence no moral choice.

Although Bellow's *Herzog* appears to be a more philosophical work, it is nevertheless just as clinical as *Letting Go*. The mind of Moses Herzog is a willed chaos—a chaos that is death to human relationships; his utterances are piffle rather than philosophy. He is frustrated, angry, defeated, or more to the point, self-defeating. He wallows in emotional and intellectual sludge. He thinks freedom is only "a howling emptiness." He, too, has "let go" of traditional values, and he has nothing with which to replace them. The best he can do is to investigate "the social meaning of nothingness." Man has made his bed of neuroses, and he must lie in it. Herzog's definition of truth reveals his distorted sense of life. "Truth is true only as it brings down more disgrace and dreariness upon human beings," he writes, "so that if it shows anything except evil it is illusion." Is Herzog searching for truth or succumbing to chaos? What is evident in his neurotic epistoloquacity is something other than rebellion, skepticism or iconoclasm. It is his failure to accommodate to the human community. The world of Herzog is first bent and then broken.

Alienation is the child of nihilism. Paradoxically, these writers regard alienation as the condition of being Jewish. Leslie Fiedler has stated this pointedly: "Jewishness means . . . not to belong; to be alienated." This, in essence, is a new kind of *galut*, a *galut* that rejects everything including the Jewish doctrine of *galut*. No wonder the alienationist writers regard Judaism as an anachronism. Knowingly or not, they are engaged in devaluating all human values. They are unable to believe in a reality that is not physical, sexual, or visceral. If the identification of Jewishness with nihilism has a precedent in the 3,500 year tradition of Jewish literature, I do not know of it.

II

If the apostles of the doctrine of alienation have expressed the dejudaization of the American Jew, certain other novelists in vogue can see the Americanization of the Jew in the light of what amounts to caricature. Writers who came to the fore in the fifties and sixties seem to expressed the condition portrayed in Meyer Levin's *The Old Bunch* (1937), showing perhaps a deepening of the process of accommodation to American mores and morality. Two instructive examples are Marjorie Morningstar, the coed who wants to make the borscht circuit and have suburbia too, and Richard Amsterdam, a kind of male Marjorie Morningstar and Harvard playboy whose ideals are the Hasty Pudding Club and having a beautiful gentile wife and ten thousand a year (*Remember Me To God,* 1957). The worlds of Herman Wouk and Richard Kaufmann swarm with Americanized versions of *schlemeils, schleppers,* and *paskudnyaks.* Those who speak for traditional Jewish ideals, like Richard's father and Marjorie's uncle, are the only characters who win the reader's sympathy.

But their views are deprived of any intellectual or moral force.

Few observers will deny the impact of American mores upon Jews, as portrayed by Wouk, Kaufmann and dozens of other popular novelists. Richly illustrative in this regard is Broadway's fiddling with Sholom Aleichem. *Fiddler on the Roof,* certainly an amusing, successful musical, is nevertheless false to Sholom Aleichem's *Tevye the Milkman.* The Broadway Tevye is made over into a permissive father who blesses the marriage of his daughter to an apostate. The original Tevye would neither have blessed nor condoned the marriage, however painful his decision. The Broadway Tevye is transformed into an oafish, peasant-like, hip-swinging, hen-pecked fellow whose faith is tailored to titillate the *amharazus de luxe* of the devotees of musicals. He is a purveyor of wise-cracks rather than sober wisdom. The line spoken to God on Broadway, "I don't have to tell you what the Good Book says," is jazz for "I don't have to tell you what the *Gemora* says." The original Tevye is a spiritual descendant of the Biblical Job, protesting life's injustice and affirming man's moral integrity—an affirmation enshrined in Jewish tradition and traceable to Mt. Sinai, as Tevye knows and his bellowing Broadway counterpart does not.

We shall have to look elsewhere for that part of American reality which reveals the attempt by Jews to establish traditional Jewish values on American soil. An illuminating example is the series of engrossing novels by Charles Angoff, which began with *Journey to the Dawn* in 1951 and passed its middle point with the sixth volume, *Summer Storm,* in 1963. The protagonist, David Polansky, and his proliferating family emigrate from Russia to Boston, where they endure the trials of economic hardship and social adjustment. Angoff is no less aware than Bellow and Roth of the corrosive effect of American life upon the Jewish family and tradition. Yet the Polanskys, for all the diversity of their viewpoints and the new roles of the second and third generations, remain rooted in Jewish life. They have regard for the Puritan-oriented culture of Boston. They revere the great representatives of American liberalism—figures like Woodrow Wilson and Louis D. Brandeis. In no way does this accommodation to American life obscure or downgrade Jewish culture and values. The Polanskys maintain their family integrity, employ Hebrew and Yiddish as living tongues, venerate education, respect law and justice, and are deeply mindful of human dignity. By a natural and healthy identification with Jewish values, the Polanskys are, according to their endowments and talents, conservators of Jewish cultural values.

Moreover, the Polanskys are not grotesque aberrations or wistful abstractions. Whether they are secularist or religious, their lives are informed and inspired by the traditional values—freedom, justice, law, goodness, learning, and compassion with its religious and moral bearings. These values are real and are expressed in human and communal relationships. Ben Gurion and Eric Fromm notwithstanding, the perpetuation of the structure of Jewish values requires something more than that we be upright and humane. The moral essences of Jewish culture, whether sanctioned by religion or humanism, require an institutional expression of shared beliefs and values.

How these values become merely verbal labels, emptied of their essence, can be illustrated by the present vogue of "compassion" in American fiction, especially in the tough, realistic novels. It would seem that compassion is lavished on the neurotic, the hipster, the whore, and an assortment of "sad cryptograms." What these practitioners of realism suggest is a phony compassion for ineffable delinquents. This amounts to the exploitation of human degradation for commercial ends rather than the sense of human tragedy. For compassion, in the traditional sense, is *rachmanut:* derived from *rechem,* the womb, the very matrix of life, compassion is a discriminating sympathy for human suffering, tempered by an understanding of pain and tragedy. True compassion requires a generous view of life and a standard of values. The compassionate man lives within a moral framework. He recognizes the gap between the man that he is and the man he can be.

All this is especially evident in the stories of Bernard Malamud. His characters are inept, hard-pressed, and sometimes obnoxious, yet they rise above the cruel pressures of their existence. They have an indomitable will to survive. Malamud invests these sad failures with pathos and dignity. His writing is instinct with the profoundest virtue of the Jewish spirit—a healing tenderness and loving compassion.

III

The world of Isaac Bashevis Singer's novels and stories is rooted in the soil of Jewish tradition. His symbolism is of a pre-modern culture, but his themes are as fresh as the dialogues of our time. The major characters of his stories and novels, despite the blend of mysticism, superstition, and eroticism in them, are deeply religious and moral. Singer has come to terms with himself; he is committed to the hallowing of man and life. In his novel *The Slave,* Jacob, a pious scholar of Josefov, is sold as a slave to a Polish peasant. At first Jacob regards the peasants as debauched and soulless creatures. But in time he discovers that they are in reality human beings, created like himself in the image of God. In this way he learns from actual life his own affinity with "all living things: Jews, Gentiles, animals, even the flies and gnats." As a consequence he eats no flesh, "neither meat nor fish nor anything else from a living creature, not even cheese or eggs." He is ultimately ransomed and busies himself obsessively with the 248 commandments and 365 prohibitions of the Law. But he sees all around him Jews obeying every injunction and practicing every ritual, yet mistreating their fellow men. Ripening into an inner maturity, Jacob discovers that the essence of his religion is the relation between man and his fellows. Singer's theme, then, is the Jew and his faith in their universal character; his message is that all creatures, man and beast, are God's chosen. Singer's allegory of man enshrines other essential Jewish values. Jacob's marriage to a Gentile woman made him subject to excommunication and subject to death by burning. But Jacob and his wife loved each other, hoped, endured, and kept their faith. Like Job and the Berditchever Rabbi, he engaged in a perpetual debate with the Almighty. Despite the evil he

saw in his fellow Jews, he recognized that there were many kind and good Jews. No matter how cruel he found the Gentiles, he found that there were many good Gentiles. It is the practice of human goodness that gives nobility to the religion they all profess. Singer shows, by way of acts of faith and kindness, that the mind and the heart are human instruments which must be played upon together in order to produce the true music of life, that the secrets of the heart are as real and powerful as the secrets of the atom. The words are the words of Singer, but the message is the message of Judaism.

A similar validation of Jewish values, based upon the experience of the present, may be found in the fiction bequeathed to us by Edward Lewis Wallant (1926-62). Deeply concerned with the problems of human guilt and responsibility, Wallant's stories of emotional crises penetrate to the essence of the human personality. The hero of *The Human Season* is a hero and not a victim. Joe Berman is a plain, roughhewn, unselfconscious Jew. He exults in being alive. He accepts hard labor with equanimity. His Irish boss is a bully, but Joe does not crawl or cringe before him. Nor is he overawed by the bully's physical prowess. He meets insult and challenge head-on, without fear of the mauling he knows awaits him. Berman's head is bashed, and he loses a finger. When he awakes and discov-

Isaac Bashevis Singer.

ers that his head is swathed in bandages and his finger gone he laughs. His brother thinks the beating has affected his head. "It's affected my head and my hand, too," Joe says, "but you should see the other guy." His humor is an expression of his love of life. "His heart sang with that mysterious exaltation that had no basis in reason." Later, in the face of the death of his wife, he is driven to the depths of melancholic grief and suffers the torments of what Freud calls "the work of mourning." He rises out of his bewildering sorrow with a deepened sense of family and faith, and achieves a dignity hewn out of a poignant encounter with life and man, with death and God. There is no ambiguity about his ultimate affirmation of life. Joe Berman is an imperfect man whose very imperfection gives the reader hope that the good in man as well as the evil is amenable to human need. Wallant's view of man, as expressed through Berman, makes man comprehensible without making him contemptible, just as Wallant's view of life makes life compassionate without making it cruel.

Nothing has been more corrosive of traditional values than modern science, and its offspring, technology. In this regard, it is science fiction that portrays the struggle of God versus Golem. In his gem of a story, *The Golem,* Avraham Davidson pictures a humanoid robot, which a scientist has created to displace mankind, making his first assault on a plain, middleclass Jewish couple, the Gumbeiners. They are unimpressed by his highfalutin scientific vocabulary and his pretensions to mastery. Their main concerns are the ordinary problems of everyday life. They quickly recognize a *golem* when they see one. Mr. Gumbeiner, drawing on his knowledge of Jewish folklore, employs the old device of marking a mystical formula on the robot's forehead and then puts the robot to work on household chores. The author mixes humor with satire to expose the intellectual smugness of technology. The use of ordinary people to project the conflict between man and technics is an expression of faith in the capacity of plain people to expose the protective devices of intellectual humbug. Davidson reasserts the Jewish belief that humor is the great solvent of life.

More than any other contemporary American writer Meyer Levin has explored the Jewish psyche in all of its bearings. Very early in youth he discovered his roots in Zionism and Hasidism and employed his art in the service of his American and Jewish heritage. One of his early novels, *Yehuda,* is a splendid evocation of life in a Palestinian kibbutz in the twenties. *The Golden Mountain,* published in 1932 before Buber's books were available in English, beautifully brought to life the legends of Israel Baalshem and Nachman Bratzlaver. His realistic portrayal of second-generation American Jews in *The Old Bunch* reveals clearly and memorably the paradoxes of American Jews. During the past two decades Levin has plumbed the psychopathology of violence in crime and war and their consequence for his own people and mankind. He sees in the emergence and growth of the state of Israel a catalyst for Jews and Jewish culture and feels that Jewish fate is bound up in the development of an organic relation between American Jews and Israel. Fostering such a relation is therefore a work of supreme importance. He writes: "If there was a Messianism in the Jewish folk that enabled it

to rise out of death to attain Israel, then humanity as a whole must possess the fuller Messianism, and contain within itself the force to attain universal peace and justice."

Levin's recent novel, *The Stronghold,* continues this grand theme. In a Bavarian castle a dozen renowned Allied hostages, including a Jewish ex-Premier of France, await liberation by the American forces. During the few days when they are suspended between life and death, there is a dramatic confrontation between the prisoners and their Nazi jailors. All the subconscious forces in the protagonists come to the surface, and the questions of motive, responsibility, identity, and faith are explored. The book is a consummation of Levin's personal and moral quest and of the meaning of the Jewish experience in our time. "The story is developed," he writes, "as a thriller, but it is in reality a confrontation, a distillation, I hope, of the morality of Judaism, Christianity, and Nazism. The story is as far as I have got, in my sixty years, to an understanding of what we in our amazing time have lived through, in relation to our Jewish tradition and history, and in relation to the behavior of mankind." Levin has made his home in a villa in Israel, overlooking the Mediterranean. His odyssey over the past forty years, from Chicago to Herzliya, has deepened his Jewish roots and enlarged his vision. The humane values of Jewish culture, which inform his life and art, work to offset the barbarities of alienation and to transform the suffering of our time into something tonic and healing.

IV

By way of conclusion, I shall try to point out objectively a few of the implications of the changes of values described above. But being objective does not mean being impartial.

The novelist is neither scientist nor philosopher nor sociologist. He is primarily an artist, and as such he must remain a stranger within our gates. He has his own net and his own draught of fishes. The images of Jews enshrined or embalmed in his writing are in part the image of the writer himself and in part the composite image of the people and the world he knows—and hates or loves, debases or ennobles. Either the novelist is confused, bitter and ill at ease ("alienated") in Zion; or he has come to terms with himself and his moral and spiritual tradition. In the one case he tells us what it is that makes our Sammies run; in the other, what makes our Davids and Ruths walk and think, despair and hope.

It is significant that writers like Angoff, Singer, and Wallant, whose writings convey a sense of immediacy and warmth in human association, were rooted in Jewish tradition in their childhood. They were reared in a milieu where the passion for kindness and justice took precedence over the lust for wealth and success. Jewish education taught them, not merely about Judaism, but, above all, to be a Jew. In a sense, they are the true rebels. The true rebel is a person who refuses to be what he is and attempts to become what he can be. This means, not copulating with death but coping with life, and this, in turn, means facing the crises and paradoxes of existence and making hard decisions on questions of right and wrong.

Most of the living novelists, whether specialists in tradition or alienation, are dissenters, and on this count they deserve the attention especially of those who live within the fortress of convention. What are the implications of the reality they describe? Their charge is that Jews live on the principle of When-in-Romism, and their adoption of American mores is so complete that they have become indistinguishable from their non-Jewish neighbors; and that this attenuation of the cultural and religious values of the Judaic tradition is brining about a spiritual abortion. Within the Jewish establishment, one notes everywhere a Gallup-poll mentality, a reliance on quantity rather than quality, a yielding to expediency instead of an embracing of faith, a substitution of research for fact rather than a search for values. Like other Americans, Jews are satisfied with a slip-cover religion and confuse mores with morality. And finally, they tell us that Jewish values, like the Jewish faith, once a substantial part of life, are now a ceremonial aspect of it.

It will serve no purpose to look upon the alienationist writers with an oblique eye or to turn from or on them in anger. To call them "self-hating Jews" is neither honest nor useful. Of course, the process of alienation is a fact of life in our technologized, middle-class society. It is expressed by American novelists of every background and persuasion—perhaps most poignantly by Negro novelists—for example, in Ralph Ellison's superb novel, *The Invisible Man.* For Jews, alienation is part of the process of the recent naturalization of Jews and Judaism in American society, and committed Jews should consider seriously what these gifted, free-wheeling writers are saying. They should be faced with historical and psychological candor.

It is our obligation to counter their doctrine of nothingness and meaninglessness on rational and moral grounds. The principle that all men are strangers is no adequate substitute for the principle that all men are brothers. To hallow human estrangement and to sanctify the emptiness of life is, in terms of the consequences of this doctrine, to justify inhumanity. A writer cannot be absolved of the responsibility for the consequences of his ideas any more than the scientist can be absolved for the consequences of nuclear fission.

There is in our best fiction an indefinable note whose burden is that the inhuman and destructive elements in life today are evidence of human inadequacy and moral failure. Even the philosopher of the absurd, Albert Camus, has written, "The meaning of life is the most urgent of all questions." And he has carried the thought further. Here is a passage from an address delivered in New York in the spring of 1946, a little less than two years after he emerged from the French underground:

> We all sanctify and justify [murder and terror] when we permit ourselves to think that everything is meaningless. This is why we have sought our reasons in our revolt itself, which has led us without apparent reasons to choose the struggle against wrong. And thus we learned that we had not revolted for ourselves alone, but for something common to all men. . . . There was in this absurdity the lesson that we were caught in a collective tragedy, the stake of which was a common dignity, a communion of men, which it was important to defend and sustain.

Thus speaks a voice of honesty, courage, and moral vision. And a voice which should remind us that the latest literary fashion is not necessarily the last word.

S. Lillian Kremer

SOURCE: "Post-alienation: Recent Directions in Jewish-American Literature," in *Contemporary Literature,* Vol. 34, No. 3, Fall, 1993, pp. 571-91.

[*In the following essay, Kremer appraises the work of contemporary Jewish-American authors, citing a revitalized interest in such previously underrepresented subjects as the Holocaust, the Israeli state, and Jewish history and literature.*]

The years since World War II have been good for Jewish-American writers. During recent decades they have joined the mainstream of American fiction. Their works, reviewed regularly and often lauded in the critical press, are popular with the reading public and are incorporated into university curricula. Yet some critics have been anticipating the end of the Jewish-American novel. Irving Howe claimed in 1977 that "Jewish fiction has probably moved past its highpoint," insofar as it is dependent on the immigrant experience. Leslie Fiedler asserted in 1986 that Jewish-American literature's dominant themes of marginality, alienation, and victimization, which had become associated in Western literature with the Jew, had peaked.

Instead of the predicted demise, however, Jewish-American writers are building on the legacies of the older generation and, as Ruth Wisse observes, "Having no longer to defend themselves from real or imagined charges of parochialism, the new Jewish writers . . . are freer to explore the 'tribal' and particularistic aspects of Judaism." Saul Bellow, Bernard Malamud, and Philip Roth in his early work employed Jewish literary influences allusively and introduced Jewish history sparingly, only occasionally placing them in the forefront of their fictional worlds. Now, Jewish thought, literary precursors, and history are often at the center of a fictional universe.

A significant portion of contemporary Jewish-American fiction is pervasively Jewish in its moral insistence and its reference to Judaic texts. Jewish religious thought and values, the trauma of the Holocaust, and the establishment of a Jewish nation in Israel are among the most significant themes of Cynthia Ozick, Arthur Cohen, and Hugh Nissenson. Even those, like Leslie Epstein and Richard Elman, whose Jewish religious values are minimal focus on recent Jewish history, positioning it centrally in their novels. Pervasive treatment of Jewish subjects and values, reference to Judaic texts, and introduction of the midrashic narrative mode, in which a familiar story or theme is given a new reading, are simultaneously making a profound mark on American thought and literature and heralding a Jewish-American literary renaissance.

1

Throughout their careers, Bellow and Malamud denied

that they were "Jewish writers," as has Roth, despite the centrality of Jewish subjects to their fiction. Cynthia Ozick, the acknowledged leader of a revitalized Jewish-American literary movement, self-consciously defines herself as a Jewish writer. She writes about Judaism and Jewish history with a high level of erudition and advocates Judaic affirmation, renewal, and redemption. Sociological observation of contemporary Jewish life does not characterize the Jewish content of her fiction as it does that of many other contemporary Jewish-American writers. Instead, she infuses her narratives with the values of Judaism. Her work reflects and contributes to the Jewish textual tradition.

In "Toward a New Yiddish," Ozick advocates creation of an indigenous American Jewish literature in English, one "centrally Jewish in its concerns" and "liturgical in nature," not a "didactic or prescriptive" literature but "aggadic," in style, "utterly freed to invention, discourse, parable, experiment, enlightenment, profundity, humanity." Invoking Yavneh, the academy of learning built to sustain Jewish civilization in the post-Temple period, as a metaphor of renewal, Ozick exhorts American Jewish writers to preserve Judaic culture and to make New Yiddish, a creative union between Yiddish and English, its medium, to "pour not merely the Jewish sensibility, but the Jewish vision, into the vessel of English."

Among Ozick's recurrent Judaic themes are *tikkun* ("repair") and *t'shuva* ("redemption"). In the essay "Innovation and Redemption: What Literature Means," Ozick argues against the theory of art for art's sake, literature that is merely self-referential, which she judges as amoral. She instead advocates a redemptive literature, writing that insists on freedom to change one's life, that celebrates creative renewal. Representative of the novelist's approach to repair and redemptive themes are her Puttermesser stories, which reverberate with these principles and simultaneously exemplify Ozick's organic integration of Jewish myth to enhance a contemporary moral quest. The first narrative, "Puttermesser: Her Work History, Her Ancestry, Her Afterlife," introduces the repair theme in the lawyer's activism on behalf of Soviet Jews, her work for political reform, and her dream of bettering the world. Central to Ruth Puttermesser's character is her passion for Jewish values. She strives to enhance her knowledge of Judaic civilization by studying Hebrew and reading Judaic writings. In these studies she discerns a civilization, a value system, a distinctive culture and forges her link to the history of the Jews.

This redemptive theme appears again in "Bloodshed." In the narrative's climactic scene, set in a prayer and study session, Ozick explores a lapsed Jew's spiritual return, invoking Yom Kippur atonement through biblical allusion to sacrifice symbolic of self-surrender and devotion to the will of God. The narrative's Hasidic leader, a Buchenwald survivor, counters the nihilism of the apostate, Bleilip, by making him the subject of a Hasidic exemplum revealing the theological and human implications of the Holocaust. The spiritual guide leads the skeptic to redemption by helping him understand that often the believer and doubter are one. Bleilip's redemption is intimated as he discovers the values of collective memory, tradition, and communal responsibility. Acknowledging his belief in God despite Holocaust history, the suicidal skeptic has metamorphosed into the identity he had earlier misappropriated, "A Jew. Like yourselves. One of you." Arriving at the Hasidic colony in scorn, Bleilip concludes his visit in praise, recognizing that he had unconsciously come "for a glimpse of the effect of the rebbe [the Hasidic spiritual leader]. Of influences" and sensing that "The day . . . felt full of miracles." Ozick's redemptive theme also intersects with her treatment of the Holocaust in *Trust*. A recorder of Holocaust history, her American protagonist, Enoch Vand, adopts the Lurianic Hasidic belief in man's restorative task in history. Beyond his compulsion to bear witness to the Holocaust, Vand seeks to reinvigorate the Jewish people and to rebuild Judaism. He commits himself to the traditional Jewish life of prayer and study. Under the guidance of a Holocaust survivor, he learns Hebrew and studies the Bible, the Talmud, and *Ethics of the Fathers*. Vand's motivation for the study of Jewish texts is comparable to Ozick's, to know "what it is to *think* as a Jew" ("Toward a New Yiddish"). By insisting on bearing witness to the Holocaust and affirming his commitment to Judaism, Vand, like Ozick, embraces the task of finding meaning and purpose through the historic event.

As in the work of Cynthia Ozick, Jewish religious values are intrinsic to and permeate Hugh Nissenson's fictional universe. Ozick has observed, in her review of *In the Reign of Peace*, that Nissenson's stories are essentially *midrashim*, revelatory commentaries, fictional commentaries on religious texts. His first collection of short stories, *A Pile of Stones*, explores the problem of religious belief in modernity. Nissenson demonstrates how the forces of secularism and external oppression have made it hard for modern Jews to remain faithful to their religious heritage, to obey God's commandments and thereby to sanctify themselves. Illustrative of the Jew persecuted for religious adherence is the hero of "The Groom of Zlota Street." An observant Jew who wears the obligatory beard is plagued by a Gentile with whom he has a standing agreement: the Gentile will purchase the Jew's wares on the condition that he may pull his beard. To demonstrate the significance of free choice, a central principle of Jewish ethical teaching, the impoverished Jew forgoes a sale and willingly endures a vicious beating for refusing the Gentile his customary pleasure.

The influence of secular movements that have usurped the loyalty Jews had historically reserved for religious piety is Nissenson's subject in "The Prisoner." Nissenson recounts the career of a religious Jew who abandons Judaism because he is unable to reconcile the horror of a pogrom with the holiness of God. Convinced that God and religion are ineffectual in the face of such violence, the apostate transfers his hopes for universal peace and an end to human suffering from God and Judaism to political revolution. Finally, as a political prisoner of the czar's regime, he exchanges the ritual garb of striped prayer shawl and phylacteries for the prisoner's striped vest and wrist chains bound to a leather waist strap. When his deportation is imminent, the prisoner has a vision of a world order that includes human suffering. He now understands that man alone cannot end human suffering, that although people are morally obligated, according to Jewish law, to help improve the world, their efficacy is limited. Bringing about the end of human suffering is reserved for God.

Whereas Jewish culture has often been the subject matter of fiction by Jewish writers, seldom have Jewish religious values been as fundamental and intrinsic to a literary work by an American Jew as they are in Nissenson's short story "The Law." Covenantal affirmation is at the heart of the story. This narrative fuses two central subjects of Nissenson's fiction, the foremost tragedy of Jewish history in the modern era, the Holocaust, and Judaic religious belief and practice. Nissenson affirms the validity of adherence to the ancient edict that Jews should consider themselves symbolically present at Sinai to receive the Law. Dramatic tension emerges in a family's deliberation on whether the son, a severe stutterer, ought to under-take the rigors of public recitation of the traditional bar mitzvah service, the occasion when the observant accepts the obligations of Jewish law. Nissenson complicates and heightens the drama by juxtaposing the memory of the father's youthful indifference to Jewish law and ritual with his son's voluntary assumption of responsibility. The significance of the youth's insistence is heightened by family history. Assimilated German Jews, they had abandoned Judaism but had Jewish identity thrust upon them by Nazi racial decree. Post-Holocaust consciousness motivates the father to reject his own father's assimilationist agenda in order to pass on the Judaic legacy to his willing son. The lesson the survivor took from his Holocaust experience—the futile nature of assimilation gained at the expense of repudiation of one's own heritage—is the author's lesson to contemporary Jews and a principal theme in the writings of self-affirming Jewish-American writers.

In contrast to immigrant Jewish-American writers like Abraham Cahan and Anzia Yezierska, whose protagonists' goals were assimilation at any cost, the moral heroes of Ozick and Nissenson assert the worth of life lived according to Jewish values and religious law. Unlike those writers whose Jewish material enriched only their novels' sociological texture, Ozick and Nissenson imbue their work with Judaic religious, textual, and historic content. They often replace the secular Jews of Bellow and Roth and the Jewishly uneducated figures in Malamud with characters steeped in Jewish learning. The resulting literature captures the essence of Jewish experience as deeply and intricately as Christian sensibility is conveyed in the work of James Joyce and Flannery O'Connor.

2

Beyond the Judaic thought that characterizes contemporary Jewish-American writing is its distinctive memory of the two critical events of twentieth-century Jewish history, the Holocaust and the establishment of the Israeli State. The 1963 trial of Adolf Eichmann and the 1967 Arab-Israeli Six-Day War are the most probable twin stimuli for revived American literary interest in the Holocaust and engagement with Israel. The intellectual debate aroused by Hannah Arendt's assessment of the Eichmann trial and Jewish leadership during the Holocaust again brought Holocaust crimes to the forefront of American Jewish thought. The 1967 Arab attack on Israel, accompanied by Nazi-like threats to annihilate the Jewish state, elevated Jewish concerns about Israel's survival and security and affected the Jewish-American literary imagination. In contrast to earlier Jewish-American fiction, whose characters were minimally shaped by ethnic history, new works often include characters molded by Holocaust experience or Holocaust knowledge.

American Jews have adapted documentary materials to the fictional universe, incorporating historic figures and relying heavily on evidentiary matter to create a fictional Holocaust universe. Among the writers who have embraced this strategy are Susan Fromberg Schaeffer, who conducted many interviews with survivors for her presentation of the Vilna ghetto and Kaiserwald labor camp in *Anya;* Norma Rosen, who incorporated documentary materials from the Eichmann trial in *Touching Evil;* Cynthia Ozick, whose description of the roundup of Parisian Jews in *The Cannibal Galaxy* owes much to *Vichy France and the Jews* by Michael R. Marrus and Robert O. Paxton; Richard Elman, whose treatment of the Hungarian Jewish catastrophe in *The 28th Day of Elul* and *The Reckoning* reflects close reading of Raul Hilberg's *The Destruction of the European Jews;* Marge Piercy, whose epic war novel *Gone to Soldiers* is a superb example of the research novel that covers multiple civilian and military fronts; and Leslie Epstein, whose *King of the Jews* is based on historic documents of the Lodz ghetto. In these works, primary loyalty is to fact presented through the prism of fiction.

Leslie Epstein combines invention and fidelity to the accounts of historians Gerald Reitlinger, Leonard Tushnet, Isaiah Trunk, and Hunnah Arendt to re-create the Lodz ghetto and explore the motivations of its Jewish elder, Chaim Rumkowski, in *King of the Jews.* Close reading of Tushnet's *Pavement of Hell* and Trunk's *Judenrat: The Jewish Councils in Eastern Europe under Nazi Occupation* suggests that Epstein draws heavily on these sources for his delineations of the ghetto elder, I. C. Trumpelman, and the Lodz ghetto. Furthermore, I would argue that these texts are the source of Epstein's collage or composite approach to character and ghetto construction. While primarily based on Lodz, elements of the Warsaw and Vilna ghettos, derived from these same sources, emerge in Epstein's Baluty suburb. Aside from embellishments of the megalomaniacal aspects of his character and a few details from the biographies of Warsaw and Vilna leaders, Epstein's Trumpelman closely resembles Mordechai Chaim Rumkowski, the most enigmatic of Jewish leaders among the *Judenrat.* Like many diarists, scholars, and novelists who try to comprehend and delineate the Rumkowski figure, Epstein is caught between sharply polarized feelings. Acknowledging the unprecedented evil under which *Judenrat* leaders functioned, he dramatizes Trumpelman's moral dilemma: balancing loyalty to his own people with obedience to the enemy that sustains his authority as long as he satisfies its demands.

Although Epstein's work began with an interest in the most eccentric and controversial of the elders, the novel's dimensions are substantially extended by ample attention to the vicissitudes of a slave labor ghetto, its overlords, police, victims, heroes, and rebels. Epstein depicts the insidious manipulation of the Jewish Council forced to accede to Nazi demands and implement orders ranging from mundane administrative detail to selections for labor and death deportations. The novel's breadth is achieved through the choral and primary voices of characters in the Holocaust trauma: administrative voices of Germans, Council members, and police officials carrying out the Hitlerian program and voices of Jews (the Bundists, the Communists, and the Orthodox) oppressed, resisting, suffering starvation, slave labor, and deportation. The novel welds history and art to evoke a grotesque kingdom, a macabre landscape revealing the essential villainy of the Nazi system.

Marge Piercy's extraordinary World War II novel, *Gone to Soldiers,* is a vast compilation of wartime experiences of civilian and military history. The segment charting the tragedy and resistance of the native-born and foreign Jews of France is faithful to survivor testimony and diaries as well as to a huge body of Holocaust and World War II scholarship, including Amy Latour's *The Jewish Resistance in France,* Vera Laska's *Women in the Resistance and in the Holocaust,* and Serge Klarsfeld's *Memorial to the Jews Deported from France, 1942-1944.* Incremental development of the ominous fate of French Jewry under the Germans, paralleled by French anti-Semitism, is the focus of the novel's early sections. Piercy is particularly strong on the theme of Jewish resistance, a topic generally ignored in American Holocaust literature. Her resisters are modeled on Jewish forces drawn from the ranks of the Jewish Scout Movement, Zionist organizations, and French Jewish immigrant communities. Debunking the myth that Jews capitulated to slaughter without protest, Piercy incorporates historical data, specific operations of French Jews active in underground groups that disrupted German projects and assisted the Allies.

Among the most prevalent themes of American Holocaust literature is examination of covenantal theodicy and the viability of Judaism in the post-Holocaust age. Called into question are the three pillars of historic Judaism: God, Torah, and the Jewish people. The Holocaust, more than any other event in Jewish history, taxes the Jew's faith in a just and merciful God and provokes questions about the nature of God, the covenant between God and Israel, and the nature of human beings. Important among the theological and philosophical responses to the Holocaust are questioning and protest of God's inaction in the face of Holocaust injustice by observant and apostate Jews and an oppositional affirmative model based on rededication to God and Judaic principles.

Richard Elman fictionalizes the plight of Hungarian Jewry in his Holocaust trilogy, concentrating on the non-observant Jew's theological quandary in the first volume. His characters rage against society and God for grave crimes against humanity and the covenant. Elman asks whether we need to revise our ideas about human nature in light of Holocaust truth, and whether the covenantal relation of the divine and human continues in the post-Holocaust era. Elman's survivor probes the meaning of God's Holocaust absence and asks whether a God of mercy and love would countenance extermination of the innocent, and whether conventional wisdom about human nature requires re-examination. His questions reflect the crises of faith and human understanding in the post-Holocaust era.

To pursue these theological and philosophical concerns, the trilogy's first volume, *The 28th Day of Elul,* is structured as the response of Alex Yagodah, a Holocaust survivor, now an Israeli citizen, to an American lawyer questioning his allegiance to Judaism. Lacking a Jewish education, Yagodah is an acculturated Jew who nevertheless raises theological questions of import. He puts man and God on trial. Denying neither the authenticity of rebellion nor the authenticity of faith, he begins his struggle in denunciation and ends in acceptance. Like the protester believers of I. B. Singer and Elie Wiesel, Yagodah simultaneously accepts God yet protests His neglect of suffering and holds Him accountable for Holocaust injustice. Yagodah wrestles with the terrifying realization of the coexistence of a just and merciful God and an evil creation. Confronting the inexplicable, he concludes, "I believe," echoing the traditional affirmation of faith many victims recited as they entered the gas chambers: *"Ani Ma'amim."*

Illustrative of contemporary writers' sensitive incorporation of the Judaic textual tradition is Elman's turn to traditional thematic and stylistic Jewish literary responses to catastrophe: providential interpretation of history, acceptance of a silent, hidden God who remains aloof from human evil to honor the principle of free will, biblical allusion and countercommentary. Elman appropriates the psalmist's construction of God's hiddenness in Psalm 44 to account for divine inaction and to distinguish between human evil and divine responsibility. Although Elman's prose echoes biblical cadence and parallelism, Yagodah's rebuke of God for crimes against the covenant parodies and reformulates the psalmist's mournful, supplicating tone: "Only He betrayed us. He profaned us. He took our prayers in vain. He mocked us. He rewarded us with cruelty. He listened but did not hear. He was there and He was not there when we needed Him. He led us into injustice." The survivor's protest subverts the original text and radically reinterprets it by articulating faith despite the terror of separation from God. In protest, the text is put to irreverent use. David Roskies accounts for classical Yiddish writers' use of liturgical parody as "their desire to imitate the sacrilege, to disrupt the received order of the text in the same way as the enemy, . . . disrupted the order of the world." Roskies' description of this traditionalist tendency "to mimic the sacrilege [thereby allowing] the individual to keep faith even as the promise is subverted" may be applied to Yagodah's reformulation of the traditional celebration of divine attributes.

Whereas Elman explores the response of an alienated Jew to the theological impact of the Holocaust, theologian Arthur Cohen joins Cynthia Ozick and Hugh Nissenson in creating a centrally Jewish literature to examine post-Holocaust theodicy. His novel *In the Days of Simon Stern* is a rich, culturally textured, complex philosophical novel dealing with the response to the Holocaust of the religiously observant. It incorporates biblical legend, theological, talmudic, and kabbalistic discourse, and dramatic enactment of the messianic redemptive theory to wrest instruction from the Holocaust. Praised by Ozick in the *New York Times Book Review* for "a brilliance of Jewish insight and erudition to be found in no other novelist," Cohen masters the sacred, theological, and mystical texts of Judaism to present a mythic odyssey of a messianic figure in the Holocaust era. Significant among the novel's contributions to American Holocaust literature is its unique exploration of the bearing of the Holocaust upon the ancient Jewish idea that messianic redemption will follow historical catastrophe.

The novel's story line chronicles the efforts of Simon Stern, a Jew informed of a prophecy proclaiming him Messiah, to rescue and rehabilitate a group of death camp survivors. As in the days after the destruction of the Holy Temple, Stern envisions and builds a fortress to house the remnant, to provide them safety from threats of assimilation and anti-Semitism, and to bear testament to the endurance of Judaism and Jewry. Parodying the Nazi death selections, Stern travels to Europe to make regenerative selections. He takes Jews—of all classes and backgrounds, all professions, all capacities—united by a passion for renewal "to . . . rebuild each other's flesh and spirit."

Affirming the restorative and regenerative approaches to Holocaust tragedy espoused by theologian Emil Fackenheim, Cohen's Jews, like Chaim Potok's survivor-scholars and rabbis, respond to Holocaust loss by undertaking a major project of repair to strengthen Judaism and Jewry. Their model is Rabbi Akiva's historic rebuilding of the remnant within the traditional Judaic system, as a distinctive and separate religious entity. Unlike I. B. Singer's apostate, socialist, and communist protesters and Elman's secularist, Cohen's Jews adhere to the tradition of the ancients who refrained from rebuking God for the destruction of the Temples, for Exile, and for the Diaspora. To blame or try God for Holocaust crimes is, for them, a futile gesture: "No need for a trial. If that were all, He'd be condemned in a trice." Rabbi Steinmann sheds no tears for humanity, but for God, because "He wants so much and can affect us so little." Steinmann has arrived at a position which marks the Holocaust as an event so different from the previous Jewish disasters that it must change our theological perceptions. To try God is to expect a participatory covenant, to expect God to respond to human petition. This judgment anticipates the theological argument of Cohen's *The Tremendum* in calling for a break from past theology. Cohen contends that "the traditional God has no connection with the Holocaust despite the palpable fact that the immensity of the *tremendum* implies a judgment upon God." Simon Stern heralds Cohen's later insistence that Jewish reality must account for the Holocaust in its view of God, the world, and man.

Spared direct experience and knowledge of the Holocaust, Jewish-American writers nevertheless bear witness articulating their recognition of the Holocaust as a turning point in history, as a catastrophe that altered the way we perceive God and humanity. These writers have addressed the Holocaust as a central reference point in their fiction and have established the Holocaust survivor as a recogniz-

able persona in our literature. By adding their voices to Holocaust testimony, these Americans join their European and Israeli colleagues to commemorate the dead, to preserve the collective memory, and to offer warnings for the future.

. . . . .

Israel has been of considerably less interest to the Jewish-American literary imagination than has the Holocaust or than might have been anticipated given the increasingly overt treatment of Jewish themes. It has, however, periodically emerged in connection with Holocaust themes and in regard to Jewish characters' exploration of personal identity and their attachment to the spiritual center of Judaism. Examples of the first theme include Bellow's *Mr. Sammler's Planet* and *To Jerusalem and Back,* Potok's scenes of Americans working on behalf of Israeli independence in *The Chosen,* and Piercy's Holocaust-wrought transformation of a French assimilationist to staunch Zionist in *Gone to Soldiers.* Illustrative of the latter are Anne Roiphe's *Lovingkindness* and Philip Roth's *Counterlife* delineating characters on a redemptive search to Israel where they seek, to the dismay of relatives, a religiously disciplined life to counteract the self-indulgence and self-destruction of their American existence.

Among the many turns and topics of Roth's *Counterlife* are Jewish and Israeli identity. When Nathan Zuckerman travels to Israel to retrieve his brother from a West Bank settlement where he is a follower of a zealot rabbi, he encounters a lengthy debate on the nature of Jewishness and Israeli statehood. Nathan asks, "What is a Jew?" and learns the Israeli perspective, the Jew of the Diaspora superseded by the Israeli who can live "free of Jewish cringing, deference, diplomacy, apprehension, alienation, self-pity, self-satire, self-mistrust, depression, clowning, bitterness, nervousness, inwardness, hypercriticalness, hypertouchiness, social anxiety, social assimilation—a way of life absolved, in short, of all the Jewish 'abnormalities,' those peculiarities of self-division." In his brief visit he sees in Israel "every Jewish dilemma there ever was" and hears a chorus of voices, including a liberal Tel Aviv journalist fearful that Israel is becoming an "American-Jewish Australia," a West Bank promoter of Jewish might, and an El Al security agent lecturing on Jewish history and anti- Semitism. Always the adversary, Nathan looks at the psychosocial dynamics of Zionism as "The construction of a counterlife that is one's own anti-myth . . . All over the world people were rooting for the Jews to go ahead and un-Jew themselves in their own little homeland. . . . that's why the place was once universally so popular—no more Jewy Jews, great!" Nathan's brother, Henry, has an equally convincing argument. He rejects Nathan's psychological profundities to advocate "a larger world, a world of ideology, of politics, of history." Compelling arguments are voiced on both sides, but the Israeli debate remains unresolved by the Zuckerman brothers.

Unlike Roth's American quester seeking personal fulfillment in the Israeli setting, Hugh Nissenson's characters are Israeli citizens bound to the collective history of the Jewish people. Nissenson's work (concordant with Bellow's *To Jerusalem and Back* in its historic perspective and with the Six-Day War segment of *Mr. Sammler's Planet* in its connecting links between Holocaust tragedy and Israeli security) emphasizes the political and spiritual dimensions of its Israeli characters. Less concerned with the individual psyche than Roth, Nissenson exhibits an interest in the individual that is deeply bound to his primary regard for Jewish political and spiritual community, the national polity.

In the Reign of Peace reinforces Nissenson's Judaic theme of humanity's need for redemption initially established in *A Pile of Stones.* Six of its eight tales employ Israeli settings in dramatizing the tensions of the religious/secular dichotomy in the modern state. Central in this collection is the paradox of exile from God and the quest for redemption. Several stories focus on the establishment and security of Israel and address issues of peace and justice in a land surrounded by militant enemies dedicated to its destruction. "The Throne of Good," set in the period prior to statehood, relates the story of a young Stern Gang member who employs the military training he received as a Holocaust era partisan to fight against the British for Israeli independence. Like other Holocaust survivors, the boy believes that he was saved for a purpose. Whereas for many survivors that purpose is manifested in bearing witness to the Holocaust, for this survivor the belief is embodied in his militant contribution to the birth and security of a modern state in the ancient Jewish homeland. During an interview with Harold Ribalow, Nissenson asserted that he had erred in narrating the story from the perspective of a Stern Gang critic. The decision to employ that point of view, however, allowed Nissenson to explore difficult questions about protecting Jewish life in the post-Holocaust period. His tale turns on the moral dilemma of whether ends can justify means, whether committing acts of terror against the British rulers to achieve the good of Jewish statehood and security is morally defensible.

Themes of messianic redemption and Israeli survival, dismissed as too parochial by many Jewish writers, are at the center of Nissenson's vision and illustrative of new directions Jewish-American writers are taking to explore Judaic content. The title story, "In the Reign of Peace," set on an Israeli kibbutz, involves an argument between the narrator, a secular member, and an observant immigrant from Morocco, who works on the kibbutz. The observant Middle Eastern Jew is astonished by *kibbutzniks* who believe neither in God nor the redemptive Messiah and fail to revere the commandments governing Sabbath celebration and the dietary laws. Rejecting the traditional Jewish messianic view, the secularist embraces an alternative redemptive vision, one that affirms the socialist ideal of members sharing the labor and benefits of the community. This claim is insufficient for the religious Jew. He believes even the achievement of a just society is not redemption; redemption is not realized until the universe is just.

The extensive body of American Holocaust literature and the emerging fiction exploring Israeli themes signify the end of a period when American writers of Jewish extraction feared that focus on Jewish interests would hinder their acceptance with publishers and readers and signal another component in the reaffirmation of Jewish values in American literature.

3

Intertextuality in Jewish-American fiction has often gone unnoticed, for it has been presented in a manner that discourages recognition. A case in point is Saul Bellow's appropriation of an anti-Hasidic text to inform the character of his holy conman, Tamkin, in *Seize the Day.* Although derivative aspects play a major role in Tamkin's character construct, Bellow's allusions to and appropriations from an obscure anti-Hasidic satire remain virtually unrecognized by the critics. In an America that increasingly values cultural diversity, writers are now freer than Bellow was to celebrate their cultural heritage overtly. Jewish intertextuality and the midrashic mode are sources of intellectual, moral, and aesthetic delight for readers and heighten the vibrancy of Jewish-American literature.

A significant mark of the revitalization of Jewish-American writing is its incorporation of and play on classical Jewish sources. Text-centeredness, as Harold Bloom makes evident in *Agon*, is the essence of Jewish learning. One might add that it is the essence of the best of contemporary Jewish-American literature. Writing infused with precursor literary and ideational concepts reveals the contemporary pertinence of those influences and heightens the cultural breadth of American literature.

In "Literature as Idol: Harold Bloom," Ozick argues that the critic treats the poem as literary idol. She faults Bloom for contributing to "discontinuity of tradition," for an interpretive system founded on breaking with the literary precursor in its suggestion that the new poet treat the old as sacrificial victim, in its insistence that "a poem comes into being out of its reading of an earlier poem, i.e., out of its own 'swerving' from the influence of a powerful precursor-poem." Ozick identifies this approach as un-Jewish and advocates instead the validity of the midrashic textual approach because it is "set against the idea of displacing the precursor. . . . [Jewish] interpretation never came to stand for disjunction, displacement, . . . revisionism. Transmittal signifies the carrying-over of the original strength." In the classic midrashic mode of the later text adding an interpretive gloss to earlier ones, Ozick affirms and contributes to the Judaic legacy. Throughout her work, she draws on the rich store of historic Jewish texts and memory to celebrate the continuity of Judaic civilization. She honors the culture and contributes to its vibrancy by creating literature exhibiting the attributes she advocates in "Toward a New Yiddish," writing that is "centrally Jewish in its concerns," "liturgical in nature," and distinguished by a "sacral imagination." By so doing, Ozick enriches both Jewish writing and American literature.

Text-centeredness, a hallmark of the midrashic mode, appears in Ozick's supernatural fantasy "The Pagan Rabbi." This narrative elaborates an epigraph from *Pirke Aboth: The Ethics of the Talmud: Sayings of the Fathers* advocating concentration on and dedication to religious study to explore the conflicting lures of Hellenism and Hebraism, one of Ozick's recurrent themes. In this instance, Ozick pits monotheistic Judaism against the temptations of nature in the conflict of a rabbi so enamored of the beauties of nature that he is distracted from sacred study and worship. The rabbi's soul takes the shape of a studious old Jew indifferent to the glories of nature to denounce his excursion into paganism. Whereas the midrashic mode is somewhat limited to a fantastical elaboration of an epigraph in this early story, Ozick advances the method for the second Puttermesser story and achieves a thematically and structurally integrated midrashic tale.

"Puttermesser and Xanthippe," derived from the folktale of the golem (a figure constructed in human form and endowed with life), owes its twelve-part structure to the pattern of construction and destruction employed in Gershom Scholem's essay "The Idea of the *Golem,*" which Ruth has been studying. Reacting to the corruption and mediocrity of city government, Puttermesser performs the rituals described in Scholem's essays and breathes life into a creature fashioned from earth to do her bidding and repair a flawed world. Following the commandment of Deuteronomy, "Justice, justice shalt thou pursue," Puttermesser's golem implements an urban reform plan and assists her master's ascent to the mayoralty. Indicative of the contemporary writer's appropriation of and contribution to the literary heritage is Ozick's extension of the golem's beneficence to a nonsectarian population and her endowment of the creature with female gender and sexual and procreative desires. Characteristic of the legendary golem that becomes a destructive agent despite its creator's intent, Xanthippe eventually rejects her role as an instrument of reform. She destroys Puttermesser's political career and the municipal reforms she instituted. Compounding the legendary disorder associated with the golem, Ozick adds the sin of idolatry to enlarge the legend's moral and aesthetic dimensions. Sarah Blacher Cohen contends that Ruth "is guilty not only of usurping God's role as a lifegiver, but she also unlawfully appropriates God's function of creating a paradise on earth." Puttermesser invokes the ritual of reversal to destroy the golem. Xanthippe fails to achieve permanent reform, yet she and the mayor amply demonstrate the need and potential for improvement and repair.

Just as T. S. Eliot's work is enriched by the texts and texture of Christianity, Ozick's writing is enhanced by her counterpoint of contemporary Jewish history and ancient Judaic text in *The Cannibal Galaxy.* Her juxtaposition of the roundup of Parisian Jews, their inhumane incarceration, and their eventual deportation to Auschwitz with references from the Mishnah that focus on communal fasts commemorating deliverance from destruction broadens reader perspective in a way that nontextually or historically referential Holocaust fiction does not. Paralleling the fury and tumult of Nazi Europe with allusion to a text recounting themes of national destruction and redemption and legends of divine and human response to tragedy effectively connects the present to other periods of persecution and intimates the eventual analogous deliverance of the Jewish remnant. Ozick extends this textual construct in Hester Lilt's story of Rabbi Akiva's commentary on biblical prophecies of Zion's destruction and restoration. The redemptive legends in conjunction with Ozick's reference to later texts affirming post-Holocaust Jewish regeneration in Israel should be interpreted as celebration of Jewish survival and renewal in a Jewish homeland. Furthermore, the concurrence of the Akiva narrative with advice to read André Neher on Edmond Fleg is wholly consistent with midrashic methodology. The dense Judaic intertextual connections that characterize Ozick's midrashic mode add a level of intellectual rigor that carries the narrative to aesthetic and moral heights surpassing the Jewish novel of alienation and sociological insight that earned popular and critical acclaim in recent decades.

Ozick's fascination with incorporation of the Jewish heritage in American fiction is paralleled by Curt Leviant's. At the heart of Jewish religious experience as expressed liturgically and textually, from the ancient world to the contemporary, has been the longing for the Messiah and interest in the conditions for his arrival. Leviant's novel *The Man Who Thought He Was Messiah* is a modern midrash on this subject, a fantasy based on Nachman of Bratslav, Hasidic leader and devotee of prayer and music, believed by his disciples to have had the soul of the Messiah. In a tale Elie Wiesel characterizes as "an enchanting spiritual universe—filled with imagination, humor, and warmth," Leviant presents a year in Nachman's life, a year of self-exile and spiritual quest. He juxtaposes Nachman's subjective view of an illicit sexual encounter, his subsequent loss of the Hebrew alphabet (to which he compared the woman's beauty), and his redemptive goals with the objective diary reports of his scribal assistant, Nathan.

Traditional themes of aspiration to messianic ascension and false messiahs are employed by Leviant to fabricate a stirring tale of spiritual longing, a metafiction in the midrashic mode that introduces one tale to interpret another. While Leviant read extensively in the biographical and historical accounts of this charismatic leader and familiarized himself with the tales that are attributed to him, he discards much biography in favor of invention based on the authentic life. Although the historic Nachman was a famous storyteller whose narratives were transcribed and remain readily available, Leviant noted in his acceptance speech for the Edward Lewis Wallant Prize for the novel that he composed his own stories for the Hasid.

Increased attention to Jewish tradition and liturgy is also evident in the work of Jewish feminists who are composing new texts to articulate their claim for a place in what has been a patriarchal tradition. Cathy Davidson lauds E. M. Broner for "finding new forms for fiction . . . [that] encompass a radical feminist reordering of social and fictional hierarchies[,] . . . [for] the way in which she employs an inheritance of Yiddish and Hebrew themes and tones in an experimental fictional mode that celebrates the female hero." Broner has not rejected Judaism for the humiliation she feels the patriarchy has visited upon women but has decided, instead, to refashion Judaism in a feminist mode. Echoing the rebellious voice of Anzia Yezierska, who found the patriarchal hierarchy oppressive and exclusive, but reaching beyond her to constructive and creative confrontation and engagement, Broner's novels *Her Mothers* and *A Weave of Women* move from secular feminism to feminist Judaism. *A Weave of Women* is a

Jewish feminist declaration of independence from the constraints of Jewish patriarchy. Broner's multinational women, living together in Israel, create a feminist Jewish ritual, resulting in an articulate, active role for women where they had been silent and passive. Their rituals parallel, but are distinguished from, Jewish male rituals in order to demonstrate women's Jewish cultural identity and authenticity. The new liturgy is a celebration of women's lives and a contribution to a dynamic and vibrant Judaism. Broner's work has encouraged other Jewish women to appropriate their rightful place in synagogues and libraries and to begin to write on subjects long considered the male province.

. . . . .

A generation of Jewish-American writers has emerged that is freer than Saul Bellow initially thought he was to explore the particularity of Jewish literature, religious experience, and history. This is a self-emancipated generation, liberated to express its artistic visions in Jewish terms—a generation unwilling to accept either the constraints of the immigration/assimilation theme or the popular Roth school of social satire with its cast of stereotypical suburban Jews composed of domineering mothers, ineffectual fathers, pampered daughters, and whining sons. On the contrary, the literary school Bellow initiated and Cynthia Ozick brings to fruition illuminates Jewish themes and judiciously appropriates precursors to extend the significant contribution of Jewish writers to American letters.

No, in thunder, Mr. Fiedler. Jewish-American fiction is not dying; it is enjoying a renaissance. Jewish-American literature is a vibrant, flourishing literature, more assertive than it was in the fifties and sixties, more essentially Jewish. Literary critics will need to broaden and extend their knowledge of Judaic thought if they are to explicate this new Jewish-American fiction with the discernment it merits.

Ruth Adler

SOURCE: "Mothers and Daughters: The Jewish Mother as Seen by American Jewish Women Writers," in *Modern Jewish Studies,* Vol. 6, No. 4, 1987, pp. 87-92.

[*In the following essay, Adler evaluates the complex portrayals of Jewish mothers by American Jewish women writers, contrasting these to the often stereotypical depictions offered by male writers.*]

The stereotype of the Jewish Mother, while frequently filling everyday banter, has also entered serious literature and become, in recent years, one of the most hackneyed and overplayed of literary themes. Most stereotypes have appeared and have subsequently been discredited as a result of their inherent limitations—the ignoring of individual differences and imposition of rigid and outmoded patterns on complex and fluid reality. The stereotype of the Jewish Mother, however, thrives, nurtured by an apparently deep-seated contemporary need.

Dan Greenburg's farcical book *How to be a Jewish Mother* typifies the stereotype. He describes the Jewish Mother as nurturing to a fault, martyr-like in her self-sacrifice, demanding, controlling, and manipulative through guilt. Forever occupied with housework, she is garrulous and unrelenting in her efforts to convince her offspring to marry within the fold, always in accordance with (or rather, above) their station.

This popularized image has been articulated almost exclusively by Jewish American male writers over the past three decades and is, as I have observed in previous works, notably absent from the Hebrew and Yiddish literature of the shtetl. One perspective, however, has been largely overlooked by modern criticism. This is the view of the Jewish Mother as she appears in the works of female Jewish American authors. In the works of most of these writers, the Jewish mother does not conform to the stereotype. Absent is the overly-solicitous, self-denying woman constantly suffusing her brood with chicken soup who has come to be identified as the quintessential Jewish mother. In her stead we find, for the most part, a harried victim of circumstance, frequently rejecting and neglectful, too drained of energy by her circumstances to be of comfort to others. There are even portrayals akin to the fairytale type of wretched and vindictive stepmother. If this appears strange and totally at odds with the prevailing view, a survey of the writings of a number of contemporary American Jewish women writers will acquaint the reader with a point of view that has been significantly obscured. What follows is a leafing through the pages of some of these works to study the portrayal of the Jewish mother from the daughter's perspective.

Some of the most extreme examples of maladaptive maternal coping are probably found in the works of Cynthia Freeman and Susan Fromberg Schaeffer. Freeman's saga *Portraits* describes Sara, an immigrant mother who dominates the lives of her children. She imposes a loveless marriage on one daughter and destroys the marriage of another. While indulging her whim for both the sensuous and the material (massages, fine clothing, and other luxuries), she heaps verbal abuse on her children and refuses, in later years, to share her affluence with a needy daughter. She is almost malevolently caricatured in her insidious plot, to frame a devoted daughter, as a ploy to redeem her own suspect virtue in her husband's eyes.

Susan Fromberg Schaeffer, in *Falling,* presents us with a second-generation American mother who is not only domineering and controlling but also physically abusive of her young child. (Is it mere coincidence that Schaeffer's mother is also named Sara, the archetypal Jewish mother?) On two occasions Elizabeth the youngest daughter, is forced out of the family car and temporarily abandoned on a cold night in a desolate area as punishment for minor misconduct. In another scene, Sara pursues the terrified child and strikes her with a wire hanger, blackening her eye and badly lacerating her cheek. Schaeffer depicts maternal abuse of a young child in a second novel, *Love.* Here the mother, when forced to remarry, abandons her child. A pathetic scene describes the little boy clinging to his mother's departing wagon, pleading to be taken along as she leaves with her new husband. Even greater injury is done the boy when, prompted by a combination of desperation and vehemence, the mother repeatedly pounds and bloodies his hand in order to release his grip.

While the maternal malevolence in these works may be extreme or exaggerated, lack of nurturance is a dominant characteristic of many contemporary women authors' descriptions of the mother. Whether in the image of the immigrant or second-generation American mother, whether of the bourgeoisie or the working class, maternal rejection, abandonment, and reluctance to assume the mothering role are frequently repeated themes.

A number of authors describe mothers who, while not malevolent or physically abusive of their offspring, offer little to generate the sympathy of the reader. These women are narcissistic or choose to place career or self-interest above the mothering function. This is the type of mother described by Lois Gould in *Necessary Objects*. Elly, an upper-middle-class Jewish woman, is too engrossed in her spa to see her son after the boy is nearly drowned in camp. Her sister, Alison, reluctantly becomes a mother only after first undergoing an abortion and another sister, Celine, "has a terrible aversion to children." *Leah's Journey*, a work by Gloria Goldreich, describes an immigrant mother who is depicted as having little compunction in favoring union activities, a lover, or travel to Europe over care of her young. Her child is left at home while Leah pursues her varied interests. The mother in *Long Division* by Ann Roiphe considers abandoning her daughter to the custody of her kidnappers—a band of gypsies—"I don't need her like an albatross around my neck." The feminist Erica Jong bemoans her mother's inadequate nurturing of her in *Fear of Flying* and ironically states, "If only I had a *real* Jewish mother."

A third category are mothers who are neither malevolent nor narcissistic, but are unable to give to their offspring because they are drained of energy by life's circumstances. They evoke the reader's empathy despite their non-nurturance. In *Heirlooms* by Carole Morgan, the immigrant mother Nehuma rejects and remains detached from her daughter Liebe. The role of the nurturing parent is assumed by the father, Morris. As Liebe matures and raises her own family, she patterns the mothering role after her own formative experiences. Liebe was glad that "She didn't have to look after her daughter day after day, tending to countless needs. Liebe was glad that others did it at the center. Weekends were terrible enough." Nehuma's other daughter, Rose, also finds child-rearing a burden. She falls into a depression after the birth of her son, is vexed at her inability to care for him, and finally commits suicide. In *Family Feeling* by Helen Yglesias, Anne, the youngest of seven children, writes of her immigrant mother, "She didn't want me and tried to get rid of me but I stuck, draining the last drops of warmth and calcium. She had no time and place for me." In "I Stand Here Ironing," Tillie Olsen describes a mother's remorse at not having offered her daughter the necessary love and emotional support when the child was young. Her work "Tell Me a Riddle" describes a sick grandmother incapable of showing physical affection for her grandchild: "Unnatural grandmother not able to make herself embrace a baby." Despite these mothers' inability to address the needs of their off-

spring, their daughters regard them with compassion and understanding. This is already evident in the writings of Anzia Yezierska, one of the earliest female Jewish American writers, who in the 1920s describes a taskmaster of a mother who chastises her undernourished fourteen-year-old daughter for allowing herself to be dismissed from the sweatshop. Yezierska, nonetheless, describes the mother with pathos and understanding, recognizing that her actions were due to desperation rather than malevolence.

Literature, as life itself, defies facile and rigid categorization, and several works by female authors describe positive mothering types as well as doting, overprotective mothers resembling the popular stereotype. Joanne Greenberg, Sylvia Tenenbaum, and Violet Weingarten give us glimpses of the latter cases. These, however, appear to be exceptions that attest to the general rule.

Similarly, not all Jewish male authors resort to the stereotype of the Jewish mother. In works by Bellow, Malamud, and others, we are given realistic descriptions of mothers as vulnerable, concerned beings. In *Herzog*, for example, Bellow lovingly describes the nurturing aspects of motherhood. He writes, "All children have cheeks and all mothers spittle to wipe them tenderly." Herzog's mother spoiled her children and even his stepmother, Taube, is described affectionately. Malamud's Ida Bober in *The Assistant* is an oversolicitous, anxious, but genuinely caring mother who follows her daughter in her concern that no harm befall the girl. One notes, however, the minor role assigned to the "real life" mother in the works of these authors as compared to the center stage occupied by the stereotype in the works of Philip Roth, Bruce Jay Friedman, Herbert Gold, et al. It would appear that in instances where the Jewish male author casts the mother in a position of central importance, her protective qualities are generally caricatured. The positive nurturing mother rarely appears or is relegated to a minor role. The non-nurturing mother is virtually nonexistent.

How is one to account for these differences? Literary analysis does not readily lend itself to rigorous scientific analysis. One can, however, attempt some tentative assessments. The fairly distinct descriptions of the mother emerging from the pens of male and female authors suggest that there may, indeed, be different gender-linked relations between mothers and their children that male and female authors experience and express in their works. The daughter's experience of her mother may differ from and contradict the son-mother relationship. A dynamic interplay of socio-cultural and socio-psychological factors may underlie these differences. Jewish culture, from time immemorial, has valued the male child. The birth of a son in Jewish tradition has been heralded with great rejoicing in contrast to the sometimes equivocal reception given to the arrival of the daughter. Contemporary society has lent its weight in favor of a male bias, and the immigrant or second-generation American mother may have found it difficult to cast off a favored tradition bolstered by the norms of her new-found American shores. Culturally sanctioned values subtly ingraining themselves into the psyche of the Jewish American mother may, indeed, have inclined her to respond with favoritism toward her son while shunning and sometimes neglecting the daughter. This notion finds kinship in the psychoanalytic postulate of penis envy, which sees the male child as the crux of maternal fulfillment. While only the most rigid Freudians interpret penis envy in a literal sense, it is generally viewed by many neo-Freudian analysts, in a larger cultural context, as symbolic of the deference accorded to the male by contemporary society. The daughter, while perhaps perceiving that she was accorded less favored treatment than her brother, responded somewhat paradoxically. On the one hand, the neglect and injury inflicted upon her were magnified in her eyes and seen at times as being more malicious and spiteful than in actuality—what child does not perceive a hurt as larger than life? On the other hand, in her sex-related kinship with her mother and in her actual or potential role as mother, she is generally able to accept this injustice with equanimity. At its worst, the mother's mistreatment is seen as a human failing. In its more benign aspects it is understood with pathos. In the daughter's eyes, the mother is sometimes faltering and imperfect and judged harshly but is rarely a caricature. The son, in contradistinction, cannot readily vilify the mother and deny his favored status. Yet, impelled to sever his maternal ties and assert his manhood and independence, he frequently resorts to sardonic humor to exaggerate and distort the mother's nurturing virtue. Hence, the stereotype of the oversolicitous Jewish Mother perpetuated by male authors.

Other factors may also contribute to the different perceptions of male and female authors. Motherhood, with its attendant child-bearing and child-rearing responsibilities, inclines the mother to respond ambivalently to her child. What mother has not at some time uttered "Who needs this?" in anger which does not truly emanate from the depths of her being? The readiness with which American-born Jewish mothers are able to acknowledge that children are a burden that they sometimes resent has been noted by psychoanalysts. Women, as actual or potential mothers, are doubtlessly more sensitive to this ambivalence and able to articulate it more freely. The plethora of rejecting mother types in the works of female authors may thus be a by-product of woman's sensitivity to the mother's ambivalent feelings, whereas the male may be more inclined to perceive the mother's nurturing features and gloss over her ambivalence.

These attempts to explain the conflicting portrayals of the mother from the male and female perspectives are by no means definitive. There may, indeed, be other socio-psychological factors that can account for these differences. However, in the light of this evidence, we can no longer adhere to an uncritical acceptance of the Jewish mother as a unidimensional Sophie Portnoy caricature. The Jewish mother emerges, for all her imperfections, with greater complexity and dignity. It would be interesting to ascertain how the mother is depicted by male and female authors in other ethnic literatures.

Rita K. Gollin

SOURCE: "Understanding Fathers in American Jewish Fiction," in _The Centennial Review,_ Vol. XVIII, No. 3, Summer, 1974, pp. 273-87.

[_In the following essay, Gollin argues that "the Jewish father remains at the moral center of Jewish fiction" even if he is not typically at its narrative center._]

I

A widespread misapprehension about fathers and mothers in American Jewish fiction hides from us some profound truths about their roles as apprehended by that fiction. Harold Fish's recent statement in _Midstream_ is representative: he speaks of "the rejection of the father," and says that his replacement "by the Jewish mother is in a way the most important event in twentieth century Jewish life and letters." But the truth is much more complicated than Fish's statement implies. Fathers in recent American Jewish fiction are never finally rejected, and Jewish mothers do not replace them. Whether the father plays a major or a minor role, whether he earns respect or ridicule, his role as a father makes him the transmitter of a moral tradition he can teach even when he has failed to master it himself. The lesson is rarely formal, and rarely involves formal Jewish laws or traditions; nor is it a pragmatic lesson in social utility and material reward. It is concerned with compassion and comprehension of human limits; and whether or not he is at the center of the narrative, the Jewish father remains at the moral center of Jewish fiction.

The two examples Fish cites from recent American Jewish fiction, _Call it Sleep_ and _Portnoy's Complaint,_ may at first seem to support his hypotheses about parents' roles, since in these novels the fathers are indeed weaker than the mothers. As he puts it,

> With the rejection of the father the Jewish mother has now come into her own. At the close of the novel [_Call it Sleep_] when David has achieved his final epiphany and is slumbering in the arms of his mother, the father, Albert, is seen skulking off, after having been thoroughly chastised and humiliated. His symbolic departure from the household marks the virtual disappearance of the Jewish father from modern literature. In _Portnoy's Complaint_ father Portnoy has become a totally ineffective and tangential figure. . . . Portnoy senior is nothing but a victim, and not even a victim of infidelity which might have lent him a touch of the heroic, but a victim of constipation.

Yet even for these novels such statements do not stand up; the situations are more intricate. Henry Roth's _Call it Sleep_ does not reject Albert Schearl as a father but as a man of violent rage, whether directed against his son, against his own father, or against an employer. At the end of the novel, Albert is not "skulking off"; rather, he is going to buy medicine to ease David's burnt foot, for the first time confronting his own responsibility for David's distress. Albert is "chastised" only tentatively by himself, and he is making no "symbolic departure." He will return: "I'll go get it" are his last words in the novel. Equally important is David's response to his father's change: for the first time he feels for his father "a vague, remote pity."

Genya Schearl cannot guide David through the alien

world of the street. David necessarily moves away from her as he ventures beyond home and family—playing with other boys; encountering gentiles; startled by power he cannot yet understand, whether the mystery latent in the Hebrew words of Isaiah, or the electricity of the third rail. Nor is he "slumbering in the arms of his mother" at the end of the novel. She is indeed sitting on his bed, speaking words of comfort. But her final question, "Sleepy, beloved?" moves David into the transcendent vision of life which concludes the novel and provides its title. He has grown past her; his mind ranges over the stream of city life, pondering questions beyond his mother's reach. His father may not be an adequate guide either, but Albert is no longer a source of terror, and David's ability to pity him attests to the growth of both father and son.

Fish's interpretation of Jack Portnoy must also be challenged. Certainly he is ridiculously ineffective—as an insurance salesman, as the husband of Sophie, as a strong male model for his son, even in dealing with his own constipation. But he is not altogether "ineffective and tangential." Alex identifies with him: "I wear his hair," he says; and he remembers his boyish pride in his father's nakedness at the Turkish baths. His own humanitarian profession as "Assistant Commissioner of Human Opportunity for the City of New York" echoes his father's dedicated job selling ghetto blacks life insurance from the Boston and Northeastern Insurance Company, a company that bills itself as "the most benevolent financial institution in America." Alex knows that the company exploited his father, and he describes his affair with Sarah Abbot Maulsby, paragon of New England's aristocracy, as an act of vengeance: "it was something nice a son once did for his dad." Alexander Portnoy is always aware of his father's love, and in devious ways, he returns it. Further, as he is about to visit Israel, he realizes that in one sense, all he ever wanted to be was a grown-up Jewish man. His grown-up father, Jack Portnoy, is indeed a victim (and of much more than constipation), but he is not merely a victim: he is a continuing influence on his son's development.

Sophie Portnoy is indeed the dominant parent in this novel. She is a vintage version of that stereotyped mother who recurs in Jewish humor, clearly similar to strong Jewish mothers such as Bessie in Clifford Odets' "Awake and Sing," or the engulfing mother of Bruce Jay Friedman's *A Mother's Kisses*. Smothering mothers, of course, occur in the literature of other religious and ethnic groups, but the figure of Sophie, urging her son to eat with loving concern and uplifted knife, seems recognizably Jewish.

Yet this kind of domineering mother has rarely interested the major American Jewish writers. In the most important American Jewish fiction, that of Malamud, Bellow, Philip Roth, and I. B. Singer, the father poses the most serious and moral problems for his child. The child may refuse to follow his father's footsteps, but he is profoundly ambivalent about his refusal; and usually by the end of the narrative, he reaches a new level of acceptance of his father and himself. The father is not rejected, not replaced. It is the mother who seems increasingly irrelevant.

II

The gulf between father and child is caused not only by archetypal rivalries between them, but also by the cultural distance between most first generation American Jewish parents and their children. Yet deep within the Jewish tradition is a double standard of respect that often helps to bridge the gulf. From Biblical times to our own, the Jewish man who achieves wealth or social power wins society's respect, but the man of piety and learning commands even greater respect. On the basis of this value system, shtetl fathers are proud to support sons-in-law who studied Talmud; thus an immigrant pants-cutter would be honored for Talmudic learning by more affluent *landsleit*. Accommodation to American experience in recent American Jewish fiction has produced secular variants of this dual standard. A father who has not succeeded in business, even one who has relaxed or relinquished formal religious practices, may still merit respect as moral guide for his more Americanized child.

Such guidance of a son by a father is never simple and rarely direct. One group of fathers, like Jack Portnoy, like other fathers in the fiction of Philip Roth, Herbert Gold, and most important, Bernard Malamud, is a schlemiel, a comic but lovable bungler; but he nevertheless conveys through his behavior the important lessons of parental love. A second group of fathers, such as Albert Schearl, command and expect obedience. Like the more traditional and more admirable patriarchs of Chaim Potok, I. B. Singer, and Saul Bellow, Schearl provokes his son to reach on his own a new level of understanding and self-reliance. Each kind of father exerts vastly different emotional pressure, but the end result, surprisingly, is almost the same.

Before writing *Portnoy's Complaint*, Philip Roth had already explored problems of inadequate fathers in three short stories of *Goodbye, Columbus* as well as in the novel *Letting Go*. Superficially, no two of his fathers are alike; yet however shallow or emotionally undeveloped, each reveals a capacity for love and anguish that his wife fails to demonstrate. Mr. Patimkin of "Goodbye, Columbus" is vulgar and insensitive, yet his love for his daughter Brenda remains generous and solicitous, especially by contrast with his wife's rigidity and recriminations. The father in "Epstein" is more pathetic: he is unsuccessful in business; his only son died years ago; and his wife and daughter give him neither love nor respect. He has become an adulterer, but only because he needs love. The young lawyer in "Eli the Fanatic" is even more anguished, overwhelmed by the Jewish heritage of suffering he apprehends through a group of refugee children and their surrogate fathers; and this heritage Eli plans to transmit to his newborn son. Eli may be deranged, but his empathetic anxiety reveals a moral awareness his wife will never achieve through her psychological theories.

The emotional interdependence of fathers and children Roth developed more fully in *Letting Go*, commencing with an epigraph from Wallace Stevens: "The son/and the father alike and equally are spent." Both Paul Herz and Gabe Wallach are sons who have wounded their fathers through inadequate understanding and love; they move through this knowledge toward the ability to themselves assume roles as fathers. None of the fathers or sons in Roth's fiction is complete or well-balanced, yet like the Portnoys, each seems admirable to the extent that he feels and offers compassionate love.

As a bizarre example of this mutual compassion, the narrator of Roth's *The Breast* praises his father's heroic effort to communicate compassion and affection for his horribly metamorphosed son without indicating distress. His father talks of people both used to know, sustaining a semblance of their former relationship. "My father's bravery has been staggering," Kepesh says, praising "this self-possession in the face of horror." His mother is dead: "if she wasn't, this would have killed her." Realizing that his father's composure is a kind of performance, Kepesh concludes that he is a "great and novel man."

The same lesson is taught with more affection and less mockery in the avowedly autobiographical fiction of Herbert Gold. The son in "The Heart of the Artichoke" and the novel-memoir, *Fathers,* resents working in his immigrant father's grocery store when he might be reading or taking trips with school friends. The story's climax is a fierce fight between father and son which both lose: the father pins down his son but relaxes his guard just long enough for the son to throw him. From the vantage point of maturity, the son regrets his victory: his father permitted too much; "to fight back was all I needed." Despite his antagonism, he feels physical pride in his father, clearly asserted as in *Portnoy's Complaint* in the all-male world of the Turkish baths. By the end of *Fathers,* the son has come to admire his father for more important attributes, despite his increasingly separate cultural identity. *Fathers* ends with Gold's praise for his father's courage and integrity on the way "to the common end, carving his will out of the dreadful void, and may I and other fathers do as much." This the grocer taught the writer, by the example of his life.

Malamud's fiction contains the widest range of such fathers, low on the social scale but elevated by devoted love for their children. "Idiots First" is an especially poignant statement about a father's love for his vulnerable child: Mendel desperately tries to put off an emissary of death only long enough to arrange to send his idiot son to the protection of a California relative. The fathers in "The Lady of the Lake," "The Magic Barrel," and "The First Seven Years" also put their children's welfare ahead of their own. If a mother appears in these stories, she is practical but ineffective; and there is no mother at all in "Idiots First" or "The Lady of the Lake." Each father is essentially a good man; but frequently during the course of the story, he becomes more aware of his child's needs. The shoemaker father of "The First Seven Years" finally accepts his ugly assistant as a prospective son-in-law not only because he wants help in the store, but more important, because he becomes aware of his daughter's response to Sobel's devoted love. In a more ambiguous narrative of a father's change, the marriage broker of "The Magic Barrel" at first refuses to introduce his wayward daughter to the rabbi who has fallen in love with her picture. Yet in the end Salzman arranges the meeting; perhaps marriage can effect a rebirth for the daughter he mourns as dead.

The central figures of Malamud's novels, *The Fixer* and *A New Life,* are also essentially good men who grow until they modify or reject their own prior standards for better ones. Yakov Bok in *The Fixer* is moved by his father-in-law's compassion to perform a compassionate act for his estranged wife and her illegitimate child: he formally announces the child is his. S. Levin in *A New Life* forfeits his role as bachelor and college teacher and acquires two children by accepting responsibility for their mother and thus for them. Levin's reward for shouldering this burden is the novel's final surprise, that Pauline is pregnant with his child. Both Bok and Levin learn to act selflessly, becoming fathers in the process.

Of these schlemiel fathers who are also moral heroes, Morris Bober of Malamud's *The Assistant* is the most fully developed. He is a poor grocer, a man still mourning his long-dead son (like Roth's Epstein), a man longing for "the best" for his daughter Helen. He is finally able to give her (and Frankie Alpine, the Italian drifter who adopts him as a surrogate father) only the example of his own selfless humanity; yet that example is crucial. Morris, who does not feel bound by orthodox Jewish laws, firmly adheres to the fundamental Jewish law as he interprets it: "to do what is right, to be honest, to be good. This means to other people. Our life is hard enough. Why should we hurt somebody else?" This is the Jewish "law" that governs even those Jewish fathers in recent fiction who do not adhere to it; and the law is taught by the fathers rather than the mothers. Although Morris' wife Ida also wants "the best" for her family, her approach is narrowly practical and self-oriented; and she has little influence on Helen's attitudes or actions. Helen learns in the end to value her father's morality. Her willingness to accept Frankie's help for her college education proves both of them are conforming to Morris's example.

III

The second group of fathers differs from the first in their direct exertion of parental authority; a child's challenge of that authority brings distress to both. These fathers are more emotionally dominant than the first group, more conscious of the respect they should command.

The fathers in Chaim Potok's novels, *The Chosen, The Promise,* and *My Name is Asher Lev,* are the clearest exponents of parental authority, and further, they are dedicated to the patriarchal activities traditionally accorded the highest respect: one is a Hasidic rabbi, one a teacher of Talmud, one a philosopher, one a religious administrator. The sons' most painful problems of identity center on the father, even when as in *My Name is Asher Lev,* the mother is important to the narrative. But only the scholar's son (in *The Chosen* and *The Promise*) is from the start bound to his father by mutual understanding and sympathy, and only he will follow his father's professional path. His friend Danny Saunders is the brilliant son of a Hasidic rabbi who has raised his son in a discipline of silence except during religious study. Eventually Danny understands and condones his father's educational method, but he will never succeed him as leader of their Hasidic sect: Danny will become a psychologist. The central figure of *My Name is Asher Lev* is even more separated from his father. Asher is a talented artist whose father rejects his paintings as violations of orthodox Jewish tradition. Eventually Asher comes to respect his father's career—establishing yeshivas, helping Jewish refugees; but like Danny Saunders, he feels bound to a completely different way of life. Through understanding their fathers, the sons win the possibility of self-respect without expending themselves in rage and rebellion. Finally, each comes to realize that despite their differences, father and son are bound by love and mutual concern.

To the extent that I. B. Singer affirms the traditional values of the shtetl, he affirms its ideal of the father as the patriarch who teaches his children practical and spiritual wisdom, and of the mother as wholly submissive and subordinate to her husband. This ideal is fully realized in "The Little Shoemakers," which crosses from the shtetl to America and from before to after World War II, ending as the old shoemaker's financially successful Americanized sons rediscover from him the joys of working together, singing traditional songs of praise. Singer's most famous story, "Gimpel the Fool," affirms the patriarchal ideal even though Gimpel's wife betrays and insults her husband: the story condemns her even if Gimpel will not.

Singer's stories set outside the shtetl and in our own time suggest that violations of patriarchal tradition are bound to bring distress. Friedl in "The Mentor" is a neurologist whose husband and daughter live apart from her on an Israeli Kibbutz. She has not replaced the Jewish father, although in a way he has replaced her. She has rejected life with her husband as stultifying; but she cannot accept her daughter's hostility. As a mother, she is bereft of love; having denied it to her daughter, her daughter denies it to her. The daughter has learned from her mother a lesson of constriction rather than growth. But in a recent (apparently autobiographical) story called "The Son," Singer affirms that the strong bond between parent and child can survive long separation. After twenty years, the narrator is visited by the son he last saw at the age of five. With wondering surprise, the two leap to recognition and intuitive understanding. The story suggests such gratification is available to any parent and child, to any father and son: any abyss between them can be bridged by affection and sympathy.

Most of these stories of conflict between father and son end in some measure of compassionate recognition and understanding, even if at the minimal level of Henry Roth's recent short story, "The Final Dwarf." Roth recounts the petty hostilities of a man past middle age on a shopping trip with his bigoted old father. After Kestler collects his mail-order eyeglasses from Sears, proud of his bargain, he grudgingly chauffeurs his old father on a round of penny-saving errands. Kestler is scornful of Pop's economies and of his social prejudices. Pop resents the resentment. Yet in the end, driving home, Pop fastens his seat belt though he had previously refused to do so, subtly acknowledging mutual concern beneath the hostility. Such concern does not deny or erase ambivalence, nor the cultural gap between father and son; and there is no pretense that father or son is perfect, infallible, or even necessarily admirable. But the strong bond between father and son generates strong emotion that can lead to mutual understanding, even if not always love.

Such problems of understanding are most fully explored in the fiction of Saul Bellow. From his earliest novels to his most recent, Bellow has scrutinized relationships between fathers and children, questioning what each should give and expect from the other. In *Seize the Day, The Victim, Herzog,* and *Mr. Sammler's Planet,* the children are adults who feel their fathers have denied them understanding and love. Their fathers may speak from positions of social respect the children may never attain, and they may offer good advice but nonetheless prove inadequate parents. Conversely, a son may learn to be a good father without—or even despite—the example of his own father. By the endings of all four novels, the central characters begin to practice the selfless compassion required of effectual fathers. The values are the same as Malamud's, though Bellow usually projects them on loftier intellectual and social planes. As in most American Jewish fiction, the mothers in these novels are either minor figures or else long since dead: the father bears a parent's moral burdens alone.

Tommy Wilhelm in *Seize the Day* is a fat, middle-aged man without a job; he is separated from his wife and children; his mother is dead. Self-pityingly, he seeks assistance from his proud and proper father. But Dr. Adler condemns Tommy's sloppy behavior; he refuses not only money but understanding, sympathy, and love. The novel's other wisdom figure, Dr. Tamkin, offers the good advice which provides the book's title; but he advises badly on the stock market and may in fact be a self-seeking cheat. These "fathers" are not wholly admirable or trustworthy; the son must learn not to depend on them. Throughout his day of emotional catastrophes, Tommy moves toward emotional independence from these fathers through an increasing ability to feel pity for other people; and thus he moves toward the possibility of becoming more adequate as a human being himself.

Asa Leventhal in *The Victim* is another man who must learn to be a father unlike his own. He remembers his father as an angry, self-centered man, and many of Asa's problems can be attributed to his own anger and self-centeredness. His mother he recalls only as a passive woman who presumably died insane. Like Tommy, Asa moves to maturity through compassion. He learns to control his resentments, and he is willing to assume responsibility for his young nephews until his brother returns to his proper role. On the novel's last page we learn that Asa is about to become a father.

An old man named Schlossberg has a minor role in the narrative which looks back to Tamkin and forward to Sammler: he speaks the novel's central advice to be "exactly human" and to "choose dignity"; yet his own son is "good-for-nothing." Thus, through Schlossberg, Bellow again questions what is necessary and what is sufficient to a good father.

In *Herzog,* the central figure is a father who learns to fulfill that role more adequately. The novel begins and ends with Moses Herzog, a twice-divorced philosopher, in the Berkshires house bought with his "heritage"—the hard-earned money of his immigrant father who "the year before his death, had threatened to shoot him" for making such a mess of his life. In the course of the novel, Herzog comes to appreciate his father as a courageous man whose primary concern was for his family, whether he was an unsuccessful bootlegger or a successful businessman. This understanding also becomes part of the Herzog heritage. Finally, Herzog is able to move beyond confusion and rage and act like a man of courage. He plans to share his life with his children: he will write a book for his daughter, and he is painting a piano for her; he will invite his son for a month's visit. He may yet become a father who deserves respect.

Bellow's most recent novel, *Mr. Sammler's Planet,* focuses more sharply on the problem of men who have earned society's respect yet fail as fathers. Mr. Sammler is one such man; his dying nephew, Dr. Gruner, is another. Both are honorable men; both have lost their wives. Although Mr. Sammler, the novel's central wisdom figure, is past seventy, he still has lessons to learn. He must recognize the full human value of Dr. Gruner, yet acknowledge Gruner's failure as father of two grown, self-indulgent children. Then Mr. Sammler can confront his own failings as a father. By the novel's end, he is able to offer his middle-aged daughter the words of love and praise she has long required. Even a middle-aged child needs a father's tenderness; unless he has learned this, even a good and wise man cannot be a good father.

IV

In these American Jewish novels, not the mother but the father is ultimately the dominant parent, teaching values of the heart and spirit even when he does not directly embody them. Rare is the mother who is tender and generous like Genya Scheral of *Call it Sleep,* or the mother Moses Herzog lovingly recalls pulling him on a sled. More frequently she is ambitious, hard-headed, and demanding. This Jewish mother may be explained as a complement to her more idealistic mate. In a way a Sancho Panza to his Quixote, she desires the immediate goods of this world, at least nominally for the sake of her children. But most surprising is how frequently the mother is simply eliminated from the fictional picture. American Jewish authors have been most concerned about the relations of father to child, and especially of the father to the son who is—or will become—a father himself.

The father-son relationship has of course interested other writers, but not in the same way. The southern fathers of Faulkner's *Absalom, Absalom* and Tate's *The Fathers,* for example, try to adhere to a rigid code of honor and a precise code of manners as the only means to get across life's abysses, including those that separate them from their sons. The Jewish fathers, by contrast, rarely worry about honor or codes of manners. If they do manage to pass over the gulfs between them and their sons, it is usually by some more intuitive route based on the love latent in relations between parents and children, and based on mutual awareness of human fallibility.

Few of these Jewish fathers (except for Potok's and some

of Singer's) have retained firm ties to Jewish ritual or orthodox belief. And whether they are immigrants or simply residents of urban America, few have roots in a particular place. Questions of political affiliation or sexual appetite are irrelevant. It does not seem especially important whether a father makes his living as a doctor or a storekeeper, whether he is better educated than his son or not, whether he has clearer career goals or not. Even if a father's problems are initially practical, like these of making a living, their resolution always has to do with the larger problem of making a life. Repeatedly, the father moves to a moral arena where value is measured in terms of integrity, dignity, responsibility, and compassion.

The fathers tend to play three kinds of roles in the fiction, whether they are schlemiels or patriarchs, and whether major or minor characters. The roles are not mutually exclusive. First, the father remains essentially the same throughout the story, but his child must learn to value him. He may be ineffectual, or even worse, tyrannical; yet the child learns to accept, to pity, and sometimes to love. Thus the children of Albert Schearl, of Jack Portnoy, of Morris Bober. Sometimes the father teaches a lesson the child prefers not to learn: Dr. Adler in *Seize the Day* and Jonah Herzog in *Herzog* are enraged by their sons' requests for money; but the novels' endings suggest the sons are beginning to understand the value of independence. Sometimes, as at the endings of Malamud's *The Assistant* and Gold's *Fathers,* a skeptical child comes to praise the father's moral heroism.

Second, the father may learn to play the role of father more properly by learning to accept responsibility and express compassion. This applies to Albert Schearl, to Eli the fanatic, to the father of Singer's "The Son," to many of Malamud's fathers, to Asa Leventhal, Herzog, and most especially Artur Sammler. By breaking out of their selfish constraints, they free themselves to express the concerned love their children require. Thus, Mr. Sammler expresses pity and contempt for his daughter Shula throughout *Mr. Sammler's Planet,* but by the end he acknowledges her devotion and rewards it by praising her as a good daughter, none better.

As a third variant, a son who is also a father may learn to understand his own father, and become a better father himself. This is true of Tommy Wilhelm, of Moses Herzog, and of Asa Leventhal. The father is traditionally a conveyor of moral wisdom; sometimes he must also become wise.

Father and children are both fallible: such is the human condition. Both must learn to accept willingly the tie that binds them, to praise and so foster in each other whatever seems to merit praise. Ambivalent feeling about the father is to be expected: Alex Portnoy scorns his father's ineffectuality as Helen regrets Morris Bober's impracticality; they learn in time to acknowledge the love offered them. Repeatedly in American Jewish fiction, affection for a father is initially mixed with contempt, but develops into a deeper affection and often into admiration. Finally, the child accepts the father not only as a single individual but as a representative of the human condition in all its absurdity yet with all its possibilities for dignity and growth.

Victoria Aarons

SOURCE: "The Outsider Within: Women in Contemporary Jewish-American Fiction," in *Contemporary Literature,* Vol. 28, No. 3, Fall, 1987, pp. 378-93.

[*In the following essay, Aarons explores the "paradox of simultaneous exclusion and inclusion" from tradition and heritage that women in Jewish-American literature face.*]

For quite some time now the issue of ethnic identity in Jewish-American fiction has posed a central concern for critics and writers alike, a concern bred from the necessity to identify the place of Jewish fiction within the broader scope of American literary culture. Not unlike other literatures that we have come to call "ethnic," black or chicano fiction, for instance, or even those which comprise the "immigrant experience" in fiction (such as Maxine Hong Kingston's novels of Chinese-Americans), Jewish-American writing emerges as yet another example—if not the primary paradigm—of both an "ethnic" and an "immigrant" fiction. Certainly the Jewish-American literature that directly grew out of the early immigrant experience in America, Abraham Cahan's *The Rise of David Levinsky* (1917), and Anzia Yezierska's *Hungry Hearts* (1920), for example, yielded to such literary concerns as dialect and a preoccupation with themes of assimilation and ethnic identity. Perhaps the best-known novel of the Jewish immigrant's journey from steerage to New York tenement life, Henry Roth's *Call It Sleep* (1934), self-consciously calls attention to the problematic mingling of languages and customs that characterized the "greenhorn's" struggle to integrate into American culture. This novel in many ways stands as a beacon to the immigrant's epic survival, much as Roth's metaphorical description in the prologue of the towering statue in New York's harbor ironically illuminates the immigrant's precarious passage into mainstream America: "the rays of her halo were spikes of darkness roweling the air; shadow flattened the torch she bore to a black cross against flawless light—the blackened hilt of a broken sword. Liberty." By its very nature, then, early Jewish-American fiction was relegated to a certain *outsider* status. Both the writers and their fictions were situated on the outskirts of our perceived notions of the American literary heritage.

For post World War II Jewish writers, however, this outsider posture seemed no longer a requirement. Bellow, Malamud, and Philip Roth merge into the mainstream of American literature to stand alongside Faulkner, Hemingway, and Steinbeck. More and more, Jewish writers speak about and within American culture, transcending an earlier "immigrant" identity imposed by an alien culture. In *Jewish Writing and Identity in the Twentieth Century,* Leon Yudkin suggests such a shift in the place of American Jewish writers from the outskirts to the mainstream of literary culture when he argues that:

> By the 1940's, a substantial native-born generation considered itself as much a part of the national fabric as any other element, religious or ethnic. To be an American Jew became increasingly one of the ways of being an American. . . . This did not mean that there was no longer a characteristically Jewish literature but

its form of expression changed. The Jew could not easily see himself as an immigrant if he was of local provenance and an English-speaking American national. He was already, on the whole, commercially successful, socially established if not totally integrated, and did not have another mother country to look back to nostalgically or to summon as a measure.

Yudkin's point here seems particularly significant in light of our attention to defining literature in terms of its ethnic origins. He argues even further that in American literature since the 1940s,

> the Jewish voice is not only heard but increasingly accepted as the norm. Jewish terminology, except in certain instances of specialist exposition, is no longer explained to the reader. Yiddish has entered the American language, and the Jewish type with the implication of his cultural, social and historical background is understood as part of the scene. Bellow does not have to translate to the extent that Cahan did. And the Jew is not seen on the fringes of society, trying to edge his way in. In many ways, he exemplifies that society. And Jewish literature is peculiarly American literature.

Yet Jewish women writers, at least in our formal recognition of them, remain beyond the pale of established critical acclaim. Less recognized than their male counterparts, yet nonetheless emerging in the American literary scene, contemporary Jewish women writers continue to be faced with issues of ethnic identity and self-definition, reinforcing the "immigrant" status that defined earlier Jewish fiction in America. For, if Jewish fiction in America has been marked by a certain outsider status, it may be all the more so for Jewish women writers, who are outsiders to the traditional, male-dominated literary culture, as well as to the more traditional Jewish laws, which limit women's roles in public worship and in institutional power.

What we find in the writing of many contemporary Jewish women, such as Grace Paley, Tillie Olsen, Cynthia Ozick, and Hortense Calisher, is a self-conscious recognition of an outsider position in both American culture and Judaism. When coupled as oft-perceived products of a literary subculture, Jewish ethnic identity and an emerging "women's fiction" become finally questions of voice, a voice that is at once a source of richness and tension in the fiction of contemporary Jewish-American women. In defining that voice, we come somewhat closer, I believe, to securing a coherent vision, a common world view, shared by many Jewish women writers in America.

I do not mean to suggest that literary concerns of ethnicity no longer remain central to the more established male Jewish writers. Indeed, the ethnicity of writers such as Malamud and their categorization as Jewish writers result in critical debate still. Robert Alter, in *After the Tradition,* suggests this tension:

> It is by no means clear what sense is to be made of the Jewishness of a writer who neither uses a uniquely Jewish language, nor describes a distinctively Jewish milieu, nor draws upon literary traditions that are recognizably Jewish.

Here the complexity of the issues surrounding Jewish identity in the fiction of American writers crystallizes. Unlike other literary subgenres that call attention to questions of ethnicity and identity (such as black, hispanic, native American, or lesbian literatures), Jewish-American fiction seems to raise issues of a distinctively different nature. Because the Jews assimilated so quickly (unlike other minority groups still pursuing their rights and fashioning their American identities), Jewish identity has been complex enough to force itself upon the design of American fiction. While group affiliation would be the apparent linking concept of minority literatures, such *public* matters of identity give way to more *private* concerns with personal identity for the Jew in America. Jewish-American literature is still an "immigrant fiction" because of the complexities of the question of what it means to *be* a Jew in America. Can one *remain* a Jew in a secular "melting pot" and still feel at home there, still maintain a posture of economic and social success? This is the essential focus for contemporary Jewish-American writers. The question of whether one can remain a Jew in America, that is, can remain connected to the faith, underlies the thematic tensions in works as diverse as I. B. Singer's "The Son from America," Grace Paley's "The Loudest Voice," and Philip Roth's "Defender of the Faith." As one might expect, however, the issue of whether one can remain a Jew in America is not only a matter of faith, but involves an even deeper connection to the heritage, to the past, to the disappearing world of the "fathers."

Can one *remain* a Jew in a secular "melting pot" and still feel at home there, still maintain a posture of economic and social success? This is the essential focus for contemporary Jewish-American writers.

— *Victoria Aarons*

Because of these complexities, a singular "Jewish" voice is untenable. Before one could identify *a* Jewish voice, one would have to answer some very vexing questions: How does one define the ethnicity of a writer: by his or her direct political statements? By his or her depiction in fiction of Jewish characters, environment, and issues? By his or her birth alone? Must a writer address particular Jewish issues or situations to be considered a Jewish writer? These questions are difficult because of the uncertainty in the definition of a uniquely Jewish character or context in America, where the character is as much American as Jewish and the context grounded in an American ethos. Questions of Jewish identity in writing are not unlike those currently faced by contemporary women writers, who have often felt compelled to address the issue of a "women's fiction," whether or not they consider themselves advocates of the genre. The current controversy among feminist critics and writers highlights this concern.

As Adrienne Rich and others have argued, how we define ourselves involves complex personal and political issues. This process of self-definition—especially for women who have been alienated historically from the Western literary heritage—presents itself in the literature by women as more than a search for identity, for a fixed personal identity. (I make the distinction here, knowing that it is a controversial one, between feminist writers, unified by a political ideology, and writers who are women.) Rather it seems to me that the attempts at self-definition through literature become a process of self-fashioning, of forging an identity. For contemporary Jewish-American women writers, faced with dual issues of sexual and ethnic identity, the process of self-definition is further complicated.

Can we make certain assumptions about Jewish women writers that will not simply reinforce well-worn stereotypes about both Jews and women? Does a self-perceived "ghettoization," the formative influence in the development of the Jew as "outsider," keep Jewish women writers on the margin of American literary culture? Such self-conscious distinctions go no little way in reinforcing an outsider status, despite, for example, Leon Yudkin's contention that the Jew in literature has secured a firm place by moving "from the periphery to the centre" of American literary tradition.

The motif of the outsider as fictional stereotype has been overly simplified in much of the writing about Jewish literature. To call the Jewish writer simply an outsider, distanced from both the American experience and from his or her Jewish heritage, ignores the dichotomy that lies at the heart of the problems of ethnic identification in fiction. As outsider, the Jew—as fictional character and as writer—becomes much more than a stereotype. The very tension in the fiction of Jewish-American writers is the insider-outsider *paradox,* the ability of the Jew to be at once insider and outsider, in terms of both America and Judaism.

Nonetheless, Jewish-American writers, I would maintain, remain in many ways on the periphery of the literary culture still, in no little part as a result of their own self-consciousness of their position in the literary community. Cynthia Ozick defines this troublesome position well when she depicts herself as "a third-generation American Jew (though the first to have been native-born) perfectly at home and yet perfectly insecure, perfectly acculturated and yet perfectly marginal." Ozick's description of the Jewish writer as defined by a precarious balance between acculturation and estrangement reflects a self-consciousness on the part of the Jewish writer, a self-conscious Judaism that extends to the characters' visions of themselves and to their perceived place in America.

Tillie Olsen's famous story, "Tell Me a Riddle," depicts a woman, an immigrant, who has spent her adult years struggling for equilibrium and comfort in America, who finally when her children are grown, when her death is imminent, renounces Judaism, renounces a connection to any specific faith. In the hospital, when told she is on the Jewish list for visiting rabbis, she proclaims: "Not for rabbis. At once go and make them change. Tell them to write: Race, human; Religion, none." For this old woman, Judaism—the religion and inherent traditions—represents backwardness, persecution, and restriction. Her daughter, American-born, tries to recreate tradition, ritual. She looks to her mother for a key to the past, for a link to Judaism, hoping to enrich the present. However, instead of being drawn to the tradition of her youth, the dying woman regards such rituals as the lighting of candles as "Superstition! From our ancestors, savages, afraid of the dark, or of themselves: mumbo words and magic lights to scare away ghosts." Her vision of Judaism militates against her principles of humanity, principles for which she fought in Olshana, in the old country, principles that flew in the face of a centuries-long stronghold of oppression. In a bitter recollection of what it meant to be Jewish, Olsen's protagonist decries the faith of her "fathers":

> Candles bought instead of bread and stuck into a potato for a candlestick? Religion that stifled and said: in Paradise, woman, you will be the footstool of your husband, and in life—poor chosen Jew—ground under, despised, trembling in cellars. And cremated. And cremated. . . .
>
> Heritage. How have we come from our savage past, how no longer to be savages—this to teach. To look back and learn what humanizes—this to teach. To smash all ghettos that divide us—not to go back, not to go back—this to teach.

Olsen's protagonist rebels against a determined adherence to a faith that persecutes and against long-ingrained gender expectations that reinforce her alienation from a religion that persecutes even more because of her status as a woman. To the amazement of her family, she cannot respond to her grandchildren. Her husband scolds her: "Unnatural grandmother, not able to make herself embrace a baby." The kind of isolation felt by the protagonist in "Tell Me a Riddle" is derived from the pressure to be what she is not, to live up to an externally defined posture of doting Jewish grandmother, solicitous wife, acquiescent old woman, content with the passage of age. She views these predetermined roles as denials of the progressive secular humanist she sees herself to be. She tells her granddaughter, " 'it is more than oceans between Olshana and you,' " and yet her hopes for equality and freedom, values symbolized by America, plummet in the face of continued oppression. Those socialist ideologies of her youth in the old country—ideologies that gave her life-blood—failed to materialize in the "land of the free," and so she remains an immigrant still, ghettoized, as she was in the *shtetl,* by her refusal to "move to the rhythms of others," to accept the diminished circumstances willed to her. The old woman's husband finally comes to understand his wife's longing and loss, and remembering the ideals of the past, sees them now in the light of betrayal and failure of the twentieth century: " ' ' "in the twentieth century ignorance will be dead, dogma will be dead, war will be dead, and for all humankind one country—of fulfillment?" Hah!' "

The immigrant's distance from his or her homeland, the "outsider" status, provides us with a vision of loss, disappointment, and disillusion. In Cynthia Ozick's brilliant short story, "Envy: Or, Yiddish in America," the main character, Edelshtein, must forever remain unnoticed because he writes his poetry in Yiddish and has no English translator. He derides America as "the empty bride,"

without dowry, without history, without identity. The wry humor with which he is portrayed by Ozick is constantly checked by our sympathies for him. Edelshtein's despair over the fate of Yiddish in America is momentarily arrested by his delight in finding a young woman, American-born, who reads Yiddish. Edelshtein's delusion that he has finally found a translator who will make him famous, will make his works known in America, founders when he discovers that Hannah, the would-be translator of his work, will not translate poems of the "ghetto." She is interested only in poetry that reflects universal concerns, poetry in the mainstream, " 'In the world. . . . Not in your little puddles.' " Edelshtein's response to Hannah's attack demonstrates the enormous gap between the immigrant and the American-born Jew, the latter a Jew by descent only:

> "Again the ghetto. Your uncle stinks from the ghetto? Graduated, 1924, the University of Berlin, Vorovsky stinks from the ghetto? Myself, four God-given books not one living human being knows, I stink from the ghetto? God, four thousand years since Abraham hanging out with Jews, God also stinks from the ghetto?"
>
> "Rhetoric," Hannah said. "Yiddish literary rhetoric."

Hannah, unlike the American-born daughters in Tillie Olsen's "Tell Me a Riddle," perceives her "heritage" not as a source of richness and continuity, but rather as a preoccupation with suffering, as a curse: " 'Suffer suffer,' she said. 'I like devils best. They don't think only about themselves and they don't suffer.' " Hannah seeks a universal—not a peculiarly Jewish—history, much in fact like Olsen's protagonist, a history without the emotional vestiges of the "old country," free from suffering, from defeat, from self-delusion. Edelshtein's outrage at Hannah's neglect of the past emphasizes the chasm between generations, between cultures. He, in turn, denies her a past, curses her: " 'Forget Yiddish!' he screamed at her. 'Wipe it out of your brain! Extirpate it! Go get a memory operation! You have no right to it, you have no right to an uncle, a grandfather! No one ever came before you, you were never born! A vacuum!' "

As Edelshtein cries out, it ultimately may be a matter of "rights," that the birthright, the right of identity, a connection to the past, to Judaism, carries with it the emotional baggage of the outsider. However, being a Jew in twentieth-century America takes on a decidedly different meaning from what it meant to be a Jew in the Eastern European shtetls. This difference in definition finally prevents Hannah and Edelshtein, Tillie Olsen's dying mother and her American-born children, and the host of Jewish characters separated by generations, from residing comfortably under the same "roof."

Problems with generational differences and with "place" are deeply connected to issues of identity and ethnicity. Grace Paley's protagonists, especially the women, struggle with identity, with their physical place in the world, and in relationships with other people—parents, husbands, children, peers. For Paley, Judaism often appears in her short stories as a nagging reminder of the past, a loss, a constant source of disquiet for many of her characters. The main character, Faith, in Paley's short story, "Faith in the Afternoon," for example, is caught between differing visions of the world. On the one hand, she remains connected to the world of the "fathers," as characterized by her parents, and on the other, she lives in a more modern America, a world seemingly free from the bonds of historical and religious dictates. Having left Judaism in a formal sense, reinforced by her marriage to a gentile, a union that finally—acrimoniously—leaves her to raise her children on her own (" 'I love their little goyish faces,' " her father says of his grandchildren), Faith attempts to bridge the two worlds. Although she has abandoned the old neighborhood of her childhood, she nostalgically turns to her mother in search of information of people from her past, and feels connected to them; their *tsouris,* their suffering, is akin to her own. Yet she remains inevitably outside of both worlds, her predicament ironically similar to the very immigrant parentage against which she shields herself:

> Her grandmother pretended she was German in just the same way that Faith pretends she is an American. Faith's mother flew in the fat face of all that and, once safely among her own kind in Coney Island, learned real Yiddish, helped Faith's father, who was not so good at foreign languages, and as soon as all the verbs and necessary nouns had been collected under the roof of her mouth, she took an oath to expostulate in Yiddish and grieve only in Yiddish, and she has kept that oath to this day.

> Faith has only visited her parents once since she began to understand that because of Ricardo she would have to be unhappy for a while. Faith really is an American and she was raised up like everyone else to the true assumption of happiness.

Yet in her failure to achieve the American image of happiness—the immigrant's dream—Faith can neither reconcile herself to her family, which is her past, nor adjust to the present. So her relationship with both parents, but especially with her father, is wrought with emotional turbulence; her "Judaism" becomes self-conscious, very much on the surface of her actions and responses.

While the father figure in Jewish literature is a powerful force with whom to be reckoned, the figure of the mother provides a deep connection to the past. Unlike Olsen's protagonist in "Tell Me a Riddle," it is often the mother who, because of her garrulity and penchant for participating actively in the lives of her neighbors and friends (frequently depicted humorously), is a rich source of information and continuity. It is not surprisingly the mothers who strongly adhere to the "world of the fathers," the mothers to whom the American-born children return time and time again. The tradition of the mother in Jewish literature—a tradition that unfortunately often lends itself to the worst kind of stereotyping—has a long history for both male and female Jewish writers. Shenandoah Fish, for instance, in Delmore Schwartz's short story, "America! America!," suffers from a loss of identity while traveling abroad and returns home to his mother's kitchen where, almost despite himself, he listens and is drawn to his mother's stories of old family ties. In them he recognizes his connection to the people in his past, not without a good deal of self-recognition and guilt, born from his conscious attempt to distance himself from his mother's immigrant history and to intellectualize his family's past. He comes to recognize his condescension toward his family and their friends with no little self-disgust:

> Shenandoah was exhausted by his mother's story. He was sick of the mood in which he had listened, the irony and the contempt which had taken hold of each new event. He had listened from such a distance that what he saw was an outline, a caricature, and an abstraction. How different it might seem, if he had been able to see these lives from the inside, looking out.

> And now he felt for the first time how closely bound he was to these people. His separation was actual enough, but there existed also an unbreakable unity.

Despite Shenandoah's recognition of his unbreakable connection to his heritage, an insight he has not come upon without considerable turmoil, he remains an outsider still: " 'I do not see myself. I do not know myself. I cannot look at myself truly.' " Shenandoah, like many of the fictive American-born children of immigrant parentage, suffers from a self-imposed but equally uncomfortable "immigrant" condition. He *is* and is *not* a part of his parents' world. Thus in characters like Shenandoah and Faith, we see, not a transcendence of traditional values, but a fragmentation of identity resulting from, on the one hand, a guilt-ridden attraction to the old ways and, on the other, the realization that the attraction, both curiosity and instinct, is felt inevitably from the "outside."

The outsider's sense of difference often results in a perceived failure to live up to the expectations of one's parents—a theme itself consistently found in the literature. We find it, for example, in such works as Chaim Potok's *The Chosen,* Bernard Malamud's *The Assistant,* Susan Fromberg Schaeffer's *Falling,* and Herbert Gold's "The Heart of the Artichoke," in which the conflict of values and choices between children and their parents—mothers who know intimate details of the lives of their neighbors, fathers who ascribe to postwar American notions of success, parents who believe in fixed absolutes, such as family loyalty, hard work, and the like—creates considerable ambivalence for the protagonists. This tension manifests itself, I believe, most strikingly in the depiction of the "modern" Jewish woman, who is, in many ways, expected to carry on the tradition. In Hortense Calisher's short stories this ambivalence manifests itself in a quiet recognition, but by no means an unqualified acceptance, of change. In "The Rabbi's Daughter," for example, Calisher's protagonist leaves the refined "world of the fathers," for her the relatively genteel world of the Jewish middle class, surrenders her career as a pianist for marriage to a man who works with his hands, yields finally to a style of dress and decorum unlike those to which she is accustomed, and takes up a life of transience. The difference in the rabbi's daughter's two hands, one more roughened than the other, reflects with understated power the dual nature of her existence. Gazing at her hand, she proclaims: "This one is still 'the rabbi's daughter,' " the hand unmarred by work, unblemished by worries about finances and domestic concerns.

Characteristic of many of the protagonists uncovered in the fiction of Jewish-American women, the rabbi's daughter breaks from the tradition, the life, but can never entirely leave the world of her "father," that world so ingrained, so very much at the heart of her identity and her struggle. This kind of ambivalence prevents the female protagonists from living comfortably in either world. For the rabbi's daughter, it breeds resentment, dissatisfaction, a sense of self as "visitor." The rabbi's daughter, upon leaving her family and moving into new temporary lodgings found by her husband, "heard her own voice, sugared viciously with wistfulness. 'Once I change [my attire] I'll be settled. As long as I keep it on . . . I'm still a visitor.' " Shedding her "travel" clothes—an adornment of past luxury—becomes a metaphor for relinquishing a past life for a much less certain future, a future without the fixed values and traditions of the "fathers."

Similarly, Paley's character Faith is equally infused with an ambivalence that causes both shame and anxiety, manifested by an uneasy love for her father, whom she can no longer look in the eye:

> He leaned over the rail and tried to hold her eyes. But that is hard to do, for eyes are born dodgers and know a whole circumference of ways out of a bad spot. . . .
>
> Mr. Darwin reached for her fingers through the rail. He held them tightly and touched them to her wet cheeks. Then he said, "Aaah . . ." an explosion of nausea, absolute digestive disgust. And before she could turn away from the old age of his insulted face and run home down the subway stairs, he had dropped her sweating hand out of his own and turned away from her.

The image presented here is strikingly visual; Faith's father virtually pulls on her, drawing his daughter to him, begging her to return to the fold. A tug of war ensues, from which neither emerges as victor.

Paley's characteristically ironic—often tentatively humorous—voice balances the pathos of her characters and situations. This voice might best be characterized as a kind of self-irony, born perhaps from the inherent problems of self-definition and from the recognition of the precarious posture of the American Jew. Jewish writers thus are ironically detached from, yet identify with, their characters.

As distanced from traditional Jewish values and culture as many of the characters are—Hannah, the rabbi's daughter, the dying old woman who denounces a faith that denies humanity, the young mother in Paley's story who recognizes the disparate needs of her father and herself—they have nonetheless a bond, a haunting connection to Judaism, an obsession with the past, an often unspoken alliance with "the fathers." Susan Fromberg Schaeffer metaphorically suggests this link to a collective sense of identity:

> they remembered with wonder, how their lives, and their characters, and their morals and their

fates had always hung there like long clothes in the closet, waiting for them to grow into them.

This compelling link to the past, a past experienced often elusively as a sort of collective memory for the American-born children, is nowhere more apparent than in the fiction that draws heavily upon the tension between the immigrant parent and his or her American-born child. This reliance on collective memory is what allows Grace Paley's narrator in "Mom" to relate the images of her childhood memory of her mother, like all mothers, who calls to the child from the window to come in off the street: "I am not the child. She isn't my mother. Still, in my head where remembering is organized for significance (not usefulness), she leans far out." For the American-born children of Jewish immigrants, life in America is both a blessing and a curse, ironically for the same reason: because one is not in Europe. Paley, in "The Immigrant Story," establishes this paradox, when a young couple attempt to grapple with their parents' lives, and with their own childhoods (a common theme in Paley's works):

> Jack asked me, Isn't it a terrible thing to grow up in the shadow of another person's sorrow?
>
> I suppose so, I answered. As you know, I grew up in the summer sunlight of upward mobility. This leached out a lot of that dark ancestral grief. . . .
>
> What if this sorrow is all due to history? I asked.
>
> The cruel history of Europe, he said. In this way he showed ironic respect to one of my known themes.

The narrator of the story remembers her childhood perception of America, reflected by an incantation: "I made an announcement to the sixth-grade assembly thirty years ago. I said: I thank God every day that I'm not in Europe. I thank God I'm American-born and live on East 172nd Street where there is a grocery store, a candy store, and a drugstore on one corner and on the same block a shul and two doctors' offices." Yet as the narrator itemizes the gains, her luck in being an American, Jack recounts the losses of the immigrant experience, of his parents' past. For him, America symbolizes the ultimate sacrifice, that of parents for children who constantly deny the promise. The misery, the guilt, and the confusion Jack feels stem primarily from his own sense of failure. Jack remembers the comparative ease of his life in juxtaposition with his pieced-together fictional picture of his parents' struggle, a picture that comes together in his "memory" of likely events:

> My mother and father came from a small town in Poland. They had three sons. My father decided to go to America, to 1. stay out of the army, 2. stay out of jail, 3. save his children from everyday wars and ordinary pogroms. He was helped by the savings of parents, uncles, grandmothers and set off like hundreds of thousands of others in that year. . . . Mostly he put his money away for the day he could bring his wife and sons to this place. Meanwhile, in Poland famine struck. Not hunger which all Americans suffer six, seven times a day but Famine, which

tells the body to consume itself. . . . My father met my mother at the boat. He looked at her face, her hands. There was no baby in her arms, no children dragging at her skirt. . . . She had shaved her head, like a backward Orthodox bride, though they had been serious advanced socialists like most of the youth of their town. He took her by the hand and brought her home. They never went anywhere alone, except to work or the grocer's. They held each other's hand when they sat down at the table, even at breakfast. Sometimes he patted her hand, sometimes she patted his. He read the paper to her every night.

Their story is the immigrant's story, and their sorrow, their loss, becomes that of their children, American-born, both finally outsiders. Jack's efforts to explain his parents' lives in America, like the obsessive queries made of Olsen's resistant protagonist—"Day after day, the spilling memories. Worse now, questions, too. Even the grand-children: Grandma, in the olden days, when you were little"—speak to, I think, an attempt at alleviating the fragmentation that has become the by-product of contemporary Jewish-American life. Such attempts often fail, however, because of the tensions inherent in the outsider's relation to his or her culture, expressed again by Shenandoah Fish:

> Shenandoah tried to imagine their arrival in the new world and their first impression of the city of New York. But he knew that his imagination failed him, for nothing in his own experience was comparable to the great displacement of body and mind which their coming to America must have been.

It is not so simple to argue that what we finally uncover in Jewish-American writing is a conflict of generations, a struggle between the immigrants and their American-born children. A struggle, certainly. However, it is a struggle that connects as well as divides. For such children in fiction, even those long since grown, the oral history embedded in their memories remains paradoxically a source of both connection and estrangement. Despite the host of characters caught in an ambivalent, often warring posture with their heritage, the guiding voice of the writer, almost without exception, tempers the conflict, makes sense of the tension through empathy. It is no wonder, then, that this conflict has as its center the family, for, as Robert Alter has recently argued, "the family, after all, is the matrix of our psychological lives, of our political, moral, and theological imaginings."

While this ambivalence is articulated most pronouncedly in the language of the vanishing immigrant in Jewish-American literature, the insidiousness of separateness, of identity by ethnicity, appears also in that literature remote from the immigrant experience. Hortense Calisher's short story, "Old Stock," for example, suggests a different vision of the outsider. The assimilated and refined Mrs. Elkin, who considers herself and her daughter removed from those "Jews whose grosser features, voices, manners offended her sense of gentility all the more out of her resentful fear that she might be identified with them," finds herself the very burnt of anti-Semitism, all the more disturbing because of her own anti-Semitic inclinations. While va-

cationing in the Catskills, where she considers herself beyond reproach, Mrs. Elkin tries her best to shun the other Jews staying at her lodgings; she considers any such association intrusive and presumptuous. Much to her embarrassment, however, Mrs. Elkin's "disguise" is exposed by an elderly local woman, and her unease, finally out in the open, reflects the denial of her own and her daughter's Jewish lineage and ironically causes her daughter to seek such a connection:

> "I told Elizabeth Smith," Miss Onderdonk said. "I told her she'd rue the day she ever started taking in Jews." . . .
>
> Mrs. Elkin, raising her brows, made a helpless face at Hester [her daughter], as if to say, "After all, the vagaries of the deaf . . . " She permitted herself a minimal shrug, even a slight spreading of palms. Under Hester's stare, she lowered her eyes and turned toward Miss Onderdonk again.
>
> "I thought you knew, Miss Onderdonk," said her mother. "I thought you knew that we were—Hebrews." The word, the ultimate refinement, slid out of her mother's soft voice as if it were on runners.
>
> "Eh?" said Miss Onderdonk.
>
> Say it, Hester prayed. She had never before felt the sensation of prayer. Please say it, Mother. Say *"Jew."*

Her mother's obvious distress paradoxically causes Hester to define herself once and for all as Jewish, and so to put an end to her mother's attempts to be what she is not.

We finally return to the question: can one remain a Jew in America? This question, born of the Jewish immigrant experience, depends for its answer on the definition of Judaism, which in many ways "looks different" in America, and on the acceptance of change, the tolerance of an evolving Jewish character in the literature of Jewish-American writers, the denial of old stereotypes and archetypal patterns.

How does one reconcile the Jewish-American experience with its past, with its immigrant origins? The steerage across the waters left behind more than miles. And the sense of loss is increasingly perceptible as the generations turn for American Jews, creating a need for a new identity, a new sense of what it means to be Jewish, a need intensified for women by the inevitably transformed feminine postures available in the "new" culture of America. In the fiction I've examined, a new vision of what it means to be Jewish in America emerges. No longer do we find, as we did with the earlier immigrant fiction and even with that which came after World War II, characters who feel excluded from and at odds with American socioeconomic ideals. Malamud, Bellow, and Philip Roth, it might be argued, worked through the evolution of the Jewish male character who, always a step out of line with the rest of America, struggled unsuccessfully to merge with the American mainstream, to shed the weighty baggage of his heritage. Contemporary Jewish-American women writers present a different sense of the "outsider." No longer on the outskirts of American culture, nor even of the literary tradition, the characters find themselves paradoxically alienated from and drawn to a heritage from which they are excluded, and yet in which they play an important function—the silent foil of a male-dominated tradition. This paradox of simultaneous exclusion and inclusion results in the fragmentation of identity we've seen in these stories, a fragmentation that causes the characters to seek to resolve their ambivalent feelings toward their pasts by trying to recreate them. Often, such characters are torn between a longing for the past, for a sense of absolutes (rituals, traditions, beliefs), and a determination to forge ahead, to fashion an identity that "fits" for this time and this place. Though their defiance of the "world of the fathers" results in new possibilities for the Jewish-American woman, it remains a vision fraught with ambivalence, with mistrust of one's "place," yet with an "insider's" instinct for continuity and the potential reaffirmation of identity. It is in this way that the Jewish-American woman, and perhaps, even more so, the Jewish-American woman writer, is the "outsider within."

Sylvia Huberman Scholnick

SOURCE: "Money Versus *Mitzvot:* The Figure of the Businessman in Novels by American Jewish Writers," *Modern Jewish Studies*, Vol. 6, No. 4, 1987, pp. 48-55.

[*In the following essay, Scholnick investigates the thematic loss of Judaistic ethics in exchange for the worship of profit as dramatized in the works of several Jewish-American writers.*]

In the thirty-one years from 1899 to 1930, nearly two million Jewish people arrived in the United States from Eastern Europe, joining the approximately 500,000 who had already arrived since 1621—first Sephardic Jews of Spanish and Portuguese origin and then, from about 1820 to 1880, Ashkenazic Jews from Germany. Most of the Eastern European Jews came to this country without money or salable skills. To review the statistics, 60 percent of these Jews in 1900 were blue-collar workers, half employed in the garment industry; 20 percent were in business, half as owners of retail stores, one-fifth as peddlers and hucksters; and 2.6 percent were professionals. Dramatically, by the 1960s in many cities, only 15 percent of the Jewish population were working class, 40 percent were in business, and 32 percent were professionals. While the immigrants found immediate employment in blue-collar jobs, their children and grandchildren turned to business and professions in remarkable numbers.

Sociologists have compiled statistics to describe this rapid transition from poverty to middle-class prosperity and the resultant changes in the character of official Judaism. But demographic statistics cannot, nor are they intended to, provide an understanding of the human dimension of the immigrant's adjustment to American life. Fiction, on the other hand, can illuminate the experience of living during this period of upheaval in the Jewish community, the personal experience of moving from poverty to wealth. And fiction succeeds in dramatizing the conflict between the traditional Jewish values and business ethics.

Among the many novels by American Jews that treat this subject are: *The Rise of David Levinsky* by Abraham Cahan (1917); *Haunch Paunch and Jowl* by Samuel Ornitz (1923); *Summer in Williamsburg* by Daniel Fuchs (1934); and *What Makes Sammy Run?* by Budd Schulberg (1941). In each of these novels a businessman of Eastern European Jewish descent figures prominently. *The Rise of David Levinsky* and *Haunch Paunch and Jowl* are written in the first person as confessions about the rise from poverty to wealth. *What Makes Sammy Run?* tells of Sammy Glick's rise to wealth and power but from the point of view of a colleague trying to understand the meaning of Sammy's life. *Summer in Williamsburg* does not follow the rags-to-riches pattern, but instead tells the story of Philip Hayman's late adolescent struggle with the question of what to do with his life—whether to follow his father's example of living a poor but ethical life in the tenements or to follow his Uncle Papravel's example of struggling for wealth at the cost of moral integrity. These works deal with a common problem: How is it possible to become a successful businessman in America and still retain the traditional Jewish values? Although these novels differ in many ways, by treating their similarities, a pattern emerges of the high cost of abandoning traditional Judaism and Jewish *mitzvot* in order to make money and escape the poverty of New York's ghetto tenements.

All four of these novels have a common understanding of the ethical foundation of Judaism. Success for Jewish people when they lived in Eastern Europe was measured by *yikhus* (prestige) achieved first and foremost through a moral life based on doing *mitzvot* (technically, commandments of both biblical and rabbinic origin, but commonly translated "good deeds"); second, *lomdes* (scholarship); and last but least important, wealth. There are 613 *mitzvot* directing all areas of life. But the key to the entire Torah, as identified in the first century B.C.E. by the scholar Hillel, was the concern of man for his fellows. When he was asked by a potential proselyte to teach the whole Torah while standing on one foot, he replies: "What is hateful to you do not do to your neighbor: that is the whole Torah; the rest is commentary, go study." From Hillel's time, this *mitzvah,* tucked away in Leviticus, has been acknowledged as the foundation of Jewish ethics: "Love your neighbor as yourself: I am the Lord" (Lev. 19:18). But as Hillel emphasized in his lesson to the proselyte, it is essential to enrich this understanding of the core of Judaism with study.

Abraham Cahan, an immigrant from Russia and consequently close to the Eastern European Jewish values, clearly articulated in *The Rise of David Levinsky* the centrality of *mitzvot* in orthodox Jewish life where action has a divine dimension. The novel tells the story of a young man's poverty-stricken early life in Russia where he studies Talmud and then, after his immigration to the United States, his rise to wealth in the garment industry. Reb Sender, David's mentor in the synagogue in Russia, advises him:

> Study the word of God. . . . There is no happiness like it. What is wealth? A dream of fools. What is this world? A mere curl of smoke for the wind to scatter. Only the other world has substance and reality. Only *good deeds [mitzvot]* and

holy learning [lomdes] have tangible worth. (emphases and brackets mine)

For the most pious Jew, like Reb Sender, wealth is not a worthy measure of human value or success, which leaves *mitzvot* and *lomdes* as the only acceptable criteria.

Scholarship in the Eastern European pious Jewish community is clearly limited to Jewish subjects, especially the Talmud, and is valued as a *mitzvah* in itself. Mrs. Levinsky dreamed of having her son study at a Talmud seminary so that he might become "a fine Jew": "This is the trade I am going to have you learn, and let our enemies grow green with envy." David was well-learned in his "trade" when he arrived in New York with four cents in his pocket, but of course, he finds that being "a fine Jew" was not a marketable skill.

Ghetto life in New York is portrayed in these novels as harsh and unacceptable. David brought to the land of Columbus the image of the American street as "a thoroughfare strewn with nuggets of the precious metal," gold, but upon his arrival found poverty. Meyer Hirsch, the protagonist in *Haunch Paunch and Jowl*, Philip Hayman in *Summer in Williamsburg*, and Sammy Glick in *What Makes Sammy Run?* are portrayed as second-generation Jews born in New York City ghettos. All resemble Philip, Meyer Hirsch's uncle in *Haunch Paunch and Jowl*, who "growls and curses at the meanness of our living . . . no better than roaches."

The growls and curses of these protagonists express their determination to leave the tenements. They all realize that the way is through financial gain. Harry Hayman in *Summer in Williamsburg* expresses this conclusion when he says:

> I'm not going to stay in this place, in the hot filth, squeezed in small dark rooms, one among a pack of dried out walking stiffs. . . . And the only way anybody can get out of this hold is to make money.

David Levinsky works his way to wealth in the garment industry, Meyer Hirsch becomes a rich, powerful lawyer, Philip Hayman's Uncle Papravel struggles to wealth in transportation, and Sammy Glick becomes the head of a leading Hollywood movie studio.

In the world that these novels portray, success is judged on the basis of wealth, while the old Jewish measures of *mitzvot* and *lomdes* lose their significance. As both David Levinsky and Meyer Hirsch are coincidentally advised, "money talks" in America. The characters who retain Jewish traditions and values are portrayed as failures unable to work their way out of the tenements. One of these characters is Max Hayman in *Summer in Williamsburg*, who is said to have "a Hebraic sense of propriety." He advises his sons, Philip and Harry, that

> a man must be honest, must do no harm to anyone, but work at his trade, justly and honestly . . . like the old days when friendship . . . meant everything. These times people care only about making money, and they don't care who gets ruined or hurt so long as they make it.

Max remains stuck in the poverty of the tenements, which leads his younger son, Philip, to see him as a "schlemiel, a dreamer, a fool who had no common sense" and his older son, Harry, to ask: "Who cares about ethics? While you're worrying about treating the other fellow right, somebody will be stepping all over your neck." Sammy Glick, who from the age of five works to help support his family, asks his father contemptuously: "While you were being such a goddam good Jew, who was hustlin' up the dough to pay the rent?" In the ghetto world that Cahan, Ornitz, Fuchs, and Schulberg write about, observant Jews appear as losers.

Jewish laws regulating diet and Sabbath observance and customs about dress and sexual activity are tossed aside by the protagonists in these novels. Sammy Glick, for example, breaks the prohibition about handling money on the Sabbath and refuses to study at the *cheder*, the Hebrew school. His break from Judaism with its Mosiac commandments is complete and he concludes: "Moses was a sap . . . they've been playing him for a sucker for two thousand years." Sammy Glick's mother evaluates her son in a brief statement that could as well be applied to Cahan's Levinsky, Ornitz's Meyer Hirsch, or Fuchs's Papravel:

> Sammy was not a real Jew any more. . . . [He] cursed and fought and cheated. Sometimes she could not believe he grew out of her belly. He grew out of the belly of Rivington Street.

Ornitz makes the same point about Meyer Hirsch when the hero as a child says of himself and his friends that they are "pagans of the city wild." The poverty of the tenements gnaws at these characters and they hunger to escape at any cost. And the cost includes the rejection of the religion of their parents and the acceptance of the ethos of the streets.

These authors dramatize the rejection of Judaism by the rising young businessman, a rejection not simply of specific laws and practices, but of the essence of the religion. Cahan through the teaching of Reb Sender and Schulberg by referring to the words of Rabbi Manheim define in their novels the core of Judaism as "love thy neighbor as thyself " or "as thy brother." But this key commandment is tossed aside by David Levinsky, Meyer Hirsch, Sammy Glick, and Papravel, whose preoccupation with themselves precludes any genuine concern for others. As Fuchs's Papravel says: "Everybody who makes money hurts people." Ornitz's Uncle Philip, who makes a fortune in the garment industry, expresses outright contempt for his immigrant employees: "It's a good thing . . . this is a free country and I can exploit whom I like." Another businessman in Fuchs's novel gives his philosophy for success: "In order to make a nickel you simply had to go out and cut the next man's throat before he cut yours. That was the only way to make money in this country." These characters replace the quintessential Jewish commandment with the business command: "Cut your neighbor's throat as he would cut yours." Ironically, the only value Judaism has for the fictional businessman is what appears to further his progress in amassing a fortune. David Levinsky, then, appreciates his Talmud education for the mental training it had given him for business. An atheist as an adult, he belongs to a German Jewish synagogue simply because it is "fashionable." Meyer Hirsch in *Haunch Paunch and Jowl* serves as legal counsel for a synagogue "to put as many people as I can under obligation to me."

The protagonists replace Judaism with a different belief system, the profit motive. As Meyer Hirsch confesses, he follows a policy that "every situation return a profit." For these businessmen, the profit motive becomes a new religion. David Levinsky calls success "the Almighty Goddess of the hour. Thousands of fortunes were advertising her gaudy splendors . . . and he who found favor in her eyes found favor in the eyes of man." The Hebrew God promises prosperity in Deuteronomy: "The Lord will give you abounding prosperity in the issue of your womb, the offspring of cattle, and the produce of your soil. . . . You will be creditor to many nations, but debtor to none" (Deut. 28:11-12). But this promise of financial success is made only to those who follow the elaborate laws given through Moses. The Goddess of Success, however, makes no such restrictive contract. In fact, each novelist tells tales of money made through illegal and unethical practices. Papravel hires strongmen to terrorize a competitor, resulting in the murder of his employee and the closing of his business; Sammy Glick takes credit for another writer's story; Meyer Hirsch finagles a judgeship by agreeing to have his client drop a case she could easily win in court; and David Levinsky cheats the union and misrepresents his business to deceive a designer into working with him. Social Darwinism, the survival of the fittest, could be called the creed of the new religion of success, a creed acknowledged by the businessman character in the novels of Cahan, Ornitz, and Schulberg. For example, David Levinsky confesses that "the only thing I believed in was the cold, drab theory of the struggle for existence and the survival of the fittest."

Curiously, the protagonists in these novels who worship the Goddess Success experience patriotism for America, which takes on the aura of the holy land in this new religion. When Sammy Glick is asked at the pinnacle of his career how it feels to have everything, he answers: "It makes me feel kinda . . . patriotic." And Levinsky, vacationing in the Catskills when he hears a band play "My Country," says that "Love for America blazed up in my soul." Papravel praises America as the one place in the world where a Jew can "make such a man of himself." America provides the freedom that allows a businessman to accumulate wealth.

Unlike Jewish ethics, which emphasize concern for the welfare of others, the American business ethic stresses personal gain to the exclusion or detriment of others. It is not surprising then to find that these entrepreneurs are portrayed as experiencing loneliness at the height of their success. Cahan's Levinsky fails to find a wife and has "a brooding sense of emptiness and insignificance," which he connects with his loss of Judaism: "My past and present do not comport well. David the poor lad swinging over a Talmud volume . . . seems to have more in common with my inner identity than David Levinsky, the well-known cloak manufacturer." Ornitz's Meyer Hirsch, rejected by

the woman he hopes to marry and settling instead for a marriage with his long-time mistress, calls himself "bitter and sore . . . a hulking pachyderm, gross, flesh-odorous." Schulberg's Sammy Glick, who desperately wants a devoted wife, finds himself married to an adulteress and "in his mouth was the thick, sour taste of defeat." It is no coincidence that these characters, who have abandoned the Jewish ethic of love for other people and have replaced it with a self-centered business ethic, fail to achieve the most significant and deepest of human relationships, the love between a man and a woman.

The poverty of the ghetto was so severe, it is no wonder the protagonists of these novels wish to escape the tenements. But the cost of the escape is too high. The old world Jewish values are shed in the rush for financial success. But in taking on the new world's business ethics, which turn them in on themselves and isolate them from other human beings, these characters feel betrayed. The novelists test the business values and find them hollow.

In Saul Bellow's *Mr. Sammler's Planet,* a novel about a wealthy real-estate investor/doctor, Arnold/Elya Gruner is able to approach a resolution of the problem of being a successful businessman in America and retaining Jewish values. An immigrant from Poland in the years before the Second World War, Gruner grew up "a kid from a rough neighborhood" in New York to become an extremely wealthy man. There is no question that he used illegal practices to achieve his position, performing abortions for the Mafia and hiding the undeclared income in his home. However, through old Artur Sammler's observations, the reader is led to view Gruner as a person with deep love and concern for his family. Sammler makes the distinction that his nephew Gruner, although a businessman, was not "ruled by business considerations. He was not in that insect and mechanical state. . . . Elya was accessible . . . not one of these sealed completed impenetrable systems." Gruner had rescued Sammler and his daughter in 1947 from a displaced persons camp in Salzburg, brought them to New York, and was supporting them generously. After Gruner dies of an aneurysm, Sammler prays to God for his nephew, praising him as a man "aware that he must meet, and he did meet . . . the terms of his contract. The terms which, in his inmost heart, each man knows." And although Sammler is using a business term, the contract he speaks of in the context of a prayer may well be the one that has served the Jewish people since the time of Moses, the covenant between man and God. Bellow does not explicitly identify Gruner's values as Jewish, but the implication is certainly there with Sammler speaking in a religious context. And Gruner is portrayed in the novel not only as a successful businessman, but one who loves his fellow man, living according to the essential Mosaic *mitzvah.* Sammler says Gruner is "a dependable man—a man who took thought for others." Later he comments, "Feeling, outgoingness, expressiveness, kindness, heart. . . . Anyway there's Elya's assignment, that's what's in his good face." Cahan, Ornitz, Fuchs, and Schulberg dramatize the discontinuity between the traditional Jewish values and American business ethics in the life of the rising young businessman. But Bellow in *Mr. Sammler's Planet* points the way to an integration between financial success and essential Judaism. Even in the promised land of America, the Jew is challenged as he always has been to find a way to continue his ancestral religion.

Leslie Field

SOURCE: "Israel Revisited in American Jewish Literature," in *Midstream,* Vol. XXVIII, No. 9, November, 1982, pp. 50-54.

[*In the following essay, Field discusses the subject of Israel as an invigorating force in contemporary Jewish-American literature.*]

A few years ago Joyce Field and I interviewed Bernard Malamud. One exchange went as follows: "Characters in your fiction wrestle with their Jewishness. In response to a question, Morris Bober defines *his* Jewishness. Yakov Bok ultimately feels he must rejoin *his* people. But these characters and others seem to adapt as minority people to the pluralistic societies they find themselves in.

"One of our students recently noted that the current writers who frequently people their works with Jews—Saul Bellow, Philip Roth, I.B. Singer, etc.—and who explore serious matters concerning Jewishness, probe or suggest a variety of possible identities. These may involve religion, assimilation, acculturation, Bundism, social action, and so on.

"But Zionism—specifically seeking one's Jewish identity with Israel—is quite conspicuous by its absence. As a matter of fact, this student further observed that the real indepth American Zionist novel has not only *not* been written, but probably will never be undertaken by a major American writer.

"Do you agree, Mr. Malamud? Why has Zionism played such a minor role for the Jewish characters who have populated so much of our fiction during the last two decades?"

And now Malamud's brief reply to that overlong question: "I agree. Writing about Zionism wouldn't interest me. I'd rather write about Israel if I knew the country. I don't, so I leave it to the Israeli writers."

I've put this question to other major American Jewish writers. It always evokes a similar response. Israel is not their milieu. Let's leave it to someone else, preferably the Israelis.

Nevertheless, some American Jewish writers have drawn upon Israel. And it was with that notion that Sarah Cohen first mentioned the idea to me and then was instrumental in orchestrating a panel for the prestigious Modern Language Association. MLA had never had such a session. True, in recent years papers were given on the more popular American Jewish writers. Now and then an earlier American Jewish writer would be included, and even an Israeli or Yiddish writer whose work happened to be considered significant for modern language research.

But investigating the role of Israel in American Jewish literature has simply not been a priority for the 15,000 members of the Modern Language Association or, for that matter, for their academic departments anywhere throughout the land. So this special session was a departure from the norm.

As moderator, I was to limit the scope of the meeting. Three papers would be offered, each on a specific author. The panelists, as it turned out, unlike Malamud, were eager to address themselves to the Israeli experience in American Jewish literature, and their credentials were first-rate.

Alvin Rosenfeld, Director of Jewish Studies at Indiana University, writes extensively on American Jewish writers and Holocaust literature. He chose to discuss Hugh Nissenson. Irving Halperin of San Francisco State is also a specialist in American Jewish literature and literature of the Holocaust, but his other interest is creative writing. And although he agreed to talk on Meyer Levin, he had serious misgivings about Levin's literary style. Finally, Sarah Blacher Cohen of SUNY at Albany, who originally suggested the idea, is no stranger to American Jewish literary figures. She would work with Bellow's *To Jerusalem and Back.*

Thus was the stage set for our discussions on "Israel Revisited in American Jewish Literature." The competition for an audience was keen at the New York Hilton during the cocktail hours of that winter afternoon. At the same time in 34 rooms scattered around the Hilton and the Americana other groups discussed "British Romanticism and British Romantic Fiction," "Perspectives of Language Theory," "Folklore as Process in Afro-American Literature," "Methodological Problems in Monolingual and Bilingual Lexicography," and so on. However, the Israel Revisited session more than held its own. Hugh Nissenson himself was in the audience, as was Cynthia Ozick, who had taken part in an early morning panel on Bellow, Malamud, and Philip Roth.

My own tentative characterization of what we were about that day and where Israel fits into American Jewish literature follows: Irving Howe has portrayed American Jewish literature as a literature of discontinuity, of nostalgia, a literature documenting a life that has passed. This focus on American Jewish literature has been with us for a long time.

Howe points out that the Jews in the Diaspora have been "multilingual." But the American Jewish writer is a special case. "The migration to America all but destroyed the internal bilingualism of Jewish life and thereby the historical complexities and religious balances that had contained it." Howe sees in the American Jewish writer a "rupture, break dissociation" with his roots. His "Jewish side" became "fragmented." What developed for the American Jewish writer, according to Howe, was that "the tradition of the Jews has figured more and more as lapsed rather than available possibilities." Thus our major American Jewish writers, Howe says, have made "the experience of loss as impetus to self-renewal" their central theme.

> **Irving Howe and others explicitly or implicitly have made a good case for the death of the American Jewish novel. But one is reminded of Isaac Bashevis Singer's often-reiterated comments on the death of Yiddish.**
>
> — *Leslie Field*

In Howe's view this syndrome has affected the works of Abraham Cahan, Daniel Fuchs, Delmore Schwartz, and Henry Roth, as well as the popular trio of Saul Bellow, Bernard Malamud, and Philip Roth. In conclusion, Howe poses a frustrating and almost devastating question concerning our current American Jewish novelists: "What remains for a novelist once the world of his youth has been destroyed, that world which overwhelms his every page even though, and perhaps just because, he is turning away from it?"

Irving Howe and others explicitly or implicitly have made a good case for the death of the American Jewish novel. But one is reminded of Isaac Bashevis Singer's often-reiterated comments on the death of Yiddish. When Singer came to America he felt Yiddish was on its deathbed. He had left Poland where people still spoke Yiddish, but even there the condition of Yiddish was miserable. Just before he left for the United States Singer put it this way: "I am going to the United States, where Yiddish is dying. My language is dying. In Poland, half-dead. In the United States, three-quarters dead." But finally Singer came to this conclusion about the revival of Yiddish: "If we would be normal people, I would say impossible . . . But with the Jews—anything can happen. Because they are so meshugeh." He then asks: "What other people would have revived a language like Hebrew after two thousand years?"

To be sure, on the one hand we have Singer's pixyish discussion about the survival of Yiddish in America and on the other a sober Howe arguing forcefully about the disappearance of Jewishness in the American novel. But both are discussing an interchangeable part of Jewish life and literature—past, present, and future. Howe seems to have shut off all options for the continuance or revival of American Jewish literature, but Singer, as usual, departs from logic as he says anything is possible. Perhaps there are factors that neither Singer nor Howe has taken into account; one, I believe, as we move closer to the end of the 20th century, is the Israeli-American-Jewish experience.

Of course American Jews and others *have* written about modern Israel as well as about pre-Israel dispersed Jewry. Every year the bibliographies in the *American Jewish Year Book* and the *Jewish Book Annual* attest to that. Some works are delightful but frothy stories with a setting in a northern kibbutz or an apartment in Tel Aviv. Some are simply potboilers using James Bond-like versions of Entebbe and mysterious cafés in Jerusalem. Still others are somewhat sober semi-autobiographical confessionals.

Much is tangential. That is, American Jewish books which combine a bagels-and-lox view of American Jewishness with a like approach to the Israeli experience. In one of Harry Golden's books he recalls his first visit to Israel. As his El-Al plane flew into the Tel Aviv area, he knew it was Friday because newspapers covered the spotless runway in preparation for the Sabbath.

But the question posed at the MLA conference was not about Harry Golden's use of Israel, but about the others, those who by many criteria are accepted as serious American Jewish writers—the Bellows, the Levins, the Nissensons, etc.

Sarah Cohen moved back and forth between Bellow's non-fictional *To Jerusalem and Back* and his fiction. She pinpointed Bellow's involvement with Jerusalem—"its peril," the fact that it is "threatened by everpresent evaluation." She saw parallels to characters and situations in Bellow's early fiction.

She said: "Israel as nation is thus subjected to the same maddening paradox of anti-Semitism which Asa Leventhal, the second generation Jewish urbanite of Bellow's *The Victim*, experiences at the hands of Kirby Allbee, the WASP descendant of the original settlers of the country."

For Cohen, Bellow linked the fate of Israel and Diaspora Jewry. In *To Jerusalem and Back*, she noted Bellow's sense of mystery and awe as he becomes immersed in the ancient city. Bellow in Jerusalem, she said, acquires the spiritual transcendence that eludes him when he attempts to capture the flavor of other important cities—Chicago or New York, for example. True, she noted some typical *Herzog* and *Humboldt's Gift* humor in this non-fiction book, but mainly she felt Bellow's involvement with Israel. He may be as baffled by Jerusalem as Herzog, Sammler, and Citrine were baffled by their 20th-century cities—before they put these cities behind them. Moreover, one can go back to much earlier novelists. A Twain or a Melville could view arid Jerusalem and dismiss it. Not Bellow. Even when he returns home to Chicago he "cannot evict Jerusalem from his thoughts." Bellow broods. "In America he continues to be ill at ease about Zion." For Bellow, Israel is or has become *special*.

Irving Halperin viewed Meyer Levin as another American writer who is serious about Israel. Halperin admitted that Levin in *The Settlers* and *The Harvest* "apparently intended to encompass no less than the entire Jewish experience of our time, to write a chronicle of the Chaimovitch family and their interactions with strands of history, from the turn of the century to the founding of the State of Israel." Thus in Levin we apparently find an even greater involvement with Israel than in Bellow. But for Halperin the large novels failed because of their pedestrian, wooden, "bloated prose." Levin's fiction, Halperin said, is second rate. It is "thin and uninteresting" despite Levin's earnestness.

How can one argue with Halperin's dismissal of Levin's prose? After all, as Halperin points out, if one wants simple documentation one has ample non-fiction available—journalism, history, etc. And he is not alone in these strictures about Levin's fiction. But I do believe Halperin was a bit hard on Meyer Levin. I find myself defending Levin's prose in much the same way I've defended Theodore Dreiser's or Thomas Wolfe's.

In the same vein, critic Ben Siegel characterized Sholem Asch's prose. Asch, he said, had many shortcomings. He was often cumbersome and careless in his use of language. He was frequently melodramatic and sentimental in his depiction of situation and character. But Asch, Siegel noted, was also a master of the panoramic scene, the great social, political, and religious upheavals of the 19th- and early 20th-century Western civilization. He was given to chronicling the "wide-spectrum," to capturing moods and impressions of eras.

As for Levin specifically, Midge Decter and Norman Podhoretz once hailed Levins' early work, *The Old Bunch,* as a landmark in the American Jewish novel despite its infelicitous prose. *The Old Bunch,* they insisted, did for Jewish Chicago of the thirties what James T. Farrell did for Irish-Catholic Chicago of the same period. It captured these milieus as few other works did. In a like manner Levin evokes the Israeli immigrant and settlement drama and the Israeli-American-Jewish ambience.

Decter and Podhoretz dealt not only with Levin. In an *Eternal Light* radio series a few years ago they cited several American Jewish books as "landmarks": Abraham Cahan's *The Rise of David Levinsky,* Ludwig Lewisohn's *The Island Within,* Henry Roth's *Call It Sleep,* Daniel Fuchs' *Summer in Williamsburg,* Saul Bellow's *The Adventures of Augie March,* Bernard Malamud's *The Assistant,* Chaim Potok's *The Chosen,* Philip Roth's *Portnoy's Complaint,* and Cynthia Ozick's *Envy, or Yiddish in America.*

Cahan in 1917 was the first modern American Jewish novelist. He depicted the immigrant Jewish experience in all its contradictions and paradoxes as no previous writer had done. In 1934, Henry Roth provided the Freudian/Joycean analysis to the immigrant experience sifted through the consciousness of a young boy. By 1953, Bellow had created Augie March, our first fictional unselfconscious American Jew who would stride through the streets of Chicago proclaiming his American Jewishness for all to hear. In 1957, we had in Morris Bober the alienated transplanted Jew depicted by Malamud. A decade later Potok wrote from within a comfortable, self-assured Orthodox Jewish community, a first for popular American fiction. In 1969, Philip Roth was even more strident than Bellow as he ran his Jew through a series of hilarious scatalogical exercises.

Although the works discussed by Decter and Podhoretz were "landmarks" signalling new departures in American Jewish fiction, nowhere do Decter or Podhoretz develop the possibility of a new Israeli dimension in the American Jewish experience and consequently in the American Jewish novel. They do touch on the Israeli experience here and there; they even go into some detail in their discussion of Lewisohn's *The Island Within,* but they apparently do not see Israel as the catalyst for the new American Jewish novel. Perhaps had they drawn upon a few other samples of recent American Jewish fiction, their landmarks, as perceptive as they are, could have been expanded somewhat. Hugh Nissenson, I believe, is a case in point.

I doubt that anyone would label Nissenson's prose "bloated" as Halperin did Levin's. On the contrary, it is often described as terse, sinewy, spartan, elliptical. But Nissension, one of the more important younger American Jewish writers, is noteworthy for his subject as well as his style. It is significant that Alvin Rosenfeld at the MLA panel introduced his discussion this way: "By common agreement, the most momentous events in Jewish life in the modern period are the destruction of European Jewry and the rebirth of the Jewish state." Yet, as Rosenfeld pointed out, "within the context of American literature the Holocaust and Israel have been slow to emerge into prominence and in most cases still play only an occasional or peripheral role." Hugh Nissenson, he felt, is an exception.

Nissenson has not written much. But in his few works (especially *Notes from the Frontier* and *A Pile of Stones*) he demonstrates the centrality of Israel to the Jewish people. Rosenfeld categorized this centrality in three ways: first are Nissenson's "efforts to translate Hemingway into Jewish national terms"; second is Israel as "home, or . . . depository for those who still hug close to God"; and, finally, Israel in a way represents the future for Jews insofar as the kibbutz ideal can be realized.

Rosenfeld depicted a Nissenson who is certainly involved with Israel—as are Bellow and Levin—But as Rosenfeld analyzed Nissenson's stories what seemed to emerge was more than involvement. It is rather a Talmudic dialogue or even Job-like confrontation with Israel. Nissenson seems to be asking many of the important questions, perhaps the most essential being: "Is it possible to create a humane civilization without God?"

It does seem clear that these three contemporary American Jewish writers—Bellow, Levin, Nissenson—have revealed their serious involvement with Israel.

In some respects, American Jewish writers have echoed their Israeli counterparts. That is, American Jewish writers, when they have taken Jewish themes seriously, have treated the Holocaust and Israel as peripheral elements in their writings, even though, paradoxically, these two subjects seem to be central to Jews everywhere today.

Israeli writers have run a parallel course. A few years ago Robert Alter singled out four Israeli writers who did depart from traditional Israeli themes as they linked Israel and the Holocaust. Alter drew upon Yehuda Amichai's *Not of This Time Not of This Place,* Haim Gouri's *The Chocolate Deal,* Hanoch Bartov's *Wounds of Maturity* (or *The Brigade*), and, finally, S.Y. Agnon's *A Guest for the Night.*

Alter conceded that Israelis often fictionalized the Zionist experience. But rarely did they tie it to its predecessor—the European or Diaspora experience. In these novels, however, they did tunnel back and forth between Europe and Israel in order to probe the very depths of Jewishness.

Some Jewish writers are now beginning to put things together. The pieces of the Jewish experience are starting to fall into place: Israelis are beginning to recognize their past in Europe and elsewhere; American Jews are beginning to recognize their present and future as part of Israel.

Meyer Levin, style notwithstanding, captured the essence of the experience perfectly as he discussed the Jewish writer a few years ago: "No American Jew, no Jew, can get through a single day without somewhere reverberating in his mind some problem, question, attitude in the relation to the Holocaust and in relation to Israel." He concluded that fiction which purports to depict the Jew today realistically must include this fundamental context.

Herbert Gold and Henry Roth nicely illustrate the born-again-Jew-syndrome. In *Fathers* Gold fictionalized the traditional story of the Jew transplanted from Europe to America. In *My Last Two Thousand Years,* he brought the story up to date. He opened his book by saying: "By a wide and narrow road I found my way back to an allegiance I didn't possess." And concluded this way: "I found myself bound both to Cleveland and Jerusalem, the American idea and the history of Israel, each of them seeking through intention and divine favor a salvation on earth, right now; not in heaven, but today."

Roth's new-found Israeli allegiance dated from the Six-Day War: "I felt a greater and greater sense of sympathy with Israel. Now, whether the Holocaust had something to do with it or not, I don't know. . . . For the first time I began to write along entirely different lines. [I began to ask] . . . what . . . do I feel about Communism, what do I feel about Israel, what do I feel about Judaism, and why. That marked the beginning of the resurgence of my own writing. . . . My conversion reminds me of Eliot's conversion.

Henry Roth's conversion more and more involves a rejection of the "old" Jew and an eager acceptance of the "new" Jew who identifies strongly with Israel. In segments from a diary-like account published in a special Henry Roth issue of *Studies in American Jewish Literature* (1979), Roth reveals his new awakening, his new thrust into American Jewish life and literature this way: "What I do read, especially of modern writing, generally concerns Israel—the *Jerusalem Post, Midstream,* and the like." Roth then goes on to take Bellow to task for settling for the safe, affluent life of a Diaspora Jew instead of taking risks to identify powerfully with Israel. (Roth deals primarily with a talk entitled "I Took Myself as I Was" that Bellow delivered before the Anti-Defamation League of B'nai B'rith in 1976. *To Jerusalem and Back* does not enter into Roth's discussion.) Roth has contempt for Bellow's view that *he is an American who happens to be a Jew.* Roth insists that we must be Jews first and Americans second. And rejecting what he sees as Bellow's denigration of aliyah, Roth concludes: "Contrary to Bellow, it is the going [to Israel] and not the staying [in the United States] that is an act of piety and valor."

If one places *To Jerusalem and Back* alongside the bulk of his published statements on Jews and Jewish literature, Bellow emerges ambivalently. Henry Roth too may have been ambivalent once, but no more: "I feel that the Diaspora is headed for assimilation, and all that is left for Juda-

ism in the future will be the State of Israel. And that is the one thing we should try to preserve."

Henry Roth is not alone in his "conversion." There seems to be a new stirring, a movement which emphasizes the present and future rather than the past. If I read Irving Howe and others correctly, "tradition as discontinuity" has been an accepted and organic characterization of American Jewish literature. But now we may have the genesis of a new thrust in American Jewish writing. Discontinuity is now being replaced, however tenuously, by continuity in a way few people imagined as the Jewish settlers came to Ellis Island and Halifax in the 1920s. And continuity in whatever form it may take begins with Ben-Gurion Airport.

JEWISH-AMERICAN WOMEN WRITERS

June Sochen

SOURCE: "Identities within Identity: Thoughts on Jewish American Women Writers," in *Studies in American Jewish Literature,* No. 3, 1983, pp. 6-10.

[*In the following essay, Sochen describes the defining quality of the Jewish-American woman writer as her continual effort to forge a personal and creative identity.*]

It is said that the twentieth century is the time in which artists and philosophers are preoccupied with the issue of identity. Perhaps so, but one could argue that Jews have always been obsessed with the question: "who am I?" Living as marginal, separate people throughout most of their history, they have always been required to be introspective collectively and individually. Identity has been an especially vital, active issue in the life of Jewish Americans where the interaction with Gentiles is commonplace. Jews raised within the Jewish tradition must question, test, and confirm their identities, their links to the Judaic past and present, and their connections to American culture as well. Jews who only had nominal or no Jewish upbringing had to create their identities in heterogeneous America.

For Jewish American women, the identity problem becomes multi-layered. Until very recently, the role of women in both the Jewish and American cultures prescribed behavior patterns and values different from that planned for men. Where the public world of work and prayer featured Jewish men, while the Jewish woman's sphere was confined to the home, it was very difficult for Jewish women to identify themselves in ways other than the traditionally prescribed one. Jewish American women writers faced the additional identity crisis of entering the male domain of literature and creativity. While women writers have always been part of the American cultural landscape, Jewish women writers become a sociological phenomenon only in America and largely in the twentieth century. Because they did not enter a socially acceptable identity role, they had to define themselves and create their own identity.

Jewish American women writers had to, and have to, wrestle with each and all of the components of their being. They have to sift through their personal experiences and their philosophical views to determine which aspect of their being will be highlighted in their work. This problem, of course, is universal to all artists. The particular dilemma for Jewish women is the merging of the various parts, the creation of a new identity type, one rarely seen in society. For some women writers in this genre, their Jewishness leads the list of identity traits; their writing reflects their primary interest in being Jewish in America. For others, being female is the defining feature of their being; and for still others, it is the successful merger of American and Jewish values that predominates. During the writer's career, each, or all, of these themes may emerge and occupy some of her work.

It is assumed herein that there is an intimate connection between the personal biography of a writer and her writings. That is not to say that it is a one to one relationship, but rather that a writer's imaginative work expresses, in however transformed a manner, governing themes and images that concern her own mind and being. The artistic process, of course, is a transforming one, but if identity, as I contend, is a major concern for all creative artists, then determining her identity will be a major personal and creative activity of a Jewish American woman writer.

Indeed, it is possible to survey the work of major Jewish American women writers of this century within this concept: identities within identity. Edna Ferber (1887-1968), for example, displayed interest in being a strong female, a Jew, and an American. Her personal preoccupation with these issues was reflected in her creative works. In her autobiographical novel *Fanny Herself* (1917), she selects perseverance as one of the Jews' most admirable traits and lauds the majesty and mystery of the Jewish ritual in the synagogue. But the bulk of her creative work focuses upon a strong woman overcoming enormous odds to succeed. She incorporates the growing experiences of America with the growing experiences of a woman and juxtaposes her major themes of women's strength with the greatness of America. In *Cimarron, Giant, So Big,* and the Emma McChesney stories, she portrays able, dynamic women in the newspaper business, in the Texas oil fields, in the prairies of Illinois, and in the business world. The harmonious identity she creates is that of a woman experiencing the success of American enterprise and American family. Though Ferber's women often express feminist sentiments, they usually marry and have a family—the necessary structure within which to experience personal success.

Fannie Hurst (1889-1968), who along with Ferber created some of the most popular fiction in America in this century, also focused more on her women characters' development than on other themes. In her autobiography, she commented that the label woman writer meant that she was fascinated with women; living in the suffrage days of the 1910s in New York, Hurst believed that "It is excitingly possible that, as her (woman's) participations and experience widen, the creative golden era of woman is about to begin." Hurst's women, however, often meet more trag-

ic ends than Ferber's precisely because they seek roles and identities previously reserved for men. While men do not have to pay for their sexual adventures, women end up determined by their sexual indiscretions. Hurst's back streets became the home for the discarded mistresses whose tragic end is melodramatically told by both Hurst and her many imitators.

Both Ferber and Hurst would be good examples of Jewish American women writers for whom the Jewishness is a pale adjective describing American women's lives in the twentieth century. Their fictional characters' identities did not contain large doses of Jewishness but rather their femaleness defined and determined their destinies. For Hortense Calisher (b. 1911) and Grace Paley (b. 1922), born a generation later, the multiple identities take on different emphases. Their experiences, growing up in the 1920s and 1930s, as opposed to the 1890s and early 1900s, played an important role in their interpretations of their parents' backgrounds. Their parents seemed to have done a lot of assimilating so that the daughters' search for identity took different turns.

In Paley's case, her parents' Socialism was more important than their Judaism. Indeed, it was to the secular Yiddish culture that she identified as a Jew, not to synagogue Judaism. The Depression, of course, became the dramatic event in her growing years and the idealistic commitment to a democratic Socialist future to override the evils of capitalism became an important part of her intellectual

Edna Ferber.

heritage. Paley's stories about the Darwin family portray three generations in which the eldest had the Socialist faith, the middle (as represented by the daughter Faith), became a social activist for black peoples' rights, and the youngest, Faith's children, became street children who visit their friends in various institutions on the weekends. The characterizations of the elder Darwins' commitment to Socialism and Zionism is lovingly and respectfully presented but the next two generations show no comprehension or commitment to the same faiths.

Calisher also displays her cool dismissal of the Jewish ingredient in her identity in some of her stories. In "The Rabbi's Daughter," for example, neither Judaism nor the Jewish culture was discussed. The focus of the story was upon the daughter, Eleanor Goodman, and her yearnings for a return to her career as a pianist after her marriage and the birth of a child had taken her away from her music. Eleanor muses: "A man, she thought jealously, can be reasonably certain it was his talent which failed him, but the women, for whom there are still so many excuses, can never be so sure." The fact that Eleanor was the daughter of a rabbit merely established her background, her context, but it played no role in her dilemma, in her struggle for selfhood. It is marriage and motherhood, the fate of women, that decided her future.

For some Jewish women writers, of course, the Jewish content within the author and her protagonist is critical. In Hannah Arendt's nonfictional biography of Rachel Varnhagen, an assimilated 18th century German Jew, the dilemma of self-denial fascinated Arendt. Varnhagen devoted her life to separating herself from Judaism and the Jewish people. But her constant disavowal of Judaism never achieved the desired effect. The Gentile society within which she lived, knew of her Jewish origins and she never found an adequate substitute identity to replace Judaism. Arendt noted that "Without a stage-set, man cannot live. The world, society, is only too ready to provide another one if a person dares to toss the natural one, given him at birth, into the luberroom." But in Varnhagen's case, the role provided by society was not able to replace the natural one. Arendt's conclusion seemed to suggest that no substitute could ever be adequate.

All writers choose subjects that speak to them, that engage their interests, their values, and their very essences. Whether nonfictional or fictional, the creatures created, the situations described, and the struggles enacted all reflect aspects of the writer's own being. Writing is both a self-identifying and a self-clarifying process. When a Jewish American woman writer, for example, writes a rags-to-riches novel, albeit with a Jewish immigrant rather than an Irish immigrant protagonist, she is operating within a tried and true genre. She is identifying with a literary tradition in America and in so doing allying herself with a whole set of American cultural beliefs. She is accepting the view that progress is a real phenomenon for newly arriving immigrants, that all of them must struggle, and that many will succeed if they observe the Protestant values of hard work, self reliance, and patience.

The tension of preserving the old in the new setting, of assimilating and of retaining aspects of the old culture, is an-

other accepted theme in the rags-to-riches genre. The conflict between the generations adds yet another ingredient. In the plethora of immigrant novels written by contemporary Jewish women, these themes inevitably play a major role. The process of writing also is a self-clarifying experience. It enables the writer to examine, in concrete form, her own values, her own conflicts, and her own resolutions. She must struggle with the problems of her heroines and heroes and emerge with conclusions that are both artistically and personally satisfying. The gift is often harmonizing these two dimensions. Unsatisfying ends often reflect the ambiguous views of the author. Unhappy conclusions mark the emotional state of the writer at the time of the work's completion. Distancing, a very desirable trait for writers and people in general, is more wished for than achieved. Because a story requires a beginning, middle, and end, the story's end may well be a tentative solution, one adequate for that moment only.

A writer's identity may change many times during a life time. In youth, she may reject the Judaic part of her identity only to reexamine it, and reintegrate it, at a later point in life. Or she may attempt to create a multidimensioned character who successfully (or unsuccessfully) grapples with each and all parts of herself. Just as in life, fiction is often sloppy and inconclusive. Gail Parent, for one, can only deal with the Jewish part of herself in a mocking, often sick joke form. Perhaps she will move from this pose to a more sympathetic one as she ages. The process of discovery and rediscovery is life long. That is the hope, the frustration, and the excitement that accompanies the experience of being a Jewish American woman writer.

Sylvia Barack Fishman

SOURCE: "The Faces of Women: An Introductory Essay," in *Follow My Footprints: Changing Images of Women in American Jewish Fiction*, edited by Sylvia Barack Fishman, University Press of New England, 1992, pp. 1-60.

[*In the following essay, Fishman explores the roles of Jewish-American women as the creators and subjects of fiction in the twentieth century.*]

OUR LITERATURE, OURSELVES

Literature shapes and reflects popular conceptions of the nature and capacities of women, and the self-images of many contemporary American girls and women are influenced not only by changing political, social, and economic conditions but also by a lifetime of contact with literary portrayals of female characters. Such portrayals exist on many brow levels and are derived from diverse religious, cultural, folkloric, and mythic traditions. Many have been nurtured by images from ancient heritages, such as classical Greek and Latin myth and drama, and by narrative characters and allegorical women in the Old and New Testaments.

In the open environment of modern American society the mix of literary heritages describing female nature is rich indeed, including widely divergent pictures. Some have become so familiar that their very names evoke an emotional ambiance: the earnest and spunky problem-solving heroines of books for young girls; the orphan told she "should have been a boy" who surmounts the limitations of her environment through her intense imagination (*Anne of Green Gables*); empowered and powerless Shakespearean characters such as Lady Macbeth, Portia, Juliet, and Desdemona; the independent heroines of novels by Jane Austen, the Brontë sisters, and George Eliot; the pure-hearted martyr doomed and betrayed by honorable and dishonorable men alike (*Tess of the D'Urbervilles*); the bitchy, manipulative survivor (Scarlett O'Hara in *Gone with the Wind*); the fickle, shallow love-object with money in her laughter (Daisy in *The Great Gatsby*); the grasping, greedy wives of Philip Wylie and the overbearing mothers of Philip Roth. In the late 1960s and 1970s, feminism opened the doors for new themes, and readers encountered the courageous experiments in integrity of Doris Lessing's protagonists, embattled modern women struggling with *Small Changes* and attempting to break out of *The Women's Room,* and the sexual adventures of women trying to conquer their *Fear of Flying.* . . .

DISLOCATION AND SURVIVAL IN IMMIGRANT AMERICA

When European Jewish women and their families emigrated to America, the contexts of Jewish life were radically altered. Although many immigrants came to the New World hoping for comfort and opportunity, they found confusion, poverty, and exploitation instead. Society was often turned upside down, as formerly middle-class, well-educated families found themselves plunged into abject poverty, while formerly impoverished and ignorant emigrés became entrepreneurial successes. Most jobs demanded a six- or seven-day work week, and religious traditions were quickly or reluctantly abandoned by immigrants who faced starvation if they did not meet the requirements of their employers.

Life for immigrant women was especially difficult. Few families were able to survive on the earnings of the husband alone, and both girls and married women worked long hours. Women who came at the beginning of the mass emigration period (1880-1924) often worked as seamstresses at home or peddled food or worked in a small family store. Many took in boarders, further increasing the congestion of their tenement domiciles and decreasing any hope of privacy. Later immigrants provided the major work force in the mushrooming garment industry, with girls typically working in the factories and married women doing piecework at home. In his memoirs, Alfred Kazin describes the pivotal role of the mother, which was typical of many immigrant households:

> The kitchen gave a special character to our lives: my mother's character. All my memories of that kitchen are dominated by the nearness of my mother sitting all day long at her sewing machine, by the clacking of the treadle against the linoleum floor, by the patient twist of her right shoulder as she automatically pushed at the wheel with one hand or lifted the foot to free the needle where it had gotten stuck in a thick piece of material. The kitchen was her life. Year by year, as I began to take in her fantastic capacity

for labor and her anxious zeal, I realized it was ourselves she kept stitched together.

Ironically, laws enacted to do away with home sweatshops actually imposed greater privations on the family, for poor women were forced to leave very young children so that they could work in the factory, rather than working at the kitchen table and caring for young children at home. A vignette from Samuel Ornitz's novel *The Bride of the Sabbath* describes the mother of a nursing infant called back to work. An older child carries his baby sister and a pot with his mother's dinner up five flights to the factory loft. His mother nurses the baby while she eats, and when the baby is satisfied, so is she. She turns back immediately to her work, without the time to look back at her children as they leave.

Jewish immigrants found themselves in an environment where few of the traditional values seemed to apply. Contemporaneous nonfiction pieces such as the memoirs of women like Mary Antin and E. G. Stern (alias Leah Morton), as well as the descriptive essays of observers such as Hutchins Hapgood, William Dean Howells, Henry James, Lincoln Steffens, and Jacob Riis, provide us with pictures of a society in the midst of violent transitions, with enormous cultural gaps often opening up between one generation and the next. American-born or -raised Jewish daughters and sons often longed fiercely to blend in with the American landscape and were mortified by the European accents and habits of their parents. American Jewish writers during the period of mass immigrations described a world in which female strength and aggressiveness was still needed but was already beginning to be derided. In immigrant settings characterized by poverty and danger, to be an enabler was a calling requiring intelligence, skill, and shrewdness as well as great reserves of physical and emotional strength; however, in this caldron of dislocation and adaptation, both societal and literary attitudes toward the competent, forceful soldier woman—in particular the Jewish soldier woman—began to change.

Many immigrant women felt confused and almost powerless in this strange new society. Their clothes, their language, and their attitudes toward life did not seem to fit their new homes. Those who did not find employment outside the home often learned English slowly and found their way around their new cities more slowly still. Late-nineteenth- and early-twentieth-century American Jewish writers often described the plight of such immigrant American Jewish women with great sympathy and sensitivity. Abraham Cahan's Gitl in "Yekl" (upon which the movie *Hester Street* is based) is an innocent creature who loses her vulgar husband to the assimilated charms of another woman but eventually finds a better man.

Cahan's Flora, in "The Imported Bridegroom," on the other hand, is a bright, ambitious, and manipulative girl who schemes to achieve her goals. The sophisticated, elegant daughter of a wealthy and seemingly Americanized Jew, Flora has a very clear sense of what she wants from life; however, like most women of her time, she must accomplish her goals vicariously, by manipulating the men in her life. Although manipulation is not a much-admired behavior in postfeminist America, for American Jewish women who aspired to marriage and a traditional life-style at the turn of the century, there were basically two choices: to act upon others or to be acted upon by others. Existence, therefore, often became a power struggle between husband and wife and between parents and their children. The third option—to pursue an independent and often single course in life—was too intimidating for women like Flora to contemplate. Flora yearns to marry an uptown doctor, and it seems for a time that she will be able to trick her father and her fiancé into fulfilling her dreams. In the end, however, she is defeated by circumstances and the equally strong wills of the men, and she may have lost them both.

One of the most lyrical descriptions of a disoriented and yet heroic Jewish mother is found in Henry Roth's *Call It Sleep,* a novel that movingly exposes the way in which dysfunctional families sometimes survive through the sacrificial efforts of women. Genya, the protagonist's mother, speaks an eloquent, expressive Yiddish but can barely string an English sentence together. When she wanders outside a few-block radius of her home, she gets lost and is terrified. And yet, in Roth's novel, the seemingly passive, cautious Genya is shown to be a woman with great reserves of strength and hidden sensuality. Singlehandedly, she provides an oasis of sanity and love for her sensitive, terrified son and her psychotic husband and quietly saves her family.

Genya's character is primarily revealed through the reactions of the men who desire her: her vulnerable, adoring son; her tormented, dependent husband; and Luter, the lecherous lodger. Although Genya has little use for authoritarian religious structures and homiletics or for rigid pieties, she maintains traditional Jewish customs on Sabbaths and holidays, and her identity is enriched by the imagery of the Sabbath mother in the eyes of her son. Additional facets of Genya's personality are revealed when her flaming-haired, vulgar, irrepressible sister Bertha arrives on the scene. Bertha, impulsive, openly defiant, a domineering Jewish female who would be instantly recognizable to audiences of the Yiddish theater as well as to later Jewish satirists such as Woody Allen and Philip Roth, serves as a foil for Genya. With Bertha, Genya's careful, protective reserve is dropped, and the reader learns much about Genya's tragic past and motivations. Henry Roth's portrayal of Genya, like the complex heroines of some Yiddish writers, serves as a potent reminder that the literary imagination can indeed transcend gender.

While Genya is clearly a heroine to her needy son, even in immigrant society, Jewish mothers already suffered from the belittling gaze of their American children. For some second-generation Americans, the raw energy and aggressive behavior of their mothers was suspect—it was un-American. The best chronicler of the rejection of immigrant mothers is Anzia Yezierska, herself a child of the tenements. She writes with equal skill of the agony of the mothers and the agony of the children as they faced each other across a seemingly impassable chasm.

One of Yezierska's most searing works, ironically called "The Fat of the Land," tells the story of Hannah Breineh, who manages to raise many children despite dire poverty.

When family finances improve, as her children grow older, they move uptown to the prestigious "allrightnik's row"—that is, Riverside Drive. But Hannah Breineh is wretched on Riverside Drive, despite the luxury, because she has no freedom to shop, to cook, to conduct her life as she pleases. Her children provide for her physically but do little to hide their scorn for her foreign and uncouth manner. Hannah Breineh's daughter Fanny, especially, is openly appalled and humiliated by her mother. For many daughters in immigrant Jewish literature, the major issue was becoming American. They wanted to be well-educated, soft-spoken, elegantly dressed, refined American ladies. These daughters saw their European Jewish mothers as the antithesis of all of these things. Their mothers did not dress like American women; they spoke too loudly and often with accents; they looked at the world through different eyes. Many of the daughters felt ashamed of their mothers. Moreover, they felt their mothers were ruining their chances for getting ahead. As Fanny tells her brothers, a girl is "always judged by her mother."

Similarly, Rachel Ravinsky, the protagonist of "Children of Loneliness," another Anzia Yezierska story, feels that her parents are dragging her backward "by the hair into the darkness of past ages." Thinking about the gentile man she has grown to love at college, Rachel wonders how she can "possibly introduce such a born and bred American to her low, ignorant, dirty parents." Mrs. Ravinsky, caught between her husband's rigidly righteous convictions and her daughter's scathing rejection, shrivels and grows "old with a sense of her own futility."

For Hannah Breineh and Mrs. Ravinsky, as for many impoverished immigrant mothers, the difficult acquisition and preparation of food became the focus of daily activity. For many mothers, that nurturing activity remained the one link that connected them to their increasingly sophisticated and scornful Americanized offspring. When their children, like Rachel Ravinsky, rejected even their food, such mothers were wounded to their souls: "Ain't even my cooking good no more either. . . . God from the world, for what do I need yet any more my life? Nothing I do for my child is no use no more. . . . How I was hurrying to run by the butcher before everybody else, so as to pick out the grandest, fattest piece of brust. . . . And I put my hand away from my heart and put a whole fresh egg into the *lotkes,* and I stuffed the stove full of coal like a millionaire so as to get the *lotkes* fried so nice and brown; and now you give a kick on everything I done." Yaakov Ravinsky laughs bitterly at his wife's continuing love for their daughter. He tells her, with cruel yet accurate brutality, that Rachel "makes herself so refined, she can't stand it when we use the knife or fork the wrong way; but her heart is that of a brutal Cossack, and she spills her own father's and mother's blood like water."

Michael Gold's fictionalized autobiography of life on the lower East Side describes Jewish women who drifted into lives as prostitutes and madams, as well as a vivid, energetic mother who speaks her mind on dishonesty and injustice in the best tradition of the Woman of Valor and has very definite ideas on the ingestion of proper foodstuffs:

> She woke at five, cooked our breakfast at home,

then had to walk a mile to her job. She came home at five-thirty, and made supper, cleaned the house, was busy on her feet until bedtime. It hurt my father's masculine pride to see his wife working for wages. But my mother liked it all; she was proud of earning money, and she liked her fights in the restaurant. . . . The manager there was a fat blond Swede with a *Kaeserliche* mustache, and the manners of a Mussolini. All the workers feared this bull-necked tyrant, except my mother. She told him "what was what." When the meat was rotten, when the drains were clogged and smelly, or the dishwashers overworked, she told him so. She scolded him as if he were her child, and he listened meekly.

> "Your food is *Dreck,* it is fit only for pigs," she told the manager bluntly. And once she begged me to promise never to eat hamburger steak in a restaurant when I grew up. "Swear it to me, Mikey!" she said. "Never, never eat hamburger." "I swear it, momma." "Poison!" she went on passionately. "They don't care if they poison people, as long as there's money in it."

Almost four decades later, Philip Roth would describe Sophie Portnoy making a similar demand of little Alexander in *Portnoy's Complaint,* but rather than seeing such a mother's behavior through bemused and basically admiring eyes, as Gold does, Philip Roth would see her fiery admonitions as a symptom of crippling and controlling behavior.

Interestingly, few writers in the first two decades of the twentieth century chose to focus their short stories and novels on the successful activism of Jewish women. In 1909-1910 about two-thirds of the women employed in the garment industry were Jewish; within that industry, Jewish women—described with admiration as *vunderbare far-brente meydlekh* (wonderful, fervent girls)—provided the primary leadership and support for the emerging unions, partially because many had brought socialist values with them from Eastern Europe and Russia. Newspaper reporters and other observers of the scene described the ferocity and eloquence of the Jewish girls who led the strike of twenty thousand shirtwaist workers on November 22, 1909, for example, as Howe summarizes:

> As the evening dragged along, and speaker followed speaker, there suddenly raced up to the platform, from the depths of the hall, a frail teen-age girl named Clara Lemlich. . . . She burst into a flow of passionate Yiddish which would remain engraved in thousands of memories: "I am a working girl, one of those striking against intolerable conditions. I am tired of listening to speakers who talk in generalities. What we are here for is to decide whether or not to strike. I offer a resolution that a general strike be declared—now." . . . Thousands of hands went up: "If I turn traitor to the cause I now pledge, may this hand wither from the arm I raise."

Immigrant and second-generation fiction by Cahan, Yezierska, and many others does capture, however, the tremendous importance of education in transforming the lives of American Jewish women—and in exacerbating the chasm between mothers and daughters. A study of working women in evening schools in New York City in 1910 and 1911 showed that 40 percent of the women were foreign-born Jews; 25 percent of Hunter College graduates in 1916 were Jewish women of Eastern European origin. Those who were successful were able to go on to get jobs as secretaries, bookkeepers, or salesclerks in the finer stores; these jobs were seen as highly desirable, and indeed they represented a very different life from twelve-hour days in factories. Many educated second-generation Jewish women became schoolteachers and social workers in numbers far disproportionate to their place in the immigrant population; early on, teaching and social work came to be considered "Jewish professions."

Later, American Jewish authors who wrote out of the Depression did depict the social activism of women, but much of the proletarian fiction of such writers as Tess Slesinger and Leane Zugsmith has little focus on the Jewish identity of characters or Jewish subject matter. Similarly, Jo Sinclair's (Ruth Seid) early proletarian fiction, such as "Tony and the WPA" (1938), has little direct connection to her Jewish roots as the daughter of immigrants; not until the publication of *The Wasteland* in 1946 did Sinclair incorporate Jewish themes into her fiction for general audiences.

The price of acculturation was very high, and for many Jewish women it amounted to a jettisoning of crucial areas of their inner life. The areas of loss depended on the woman. For some, traditional religious behavior was sacrificed as un-American. For others, Jewish religious ritual had long since been abandoned in the struggle for socialist equality. Some, especially those living in urban centers, were able to continue with their socialistic endeavors on American shores, and these women were extremely influential in creating and supporting union movements in the United States. For those women who were isolated from such centers of socialist struggle, however, the revolutionary fervor that was the core of their lives before emigration found no outlet in America. Women who lost the opportunity to live out their dreams found themselves bereaved, with no vocabulary to articulate their loss and grief.

Tillie Olsen writes frequently both of women who have lost their sense of direction and of strong women involved in socialist activities, but only in *Tell Me a Riddle* does the Jewish identity of her characters become obvious or salient. In *Tell Me a Riddle,* Eva, a brilliant, eloquent young Russian revolutionary, comes to this country, marries, and has seven children. Her husband, according to the American custom, is the one who is usually out of the house—at work, at meetings, at clubs—while she remains at home with the children. She is an affectionate, creative mother who takes the wash basin outside to do her laundry on a beautiful day and shows her little ones how to blow soap bubbles with the hollow stalks of wild onion in the yard.

But Eva has no time to read, no time to listen to music, no time to discuss politics with friends. As an older woman, she is very bitter, hating her husband for the way he allowed their family life to divest her of her intellectual and spiritual birthright. She withdraws emotionally from her husband and children and even her grandchildren, yearning for time before she dies to move to the rhythms of her own heart. On her deathbed, she sings snatches of songs she remembers from the revolution. One of them longs for a time when each individual will be valued for him or herself, "every life a song."

THE EVOLUTION OF LITERARY TYPES: THE JEWISH MOTHER AND THE JEWISH AMERICAN PRINCESS

It was to be a long time before American Jewish women, within and outside of novels, would be free to explore their own inner natures. Instead, the midtwentieth-century American literary scene proliferated with books that ridiculed or discouraged the ambitions of Jewish women for intellect, vocation, or self-esteem. The soldier woman qualities that were so admirable to the Yiddish writers were infuriating to midtwentieth-century American Jewish novelists. The world had changed dramatically for American Jews, and different female qualities seemed necessary and admirable in this changed world. Most American Jewish women during and after World War II lived in pleasant neighborhoods, not in grimy tenements. They had 2.8 children, not 8 or 10 children. They washed their clothes in laundromats or in their own washing machines, instead of boiling vats of water on the stove. But they were as smart and as aggressive and as articulate as ever; like Asch's Rachel-Leah, they dramatized their lives and were on the lookout for ever-present dangers that might threaten them and their families. But because the very real dangers of Jewish life in Europe had disappeared from the American Jewish environment, their level of anxiety seemed inappropriate. In lieu of outside employment and in the absence of external challenges such as war or poverty, many American women became caught up in a cycle of consumerism that was easily satirized and mocked. In the hands of American Jewish novelists, both the consumerism and the satire were given a Jewish flavor.

The attitude of Jewish authors toward Jewish women was in many ways symptomatic of their attitude toward middle-class Jewish America. Some of the most widely read midtwentieth-century American Jewish writers were second-generation American men whose lives had been permeated both with consciousness of their Jewishness and with an acute awareness of the differences between Jewish mores and values and those of the United States in its most conformist mode. Jewish women seemed to personify the foreignness of Jewish culture. Apple-pie America might be represented by a blond, sweet woman with a kind of childlike prettiness, a woman who always supported her man and seldom contradicted him; conversely, America might be embodied in the glorious, uninhibited sexuality and putative stupidity of the ubiquitous "blond bombshell" or "sex kitten."

As Philip Roth characterized the assimilative hunger of second-generation American Jewish men, "O America! America! it may have been gold in the streets to my grandparents, it may have been a chicken in every pot to my father and mother, but to me, a child whose earliest movie memories are of Ann Rutherford and Alice Faye, America is a *shikse* nestling under your arm whispering love love love love love!" And if America at its most attractive was

the sunny smile and smooth yellow hair of a non-Jewish woman, then Jewish women were both un-American and undesirable.

The problematic, distinctive nature of American Jewish women was presented in two basic stock characters: the "Jewish mother" and the "Jewish American princess." Some European Yiddish writers had already created the figure of the overbearing Jewish matron, but their actual targets were the ineffectual husbands who created the necessity for their wives' forcefulness. In America, however, the rationale for criticism shifted. The forceful Jewish woman was compared unfavorably with more restrained gentile women. In Jewish literature the aggressive, verbal, clever Jewish woman was often caricatured as pushy and unattractive compared to the refined, polite, domestic, docile, and ornamental image of the "real" American non-Jewish woman.

Interestingly, Jewish daughters came under fire first, and satirical stereotypes of unmarried Jewish women remained prevalent throughout the 1970s and 1980s. Indeed, when undergraduates in a spring 1991 class on "Women in Jewish Culture" were asked if they ever thought of the Jewish woman in terms of the stereotypical Jewish American princess the most forthright and fulsome descriptions came from Jewish females. Significantly, some students were resistant to the idea that the JAP image was fundamentally either misogynist or antisemitic, despite ample documentation. As one student put it, "I come from the Five Towns [Long Island], and where I come from calling someone a JAP is a compliment. Being a JAP means that you've made it. Being a JAP means you have money and prestige, and you know how to use both. A JAP knows and wears what is stylish—she knows exactly where to buy it and how to put things together. And a JAP knows how to get other people to do things for her. Isn't that power? What's more American than power? Being a JAP is being a powerful woman."

This unironic and remarkably naive description of the so-called Jewish American princess is a fundamentally accurate depiction of the sociological beginnings of this stereotype. The yearning to be American, to fit in, was translated in many upwardly mobile families into providing both sons and daughters with every advantage that would enable them to appear and behave as real Americans. For both boys and girls this meant acquiring secular education far beyond the norm for their non-Jewish cohort; for boys it meant being helped with a start in business or professional life as well. But for women, who in the American consumer culture that surrounded them were steered toward being attractive and being effective and conspicuous consumers, a different kind of "higher education" was necessary.

American Jewish writers satirically describe the young woman whose parents were grooming her to fit into upper-middle-class American norms, as they saw them. Although some Jewish writers satirize Jewish men as well, depicting a variety of vulgar, aggressive, materialistic Jewish males, their discomfort with Jewish family life is more often channeled into a preoccupation with Jewish women. Ironically, the negative literary stereotypes of materialistic, manipulative Jewish women that were promulgated by American Jewish writers were only the most recent in a long line of antisemitic literary stereotypes of materialistic Jews in the annals of English literature. As Francine Klagsbrun notes, "All the old stereotypes of Jews come into play in the term JAP. In this day, polite Christian society would not openly make anti-Jewish slurs. But JAP is okay. JAP is a kind of code word. It's a way of symbolically winking, poking with an elbow, and saying, 'well, you know how Jews are—so materialistic and pushy.' What is interesting is that this code word can be used in connection with women—the Jewish American Princess—and nobody protests its intrinsic antisemitism." Eventually, this stereotype was articulated in a genre of humor called JAP jokes. Such jokes, which are often vicious in nature, continue to circulate, although they have now been exposed for their intrinsically antisemitic and misogynist content; JAP humor often suggests that Jewish women are sexually manipulative or unresponsive, that they are obsessively materialistic and exploit their husbands financially, and even that they should be physically exterminated.

A gap often developed between the way Jewish women felt about their families from the inside of the experience and the way they looked from the outside. That gap is brilliantly captured by Herman Wouk in his depiction of one of the best-known Jewish princesses, Marjorie Morningstar. As Wouk's protagonist, Marjorie Morgenstern, walks down the aisle on her wedding day, she looks into the face of the man she almost married, her beloved nemesis, the playboy playwright Noel Airman. At that moment, Marjorie sees her wedding through Noel's eyes as if she were looking through a ghastly green filter, and she knows that through the filter of his perceptions her spectacular and long-awaited wedding is nothing more than "a blaze of silly Shirley glory." To view her family and the man she really loves and wants to marry through her own affectionate eyes, she must brush away the green filter of Noel's jaundiced attitudes.

It is Airman who first fully describes the princess stereotype to the young and inexperienced Marjorie early in the novel, under the generic name of "Shirley." The youthful appearances, lighthearted personalities, and ostensible career aspirations of unmarried Jewish women are all a sham, Airman insists, because they really are after what women have always wanted "and always will—big diamond engagement ring, house in a good neighborhood, furniture, children, well-made clothes, furs." Although they insist that they despise "domestic dullness," says Airman, in the end they marry "dentists, doctors, woolen manufacturers, lawyers" and settle in for a lifetime of shopping and bourgeois social events. Marjorie correctly condemns Airman's caricature of the Shirley and spiritedly tells him he is "a damned intellectual snob . . . and a bit of an antisemite."

The character of Marjorie actually has more depth than is sometimes appreciated, as does her pragmatic, dryly witty mother. Both mother and daughter would prefer to maintain control over their surroundings and other human beings, but only because they wish to accomplish certain practical ends, not simply for the acquisition of power itself. In this, each resembles the character of Cahan's Flora in "The Imported Bridegroom" (1898). Vital, brave, complicated, and charming—as well as unfailingly manipulative—Marjorie struggles valiantly with a culture that sends her mixed messages about the nature of femininity, sexuality, and the purpose of life. Marjorie takes genuine chances, sleeping with Airman and falling in love with Eden, a secretive, drug-addicted, anti-Nazi hero. However, although she clearly grows and matures through these experiences, Wouk punishes her for the chances she takes. When Marjorie finally meets and agrees to marry a solidly responsible Jewish professional, both he and she are grief-stricken and distraught that Marjorie is no longer a virgin. Marjorie confesses her affair—"every word like vomit in her mouth"—and both of them regard her sexual experience as "a physical deformity, like a crippled arm."

Wouk indicates that Marjorie has done the correct thing, that she has followed her inescapable and life-affirming destiny, when she ultimately discards inappropriate dreams of glory and chooses the traditional religion and values she has grown up with, a stable man she has grown to love, "and children, and a warm happy home." Narrator Wally Wronken comments at the conclusion of the novel that Marjorie now sounds just like her mother, a woman he has always liked. Contemporary readers may well find troubling Marjorie's abrupt abandonment of her career dreams, as well as her obsession with physical virginity, but there is no doubt that Marjorie's feelings accurately reflect normative attitudes among American Jews in the 1950s.

In contrast to searching yet practical Marjorie, Brenda Patimkin, heiress to the Patimkin plumbing fortune in Philip Roth's *Goodbye, Columbus,* loves power for its own sake and fights fairly or unfairly as the need arises to maintain the competitive upper hand over every significant person in her life. Neal, Roth's poor but intellectual protagonist from urban Jewish Newark, reflects that Brenda, who has had her nose "fixed" so that it will look less Jewish, tries to "fix" her relationships with people as well. She competes with her mother, her father, her little sister, and Neal. Through the pages of Roth's novella, the reader sees both Brenda and her younger sister being shaped by their parents into self-centered and power-hungry women. Because they are both bright and energetic, they absorb these lessons well.

Moreover, Brenda does not feel that she must be a productive person. Her parents have sent her mixed messages about what life requires of her, the primary message being that she is required only to please herself and to be a loyal daughter. Sporadically, however, her mother, perhaps remembering her own, more deprived adolescence, castigates Brenda for her parasitic behavior. In one memorable fight with her mother, Brenda angrily rejects the notion that she ought to contribute in any way to the household community:

> "When's the last time you lifted a finger to help around here?"
>
> "I'm not a slave. . . . I'm a daughter."

"You ought to learn what a day's work means."

"Why?" Brenda said. "Why?"

"Because you're lazy," Mrs. Patimkin answered, "and you think the world owes you a living."

"Whoever said that?"

"You ought to earn some money and buy your own clothes."

"Why? Good God, Mother, Daddy could live off the stocks alone, for God's sake. What are you complaining about?"

"When's the last time you washed the dishes?"

"Jesus Christ!" Brenda flared, "Carlota washes the dishes!"

The Jewish mother was the next target of the satirical efforts of Jewish men. In a epoch when psychiatrists advised women that the only road to feminine fulfillment and happiness was acceptance of a submissive and supportive role, Jewish male writers often portrayed Jewish women in a grotesque mirror image of the proverbial Woman of Valor. These fictional Jewish women had their own ideas and tried to conquer their husbands and sons; they used food, hygiene, and guilt as weapons of domination.

Fear of maternal domination was far from an exclusively Jewish preoccupation in midtwentieth-century America. Indeed, Philip Wylie's *Generation of Vipers* (1942) scathingly accused "dear old Mom" of tying all of male America to her apron strings through heavy-handed emotional manipulation. Erik Erikson in 1950 wholeheartedly accepted the notion of "Momism," the phenomenon of the pathologically dominating mother who infantalizes and emasculates both husbands and sons. Although fear and loathing of the domineering mother began as a culture-wide systemic misogynistic impulse, it soon became highly associated with the Jewish mother in particular. The Jewish mother, like the Jewish American princess, became a staple of American Jewish fiction. And, like the princess, the cartoon figure of the omniscient, omnipotent Jewish mother has enjoyed an amazingly long shelf life in the popular imagination, no doubt due partially to the talents of Jewish writers and filmmakers.

Jewish mothers were repeatedly caricatured as the apotheosis of the crippling "smothering mother," absurdly exaggerating whatever dangers she might find on the midtwentieth-century American landscape. The Jewish mother as terrorist is a peculiarly American hybrid, very assimilated and yet very Jewish. Herbert Gold's mother in *Family,* for example, is worried because her divorced son is thin, "skin and bones," so she prepares a breakfast of strangely brown scrambled eggs. When he vomits over the polished marble hallways at a job interview, his mother is puzzled: with traditional Jewish maternal solicitude—but with highly nontraditional methods—she had put quantities of religiously prohibited bacon grease in the eggs to fatten him up.

The hysterical mother par excellence is surely Roth's Sophie Portnoy in *Portnoy's Complaint.* Sophie Ginsky Portnoy is so obsessed with her son Alex that she tries to con-

trol every aspect of his life, especially those connected to the alimentary canal. When Alex is at the table or when Alex is in the bathroom, Sophie Portnoy wants to know exact details on the nature of his meal or his defecation. She feels that through knowing and controlling every aspect of his life she can protect him from as yet unknown dangers: " 'He eats French fries,' she says, and sinks into a kitchen chair to Weep Her Heart Out once and for all. 'He goes after school with Melvin Weiner and stuffs himself with French-fried potatoes. Jack, you tell him, I'm only his mother. Tell him what the end is going to be. Alex,' she says passionately, looking to where I am edging out of the room, *'tateleh,* it begins with diarrhea, but do you know how it ends? With a sensitive stomach like yours, do you know how it finally ends? *Wearing a plastic bag to do your business in!' "*

Not only is Sophie Portnoy's overprotectiveness satirized, but her intelligence, strength, and articulateness is denigrated as well. She is, the novel tells us, an intelligent woman with poetic sensibilities. She encourages Alex in his schoolwork and listens to him attentively for hours, praising him as though he were "the Pope." She is, as well, a generous woman who, like Asch's Rachel-Leah, moves about the kitchen with energy and joy and is tirelessly concerned about others, a principled woman who, like Grade's Mother Vella, expects high religious performance from her children. However, Roth pillories Sophie Portnoy for many of the same female qualities that Asch, Grade, and earlier Jewish writers admired. Few Jewish writers looked beyond the surface of women's lives. The woman of valor had fallen upon hard times.

REAL WOMEN: JEWISH MOTHERS AND DAUGHTERS EXPLORE NEW PATHS

If the typical woman in Old Order societies gained some measure of self-esteem because she knew, like Rachel-Leah, "her duty and her own value," women in the changing society of midtwentieth-century America were often unhappy partially because of confusion about their proper role. Many, no longer content to follow in their mothers' footprints, had not yet defined what they wished to be instead. For some, the exploration of new paths was further complicated by anguished feelings of resentment and guilt toward the mothers they loved and hated and, at least psychologically and often physically as well, were leaving behind. They feared to be too close to their mothers because they did not wish to become like them, but they felt that in abandoning their mothers' life-styles they were adding to the burdens that had already oppressed and diminished the older women.

Explorations of mother-daughter relationships, already an intriguing element in earlier American Jewish fiction, emerged as a major motif in mid- and late-twentieth-century novels and short stories. Indeed, although Jewish fiction shared in a culture-wide, growing American interest in the mother-daughter dyad, the Jewish presentation of the relationship had some special characteristics. Marianne Hirsch demonstrates that "the mother/daughter plot" has been a powerfully evocative motif in literature; she asks important questions that are germane to this discussion, such as "What is unique about the attachment between mothers and daughters? Do cultural, ethnic, and class differences, and differences in sexual preference shape the details of their interaction? And where are the voices of the mothers, where are their experiences with maternal pleasure and frustration, joy and anger? . . . What explains the fact that in fiction and theory we find only rarely the most common aspects of mother-daughter interaction, anger for example?"

For women who derive from distinctive ethnic groups, especially those with strong hierarchical traditions, such as traditional Jewish, Chinese, and Japanese societies, the stakes in the conflict between mothers and daughters are complicated even beyond their general psychological import. Partially because of the high cultural stakes of the struggle between American Jewish parents and their offspring, in American Jewish literature anger is a freely expressed emotion. Starting with mother-daughter relationships in the literature of Yezierska and Olsen and moving forward to works by Piercy, Gornick, Goldstein, Broner, Chernin, and Roiphe, among others, one repeatedly finds mothers and daughters confronting each other; one might easily say that anger is the signature emotion of the genre. Moreover, Jewish authors seem somewhat more likely than average to present the world as viewed through the eyes of a mother, and the mother's perspective is vividly represented in the fiction and memoirs of Peretz, Asch, Yezierska, Olsen, Chernin, and Roiphe.

The prevalence of anger and of maternal viewpoints in Jewish-authored mother-daughter stories arises partially because such motifs are powerfully symbolic of the ambivalence of American Jewish women in a transitional world. Many women find themselves caught, like Yezierska's immigrant heroines, between feelings of loyalty to their traditional Jewish mothers and attraction to their gentile lovers; that conflict is a vivid and graphic symbol of the pull of the past and the lure of the new. The painful predicament of women caught between American and Jewish values was perhaps most pronounced for those families in which poverty exacerbated the division between generations. Several outstanding pieces of fiction explore the confusion of urban women who try to straddle two worlds, without even the financial backing to assure them that they can fully enter American culture if they are willing to leave the Jewish world.

Bernard Malamud's works deal with the conflict between the humanistic values of prophetic Judaism—which he characterizes as "the Jewish heart"—and the amoral materialism that lies at the heart of capitalistic American society. However, most often women are accessories to the action in Malamud's fiction, rather than central or fully developed characters. One of the significant exceptions is the character of Helen Bober in Malamud's 1959 novel, *The Assistant.* Helen, daughter of a kindhearted, impoverished grocer, Morris Bober, is a young woman of unusual integrity, moral fiber, and intellectual and spiritual potential. However, she is trapped by her socioeconomic position and fears she will never be able to escape her "miserable Bober fate." When a love affair develops between Helen and Frank Alpine, an Italian drifter with a criminal record who becomes her father's grocery assistant, Helen

Bernard Malamud.

is torn by ambivalent feelings. Is she betraying her parents and her people by loving a non-Jew? Is she betraying her ambitions for higher education and the intellectual life by allying herself with an uneducated man?

To Helen's mother, however, the relationship between Frank and Helen is an unequivocal "tragedy." Helen's mother, Ida, confronts Morris—much as Sholem Aleichem's Golda confronts Tevye and accuses of him of bringing Pertschik into the house so that he may court Hodel—and accuses the grocer of bringing Alpine into the house for Helen. Malamud creates an affecting portrait of mother and daughter, revealing their characters both from within, through their own thought processes, and from without, in the way they are perceived by others. The ties that bind Helen and Ida together and the distances of experience and expectation that separate them from each other testify eloquently to the moral ambiguity that accompanies and complicates mother-daughter relationships in the best American Jewish literature.

Very often in American Jewish literature the intelligent, ambitious daughter feels that she has more in common with her father than with her mother; it is the father who is the kindred spirit. This alliance between father and daughter can leave the mother feeling displaced and alienated from her daughter's love when the daughter moves beyond the need for simple nurture. Thus, in E. M.

Broner's novel, *Her Mothers,* Beatrix, the protagonist, for years makes her mother feel as though she is unworthy of Beatrix's friendship and regard. Beatrix's mother is acutely aware of the way her daughter snubs her, as she complains: "You had your father sign your report card; when you told about your day, about your night, you looked at your father; when you spoke of foreign affairs, money affairs, travel affairs you looked at your father." Because Beatrix is a mother as well as a daughter, she learns through her own experience how great a gift is the reconciliation of a daughter's embrace.

One of the most effective portraits of a confused young woman who feels drawn to her father and guiltily estranged from her mother is found in Seymour Epstein's 1964 novel, *Leah.* Many readers have expressed astonishment that *Leah* is authored by a man; the book's delicate, nuanced presentation of the protagonist's psychology illustrates yet again the gender-transcending power of the literary imagination. Leah is a sensitive, thoughtful woman whose empathetic personality draws many men to her. However, none of these men seems to meet her emotional needs, partially because she finds her father's dramatic personality and ostentatious joie de vivre so compelling that all other men suffer by comparison. Leah's father gives her advice about men that is somewhat similar to the advice Marsha Zelenko gives to Marjorie Morningstar: he encourages Leah to live life to the limit, to reach for beauty, truth, and imaginative excellence, rather than for materialistic security. This is especially difficult for a woman like Leah, who works because she must—for a paycheck rather than in fulfillment of inner-directed career goals, a woman who repeatedly meets seemingly ordinary men.

Leah's relationship with her father is intensified by his desertion of her mother, ostensibly because of her mother's lack of emotional responsiveness, her "granite" nature, her paucity of imagination. Leah, like many of the daughters of abandoned mothers described in American Jewish literature, blames her mother for her father's dereliction. She has shared her father's view of her mother for most of her life. However, when an emotional crisis in her own life makes her vulnerable enough to open up to her mother, Leah discovers that her mother exhibits warmth, responsiveness, and inner resources that she had never known or appreciated. She could not have been more amazed, she says, had "pink doves flown out of my mother's mouth."

For the first time in her memory, Leah consciously and positively identifies with her mother; this new identification increases her own sense of direction and self-esteem, making it possible for her to accept a suitor who has genuinely understood and cared for her for many years. For Leah, identification with her mother is liberating. It also makes it possible for her to confront her father with his own hypocrisy, as he grasps for the materialistic security he has always derided. The words with which Leah's outburst erupts are instructive: "I have a mother!" Leah cries out to her father on a windy street corner. She is capable at last of making her own life.

Divided parental allegiances are additionally complicated when the daughters, like Epstein's Leah or Grace Paley's Faith Darwin Asbury, have more in common intellectually with their fathers than with their mothers. Faith, the frequent heroine of Paley's superb short stories in *Enormous Changes at the Last Minute* and *Later the Same Day,* is a searching, idealistic Jewish woman with two sons, whose parents have decided to take early retirement in the Children of Judea Retirement Home. Paley presents an accurate but extraordinarily gentle and balanced picture of the infantilizing mother and her impatient daughter. In "Faith in the Afternoon" Mrs. Darwin greets the news that Faith's husband Ricardo has abandoned Faith by chiding, "Oh, well, Faithy, you know you have a terrible temper." In "Dreamers in a Dead Language," Mrs. Darwin holds Faith's hand and recalls the time when Faith was a baby who sucked applesauce off her fingers. Seemingly unable to comprehend that Faith is a grown, independent woman, she urges Faith to wash her hands more carefully.

Despite the fact that Mrs. Darwin treats Faith like a little girl who has forgotten to wash, she is a sympathetically drawn figure. Faith tolerates her mother's ministrations with reasonable aplomb. What Faith can't tolerate is a revelation her father makes to her later, that he would like to divorce his wife but he can't—because he never married her. When they were young, they were socialist idealists who didn't believe in marriage, he says. Faith bursts out angrily: "Oh, *you* were idealists. . . . Well, Pa, you know I have three lovers right this minute. I don't know which one I'll choose to finally marry. . . . I'm just like you, an idealist. The whole world is getting more idealistic all the time. It's so idealistic. People want only the best, only perfection."

Faith is angry because her father is acting like Ricardo, the gentile husband who left her to pursue other women. Her father speaks as though he will leave her mother a lonely, deserted woman like herself. "So," she shouts at her father, "You and Ricardo ought to get a nice East Side pad with a separate entrance so you can entertain separate girls." Although they are very different in terms of self-knowledge and intellectual capacity, Faith and her mother are both secularized, compassionate, caring women who retain much of the Jewish cultural ethos of concern for others. It seems they may end by having a very similar fate.

This tendency of history to repeat itself in the lives of women is at the heart of much mother-daughter conflict as reported in American Jewish fiction. A common pattern—indeed, a pattern that recalls some of the immigrant fiction as well—depicts a daughter whose entire life is lived in reaction to her mother. Obsessed by the conviction that she does not want to repeat her mother's mistakes, the daughter never truly achieves independence from the past. Frequently, behind the destructive mother-daughter relationship in these contemporary works of American Jewish fiction there is a man whose expectations and demands pit women against each other.

A world of such women is evoked in Vivian Gornick's memoir, *Fierce Attachments,* which focuses on thwarted women who turn inward, blighting the lives of subsequent generations of women. The Bronx apartment of the protagonist's youth is a rich and colorful world of women, in which her mother is powerful—and yet bitterly aware that she is removed from the patriarchal power structure of the world of work. The Bronx women send mixed messages about the world of men and work to the protagonist as she grows up: men are longed for, hated, admired, and disdained. Concomitantly, the women's ghetto in the apartment building is both safe and threatening, sometimes shimmering with lesbian overtones, sometimes as claustrophobic as the grave. It partakes of the characteristics of a literary community of women as described by Nina Auerbach, in that it is a kind of matriarchal society that both empowers women yet blocks the progress of young women toward independence and maturity in an outside world that is, finally, both patriarchal and heterosexual. Each of Gornick's women struggles to establish a workable relationship with the men in her life, often unsuccessfully. Seeing their personal potential stunted by male demands, priorities, and expectations, some women react with anger, some with denial, and some with apathy and despair.

Gornick's protagonist is obsessed by her mother and by the past partially because her mother withdrew from appropriate nurturing during a pathologically extended period of grieving for her dead husband. As an adolescent, Gornick's protagonist becomes convinced that she can keep her mother alive and functioning only through the sheer strength of her presence and her will. Mothers can withdraw from their daughters for other reasons, as Daphne Merkin illustrates in her novel *Enchantment*. In Merkin's novel, Hannah Lehman grows up in an affluent German-Jewish Orthodox home on New York's Upper West Side. In contrast with the more familiar stereotype of the "smothering" Jewish mother, Hannah feels that her mother ignores her. Both infatuated with her mother—enchanted—and alienated from her, Hannah finds that all of her subsequent relationships are disturbed. Her mother's emotional withdrawal controls Hannah's life just as surely as another mother's direct manipulation.

Daughters in many pieces of recent American Jewish fiction observe their mothers being neglected or abandoned, and their first impulses are to blame the mother for "provoking" mistreatment and to distance themselves from the mother's fate by showing how "different" they are from their mothers. In *Leah* and in "Dreamers in a Dead Language," one way in which daughters distance themselves from their mothers is to identify strongly with their fathers, until life circumstances thrust gender bonds upon them. In much American Jewish fiction, another effective way in which the Jewish daughter distances herself from the Jewish mother is to marry or become sexually involved with a partner overtly quite different from the man who married—and then neglected or abandoned—mother; the most "different" type of man is frequently non-Jewish.

Anne Roiphe, in *Lovingkindness*, makes these emotional currents between mother and daughter explicit. *Lovingkindness* expands the reactive mother-daughter pattern to three generations: the grandmother, a wealthy, heavily made-up, card-playing, dependent, and conventionally Jewish woman whose husband cheats on her; the mother,

Annie, an independent, intellectual, assimilated woman who marries a non-Jew to escape the same fate her mother suffered; and the disturbed granddaughter, Andrea, an emotionally fragile girl who goes from a punk life-style to extreme religiosity in Yeshiva Rachel, a girl's school that educates and indoctrinates "born-again" Jews in Jerusalem, to escape her own mother's values system and behavior.

Roiphe's protagonist remembers her mother weeping day after day over her husband's philandering and neglect; Annie is sure it is her mother's fault: "I believed that if she tried harder she could make him kind and gentle, considerate and loving, that rosebushes could grow in our living room and that birds could fly free in our dining room. I believed that if she worked at it he would stop leaving lipstick-stained shirts on his armchair and come home for dinner and put his arms around her and whisper in her ear and they could put on a record and dance together."

Partially in order to protect herself from the emptiness of her mother's life, Annie seeks out a totally different kind of relationship. Annie determines that she will marry a spectacularly gentile man. Like Philip Roth's Jewish men who rejected Jewish women because they hope to buy American identity in the bed of a gentile, Annie too tries to buy acculturation in the arms of a true American:

> I was wanting something exotic, something American, something that spoke of picket fences, white clapboard houses, Fourth of July parades in which children sold lemonade as the Lions and Elks wearing fezzes walked past to the sound of the trumpet and the Veterans of Foreign Wars waved to their families as they marched in uniforms that stretched across stomachs greatly sucked in for the occasion. I wanted to bed with a man who had drunk in the Declaration of Independence with his mother's milk, who knew the purple mountain's majesty because he had inherited the vision from the kind of man who had made stone boulders into even fences. I wanted a man who was not a tourist in towns where the white steeples stung the sky. . . . I wanted a man who couldn't tell a Yiddish joke.

Annie's choice turns out to be a poor one, and she finds herself increasingly neglected by and then widowed by (perhaps semi- intentionally) her drunken, poetic, gentile husband. Mother-daughter history repeats itself as Annie watches her daughter, named Andrea to evoke the Aegean Isles, reject her values and life-style as definitively as she had rejected her own mother's. Annie reflects long on the nature of mother love as it is depicted in Greek myth and drama and as it plays itself out in contemporary life. Although Annie is appalled by Andrea's coup de grace in becoming a born-again Jew, after traveling to Jerusalem, Annie's negative attitude toward Judaism softens. Annie—and Roiphe—bear witness to the beauty and depth of a woman's restricted life in an ultra-Orthodox Jewish community. We have come full circle from the writings of Anzia Yezierska. Yezierska describes the daughter's longing to escape from the foreignness and restrictions of the Jewish past. Annie's daughter wants to return to them.

Stricken with ambivalence and doubt, Anne Roiphe's heroine wonders if women's liberation is after all a mere evolutionary aberration, which will be erased by the growing forces of fundamentalism. She wonders if women in the future will be relegated, as her daughter has chosen to be relegated, to the quiet byways of the domestic realm. In her questions about the past and future of the personal lives of women and the entanglement of those lives both in Jewish values and in the lives of their mother and daughters, Roiphe's Annie is emblematic of an entire generation of women struggling to find their own path in a transitional society.

CONTEMPORARY SOLDIER WOMEN IN A CHANGING WORLD

American Jewish women struggled not only with their own mothers and daughters but with a plethora of challenges in the shifting landscape of America in the 1970s and 1980s. The whole world was seemingly open to them: they could pursue education as far as their intellectual capacities and ambitions could take them; they could enter any vocational field; they could follow their sexual inclinations into numerous or monogamous, lesbian or heterosexual liaisons; they could have seven children while pursuing a career in gastroenterology or postpone or avoid having children altogether. In terms of their relationship with Judaism, they could attain rabbinical ordination or they could completely estrange themselves from Jewish life. The choices were at times bewildering.

American Jewish literature has faithfully recorded the battles undertaken by Jewish women in this extraordinary time of change. The impact of external forces on the women portrayed in Jewish fiction has shifted perceptibly from decade to decade. Thus, despite the appearance of enormous external change early in the emergence of the contemporary feminist movement, Jewish female protagonists in the early 1970s were often depicted as being victimized by society, being deluded and denuded, being left with what were in actuality "Small Changes," as Marge Piercy insists in her diligent chronicle of the stormy, experimental cultural environment of the late 1960s and early 1970s. Piercy portrays Miriam, a bright, talented, lively Jewish female professional who has affairs simultaneously with two gentile men, neither of whom accords her the respect she deserves and whose friendship with each other sometimes seems more real than their relationship with Miriam. Later she marries a seemingly stable Jewish man, but when she wants to augment motherhood with a very modest career, he is ready to leave his "pushy" "orange and purple" Jewish wife for a docile "pastel" non-Jewish subordinate.

Piercy's observation about society's punitive attitude toward vibrant Jewish women jibes with poet Adrienne Rich's essay about being half-Jewish, "Split at the Root." She recalls that the route to success for Jewish women until very recently consisted in their being able to suppress their Jewishness:

> With enough excellence, you could presumably make it stop mattering that you were Jewish; you could become the *only* Jew in the gentile world, a Jew so "civilized," so far from "common," so attractively combining southern gentility with European cultural values that no one would ever confuse you with the raw, "pushy" Jews of New York. . . . We—my sister, and I—were constantly urged to speak quietly in public, to dress without ostentation, to repress all vividness or spontaneity, to assimilate with a world which might see us as too flamboyant. I suppose that my mother, pure gentile though she was, could be seen as acting "common" or "Jewish" if she laughed too loudly or spoke aggressively.

One thinks also of Hortense Calisher's memories of growing up Jewish in the South, dealing with a mother who, despite her activity in the Temple Sisterhood, "didn't want to be Jewish," who "sneered at the name of a high school friend I had brought home, whose head of blond fuzz she had termed 'kike hair.' . . . when I went uncombed or unkempt I was accused of having the same." And yet the young Hortense understands also that she is a vehicle for familial continuity, for "when we elders die, you will be our keepers."

By the late 1970s and 1980s, women in American Jewish fiction were most often not only doing active battle with their surroundings but achieving significant triumphs as well, in the fiction of some male as well as female authors. Pushiness—that is, assertive behavior and clearly and forcefully articulated opinions—made a comeback. The soldier woman was back in style, rescued by the general women's liberation movements and by Jewish feminist writing. Interestingly, women have become frequent protagonists of American Jewish short stories and novels during these two decades, not only because far greater numbers of Jewish female authors have recently published books than in earlier historical periods but also because the extent of change in the lives of contemporary Jewish women has been dramatic and full of conflict, offering a broad spectrum of themes to writers of fiction. Thus, a focus on female protagonists and significant supporting characters is found not only in the works of female authors and new figures on the American Jewish literary scene in the 1970s and 1980s but also in the recent works of some established male literary figures, who previously did not seem much interested in women except as accessories to men's lives.

Indeed, it might fairly be stated that feminist exploration is one of the most significant new movements in American Jewish literature, as it is in American Jewish life. This literary exploration has achieved a rather startling prominence in all varieties of literature, running the entire gamut from difficult, critically acclaimed fiction to glossy, melodramatic, shallow romantic novels. As a general observation, the female protagonists in popular Jewish romances are almost always breathtakingly beautiful, and no matter how agonizing their experiences, they almost always achieve the predictable romantic and material successes that are a sine qua non of the genre. . . . [It] is significant to note that, unlike such novels in the past, today's beautiful protagonists (1) are often identifiably, proudly Jewish, and (2) achieve their goals not through the ministrations of a handsome and mysterious gentleman but through their own intelligent, energetic efforts. The image of the woman in contemporary American Jewish literature has been rehabilitated and transformed even at the most basic, grass-roots level.

Jewish women now appear as protagonists in fiction whose scope extends far beyond "the Oedipal swamp" (to borrow a phrase from Philip Roth). Among major themes that have emerged in recent American Jewish fiction focusing on women, some of the most important include the role of the Holocaust in the identity of survivors, their children, and the broader Jewish community; Israel as a focal point of American Jewish identity and as a setting for the exploration of Jewish identity; a variety of religious and cultural subgroups within Jewish life, such as Sephardi Jewish communities, ultra-Orthodox communities, and feminist groups; sexual subgroups, such as Jewish lesbians and homosexuals; and the tension between intellectual and sensual, personal and professional, Jewish and humanistic agendas in the lives of contemporary American Jewish women. Moreover, feminist themes are often linked with Israel, the Holocaust, and Jewish subgroups and societies in recent American Jewish fiction.

Some feminist literature has been experimental in theme, style, or content. A good example of the creative freedom that marks some self-consciously feminist American Jewish literature can be found in E. M. Broner's *A Weave of Women,* which describes a dozen women and three girls who dream of and plan for a feminist vision of utopia in Israel. They create their own Israeli/Jewish/feminist liturgy, together with its own ceremonial literature and myth. Broner's experimental style blends Hebrew, Yiddish, and biblical motifs within narrative, drama, and poetic forms. Her fiction is an example of what might be termed mythic exploration of feminist issues. Another example of this type of fiction is Kim Chernin's *The Flame Bearers,* which depicts a sect of Jewish women devoted to a female aspect of godhead called Chochma, the Bride. Other works by the prolific Chernin include feminist-oriented and Jewishly intense essays, such as those found in *Reinventing Eve,* and memoirs such as *In My Mother's House.* In one memorable episode in *Reinventing Eve,* Chernin experiences a spiritual epiphany with a unique Jewish "goddess" in an Israeli village, together with little girls and an aged woman, as the others pray in the synagogue on the High Holidays.

More commonly, however, feminist issues within Jewish and American culture have been explored in familiar American Jewish settings. The female protagonists of recent American Jewish fiction have had to struggle with a multiplicity of identities: they are Jewish, they are Americans, they are daughters and wives and lovers and mothers, they are moderns, they are heirs to an ancient tradition. Equally important, American Jewish women are not depicted as balancing these competing demands exclusively according to their own internal preferences; influences from sweeping historical events to the significant others in women's lives often distort the decision-making process.

The effect of history on the lives of individual women is movingly addressed in Gloria Goldreich's *Four Days.* While the novel focuses on the moral decision of Ina, a middle-aged daughter of Holocaust survivors, over whether to abort an unplanned pregnancy, an interrelated subplot examines the character of Ina's mother, Shirley Cherne. When Shirley, as a young mother, is incarcerated in a concentration camp with her little daughter, she is passionately maternal, a thin, tenderly loving, indomitable wraith of a woman who manages against all odds to keep her little girl hidden and safe. Once in America, however, Shirley metamorphoses into a plump, hard-edged, pragmatic, and phlegmatic businesswoman who has little time or energy for that same daughter. Ina puzzles over the nature of femininity and maternity and the true identity of her Holocaust mother.

The complex interaction between mothers who are Holocaust survivors and their daughters has been the subject of some of the most compelling recent literature. Rebecca Goldstein's story "The Legacy of Raizel Kaidish," for example, portrays a mother who engineers her daughter's personality through the strongest kind of emotional manipulation; she tries to create of her daughter a selfless, dispassionately altruistic saint, all in an effort to expiate her own profound moral failure within the hell of the concentration camps. Only on her deathbed does she acknowledge that she has been wrong to sacrifice her daughter's autonomy. Cynthia Ozick, in *The Shawl,* portrays a very different kind of mother, Rosa Lublin, who, like Goldreich's Shirley Cherne, struggles to hide, protect, and nurture her small daughter. But Lublin's daughter is betrayed, discovered, and killed. Rosa, like Demeter unwilling to abandon Persephone to the gods of death and darkness, wills her daughter Magda into life and existence within her own imagination. She imagines every detail of her daughter's physical and emotional existence, her talents, her attitudes, her feelings. Within Rosa's mind, her dead daughter is vital, beautiful, and fierce, "a tigress."

The Holocaust also looms in the background of Saul Bellow's 1989 novella, *The Bellarosa Connection.* Narrated by an elderly Jewish man, the brilliant and wealthy founder of the Mnemosyne Institute in Philadelphia, the narrative ostensibly describes the relationship between two Jewish men, Holocaust survivor Harry Fonstein and the Broadway producer Billy Rose, who saves Fonstein and many other Jews from the Nazis; in reality, however, the book is animated and dominated by the figure of Sorella Fonstein, Harry's wife. Sorella Fonstein seems at first glance like a character created in order to poke fun: the narrator recalls that when he first met her, "Sorella's obesity, her beehive coif, the preposterous pince-nez—a 'lady' put-on—made me wonder: What is it with such people? Are they female impersonators, drag queens?"

Significantly, the Jewish women portrayed in most of Bellow's previous novels are often misfits who display grotesque behaviors or appearances. The three main female figures in Bellow's *Mr. Sammler's Planet* (1969), for example, are each devoted to the protagonist but are regarded by him as grossly inferior in their physical, moral, and intellectual capacities. Sammler's daughter Shula is genuinely mad, a pathetic, bewigged creature who scavenges Broadway trash baskets and goes about creating havoc in her own and other people's lives. Sammler thinks that Shula's emotional instability is somehow linked to her thin hair, a quirky symbol of her twisted femininity. Sammler also thinks that the widow, Margotte, who tries to take care of him is "sweet but on the theoretical side very tedious, and when she settled down to an earnest theme, one was lost . . . because mornings could disappear while Margotte in her goodness speculated." Perhaps most egregiously, Angela Gruner, the sexually hyperactive daughter of Sammler's generous cousin, emits a plethora of sexual odors, speaks constantly of her numerous affairs, and evokes from her otherwise kindhearted father such epithets as " 'Bitch' when his daughter approached with all her flesh in motion—thighs, hips, bosom displayed with a certain fake innocence. . . . Under his breath, Gruner said 'Cow!' or 'Sloppy cunt!' "

In contrast, Sorella Fonstein, while certainly as physically grotesque as any of Bellow's previous female characters, is described with admiration, sympathy, and approval, an admiration all the more astonishing given her doorway-filling, chair-straining size; she is, as the protagonist comments succinctly, "off the continuum." Bellow characterizes Sorella as a new and totally original type of soldier woman, a woman of immense honesty and courage as well as immense bulk and a woman who triumphs morally over the powerful, womanizing Billy Rose and over the soul-killing materialism of the "Shirley" stereotype.

For decades, Bellow has effectively explored the dialectic of appetite and repulsion that female sexuality evokes in some men. Although fascinating as a psychological phenomenon, the love-hate relationship that men have with women's bodies has been the basis of profound discrimination against women at many times and in many cultures. This discrimination has attracted the attention of Jewish women writing today, who often include in their fiction male characters who project their own psychological ambivalence onto female physical characteristics and virtually convert normal female physiology into a type of pathology.

One of the most devastatingly witty and accurate satires on the male projectionist fallacy is found in Cynthia Ozick's *The Cannibal Galaxy*, which portrays Hester Lilt, a world-renowned philosopher who enters her daughter in the Jewish day school of principal Joseph Brill. Lilt suffers socially because of her dual nature—at times she is isolated or even ostracized by a society that continues to insist, "either mind or body." Initially, Lilt impresses Joseph Brill as another order of being from most women, especially from other mothers, because she is rational, honest, and direct. Brill thinks that most mothers are like frenzied creatures on a hormonal flood but that Hester—the intellectual female—is necessarily different:

> It was strange to think she had a child. Profoundly, illimitably, he knew the mothers; she was not like any of them. The unselfconscious inexorable secretion ran in all of them. From morning to night they were hurtled forward by the explosions of internal rivers, with their roar of force and pressure. The mothers were rafts on their own instinctual flood . . . that was why they lived and how: to make a roiling moat around their offspring . . . they were in the pinch of nature's vise. . . . And their offspring

too would one day be the same: aggressive, arrogant, pervicacious.

Having decided that most mothers are all body, all instinctive frenzy to protect their offspring, but that Hester is different and all mind, Brill blurts out to her that her daughter is an inferior creature and is not worth the love of her intellectual mother. He is shocked by the white fury with which Lilt answers him. Brill decides that "she was like the others: nature's trick, it comes in with the milk of the teat."

Nature's trick, of course, is that both men and women have dual natures, a duality that has been expressed via many literary formulas down through the centuries. Both men and women are pulled between the demands of intellect and rationality, on the one hand, and the demands of emotion, passion, and compassion on the other. It is out of this conflict between priorities—each necessary to civilized human life—that individuals forge their own unique answers, in the words of Olsen's revolutionary refrain, "every life a song."

But because one of the formulas used to express human duality has been gender-related, women have often been relegated exclusively to earthly concerns, in literature as in life. Sometimes women's so-called earthliness has been seen as praiseworthy, in the woman of valor mode of the radiant enabler, and sometimes it has been seen as destructive, even demonic: man would soar to spiritual and artistic heights but for women's seductiveness or interference.

Ozick plays with these and other stereotypes in her short story "Puttermesser and Xanthippe." Puttermesser, a highly rational lawyer in her thirties working as a civil servant for the city of New York, is passionately devoted to improving the life of the city, but she has a relatively undistinguished position and little power. Attorney Puttermesser actually is drawn along the lines of a male stock figure of Yiddish comic stories: the *luftmensch,* or "sky-man," the Jewish intellectual whose total lack of practical knowledge and ability cause failure at every endeavor. Although she is intellectually capable and is often given the task of training young male lawyers, she has no street smarts—her name means "butter knife"; she is not sharp—and she is never promoted.

After a series of humiliating demotions, Puttermesser unwittingly creates a female golem, a creature who insists on being called by the name of Xanthippe, Socrates' putatively shrewish wife. Just as the male golem in Jewish folktales begins by fulfilling the dreams of his creator and saving the Jews of the city, Puttermesser's lady golem begins by transforming New York. The city becomes a place of peace, joy, harmony, and prosperity. Puttermesser becomes mayor of New York City and is able to accomplish all of her goals. However, it is in the nature of the golem to continue growing and growing and to become more and more controlled by lust rather than rationality. Whereas the male golem becomes more and more destructive—all those androgens—the female golem fulfills male anxieties about the fully sexual adult female as she becomes a monster of sexuality—all those estrogens. She neglects her benign dictatorship of the city and sexually decimates all of the male civil servants. The city slips back into its old poverty and decadence. Eventually the golem—sheer, un-thinking power—always threatens to destroy its superra-tional creator unless it itself is destroyed. Puttermesser must assume the agonizing task of destroying her female golem, and the overintellectualized female *luftmensch* is left without power or progeny.

American Jewish women still struggle with a variety of male power structures, according to recent American Jew-ish fiction. In another response to perceived misogyny and patriarchal oppression, some Jewish authors have champi-oned lesbianism as both a physical/social orientation and a political statement. Such authors describe the worldview and experiences of those Jewish women who reject male-identified gender behavior and identify primarily with other women. Fiction depicting the lives of Jewish lesbi-ans, once difficult to find, has begun to appear more fre-quently now: interested readers may enjoy Alice Bloch's novel *The Law of Return;* Leslea Newman's collection of short stories, *A Letter to Harvey Milk;* and Edith Ko-necky's *A Place at the Table,* among other fictional explo-rations of Jewish lesbian life. Although some Jewish lesbi-an writing is highly critical of Jewish tradition, which it perceives as hostile to its very existence, a significant amount of Jewish lesbian writing is deeply committed to Jewish peoplehood and Jewish survival, and several an-thologies have been largely dedicated to Jewish-content feminist and lesbian writing.

Gloria Kirchheimer's story, "Food of Love," is drawn from one such anthology, *The Tribe of Dina.* Kirch-heimer's story focuses on yet another subgroup in Ameri-can Jewish life, the large Sephardi community of Ameri-can Jews. Sephardi women have their own special rela-tionship with patriarchal family and community systems. Many Sephardi Jewish women have stated that women in Sephardi society have been far more cloistered and re-stricted in their activities than women deriving from Ger-man or Eastern European Jewish societies. Beyond the boundaries of the Sephardi community, Sephardi Jewish women often suffer from a double discrimination: they are suspect because they are women and because they are not of Ashkenazi derivation. Ruth Setton, in her story "Street of the Whores" presents the struggles of a young Sephardi woman to find her own path and to survive repeated on-slaughts upon her self-esteem. Both her femaleness and her Moroccan heritage are regarded by other characters as intrinsically dirty and unreliable. She must not only deal with their attacks but keep her inner life free from the temptation to internalize these destructive images.

The theme of continuing attacks on the self-esteem of Jew-ish women emerges as an important motif in recent Amer-ican Jewish fiction. As in the past, discomfort with the fully sexual adult female presence is sometimes absorbed by women themselves. The framework of fear of the overt-ly female has, of course, shifted with time and changing mores: Peretz's overbearing matron warned her daughter that female sexuality could lure men and women into sin, which men could overcome through scholarship and piety but which would surely doom the careless woman; today the religious scaffolding of misogyny is far from ubiqui-tous. However, some women in contemporary American Jewish literature still exhibit squeamishness about their fe-male nature.

Rebecca Goldstein's *The Mind-Body Problem* wittily cap-tures many facets of the discomfort American Jewish women can still feel about themselves. That discomfort ranges from a lack of self-esteem, in which a woman is made to feel deficient because she is both attractive and in-telligent, to a real revulsion against female physiology. In Goldstein's book, one woman comes to see her mind as the enemy that threatens her chances for a happy marriage. Another woman articulates the pathological attitudes to-ward the female body that both Bellow and Ozick put into the mouths of men; here, women have absorbed destruc-tive male attitudes so thoroughly that they see their bodies as the enemy.

Goldstein surveys the many prejudices that confront the brilliant, multifaceted woman. Her female protagonist, Renee Feuer, is a beautiful young woman who goes to Princeton to get a Ph.D. in philosophy and studies philo-sophical approaches to the dichotomy between the intel-lect (the mind) and the senses (the body). Her professors do not take her seriously—she is too beautiful—until she gains legitimacy by marrying a world-famous mathemati-cal genius. The genius wants Renee to abandon her career and make herself his organizer and enabler. Renee's best friend, Ava, an attractive classmate from Barnard who has now become an intentionally ugly academic, reinforces the idea that femininity and intellectualism are mutually ex-clusive, that "feminine is dumb," and that a woman who hopes to be taken seriously as a scientist must "stamp out all traces of girlishness."

Ava's insistence that she cannot see herself both as a woman and as an intellectual is true not only of women in the sciences but often of women in the arts as well. Hor-tense Calisher argues that many female writers and paint-ers have absorbed the judgments of their male colleagues. They are terrified that if they are perceived as female art-ists their art will be somehow trivialized or diminished: "She knows her own capacity for the universal, and will not have it contaminated with the particular—if the par-ticularity is feminine. Looking abroad, it can be seen what happens to women who do ride their femininity in the lit-erary races: Doris Lessing, tied to psychiatry, suffragett-ism, and the vaginal reflex." It is their flight *away* from overt femaleness, however, that actually does reduce the power of some female writers, Calisher suggests. Only by speaking out with their own voices can the full power of their artistic vision be realized.

For many years, some female writers suppressed aspects of their experience in order to assimilate into the domi-nantly patriarchal literary environment. Similarly, Jewish writers for many years catered to the predominantly non-Jewish literary establishment either by ignoring Jewish subject matter or by treating Jewish characters as a species of precocious "others," existential heroes or court jesters, whose value consisted in their standing both inside and outside Christian or secular societies and commenting on them. Few American Jewish writers prior to 1965 ex-plored what being Jewish meant for the Jews themselves. Just as female writers today are reclaiming their own womanly voices, Jewish writers are regaining their Jewish voices. Jewish female writers, doubly marginal, for many years disguising two primary aspects of their identity, are at last writing out of their full vision. Writers such as Cynthia Ozick, Rebecca Goldstein, and others draw on the full, complex, often contradictory and conflicting particularisms of their female Jewish American experience and vision.

Contemporary American Jewish writers often focus specifically on women's struggles to be treated as multifaceted individuals. Their works illustrate the fact that the battle is far from over. As surely as is I. B. Singer's Yentl the yeshiva boy, Rebecca Goldstein's Ava is convinced that she must dress, act, and think like a man in order to be considered, by others and by herself, a bona fide intellectual. She must reject her female nature, mind *and* body, to participate in the discipline she loves, albeit it is physics rather than the Talmud that she studies, and it is drab, androgynous clothing rather than a *taalith* that she dons. As keenly as did Jewish heroines of past decades, Renee Feuer rejects the rigid pieties of her mother's life, but she longs for the melodies and flavors, the spiritual and communal richness of traditional Jewish culture. Depictions of Jewish women have become broader, deeper, and more believable than they had been in recent decades, but the problems Jewish female protagonists face bear more than a passing resemblance to the problems of Jewish women in the past.

A new and yet curiously traditional protagonist has emerged in contemporary American Jewish fiction: the strong, intelligent woman who struggles with conflicts arising from within and from without. The scope of female protagonists in American Jewish fiction is more diverse than it has been for decades, reflecting changing economic and societal conditions for American women. Despite radical changes in the social realities and in the literary depictions of women in recent American Jewish literature, however, the ancestry of the contemporary soldier woman remains a venerable one, enriched immeasurably by historical and literary precedents.

THE HOLOCAUST AND JEWISH-AMERICAN FICTION

Edward Alexander

SOURCE: "The Holocaust in American Jewish Fiction: A Slow Awakening," in *The Resonance of Dust: Essays on Holocaust Literature and Jewish Fate,* Ohio State University Press, 1979, pp. 121-46.

[*In the following essay, Alexander discusses the Holocaust as a long-neglected subject among Jewish-American writers not truly addressed in literature until the late 1960s.*]

During World War II, American policy toward rescuing Jews from Europe could have been the occasion of a tragic conflict of loyalties for the American Jewish community. Yehuda Bauer has succinctly described that policy as follows: "Every humanitarian consideration was dropped, and the slogan 'rescue through victory' became the statement of official policy. This policy did not take into ac-

count that few Jews would remain to be rescued after victory." The conflict never occurred: the Jews of Europe were left to be murdered, and their brethren in the United States, who barely thought of allowing their Jewish loyalties to "interfere" with the war effort, remained largely undisturbed by tragedy or divided loyalties.

If one large segment of American Jews, descended either actually or spiritually from the German Reform movement, had always believed that they were Americans of the Jewish persuasion rather than members of the Jewish people, another large and vocal group, those descended from Eastern Europe and imbued with the ethos of Jewish radicalism and socialism, believed themselves to be, not Americans of course, but internationalists first, and Jews second (if Jews at all). Irving Howe has pointed out the way in which Eastern European Jewish socialists, from the beginning of their life in America, "yearned to bleach away their past and become men without, or above, a country." They stubbornly denied that there could be any problems peculiar to Jews as a people and worth addressing as such. To admit this possibility was for them particularism, provincialism, nationalism. "Rebelling against the parochialism of traditional Jewish life," says Howe, "the Jewish radicals improvised a parochialism of their own— but with this difference: they called it 'universalism.'" By the time of the Holocaust, socialism no longer held so compelling a sway over American Jews as it once did. Yet their loyalty to, and enthusiasm for, President Roosevelt derived largely from a belief that, even though he retained the capitalist structure of American society, he had done much to realize their old socialist program through piecemeal reform. At the very time, therefore, that Franklin Roosevelt was, by doing nothing to admit Jewish refugees to the United States, sending hundreds of thousands of Jews to their death, American Jews were his most fervent, uncritical, and reliable bloc of supporters. Even when the war was over and the full extent of Roosevelt's shameful guilt became known, the long-standing conviction of the American Jewish community that the best way to ameliorate the condition of Jews was to ameliorate American society at large was unshaken.

Not long after the war, a generation of American Jewish writers arose who purported to satirize every aspect of American Jewish life. Every American Jewish malady, still more any American malady that could with any plausibility be labeled Jewish—suffocating maternal affection, suburban vulgarity, materialism, kitchen religion—was mercilessly pilloried. But the fact that the most powerful, or at any rate, least powerless, Jewish community in the world had abnegated responsibility for its helpless brethren during their hour of utmost need did not, apart from a few isolated instances, provoke moral satire. Another malady from which the Jewish satirists studiously withheld their irony was the Jewish infatuation with leftist political movements, a delusion that gives every indication of being the most damaging to Jewish existence, the most permanent in its destructiveness, since the seventeenth-century delusion with Sabbatai Zevi.

These two great avoidances were connected with each other in more than an accidental way. It is not the fashion of any satirist to select as his primary subject precisely those moral evasions of which he has himself been guilty or those false idols after which he has himself been lusting. It is a hero and not a clod who declares for himself and his author Norman Mailer that " 'the massacres and progroms, the gas chambers, the lime kilns—all of it touched no one, all of it was lost.' " The imagination of American Jewish writers was not effectively touched by the Holocaust either during its occurrence or for two decades afterward (this despite the fact that detailed information about the massacres was available to those who could read newspapers from December 1942). One of Saul Bellow's characters in his 1944 novel *Dangling Man* provides the exception that tests the rule. Awaiting induction into the army, the hero Joseph dreams that he is in a low chamber surrounded by rows of murdered people, one of whom he has been charged with identifying and reclaiming. His charnel-house guide reads from an identity tag a place name which reminds Joseph that "in Bucharest . . . those slain by the Iron Guard were slung from hooks in a slaughterhouse. I have seen the pictures." In horror, he jumps back "in the clear," and claims that "I was not personally acquainted with the deceased. I had merely been asked, as an outsider." He wonders why he and his friends have so easily accustomed themselves to the slaughter in Europe and why they have so little pity for the victims. But his answer does not venture beyond the most charitable of explanations: "I do not like to think what we are governed by. I do not like to think about it. It is not easy work, and it is not safe. Its *kindest* revelation is that our senses and our imaginations are somehow incompetent."

The causative link that, in my view, exists between the absence of the Holocaust and the absence of satire of the American Jew's love of leftist humanitarianism from American Jewish fiction is also hinted at in this literally exceptional novel. The eventual induction of Bellow's hero into the army not only takes him away from the dreamworld of American freedom back to the European world of limited choice and unlimited bloodshed; it also forces him to give up his scholarly work on the Enlightenment. In fact, however, his fascination with this subject had already begun to wane, for reasons that are evident in his explanation of why he quit the Communist party: " 'You see, I thought those people were different. I haven't forgotten that I believed they were devoted to the service of some grand flapdoodle, the Race, *le genre humain*. Oh, yes, they were! By the time I got out, I realized that any hospital nurse did more with one bedpan for *le genre humain* than they did with their entire organization. It's odd to think that there was a time when to hear that would have filled me with horror.' "

The Enlightenment and the French Revolution granted Jews equal rights simply because they belonged to *le genre humain*. Despite the Enlightenment's unconcealed hatred of Judaism (and often of Jews), no group believed more fervently than the Jews that the Christian Trinity had been supplanted as a motive force in the European mind by the new Trinity of Liberty, Equality, and Fraternity. The revolutionists would grant everything to the Jews as individuals, but nothing to them as a people or a distinct group. Jews impressed by the new dispensation came to believe

that they must relinquish their national character in order to assimilate with "humanity." They were not noticeably disturbed by the fact that in practice their assimilation was not with all humanity but with the particular people among whom they lived. Thus, while the People Israel was rapidly improving itself out of existence, the other peoples—the French, the Poles, the Germans—were asserting their national rights more boldly than ever.

But no conviction has ever been more resistant to negative evidence than the belief of the Jewish leftist in the promises held out to him by declarations of human rights. The leftist-supported pogroms in Russia in the 1880s; the espousal by every left-wing party in nineteenth-century France of antisemitism; the Dreyfus Affair; the refusal of the German Socialists to condemn antisemitism during the 1930s; the destruction of European Jewry amidst worldwide indifference: such an accumulation of horrors might have been thought finally destructive of the delusory belief in emancipation, equality, assimilation, and enlightenment. A non-Jewish observer like Francois Mauriac, when he witnessed trainloads of Jewish children standing at Austerlitz station in Paris awaiting deportation to the death camps, knew that "the dream which Western man conceived in the eighteenth century, whose dawn he thought he saw in 1789, and which . . . had grown stronger with the progress of enlightenment and the discoveries of science—this dream vanished finally . . . before those trainloads of little children." But the faith of the Jewish universalist has proved more immune to the evidence of mere experience than that of the French Catholic; and everything we know of Jewish life in the United States shows that this faith has survived the Holocaust itself. Here a majority of Jews do not merely look upon the varied offspring of Enlightenment universalism as conducive to Jewish existence but actually believe Judaism itself to be coextensive with them.

In the aftermath of the Holocaust, it is not enough for the American Jew simply to be an American, or even simply "to be." He must embrace the particularity of his Jewish identity, an identity that is forevermore inseparable from the experience of the Holocaust.

— *Edward Alexander*

The persistence of the universalist-humanist delusion among American Jews even in the wake of the Holocaust is nowhere represented with more symbolic force than in Bernard Malamud's story "The Lady of the Lake" (1958), one of but two stories in his work dealing directly with the Holocaust. The protagonist comes into a small inheritance and decides to go abroad "seeking romance." In the States, where "a man's past was . . . expendable," he was Henry Levin, but once in Europe Levin takes to calling himself Henry Freeman, thus symbolically severing his

Jewish ties. When he meets an attractive Italian girl named Isabella he identifies himself as an American but denies his Jewish identity. He wonders, since "he absolutely did not look Jewish," why she should ask the question of him, but quickly dismisses it as a quirk. "With ancient history why bother?" One of her attractions, to be sure, is precisely a face that carries "the mark of history," that is, of "civilized" Italian history. But at the crucial moment, when he comes to propose marriage to Isabella, she reveals her breasts, on whose "softened tender flesh" he recognizes the tattooed blue numbers of the concentration-camp inmate that show her Jewish identity. " 'I can't marry you. We are Jews. My past is meaningful to me. I treasure what I suffered for.' " Levin-Freeman suddenly discovers the emptiness of his freedom and, having deprived himself by his deception of what he most desired, can only stammer, " 'Listen, I-I am—.' " But before he can supply the missing label, Isabella disappears into the night. In the aftermath of the Holocaust, it is not enough for the American Jew simply to be an American, or even simply "to be." To embrace the fullness of life that Isabella here represents, he must embrace the particularity of his Jewish identity, an identity that is forevermore inseparable from the experience of the Holocaust.

Levin-Freeman is symbolic not only of the American Jew who has evaded his moral responsibility and impoverished his life by cutting himself off from the Jewish past. He may also be taken as a symbol of the American Jewish writer who, in embracing what Cynthia Ozick has called the "Diaspora of freedom," has doomed himself to the obscurity of a perpetual involvement "with shadow, with futility, with vanity, frivolity, and waste." He has denied the novelist's responsibility to engage and extend his readers' imaginative sympathy, and he has impoverished his own art by separating his Jewish characters from their history, which could have provided him with that norm of behavior without which satire becomes sterile.

Thus the "silence" of most American Jewish writers on the Holocaust was not (as has sometimes been urged in their defence) an awed acknowledgement of the unspeakable and unimaginable character of the evil that occurred, or the implicit admission that what is absolutely unprecedented in human affairs cannot be imitated in a literary action. American Jewish writers have hardly been struck dumb in the face of various evils that (however mistakenly) they consider on a par with Auschwitz and Treblinka. Carlyle once spoke of the unique eloquence of "the SILENCE of deep Eternities, of Worlds from beyond the morning-stars." But the long silence of American Jewish literature on the Holocaust was eloquent only of its own failure to shake off the incubus-like ideological superstitions of modern Jewry and grasp its proper subject—even though to do so would have been to admit that Jewish suffering had been not merely an indiscriminate part of man's inhumanity to man but unique, and that the human rights granted to Jews as "freemen" and individuals had been an invitation to self-destruction. As Norma Rosen recently wrote, "The Holocaust is the central occurrence of the Twentieth century. It is the central human occurrence. It cannot therefore be more so for Jews and Jewish writers. But it ought, at least, to be that."

Among the best-known American Jewish writers, with the exception (again) of Saul Bellow, this silence even today has not been broken. But if we now turn from speculation about why we have not had, in America, a substantial literature of the Holocaust to evaluation of what we do have, we will notice a gradual awakening in our literary culture that seems to have been spurred by the Eichmann trial and the Six-Day War. Since the sixties, a number of American Jewish writers, including some of the most gifted, have sought to rediscover for us in the Holocaust our own buried life.

We still frequently notice, in this literature, the deep-seated reluctance to conceive of specifically Jewish suffering, as well as a compulsive desire for discovering analogies between Jewish suffering and that of whatever oppressed or allegedly oppressed group (not excluding the Arabs) is at the time of writing the special beneficiary of liberal-left benevolence. The most hideous example of this tendency is probably Richard Elman's pseudo-documentary novel *The 28th Day of Elul* (1967). The novel's hero is a survivor who writes from Israel to the lawyer of a deceased American uncle to prove that he is truly a Jew and therefore deserving of his uncle's legacy. By way of explaining to the lawyer what Hitler's victims endured, the best he can do is say "they were treated like niggers." The worst he can think to say of the German murderers themselves is that they are like Americans, who are "just as guilty" because they dropped bombs on Hamburg and Dresden—or like (to this point does egalitarian nihilism invariably lead us) Israeli army officers. The German organizers of mass killing were, according to the moral and historical perspective of this writer who is all knowingness and no knowledge, just like bourgeois functionaries everywhere. " 'We even have them in Israel . . . with patches over their eyes.' " This book, whose narrator-hero says he is no more a conscious member of the Jewish religion than of the "human race," bears out in a truly remarkable way Cynthia Ozick's further observation that "whoever thinks it necessary to declare the Jews members of 'mankind' is not quite sure of the very proposition he finds it necessary to declare; and, like Shakespeare, he can end by confusing the victim with the victimizer."

Even in works infinitely superior to Elman's in literary tact and moral imagination, we often encounter the desire to make the Jew into "an archetype of the eternal oppressed." This may begin with the understandable intention to relate the Holocaust to what is readily available in the experience of the author and his imagined audience. But it can end by transfusing the blood of Jewish culture and Jewish experience into the *caput mortuum* of universalist ethical demonstrations.

In Edward Wallant's *The Pawnbroker* (1962), the hero is Sol Nazerman, who lost his wife and children during the Holocaust and himself suffered mutilation through medical experimentation. Formerly a professor in Poland, in his American incarnation he is a pawnbroker whose shop exists to subserve the interests of a Mafia gangster. He believes that all life has been gassed and burned in those crematoriums where he had himself been forced to work. His hopes amputated long ago, his greatest wish now is to be free of human relationships beyond the formal ones required by his home life with the shallow, assimilated "American" family of his sister, and by his business transactions with the derelicts who frequent his shop. To satisfy his biological needs, he occasionally sleeps with a survivor, named Tessie Rubin. The act is a form of necrophilia, a consummation not of tenderness or love but of the desperation and anguish of people who have lost the will to live. He resents the attempted intrusion upon his privacy and unfeelingness by a well-intentioned social worker, Miss Birchfield. His true life is among the dead, and comes to him in dreams of his murdered family and people. Wallant conveys very powerfully the spiritual distance that separates Nazerman from his mindless relatives, his hostile black and Puerto Rican customers, and the woman who loves him yet wishes the blue numbers on his arm and the memories they represent would disappear altogether. " 'There is,' " he tells Miss Birchfield, " 'a world so different in scale that its emotions bear no resemblance to yours; it has emotions so different in degree that they have become a different *species*!' "

Finally, however, Wallant proves as unwilling to accept this wall of separation and distinction as the naïvely well-intentioned social worker, who hopes to "cure" Sol of his "bitterness" and make him a *"human being"* again. Sol has refused emotional relationship not only with her but also with his black Puerto Rican assistant, Jesus Ortiz, who emulates Sol in what he takes to be the peculiarly Jewish magical power of pawnbrokerism. When Jesus asks about those same blue numbers, " 'Hey, what kind of tattoo you call that?' " Sol replies, " 'It's a secret society I belong to. . . . You could never belong. You have to be able to walk on the water.' " Jesus has some vague sense of, and curiosity about, the suffering that is evident in Sol's face and manner: " 'Niggers,' " he complains, " 'suffer like animals. They ain't caught on. Oh, yeah, Jews suffer. But they do it big, they shake up the worl' with their sufferin'.' " But Jesus is entirely ignorant of the specific sources of that suffering, the Holocaust not being one of those irritants to the feelings of minorities for the alleviation of which the American educational system offers its famed "sensitivity" training. Sol has no desire to enlighten Jesus, and neither does Wallant himself. Indeed, it is characteristic of American Jewish writing, drawn compulsively to the relationship between blacks and Jews, invariably to assume that although Jews are under the most compelling of obligations to fathom black suffering, blacks are under no obligation whatever to fathom Jewish suffering, much less to have heard about it. (It is truly a wonderful example of liberal condescension which assumes that blacks may be complete human beings without achieving imaginative sympathy with their neighbors, whereas their neighbors are absolutely required to identify with the plight of blacks if they are to live lives that are both moral and fully integrated.)

It is only when Sol can be made to suffer for Jesus that Sol's icy encasement will melt away, that his rehabilitation will be possible, and that his own suffering will be subsumed within the general suffering of humanity. The curative process begins when he discovers that his Mafia em-

ployer also runs the house of prostitution where one of his black customers works. He remembers the sexual enslavement of his wife by the Gestapo, and, even though he has always taught Jesus that belief in money is the only absolute in this world, he now refuses to be paid with money from the whorehouse and is brutally beaten for his new finickiness. The barriers to memory are now down, and Sol's nightmare visions begin to penetrate his waking life and crack his unfeeling armor.

Heavy symbolic operations now come into play, all of them intended to validate Jewish suffering by linking it, through Christian Symbolism, with the plight of dark-skinned Americans. Jesus, who has been conspiring with a gang of black hoodlums to rob the shop of his employer, goes into a church before joining his comrades. Looking at a statue of Jesus Christ, he is struck by the vague recognition that this savior of his was not only a white man and therefore incapable of knowing what blacks must endure, but also a Jew and therefore linked with the pawnbroker. "And He was a Jew, too, like the Pawnbroker; there's a laugh for you. He tried to imagine the Pawnbroker in a position like that, nailed up on a cross. . . . He began to chuckle, harshly. Wouldn't everybody be shocked to see Sol Nazerman up there, his arm with the blue numbers stretched out to the transfixed hand?" At last illumination has come to Jesus Ortiz on this little matter of the blue numbers; it is in truth a property of crucified humanity. Sol Nazerman, whom Ortiz knows to be a possible, albeit not intended, casualty of the armed robbery, becomes fixed in his mind's eye as Jesus Christ crucified. The old literary-psychological device of the "double" asserts the interdependent existence of the Puerto Rican and the Jewish Jesus, whose surname, it now dawns on us, bears a strong resemblance to "Nazarene." In the robbery, it is Jesus Ortiz who literally "dies for" Sol Nazerman by stepping in the line of a bullet. With his death, Sol's long-dead emotions burst into life.

The symbolism may at first seem imprecise, working to conceal rather than reveal meaning. But in truth the symbolism of the doubling has its own logic, however unappealing. Jesus Ortiz has been sacrificed on behalf of Sol Nazerman, in that his death serves to bring Sol back to life. But Sol too has been sacrificed, not so much for Ortiz as for the suffering humanity he represents, not so much in his body as in the uniqueness of his memories and of the Jewish people's suffering. In his final dream, Sol walks over the desolate grounds of the death camp, "monument to a forgotten race." He meets an S.S. officer who turns out to be the Mafia gangster, and informs Sol, " 'Your dead are not buried here.' " The tears that signify Sol's return to life are at first mysterious to him, "until he realized he was crying for loss of one irreplaceable Negro who had been his assistant and who had tried to kill him but who had ended by saving him." The dilution of the Jewish literary imagination brings even a fine writer like Wallant to the point where the Jews are asked not merely to give up their lives for the benefit of downtrodden minorities but their deaths as well.

Touching Evil (1969), by Norma Rosen, is a novel whose reach far exceeds its grasp. It tries to imagine how Americans, specifically non-Jewish American women, who have been touched by the evil of the Holocaust might try to think and feel and imagine their way into the lives of those who had been tortured and killed. The two crucial dates of the story are 1944, when the older of the two women central to the story, having been shown photographs of the death camps at the very moment when she is being seduced, vows she " 'will never marry or have children,' " and 1961, when the younger woman, Hattie, dutifully follows the Eichmann trial on television during her pregnancy. She too has misgivings about propagating the species because, in her view, the Germans have poisoned the very process of generation. But her burgeoning into motherhood is vital to her spiritual existence because it is the path by which she enters into the lives of those whose blood will otherwise be covered by the earth. She suspends her personal rhythms of existence and identifies herself with those "far-gone pregnant women in their forced march; the woman giving birth in the typhus-lice-infested straw; the woman who was shot but did not die, and who dug her way from under a mountain of corpses that spouted blood. . . ."

Unfortunately, Norma Rosen has not pursued this striking central idea with sufficient concentration. She too allows herself to be diverted by the temptations of analogy, of heavy symbolism, and feminist topicality. In fact, the book concludes with the older woman "looking for Jesus," who, precisely like Wallant's character of the same name, is a Puerto Rican misled by his evil friends into criminal actions, and aspiring to take him in as Hattie has taken in the pregnant Jewish woman of the Holocaust during the process of childbirth. Even the crucial scenes in which the hysterical Hattie compares the labor room of a New York hospital to a concentration camp are so enveloped in feminist rhetoric that many a reader (especially today) will forget that their point (as the author herself has felt obliged to explain) is to finalize the identification between Hattie and the women whose stories she has heard in the Eichmann trial, not to present women as the oppressed race.

Daring, even brilliant, as is the central idea of *Touching Evil,* it would have been far more daring if Rosen had made the heroine who seeks to identify with the Jewish victims of Hitler through the shared burden of motherhood a Jew herself. For in no respect has the refusal of most American Jewish writers to allow their awareness of Jewish history and of the Holocaust to impinge on their depiction of American Jewish life shown itself so glaringly as in their relentless attack upon "the Jewish mother." This well-known monster of American fiction, who suffocates her offspring with egoism parading as affection, was created not merely in willful ignorance of what Singer calls "the generations-old dolor of the Jewish mother . . . who bled and suffered so that murderers should have victims of their knives," but with a stolid, almost stupid refusal to consider that the paralyzing dilemmas faced by hundreds of thousands of Jewish mothers in Hitler's Europe might just possibly have touched the consciousness and affected the behavior of at least a few of their American counterparts.

Just how great was the failure of awareness, how mon-

strous the thoughtlessness, of the Jewish writers who invented this caricature should be evident to anyone who reads *Anya* (1974), by Susan F. Schaeffer. The extraordinary achievement of this novel, probably the best American literary work on the Holocaust, cannot be conveyed by a description of just one of its themes; but nowhere is its special power to convey the enormity of Jewish suffering during the destruction process more evident than in its depiction of the agony of Jewish mothers. Susan Schaeffer has given to all those nameless and unremembered women who were forced to choose between life and a mother's loyalty to her child, or—more horrible yet—between the relatively "easy" death of the gas chamber and that death in the burning pit which she would share with her child if she did not abandon him, "a monument and a memorial."

Anya is a historical novel in the form of a memoir written by Anya Savikin some years after she is brought to New York from the D.P. camps. It is truly historical—and uniquely dignified—in that the author refuses to distance herself from the woman who tells the story through irony or the wisdom of hindsight. Rather, she tries to view the events of the Holocaust cataclysm as they would have appeared to an ordinarily intelligent person caught up in them. In fact, not only Susan Schaeffer, but the fifty-two-year-old woman who tells her own story, in 1973, resists the temptation to separate herself from the young woman who endures the war years. We are made to feel how an eighteen-year-old assimilated Jewish girl spending her summers at elegant resorts and reading *Mein Kampf* in a hammock might very well dismiss it, as Anya does, as "a fairy tale." The novel takes us over much of the familiar Holocaust terrain—prewar pogroms in Poland, the invasion and bombardment of Warsaw, selections, killing by shooting and killing by gas; yet invariably the writer makes us feel that we are experiencing these things afresh, seeing them with new eyes. She tells, with a wealth of detail that is part of the novel's meaning, of the life of her wealthy, assimilated family in Poland before the war, of the arrest, torture, and murder of her father, sister, brothers, husband, and, finally, mother; of her own suffering in the camps, and of her miraculous escapes and survival, made possible by her determination to save her daughter.

The novel is as much about memory as about the Holocaust. Anya tells us that her great wish had always been to be taken over by "the continuity of life": to marry, to bear children, to accumulate the physical record of family memory in pictures and furniture and jewelry; then, at the last, to die a normal death. Perhaps no writer since Thomas Hardy (as poet) has expressed so well as Schaeffer the paradoxical way in which material possessions form the texture of a life, and make us human. When she and her family are brought to the killing center at Ponary, Anya feels that their lives depend most of all on her ability to retain through memory the world—only ten blocks away in their apartment in Vilna—from which they are now separated by what seem "huge deep cliffs filled with violent water." "I started to picture the stove. It seemed very important that I remember every detail, as if all our lives depended on it." That in some sense they *do* depend on it is recognized by the Germans as well. Thus, when Anya visits a ravaged Warsaw much later in the story, a Polish cart-driver tells her how the Germans killed not only people, but the trees and the furniture. " 'Kill all the furniture?' I echoed helplessly. 'You know, couches, chairs, credenzas, kill them. There should be nothing left for anyone to come back to.' " When you are living in what Anya's mother taught her to call "biblical times," the boundaries between what is living and what is dead are obliterated. For Anya, at the end of the war, the dead are more real than the living, and memory serves not to retain that which still exists but to recover that which is no more. It is a dangerous but indispensable faculty: "Then I opened the box: There was Momma's big diamond ring, and Poppa's diamond ring, and her pin, my diploma, my index from medical school, the pictures of Stajoe and me near the rock at Druzgeniekie. . . . But something had escaped from the box like a dangerous gas. It was time, old time. I had to take care not to breathe it in." That massive infusion of the details of everyday life that has characterized the realistic novel since Thackeray finds in this novel its true justification. By conveying so richly the fullness of an individual life, Schaeffer, without more than glancing at the dimensions of the Holocaust, makes us see how far beyond imagining is the loss of six million lives, each of them a treasure house of association and memory.

When she has lost almost everything and everyone, Anya must be taught by her mother how and why to survive. The elder Mrs. Savikin, a splendid character who both understands and embodies the naturalness of custom, insists that even in the Vilna ghetto her daughter must comb and wash and put on lipstick if she wants to retain the human image and survive. When the ghetto is being liquidated, the order goes out that all women with children are to be killed. "Some of the women heard it and ran away from their children. 'How could they do it?' I asked Momma. 'Everything for life,' she answered dully; 'everything to live.' " Then Anya and *her* mother are sent in opposite directions at the segregation point, the younger to live, for a while, the older to die at once. Anya tries to stay with her mother, but to no avail; and the last words of the mother whom she will never see again are: " 'You will live! You have someone for whom to live!' " This is her way of reminding Anya of what she has already taught her by example: that the continuity of life for which she had hoped now resides in the daughter Ninka, who has been hidden with a Christian family. The little girl has become the repository of all those destroyed lives. " 'She is the photograph album,' I thought, seeing myself turn the pages with Momushka."

The last segment of the novel takes place in the United States, where Anya has settled with her second husband, a survivor of Auschwitz. When the war ended, she had decided at once: " 'I am going to Palestine, or America.' " But her choice was made for her by the Communists, NKVD parading as Zionists, who arrested her and so blocked her way to Palestine. America threatens, actually and symbolically, the desecration of her experience and the spoliation of her memories. Having escaped the European inferno, she must now be plagued by the predators on the streets of New York. On Yom Kippur, the family's apartment is burglarized and the treasured family photos

stolen: "It was a tragedy for me, a real tragedy. I had so little of them left." Worse still, she is disappointed in the daughter, the recipient of all her love who now turns out to be herself unloving. But the memories are by now fixed in her mind, independently of the photos. Her dismay over her daughter is lessened when she recalls two women living in California who had saved themselves by hiding when Gestapo officers held up their children and asked the mothers to step forward. She cannot understand mothers who could abandon their children, but she does not condemn them, for "there were no normal lives during the war, no ethical lives." Nevertheless, when she says that even now, in the safe haven of the United States, "I cannot even leave my living child alone for one second," Susan Schaeffer does not invite us to sneer but to see and understand.

It is in the United States that Anya reflects (virtually for the last time) on the meaning of all that has happened, to her and to the Jewish people. Although her Jewish illiteracy ran deep, she had begun to feel her way toward a belief in God from the time when, as a girl in medical school, she had been saved by an accident of fate from a horrible pogrom perpetrated against Jewish girls by the other medical students. She sat in perplexity with her mother after the event, thinking " 'What for, the chosen people, what for? Chosen for what? For this, to be endlessly persecuted, just because we are Jewish?' And it was then I began to believe. Even the endless persecution was a form of being chosen." Why, she now asks, was she saved when all the rest of her family went under? "Always I felt this hand over me. Always, I was the lucky one." But her world was obliterated, "destroyed, erased, as if it were less than a spelling lesson on the blackboard," and now the Jews are reduced to the humiliation of accepting reparation money, as if one could offer compensation for a whole world, "nothing less than the globe my father's hand rested on."

If her own survival remains a mystery to her, the Holocaust itself remains a greater one. Was the Holocaust perhaps a punishment for intermarriage? "Sometimes I think it is a payment for our new country, for Israel." Anya can never come to any definite conclusions. Her reflections are presented not for their profundity but for their conformity to her experience, with which they keep pace. She has no interest whatever in finding out what "other, wiser people" think it all meant, for "Who can know what it meant? I don't believe anyone can. So I satisfy myself with simple answers that suit the weather of the day." Anya's impulse to understand her experience comes to rest not with what Bellow's Mr. Sammler contemptuously refers to as "explanations" but with her sitting down to put her feelings on paper. In the last page of the book, she re-creates and recovers her destroyed family in a dream, in a new house, which will not vanish, and which in fact comprises the novel that stands before us, a triumph over time.

American Jewish Holocaust writing concentrates most of its attention on the problems of individuals, whether they are survivors, like Anya or like Bellow's Artur Sammler, or American Jews who belatedly react to what they had watched from a distance, or perhaps not watched at all. For the most part, its characters are not participants in a process of rebirth and recovery that involves them with the Jewish people as a whole or even with the Jews of their own country. When the hero of Bellow's *Mr. Sammler's Planet* (1970), upon hearing news of the outbreak of the war in 1967, hastens to secure a journalistic assignment that will take him to Israel, he is fleeing what suddenly strikes him as the historical irrelevance of Jewish America. The contrast here with the literature of Israel may seem unsurprising. Yet it requires some explanation if we take at all seriously the claims made by American Jewry, usually implicitly but sometimes explicitly, that the American Jewish community, by far the largest in the world in numbers since the destruction of European Jewry, is a continuator and an inheritor of that ravaged civilization as much as Israel is, and has if not an equal then at least a unique role to play in the Jewish future. Only two American Jewish writers have tried to grapple with this question, and to imagine a communal response to the Holocaust that is creative and that does not consist of the answer: Israel. The alternative answers can also be identified by place-names: Yavneh and Bene Brak.

In 1969 and 1970, Cynthia Ozick published, within a period of a few months, a short story and an essay that defined two American Jewish responses to the Holocaust and the relation between them. The story, a small masterpiece, was entitled "Envy; or, Yiddish in America." In it she ironically but affectionately re-created the ambience of American Yiddish writers, for whom continuation of Yiddish, the language of the majority of the victims of the Holocaust, constitutes the most meaningful form of Jewish survival. "A little while ago," writes one of the story's characters, "there were twelve million people . . . who lived inside this tongue, and now what is left? A language that never had a territory except Jewish mouths, and half the Jewish mouths on earth already stopped up with German worms. The rest jabber Russian, English, Spanish, God knows what. . . . In Israel they give the language of Solomon to machinists. Rejoice—in Solomon's time what else did the mechanics speak? Yet whoever forgets Yiddish courts amnesia of history." The story conveys its author's profound dissatisfaction with what one of the characters archly refers to as "so-called Amer.-Jewish writers." It conveys too the sense that Yiddish and Hebrew have now, because of the Holocaust and the establishment of the State of Israel, exchanged their traditional roles within Jewish life, with Yiddish, now the language of martyrdom, acquiring a sacred status, and Hebrew, used (often badly) by bus-drivers and peddlers of unkosher meat in Tel Aviv, becoming the language of the folk and the street. Yet this very transformation and elevation of Yiddish into the language of a coterie, who seek meaning and salvation through continuing to write in it, would itself seem the final confirmation that Yiddish language and literature, which for centuries actually did perform many of the functions of a homeland for people who had none, can no longer do so. The elegiac note in this mainly comic story can be deeply moving: " 'In Talmud if you save a single life it's as if you saved the world. And if you save a language? Worlds maybe. Galaxies. The whole universe.' " But how can a language itself in need of salvation save others?

Cynthia Ozick sought an answer to this question in her lecture/essay of 1970 entitled "America: Toward Yavneh." Yavneh traditionally and literally, of course, refers to the place in which, in the year 70, following the fall of Jerusalem to the Romans, the sage Yohanan ben Zakkai established an academy that became the spiritual center of Judaism after the nation ceased to be an independent political entity. Yavneh continued to flourish as a religious center: in it the canon of the Bible was formulated and the Mishnah was begun. Thus Judaism could be said to have survived and, in one sense, flourished even after the Jewish Commonwealth was no more.

By applying, however tentatively, the term *Yavneh* to America, Ozick does not, like some subsequent exploiters of this metaphor, intend to congratulate American Jewry on a moral or intellectual character superior to that of Israeli Jews. On the contrary, she makes clear that American Jews for the most part remain in their corner of the Exile because they love to be flattered for having those very traits that are so easily (and often fraudulently) claimed by people without power or responsibility, their devotion to "Mankind" (rather than to Jews), their pacific character, their widespreading, indiscriminate philanthropy. "In America . . . the fleshpots are spiritual. The reason we do not Ingather is not because of our material comforts, but because of our spiritual self-centeredness." Indeed, her whole thrust up to this point in her essay is that when the Jews went into Exile their capacity for literature seemed to abandon them, especially when they chose to address, as most American Jewish writers still do address, the principle of "Mankind" rather than the culture and problems of their own people. Nevertheless, she finally expresses the hope that just as Spain was for a time in the Middle Ages a sort of Jerusalem Displaced, so can America be.

" 'Yavneh,' " she says, "is an impressionistic term, a metaphor suggesting renewal. The original Academy at Yavneh was founded after the destruction of the Temple; the new one in prospect coincides with the restoration of Zion." She expresses the hope that the Yavneh of America can share responsibility for Jewish destiny with the Jews of Israel. In a kind of division of labor scheme for the reconstruction of a shattered people, she envisions Jerusalem as the healer of wounds, the bringer of health, the safekeeper, and Yavneh America as "the Aggadists, the makers-of-literature." Although most of her essay has demonstrated, rather conclusively, that Diaspora culture has been largely a disaster, and that "there are no major works of Jewish imaginative genius written in any Gentile language, sprung out of any Gentile culture," she now makes a declaration of faith in the ability of American Jewry to preserve itself by making a new culture. This culture will itself be partly the result of the restoration of Israel, partly the result of the Holocaust, and yet it will have its own character, its own principle of life.

The main instrument of this reconstruction will be a creative union between Yiddish and English that Ozick labels New Yiddish, and that she hopes will become, just as "old" Yiddish was, "the language of multitudes of Jews, spoken to Jews by Jews, written by Jews for Jews." If doubters ask who is to invent such a language, her answer is that it has already been invented, that her essay itself is written in it, that Norma Rosen's *Touching Evil* and Saul Bellow's *Mr. Sammler's Planet* are novelistic examples of it. Just as a dialect of Middle High German was once changed into Yiddish by being made the instrument of Jewish peoplehood, Jewish necessities, so too can English be transformed into New Yiddish by Jewish writers who have found their proper subject—the Holocaust and Jewish fate—and can transmute the characteristic rhythms and intonations of Yiddish into English.

Although few readers have failed to be impressed by Cynthia Ozick's brilliance of mind and style, many come away from the essay feeling that she is something like the magician who puts eggs into a hat and brings forth—eggs. Her procedure is similar to that of the Gothic revivalists of the nineteenth century who thought to recreate the civilization of the Middle Ages by imitating its architecture, even as they maintained that all architecture was inevitably an index of the ethical values of the civilization that produced it. But if criticism cannot create a new culture, perhaps it can, as Matthew Arnold believed, create a new literature. Cynthia Ozick's call for American Jewish culture to assume, alongside Israeli Jewish culture, responsibility for the reconstruction of Jewish life, has already stirred a response among younger writers, most notably in Arthur A. Cohen's *In the Days of Simon Stern* (1973). This novel, garrulous, pedantic, and badly structured, is nevertheless rich in idea and imaginative power, and unique among the works of American fiction we have surveyed in two respects. It views the Holocaust from the perspective of Jewish religion, and it attempts to imagine, in America, a collective rather than individual response to the destruction of European Jewry.

The novel's narrator is blind Nathan Gaza, a survivor of Auschwitz whose name calls up that of the prophet of Sabbatai Zevi, the false messiah of the seventeenth century who appealed to the desperate hopes of masses of Jews in the aftermath of unprecedented massacre. Nathan tells his story in English, but deplores its inadequacy as a language of prophecy and says he uses it only because Simon Stern, who thought English second only to Hebrew, demanded it. Nathan tells the story of Simon Stern, whose parents were informed, before his birth in 1899, that their son would be the Messiah, but that his emergence would be contingent on their own death. Simon does not learn of his identity until much later, in fact, just after he learns from the modern Elijah, Chaim Weizmann, in his Madison Square Garden speech of 1943, that two million Jews have already been killed. No sooner does Weizmann say that " 'we are being destroyed by a conspiracy of silence' " than Simon is stricken with impotence, forever incapable of physical love because his creative destiny must be fulfilled in other realms. He now receives the letter than his father had written him in 1899 telling him that he is the Messiah. The linkage between the death of his parents by fire in the previous year and the death of two million Jews quickens his sense of mission. "Why is it always so," asked Simon's father in his revelatory letter, "that good should come out of evil?" Up to this time in his life, Simon's messianic energies have gone into the accumulation of sixty

million dollars' worth of real estate. But the simultaneous revelation of his messianic destiny and of the destruction of the Jews of Europe raises the question of whether what the Book of Daniel calls "the time of beating wings" is at hand. Nathan, true to his prophetic role, reflects: "*The world, it is said, will be saved either when it has become so transparently magnificent that the Messiah appears as a reward or when it aches so from misery that the Messiah comes like a medicine. But there's a third way. The Messiah comes into our midst when men are speechless.*"

Although Simon and his friends do place advertisements in the *New York Times* informing the nation of the details and magnitude of the slaughter and urging the Allies to bomb the death camps, they do not undertake political action. Simon dreams of confronting Roosevelt over his callous refusal to ransom the Jews and take them in, but his dream is not translated into action. Simon gives five million dollars to endow a Society for the Rescue and Resurrection of the Jews, whose actions during the war are fictional confirmation of the accusation (made by Hilberg and others) that in the midst of the slaughter American Jews thought, when they thought at all, not of political action to effect rescue but of postwar salvage operations. Simon's society has as its primary purpose the preparation of centers and domiciles for the restoration to the remnant—for, as the Bible says, there always *is* a remnant—of their souls as well as their bodies.

Cohen himself is more interested in pursuing the idea of a separate destiny for post-Holocaust American Jewry than in a political critique of the American Jewish community during the war. Whereas in *Anya* the heroine ends up in America purely by accident, here the decision to go to America rather than to Eretz Israel is a conscious one, forced by Simon Stern. Simon actually goes to the D.P. camps to select the choice survivors and urge them to go to New York with him rather than to Palestine. " 'Some will want to go and cannot. Others will not want to go and I will persuade you to come.' " As if to emphasize the competitive character of the choice, Cohen shows Simon's speech to the survivors precipitating a battle between the two factions. "There was a momentary silence as the assembly considered his invitation and then a cry went up: 'To America. To America.' And others replied, 'To the Land. To the Land. *Eretz Yisrael.*' Fists hit against the air and arms struck out against others."

Eventually the refugees are brought to New York, and the process of rehabilitation begins. Simon Stern envisions, not exactly a Yavneh, but "a small Bene Brak as in the days after the destruction of the ancient temple," a Bene Brak in New York City that will bear witness that " 'despite all, everything, Jews will endure.' " The original Bene Brak, like the original Yavneh, became important only in the first century of this era, when, following the destruction in Jerusalem, a group of sages moved there and made it into a famous seat of learning, where Rabbi Akiva established his great academy. The very idea that a Bene Brak could arise in New York City after the Holocaust constitutes an audacious challenge to modern Israel's role as the rightful inheritor of the destroyed Jewish civilization of Europe.

The task of giving a semblance of civility to a community of survivors of bestiality is engaged with energy. Simon is proclaimed Messiah at a meeting of the Society, and the "endurers" begin to rebuild a Temple replica as well as to regain the pride, courage, and tenacity of the Jews who built the original. But from this high point all is decline and dissolution: we have had no more than what Nathan calls "a fulfilled moment." The same may be said of the novel itself, for the idea of building a restored Jewish civilization in New York City is even more quixotic than that of building it on a new literary language. Cohen is prepared for this objection, which is met by one of his characters, who says that really there is "no difference between Simon Stern and David Ben-Gurion. He drew none of the haughty distinctions between those who build castles in the sky and those who build castles in the sand." Once again, we meet the notion of a division of labor between the two inheritors of the Jewish remnant, Israel and Diaspora. But here the idea has an enormous arrogance absent from Cynthia Ozick's formulation. For in truth the speaker asserts not equality between the partners but the superior spirituality of the partner whose castles are built *only* in the air. True, the castles in the sky built in New York and those in sand built in Eretz Israel are both shaky and unstable, but "the former were the constructions of visionaries and the latter the constructions of unskilled engineers. The fact that the visionaries had kept the People alive for thousands of years was proof enough that the engineers would in time learn their trade." There could be no more stunning illustration than this of what Hillel Halkin has called the tendency of some American Jewish intellectuals to imagine the entire Jewish people "with its body in the East and its soul in the West."

The Holocaust has, then, finally become a subject of American Jewish fiction, finally made itself felt as an event of Jewish history and significance.

— *Edward Alexander*

Despite its shortcomings, *In the Days of Simon Stern* asks important questions about the political and theological implications of the Holocaust, questions either prohibited or tacitly avoided by most American Jewish writing. It forces us to look back at the conduct of American Jewry and of Jewry's favorite senators and president during the Holocaust and to ask whether, in Simon's words, "the murderers are . . . the ones who do not pay attention." It also explores, with more audacity than perhaps any work except Moshe Flinker's diary and Nelly Sachs's poetry the bearing of the Holocaust upon the ancient Jewish idea that messianic redemption will come through historical catastrophe. Above all, it suggests a new future for American Jewish writing by opening the question of how to reorganize Judaism in the Diaspora after the European Diaspora has been destroyed, and of how American Jew-

ish culture can assume, alongside Israeli Jewish culture, responsibility for the reconstruction of Jewish life.

The Holocaust has, then, finally become a subject of American Jewish fiction, finally made itself felt as an event of Jewish history and significance. This ought to be a cause of satisfaction, even if it is a strange satisfaction that comes from assimilating to the imagination a catastrophe that befell us over three decades ago. But, alas, we have no time to enjoy even this qualified satisfaction, for the Jews do not seem able to extricate themselves from the storm center of modern history. If world events and American policy continue on their present course, American Jews may once again find themselves faced with a tragic choice between their identity as members of the Jewish people and their identity as American citizens. If our writers have at last begun to equip us for tragedy, they will at least have saved us from the worst calamity.

Susanne Klingenstein

SOURCE: "Visits to Germany in Recent Jewish-American Writing," in *Contemporary Literature*, Vol. 34, No. 3, Fall, 1993, pp. 538-70.

[*In the following essay, Klingenstein studies the Holocaust and the theme of Jewish-American visits to Germany as exemplified in the writings of Cynthia Ozick and Rebecca Goldstein.*]

The question of Germany—how to view it, how to respond to it, how to cope with its apparent return not just to normal life but to power and influence in Europe—begs the question of one's attitude toward the Holocaust. It induces even the most American of Jewish writers to think as Jews. It was only a matter of time until the theme of responses to Germany should make its appearance in fiction. This motif has recently emerged in Jewish-American writing in the form of visits to Germany as steps onto Shoah territory. In this essay I examine some very different examples of this new motif, beginning with Cynthia Ozick's early novel *Trust*. I will then go on to discuss some autobiographical accounts before turning to Rebecca Goldstein's novels *The Mind-Body Problem* and *The Late-Summer Passion of a Woman of Mind*, which use the theme of return to illuminate the validity of certain philosophical positions adopted by her protagonists. The preoccupation with Germany in fiction and autobiography reveals how Jewish-American writers have taken on the liturgical task of *Vergangenheitsverarbeitung*, of weaving the past into the Jewish present.

HIEROGLYPHS OF EUROPE

Few American authors have revered and trusted the chronicler of the American enchantment with Europe, Henry James, as much as Cynthia Ozick. He became the literary master of her apprentice years:

> In early young-womanhood I believed, with all the rigor and force and stunned ardor of religious belief, in the old Henry James, in his scepter and his authority. I believed that what *he* knew at sixty I was to encompass at twenty-two; at twenty-two I lived like the elderly bald-

headed Henry James. I thought it was necessary—it was imperative, there was no other path!—to be, all at once, with no progression or evolution, the author of the equivalent of *The Ambassadors* or *The Wings of the Dove,* just as if "A Bundle of Letters," or "Four Meetings," or the golden little "The Europeans" had never preceded the great late Master. ["The Lesson of the Master"]

In 1950, at the age of twenty-two, Cynthia Ozick began to write what she would later call "a cannibalistically ambitious Jamesian novel." She abandoned it almost seven years later after a futile three hundred thousand words. "Rapture and homage," she would come to see, "are not the way. Influence is perdition." When Ozick began her second novel in 1957, the splendor of James was still the light by which she wrote. But in November 1963, when she finished the immense, intricate prose poem *Trust,* published uncut in 1966, "the stupendous Jamesian lantern" had been outshone by the lightning of history. The moral obligations resulting from historical insight modified Ozick's single-minded dedication to art. It is true that the stories Ozick published just after *Trust,* such as "The Pagan Rabbi" (1966) or "Envy; or, Yiddish in America" (1969), still focus on language, style, and the *art* of writing. But in the message those tales convey, history asserts itself vigorously over art.

Ozick's shift of emphasis from art to history is reflected in the development of Enoch Vand, the only Jewish character in *Trust.* He is an American government official who visits Europe in 1945 to sort out, count, and bury the dead. His mission reveals to him the full extent of Europe's evil. *Trust* thus plays with the Jamesian theme but finds the Jamesian perception of Europe to be naive in light of the human capacity for evil revealed to the world in 1945. It was as response to history that art became significant. Ozick had learned this toward the end of writing *Trust.* Her insight is reflected in Enoch Vand's reaction to the devastation of Europe in 1945. The Chicago-born Enoch is one of three father figures in *Trust.* The other two are Gustave Nicholas Tilbeck, former lover of Allegra Vand (Enoch's wife), and William, Allegra's first husband. The three men stand for mutually exclusive realms: William represents business, money, thrift, solidity, society; Enoch stands for history, justice, ethics, redemption; and Nick celebrates nature, love, music, genius. Nick is an opportunist—unreliable, greedy, unprincipled, and disruptive. He is the antithesis to William and Enoch, who regard him as their enemy. In short, Nick represents the unbridled imagination, which Goethe defined as an elementary constant that not only resists the process of civilization but, occasionally, breaks through all barriers to disrupt and upset the respectable world with its rawness and brutality.

It is precisely this elementary force—the imagination, which the novel regards as a libidinal drive ("the god Pan")—that Enoch wants to vanquish. Not quite grasping Enoch's new Jewish mission, Allegra tells her daughter at the end of the novel, when an ambassadorship has failed to materialize: "He'll do *some*thing. He has this idea for an essay—actually it's a Jewish sort of essay. . . . It's

Cynthia Ozick.

called Pan Versus Moses. It's about Moses making the Children of Israel destroy all the grotto shrines and greenwood places and things. It's about how Moses hates Nature." Enoch's new project constitutes some progress over his earlier endeavor "to demonstrate how creation is an unredeemed monstrosity," insofar as Enoch now seems to believe that the ethical principles of Moses can keep in check the libidinal drives which, uncontrolled, lead to excess and destruction. On the last page of the novel, we learn that Enoch has read the Bible in Hebrew and studied the Ethics of the Fathers, which has led him to ask "for the whole Talmud."

The novel's punch line, however, should not be read as Enoch's "walking with God" (Gen. 5:24). "Faith in God," Enoch had said earlier, "rewards with the power of complacency, which is exactly why I find most piety obnoxious." What he turns to is a form of history, one tempered by ethical insight, more civilized than the ferocious belief in history he had developed as a witness to the Nazi crimes. Speaking with Allegra's daughter about the Germans' atrocities, Enoch tells her:

There are crimes which time chooses to memorialize instead of mitigate.

Human crime is a bloated craw, there's no waiting for it to finish because no matter how full it seems to be it only stretches for more, it's tremendous, both in itself and cumulatively, it's turned into an enormity of enormities—it's left the human dimension, it's vanished out of politics and gone to fertilize history, that's the thing!

> I don't believe in politics. I believe in history. . . . I believe in vengeance and history. Vengeance belongs to history and not to men. Vengeance is a high historical act. . . . [History] isn't simply what has happened. It's a judgment on what has happened!

Enoch formed these views in 1945, when he inspected piles of corpses for the American government and listed the names of the dead in black ledgers. His wife "equated Enoch with Europe," but she hardly suspects that it is no longer the Europe of *The Ambassadors*. Enoch's Europe has become a goddess of slaughter.

> She was war, death, blood, and spilled the severed limbs of infants from her giant channel in perpetual misbirths; she came up enlightened from that slaughter like a swimmer from the towering water-wall with his glorified face; she came up an angel from that slaughter and the fire-whitened cinders of those names. She came up Europa.

This Europe does not invite Jamesian subtleties; gossamer art and "practiced hesitation" are no longer adequate responses. Enoch grasps the reality of Europe; hence the "worship" of his goddess does not consist in the creation of art, but in the precise recording of history with the help of two assistants. Twelve years later, in 1957, with his hopes of an ambassadorship shattered, Enoch returns to precisely this occupation, much to the annoyance of his wife, who shouts to her daughter: "He'll do something. . . . Nothing public. Something personal. Something with me left out of it. . . . He'll write history." Allegra is annoyed, because she equates history with death: "I don't want to just get *into* history, that's what I call burial, I want to climb up *out* of it, I want to survive!" But her daughter, the product of amnesia and imagination, is helpless vis-à-vis the riddle of Europe; for her "the cadenced psalmings of the deathcamps" become "a hieroglyph of Europe."

In most of the fiction Cynthia Ozick published after *Trust* (but rarely in her essays), the Europe of James and high art disappears under a layer of death camp hieroglyphs. This is not to say that Ozick has become a "Holocaust writer." The recent claim of an annoyed German scholar that "the Holocaust is . . . unquestionably a major thematic preoccupation in her work and it is in keeping with her self-image as a Jewish writer that this should be so" is an exaggeration born of frustration with the negative role of Germans in Ozick's fiction. It is difficult for Germans—particularly for academic Americanists, who thought they had escaped the past at least intellectually—to be confronted time and again not with the cultural achievements of their country but with its crimes. For many artists, including Ozick, however, it is simply impossible to overlook that the face of Europe is now riddled with the pockmarks of the camps. At the end of *Trust,* Ozick concludes that fiction touching on post-1945 Europe cannot mimic the style of James; if it wants to be serious as art it needs to take history into account, which

means to include, in one way or another, the still enigmatic hieroglyph of the camps.

As a metaphor, "hieroglyph of Europe" has a certain ingenuity. We associate the Egyptian pictograph with death and a pagan culture inimical to Jews. Moreover, a hieroglyph or pictograph is defined as a picture representing an idea. The death camps spell out the racial aspects of National Socialist ideology; pushed further, we might say that the picture of a camp represents Nazi ideas. Ozick never used "hieroglyph of Europe" in that crude sense; but the association of pictorial writing and barbarism (which, for her, comprises both the paganism of antiquity and the fascism of modernity) became a motif in her work. The most lavish example of her metaphoric train of thought that connects writing, imag(in)ing, image, art, annihilation can be found in her last novel to date, *The Messiah of Stockholm*. When Lars Andemening, the novel's protagonist, gets to read *The Messiah,* the lost manuscript of a novel by Bruno Schulz, whom Lars believes to be his father, he is drawn into a phantasmagoric world of destruction. At one point the Messiah itself is described. More than anything else, he resembles a book with seemingly organic leaves:

> The flippers did indeed have the moist texture of petals . . . , and their peculiar tattoos certainly put one in mind of some postulate recorded in an archaic signification—a type of cuneiform, perhaps, though it was impossible to say what this unreadable text might be proposing as thesis or axiom. When examined with extreme attention . . . the inky markings showed themselves to be infinitely tiny and brilliantly worked drawings of these same idols that had taken hold of the town of Drohobycz. It was now clear that Drohobycz had been invaded by the characters of an unknown alphabet.

We know that in reality Drohobycz was invaded by the Wehrmacht and occupied by the SS, whose emblem is two archaically shaped letters. In this passage about Bruno Schulz's supposed novel *The Messiah,* Ozick links visionary fiction, paganism, idolatry, and Nazism in one gigantic sweep, thus elaborating her earlier metaphor of the hieroglyph. Toward the end of *The Messiah,* the idolatrous world of Drohobycz is reduced to ash, just as in Ozick's novel *The Messiah of Stockholm* Schulz's manuscript goes up in flames. This conflagration has a double meaning: it stands for the fires of the Shoah as much as for the messianic expectation of fulfillment expected from a führer cult. From a Jewish perspective the two are, of course, identical. For Jews, the advent of any messiah in history has so far spelled only one thing—death.

In her elaborate metaphor, Ozick also plays with an old theme in mystic and messianic writing that connects it to the modern *l'art pour l'art,* which is that fulfillment is identical with the annihilation of the self. This theme that art as end in itself spells the end of the self goes back to one of Ozick's earliest fictions. In 1971, five years after *Trust,* Ozick published a short story titled "The Suitcase" in her collection *The Pagan Rabbi,* in which she indicts an abstract art-for-art's-sake as dehumanizing. Significantly, the artist in the story, the painter Gottfried Hencke (the

German *Henker* means "hangman"), is the son of a German immigrant. The father, Arthur Hencke, a Fokker pilot for the kaiser turned American architect, does not know what to think about his son's art:

> His canvases were full of hidden optical tricks and were so bewildering to one's routine retinal expectations that, once the eye had turned away, a whirring occurred in the pupil's depth, and the paintings began to speak through their afterimage. Everything was disconcerting, everything seemed pasted down flat—strips, corners, angles, slivers. Mr. Hencke had a perilous sense that Gottfried had simply cut up the plans for an old office building with extraordinarily tiny scissors.

Genevieve, the artist's Jewish lover, translates the son's abstract paintings into historical significance: " 'Shredded swastikas, that's what,' Genevieve announced. 'Every single damn thing he does. All that terrible precision. Every last one a pot of shredded swastikas, you see that?' " Ozick's point in comparing abstract art to the murderous idolatry of Nazism is an indictment of art-for-art's-sake as dehumanizing and destructive. The common denominator of *l'art pour l'art* and the führer-worship of Nazi Germany with its disastrous consequences, as Ozick sees it, is the erasure of the recognizably human. In art, such erasure creates satiation. The art critic invited to speak at the opening of Gottfried's show calls the paintings "The Art of Fulfillment." The fulfillment consists in the completeness of the erasure which ends all desire. Hence Gottfried's art, concludes the critic, "is an art not of hunger, not of frustration, but of satiation. An art, so to speak, for fat men." Is it entirely wrong to think here of Hermann Göring and his greed for modern art?

The presence of the motif is important: art that refers to nothing but itself is self-satisfied; it is an art of fulfillment in the terrible, ambiguous sense of the word that includes the destruction of the human; it is an art of satiation because it excludes the confusing realm of history which upsets its neatly constructed patterns. Such art erases the human face. It was precisely the potential to bring about such erasure that Ozick feared about high art, even about a creativity such as Henry James's. Academics of that period describe the art of *The Ambassadors* indeed as a fearful thing "where the creative delight lay solely in the forms and patterns of the literary work . . . which were developed not only at the expense of any sense of reality or human content . . . [but] to conceal, deform or destroy the human content for the sake of the deceptive literary form." These words were written in 1963 by the now almost forgotten critic Maxwell Geismar, just as Ozick finished *Trust*. By then she had left the world of such worship behind, recognizing that literary art needed an objective correlative against which to measure itself—history. Ozick's increasing awareness of the recent events in Europe during her work on *Trust* caused the world of Henry James to recede and Jewish history and its cursed shadow, Germany, to emerge in her subsequent fiction. That it did not induce her to pay a visit to the Shoah territory depicted in her writing has much inflamed German critics of her work.

VISITS TO GERMANY

To construct parallels between a writer's life and work is a notoriously dangerous enterprise. Yet since I have claimed, a bit brashly perhaps, that the significance of *Trust* as a launching pad for Ozick's development as a writer lay in the author's shift of focus from art to history and in the concomitant abdication of Henry James as intimate literary mentor, it seems permissible to follow up with some remarks about the writer's intellectual life supporting the thrust of these claims.

At the age of twenty-two, Ozick read Leo Baeck's essay "Romantic Religion." It pried her loose from her fascination with English romantic poetry, and "it began for me a sustained period of intellectual crisis and turning. . . . Almost immediately after Baeck, the six volumes of Graetz came luckily into my hands; and I fell into the furnace of Jewish history, where one burns and burns, and is never consumed. And after that, the bottomless voice of the Holocaust testimony, volume after volume after volume. For me it began with Raul Hilberg's *The Destruction of the European Jews*." What began to emerge during her reading was a sense of "the inescapable nature of 'paganism' (a word I isolate in quotation marks because I mean it to include not only classical time, but present time)." As a writer, Ozick knew that she could not take Enoch's path and immerse herself in the study of Talmud to escape paganism: "The rest of us are either suffocated or seduced by it, returned now and then, by a single insight of human clarification, to where Abraham stood." Aware of the inescapable nature of paganism and yet inescapably tied to the ethics of monotheism ("the cult of a single idea" [*Trust*]), she set out to write stories like "The Pagan Rabbi." Today this is Ozick's favorite story, not because the narrative voice comes down on the side of history, but, as she said in a recent conversation with me, because she succeeded in finding a poetical voice for a dryad.

Another concession Ozick has never made, however: she has refused to this day to set foot in Germany. Some of her reasons are stated by Enoch: "Nobody has a right to look at the ash and the bones and say: I am merciful, therefore I forgive this crime. . . . You want to know why? Because the crime is too big for us, in our human littleness, to presume to forgive it or avenge it." In 1972, Ozick received in the mail a book by the German writer Dieter Wellershoff with a request for a favorable comment. She replied to the publisher: "A book by a German is not for me. . . . The point is that I, in my generation, will not perpetuate the *connectedness* of speaking to, for, or about a German." Her refusal to go to Germany Ozick considers a "negative memorial act" and more effective than Germany's *Gedenkstätten* ("memorial monuments"): "What stands in witness for Germany is not the Germans, but an emptiness, an absence—the ones who are not there."

In 1988, Ozick published a letter which attracted enormous attention and was sneeringly summarized in the conservative German daily *Frankfurter Allgemeine Zeitung*. In this letter she reaffirmed her memorial: "I am a Jew who does not, will not, cannot set foot in Germany. This is a private moral imperative; I don't think of it as a 'rule,' and I don't apply it to everyone, particularly not to German-born Jews, who as refugees or survivors have urgencies and exigencies different from my own." But for her, participation in a conference on current German-Jewish relations was impossible:

> When Germans want to reflect on . . . German-Jewish "relations," it seems to me they are obligated to do it on their own. . . . The Germans must undertake memorial explorations under their given condition of scarcity—the absence of native Jews. Why must an American writer, a Jewish citizen of the United States, be imported for a conference on "German-Jewish relations"? Only because there is no German-born Jewish writer of her own age who is alive to speak.

Importing Jews creates the illusion of a normality that is not within reach.

Ozick's misgivings about the presence of Jews in Germany were recently confirmed in a book by Susan Neiman, now a philosophy professor at Yale. She went to Germany as a student on a Fulbright scholarship in 1982 to write a dissertation on reason. She stayed for six years and left with serious doubts about the effectiveness of *Vergangenheitsverarbeitung.* Gradually, Neiman, who is an American Jew, began to understand her usefulness to the country. "The German Jewish Community played a remarkable role in the history of the Federal Republic. The government needs them. Their protected existence serves to belie continuity between the postwar government and the Third Reich." But hyperprotection proved counterproductive. "The fragility of it all was overpowering. Being Jewish in Berlin is something precious and secret, to be shared, alone, with someone you trust." When Neiman sought to organize a cultural project on contemporary Jewish life in Berlin, she was overwhelmed by the facticity of Jewish absence. "Why in the world should we celebrate Jewish life in Berlin by inviting writers from Israel and London?" When no contemporaries could be found, her husband advised her to give it up, because "There is no Jewish culture in Berlin nowadays, literary or otherwise. And nobody really wants it either."

A sense of finality eventually catches up with those who attempt to live as Jews in Germany; the country has no Jewish future, only a past. Young Jews come and leave; old Jews return to visit their childhood haunts. There can be little doubt about the overall success of the Final Solution, planned at an idyllic villa on the banks of Berlin's Wannsee on January 20, 1942. Fifty years later, the government of Berlin funded an exhibit, Jüdische Lebenswelten, about Jewish life and culture in Europe. Ferdinand Gottlieb, a German Jew born in Berlin in 1919 who left hurriedly in 1934 and vowed never to return, finally accepted a government-sponsored invitation to Berlin to see some of his "old school buddies after 58 years." About Jüdische Lebenswelten he wrote to the *New York Times:* "My wife and I were astonished at the vast numbers of Germans attending the exhibition and their fascination with Jewish culture. We were reminded of Hitler's desire to have a museum of dead people." Or as Susan Neiman puts it: "Germans love dead Jews, and they know all their names." Conversely, there is the German publisher who,

after a conversation with Ozick in New York, wrote to her "a warmly intended letter: My time with you was different from any other experience; it was like a visit to a museum."

. . . . .

The urge to visit the past—to return to one's place of origin, or to see the site of a heinous crime against one's people—is a recurring motif in recent Jewish writing. Those who come for the camps and cemeteries, however, often find themselves disappointed. Visiting Dachau, Leslie Fiedler does not feel like "a pilgrim to a place of martyrdom but a tourist in some horrific Disneyland." But those who come because of personal ties to pre-Shoah Germany or Austria often find themselves shaken; unsurprisingly, their essayistic or fictional accounts are often quite restrained. One scene in particular recurs so often that one might call it the archetypal scene of return. It is the visit to one's former apartment or to the former home of a close relative.

Here is such a scene from Lore Segal's novel *Her First American* (1985). Ilka Weissnix, a woman in her twenties, and her mother, both refugees from Austria, have traveled back to Vienna to look over the past. They are now standing outside their old apartment.

> "What are we going to say?"
>
> Ilka rang and listened. She said, "The kitchen is immediately on the left, with the maid's room behind. The foyer goes to the right, past the dining room, past the bathroom, and makes an ell to your and Vati's bedroom. There's nobody home. . . .
>
> "There they are." The slurp of slippers approached from the left. The kitchen.
>
> "What are we going to say?"
>
> An eye in the peephole. A woman's voice—not a young voice—said, "Ja?" and Ilka asked for her father: "Please I want to speak with Herrn Max Weissnix?"
>
> "There is no Weissnix. Here lives Hohenzoll. You can enquire from the superintendent on the first floor."
>
> Ilka said, "Danke schön," which means "Thank you beautifully."
>
> The woman said, "Bitte schön," which means "Beautifully please," and clicked the peephole shut and slurped to the right around the ell into Ilka's parents' bedroom.

It turns out that Ilka's exact memory is a delusion. Life in America has changed her habit of thinking. "In the plane home Ilka's mother said, 'That was not our doorbell we rang.' 'Yes it was. Door nine, first stairway, second floor.' 'Aha!' said Ilka's mother. 'In Vienna the second floor is the mezzanine and the third floor is the second floor. The door we rang was mezzanine door nine.' " It is characteristic of Segal's writing that the incident so charged with emotion—the near miss of an encounter with the past—receives no narrative comment. It is left to the reader to determine whether the inexactness of memory constitutes a painful loss, because it finally severs ties to a family member who perished in the Shoah (Ilka's father was shot by Nazis on a road outside Vienna), or whether mnemonic errors are indicators of the healing power of time. Ilka's expectation was that exact place-recognition would put the haunting ghosts to rest. "I'm taking my mother to Austria," Ilka says to one of her American friends; "if she sees that road and sees the spot where she left my father maybe she might put it behind her."

But the resurrection of the dead does not occur because Ilka's mother, who also fancies that she remembers exactly, cannot find or recognize the spot where she parted from her husband. This scene in Segal's novel has a real-life counterpart. In an autobiographical essay, Segal describes her first visit to Austria in 1968, which she left as a ten-year-old girl thirty years earlier on a children's transport to England. In 1968, Segal's American husband "insisted—against my own wishes—that I owed myself a return to my childhood. I cried the whole week in Vienna." The couple travels to St. Gilgen. "There was a lovely lake where we spent my father's last vacation the summer before Hitler." The next day, Segal tries to verify her memory. She lives through the experience described for Ilka's mother in *Her First American:*

> I got up in the morning . . . and went to look for the green house with the steep field. I remembered the contour of the mountain in back like a man with one shoulder higher than the other. But there was no lake. I turned around and walked in the other direction until a brand-new six-lane highway laid itself across my path. There were so many houses! Some fields were steeper than others. Mountains humped. Could the lake I remembered have been in Mallnitz, a different summer? And so my father continued dead.

That life goes on even after human tragedies, that life unfolds and ensnares the mourner with its "post-mortem possibilities," Segal emphasized in her review of A. B. Yehoshua's novel *Five Seasons,* which is about overcoming *Abschiedsschmerz,* the pain in mourning. Like Segal in *Her First American,* Yehoshua integrates a scene of return into the process of mourning. It speaks for Segal's courageous embrace of life's post-mortem possibilities that she does not dwell in her review of *Five Seasons* on Yehoshua's version of a visit to the site of a tragically abbreviated childhood. Yehoshua's protagonist, Molkho, is a Sephardic Jew who is mourning the recent death of his wife from cancer. She had left Berlin as a child in the late thirties after her father had committed suicide. Toward the end of the novel Molkho, now in his fifth season of mourning, is in Berlin for the second time and finally ready to search for the house in which his wife spent her childhood. He finds it accidentally as he steps into one of the houses on her street to escape the rain. Because of its fictional nature, Yehoshua's scene of return (by proxy) is fraught with indicators of loss and return, and of journeys that finally come full circle. Molkho stands in the hall on the ground floor waiting for the elevator:

He waited in vain for it to return, its caller having apparently vanished. At last, he pressed the button himself. With a jerk and a wheeze the gray tail slid past, followed by the red cage. Molkho opened the two doors of ancient grillwork, entered the malignant cell, and pressed a button, watching the apartment slip by. Once, long ago, her faith in life already shattered, a young girl had stepped forth from one of those doors on her way to Jerusalem. But did I really kill her? he wondered. The elevator stopped, letting him out in a hallway, where he first looked for a door without a name and then knocked on one that had several. There was silence, followed by the scrape of a chair across a floor. A child clambered up to reach the high lock and opened the door a crack, peering earnestly out at the stranger. "Doctor Starkmann?" Molkho asked the wide-eyed little boy, who was apparently all alone. "Doctor Starkmann?" The boy frowned adorably, as if trying to recall the man who had killed himself here fifty years ago, and made a move to shut the door. For a second Molkho tried stopping him, flattening himself sideways as if to slip through the crack; then, with a quick backward step, he turned and dashed down the stairs and into the rainy street to the underground, by which he returned to the Alexanderplatz, which now seemed safely familiar, despite the falling night.

Like all callers on the past, Molkho seems to have accomplished nothing; but this is not true. The visit confirmed his loss: his wife *is* irretrievable. It is this confirmation which finally sets Molkho free to find another wife, because, as the novel claims in its last sentence, "a man has to be in love." This development is foreshadowed in Molkho's first visit to Berlin a year earlier. One night he has tickets for Mozart's opera *Don Giovanni.* He is particularly eager to hear it, since he wants so much to fall in love to overcome the recent loss of his wife. Arriving at the Berlin opera he learns "that the man who was to play Don Giovanni was sick and that . . . the opera tonight would be Gluck's *Orpheus and Eurydice.*" Molkho is disappointed but attends the performance nevertheless. "The curtain rose, revealing a minimal, almost symbolic set that Molkho stared at resentfully. It seemed ugly to him, and as the music resumed again, dusky and constrained, he grieved inwardly for his lost *Don Giovanni.*" Gradually, Molkho is caught up in the action and the music of the opera, even though the audience, which he imagines to be a mixture of Germans and camp survivors, repeatedly forces itself on his attention.

In the final act, Orpheus, who has searched for Eurydice among the dead, begins his ascent from Hades followed by Eurydice. "Molkho knew that Orpheus mustn't look back as he led Eurydice after him, but he also knew, anxiously waiting for it to happen, that Orpheus would forget." When he does and Eurydice disappears forever, the audience dissolves in grief. A man whom Molkho takes for a Jewish survivor mourns uncontrollably, "tears running down his cheeks. . . . and Molkho knew with an inner pang that the man was crying for him too. Even the German on his right was sitting on the edge of his seat." Molkho, however, will not venture into Hades until his next visit to Berlin, almost a year later. The scene's last sentence, quoted here, which also ends the chapter, is odd and not further illuminated by Yehoshua. What does it imply about the German? Capacity for grief? That an opera, at least, penetrates Germans' armor? Or that even at the opera Germans do not permit themselves to mourn? Taking the opera now as a symbol for efforts at *Vergangenheitsverarbeitung,* does Yehoshua imply increasing self-consciousness among Germans? Or does he indict the German inability to mourn? The ambiguity of Yehoshua's last sentence reflects the opaqueness of the German mask.

It is an opaqueness that is rarely dispelled, not even when the Germans are as young and talkative as Heinrich and Elsa in Norma Rosen's essay "Notes toward a Holocaust Fiction." Protected by the mask of fiction, Rosen describes her visit to Austria in the company of her husband Robert. Rosen's fictional persona confesses to the German couple: "Sometimes, my husband and I have trouble looking at Germans or Austrians of a certain age. We think of what they were doing during the Hitler years." The light-hearted, pleasure-seeking Germans give only the tiniest indication of uneasiness and then cry out together, "Yes, yes, that is natural, understandable!" But fundamentally, they are untouched. They do not ask the American couple what brought them to Austria. For Robert, it was a return to the sites of childhood. He had left Vienna as a fourteen-year-old boy on the same *Kindertransport* that took Lore Segal and six hundred other children to safety. Norma Rosen describes their walk through Robert's Vienna:

> In silence they stood before the doorway of the house where he had lived; in silence followed his path to school through the tree-shaded alleys of the *Augarten* . . . ; in silence sat on a bench beside the broad road called the *Hauptallee,* where his parents rested in the open air on Sundays and his little-boy self, untouched by sadness then, played with friends. When the bench sent forth too many emanations, he got up and walked rapidly away.

The couple's silence does not break until their visit to the Jewish cemetery, where Robert Rosen says Kaddish (a prayer of mourning) for the parents he lost in the death camps. When the Rosens meet the German couple a few days later, the silence that we might expect to befall the Germans is buried under an easy chatter. Is it a mask? Does it hide shame? Or is there none? The Germans remain opaque, unperturbed, while Jews, who step on Shoah territory, enter a state of heightened self-consciousness, which eventually prompted Susan Neiman to cry out in Berlin: "A Jew can't live here without going crazy. Sooner or later."

CONSTRUCTIONS OF THE PAST AS MIRRORS OF THE SELF

Occasionally, however, young Germans, too, think they are going crazy. Some of them, paradoxically those most attuned to the inescapability of the past, have become refugees, hoping that America, Allegra's country of amnesia, will help them to live in peace. "I was running away from a father figure and a fatherland," writes Sabine Reichel, a New York citizen born in Hamburg in 1946, "and America helped me carry out the escape. Wanting to leave Germany meant wanting to free myself from that sticky legacy; this had always been a subconscious desire, almost a logical conclusion to the distressing facts and negative image I had to face about my homeland."

The protagonist of Rebecca Goldstein's second novel, *The Late-Summer Passion of a Woman of Mind* (1989), is such a refugee from the past. Eva Mueller comes to America because "it was far from Germany." When the novel opens she is forty-seven years old, a successful professor of philosophy at Cornell, and currently at work on a book titled *Reason's Due.* In the course of the novel, however, Eva's armor of rationality is dismantled by a passionate young student who approaches her without fear. Gradually, Eva responds to his love and enthusiasm. Her opening up becomes a journey to the core of her self. She begins to realize the degree of her self-deception.

In the most interesting section of the novel, Goldstein shows how the failure of Eva's brave effort to confront her father's involvement in the cultural politics of the Third Reich is transformed into yet another layer of self-deception. Eva's investigation of her father's Nazi past culminates in a surprising variant of the theme of return to Shoah territory.

Before examining Goldstein's compelling invention of the German variant, I would like to turn briefly to her rendition of the more familiar Jewish version in her first novel, *The Mind-Body Problem* (1983). Scenes of return are smoothly integrated into the novel's overall philosophical argument about the relation of body to mind. Defining the mind-body problem is essential to developing concepts of identity, the classic theme of the bildungsroman. Like Ozick's *Trust,* however, Goldstein's novels are often more interested in the philosophical positions they expose than in psychological realism.

The Mind-Body Problem is the story of a failing marriage. The narrator, Renee Feuer, is an attractive, body-conscious philosophy student at Princeton, who marries the math genius Noam Himmel in order to compensate for her doubts about her philosophical abilities: "If I couldn't find any affirmation of my worth in the mind, I would seek it in the body." While there can be little doubt that the metaphysically named Noam Himmel ("heaven") represents the life of pure mind, matters are less clear in the case of the passionate Renee Feuer ("fire"), named for the philosopher René Descartes, a dualist, who split reality into objectivity and subjectivity, that is, body and soul. Renee's last name reflects not only the fact that she loves the heat of sex, but also her idea that "the process of thinking about philosophy always reminds [her] of fireworks." Renee combines body and mind; and it is only after the antimetaphysical turn of Princeton's philosophy department makes her doubt her mental capacities that she takes up "doing philosophy of body," that is, seducing academics.

In fact, like her philosophical namesake Descartes, Renee negotiates between polar extremes: she feels Jewish but doesn't look it. She grew up Orthodox but discarded observance while studying philosophy at Barnard; hence she can make sense of orthodox Lakewood as well as goyish Princeton, although she is not at home in either world. She conducts her early love affairs by dissociating herself from her body. "*I* remained untouched and unpenetrated, a bloodless virgin in spirit through all my promiscuity." When she finally falls in love, it is with a math genius. Renee's friend, the physicist Ava Schwartz (a scholar of physical facts, who loves platonically another physicist by the name of Daniel Korper ["body"]), sums up Renee's predicament: " 'The problem with you, Renee,' she finally said, 'is that you think the male sexual organ is the brain.' "

As Renee's marriage to Noam Himmel progresses, the couple's polar positions emerge more clearly. Renee becomes increasingly confined to the limited possibilities of her body, whereas Noam isolates himself in the incorporeal world of mathematics. This world provides him with celestial refuge: " 'I discovered early on that I liked ideas much better than people, and that was the end of my loneliness. For one thing, ideas are consistent. And you can control them better than people.' He smiled. 'Hell, to be honest, I've just always found them more interesting. Logical relations are transparent and lovely. Human relations, from what I can tell, always seem pretty muddy.' " The last image is Kafka's, who consistently characterized physical relations as "dirty," that is, as containing the element "earth" that muddies the pure spirituality he longed to attain. Or, as Noam puts it succinctly, "matter muddles."

Like Kafka, Noam reaches for transcendence. " 'I wanted to hit a number no one else ever had, to be the first to get to it.' He laughed. 'And then, you know, with the supernaturals I really did it. A whole new realm, beyond any of the others.' His voice was uncharacteristically soft. 'Numbers so big. A beautiful vast infinity of them, waiting there in the great solemn silence, waiting there for me.' " For Noam, numbers are not simply creations, figments of the imagination. They are a reality waiting to be discovered. "He holds," Renee realizes, "as so many great mathematicians have, the Platonist point of view. For him mathematical truths are descriptions of a suprasensible reality, an objective reality that exists independent of our perceptions of it." This reality, which exists absolutely (that is, severed from immanence), is identical with the True and the Beautiful. "So many people," Noam claims, "have no sensibility whatsoever for mathematical beauty, are even arrogantly skeptical of its existence. But of course beauty is what math is all about, the most pure and perfect beauty." Noam's aesthetic sense, however, is not visual, as is that of his wife, who thinks in images. Bored by art, he sighs, "I am just not interested in the qualities of appearances, mine or anybody else's. It's the reality out there, not as it appears from within any point of view, but as it *is* from no point of view at all, that interests me."

As Platonist, Noam quickly assigns his wife "the role of the empiricist enemy, the positivist skeptic." The philosophical positions of husband and wife, Platonist and empiricist, are put to the test most severely during the couple's honeymoon in Europe (Rome, Vienna, Budapest). The significance of transporting Feuer and Himmel to Europe during their first period alone together is to add the

dimension of time. Time is the philosophical challenge. How do the two positions cope with time, and particularly with its human aspect, remembered time? During the honeymoon, ideally a period of sweet mingling of bodies and minds, the couple's notions of reality and personal identity are getting worked out. It is within this context that Goldstein constructs some remarkable scenes of return.

The honeymoon begins badly. In Rome, the summit of the European experience, where past and present, history and sensuality coalesce, where heroines like Isabel Archer and Daisy Miller met their fates, Noam goes off to do math with colleagues at the university, while Renee strolls aimlessly around the city, annoyed rather than stimulated by the advances of Italian men. On the train from Rome to Vienna, Noam files into a creative frenzy, and Renee learns that for Noam the intense act of mental creation (rather than sex) provides the ultimate pleasure. He explains his immersion into pure thinking: "I feel like I'm walking out in some remote corner of space, where no mortal's ever been, all alone with something beautiful." Renee concludes that in moments of creative frenzy, "Noam was off in Plato's heaven. I must remember, I told myself fervently, that Noam is not always where his body is."

Noam's complete dissociation of body and mind, phenomena and essences, appearance and reality, subjectivity and objectivity, and his idealist's disdain for the first term in these sets, is taken one step further during the couple's visit to Vienna. When Renee wakes up in their hotel room, Noam is gone. He returns many hours later and announces that he once lived in Vienna, "I just have to discover when it was." Knowing well that her husband has never before set foot in Vienna, Renee asks Noam to explain his *meshugas*. "I've always known that I lived before, that this particular persona wasn't my first. All of us probably have. I don't see any reason why I should be special. I've known since I was a child." For proof he cites his stunning mathematical gifts as a child. "I saw things so easily. Mathematical truths, I mean. I just knew things. Before I'd see why, before I'd have any inkling of the proofs, I'd know the results. I knew exactly what to look for . . . . It's very hard to describe, but I knew these things because I was remembering them."

Renee argues that this is simply straightforward Platonism. "Plato said that all learning is recollection, . . . that our souls knew everything before birth." Although Noam counters that Plato's thinking does not accommodate the obvious progress made in human knowledge (the dynamics of time), he agrees with the Greek:

> He was right about the independent existence of the soul and its survival of the body. And he was right about the obscuring influences of the body. Matter muddles. When we become attached at birth to a corporeal existent, our memories and knowledge are largely canceled. Almost the entire contents of consciousness is emptied. It probably has to be that way. Most people would probably feel that their precious individualities were undermined if they knew they'd existed before. They'd be jealous of that former existence.

But the uniqueness of the self is inviolate. It's always the same self, just a different life.

Hence it is not one's physical appearance in history (a specific body at a specific time and place) that defines a person; rather, the uniqueness of the self, one's identity, is transhistorical or metaphysical. "I think," Noam concludes, "the identity of the self consists primarily in its moral and intellectual attributes, interpreted as dispositions, potentialities." It is precisely this definition of identity that will lead to Noam's downfall at the end of the novel, when he loses his mathematical gift and is thus deprived (in his view) of his uniqueness.

Toward the end of their stay in Vienna, Noam has discovered through anagnorisis that his particular constellation of moral and intellectual attributes formerly inhabited the body of a Viennese Jew, probably a child, murdered by the invading Nazis in 1938, the year Noam was born in America. Once the matter is settled, Noam's idealistic indifference toward appearances reasserts itself. Whistling Wagner's "Ride of the Valkyries," he remarks to Renee, "I've really been somewhat absurd. . . . I shouldn't be overly concerned with the identity of one particular individual, even if that individual is me. It's the general facts that are important."

Noam is absurd indeed. Renee's anagnorisis in Hungary brings into relief not only the absurdity but the cruelty of Noam's idealism. While Noam is at a conference in rural Hungary, Renee drives to Budapest with a math colleague's wife. Barbara wants to visit the children of the one family member who survived the camps and the small pogroms after the war. Having dropped off Barbara, Renee drives around the city and discovers a building decorated with Jewish stars. She enters and finds a museum displaying liturgical objects in what was once the second largest synagogue in Europe. A small room is devoted to the destruction of the Hungarian Jews; it contains maps, official documents, and a body's shell: "a faded pair of the black and white striped inmate's uniform and a pile of tattered boots." The courtyard is a cemetery for Nazi victims; the engraved names yield little about the identities of their bearers.

Wandering through the neighborhood, Renee finds signs of life in a Jewish soup kitchen—a dwarf and an old woman with a damaged face; both are tattooed with blue numbers. They invite her to share a meal or a cup of coffee. Renee is uneasy, but the dwarf, Janos Seifert, chats amicably with her. What the museum, the cemetery, the encounter with the two survivors signify is the irreplaceability of those murdered in the Shoah. With their bodies disappeared their culture. The murdered were not just bodies—they were persons, unique selves located in a particular time and place. What made them unique does not migrate from body to body, from culture to culture. Personal identity is tied to a specific body, just as consciousness is shaped (made specific) by historical circumstances. This means "we are our bodies, we die with our bodies." Or, as Ava Schwartz, the physicist, puts it: "Physical facts come first. Logic has to conform to them." Hence mourning someone's death is a process of serious leave-taking. There are no returns, no resurrections. Remembering is

different, since it "raises the dead without reviving them" (*Trust*). Noam's odd belief in reincarnation, Goldstein shows, is a logical outgrowth of idealism. High-minded idealism, much cherished in German culture, dissolves specificity and, consequently, releases perpetrators from personal responsibility ("we were only following orders"). Janos Seifert's inquiry about "the name of the French bishop, who said that reality exists in the individual sensorium" is precisely to the point. As former inmate of the camps and subject of medical experiments, Seifert knows better than Noam that reality is located in the physical facts.

As Renee leaves the precinct of the synagogue she sees a man rushing to Maariv, the evening prayer, and intense longing transports her back into the world of her beloved late father. She associates his world with the suspended time of Shabbat. "I was back inside its space, enfolded in its distances, feeling the enforced but real sense of serenity, bounded round by prohibitions. The appearances of things were softened, muted, subtly but thoroughly transformed." But she knows that she has to leave that realm and step back into real time. "As I got into my car, the noise and hard outlines of the world reasserted themselves. I had broken through the cobweb borders, had stepped outside of Shabbos, was on the far side again of *Havdalah,* the separation between the sanctified and secular." Jewish observance creates a rhythm of doing and thinking (*mitzvot* are thoughts put into action) that orders the relation of transcendence and immanence and occasionally condones, for a suspended moment, the intermingling of the two.

But Renee has long ago left that world of intellectual safety. When she picks up Barbara, she learns that her friend has not been able to communicate with her Hungarian cousins: they no longer share a common language. The two women drive back in silence, "both of us brooding over the worlds out of which we had been shut, the pasts from which we were cut off. There's no going back, I kept thinking. You've made your choice, now that life is dead to you." The passing of time has created incompatible realities that can be brought into communication only with great difficulty. This theme is explored further in *The Late-Summer Passion of a Woman of Mind.*

. . . . .

Eva Mueller, the protagonist of Goldstein's second novel, is not aware, at first, of the deep chasm history has created between herself, a philosophy student from Germany, and Martin Weltbaum, a Jewish instructor at the Columbia Law School. The two become involved in an eleven-month relationship, in which the flow of passion, love, outrage, hatred is dictated by history. Martin is the son of survivors; his parents lost their first spouses and children in the Shoah. After the war they met in Berlin, married, and moved to New York. Martin grew up in Washington Heights harboring an intense, pathological hatred of all manifestations of death; and most of all he hates his parents because they "carried death within them."

What attracts Martin to Eva Mueller is her German origin. She is the child of perpetrators. Martin insistently in-quires into her parent's past. He urges Eva to write to Yad Vashem for information about her father's role in the Third Reich. A letter from Jerusalem confirms that Herbert Mueller, now a retired professor of musicology in Münster, was appointed assistant to the president of the Reich Music Chamber in 1937 upon publication of his book *The* Ring *Cycle of Wagner and the Critical Moment in the History of the Fatherland.* Martin is disappointed that Eva's father has not turned out to be a thug: "Still, I suppose one shouldn't underestimate the power of culture. Maybe Papa even managed to get in a few kicks at enemies of the state like Bruno Walter and Otto Klemperer."

The relationship between Eva and Martin turns into torture. Martin abuses Eva emotionally, psychologically, and sexually. Eva accepts the abuse as if it were a necessity. "Everything within her, even her own voice, had been stilled. . . . She knew that all that was happening had to happen, and thus was absolutely right." The relationship breaks, and releases the lovers from their stagnant hell, when Eva becomes pregnant. Forced into action by the time bomb in Eva's belly, Martin finally sides with his parents against Eva, severs the relationship, and pays for the abortion. Eva realizes that "it was she whom he had hated all along."

At this point the narrative flow of the novel breaks. After two blank pages chapter three begins with Eva's reflection "that there *was* something seriously amiss with her book." The narrative is back in the present, in Eva's Cornell office in 1985. Eva's new manuscript, *Reason's Due,* the fruit of ten years of labor, has been criticized by her editor. Eva believes that she has discovered her error: "Time, Eva now thought. It was time that contained the ambiguity. . . . She had known instinctively that time posed problems that might well overwhelm her, unravel the tight little pattern of her ideas. She had ignored it because she had not understood it. It was her minotaur, and she had built a system of labyrinths to try to contain it. It had been an act of intellectual cowardice."

Here, perhaps, Eva is too harsh on herself; her intellectual efforts were more than sufficient; it was her emotions she feared. Like Martin Weltbaum, Eva Mueller is arrested in time because she is incapable of mourning. She cannot acknowledge that the passing of time causes loss and that it seals off past acts in an unreachable distance. The minotaur around whom Eva built her labyrinth of logic is her father, whose image as the best, sweetest, and "the most loving of all parents" she preserved untouched. And yet she learned about his involvement with the Nazi regime in 1951, when she was fourteen and began to connect her early memories, her *Traumbilder,* with the facts she studied in school about recent German history.

Like many young Germans, Eva is unable to confront her parents. This inability to ask questions—an emotional cowardice that avoids uncovering the unbearable, namely that the loving parent is really a monster—became known in Germany as *das grosse Schweigen,* or, in the terminology of the psychologist Dan Bar-On, the legacy of silence. After the student rebellion of the late sixties, which in Germany took the form of aggressive outbursts against a

generation of parents that had acquiesced to the Nazi regime, the lid was once more clamped down on the past; the lid stayed screwed on for some twenty years. Since 1987, however, as the postwar generation began to reach the watershed age of forty, a flood of essays and books has broken the silence. Oddly enough, one of these books, *What Did You Do in the War, Daddy?* appeared in America. Its author, Sabine Reichel, is, as I noted earlier, an escapee from the past. Unlike her fictional counterpart, Eva Mueller, however, she did once try to find out what had happened:

> When I was finally able to ask my father, "What did you do in the war?" it was a small victory over fear and obedience. By putting the ghosts of the past into perspective, I was able to keep them alive without feeling threatened by them. But asking questions was more than the triumph of curiosity over authority, and of the awakening of historical consciousness over social amnesia. It was a form of liberation, a step out of childhood and into a more equal relationship between a father and a daughter.

Goldstein's Eva Mueller is not capable of such a confrontation, not, at least, while she is living at home. "To face her father directly and demand the knowledge which was by some right her own was impossible for her. Whatever the expression on his face that would have greeted her questions, she would not have been able to look on it, neither his remorse nor his lack of it." Was Eva Mueller afraid that she would acquiesce *post factum* to her father's cowardice, as Sabine Reichel did when she wrote about her father, an actor in theater performances for the Wehrmacht and since 1943 an announcer and entertainment producer at the Reichs Rundfunk in Berlin, "I have admiration and respect for the way he tried to live his life during a time I am forever grateful for having escaped"?

Instead of asking, Eva Mueller ran away, saving herself from having to take a position and freezing her relationship with her father in time. Eva escaped to America and buried her hurt: "Eventually a kind of escharotic hardness had grown up over the hurtful place, resulting perhaps as much from the great stretch of the Atlantic Ocean she had placed between herself and her father as from the passage of time." After her escape, Eva begins to construct a cage for the minotaur, a process which Martin briefly disrupts:

> And then of course there had been her study of philosophy, by means of which she had managed to wrap herself in the sterile gauze of genuine high-mindedness. She had found her salvation in the work of that excommunicated Jew from Amsterdam who, in the grandeur of his modesty— oh, how unlike the Bayreuthian beast of egoism who had claimed her father's reverence!—had quietly gone about the business of revealing the logical structure of truth, and with it the secret of making our peace with the tragic possibilities of life.

But as she is about to bury herself in Spinoza, time catches up with Eva—as earlier her progressing pregnancy had yanked Martin out of the constant torture he had devised for the two of them. Two years after her first inquiry, another letter arrives from Jerusalem stating that Yad Vashem now has a copy of Herbert Mueller's book on Wagner. Eva's journey to Jerusalem in the summer of 1967 to read her father's book in a tiny office at Yad Vashem is a displaced visit to Germany—an encounter with her father's thoughts in 1937 in the setting that documents the devastation to which these thoughts contributed in their minor yet significant way.

When she arrives, Dr. Friedlander, a refugee from Berlin, hands her the book and clears a reading space for her at his desk. Absorbed in the pages before her, Eva hardly notices how Dr. Friedlander attends to her physical needs: he brings her food, turns on the light, keeps her space undisturbed. In the book before her Eva learns the thoughts of the man whose goodness she had assumed: "It was [her father's] voice she heard, heard it as she had not heard it for years. . . . And, even more difficult to take in, the very qualities for which she had once so adored and revered him were apparent in his work. Yes, it was true. His idealism and high-mindedness, his scholarship and culture: they were here, like poetry in the poison."

These are also the qualities for which George Eliot and George Lewes admired the Germans, and which Henry Adams in his cantankerous remarks about mid-nineteenth-century Berlin in his *Education* did not consider real. Yet if the high-mindedness and idealism *were* real—and German culture of the nineteenth century hardly permits us to doubt it—was not the crime of destruction all the greater? As Cynthia Ozick remarks: "We condemn the intelligent man of conscience because there *is* a difference [from the brute]; because, though at heart not a savage, he allowed himself to become one, he did not resist. It was not that he lacked conscience; he smothered it. It was not that he lacked sensibility; he coarsened it. It was not that he lacked humanity; he deadened it." What indeed does the career of a Herbert Mueller or Karl-Heinz Reichel say about the humanizing, educational effects of culture? What are we to think when Susan Neiman concludes, after six years in Berlin, that "the land of *Dichter* and *Denker* has no imagination?"

"German dreamers," Neiman writes, "do not put themselves in the place of the Jews." They don't; and yet they do—as usurpers. Before her visit to Yad Vashem, Eva

> could never picture to herself a single victim. She could even conjure up an image of the black-and-white striped pajamas they wore. But they too hung limp and empty.
>
> Well no, not always empty. In the grotesquely cruel and mocking joke her mind sometimes played on her, she would see a face above the prison clothes, staring out, dazed and vacant, from between barbed wire.
>
> The face was her father's.

As Eva emerges from Yad Vashem, from her visit to the past housed in the ruins of the present, she loses her father. She speaks of him in the past tense. She has learned to place her father in history, and thus to release herself from their fixated relation. He is no longer the timelessly good father, even though she is still condemned to love him. As

she emerges from his book, she places her father in the prison of time by holding him responsible for his acts. She begins to see him as "a victim of the inexorable logic that binds one's action to the determining causes, historical and personal." It was his misfortune to have been "present at that place at that time." Her dream-image takes on a new meaning. Lacking the courage and the greatness to go against the zeitgeist, to transcend the vision of his time, her father became a prisoner of his time. Like Sabine Reichel, Goldstein's Eva Mueller does not condemn her father for his lack of vision and personal courage. "To be evil," the philosophy professor concludes, "is to suffer perhaps the worst kind of misfortune that can possibly befall one," because there can be no forgiveness. Who could administer the forgiveness—and in whose name? Although she acknowledges "the truth behind her childhood image: her father did indeed wear the black-and-white pajamas of bondage and stare out, dazed and vacant, from between barbed wire," Eva does not realize that she is his keeper. She remains in a state of secondary bondage from which no late-summer passion of the forty-seven year old for an all-American philosophy student can release her. Susan Neiman's Jewish notes from Berlin are relevant to Eva's situation:

> It is not much to live for, keeping the dead. History imposed an impossible task. . . . Germans devoted to working through the past seem bound to succumb to blind pathos or morbid fascination. Those who, like Helmut Kohl invoking the mercy of a late birth, call for an end to vergangenheitsverarbeitung, risk becoming Nazi apologists. They are damned if they do, they are damned if they don't. They are, quite simply, damned.

EPILOGUE: SOME CULTURAL REFLECTIONS

It is difficult to find the right closure for an essay on the emerging theme in recent Jewish writing of visits paid to Germany. Much as one might feel the rightness of Susan Neiman's remarks about the intolerable task of *Vergangenheitsverarbeitung,* one would not want such an essay to end with the word "damned." Who is to say whether the Germans are damned or not? They may yet prove themselves a new nation endowed with moral strength.

Meanwhile, as Ian Buruma recently reported in "Ways of Survival," a review of two post-Shoah novels that appeared in *The New York Review of Books,* German ingenuity has devised a third road between the aporia of working through the past and declaring the end of this noxious task, and that is to substitute for self-examination and national introspection an obsession with things Jewish, an obsession that ranges from a distant fascination with Jewish culture to the usurpation of the still-vacant space once occupied by German Jews. Buruma mentions a German journalist "who made some excellent films on the Nazi period, [and] went so far as to adopt a Hebrew name." And he refers to "a fashionable new café in east Berlin where blond, young, blue-eyed Germans sit around in *kippas* eating falafel." There are a hundred other examples, which I cannot mention here, of the truly astonishing ways in which Germans not only attempt to obliterate the human and cultural gaps left by the Shoah but also manage to create new, painless ways of atonement.

In his article Buruma describes how the preferred German attitude toward the Shoah, *Betroffenheit,* "a state of speechless embarrassment" as a result of having been physically struck, has produced of late "a wave of interest in Jewish matters, especially in Berlin, and most especially among young people." This phenomenon is paralleled on the national level by an imagined need to feature Jewish spokespersons on all sorts of occasions. "It is as though German public opinion needs the moral approval or castigation of famous Jews," writes Buruma, "before it can make up its mind about anything, especially about the state of being German." Hence the stream of Jewish visitors—most of them Americans, among them survivors, businessmen, scholars, conference participants, and ordinary tourists—is one of the most welcome developments in recent years. The German government takes good care that the stream keeps flowing, because it is this stream that creates the impression that Germany has rejoined the family of man, while it obfuscates the fact that the Germans face an unsolvable problem. Cynthia Ozick, for one, blames American Jews for contributing to the obfuscation: "When Jewish Americans go to Germany to 'help'— i.e., to supply Jewish representation at a Holocaust conference—they aren't making it easier for the Germans to see into the soul of the dilemma, namely the loss of *German-Jewish* representation; the Americans are confusing the question by abetting the tragic and degrading falsehood of human interchangeability."

But does that mean American Jews should not visit Germany? "German-born Jews," Cynthia Ozick concedes, "as refugees and survivors have urgencies and expediencies" of their own; and so do their children. I remember a stunning report in *Die Zeit* in the late seventies about a young Jewish woman by the name of Jane Gilbert whose parents had survived the death camps. Jane decided to leave America and settle in Germany in order to learn to cope with the traumatizing image inherited from her parents of a ghoulish Germany, which had seriously begun to haunt her. In a more moderate way, this is precisely what Jewish writing of the kind described in this essay is trying to do. There is a need among certain groups of American Jewish intellectuals to rethink the issue of Germany.

Excepting some early flukes, it took nearly forty years for this theme, Jewish visits to Germany, to emerge in fiction and essays. The figure is reminiscent of the time the Israelites spent wandering in the desert after their flight from Egypt. During that period a new generation was supposed to reach maturity that had not known slavery and hence was ready to take possession of the promised land with the souls and minds of the freeborn.

Indeed, during the past forty years, a new generation has sprung up in Germany; but there is no new generation of Jews, because in a profound way (*Exodus* not withstanding), Jewish thought does not recognize the concept of passing generations. What happens to a specific group of Jews at a specific time is happening to all Jews. In Jewish thought, history is not sequential but simultaneous. The

revelation of the Torah on Mount Sinai is celebrated, the two destructions of the Temple are lamented, the victims of the Crusades are mourned as if these events had happened to the now living.

While Germans naturally prefer to think of history as sequential (one generation replaces another), Jews think of historical events as always present. An awareness of this clash in the perception of history emerges forcefully in an essay by Lucy Dawidowicz titled "In Berlin Again" (1986). Dawidowicz had been in Berlin briefly on August 26, 1939, to change trains in her transit from Vilna to Copenhagen. She returned in February 1947 as an education officer with the American Joint Distribution Committee. And in October 1985 she came for the third time in order to attend "a scholarly conference about the life of the Jews in National Socialist Germany in the years between 1933 and 1939" organized by the Leo Baeck Institute. "Unnerved" by the thought of returning to Germany, she wondered how she could be "an objective observer in the land of the murderers of the Jews." Arriving in Berlin she encountered something for which she was not at all prepared:

> What I expected to see or hear I can't now imagine. But it was the youthfulness of the crowds that disconcerted and even disoriented me. These were not the Germans I had expected to confront. All of them were obviously born after 1945 and most were probably born after the Berlin Wall was erected [in 1961]. They were ordinary young people, too young to be charged with the burden of Germany's terrible history. They were not the ghosts of the Nazi past.

Dawidowicz was shocked by an intense sense of discontinuity. "Could I have really supposed that the Berlin of 1985 was a continuation of the Berlin of 1935? Could I have thought that the Germans on the street were the same Germans who had jeered at Jews on the streets of Berlin in 1938?" In Germany and confronted with the fact and facticity of a new generation, she became confused as to what perception of history to adhere to. Although Dawidowicz was overwhelmed at first by "the reality of contemporary Germany," the *Jewish* historian in her eventually dominated. What she saw and encountered did not gain any "real presence" because her "consciousness of Germany as Nationalist Socialist Germany totally preempted any other idea." But almost immediately she recognized that she was not really thinking of Nazi *Germany,* which is a closed chapter in history; the Germans of today are not Nazis. What really preoccupied her was "the murder of the six million European Jews." Although Nazi Germany conceived and carried out the killings, Dawidowicz concluded that the two phenomena did not share the same historical status: "the place of Nazi Germany in history is not the same as the place of the murder of the European Jews. One belongs to the transient past, the other to the enduring past. . . . Except for the murder of the European Jews, Nazi Germany left no lasting heritage."

For a gentile historian that may not be so obvious. But when Dawidowicz's confusion cleared, the Jewish historian spoke as a *Betroffene,* as one who was "as if physically struck" by something that had actually happened to others. Jewishly speaking—that is, according to the principle of simultaneity—it had indeed happened to her too, and thus *contemporary* Germany could not take on reality for Dawidowicz. While Germany's chancellor Helmut Kohl, who claims the grace of belated birth (*Gnade der späten Geburt*), embraces history as sequential (transient past), the American Jewish scholar Dawidowicz regards history as simultaneous, as happening now and to her and to subsequent Jewish generations.

It is precisely because of this principle of simultaneity that "visits to Germany" will be increasingly one of the most powerful themes in Jewish writing. In this theme ongoing life and history interconnect in fictional conjecture and aim right at the heart of Jewish identity. By dealing with Jews returning to or visiting Germany, fiction enters the realm of Jewish historical myth-making. Such fiction attempts, in part, to answer the question of how Jews should relate to Germany and to the Germans. The question is a difficult one, because on its deepest level the answers reflect what status and stature the writer accords the Shoah. Is it part of the transient or the enduring past? Can it be forgiven, and, if not, what does that mean about Jewish-German relations? These questions are still open: they are only just now beginning to be broached in fiction.

The principle of simultaneity has yet another effect: it lifts even the most personal Jewish visit to Germany beyond the sphere of the ephemeral. Because visits to Shoah territory *betreffen* ("touch on, concern") the sphere of the enduring past, such visits are paid by individual Jews as representatives of and on behalf of all Jews. They become collective, historical acts and hence have restitutional power. That is why they are so intensely desired by the Germans and so hotly debated among American Jews. Confining their visits to fiction, some writers have been allowed to participate in the current debate without creating a *fait accompli*. Such caution seems still to be in order.

FURTHER READING

Anthologies

Antler, Joyce, ed. *America and I: Short Stories by American Jewish Women Writers.* Boston: Beacon Press, 1990, 355 p.
    Stories from throughout the twentieth century about the Jewish-American experience from the female perspective.

Chapman, Abraham, ed. *Jewish-American Literature: An Anthology of Fiction, Poetry, Autobiography, and Criticism.* New York: New American Library, 1974, 727 p.
    Represents a diversity of cultural, intellectual, and political viewpoints found in Jewish-American literature.

Fishman, Sylvia Barack, ed. *Follow My Footprints: Changing Images of Women in American Jewish Fiction.* Hanover, N. H.: University Press of New England, 1992, 506 p.
    Sampling of short stories and excerpts from novels by authors ranging from Abraham Cahan to Cynthia Ozick, that portray Jewish-American women.

Malin, Irving, and Stark, Irwin, eds. *Breakthrough: A Treasury of Contemporary American-Jewish Literature.* Philadelphia: The Jewish Publication Society of America, 1964, 376 p.
    Collection of short stories, poetry, and nonfiction by prominent Jewish-American writers.

Solotaroff, Ted, and Rapoport, Nessa, eds. *Writing Our Way Home: Contemporary Stories by American Jewish Writers.* New York: Schocken Books, 1992, 380 p.
    Consists of short stories that focus on the eclectic themes of post-immigrant Jewish literature, including those related to the Israeli state, the Holocaust, and the status of Jews in America.

Secondary Sources

Berger, Alan L. *Crisis and Covenant: The Holocaust in American Jewish Fiction.* Albany: State University of New York Press, 1985, 226 p.
    Surveys Jewish-American novelists' religious, ethical, and symbolic responses to the Holocaust.

Bilik, Dorothy Seidman. *Immigrant Survivors: Post-Holocaust Consciousness in Recent Jewish American Fiction.* Middletown, Conn.: Wesleyan University Press, 1981, 216 p.
    Examines the new immigrant/Holocaust-survivor novel as one "that is more concerned with the tragedy of the Jewish historical past than the comic sociology of the American Jewish present."

Cronin, Gloria L.; Hall, Blaine H.; and Lamb, Connie, eds. *Jewish American Fiction Writers: An Annotated Bibliography.* New York: Garland Publishing, Inc., 1991, 1233 p.
    Comprehensive bibliography that includes books and articles offering surveys and overviews as well as entries devoted to major authors.

Donald, Miles. "The Minorities: Black Fiction and the Jewish-American Novel." In his *The American Novel in the Twentieth Century,* pp. 141-75. Newton Abbot, England: David & Charles, 1978.
    Historical overview of prominent figures in Jewish-American literature, such as Nathanael West, Bernard Malamud, and Saul Bellow.

Fine, David M. "Immigrant Ghetto Fiction, 1885-1918: An Annotated Bibliography." *American Literary Realism, 1870-1910* 6, No. 3 (Summer 1973): 169-95.
    Includes citations for novels, stories, secondary sources, and reviews pertaining to early Jewish-American fiction.

Finkelstein, Norman. *The New Ritual of Creation: Jewish Tradition and Contemporary Literature.* Albany: State University of New York Press, 1992, 162 p.
    Argues that a pervasiveness of tradition, religion, and intertextuality exists in the writings of contemporary Jewish-American authors.

Fried, Lewis. *Handbook of American-Jewish Literature: An Analytical Guide to Topics, Themes, and Sources.* New York: Greenwood Press, 1988, 539 p.
    Survey designed to "acquaint the general reader with the major subjects and themes of American-Jewish literature" that includes essays on the three principal periods in American-Jewish fiction: 1880-1930, the Depression era and World War II, and the postwar period.

Friedman, Alan Warren. "The Jew's Complaint in Recent

American Fiction: Beyond Exodus and Still in the Wilderness." *Southern Review* VIII, No. 1 (January 1972): 41-59.
> Investigates the ambiguous consequences of Jewish assimilation into American culture.

Gittleman, Sol. *From Shtetl to Suburbia: The Family in Jewish Literary Imagination.* Boston: Beacon Press, 1978, 209 p.
> Studies the changes in Jewish culture following "the disintegration of East European life in Czarist Russia after 1881" and the near-total loss of the Yiddish language over the next century.

Guttmann, Allen. *The Jewish Writer in America: Assimilation and the Crisis of Identity.* New York: Oxford University Press, 1971, 256 p.
> Discusses the cultural and existential crises of Jews in North America.

———. "The Conversion of the Jews." In *The Cry of Home: Cultural Nationalism and the Modern Writer*, edited by H. Ernest Lewald, pp. 245-67. Knoxville: University of Tennessee Press, 1972.
> Traces the acculturation of Jews in America as dramatized by Jewish-American writers.

Harap, Louis. *The Image of the Jew in American Literature: From Early Republic to Mass Immigration.* Philadelphia: The Jewish Publication Society of America, 1974, 586 p.
> Examines portrayals and stereotypes of Jews and Jewish life in America prior to the large-scale acculturation of Jews in the twentieth century.

———. *In the Mainstream: The Jewish Presence in Twentieth-Century American Literature, 1950s-1980s.* New York: Greenwood Press, 1987, 204 p.
> Discusses the work of important critics and novelists, including Philip Rahv, Alfred Kazin, Saul Bellow, and Bernard Malamud, during a period of strong Jewish influence in American literature.

Lewis, Stuart A. "The Jewish Author Looks at the Black." *The Colorado Quarterly* XXI, No. 3 (Winter 1973): 317-30.
> Investigates Jewish perceptions of African-Americans, including those marked by animosity and racism.

Lewisohn, Ludwig. "A Panorama of a Half-Century of American Jewish Literature." *Jewish Book Annual* 9 (1950-51): 3-10.
> Brief history of Jewish-American literature in the first half of the twentieth century.

Lichtenstein, Diane. *Writing Their Nations: The Tradition of Nineteenth-Century American Jewish Women Writers.* Bloomington: Indiana University Press, 1992, 176 p.
> Focuses on the problems of marginality and the search for reconciliation in the experience of Jewish women in America.

Liptzin, Sol. *The Jew in American Literature.* New York: Block Publishing Company, 1966, 251 p.
> Outlines "the principal layers of the image and self-image of the American Jew" by examining these within their historical and cultural contexts.

Malin, Irving. *Jews and Americans.* Carbondale: Southern Illinois University Press, 1965, 193 p.
> Explores significant aspects of the Jewish-American experience, including questions of heritage, tradition, and cultural change.

———, ed. *Contemporary American-Jewish Literature: Critical Essays.* Bloomington: Indiana University Press, 1973, 302 p.
> Collection of essays on works by Jewish-American writers, many of which study their subjects from a theological or religious perspective.

Mersand, Joseph. *Traditions in American Literature: A Study of Jewish Characters and Authors.* Port Washington, N. Y.: Kennikat Press, Inc., 1939. Reprint, 1966, 247 p.
> Observes the Jew as both the creator and subject of fiction in the nineteenth and twentieth centuries, highlighting some of the most influential and enduring figures.

Pinsker, Sanford. *The Schlemiel as Metaphor: Studies in the Yiddish and American Jewish Novel.* Carbondale: Southern Illinois University Press, 1971, 172 p.
> Researches the origins of the *schlemiel* (fool) character in the Old Testament and traces his appearances in Yiddish fiction and the works of such contemporary novelists as Isaac Bashevis Singer, Bernard Malamud, and Saul Bellow.

———. "The Rise-and-Fall of the American-Jewish Novel." In his *Between Two Worlds: The American Novel in the 1960s*, pp. 29-57. Troy, N. Y.: The Whitston Publishing Company, 1980.
> Analyzes Philip Roth's *Portnoy's Complaint* within the context of 1960s American culture.

———. *Jewish-American Fiction: 1917-1987.* New York: Twayne Publishers, 1992, 167 p.
> Concentrates on several major writers and their works to illustrate the development of Jewish-American literature in the twentieth century.

Ribalow, Harold U. *The Tie That Binds: Conversations with Jewish Writers.* San Diego: A. S. Barnes & Company, 1980, 236 p.
> Interviews of nine notable Jewish-American authors, including Susan Fromberg Schaeffer, Chaim Potok, and Isaac Bashevis Singer.

Schulz, Max F. *Radical Sophistication: Studies in Contemporary Jewish-American Novelists.* Athens, Oh.: Ohio University Press, 1969, 224 p.
> Probes "the humanistic exploration of man's place in society" evident in the works of Jewish-American novelists.

Shapiro, Ann R., ed. *Jewish American Women Writers: A Bio-Bibliographical and Critical Sourcebook.* Westport, Conn.: Greenwood Press, 1994, 557 p.
> Exhaustive listing of sources that provide biographical and bibliographic information on a variety of Jewish-American women writers of the twentieth century.

Shechner, Mark. *After the Revolution: Studies in the Contemporary Jewish American Imagination.* Bloomington: Indiana University Press, 1987, 261 p.
> Investigates common themes associated with the political, social, and psychological changes of the twentieth century on which renowned Jewish-American writers have focused.

Sherman, Bernard. *The Invention of the Jew: Jewish American Education Novels (1916-1964).* New York: Thomas Yoseloff, 1969, 256 p.

Traces "the evolution of the education novel as a sub-genre within Jewish-American fiction."

Uffen, Ellen Serlen. *Strands of the Cable: The Place of the Past in Jewish American Women's Writing*. New York: Peter Lang, 1992, 193 p.

A decade-by-decade look at the Jewish woman writer's experience of history in twentieth-century America.

Wisse, Ruth R. *The Schlemiel as Modern Hero*. Chicago: University of Chicago Press, 1971, 134 p.

Analyzes the character of the *schlemiel* as a figure that embodies the follies and weaknesses of his culture.

Yudkin, Leon Israel. *Jewish Writing and Identity in the Twentieth Century*. New York: St. Martin's Press, 1982, 166 p.

Examines the quality and nature of Jewishness as portrayed in literature.

Music and Modern Literature

INTRODUCTION

Music and literature have existed in collaborative form since ancient times, and have invited comparison because of their fundamental similarity in form: unlike the visual arts, which exist in space, music and literature are primarily temporal in nature—dependent on the medium of time for their meaning. Scholars believe that performance of music and recitation of literature first arose as a single activity with the tradition of oral storytelling that was accompanied by music. However, as music and literature began to develop into separate art forms—with the predominance of written text over the oral tradition—the connection between them lessened, and throughout history their interrelationship has varied depending on time period and geographic locale. Poets have always cast their verses into structures with musical origins, such as the sonnet, the hymn, the ballad, the ode, and the lyric. In addition, they have attempted to use language to emulate the cadences of music. This is particularly true of the Symbolist poets, for whom the sound of words was much more important than the sense. Prose writers, although to a lesser extent than poets, also have adopted musical structures, such as the sonata and the leitmotiv, and their works have been inspired by or based on musical compositions and subjects. Additionally, music and musical performance often appear in works of prose fiction as elements of plot, setting, character, and theme, particularly in works of the late-nineteenth and early-twentieth centuries. More recently, the Beat poets of the 1950s and 1960s infused their works with the rhythms and improvisational nature of the bebop jazz pioneered by such musicians as John Coltrane, Charlie Parker, and Dizzy Gillespie, and rock musicians such as the Beatles and Led Zeppelin added poetic and operatic elements to their music. Both literary critics and musicologists acknowledge the historical and aesthetic importance of the relationship of the two art forms, frequently citing the continued popular appeal of the music-literature union as evidence of its social influence as well.

OVERVIEWS

J. A. Fuller-Maitland

SOURCE: "Music and Letters," in *Essays and Studies*, Vol. XVII, 1932, pp. 44-55.

[*In the following essay, Fuller-Maitland traces the relationship between the musical and literary arts in England from the Elizabethan age to the twentieth century.*]

Once upon a time the world of letters included Music among its departments. The education of the average Englishman in the Elizabethan days would not have been thought complete if he had not been taught something concerning the art, or at least something in the way of what we now call appreciation. The often-quoted passage in Morley's *Plaine and Easie Introduction to Practicall Musicke* (1597), telling how a guest was put to confusion when the part-books were brought out and he was expected to join in madrigal-singing, may have been a little too highly coloured to be accepted as a literal statement of fact, since the treatise naturally gives an awful warning against ignorance of what it undertakes to teach. But Shakespeare's many references to music may surely be taken to imply a certain amount of musical knowledge in the audience, for if the technicalities which Bianca had to learn had been quite unintelligible to the bulk of the spectators, would they have endured their length and minuteness? At any rate, the sixteenth-century hearer who was conscious that he had 'no music in himself' would not like to find that he was unworthy of confidence, and would probably keep quiet about his disability. He would not take pride in 'not knowing one tune from another', as many an otherwise educated man has been known to boast in fairly recent times.

Throughout the seventeenth as through the sixteenth century, music was recognized, if not actively practised, by educated people in general. Down to the Restoration, as we are apt to forget, musical performances took place almost exclusively in private houses or in church. 1665 is the earliest date that has been found for a public concert in England (a subscription concert at Oxford), and this date is considerably earlier than any notice of public concerts on the continent. No doubt it often happened that musicians were paid for their services on special occasions; and it is likely that among the nobility there were some who emulated the 'King's Band of Musick' and employed musicians of their own, thus befriending the art in a way that resembled the beneficent patronage exerted at so many small courts abroad, the influence of which was powerful on the development of the art in the classical days. But the bulk of the music that was to be heard must have been of the domestic kind, and its executants what we should now call amateurs.

Somewhere about the end of the seventeenth century Milton's sphere-born sisters ceased to be harmonious; we can only guess at the severance between their divine sounds; but the wedding celebrated in the poet's immortal words had to wait for its final consummation until the breach had been healed, and Parry's music could glorify the union.

Even after this splendid epithalamium, the arts of Music and Poetry were often treated as if they were in opposition; as late as 1912, W. H. Hudson, in *A Hind in Richmond Park*, closed a beautiful comparison between the two, with these words: 'As they grew to womanhood they changed, and progressing from beauty to beauty, they grew less and less alike until, their sisterhood forgotten, they were become strangers to one another and drew further and further apart; and finally, each on her own throne, crowned a queen and goddess, and worshipped by innumerable devoted subjects, they dwell in widely-separated kingdoms.'

It is tempting to lay the blame for the separation between music and literature upon the fashionable adoration of foreign performers of whom such a torrent swept over the country not long after the Hanoverian Succession. This suggestion is perhaps less paradoxical than appears at first; we all know how common it is for games and sports to become professionalized and to lose their charm for those who were fond of them in a quiet way, and who, finding themselves so easily surpassed by the professors, lost their interest as actual participants and took to watching players who were paid for their exertions. What happened soon after the advent of Italian Opera followed exactly this course; music left the home for the theatre and concert-room, and from about this time musical references become rarer and rarer in the general literature of the day, being almost entirely confined to easy sneers at the operatic conventions and makeshifts. The rivalries between Cuzzoni and Faustina, the combat of Nicolini with the property lion, cannot have excited much interest among those who did not frequent the Opera; and the two papers in *The Tatler* (nos. 153, 157) in which Addison likens various types of people to various musical instruments do not show much more than that the general characteristics of the mediums of sound were recognized. When Fielding's Amelia goes 'to the oratorio' (name not specified) she has to wait two hours before catching sight of 'Mr. Handel's back', a passage which incidentally helps us to realize some of the conditions under which such concerts were given, for it is evident that seats were not reserved, and also that Handel conducted in the way to which we are now accustomed, not seated at the harpsichord (unless, indeed, the party's seats were at the side of the auditorium). But musical allusions such as this are comparatively rare during the Augustan age of our literature. Appreciation of music was ever more and more closely confined to a small body of *cognoscenti,* and the art gradually lost its interest for those who were not specialists, whether professional or amateur. Goldsmith, whose references to music are always to the point and accurate, seems to be the latest of the distinguished writers of the eighteenth century to make any allusion to music as if it were part of ordinary education.

It is not impossible that even the superficial knowledge of the Italian language which was needed for the enjoyment of the Opera may have done something to widen the gulf between general literature and music. That gulf remained yawning till well on in the nineteenth century, to the great disadvantage of musical progress, while to some extent letters suffered too.

As the musical forms became more and more highly organized, and the 'classical' ideals more and more widely recognized, a fresh obstacle arose to keep literary and musical people apart; for the former there was yet another language to be learnt before the more elaborate patterns of construction could be assimilated, and those who had not

time or opportunities for undertaking the trouble involved in the attempt to grasp the elements of musical form very naturally enrolled themselves among the really unmusical people, and were very properly angry when the few who had mastered what they themselves had shirked spoke a language to which they had no key.

It would probably be quite wrong to suppose that the period during which music was virtually banished from the world of letters was sterile in musical talent. The wind of artistic genius bloweth where it listeth, and it may well be that even in the eighteenth and nineteenth centuries there were born in England some who in the more favourable conditions of Germany would have made a name for themselves as musicians; and here reference may be made to such careers as those of Pearsall and Pierson, the former of whom preferred to expatriate himself for reasons not unconnected with ambitions other than artistic, while he did obtain a considerable degree of recognition in England by his part-songs, which became household words among English amateurs. The latter, a son of 'Pearson on the Creed', sought in Germany (where he changed the spelling of his name) a congenial atmosphere he could not find at home, and eventually became eminent as a German composer, whose music to *Faust* was regularly employed whenever Goethe's drama was revived. As things then were in England, the exercise of music as a serious branch of art was completely discredited as an occupation for male children, though the daughters of any well-to-do family were compelled to learn pianoforte pieces whatever their natural propensities might be, and any young woman who could boast a shapely arm was similarly enjoined to play the harp. These performances of course went in and out of fashion, just as the custom of playing the flute was at one time quite normal among young men, so much so that, when the Cambridge University Musical Society was first started, the difficulty was to find employment for the very numerous amateur flautists, and to discover any undergraduate students of stringed instruments. Though domestic performances are often referred to by Jane Austen, who often makes one of her characters go to 'the instrument', and be accompanied by some gentleman on the flute, she is careful not to give us any details, and it is evident that the music was rather a convenient way of disposing of characters that for the moment were not wanted, than an episode in the story. When we consider what was the standard probably attained on such occasions, it is impossible to be surprised that the number of professedly unmusical people should have been so markedly increased. In fact, the more delicate the musical sensibilities were, the greater the certainty that those who felt tortured by these displays would seek the company of others similarly afflicted, and would establish themselves as haters of music. Jane Austen wisely did not commit herself to any musical details and avoided the trap into which so many of the Victorian novelists fell, although we must not forget that Thackeray gives us a memorable picture of the performance of Mme. Schroeder-Devrient in *Fidelio,* while at the other end of the scale he created the celebrated 'finger' of Miss Wirt, a member as famous as Sir Willoughby Patterne's 'leg'. Those variations on 'Sich a gettin' upstairs' must surely have had an actual, audible existence before they reached immortality in one of the indisputably admirable passages in *The Book of Snobs.*

It is curious that George Eliot, who had a more definite musical training than the average lady of her time, should have committed herself to such a blunder as the passage in *Mr. Gilfil's Love Story:* 'Handel's "Messiah" stood open on the desk, at the chorus "All we like sheep", and Caterina threw herself at once into the impetuous intricacies of that magnificent fugue'; but she makes ample amends in *Middlemarch* and must evidently have made a complete study of the usual view of music held by two types of English gentlemen and one typical English lady. Mr. Brooke remarks, ' "There is a lightness about the feminine mind—a touch and go—music, the fine arts, that kind of thing—they should study those up to a certain point, women should; but in a light way, you know. A woman should be able to sit down and play you or sing you a good old English tune. That is what I like; though I have heard most things—been at the opera in Vienna: Gluck, Mozart, everything of that sort. But I'm a conservative in music—it's not like ideas, you know. I stick to the good old tunes." "Mr. Casaubon is not fond of the piano, and I am very glad he is not," said Dorothea, whose slight regard for domestic music and feminine fine art must be forgiven her, considering the small tinkling and smearing in which they chiefly consisted at that dark period.

' "I never could look on it in the light of a recreation, to have my ears teased with measured noises," said Mr. Casaubon. "A tune much iterated has the ridiculous effect of making the words in my mind perform a sort of minuet to keep time . . . As to the grander forms of music, worthy to accompany solemn celebrations, and even to serve as an educating influence according to the ancient conception, I say nothing, for with these we are not immediately concerned."

' "No; but music of that sort I should enjoy," said Dorothea. "When we were coming home from Lausanne my uncle took us to hear the great organ at Freiberg, and it made me sob."

' "That kind of thing is not healthy, my dear," said Mr. Brooke.'

The attitude of the average Englishman of the early nineteenth century, so well indicated by George Eliot, is illustrated in Charles Lamb's well-known lines beginning

> Some cry up Haydn, some Mozart,
> Just as the whim bites; for my part,
> I do not care a farthing candle
> For either of them, or for Handel.

One wonders how such a poem, if it could have been perpetrated, *mutatis mutandis,* in the spacious Elizabethan days, or at any moment when music was at peace with letters, would have been received, or what punishment would have been thought appropriate for such ribaldry.

Another instance of the width of the separation between literature and music is to be found in the popularity and no doubt financial success of an absurd novel called *Charles Auchester,* in which the scarcely-disguised por-

traits of Mme. Sainton-Dolby, Mendelssohn, and Sterndale Bennett are framed in a mass of high-falutin' stuff that reveals an uncommonly superficial knowledge of the art to whose lovers it appeals.

Though the vogue of this book cannot be taken as a completely trustworthy sign of the average English reader's attitude towards music, it might be profitable to compare it with such a story as *Facing the Music* if an illustration were wanted of the change in public appreciation.

In the comfortable days of Queen Victoria, when the words 'glimpse' and 'sense' were still content with their position as nouns substantive, the graphic arts, unlike that of music, were not banished from literature or from general conversation, for among the small change of talk in the London season, one of the commonest conversational openings was 'Have you been to the Royal Academy?'; but it would have been a solecism to ask one's neighbour if she had been to such and such a concert without first ascertaining whether she was musical or not.

Yet another indication of the width of the chasm between music and letters may be found in the condition of the song-writing of the period. Down to the time of Purcell, the words chosen by composers for musical treatment were such as were likely to be accepted by educated people, and these were set with due appreciation of the natural inflection or accentuation intended by the poet. In the days of the estrangement I have spoken of, the purveyors of songs either chose words of exquisite ineptitude, or, when they ventured to embark upon snatches of real poetry (as was occasionally done by men like Stevens, Bishop, Balfe, and others) they ignored the obvious accent and even the meaning of the words, or tortured them to fit their silly little tunes. Of the art that is sometimes called 'declamation', or more properly 'accentuation', there is hardly a trace until we come to the work of a great man like Parry, to whose skill, in this regard, Milton's sonnet to Henry Lawes is entirely appropriate.

The case of Tennyson is very curious, for the ear that was so delicately attuned to the music of words was completely deaf to that of notes. He was aware of his deficiency, for he said to Hubert Parry: 'Browning is devoted to music, and knows a good deal about it; but there is no music in his verse. I know nothing about music, and don't care for it in the least; but my verse is full of music.' (The words are reported by Sir Mountstuart Grant Duff, in his *Victorian Vintage.*) Yet he must have had an instinctive appreciation of what musicians call 'height' and 'depth'; for, when Stanford played through to him an album of settings of his songs by various writers, the poet made singularly apt comments on the way in which the melodies went up or down, and the songs he elected to praise on this account were exactly those which a musician would have picked out as coming from the pens of distinguished composers. The queer orchestra of 'flute, violin, bassoon', to which the dancers in *Maud* contrived to dance 'in tune', may be contrasted with Hardy's delicious descriptions of village music of the old type, and of the little groups of instruments that were used in country churches. The quarter of a century that separates *Maud* from the early books of

Hardy did actually see the beginnings of the bridge that was to unite letters and music once more.

Browning, whose practical knowledge of music was considerable, is the most satisfactory of the Victorian poets who have dealt with music, and his words are sometimes so apt that the music he describes can be almost literally translated into notes; still, there is always that stumbling-block of 'the mode Palestrina' which neither Pope Gregory nor the authorities of the Solesmes chant could possibly identify. By a strange perversity, the most easily accessible edition of his complete works is a treasure-house of musical 'howlers', as indeed it is of blunders other than musical. For example, the editors' definition of fugue as 'a kind of melody', of 'girandole' as 'a dance', and of a toccata as 'an overture—a touch-piece' can never be forgotten now that the chasm has been bridged and most people know enough to be amused, not misled, by these wonderful statements. One of the best musical 'howlers' was perpetrated after the breach between music and letters was healed. A well-known clerical poet in the North of England, in a pamphlet telling of the formation of some local industry and the opposition the committee met with, wrote 'A tumult arose, wild as a *Parsifal* chorus'. Some female novelist, whose book has passed into a well-merited oblivion, said: 'She roguishly played on her violin some short piece of Palestrina.'

Robert Browning, whose practical knowledge of music was considerable, is the most satisfactory of the Victorian poets who have dealt with music, and his words are sometimes so apt that the music he describes can be almost literally translated into notes.

—*J. A. Fuller-Maitland*

If there were faults on the literary side, the musicians were perhaps even more to blame. Through the earlier half of the Victorian era, most of the professional musicians were apt to look upon their art as a mere trade, and few indeed were those who had enough imagination to consider it from a higher point of view. Of course there were some brilliant exceptions, but the bulk of cathedral organists and professional musicians were content to go on in their narrow groove of work, and it must be remembered that to become an expert musician is a 'whole-time job', what with the necessary technical practice and the education of others in the same branch of knowledge and skill. It must be remembered, too, that music stands apart from the other arts, since it alone, in Lord Balfour's words, 'is without external reference'. Still, when all allowances have been made, the fact remains that, as a body, the practitioners of music had not much general culture, or indeed much reverence for the ideals they were supposed to profess.

The typical Victorian organist would go to his desk and turn out an anthem because his wife wanted a new bonnet; and the remark made by the wife of a well-known conductor during the first season of the Richter Concerts is hardly an exaggeration: 'Don't talk to me about Richter; me and———, we've conducted the Philharmonic these twenty years and we don't want any foreigners coming to teach us how to conduct.' Whether or not such instances of a trade view of the art are actually true, it must be confessed that the Germans of that time did take a higher view of the art in which their nation had so long been eminent, and I am inclined to think that their artistic attitude, whether real or assumed, had something to do with the preference shown for so many years to everything that came out of Germany, so that a fifth-rate foreign performer was more highly paid and more warmly applauded than a first-rate English one.

The professional writers on music had little or no literary taste, and the jargon they used was calculated to disgust any educated reader who might chance upon the musical notices in the daily papers. This jargon was in some degree excusable when we remember how very few synonyms there are for the definite technical terms that must be used if any useful impression is to be conveyed. But the *clichés* we critics used were even farther removed from anything like a literary style; a favourite opening to an article upon any of the provincial festivals in the autumn was: '——— was *en fête* to-day. The show of bunting, though not so abundant as on former occasions', &c., &c. In the end of the nineteenth century we should not have been shocked by such a sentence as 'The rendition of this item, and which was reminiscent of the palmy days of the lyric stage', &c.

How and when was the chasm bridged over? It is not easy to say very definitely, but it is probable that the first pier of the bridge was firmly planted when Sir George Grove, whose place in the world of letters was assured,—was he not editor of *Macmillan's Magazine?*—allowed his musical enthusiasms full play in his work at the Crystal Palace and the inception of his great *Dictionary of Music*. If he was not the actual beginner of the musical renaissance in England, he used his great influence in the encouragement of that movement, and it was mainly due to him that the musical education of the country reached a point at which literary people were compelled to recognize the tuneful art.

An important part in this bridge-building was played by certain official appointments, like Parratt's connexion with Oxford, Stanford's with Cambridge, and Harford Lloyd's with Eton. Each of these succeeded men whose ideals, such as they were, were bounded by the limits of the professional attitude already referred to. Each started a tradition of general cultivation, so that to-day it would be hard to find among cathedral organists any specimens of the old type, who would admit that they took no interest in general literature. Not only the standard of musical tuition in our great public schools, but the conditions in which it is given, have so marvellously improved that it is possible to believe in the recorded fact that the greatest masterpiece of music, Bach's Mass in B minor, was actually performed at Oundle School without extraneous help. Among those who 'assisted' at such a performance, whether as listeners or executants, there must have been many boys who would be classed as 'unmusical', but even these can no longer ignore music in the way their forefathers did, or echo their ancestors' favourite gibe: 'Musicians' heads are as empty as their fiddles.'

In many ways the institution of Musical Competition Festivals has done much to bring music into line with the other arts and with literature. For on the one hand the pattern of the festivals devised by Miss Mary Wakefield has given useful employment in their organization and direction to a very large number of intelligent people all over the country whose interest in music had been largely wasted in the old-fashioned amateur efforts, and whose friends, if not 'musical' themselves, are bound to recognize something of the importance of the art; and, on the other hand the improved culture of the young composers has led them to choose for their part-songs words of lasting beauty instead of the trumpery that was formerly thought good enough to be set to music.

The admirable catholicity of the Broadcasting programmes is another element in the healing of the old breach, as well as a sign of the reality of the healing process. To refer only to one side of its work; the weekly performance of the Bach cantatas, that series of masterpieces buried for so long, is not only an inestimable boon to musical hearers, but is an education in itself for the young people who have to learn them. It may be surmised that the mere neglect to switch off the current has often compelled literary and musical listeners respectively to hear parts at least of each other's delights.

It may be a mere coincidence that so many of the old dichotomies, such as that between Science and Religion, are in course of being brought into agreement, and it stands to reason that every effort of the kind is to the manifest advantage of both sides.

As I have already said, it is inconceivable that Charles Lamb's ribald rhymes could have been accepted in the earlier days when music was the property of all men; and it is just as impossible to imagine *The Testament of Beauty* as existing before the fulfilment of the revival of music and its restoration to the world of letters:—

> And if the Greek Muses wer a graceful company
> yet hav we two, that in maturity transcend
> the promise of their baby-prattle in Time's cradle,
> Musick and Mathematick: coud their wet-nurses
> but see these foster-children upgrown in full
>   stature,
> Pythagoras would marvel and Athena rejoice.

James Anderson Winn

SOURCE: "The Condition of Music," in *Unsuspected Eloquence: A History of the Relations between Poetry and Music*, Yale University Press, 1981, pp. 287-346.

[*In the following essay, Winn explores similarities and differences between poetry and music within the context of* nineteenth- and twentieth-century movements toward autonomy in both arts, with particular emphasis on the efforts of the Parnassian and Symbolist poets to make the language of poetry independent of everyday meaning by emulating the effects of music.]

INTRODUCTION

Wagner's ideas, not to mention his success and his arrogance, were bound to produce opponents, whose works, whether in music or in words, were just as certain to be dismissed as reactionary by his convinced followers. So when Eduard Hanslick published his slender volume *Vom Musikalisch-Schönen (The Beautiful in Music)* in 1854, it was possible for Wagnerites to dismiss it as mere polemic, the product of Hanslick's known antipathy to Wagner and friendship for Brahms. But the importance of Hanslick's work transcends not only these personal relations but the immediate concerns of nineteenth-century music as well; as Morris Weitz argues, "it is to music what Hume's *Inquiry Concerning Human Understanding* is to speculative philosophy, a devastating critique of unsupportable views and an attempt to state clearly and precisely the territories and boundaries of the areas they discuss." More than that: *The Beautiful in Music* separates and dismisses the various imitative and emotive notions about the function of music which Romantic thought had impressionistically blurred together; it boldly insists on music's autonomy, its independence not only from words (a battle already won in the eighteenth century) but from verbally definable feelings as well. The aesthetic position it stakes out is not only fundamental to twentieth-century thought about music, but strikingly similar to the literary aesthetics of I. A. Richards and the American New Critics.

For musicians, the idea of autonomy would prove a means of liberating themselves from all kinds of imitative demands; as the coherence of classical Viennese instrumental music had given the quietus to the Renaissance claim that music's function was to serve or express words, Hanslick's doctrine would still the Romantic claim that its function was to express or imitate some specific emotion. Thus, in the course of his argument, Hanslick finds the recitative, the legacy of the Musical Humanists, a particularly convenient target:

> In the recitative, music degenerates into a mere shadow and relinquishes its individual sphere of action altogether. Is not this proof that the representing of definite states of mind is contrary to the nature of music, and that in their ultimate bearings they are antagonistic to one another? Let anyone play a long recitative, leaving out the words, and inquire into its musical merit and subject.

Two birds with one stone: not only does music "degenerate" when it makes itself the slave of words, but "the beautiful tends to disappear in proportion as the expression of some specific feeling is aimed at."

Poets, too, were interested in autonomy, though the word necessarily had a different meaning for them. As Hanslick proclaimed the independence of music from the demands of words or specific emotions, Edgar Allan Poe, in an essay first published in 1850, "allude[d] to the heresy of

The Didactic," the claim that "the ultimate object of all Poetry is Truth." The old doctrine that poetry had a duty to instruct as well as to please, like the doctrine that music had a duty to imitate something, took a variety of forms in the nineteenth century; W. K. Wimsatt distinguishes three—"the Shelleyan and Carlylean rhapsodic retort to scientism," a vigorous assertion that poetry also dealt in truth; "the Arnoldian neo-classic idealism," a prophecy that poetry would assume the functions of religion and philosophy; and "the sociorealistic propagandism" that would eventually harden into Soviet demands for "socialist realism." Concerned to make a quite different claim for poetry, Poe argues that it has nothing to do with truth:

> The demands of Truth are severe. She has no sympathy with the myrtles. All *that* which is so indispensable in Song, is precisely all *that* with which *she* has nothing whatever to do. It is but making her a flaunting paradox, to wreathe her in gems and flowers. In enforcing a truth, we need severity rather than efflorescence of language. We must be simple, precise, terse. We must be cool, calm, unimpassioned. In a word, we must be in that mood which, as nearly as possible, is the exact converse of the poetical.

A familiar ancient distinction, if one more or less absent from Western aesthetics since the Renaissance; it might be Plato or Augustine on music and rhetoric, with the striking difference that Poe chooses Song rather than Truth. His Greek and patristic forbears, arguing that eloquence and melody were incompatible with truth, had sought in vain to control the claims of beauty, even in their own writings, but Poe "define[s] . . . the Poetry of words as *The Rhythmical Creation of Beauty*." And like many who would follow him, including (in their several ways) Pater, Wilde, Mallarmé, Verlaine, Pound, and Auden, Poe links poetry to music in the same gesture with which he separates it from didacticism:

> Contenting myself with the certainty that Music, in its various modes of metre, rhythm, and rhyme, is of so vast a moment in Poetry as never to be wisely rejected—is so vitally important an adjunct, that he is simply silly who declines its assistance, I will not now pause to maintain its absolute essentiality.

Twenty-three years later, in an essay on the painter Giorgione, Walter Pater would maintain that "*all art constantly aspires towards the condition of music.*"

There were powerful conceptual similarities between the musical and literary movements toward "autonomy." Central in both cases was the positing of some aspect of the mind between intellect and feeling, a three-part scheme where older accounts had only two. Thus Hanslick:

> It is rather curious that musicians and the older writers on aesthetics take into account only the contrast of "feeling" and "intellect," quite oblivious of the fact that the main point at issue lies halfway between the horns of this supposed dilemma. A musical composition originates in the composer's imagination and is intended for the imagination of the listener.

And Pater:

> Art . . . is always striving to be independent of the mere intelligence, to become a matter of pure perception, to get rid of its responsibilities to its subject or material; the ideal examples of poetry and painting being those in which the constituent elements of the composition are so welded together, that the material or subject no longer strikes the intellect only; nor the form, the eye or the ear only; but form and matter, in their union or identity, present one single effect to the "imaginative reason," that complex faculty for which every thought and feeling is twin-born with its sensible analogue or symbol.

Yet even in these obviously similar passages we see equally important differences: Hanslick is concerned to *separate* the imagination from feeling on the one side and intellect on the other, to establish an area of the mind from which music can be said to arise in the composer and to which it can be said to appeal in the listener, without either the claim that music is an intellectual language or the claim that it is a language of the feelings. Pater, by contrast, is concerned to *fuse* intelligence and sensuality, the mind and the ear, to produce his "imaginative reason." The movement toward musical autonomy was a movement toward abstraction, a declaration of independence from imitative demands; the movement toward poetic autonomy saw and admired in music not only its physical sensuality, but its abstraction as well. For Pater, music "most completely realises" his combining ideal, the "perfect identification of form and matter"; therefore "music, . . . and not poetry, as is so often supposed, is the true type or measure of perfected art." Hanslick, denying the capacity of musical form to express an external subject, makes a simpler claim: "the form (the musical structure) is the real substance (subject) of music—in fact is the music itself."

Hanslick's definition of autonomy can be more abstract than Pater's because the art he describes is finally more abstract; he can claim that structure simply *is* meaning, while Pater must necessarily talk about "welding" the two together. If, with Hanslick, we define the condition of music as the abstraction resulting from the essential neutrality and plasticity of its materials, we must recognize, as Pater's verb suggests, that poetry may *aspire* to that condition but cannot reach it. Words . . . resist attempts to empty them of their ordinary morphemic content. I may write a poem in which the word "swan" comes to function as a symbol for some larger abstraction, but even a reader who understands my method will find it hard to read that word without some notion, however fleeting, of a large, white bird with a curved neck. By contrast, I may change utterly the meaning of a note or even a chord in a composition; I may do so within a theoretical system or (more radically) by changing the entire system. The note G may be the tonic of one tonal piece, but in another piece in another key, it will take on another function; and since, in music, function *is* meaning, the fact that G has been the tonic of some other piece will be entirely irrelevant. As Hanslick compactly puts it,

> The fundamental difference consists in this; while sound in speech is but a sign, that is, a

means for the purpose of expressing something which is quite distinct from the medium, sound in music is the end, that is, the ultimate and absolute object in view.

W. H. Auden, in a poem entitled "The Composer," makes the same distinction from a poet's point of view:

> All the others translate: the painter sketches
> A visible world to love or reject;
> Rummaging into his living, the poet fetches
> The images out that hurt and connect.
> From Life to Art by painstaking adaption,
> Relying on us to cover the rift;
> Only your notes are pure contraption,
> Only your song is an absolute gift.

Just how absolute or pure music could be has been proved in our century by a development Hanslick only dimly foresaw: the waning of the tonal system. Hanslick does acknowledge the speed with which music "uses up" its forms:

> Modulations, cadences, intervals, and harmonious progressions become so hackneyed within fifty, nay, thirty years, that a truly original composer cannot well employ them any longer, and is thus compelled to think of a new musical phraseology.

But he imagines, as anyone would have in 1854, that triads "will ever remain the indestructible foundation upon which all future development must rest." The first perception proved more accurate than the second: as a result of the harmonic innovations of Hanslick's arch-enemy Wagner, among others, triadic progressions, stable keys, and ordinary cadences began to seem "hackneyed." By the turn of the century it was possible to hear, in the music of composers all over Europe (Debussy and Scriabin, for example) such powerful motion away from tonality that triadic conclusions, when employed, seemed hollow gestures toward convention. And by 1910, Arnold Schönberg was announcing his abandonment of tonality in language which still echoes Pater's notion of a fusion of expression and form, and which sounds positively Romantic in its acknowledgement of an "inner compulsion":

> With the *George* songs I have for the first time succeeded in approaching an ideal of expression and form which has been in my mind for years. Until now, I lacked the strength and confidence to make it a reality. But now that I am conscious of having broken through every restriction of a bygone aesthetic; and though the goal toward which I am striving appears to me a certain one, I am, nonetheless, already feeling the resistance I shall have to overcome; I . . . suspect that even those who have so far believed in me will not want to acknowledge the necessary nature of this development . . . I am obeying an inner compulsion which is stronger than any upbringing.

The revolutionary changes wrought by Schönberg and others exposed as never before the limitations of the metaphorical description of music as a language. As Charles Rosen explains in his little book about Schönberg,

> The so-called "breakdown of tonality" at the end of the nineteenth century revealed to what extent this exterior stability [of the tonal system] was an illusion; more precisely, it was a construction that depended substantially on the individual works of music much more than a linguistic system depends on individual acts of speech. Music is only metaphorically a language; a single work of music may transform and even create an entire musical system, while no act of speech may do more than marginally alter language.

> If an individual work of music may alter and even create "language," then the conditions for understanding it must—at least partially—be made evident in the work itself.

Thus, to adopt for a moment the famous distinction of the linguist Saussure, the relation between a *parole*, an individual speech act, and the *langue*, or larger system, is quite different in poetry and in music. A word in a particular *parole*, even if that *parole* is a poem, will seem to most readers to refer inevitably to its dictionary meaning in the *langue*. But in music, each *parole*, each piece, must establish *within itself* the "conditions for understanding it." This was actually as true for Mozart as for Schönberg, but the familiarity of the tonal *langue* implied by Mozart's *parole* made it possible to adopt the comforting but false assumption that the tonal system was a stable language in which individual pieces might be written. One could thus believe that even if music did not express words or feelings, it followed dependable syntactic rules, and thus had some kind of extrinsic referent. Atonal music, by depriving us of the comfort of triads and cadences, scalar and chordal relations, all that Rosen aptly terms "prefabricated material," forces us to confront and acknowledge the uniqueness of each piece. It fully validates Hanslick's claim that musical structure is musical meaning.

Hanslick's prophetic assertions, especially as validated by the ever more apparent autonomy of individual musical works, would thus seem to indicate a final unbridgeable gap between poetry and music. But in the very crisis brought on by the abandonment of "prefabricated material," Schönberg drew on poetic form to solve the urgent problems of length and organization. And when he finally solved those problems in a more purely musical way by devising the "twelve-tone" or "serial" method of composition, he employed some procedures closely related to older kinds of poetic construction: the retrograde, for example, one of the basic operations performed upon a twelve-tone row, is the "crab" or backwards ordering . . . in the music of Machaut, which Schönberg heard in an early revival and praised for its constructive craft, a craft precisely paralleled in the anagrammatic devices of Machaut's poetry.

In poetry itself, Pater's words have not lost their validity: many of the nameable movements in French and English poetry of the late nineteenth and twentieth centuries may be usefully described as attempts to attain various metaphorical versions of the condition of music, motions toward musical technique along various axes; the poets and theorists of these movements, though not all of them have understood music with real precision, have usually acknowledged their desire to make poetry more like it.

Richard Wagner in 1860.

The Parnassian poet Théodore Banville, for example, believed that poets should recover intricate medieval forms—rondels, rondeaux, ballades, and villanelles—forms with such demanding technical requirements that content would become subservient to "the implacable richness of the rhyme." Since rhyme depends upon an accidental likeness between words, not a syntactic or morphological one, the French Parnassians and their English admirers were aspiring to the condition of music along the old axis of construction, the axis along which Schönberg would later proceed in borrowing formal hints from poetry. Writing a rondel necessarily entails choosing words for their rhymes and adjusting both syntax and content to accommodate words thus chosen; Swinburne's rondels provide some familiar examples of the possibilities and limitations of this kind of aspiration toward music, but it has been a method infrequently employed in the twentieth century, where the ideal of "sincerity" has made it difficult for poets to accept the constraints of intricate forms. But W. H. Auden, perhaps the preeminent virtuoso among modern English poets, not only mastered numerous older forms but invented equally difficult new ones, some of which show curious affinities with serial techniques; these poems demonstrate the continuing possibility for a technical influence between music and poetry, the usefulness of "contraption" even in a century whose characteristic poetic style is, as Auden admits, "Good Drab."

The much more important Symbolist movement placed even greater emphasis on sound; James Robinson argues

that "Mallarmé went on from Banville to conclude that the value of poetry lay more in the sound of words than in their sense," but Mallarmé's position was much more revolutionary than Banville's: given a choice between suggestiveness and clarity, Mallarmé chose suggestiveness; he even attacked the Parnassians as "deficient in mystery," apparently because their poems sometimes named objects:

> The Parnassians take something in its entirety and simply exhibit it; in so doing, they fall short of mystery; they fail to give our minds that exquisite joy which consists of believing that we are creating something. To *name* an object is largely to destroy poetic enjoyment, which comes from gradual divination. The ideal is to *suggest* the object. It is the perfect use of this mystery which constitutes symbol.

For the Symbolists, the poem becomes a closed system, whose elements derive their meaning as much as possible from their place in that single formal structure, as little as possible from their everyday functions as names of things. Small wonder that Paul Valéry described Symbolism as the "intention of several groups of poets (not always friendly to one another) to recover from music the heritage due to them." In its fascination with sound, its hostility to ordinary syntax, and most of all its attempt to make the poem a self-contained world, Symbolism was one of the most thorough and serious attempts in history to push poetry in the direction of music. The final, summarizing document of the movement is aptly entitled *Four Quartets*.

So argues Hugh Kenner, explaining how Eliot and Pound, both influenced by the Symbolist movement, developed in different directions:

> One poet moved out of Symbolism, one deeper into it. Commencing from the post-Symbolist nineties, Pound worked his way clear of systematized suggestiveness until his chief point of contact with 19th-century French verse was Théophile Gautier of the direct statement ("Carmen is thin") and his most Symbolist procedure an isolating of single words, not necessarily English. Eliot . . . worked more and more deeply into the central Symbolist poetic.

But Pound's hygienic program for clearing away the Symbolist mists was the use of the "image" (later the "vortex"), which he defined as "that which presents an intellectual and emotional complex in an instant of time." In that definition we may still hear the voices of Hanslick and Pater, the idea of an instantaneous fusion of intellect and emotion in a single image. Simultaneity is the axis along which this kind of poetry—whether we call it Imagism, Vorticism, or (more simply) the procedure of Pound—aspires to the condition of music. Pound's fascination with Chinese ideograms, beyond their alleged visual expression, lay in the fact that one ideogram might be made be out of several others like a chord out of several notes. Joyce's *Finnegans Wake*, forging new words (new chords) from disparate linguistic elements, strains toward this kind of harmony, and Pound's *Cantos*, assembling the melodies of many times and tongues, strain toward a more contrapuntal simultaneity. Again Kenner has caught it: "A polyphony, not of simultaneous elements which are impossible in poetry, but of something chiming from something we remember from earlier, earlier in this poem and out of earlier poems, such is Arnaut's way—and such Pound's."

As Kenner's aside acknowledges, actual polyphonic simultaneity is impossible in poetry, but the results of Pound's search for an equivalent are often impressive, as are the results of Mallarmé's attempt to make the poem a closed system, or the results of Auden's formal virtuosity. Hanslick's claim that music is not finally a language is correct, but these poets (like many of their predecessors) have seen in the musical possibilities for simultaneity, density, and design attractive models for poetry.

Similarly, the greatest of twentieth-century composers, while convinced of the autonomy of music, not by any means cut themselves off from the expressive possibilities we associate with poetry. At the simplest level, we ought to remember that the revolutionary works of Schönberg's "Expressionist" period—the *George Lieder, Erwartung,* and *Pierrot Lunaire*—all employ texts, and that the *Sprechstimme* introduced in *Pierrot Lunaire*, while it dramatizes the difference between speech and song, acknowledges the expressiveness of spoken poetry by incorporating its shifting and uncertain pitch into a carefully designed musical setting. Schönberg was neither naive nor sentimental about the relations between music and poetry; many of his pronouncements on the subject sound the orthodox Hanslickian doctrine of autonomy. But his greatest scorn was reserved for music he took to be empty of expression; he was no cold-blooded mathematician.

The other giant among twentieth-century composers, Igor Stravinsky, chose a path often followed by poets: the renewal of past techniques. Reaching back past Romanticism, he regained some of the compression, wit, and irony of eighteenth-century art. But even when writing in a strictly diatonic idiom, Stravinsky manages to indicate that that idiom is a mask, a *persona*; he is arguably the most rhetorical composer who ever lived. Because older music was more frequently heard in the twentieth century than in the nineteenth, thanks to recording and greatly expanded publication, neo-classic procedures which had been available to poets for centuries—allusion, parody, burlesque—were newly available to twentieth-century composers, a situation brilliantly exploited by Stravinsky. But like Pound and Eliot, similarly eclectic poets, Stravinsky remains recognizably himself no matter what mask he assumes. The ultimate example of the power of his compositional personality to transcend convention is the marvelous twelve-tone music he wrote after the death of Schönberg, music in which he masters a new idiom just as deftly as he had earlier mastered the idioms of Gesualdo, Haydn, and American jazz. And if, like Schönberg, Stravinsky made severe claims for musical autonomy, he too continued to set texts. His *Shakespeare Songs*, for example, are at once explorations of serial technique and witty examples of imitative word-painting.

> **In its fascination with sound, its hostility to ordinary syntax, and most of all its attempt to make the poem a self-contained world, Symbolism was one of the most thorough and serious attempts in history to push poetry in the direction of music.**
>
> **—*James Anderson Winn***

Indeed, the great danger for poets and composers in our time may be the tendency to respond to our recognition of the gap between music and poetry by exaggerating it, by withdrawing into isolation. The weakest twentieth-century music, the dead academic serialism of the 1950s, results from a rigorous working out of constructive principles and an ascetic disregard for expression; in aleatoric music, where some elements are determined by chance, this asceticism has become a kind of despair. The weakest twentieth-century poetry, the self-indulgent amoebic "free verse" of the little magazines, so values its supposed expressive "authenticity" that it abhors even minimal craft and construction. If there is one central lesson in the history traced in [*Unsuspected Eloquence*], it is that great music and great poetry invariably involve both construction and expression. The healthy and accurate recognition by modern theorists of the fundamental gap between the two arts—the fact that music has by nature greater constructive resources, and poetry greater expressive resources—need not mean that analogies between musical and poetic procedures are pointless. The pursuit of such analogies, whether true or false, has been a factor in the making of great works in both arts, and may in turn enrich our understanding of them.

VERSIONS OF AUTONOMY: HANSLICK AND THE NEW CRITICS

Richard Wagner's enterprise, as Hanslick recognized, was not a pursuit of analogies between distinct arts but a thoroughgoing attempt to merge the arts in a *Gesamtkunstwerk*. In a pointed personal version of the myth of Beethoven as "tone poet," Wagner argued that Beethoven finally turned to texts, specifically to Schiller's "Ode to Joy" in the final movement of the Ninth Symphony, because he had come to recognize that only the word could give music the precise expressive meaning for which (according to Wagner) his earlier work had been searching. With reverent gestures in the direction of ancient Greek tragedy, Wagner declared that the music of the future must be combined with poetry and dramatic spectacle. His opinions . . . sometimes resembled those of the Renaissance musical humanists, though there is no evidence that Wagner knew their work; in any case, Wagner was a much more influential spokesman for these ideas than Bardi or Baïf: not only was he an able propagandist, but he was an important composer whose significant musical innovations suggested that his opinions should be taken seriously.

For Hanslick, however, Wagner's operas were a "violation of music by words," and the metaphor of rape seems intentional. In order to explain his opposition to Wagner without seeming merely personal, Hanslick constructs a careful and skeptical philosophy of music, a philosophy whose main points are negative: he denies the validity of a number of conventional ways of discussing music, insisting instead on an aesthetic perspective which acknowledges music's autonomy and discusses music in musical terms. Some of his main points reappear in the equally skeptical, negative, and liberating literary aesthetics of the so-called New Critics.

Romantic composers of program music, like the Musical Humanists of the Renaissance, couched much of their talk about music in the language of emotion; they spoke of the power of music to express a composer's emotions or to arouse a listener's emotions. Hanslick, while quite careful to acknowledge that "music operates on our emotional faculty with greater intensity and rapidity than the product of any other art", nonetheless insists that "definite feelings and emotions are unsusceptible of being embodied in music." He separates and rejects what the New Critics would call the "intentionalist" and "affectivist" arguments:

> On the one hand it is said that the aim and object of music is to excite emotions, i.e., pleasurable emotions; on the other hand, the emotions are said to be the subject matter which musical works are intended to illustrate.

> Both propositions are alike in this, that one is as false as the other.

> Aesthetic investigations must above all consider the beautiful object, and not the perceiving subject.

Even though Hanslick claimed (perhaps disingenuously) that the principle of concentration on the object had already been established in the aesthetics of the other arts, it took many years for literary critics to achieve a similarly rigorous insistence on separating the aesthetic object from the responses of its perceiver or the intentions of its maker. And when Monroe Beardsley and W. K. Wimsatt gave those principles their most exacting formulation—in the essays on "The Intentional Fallacy" and "The Affective Fallacy"—they acknowledged their indebtedness to Hanslick by choosing as an epigraph for the latter essay a cutting *reductio ad absurdum* from Hanslick's attack on musical affectivism: "We might as well study the properties of wine by getting drunk." The essay on intentionalism contains no explicit quotations from Hanslick, but closely follows the opinions he expressed in passages like these:

> The beautiful, strictly speaking, aims at nothing.

> In music there is no "intention" that can make up for "invention."

> The limits to which a musical composition can bear the impress of the author's own personal temperament are fixed by a preeminently objective and plastic process.

Neither Hanslick nor his New Critical heirs would want

to deny that poets and composers have intentions, or that their works may affect us powerfully; they are united in recognizing that neither of these phenomena "possesses the attributes of inevitableness, exclusiveness, and uniformity that a phenomenon from which aesthetic principles are to be deduced ought to have."

Hanslick takes a similar position about pleasure; he acknowledges its occurrence but denies its relevance to aesthetic investigation:

> If the contemplation of something beautiful arouses pleasurable feelings, this effect is distinct from the beautiful as such. I may, indeed, place a beautiful object before an observer with the avowed purpose of giving him pleasure, but this purpose in no way affects the beauty of the object. The beautiful is and remains beautiful though it arouse no emotion whatever, and though there be no one to look at it.

Here the most striking literary analogue comes in the *Principles of Literary Criticism* of I. A. Richards (1928):

> It is no less absurd to suppose that a competent reader sits down to read for the sake of pleasure, than to suppose that a mathematician sets out to solve an equation with a view to the pleasure its solution will afford him. The pleasure in both cases may, of course, be very great. But the pleasure, however great it may be, is no more the aim of the activity in the course of which it arises, than, for example, the noise made by a motorcycle—useful though it is as an indication of the way the machine is running—is the reason in the normal case for its having been started.

For both Hanslick and Richards, pleasure is at least as unsatisfactory a basis for aesthetic principle as intention or affect; it is a by-product of musical or poetic objects they would advocate studying in a more purely analytical way.

But Hanslick's most important point was one which could have no literary analogue: the denial of past and present attempts to describe music as a language. In a passionate conclusion to a long discussion of this point, Hanslick points to the "mischievous practical consequences" of

> . . . those theories which try to impose on music the laws of development and construction peculiar to speech, as in former days, Rameau and Rousseau, and in modern times the disciples of Richard Wagner, have endeavored to do. In this attempt the life of the music is destroyed, the innate beauty of form annihilated in pursuit of the phantom "meaning." One of the most important tasks of the aesthetics of music would, therefore, be that of demonstrating with inexorable logic the fundamental difference between music and language, and of never departing from the principle that, wherever the question is a specifically musical one, all parallelisms with language are wholly irrelevant.

This stringent denial of all metaphorical attempts to describe music as a language is central to Hanslick's stated purpose: the establishing of musical "autonomy." But advocates of poetic "autonomy," as we have seen, made much of metaphors comparing poetry to music; here we confront a semantic inconsistency at least as ironic and re- vealing as those conflicting definitions of "imitation" in the eighteenth century. For Hanslick and the twentieth- century musicians who came to accept his doctrine, musi- cal autonomy meant an escape from the extraneous re- quirement that music "mean" something which might be verbalized; for Poe, Wilde, and Pater, poetic autonomy meant an escape from a criticism centered on subject mat- ter, and one of the most common and powerful ways to express what that escape might mean for poetry was to talk of aspiring to the condition of music. Even Richards, whom we hardly think of as a pale aesthete, sounds very much like Poe in drawing a clear line between poetry and truth:

> It is evident that the bulk of poetry consists of statements which only the very foolish would think of attempting to verify. . . . Even when they are, on examination, frankly false, this is no defect.

And in seeking to explain why T. S. Eliot's poems were misread by those seeking a logical or intellectual structure, he falls back on the analogy to music:

> If it were desired to label in three words the most characteristic feature of Mr. Eliot's technique, this might be done by calling his poetry a "music of ideas." The ideas are of all kinds, abstract and concrete, general and particular, and, like the musician's phrases, they are arranged, not that they may tell us something, but that their effects in us may combine into a coherent whole of feel- ing and attitude and produce a peculiar libera- tion of the will.

Ironically, the analogy leads Richards into an affectivist account of music that Hanslick would surely have reject- ed: another example of the tendency for poets and critics marching under the banner of autonomy to encourage loose analogies to music, while musicians marching under a similarly labeled banner have discouraged descriptions of music as a language. This inconsistency is not merely amusing; it ultimately confirms a basic difference between the arts, as does the fact that Hanslick's position has be- come something like orthodoxy among twentieth-century composers, while the tough Hanslickian positions of Beardsley and Wimsatt have met a constant and ingenious opposition from poets and literary critics. To put it as sim- ply as possible, most people cling more tightly to inten- tional and affective claims as ways of discussing poetry than as ways of discussing music, and they think of subject matter as a primary category for describing a poem. If you tell me that you have just read an interesting poem, I am likely to ask you what it was "about," and your answer may well include some remarks about what the poet was "trying to do" and how the poem moved you; if you tell me that you have just heard an interesting piece of music, I cannot so easily inquire about its subject matter, and your only satisfactory answer to such an inquiry would be to sing or whistle some remembered portion of the musical material. Nor would claims about the composer's inten- tions or the music's emotional impact on you tell me very much about the piece; its notes would remain "pure con- traption." And even the coiner of that phrase, for all his

respect for composers, recognized the limits on poetry's aspirations toward music, its ultimate duty to say some- thing. In "The Cave of Making," he admits to the ghost of Louis MacNeice:

> I should like to become, if possible,
> a minor atlantic Goethe,
> with his passion for weather and stones but with-
> out his silliness
> re the Cross: at times a bore, but,
> while knowing Speech can at best, a shadow
> echoing
> the silent light, bear witness
> to the Truth it is not, he wished it were, as the
> Francophile
> gaggle of pure songsters
> are too vain to. We're not musicians: to stink of
> Poetry
> is unbecoming, and never
> to be dull shows a lack of taste.

Poetry, by this account, is not truth, but its aspirations to- ward truth-telling are as much a part of its problematic identity as its aspirations toward musical purity. Auden is making at the level of the whole art the same point Han- slick made earlier at the level of fundamental materials: that notes are plastic and neutral, while words mean things, even if we wish they did not. . . .

THE AXIS OF CONSTRUCTION

When modern poets have sought to emulate music along constructive lines embracing various kinds of formal com- plexity, they have often wished to escape critical fixations on the politics, morality, truth, or "sincerity" of their sub- ject matter. We have already seen how that kind of analo- gy to music helped Poe attack "the heresy of *The Didac- tic*," and in France, where Poe's influence was to prove most powerful, Gautier had declared as early as 1835 that "form is everything." A group of poets called the Parnas- sians, formed in the 1860s, built an entire aesthetic theory on that principle. Reaching back to Villon and Ronsard, as Schönberg later reached back to Machaut, Théodore Banville devoted himself to virtuoso forms ultimately de- rived from the troubadour tradition. The title page of his *Améthystes* (1862) describes the contents as "composed according to the rhythms of Ronsard," and since those rhythms were musical in origin, we may think of Banville as cheerfully writing new words to an old tune, insisting on the primacy of form in order to deflect critical attention from the contents of such lines as these:

> Vois, sur les violettes
> Brillent, perles des soirs,
> De fraîches gouttelettes!
> Entends dans les bois noirs,
> Frémissants de son vol,
> Chanter le rossignol.
>
> Reste ainsi, demi-nue,
> A la fenêtre; viens,
> Mon amante ingénue;
> Dis si tu te souviens
> Des mots que tu m'as dits
> Naguère, au paradis!
>
> [Look, on the violets / Sparkle, pearls of the eve- ning, / Fresh dewdrops! / Hear from the dark

woods / Trembling in his flight, / The nightingale singing. / Stay that way, half-naked, / At
the window; come, / My innocent lover; / Say
if you remember / The words you said to me /
Before, in paradise!]

In the troubadour tradition, . . . a similar concentration
on form produced a similar freezing of content, but in Victorian England, where the moral criticism of Arnold and
Ruskin was dominant, the issue was not the conventional
emptiness of the first stanza but the "indecency" of the
second, for which the perfection of the rhyme between
"demi-nue" and *"ingénue"* was no justification. When
Swinburne, among others, began to employ such old
French forms, he did so (as Robinson puts it) "defiantly,
with accusations of indecency and atheism exploding in
his ears." Tennyson referred to the intricate stanzas as
"poisonous honey stol'n from France," a phrase in which
we may hear not only Victorian prudishness but a distant
echo of eighteenth-century British attitudes toward seductive "foreign" music; this suspicion of continental "art for
art's sake" was apparently still alive in 1964, when Auden
glanced disparagingly at the "Francophile gaggle of pure
songsters."

But the real aesthetic issue raised by Parnassian poetry is
neither moral nor national: it is the poetic imbalance between form and content produced when a poet commits
himself to a stanza requiring repeated rhymes on the same
syllable. Under these circumstances, the poet must find
not only a number of words for each of his rhyming
sounds, but a structure of meaning in which he may logically use the rhymes he has found; as Banville's phrase
about the "implacable richness" of rhyme suggests, formal
considerations may alter or even control the poem's content. The metaphor of "organic form," plausible enough
when applied to Wordsworth's blank verse, cannot apply
to any rondel, though the successful rondel will minimize
the strain between form and meaning. Consequently, such
poems often work best when taking poetic form itself for
a subject, as in this example of Swinburne at his best:

"The Roundel"

A roundel is wrought as a ring or a starbright
   sphere,
With craft of delight and with cunning of sound
   unsought,
That the heart of the hearer may smile if to pleasure his ear
                    A roundel is wrought.
Its jewel of music is carven of all or of aught—
Love, laughter, or mourning—remembrance of
   rapture or fear—
That fancy may fashion to hang in the ear of
   thought.

As a bird's quick song runs round, and the
   hearts in us hear
Pause answer to pause, and again the same strain
   caught,
So moves the device whence, round as a pearl or
   tear,
                    A roundel is wrought.

Here Swinburne's own craft and cunning make the
rhymes successful; even "tear," perhaps the word most

distant from the basic subject of the poem, is neatly
worked in through the witty, almost "Metaphysical" play
on its roundness. But the claim of the second stanza, that
a rondel may accommodate any subject, even strong emotion, is not borne out in Swinburne's other poems in this
form. The series on the death of a baby, in which the ingenuity of the form makes the expression of grief almost grotesque, exemplifies the problem. Here is the worst of those
poems:

"Etude Réaliste"

A baby's feet, like sea-shells pink,
   Might tempt, should heaven see meet,
An angel's lips to kiss, we think,
   A baby's feet.
Like rose-hued sea-flowers toward the heat
They stretch and spread and wink
Their ten soft buds that part and meet.

No flower-bells that expand and shrink
   Gleam half so heavenly sweet
As shine on life's untrodden brink
   A baby's feet.

Here the strain to rhyme is everywhere evident; the extended comparison to flowers is forced by the need to accommodate such implausible words as "heat" and
"wink," which seem tenuously connected to a baby's feet
despite the metaphor, and the superfluous phrase "we
think" in the first stanza serves only to slip in a rhyme.

Our sense of a poor fit between the formal music of this
poem and its sentimental matter is analogous to the discomfort we may feel in the church music of Haydn and
Mozart, where a solemn text like the *Kyrie* is frequently
set as a bright operatic quartet. But in that case, we can
ignore the inappropriateness of the setting and enjoy the
music on its own terms, while we cannot (alas) ignore the
content of Swinburne's poem. The demands of meaning
constrain the constructive ingenuity of poets, but also
make possible their most dazzling feats of virtuosity; we
are impressed with "The Roundel" because it succeeds
where it might easily have failed. During the tonal period,
harmonic demands provided similar constraints and opportunities for composers employing canonic constructions; the thrill of a Bach fugue lies in the way the strictly
canonic lines nonetheless produce plausible voice-leading
and clear harmony. An atonal canon, by contrast, free
from the requirements of tonality, is somewhat one-
dimensional. As Rosen puts it, "the ingenuity of design of
Schönberg's canons may dazzle and charm, [but] the
virtuosity . . . has vanished with the disappearance of
tonal harmony."

If poets could escape from meaning as composers had escaped from tonality, they might gain a similar freedom of
construction, while risking a similar loss of virtuosity. Not
surprisingly, there were such experiments among the Dadaists: in 1913 the Russian Futurist poet Kruchonykh
published a series of vowels entitled "Heights (Universal
Language)," and a few years later Hugo Ball, leader of the
Zurich Dada circle, published a number of poems containing virtually no words in any language. Here is one:

"Seepferdschen und Flugfische"
[Sea-horses and Flying Fish]

tressli bessli nebogen leila
flusch kata
ballubasch
zack hitti zopp

zack hitti zopp
hitti betzli betzli
prusch kata
ballubasch
fasch kitti bimm

zitti kitillabi billabi billabi
zikko di zakkobam
fisch kitti bisch

bumbalo bumbalo bumbalo bambo
zitti kitillabi
zack hitti zopp

tressli bessli nebogen grügrü
blaulala violabimini bisch
violabimini bimini bimini
fusch kata
ballubasch
zick hiti zopp

Much of the charm of this poem is purely musical. It has strong rhythm ("bumbalo bumbalo bumbalo bambo"), marked cadences ("zack hitti zopp"), variation ("flusch . . . prusch . . . fusch"); we might even describe it as an imprecisely notated, percussive, vaguely pitched piece of minimal music. But even this radical attempt to attain the condition of music cannot escape problems of meaning: it has a title; it includes at least one real word ("fisch"); its coinages (e.g., "violabimini") frequently suggest real words; and it even includes a poetic allusion ("leila" and "blaulala" sound like distortions of the song of Wagner's Rhine maidens, "Weialala leia"). It is at least as impure as a piece of program music; we are encouraged to seek for some kind of meaning, despite the obvious lack of syntax. And this "impurity" is inevitable, for meaning in poetry, unlike tonality in music, is not a system which can be replaced, but a central and inescapable element.

The contemporary inheritors of the Dadaists and the Parnassians, the OuLiPo group in Paris, seem for the most part to recognize this fact. Their leader, George Perec, claims to "reject the noble image of literature as a divine inspiration," preferring to believe that "language is a kind of putty that we can shape," but Perec's shapes, which include a 5,000-letter palindrome and a substantial novel (*La Disparition*) without a single occurrence of the letter *e*, have meaning; indeed, some reviewers of the novel failed to notice its technical trick. Another production from the same group, *Cent Mille Milliards de Poèmes* by Raymond Queneau, shows obvious affinities with serial methods in music. It is a book containing 10 sonnets, each cut into 14 one-line strips; by turning over these strips, the reader may produce 10 different poems, all making sense! Machaut and Compiègne would be proud, for this kind of production is more like their work than like that of Hugo Ball; its ultimate accomplishment is intelligibility.

Despite their ingenuity and charm, the constructive experiments we have been examining were not and are not part of the main stream of Western poetry, in which there has been, on balance, a turning away from virtuosity of all kinds. In 1968, W. H. Auden spoke at the opening of the Salzburg festival, acknowledging his great fondness for music and opera. He said in part:

> . . . In the contemporary world, opera is the only art-form involving words which can still employ the High or Sublime Style. In days gone by, the poet could write in a High Style all by himself. This seems to be no longer possible. The characteristic style of modern poetry, or of the modern poetry I admire, is what Professor C. S. Lewis has termed Good Drab. It is a quiet intimate tone of voice, the speech of one person addressing one person, not a large audience: whenever a modern poet raises his voice, he seems phoney, like a man wearing elevator shoes.

The nostalgia for the High Style here is as real as the recognition of its difficulties. And if Auden seems to be thinking mainly of diction, we should remember that choice of words powerfully affects form and meter, as Edward Sapir argues in a seminal essay on "The Musical Foundations of Verse":

> Whatever be our favorite theory of the nature of diction in poetry, it must be granted unreservedly that any lexical, grammatical, or stylistic peculiarity that is not current in prose helps to accentuate the rhythmic contour if only because the attention is more or less forcibly drawn to it.

Constrained by his perception of modern life to employ a vocabulary and grammar "current in prose," Auden was not unlike Schönberg, who was constrained by his perception of musical truth to abandon the tonality he loved.

But neither composer nor poet yielded to the formless. . . . [Schönberg] eventually won through to a music at once highly formal and uncompromisingly modern, in part through renewing old techniques, in part through inventing new ones. Auden's career involved parallel achievements. He could imitate Anglo-Saxon alliterative verse, Skelton, Swift, or Hardy; he could write short lines, long lines, or lines scanned syllabically; he made such forms as the *ballade,* the *rondeau,* the *villanelle,* the *sestina,* and the *canzone* his own without producing a sense of artificial High Style, using them to accommodate wryly modern comments on politics, theology, and sex. He was rarely guilty of an empty line, preferring the true virtuosity in which formal song enhances expression to the hollow chiming of the "Francophile gaggle of pure songsters." And in a century where, as Sapir complains, "only a very small number of possible forms have been at all frequently employed," Auden invented a number of stanza-forms and rhyme-schemes, some of them as intricately new as serial procedures in music. . . .

THE AXIS OF SYMBOLISM

It is another striking irony that the most thoroughgoing modern attempt to push poetry in the direction of Hanslick's kind of autonomy was perpetrated by a group of poets devoted to his enemy Wagner. In 1887 a group of French Symbolists, normally a mild-mannered lot, actually engaged in a street riot when a performance of *Lohen-*

grin was forbidden by the police. As early as 1861, when Baudelaire published an admiring essay on *Tannhäuser,* there had been interest in and enthusiasm for Wagner among French poets. Wagner's *Lettre sur la Musique* (also 1861), a greatly condensed and somewhat misleading statement of his aesthetic principles, seems to have been the main point of contact, though there were occasional performances of his works in France. Some poets traveled to Germany to hear the operas or meet the great man: Villiers de l'Isle-Adam was such an enthusiast, visiting Wagner in 1869 and 1870. And when Wagner died in 1883, his mythic stature was assured: in the next year Edouard Dujardin organized a new periodical to be called the *Revue Wagnérienne* and secured a promise of a contribution from Stephane Mallarmé.

Mallarmé's contribution, entitled *Richard Wagner, Revery of a French Poet,* appeared in August, 1885; five months later, Mallarmé distilled from its already suggestive imagery a dense and mysterious sonnet on Wagner. In these works, and in the poet's famous Oxford speech, *Music and Literature* (1894), we encounter in all its complexity the "simultaneous need for, and distrust of, music" which Bradford Cook has identified as an important part of the Symbolist movement.

There were real affinities between Wagner and Mallarmé: Mallarmé's interest in producing an all-embracing, dramatic work of art, thought of simply as *"L'OEuvre,"* the work, suggests Wagner's grandiose concept of the *Gesamtkunstwerk;* Wagner's dissolution of tonality and embracing of a fluid and continuous chromaticism suggests Mallarmé's extraordinary treatment of French syntax. But Mallarmé seems not to have understood the drive toward mimesis and literary precision apparent in the device of the *leitmotif;* indeed, his praise of Wagner suggests a view of music somewhat closer to Hanslick's:

> Now at last we have music which is obedient only to its own most complex laws, above all to the vague and the intuitive.

If the sentence ended at the word "laws," we would have a plausible statement of autonomist doctrine, but Mallarmé goes on to celebrate "the vague and the intuitive" as *laws.* This attitude, applied to language, lies at the heart of the Symbolist movement, as Hugh Kenner perceives:

> Mallarmé and Valéry and Eliot felt words as part of that echoing intricacy, Language, which permeates our minds and obeys not the laws of *things* but its own laws, which has an organism's power to mutate and adapt and survive, and exacts obligations from us because no heritage is more precious. The things against which its words brush are virtually extraneous to its integrity. . . . By the end of the [nineteenth] century, in France, whole poems have been made "too subtle for the intellect," held together, as effects are, by the extrasemantic affinities of their words.

Ignoring the musical attempt to name or describe objects, the *leitmotif,* Mallarmé praised Wagner's music, and music in general, for its imprecise, evocative effects. He had attacked the Parnassians for naming objects in poetry,

and he heard in music the suggestiveness he hoped to achieve in words. The speech on *Music and Literature* includes a typical statement of this theme:

> It is not *description* which can unveil the efficacy and beauty of monuments, seas, or the human face in all their maturity and native state, but rather *evocation, allusion, suggestion.*

The Symbolist movement reenacts and extends the Romantic tendency to celebrate and emulate the supposed vagueness of music; Kenner contends that "Symbolism is scientific Romanticism," and the scientific thoroughness with which the Symbolists explored "extra-semantic" devices of sound, undermined syntax, and sealed off their poems from the exterior world of things bears out his claim. In all these activities, the Symbolists imagined that they were moving closer to music.

At the level of basic materials, Mallarmé laments the fact that the sounds of words are not always appropriate to their meaning:

> I am disappointed when I consider how impossible it is for language to express things by means of certain keys which would reproduce their brilliance and aura—keys which do exist as a part of the instrument of the human voice, or among languages, or sometimes even in one language. When compared to the opacity of the word *ombre* [shadow], the word *tenebres* [darkness] does not seem very dark; and how frustrating the perverseness and contradiction which lend dark tones to *jour* [day], bright tones to *nuit* [night]! We dream of words brilliant at once in meaning and sound, or darkening in meaning and so in sound, luminously and elementally self-succeeding.

In poetic practice, this longing for a more musical language led Mallarmé, Valéry, and most of all Verlaine to an intense emphasis on sound. Like older poets, they employed imitative devices: in Mallarmé's sonnet on Wagner (of which more presently), the hero makes his entrance in a noisy fanfare of trumpets achieved by crowding the line with dentals and plosives:

> Trompettes tout haut d'or pâmé sur les vélins . . .
>
> [Trumpets high of gold fainted on velum . . .]

But Symbolist manipulation of sound moved well beyond mere onomatopoeia. In Mallarmé's mature work, subtle patterns of organization by sound are more important than syntax. These patterns are not complex and orderly constructions . . . but unique and particular creations in whose mysterious power to suggest and evoke Mallarmé believed intensely. It is difficult to provide examples because these effects, almost by definition, defy analysis. Perhaps the strongest evidence of their presence is the continued capacity of the best Symbolist poetry to move us, even when we cannot parse it. "Genuine poetry can communicate before it is understood," wrote T.S. Eliot in 1929, thinking of Dante, and in 1942 he applied that highly Symbolist principle explicitly to Mallarmé:

> One of the most obscure of modern poets was

the French writer Stephane Mallarmé, of whom the French sometimes say that his language is so peculiar that it can be understood only by foreigners. . . . If we are moved by a poem, it has meant something, perhaps something important, to us . . . If, as we are aware, only a part of the meaning can be conveyed by paraphrase, that is because the poet is occupied with frontiers of consciousness beyond which words fail, though meanings still exist.

In its resistance to paraphrase, Symbolist poetry attains one aspect of the condition of music. Its dependence on the specific sounds of deliberately selected words, its distaste for naming objects and making statements, its fragmentation of syntax . . . , its tendency to employ words and phrases with a gestural rather than a lexical significance—all the features that make it impossible to translate or paraphrase—produce a close poetic analogue to that feature of music which Hanslick perceived so clearly: that its sounds are not signs of exterior objects but objects in their own right. Thus Cleanth Brooks:

> In the Mallarmean poem the words acquire something of the bulk and density of things; the poem is treated almost as if it were a plastic object with weight and solidity and with even a certain opacity. For the words are not *signs,* transparently redacting ideas. Instead they have acquired something like bulk and mass.

The kind of bulk and mass, we might add, possessed by notes and chords.

All these aspects of Symbolism appear in Mallarmé's sonnet on Wagner:

> Le silence déjà funèbre d'une moire
> Dispose plus qu'un pli seul sur le mobilier
> Que doit un tassement du principal pilier
> Précipiter avec le manque de mémoire.
> Notre si vieil ébat triomphal du grimoire
> Hiéroglyphes dont s'exalte le millier
> A propager de l'aile un frisson familier!
> Enfouissez-le moi plutôt dans une armoire.
> Du souriant fracas originel haï
> Entre elles de clartés maîtresses a jailli
> Jusque vers un parvis né pour leur simulacre,
> Trompettes tout haut d'or pâmé sur les vélins,
> Le dieu Richard Wagner irradiant un sacre
> Mal tu par l'encre même en sanglots sibyllins.

> [The silence already funereal of a veil / Covers with more than a fold over the furniture / Which a collapse of the principal pillar / Will efface with the loss of memory. / Our so old triumphant exercise of the conjuror's book, / Hieroglyphs with which the crowd is excited / At propagating on its wing a familiar thril / Rather hide it for me in a closet. / Hated by the original smiling noise / There burst forth from master lights / To the stage born for their representation, / Trumpets high of gold fainted on velum, / The god Richard Wagner radiating a consecration / Ill-silenced by the very ink in sibylline sobs.]

The Symbolist reluctance to name objects is evident here. A dark theatre is evoked without being overtly described;

Mallarmé's embarrassment about the state of poetry appears obliquely in the desire to conceal the hieroglyphic conjuror's book; and Wagner appears less as a sound piercing the silence than as a light piercing the darkness. The climax of the poem is unquestionably the word *"Trompettes,"* but naming a musical instrument is the least important function of that word. The trumpets stand for Wagner; they delay still further the appearance of his name and stand in grammatical apposition to that name, which is the long-delayed subject of the poem's strongest verb (*"a jailli,"* burst forth); they are golden in color, so as to participate fully in the poem's most basic opposition, that between darkness and light; their gold, in the poem's strangest construction, has "fainted" onto parchment, and the force of that fainting or swooning surely attaches to the speaker as well, for whom Wagner's appearance in a flourish of trumpets is an overwhelming experience. One might mechanically line up the imagery of the poem this way: Wagner's music illuminates poetry as the "master lights" illuminate a dark theatre as gold trumpets illuminate an old manuscript. But the first part of that formula remains entirely unstated, and the other images are not discrete, one-to-one allegory but interpenetrating, fluid symbolism. Our paraphrase does violence to the poem by attempting to restate what Mallarmé evokes or suggests.

But we paraphrase because we need to find meanings

Robert Browning the year of his death.

in poems, just as, at the level of the individual word, we cannot entirely ignore the ordinary significance of *"Trompettes,"* even though that meaning is less important here than the unique symbolic meanings built into this poem, in which the trumpets represent Wagner, shine like gold, and burst forth from the stage lights. Symbolist poetry can effect this kind of shift or enrichment of a word's meaning because a symbolist poem, like a piece of music, is a closed system, in which context is a primary determinant of meaning. Thus T. S. Eliot, in *Four Quartets,* relentlessly repeats his central symbols ("fire," "rose") until we think of them primarily as compressed allusions to their previous contexts, not as names of elements or flowers. When the fire and the rose become one, in the last line of that poem, the effect is like a musical conclusion in which two previously separate themes are shown to be harmonically compatible. That musical effect, not some analogy by form to any particular piece, earns the poem its title. Once we get past the "file-card" approach to Wagner's operas, something quite similar can happen: we may hear a *leitmotif* less as a phrase arbitrarily designating some object or concept ("the sword," "fate") than as a phrase we have heard before in other contexts and are now hearing, aware of its past, in a new context.

Perhaps Mallarmé heard these effects in Wagner, despite his relative ignorance of musical technique. But even in the enthusiastic *Revery* there are uncertainties, jealousies, reservations. Mallarmé points to the "strange defiance hurled at poets by him who has usurped their duty," and to the way the music "penetrates, envelops, and joins [the drama] by virtue of the composer's dazzling will." And the conclusion, from which he drew some of the imagery of the sonnet, depicts the poet as climbing only part of the way up the mountain of abstraction, for a curious reason:

> Oh Genius! that is why I, *a humble slave to eternal logic,* oh Wagner!—that is why I suffer and reproach myself, in moments branded with weariness, because I am *not among those* who leave the universal pain and find lasting salvation by going directly to the house of your Art, which is their journey's end. . . . May I at least have my share in this delight? And *half-way up* the saintly mountain may I take my rest in your Temple, Whose dome trumpets abroad the most extensive dawning of truths ever known and, as far as the eye can reach from the parvis, urges on the steps of your elected as they walk upon the lawns?

That Mallarmé, the chief celebrant of Symbolist aspiration toward music, should find himself, by contrast with Wagner, a slave to *logic* indicates that even he was finally aware of the limits of that aspiration. In the later speech, he describes literature as "our mind's ambition (in the form of language) to define things," and if the method of that defining, for Mallarmé and his inheritors, was a sonorous suggestiveness which owed much to music, the sonnet to Wagner, hazy as it is, achieves a degree of defining much more exact than that achieved by any piece of music—even a Wagnerian *leitmotif.* Eliot would later " . . . insist that a 'musical poem' is a poem which has a musical pattern of sound and a musical pattern of the secondary meanings of the words which compose it, and that

these two patterns are indissoluble and one." This definition, if somewhat clearer than any of Mallarmé's utterances on the subject, remains fundamentally Symbolist in its concentration on sound and secondary meaning; by implication, it also recognizes that *primary* meaning, with its capacity to define things, is the area where analogies between poetry and music fail.

THE AXIS OF POLYPHONY

[A] composer gives meaning to an otherwise neutral or meaningless note by giving it a function in a system: in tonal music, he chooses a key; in twelve-tone music, he devises a row. Symbolist poets, seeking similar control over their words, loaded them with so many functions and meanings that their ordinary denotative functions were obscured, and became less important than particular functions taken on by words in a particular poetic context, a context held together by "extra-semantic affinities" of sound and suggestion. But when a tonal composer wants to alter the function of a note, he tends to isolate it, to state it without harmonic support . . . , while a Symbolist poet alters the meaning of a word by multiplying its secondary associations in order to drown out the dictionary definition, as Mallarmé turns *"Trompettes"* into an explosion of Wagnerian light. The Symbolist poet makes his words more flexible by turning them into simultaneities, polyphonic intersections of multiple meanings.

Twentieth-century advances in linguistics have made all of us more aware of the extent to which all words are simultaneities. A word has a history; it may once have meant something else; it may once have been more overtly or physically metaphorical; it has cousins in the great linked family of languages, brothers within its own. What the Symbolists were trying to do to words—to enrich them, to complicate them, to make them more flexible, to free them from one fixed significance—was an intuition of a feature now recognized as pervasive in language, a feature explored in all its complexity by a poet who treated all languages as a part of Language: Ezra Pound.

Symbolism was an important part of Pound's heritage, to be sure; it alerted him to these matters. Even when writing a brief for increased technical precision by poets, Pound makes a generously inclusive gesture toward Symbolist aesthetics:

> . . . I do not by any means mean that poetry is to be stripped of any of its powers of vague suggestion. Our life is, in so far as it is worth living, made up in great part of things indefinite, impalpable.

But this genuine respect for the indefinite was affected, inevitably, by Pound's close study of troubadour poetry, which he understood far more fully than Swinburne did. In the same essay, "I Gather the Limbs of Osiris" (1911-12), he recognizes the "polyphonic" quality of Arnaut's rhyming technique, as well as the fundamental difference between collaborations in which a composer sets a poem and those in which a poet writes words for a tune:

> It is my personal belief that the true economy lies in making the tune first. We all of us compose verse to some sort of tune, and if the 'song'

is to be sung we may as well compose to a 'musician's' tune straight away.

By 1918, echoing Dante, he has become quite dogmatic:

> Poetry is a composition of words set to music. Most other definitions of it are indefensible, or metaphysical. . . . Poets who will not study music are defective.

During the same period, he was also learning about Chinese poetry, a poetry in which each word was a visible combination of meanings, not adequately describable in the Western notion of "parts of speech." His mentor, Ernest Fenollosa, had written:

> A true noun, an isolated thing, does not exist in nature. Things are only the terminal points, or rather the meeting-points of action, cross-sections cut through possible actions, snapshots. Neither can a pure verb, an abstract motion, be possible in nature. The eye sees noun and verb as one, things in motion, motion in things.

The word as chord in a fused, organic fashion: if Symbolism was scientific Romanticism, the Imagism with which Pound briefly flirted in 1912 was compressed Symbolism. Heinrich Schenker, penetrating to the essence of tonality as tonal music wanted, reduced sonata movements to statements of a triad; his analytical method distinguishes ruthlessly between "foreground" and "background" levels of composition, between decorative "passing tones" or "neighbor notes" and more essential or structural events. But Schenker's reductions appear as analytical charts, while Pound's similar reductions of Symbolism appear as poetry:

"In a Station of the Metro"

The apparition of these faces in the crowd;
Petals on a wet, black bough.

A poem distilled from a much longer draft. The *Cantos* would carry this process further in one way, using Chinese characters and brief phrases in Greek, Italian, and Provençal as allusive reductions of other poetic and historical worlds. Kenner's assertion that this "isolating of single words, not necessarily English" was Pound's "most Symbolist procedure" identifies the source of the notion of the word as chord, but also acknowledges that Pound was to move beyond that notion, though not away from techniques derived from music; indeed, it was by means of his serious study of music that he progressed from the chordal, separate sonorities of Imagism to the intersecting melodic and contrapuntal lines of the *Cantos*. His opinions about music were as definite and cranky as his opinions about literature, and as honestly earned. Learning by doing, just as he taught himself languages by translating their literature and carpentry by building his own furniture, he composed a sort of opera (*Villon*), attempted to play the bassoon (a perfect instrument for him, with its rich, often awkward assortment of overtones), and wrote in 1924 a "Treatise on Harmony" which Kenner has accurately identified as one of the important keys to the *Cantos*.

The most important assertion of the "Treatise" is its Bach-like insistence on the primacy of the horizontal line: chords are not thought of as units (as in Rameau) but as intersections of contrapuntal lines:

> The early students of harmony were so accustomed to think of music as something with a strong lateral or horizontal motion that they never imagined any one, ANY ONE could be stupid enough to think of it as static; it never entered their heads that people would make music like steam ascending from a morass.

This opinion represents more than a prejudice against nineteenth-century chordal practice (though it is certainly that, as Pound's concurrent distaste for the piano and fondness for antique instruments suggests): properly understood, it explains why Pound eventually broke free from Symbolist practice to achieve a contrapuntal poetry. Chordal moments remain, as emphatic chords sometimes punctuate an otherwise linear fugue of Bach, but the *Cantos* are made from "strong lateral or horizontal motions," including the narrative line of the *Odyssey*, the sexual energy of Ovid and Arnaut, the correspondence of early American presidents, and the misguided economics of Mussolini. It is an index of Pound's achievement that no single sample can serve as a touchstone, any more than a few isolated bars can tell us much about a fugue; in both cases, the manipulation of the lines in the total construct is the central accomplishment.

Here as in other areas, Pound stands revealed as the quintessential modern, for twelve-tone music, relentlessly linear, recovers true polyphony from the chordal mists of Impressionism. . . . [Polyphony originated] in the combining of distinct tunes, and no music centered on chords as chords has been able to sustain real development: Debussy's harmonies, as Schönberg realized, were "without constructive meaning" and so served only a "coloristic purpose." Impressionist music, starved of linear motion, had to be outgrown, though even Schönberg profited from its lessons in the handling of color; Symbolist poetry, starved of linear statement, had to be outgrown as well, though Pound salvaged from it some of his most memorable techniques. James Joyce, in prose, moved in the opposite direction: *Ulysses* constructs a giant counterpoint of ancient myth and tawdry Dublin reality, but in *Finnegans Wake* those elements have been fused, at the level of the individual word, into chords. On the first page, "Sir Tristram, violer d'amores," arrives "from North Armorica . . . to wielderfight his penisolate war," and in one word we hear "penis," "penultimate," "peninsular," "isolate," and perhaps "desolate." Other Joycean coinages involve several languages, performing chordally the combinations the *Cantos* perform contrapuntally.

The contrapuntal method . . . is the more authentically musical, not only in terms of the past, but in terms of the present: according to Roger Sessions, in 1960, "composers by and large no longer interested in chords as such," since atonality allows any vertical combination and finds its grammar in the ordering of intervals, not in chordal inflections. It is also a superior literary method, as we may discover by comparing the rewards of rereading the *Cantos* with those of rereading the *Wake*: rereading Joyce, we will gain local explosions of understanding, many of them comic, as we hear more of the component notes in the chordal words from which the work is forged; rereading Pound, we will begin to hear the "long lines" of thought, argument, and design which cross each other in every canto. For Pound had no Symbolist distaste for statement, narrative, opinion; like the Goethe Auden admired, he wished his poetry were truth: "I have tried," he confessed at the end, "to write Paradise." . . .

CONCLUSION

Just as both arts need Romantics and rhetoricians, both need the renewal that comes from aspiration toward each other. Aesthetics is a notoriously imprecise and subjective area, and the relative consensus in the twentieth century about the distinctions between music and poetry is an example of progress; no composer I know of now advocates a return to program music, nor do poets aspire to a hidden medieval complexity of form. But the most characteristic modern problems in both arts may be described as withdrawals into their own conditions. Thus Ernst Krenek, an advocate of "total serialization," in which the composer abdicates his decision-making capacity and allows chance procedures to dictate pitches and rhythms, alleges that what composers have always called inspiration is really chance:

> Generally and traditionally "inspiration" is held in great respect as the most distinguished source of the creative process in art. It should be remembered that inspiration by definition is closely related to chance, for it is the very thing that cannot be controlled, manufactured, or premeditated in any way. This obviously answers the [dictionary] definition of chance as "the absence of any known reason why an event should turn out one way rather than another." Actually the composer has come to distrust his inspiration because it is not really as innocent as it was supposed to be, but rather conditioned by a tremendous body of recollection, tradition, training, and experience. In order to avoid the dictations of such ghosts, he prefers to set up an impersonal mechanism which will furnish, according to premeditated patterns, unpredictable situations.

This is the counsel of despair, and its results, whether generated by humans or machines, are contemptible. Meaning in music is a profound mystery, not finally susceptible to verbal accounts, but surely the "body of recollection, tradition, training, and experience" that a composer brings to his work is a central part of the process that generates meaning. The success of composers like George Crumb in an eclectic, collage style that alludes explicitly to parts of that tradition is only one of many current attempts to leave behind the grimly academic music that resulted from the principles laid out by Krenek and his allies. Some have overreacted, alleging that only by a return to tonality can music regain emotional meaning; this is nonsense. Expressive power in music has survived other changes of the musical language . . . and in the works of Schönberg and Stravinsky, it survives the death of tonality. Nor is the twelve-tone system the only possibility: the stunning music of Krysztof Penderecki is neither tonal nor Schönbergian, but it achieves a dramatic expression of its composer's "recollection. . . . and experience."

On the poetic side, the equivalent problems result from an exaggeration of Auden's healthy perception that the High Style is no longer possible. Some poets have evidently concluded that no style is possible, that a group of words becomes a poem when its author declares it one. The notion that formlessness guarantees authenticity, the apparent principle behind much "little magazine" verse, is as serious an abdication of artistic responsibility as Krenek's reliance on chance. An art that began as one part of *mousike* cannot so abandon its past as to break entirely with construction. Again there is a possible overreaction, the allegation that only a return to rhyme and regular metrics can save poetry; but this notion, like the equivalent advocacy of a return to tonality for music, misses the point. If contemporary poetry has a serious need, it is the need for formal innovation, for *new* principles of construction which can help poets shape, order, and control the expression which is their high calling.

Finally, as I have tried to show here, analogies between poetry and music can help those of us who read and listen as well as those of us who create: by recasting poetic problems in musical terms, or musical problems in poetic terms, we may gain a fresh perspective. The naive student who demands of poetry a breathless enthusiasm, and so suspects any highly formal poetry of infidelity to feeling, may find it hard to cling to his reductive aesthetics if asked to apply them to music. And the advanced literary theorist may also profit from thinking about the relations we have been studying, as W. K. Wimsatt realized:

> A theorist of poetry, being inevitably a person who subscribes to metaphoric and analogical ways of thinking, is in a good position to avoid both the fault of running the arts confusedly together by metaphors which become literal and the opposite fault of cutting the arts off from one another too completely by the denial of all such relations. There are poetic dimensions which can never be described except metaphorically, and to keep open, if only tentatively, the time-honored metaphoric avenues may do something to prevent theoretical discussion from declining into the literalism of a quasi-scientific semantics.

My purpose in this history has been to demonstrate the origins of those "time-honored metaphoric avenues" in the explicit intersections of the histories of music and poetry.

Alex Aronson

SOURCE: "Musical Correlatives," in *Music and the Novel: A Study in Twentieth-Century Fiction*, Rowman and Littlefield, 1980, pp. 1-36.

[*In the following essay, Aronson explores musical analogies in various works of literature and art that can be traced to Pythagoras's concept of universal harmony, and examines how a number of nineteenth- and twentieth-century poets and novelists have attempted to capture the experience of music in their writings.*]

1

In Aldous Huxley's *Point Counter Point*, published in 1928, there occurs a description of a concert at the house of Lord and Lady Tantamount before an audience of invited guests. The orchestra is playing Bach's suite in B-minor, for flute and strings. It is a festive occasion. Conductor, soloists and orchestra perform with gusto and precision. Some of the listeners present respond to the musical ritual by closing their eyes and by a willing surrender to visual associations of a vaguely disturbing though not unwelcome ambiguity. Others, less given to musical rapture, are irritated by what they consider to be either hypocrisy or self-indulgence or both and pass their time observing their variously entranced neighbors. It is a heterogeneous audience portrayed with considerable ironic detachment.

The reader is disconcertingly aware of this sense of aloofness when Huxley comes to describe the music itself. Evidently realizing the inadequacies of language to say anything of any validity whatever about the emotional content of the music, he is being facetiously scientific about it. The flautist "blew across the mouth hole and a cylindrical air column vibrated." The violinists produced a similar kind of vibration in the air when they "drew their rosined horse-hair across the stretched intestines of lambs." While Bach, in Huxley's words, was meditating on the beauty, goodness, and oneness of things, Huxley meditates on music or rather on "the universal concert of things."

The meditation takes place in the mind of Lord Edward who knows a great deal about chemistry and biology and the mathematical relation between them and is not without musical erudition. As an expert in osmosis he is especially interested in, if not actually obsessed, by the problem of "natural harmony" of which musical harmony may be said to be only a small part. In the "total life of the universe", as he likes to call it, the individual life of man or beast is being compared to a melody whose modulations are open to chemical and mathematical analysis. "It's all like music," meditates Lord Edward in his laboratory while performing an experiment on a newt and listening to Bach being played downstairs, "harmonies and counterpoint and modulations."

The composer who creates these melodies is equally exposed to this disconcerting osmotic process. When he dies he is, predictably, "transformed into grass and dandelions, which in their turn had been transformed into sheep" whose intestines, in due time, will be made into strings of various lengths on which these melodies are going to be played all over again. It is an alarming and inhuman prospect. In the course of this osmotic process music is being reduced to air vibrations which in turn shake the *membrana typani*, the interlocked *malleus, incus* and stirrup bones of the ear, "raise an infinitesimal storm in the fluid of the labyrinth", and finally make the hairy endings of the auditory nerve "shudder like weeds in a rough sea." All these complex auditory phenomena, the result of Bach's variously solemn or gay meditations on life can be summed up—and Huxley has no compunctions about doing so—by referring to "Euclidian axioms" which "made holiday with the formulae of elementary statistics. Arithmetic held a wild saturnalian kermesse; algebra cut capers". When, finally, the *Badinerie* with which the suite

in B-minor ends reaches its joyful conclusion the music terminates "in an orgy of mathematical merry-making."

Huxley, who had had a scientific education and possessed considerable musical knowledge, sets his osmotic description of biochemistry, translated into musical terms, and the music of Bach, explored in statistical terms, at the beginning of his novel. It is one of his counterpoints. There will be other forms of osmosis in his novel, based on the relationships between human beings, between the various arts, between the individual and the society he inhabits, between moral compulsions and the political life. The "universal concert of things," defined in parodied scientific terms, but understandable to the lay reader and applied to a well-known piece of music with which most educated readers may be assumed to be familiar, acquires comic dimensions. For what Huxley attempts in this episode, deliberately assuming the role of the all-knowing scientist who rejects the imaginative appeal of music for biochemical formulas, is to shock the reader out of his smug acceptance of music as a convenient release for repressed emotions and irrelevant mental or visual associations, and as a form of exuberant self-indulgence.

The reader is startled as he might well be. He does not know that Huxley's detached objectivity when portraying composer, musician and listener "osmotically" is founded upon a theory of numbers as old as humanity itself and that "the vibrating air columns" in the flute and "the stretched intestines of lambs" had been used for scientific measurements by Pythagoras two thousand five hundred years ago. The reader, ignorant of Pythagoras's discovery that the perceived harmony of musical intervals is paralleled by the simple numerical ratios of spatial distance on the string and the flute, to which may be added the present-day knowledge of the simple relations between the wave frequencies of musical sound, is thus liable to miss the ironic implications inherent in Huxley's veiled reference to ancient theories of measurable harmony in the absurd upper-class setting of twentieth-century London.

Pythagoras's theory of proportion is equally applicable to mathematical measurements, to the movement of stars and to the definition of musical harmony. It may not help the reader of Huxley's novel to achieve a deeper insight into the novelist's concern with osmosis. But it may open up revealing perspectives into the history of ideas—of special interest to the reader puzzled by the recurrent metaphor of harmonious music in the art and literature of all times. For in the language of symbols, created by Pythagoras and the Pythagoreans, harmony is determined by the mathematical relation between numbers and tones, made visible by diagrams and, when recreated on strings of various lengths, translated into chords.

One further dimension is added to this definition of harmony when this system of auditory and visual proportions is found to be embodied in certain planetary constellations and the motions of the spheres with which each planet follows its predetermined course. The belief that this movement of the spheres produces harmonious sound remained intact throughout the Renaissance, accepted as an unquestioned axiom by scientist, musician, artist and poet.

Huxley who by temperament and innate gifts was better qualified for scientific than literary explorations knew all this. He must also have known that his "universal concert of things," meditated upon first by Bach and then by Lord Edward Tantamount, was a parody of the humanist revival in the belief in Pythagoras's "music of the spheres." What he so mockingly resurrected were ancient and medieval analogies according to which scientist and artist alike were assumed to share a common body of musical knowledge and experience.

Huxley thus adds an ironic dimension to the tradition of past great masters of literature among whom Shakespeare comes to mind first of all. Shakespeare's preoccupation with the "universal concert of things" is of the very stuff of which his plays are made. By a curious coincidence he was equally startled at the apparently incongruous relation between the intestines of sheep and the creation of harmony in the soul of man. "Is it not strange," exclaims Benedick, "that sheeps' guts should hale souls out of men's bodies?" Shakespeare, in all likelihood, knew a good deal less about Pythagoras than Aldous Huxley. But from Boethius or possibly Montaigne he had acquired a general, if vague, knowledge of the movement of the planets which, says Montaigne, "in their rolling motion, touching and rubbing against another, must of necessitie produce a wonderful harmonie." Shakespeare also knew that this music of the spheres remained inaudible to men's ears and, thus, could not directly affect their souls. Though constantly reaching out towards harmony man's soul remained insensible—except by indistinct reflection—to those heavenly chords which, according to contemporary belief, determined the "Nativitie of Mortals."

In *The Merchant of Venice,* Lorenzo, an otherwise unprepossessing figure, is heard meditating on music and, in six lines of impassioned poetry, sums up the Pythagorean system of spherical music. Harmony, he declares—and this is quite in line with Pythagorean ways of thinking—is confined to "immortal souls" only. As long as the soul of man is closed in by "this muddy vesture of decay" (V, 1, 64-5), harmony as a universal musical chord, may be at best an aspiration, a spiritual ideal beyond the reach of man. In very exceptional circumstances an echo reaches mortal ears when it may be heard in the speaking voice of a particularly well-integrated person. When Cleopatra describes Antony's voice as being "propertied as all the tuned spheres" she communicates to those around her a sense of personal completeness derived from what, at a later stage, Huxley will rather more prosaically call "the universal concert of things."

In Shakespeare's vision of the harmonious relation between animate and inanimate elements in nature, only man constitutes a sometimes perplexing but mostly agonizing discord. It is man's propensity to think evil and to do evil which is taken as a pretext for "planetary" explanations. Ulysses, in *Troilus and Cressida,* in his speech on degree, blames the planets when they "in evil mixture to disorder wander" (I, 3, 94-5) for political and social upheavals. Jaques's melancholy in *As You Like It,* which threatens the prevailing harmony among the exiles in the Forest of Arden is compared to "discord in the spheres" (II, 7,

6). Iago blames "some planet" that has "unwitted men" (II, 3, 182) for the quarrel which woke Othello and tore him from Desdemona's side. Leontes, in *The Winter's Tale,* in search for a rational motive to justify his sudden and inexplicable fit of jealousy, ominously points at "a bawdy planet that will strike / When 'tis predominant" (I, 2, 201). The most explicit of them, Edmund, in *King Lear,* dismisses any sort of "spherical predominance" as a mere excuse for "knaves, thieves, and treachers" to indulge in their crimes as if, he mockingly observes, they acted "by heavenly compulsion", while "drunkards, liars, and adulterers" consider themselves at liberty to commit their sins "by an enforc'd obedience of planetary influence" (I, 2, 127).

Aldous Huxley who felt at home in Shakespeare's plays no less than in biochemistry knew that the drawing of musical analogies—whether in terms of planetary motion or simple mathematical measurements—was a commonly accepted practice among writers and artists throughout the Renaissance. Both concord and discord could be conceived visually in keeping with Pythagoras's diagrams. They could also be recreated, as it were, by painters who, assuming the existence of the universal harmony of things, might and indeed did attempt a reflection of it through the application of color and design on canvas. Thus, in Ficino's theory of the image, the Pythagorean belief in the music of the spheres is being transposed from the realm of music to that of art. For according to Ficino, "the number and proportions of a thing preserved in the image something of the power of the spiritual essence which it embodies."

The artist in search of visual perfection frequently looked in music for valid analogies. Pythagorean theories provided the mathematical foundation. Spherical music stood for a symbolic representation of the essence of harmony. All that could be measured and divided into numbers and proportions, whether of visual or auditory import, became part of the universal harmony. If, as Shakespeare implied, man is the only discordant element in nature, then it is the artist's business to recreate harmony in the very teeth of man's attempts at self-destruction. Leonardo da Vinci, in one of his *Notebooks,* establishes this analogy between painting and music in terms of measurement and proportion. "Although objects observed by the eye touch one another as they recede, I shall nevertheless found my rule on a series of intervals measuring 20 *braccia* [about 28 inches] each, just as the musician who, though his voices are united and strung together, has created intervals according to the distance from voice to voice, calling them unison, second, third, forth, and fifth, and so on, until numbers have been given to the various degrees of pitch proper to the human voice . . . If you say that music is composed of proportion, then I have used similar meanings in paintings, as I shall show."

Such analogies abound in the history of art and art criticism. Each age developed a different musical criterion appropriate to the new cultural context. Thus, Poussin in the seventeenth century relates his paintings to Greek "modes" of musical composition and, in a well-known letter, promises his friend that "before a year is out I hope to paint a subject in [this] Phrygian mode" which, he believes, is particularly suitable for "horrible subjects." Whistler, some two centuries later, insists on designating his works as "arrangements" or "harmonies" and, finally, decides to call them "symphonies" or "nocturnos." In more recent times abstract painters found no difficulty in establishing even closer analogies between the abstract patterns of sound and design by merely calling a painting by the name of a musical composition. Familiarity with the music, represented on the canvas as an abstract configuration of lines, shapes, and colors, would enable the spectator to respond in a predictable and desirable way. When Mondrian labelled a painting *Broadway Boogie-Woogie* (painted in 1942/43) he aimed at an "orchestration" effect with its popular dance rhythm, pitch, and volume. However, the music remains unheard. Shapes and colors cannot be made to sing. The spectator who has never witnessed the playing of a boogie-woogie may conceivably associate this painting with the first of Bach's Brandenburg Concertos. The deliberate avoidance of any actual likeness leaves all aesthetic options open. Similar doubts arise when one looks at Kandinsky's abstract paintings which were supposed to be attempts at translating Wagner's music into visual terms.

Pythagoras's system of numbers and proportions continues to haunt the artist in his search for harmonious structure. More even than the painter, the architect may discover analogies "in depth" between his planning an edifice and musical composition. Both arts assume the existence of a "third" dimension which in music is called an interval and in architecture free, unused space. This relation between mass and intervals establishes a criterion of harmony depending on spatial measure very close to the original Pythagorean assumption of a "universal concert of things." Le Corbusier who came from a family of musicians accepts the Renaissance view that architects should go to school to study science as well as music. "More than these thirty years past," he wrote, "the sap of mathematics has flown through the veins of my work, both as an architect and painter; for music is always present within me." The somewhat baffling realization that architecture exists in space while music exists in time is no obstacle to analogical thinking of this kind. In mathematical terms both interval and silence are alike measurable. Music has been called "architectural" on more than one occasion. And if the analogy is not extended into extravagant absurdity (as in Huxley's novel which started this whole train of thought), the listener to music, responsive to geometric form and algebraic progression, may indeed receive an auditory image of some harmonious essence beyond anything that ordinary everyday life can provide. Within the context of the history of ideas the Pythagorean concept of harmony—though modified by modern scientific thought—is still with us.

2

Color and sound as used by the artist have this in common that they tend away from reality as a mere sense impression. A painting which does not go beyond a true-to-life imitation of reality ceases to be art however exact the measurements and proportions. Sound which merely imitates nature is not music even if pitch, volume, and interval approximate as closely as humanly possible to the various noises originating in man's natural surroundings. What painter and musician, then, create is an illusion of reality as perceived through the imagination. What the eye sees and the ear hears—the painting or the piece of music—is thus retranslated by the spectator and listener through a variety of sense impressions into the language of the mind. Frequently—and by a process which Pythagoras was the first to suggest—the illusion created by a painting evokes musical analogies while a piece of music is made "visible" through visual associations originating in the listener's memory. As long as the two arts keep within the framework of illusion the likelihood of their actual fusion into a compound work of art remains a distinct, if theoretical, possibility.

Throughout the nineteenth century, writers, both in poetry and prose, explored this likelihood as a matter of increasing practical application. As their medium was language they made use of discursive speech to rationalize the need for the fusion of the arts. The logic of their argument was indeed unassailable. What other medium but the word could establish a significant link between color and sound by a detailed analysis of the "complete," if illusory, work of art? Only human speech could supply, in terms of intellectual concepts, a new meaning to harmony in the arts considered as the most accomplished of all illusions.

One of the earliest and most curious attempts at describing such a fusion of the arts of painting and music occurs in a novel by Balzac, called after its protagonist, *Gambara*. Gambara is a failed musician who, provoked into telling the story of his life, expounds his theories of music in a remarkable mixture of Pythagorean and Bergsonian concepts. "Nature" is, indeed, the criterion applied to both arts. The human and the nonhuman, according to him, are interchangeable because "music is both a science and an art. Its roots plunge into physics and mathematics, and this makes it a science." Like Huxley a hundred years after Balzac he is also concerned with the vibrations of air columns which "find in us corresponding elements that answer, that vibrate sympathetically, and that are capable of enhanced significance by the application of thought." This explains, continues the musician, why the physical phenomena of sound "match ideas within us according to our capacities." Proust who will elaborate upon this in a somewhat subtler way and with greater psychological insight will add little to the musical theories of Balzac's frustrated musical hero.

But this is merely the beginning of the story. Warming up to his subject he provides a popularized version of the synesthetic effect of music on the visual imagination of composer and listener. For, he asserts, "in music the instruments play the role of colors used by the painter," because mathematical laws apply to both the arts alike. The ideal composer, says Gambara, would translate "the phenomenon of light, vegetation, and life itself" into harmonious sound. He repeatedly refers to the listener's "dormant memories," a very Bergsonian concept indeed, which would be awakened to a new life by the fusion of auditory and visual elements. What this new life will be like is not spelt out in so many words. The reference here is evidently to the synesthetic effect of music, the evocation of a different kind of sense impression from that which one commonly associates with the experience of listening to a melody played on an instrument or sung by a human voice.

It is this evidence of fused sense impressions that De Quincey tried to provide in his *Dream-Fugue,* published as part of his *English Mail Coach* in 1849. Conceivably his addiction to opium had something to do with this remarkable dream-vision of man's mortality on earth. De Quincey's inspired piece of writing eliminates any distinction between what the ear hears or the eye sees, between actual and imaginative listening, between sight and insight. The dream which is the subject of this "fugue" releases the dreamer from the prison in which reason holds him captive. Thus he is enabled to experience sense impressions on a multiplicity of levels at a time. Music is at the very center of the experience. It evokes the response of all the senses simultaneously, as it were, and is equally assimilated by the sense of sight, smell, taste, and touch. Music is all-pervading because it is the stuff of which dreams are made. While reading the dream fugue, the reader becomes aware of an uncanny sensation, that of listening to a piece of music that has never been composed and of seeing visions that have never been painted except in the writer's overwrought imagination. This creation of a synesthetic universe provides the most coherent illusion of an ideal work of art. Such transcendental experiences had already, a few years earlier, been defined by another opium addict, Edgar Allan Poe, in terms of the poetry he wished to write. In a letter, probably written to his publisher in 1831, Poe defines poetry as consisting of "indefinite sensations, to which end music is an *essential,* since the comprehension of sweet sound is our most indefinite conception. Music, when combined with pleasurable ideas, is poetry."

No one could have agreed more readily than Baudelaire who adapted and translated the work of De Quincey and Poe into French. In his own poetry, perfumes, colors, and sounds establish confusing correspondences, sense impressions are no longer what they seem to be, and the harmonies thus created are of an esoteric nature. In his various essays on Poe he praises the American poet for having revealed new possibilities of self-realization through his exploration of the kinship of poetry and music. The following passage chosen at random reflects the enthusiasm with which Baudelaire greeted this revelation of a "paradis artificiel" where the poet and the musician would share in equal measure an intimation of immortality. "It is at the same time through poetry and beyond poetry, through and beyond music, that the soul perceives the splendors that lie beyond the grave." When, some years later, Baudelaire discovers the music of Wagner he sees in the multiple associations of word and sound as part of a stage-representation, the fulfillment of his own dream of a synesthetic experience through art. While, on the one hand, Wagner's operas remind him of medieval Mystery-plays they also evoke the masterworks of painters, "those great visions which the Middle-Ages spread across the walls of its churches or wove into its magnificent tapestries." This was written in 1857. Some thirty years later Walter Pater in England, without referring to Wagner and his synesthetic vision of a new form of art and drama, made music the ultimate criterion by which the excellence of art—be it poetry or painting—would be judged.

According to Pater not only does "all art constantly aspire towards the condition of music," music itself is assumed to be a principle of integration compelling the poet or painter to strive for that unity of matter and form which is most completely realized in a musical work. "In its consummate moment," continues Pater, "the end is not distinct from the means, the form from the matter, the subject from the expression; they inhere in and completely saturate each other, and to it, therefore, to the condition of its perfect moments, all the arts may be supposed to tend and aspire. In music, then, rather than in poetry, is to be found the true type or measure of perfected art." We do not know, nor does Walter Pater tell us, what kind of music he had in mind when he wrote this. He certainly was influenced by the French *Parnassiens* and the esthetic theories advanced by Baudelaire a generation earlier. But taken out of its historical context Walter Pater's insistence on music as the ultimate criterion of beauty repeats in the language of late nineteenth-century estheticism what humanist writers on art had said centuries before: painting and music are a transmutation of nature in terms of proportion and measurement, while poetry is speech attuned to some transcendental universal harmony. All the arts alike express man's attempt at translating the discord prevailing in the quotidian experience of life into harmonious proportions.

Twenty years after Pater's essay on Giorgione where these lines occur, Mallarmé, in language visionary and obscure, dreams of an art "which shall complete the transposition into the book of the symphony," an art, he implies, which would encompass all that is most perfect in speech and in sound, "drawing to itself all the correspondences of the universe, the supreme Music." This dream was shared by a whole generation of writers both on the continent and in England. John Synge who, in all likelihood had met Mallarmé during his stay in Paris imagined a new type of writer who would write of human life as "a symphony and the translation of this sequence into music, and from music again, for those who are not musicians, into literature."

The temptation to find in music a universal criterion for *all* sense-impressions was particularly hard to resist whenever a writer's surrender to physical sensations became an end in itself. Baudelaire had pointed the way. Others followed, convinced that music had the power of transforming any sensation into sound. Thus one finds Huysmans in his notorious *A Rebours (Against Nature)* describing Des Esseintes' collection of liqueurs as a musical instrument "providing his palate with sensations analogous to those which music dispenses to the ear." To give but one example, "Dry curacao . . . was like the clarinet with its piercing, velvety note." The analogy is carried to absurd lengths. String quartets might be played by a subtle combination of various liqueurs. Major and minor keys were equally at his alcoholic disposal. And, to crown it all, "he even succeeded in transferring specific pieces of music to his palate, following the composer step by step, rendering his intentions, his effects, his shades of expression, by mixing or contrasting related liqueurs, by subtle approximations and cunning combinations."

The symbolist movement in poetry and in prose used music as a catalyst. The least tangible of all the arts, it was therefore open to a larger variety of emotive associations than painting, sculpture, or architecture. It enabled the artist to fuse sound and color, melody and design, volume and shape, evoke more complex responses than any single art could ever produce, and, finally, directly appeal to sense impressions in such a way that the whole of the human personality was involved in the esthetic experience. Symbolism, as understood around the turn of the century, on the continent and in England, implied an intricate set of musical significances which neither poet nor novelist could do without. Speech itself had to be musically oriented. The poetic line as a melody, the novel as a sonata, became commonplaces of literary criticism. Literary and musical structures were found to originate in some common primordial principle of artistic creation. The "universal concert of things" underlying all symbolist doctrines on art was being trivialized until any analogy, however absurd, between music and the other arts was found to possess an innate validity no longer subject to rational argument. Huysmans' digression into the musical equivalents of the various liqueurs is as good an evidence as any for the symbolist claim of some ultimate harmony based on sense impressions rather than on Pythagorean mathematical insight.

3

W. B. Yeats who started his poetic career as a disciple of Walter Pater and an admirer of Mallarmé was the first to realize the pitfalls of a symbolist vision of art founded on the predominance of music over the other arts. Repeatedly he looked upon music as a threat to the poet's spoken word. He "would have no one write with a sonata in his memory," he wrote in 1906, for "music is the most impersonal of things and words the most personal, and that is why musicians do not like words." In the same essay he asserts that there should be only so much music in poetry "as [the poet] can discover on the wings of words." Being himself tone-deaf he warns the reader against what he considers to be the illusory perfection of the musician's art. And when, still in the same essay, he compares the "spoken" music of Villon's verse when recited to the accompaniment of a guitar to a professional musician performing on a piano, "it is the piano, the mechanism, that is the important thing, and nothing of you means anything but your fingers and your intellect."

In earlier writings Yeats visualized a kind of poetry recital in which the meaning of the word would be stressed by the use of a musical instrument in the background. For though poetry and not music is the object of such experiments, as he calls them, he dreams of some primordial scene where the distinction between word and music had not yet become established in the minds of the listeners, a scene "of wild-eyed men speaking harmoniously to murmuring wires while audiences in many-colored robes listened, hushed and excited." The "wires" are those of a "psaltery"—"a beautiful stringed instrument" producing

what Yeats called "natural" music to which he had been introduced by Arnold Dolmetsch who at the turn of the century was one of the first to revive interest in old musical instruments and their music.

A few years before his death, Yeats was still convinced of the superiority of poetic speech over musical intonation. In October 1936, shortly before a BBC broadcast of some of his poems, he discussed the possibility of using a drum or other musical instrument between stanzas or between poems. The idea was "to heighten the intensity of the rhythm, but never behind the voice," for, he explained, "there must never be an accompaniment, and no words must be spoken through music." The musical notes "must never be loud enough to shift the attention of the ear."

In spite of all misgivings Yeats's preoccupation with music and particularly the singing voice never ceased. Some of his most accomplished poems make use of musical metaphors in a context of significant human experience, not a mere accompaniment but the very stuff of which poetry itself is made. "Sailing to Byzantium" (1926) is, very largely, a poem about the life of the poet translated into musical terms. It begins with the "sensual music" of "generation," leading up to the poet's own attempt at "singing" and his conviction that there is no "singing school but studying / Monuments of its own magnificence." The poet, therefore, decides to sail to Byzantium to meet there his "singing masters" who will teach him how to translate his anguish and desires into an "artifice of eternity." Such an artifice is the golden nightingale singing of the passing of time to the lords and ladies of Byzantium. This appears to be the subtlest attempt made by a poet to realise Mallarmé's vision of an art that would draw to itself "all the correspondences of the universe, the supreme Music." For though Yeats certainly knew little enough of Byzantine music, his "Sailing to Byzantium" traces the transformation of poetry into music as part of his own experience of growing old, an expression of his awareness that in order to outlast time the sensuous music of youth must be replaced by the immutable, timeless singing of the golden bird.

When, at a still later stage, Pythagoras is introduced into Yeats's poetry, it is as a mathematician and philosopher rather than as the discoverer of the "music of the spheres." He appears in three of Yeats's major poems. In the first "Among School Children," he is rejected outright, together with Plato and Aristotle. Yeats contemptuously refers to their teaching as "Old clothes upon old sticks to scare a bird" and chooses "passion, piety, or affection" instead. Within the context of a poem written in praise of "the great rooted blossomer," this rejection of all philosophical systems has an inner consistency of its own. There is no place for "golden thighed Pythagoras" who "fingered upon a fiddle-stick or strings / What a star sang and careless Muses heard" among Yeats's images of "labour" which is both blossoming and dancing. Yet, the body of the dancer is "swayed to music." Conceivably, the reader of the poem may think there would have been no dance had there been no music. And if it is in music that all dance originates, would this not be true as well of all the other arts, of which dance is the most perfect physical embodiment?

Six years later Yeats writes one of his most humorous, but also one of his most disturbing poems, "News from the Delphic Oracle" (1934). Here Pythagoras is found in the company of Plotinus but also of Niamh and Oisin, transplanted without any more ado from Irish mythology to classical Greece. What these four have in common is that they are bored and in great need of love. "Tall Pythagoras," no better than the other "golden cadgers," "sighed amid his choir of love" (possibly an ironic reference to the music of the spheres), yawned and apparently fell asleep. It is against the background of this spectacle of sterile longing that Yeats resurrects the "dolphin-torn and gong-tormented sea" of an earlier poem ("Byzantium"), a paradise of sexual promiscuity ruled over by a different sort of music. For

> Down the mountain walls
> From where Pan's cavern is
> Intolerable music falls.

The implication of how "intolerable" this music is, is made fairly clear in the lines that follow. It is a music of the body rather than the spirit, no more measurable in terms of numbers. Pythagoras, defeated by the intensity of lust, is contrasted to the god Pan, mathematical contemplation to the laughter of the "ecstatic waters" where nymphs and satyrs "copulate in the foam."

A year before his death, in his poem "The Statues," Yeats returns once more to ancient Greece. Tormented by his vision of "The Second Coming," by the threat of "Asiatic vague immensities" overcoming all that Western Europe has created in art and literature, he writes a poem on the origin of the European sculptural tradition which, he now believes, must be preserved. The basis of that tradition is to be found in the Pythagorean theory of numbers which provided sculptors with a mathematical basis for their work.

> Pythagoras planned it. Why did the people stare?
> His numbers, though they moved or seemed to move
> In marble or in bronze, lacked character.

One remembers Yeats's dislike of "character" as part of the vocabulary of psychological realism. It is in keeping with his worship of the body "swayed in music" that "passion" is now substituted for character. Pythagoras, in this remarkable poem, achieves a kind of paradoxical resurrection. He helped sculptors to model "with a mallet or a chisel . . . these Calculations that look but casual flesh" and thus created "live lips upon a plummet-measured face." By making the creation of these statues possible Pythagoras also "gave women dreams and dreams their looking-glass."

During the last year of his life Yeats expressed, this time in prose, his belief that only a reborn affirmation of harmony as the sole criterion of Western art can save Europe from final self-destruction. "There are moments when I am certain that art must once again accept those Greek proportions which carry into plastic art the Pythagorean

number, those faces which are divine because all there is empty and measured. Europe was not born when Greek galleys defeated the Persian hordes at Salamis; but when Doric studios sent out those broad-backed marble statues against the multiform, vague, expressive Asiatic sea, they gave to the sexual instinct of Europe its goal, its fixed type." "The Statues" of which this passage is an exact comment reflects Yeats's final return to mathematical proportion as the first step to be taken by the artist on his way towards perfection. What is being reaffirmed here is an archetypal vision of the oneness of all created life whether it be in painting, sculpture, or indeed in music. There is here that affirmation of stillness which pertains to music no less than to statuary, to poetry no less than to the visual arts. If Yeats does not mention music in this remarkable poem it is because his preoccupation with the human body as a criterion of perfect living proportion precluded all that is abstract and impersonal, and devoid, as he then thought, of powerful instinctual urges. By the time he wrote this poem he must have become aware of the perils to the human soul in Pan's "intolerable music." Like the waters which echoed this music it is "ecstatic," and like the dolphins on whose back the slim adolescents had come to play in the sea it is "brute."

T. S. Eliot's poetry is less visually oriented. In his poetry musical images and metaphors abound. The musical experience furnishes him with some of his most persuasive "objective correlatives." Thus human beings and their response to the environment in which they live come to life as if they were musical themes, counterpoints of thinking and feeling, harmonious chords or shrill dissonances in an orchestral piece of always surprising and, at times, bewildering variety. Thus Eliot's use of music in his poetry leads to a widening of the reader's range of response in terms of both formal and thematic significances.

Eliot's critical pronouncements reveal an equal preoccupation with musical patterns and content. Not altogether surprisingly, a survey of musical analogies in Eliot's critical work discloses his suspicion of inadequacy on the part of the man of letters who goes to music in order to find critical support in his attempt at perfection in art for which literary criticism has not yet developed a suitable vocabulary. Thus, in the winter of 1933, Eliot in an unpublished lecture delivered in New Haven, Connecticut, is supposed to have said that he had in his own poetry, attempted "to get beyond poetry as Beethoven, in his later work, strove to get beyond music." What Eliot meant by getting "beyond poetry" is unambiguously stated in the same lecture: it is an attempt to let poetry speak for itself "with nothing poetic about it," or poetry "so transparent that we should not see the poetry." Eliot does not tell the reader what Beethoven was doing when he "strove to get beyond music." But the analogy clearly refers to a criterion of absolute esthetic purity where poetry—as Eliot would like to write it—would "stand naked in its bones," combining within itself the ideal perfection of both poetry and music.

Neither words nor ideas need be sacrificed to this perfection. Meanings may not only be preserved but may acquire additional levels of significance. In an early essay on "Ezra

Pound, his Metric and Poetry" (1917) Eliot makes his position clear. Dismissing the merely emotional appeal of music in the poetry of Shelley or Swinburne as being nearer rhetoric "than to the instrument," he concludes, "For poetry to approach the condition of music (Pound quotes approvingly the dictum of Pater) it is not necessary that poetry should be destitute of meaning" as long as there is "a definite emotion behind it." Frequently, when speaking of Shakespeare's plays Eliot implies the existence of a significant relation between musical pattern and poetic response, between a formal structure, musically conceived, and the moods, emotional disposition or frame of mind it evokes in those who witness a performance of the play.

Thus, in 1951, in a lecture entitled "Poetry and Drama" Eliot visualizes "a kind of mirage of perfection of verse drama, which would be a design of human action and of words, such as to present at once the two aspects of dramatic and of musical order." Referring, in particular, to the garden scene in *Romeo and Juliet* he discovers there "a musical pattern . . . as surprising in its kind as that in the early work of Beethoven." Though Eliot is concerned here with the poetry spoken on the stage rather than with plot or character, he finds a kind of musical perfection in the scene which is the result of Shakespeare having discarded "the stiffness, the artificiality, the poetic decoration, of his early verse," thus achieving "a simplification of the language of natural speech" and a perfection of poetry brought about by the integration of the musical pattern into the poetry of this scene. Already in an earlier essay, "The Music of Poetry," Eliot had advised the poet to go to music in order to acquaint himself with musical techniques and, in particular, with the effect that such techniques may have on the reader of poetry. Eliot here stresses "possibilities for verse which bear some analogy to the development of a theme by different groups of instruments; there are possibilities of transitions in a poem comparable to the different movements of a symphony or a quarter; there are possibilities of contrapuntal arrangement of subject-matter."

The poet whose only tool is the word may find it impossible to compete with the multiplicity of thematic variations inherent in the use of diverse instruments to express a large variety of musical ideas or emotions. Musical analogies which refer poet or reader to musical patterns, communicating no meaning beyond what the sounds themselves express, may ultimately convey a sense of the inadequacy of all speech when measured by musical criteria. For this sense of the completeness of revelation that great music transmits finally silences even the most articulate among literary critics. Nothing of any intellectual validity whatever can be said about such music. Words themselves appear irrelevant, and the most erudite commentary merely a trivial appendage to the wordless message of perfection conveyed through the musical experience. Northrop Frye, for instance, confesses to such "a feeling of definite revelation" after listening to a Palestrina motet or a Mozart Divertimento. "Here," he says, "is a simplicity which makes us realize that the simple is the opposite of the commonplace, a feeling that the boundaries of possible expression in art have been reached for all times." And T. S.

Eliot wrote, in answer to a letter by Stephen Spender who was reminded of Beethoven's posthumous music when reading "Ash Wednesday," "I have the A-minor Quarter on the gramophone and find it quite unexhaustible to study. There is a sort of heavenly or at least more than human gaiety about some of his later things which one imagines might come to oneself as the fruit of reconciliation and the relief after immense suffering; I should like to get something of that into verse before I die."

4

The novelist's concern with the musical experience is necessarily and for similar reasons of an equivocal nature. As long as he could portray the thoughts, feelings, and sense impressions of his fictitious characters without recording the inwardness of this experience, the musician or the listener to music differed from other characters only in so far as they were "musically" oriented. The way they listened and responded to music could still be described "realistically" and in the language of everyday life. In this way the musical experience, just like any other esthetic experience, could be absorbed by the reader's imagination. There was no need to render it as pertaining to different levels of consciousness which partook of this experience.

Musical analogies which refer poet or reader to musical patterns, communicating no meaning beyond what the sounds themselves express, may ultimately convey a sense of the inadequacy of all speech when measured by musical criteria. For this sense of the completeness of revelation that great music transmits finally silences even the most articulate among literary critics.

—Alex Aronson

Increasingly the novelist, at the beginning of the twentieth century became aware of states of consciousness where sensory impressions and thought are inextricably intermingled, a pleasing twilight of indefinite sensations which pertains more to the realm of poetry than of prose. Language itself had to undergo a process of transformation in order to integrate this newly discovered reality. Realizing that all human speech, instead of communicating the true nature of experience, introduces an inevitable element of alienation, the novelist in the early decades of this century attempted the almost impossible: to capture the moment of emotional intensity (for example, when listening to music) at the very instant of sudden and inexplicable revelation. Time itself, the fleeting moment of experience, the instant of perception, had to be given verbal permanence.

The challenge the modern novelist had to face was to render the time-bound nature of music and thought into speech which (though itself part of the flow of time) would be "always present." Eliot's self-evident assertion, in

Burnt Norton, that "Words move, music moves / Only in time" appears to establish a common denominator applicable to both writer and musician. For the patterns formed by words and the patterns formed by music originate in the same silence that existed before and will again be after the words and the music have reached the listener's consciousness. It is, says Eliot, the "stillness" out of which all art grows. He compares it to a Chinese jar which "still / Moves perpetually in its stillness." "Not," he adds, "the stillness of the violin, while the note lasts" but rather the "co-existence" of past, present and future in both music and poetry. The true predicament of the artist, then, is to render simultaneously "the moment in and out of time," that is the moment experienced first as time passing and then as a still point in time. In "The Dry Salvages," Eliot, attempting to formulate the predicament, refers to music "heard so deeply / That it is not heard at all, but you are the music / While the music lasts." There is, thus, no common criterion applicable to both musical time and the time it takes to "describe" it, and the time needed to read such a description. Different levels of consciousness are involved. The poet rightly assumes that sound actually heard and sounds echoing in the memory may evoke different responses. It is the novelist's rather than the poet's business to disentangle stillness from movement, silence from sound, memory from experience. Eliot is a dependable guide in this apparently contradictory welter of incompatibilities. For when, at the end of *The Four Quartets,* he concludes that "Every phrase and every sentence is an end and a beginning," he may well mean the musical phrase and the sentence spoken by the poet, both equally and in the same proportion moving perpetually in their stillness, time-bound as well as timeless, existing in a present no longer measurable by the clock.

As far as the novelist is concerned this implies a re-assessment of visual reality in terms of sounds heard in time or remembered "out of time." Eyesight is replaced by daydream, the world of objects by the imaginative recreation of a universe in which material phenomena undergo a seachange and are transformed into fantasy. Human beings, landscapes and the sensations they evoke are "seen" as through a mist, floating on the surface of memory, no longer subject to the controlling authority of the conscious mind. Finally, a sequence of sounds played or sung at a certain pitch and rhythm or a change from major to minor key are found to evoke a variety of associations and memories, frequently, though not always, related to sense impressions received in the past. It is this complex interrelationship between the musical experience and the mental process it initiates that stimulates the novelist to investigate the twilight where the encounter between music and human consciousness takes place.

Novelists, repeatedly and in growing numbers ventured into that no man's land of the mind although they realized, sooner or later, that what had been initially composed as a sequence of sounds, for instance a melody which could be musically defined by such simple concepts as key, pitch, or rhythm, did not lend itself easily to transposition into even the most imaginative and expressive of prose-fictions. Though words may be used "musically," in the sense in which symbolist poets attempted to supply a musical equivalent for an experience without altogether dispensing with language, they cannot transform time-bound reality into a timeless continuum. Yet novelists in search of linguistic correspondences for human experiences inaccessible to logical analysis, were increasingly attracted to that borderland of the mind where concepts, values, and attitudes, acquired, as it were, musical features, where a sequence of thoughts was shown to be related to some imaginary modality of sounds and an emotion could be rendered through consonance or dissonance or in a minor or major key. Underlying this search was the assumption that the semantics of human speech correspond in some intangible way to the semantics of musical composition, that it might, after all, be possible to translate the meaning of a melody into linguistic terms. As far as psychic processes were concerned it seemed almost self-evident that especially through music could significances be revealed which lay below the threshold of consciousness.

Yet language is a singularly inept vehicle of expression when it is called upon to say something adequate about the content of a musical work. The modern novelist whose concern with music grew out of his preoccupation with mental processes could hardly have recourse to technical language and write a musicologist's novel. Any attempt at transposing musical content into a prose freed of semantic rigidity and thus approaching the fluidity of musical progression, turned the musical experience into an objective correlative used by the novelist to portray states of mind or a particular emotional setting which everyday language was unable to convey. The musical experience was thus used as a mirror with the help of which a character could be viewed, a relationship portrayed, an idea realized through the sounds that were found to be most expressive of what this idea stood for within the context of the novel. Musical content appeared to be the obvious equivalent for the vague and amorphous psychic states for which language had not evolved any adequate vocabulary. The novelist who aimed at unravelling the complexities of the human soul discovered in music an esthetic equivalent for the interior monologue, expressiveness uncontaminated by the ambiguity of verbal communication.

This discovery led to a dilemma that no novelist could solve in a satisfactory way: the writer of fiction had no other means of communicating the pure expressiveness of music but through linguistic equivocation. If music was indeed an objective correlative for experiences that could only be expressed in nonverbal terms, the novelist became increasingly aware of the fact that—as Susanne Langer puts it—though music is indeed the "logical expression" (though not the cause or cure) of feelings, yet "it has its special ways of functioning that make it incommensurable with language." The writer's experiments with musical content translated into the prose of his fiction were, thus, from the outset, of a most problematic nature.

No one was more troubled by the absence of an objective correlative which would denote musical meaning than Marcel Proust. Throughout his monumental novel he makes it abundantly clear that though various individuals may indeed associate a musical phrase with memories of experiences colored by sense impressions of a nonmusical nature, these memories need not in any way correspond to the musical statement made by the composer but be mere approximations to the "meaning" underlying the music. The reader may easily be misled by Proust's concern with the effect of Vinteuil's "petite phrase" on Swann and Marcel into assuming that Proust's impressionistic technique of transcribing the musical phrase into a literary image served as an end in itself. For the music that accompanies the reader from volume to volume is generally interwoven in a stream of only partially controlled memories. The melody repeatedly appears as an indistinct floating image, wrapped in a mist of associations derived from the hearer's past. In Proust's imagination this melody is "ensevelie dans la brume" (entombed in fog) or "noyée dans le brouillard" (drowned in mist). Already at the beginning of the novel after having heard Vinteuil's sonata only once "it remained almost wholly invisible to me, like a monument of which its distance or a haze in the atmosphere allows us to catch but a faint and fragmentary glimpse."

Images of indistinctness that crowd in on Swann's mind when he remembers Vinteuil's music have no material equivalents in reality. Their frame of reference is and remains throughout the book the hearer's memory. Thus, he would like to remember the music as one recalls any other sense impression "of light, of sound, of perspective, of bodily desire." Similarly, Marcel, long after the little phrase had been absorbed in his waking consciousness, remembers it as "the expression of certain states of the soul analogous to that which I had experienced when I tasted the madeleine that had been dipped in a cup of tea." If we compare this passage with a much earlier one where the effect of the little phrase on Swann is described as being "closely akin . . . to the pleasure which he would have derived from experimenting with perfumes" there is little to differentiate between Proust's various uses of the musical correlative in terms of either taste or smell or sight. Memories resurrected through musical associations, may differ in intensity of sensuous perception, one sense impression being replaced by another, the indistinctness of a monument perceived from far away in a haze may be substituted by the dreamlike vision of a woman, "this invisible creature whose language I did not know and whom I understand so well—the only stranger that it has ever been my good fortune to meet"; it is with such impressions as these that the reader may place Vinteuil's little melody in a world of experiences which constitutes at best only an image, "a reflection, like water or glass" (these are Swann's words), the shadow of a shadow, and, more often than not, a memory remembered, a dream recaptured an infinite number of times.

An objective correlative, however, does not cease to carry manifold significances because of its indistinctness. In memory, as in dreams, relation between things and people assume blurred and confused shapes. The memory of a melody may indeed appear at one time as the scent of "roses in the evening," at another as "the cooing of a dove," and again as "an invitation to partake of intimate pleasures." What these memories have in common constitutes the dimly perceived reality of the melody in so far

as remembered sense impressions may at all correlate music with actually experienced events in one's life. Proust is naturally inclined towards metaphorical speech—as if in memory there is no place for any sort of explicit analogy—enabling the reader to reexperience the event itself though in a somewhat modified and distorted way. Thus while Vinteuil's sonata is described with the help of such adjectives as "slender, frail, tender, rustic, pale, candid, and timid," the first bars of the septet by the same composer recall the image of "continuous, level surfaces like those of the sea, in the midst of a stormy morning beneath an already lurid sky . . . in eery silence, in an infinite void . . ." The transition from adjectival writing to the evocation of an objective correlative implies a greater maturity of expression on the part of the composer and of receptivity on the part of the hearer. The homeliness of the earlier work has grown into the complexity of Vinteuil's old-age composition. Obscurity and indistinctness have been transformed into a clarity of vision which, as in a flash of lightning, illumines a world "so harsh, so supernatural, so brief, setting athrob the still inert crimson of the morning sky above the sea."

Proust's observations on the musical experience and the way it affects the central characters in his novel create a psychological universe of considerable complexity. Listening to music, and especially to the kind of music represented by Vinteuil's little melody, produces an intensely emotional response from which the rationality of the thinking mind is excluded. The melody, from this moment onward, is a haunting presence which takes possession of the hearer's memory. All those events of his life that are overshadowed by violent emotions such as jealousy or physical desire, the fear of losing a beloved person or the anguish caused by such a loss, become entangled in the web woven by the melody. With the regularity of a conditioned reflex the emotion may be provoked by the music just as the emotion itself may arouse the memory of the corresponding musical phrase. Emotional and musical arousal are thus almost identical. In memory they become one and indivisible—so much so that when a particular piece of music ceases to exercise its fascination upon the hearer, the emotion usually associated with it is no longer found to be of any validity. The hearer, in effect, asks himself how it could have happened that at any one time this music represented the unbearable anguish of jealousy and cannot remember how the association between the musical phrase and his jealousy came into existence.

Considerations such as these are liable to interfere with the even flow of the narrative. The problem that Proust faced—and Joyce was going to solve in his own way—was how to transcribe not merely the melody but the memory of it and the meaning it acquired when being remembered in reasonably intelligible prose. If as Proust says at the beginning of the novel, all musical impressions are *"sine materia"* and speaks of the memory of these impressions as "the presence of one of those invisible realities," he thereby implies that the novelist has no way of translating this immaterial and invisible reality which is music into the language of fiction except in terms of subjectively experienced sense impressions.

This is what Proust repeatedly and insistently does. As the novel progresses these images, scents, and tastes become progressively more lucid. As Vinteuil's music grows more complex under the shadow of his approaching death, his melodies communicate a message which requires no material explanation as it provides what Proust calls "the profound equivalent . . . of how the composer heard the universe and projected it far beyond himself." The novelist's attempt to render this profound yet invisible "equivalent" in words makes Proust speculate as to the possible relationship between the composer's musical and the novelist's literary projection of reality into the work of art.

The first of what might be called the major post-Wagnerian novelists, he was also the first to formulate what happens when the novelist adapts musical content to the writing of a work of fiction. Beginning and end of the novel no longer depend on the chronological development of plot and characters but on the introduction of themes, *le leitmotif* as Proust so characteristically calls it, which prepare the reader for what is to come. It is through the elaboration of a given theme that duration in the novel acquires depth and substance. The transposition of musical into literary themes involves the writer in a process of "musicalization." "It is impossible," writes Proust, "to foresee the total work by the first volume alone which makes sense only in terms of those that follow . . . It's similar to those [musical] pieces which one does not realize to be leitmotifs when one listens to them in isolation at a concert in an overture."

Proust unquestionably assumes that musical themes originate in the unconscious and that, therefore, the writer of fiction by introducing leitmotifs into his novel has to make them intellectually accessible to the reader. This may explain the following remark made by him in an interview: "If I presume thus to reason about my book, it is because the book is in no way a work of reason: it is because its most trifling details have been supplied to me through feeling; because I first of all noticed them deep down within myself, without understanding them, having as much trouble to change them into something intelligible as if they were foreign to the work of the intellect just as is—how shall I put it?—a theme of music."

Marcel's desire to write a novel different from any work of fiction written previously is mentioned for the first time in the last volume of *A La Recherche* which, Proust tells a friend in a letter, "was written immediately after the first chapter of the first volume. All the 'inbetween' part was written subsequently." The inspiration to write the novel came to him while listening to Vinteuil's music which, in effect, is first mentioned in the first volume (when Swann hears "la petite phrase") and occurs again in the last volume when Marcel listens to Vinteuil's septet in which the same musical phrase has acquired greater complexity and significance. The idea which progressively takes possession of Proust's mind was thus already there, at the very beginning of *A La Recherche*. The growth of that idea to its final realization, the writing of a work of fiction, is what this novel is all about. It is also a deliberate attempt on the part of the novelist to prove to himself and his prospective readers that music can aspire to the "condition of language," and this not necessarily by a contrapuntal modulation of themes or a set of variations, but rather by transposing the novelist's (in this case Marcel's) experience of reality—within the limitations imposed by time, place, social context and the writer's own temperamental predilections—into music.

By the time the reader finishes reading Proust's novel, he may well ask himself whether any dividing line can be drawn between music remembered and music heard, and between sense impressions evoked by music and a musical theme emerging from any one of these impressions. Such questions are themselves valid critical comments on the relationship between the art of the story-teller and that of the musician in an age where clear distinctions between the two are no longer called for. When, for example, Proust writes that "a prolonged smile is like a sustained G sharp" he relates a psychological observation to the tonal quality of a particular sound or chord as if the two—his observation of the smile and his awareness of the singular effect produced by the playing of a chord in G sharp on an instrument—constituted one and the same kind of tonality. Such a correlation may be indefensible by either musicological or psychological criteria, yet it paves the way for further experiments with language when the G sharp will not "stand for" or be "like" a prolonged smile but *be* the smile itself. Proust indeed asks himself whether this is not what might have happened "if there had not come the invention of language, the formation of words, the analysis of ideas, the means of communication between one spirit and another." Remembering the precision with which music could express what lies below the threshold of consciousness, Proust describes his return to language "from the unanalyzed" as "so inebriating, that on emerging from that paradise [i.e. music], contact with people who were more or less intelligent seemed to me of an extraordinary insignificance."

Once the novelist claims the validity of musical equivalents for words and thus transcribes the reality he perceives around him by way of tonality or atonality, there is nothing to stop him from rendering his observation of human nature in terms of sound symbols. Such a musical correlative will be—like sounds themselves—immaterial and invisible. No objective correspondences will help the reader in his search for a valid psychological frame of reference. The only significance that can be attributed to such sound symbols will emerge from the way "the composer [and now also the writer] heard the universe and projected it far beyond himself."

E. M. Forster, in an early novel, does precisely this. At a loss for the right word when describing the effect of a musical composition, in this case Beethoven's last piano sonata, opus 111, on performer and listener, he can only suggest with the help of nonmusical allusions what this music meant to those "whom breeding and intellect and culture have alike rejected," the outsider, the misfit, and the rebel. He, first of all, admits his inability to "translate [the composer's] visions into human words, and his experiences into human action." He realizes that there is passion, "but it could not be easily labelled." Yet, having ventured so far, he makes Lucy, in *A Room With a View* (1908), play the first movement of this extraordinary sonata before a musically indifferent audience, remarking, however, that while she was playing she divested herself of her everyday identity and entered "a more solid world" where "she was then no longer either deferential or patronizing; no longer either a rebel or a slave." She became what Forster designates as "tragical," in the sense that she extracted from the music she played a conviction of ultimate victory. For, adds Forster, Beethoven's sonatas "can triumph or despair as the player decides, and Lucy had decided that they should triumph." In its final analysis it is not Lucy but Forster who decides that Beethoven's last piano sonata should embody the "victory" with which this novel ends. The reader who is assumed to be familiar with this piece of music may, after some hesitation, approve of Forster's choice and will ask no more questions. He is, however, left with a literary statement of considerable ambiguity.

A Room With a View was written long before Forster became acquainted with Proust's work. When, in 1927, his *Aspects of the Novel* was published Proust's concern with music is given a very prominent place. The "little phrase," according to Forster, creates "a homogeneous world" as it provides the reader with "complete orientation"—"stitching Proust's book together from the inside" as part of the protagonist's memory. When Forster writes about novels and the part music plays in them he is more concerned with "rhythm" than with the actual content of any given musical piece. It is the relation between various "blocks of sounds" that he calls rhythm. It enters the mind without being actually audible. To recreate this rhythm in the writing of a novel, "this common entity, this new thing . . . the symphony as a whole" is Forster's ideal of fiction-writing. "Music," he continues, "though it does not employ human beings, though it is governed by intricate laws, nevertheless does offer in its final expression a type of beauty which fiction might achieve in its own way." Forster calls this new type of literary structure "expansion," a new way of looking at people which will emphasize the inwardness of all conscious response to music. The musical experience is the essence of this "expansion" which will lead the novelist away from mere story-telling and characterization towards a deeper psychological truth which no novelist in the past ever ventured to portray.

The more the writer realized the need for increasingly subtler forms of evocation than the prose of everyday life was capable of expressing, the more was he likely to look in music for an objective equivalent for emotions that might have been more adequately expressed through poetry as they were too complex to be conveyed in conventional speech. Virginia Woolf, in an early story, probably written in 1921, before she became acquainted with Proust's work, illustrates this search for a new language when she describes the effect of a string quartet by Mozart on a listener, evidently herself, tortured, as she then was, by a sense of loss and inner division. Here, the writer intentionally dispenses with description of the music in such ambiguous terms as "victory" or "despair," but evokes the texture of the music through images relating to her own past. Thus the prose she employs shifts from interior monologue—"How lovely goodness is in those who, stepping lightly, go smiling through the world"—to nature associations originating in the hearer's memory—"Fountain jets; drops descend . . . washing shadows over the silver fish . . . leaping, splashing, scraping sharp fins"—to encounters in the past charged with intense emotion—"I see your face, I hear your voice . . . What are you whispering? Sorrow, sorrow. Joy, joy. Woven together, inextricably commingled, bound in pain and strewn in sorrow."

The experimental nature of this short, fragmentary sketch is of considerable interest to anyone concerned with the gradual dissolution of conventional thematic structure and its effect on the portrayal of human thought in contemporary fiction. The novelty of this approach to the hearer—the music being the medium through which human consciousness is portrayed—points backwards to Proust's impressionistic literary experiments with music as well as towards Joyce's more daring representation of the stream of consciousness still to come. In later novels Virginia Woolf frequently refers to the virtually unrestricted expressiveness of music as contrasted to the limiting syntactical speech patterns employed by writers attempting to render emotions which elude the dictionary meaning of words. How, indeed, she asks herself in *The Waves,* can "falling in love for the first time" be denoted by words? Admitting the novelist's inability to say anything worth saying about the emotions aroused by first love, she calls for music to help her in her task. "Here again there should be music . . . a painful, guttural, visceral, also soaring, lark-like, pealing song to replace these flagging, foolish transcripts—how much too deliberate! which attempt to describe the flying moments of first love."

More disillusioned than in 1921 Virginia Woolf now knew that this desire for a linguistic transformation of sounds into words must remain unfulfilled. Yet a few pages later she once more returns to a musical image, this time to evoke characters rather than emotions. Are not, she asks, characters as they appear to us in life open to musical definitions, each one standing for a different instrument, a melody or chord? How much simpler it would be, Virginia Woolf meditates, to render the complexity of human nature in terms of a musical composition, thereby preserving the immediacy of musical communication in the face of the corrupting effect of all human speech? Thus she desires nothing better than to "compose" her characters until the imprecision of their human qualities is transformed into the exact polyphonic pattern of a symphony. Again in *The Waves* Virginia Woolf lets a character (Bernard) deliberate upon this form of musical revelation claiming for music a wider imaginative scope than descriptive prose can provide. "How impossible to order them rightly, to detach one separately, or to give the effect of the whole—again like music. What a symphony with its concord and discord, and its tunes on top and its complicated bass beneath, then grew up! Each played his own tune, fiddle, flute, trumpet, drum or whatever the instrument might be." This passage was written, Virginia Woolf notes in her *Diary,* after she had listened to a Beethoven quartet one night and had felt the need to "merge all the interjected passages into Bernard's final speech." Music, actual or imaginary, rounds up a novel the rhythmic quality of which very nearly approaches the pattern of a musical composition, the ebb and tide of the sea, the coming and going of the waves.

Proust's experiments in the use of musical material in the thematic structure of his fictitious universe became known to the English reading public while E. M. Forster and Virginia Woolf were writing their novels. There seems little, if any, actual influence on the part of the French writer on either of them. When they *did* read him they felt over-awed by the gigantic dimensions of his work. They also discovered in *A La Recherche* a similar concern with musical form and content as had been tentatively expressed in their own novels. The one writer—hardly at all familiar with Proust at that time—who had become even more deeply aware of the need to turn the writing of fiction into something resembling musical composition—was Thomas Mann. Even before Proust had finished writing his novel Mann had already published a number of short stories dealing with the devastating effect of music on individuals of an artistic temperament.

As early as 1918, Thomas Mann who called himself a man of letters (*ein Literat*) characterized his work as that of a musician, comparing it to the writing of Schopenhauer and Nietzsche who were "men of letters as well as musicians, but the latter more than the former." As for his own writings, "they were good scores (*Partituren*), everyone of them." Not without pride Mann added that "musicians also loved them; Gustav Mahler, for example, loved them." When, in 1938, Thomas Mann was asked to write an introduction to an American edition of his stories, he insisted on the need for a musical interpretation of his early work. He traced the development in his use of musical themes which, as a true Wagnerian, he calls *leitmotifs*, from being a mere structural device to a psychological concept underlying all his later prose fiction. In *Tonio Kröger*, he says, "I first learned to employ music as a shaping influence in my art. The conception of epic prose-composition as a weaving of themes, as a musical complex of associations, I later on largely employed in *The Magic Mountain*, only that there the verbal leitmotif is no longer as in *Buddenbrooks* employed in the representation of form alone, but has taken on a less mechanical, more musical character, and endeavours to mirror the emotion and the idea." Once more, in 1953, Mann, writing an introduction to the American edition of *The Magic Mountain*, emphasizes the specifically musical enjoyment which the awareness "of the structural coherence of the thematic fabric" gives the reader. In order to derive the greatest benefit from the novel, Thomas Mann, in effect, suggests that the book should be read twice. For only the second time is the reader able to "really penetrate and enjoy its musical associations of ideas. The first time the reader learns the thematic material; he is then in a position to read the symbolic and allusive formulas both forwards and backwards." Finally, in a letter to Theodore Adorno whose advice proved so helpful in the writing of *Doctor Faustus*, Mann returns to his first assertion made in 1918, that he has "always been adept at literary music-making, [has] felt myself to be half-and-half of a musician" and has "translated the technique of musical interweaving to the novel."

The concern with musical form and content on the part of such different novelists as Proust, Forster, Virginia Woolf and Thomas Mann, in the first half of the twentieth century is no coincidence. Nor can it be attributed to such purely musical influences as Wagner's music and the impressionism of Debussy and his school. All of them alike turned to the musical experience as embodying a primordial vision of human life expressed through rhythm or melody, pitch or volume, concord or discord. In their search for a faithful representation of the inwardness of experience, be it through individual consciousness or through the awareness of social identity, they discovered in music a metaphor of harmonious coexistence. As in the modern novel the Pythagorean planets increasingly drift "in evil mixture to disorder," the wish to make sense of that disorder impelled the novelists to apply a musical perspective to the mind of man. Thus the musical experience in the modern novel is no longer a merely literary device to create a congenial background to events and characters, but has itself become an essential ingredient of contemporary fiction writing. The vibrating air column of the flute and the vibrating strings on the violin acquired an almost metaphysical significance. What was involved was not only the application of scientific theories to the esthetic laws governing the creation and performance of music, but a new vision of the way human consciousness functions, expressed in the novel through a fusion of sense impressions and thought, the texture of sounds and the texture of words, music and speech.

MUSICAL FORM/LITERARY FORM

Steven Paul Scher

SOURCE: "Notes Toward a Theory of Verbal Music," in *Comparative Literature*, Vol. XXII, No. 2, Spring, 1970, pp. 147-56.

[*In the following essay, Scher uses a passage from Aldous Huxley's* Point Counter Point *to illustrate his conception of verbal music, and he also describes the characteristic features of verbal music in prose.*]

Aesthetic speculation about the interrelationship between literature and music has been regarded as a fascinating and elusive, if somewhat suspect, border area of literary criticism. In their influential *Theory of Literature* René Wellek and Austin Warren voiced particularly strong scepticism concerning the possibility of successfully combining the "sister arts." Yet the numerous examples of "great artists in the field of literature [who] also feel a need for going beyond the limits of their art and striving after a symbiosis with the other art" cannot be ignored; and today more and more scholars agree that musico-literary relations promise a rewarding territory for critical exploration within the larger framework of the study of literature and the other arts. It is another matter that the legitimacy of such study as an integral branch of comparative literature continues to be contested. Many comparatists still only recognize investigations which deal with comparison of literary works "beyond national boundaries." Controversy concerning the legitimacy of critical treatments of literature and the arts will hopefully subside as more comparatists endorse Henry H. H. Remak's broader definition, according to which

> Comparative literature is the study of literature beyond the confines of one particular country, and the study of the relationships between literature on the one hand and other areas of knowledge and belief, such as the arts . . . philosophy, history, the social sciences, the sciences, religion, etc., on the other. In brief, it is the comparison of one literature with another or others, and the comparison of literature with other spheres of human expression.

With the publication of Calvin S. Brown's *Music and Literature: A Comparison of the Arts* (1948), the comparative investigation of the sister arts was given a thorough theoretical foundation. In view of the variety of recent contributions no doubt largely inspired by Brown's comprehensive study, there is every reason to assume that critical attention to the relations of literature and music will continue to grow. In spite of such promising prospects, however, relevant contributions still appear which are disappointingly limited in scope. For instance, in a recent publication by the Modern Language Association aimed at informing a wide audience, *Relations of Literary Study: Essays on Interdisciplinary Contributions* (1967), Bertrand H. Bronson reveals an astonishingly narrow conception of the future tasks of musico-literary criticism. He concludes his article, "Literature and Music":

> We need studies of forms poetico-musical, with equal attention to both sides wherever possible, and of individual examples of such forms: masques, operas and oratorios, odes, songs. We need readable studies of musical theory and musical history. We need musical criticism written responsibly but with a sense of style, for the non-professional reader. . . . And finally, we could do with more, and more scholarly, biographies both of musicians and literary men with a strong musical concern.

However general in formulation, most of Bronson's desiderata strike me as belonging to the domain of musicologists rather than of literary scholars. In addition to the topics suggested by Bronson involving music *and* literature (vocal music), literature *in* music (program music), and musical biography, there are indeed many other areas which would benefit more from further exploration by literary critics. I am referring particularly to manifestations of musical influence in literature such as word music, structural and formal parallels between the two arts, musical influences on literary periods and on individual authors, and literary synaesthesia.

In the following I shall focus on a hitherto largely neglected aspect of the problem of music *in* literature, the phenomenon of verbal music. . . . [I will use the definition of verbal music] developed in my *Verbal Music in German Literature* (1968) as a point of departure. . . .

I.

By verbal music I mean any literary presentation (whether in poetry or prose) of existing or fictitious musical compositions: any poetic texture which has a piece of music as its "theme." In addition to approximating in words an actual or fictitious score, such poems or passages often suggest characterization of a musical performance or of subjective response to music. Although verbal music may, on occasion, contain onomatopoeic effects, it distinctly differs from word music, which is exclusively an attempt at literary imitation of sound.

The above definition indicates that verbal music is a *literary* phenomenon. Its texture consists of artistically organized words which relate to music only inasmuch as they strive to suggest the experience or effects of music, while necessarily remaining within the boundaries of the medium of literature. Realizing the ultimate impossibility of a transformation in basic artistic material, poets and writers who nevertheless attempt verbalizations of music must be content if they succeed in achieving a relatively true verbal semblance of the musical medium.

As an illustration of the type of literary texture I have in mind, I shall quote the following passage of verbal music from Aldous Huxley's *Point Counter Point:*

> Meanwhile the music played on—Bach's Suite in B minor, for flute and strings. Young Tolley conducted with his usual inimitable grace, bending in swan-like undulations from the loins and tracing luscious arabesques on the air with his waving arms, as though he were dancing to the music. A dozen anonymous fiddlers and cellists scraped at his bidding. And the great Pongileoni glueily kissed his flute. He blew across the mouth hole and a cylindrical air column vibrated; Bach's meditations filled the Roman quadrangle. In the opening *largo* John Sebastian had, with the help of Pongileoni's snout and the air column, made a statement: There are grand things in the world, noble things; there are men born kingly; there are real conquerors, intrinsic lords of the earth. But of an earth that is, oh! complex and multitudinous, he had gone on to reflect in the *fugal* allegro. You seem to have found the truth; clear, definite, unmistakable, it is announced by the violins; you have it, you triumphantly hold it. But it slips out of your grasp to present itself in a new aspect among the cellos and yet again in terms of Pongileoni's vibrating air column. The parts live their separate lives; they touch, their paths cross, they combine for a moment to create a seemingly final and perfected harmony, only to break apart again. Each is always alone and separate and individual. "I am I," asserts the violin; "the world revolves round me," calls the cello. "Round me," the flute insists. And all are equally right and equally wrong; and none of them will listen to the others.

> In the human fugue there are eighteen hundred million parts. The resultant noise means something perhaps to the statistician, nothing to the artist. It is only by considering one or two parts

at a time that the artist can understand anything. Here, for example, is one particular part; and John Sebastian puts the case. The Rondeau begins, exquisitely and simply melodious, almost a folk song. It is a young girl singing to herself of love, in solitude, tenderly mournful. A young girl singing among the hills, with the clouds drifting overhead. But solitary as one of the floating clouds, a poet had been listening to her song. The thoughts that it provoked in him are the Sarabande that follows the Rondeau. His is a slow and lovely meditation on the beauty (in spite of squalor and stupidity), the profound goodness (in spite of all the evil), the oneness (in spite of such bewildering diversity) of the world. It is a beauty, a goodness, a unity that no intellectual research can discover, that analysis dispels, but of whose reality the spirit is from time to time suddenly and overwhelmingly convinced. A girl singing to herself under the clouds suffices to create the certitude. Even a fine morning is enough. Is it illusion or the revelation of profoundest truth? Who knows? Pongileoni blew, the fiddlers drew their rosined horsehair across the stretched intestines of lambs; through the long Sarabande the poet slowly meditated his lovely and consoling certitude.

In this excerpt, which constitutes an early high point of his novel, Huxley focuses on a performance of Bach's Suite in B minor, the central event of a musical soirée given by Lady Edward Tantamount. Through its metaphorical content this interpretive description of orchestral music also provides a symbolic moment of reference for the developing plot structure. Just as Proust renders in words the recurrent "petite phrase" from the Andante movement of Vinteuil's (?) sonata for violin and piano in *A la recherche du temps perdu,* Huxley describes a musical experience as a significant instant in the narrative sequence of *Point Counter Point.* He creates a multidimensional spatial-temporal impression of the music which—after this initial detailed description—he takes up later in the novel and develops further in its spiritual and emotional impact. . . .

To create literary works of art, the poet (in this designation I include the writer of poetry as well as of prose) projects his imagination to his readers by means of conventional or innovative literary structures and techniques. In all literary evocations of music the poet supplements his ordinary source (i.e., poetic imagination) with direct musical experience and/or a score, or allows his imagination to be inspired by music; he thus assumes the role of transmitter, rendering (suggesting, describing, or creating) music in words.

In word music, which aims at poetic imitation of musical sound, onomatopoeia—broadly defined—serves as the poet's primary technique of verbalization. The poet who chooses to imitate musical structures and devices achieves his goal through attempting the superimposition of musical structures on a literary work or through experimenting with musical devices in a literary medium.

Rather than capturing a poetic semblance of musical sound or imitating musical form, verbal music aims primarily at poetic rendering of the intellectual and emotional implications and suggested symbolic content of music. Two basic types of verbal music can be distinguished. When the poet draws on direct musical experience and/or a knowledge of the score as his source we may speak of *re-presentation* of music in words: he proceeds to *describe* either a piece of music which he himself identifies or which is identifiable through inference (e.g., the Huxley passage cited above). Poetic imagination alone, inspired by music in general, serves as the source of the second type of verbal music; and it involves direct *presentation* of fictitious music in words: the poet creates "a 'verbal piece of music,' to which no composition corresponds."

II.

In his *Sound and Symbol,* Victor Zuckerkandl observes: "The encounter with the tonal world includes the three fundamental experiences of motion, time, and space." His statement holds true, I believe, not only for the listener's encounter with the world of music, but also for the poet's attempt to capture this encounter and communicate it to his readers in passages of verbal music, especially in prose.

Gotthold Ephraim Lessing's pioneering efforts to compare literature and the plastic arts are well known; and the distinctions in his *Laokoon oder über die Grenzen der Malerei und Poesie* (1766) are considered fundamental to modern aesthetics and art criticism. Less common knowledge, however, is that he also planned to complete a similar treatise on the relations between literature and music. It is not inconceivable that he might have included considerations of musico-literary phenomena such as verbal music.

In his persuasive article, "Spatial Form in Modern Literature," Joseph Frank describes Lessing's conclusions about the limitations of the respective artistic media (*Laokoon,* chapter 26) as follows:

> Form in the plastic arts, according to Lessing, is necessarily spatial because the visible aspect of objects can best be presented juxtaposed in an instant of time. Literature, on the other hand, makes use of language, composed of a succession of words proceeding through time; and it follows that literary form, to harmonize with the essential quality of its medium, must be based primarily on some form of narrative sequence.

And comparing the media of music and the plastic arts, Susanne K. Langer summarizes:

> Music unfolds in virtual time created by sound, a dynamic flow given directly and, as a rule, purely to the ear. This virtual time, which is an image not of clock-time, but of lived time, is the primary illusion of music. In it melodies move and harmonies grow and rhythms prevail, with the logic of an organic living structure. Virtual time is to music what virtual space is to plastic art: its very stuff, organized by the tonal forms that create it.

I suggest that, as a result of a unique set of aesthetic conditions, instances of verbal music, especially in prose, are capable of transcending the limitations of the literary medium and are able to create a semblance of several artistic media combined while actually confined to only one, the literary.

Effective attempts to express literature in the medium of music generally accomplish a quasi-visual representation of "literary" space within the temporal confines of music. Effective attempts to express music in the medium of literature, on the other hand, generally accomplish a representation of the illusion of "musical" space (i.e., the impression of space invoked by a musical composition) through visual and spatial imagery within the temporal confines of literature.

—Steven Paul Scher

Painting, sculpture, architecture, music, and literature, generally considered the major fine arts, may be classified into two types: visual and auditory. The visual arts (painting, sculpture, and architecture) are static and primarily exist in space. Though essentially spatial in nature, they also strive to be comprehended in time, i.e., they try to create the illusion of time. The auditory arts (music and literature) are dynamic and primarily exist in time. Though essentially temporal in nature, they also strive to be comprehended in space, i.e., they try to create the illusion of space. Thus each of the two types of art attempts to overcome the ontological restrictions of its own mode and tends toward the aesthetic conditions of the other type.

However unrealizable the reciprocal tendencies of the various arts may be, their realization can at least be attempted or approximated by one type of art in the medium of the other. In this sense we may speak of an essential affinity between the visual and the auditory arts as reflected in the numerous mixed categories and interrelations possible between the arts such as painting in literature, music as painting, painting in music, literature in painting, etc.

Both literature and music are temporal art forms and thus share an intrinsic aesthetic impulse to be comprehended in space. Approximation of the one art in the medium of the other might well enhance the degree of successful "spatialization" under primarily temporal conditions and relationships. With these assumptions in mind, tentative conclusions may be drawn, I think, concerning the phenomenon of reciprocal evocability in the sister arts. Effective attempts to express literature in the medium of music generally accomplish a quasi-visual representation of "literary" space within the temporal confines of music (cf. the phenomenon of program music). Effective attempts to express music in the medium of literature, on the other hand, generally accomplish a representation of the illusion of "musical" space (i.e., the impression of space invoked by a musical composition) through visual and spatial imagery

within the temporal confines of literature (cf. the phenomenon of verbal music, creating "the illusion of 'musical' motion within a 'musical landscape' ").

What concrete aesthetic implications for verbal music can be inferred from the preceding speculations? As demonstrable in the Huxley passage quoted above, instances of verbal music are most effective if they are able to conjure up unique combinations of spatial and temporal relations while firmly anchored in the narrative context. Successful authors of verbal music achieve an ingenious intermingling of the basic principles of spatial and temporal perception to a degree of simultaneity which ultimately creates a verbal semblance of a pictorial (three-dimensional) artistic medium beyond the limitations of aesthetic perception characteristic of any one art form.

A definite retarding effect on the narrative movement in a given work emerges as a characteristic feature of prose passages of verbal music. In context the result of such retardation consists in the creation of a literally static moment which tends to arrest and suspend the narrative flow for the duration of the verbal evocation. This moment effects a temporary rest in the progressing, horizontal sequence of the narrated events. In fact, within the confines of the particular instance, the horizontal narrative sequence tends to slow down to a vertical standstill and assume spatial dimensions, suggesting a semblance of "literary" and "musical" space combined.

A passage from Thomas Mann's *Buddenbrooks,* the presentation of Hanno Buddenbrook's final ecstatic improvisation on the piano concluding his interminably long day at school, may serve as an example for such a retarding effect of verbal music. This music description toward the end of the novel is strategically situated to convey symbolic significance in structure as well as in theme. Structurally, it constitutes the culmination of the long process of artistic refinement in the Buddenbrook family; the intrusion of musical influence gradually destroys the vitality of the competitive commercial spirit of the family and signifies irreversible decline. In the form of a musical allegory, full of erotic overtones and reminiscent of the "Liebestod" music of Wagner's *Tristan,* Hanno's improvisation directly anticipates the agony of the chilling penultimate chapter describing the symptoms of typhus, the boy's fatal illness. And thematically, for the last time before the final catastrophic events—Hanno's death and the subsequent collapse of the Buddenbrook household—the passage reiterates the major motifs of the novel which bring about the disintegration of the family.

Are retardation, spatiality, verticality, and a generally static quality characteristic only of passages of verbal music? Nature descriptions, evocations of specific paintings, detailed portrayals of objects, essayistic digressions, philosophical speculations and the like also seem to accomplish a similar illusion within the narrative sequence of fiction. In successful verbal evocations of music, however, the chief distinguishing trait might be that the created feeling of spatiality mingles simultaneously with a definite impression of progressive movement. Simultaneity, i.e., the momentary fusion of movement in "musical" space (horizontality) and standstill in narrative time (verticality), may be said to provide a linguistic framework which lends itself more readily to symbolic representation than the other constituents of narration capable of retardation. By force of a virtually unlimited potentiality for symbolic reference, instances of verbal music possess a greater synthesizing power. Authors can utilize this potentiality in order to integrate retrospective as well as anticipatory allusions and other correspondences present in narrative structures.

Nathaniel Mackey

SOURCE: "Sound and Sentiment, Sound and Symbol," in *Callaloo,* Vol. 10, No. 1, Winter, 1987, pp. 29-54.

[*In the following essay, Mackey analyzes writings by Jean Toomer, William Carlos Williams, Ralph Ellison, and Wilson Harris—in whose work music is an important element—largely basing his analysis on the ideas about music expressed in Steven Feld's* Sound and Sentiment, *in which music is associated with loss and social dislocation, and Victor Zuckerkandl's* Sound and Symbol, *in which music is accorded mystical significance.*]

Senses of music in a number of texts is what I'd like to address—ways of regarding and responding to music in a few instances of writings which bear on the subject. This essay owes its title to two such texts, Steven Feld's *Sound and Sentiment: Birds, Weeping, Poetics and Song in Kaluli Expression* and Victor Zuckerkandl's *Sound and Symbol: Music and the External World.* These two contribute to the paradigm I bring to my reading of the reading of music in the literary works I wish to address.

Steven Feld is a musician as well as an anthropologist and he dedicates *Sound and Sentiment* to the memory of Charlie Parker, John Coltrane, and Charles Mingus. His book, as the subtitle tells us, discusses the way in which the Kaluli of Papua New Guinea conceptualize music and poetic language. These the Kaluli associate with birds and weeping. They arise from a breach in human solidarity, a violation of kinship, community, connection. *Gisalo,* the quintessential Kaluli song form (the only one of the five varieties they sing that they claim to have invented rather than borrowed from a neighboring people), provokes and crosses over into weeping—weeping which has to do with some such breach, usually death. *Gisalo* songs are sung at funerals and during spirit-medium seances and have the melodic contour of the cry of a kind of fruitdove, the *muni* bird. This reflects and is founded on the myth regarding the origin of music, the myth of the boy who became a *muni* bird. The myth tells of a boy who goes to catch crayfish with his older sister. He catches none and repeatedly begs for those caught by his sister, who again and again refuses his request. Finally he catches a shrimp and puts it over his nose, causing it to turn a bright purple red, the color of a *muni* bird's beak. His hands turn into wings and when he opens his mouth to speak the falsetto cry of a *muni* bird comes out. As he flies away his sister begs him to come back and have some of the crayfish but his cries continue and become a song, semiwept, semisung: "Your crayfish you didn't give me. I have no sister. I'm hungry. . . ." For the Kaluli, then, the quintessential source

of music is the orphan's ordeal—an orphan being anyone denied kinship, social sustenance, anyone who suffers, to use Orlando Patterson's phrase, "social death," the prototype for which is the boy who becomes a *muni* bird. Song is both a complaint and a consolation dialectically tied to that ordeal, where in back of "orphan" one hears echoes of "orphic," a music which turns on abandonment, absence, loss. Think of the black spiritual "Motherless Child." Music is wounded kinship's last resort.

In *Sound and Symbol,* whose title Feld alludes to and echoes, Victor Zuckerkandl offers "a musical concept of the external world," something he also calls "a critique of our concept of reality from the point of view of music." He goes to great lengths to assert that music bears witness to what's left out of that concept of reality, or, if not exactly what, to the fact that something *is* left out. The world, music reminds us, inhabits while extending beyond what meets the eye, resides in but rises above what's apprehensible to the senses. This coinherence of immanence and transcendence the Kaluli attribute to and symbolize through birds, which for them are both the spirits of the dead and the major source of the everyday sounds they listen to as indicators of time, location and distance in their physical environment. In Zuckerkandl's analysis, immanence and transcendence meet in what he terms "the dynamic quality of tones," the relational valence or vectorial give and take bestowed on tones by their musical context. He takes great pains to show that "no material process can be co-ordinated with it," which allows him to conclude:

> Certainly, music transcends the physical; but it does not therefore transcend tones. Music rather helps the thing "tone" to transcend its own physical constituent, to break through into a nonphysical mode of being, and there to develop in a life of unexpected fullness. Nothing but tones! As if tone were not the point where the world that our senses encounter becomes transparent to the action of nonphysical forces, where we as perceivers find ourselves eye to eye, as it were, with a purely dynamic reality—the point where the external world gives up its secret and manifests itself, immediately, *as symbol.* To be sure, tones say, signify, point to—what? Not to something lying "beyond tones." Nor would it suffice to say that tones point to other tones—as if we had first tones, and then pointing as their attribute. No—in musical tones, being, existence, is indistinguishable from, *is,* pointing-beyond-itself, meaning, saying.

One easily sees the compatibility of this musical concept of the world, this assertion of the intrinsic symbolicity of the world, with poetry. Yeats's view that the artist "belongs to the invisible life" or Rilke's notion of poets as "bees of the invisible" sits agreeably beside Zuckerkandl's assertion that "because music exists, the tangible and visible cannot be the whole of the given world. The intangible and invisible is itself a part of this world, something we encounter, something to which we respond." His analysis lends itself to more recent formulations as well. His explanation of dynamic tonal events in terms of a "field concept," to give an example, isn't far from Charles Olson's "composition by field." And one commentator, to give another, has brought *Sound and Symbol* to bear on Jack Spicer's work.

The analogy between tone-pointing and word-pointing isn't lost on Zuckerkandl, who, having observed that "in musical tones, being, existence, is indistinguishable from, *is,* pointing-beyond-itself, meaning, saying," immediately adds: "Certainly, the being of words could be characterized the same way." He goes on to distinguish tone-pointing from word-pointing on the basis of the conventionally agreed-upon referentiality of the latter, a referentiality writers have repeatedly called into question, frequently doing so by way of "aspiring to the condition of music." "Thus poetry," Louis Zukofsky notes, "may be defined as an order of words that as movement and tone (rhythm and pitch) approaches in varying degrees the wordless art of music as a kind of mathematical limit." Music encourages us to see that the symbolic is the orphic, that the symbolic realm is the realm of the orphan. Music is prod and precedent for a recognition that the linguistic realm is also the realm of the orphan, as in Octavio Paz's characterization of language as an orphan severed from the presence to which it refers and which presumably gave it birth. This recognition troubles, complicates and contends with the unequivocal referentiality taken for granted in ordinary language:

> Each time we are served by words, we mutilate them. But the poet is not served by words. He is their servant. In serving them, he returns them to the plenitude of their nature, makes them recover their being. Thanks to poetry, language reconquers its original state. First, its plastic and sonorous values, generally disdained by thought; next, the affective values; and, finally, the expressive ones. To purify language, the poet's task, means to give it back its original nature. And here we come to one of the central themes of this reflection. The word, in itself, is a plurality of meanings.

Paz is only one of many who have noted the ascendancy of musicality and multivocal meaning in poetic language. (Julia Kristeva: "The poet . . . wants to turn rhythm into a dominant element . . . wants to make language perceive what it doesn't want to say, provide it with its matter independently of the sign, and free it from denotation.")

Poetic language is language owning up to being an orphan, to its tenuous kinship with the things it ostensibly refers to. This is why in the Kaluli myth the origin of music is also the origin of poetic language. The words of the song the boy who becomes a *muni* bird resorts to are different from those of ordinary speech. Song language "amplifies, multiplies, or intensifies the relationship of the word to its referent," as Feld explains:

> In song, text is not primarily a proxy for a denoted subject but self-consciously multiplies the intent of the word.
>
> . . . Song poetry goes beyond pragmatic referential communication because it is explicitly organized by canons of reflexiveness and self-consciousness that are not found in ordinary talk.

The uniqueness of poetic language is unveiled in the story of "the boy who became a *muni* bird." Once the boy has exhausted the speech codes for begging, he must resort to another communication frame. Conversational talk, what the Kaluli call *to halaido,* "hard words," is useless once the boy has become a bird; now he resorts to talk from a bird's point of view. . . . Poetic language is bird language.

It bears emphasizing that this break with conventional language is brought about by a breach of expected behavior. In saying no to her brother's request for food the older sister violates kinship etiquette.

What I wish to do is work *Sound and Sentiment* together with *Sound and Symbol* in such a way that the latter's metaphysical accent aids and is in turn abetted by the former's emphasis on the social meaning of sound. What I'm after is a range of implication which will stretch, to quote Stanley Crouch, "from the cottonfields to the cosmos." You notice again that it's black music I'm talking about, a music whose "critique of our concept of reality" is notoriously a critique of social reality, a critique of social arrangements in which, because of racism, one finds oneself deprived of community and kinship, cut off. The two modes of this critique which I'll be emphasizing Robert Farris Thompson notes among the "ancient African organizing principles of song and dance":

> *suspended accentuation patterning* (offbeat phrasing of melodic and choreographic accents); and, at a slightly different but equally recurrent level of exposition, *songs and dances of social allusion* (music which, however danceable and "swinging," remorselessly contrasts social imperfections against implied criteria for perfect living).

Still, the social isn't all of it. One needs to hear, alongside Amiri Baraka listening to Jay McNeely, that "the horn spat enraged sociologies," but not without noting a simultaneous mystic thrust. Immanence and transcendence meet, making the music social as well as cosmic, political and metaphysical as well. The composer of "Fables of Faubus" asks Fats Navarro, "What's *outside* the universe?"

This meeting of transcendence and immanence I evoke, in my own work, through the figure of the phantom limb. In the letter which opens *From A Broken Bottle Traces of Perfume Still Emanate* N. begins:

> You should've heard me in the dream last night. I found myself walking down a sidewalk and came upon an open manhole off to the right out of which came (or strewn around which lay) the disassembled parts of a bass clarinet. Only the funny thing was that, except for the bell of the horn, all the parts looked more like plumbing fixtures than like parts of a bass clarinet. Anyway, I picked up a particularly long piece of "pipe" and proceeded to play. I don't recall seeing anyone around but somehow I knew the "crowd" wanted to hear "Naima." I decided I'd give it a try. In any event, I blew into heaven knows what but instead of "Naima" what came out was Shepp's solo on his version of "Cousin

Mary" on the *Four for Trane* album—only infinitely more gruffly resonant and varied and warm. (I even threw in a few licks of my own.) The last thing I remember is coming to the realization that what I was playing already existed on a record. I could hear scratches coming from somewhere in back and to the left of me. This realization turned out, of course, to be what woke me up.

Perhaps Wilson Harris is right. There are musics which haunt us like a phantom limb. Thus the abrupt breaking off. Therefore the "of course." No more than the ache of some such would-be extension.

I'll say more about Wilson Harris later. For now, let me simply say that the phantom limb is a felt recovery, a felt advance beyond severance and limitation which contends with and questions conventional reality, that it's a feeling for what's not there which reaches beyond as it calls into question what is. Music as phantom limb arises from a capacity for feeling which holds itself apart from numb contingency. The phantom limb haunts or critiques a condition in which feeling, consciousness itself, would seem to have been cut off. It's this condition, the non-objective character of reality, to which Michael Taussig applies the expression "phantom objectivity," by which he means the veil by way of which a social order renders its role in the construction of reality invisible: "a commodity-based society produces such phantom objectivity, and in so doing it obscures its roots—the relations between people. This amounts to a socially instituted paradox with bewildering manifestations, the chief of which is the denial by the society's members of the social construction of reality." "Phantom," then, is a relative, relativizing term which cuts both ways, occasioning a shift in perspective between real and unreal, an exchange of attributes between the two. So the narrator in Josef Skvorecky's *The Bass Saxophone* says of the band he's inducted into: "They were no longer a vision, a fantasy, it was rather the sticky-sweet panorama of the town square that was unreal." The phantom limb reveals the illusory rule of the world it haunts.

Turning now to a few pieces of writing which allude to or seek to ally themselves with music, one sense I'm advancing is that they do so as a way of reaching toward an alternate reality, that music is the would-be limb whereby that reaching is done or which alerts us to the need for its being done. The first work I'd like to look at is Jean Toomer's *Cane*. Though *Cane* is not as announcedly about music as John A. Williams's *Night Song*, Thomas Mann's *Doctor Faustus,* or any number of other works one could name, in its "quieter" way it's no less worth looking at in this regard. First of all, of course, there's the lyricism which pervades the writing, an intrinsic music which is not unrelated to a theme of wounded kinship of which we get whispers in the title. Commentators have noted the biblical echo, and Toomer himself, in notebooks and correspondence, referred to the book as *Cain* on occasion. His acknowledged indebtedness to black folk tradition may well have included a knowledge of stories in that tradition which depict Cain as the prototypical white, a mutation among the earlier people, all of whom were up to that point black: "Cain he kill his brudder Abel wid a great big

club . . . and he turn white as bleech cambric in de face, and de whole race ob Cain dey bin white ebber since." The backdrop of white assault which comes to the fore in "Portrait in Georgia," "Blood-Burning Moon," and "Kabnis" plays upon the fratricidal note struck by the book's title.

Indebted as it is to black folk tradition, *Cane* can't help but have to do with music. That "Deep River," "Go Down, Moses," and other songs are alluded to comes as no surprise. Toomer's catalytic stay in Georgia is well-known. It was there that he first encountered the black "folk-spirit" he sought to capture in the book. Worth repeating is the emphasis he put on the music he heard:

> The setting was crude in a way, but strangely rich and beautiful. I began feeling its effects despite my state, or, perhaps, just because of it. There was a valley, the valley of "Cane," with smoke-wreaths during the day and mist at night. A family of back-country Negroes had only recently moved into a shack not too far away. They sang. And this was the first time I'd ever heard the folk-songs and spirituals. They were very rich and sad and joyous and beautiful.

He insisted, though, that the spirit of that music was doomed, that "the folk-spirit was walking in to die on the modern desert" and that *Cane* was "a swan-song," "a song of an end." The elegiac weariness and weight which characterize the book come of a lament for the passing of that spirit. In this it's like the music which inspired it, as Toomer pointed out in a letter to Waldo Frank:

> . . . the Negro of the folk-song has all but passed away: the Negro of the emotional church is fading. . . . In my own . . . pieces that come nearest to the old Negro, to the spirit saturate with folk-song . . . the dominant emotion is a sadness derived from a sense of fading. . . . The folk-songs themselves are of the same order: the deepest of them, "I aint got long to stay here."

So, "Song of the Son":

> Pour O pour that parting soul in song,
> O pour it in the sawdust glow of night,
> Into the velvet pine-smoke air to-night,
> And let the valley carry it along.
> And let the valley carry it along.
>
> O land and soil, red soil and sweet-gum tree,
> So scant of grass, so profligate of pines,
> Now just before an epoch's sun declines
> Thy son, in time, I have returned to thee,
> Thy son, I have in time returned to thee.
>
> In time, for though the sun is setting on
> A song-lit race of slaves, it has not set;
> Though late, O soil, it is not too late yet
> To catch thy plaintive soul, leaving, soon gone,
> Leaving, to catch thy plaintive soul soon gone.
>
> O Negro slaves, dark purple ripened plums,
> Squeezed, and bursting in the pine-wood air,
> Passing, before they stripped the old tree bare
> One plum was saved for me, one seed becomes
>
> An everlasting song, a singing tree,
> Caroling softly souls of slavery,
> What they were, and what they are to me,
> Caroling softly souls of slavery.

Cane is fueled by an oppositional nostalgia. A precarious vessel possessed of an eloquence coincident with loss, it wants to reach or to keep in touch with an alternate reality as that reality fades. It was Toomer's dread of the ascending urban-industrial order which opened his ears to the corrective—potentially corrective—counterpoint he heard in Georgia. In the middle section of the book, set in northern cities, houses epitomize a reign of hard, sharp edges, rectilinear pattern, fixity, regimentation, a staid, white order: "Houses, and dorm sitting-rooms are places where white faces seclude themselves at night." The house embodies, again and again, suffocating structure: "Rhobert wears a house, like a monstrous diver's helmet, on his head. . . . He is sinking. His house is a dead thing that weights him down." Or: "Dan's eyes sting. Sinking into a soft couch, he closes them. The house contracts about him. It is a sharp-edged, massed, metallic house. Bolted." Compare this with Kabnis's fissured, rickety cabin in the south, through the cracks in whose walls and ceiling a ventilating music blows:

> The walls, unpainted, are seasoned a rosin yellow. And cracks between the boards are black. These cracks are the lips the night winds use for whispering. Night winds in Georgia are vagrant poets, whispering. . . . Night winds whisper in the eaves. Sing weirdly in the ceiling cracks.

Ventilating song is what Dan invokes against the row of houses, the reign of suffocating structure, at the beginning of "Box Seat":

> Houses are shy girls whose eyes shine reticently upon the dusk body of the street. Upon the gleaming limbs and asphalt torso of a dreaming nigger. Shake your curled wool-blossoms, nigger. Open your liver lips to lean, white spring. Stir the root-life of a withered people. Call them from their houses, and teach them to dream.
>
> Dark swaying forms of Negroes are street songs that woo virginal houses.

Thirty years before the more celebrated Beats, Toomer calls out against an airtight domesticity, a reign of "square" houses and the domestication of spirit that goes with it, his call, as theirs would be, fueled and inflected by the countering thrust of black music.

Not that the beauty of the music wasn't bought at a deadly price. Its otherworldly reach was fostered and fed by seeming to have no home in this one ("I aint got long to stay here"). What the night winds whisper is this:

> White-man's land.
> Niggers, sing.
> Burn, bear black children
> Till poor rivers bring
> Rest, and sweet glory
> In Camp Ground.

The singing, preaching and shouting coming from the church near Kabnis's cabin build as Layman tells of a lynching, reaching a peak as a stone crashes in through one of the windows:

> A shriek pierces the room. The bronze pieces on the mantel hum. The sister cries frantically: "Jesus, Jesus, I've found Jesus. O Lord, glory t God, one mo sinner is acomin home." At the height of this, a stone, wrapped round with paper, crashes through the window. Kabnis springs to his feet, terror-stricken. Layman is worried. Halsey picks up the stone. Takes off the wrapper, smooths it out, and reads: "You northern nigger, its time fer y t leave. Git along now."

Toomer put much of himself into Kabnis, from whom we get an apprehension of music as a carrier of conflicted portent, bearer of both good and bad news. "Dear Jesus," he prays, "do not chain me to myself and set these hills and valleys, heaving with folk-songs, so close to me that I cannot reach them. There is a radiant beauty in the night that touches and . . . tortures me."

Cane's take on music is part and parcel of Toomer's insistence on the tragic fate of beauty, the soul's transit through an unsoulful world. This note gets hit by the first piece in the book, the story of "Karintha carrying beauty," her soul "a growing thing ripened too soon." The writing is haunted throughout by a ghost of aborted splendor, a spectre written into its much-noted lament for the condition of the women it portrays—woman as anima, problematic "parting soul." These women are frequently portrayed, not insignificantly, singing. The mark of blackness and the mark of femininity meet the mark of oppression invested in music. Toomer celebrates and incorporates song but not without looking at the grim conditions which give it birth, not without acknowledging its outcast, compensatory character. "Cotton Song," one of the poems in the book, takes the work song as its model: "Come, brother, come. Lets lift it; / Come now, hewit! roll away!" Like Sterling Brown's "Southern Road," Nat Adderley's "Work Song," and Sam Cooke's "Chain Gang," all of which it anticipates, the poem excavates the music's roots in forced labor. Music here is inseparable from the stigma attached to those who make it.

This goes farther in fact. Music itself is looked at askance and stigmatized in a philistine, prosaic social order: "Bolted to the endless rows of metal houses. . . . No wonder he couldn't sing to them." Toomer's formal innovations in *Cane* boldly ventilate the novel, a traditional support for prosaic order, by acknowledging fissures and allowing them in, bringing in verse and dramatic dialogue, putting poetry before reportage. This will to song, though, is accompanied by an awareness of song's outlaw lot which could have been a forecast of the book's commercial failure. (Only five hundred copies of the first printing were sold.) *Cane* portrays its own predicament. It shows that music or poetry, if not exactly a loser's art, is fed by an intimacy with loss and may in fact feed it. This comes out in two instances of a version of wounded kinship which recurs throughout the book, the thwarted communion of would-be lovers. Paul, Orpheus to Bona's Eurydice, turns back to deliver an exquisitely out-of-place poetic address to the doorman, then returns to find Bona gone. Likewise, the narrator holds forth poetically as he sits beside Avey in the story which takes her name, only to find that she's fallen asleep. A play of parallel estrangements emerges.

His alienation from the phantom reign of prosaic power—the Capitol dome is "a gray ghost ship"—meets her detachment from and immunity to prepossessing eloquence:

> I talked, beautifully I thought, about an art that would be born, an art that would open the way for women the likes of her. I asked her to hope, and build up an inner life against the coming of that day. I recited some of my own things to her. I sang, with a strange quiver in my voice, a promise-song. And then I began to wonder why her hand had not once returned a single pressure. . . . I sat beside her through the night. I saw the dawn steal over Washington. The Capitol dome looked like a gray ghost ship drifting in from sea. Avey's face was pale, and her eyes were heavy. She did not have the gray crimson-splashed beauty of the dawn. I hated to wake her. Orphan-woman. . . .

Beauty apprised of its abnormality both is and isn't beauty. (Baraka on Coltrane's "Afro-Blue": "Beautiful has nothing to do with it, but it is.") An agitation complicates would-be equanimity, would-be poise. "Th form thats burned int my soul," Kabnis cries, "is some twisted awful thing that crept in from a dream, a godam nightmare, an wont stay still unless I feed it. An it lives on words. Not beautiful words. God Almighty no. Misshapen, split-gut, tortured, twisted words." The tormenting lure of anomalous beauty and the answering dance of deformation—form imitatively "tortured, twisted"—also concern the writer I'd like to move on to, William Carlos Williams. The harassed/harassing irritability which comes into the "Beautiful Thing" section of *Paterson* recalls Kabnis's "Whats beauty anyway but ugliness if it hurts you?" In black music Williams heard the "defiance of authority" he declares beauty to be, a "vulgarity" which "surpasses all perfections."

Williams's engagement with black music was greatly influenced by his sense of himself as cut off from the literary mainstream. At the time the two pieces I'd like to look at were written Williams had not yet been admitted into the canon, as can be seen in the omission of his work from the *Modern Library Anthology of American Poetry* in 1945, at whose editor, Conrad Aiken, he accordingly takes a shot in *Man Orchid*, the second of the two pieces I'll discuss. His quarrel with T. S. Eliot's dominance and influence doesn't need pointing out, except that it also comes up in *Man Orchid*. Seeing himself as a victimized poet, Williams celebrated the music of a victimized people. In a gesture which has since been overdone ("the white negro," "the student as nigger," analogies between "women and blacks"), he saw parallels between their lot and his own. This can also be seen, though in a slightly more subtle way, in the first of the two pieces I'd like to turn to, "Ol' Bunk's Band."

Both pieces grew out of Williams's going to hear New Orleans trumpeter Bunk Johnson in New York in 1945. A revival of interest in Johnson's music was then going on and Williams caught him during a 3 1/2-month gig at the Stuyvesant Casino on the lower east side. He soon after wrote "Ol' Bunk's Band," a poem whose repeated insistence "These are men!" diverges from the dominant culture's denial of human stature to black people. He goes against the grain of accepted grammar in such things as the conscious "vulgarity" of the triple negative "and / not never / need no more," emulating a disregard for convention he heard in the music. The poem in full:

> These are men! the gaunt, unfore-
>   sold, the vocal,
> blatant, Stand up, stand up! the
>   slap of a bass-string.
> Pick, ping! The horn, the
>   hollow horn
> long drawn out, a hound deep
>   tone—
> Choking, choking! while the
>   treble reed
> races—alone, ripples, screams
>   slow to fast—
> to second to first! These are men!
>
> Drum, drum, drum, drum, drum,
>   drum, drum! the
> ancient cry, escaping crapulence
>   eats through
> transcendent—torn, tears, term
>   town, tense,
> turns and back off whole, leaps
>   up, stomps down,
> rips through! These are men
>   beneath
> whose force the melody limps—
>   to
> proclaim, proclaims—Run and
>   lie down,
> in slow measures, to rest and
>   not never
> need no more! These are men!
> Men!

The "hound deep / tone," reminding us that Johnson played in a band known as the Yelping Hound Band in 1930, also conjures a sense of underdog status which brings the orphaned or outcast poet into solidarity with an outcast people. The repeated assertion "These are men!" plays against an implied but unstated "treated like dogs."

Threaded into this implicit counterpoint are the lines "These are men / beneath / whose force the melody limps," where "limps" reflects critically on a crippling social order. The musicians do to the melody what's done to them, the social handicap on which this limping reports having been translated and, in that sense, transcended, triumphed over. Williams anticipates Baraka's more explicit reading of black music as revenge, sublimated murder. Looking at *Paterson*, which hadn't been underway long when "Ol' Bunk's Band" was written, one finds the same complex of figures: dogs, lameness, limping. In the preface to Book 1 the image conveyed is that of a pariah, out of step with the pack:

> Sniffing the trees,
> just another dog
> among a lot of dogs. What
> else is there? And to do?
> The rest have run out—
> after the rabbits.
> Only the lame stands—on
> three legs. . . .

This leads eventually to the quote from John Addington Symonds's *Studies of the Greek Poets* which ends Book 1, a passage in which Symonds comments on Hipponax's choliambi, "lame or limping iambics":

> . . . Hipponax ended his iambics with a spondee or a trochee instead of an iambus, doing thus the utmost violence to the rhythmical structure. . . . The choliambi are in poetry what the dwarf or cripple is in human nature. Here again, by their acceptance of this halting meter, the Greeks displayed their acute aesthetic sense of propriety, recognizing the harmony which subsists between crabbed verses and the distorted subjects with which they dealt—the vices and perversions of humanity—as well as their agreement with the snarling spirit of the satirist. Deformed verse was suited to deformed morality.

That Williams heard a similar gesture in the syncopated rhythms of black music is obvious by Book 5, where, after quoting a passage on Bessie Smith from Mezz Mezzrow's *Really the Blues,* he makes his well-known equation of "satiric" with "satyric":

> a satyric play!
> All plays
> were satyric when they were most devout.
> Ribald as a Satyr!
>
> Satyrs dance!
> all the deformities take wing.

This would also be a way of talking about the "variable foot," less an aid to scansion than a trope—the travestied, fractured foot.

Williams here stumbles upon, without naming and, most likely, without knowing, the Fon-Yoruba orisha of the crossroads, the lame dancer Legba. Legba walks with a limp because his legs are of unequal lengths, one of them anchored in the world of humans and the other in that of the gods. His roles are numerous, the common denominator being that he acts as an intermediary, a mediator, much like Hermes, of whom Hipponax was a follower. (Norman O. Brown: "Hipponax, significantly enough, found Hermes the most congenial god; he is in fact the only personality in Greek literature of whom it may be said that he walked with Hermes all the days of his life.") Like Hermes's winged feet, Legba's limp—"deformities take wing"—bridges high and low. Legba presides over gateways, intersections, thresholds, wherever different realms or regions come into contact. His limp a play of difference, he's the master linguist and has much to do with signification, divination, and translation. His limp the offbeat or eccentric accent, the "suspended accentuation" of which Thompson writes, he's the master musician and dancer, declared first among the orishas because only he could simultaneously play a gong, a bell, a drum, and a flute while dancing. The master of polyrhythmicity and heterogeneity, he suffers not from deformity but multiformity, a "defective" capacity in a homogeneous order given over to uniform rule. Legba's limp is an emblem of heterogeneous wholeness, the image and outcome of a peculiar remediation. "Lame" or "limping," that is, like "phantom," cuts with a relativizing edge to unveil impairment's

power, as though the syncopated accent were an unsuspected blessing offering anomalous, unpredictable support. Impairment taken to higher ground, remediated, translates damage and disarray into a dance. Legba's limp, compensating the difference in leg lengths, functions like a phantom limb. Robert Pelton writes that Legba "transforms . . . absence into transparent presence," deficit leg into invisible supplement.

Legba's authority over mix and transition made him especially relevant to the experience of transplantation brought about by the slave trade. The need to accommodate geographic and cultural difference placed a high premium on his mediatory skills. He's thus the most tenaciously retained of the orishas among New World Africans, the first to be invoked in vodoun ceremonies, be they in Haiti, Cuba, Brazil, or elsewhere. There's little wonder why Williams's work, concerned as it is with the New World as a ground for syncretistic innovation, would be paid a visit by the African bridge between old and new. What he heard in Bunk Johnson's music was a rhythmic digestion of dislocation, the African genius for enigmatic melding or mending, a mystery of resilient survival no image puts more succinctly than that of Legba's limping dance.

Legba has made more straightforward appearances in certain works written since Williams's time, showing up, for example, as Papa LaBas (the name he goes by in New Orleans) in Ishmael Reed's novels. Or as Lebert Joseph in Paule Marshall's *Praisesong for the Widow,* a novel whose third section is introduced by a line from the Haitian invocation to Legba and in which one comes upon such passages as: "Out of his stooped and winnowed body had come the illusion of height, femininity and power. Even his foreshortened left leg had appeared to straighten itself out and grow longer as he danced." One of his most telling appearances in the literature of this country, though, is one in which, as in Williams's work, he enters unannounced. In Ralph Ellison's *Invisible Man* one finds adumbrations of Legba which, bearing as they do on the concerns addressed here, deserve more than passing mention.

Invisible Man, like *Cane,* is a work which draws on black folk resources. While collecting folklore in Harlem in 1939 for the Federal Writers' Project, Ellison was told a tale which had to do with a black man in South Carolina who because he could make himself invisible at will was able to harass and give white people hell with impunity. This would seem to have contributed to the relativizing thrust of the novel's title and its long meditation on the two-way cut of invisibility. On the other side of invisibility as exclusion, social death, we find it as revenge, millenarian reversal. The prominence of Louis Armstrong in the novel's prologue brings to mind Zuckerkandl's discussion of the case music makes for the invisible, as invisibility is here both social and metaphysical. The ability to "see around corners" defies the reign of strict rectilinear structure lamented in *Cane* by going outside ordinary time and space constraints. Louis's horn, apocalyptic, alters times (and, with it, space):

> Invisibility, let me explain, gives one a slightly
> different sense of time, you're never quite on the

beat. Sometimes you're ahead and sometimes behind. Instead of the swift and imperceptible flowing of time, you are aware of its nodes, those points where time stands still or from which it leaps ahead. And you slip into the breaks and look around. That's what you hear vaguely in Louis' music.

This different sense of time one recognizes as Legba's limp. It leads to and is echoed by a later adumbration of Legba, one in which Ellison hints at a similarly "offbeat" sense of history, one which diverges from the Brotherhood's doctrine of history as monolithic advance. Early on, Jack describes the old evicted couple as "already dead, defunct," people whom "history has passed . . . by," "dead limbs that must be pruned away." Later "dead limbs" plays contrapuntally upon Tarp's contestatory limp, a limp which, as he explains, has social rather than physiological roots. It was caused by nineteen years on a chain gang:

> You notice this limp I got? . . . Well, I wasn't always lame, and I'm not really now cause the doctors can't find anything wrong with that leg. They say it's sound as a piece of steel. What I mean is I got this limp from dragging a chain. . . . Nobody knows that about me, they just think I got rheumatism. But it was that chain and after nineteen years I haven't been able to stop dragging my leg.

Phantom limb, phantom limp. Tarp goes on, in a gesture recalling the protective root Sandy gives Frederick Douglass in the latter's *Narrative,* to give Invisible Man the broken link from the leg chain he dragged for nineteen years. Phantom limb, phantom limp, phantom link: "I think it's got a heap of signifying wrapped up in it and it might help you remember what we're really fighting against." This it does, serving to concentrate a memory of injustice and traumatic survival, a remembered wound resorted to as a weapon of self-defense. During his final confrontation with the Brotherhood, Invisible Man wears it like a set of brass knuckles: "My hand was in my pockets now, Brother Tarp's leg chain around my knuckles."

"The trouble has been," Olson writes, "that a man stays so astonished he can triumph over his own incoherence, he settles for that, crows over it, and goes at a day again happy he at least makes a little sense." Ellison says much the same thing towards the end of *Invisible Man* when he cautions that "the mind that has conceived a plan of living must never lose sight of the chaos against which that pattern was conceived." This goes for both societies and individuals, he points out. Legba's limp, like Tarp's leg chain, is a reminder of dues paid, damage done, of the limbs which have been "pruned away." It's a reminder of the Pyrrhic features every triumph over chaos or incoherence turns out to possess. The spectre of illusory victory and its corollary, the riddle of deceptive disability or enabling defeat, sit prominently among the mysteries to which it witnesses. "No defeat is made up entirely of defeat," Williams writes in *Paterson.*

In *Man Orchid,* the second piece which grew out of Williams's going to hear Johnson's band, the stutter plays a significant role. What better qualification of what can only be a partial victory over incoherence? What limping, staggering, and stumbling are to walking, stuttering and stammering are to speech. "*To stammer* and *to stumble,* original *stumelen,* are twin words," Theodore Thass-Thienemann points out. "The use of the one and the same phonemic pattern for denoting these two different meanings is found in other languages too. Stammering and stuttering are perceived as speech *im-pedi-ments.*" The stutter enters *Man Orchid* largely because of Bucklin Moon, the author of a novel called *The Darker Brother.* Moon was at the Stuyvesant Casino on the night of 23 November 1945, the second time Williams went to hear Johnson's band. He ended up joining Williams and his friends at their table, among whom was Fred Miller, editor of the thirties proletarian magazine *Blast* and one of the co-authors of *Man Orchid.* Because of his novel and his knowledge of black music, Moon was incorrectly taken by them to be black, though Miller asked Williams in a letter two days later: "Would you ever think that Bucklin Moon was a Negro, if you passed him—as a stranger—in the street? He looks whiter than a lot of whites." Moon evidently spoke with a stutter whenever he became nervous and unsure of himself, which was the case that night at the Stuyvesant Casino. Miller goes on to offer this as a further peculiarity: "a stuttering or stammering Negro is a pretty rare bird indeed: your darker brother is articulate enough, when he isn't too frightened to talk." Like Legba's limp, Moon's stutter would come to symbolize a meeting of worlds, a problematic, insecure mix of black and white.

At the Stuyvesant Williams suggested that he and Miller publish an interracial literary magazine. Miller was enthusiastic at the time but soon lost interest. He suggested within a couple of weeks, however, that he and Williams collaborate on an improvisatory novel which was to be written as though they were musicians trading fours: "You write chap. I, send it to me, I do the 2d Chap., send mess back to you, you do 3—and so on." Williams liked the idea and *Man Orchid* was launched. They spent the next year working on it, off and on, bringing in a third collaborator, Lydia Carlin, in March. The work was never completed and what there is of it, forty pages, remained unpublished until 1973. It's going too far to call it a novel and outright ludicrous to call it, as Paul Mariani does, "Williams's black novel," but the piece is interesting for a number of reasons, not the least of them being its anticipation of the bop-inspired attempts at collaborative, improvisatory writing which became popular among the Beats a decade later.

Wray Douglas, *Man Orchid's* black-white protagonist, is based in part on Bucklin Moon and intended to embody America's yet-to-be-resolved identity. As Williams writes: "To resolve such a person would be to create a new world." But other than his presumed black-white mix and his stutter not much of Moon went into the figure. Wray Douglas is clearly his creators' alter ego, the narrated "he" and the narrator's "I" in most cases the same. Want of resolution and the stubborn problematics of heterogeneity are what *Man Orchid* most effectively expresses, the latter symptomized by the solipsistic quality of the work and the former a would-be flight from the resolute self (false resolution) which the solipsism indulges even as it eschews. Two white writers sit down to create a black protagonist whose model is another white writer. The ironies and contradictions needn't be belabored.

The stutter thus becomes the most appropriate, self-reflexive feature of an articulation which would appear to be blocked in advance. Williams's and Miller's prose in *Man Orchid* both stutters and refers to stuttering. Here, for example, is how Williams begins Chapter 1:

> Is it perchance a crime—a time, a chore, a bore, a job? He wasn't a musician—but he wished he had been born a musician instead of a writer. Musicians do not stutter. But he ate music, music wrinkled his belly—if you can wrinkle an inflated football. Anyhow it felt like that so that's what he wrote (without changing a word—that was his creed and always after midnight, you couldn't be earlier in the morning than that). All good writing is written in the morning.
>
> Is *what* perchance a crime? (One) (or rather two) He ate and drank beer. That is, he ate, he also drank beer. A crime to be so full, so—so (the thing the philosophers hate) poly. So p-p-poly. Polypoid. Huh?

Thinking, perhaps, of the use of singing in the treatment of stuttering, Williams identifies writing with the latter while looking longingly at music as the embodiment of a heterogeneous wholeness to which his writing will aspire, an unimpeded, unproblematic wholeness beyond its reach. Miller's contribution to *Man Orchid* is likewise touched by a sense of writing's inferiority to music. Early on, referring to Bessie Smith's singing, he asks: "What were the little words chasing each other like black bits of burnt leaves across the pages he held—[compared] to that vast voice?" Two pages later he answers:

> More printed words like black bits of burnt leaves. They had the right keyhole, those guys, but the wrong key. The only words that could blast like Bunk's horn or smash like John Henry's hammer were the poet's, the maker's, personal, ripped out of his guts: And no stuttering allowed.

Throughout *Man Orchid,* however, the writer's emulation of the musician causes rather than cures the stutter. Imitating the spontaneity of improvisatory music, Williams and Miller approach the typewriter as a musical keyboard on which they extemporize "without changing a word." Wrong "notes" are left as they are rather than erased, though the right ones do eventually get "played" in most cases. This results in a repetitiveness and a halting, staccato gesture reminiscent of a stutterer's effort to get out what he wants to say. Thus Williams: "American poetry was on its way to great distinction—when the blight of Eliot's popular verse fell pon—upon the gasping universities—who hadN8t hadn8T hadn't tasted Thames water for nearly a hundred years." By disrupting the fluency and coherence available to them Williams and Miller attempt to get in touch with what that coherence excludes, "the chaos against which that pattern was conceived." This friendly relationship with incoherence, however, constitutes a gesture towards but not an attainment of the otherness to which it aspires, an otherness to which access can only be analogically gotten. *Man Orchid,* to give the obvious example, is a piece of writing, not a piece of music. Nor, as I've already noted, is the color line crossed. The stutter is a two-way witness which on one hand symbolizes a need to go beyond the confines of an exclusionary order while on the other confessing to its at best only limited success at doing so. The impediments to the passage it seeks are acknowledged if not annulled, attested to by exactly the gesture which would overcome them if it could.

One measure of *Man Orchid's* flawed embrace of otherness is the prominence in it of Williams's all too familiar feud with Eliot, a feud into which he pulls Bunk Johnson. Johnson's music is put forth as an example of an authentic American idiom, "the autochthonous strain" whose dilution or displacement by "sweet music" paralleled and anticipated that of a genuine "American poetry [which] was on its way to great distinction" by *The Waste Land:*

> Eliot would not have been such a success if he hadn't hit a soft spot. They were scared and rushed in where he hit like water into the side of a ship. It was ready for it a long time. Isn't a weak spot always ready to give way? That was the secret of his success. Great man Eliot. They were aching for him, Aiken for him. He hit the jackpot with his popular shot.
>
> But long before that, twenty years earlier ol' Bunk Johnson was all washed up. Sweet music was coming in and jazz was through. But I mean THROUGH! And when I say through, I mean through. Go ahead, quit. See if I care. Take your band and go frig a kite. Go on back to the rice swamps. See if I care. Sell your ol'd horn. See if I care. Nobody wants that kind of music any more: this is a waste land for you, Buddy, this IS a waste land! I said Waste Land and when I sez Waste land I mean waste *land.*
>
> . . . Thus American poetry, which disappeared about that time you might say, followed the same course New Orleans music had taken when sweet music displaced it about in 1906 or so.

Fraternity with Johnson is less the issue than sibling rivalry with Eliot, a literary quarrel in which Johnson has no voice but the one Williams gives him. What it says is sample: "Black music is on Williams's side." (The Barbadian poet Edward Kamau Brathwaite provides interesting counterpoint, picturing Eliot and black music as allies when he notes the influence of Eliot's recorded readings in the Caribbean: "In that dry deadpan delivery, the riddims of St. Louis . . . were stark and clear for those of us who at the same time were listening to the dislocations of Bird, Dizzy and Klook. And it is interesting that on the whole, the Establishment couldn't stand Eliot's voice—far less jazz!")

The possibility that otherness was being appropriated rather than engaged was recognized by Miller and for him it became an obstacle to going on. When he began to voice his misgivings Williams brought in Lydia Carlin, who not only added sexual otherness to the project but a new form of ethnic otherness as well, in that, though she herself was English, one of the two chapters she contributed was about a Polish couple, the Czajas. Her two chapters are much more conventional, much less improvisatory than Williams's and Miller's and tend to stand apart from rather than interact with theirs. Her taking part in the project did nothing to solve the problem and as late as Chapter 7 Miller is asking:

> Now returning to this novel, Man Orchid. Why the orchid?—to begin with. There's the old, tiresome and at bottom snobbish literary assumption that the Negro in America is an exotic bloom. Negro equals jungle. Despite the fact that he has been here longer than the second, third, even ninth generation Eurp European—Negro equals jungle. Then why doesn't the ofay bank president of German descent equal Black Forest? The Rutherford doctor of Welsh descent equal the cromlechs? or Welsh rarebit?

As bad if not worse is the fact that the choice of that particular orchid because of its phallic appearance plays upon a stereotypic black male sexuality. The distance from this to Norman Mailer's "Jazz is orgasm" isn't very great, which is only one of a handful of ways in which *The White Negro* bears upon this predecessor text.

Miller, though he could agonize as above, was no more free than Williams was of stereotypic equations. To him Johnson and his music represent a black essence which is unselfconscious and nonreflective: "Only the Bunks're satisfied to be Bunks, he told himself enviously. Their brain don't question their art. Nor their left hand their RIGHT. Their right to be Bunk, themself." The vitiation of "black" non-reflective being by "white" intellectuality is largely the point of his evocation of Wray Douglas and the trumpeter Cholly Oldham. The latter he describes as having "too much brain for a musician." Oldham stutters when he plays and wants to be a painter:

> There was between Cholly and Bunk—what? a difference of thirty, thirty-five years in age, no more. But the difference otherwise! Hamlet son of Till Eulenspiegel. Showing you what the dry rot of intellectuality could do to the orchid in one generation. Progress (! Up from Slavery. That night-colored Hamlet, he wants to paint pictures now.

Black is nonreflective, white cerebral. So entrenched are such polarizations as to make the notion of a black intellectual oxymoronic. In May, Miller wrote to Williams that it had been a mistake to model their protagonist on Bucklin Moon: "I don't know enough about him and his special type, the colored intellectual (although I've been acquainted with and 've liked lots of ordinary Negro folk, laborers, musicians et al)." Small wonder he questioned the idea of an interracial magazine by writing to Williams:

> Is there sufficient Negro writing talent—of the kind we wd. have no doubts about, AS talent, on hand to balance the white talent? I don't believe any more than you that publishing second-rate work with first-rate intentions would serve any cause but that of bad writing.

To what extent was being looked upon as black—as, even worse, that "rare bird," a black intellectual—the cause of Moon's nervousness that night at the Stuyvesant? Could a sense of distance in Williams's and Miller's manner have caused him to stutter? Miller's wife recalls in a letter to Paul Mariani:

> Moon began with easy speech and there was talk at first of the interracial magazine but Moon soon took to stammering. To me Williams was always a warm congenial person, but he would become the coldly analytical surgeon at times and the effect it had on those around him at such a time was quite devastating.

That "coldly analytical" scrutiny would seem to have been disconcerting, making Williams and Miller the agents of the disarray about which they would then go on to write—as good an example as any of "phantom objectivity," the social construction of Moon's "mulatto" self-consciousness.

What I find most interesting about *Man Orchid* is that it inadvertently underscores a feature which was then coming into greater prominence in black improvised music. With the advent of bebop, with which neither Williams, Miller, nor Carlin seem to have been much engaged, black musicians began to assume a more explicit sense of themselves as artists, conscious creators, thinkers. Dizzy Gillespie would don a beret and a goatee, as would, among others, Yusef Lateef, who would record an album called *Jazz for the Thinker*. Anthony Braxton's pipe, wire-rim glasses, cardigan sweater, and diagrammatic titles are among the present-day descendants of such gestures. The aural equivalent of this more explicit reflexivity would come at times to resemble a stutter, conveying senses of apprehension and self-conscious duress by way of dislocated phrasings in which virtuosity mimes its opposite. Thelonious Monk's mock-awkward hesitancies evoke an experience of impediment or impairment, as do Sonny Rollins's even more stutterlike teasings of a tune, a quality Paul Blackburn imitates in "Listening to Sonny Rollins at the Five Spot":

> There will be many other nights like
> me standing here with someone, some
> one
> someone
> some-one
> some
> some
> some
> some
> some
> some
> one
> there will be other songs
> a-nother fall, another————spring, but
> there will never be a-noth, noth
> anoth
> noth
> anoth-er
> noth-er
> noth-er
> 　　　　　other lips that I may kiss,
> but they won't thrill me like
> 　　　　thrill me like
> 　　　　　　like yours
> used to

dream a million dreams
but how can they come
when there   never be
a-noth———

Though Williams and Miller insist that Bunk Johnson doesn't stammer, the limp he inflicts on the melody is ancestral to the stutter of Monk, Rollins, and others.

As among the Kaluli, for whom music and poetry are "specifically marked for reflection," the black musician's stutter is an introspective gesture which arises from and reflects critically upon an experience of isolation or exclusion, the orphan's or the outsider's ordeal, the "rare bird's" ordeal. Like Tarp's leg chain, it symbolizes a refusal to forget damage done, a critique and a partial rejection of an available but biased coherence. Part of the genius of black music is the room it allows for a telling "inarticulacy," a feature consistent with its critique of a predatory coherence, the cannibalistic "plan of living" and the articulacy which upholds it. *Man Orchid,* where it comes closest to the spirit of black music, does so by way of a similar frustration with and questioning of given articulacies, permissible ways of making sense. In Chapter 6 Williams attempts to make racial distinctions meaningless, the result of which is part gibberish, part scat, part wisdom of the idiots ("the most foolishest thing you can say . . . has the most meaning"). His inability to make sense implicitly indicts a white-dominated social order and the discourse of racial difference by which it explains or makes sense of itself:

> Not that black is white. I do not pretend that. Nor white black. That there is not the least difference is apparent to the mind at a glance. Thus, to the mind, the eye is forever deceived. And philosophers imagine they can have opinions about art? God are they dumb, meaning stupid, meaning philosophers, meaning schools, meaning—learning. The limits of learning are the same as an egg to the yolk. The shell. Knowledge to a learned man is precisely the sane— that's good: sane for same—the same as the egg to the hen. No possibility of interchange. Reason, the shell.
>
> No matter how I try to rearrange the parts, to show them interchangeable, the result is always the same. White is white and black is the United States Senate. No mixing. Even if it was all black it would be the same: white. How could it be different?

The very effort to talk down the difference underscores the tenacity of the racial polarization *Man Orchid*'s liberal mission seeks, to some degree, to overcome—a tenacity which is attested to, as we've seen, in other ways as well, not the least of them being the authors' preconceptions.

The play of sense and nonsense in Wilson Harris's *The Angel at the Gate* is more immediately one of sensation and nonsensation, a complex mingling of endowments and deprivations, anesthetic and synesthetic intuitions. One reads, for example, late in the novel:

> Mary recalled how deaf she had been to the voice of the blackbird that morning on her way to Angel Inn and yet it returned to her now in the depths of the mirror that stood beside her. Half-reflected voice, shaded sound, silent echo. Was this the source of musical composition? Did music issue from reflections that converted themselves into silent, echoing bodies in a mirror? Did the marriage of *reflection* and *sound* arise from deaf appearance within silent muse (or was it deaf muse in silent appearance) from which a stream of unheard music rippled into consciousness?

In dialogue with and relevant to such a passage is a discussion in Harris's most recent critical book, *The Womb of Space,* a discussion which touches upon Legba as "numinous shadow." Harris writes of "metaphoric imagery that intricately conveys music as the shadow of vanished but visualised presences": "Shadow or shade is alive with voices so real, yet strangely beyond material hearing, that they are peculiarly *visualised* or 'seen' in the intricate passages of a poem. *Visualised presence* acquires therefore a *shadow and a voice* that belongs to the mind's ear and eye." Music described in terms pertaining to sight is consistent with inklings of synesthetic identity which run through *The Angel at the Gate.* It's also part and parcel of Harris's long preoccupation, from work to work, with an uncapturable, ineffable wholeness, a heterogeneous inclusiveness evoked in terms of non-availability ("silent echo," "unheard music") and by polysemous fullness and fluency ("a stream . . . rippled").

The Angel at the Gate's anesthetic-synesthetic evocations recapitulate, in microcosm, the translation between media—aural and visual, music and writing—it claims to be. The intermedia impulse owns up to as it attempts to advance beyond the limits of a particular medium and is a version of what Harris elsewhere calls "a confession of weakness." The novel acknowledges that its particular strength can only be partial and seeks to "echo" if not enlist the also partial strength of another art form. Wholeness admitted to be beyond reach, the best to be attained is a concomitance of partial weaknesses, partial strengths, a conjunction of partial endowments. This conjunction is facilitated by Legba, upon whom *The Womb of Space* touches as a "numinous frailty" and a "transitional chord." In *Da Silva da Silva's Cultivated Wilderness,* an earlier novel which likewise leans upon an extraliterary medium, the painter da Silva's advertisement for a model is answered by one Legba Cuffey, whose arrival infuses paint with sound: "The front door bell pealed it seemed in the middle of his painting as he brooded on past and future. The sound of a catch grown sharp as a child's cry he thought in a line of stroked paint." In this case painting, like music in *The Angel at the Gate,* is an alternate artistic arm with which the novel extends or attempts to extend its reach. "So the arts," Williams writes in *Man Orchid,* "take part for each other."

Music figures prominently at the end of Harris's first novel, *Palace of the Peacock,* where Legba's limp, the incongruity between heaven and earth, is marked by the refractive obliquity and bend of a passage from one medium to another. The annunciation of paradise takes the form of a music which issues through the lips of Carroll, the black namesake singer whose father is unknown but whose mother "knew and understood . . . [that his] name involved . . . the music of her undying sacrifice to make and save the world." The narrator notes a discrepancy between the sound Carroll's lips appear to be making and the sound he hears: "Carroll was whistling. A solemn and beautiful cry—unlike a whistle I reflected—deeper and mature. Nevertheless his lips were framed to whistle and I could only explain the difference by assuming the sound from his lips was changed when it struck the window and issued into the world." The deflection from apparent sound reveals not only the insufficiency of the visual image but that of any image, visual, acoustic or otherwise. Heaven is wholeness, meaning that any image which takes up the task of evoking it can only fail. Legba's limp is the obliquity of a religious aspiration which admits its failure to measure up to heaven, the bend legs make in prayer. As in the *Paradiso,* where Dante laments the poem's inability to do heaven justice by calling it lame, the narrator's evocation of Carroll's music is marked by a hesitant, faltering gesture which whenever it asserts immediately qualifies itself. It mimes the music's crippling, self-correcting attempts to register as well as redeem defects. The music repeatedly breaks and mends itself—mends itself as a phantom limb mends an amputation:

> It was an organ cry almost and yet quite different I reflected again. It seemed to break and mend itself always—tremulous, forlorn, distant, triumphant, the echo of sound so pure and outlined in space it broke again into a mass of music. It was the cry of the peacock and yet I reflected far different. I stared at the whistling lips and wondered if the change was in me or in them. I had never witnessed and heard such sad and such glorious music.

This is the ongoingness of an attempt which fails but is repeatedly undertaken to insist that what it fails to capture nonetheless exists. Legba's limp is the obliquity of a utopian aspiration, the bend legs make preparing to spring.

Inability to capture wholeness notwithstanding, *Palace of the Peacock* initiates Harris's divergence, now into its third decade, from the novel's realist-mimetic tradition. The accent which falls upon the insufficiency of the visual image is consistent with the novel's earlier suggestions of an anesthetic-synesthetic enablement which displaces the privileged eye: "I dreamt I awoke with one dead seeing eye and one living closed eye." And again: "I had been blinded by the sun, and saw inwardly in the haze of my blind eye a watching muse and phantom whose breath was on my lips." That accent encapsulates Harris's quarrel with the cinematic pretense and the ocular conceit of the realist novel, a documentary stasis against which he poses an anesthetic-synesthetic obliquity and rush. This obliquity (seeing and/or hearing around corners, in Ellison's terms) is called "an angled intercourse with history" in *The Angel at the Gate,* the medium for which is the Angel Inn mirror, described at points as "spiritual" and "supernatural." Mary Stella is said to perceive the world "from a meaningfully distorted angle in the mirror," a pointed subversion of the mirror's conventional association with mimesis. Angularity cuts with a relativizing edge: "How unreal, yet real, one was when one saw oneself with one's own eyes

from angles in a mirror so curiously unfamiliar that one's eyes became a stranger's eyes. As at the hairdresser when she invites one to inspect the back of one's head."

Late in the novel Mary Stella's "automatic codes" are said to have "propelled her pencil across the page of a mirror"—clear enough indication that the novel sees itself in the Angel Inn mirror, that reflection and refraction are there the same. Angled perception is a particular way of writing—writing bent or inflected by music. *The Angel at the Gate* is said to be based on Mary Stella's automatic writings and on notes taken by her therapist Joseph Marsden during conversations with her, some of which were conducted while she was under hypnosis. In the note which introduces the novel mention is made of "the musical compositions by which Mary it seems was haunted from early childhood," as well as of "a series of underlying rhythms in the automatic narratives." Like the boy who became a *muni* bird, Mary Stella, an orphan from the age of seven, resorts to music in the face of broken familial ties—those with her parents in the past and in the present her troubled marriage with Sebastian, for whom she's "the same woman broken into wife and sister." Louis Armstrong's rendition of "Mack the Knife," the song her mother frequently sang during her early childhood, animates a host of recollections and associations:

> . . . the music returned once again coming this time from an old gramophone her mother possessed. It was "Mack the Knife" sung and played by Louis Armstrong. The absurdity and tall story lyric, oceanic city, were sustained by Armstrong's height of trumpet and by his instrumental voice, hoarse and meditative in contrast to the trumpet he played, ecstatic cradle, ecstatic childhood, ecstatic coffin, ecstatic grieving surf or sea.

> . . . Stella was shivering. The fascination of the song for her mother was something that she grew up with. Mack was also the name that her father bore. Mack was her mother's god. And her mother's name? *Guess,* Stella whispered to Sebastian in the darkened studio. Jenny! It was a random hit, bull's eye. It struck home. Jenny heard. She was weeping. It came with the faintest whisper of the sea, the faintest whisper of a flute, in the studio. Mack's women were the Sukey Tawdreys, the sweet Lucy Browns, of the world. Between the ages of four and seven Stella thought that the postman was her father. Until she realized that he was but the middleman between her real father and Jenny her mother. He brought the letters from foreign ports with foreign stamps over which Jenny wept. On her seventh birthday the last letter arrived. Her father was dead, his ship sunk. It was a lie. It drove her mother into an asylum where she contemplated Mack clinging for dear life to sarcophagus-globe even as she vanished into the arms of god, bride of god.

> Stella was taken into care by a Social Welfare Body and placed in an orphanage in East Anglia.

Mary Stella's automatic narratives, prompted by her thirst for connection and by "her longing to change the world," instigate patterns of asymmetric equation into which characters named Sukey Tawdrey, Mother Diver, Lucy Brown, and so forth enter. The song, it seems, populates a world, an alternate world. Her music-prompted hand and its inscription of far-flung relations obey intimations of unacknowledged wholeness against a backdrop of social and psychic division. "To be whole," we're told at the end, "was to endure . . . the traffic of many souls."

The novel's concern with heterogeneous wholeness invokes Legba repeatedly—though, significantly, not by that name. As if to more greatly emphasize Legba's association with multiplicity, Harris merges him with his trickster counterpart among the Ashanti, the spider Anancy, tales of whose exploits are a prominent part of Caribbean folklore. An asymmetric equation which relates deficit leg to surplus legs, lack to multiplicity, brings "a metaphysic of curative doubt" to bear on appearances. Apparent deficiency and apparent endowment are two sides of an insufficient image. When Sebastian discovers Mary Stella's attempt at suicide "his legs multiplied," but later "there was no visible bandage around his ankle but he seemed nevertheless as lame as Anancy." Other such intimations occur: Marsden described as a cane on which "something, some invisible presence, did lean," Sebastian asking of the jockey who exposed himself to Mary Stella, "Did he, for instance, possess a walking stick?," and Jackson, Mary Stella's "authentic messenger," falling from a ladder and breaking his leg. The most sustained appearance occurs when Mary Stella happens upon the black youth Anancy in Marsden's study. The "funny title" of a book has brought him there:

> . . . He turned his eyes to the desk. "The door was open and I saw the funny title of that book." He pointed to the desk.

> "Sir Thomas More's *Utopia*," said Mary, smiling against her fear and finding her tongue at last. "I put it there myself this week." His eyes were upon hers now. "I put it . . ." she began again, then stopped. "I brought you here," she thought silently. *"Utopia was the bait I used."* The thought came of its own volition. It seemed irrational, yet true. There was a ticking silence between them, a deeper pull than she could gauge, a deeper call than she knew, that had sounded long, long ago, even before the time when her father's great-great-grandmother had been hooked by an Englishman to bear him children of mixed blood.

Mary Stella's pursuit of heterogeneous relations carries her out as well as in. She discovers an eighteenth-century black ancestor on her father's side. That discovery, along with her perusal, in Marsden's library, of seventeenth- and eighteenth-century parish accounts of money spent to expel children and pregnant women, several of them black, arouses her desire for a utopian inclusiveness, the "longing to change the world" which "baits" Anancy. The world's failure to comply with that desire leads her to distance herself from it, to practice a kind of cosmic displacement. Her schizophrenia involves an aspect of astral projection, as she cultivates the "capacity to burn elsewhere" suggested by her middle name: "Ah yes, said Stella, I am

a mask Mary wears, a way of coping with truth. We are each other's little deaths, little births. We cling to sarcophagus-globe and to universal cradle."

Displacement and relativizing distance account for the resonances and agitations at work in the text, an animated incompleteness whose components tend towards as well as recede from one another, support as well as destabilize one another. The pull between Mary Stella and Anancy is said to arise from "a compulsion or infectious Cupid's arrow . . . related to the target of unfinished being." Some such pull, together with its other side, aversion, advances the accent on relationality which pervades the novel and has much to do with Harris's distinctive style. The sought-after sense of dispersed identity makes for staggered equational upsets and elisions in which words, concepts, and images, like the characters, are related through a mix of contrast and contagion. The musicality of Harris's writing resides in its cadences, imaginal concatenations and poetic assurance, but also in something else. *The Angel at the Gate* offers a musical conception of the world whose emphasis on animate incompleteness, "unfinished being," recalls Zuckerkandl's analysis of tonal motion:

> A series of tones is heard as motion not because the successive tones are of different pitches but because they have different dynamic qualities. The dynamic quality of a tone, we said, is a statement of its incompleteness, its will to completion. To hear a tone as dynamic quality, as a direction, a pointing, means hearing at the same time beyond it, beyond it in the direction of its will, and going toward the expected next tone. Listening to music, then, we are not first *in* one tone, then in the next, and so forth. We are, rather, always *between* the tones, *on the way* from tone to tone; our hearing does not remain with the tone, it reaches through it and beyond it . . . pure betweenness, pure passing over.

A mixed, middle ground which privileges betweenness would seem to be the realm in which Harris works. He alludes to himself as a "no-man's land writer" at one point and later has Jackson say, "I must learn to paint or sculpt what lies stranded between earth and heaven." An "attunement to a gulf or divide between sky and earth" probes an estrangement and a stranded play in which limbs have to do with limbo, liminality, lift:

> The women were dressed in white. They carried covered trays of food and other materials on their head. There was a statuesque deliberation to each movement they made, a hard-edged beauty akin to young Lucy's that seemed to bind their limbs into the soil even as it lifted them very subtly an inch or two into space.

> That lift was so nebulous, so uncertain, it may not have occurred at all. Yet it was there; it gave a gentle wave or groundswell to the static root or the vertical dance of each processional body.

What remains to be said is that to take that lift a bit farther is to view the outsider's lot as cosmic, stellar. Social estrangement is gnostic estrangement and the step from Satchmo's "height of trumpet" to Sun Ra's "intergalactic music" is neither a long nor an illogical one. In this respect, the film *Brother from Another Planet* is worth—in what will serve as a closing note—mentioning briefly. That it shares with *The Angel at the Gate* a theme of cosmic dislocation is obvious enough. That the Brother's limp is the limp of a misfit—the shoes he finds and puts on don't suit his feet—is also easy to see. An intermedia thread is also present and bears on this discussion, especially the allusions to Dante (the Rasta guide named Virgil) and *Invisible Man* (the Brother's detachable eye), where it would seem the film were admitting a need to reach beyond its limits. What stronger suggestion of anesthetic-synesthetic displacement could one want than when the Brother places his eye in the drug dealer's hand? Or than the fact that the movie ends on a seen but unsounded musical note as the Brother gets aboard an "A" train?

Daniel Melnick

SOURCE: "Fullness of Dissonance: Music and the Reader's Experience of Modern Fiction," in *Modern Fiction Studies,* Vol. 25, No. 2, Summer, 1979, pp. 209-22.

[*In the following essay, Melnick explores the ethos of dissonance in modern fiction, by which he means the capacity of the modern novel to evoke the reader's creative response to the disordered vision of reality it presents.*]

Dissonance, as a critical term, is conventionally used to characterize a particular tone or "musical" style in fiction; yet the bearing of the idea of dissonance on modern fiction is profounder and more far-reaching than that use supposes. Dissonance—with its revelation of disorder—can be understood as a means by which modern fiction offers the reader the opportunity actively to engage a vision of disintegrating experience. Joyce's *Ulysses,* in this conception, invites and requires the reader's active, creative response, and the novel's dissonance is its capacity so to involve and affirm the reader's freedom of imaginative perception and judgment. It is this meaning of the term dissonance which, for example, underlies Frank Kermode's remark that the reader searches for "the discoveries of dissonance" in the modern novel. Nietzsche's idea of dissonant art shapes this sense of the term so richly relevant to the nature of fiction in our century, and it is that sense of dissonance which I want to explore here.

My intention is to describe the bearing of the idea of dissonance on the aesthetic aims of modern fiction and on the common critical views of them. Though I trace the richly involuted connection between the aesthetics of music and how modern novelists view their art, my crucial interest is not in the sensuous musical effects certain narratives achieve. My concern is, rather, with the Nietzschean idea of dissonance as it offers an approach to meaning in fiction; for the concept of dissonance illuminates both the nature of modern culture and the reader's experience of the spirit and intentions of modern fiction. As I re-examine not unfamiliar patterns of literary thought, my hope is finally to lay bare their aesthetic and ethical basis in the light of the idea of dissonance.

A dissonant sensibility underlies the work of twentieth-century composers, and such a sensibility also shapes how literary artists in our century confront the modern predic-

ament of the imagination. A dissonant art, in Nietzsche's view, voices the disintegration besetting human experience and so finds a paradoxical fertility in the face of disaster. A most significant feature of dissonance, in this view, concerns the perceiver's experience. As the reader penetrates the life-like disharmony and subversive ambiguities of dissonant fiction, he finds delight and solace in his own creative response, in the investment of imaginative energy which the difficulties of the form itself stir into life in him. The aim and the distinctive power of dissonance are, then, to involve the perceiver in the processes of perception and judgment by which human life may endure in a disordered world, and that aim helps to define the vital, distinguishing function of fiction in the twentieth century.

I

A forceful explanation for music's value to modern novelists and poets is suggested by Erich Heller:

> After the seventeenth century, Europe no longer dwelt or worshipped or ruled in buildings created in the image of authentic spiritual vision. For all that was real was an encumbrance to the spirit who, in his turn, only occasionally called on the real, and even then with the embarrassment of an uninvited guest. He was most at home where there was least "reality"—in music. The music of modern Europe is the one and only art in which it surpassed the achievement of former ages. This is no accident of history: it is the speechless triumph of the spirit in a world of words without deeds and deeds without words.

The relation of the modern spirit to reality appears embattled, defensive, disordered by violence and imaginative impotence; man's withdrawn and disintegrating inner life can, it seems, be rendered only, or most richly, by music with its ambiguous "reality." These perceptions of music's value—as an art which can endure the gap between spirit and experience—underlie what is, in Nietzschean terms, the sensibility of dissonance. Such a sensibility shapes both how Mann, Proust, and Joyce view music's meaning and their attempts to imagine the difficult connection between words and modern experience.

Nietzsche develops the idea of dissonance in *The Birth of Tragedy from the Spirit of Music,* published in 1872. There, Nietzsche shows that the perceiver's actively engaged response is an integral component of dissonant form and that his response is closely tied to the consciousness of human possibility the form itself stirs within him. A main purpose of *The Birth of Tragedy,* with its complex avowal of Wagner's music, is to analyze the significance of dissonance by describing how it relates to the two opposed forces at work in Greek tragedy. The Apollonian element in tragedy is art's perfect and dream-like form which imagines an ideal existence. The Dionysian element is the audience's store of emotional response; the emotional force of their tragic desire for the perfected Apollonian images is formulated by the sung chorus of the tragedy.

> **A dissonant sensibility underlies the work of twentieth-century composers, and such a sensibility also shapes how literary artists in our century confront the modern predicament of the imagination. A dissonant art, in Nietzsche's view, voices the disintegration besetting human experience and so finds a paradoxical fertility in the face of disaster.**
>
> **—Daniel Melnick**

What is beautiful is a fiction, and man's relation to this imaginative act must be a function of the ceaseless creativity—what Nietzsche terms the dissonance—of his Dionysian response. Dissonance subverts a harmonious ideal in order to reveal the perceiver's response to tragedy's informing insight, that all ideal appearance—all human order—is illusion. "What is man," Nietzsche asks, "but a dissonance?" In terms of the dynamics of modern fiction, the risk of encountering a dissonant narrative is disillusionment; as dissonance "tears the veil of illusion," it can subvert the ideals and cultural order which sustain the reader. Yet, the profound understanding Nietzsche offers us is that dissonance enables the reader to encounter this risk and to endure it through the opportunity for creative response and judgment it offers. That opportunity is achieved by the revelation—that *Heart of Darkness* for instance offers—of the clashing possibilities and implacable contradictions struggling to survive, raging to exist, in our world.

It is illuminating and important to consider the rigorously dissonant music of Arnold Schoenberg both as an expression of the sensibility Nietzsche defines and as a musical analogue to the modern novel with its "dissonant" qualities—difficult, ironic, often parodic, oblique and idiosyncratic, apocalyptic, or at times intentionally silent. The risk that both this music and the novels, for example, of Mann and Joyce contain is that their formulation of the inner life will be negated by the incommunicability or vacancy of the withdrawn and diminished spirit they envision. Schoenberg's music as well as *Doctor Faustus* and *Ulysses* meet this risk by creating a perilous balance between their innovative, humanly valuable but always threatened forms and the subversive vision these forms are made to reveal.

The reader or listener is implicated in the effort to sustain that balance in an extraordinary way; such art offers him the Dionysian opportunity to take up a creative role. Modern music—with modern fiction—relies on his creative engagement (and not on traditional symbols and their meaning) to disclose and affirm the value and meaning of the distorted vision communicated through its intentional disintegration of the received language of art. In other words, the difficulty of the modern novel and of Schoenberg's dissonance results not from a denial of art's role of communicating the condition of man's inner life, but from the ex-

pression of the very form in which that life endures. The difficult and dangerous task of spiritual survival finds in the modern novel a similarly dangerous, symbolically difficult but still expressive formulation—still vital because fiction like Joyce's and Lawrence's taps the energy of the perceiver's disillusioned yet enduring and creative response.

The aesthetic and the implicit ethic of dissonant art help us, then, to locate a shaping principle of modern narrative; they help to define the reader's experience as a renewing drama of self-discovery and self-judgment. It is the principle of dissonance, and not the more conventional formalist notion of a musical analogy, which illuminates the underlying function of modern fiction—the value and the risk for the reader of *Heart of Darkness, Remembrance of Things Past, Doctor Faustus, Ulysses,* or *Women in Love.* On the one hand, to perceive these novels in purely formal terms as dissonant helps us certainly to grasp what is already well established: that modern fiction formulates the disintegrating shape of human *time,* with its analogously musical patterns—allusive and suggestive, open-ended and ambiguous, rhythmic and charged with meaning. On the other hand, however, the profounder insight of the dissonant sensibility is that the modern novel would draw the reader into a new relationship to fiction. No longer does the novel serve fiction's traditional ends and lead the reader to an affirmation of now fragmented received values. The dissonant imagination of modern novelists—with all the cunning artifice of their efforts to create a human order—exists amid the disordered ruin of social and moral experience. Their novels find their justification and fulfillment, finally, in evoking from the reader a special investment of imaginative energy, a self-challenging and self-implicating response of understanding and judgment.

There is a vital connection between the assumptions of dissonance and, for example, Conrad's view of his art. In his finest statement on fiction, the "Preface" to *The Nigger of the "Narcisus,"* he initially offers a conventional symbolist view of music's special expressivity; that art's "magic suggestiveness" (its "perfect blending of form and substance") is a means to make perceptible "the moral, the emotional atmosphere" and the "secret truth" of the observed moment. More important, however, than his use of a musical, and later a visual, analogy is Conrad's avowal of the aims of the dissonant sensibility. He would assault the complacent reader with the subversive and ambiguous "glimpse"—with the "fragments"—of truth for which the reader has "perhaps forgotten to ask." Dissonance in fiction is precisely this challenge to the reader's own temperament, a challenge which elevates his role to its new position at the center of aesthetic intention; the fiction becomes an appeal to his capacity for imaginative perception and judgment.

The aim of *Remembrance of Things Past,* Proust similarly suggests, is to reveal to the reader the "purely musical impressions, non-extensive, entirely original," which make up the novelist's conception of embattled human time; and Proust's crucial hope for his novel is that the work would become the reader's own "book of his inner being." With equal commitment, Mann views his fiction as a musical organism of which the reader would be a conductor integrating the structure of dissonant and paradoxical ironies in the fiction. Thus, Mann intentionally relies on the reader to implicate himself in—and indeed to achieve—the novel's meaning and impact. Joyce's art is also influenced and, most important, illuminated by the ethos of dissonance; an early essay of his asserts, for example, that a perfected art is like life "not to be criticized, but to be faced and lived." The mental and emotional challenge of Joyce's fiction assaults the reader, and demands of him an active response.

In noting the place of dissonance in modern narrative, I am not merely reiterating the critical perception of a "musical" prose and oblique, fertile symbolism in fiction; such are, of course, the traditional hallmarks of a musical aesthetic, and, in these terms, Conrad's and also Lawrence's technique does appear to approach "the condition of music." But in Lawrence, for example, these quasi-musical techniques are only some among many narrative tools he uses to accomplish the profounder aim of the dissonant imagination. Mark Schorer suggests of Lawrence that "no novelist speaks more directly to us, and if we can't hear him, we are, I quite believe, lost." It is the redemption of his readers which Lawrence would achieve; precisely as in the drama of dissonant art, the novelist asks the reader to rise to the Dionysian challenge of healing himself, of stirring himself to a creative affirmation in the face of death—the death even of conventional narrative itself. The strategy of dissonance requires not just that these novelists create structures of dissonance, but that each of them makes the value and meaning of his work depend on the reader's creative response.

II

I mentioned criticism's formal attempt to take up a musical analogy in order to analyze a literature of suggestive and sensuous effects. The roots of that attempt are, of course, in the symbolist movement in France, before that in the philosophy of Schopenhauer and in Romantic thought generally. Modern novelists were as strongly as they were variously influenced by the legacy of French and German aesthetics. When considered in the light of the assumptions of dissonance, however, Schopenhauer—with Wagner—and the French symbolists and England's Pater do not merely offer the rationale for technical experiment, for a "musical" prose; their ideas represent steps in the evolution of the modern novel's challenge to the reader that he in effect become the meaning of fiction.

To understand that complex development—and even, at times, a betrayal—of the insights of dissonance in fiction, we should first consider Schopenhauer's influential assertion of the value of music's "will-less" formulation of the inner life. Reality, in his view as in Conrad's, is implacably hostile to man, for it is a manifestation of irrational Will—impossible to satisfy and the source of the pain and evil of existence. In this pessimistic and ennervated conception, art's function for the perceiver is to achieve the absence of pain; art here provides the only genuine human pleasure, for it is the only human activity not at the service of the Will's remorseless striving. Music, for Schopenhauer as for the symbolists, stands above all the other arts. Its

formulation of feeling is a direct rendering of the Will, not simply as in the other arts a "representation of Ideas"—that is, of particular experiences. The contemplation of music is, to the philosopher, the transcendent achievement of the human mind and a crucial means of surviving the destructive world of the Will. Schopenhauer's view here has a significant bearing on Proust, Woolf, Conrad, and other novelists; even as they move beyond its limits, their works are shaped by a similar vision of art's transcendent role in a destructive and disintegrating world.

In the narrow perspective of the formalist use of a musical aesthetic, what to the philosopher is music's direct revelation of inner experience offers a rationale for the modern novel's exploration of the flux of perception. In these terms, a musical analogy illuminates how fiction complicates and transcends its traditional role of "representing" the world of social and moral conventions; instead, modern fiction provides the reader's imagination with the opportunity directly to encounter and comprehend the irrational flow of human time itself. In the larger perspective of a dissonant sensibility, however, a qualification complicates the remarkable parallels between modern fiction and a Schopenhauerian view of art. In the latter view, the aim of our experience as readers, as will-less subjects of a musically-conceived narrative, would be that we are "relieved of our suffering selves" and, thus, are in resigned sympathy with the suffering of all existence. Given the demand for our active engagement, like that in *Heart of Darkness,* the passive nature of the reader's experience in Schopenhauer's view gives rise to the crucial ambiguity qualifying his influence and also, we will see, that of the symbolists (who—in terms of both vision and experience—would, in Edmund Wilson's phrase, "rather drop out of common life than struggle to make themselves a place in it").

The assumptions—and also the limitations—of Schopenhauer's conception of music shape the view of art developed by Mallarmé, the central theoretician of symbolism. In Mallarmé's attempt to formulate the universe of Schopenhauerian "Ideas," he laid the groundwork for the modern formalist belief that poetry strives to achieve music's self-sustaining transcendence of modern reality, that poetry should imitate what is considered music's melodious, suggestive, and—in terms of content—infinitely ambiguous evocation of feeling's form. This article of the symbolists' faith reveals both the power and the limits of their aesthetic, particularly in its influence on the fiction of Joyce and Proust. Mallarmé's contemporary, Dujardin, first made the symbolist effort to bring to fiction a sense of music's "simultaneity, its development in time," and the resulting creation of an interior monologue prefigures in Joyce's view his own experimental rendering of the temporal flow of consciousness. Dujardin, as a symbolist novelist, thought of his musical fiction as a quasi-religious elevation of inner time, and this precise conception later gives rise to Proust's vision of the moments of spiritual time which enliven and redeem the chaotic mechanical flux of real experience. Yet these connections between a symbolist musical aesthetic and the great masterpieces of modern fiction emphasize the inability of that aesthetic to account for the creator's and the perceiver's fertile relationship to such fiction.

When fiction aspires merely to be a sensuous music, an art of pure "evocation, allusion and suggestion," the result is the often life-less and shallow symbolist efforts at the end of the nineteenth century. An ennervating desperation of intent indeed shapes the Mallarméan hope that a symbolist fiction would enable "the mind to seek its own native land again." Mistakenly, from the standpoint of modern fiction's rich confrontation both of the reader and of experience, the symbolist chooses the dream above disintegrating reality; a musical transcendence is his vocation, and necessarily that of his reader. The reader's role is fulfilled only by his entry into the world of symbolic forms the artist creates. Both the writer's and the reader's exploration of this "dream-like" inner world which a symbolist fiction would achieve leads not to the vital challenge and engagement of the reader in *Ulysses* and *Remembrance of Things Past,* but to the contemplation of "lyric forms" of "pure musicality"—the static forms of "self-sufficient" expressivity.

The strengths and failures of the symbolist aesthetic are found also in the work of Walter Pater; his views with those of the French writers are given a crucial, powerfully stylized expression in Arthur Symons' influential study of the symbolists. Pater's work forms an important aspect of the cultural milieu within and against which novelists in English, Joyce and Conrad for example, defined their art. In Pater's classic description of music in *The Renaissance,* he presents the formal ideal of music's pure expressivity. "It is the art of music which most completely realises the artistic ideal of the perfect identification of matter and form. In its consummate moments, the end is not distinct from the means, the form from the matter, the subject from the expression." Even as Conrad and Joyce move beyond the limits of this conception, their views of music and the later novelist's youthful celebration of the "rhythm phrase" as the perfected mode of literary expression echo Pater's statement and, indeed, his style of polished abstraction, repetition, and passive ambiguity. Such a style is itself "musical," for its assured and abstract artifice and its artful incantations seem to evoke and embody a higher, purer spiritual alternative to the demeaned prosaic world.

The suggestive ambiguity of his style "perfectly" renders the ambiguity of his meaning. What is Pater's central ambiguity, the source of both his power and his limitations? His idea of music as a model for art's "consummate moments" obscures the distinction between aesthetic form and the "aesthetic life"; the living subject and the formal expression are identical, Pater implies, and should equally "burn with a hard gem-like flame." The "Conclusion" to *The Renaissance,* which most fully develops this ambiguity, seems at times to mistake surface for depths, spectacle for substance, and it is this characteristic error which keeps Pater from fully achieving the insights of the dissonant sensibility.

Conrad and Joyce take up the Paterian sense of how life and art may be musically conjoined, but they transform it into a dissonant strategy by which the modern novel challenges the reader to explore its revelation of experience. At best, the ambiguity of Pater's conception becomes a vital means for these novelists to create an intentionally open-ended and challenging aesthetic encounter, an encounter which—in Pater's later view—is the aim of great art; their intentionally ambiguous narrative visions are made both to assault the reader and to endure—tempered and still expressive—through the reader's own response to that assault. At worst, however, Pater's aesthetic became a rationale for a style of over-wrought, gem-like effects, as well as for a shallow but consuming Wildean self-fabrication; and Joyce and Conrad view with transfiguring irony that paradoxical legacy of symbolism which Pater independently brought to English literature. The dangers of the legacy of his aesthetic led Yeats to remark that Pater taught the "tragic generation" at the *fin-de-siècle* to "walk upon a rope, tightly stretched through serene air, yet we were left to keep our feet upon a swaying rope in a storm."

The composer who, with Pater and the symbolists, encouraged such fateful aesthetic feats was Richard Wagner, and his thought and art can help us more precisely to define the ambiguous fertility of the late nineteenth-century idealization of music. Partly like Schopenhauer, Wagner was—in Mann's words—"the most glorious brother and comrade of all the sufferers from life, given to pity, seeking for transport, these art-mingling symbolists, worshippers of *l'art suggestif.*" Among these symbolists was the novelist Dujardin, editor of the *Revue Wagnerienne,* who was naturally attracted to Wagner's opera, for their extended forms spoke, in part like the genre of fiction, to and of a culture and a people. For Dujardin, Wagner's use particularly of chromatic dissonance and the leitmotif was an exemplary disintegration and restructuring of traditional form and provided the self-conscious model for his stream-of-consciousness experiment. Modern novelists, however, express a highly qualified admiration for the legacy of Wagner's art, and Dujardin himself vacillated radically in his judgment of the composer's example.

The basis of qualification concerns the central issue of the dissonant imagination, the question of the perceiver's experience of Wagner's operas. In a sense, Wagner's conception of the listener's role seems to involve no Schopenhauerian passivity of the individual perceiver's will. He saw his art as "an appeal to the feelings of the people"; he would mythologize their emotion with its natural and "healthy sensuality" (to use Nietzsche's ironic phrase). Wagner asserts that his art would be "religion brought to life," transforming the emotional life of humanity into "a mythic cry." Wagner, thus, wanted to give voice and religious, mythic sanction to what Schopenhauer thought art should transcend, a race's instinctual will. For the composer, the life and death of that will became a tragic myth. The underlying point here is that Wagner wants his music to hold the perceiver in its embrace; this is the case both when he glorifies the inner world of suffering and transport, and when he transforms "the people's" feelings into myth. Wagner's listener is the fulfilled yet fundamentally still passive recipient of the music's embrace, of feeling's grasp.

The views of art and experience developed by Wagner, Schopenhauer, and the symbolists are challenged by

Nietzsche's thought. In Mann's understated phrase, the philosopher was "irritated by a certain lack of clarity" particularly in Wagner's understanding of "psychological matters." Late in Nietzsche's life, the "enthusiasm of Mozart's dance" became a truer, more subtle expression of a dissonant sensibility than Wagnerian opera and more truly Dionysian and tragic in the face of man's impoverished inner life. Wagner's "frenzied" efforts seemed to him a blind and self-indulgent surrender to the awe and impotent rage of a falsely Dionysian spirit. Even in the advocacy in *The Birth of Tragedy* of those efforts, Nietzsche yet moves beyond the composer's myth-embracing view and asserts the role of the *individual's* imagination in the processes of dissonance.

In the dissonant conception of modern fiction, the reader is the ultimate subject of the narrative's formulation of existence, but not the ambiguously passive subject of "mythic" or "self-less" knowledge. In the face of disintegrating experience, the Dionysian effect of the modern novel is yet to stir in the reader a creative, self-realizing "delight" and "desire for existence." Dissonant fiction does not embody a Schopenhauerian resignation and neither does it voice the Wagnerian certainties of myth. Its central assumption is that the reader must independently comprehend and judge how its vision is "life-furthering." *Ulysses* or *Doctor Faustus,* Nietzsche can remind us, are fictions which one actively engages; only in that way do their illusions enable the reader to escape not time and suffering, but a passive stance towards the world of time and suffering. This is Nietzsche's crucial insight into the nature of the modern imagination.

The profound bearing of the dissonant aesthetic on Conrad's art, for example, is clear in *Heart of Darkness* with the suggestive disintegration of Marlow's perceptions there. In a statement which embodies the insights of dissonance (and which foreshadows E. M. Forster's—among others'—hope for a musical "expansion" and open-endedness in fiction), Conrad writes that *Heart of Darkness*

> was like another art altogether. That sombre theme had to be given a sinister resonance, a tonality of its own, a continued vibration that, I hoped, would hang in the air and dwell on the ear after the last note had been struck.

The voices Marlow hears and that he projects form this sinister and assaulting dissonance. Kurtz's voice, he says, has " 'the gift of expression, the bewildering, the illuminating, the most exalted and the most contemptible, the pulsating stream of light, or the deceitful flow from the heart of an impenetrable darkness.' " Marlow's voice—driven thus into anxious paradox and even silence—embodies the aim and effect of dissonance: like each element of symbol and event here, Marlow's self-challenging narration relies on the reader to transcend its limitations of piety and anxiety, to engage the unfinished task of insight and judgment, and so to take up that creative and, for Conrad, heroic role central to the novel's aim and meaning.

The dissonant aesthetic also bears—even more overtly—on Joyce's art in *Ulysses*; that crucial bearing concerns the

impact on the reader of the work's narrative artifice, rather than the novel's experimental, quasi-musical structures with their attempt at—among other things—a Wagnerian union of the arts. The significance of dissonance here can be seen in "Sirens" which indeed helps us to draw the distinction between a "prose music" and the effects achieved by the dissonant imagination. Take, for example, Bloom's perception of the high tenor note Simon Dedalus sings in the aria "M'appari":

> —Come!
>
> It soared, a bird, it held its flight, a swift pure cry, soar silver orb it leaped serene, speeding, sustained, to come, don't spin it out too long long breath he breath long life, soaring high, high resplendent, aflame, crowned, high in the effulgence symbolistic, high, of the ethereal bosom, high, of the high vast irradiation everywhere all soaring all around about the all, the endlessnessnessness.
>
> —To me!
>
> Siopold!

That the passage presents and parodies a self-consciously musical prose is not my point here; the profounder function of the passage is to confront the reader with the strategic complexity of Joyce's vision. Bloom's experience is enclosed within a structure of comic inflation and deflation which both victimizes and enchances the flow of his consciousness. Joyce's dissonant aim is to place the reader in the crucial position of perceiving and judging how the vitality of Bloom's experience endures within and despite the distortions of the very form which brings it to life. Bloom's experience of the music here issues in his creative identification with the operatic character Lionel and the singer Simon: "Siopold!" Such a response offers us an image for the reader's creative relationship to the strategy of dissonance in *Ulysses*. Our engagement of *Ulysses*—an involvement of perception and human judgment on which the work's value depends—is a version of Bloom's involvement with music above, only conscious of the distortion, the vitality, and the imaginative risk of self involved in our response: "Siopold!"

The value of a dissonant conception of the modern novel is, then, not to offer a paradigm for a "pure" symbolist narrative; the analogy between fiction and dissonance indeed suggests how our fiction would enable the reader to encounter the subversive realities from which the symbolists withdrew. Nor does dissonance merely provide one among several models for technical experiment, or for the effort "to complete the work of Wagner" in the novel. The idea of dissonance offers, rather, an insight into the creative role of the reader as he encounters the assaulting complexity, the ironic obliquity, and ambiguity of fiction in our century.

III

Criticism has in the past focused attention on the structural relationship between music and experiments in fiction. Such purely textural analyses of musical form in fiction make the assumption that the novel unfolds in time. In the words of one critic of Conrad, Woolf, and Joyce, when a "musical" fiction experiments "with the linear progression of language," it attempts to convey "the temporal multiplicity of inner experience." As such experiments render the temporal richness of consciousness, however, do they make it possible for the reader himself to enliven his sense of time? Modern fiction appears to abandon the traditional idea that imaginative communication with the reader is a direct and coherently expressive process, and it is commonly held that such experimental fiction, adapting the symbolist musical ideal, presents itself as a pure self-sustaining formal texture to the reader. In this way, for example, Joyce's fiction is often seen as a linguistic experiment in ambiguity. Yet that view can obscure strategic implications for the reader's experience.

The effort to explore the modern novel's value for the reader has been carried on in the searching criticism of, for example, Frank Kermode and W. J. Harvey; both analyze how in part musically-conceived form (the "virtual time" of *Ulysses* or the "reader's time" in *The Magic Mountain*—what Kermode, as we saw, called the reader's "discoveries of dissonance") is central to modern fiction's aesthetic and ethical intentions. The value to criticism of the musical analogy is the illumination it brings to the study of the narrative's crucial impact and reliance on the reader. Indeed, the connection between the frequent use of the analogy and the critical emphasis on ambiguity in fiction points to the insight which Nietzsche's view of disharmony can offer us—that dissonance ultimately formulates the responsive voice of the perceiver in art. Modern dissonant fiction becomes a means for the reader to declare and to explore his own freedom in time, in short to become the novelist of himself; novels as different as *Doctor Faustus* and *Women in Love* assume and achieve a new identity and partnership between the creator and the perceiver to wrest meaning out of a disintegrating time and culture.

To speak of the perceiver's opportunity in the face of fragmented and self-disintegrating form is, then, what modern fiction compels us to do; it forces us carefully to examine the experience of the reader. Fiction in our century renders the relentless and ambivalent tension between reality and human aspiration, and it stirs to life in us a sense of opposed emotional possibilities, a fullness of possibility—this is the perceiver's response of Dionysian emotion central to the definition of modernism in the arts. The dissonance of modern fiction dramatically heightens what is in Suzanne Langer's terms the central characteristic of musical utterance: an ambivalence of emotional reference. The idea of dissonance in fiction shows us how such heightened ambivalence of content challenges the reader to become the free yet obligatory explorer of the world of possibility—of disordering contradiction—modern fiction imagines. The reader's fascinated responsibility, central to the profound and distinguishing aims of the novel in our century, is to confront and choose among those possibilities for meaning. Fiction's adaptation of the sensibility of dissonance assaults the reader's sense of self and depends centrally on the depth and energy of the response that its self-challenging form stirs within him. That engagement of the reader—the demand, finally, that he become fic-

tion's meaning—is the aim underlying the idea of dissonance in modern fiction.

MUSIC IN LITERATURE

Carl Van Vechten

SOURCE: "Modern Musical Fiction," in *Interpreters and Interpretations,* Alfred A. Knopf, 1917, pp. 299-353.

[*In the following essay, Van Vechten comments on novels that have musical themes, giving particular consideration to Gertrude Atherton's* Tower of Ivory, *Bernard Shaw's* Love among the Artists, *and Henry Handel Richardson's* Maurice Guest.]

I

It has been the fashion for musicians to sneer at the attempts of literary men and women to celebrate their fellow-craftsmen. Novels which float in a tonal atmosphere frequently do contain a large percentage of errors, but is this not as true of novels which deal with electrical engineers, book-binders, painters, politicians, or clowns of the circus? Perhaps not quite. To learn the technical phraseology, the bibliography, the iconography, the history, the chronology of music, a man must devote a lifetime to its study. Happy the musical pedant who does not make blunders now and again. They cannot be avoided. Even our accredited music critics, be they ever so wary, occasionally fall into traps. In the circumstances we should smile leniently on the minor and major mistakes of our minor and major novelists. To a musician, to be sure, these are frequently ludicrous. One of Ouida's characters has the habit of playing organ selections from the masses of Mendelssohn, and the tenor in *Moths* goes about singing melodies from Palestrina! In *Les Misérables* Victor Hugo allots one of Hadyn's quartets to three violins and a flute. In *Peg Woffington* Charles Reade describes the actress as whistling a quick movement and then tells how Mr. Cibber was confounded by "this sparkling *adagio*," and the following passage from Marie Corelli's *The Sorrows of Satan* deserves what notoriety this page can afford it: "An amiable nightingale showed him (Prince Rimanez) the most elaborate methods of applying rhythmed tune to the upward and downward rush of the wind, thus teaching him perfect counterpoint, while chords he learnt from Neptune." Even George Moore, whose *Evelyn Innes* is generally regarded as one of the most successful attempts of a novelist to describe musicians and music, in *Ave* speaks of Anton Seidl as a broken old man who looked back upon his life as a failure. However, it is easy to paraphrase a happy remark made by Andrew Lang in his preface to *A Tale of Two Cities*: "The historical novelist is not the historian." So we may say that the musical novelist is not the musician.

In Europe writers of fiction have frequently chosen musical subjects. Balzac's *Gambara* and *Massimilla Doni,* the tale of a musical degenerate whose chief pleasure it is to hear two tones in perfect accord, come to mind. Other more or less familiar French examples are Camille Selden's *Daniel Vlady* (1862), Guillaume Edouard Désiré Monnaie's *Les Sept Notes de la Gamme* (1848), George Sand's *Consuelo*, and Romain Rolland's *Jean-Christophe*. Nor should one forget Saint-Landri, composer and conductor, who figures prominently in Guy de Maupassant's *Mont Oriol*. Listen to him: "Yes, my dear friend, it is finished, finished, the hackneyed style of the old school. The melodists have had their day. This is what people cannot understand, music is a new art, melody in its first lisping. The ignorant ear loves the burden of a song. It takes a child's pleasure, a savage's pleasure in it. I may add that the ears of the people or of the ingenuous public, the simple ears, will always love little songs, airs, in a word. It is an amusement similar to that in which the frequenters of café-concerts indulge. I am going to make use of a comparison in order to make myself understood. The eye of the rustic loves crude colours and glaring pictures; the eye of the intelligent representative of the middle class who is not artistic loves shades benevolently pretentious and affecting subjects; but the artistic eye, the refined eye, loves, understands, and distinguishes the imperceptible modulations of a single tone, the mysterious harmonies of light touches invisible to most people. . . . Ah! my friends, certain chords madden me, cause a flood of inexpressible happiness to penetrate all my flesh. I have to-day an ear so well exercised, so finished, so matured, that I end by liking even certain false chords, just like a virtuoso whose fully developed taste amounts to a form of depravity. I am beginning to be a vitiated person who seeks for extreme sensations of hearing. Yes, my friends, certain false notes. What delights! How this moves, how this shakes the nerves! how it scratches the ear—how it scratches! how it scratches!"

Hans Andersen has written at least two musical tales, *The Improvisatore* and *Only a Fiddler*. Another Norse story is Kristofer Janson's *The Spell-bound Fiddler*. In D'Annunzio's *Il Fuoco* there are long passages devoted to a discussion of music; Richard Wagner is a figure in this novel and there is an account of his death in Venice. There should be mention of Henryk Sienkiewicz's *Yanks the Musician and Other Tales*. Tolstoi made music rather than a musician the hero of *The Kreutzer Sonata*. It is the first and last time that this celebrated sonata for violin and piano has performed the offices of an aphrodisiac.

German literature is full of examples: Gustav Nicolai's *Arabesken* (1835) *Die Geweihten* (1836), and *Die Musikfeind,* G. Blaul's *Das Musikfest* (1836), August Kahlert's *Tonleben* (1838), G. A. Keferstein's *König Mys von Fidibus* (1838), Julius Becker's *Der Neuromantiker* (1840), Ludwig Bechstein's *Clarinette* (1840), Wilhelm Bachmann's *Catinka Antalani* (1845), Karl Goldmick's *Der Unsterbliche* (1848), Edward Maria Oettinger's *Rossini* (1851), Daniel Elster's *Des Nachtwächters Tochter* (1853), Eduard Mörike's *Mozart auf der Reise nach Prag* (1856), A. E. Brachvogel's *Friedemann Bach* (1859), and H. Rau's *Beethoven, Mozart,* and *Weber* are a few. Elise Polko's *Musical Tales* have been translated into English. One of the best of the German musical novels is comparatively re-

cent, Ernst von Wolzogen's *Der Kraft-Mayr,* translated by Edward Breck and Charles Harvey Genung as *Florian Mayr*. The book gives an excellent picture of the Liszt circle at Weimar; the composer is one of the leading figures of the story and James Huneker asserts that it is the best existing portrait of Liszt. Of course he is only presented as a teacher in his old age. Von Wolzogen, it will be remembered, supplied Richard Strauss with the book for his music drama, *Feuersnot,* yet to be given in America.

Elizabeth Sara Sheppard's *Charles Auchester,* with which both the names of Mendelsohn and Sterndale Bennett are connected, is generally spoken of as the first musical novel in English. This is not strictly true. There were earlier attempts. The fourth edition of *Musical Travels Through England*—by the late Joel Collier (George Veal) was issued in 1776 and *The Musical Tour of Dr. Minim, A. B. C. and D. E. F. G. with a description of a new invented instrument, a new mode of teaching music by machinery, and an account of the Gullabaic system in general* appeared in London in 1818. There is further *Major Piper; or the adventures of a Musical Drone* in five volumes by the Reverend J. Thompson, the second edition of which appeared in 1803, but there is less about music in this novel than the title would imply. Since *Charles Auchester* there has been indeed a brood of musical novels. *Alcestis,* dealing with musical life in Dresden in the time of Hasse, appeared in 1875. Jessie Fothergill's sentimental story, *The First Violin* was published in 1878. Sometime later it was made into a play for Richard Mansfield. There are many others: George Meredith's *Sandra Belloni* and *Vittoria,* Kate Clark's *The Dominant Seventh,* J. Mitchell Chapple's *The Minor Chord,* Edna Lyall's *Doreen,* Rita's *Countess Daphne,* Marion Crawford's *A Roman Singer,* Edward L. Stevenson's *A Matter of Temperament,* George Augustus Sala's *The Two Prima Donnas,* J. H. Shorthouse's *A Teacher of the Violin,* A. M. Bagby's *Miss Träumerei,* Jane Kingsford's *The Soprano,* Henry Harland's *As It was Written,* Henry Fothergill Chorley's *A Prodigy* (in three volumes, dedicated to Charles Dickens), William Kennedy's *The Prima Donna,* Mrs. S. Samuel's *Cherry the Singer,* Hall Caine's *The Prodigal Son,* Allen Raine's *A Welsh Singer,* Lucas Cleeve's *From Crown to Cross,* E. F. Benson's *Sheaves,* George du Maurier's *Trilby,* Anne Douglas Sedgwick's (Mrs. Basil de Sélincourt) *Tante,* made into a play for Ethel Barrymore, Arnold Bennett's *The Glimpse,* John Philip Sousa's *The Fifth String,* Gustave Kobbe's *All-of-a-Sudden Carmen,* Della Pratt Grant's *Travelli, The Sorceress of Music,* J. Meade Falkner's *The Lost Stradivarius,* Myrtle Reed's *The Master's Violin,* and H. A. Vachell's *The Other Side.* At least one of Walter Pater's tales, "Denys l'Auxerrois," is based on a musical theme, of a pagan boy who builds an organ, a pretty fable told with emotion and rhythm. Two of James Huneker's twelve volumes, *Melomaniacs* and *Visionaries,* are devoted to short stories on musical subjects.

Robert Hichens has written one musical novel, *The Way of Ambition.* The story is that of an English composer, Claude Heath, married to an ambitious young woman, Charmian, who determines to "make him." In this attempt she almost wrecks his career but after the complete failure of the opera she has urged him to write, he asserts himself and makes her see the folly of trying to direct the course of an artist. The beginning of the struggle is most amusingly depicted:

"On the morning after the house-warming, when a late breakfast was finished, but while they were still at the breakfast-table in the long and narrow dining-room, which looked out on the quiet square, Charmian said to her husband:

" 'I've been speaking to the servants, Claude. I've told them about being very quiet to-day.'

"He pushed his tea-cup a little away from him. 'Why?' he asked. 'I mean why specially to-day?'

" 'Because of your composing. Alice is a good girl, but she is a little inclined to be noisy sometimes. I've spoken to her seriously about it.'

"Alice was the parlour-maid. Charmian would have preferred to have a man answer the door, but she had sacrificed to economy, or thought she had done so, by engaging a woman. As Claude said nothing, Charmian continued:

" 'And another thing! I've told them all that you're never to be disturbed when you're in your own room, that they're never to come to you with notes, or the post, never to call you to the telephone. I want you to feel that once you are inside your own room you are absolutely safe, that it is sacred ground.'

" 'Thank you, Charmian.'

"He pushed his cup farther away, with a movement that was rather brusque, and got up.

" 'What about lunch to-day? Do you eat lunch when you are composing? Do you want something sent up to you?'

" 'Well, I don't know. I don't think I shall want any lunch to-day. You see we've breakfasted late. Don't bother about me.'

" 'It isn't a bother. You know that, Claudie. But would you like a cup of coffee, tea, anything at one o'clock?'

" 'Oh, I scarcely know. I'll ring if I do.'

"He made a movement. Charmian got up.

" 'I do long to know what you are going to work on,' she said, in a changed, almost mysterious, voice, which was not consciously assumed.

. . . . .

"Claude went up to the little room at the back of the house. At this moment he would gladly, thankfully, have gone anywhere else. But he felt he was expected to go there. Five women, his wife and the four maids, expected him to go there. So he went. He shut himself in, and remained there, caged."

We subsequently learn that he passed the time that day, and many thereafter reading Carlyle's *French Revolution.* Now this is amusing.

Heath has a leaning towards Biblical subjects for his inspiration but Charmian urges him to write an opera; she succeeds, indeed, in making him do so and she also succeeds

in disposing of it to Jacob Crayford, an American impresario who seems faintly modelled after Oscar Hammerstein. A good part of the book is taken up with descriptions of the writing of this opera (there is a striking passage descriptive of oriental music), its rehearsals, its performance, and its failure. Robert Hichens knows music (he was at one time a music critic) and he knows the stage. These scenes are carefully done, but he asks the New York music critics to pass judgment on Heath's opera without having seen or heard the rehearsals. This is an inaccuracy. . . . One of the characters, a Frenchwoman, says, "English talent is not for opera. The Te Deum, the cathedral service, the oratorio form in one form or another, in fact the thing with a sacred basis, that is where the English strength lies." Mme. Sennier probably overlooked the fact that England's two greatest composers, Purcell and Sir Arthur Sullivan, did write operas and that most of the oratorios popular in England were written by Germans. Heath desires to write music for Francis Thompson's "The Hound of Heaven" to the dismay of his wife who reads him other poetry in an attempt to set his muse on the right road. "She re-read Rossetti, Keats, Shelley, dipped into William Morris,—Wordsworth no—into Fiona Macleod, William Watson, John Davidson, Alfred Noyes." In the end, we are led to believe, Heath was well on the road towards becoming another Elgar.

W. J. Henderson's musical romance, *The Soul of a Tenor,* is particularly wooden and lifeless. The characters are but puppets at the behest of a not very skilful manipulator. The story concerns Leandro Baroni (originally Leander Barrett of Pittsburg), a tenor at the Metropolitan Opera House, who through a love affair with a gypsy soprano, Nagy Bosanska, finds "his soul," becomes a great Tristan, and returns to his puritanic and faithful American wife, from whom he had become estranged. There are glimpses of other singers, of rehearsals at the Metropolitan Opera House, of performances of *L'Africaine* and other operas. The author disclaims any intention of painting portraits of living models, with a brief exception in favour of magnificent Lilli Lehman rehearsing and singing *Don Giovanni* at Salzburg (Baroni is the Ottavio), but surely Mrs. Harley Manners, who attends morning musicales and rehearsals at the Opera, is an almost recognizable character. There are amusing pages; that in which the critics' views of Baroni are exposed is the most diverting: "It was universally conceded that he was in some ways the most gifted tenor since Jean de Reszke. The *Boston Herald* declared that he was far greater because one night, when he had a cold, he sang out of tune, and this the Boston man declared showed that he was not a mere vocal machine. The *Evening Post* of New York fell at his feet because, when made up for Lohengrin, he was the image of Max Alvary. That he sang it like Campanini was not mentioned. The *Tribune* published a deprecatory essay two columns long after he sang Don Ottavio in Mozart's inaccessible *Don Giovanni* and a sprightly weekly printed eight pictures of him and his shoes and stockings, with a Sunday page giving an intimate account of his manner of taking his morning bath and dressing for the day. The *American* expressed regrets about him because, being an American, he did not advocate opera in English. The *Sun* went into a profound analysis of his vocal method and his treatment of recitative in all schools of opera, showing thereby that he was a greater master of the lyric art than Farinelli or Garat, singers of whom the readers of the article had never heard, and about whom, therefore, they cared absolutely nothing. The *Times* asserted that he had no method at all, and that this was what made him a truly great singer." Erudition steeps this pen, but why does Mr. Henderson, himself a music critic, and therefore not liable to error, spell Bruckner with an *umlaut*?

There are points of interest about Willa Sibert Cather's recent musical novel, *The Song of the Lark,* although I do not think the book as a whole can be considered successful. The Swedish-American singer who plods through its pages at the behest of the eyes of the reader was undoubtedly suggested by Olive Fremstad. The first hundred pages of the book are the best. Thea Kronborg growing up in Moonstone, Colorado, and her childhood friends are thoroughly delightful. The study years in Chicago and the love scenes in the home of the Cliff Dwellers are neither so interesting nor so true. Kronborg, the artist, does not seem to be realized by Miss Cather. The outlines of the completed figure are much more vague than those of the original rough sketch. Indeed as Thea grows older she seems to elude the author more and more. . . . Thea's artistic soul is born before Jules Breton's picture in the Chicago Art Institute; hence the title. . . . The fable is weak and the men who fill in the later pages are mere lay figures. There is a brief glimpse of Theodore Thomas and an arresting description of Pauline Viardot as Orphée. H. R. Haweis's *Musical Memories* play a part in Thea's early life. A Chicago soprano is drawn rather skilfully. . . . Thea at the Metropolitan Opera House sings Elsa, Sieglinde, Venus and Elizabeth, Leonora (in *Trovatore*), and Fricka in *Das Rheingold.* Here is a passage which describes Olive Fremstad as well as it does Thea Kronborg: "It's the idea, the basic idea, pulsing behind every bar she sings. She simplifies a character down to the musical idea it's built on, and makes everything conform to that. The people who chatter about her being a great actress don't seem to get the notion of where *she* gets the notion. It all goes back to her original endowment, her tremendous musical talent. Instead of inventing a lot of business and expedients to suggest character, she knows the thing at the root, and lets the musical pattern take care of her. The score pours her into all those lovely postures, makes the light and shadow go over her face, lifts her and drops her. She lies on it, the way she used to lie on the Rhine music. Talk about rhythm!"

There are many plays on musical subjects: *The Broken Melody, La Tosca, The Greater Love, The Music Master, The Climax, The Tongues of Men,* Edward Knoblauch's *Paganini,* Hermann Bahr's *The Concert,* and René Fauchois's *Beethoven* are a few. Frank Wedekind has written two plays which may be included in the list: *Der Kammersänger,* presented as *The Tenor* by the Washington Square Players, and *Musik.*

II

Tower of Ivory

It was to have been expected that Gertrude Atherton, who allows no ink to drop idly from her pen, would turn her attention to the American girl as opera singer; in a flamboyant and breathless romance, *Tower of Ivory,* she has done so, on the whole creditably. There is considerably of reality about Margarete Styr, once Peggy Hill of New York. Mrs. Atherton has wisely set her history back in the last days of the mad Ludwig of Bavaria, for there might have been recognition scenes if she had made it contemporaneous. The author has admitted that Mottl-Fassbender was her model, but she has allowed her imagination full rein. Mottl-Fassbender is not an American, nor has she ever suggested a "tower of ivory"; however, she cannot be held responsible for Styr's early life. Mrs. Atherton's heroine was born in a mining camp, the daughter of a poor miner, and passes her childhood in dirty drudgery. Seduced by a drummer, she is taken to New York where she passes from one man to another until she falls into the hands of a millionaire who begins her musical education. By this time, however, she is so disgusted with the male sex that she runs away presently to join a travelling theatrical troupe. In a short Pacific voyage, from one town to another, she suffers shipwreck and her life is saved by a boy who ties her to a floating mast, projecting above the angry waves, and who clings to it desperately himself as there is no more rope. After several hours she sees him drop below where he is washed away, the helpless prey of the sea. At this moment her soul is born, what Mrs. Atherton calls the "Soul of an Artist." Remembering her voice she goes to Europe. She begins to read. One of the few books mentioned is *A Rebours.* These study years or months are elided. They are dangerous ground for a novelist. It will be remembered that George Moore neglected to furnish them in *Evelyn Innes.* When we first meet the Styr, indeed, she has erased her past, has become the reigning Wagnerian singer in Munich, the favourite artist of Ludwig, and an ascetic. She lives alone and is rarely to be seen except on the stage. Shut up in her tower over the Isar her personal life becomes a mystery. Through this isolation a young Englishman, charmingly characterized, much better done on the whole than the Styr herself, breaks. As he enters her house Mrs. Atherton describes it to us. It is a relief to discover that the Styr has as bad taste in house decoration as most singers. Have you ever been in a prima donna's apartment?

"She felt some vanity in displaying her salon to one she knew instinctively possessed a cultivated and exacting taste. It was a large room on the right of the entrance, with a row of alcoves on the garden side, each furnished to represent one of the purple flowers. The wood-work was ivory white; the silk panels of the same shade were painted with lilacs, pansies, asters, orchids, or lilies, as if reflecting the alcoves. There was but one picture, a full-length portrait of Styr as Brynhildr, by Lenbach. The spindle-legged furniture was covered with pale brocades and not aggressive of any period. It was distinctly a 'Styr Room,' as her admirers, who were admitted on the first Sunday of the month, had long since agreed, while sealing it with their approval."

Styr's répertoire includes the Brünnhildes, Isolde, Kundry, Elizabeth and Venus, Iphigenia, the Countess in *Figaro,* Katherina in *The Taming of the Shrew,* Leonora in *Fi-*

delio, Donna Anna, Aida, and Dido in *Les Troyens.* She is indeed the "*hochdramatisch*" of the Hoftheater in Munich. She gives command performances of *Parsifal, Götterdämmerung,* and *Tristan* before Ludwig, always at midnight, the favourite hour of that remarkable monarch. On one occasion she smuggles her young Englishman in and he hears the king heave a deep sigh, presumably because after death he will have no further opportunities for enjoying the music of Wagner. . . . When we first meet the Styr she sings alone, by command, at Neuschwanstein, the country palace of Ludwig, at midnight and out of doors, on a bridge which crosses a mountain torrent. Her selections, chosen by the monarch, include Kundry's appearance to Klingsor, Act II, Scene I of *Parsifal,* part of the ensuing scene, the Cry of the Valkyries, and finally a group of songs. This reads very much like a description of Mme. Gadski appearing with the Philharmonic Society. The Styr, however, sings unaccompanied, without orchestra or piano!

There is a long account of her Isolde. We are told that by the expression of her eyes alone she can fix the mood of her audience. Her powers of suggestion are uncanny. On one occasion she shows the Englishman how she would play Mrs. Alving:

" 'I won't permit you to question my right to be called an actress! You remember the scene in *Ghosts* in which Mrs. Alving listens to Oswald's terrible revelation?'

"He nodded, holding his breath. She did not rise, nor repeat a word of the play, but he watched her skin turn grey, her muscles bag, the withering cracking soul stare through her eyes. Every part of her face expressed a separate horror, and he could have sworn that her hair turned white."

Mrs. Siddons, according to report, could move a roomful of people to tears merely by repeating the word, "Hippopotamus" with varying stress.

As Isolde the Styr gives another example of this power, "staring at the phials in the casket while the idea of death matured in her desperate brain,—death for herself as well as for the man that betrayed her,—raised her head slowly, her body to its full height. She looked the very genius of death, a malign fate awaiting its moment to settle upon the ripest fruits, the blithest hopes. A subtle gesture of her hand seemed to deprive it of its flesh, leave it a talon which held a scythe; by the same token one saw the skeleton under the blue robe; her mouth twisted into a grin, her eyes sank. It was all over in half a minute, it was but a fleeting suggestion, but it flashed out upon every sensitive soul present a picture of the charnel house, the worm, death robbed of its poetry, stripped to the bones by the hot blasts from that caldron of hate."

We learn that "No other Isolde has ever been as great as Styr, for no other has been able to suggest this ferocious approach of a devastating force, this hurricane sweeping across the mind's invisible plain, tearing at the very foundations of life. And all this she expressed before singing a note, with her staring moving eyes, her eloquent body, still and concealed as it was, a gesture of the hand. . . . When she started up, crying out to the wind and waves to shatter the ship the passion in her voice hardly expressed the rage consuming her in plainer terms than that first long silent moment had done."

Brain, says Styr, all brain: " 'You give no stage artist the credit of a brain, I suppose? Can you imagine a born actress—born, mind you—living her part, yet never quite shaking loose from that strong grip above? That is what is meant by "living a part." You abandon yourself deliberately—with the whole day's preparation—into that other personality, almost to a soul in possession, and are not your own self for one instant; although the purely mental part of that self never relaxes its vigilance over the usurper. It is a curious dual experience that none but an artist can understand. Of course that perfect duality is only possible after years of study, work, practical experience, mastery of technique. . . . Most singers have no brain, no mental life; they must be taught their rôles like parrots, they put on a simulation of art with their costumes which deceives the great stupid public and touches no one. Mere emotionalism, animal robustness, they call temperament. I strengthened and developed my brain during those terrible years to such an extent that I now act out of it, think myself into every part, relying not at all upon the instructions of the uninspired, nor upon chance.' "

However, even brainy prima donnas with disgust for all men in their hearts are occasionally exposed to emotional storms, thinks Mrs. Atherton. The departure of Ordham for England and his subsequent marriage (there had never been talk of love or marriage between Ordham and Styr; their relationship up to this time had been idealistic) threw Styr into a frightful state. The bad news came to her on a *Tristan* night. She flung aside her carefully studied gestures, her prepared effects, and stormed through the music drama. Afterwards she felt that this performance had been so electrifying that any return to her original conception of the rôle would be considered as an anti-climax. So she steadfastly refused to sing Isolde in Munich again. As a matter of fact this was probably the worst performance she had ever given.

There are descriptions of the singer as Brünnhilde: "In *Die Walküre* she made her alternately the jubilant sexless favourite of Wotan, shadowed subtly with her impending womanhood, and the goddess of aloof and immutable calm, Will personified, even when moved to pity. In *Götterdämmerung,* particularly of late, she had portrayed her as woman epitomized, arguing that all great women had the ichor of the goddess in their veins, and that primal woman was but the mother of sex modified (sometimes) but not remade. In the last act of *Siegfried* her voice was wholly dramatic and expressed her delight at coming into her woman's inheritance in ecstatic cries, almost shouts, which were never to be forgotten by any that heard them, and stirred the primal inheritance in the veriest butterfly of the court. In this beautiful love scene of *Götterdämmerung,* the last of the tetralogy, her voice was lyric, rich and round and full, as her voice must always be, but stripped of its darker quality, and while by no means angelic, a character with which she could invest it when portraying the virgin Elizabeth, was as sweet and clear and triumphant as if bent upon giving the final expression to the first love of woman alloyed with knowledge." Somewhere else in the book there is another clue to her conception of the rôle of Brünnhilde: "Of late Styr had played the character consistently to the end as a woman. But to-night she appeared to defer once more to Wagner—possibly to the King—and to be about to symbolize the 'negation of the will to live,' the eternal sacrifice of woman, the immolation of self; although she had contended, and for that reason sang no more at Bayreuth, that such an interpretation was absurd as a finale for Brünnhilde, no matter what its beauty and truth in the abstract. The gods were doomed, her renunciation of life did not save them, and as for the sacrifice of woman to man, that she had accomplished twice over. Brünnhilde died as other women had died since, and doubtless before, in the hope of uniting with the spirit of her man, and because life was become abhorrent."

In the scene with Siegfried disguised as Gunther Styr made another of those physical transformations which so startled her audiences; at the close of the drama she mounted her horse and rode straight into the flames. Mrs. Atherton says that only "Vogel" had done this before her. Probably she refers to Therese Vogl, a favourite Wagnerian singer in Munich in the Eighties and early Nineties. According to report Vogl (or was it Rosa Sucher?) did indeed mount the horse and charge into the wings, whereupon a dummy mounted on a *papier maché* horse was swung across the back of the stage into the flames. A substitution of this sort is in vogue in the Witch's ride in *Hänsel und Gretel* at the Metropolitan Opera House. There have been those who have danced the Dance of the Seven Veils in *Salome;* there have been tenors who have taken the terrific falls of Fra Diavolo or of Mâtha in *Salammbô,* but I have never heard of a Brünnhilde who has been brave enough to ride her Grane into the flames. Not trusting my own memory I asked Tom Bull, who has seen all the performances of the Wagner dramas at the Metropolitan since they were first produced there. He said that no soprano had ever attempted the feat at that house. "We've had but one Brünnhilde that would dare do it and that's Fremstad. She never did, however. No one ever did here. Why, we've had the same horse for years, a tame old creature, and even now he baulks on occasion." As luck would have it that very day this nag gave the occupants of the stage some trouble!

There is an amusing scene depicting the effect of Wagner on the artistic temperament. Those of us who have been unfortunate enough to have visited singers in their dressing-rooms on such occasions will appreciate the following account:

"He (Ordham) had made his way across the back of the stage, passed opened doors of supers who were frankly disrobing, too hungry to observe the minor formalities, and was approaching the room of the prima donna, when its door was suddenly flung open, a little man was rushed out by the collar, twirled round, and hurled almost at his feet. The Styr, her hair down, her face livid, her eyes blazing shouted hoarsely at the object of her wrath, who took to his heels. The *intendant* rushed upon the scene. Styr screamed out that the minor official had dared come to her dressing-room with a criticism upon the set of her wig, and

that if ever she were spoken to again at the close of a performance by any member of the staff, from the *intendant* down, she would leave Munich the same night. The great functionary fled, for she threatened to box his ears unless he took himself out of her sight, and the Styr, stormed up and down, beat the scenery with her hands, stamped, hissed, her pallor deepening every second, until it was like white fire. Ordham half fascinated, half convulsed, at this glimpse of the artistic temperament in full blast, stared at her with his mouth open. She looked like some fury of the coal-pit, flying up from the sooty galleries on the wings of her voice. Her words had been delivered with a strange broad burring accent, which Ordham found more puzzling than her tantrum.

"Suddenly she caught sight of him. If possible her fury waxed.

" 'You! You!' she screamed. 'Go! Get out of here! How dare you come near me? I hate you! I hate the whole world when I have finished an opera! They ought to give me somebody to kill! Go! I don't care whether you ever speak to me again or not—' "

Later she apologizes and explains: " 'It is all over a few hours later, after I have taken a long walk in the Englischergarten, then eaten a prosaic supper of cold ham and fowl, eggs perchance, and salad! But for an hour after these triumphs I pay! I pay!' " Mrs. Atherton, perhaps, has idealized her heroine when she gives her better manners in private life: " 'Tantrums do not hurt a prima donna; in fact they are of use in inspiring the authorities with awe. But in private life—well, the price I sometimes had to pay was too high. I soon stopped throwing things about like a fishwife; and all the rest of it.' "

Evelyn Innes, it will be remembered, gave herself to Ulick Dean after a performance of *Tristan.* One of the characters of *The Way of Ambition* says: "The Empress Frederick told a friend of mine that no one who had not lived in Germany, and observed German life closely, could understand the evil spread through the country by Wagner's *Tristan.*" "It is no wonder," says Mrs. Atherton, "the Germans keep on calling for more sensation, more thrill with an insatiety which will work the ruin of music and drama in their nation unless some genius totally different from Wagner rises and diverts them into safer channels. Beyond Wagner in his own domain there is nothing but sensationalism. Rather he took all the gold out of the mine he discovered and left but base alloy for the misguided disciples."

Margarete Styr was not engaged by Walter Damrosch to sing in New York although there seems to have been correspondence between them. But she did sing in London under Hans Richter and made a great success there. Her rôles seem to have been the three Brünnhildes, Isolde, and Elizabeth. It was not felt that London was sophisticated enough to sit through her very voluptuous representation of Venus; so an older, fatter singer was put in the part and much of the scene was cut. Styr made her appearance as Elizabeth in the second act after the boxes were filled. Queen Victoria, having heard rumours of Peggy Hill's life in New York, refused to meet the Styr socially, did not entertain her at Buckingham or Windsor, but everybody else in London seems to have invited her.

III

Love Among the Artists

Bernard Shaw wrote *Love Among the Artists* in 1881, but of all his published novels (the first of the five has never been printed) it was the last to reach the public; it was published serially in *Our Corner* in 1887-8. The author has never professed admiration for any of these early works. Dixon Scott calls Shaw the "son of Donizetti's *Lucrezia Borgia*," and the Irishman concedes the truth of this description when he says "I was brought up in an atmosphere in which two of the main constituents were Italian opera and complete freedom of thought." He has written musical criticism and one complete book on music, *The Perfect Wagnerite;* all through his work run references to the tonal art, expertly expressed and adroitly placed. *Love Among the Artists* is far from being a completely satisfactory novel but on its musical side, at least, it is very diverting, and it is much more modern in its comments than most of the musical novels of a couple of decades later. In a preface the author explains his purpose, "I had a notion of illustrating the difference between the enthusiasm for the fine arts which people gather from reading about them, and the genuine artistic faculty which cannot help creating, interpreting, or at least unaffectedly enjoying music and pictures." There are actresses and painters in the book but the most clearly outlined characters are musicians, an English composer (did such a good one ever exist?) and a Polish pianist. Both are delightfully limned and although it has been my misfortune up to date to meet softer-spirited and less noble-minded composers than Owen Jack who is done in the grand manner, modelled somewhat after Beethoven, at least the lady pianist is like the average interpretative instrumental artist.

We first meet Mme. Aurélie Szczympliça at the rehearsal of Jack's *Fantasia* by the Antient Orpheus Society. She has consented to introduce the new music to England; indeed so highly does she regard the composition, although she does not know the composer, that she has prevailed upon the directors of the Society to reverse their unfavourable decision in regard to its performance. Accompanied by her mother she comes in bundled in furs, and asks the conductor to rehearse the *Fantasia* first, although she avows her intention of remaining to hear the orchestra go through with the rest of the programme. Jack is allowed to conduct his own work. The first section goes pretty well.

"But when a theme marked *andante cantabile,* which formed the middle section of the fantasia, was commenced by the pianist, Jack turned to her; said 'Quicker, quicker. *Plus vite*'; and began to mark his beat by striking the desk. She looked at him anxiously; played a few bars in the time indicated by him; and then threw up her hands and stopped.

" 'I cannot,' she exclaimed. 'I must play it more slowly or not at all.'

" 'Certainly, it shall be slower if you desire it,' said the elder lady from the steps. Jack looked at her as he sometimes looked at Mrs. Simpson. 'Certainly it shall not be slower, if all the angels desired it,' he said, in well pronounced but barbarously ungrammatical French. 'Go on; and take the time from my beat.'

"The Polish lady shook her head; folded her hands in her lap; and looked patiently at the music before her. There was a moment of silence, during which Jack, thus mutely defied, glared at her with distorted features. Manlius rose irresolutely. Jack stepped down from the desk; handed him the stick; and said in a smothered voice, 'Be good enough to conduct this lady's portion of the fantasia. When *my* music recommences, I will return.' "

After the lady has had her way Jack is convinced that it is better than his!

She plays at the concert, appears in society, and immediately fascinates the stupidest young man in the book, Adrian Herbert, who breaks his engagement with an English lady to marry her. He paints very badly and his favourite composer is Mendelssohn. He sees nothing in Jack and his artist-wife acquires a great contempt for his opinions. They begin to quarrel soon after they are married; and each quarrel is usually followed by a passionate reunion. There is no question about her preferring her piano to her husband. Her mother is a mere automaton. Aurélie's world revolves around her ambition. Yet she is a lady. She would not promise to marry Adrian until he had secured his release from his engagement with the English girl; her manners in general are good. She is always, however, coldly self-sufficient. She does not speak English very fluently and like all artists she is susceptible to flattery, so that when an American utters some stupid commonplaces in the language she only half understands she gives him credit for possessing a high degree of intelligence. A baby is born to this ill-assorted pair and this baby provides the occasion for one of the most deliciously humorous scenes in the book:

"Mary was in the act of handing the child carefully back to Madame Szczympliça, when Aurélie interposed swiftly; tossed it up to the ceiling; and caught it dexterously. Adrian stepped forward in alarm; Madame uttered a Polish exclamation; and the baby itself growled angrily. Being sent aloft a second time, it howled with all its might.

" 'Now you shall see,' said Aurélie, suddenly placing it, supine, kicking and screaming, on the pianoforte. She then began to play the Skaters' Quadrille from Meyerbeer's opera of *The Prophet*. The baby immediately ceased to kick; became silent; and lay still with the bland expression of a dog being scratched, or a lady having her hair combed.

" 'It has a vile taste in music,' she said, when the performance was over. 'It is old fashioned in everything. Ah yes. Monsieur Sutherland: would you kindly pass the little one to my mother.' "

Owen Jack is the type of high-tempered, ridiculously natural (without a trace of self-consciousness) composer, with, it must be added, a strong strain of romanticism in his blood. He does not resemble Percy Grainger, Cyril Scott,

Claude Debussy, Giacomo Puccini, or Engelbert Humperdinck. He is discovered on a park bench in the first chapter of the book, where, overhearing an old gentleman bemoaning his inability to find a tutor for his son, he applies for the position. Thus the author describes his first appearance: "He was a short, thick-chested young man, in an old creased frock coat, with a worn-out hat and no linen visible. His skin, pitted by smallpox, seemed grained with black, as though he had been lately in a coal-mine, and had not yet succeeded in towelling the coal-dust from his pores. He sat with his arms folded, staring at the ground before him. One hand was concealed under his arm: the other displayed itself, thick in the palm, with short fingers, and nails bitten to the quick. He was clean shaven, and had a rugged, resolute mouth, a short nose, marked nostrils, dark eyes, and black hair, which curled over his low, broad forehead." Jack is engaged, after queries have been made and more or less satisfactory replies have been received in regard to his past, and goes to the Sutherland home at Windsor where he proceeds to pound the spinet into bits, to rag the servants, to express his frank opinions of Adrian's vile painting, and finally after he has alienated most of the household, to precipitate a situation of ejection by bringing a drunken soldier to the house to play the clarinet. On the way to London he bursts into a first class compartment, occupied by an old man, who has bribed the guard to be allowed to travel alone, and his daughter, Magdalen, who is being taken home a prisoner from the delights of life on the stage. A most outrageous squabble follows. Once in the London station the girl sees a chance to escape and presses Jack to accept a ring in return for cab fare. He empties his pockets into her hands, with a gesture of gallantry, gold, silver, copper, about four pounds altogether, and refuses the ring, but she sends a porter after him with it. Later Jack gives Magdalen lessons in speaking, teaches her how to use her voice, and she becomes a successful actress, a state of affairs which her family accepts with resignation. Jack also enters into an engagement to teach singing to a class of young ladies, who arouse his deepest ire. Genius in its old age is sometimes able to give instruction without losing its temper; never in youth. As a matter of fact great interpretative artists, great composers, are never the best teachers. Jack as a teacher is impossible. On one occasion he interrupts a lesson to leave the room in a rage; asked when he will return he snaps, "Never!" But he comes back for the next lesson as if nothing had happened, and indeed, so far as he was concerned, nothing had. His landlady gives a further illuminating description of Jack as a teacher:

" 'I got him a stationer's daughter from High Street to teach. After six lessons, if you'll believe it, Miss, and she as pleased as anything with the way she was getting along, he told the stationer that it was waste of money to have the girl taught, because she had no qualification but vanity. So he lost her; and now she has lessons at four guineas a dozen from a lady that gets all the credit for what he taught her. Then Simpson's brother-in-law got him a place in a chapel in the Edgeware Road to play the harmonium and train the choir. But they couldn't stand him. He treated them as if they were dogs; and the three richest old ladies in the congregation, who had led the singing for forty-five years, walked out the second night, and said they wouldn't enter the chapel till he was gone. When the minister rebuked him, he up and said that if he was a God and they sang to him like that, he'd scatter 'em with lightning!' "

In a sudden outburst Jack explains himself to a lady who has been instrumental in getting him pupils: " 'Here am I, a master of my profession—no easy one to master—rotting, and likely to continue rotting unheard in the midst of a pack of shallow panders, who make a hotch-potch of what they can steal from better men, and share the spoil with the corrupt performers who thrust it upon the public for them. Either this, or the accursed drudgery of teaching, or grinding an organ at the pleasure of some canting villain of a parson, or death by starvation, is the lot of a musician in this country. I have, in spite of this, never composed one page of music bad enough for publication or performance. I have drudged with pupils when I could get them, starved in a garret when I could not; endured to have my works returned to me unopened or declared inexecutable by shop-keepers and lazy conductors; written new ones without any hope of getting even a hearing for them; dragged myself by excess of this fruitless labour out of horrible fits of despair that come out of my own nature; and throughout it all have neither complained nor prostituted myself to write shopware. I have listened to complacent assurances that publishers and concert-givers are only too anxious to get good original work—that it is their own interest to do so. As if the dogs would know original work if they saw it: or rather as if they would not instinctively turn away from anything good and genuine! All this I have borne without suffering from it—without the humiliation of finding it able to give me one moment of disappointment or resentment; and now you tell me that I have no patience, because I have no disposition to humour the caprices of idle young ladies.' "

This is most excellent stuff and there is more of it. Of Jack as a composer we have several glimpses, but from the scene in which he pays the drunken clarinettist to play a part in his *Fantasia* so that he may know how it will sound, it is foreordained that he will become a great figure. I must omit the very amusing preliminary negotiations, the prolonged exchange of notes, which prelude the performance of Jack's *Fantasia* by the Antient Orpheus Society. But an incident of the rehearsal is too good to leave unquoted, especially as it will remind readers of a similar incident in the life of Hugo Wolf, used by Romain Rolland in his novel, *Jean-Christophe*. But Shaw imagined the scene before it happened to Wolf! To be sure with a happier ending. The Antient Orpheus Society is any Philharmonic Society, conductor, board of directors and all, to the life. I suppose they are like that in Abyssinia if they are so unfortunate as to have philharmonic orchestras there. The plot of Wagner's *Die Meistersinger* is enacted season after season at the meetings of the doddering old fools who control the destinies of the society. The fussy old idiots take creaking cautious steps towards the future. These are fully described . . . and finally the rehearsal in the great Chapter IX:

"Jack had rapped the desk sharply with his stick, and was looking balefully at the men, who did not seem in any hurry to attend to him. He put down the stick; stepped from the desk; and stooped to the conductor's ear.

" 'I mentioned,' he said, 'that some of the parts ought to be given to the men to study before rehearsal. Has that been done?'

"Manlius smiled. 'My dear sir,' he said, 'I need hardly tell you that Players of such standing as the members of the Antient Orpheus orchestra do not care to have suggestions of that kind offered to them. You have no cause to be uneasy. They can play anything—absolutely anything, at sight.'

"Jack looked black, and returned to his desk without a word. He gave one more rap with his stick, and began. The players were attentive, but many of them tried not to look so. For a few bars, Jack conducted under some restraint, apparently striving to repress a tendency to extravagant gesticulation. Then, as certain combinations and progressions sounded strange and farfetched, slight bursts of laughter were heard. Suddenly the first clarinettist, with an exclamation of impatience, put down his instrument.

" 'Well?' shouted Jack. The music ceased.

" 'I can't play that,' said the clarinettist shortly.

" 'Can *you* play it?' said Jack, with suppressed rage, to the second clarinettist.

" 'No,' said he. 'Nobody could play it.'

" 'That passage *has* been played; and it must be played. It has been played by a common soldier.'

" 'If a common soldier ever attempted it, much less played it,' said the first clarinettist, with some contemptuous indignation at what he considered an evident falsehood, 'he must have been drunk.' There was a general titter at this.

"Jack visibly wrestled with himself for a moment. Then, with a gleam of humour like a flash of sunshine through a black thundercloud, he said: 'You are right. He *was* drunk.' The whole band roared with laughter.

" 'Well, *I* am not drunk,' said the clarinettist, folding his arms.

" 'But will you not just try wh—' Here Jack, choked by the effort to be persuasive and polite, burst out raging: 'It can be done. It shall be done. It must be done. You are the best clarinet player in England. I know what you can do.' And Jack shook his fists wildly at the man as if he were accusing him of some infamous crime. But the compliment was loudly applauded, and the man reddened, not altogether displeased. A cornist who sat near him said soothingly in an Irish accent, 'Aye do, Joe. Try it.'

" 'You will: you can,' shouted Jack reassuringly, recovering his self-command. 'Back to the double bar. Now!' The music recommenced, and the clarinettist, overborne, took up his instrument, and when the passage was reached, played it easily, greatly to his own astonishment. The brilliancy of the effect, too, raised him for a time into a prominence which rivalled that of the pianist. The orchestra interrupted the movement to applaud it; and Jack joined in with high good humour.

" 'If you are uneasy about it,' he said, with an undisguised chuckle, 'I can hand it over to the violins.'

" 'Oh, no, thank you,' said the clarinettist. 'Now I've got it, I'll keep it.' "

There are many, many more delightful pages in this very delightful book. We see Jack, at the request of a young lady that he play Thalberg's *Moses in Egypt*, satisfying her with improvised variations of his own on themes from Rossini's opera; on another occasion he improvises on themes from the second symphony of an old second-rate English composer, one of the patrons of the Antient-Orpheus Society. Finally we see him the completely arrived master with his music for Shelley's *Prometheus Unbound*: "four scenes with chorus; a dialogue of Prometheus with the earth; an antiphony of the earth and moon; an overture; and a race of the hours."

IV

Maurice Guest

Henry Handel Richardson's *Maurice Guest* was issued by Heinemann in London in 1908. Sometime later an American edition appeared. Otto Neustätter's German translation was published in Berlin by G. Fischer in 1912. The book seems to exist in the New York Public Library only in its German form. A search through the English *Who's Who?* and kindred manuals of biography revealed no information about the author. Lately I have learned that Henry Handel Richardson is a pseudonym, assumed with much mystery by a Australian lady, herself a musician and at one time a music student at Leipzig. She has already published a second novel and a third is on the press, I believe.

Mr. Richardson (for convenience I retain the author's symbol) has dealt with what is generally ignored in imaginative works about musicians, the study years. *Maurice Guest* is a novel of music student life in Leipzig. With unfaltering authority and a skilful pen he has drawn such a hectic picture of this existence (from my knowledge of a similar life in Paris I should say that it is not overdrawn) as should frighten any American mother to the point of preventing her off-spring from embarking on a musical career which shall require any such preparation. Indeed if mere students in Germany indulge in such riots of emotion what can be expected of *virtuosi* I should like to know!

The character of the title is an English boy, no colossal exception, no abnormality . . . rather the average boy who takes up music for a vocation without having much reason for doing so. His somewhat negative, romantic, sentimental, but very serious temperament quickly involves him in the maelstrom of student sex life, in which, for him, there is no escape. He fails in his piano studies while others, more brilliantly equipped for the career of an artist, quickly speed to their goals, at the same time living disordered and drunken existences. It is the tragedy of the real artist and the man who thinks he is one written in terms of the student. Tchekov in one of his greatest plays, *The Seagull*, compares the two types, as Trigorin and Treplieff, on another plane, of course. Frank Wedekind, too, in *Musik*, has dealt with the subject. Of the thousands of music students in Germany only a comparatively few develop into artists, while of those who master the art, still fewer are capable of profiting financially by it. The central character of *Musik,* Klara Huhnerwadel, is a neurotic girl, insanely in love with her singing teacher. The play has a tragic and, according to Wedekind's wont, a bitterly ironic ending. In Mr. Richardson's book, Maurice, who is not unlike Octavius in *Man and Superman,* indeed not unlike Hamlet, is contrasted with a brilliant and unscrupulous Polish violinist, Schilsky, successful in love, successful as a *virtuoso,* successful as a composer. He not only plays the violin like a master, but we are told he plays a dozen other instruments better than well; we are given a description of his piano playing. Like Richard Strauss he has written a tone-poem suggested by Nietzsche's "Zarathustra." He is an excellent *chef d'orchestre.* His amatory adventures are conducted with an unscrupulous eye on the pocket books of his conquests. He lives on women, especially one woman, who, however, cannot hold his attention, even by paying freely. Despised by the town, there is scarcely a woman who is not in love with him, scarcely a man who is not his friend. All admire his genius. Here is a picture of the man, which you might place next to the conventional description of the musician composing in a garden, surrounded by nightingales and gardenias, dreaming of angels. Regard this Saint Cecil:

"In the middle of the room, at the corner of a bare deal table that was piled with loose music and manuscript, Schilsky sat improving and correcting the tails and bodies of hastily made notes. He was still in his nightshirt, over which he had thrown coat and trousers; and, wide open at the neck, it exposed to the waist a skin of the dead whiteness peculiar to red-haired people. His face, on the other hand, was sallow and unfresh; and the reddish rims of the eyes, and the coarsely self-indulgent mouth, contrasted strikingly with the general youthfulness of his appearance. He had the true musician's head: round as a cannonball, with a vast, bumpy forehead, on which the soft fluffy hair began far back, and stood out like a nimbus. His eyes were either desperately dreamy or desperately sharp, never normally attentive or at rest; his blunted nose and chin were so short as to make the face look top-heavy. A carefully tended young moustache stood straight out along his cheeks. He had large slender hands and quick movements.

"The air of the room was like a thin grey veiling, for all three puffed hard at cigarettes. Without removing his from between his teeth, Schilsky related an adventure of the night before. He spoke in jerks, with a strong lisp, and was more intent on what he was doing than on what he was saying.

" 'Do you think he'd budge?' he asked in a quick sputtery way. 'Not he. Till nearly two. And then I couldn't get him along. He thought it wasn't eleven, and wanted to stop at every corner. To irritate an imaginary bobby. He disputed with them too. Heavens, what sport it was! At last I dragged him up here and got him on the sofa. Off he rolls again. So I let him lie. He didn't disturb me.'

"Heinrich Krafft, the hero of the episode, lay on the short, uncomfortable sofa, with the table-cover for a blanket. In

answer to Schilsky, he said faintly, without opening his eyes: 'Nothing would. You are an ox. When I wake this morning with a mouth like gum arabic, he sits there as if he had not stirred all night. Then to bed, and snores till midday, through all the hellish light and noise.'

"Here Fürst could not resist making a little joke. He announced himself by a chuckle—like the click of a clock about to strike.

" 'He's got to make the most of his liberty. He doesn't often get off duty. We know, we know.' He laughed tonelessly and winked at Krafft.

"Krafft quoted:

" 'In der Woche zwier.'

" 'Now you fellows, shut up!' said Schilsky. It was plain that banter of this kind was not disagreeable to him; at the same time he was just at the moment too engrossed, to have more than half an ear for what was said. With his short-sighted eyes close to the paper, he was listening with all his might to some harmonies that his fingers played on the table. When, a few minutes later, he rose and stretched the stiffness from his limbs, his face, having lost its expression of rapt concentration, seemed suddenly to have grown younger."

The conflict in this novel is expressed through Louise, one of those young women with a certain amount of money who find food for the gratification of their sex desires in the atmosphere of a music school town. She it is who, thrown aside by Schilsky, creeps back literally on her knees to beg him to renew their love; she it is who lavishes attention and money on his quite careless indifference; and she it is to whom Maurice Guest devotes his love. Schilsky goes away without a word, and Louise, abandoned, in utter grief accepts the attentions of Maurice, at first without enthusiasm, later at least with gratitude, but when she has at length become his mistress the shadow of her past continually haunts Maurice; continually he drags it over their altar of love, polluting the oblations with his frantic suspicions. The psychology of these scenes, protracted to the wearying point, is so completely satisfying that they seem almost autobiographical. Here is a typical scene in which the comparison is laid bare:

" 'Or tell me,' Maurice said abruptly with a ray of hope; 'tell me the truth about it all for once. Was it mere exaggeration, or was he really worth so much more than all the rest of us? Of course he could play—I know that—but so can many a fool. But all the other part of it—his incredible talent, or luck in everything he touched—was it just report, or was it really something else?—tell me.'

" 'He was a genius,' she answered, very coldly and distinctly; and her voice warned him once more that he was trespassing on ground to which he had no right. But he was too excited to take the warning.

" 'A genius!' he echoed. 'He was a genius! Yes, what did I tell you? Your very words imply a comparison as you say them. For I?—what am I? A miserable bungler, a wretched dilettant—or have you another word for it? Oh, never mind—don't be afraid to say it!—I'm not sensitive tonight. I can bear to hear your real opinion of me; for it could not possibly be lower than my own. Let us get at the truth at once, by all means!—But what I want to know,' he cried a moment later, 'is, why one should be given so much and the other so little. To one all the talents and all your love; and the other unhappy wretch remains an outsider his whole life long. When you speak in that tone about him, I could wish with all my heart that he had been no better than I am. It would give me pleasure to know that he, too, had only been a dabbling amateur—the victim of a pitiable wish to be what he hadn't the talent for.' "

At length Schilsky returns and Maurice becomes in truth Don José, to the Carmen (her favourite opera) of Louise. She frankly admits that the Pole is her only passion, and Maurice, who lacks the stamina of his Spanish prototype, brings the book to a satisfactory conclusion by killing himself. . . . There is a short final scene in which we get a glimpse of Louise as Mme. Schilsky.

There is nothing jerky about the telling of this sordid story; nothing jars. It is done with a direction and a vivid attention to the matter in hand which is very arresting, and such atmospheric episodes as decorate its progress only aid in the elaborate development of the main theme. For example Schilsky is the recipient of homosexual affection from one Heinrich Krafft, who plays Chopin divinely and keeps a one-eyed cat named Wotan. This character is sharply etched with a few keen strokes. He in turn is under the subjugating amorousness of a masculine young lady named Avery Hill. There is an American girl, Ephie Cayhill, who pursues Schilsky and whom he seduces as he might munch a piece of cake, the while he is playing, composing, drinking, and continuing his affair with Louise. Her sister discovers her secret at a crucial moment, and she is carried away from Leipzig and drops out of the book, having served her purpose in denoting Schilsky's unlimited capacity.

The American colony is sketched, not at length, but the details catch the eye like the corners of a battle field in a Griffiths's picture. Mr. Richardson here, however, has almost verged on caricature at times. We have all of us heard Americans who go abroad talk but this perhaps is a little strong: "I come to Schwartz (a piano teacher) last fall and he thinks no end of me. But the other week I was sick, and as I lay in bed, I sung some—just for fun. And my landlady—she's a regular singer herself—who was fixing up the room, she claps her hands together and says: 'My goodness me! Why *you* have a voice!' That's what put it in my head, and I went to Sperling to hear what he'd got to say. He was just tickled to death, I guess he was, and he's going to make something dandy of it, so I stop long enough. I don't know what my husband will say though. When I wrote him I was sick, he says: 'Come home and be sick at home'—that's what he says." And here's another American lady: "Now Mr. Dove is just a lovely gentleman, but he don't skate elegantly, an' he nearly tumbled me twice. Yes, indeed. But I presume when Miss Wade says come, then you're most obliged to go." But there isn't much of this sort of thing. The piano teachers of the colony, with their small petty jealousies, their sordid family lives, are painted. Pension life is depicted on

the canvas, and the average family of Leipzig that takes in music students to board and room. A typical figure is Frau Fürst, the widow of an oboe player in the Gewandhaus orchestra who died of a chill after a performance of *Die Meistersinger*. In her youth she had a good soprano voice and Robert Schumann often sent for her to come to his house in the Inselstrasse to try his songs, while Clara Schumann accompanied her. During her husband's lifetime she had become accustomed to remaining in the kitchen during musical evenings at the house, and she continues to do so when her son, who is a pianist and teacher, has friends in. On the same fourth floor with the Fürsts "lived a pale, harassed teacher, with a family which had long outgrown its accommodations; for the wife was perpetually in childbed, and cots and cradles were the chief furniture of the house. As the critical moments of her career drew nigh, the 'Frau Lehrer' complained, with an aggravated bitterness, of the unceasing music that went on behind the thin partition; and this grievance, together with the racy items of gossip left behind the midwife's annual visit, like a trail of smoke, provided her and Fürst's mother with infinite food for talk. They were thick friends again a few minutes after a scene so lively that blows seemed imminent, and they met every morning on the landing, where, with broom or child in hand, they stood gossiping by the hour."

There are several descriptions of the students in the cafés, students with their blasphemous, obscene gossip, mingled with technical small talk. All through the book we are reminded why these young people are foregathered in these strange relations. That there are men and women of small talent who escape the weakening influences of such a circle I am too ready to admit, but Mr. Richardson has not gone to extremes. The life of vocal students in Paris is similar.

John F. Szwed

SOURCE: "Josef Škvorecký and the Tradition of Jazz Literature," in *World Literature Today*, Vol. 54, No. 4, Autumn, 1980, pp. 586-90.

[*In the following essay, Szwed first discusses American jazz fiction dealing with race relations and then turns his attention to the jazz fiction of the Czechoslovakian writer Josef Škvorecký, illustrating how Škvorecký uses jazz as a metaphor for revolution.*]

The idea of the universality of the black experience in the West is so common that it seems too banal to mention. It comprises a subtext in the writings of Twain, Melville, Faulkner, maybe half of American literature. A smaller group of writers—DuBois, those of the Harlem Renaissance, Norman Mailer—have told us that part of this experience is its ability to be communicated indirectly, through images of the body, through art, music, dance. The theoretical appeal of blacks also represented for late nineteenth- and twentieth-century artists an escape from industrialization and the rise of the middle class: one thinks of slumming literati such as Rimbaud in his *A Season in Hell*, his "pagan book, nigger book"; André Gide and Picasso in Africa; D. H. Lawrence in New Mexico, Australia and those other Harlems of the European mind.

(So Rimbaud may have been dealing in the slave trade in East Africa; Gide and Picasso could scarcely be called boosters of a *black* Africa; and Lawrence so hated Bessie Smith's "Empty Bed Blues" that he broke the record against Harry Crosby's wall. So what else is new?)

But there was a special attraction in the life and appearance of the black jazz musician: the double alienation of the artist and color. Whatever his occupation itself might be like, the jazz musician provided perhaps the first truly nonmechanical metaphor for the twentieth century. Not since the English Gentleman, with his modality of poise, authority and how-one-should-be, has such an image dominated the world. Some abstraction or other of the lives of jazz performers and their followers now gives shape to the mores of street punks and media executives; it informs the muscles of professional dancers as well as the timing of stand-up comedians; and it feeds the languages and moves of fashion designers, basketball players, soldiers and others. Now, whether one has heard of Charlie Parker or not, one inherits a notion of cool, an idea of well-etched individuality, a certain angle of descent. Such is the detachability and resale value of race and culture in our times.

Jazz has touched literature in a strange variety of ways. Sometimes the musicians and their followers have provided a rich background for period pieces such as Claude McKay's *Home to Harlem* or Langston Hughes's *Not Without Laughter,* or they have supplied allusions and intertextual shape (Ellison's *Invisible Man,* Joyce's *Finnegans Wake,* Malcolm Lowry's *Under the Volcano*), maybe even a controlling figure (Ishmael Reed's *Mumbo Jumbo*). Others have found in jazz a model for improvisatory and antiphonal writing; and some have seen in the speech and writing of musicians a special kind of oral rhythm and dynamics of imagery. Yet curiously, the jazz life itself has seldom provided the basis for first-rate fiction. Perhaps the subject is at once too arcane and too restricted, too confined. What we most often see in fictional representations of jazz musicians' lives is either conventional sociological wisdom or local color dominating character.

Still, some jazz fiction is not without interest. More often than not it seems to be about relations between blacks and whites. And some very interesting fiction has been done by those who have used jazz as a keystone for constructing novels of manners that deal with race relations. Needless to say, the writers of this genre are usually white, and the white personae they create in their books are means by which the authors legitimize their creation of black characters. Here we see some justification for Mailer's remark that "it is moot if any white who had no ear for jazz can know the passion with which some whites become attached to the Negro's cause." The best documentation of the twice alienated is in the novel of the hipster. Chandler Brossard's *Who Walk in Darkness* (1952) leads into the Village and Uptown in the late 1940s, to those places where jazz and Latino musics mixed along with black and white; the book's central figure is a black man passing for white, but that fact was edited out of the first edition—a nice, reflexive fifties touch. John Clellon Holmes's *Go!* (1952) and *The Horn* (1958) also witness the period, as do

Jack Kerouac's many novels, especially *Desolation Angels* (1965) and *The Subterraneans* (1958). Kerouac's books are lame in some fundamental ways, but there is a sweetness in his documentation of postwar underlife that makes him hard to resist. Jazz is everywhere in his work, and musicians such as Brew Moore, Allen Eager and Richie Kamuca make appearances under pseudonyms, along with the legendary fan, Jerry Newman. (In a favorite passage of mine in *Visions of Cody* Jack himself secretly trails his idol, saxophonist Lee Konitz, across New York City.)

> Curiously, the jazz life itself has seldom provided the basis for first-rate fiction. Perhaps the subject is at once too arcane and too restricted, too confined. What we most often see in fictional representations of jazz musicians' lives is either conventional sociological wisdom or local color dominating character.
>
> —*John F. Szwed*

There was other hipster fiction, and a wonderful level of excess was reached in the novels of Bernard Wolfe and the short stories of Terry Southern. Wolfe is a man of remarkably diverse interests—a psychologist, a screenwriter, an associate of Trotsky in Mexico, a theorist of race relations—who first became known for the book he coauthored with white clarinetist Mezz Mezzrow, *Really the Blues* (1946). Though avowedly Mezzrow's autobiography, the book rather crudely uses blacks as ciphers for white fantasy, and as in minstrel shows, the medium is a white man boasting of his competence in black culture by taking observers on a guided tour, complete with a glossary of native hip terms. Although Mezzrow does the talking, Wolfe's interest in Nietzsche's polarities and *The Birth of Tragedy* is always in the wings. (Nietzsche's is "the only book I know which says something about bebop," Wolfe once wrote.)

In some later essays, especially "Uncle Remus and the Malevolent Rabbit"—an essay that influenced Franz Fanon—Wolfe reversed himself (or Mezzrow, whatever) on blacks with a vengeance. Now black culture was to be *nothing* but white fantasies or the product of black reaction to those fantasies. Then, in two novels, *The Late Risers* (1954) and *The Magic of Their Singing* (1961), he introduced the hipster as the latest in a long series of literary white America's wise psychopaths. Although at times fragmented by a forced didacticism, there are some strong moments in Wolfe's books. In *The Late Risers,* for instance, there is a fine composite black character named Movement, a man who has appeared in *Carmen Jones, Cabin in the Sky, Green Pastures* and the Katherine Dunham dance company, but who now dresses Brooks Brothers with a single gold earring and deals drugs and sundries. Hearing of the terminal illness of an aging German professor of *Afro-Amerikanische* who is seeking the help of a

Haitian voodoo adept, Movement volunteers to impersonate a *houngan* with the aid of Folkways recordings and burnt cork ("I do not have to cross color lines, only observe them"). This deviation from his usually correct appearance in aid of a white man who is a professional student of the incorrect puzzles Movement's friends and leads him to justify his behavior by a weird reinterpretation of Sartre's *Anti-Semite and Jew* and Melville's *The Confidence Man*. (Concerning the professor's obsession with black culture, Movement observes, "I understand a man caught between conjure and *Das Kapital*.")

Wolfe has dozens of passages such as this, most of them amounting to a vicious satire on hipster race relations in mid-century. Even so, there is nothing in Wolfe that even approaches the viciousness of Terry Southern's treatment of the same subject in *Red Dirt Marijuana and Other Tastes* (1967). In "The Night Bird Blew for Dr. Warner" a white professor of music turns ethnographer to experience bebop in the manner of the natives. Schooled for his field trip in hip argot and eager to experience serious drugs, Dr. Warner sets out for certain neighborhoods to seek truth but ends up having his head beaten in. And in "You're Too Hip, Baby" a white fan solicits the friendship of an expatriate black musician in Paris with ultimate cool and studied restraint, only to have the tenor saxophonist offer him music lessons, his wife and finally himself sexually in exchange. When each is rejected in turn, the musician asks what it is the white man *really* wants; when he learns that it's merely "the scene" and the "sounds," he rejects him as a "hippy and a professional nigger lover."

The metaphysics of race relations take a different turn in the jazz fiction of black writers. Where whites see jazz as a way out and treat its practitioners with a form of New Sentimentalism, blacks look to the music as a means of unifying their situation in a white-dominated society with a black collective tradition and a meaningful group history. James Baldwin, in his short story "Sonny's Blues" (1957), brings his characters in line with their culture through a moment of ritualized musical affirmation. Much the same project pervades John Williams's *Night Song* (1962) and William Melvin Kelley's *A Drop of Patience* (1965). And just such a ritual music scene is the totality of LeRoi Jones's "The Screamers" (1967). The purest version of this use of jazz as metaphor occurs in Rudolph Fisher's "Common Meter" (1930), wherein a cutting contest between two bands at the "Arcadia Ballroom" offers the winner the "jazz championship of the world" and, on a side bet, the favors of a fine dance hostess. When one band tricks the other by cutting the skins on the drum heads, denying them rhythm, the victims triumph by collective foot stomping, turning "St. Louis Blues" into a *shout*.

> They had been rocked thus before, this multitude. Two hundred years ago they had swayed to that same slow fateful measure, lifting their lamentation to heaven, pounding the earth with their feet, seeking the mercy of a new God through the medium of an old rhythm, zoomzoom. They had rocked so a thousand years ago in a city whose walls were jungle.

Of course it's possible to pass over this sort of thing as yet

another example of the Negro as Exotic Primitive. But in the 1930s, when Sterling Brown criticized the stereotype of the exotic as a departure from the American social norm, the act of departure had considerably different significance. At their best, these books treat the exotic as an assertion, as a transvaluation of the norm, rather than as an act born of weakness and the necessity of failure.

By the same token, when jazz fiction amounts to mere social-science melodrama, it deserves to be neglected—as has been "Blue Melody" (1948), a soggy bagel by J. D. Salinger. Here two Southern white children are befriended by a black pianist and his blues-singing niece, but their urban pastoral cannot override reality when the niece dies from a ruptured appendix (yes, cf. "The Death of Bessie Smith" by Edward Albee too!). But jazz fiction that comes anywhere near its living originals has had a certain mediating force, standing between the public on one side and those peculiar moral tracts about black folks put out by sociologists and urbanologists on the other. The simple fact is that it has been difficult to reduce, say, a Charles Mingus or a Duke Ellington to crude and broken ruins of racism, or to treat a Billie Holiday or Lester Young as nothing more than—to use Ralph Ellison's phrase—the sum of their brutalization. Jazz fiction in this sense has been an ongoing refutation of the sociology of pathos.

. . . . .

It might seem easy to dismiss European novels on jazz as being more of the same with less detail and style. But truth be told, novels such as Ernest Borneman's *Tremelo* (1948), W. Clapham's *Come Blow Your Horn* (1958), Bennie Green's *Blame It on My Youth* (1967), A. Mitchell's *If You See Me Comin'* (1962) or John Wain's *Strike the Father Dead* (1962) are no worse and sometimes better than the American average. Yet one should treat with care jazz followers on the Continent, where the music has suffered special constraints, where some have gone to concentration camps for jazz, where some have indeed died for jazz. Many East Europeans have now suffered musical censorship under both the Nazis and nominally socialist governments with little or no difference in policy. Accounts of this repression are curiously rare in the West, so that the publication of Josef Škvorecký's "Red Music" (which is included as a preface to his two novellas published together under the title *The Bass Saxophone* [1979]) is doubly important: it serves as both a political revelation and a necessary introduction to Škvorecký's jazz literature, a literature which is surely the most important, the best fiction we have, and in which the music has been used both as a subject for description and as a stylistic means.

When Škvorecký undertook to write about jazz beyond the American context, he was in effect freed of the burden of the racial conflict which partially motivates American jazz literature; he nonetheless inherited the esthetic oppositions and social implications of the organization of the music. The esthetics of jazz demand that a musician play with complete originality, with an assertion of his own musical individuality. (Regardless of the public's acclaim for some noted imitators, musicians give only the meanest of rewards to camp followers.) At the same time jazz re-

Tommy Potter, Charlie Parker, Dizzy Gillespie, and John Coltrane at Birdland, New York, 1951.

quires that musicians be able to merge their unique voices in the totalizing, collective improvisations of polyphony and heterophony. The implications of this esthetic are profound and more than vaguely threatening, for no political system has yet been devised with social principles which reward maximal individualism within the framework of spontaneous egalitarian interaction. Thus when Europeans and white Americans embrace the music, they also commit a political act of far more radical dimensions than that of simply espousing a new political ideology. (True radicalism, someone once said, lies not in telling someone his politics are wrong, but in telling him his shoes are tied wrong.)

Škvorecký's fictional world is divided into those who have made this musical commitment and those who haven't, and the music becomes a metaphor for a greater revolution than one we have lived to see. *The Cowards* (1958) begins with an epigraph from Mezzrow and Wolfe's *Really the Blues* to the effect that behind the jazz played by white Chicagoans of the 1920s was a revolution in bourgeois values, a revolution carried forth by the optimism and creativity of youth. Early on in *The Cowards*, the narrator Danny says:

Some old geezer stood planted in the doorway with a half pint of beer in his hand, staring at us. I could read his mind. His eyes looked like two bugles and he had a mouth like a tuba. He certainly didn't think the stuff we were producing was music. We didn't either, really. Not *just* music. For us it was something more like the world. Like before Christ and after Christ. I couldn't even remember what it has been like before jazz. I was probably interested in soccer or something—like our fathers who used to go to the stadium every Sunday and shout themselves hoarse. I wasn't much more than a kind of miniature dad myself then. A dad shrunk down to about four foot five. And then along came Benno with his records and jazz and the first experiments in Benno's house with a trumpet, piano, an old xylophone I'd dug up in the attic and two violins that Lexa and Haryk were learning to play because their parents wanted them to. And then Jimmy Lunceford and Chick Webb. And Louis Armstrong. and Bob Crosby. And then everything else was After Jazz. So that it really wasn't just music at all. But that old geezer over there couldn't understand that. He'd been ruined a long time ago by soccer and beer and brass band music.

The Cowards is an account by jazz-living youth of the events of 4-11 May 1945, the period when the Germans were withdrawing from Czechoslovakia and the Russians were moving in. Though it is in many respects a scrupulously realistic account of the times, it is also something of manifesto of a specific cultural continuity in a period of change, a counter-continuity of anti-bourgeois values, a revolution within a revolution, a critique of the falsity of the revolution as seen from behind dark glasses and music stands. (Whatever else was happening during those days on the political front, the book opens with the playing of Jimmy Lunceford's "Annie Laurie" and ends with his "Organ Grinder's Swing.")

Škvorecký's short story "Song of the Forgotten Era" follows other jazz children forward to an incident in 1951, as reflected upon by one of them in the early 1960s. Here the act of playing a Russian military march in swing time brings the wrath of the government down upon them and permanently alters the direction of their lives. The story ends with one of the postwar youths, now an adult, singing a jazz version of "Annie Laurie," reaching back to the optimism of youth and a momentarily liberated Czechoslovakia.

> I closed my eyes. It was so long ago. So terribly long ago. It was a blood sacrifice, a different, less conspicuous kind of sacrifice, for a better life of that generation of twist-crazy chicks and youths up there. . . . Venus . . . was singing, in that forgotten voice, the song of the quickly forgotten years.

In "Pink Champagne" (1969), another short story set in Prague during the same period, the period Škvorecký calls the "very intense, very underground and generally crazy" period of his life, jazz is only a small part of the theme; it surfaces when a group of university students pass themselves off as English peace marchers by singing a Jimmy Rushing blues. Later they find themselves singing the song again, now in private, not as a trick, but as an act of unity. At first glance, "Emöke" would seem to be something of a departure from this theme, since the blues appear as part of a young man's scheme to seduce a Hungarian woman who has retreated from the war and her own personal tragedies into a spirituality which she wears like a widow's mourning garb. Here the blues the young man improvises to crack her resistance while dancing is a homemade, very Czech version of the blues, but one which calls upon some ancient secrets from distant mystical sources.

> But now she was hearing it, a poem composed just for her by a man, a poem flowing from a man's heart, borne by the strange magic of this crazy age of telecommunications from the heart and throat of a half-stoned black shouter of the Memphis periphery to the vocal chords [*sic*] of a Prague intellectual in this social hall in a recreation center in the Socialist state of Czechoslovakia.

Škvorecký has discovered the very unifying and affirming ritual qualities of the music which black writers had discovered in the United States. In "Red Music" he states it again, now in opposition to a writer of brilliant jazz criticism who could finally never get the music squarely in line with what he calls his own "Marxist-Leninist" orientation.

> And no matter what LeRoi Jones says to the contrary, the essence of this music, this "way of making music," is not simply protest. Its essence is something far more elemental: an *élan vital,* a forceful vitality, an explosive energy as breathtaking as that of any true art, that may be felt even in the saddest of blues. Its effect is cathartic.

Škvorecký comes very close here to what Sidney Bechet, in his autobiography *Treat It Gentle,* said jazz was all about. Bechet explained that the music invented by ex-slaves was something which transcended the conditions of race and servitude: "It wasn't just white people the music had to reach to, nor even their own people, but straight out to life and to what a man does with his life when it finally *is* his."

"The Bass Saxophone," the latest of Škvorecký's works to appear in English translation, returns again to the occupation, now to an incident in which a young musician crosses political lines and risks everything in order to have a chance to play a bass saxophone in a strange German band. Realism is kept to a minimum: there are no accounts of suppressed newspapers, forced labor, gas chambers and the rest. In this war there is first and only the ban against jazz and the underground which manages to keep the music alive. Czechoslovakia thus becomes a landscape of hidden music, where apparently innocent peasant gatherings could, at the signal of a lookout, begin trucking to a Basie tune; where German *Offizierschule* bands rehearsed smuggled Chick Webb arrangements; where the Jews of Terezín had a band called the Ghetto Swingers (all but one of them to die finally in the camps); and where even in the camps other bands kept playing what the Nazis called *Judeonegroid* music. Škvorecký's obsession with this single suppressed art gives "The Bass Saxophone" a suffocating closure and an amnesiac structure. Only his sense of the absurd and the richness of his descriptions of the music keep it moving. And one does not easily forget his image of Kansas City riffs in Buchenwald.

Jazz may be something of a general motif in modern Czech fiction; Škvorecký himself has mentioned its presence in films such as *Hijacking* (1952) and *Music from Mars* (1964). I have not read Škvorecký's "The End of the Nylon Age" or "A Word I Shall Not Withdraw," but I have read Milan Kundera's *The Farewell Party* with its crude handling of jazz as exotic background and local color. What finally is unique and appealing in Škvorecký's writing is its Europeanness, the very distance between his characters' love for jazz and the sources of the music. They may live and die for jazz, but it is always someone else's music, heard through imported records and badly translated song lyrics. Readers of the fiction of jazz are not musicians, and this distance between author and subject echoes the distance between reader and living musicians. Somehow, in speaking from deep continental Europe, Škvorecký has caught the excited detachment that one once felt in looking at faded and awkwardly posed pictures of jazz heroes in old issues of *Metronome* magazine.

Anthony DeCurtis

SOURCE: "The Product: Bucky Wunderlick, Rock 'n Roll, and Don DeLillo's *Great Jones Street*," in *South Atlantic Quarterly*, Vol. 89, No. 2, Spring, 1990, pp. 369-79.

[*In the following excerpt from an essay on Don DeLillo's novel* Great Jones Street, *DeCurtis explores how the novel's main character—the rock star Bucky Wunderlick—his music, and the people with whom he associates reflect the dominant culture and counterculture of the 1960s and 1970s.*]

Perhaps the best-known passage in Don DeLillo's *Great Jones Street,* not one of his more highly regarded novels, occurs at the beginning of the book. As the novel kicks off, rock star Bucky Wunderlick is holed up in an apartment in a desolate industrial section of Manhattan—this is the early seventies; Manhattan had industrial sections then—having abandoned his band midtour in Houston. Bucky's reflections on his celebrity, which he is seeking to escape and examine, start the novel:

> Fame requires every kind of excess. I mean true fame, a devouring neon, not the somber renown of waning statesmen or chinless kings. I mean long journeys across gray space. I mean danger, the edge of every void, the circumstance of one man imparting an erotic terror to the dreams of the republic. Understand the man who must inhabit these extreme regions, monstrous and vulval, damp with memories of violation. Even if half-mad he is absorbed into the public's total madness; even if fully rational, a bureaucrat in hell, a secret genius of survival, he is sure to be destroyed by the public's contempt for survivors. Fame, this special kind, feeds itself on outrage, on what the counselors of lesser men would consider bad publicity—hysteria in limousines, knife fights in the audience, bizarre litigation, treachery, pandemonium and drugs. Perhaps the only natural law attaching to true fame is that the famous man is compelled, eventually, to commit suicide.
>
> (Is it clear I was a hero of rock 'n' roll?)

When I read that passage to a friend of mine—a friend who is, like me, a rock fan and a reader—he said, "That's exactly what a writer would think a rock star thinks like." He wasn't being complimentary. My friend knows that rock stars' thoughts more often read like a Don DeLillo parody of an interview—of which *Great Jones Street* contains several funny examples—than like the sort of sociocultural analysis at the heart of the passage I just quoted. Even Bob Dylan, who has made albums that move me as much as any works of art I know and who is one of the figures on whom DeLillo's portrayal of Wunderlick seems to be based, typically doesn't seem to have very much to say about his own work. In fact, in interviews, he often doesn't even seem to understand his own work, or at least he affects not being able to understand it, let alone the context that helped produce it. For example, here is an exchange between Dylan and former *Rolling Stone* writer Kurt Loder that appeared in *Rolling Stone* in 1986. They are discussing Dylan's sixties albums, virtually every one of which is riveting and virtually every one of which seems to scream self-conscious intent:

> Did you feel that you had tapped into the Zeitgeist in some special sort of way?
>
> With the songs that I came up with?
>
> Yeah.
>
> As I look back on it now, I am surprised that I came up with so many of them. At the time it seemed like a natural thing to do. Now I can look back and see that I must have written those songs "in the spirit," you know? Like "Desolation Row"—I was just thinkin' about that the other night. There's no logical way that you can arrive at lyrics like that. I don't know how it was done.

Not even "I don't know how I did it," but "I don't know how it was done." Dylan goes on to describe how he feels his songs of that time came "through" him, which is about as characteristic a declaration from a rock songwriter as you will find. This mystical notion of creativity is one of the stances artists adopt to keep their own creative processes concealed from themselves, protected from a self-consciousness that they fear might prove paralyzing. It is also a way to maintain distance from audience expectations—one of the central, ongoing preoccupations of Dylan's career. Since artists have no control over what comes "through" them, the reasoning would seem to run, they can hardly be held accountable for deviating from the styles they previously worked in.

Wunderlick's relationship to his audience, and to the entire culture that is playing him, is central to *Great Jones Street*. . . . [In an interview], DeLillo says about Wunderlick: "The interesting thing about that particular character is that he seems to be at a crossroad between murder and suicide. For me, that defines the period between 1965 and 1975, say, and I thought it was best exemplified in a rock-music star." My friend's comment aside, Wunderlick, like so many of DeLillo's characters, is not meant to seem like a realistic, three-dimensional person; he is a notion around which DeLillo collects his ideas about how the culture was functioning at the time in which his novel is set. Wunderlick's actions, thoughts, and speech reflect those ideas, rather than anything that might conventionally be considered his own "motivations."

The interplay between murder and suicide that DeLillo mentions would seem to suggest the movement of American society from the political upheavals and turmoil of the late sixties to the dreadful cynicism, deep alienation, and desperate privatism of the seventies. Wunderlick's writing traces a similar pattern of drawing inward. His first album, a "special media kit" included in the novel informs us, is called *Amerikan War Sutra*—it's from 1968, natch, and his second, from 1970, is *Diamond Stylus,* an evident movement from political protest to a kind of aestheticism. By the time of his third album, *Pee-Pee-Maw-Maw,* in 1971—a "landmark work" in the estimation of one of the novel's characters—Wunderlick is trying to defeat language itself with a kind of minimalist gibberish.

Wunderlick's desire to strip away the rational meanings

of language is related to his urge for self-attenuation—a response to the failure of the sixties' promise of ever-expanding utopian possibilities, and the suicidal pole of the dichotomy DeLillo mentioned in discussing *Great Jones Street*. He speaks of himself as potentially becoming "the epoch's barren hero, a man who knew the surest way to minimize." Near the end of the book, his desire to elude the tyranny of language and achieve a pure, perfectly unimpeded relationship with his audience reaches the point of a desire to be disembodied: "I'm tired of my body. I want to be a dream, their dream. I want to flow right through them." He speaks of wanting to become "the least of what I was." In virtually the only comprehensible lyrics on *Pee-Pee-Maw-Maw*'s title track—DeLillo provides the full lyrics—Wunderlick states, in an eerie combination of Yeats and the depressed, pragmatic wisdom of the seventies, "The beast is loose / Least is best."

What Wunderlick learns in his withdrawal is that it is finally impossible to withdraw. Great Jones Street is no different from Main Street or Wall Street; it offers no haven, no safe retreat. When he jumped off what he calls his "final tour"—though near the end of the novel he, like all good rockers with savvy managers, is contemplating going on the road again—Wunderlick had become convinced that suicide was the only meaningful performance still available to him. The basic rock-star paranoid fantasy—that the fans' wild love would somehow transform itself into murderous rage (a fantasy that proved all too real in the case of John Lennon and that is captured brilliantly on David Bowie's album, *The Rise and Fall of Ziggy Stardust*)—is turned around in Wunderlick's case.

On the "final tour," the mayhem Wunderlick's group could routinely inspire tapered off; the fans themselves withdrew, creating a vacuum that they expected Wunderlick to fill, or to internalize. "There was less sense of simple visceral abandon at our concerts during these last weeks," Wunderlick says, stricken with wonder. "Few cases of arson and vandalism. Fewer still of rape." He attributes this lessening of violence to his audience's realization that "my death, to be authentic, must be self-willed—a successful piece of instruction only if it occurred by my own hand, preferably in a foreign city"—that last detail, evidently, an allusion to the mysterious death of Jim Morrison in Paris. "It's possible the culture had reached its limit," Wunderlick speculates, "a point of severe tension."

This lessening of the fans' violence triggers a dual response in Wunderlick. The first is his suicidal, self-attenuating retreat to his room; he is one of the earliest of the "men in small rooms" that populate DeLillo's novels. The other response turns the violence toward the audience: "What I'd like to do really is I'd like to injure people with my sound," he says at a hilarious symposium at a prominent think tank, at which he is the featured guest. "Maybe actually kill some of them." Later on he says, "It's murder I've been burning to commit. I'm way beyond suicide."

But once Wunderlick retreats to the room on Great Jones Street, having reached his own limit within the context of the general cultural dissolution, it quickly becomes clear that the forces that really control events—quite independent of the whims of pop stars—have not relaxed their

grip simply because he has decided to drop out. What happens is that the void he creates by his withdrawal makes the functioning of those forces more apparent—and more frightening—to him.

The first evidence of this is that Globke, Wunderlick's manager, turns up at the apartment even though Wunderlick has informed no one of his whereabouts. The very permeability of Wunderlick's room—the ultimate room of his own, an image of the sacrosanct internal world of the artist—is testimony to the failure of alternatives and escapes in this novel. On his visit, Globke informs Wunderlick that his management firm, Transparanoia, will stand by Wunderlick through this weird period—"What the hell, an artist's an artist," Globke reasons with the wisdom of a businessman who knows his product and which side his check is signed on. He also reveals that Transparanoia owns the building Wunderlick is living in. So much for escape; real estate never sleeps. Globke clearly does not share Wunderlick's desire to minimize: "It's a business thing. . . . Diversification, expansion, maximizing the growth potential. Someday you'll understand these things. You'll open your mind to these things." Transparanoia, it should be noted, is run exclusively on Wunderlick's earnings and investments. For Wunderlick's own purposes, of course, his money is "spent" or "tied up."

As in Pynchon's novels, the various undergrounds in *Great Jones Street* begin to intersect—and begin more and more to resemble flaky, sinister spin-offs on the dominant culture, rather than rebellious or subversive alternatives to it. Globke proves to be only the first of an endless series of visitors to what was supposed to be Wunderlick's secret hideaway. In the most important of those visits, Bucky, the messianic rock star turned urban hermit, is visited by a member of the Happy Valley Farm Commune—"a new earth-family on the Lower East Side that has the whole top floor of one tenement"—the book's major image of counterculture idealism gone beserk.

The Commune, whose members fled the rural life to try to find themselves in the city, holds Wunderlick in esteem for "[r]eturning the idea of privacy to American life," and asks him to stash a drug—alternately referred to as the "package" or the "product"—in his apartment. The product, as it happens, is "the ultimate drug," a drug that destroys the ability of people to speak. It was originally designed by the federal government to silence dissenters. "You'll be perfectly healthy," one character explains to Wunderlick, who eventually takes the drug. "You won't be able to make words, that's all. They just won't come into your mind the way they normally do and the way we all take for granted they will. Sounds yes. Sounds galore. But no words." In the desperate environment of a culture that has reached the breaking point, all extreme experience is desirable: "Everybody's anxious to get off on this stuff. If U.S. Guv is involved, the stuff is bound to be a real mind-crusher. . . . People are agog. It's the dawning of the age of God knows what."

More to the point: however many people want to get off on it, at least as many want to get their hands on it and sell it—or is that a false distinction? A culture under siege creates its own vital markets. The drug product becomes like the pornographic movie allegedly filmed in Hitler's bunker in *Running Dog:* an imagined commodity that, independent of its value or even its status as an object of desire, serves as a lightning rod for the greed and acquisitiveness pervading the cultural atmosphere. When the drug package becomes confused with another package containing Wunderlick's "mountain tapes"—a cache of songs Wunderlick had recorded in his remote mountain home a little over a year before his "final" tour (and based on the "basement tapes" Dylan made in Woodstock after his motorcycle accident in 1966)—the thematic center of the novel becomes clearly defined. The drug and Wunderlick's music, no matter how authentically conceived or individually created, are both products, and the buying and selling of products is what makes the world of *Great Jones Street* turn.

Eventually, every character in *Great Jones Street* is pursuing either the package containing the so-called "ultimate drug" or the one containing Wunderlick's mountain tapes. And every relationship that Wunderlick thought he had is finally seen to revolve around the possibility of business deals (legitimate or illegal, underground or mainstream, related to drugs or music: distinctions among these pairings are purely conceptual, finally) and profits. Each person is simultaneously on the make for himself and representing shadowy others. Azarian, a member of Wunderlick's band, appears one day and, after quizzing Bucky about his intentions for the group, gets around to his real point: "Happy Valley Farm Commune is holding something I'm willing to lay out money for. I represent certain interests. These interests happen to know you're in touch with Happy Valley. So they're making the offer to you through me."

When Opel Hampson, Bucky's girlfriend and the person who normally lives in the apartment on Great Jones Street, returns from her travels in "timeless lands," it is, she says, because "I've got business." That business is, of course, the product. Like Azarian, she is representing "people." "I'm bargaining agent for Happy Valley," she explains. "I have bargaining powers. I wheel and deal." Azarian and Opel eventually die for their troubles.

Fenig, the funny, failed writer who lives above Wunderlick, is likewise on the make, continually seeking to figure out the literary market—this, despite the wonderful fact that his one-act plays "get produced without exception at a very hip agricultural college in Arkansas." In the course of the novel, Fenig's wanderings through the world of genres take him through science fiction to pornographic children's literature ("Serious stuff. Filthy, obscene and brutal sex among little kids"). The object of his obsession is fame. His meditations on the subject are somewhat less penetrating than Wunderlick's: "Fame. . . . It won't happen. But if it does happen. But it won't happen. But if it does. But it won't." But if it does: "I'll handle it gracefully. I'll be judicious. I'll adjust to it with caution. I won't let it destroy me. Fame. The perfect word for the phenomenon it describes." The final genre that captivates Fenig is, needless to say, "[f]inancial writing. Books and articles for millionaires and potential millionaires." This money literature is his "fantastic terminal fiction."

The urge to entrepreneurship also infects Hanes, a messenger for Transparanoia and an emissary for the Happy Valley Farm Commune. He takes the drug package from Wunderlick and, drugged with the power of possessing such a precious object, attempts to double-cross the Commune and make a deal for the drug on his own. As does Dr. Pepper, the scientific genius of the underground whose name is a clever conflation of the counterculture utopianism of the Beatles' *Sgt. Pepper's Lonely Hearts Club Band* and the soft-drink commodity. Pepper first signs on to analyze the drug for the Commune and then attempts to obtain and market it himself. "Everybody in the free world wants to bid," is how Pepper describes the drug's desirability. Bohack, a representative of the Commune whose name derives from a supermarket chain, threatens Wunderlick when he cannot produce the drug. Meanwhile Globke steals the mountain tapes from his own client and plots to release them. Finally, the double-dealer Hanes, in order to save his own life, informs the Commune of the whereabouts of the mountain tapes, which the Commune then destroys. The members of the Commune are angry that Wunderlick, who, after all, had restored the notion of privacy to American life, was planning to violate his own privacy and tour again.

The character who has the most to say to Wunderlick about what his life has been—and what it has become, and what determines it—is Watney. Watney is a former pop star—he pulls up to Wunderlick's building in a limousine that includes "[t]hree rooms and a dining alcove. But at the same time fairly inconspicuous"—and stands as a kind of Alice Cooper figure, an image of the decline of rock into shock spectacle, as opposed to Wunderlick's Dylan/Jagger fusion. Watney's wild, androgynous band, Schicklgruber, epitomized the notion of rock 'n roll as a mad, pointless threat to the social order: "wherever they went the village elders consulted ordinances trying to find a technicality they might use to keep the band from performing or at the very least to get the band out of town the moment the last note sounded." When he visits Wunderlick, however, it turns out Watney is done with rock 'n roll and is—in a perfect transition—"into sales, procurement and operations now. I represent a fairly large Anglo-European group." Like everyone else, he visits the former band leader to bid on the drug product.

In the course of his discussion about the product with Wunderlick, Watney explains the reasons for his move into sales:

> I had no real power in the music structure. It was all just show. This thing about my power over kids. Watney the transatlantic villain. Schicklgruber the assassin of free will. It was just something to write, to fill up the newspapers with. I had no power, Bucky. I just dollied about on stage with my patent leather pumps and my evil leer. It was a good act all right. But it was all just an act, just a runaround, just a show.

Later on in the novel, Watney explains to Wunderlick how real power works.

> Bucky, you have no power. You have the illusion of power. I know this firsthand. I learned

this in lesson after lesson and city after city. Nothing truly moves to your sound. Nothing is shaken or bent. You're a bloody artist you are. Less than four ounces on the meat scale. You're soft, not hard. You're above ground, not under. The true underground is the place where power flows. That's the best-kept secret of our time. You're not the underground. Your people aren't underground people. The presidents and prime ministers are the ones who make the underground deals and speak the true underground idiom. The corporations. The military. The banks. This is the underground network. This is where it happens.

By the end of the novel, Wunderlick takes the ultimate drug, which provides him with "weeks of deep peace," but proves "less than lasting in its effect." Like all consumer goods, it is ultimately disappointing. The failure of the drug to transport him to a place beyond language—its failure to achieve a kind of suicide for him—is part of what Wunderlick calls his "double defeat." The other part of that defeat is the frustration, with the destruction of the mountain tapes, of his murderous desire to get back on the road. As Wunderlick himself frames the dichotomy of his failure: "first a chance not taken to reappear in the midst of people and forces made to my design and then a second enterprise denied, alternate to the first, permanent withdrawal to that unimprinted level where all sound is silken and nothing erodes in the mad weather of language." As the rumors surrounding his disappearance continue to swirl, he is back in numb isolation on Great Jones Street, sounding almost like a character out of T. S. Eliot: "When the season is right I'll return to whatever is out there. It's just a question of what sound to make or fake."

"Your life consumes itself," Watney tells Wunderlick, and the revelation of Wunderlick himself, and all artists, as objects of consumption, commodities like the ultimate drug or the mountain tapes, is part of the point of *Great Jones Street*. Like the Happy Valley Farm Commune, which moves from utopian ruralism to vicious drug dealing, each of the book's characters, with the exception of Wunderlick, who is essentially paralyzed, abandons whatever alternative seemed to be available and willfully enters the market economy. In 1990 it may not seem like much of an exercise to explore how much the sixties counterculture and its utopian hopes did or did not threaten the dominant culture. In 1973, however, such an exercise was well worth undertaking, and may still have value today. What DeLillo depicts in *Great Jones Street* is a society in which there are no meaningful alternatives, in which everyone and everything is bound in the cash nexus and the exchange of commodities, outside of which there stands nothing. Everything is consumed, or it consumes itself: murder or suicide, exploitation or self-destruction. After a decade of rampant market economics and amidst regular announcements of the worldwide triumph of capitalism—smug, dumb declarations of how the West has won—can the world DeLillo portrays in *Great Jones Street* not seem painfully familiar?

In a recent interview in *Rolling Stone*, Axl Rose, lead singer of Guns n' Roses, the fuck-you, rebellious band of the moment—and one of the most popular bands in the world—made questionable remarks about gays, blacks, women, and immigrants, and then offered these observations about his artistic life: "I was figuring it out, and I'm like the president of a company that's worth between $125 million and a quarter billion dollars. If you add up record sales based on the low figure and a certain price for T-shirts and royalties and publishing, you come up with at least $125 million, which I get less than two percent of." A little while later Rose advises youngsters aspiring to his lifestyle of rock 'n roll revolt: "What I'd tell any kid in high school is 'Take business classes.' I don't care what else you're gonna do, if you're gonna do art or anything, take business classes."

Is it clear he is a hero of rock 'n roll?

THE INFLUENCE OF MUSIC ON LITERATURE

Calvin S. Brown

SOURCE: "Fiction and the Leitmotiv," in *Music and Literature: A Comparison of the Arts,* University of Georgia Press, 1948, pp. 208-18.

[*In the following essay, Brown argues that the compositions of Richard Wagner have been the principal musical influence on the novel, and he illustrates how Gabriele d'Annunzio and Thomas Mann used the musical device of the leitmotiv, as Wagner developed it, in their novels.*]

For fairly obvious reasons, music has exerted considerably more influence on poetry than on prose fiction. By its very nature, poetry demands a constant attention to problems of sound, and thus is likely to suggest musical analogies to its creators. Also, except for narrative poetry (in which musical influence is slight) poetry demands the conscious search for form to a much greater degree than does fiction. Even if we ignore the great mass of fiction which is really a commodity on the market rather than a type of literature, the fact still remains that any narrative tends to become a framework in itself and to impose the form of its own characters, incidents, and relationships on the work which presents it. The writer must, of course, invent or select his narrative in the first place, but this process rarely involves the conscious preoccupation with more or less abstract form which usually falls to the lot of the poet.

Even more important is the distinction in scale between most fiction and most music. [The] poets who attempt sonata form usually work on a much smaller scale than do composers employing the same medium. The reverse is true of fiction, which, except in the short story, usually exceeds the ambitious musical work in length. The colossal type of novel which has been in vogue during the past decade has accentuated this difference. The short novelette is comparable to the symphony in its proportions and scale, but it has never been a widely cultivated form in the English-speaking countries. As a very broad generalization, we may say that there are two general literary types, the short and concentrated, and the long and diffuse. Novels and, to a lesser extent, dramas tend to fall into the latter classification.

It has been noted that one of the baffling characteristics of Wagner's music, to a person whose standards have been formed on symphonic literature, is its slowness of development, but this slowness simply keeps the music in step with the normal pace of the drama which it accompanies. By habit, Wagner mastered this type of stately composition on a grand scale and learned to practise it even in purely instrumental works.

> In short, the *Siegfried Idyll* succeeds where practically every "Symphonic Poem," from those of Liszt onwards, fails. It is a piece of purely instrumental music, quite twice the size of any well-constructed movement of a classical symphony, and yet forming a perfectly coherent and self-explaining musical scheme. Its length, its manner of slowly building up broad melodies out of constantly repeated single phrases, and the extreme deliberation with which it displays them stage by stage in combination, are features of style that have nothing to do with diffuseness. . . . [Tovey, *Essays in Musical Analysis*]

Wagner's music is, then, almost the only music constructed on the same scale as the larger genres of literature, and, like the very few truly great literary works, it achieves this vastness with a sense of inevitability and even economy of means.

In the light of these facts it is natural to assume that Wagner will be of more use to the writers of fiction than will other composers, and the facts will bear out this assumption. The principal musical influence on the novel, and even the novelette, has been the adoption of methods of construction developed by Wagner.

Other music has, of course, been of occasional and sporadic importance. Cadilhac's efforts in the direction of the symphonic novel were largely inspired by the symphonies of Beethoven. A host of writers with a passion for music have brought it into their novels as subject matter: even the famous "musical" works of E. T. A. Hoffmann hardly achieved more than this. And this writing *about* music shows the influence of music on literature to exactly the same extent that Lamb's "Dissertation on Roast Pig" shows the influence of cookery.

A more interesting experiment was made by Aldous Huxley in *Point Counter Point*. The title, a literal translation of the *punctum contra punctum,* or "note against note," of the early theorists, gives a fair indication of what the novel sets out to do. The plan is, briefly, one of complication, sudden shifts of subject and tone, and the playing off of incident against incident. Part of the complication, including the idea of having one of the characters an author who determines to write the book in which he appears, seems to be borrowed from one of Gide's novels. Perhaps it will be as well as to let the notebooks of Philip Quarles, Huxley's fictitious author, describe the method:

> The musicalization of fiction. Not in the symbolist way, by subordinating sense to sound.

> [. . .] But on a large scale, in the construction. The changes of moods, the abrupt transitions. (Majesty alternating with a joke, for example, in the first movement of the B flat major Quartet. [. . .]) More interesting still, the modulations, not merely from one key to another, but from mood to mood. A theme is stated, then developed, pushed out of shape, imperceptibly deformed, until, though still recognizably the same, it has become quite different. In sets of variations the process is carried a step further. Those incredible Diabelli variations, for example. The whole range of thought and feeling, yet all in organic relation to a ridiculous little waltz tune. Get this into a novel. How? The abrupt transitions are easy enough. All you need is a sufficiency of characters and parallel, contrapuntal plots. While Jones is murdering a wife, Smith is wheeling the perambulator in the park. You alternate the themes. More interesting, the modulations and variations are also more difficult. A novelist modulates by reduplicating situations and characters. He shows several people falling in love, or dying or praying in different ways—dissimilars solving the same problem.

This is an exact description of the technique of the book. While Spandrell and Illidge are murdering Everard Webley in Philip Quarles' house, Philip is arriving at his parents' home to untangle the absurd situation of his fatuous and socially prominent father, whose pregnant secretary is threatening to tell all. In the affair between cheerfully amoral Lucy Tantamount and gloomily passionate Walter Bidlake we have a fine example of dissimilars solving the same problem, and the method is carried on in the tentative infidelities of Elinor and Philip, Mr. Quarles' pompous seduction (with full cooperation) of Gladys, and Burlap's *seductio ad absurdum* of Beatrice. The same principle is worked out in the deaths of Little Philip, of Webley, and of Spandrell, and the approaching death of old John Bidlake. Finally, the screeching parrot that interrupts a passionate scene between Walter and Lucy is probably a lineal descendant of the joke in the B flat major Quartet.

Early in *Point Counter Point* Philip Quarles suggests another possibility which is also mentioned further on in the passage just quoted; the author can assume various points of view about the characters and events of his story, shifting from the cynical to the sentimental, from the religious to the physiological. It is perhaps unfortunate that Huxley did not attempt this technique. As the novel stands it is a brilliant piece of work, but somewhat too ingenious, too much of a *jeu d'esprit*. The contrasts and parallelisms are cleverly managed, but the machinery is too obvious. The essential theory, of course, is Aiken's method of juxtaposition except that, by having real characters and events instead of a succession in the mind, Huxley does give a sense of continuity: an action which has been left off halfway is being continued while a new one is described. In a literal sense he thus comes closer to counterpoint than does Aiken, but the suggestion of the musical analogy is not nearly so effective. Furthermore, for all its brilliance and ingenuity, *Point Counter Point* seems to have been a blind alley and to have made no contribution to the technique of fiction.

Wagner did make such a contribution in the Leitmotiv, and writers of fiction have only begun to exploit its possibilities. In a way this device has been known since the dawn of literature, and there is a certain amount of justification for considering the regular Homeric combination of an epithet with a noun—"the many-voiced sea," "the hollow ships," "Dawn, the rosy-fingered"—as a Leitmotiv. Similarly, one critic finds that the device was used, to some extent, well before the time of Wagner and, later, independently of his influence, by such writers as Goethe and Dickens. Sometimes, as in Goethe's *Wahlverwandtschaften,* the motives have been organic, but more frequently they have been mechanical repetitions of some descriptive or characterizing trait, like Mr. Micawber's constant statement that he is "waiting for something to turn up." There is no reason to think that such repetitions as this, or as the constantly repeated phrases of the folk-tale, owe anything to musical influence or are real parallels to musical devices. With the rise of Wagner, however, a number of writers felt a distinct musical influence and deliberately began to base some of their effects on Wagnerian music. Thus there are genuine Leitmotivs here and there in Zola, and the imitation of Wagner is unmistakable in the scene in *Le ventre de Paris* which describes the shifting, blending, clashing stenches of a cheese-shop in terms of Wagnerian orchestration.

A genuine Leitmotiv in literature is hard to define, for its existence is determined more by its use than by its nature. One might say that it is a verbal formula which is deliberately repeated, which is easily recognized at each recurrence, and which serves, by means of this recognition, to link the context in which the repetition occurs with earlier contexts in which the motive has appeared. (It will be noted that this definition, written entirely for the literary use of the Leitmotiv, will apply equally well to the musical use if we merely change *verbal* to *musical*.) Perhaps we should add that in both music and literature the Leitmotiv has to be comparatively short and must have a programmatic association—must refer to something beyond the tones or words which it contains.

Both d'Annunzio and Thomas Mann, different as they are in other respects, have come strongly under the influence of Wagner. Both have spoken of him with admiration, and by a striking coincidence (for it seems to be nothing more) both have written books which use *Tristan und Isolde,* played by one of a pair of lovers to the other from a piano score, as the climax and key. It is not surprising, then, to find that both have cultivated the use of the Leitmotiv, on Wagnerian principles, so extensively that critical studies of its use by each have been published.

D'Annunzio's novel *Trionfo della Morte* (*The Triumph of Death*) illustrates very well his use of Leitmotivs. It is the story of a man and his mistress, Giorgio being something of a Hamlet-type (though a sensualist withal), and the mistress being a "prezioso strumento di voluttà" and little more. From the very opening chapter, in which they walk in the Pincio gardens and arrive at the parapet just after a man has killed himself by leaping off, Giorgio is haunted by the fascination of death. This early suicide becomes one recurring theme. Another is the recollection of the lover's uncle, who had also killed himself. A number of other motives are employed, such as the sound of men at work ramming down paving-blocks in the streets, Giorgio's mother's agonized question "*For whom* do you forsake me?" and the music (described in rather Wagnerian terms) of the sea. These themes serve to hold together the various episodes of the story, but they have an even more important purpose in keeping before the reader the state of mind of the man—the hypnotic fascination of suicide—which is a steady undercurrent and is the real subject of the book. Finally, after playing Tristan for Ippolita, Giorgio takes her for a walk by the sea, lures her to the top of a cliff, suddenly seizes her, and leaps off.

D'Annunzio's preface leaves no doubt as to the deliberateness or the ultimate source of his method. It speaks of the intention of representing the inner life of a character rather than merely a series of external events, of writing "a plastic and symphonic prose, rich in images and music." More specifically still, it says that the contemporary psychological analyst has, in the Italian vocabulary, "musical elements so varied and effective as to be able to compete with the great Wagnerian orchestra in suggesting what only Music can suggest to the modern soul."

Thomas Mann's use of the Leitmotiv is more skilful and extensive than d'Annunzio's, and worthy of more detailed treatment. Perhaps it is best seen in *Tonio Kröger,* of which Mann himself writes:

> Here probably I first learned to employ music as a shaping influence in my art. The conception of epic prose-composition as a weaving of themes, as a musical complex of associations, I later on largely employed in *The Magic Mountain.* Only that there the verbal leitmotiv is no longer, as in *Buddenbrooks,* employed in the representation of form alone, but has taken on a less mechanical, more musical character, and endeavors to mirror the emotion and idea.

The later developments here mentioned are interesting, but the germ of all of them is contained in *Tonio Kröger,* and this novelette is far more convenient for purposes of illustration than are the vast novels.

Tonio Kröger, the son of a good bourgeois north-German father and a happy-go-lucky, musical Italian mother, has, during his adolescence, two attachments. The first is to Hans Hansen, a schoolmate who likes Tonio in a way, but shares none of his literary interests—who is obliging enough to promise to read *Don Carlos* because of Tonio's enthusiasm about it, but never does. Hans is really interested in his riding lessons and his books about horses. A description of a walk taken by the two after school one afternoon indicates their relationship. After this comes Tonio's first love, for Ingeborg Holm, "the blonde Inge." She is a feminine counterpart of Hans—gay, self-confident, a complete extravert. Magdalena Vermehren watches Tonio with dreamy admiration, but not Inge—she laughs at him for an awkward mistake in dancing-class, and he retires, abashed, to stand in the darkened hall outside and vainly hope that she will miss him and come to him. He promises himself that he will be true to her, whatever she may think of him, but as time passes he is shocked to find that love passes and such faithfulness is impossible.

Tonio's father dies, the house and business are sold, his mother marries an Italian virtuoso and disappears from his life, and he leaves his provincial home town in high scorn. When we next meet him he has achieved considerable reputation as a writer. He visits Lisaweta Iwanowna in her studio, and she stops her painting to have tea with him. He does most of the talking, disburdening himself of a long series of reflections. Artistic genius is not a gift but a curse. The artist must calculate his effects coldbloodedly, and thus must shut himself off from ordinary human warmth of feeling. He is a man apart, always wanting to mingle with his fellows as one of them, but never succeeding. In fact, art is probably an escape from some failing as a human being, and the artistic temperament is highly suspect. After all this, Lisaweta gives him her answer: he himself is simply a bourgeois on the wrong path.—Some time later, Tonio again visits Lisaweta and tells her that he is setting out to visit Denmark, traveling by way of his—he almost says "home," but changes to "starting point."

He stops by his home town very briefly, but long enough to look at Ingeborg's old house, to repeat the walk taken with Hans years before, to visit his old home and find that it is now a public library, and to be detained on suspicion at his hotel and almost arrested as a swindler. (After telling Lisaweta about a criminal banker who was an excellent writer, he had drawn the conclusion that no honest banker *could* be an artist.) Then he went on to Denmark, where he soon settled down in a seaside resort. Here he witnessed a dance held by a group of excursionists. He stood in the darkened passageway and watched longingly while two youngsters remarkably like Hans and Ingeborg enjoyed themselves. A dreamy-eyed, awkward girl (Magdalena!) slipped and fell; Tonio helped her to a chair, looked once more at Hans and Inge, and went to his room. "From below floated up to him, muffled and soothing, the sweet, trivial waltz-time of life."

He sat down and wrote to Lisaweta—not a narrative, but a general statement. He sees that he is a mixture of his father's bourgeois nature and his mother's artistic temperament. "I stand between two worlds but am at home in neither, and this makes it rather difficult for me. You artists call me a bourgeois, and the bourgeoisie want to arrest me—I don't know which group wounds me more." But he goes on to say that he accepts the mixture, that if anything can make a poet out of a mere man of letters, it is precisely this attachment to the human, the living, and the ordinary. "Do not scold me for this love," he writes, and (seeing now for himself what the author had seen in him as he returned from his walk with Hans years before) he concludes: "Longing is in it, and sorrowful envy, and a tiny bit of scorn, and an utter, pure happiness."

This summary of the action is sufficient for our purposes, though many details have necessarily been omitted. Before examining the use of the Leitmotiv, we should notice that the structure is clearly sonata form, the four paragraphs of the summary including respectively the exposition, development, recapitulation, and coda. The exposition states separately the two themes of Hans and Inge. The develop-

ment is devoted largely to the conversations with Lisaweta, in which the significance of these themes for Tonio's character and life is worked out. The recapitulation is devoted to Tonio's journey, though with the addition of some new episodes. Nevertheless, in the return to Tonio's home town, the childhood recollections, and the repetition of the walk with Hans we clearly have the recapitulation of the first subject; and (after a brief account of the intervening days) in the dance at the inn, even including the accident on the dance floor, we have the second. Finally, the letter to Lisaweta is a coda which sums up the whole thing.

The fact that a work based on sonata form can be an excellent example of the literary use of the Leitmotiv shows that musical analogies in literature are never exact. Yet the combination, strange as it seems from a purely musical point of view, solves very effectively the problem of repetition. To repeat exactly the opening chapters would have been both tedious and pointless, for the significance of the mature Tonio's visit to his home and his stay in Denmark lies in the fact that he now sees from a different point of view the experiences of his childhood. Nevertheless, the repetition is close when he relives these experiences, and the basic identity must be clearly shown. This is achieved by the repetition of short passages like the conclusion of the letter to Lisaweta. In the same way, the description of the blonde dancer at the seaside resort repeats phrases from the description which introduced Ingeborg Holm. When Tonio repeats the walk taken with Hans in his childhood, Mann repeats his account of that walk in essentially the same words, but with appropriate slight differences: "Then he left the promenade along the wall not far from the station, saw a train puff by in clumsy haste, amused himself by counting the cars, and looked at the man who sat on top of the last one." As children, Tonio and Hans had waved to this man.

These passages which are repeated in order to call attention to the essential unity of superficially different experiences are necessarily somewhat long. It may even be questioned whether they should be classified as Leitmotivs at all, for, because of the nature of the story, each of them is repeated only once. There can be no such question about certain shorter phrases which occur more often. Three of these, all connected in one way or another with Tonio's good philistine of a father, will show the method. The first is, to all appearances, merely a physical description: the father was "a tall, carefully dressed man with thoughtful blue eyes, who always wore a wild flower in his buttonhole." This formula is repeated when Mann speaks of the father's death; and when Tonio, a literary man of note, lives in large cities, but finds no joy of heart there, it is suggested that perhaps his heredity from this identically-described father is responsible. Finally, when Tonio revisits his home (now a library), he thinks of his father in these same terms. Through these repetitions the motive gradually comes to stand for the bourgeois element both in the father and in Tonio. Its ramifications are seen, for example, when Lisaweta tells Tonio to sit down on a trunk in her studio, if he is not too afraid for his "patrician garments"; and he replies that as far as possible the artist ought to dress and act like a respectable person. (A similar description of "his dark and fiery mother, who played the piano and mandolin so beautifully" likewise comes to be a representation of the artistic side of his nature.)

The other two motives derived from the father both originate in an early passage which tells how young Tonio found his father's scolding of his artistic vagaries "more proper and respectable" than his mother's tendency to reward or ignore them. The boy went on to think (obviously quoting a lecture from his father), "We are not gypsies in green carts, but substantial people. . . ." This gypsy-theme returns when Tonio, startled by Hans' repugnance for his foreign Christian name, thinks that there is always something different about him which makes him not quite acceptable to his fellows. It returns again, when he recoils from the escapades of Bohemian life. It appears for the last time when he considers revealing his identity to the police in order to prove that he is no swindler, no gypsy in a green cart.

From this same original passage is derived another motive, that of finding "quite as it should be" (*sehr in der Ordnung*) the attitude of the everyday world towards art and the artist. The exact verbal formula does not appear until later, but the connection with his secret approval of his father's condemnation in this passage is clear from the fact that its first two appearances (when he first returns to his home town, and later when he visits the house itself) are connected with the recollection of his father's lectures. The third use is in connection with the bourgeois distrust shown in the suspicions of the police.

Other important motives include the reference to the living heart (used five times) to summarize the world of warm and natural human relationships; and the contrasting reference to device and effect (*Pointe und Wirkung*) for the coldblooded calculation of the deliberate artist. Minor motives abound: books about horses, for example, not only refer to Hans Hansen's literary interests, but come to represent the general way of life of the sound extravert who has no need of literature. But a full listing of such motives would extend to inordinate length without contributing any new principles.

Various critics have attempted to classify literary Leitmotivs, but the results are not very convincing. The failure is not surprising, for the device is essentially a method of economy by which a short expression comes to stand for and to recall to the reader's mind an entire and frequently complex idea, character, or situation. Because of its very economy, then, a motive will frequently accomplish several different things at the same time. Since the classifications are based primarily on the use to which a motive is put, they necessarily fall to pieces in cases of multiple significance. One suggested grouping, for example, distinguishes between characterizing and structural motives, and in some very simple cases the distinction can be made. In *Tonio Kröger*, however, such a classification is meaningless. The description of Tonio's father is, from one point of view, purely a motive of characterization. Nevertheless, it is structural in that it connects one side of Tonio's own character with his father, and it is structural in an even more mechanical way when, as Tonio sits in that part of the library which used to be his own room, he

thinks that another part now occupies the place where he sat at his father's deathbed. In this instance, the character of the father is hardly in question, and the purpose of the repeated characterization is simply to connect this visit more directly with Tonio's earlier life. Any really effective use of the literary Leitmotiv will similarly defy classification because of its multiple relevance.

The recent development of the Leitmotiv as a literary device is an example of reciprocal interaction between literature and music. The English *riding coat* was borrowed into French (with the Gallicized spelling and pronunciation) as *redingote*, and English has recently borrowed this form of the word back, Anglicizing the pronunciation and using it for something quite different from a riding coat. A similar interchange has taken place in the case of the Leitmotiv. . . . [The] musicians created it by imitating language—by giving an external significance to a group of sounds. But this group of sounds was, in most cases, longer and more impressive than a single ordinary word. Above all, it attracted attention to itself in a way that a single word cannot imitate except in such very rare cases as Macbeth's "this hand will rather / The multitudinous seas *incarnadine*." And since it thus attracted attention and called for recognition, it lent itself to a variety of uses in the handling of plot, characterization, and idea demanded by the programmatic music in which it was used. Seeing its usefulness, the writers then borrowed it back by creating, in imitation of it, a *phrase* which would be easily recognizable and could be employed in a similar way. They are still exploring its possibilities and finding new uses for it. Thus music would not have developed the Leitmotiv without certain antecedent suggestions from literature, and literature would not have developed it to anything resembling its present use without the example of music.

Kathy J. Ogren

SOURCE: "Controversial Sounds: Jazz Performance as Theme and Language in the Harlem Renaissance," in *The Harlem Renaissance: Revaluations,* edited by Amritjit Singh, William S. Shiver, and Stanley Brodwin, Garland Publishing, Inc., 1989, pp. 159-84.

[*In the following essay, which focuses on the controversy among writers and artists of the Harlem Renaissance over the morality, history, and aesthetics of jazz music, Ogren studies the works of several authors who celebrate jazz performance for its rich folk heritage and power to evoke audience participation. Ogren's essay was first presented as a paper at a conference entitled "Heritage: A Reappraisal of the Harlem Renaissance," in 1985.*]

> The Salvation Army of Cincinnati obtained a temporary injunction today to prevent the erection of a moving picture theatre adjoining the Catharine Booth Home for Girls, on the ground that music emanating from the theatre would implant "jazz emotions" in the babies at the home. The plaintiffs realize that they live in a jazz age, declared the suit, . . . "but we are loathe to believe that babies born in the maternity hospital are to be legally subjected to the im-

planting of jazz emotions by such enforced proximity to a theatre and jazz palace."

New York Times, 1926

Readers of the *New York Times* in the 1920s would not have been surprised by this news item, dateline, Cincinnati, Ohio. Throughout the decade, the *Times* as well as other newspapers recorded a growing controversy concerning the influence of jazz music. Reports came from cities across the nation and in Europe. Most of them documented fears about the spread of this new form of popular music. As the Cincinnati Salvation Army admitted, jazz was not only a popular craze of the 1920s, but was often the music that described the ambiance or mood of the decade. Indeed, this description remains a common one in present-day accounts of the 1920s.

The centrality of jazz in our historical memory is neither an accident nor a convention derived from the "roaring twenties" stereotype. Although the injunction requested by the Cincinnati Salvation Army sounds slightly comical today, it should not be dismissed lightly. Americans chose this powerful new music—characterized by improvised melodies, syncopated rhythms and a strong beat—to represent fundamental cultural changes they experienced in the early twentieth century. Detractors criticized both its musical characteristics and its origins in lower-class black culture. Jazz-lovers hailed it as everything from exciting entertainment to an antidote for repressive industrial society. In either case, Americans found jazz symbolic of fundamental changes they identified in postwar life. Participation in jazz performance provided an opportunity to experience, celebrate, and perhaps cope with change.

One aspect of the jazz controversy that has not received sufficient attention is the debate concerning popular music—especially blues and jazz—that took place among prominent Harlem Renaissance participants. Jazz musicians were among the many migrant artists who moved to New York in the mid-1910s and 1920s in search of improved job opportunities and national exposure via radio and recording contracts. Some musicians were counted among the creative artists of the Harlem Renaissance, but most of them were not jazz musicians. The musicians themselves do not seem to have paid much attention to the manifestos of artistic pride that characterized this outpouring of Afro-American arts and letters. Participants in the Harlem Renaissance, however, certainly heard—and debated—jazz.

Many Harlem Renaissance scholars point out that leaders of this cultural movement devalued blues and jazz, preferring the spirituals as a source of artistic inspiration. Some leaders also ignored jazz because of its identification with vice and crime or its association with the cult of primitivism. Nathan Huggins neatly summarizes this position:

> Harlem intellectuals promoted Negro Art, but one thing is very curious, except for Langston Hughes, none of them took jazz—the new music—seriously. Of course, they all mentioned it as background, as descriptive of Harlem life. All said it was important in the definition of the New Negro. But none thought enough about it to try and figure out what was happening. . . .

The promoters of the Harlem Renaissance were so fixed on a vision of *high* culture that they did not look very hard or well at jazz.

Huggins attributes this neglect of jazz to the Harlem Renaissance leaders' belief that blacks would prove their artistic ability by measuring up to white cultural standards and impressing white patrons. Presumably, these leaders assumed jazz could serve neither need.

More recent studies of Harlem in the 1920s also emphasize the opposition of the intelligentsia to jazz. David Levering Lewis concludes that the "talented tenth's" encouragement of the arts was a political strategy of "civil rights by copyright." Their endorsement of assimilationist values led them to reject most jazz and blues as disreputable music. Fletcher Henderson's Rainbow Orchestra gained their approval, according to Lewis, because "the funkiness and raucousness of jazz dissipated" under his direction, and he gained support from white audiences.

> The centrality of jazz in our historical memory is neither an accident nor a convention derived from the "roaring twenties" stereotype. Americans chose this powerful new music—characterized by improvised melodies, syncopated rhythms and a strong beat—to represent fundamental cultural changes they experienced in the early twentieth century.
>
> **—Kathy J. Ogren**

Although these historians have effectively explained the biases against jazz shown by some Harlem Renaissance leaders, other participants in the Harlem Renaissance found jazz a provocative challenge to their analysis of Afro-American culture and a positive stimulus to their imagination. Harlem Renaissance critics studied the striking musical features of jazz, in particular its innovative rhythms and improvisation. They noted that jazz was created in live performance, and that performer-audience interactions, particularly in the black community, helped perpetuate the participatory and spontaneous qualities of jazz. In their estimation, the music provided a valuable record of the Afro-American experience.

In addition to exploring the communicative and historical meaning of jazz, Harlem Renaissance writers pointed to jazz and blues as evidence of the Afro-American creative potential crucial to the developing renaissance. For example, even though James Weldon Johnson, Joel A. Rogers, and Alain Locke all dreamed of "more dignified" symphonic expressions of jazz, each applauded the popularity of jazz and tried to explain its salient characteristics. Literary artists such as Claude McKay, Langston Hughes, and Zora Neale Hurston used jazz and blues not only for settings and themes in their novels and poems, but also as a language expressing their particular artistic vision and containing the potential for a more general Afro-American aesthetic.

Jazz performance became not only a subject of analysis and discussion in the Harlem Renaissance; it informed debates about the Harlem Renaissance itself. This is especially clear from discussions over the appropriateness of jazz performance as an expression of the "primitive" folk, or working-class roots for black art and literature. All of these writers depicted or analyzed the participatory nature of jazz performance and its communicative strength, thereby testifying to the significant role of jazz performance in the Harlem Renaissance.

Harlem Renaissance writers analyzed the folk origins of black music in order to remind readers that it was indigenous to America and that it captured the particular experiences of Afro-Americans. James Weldon Johnson, Joel A. Rogers, and Alain Locke all commented on the folk origins of spirituals, work songs, ragtime, and blues. They were concerned with claiming a place for these musical idioms in American musical history.

James Weldon Johnson, a composer of ragtime and Broadway songs himself, used black music as a theme in much of his writing. His early novel, *The Autobiography of an Ex-Coloured Man* (1912), depicted a ragtime musician torn between composing great symphonies based on Afro-American music and passing into the white business world. The unnamed protagonist chooses to pass, perhaps expressing Johnson's pessimism for the future of black composers. Johnson published *The Book of American Negro Spirituals* (1925) and *God's Trombones—Seven Negro Spirituals in Verse* (1927), both of which made valuable contributions to black music history and folklore. Johnson explained that the trombone had "just the tone and timbre to represent that old-time Negro preacher's voice," and at the same time, "there were the traditional jazz connotations provided by the trombone." Finally, in both *The Autobiography* and *Black Manhattan* (1930), Johnson provided cultural historians with a rich description of jazz cabarets and nightclubs.

In his well-known introduction to *The Book of American Negro Poetry* (1922), Johnson asserted that the Uncle Remus stories, spirituals, the cakewalk, and ragtime "were the only things artistic that have yet sprung from American soil and been universally acknowledged as distinctive American products." Johnson's description of ragtime emphasized the ability of the music to provoke audience response and engage listeners:

> Any one who doubts that there is a peculiar hell-tickling, smile-provoking, joy-awakening, response-compelling charm in Ragtime needs only to hear a skillful performer play the genuine article, needs only to listen to its bizarre harmonies, its audacious resolutions often consisting of an abrupt jump from one key to another, its intricate rhythms in which the accents fall in the most unexpected places but in which the fundamental beat is never lost, in order to be convinced. I believe it has its place as well as the music which draws from us sighs and tears.

Johnson's adjectives—"awakening," "provoking," "com-pelling," "audacious"—show his appreciation of the communicative power of black music to evoke emotions and audience participation. These kinds of descriptions were common in the Harlem Renaissance writing on jazz. Johnson's influential introduction provided an important early recognition of the relationship between music idioms and poetic voice in Afro-American literature.

Joel A. Rogers's "Jazz at Home," which Alain Locke included in his 1925 *New Negro* anthology, offered the comprehensive statement on jazz in the early literature of the Harlem Renaissance. Rogers's perspective was typical of Harlem Renaissance critics interested in jazz. He discussed the history of jazz performance, the influence of jazz on other music and entertainment forms, and jazz as a symbol of the modern age.

Rogers attributes the distinctiveness of jazz performance to qualities derived from folk music. It is, he wrote, "of Negro origin, plus the experience of the American environment." Acknowledging the role of vernacular dance in the rhythmic development of jazz, Rogers further explains:

> It is in the Indian war dance, the Highland fling, the Irish jig, the cossack dance, the Spanish fandango, the Brazilian *maxixe,* the dance of the whirling dervish, the hula hula of the South Seas, the *dance du ventre* of the Orient, the *carmagnole* of the French Revolution, the strains of Gypsy music, and ragtime of the Negro.

By locating the origins of jazz in worldwide folk music and dance, Rogers asserts a long and dignified heritage for jazz. Furthermore, identifying jazz with dance underscores its function as an expressive entertainment form.

Rogers's historical sketch of jazz also highlights the participatory qualities of jazz performance. Ragtime band performers, for Rogers, made their own instruments and used their bodies if necessary for "patting juba" rhythms. When itinerant stride and boogie-woogie pianists played the first jazz, according to Rogers, the audience became part of the show. Rogers recounts an apocryphal story that credits the audience with inventing the word jazz:

> Then came Jasbo Brown, a reckless musician of a Negro cabaret in Chicago, who played this and other blues, blowing his own extravagant moods and risqué interpretations into them, while hilarious with gin. To give further meanings to his veiled allusions, he would make the trombone "talk" by putting a derby hat and later a tin can at its mouth. The delighted patrons would shout, "more Jasbo. More, Jas, more." And so the name originated.

Rogers points out that when performers interacted with their communities in various call-and-response formats, they helped perpetuate a performance style typical of Afro-American sacred music, as well as blues and jazz.

Rogers indicates further that the excitement and energy of jazz music and dance had inspired Broadway artists and that it continued to influence modernist European composers. "With the same nonchalance and impudence with which it left the levee and the dive to stride like an upstart conqueror, almost overnight into the grand salon," Rogers proclaims, "jazz now begins its conquest of musical Parnassus." For Rogers, these new uses of jazz illustrate that black music was finally earning the respect it deserved.

Alain Locke's own essay on music in *The New Negro* calls for a serious study of the spirituals, which he believed were "the most characteristic product of the race genius as yet in America." But his appreciation of jazz grew during the 1920s and in his 1934 essay, "Toward a Critique of Negro Music," he expresses his admiration for a range of jazz artists including Duke Ellington, Noble Sissle, Cab Calloway, and Fletcher Henderson. In this latter essay, Locke tempers his earlier and fairly elitist disregard of jazz with a deepening critique of its origins and development through Afro-American musical traditions. His study culminated in *The Negro and His Music,* published in 1936. Locke's changing ideas on the subject of music underscore the value in seeing the Harlem Renaissance as an ongoing process of creation and evaluation rather than an event fixed in time.

In all of his musical criticism, Locke argues for a painstaking analysis of how formal elements of black music are transformed in performance. His treatment of jazz was designed to show how ragtime and jazz embody "Negro rhythm and harmony" that had been lost through the dilutions of Stephen Foster, minstrelsy, and other popularizations of Afro-American music. For example, Locke used Abbe Niles's and W.H. Handy's *Blues: An Anthology* in his own history of jazz in order to emphasize the folk elements in the music. He notes that Handy attributed his inspiration for blues composition to the itinerant minstrels Handy witnessed at train crossings and to the lively responses from audiences who heard Handy play "hot."

Locke also locates jazz rhythm and improvisation in folk music practice. The "tango rhythm," he wrote, was "characteristically Negro and its popularity among Negroes becomes very plausible when it is realized that it is originally an African Rhythm," and "basic in the purest and oldest strains of the Afro-Cuban music, in the folk music of Mexico and Brazil . . . and in Negro dances of even the Bahamas and Barbados." Improvisation, Locke writes:

> . . . came rocketing out of the blues. It grew out of the improvised musical "filling in" of the gap between the short measure of the blues and the longer eight bar line, the break interval in the original folk form of three line blues. Such filling in and compounding of the basic rhythm are characteristic of Negro music everywhere, from deepest Africa to the streets of Charleston, from the unaccompanied hand-clapping of the street corner "hoe-down" to the interpolation of shouts, amens, and exclamations in Negro church revivals.

Locke aims to prove that jazz has a unique structure, history, and musical tone that originated in and continues to express the participatory traditions of black folk music—not only in America—but in Africa and much of the rest of the new world.

In addition to explaining the history and development of jazz, Johnson, Rogers, and Locke also refuted the charges of critics in the 1920s who complained that jazz was a "bunch of noise" lacking musical structure and requiring no skill or training to perform. All three of them were slightly more sympathetic to suggestions that jazz had a hypnotic effect on its listeners or that it symbolized the modern age.

For all of his alleged disdain for jazz, Locke disputes those who claimed the music was a "mere set of musical tricks by which any tune whatsoever can be 'ragged' or 'jazzed.' " Jazz had distinctive musical characteristics like other music genres, Locke insists, and could trace its lineage back to secular and sacred black folk music. He points out that it took talent and practice to play jazz and that black musicians in particular had mastered it. Accomplished jazz musicians needed to improvise, work with fellow bandsmen, and be skilled at head tunes and complex rhythms. According to Locke, jazz is characterized by a "freestyle" that "has generations of experience back of it; it is derived from the voice tricks and vocal habits characteristic of Negro choral singing." The distinctiveness of jazz, then, derives from communal and participatory performance practice and continues to be expressed through improvisation.

Locke compares jazz to an "epidemic" that spread quickly and transformed tempo, technique, and themes in popular music. Johnson suggests a similar influence for ragtime when he describes it as music that "jes grew." Similarly, Rogers attributes a narcotic quality to jazz and believed that it offered psychological relief after World War I that was "safer than drugs or alcohol." Acknowledging potentially immoral influences of jazz, Rogers insists that its impact depends on the stability of its listeners: "Jazz, it is needless to say, will remain a creation for the industrious and a dissipator of energy for the frivolous, a tonic for the strong and a poison for the weak."

Locke expressed fears that the growing commercial success of jazz undermines its folk heritage. The "common enemy" of all jazz musicianship is the "ever present danger of commercialization" as well as the "public taste," which he deemed a "notoriously poor judge of quality." Locke hoped jazz "experts" would exert more influence on public taste and encourage listeners to appreciate and thereby protect its folk roots. Likewise, Locke measured the purported immorality of jazz against its origins in folk culture. He concurred with those who found an "erotic side of jazz." But, he explained:

> . . . there is a vast difference between its first healthy and earthy expression in the original peasant paganism out of which it arose and its hectic, artificial and sometimes morally vicious counterpart which was the outcome of the vogue of artificial and commercialized jazz entertainment. The one is primitively erotic; the other, decadently neurotic.

Locke carefully defines primitivism by its relation to folk traditions, and in that context, he considers jazz a positive influence on twentieth-century society. Noting that jazz had been accused of being both "an emotional escape," and an "emotional rejuvinator" for those trying to cope with post-World War I America, Locke insists that jazz did not cause immorality. Its popularity was a symptom of larger social changes, he concludes. Much like Rogers, he sees jazz as a "spiritual child of the twenties."

James Weldon Johnson, Joel A. Rogers, and Alain Locke see black music serving a dual role in the Harlem Renaissance. Despite their proselytizing for jazz symphonies, they nonetheless consider jazz and blues repositories of Afro-American history and creativity and fascinating musical idioms in and of themselves. The various perspectives offered by Johnson, Rogers, and Locke acknowledge the power of musical performance to express emotions through spontaneity and audience participation, and each author documents the unique strengths of ragtime, blues, and jazz that depended on participatory musical traditions.

Both Rogers and Locke rebutted aesthetic and moral accusations against jazz by condemning those with a prurient or commercial interest in jazz. Because they located the controversial qualities of jazz in the white-dominated commercial music industry—not in black performance traditions—these authors shifted the terms of the jazz controversy. Furthermore, their criticism of the commercialization of Afro-American folk culture encouraged a serious analysis of the role of black music in American popular entertainment. These concerns were not typical of white jazz critics.

The poets and novelists of the Harlem Renaissance also discovered a unique creative well in jazz performance. Nathan Huggins suggests that the literary use of jazz as background was casual—almost a convention required by the cult of primitivism. But for some young artists, jazz and blues inspired new themes and language forms. Three young writers in particular—Claude McKay, Langston Hughes, Zora Neale Hurston—interpreted jazz and blues performance in provocative new ways. Black music also informed their attempts to formulate a new asthetic.

Claude McKay is perhaps the best-known Harlem Renaissance fiction writer to use primitivism self-consciously in his fiction. McKay's portrayal of exotic themes and atmospheres in *Home to Harlem* (1928), for example, drew on jazz performance. The music and the locations for its performance became a fundamental part of McKay's attempt to create a primitive urban world.

In *Home to Harlem*, the protagonist, Jake, returns to Harlem following his desertion from World War I military service. He is entranced by "The noise of Harlem, the sugared laughter. The honey- talk on its streets, and all night long, ragtime and 'blues' playing somewhere, . . . singing somewhere, dancing somewhere! Oh! the contagious fever of Harlem." McKay uses this tone throughout the novel and evokes images of epidemic diseases much as Johnson, Locke, and Rogers had. The communicability of jazz pervades McKay's Harlem.

Much of the novel is set in the cabarets and nightclubs of Harlem. McKay's descriptions of performance locations stressed the exotic and the sensational. Nevertheless, they are fairly consistent with actual cabarets in the 1920s. McKay explains that some cabarets, like Barron's, relied

"on its downtown white trade." Others, such as Leroy's, served as "the big common rendezvous shop for everybody." The "Congo" was typical of blacks-only clubs: "It was African in spirit and color. No white persons were admitted there." McKay bases his fictional Harlem nightlife on the actual clubs that existed in the 1920s, and he uses their differences to illustrate class and racial divisions.

McKay also makes effective use of the decor of clubs to evoke images of hot-house or jungle-like worlds in which dancing, drinking, fighting, and flirtation were common. The environment relaxed the restraints of everyday life, and performers and patrons responded by expressing the emotions they normally held in check.

In a typical scene from *Home to Harlem,* for example, McKay offers his vision of how musical entertainment provided a welcome release for the "common workaday Negroes of the Belt":

> The orchestra was tuning up. . . . The first notes fell out like a general clapping for merry-making and chased the dancers running, sliding, shuffling, trotting to the floor. Little girls energetically chewing Spearmint and showing all their teeth dashed out on the floor and started shivering amourously, itching for their partners to come. Some lads were quickly on their feet, grinning gayly and improvising new steps with snapping of fingers while their girls were sucking up the last of their creme de menthe. The floor was large and smooth enough for anything.

The fictional nightclub scene, like others in McKay's novel, represents the nightclub as a place where patrons enjoy themselves and where the music and its setting are conducive to participation.

For McKay, working-class and peasant cultures contained a source of beauty that was relatively untouched by the civilized world. He believed that the Harlem he created in *Home to Harlem* was "similar to what I have done for Jamaica in verse." McKay used blues and jazz music in the American setting to establish an open, emotional, and participatory ambiance—what he considered "primitive." Despite a favorable reception by some reviewers, however, others claimed that *Home to Harlem* had strayed too far from a healthy grounding in folk cultures. He was accused of pandering to the exploitative tastes of white slummers by glorifying the Harlem underworld.

McKay's portrayal of musical entertainment and its meaning for lower-class blacks challenges the assertion of Locke and others that "primitive" virtues belonged only to rural folk culture and that commercialization distorted "primitive" beauty. Likewise, McKay's suggestion that the power of music came from participatory performances located in dives and cabaret offended the more conservative Harlem Renaissance leaders. McKay later expressed his disappointment that "many of the talented Negroes regarded their renaissance more as an uplift organization and a vehicle to accelerate the pace and progress of smart Negro society." McKay's controversial treatment of blues and jazz performance and the world of black entertainment drew criticism from W.E.B. DuBois, in particular, who could not accept the moral tone of *Home to Harlem.*

McKay depicted an extreme potential of performance that challenged the norms of Renaissance leaders and set him apart from more genteel aesthetic values. As the reaction to McKay's work showed, however, black participants in the Harlem Renaissance debated the meaning and function of jazz. Theirs was not a simple argument between pro- and anti-jazz factions.

The richness of the discussion over jazz performance becomes clearer when we look at the writings of Langston Hughes and Zora Neale Hurston. Like Claude McKay, Langston Hughes found inspiration in the experiences of common people he saw in Harlem—many of them recent migrants from the South. Hughes did not try to develop a "primitive" vision. Beginning in the 1920s and continuing throughout his career, Hughes based his lyrical craft on the rich oral traditions of Afro-American folk tales and humor, blues and jazz, and sacred music. Musical performance and performers are prominent themes in Hughes's 1920s collection of poems, *The Weary Blues* (1926) and *Fine Clothes to the Jew* (1927).

Hughes used music, musicians, and dancers as the subjects of many early poems. *The Weary Blues,* for example, featured several poems that paid tribute to dancers, including: "Danse Africaine," "The Cat and the Saxophone," "Negro Dancers," and "Song for a Banjo Dance." The poems evoke various kinds of Afro-American dance, and one commentator has pointed out that "the poems are arranged in thematic pairs, each pair a contrast in mood, style, or point of view." All of them, nevertheless, capture the energy and grace of movement, and the relationship of dance to music. The poems reflect Hughes's appreciation of the richness of Afro-American dance as a performance medium.

Performance environments are also important in Hughes's poems from the first volume. "Jazzonia" and "Jazz Band in a Paris Cafe" capture the alluring world of the cabaret. In "Jazzonia," Hughes equates the effect of the performance atmosphere with that of the Garden of Eden and of ancient Africa:

> Oh! silver tree!
> Oh, shining rivers of the soul!
>
> In a Harlem cabaret
> Six long-headed jazzers play.
> A dancing girl whose eyes are bold
> Lifts high a dress of silken gold.
>
> Oh! shining tree!
> Oh, shining river of the soul!
>
> Were Eve's eyes
> In the first garden
> Just a bit too bold?
> Was Cleopatra gorgeous
> In a gown of gold?
>
> Oh, shining tree!
> Oh, shining rivers of the soul!
>
> In a whirling cabaret
> Six long-headed jazzers play.

The performance in Hughes's cabarets are seductive, and the lyrical form echoes musical compositions with stanzas and refrains. Hughes uses the images and question marks in "Jazzonia" to suggest the power of music, rather than explaining it directly.

The most innovative aspect of Hughes's jazz and blues poetry is his combination of imagery from performance with music idioms. *The Weary Blues* and *Fine Clothes to the Jew* contain a wide range of blues, and many of them express the experience of migration and disappointment, as in "Bound no' Blues," "Homesick Blues," "Listen Here Blues," and "Po' Boy Blues." Hughes attributes his affection for the blues to his first exposure to them in the poor districts of Washington, D.C. In his autobiography *The Big Sea,* Hughes described the inspiration he found in the blues:

> I tried to write poems like the songs they sang on Seventh Street—gay songs, because you had to be gay or die; sad songs, because you couldn't help being sad, sometimes. But gay or sad you kept on living and you kept on going. Their songs—those of Seventh Street—had the pulse beat of the people who kept going.

In *Fine Clothes to the Jew,* Hughes also explains the blues to his readers and notes: "The mood of the blues is almost despondency, but when they are sung people laugh."

Although Hughes would experiment a great deal in his later career with jazz forms, he offered an early example in "The Cat and the Saxophone":

> EVERYBODY
> Half-pint,—
> Gin?
> No, make it
> LOVES MY BABY
> corn. You like
> liquor,
> don't you honey?
> BUT MY BABY
> Sure. Kiss me,
> DON'T LOVE NOBODY
> daddy.
> BUT ME.
> Say!
> EVERYBODY
> Yes?
> WANTS MY BABY
> sweetie, ain't I?
> DON'T WANT NOBODY
> Sure.
> BUT
> Then let's
> ME,
> do it!
> SWEET ME.
> Charleston,
> mamma!

The alternation of capitals and lower case letters creates a syncopated cadence, and Hughes incorporates jazz song lyrics, as well as jazz dance and a sense of free improvisation. Much of Hughes's 1920s poetry used music and performance themes. The poems themselves are Hughes's own blues and jazz performances.

The publication of Langston Hughes's jazz and blues poetry did not generate the same kinds of criticism as McKay's cabaret world of *Home to Harlem*. W.E.B. DuBois praised Hughes in a 1924 *Crisis* article on "The Younger Literary Movement," and Jessie Fauset and DuBose Heyward both gave high praise to *The Weary Blues*. Locke commented that Hughes's poetry did not have "the ragged provincialism of a minstrel but the descriptive detachment of Vachel Lindsay and Sandburg . . . the democratic sweep and universality of a Whitman." Hughes's verse was often compared with that of Vachel Lindsay and Walt Whitman.

Countee Cullen also complimented his fellow poet, but offered his reservations about the qualities of jazz poetry. Cullen asked if poems like "The Cat and the Saxophone" should be counted "among that selected and austere circle of high literary expression which we called poetry." Cullen voiced his concern that Hughes would become like those writers who are "racial artists instead of artists pure and simple." Cullen's questions were echoed by other critics like George Schuyler who derided the "Negro Art Hokum" and insisted that discussions of black cultural distinctiveness were wrong-headed. According to Schuyler, folk art and folk music, including blues and jazz, could have been "produced by any group under similar circumstances." These criticisms challenged those writers who found in jazz a distinctive Afro-American poetry and voice.

Hughes published a response to Schuyler's article in *The Nation*. Hughes's essay asserted the position typical of young and experimental Harlem Renaissance writers. Hughes began by lamenting the lack of self-worth he felt was expressed by a young poet who remarked, "I want to be a poet—not a Negro poet." Hughes attributed the failure of this young man to appreciate his racial heritage to the dominance of black bourgeois cultural values. Hughes castigated the "Negro middle class" for "aping things white" and imitating "Nordic manners, Nordic faces, Nordic hair, Nordic art." Such aesthetic standards, according to Hughes, created "a very high mountain indeed for the would-be racial artist to climb in order to discover himself and his people." Hughes's essay provided an impassioned defense of the distinctive qualities of black folk art. He also insisted that the common people continued to offer the best inspiration for great art because, unlike the middle class, they had not been entirely seduced by white artistic standards.

Hughes explained that he wanted to write about those blacks who "lived on Seventh Street in Washington D.C. or State Street in Chicago and they do not care whether they are like white folks or anybody else. Their joy runs, bang! into ecstasy! . . . They are not afraid of the spirituals and jazz is their child." Hughes was proud of the "racial" themes in his poetry, and he sought to grasp and hold some of the meanings and rhythm of jazz. His art was an expression of solidarity with the folks on Seventh Street. Langston Hughes concluded the essay with one of the most influential manifestos ever proclaimed by an Afro-American writer:

> Let the blare of Negro jazz bands and the bellowing voice of Bessie Smith singing Blues penetrate the closed ears of the colored near-

intellectuals until they listen and perhaps understand. Let Paul Robeson singing "Water Boy," and Rudolph Fisher writing about the streets of Harlem, and Jean Toomer holding the heart of Georgia in his hands, and Aaron Douglas drawing strange black fantasies cause the smug Negro middle class to turn from their white, respectable, ordinary books and papers and catch a glimmer of their own beauty. We younger artists who create now intend to express our individual dark-skinned selves without fear or shame. If white people are pleased we are glad. If they are not, it doesn't matter. We know we are beautiful. And ugly too. The tom-tom cries and the tom-tom laughs. If colored people are pleased we are glad. If they are not, their displeasure doesn't matter either. We build our temples for tomorrow, strong as we know how, and we stand on top of the mountain, free within ourselves.

"The Negro Artist and the Racial Mountain" was punctuated with Hughes's "tom-tom" rhythms evoking music as a distinctive form of Afro-American culture. Hughes used music to celebrate the creativity of black people and to assert his own artistic independence. Jazz performance served as a fundamental measure of aesthetic development in his poetic vision.

Zora Neale Hurston's approach to folk culture provides a third distinctive vision of musical performance in Harlem Renaissance writing. Hurston became a legend of the Harlem Renaissance because her behavior shocked and amused contemporaries. Indeed, until recently many critics demeaned her talents and focused instead on her unconventional life. Hurston's biographer, Robert Hemenway, has pointed out that her flamboyant personal style and storytelling abilities derived in part from her childhood in the all-black town of Eatonville, Florida. More than any other Harlem Renaissance writer, Hurston had a firsthand knowledge and appreciation of folk tales and culture. This understanding set her apart from her literary contemporaries and formed the basis for her analysis of musical performance.

As Hemenway observes, Hurston did not try to preserve folk culture by advocating its transformation into "high culture." She did not see folk culture as a static object; instead, she recognized "no distinctions between the lore inherited by successive generations of folk and the imagination with which each generation adapted the tradition and made the lore its own." Hurston refined her own understanding and knowledge of folk traditions by training in anthropology with Franz Boas. She drew on her own experiences in Eatonville for some of her earlier fiction, and as a practicing anthropologist, she contributed interesting observations on black folk music to Nancy Cunard's 1934 *Negro Anthology*. Hurston delineates "Characteristics of Negro Expression" that were based on the ways blacks "modified language, mode of food preparation, practice of medicine, and most certainly religion." Hurston also describes the complicated dissemination of jazz.

> Everyone is familiar with the Negro's modification of the white's musical instruments, so that his interpretation has been adopted by the white man himself and then reinterpreted. In so many

Langston Hughes.

words, Paul Whiteman is giving an imitation of a Negro orchestra making use of white-invented instruments in a Negro way. Thus has arisen a new art in the civilized world, and thus has our so-called civilization come.

Hurston does not speculate on what *could* become of folk traditions; rather, she records their transformation and acknowledges the dynamic between popular and folk music forms.

Zora Neale Hurston also provides her explanation for the entertainment milieu in the South from whence jazz developed: the jook. Her analysis of the jook is at once a description of music, black women's social roles as entertainers, and an analysis of black aesthetics. "Jook," she wrote, "is the word for Negro pleasure house. It may mean a bawdy house. It may mean the house set aside on public works where the men and women dance, drink and gamble." Hurston records that the piano had replaced the guitar as the source for music in the jooks, and "player-pianos and victrolas" were following. The significance of the jooks, according to Hurston, was that "musically speaking, the Jook is the most important place in America. For in its smelly, shoddy confines has been born the secular music known as blues, and on blues has been founded jazz.

The singing and playing in true Negro style is called jooking!" Hurston emphasizes the communal creation of jook music that travels "from mouth to mouth and from Jook to Jook for years before they reach outside ears. Hence the great variety of subject matter in each song."

Hurston credits the jook with providing themes for black Broadway shows and noted that black audiences preferred a "girl who could hoist a Jook song from her belly and lam it against the front door of the theatre." Hurston lambasts "the bleached chorus" of some black theater reviews and concluded it was "the result of a white demand and not the Negro's." Hurston describes the effects of racism in black entertainment on black women, which was rarely noted by other Harlem Renaissance writers. Hurston also voices amusement at a famous white actress's use of blues on the stage:

> Speaking of the influence of Jook, I noted that Mae West in "Sex" had much more flavor of the turpentine quarters than she did of the white bawd. I know that the piece she played on the piano is a very old Jook composition. "Honey let yo' drawers hang low" had been played and sung in every Jook in the South for at least thirty-five

years. It has always puzzled me why she thought it likely to be played in a Canadian bawdy house.

Hurston records the creation of folk music as she saw it performed, and she notes its influence on both white and black music. Like Locke, she was concerned about the effects of commercialism on folk culture, but she did not call for it to be elevated to "high" culture.

In fact, Hurston upbraids the "Niggerati" who would have a renaissance at the expense of authentic black art:

> To those who want to institute the Negro Theatre, let me say it is already established. It is lacking in wealth, so it is not seen in the high places. A creature with a white head and Negro feet struts the metropolitan boards. The real Negro theatre is in the Jooks and cabarets. Self-conscious individuals may turn away the eye and say, "Let us search elsewhere for our dramatic art." They certainly won't find it. Butter Beans and Susie, Bo-Jangles and Snake Hips are the only performers of the real Negro school it has ever been my pleasure to behold in New York.

Hurston's aesthetic differs both from the "folk" abstractions of other Harlem Renaissance leaders and white-influenced artistic standards. Her training in anthropology enabled her to document the relationship of folk music to jazz. She also shows a unique appreciation of black women's experiences as entertainers—a sensitivity that some critics find embodied in her literary performance.

The well-documented criticism of jazz on moral values or bourgeois taste was only one response to jazz. Complex questions regarding the history and aesthetics of jazz performance also developed from the music and engaged prominent Harlem Renaissance writers. These discussions of jazz in the black community illustrated differing perspectives on music. James Weldon Johnson, Joel A. Rogers, and Alain Locke provided evidence for the existence of the New Negro by documenting the impact of folk music on ragtime, blues, and jazz. They acknowledged that participatory performance was the key to its creative power and lamented its trivialization through facile primitivism or commercial exploitation.

Claude McKay, Langston Hughes, and Zora Neale Hurston used jazz themes in their writing to communicate new and experimental ideas. Hughes, in particular, transformed the language and voice of musical performance into his poetry. These younger writers found jazz performance helpful to the creation of an Afro-American aesthetic based on folk and working-class culture. Their concerns put them at odds with more artistically conservative critics like W.E.B. DuBois and George Schuyler.

The Harlem Renaissance was pervaded by jazz performance. It was to be found on Broadway, in clubs, cabarets, rent parties, and even occasionally in early movies. Most Harlem Renaissance writers attended some or all of these performances, and it is curious that they did not say more about jazz. But even those who had reservations celebrated its popularity. A sincere appreciation of the unique participatory style of jazz performance sounds can be heard throughout Harlem Renaissance discussions of jazz. Those writers promoting the merits of jazz paid particular attention to the milieus of performance and the importance of traditions and practices in appreciating music. This understanding distinguished them from most whites debating the music in the 1920s and identified the centrality of performance in any future assessments of the cultural significance of jazz.

John Lucas

SOURCE: "Appropriate Falsehoods: English Poets and American Jazz," in *The Yearbook of English Studies*, Vol. 17, 1987, pp. 46-61.

[*In the following essay, Lucas provides a historical account of popular and literary reaction to the growth and development of jazz music in England from the 1920s to the 1950s, also comparing poems by Kingsley Amis, Phillip Larkin, John Wain, and Roy Fisher on the basis of their insight into the roots and evolution of jazz.*]

> He breathed in air, he breathed out light,
> Charlie Parker was my delight.

Adrian Mitchell's celebrated couplet defines a minority response, at least as far as English poets who claim an interest in jazz are concerned. They may not agree with Philip Larkin's even more celebrated anathematizing of the three Ps (Parker, Pound, and Picasso) but on the whole their devotion is given to the so-called traditional styles and masters, and for most of them 'modern jazz' is a contradiction in terms. The music of New Orleans and Chicago, of Armstrong, Beiderbecke, Condon, Ellington, Ory, and Waller, this is what jazz means for those predominantly middle-class, university-educated poets who, during the 1940s and 1950s, proclaimed their devotion in prose and verse. I want to offer some suggestions as to why this should be so, but before I do it will be as well to say something about the reputation of jazz in pre-war England.

The year to begin with is 1919. Before then there had been talk of 'ragtime', but I do not think that anyone had much sense of what that word really meant, and since they had little more to go on than Irving Berlin's 'Alexander's Ragtime Band' this is not very surprising. What does seem to be true is that during the war years, 1914-18, army officers home on leave or due to be sent out to the Western Front included among their diversions regular attendance at dinner-dances; at such dinner-dances, interspersed with the newly-fashionable and 'shocking' tango, and other, rather more acceptable, dance-music, there would be an occasional bow in the direction of 'ragtime'. This seems to have meant up-tempo numbers with a fairly solid four-to-the-bar rhythm which, considering that most orchestras were largely composed of violinists, must have sounded pretty excruciating.

Then, in 1919, the Original Dixieland Jazz (or Jass) Band came to England. 'Untuneful Harmonists playing Peppery Melodies', as they rather oddly styled themselves, they produced what has been called a 'phenomenal impact' on British audiences, and numbers such as 'At the Jazz Band Ball', 'Bluin' the Blues', 'Clarinette Marmalade', and above all 'Tiger Rag' soon entered the repertory of English dance bands of the period. For many people, however, even those who did not know the original meaning of the word 'jass', this was the music of a decadent society, of sexual promiscuity, of drink and drugs. Dances such as the charleston and blackbottom were widely thought to be quintessential jazz dances, and the music became a kind of do-it-yourself affair, since all you needed to make it with was a banjo or ukelele. Sheet-music, setting out simplified chord sequences for these instruments, sold in the thousands, and the Bright Young Things of the Jazz Age set about destroying themselves and others to the accompaniment of 'You're Nobody's Sweetheart Now', 'Mississippi Mud', 'Margie', and other, similar, numbers, turned out as fast as Tin-pan Alley could supply them. To put the matter this way is of course to parody it (although not outrageously, as Evelyn Waugh's *Diaries* of the 1920s and Martin Green's *Children of the Sun* between them make clear, and anyway it is difficult to parody the kinds of self-parodying people who occur in their pages). More important is the fact that the vast majority of those who jigged and hopped and crossed their hands over their knees in or out of time to 'Nagasaki', 'Has Anybody Seen My Girl?', and the rest, had no real interest in jazz as such. Nat Gonella is on record as saying that when he went to hear Louis Armstrong at the Palladium in 1930 the fashionable audience left in droves. (Gonella, a genuine enthusiast, was so enraged by this response to his hero that he did his best to trip up those who passed him on their way to the exit.)

Nevertheless, for most writers in the 1920s ragtime equalled jazz equalled decadence. Eliot's 'Shakespeherien Rag' ('It's so elegant / So intelligent') echoes eerily round the room of the neurasthenic, bored wife of 'A Game of Chess', and the syncopated speech-rhythms of *Sweeney Agonistes,* as well as the song 'Under the bamboo tree', imply a world whose devitalized routines ('You'd be bored. / Birth, and copulation, and death') can be known and judged through its devotion to ragtime, which, for Eliot, meant jazz. We know this is so because in 1924 he consulted Arnold Bennett about a 'drama of modern life (furnished flat sort of people)' which he wanted to write 'in a rhythmic prose "perhaps with certain things in it accentuated with drum beats" '. Three years later Bennett wrote to Eliot to ask what had happened 'to that Jazz play'. (A fragment, called 'Wanna Go Home Baby', had in fact been published in *Criterion* for January 1927.)

You would expect attitudes to change with the coming of a younger and politically radical group of poets, and of course they did. What had been seen as decadent now became subversive. Yet for the writers of the 1930s jazz wasn't the influence it might and perhaps should have been. Auden, for example, never seems to have been much interested in it. True, a number of his songs and the *Dance of Death* show how excited he was by the cabaret and revue work of the Weimar Republic which he had had a chance to experience at first hand, and some of that work was undoubtedly influenced by American jazz. But once you have taken note of his approval of such songwriters as Cole Porter and Rogers and Hart, and of the fact that he includes a generous selection of spirituals and bar-room and chain-gang songs in his great *Oxford Book of Light Verse* of 1938 (they include 'John Henry', 'Stagolee',

'Frankie and Johnny', 'Casey Jones', and 'This Train'), you have exhausted the matter of Auden's interest in the music. When Geoffrey Grigson commissioned various writers to contribute to *The Arts To-day* (1935) he invited Edward Crankshaw to write about 'Music'. Crankshaw's piece avoids any mention of jazz, even thought it aims to be as up-to-date as possible. At one point in his essay he notes that 'Mr Constant Lambert in his admirable book was the first to point . . . out' the parallel between the progress of Schönberg and James Joyce. He does not, however, note Lambert's remark that Duke Ellington is probably one of the finest and most influential of modern composers and arrangers. Even Louis MacNeice, the one poet you might think would be much interested in some aspects of jazz (not least in the clubs where it could be found uncertainly surviving, and where late drinking, the conducting of illicit affairs, and a general air of cigarette-ash bohemianism provided the kind of atmosphere that seems made for him), uses the word in a vague, if vaguely approbatory, way.

But at this point I need to say that I am not at all sure just how much jazz any of the writers of the 1930s could have heard or of what they could have been aware. It is not simply that confusion over the word was still widespread. (Two important details about the first sound-picture, *The Jazz Singer,* are that Al Jolson wasn't black and he couldn't or anyway didn't sing jazz.) More important, perhaps, is the fact that if you were in England it was never very easy to hear American musicians playing the new music. In the first place, from the mid-1930s there was a Musicians Union ban on visiting musicians playing with their own groups, which meant that any American jazzman booked to appear in Britain would have to be accompanied by British Musicians, an understandable move to preserve jobs but a disaster in that it led the majority of jazzmen to stay away. (Still, Fats Waller came to England in 1939 and recorded a half-hour programme for BBC television, with a group that included the trombonist George Chisholm. Unfortunately the BBC either lost or destroyed the recording.) In the second place, records of the jazz bands were not easy to come by, although those who lived in the port towns fared better than most, if only because visiting American seamen would frequently bring records ashore with them, for barter or sale. This helps to explain why cities such as Belfast, Bristol, Liverpool, and Glasgow have always been jazz strongholds, and places from which some of the best British bands and musicians have come.

All this means that anyone wanting to listen to jazz in the 1930s, whether in clubs, on records, or sitting by the wireless in kitchens in the lonely fens, would not have an easy time of it, and that what they would hear might well be no more than a parody of the real thing, especially if it came from such dance bands as those led by Jack Hylton, Ambrose, Henry Hall, and Ray Fox, which were nationally famous, had regular time on the radio, and made many records.

> They were in almost no sense 'jazz' bands, but about every sixth piece they made a 'hot number', in which the one or two men in the band who could play jazz would be heard. The classic

'hot number' was 'Tiger Rag': . . . Harry Roy had a band-within-a-band called the Tiger-Ragamuffins. Nat Gonella's stage show had a toy tiger lying on the grand piano. Trombonists and tuba-players became adept at producing the traditional tiger growl. I found these hot numbers so exciting that I would listen to hours of dance music in order to catch them when they came.

This is Philip Larkin, in the introduction to *All What Jazz* (1972), and he goes on to tell of how he slowly began to build up a record collection which could 'bear all the enthusiasm usually directed at more established arts. There was nothing odd about this. It was happening to boys all over Europe and America. It just didn't get into the papers'. At Oxford, he continues, 'my education grew. I met people who knew more about jazz than I did, and had more records, and who could even parallel my ecstasies with their own'. Larkin names no names, but among the Oxford near-contemporaries who shared his enthusiasms were Kingsley Amis and John Wain, and the 'ecstasies' of all three were to spill over into poetry and prose. There will be more to say about this, but as a way into discussing the poems I need to ask why it was that this *particular* enthusiasm was happening, if not 'to boys all over Europe and America', at least to Larkin and many of his contemporaries.

The most obvious explanation is, of course, that jazz recommended itself to Larkin's generation precisely because it wasn't seen as an established art. Since Auden's generation (among whom there would have been some who taught Larkin's) had no great interest in the music, beyond annexing its name and vaguely-understood contents in the cause of subversive social and political stances, the way was clear for Larkin and his contemporaries to strike a rebellious pose through their adoption of jazz as an art form. If they did not want to claim that much for it they could at least justify an interest in jazz because it was 'unpretentious'. This unpretentiousness is, in fact, one of the most widely-presumed characteristics of jazz and its exponents. A story (almost certainly apocryphal) which jazz-buffs of Larkin's generation never tire of telling is of Louis Armstrong (or, in some versions, Fats Waller), replying to the inevitably white, upper-class lady's enquiry as to what swing is (in some versions swing becomes rhythm): 'Lady, if you has to ask, you jest ain't got it.' And when jazz musicians tune up (usually to A natural) they famously remark, as they finish adjusting slide or string, 'near enough for jazz'.

It is worth noting that this self-deprecatory element, which could be found among jazz musicians and which, in America at least, had a great deal to do with the fact that most of the musicians were black and working for and in white men's clubs, hotels, and restaurants, becomes one of the most remarked-on elements of the generation of Movement poets. This may also explain why Larkin and others so took against Parker and the jazz musicians of *his* generation, simply because they refused to be 'unpretentious': that is, they were prepared to be aggressive champions of their music, to take pride in their great technical mastery, to scorn their (often white) audiences, to play un-

familiar tunes or radically alter familiar ones. Parker's creative or, some would say, destructive treatment of 'How High the Moon' is an obvious example.

Jazz also recommended itself simply because it was the almost private/secret possession of the young. The fact that the records were hard to come by meant that they acquired an almost legendary status; labels and matrix numbers were memorized, rare buys were jealously guarded. The fact that the wax 78 rpms were frail, easily scratched and broken, added to their rarity value. In general there was the heady feeling that in learning to appreciate jazz you were coming in on a sub-culture. Writing as someone who joined this sub-culture as late as the early 1950s I can speak with the authority of one who recalls the thrill of buying a black-Brunswick-label recording of the Hot Six playing 'Potato-Head Blues' which *must*, so my elders and betters told me, have been a pirated version. I can also recall the thrill of joining my school's Rhythm Club (I don't suppose there was a school in the country which, throughout the 1940s and 1950s, failed to have such a club) and hearing my very first jazz record: Dizzie Gillespie's 'Cognac Blues'. The music itself meant little, the title everything. It suggested a society of dimly-lit cafés, a night-life of sex and poetry, and, perhaps most importantly, an escape from the Light-Programme diet of Patti Page asking 'How Much is that Doggie in the Window?' and Donald Peers requesting 'Red Roses for a Blue Lady'. I bring my own experience in at this point in order to suggest that for at least twenty years (roughly from 1936 to 1956) jazz music was the music you could, if you were young, associate with mild rebelliousness, with striking the father dead, with an argot known only to the *cognoscenti*.

There was also the fact that jazz became increasingly admired by those who could identify it with a mild form of socialism. It was, after all, the music of the down-trodden, and was therefore ethnically respectable; there were those who claimed to hear in it the voice of the oppressed slave striking back at his or her oppressor (for the great Blues singers, Ma Rainey and, preeminently, Bessie Smith, were idolized by my generation and I suspect by Larkin's). There is a particularly nauseating moment in Osborne's *The Entertainer* (1957) when Archie Rice recalls an old negress singing her heart out, and the idea that jazz simply (very simply) spoke equally for joy, heartache, and deprivation was one of the more enduring myths of the period I am now considering. This is not to say that the music lacked social content, or that it was devoid of political comment; but it is to say that one of the motives behind the identification with jazz was that it could be seen as expressive of the admirer's political and social radicalism. It is worth adding that, although Larkin (before his comparatively late and almost parodic lurch into Thatcherism) seems never to have been prepared to declare a political point of view, Amis and Wain were milk-and-water Fabians for whom an identification with jazz might well seem appropriate to their political positions. More generally, and perhaps more seriously, jazz could be seen as the 'people's' music, a possibility which would have been strengthened by the meetings of British men-at-arms with their American counterparts, many of whom were black and some of whom were the very musicians the British had worshipped and imitated from afar. Support for and interest in jazz therefore could be seen as or adopted as a sign of political solidarity, and it is no accident that during the 1940s and 1950s the *William Morris Society Bulletin* should have carried jazz material.

To admire jazz could also be seen as a sign of intellectual daring, or of wanting to shock the bourgeoisie. The postwar euphoria will have had something to do with this heady determination of clearing out the old in order to make way for the new. After all, it *was* daring to prefer Armstrong to 'filthy Mozart', or to pretend to do so, or, more seriously, to find room for both. In addition it became another means of scorning the insular philistinism of previous generations. Jazz was eminently acceptable on the Left Bank. France had been the one country in Europe prior to the war where jazz and jazz musicians were made very welcome. Albert Nicholas, Bill Coleman, Sidney Bechet (who had first toured in a revue in 1925 which included Josephine Baker), Tommy Ladnier, and others had all made at least temporary homes in Paris; and Paris famously was famously the adopted home of Django Reinhardt and the Hot Club. After the war many of these musicians returned. Jazz was now the approved music of the literary avant-garde. Sartre and Camus regularly and casually mentioned jazz musicians and quoted the titles of their 'classic' recordings. In 1947 Henri Matisse issued a series of lithographs named, simply, *Jazz,* and although the inspiration for the title had less to do with Matisse's interest in the music than in the fact that he was responding to a renewal of hope, of light, of freshness, this in turn meant that jazz could be identified as the carefree music which dispelled the gloom and shabbiness of war-shattered Europe. It really *was* Europe which took to the music. In Paris Claude Luter's band gained extra *cachet* because Bechet so often played and recorded with it, but it attracted large audiences on its own account. There was the Dutch Swing College Band, the White Eagle New Orleans Band of Berlin, there were bands aplenty spread across Belgium; and so on.

In addition there was now a steady growth of literature on the subject. In Britain *Jazz Journal* was an established and respected magazine, *The Melody Maker* gave regular and increasing space to jazz commentators, Eric Hobsbawm wrote a jazz column in the *New Statesman and Nation* under the pseudonym of Francis Newton: Frankie Newton was a negro jazz trumpeter who had died young, of tuberculosis, just before the war. Then there were the books. Rex Harris's *Jazz* was first published by Penguin (as a Pelican book) in 1952, and by 1957 was into its fifth edition. André Hodeir's highfalutin *Jazz: Its Evolution and Essence* was translated into English in the early 1950s. As the decade wore on biographies, criticism, and general histories piled up on the bookstalls. Jazz, it seemed, was everywhere.

Yet this is an exaggeration. For although in Britain any number of jazz bands, professional and semi-professional, were being formed, and although most towns had a jazz club where local bands could perform each week and where there would be occasional guest nights featuring out-of-town musicians, these were invariably British. The

Musicians Union did not relax its ban on foreign groups until 1956. Before then, if you wanted to hear the great and not-so-great American bands, you had to cross either the English Channel or the Irish Sea. (The *Melody Maker* ran excursion specials for those wanting to hear live such orchestras as those of Woody Herman and Stan Kenton when they visited Ireland.) Then, in 1956, the Musicians Union decided on a policy of exchanges. American bands could come to England on condition that English bands were allowed to tour the United States. They got Freddy Randall and his band and we got Louis Armstrong and his All Stars. You would think that this would have increased jazz's popularity. Quite the reverse: 1956 marked the beginning of the end for the mass popular appeal of jazz. There were still many tours to come, jazz-band balls and concerts at the Festival Hall and halls throughout the country (nearly all of them sell-outs in both senses of the word), and the traddy-pop boom was as yet some years off. But George Melly recalls that in 1956 he recorded a 'novelty number' of the 1920s, 'My Canary's Got Circles Under His Eyes', which was a total flop (it deserved to be), and that the week it was released a 'boy' called Tommy Steele released a record called 'Rock with the Cavemen' (*Owning Up*). A new kind of do-it-yourself music, born from the skiffle bands which themselves had been born out of the jazz bands, was on the way.

Jazz had always been a do-it-yourself music, or so legend reported. The negroes of the deep south made guitars out of cigar-boxes and broomsticks, bought reach-me-down brass instruments from hock shops; and away they went. Of course, it wasn't at all like that, but this appropriate falsehood made it easier for young people in Britain (predominantly male) to buy up odd instruments and learn to play them (a new brass instrument could easily be 'improved' by a few well-placed dents). Philip Larkin says that after an early and brief flirtation with drumming he became a listener only, and the remarks that only one person in his circle at Oxford could play a musical instrument: the saxophone. I do not know whether this was typical of his class but it certainly wasn't typical of his generation, for many young working-class men were learning to play instruments so that they could copy the bands and music they loved.

The first British jazz bands were therefore almost entirely made up of working-class musicians, and they continued to be so throughout the 1950s. There were exceptions: Humphrey Lyttleton, of Eton and the Guards, was the most spectacular; and everyone knew that Chris Barber and Johnny Dankworth had been to the Royal College of Music, and that Sandy Brown (almost certainly the most original talent among British musicians) was Scottish and formidable in argument. On the other hand, when he played he usually wore a vest or dirty old grey V-neck sweater and in this respect looked little different from the musicians who made up his and countless other home-grown bands. The only exception to this, for a while at least, was Ken Colyer, who had a penchant for requiring his band to wear evening dress, as an act of homage to King Oliver's bands of the 1920s whose music he idolized and rather beautifully reproduced. But this did not last for long, and for most of the time his band, too, was wearing the classless uniform of cords, check-shirts or sweaters, and cracked leather shoes (they were sometimes replaced by 'desert boots') which like the rest of the outfit typically came from Millett's or the Army and Navy Stores.

For a while, at least, classlessness might even have seemed to be the crux of the matter. Everyone dressed more or less the same way and went to the same places to hear live jazz and danced in the same manner and followed the same bands and used the same forms of transport; for all of these reasons jazz fans were keen not to be identified as hooray Henries. 'Did we really talk like this, / With such absurd self-consciousness?' The question John Mole puts, wonderingly, in his charming poem 'The Jazzmen' (*The Instruments,* 1971) is directed at the fact that he and his schoolfriends, jazz *aficionados* all, did their best to disguise their public-school accents by adopting the jazz patois, speaking, for example, of 'cats' who 'grooved'. They may have been 'Young gentlemen from public school', a minor one, 'deft at turning out a bore', but they knew that the music they loved was rooted and flowered in the most underprivileged of all levels of American society; if they wanted to hear it in England ('Humph at the Conway, Ken at Mac's'), Eel Pie Island, where Sandy Brown's band played to vast, delirious audiences, or anywhere else, for that matter, it was advisable to put on a protective voice along with the protective uniform.

Yet as Mole's poem reveals, middle-class and upper-class boys were now not merely listening to the music; they were trying to play it. He and his friends formed a jazz-band:

> Honour, though, our little clique,
> That dinned the Music Room each week,
> Us practising musicians who
> Thumped as grossly as we blew;
> Authentic every turgid sound
> Issuing from that hallowed ground.

For the cornet-player authenticity meant taking pains 'Not to sound slick like Harry James'. For Mole himself it meant learning the classic Alphonse Picou solo on 'High Society'. Mole still plays clarinet, and in fact you could easily make up a jazz band from the writers of our generation who learnt to play the music they loved. Throughout the 1950s there was an annual Universities Jazz-Band championship, and jazz meant 'traditional' that is, non-modern, jazz. Oxford in 1957 had a very George-Lewis-like outfit, the Loughborough Colleges band managed a fair imitation of Eddie Condon's group, the band I played in took Bunk Johnson as hero, and so on.

The point about all this is that the amorphous classless-ness of the immediate post-war days was giving ground before the growing confidence of public-school and grammar-school products who were quite likely to be using traditional jazz as a stick with which to beat not only modernism (the three Ps) but also the vague radicalism which had earlier seemed an integral element in jazz appreciation. I need to tread carefully here. Some of my best

---

> **The social-political context in which jazz exists, at least in America, made it inevitable that musicians such as Charlie Parker and Miles Davis and their followers would turn their backs (often literally) on audiences who asked for more of the same and who, as they rightly saw, essentially wanted black musicians to go on being Uncle Toms to condescending white audiences.**
>
> *—John Lucas*

---

friends are jazzmen and most of those are on the left of the political spectrum. Some went to public school and others, like myself, came out of the grammar school system. Still others were products of secondary moderns and some of them were and are to the political right. Nevertheless, there can be no doubt that as the 1950s wore on so traditional jazz became increasingly identified as 'apolitical' (that is, conservative) and that some of its eloquent champions emerged as themselves increasingly conservative: which is why they rejected the newer jazz, for that signified a new-found confidence and aggressiveness on the part of black people which was part of the story of the emergence of black consciousness in America. And in Britain? I think it fair to say that only one kind of modern jazz ever really caught on here, and that, significantly enough, its adherents were working-class (Glasgow and London were the centres where it grew). They admired Parker but they imitated the 'cool' jazz associated with the Gerry Mulligan quartet, and their uniform featured button-down shirts and Italian suits; as far as I know, just because this jazz was working-class it was never much written about.

Traditional jazz, by contrast, never lacked for articulate middle-class supporters, who could look back to the early 'innocent' days as composing a kind of golden world before the fall into modernism and Birdland, Art Blakey's Jazz Messengers, Charlie Parker and, worse and worse, John Coltrane and free form. I have to say that the jazz I love best belongs to the period stretching from early Armstrong through to the death of Fats Waller in 1943 (this period does, after all, contain a mass of beautiful and exciting music), but I know that the social-political context in which jazz exists, at least in America, made it inevitable that musicians such as Parker and Miles Davis and their followers would turn their backs (often literally) on audiences who asked for more of the same and who, as they rightly saw, essentially wanted black musicians to go on being Uncle Toms to condescending white audiences. The uncomprehending contempt directed at modernism by Kingsley Amis is, therefore, an essential part of the condescension with which he gives his approval to the more traditional forms of jazz, as in his 'Farewell Blues', a pastiche of Hardy's great poem 'Friends Beyond':

Bongo, sitar, 'cello, flute, electric piano, bass
   guitar,
Training Orchestra, Research Team, Workshop,
   Group, Conservatoire,
Square Root, Nexus, Barbaresque, Distortions,
   Voltage—bloody row,
For Louis Armstrong, Mildred Bailey, Walter
   Page and Sidney Catlett
               lie in Brunswick Churchyard
now.

Trumpets gelded, drums contingent, saxo-
   phones that bleat or bawl,
Keyless, barless, poor-man's Boulez, improvis-
   ing on fuck-all,
Far beyond what feeling, reason, even mother
   wit allow,
While Mugsy Spanier, Floyd O'Brien, Sterling
   Bose and Henry Allen
              lie in Decca Churchyard now.

Dead's the note we loved that swelled within us,
   made us gasp and stare,
Simple joy and simple sadness thrashing the as-
   tounded air;
What replaced them no one asked for, but it
   turned up anyhow,
And Coleman Hawkins, Johnny Hodges, Bessie
   Smith and Pee Wee Russell
            lie in Okeh churchyard now.

(*Collected Poems, 1944-1979,* 1980)

A revealing point about this poem is that Amis's adherence to traditional jazz, which had earlier made him seem
faintly radical, can now go hand-in-hand with a tetchy
conservatism. 'Farewell Blues' reads almost as a parody
piece, its snarling, ignorant dismissal of the new music
very similar to the peevish anger with which Somerset
Maugham tried to dismiss the young iconoclastic post-war
writers among whom was, of course, Kingsley Amis. Another point is that in most of its claims and assertions the
poem is plainly wrong. When Amis says that 'no one'
asked for the new music he's talking nonsense. The fact
that he didn't want it hardly counts against the fact that
Charlie Parker, for example, became a hero to millions of
young blacks in America and to a sizeable number of people in Britain. The gap that Amis tries to open up between
then and now is made ludicrous as soon as you realize that
Parker's music, as he himself always acknowledged, owed
a great deal to the examples of Coleman Hawkins and
Johnny Hodges. Larkin, more astute and truthful than
Amis, had grudgingly to admit the fact of Parker's genius
when, reviewing a Parker memorial album, he wrote:

It is Parker's solos that carry these records and
have caused an alteration in the course of jazz
Granted that his technique and musical instinct
for innovation were unrivalled, what was he
like? His talent was indivisible; one cannot say
that he would have been better if he had played
more simply or with fewer rhythmic eccentrici-
ties; these are features of the wild, bubbling freedom that characterises him, and that some say

earned him his nickname. But freedom from
what? As one listens to Parker spiralling away
'out of this world', as the phrase goes, one can
answer 'humanity', and that is a fatal thing for
any artist, or any art, to be separated from. (*All
What Jazz,*)

On the other hand, the two writers are not far apart in
their prejudices. What Larkin here means by 'humanity'
can be glossed by Amis's phrase 'simple joy and simple
sadness'. Jazzmen and women are then a kind of stand-in
for a contented peasantry in Amis's vision of an ideal past
where music is the token of uncomplicated relations. But
you have to shed a great deal of history before you can arrive at the belief that there was anything simple about the
sadness of Bessie Smith or the joy of Louis Armstrong
('Laughin' Louis' was an invention of the Mafia, who
forced the great genius of the music into endless excruciat-
ingly embarrassing roles, on stage, on screen, and on record, because he was good business—at least as long as he
kept laughing, kept on pumping out the simple joy).

Like Amis and Larkin, John Wain's preference is for the
more traditional forms of jazz. Nevertheless, Wain's
'Music on the Water' (subtitled 'to Bill Coleman in Paris')
is alert to some of the historical tragedies out of which jazz
emerged:

Out at sea, the slave ships were coming.
Sound reached out across water:
dead-smack of corpse, gull-scream,
chop of the settler's axe, gun-crack and
whip-crack: in the steamy fields
the black backs bend, the long dark song goes
   up:
the American earth, no longer Eden:
and sound moves out across water.

Unfortunately, as this passage illustrates, Wain's poem is
not much more than a plodding Janet-and-John rehash of
a part of American history; his efforts to characterize
Coleman's music, and that of Django, with whom Coleman sometimes played in Paris, is clogged with the same
kind of clichés as deaden *Strike the Father Dead,* his well-
meaning novel about jazz musicians ('I brought up my
hands and let them fall on to the keys. Instinctively, they
formed a chord, . . . a lovely rich chord, which welled up
out of the piano and rolled out, in ever-widening circles,
till it filled the whole world'). I have to say that I have
never known a jazz musician who talks and thinks as
Wain's are made to do.

In their different ways both Amis and Wain want to make
absolute claim for the jazz they like. If this feels less than
convincing it is because you realize that they aren't in fact
in a position to speak with the kind of inwardness, or
knowingness, that they pretend. Their writings about jazz
therefore create some decidedly inappropriate falsehoods.
Philip Larkin, on the other hand, from whose marvellous
poem 'For Sidney Bechet' the phrase comes, knows how
to keep his distance while at the same time finding the
right way to praise the music he loves.

The note you hold, narrowing and rising, shakes
Like New Orleans reflected on the water,
And in all ears appropriate falsehood wakes,

Building for some a legendary Quarter
Of Balconies, flower-baskets and quadrilles,
Everyone making love and going shares—

Oh, play that thing! Mute glorious Storeyvilles
Others may license, grouping round their chairs
Sporting-house girls like circus tigers (priced

Far above rubies) to pretend their fads,
While scholars *manqués* nod around unnoticed,
Wrapped up in personnels like old plaids.

On me your voice falls as they say love should,
Like an enormous yes. My Crescent City
Is where your speech alone is understood,

And greeted as the natural noise of good,
Scattering long-haired grief and scored pity.
                    (*The Whitsun Weddings* 1964)

I do not know which particular record of Bechet's Larkin may have had in mind when he wrote the poem, and it is entirely possible that the description of 'the note', although it accurately catches Bechet's great powers of wide-vibrato glissand, is not meant to refer to a specific track. Nevertheless, it is worth remarking that on at least two occasions Larkin picked out 'Blue Horizon' as one of his favourites: 'six choruses of slow blues in which Bechet climbs without interruption or hurry from low to upper register, his clarinet tone at first thick and throbbing, then soaring like Melba in an extraordinary blend of lyricism and power that constituted the unique Bechet voice, commanding attention the instant it sounded'.

The title of that great recording is appropriate to the meaning of Larkin's poem, which is after all about travelling across to an entirely imaginary New Orleans, the Crescent City where jazz first began and where, so various legends had it, the good times endlessly rolled. Hence the attractions of the Latin Quarter, its fantastic creole freedoms held in check by 'Oh, play that thing!', a phrase that can be heard on one of the classic jazz records, King Oliver's 'Sugar Foot Stomp', where it is exuberantly shouted by banjoist Bud Scott, after three choruses of the master's muted cornet and as a lead into a joyous ensemble closing sequence. In the poem the phrase, placed as it is, sounds with a rueful self-mockery which reminds us of the distance between the world of those 'antique negroes' (to quote from another Larkin poem that alludes to King Oliver) and the fact that Larkin, the jazz-buff, is listening on his own to the music that seems to hold out the promise of making love and going shares.

New Orleans was also famous for the fact that in 1917 the police closed down Storeyville, the red-light district where many of the early jazz musicians were hired to entertain punters waiting their turn with the Sporting-House girls. In scripture it is, of course, a virtuous woman who is priced far above rubies. Larkin's joke testifies both to the fact that some of the Storeyville brothels were extremely lavishly got-up and very expensive, and that the solitary listener can in his licentious imagination (but only there) reissue licences to the sporting houses. The brilliant image

of the scholars *manqués* wrapped up in personnels like old plaids' points to the efforts of rival jazz historians and discographers to put a name to each musician taking part in the early recording sessions (they often went unnamed by the record companies concerned).

In the 1950s these attributions often brought the historians into sharp conflict and provided them with a no-doubt welcome opportunity to assert their erudition on record-sleeves and in the columns of the musical press. In short, Larkin evokes, generously and wittily, a number of very English preoccupations with a city and its music which have attained the status of myth. It is this which saves the poem from falling into sentimentality at the end, for, although at first glance 'the natural noise of good' may seem uncomfortably close to 'simple joy and simple sorrow', in fact Larkin is aware, as Amis isn't, of the mythicizing qualities of that 'enormous yes'. It is another appropriate falsehood, and because he knows this to be so he is free to indulge a dream of a world free of 'long-haired grief and scored pity'. In the 1950s 'long-hair' was a term of genial contempt directed by jazzmen at classical or 'serious' musicians. Larkin brilliantly puns on this to imply that Bechet's music cancels a world of sorrow, of Niobe and her misfortunes; and, in a further pun, that such improvised (that is, unscored) music dispels the deep-hatched lines of pity and suffering that mark her woes. But this dream can last for only so long as the record itself. The poem has about it the neat containment of the kind of jazz number that fits perfectly into the limitations of a 78 rpm record.

Once Larkin had written his poem it became inevitable, I think, that other poets would try to pay tribute to the virtues of their jazz heroes, or to empathize with their hard-luck lives. This will explain Michael Longley's 'Words for Jazz Perhaps', a sequence of poems contained in his first volume, *No Continuing City,* in which he writes of Fats Waller, Bud Freeman, Bessie Smith, and Bix Biederbecke, just as it will explain Douglas Dunn's rather better 'Billie 'n' Me', about the tragic life and death of Billie Holiday. 'And silent now', it ends, 'As the saxophones in Harlem pawnshops, / Your voice that meant how tough love is'. There are other such poems, but it is hardly necessary to list them here. Instead, I want to close by mentioning a far more original poem than any so far discussed: Roy Fisher's 'The Thing About Joe Sullivan'. This is the title-poem of a volume Fischer brought out in 1978, and it has been subsequently republished in his *Poems 1955-80* (1980).

Joe Sullivan was a negro pianist who, having learned much of his craft from Earl Hines, began his career with Eddie Condon before branching out into solo work and occasional recording sessions and work with other groups. (There is an affectionate account of him in Condon's *We Called It Music* [1948].) Jazzmen have always had a great respect for Sullivan, yet he never achieved the fame of other, less talented, musicians, perhaps because he never stayed for long with any one group; this was almost certainly due to his restless desire to push his music further, to test himself against harder obstacles. Sullivan, in other words, was not a 'one style' man; I imagine it was this which attracted Fisher, himself a talented pianist and very fine poet, to him. It is significant that Fisher is more aware of developments in post-war American poetry than most English poets, Charles Tomlinson and Donald Davie excepted, and both in style and subject-matter he is *sui generis*. 'The Thing About Joe Sullivan' is both a poem in praise of an outstanding pianist, a subtle probing of his art, and at the same time an example of how to write the kind of poem that, perhaps like Sullivan's own music, starts from certainties and moves off into more exploratory and tentative statements.

> The pianist Joe Sullivan,
> jamming sound against idea
>
> hard as it can go
> florid and dangerous
>
> slams at the beat, or hovers,
> drumming, along its spikes;
>
> in his time almost the only
> one of them to ignore
>
> the chance of easing down,
> walking it leisurely,
>
> he'll strut, with gambling shapes,
> underpinning by James P.,
>
> amble, and stride over
> gulfs of his own leaving, perilously
>
> toppling octaves down to where
> the chords grow fat again.

In jazz talk 'to jam' is to improvise, and in a sense the poem is improvising with possibilities of language and rhythm that Sullivan's own daring seem to have required of his admirer. You have only to compare this language, and the handling of pause, of pace, with the passage I quoted from *Strike the Father Dead* to sense how authentic Fisher's recreation of Sullivan's manner is. Yet it isn't just recreation that's at stake here; for the poem is an act of considering, a way of thinking about and enacting the daring perilousness of improvisation, while recognizing that there must always be the possibility of control. Thus when Sullivan struts, 'with gambling shapes', he is both playing and playing with the kind of music called a 'strut' (or, as variation, a 'cakewalk'), which accompanied or summoned up negro mimicry of the white man's way of walking or dancing, and at the same time gambling with ideas that might not come off were it not for the fact that he has not entirely forsaken the solid left-hand rhythm he learned from listening to James P. Johnson, the acknowledged king of 'stride' piano. As a result Sullivan can 'stride' over 'gulfs of his own leaving' (the enjambment reinforces the stride), and to do this is both an act of great daring and a way of employing artistic means that offer him a firmness of purpose.

Towards the end of the poem Fisher brings himself in. The thing about Joe Sullivan, he says, is his mood:

> a feeling violent and ordinary
> that runs in among standard forms so
> wrapped up in clarity
>
> that fingers following his
> through figures that sound obvious

> find corners everywhere,
> marks of invention, wakefulness;
>
> the rapid and perverse
> tracks that ordinary feelings
>
> make when they get driven
> hard enough against time.

The strange hesitancy of the poem's title is now justified as Fisher more deeply and personally explores Sullivan's way with music, his use of form to take risks that threaten to become formless but which are always rescued by a shaping purpose that discovers itself through the very act of creation, through the artist's mixture of daring and determination not to waste or idle with his art. At the same time he can place his trust in hard-won techniques which, traditional themselves (in the sense that Sullivan was brought up in the era of, and learnt from, a great generation of jazz pianists, especially Johnson and Hines), allow him, indeed require him, to move forward, tracking feelings that become eloquent with ideas as they are 'driven / hard enough against time': that is, the time a tune takes to be played, the musical time it is played in, and the time in which the artist lives, all of which form resistant mediums which his restless spirit must challenge.

Fisher's deep, inward understanding of how an art form cannot stand still makes 'The Thing About Joe Sullivan' not merely a far better poem than 'Farewell Blues' or several of the same breed; it also shows a far more tactful and alert awareness of how we all must live in time. Not, of course, that this will seem a recommendation to those for whom the three Ps spell the death of civilization.

Paul Oliver

SOURCE: "Can't Even Write: The Blues and Ethnic Literature," in *MELUS,* Vol. 10, No. 1, Spring, 1983, pp. 7-14.

[*In the following essay, Oliver contends that there is no interrelationship between blues music and black literature, for, as Oliver illustrates, while it is true that many black poets imitate the structure and content of blues songs, cultural and economic barriers prevent most blues singers from acquiring even an awareness of black poetry.*]

> Lord, the reason why baby, I been so long wri-
> tin' to you
> I say, the reason why baby, I been so long writin'
> to you,
> Because I been studyin' so hard, Lord how to
> sing these blues.

Sleepy John Estes' verse may not summarize the whole issue of the relationship between ethnic song and literature, but it does give us a hint of where the folk composer's priorities lie. Estes was a blues singer from Brownsville, Tennessee, one of the hundreds of such singers whose recordings have constituted one of the largest reserves of a folk literature among any ethnic group. He was Black, he was a poor farmer, and he was nearly blind; if he had sent a letter to his woman, it would have been very probably through the hand of a friend.

"Got me accused of forgery, I cain't even write my name . . ." sang another blues singer, Eddie Boyd—sang several other blues singers, in fact, for blues has its traditional stanzas and phrases which express succinctly ideas that can be drawn into new compositions. Though he lived in Chicago and eventually settled in Sweden, and though he was more sophisticated a blues singer than some, Eddie Boyd wrote with great difficulty; even as famous a blues singer as Muddy Waters, with numerous international tours behind him and many a college appearance in his yearly calendar—even he signs his name with a rubber stamp. Literacy is not unknown among blues singers: Whistling Alex Moore, who drove a junk cart and horse around the streets of Dallas for decades, had a flowing "copperplate" hand when he wrote his pencilled letters on pages of an exercise book, filling in the loops with indelible pencil to improve their decorative appearance. But he was an exception. When Garfield Akers sang his "Cottonfield Blues"

> I'm gon' write me a letter ooh, I'm gon' mail it
>   in the air . . .
> Said, I' know you'll catch it, mama in the world
>   somewhere . . .

he probably was referring to his own singing.

Blues is for singing. It is not a form of folk song that stands up particularly well when written down. Sometimes the poetic qualities of a blues verse survive the transfer to the printed page and the stark economy of the words, the occasional touches of sardonic humor or the bleakness of a despairing stanza stabs home:

> They sentenced me to ten years on Big Brazos,
>   picking cotton and corn
>   and listening to the big bell tone (twice)
> Now every time I hear a street light jingle, I start
>   aching all in my
>   bone . . .

sang Mercy Dee Walton in a long blues, "Mercy's Troubles."

> Baby next time you go out, carry your black suit
>   along (twice)
> Coffin gonna be your present; Hell gonna be
>   your brand new home . . .

—the words of King Solomon Hill in "Whoopie Blues" are no more and no less poetic, laconic or ironic than those in countless other recordings.

The elusive poetry of the blues has been the subject of separate studies by Samuel Charters and Paul Garon, anthologized by Eric Sackheim, analyzed for their formulaic structure related to meaning by Jeff Todd Titon, and as binary systems of expression by myself. But they stand as what they are: stanzas that are sometimes new, sometimes traditional, composed in forms that are predetermined,

most frequently to a threeline, twelve-bar structure, sung to a solo accompaniment of guitar or piano or to the playing of a small group of instrumentalists. Blues can be analyzed on the printed page, but they do not exist there: blues are essentially performed—they exist in the singing and the playing. The music of the blues is inseparable from the words when considered as a totality, even though the words considered in isolation from the complement of the instrumental accompaniment may still have powerful messages to convey.

So where does this leave blues in relation to an ethnic literature? The question begs others, and though they have doubtless been discussed in these pages often before, some comments on them must be made. In the first place, there is the considerable problem of whether there is such an entity as an ethnic literature, or indeed an ethnic art form at all, if by ethnic is meant "racially identifiable." Culture is not a quality of race, and races do not automatically produce identifiable cultural traits. Racial groups, by their need to retain their identity, or sometimes because of their visible separation from others of different races (by skin pigmentation or hair type), may keep together as a discrete group and in so doing evolve as cultures. In the process, an "ethnic culture" might be identified both by the group itself and by those outside it, a product of its separate life within the larger society. Whether that culture is made evident by the food it eats, the clothes it wears, the argot it speaks, the rhythms it beats or the songs it sings, it gains its strength from the reinforcement of its own identity which the cultural expression manifests. But it is not inherently racial in origin, but cultural.

Cultural here may mean, however, not merely the mores and material artifacts of a racial group, but of a part of it—of a culture within the culture. Blues is not the music of all Black Americans, many of whom consider it of low class and status, lewd, irreverent and unsophisticated. All of which it is, as a folk culture or as a popular culture, from which many middle-class Blacks are, or choose to be, alienated. Blues is an expression of a working-class subculture, or rather, of several. For the blues in the cities is different from that of the rural regions; and the blues of the 1950s is different from the blues of the 1920s. The latter issue is complex, but there is a substantial literature available for those who wish to study the regional and temporal distinctions further. Moreover, blues is not representative of the whole of Black culture in the lower economic brackets: it is regarded as the music of the Devil by the members of churches of all denominations. Even the relationship of the blues singer to his (the majority of blues singers in the folk tradition are male) group is itself ambivalent. He is often regarded as dissolute, irresponsible, and something of a clown while being admired for his music making and his capacity to speak through his blues songs for the community. And, it must be said that such opinions are often justified even though many blues singers in no way fit such stereotypical descriptions.

Because blues singers have been drawn generally from among the poorest in the Black communities, in an ethnic

> **Blues can be analyzed on the printed page, but they do not exist there: blues are essentially performed—they exist in the singing and the playing. The music of the blues is inseparable from the words when considered as a totality, even though the words considered in isolation from the complement of the instrumental accompaniment may still have powerful messages to convey.**
>
> **—*Paul Oliver***

minority which is itself largely disadvantaged, they have frequently been illiterate, educated only in the experience of a hard life. Whatever ideas may be in the literature of middle-class Black Americans, whatever poems may have been written under the inspiration of blues of one kind or another, remains entirely unknown to them. If the issue of "inter-relationship of ethnic music and literature" is the one that concerns us here then it must be accepted that any such relationship is not "inter-" but one-sided. There is no inter-relationship in the sense that the blues singer and creator of this form of ethnic music has any awareness of, or seeks any inspiration from, Black literature.

So, the position is one of the educated, literary poets and writers within the Black community looking to the blues for a source of ideas, and perhaps for a means of identification with what they may perceive as the roots of their culture. Such a perception may be romantic and insecurely based, but it is one that several Black writers have believed in. In passing, it should be mentioned that such a romantic identification is no less evident among white writers, and that literary narratives of the life of fictitious blues singers from Howard Odum's *Rainbow Round My Shoulder: The Blue Trail of Black Ulysses* (1928) to Peter Guralnick's *Nighthawk Blues* (1980) have been by authors who could claim no ethnic links with their subjects. But, that is another (in some ways, more fascinating) issue.

Blues-related poetry appeared first in the 1920s "Negro Renaissance" when the experience of blues by Black poets was mainly through recordings or the stage presentations of Harlem shows and the vaudeville performances of Bessie Smith and Clara Smith. Langston Hughes (born 1902) and Sterling Brown (born 1901) were the most sensitive to the idiom and Hughes, in particular, closely followed it:

I'm gonna walk to de graveyard
'Hind my friend, Miss Cora Lee,
Gonna walk to de graveyard
'Hind ma dear friend, Cora Lee,
Cause when I'm dead some
Body'll have to walk with me.

Brown also essayed the three-line blues form with "Tornado Blues":

Black wind came aspeedin' down de river from
de Kansas plains,
Black wind came aspeedin' down de river from
de Kansas plains,
Black wind came aroarin' like a flock of giant
aeroplanes.

Destruction was adrivin' it and close behind was
Fear,
Destruction drivin', pa'dner at his side was Fear,
Grinnin' Death and skinny Sorrow was
abringin' up de rear. . . .

Both Hughes and Brown seem to have felt their detachment from the folk community while working in the idiom and sprinkled their verses with "ma" and "de" as liberally as any plantation memories of the 1890s. The long lines of the blues form were divided by Hughes, and in "Memphis Blues," Sterling Brown shattered it:

Was another Memphis
'Mongst de olden days,
Dome been destroyed
In many ways . . .
Dis here Memphis
It may go.
Floods may drown it,
Tornado blow
Mississippi wash it
Down to sea—
Like de other Memphis in
History.

As poets, both were developing concepts that would not occur in blues. Personification of Death, Sorrow and Fear are alien to its imagery, though possibly because personification of "the Blues" embraces them all in the traditional idiom. Both poets wrote longer works like Brown's "Long Gone" in *Southern Road,* or Hughes's "Ask Your Mama" which has "the traditional folk melody of the 'Hesitation Blues' (as) the leitmotif for this poem," but Hughes's rightly termed it "Twelve Moods for Jazz"; poems to be read between or against jazz improvisation and not poems that simulated blues form or expression. Like Sterling Brown's "Ma Rainey," which was a poem about and to the singer, not an attempt at recreating her song composition, it was far more effective as poetry.

Myron O'Higgins (born 1918), a student of Sterling Brown, also wrote of one of the great figures in vaudeville blues, Bessie Smith, keeping approximately to the blues form:

Bessie lef' Chicago
in a bran' new Cad'lac Eight
Yes, Bessie lef' Chicago
in a gret big Cad'lac Eight
But dey shipped po' Bessie back (Lawd)
on dat lonesome midnight freight.
Lawd, let de peoples know
what dey did in dat Southern Town,
Yes, let de peoples know
what dey did in dat Southern Town
Well, dey lef' po' Bessie dyin'
wid de blood (Lawd) a-streamin' down.

Like Edward Albee in his play *The Death of Bessie Smith,* O'Higgins was making both a political and poetic point. Blues singer Booker T. Washington merely mourned her passing with the curious specific details that often occur in blues, but without the background of "de thunder rolled an' de lightnin' broke de sky," which O'Higgins felt necessary to his poem. Sang Booker T. Washington:

> Bessie Smith went out ridin', went out ridin' in
>   a limousine (twice)
> Well that poor girl died suddenly, it was the
>   worst I ever seen.
> Well they took poor Miss Bessie way down some
>   lonesome road (twice)
> Well that poor girl gone this morning, yessir, she
>   ain't gonna sing no more.
>
> Bessie Smith wore pearls, and she wore dia-
>   monds, gold (twice)
> Well that poor girl gone, Bessie Smith won't no
>   more.

It is arguable whether Myron O'Higgins makes a more effective comment—or poem—than does Washington with his reflection on wealth and mortality. Another poet who also wrote of Bessie Smith's death, or rather, the popularly believed version of it, was Oliver Pitcher (born 1923) in his bitter poem "Salute." He, too, has been drawn to the blues as in "Harlem: Sidewalk Icons."

> Man, in some lan
> I hear tell, tears wep
> in orange baloons will
> bus wide open with
> laughter
> Aw, cry them blues Man!

—but the last line strikes a false note. Other poets have felt the challenge of the blues and have—like James C. Morris (born 1920) tried to describe them:

> These are the blues:
> a longing beyond control
> left on an unwelcome doorstep,
> slipping in when the door is opened.
>
> These are the blues:
> a lonely woman crouched at a bar,
> gulping a blaze of Scotch and rye,
> using a tear for a chaser.
>
> The blues are fears that
> blossom like ragweeds
> in a well-kept bed of roses.
>
> (Nobody knows how tired I am.
> And there ain't a soul who gives a damn.)

In 1924, before James Morris had started school at Talladega, Alabama, blues singer Ida Cox had recorded her own definition:

> Oh the blues ain't nothin' but a slow achin'-heart
>   disease (twice)
> Just like consumption it kills you by degrees.

> Oh papa, papa, mama done gone mad (twice)
> Oh the blues ain't nothin' but a good woman
>   feelin' bad.

Few Black poets have tested their work by having it sung by a blues singer. One that did was Richard Wright who made the mistake of getting Paul Robeson to sing "King Joe" with the Count Basie Band. Robeson was too much of a concert singer to sing blues and Wright too much of a poet to write them. Its folksiness struck the wrong note when Joe Louis was the theme:

> Black-eyed pea said "Cornbread, what makes
>   you so strong?" (twice)
> Cornbread say, 'I come from where Joe Louis
>   was born.'
>
> Bull-frog told boll-weevil, "Joe's done quit the
>   ring," (twice)
> Boll-weevil say, "He ain't gone and he is still the
>   king."

Among Black poets, Wright was unusual in having been born on a plantation (1908) and having educated himself. His contact with blues was far closer than most, but he rarely essayed the form. His great poems like "I Have Seen Black Hands" or "Between the World and Me" are all the more impressive because they do not affect an artificial naivete. All the other poets quoted here had a good education; several went to Universities and one or two have University appointments: very appropriate for poetry and literature, but far removed from the milieu of the blues. Poets are trained to structure their compositions, to understand the rhythms and the resonances of words; they develop critical ears and write with fastidious hands. But the ears of blues singers are atuned to the sounds of freight trains and Martin guitars, and their hands are calloused by hoes, ice-picks and metal guitar strings.

There is little point in making further comparisons between the poets' use of blues form or the blues singers' language, and those of the blues singers' themselves. Ethnically, they may well be related, but in terms of literacy, world-view and cultural milieu, they are separated by a gulf which may perhaps be bridged, but will not be closed. Of course, this is not an argument for rejecting the blues, nor is it a way of saying that poets should not turn to blues, or anything else, for inspiration: the poet should have the creative freedom to draw his resources from where he chooses. All the same, it is worth emphasizing that this kind of choice is seldom the luxury of the blues singer.

Is there a future for an ethnic poetry of Black writers inspired by the blues? Maybe, but just as there seems little to look forward to in blues with literary pretensions, so there is little to be said for a literature with pretensions to being folk composition. The beauty of the blues resides so often in the relationship of the vocal and the words expressed to the music that is a part of it. As folk art in its origins and popular art today, it is remarkable, but, to date, it has not been a convincing source for an ethnic literature.

LITERATURE AND POPULAR MUSIC

Naomi Lindstrom

SOURCE: "Dylan: Song Returns to Poetry," in *Texas Quarterly*, Vol. XIX, No. 4, Winter, 1976, pp. 131-36.

[*In the following essay, Lindstrom calls for a reevaluation of conventional thinking about the differences between the language of poetry and the language of popular songs, crediting Bob Dylan with initiating a trend in popular music toward the composition of more complex lyrics.*]

There is certainly much to remind us that poetry was once something for people to sing to one another. We use words that hark back to the old kinship between poetry and song: *canto, cantico, lyric, sonnet* (little song). Yet we must point out to literature students that the ballads frequently singled out as sung poetry, were by no means the only poetic form to be communicated in this manner. Indeed, it seems difficult to impress this fact on our own minds, so accustomed are we to the idea that poetry is poetry and song is song. As is well known, when printing techniques allowed individual readers to go off alone, each with a copy of a poem to pore over in silence, poetry lost its old reliance on song as a means of transmission and settled into its on-the-page existence. But how permanent was this rift?

Many of us grew up with the assurance that song has lyrics—that is, that it has words which must have the feature of singability but not the sort of complex elaboration one would demand from a literary text—and that a book of poetry has poems—complexly developed works which if sung to a person would leave him with nothing but a tangled blur of images in his head and which must be studied at length and in silence. We have in recent years had our categories challenged. There can be a study entitled *The Poetry of Rock* (1969), on rock lyrics as a form of poetic expression. But one can scarcely imagine what sort of analysis might be perpetrated using for texts the words to rock and roll of the late fifties or early sixties. A good many people were startled to find Bob Dylan appearing in listings of favorite poets among college students. Now one can buy a record, pull out a sheet with the lyrics printed on it, and read something which appears to have all the features of poetry: innovative metaphors, surprising imagery, well-employed metonymy—in short, every characteristic except that of being presented to the world as poetry. A rock singer today may be a published poet, as in the case with Patti Smith, who was surprised to find herself singing rock only because, while she knew her poetic expression would eventually be triumphant, "I just didn't know it would have anything to do with my throat."

One might be surprised enough to find such demanding texts on records, which, after all, can be played repeatedly, allowing the listener to go back over a song somewhat as he would go over a poem. It is more startling to hear poetic texts played over the radio, where they are heard through once and gone, until listener and song happen to meet again. Thus we must abandon our conventional notion that poetry cannot normally be sung, that the com-pression of language and complex elaboration which make it poetry also make it too demanding to be taken in through the ear. Nor does it make sense, in the face of such occurrences, to continue to think of song lyrics as a form of verbal expression approximately on a level with football cheers, political slogans, anonymous letters, and other sometimes cleverly done but not very exalted forms.

Such a distinction held up well enough when one went from on-the-page "real" poetry straight to the ever-at-hand consolations of a reassuring, innundating spew of AM noise. There, words were worked around such well-known topics as the avowed intention to acquire a new love and thus forget the previous one; declarations of undying loyalty to rock and roll; the beloved who did not even know that the poetic *I* existed; and the possibility of partying for unbounded periods of time, for example, around the clock. However, such a song-poetry distinction is blurred by turning on the radio and hearing, say, Judy Collins singing Leonard Cohen's reworkings of such Biblical themes as Abraham and Isaac.

Naturally, not everything sung before Dylan was simplified for the ear's benefit. In the early twenties, Edith Sitwell presented *Façade* at the Aeolian Hall in London—at least one interesting example of poetry-as-song which neither antedates Gutenberg nor follows after Dylan. While sung-chanted, the work was not made less complex in the interests of accessibility to listeners. In fact, her poems were already written when, as Osbert Sitwell recounts the genesis of the work, the Sitwells became fascinated with the idea of making poetry abstract in the way sculpture and painting were abstract. Osbert Sitwell explains: "A young musician, William Walton, was then sharing a house with us, and we decided together that he should set the poems to music and that they should be presented in as abstract a manner as possible." Here Sitwell seems to be positing as an advantage the supposed problem with singing poetic texts, that a good deal of what was sung would be lost on the hearer, who could only be expected to assimilate so much at a time. The first performance of *Façade* evidently had the intended effect of becoming abstract by frustrating the listener's attempts to grasp the poetic text in its entirety, determine its rhetorical thrust, and savor the use of language. However, the audience which experienced this abstract effect did not find it much to its liking, and according to Sitwell, "At the end, my sister was warned not to leave the shelter of her dressing room until the crowd had dispersed, or she might meet with injury."

Certainly it is not possible that a mutation in the human brain caused people to be able to take in poetry just as fast as it could be sung. Yet by the sixties it was accepted, at least by those who were willing to listen to Bob Dylan, that a Dylan song might contain such a welter of images, discontinuous narrative, curious metaphors, and phrases so hermetic as to exclude every listener except Dylan, that, even after hearing it through more than once, a listener might have only a vague notion of what it was about. Lines such as "My penthouse has your Arabian drum / shall I leave it now beside your gate / or, sad-eyed lady, shall I wait?" left listeners with nothing more definite than that the poetic *I* was addressing himself, in tones of hesitation and only tentative approach, to a mysterious woman. From other lyrics one could eventually figure out that while the sad-eyed lady had had a great many men figure in her life, none of them was capable of offering her the sort of total commitment and support she demanded, an attitude on her part which might explain the singer's hesitancy to approach her. Describing the sad-eyed lady's hangers-on, an unsavory lot, the singer concluded brutally, "Who among them do you think would ever carry you?" After giving out only this much information, the song retreats into obscurity, effectively excluding the listener from deciphering it in its totality. It would be hard to think of a more effective refutation of the idea that song lyrics must render up their meanings on the spot in order to satisfy.

The reaction to, for instance, the Dylan songs on *Blonde on Blonde* was an almost overwhelming concern with thematics. One group of listeners seemed most intent on determining whether the narrative voice or any of the characters in a given song were under the influence of drugs or using drug-induced experiences as referents. Such a concern was not only somewhat reductive, but hopeless, since the lyrics were so ambiguous that various sets of referents could be plugged in. Other special-interest groups sifted through Dylan lyrics seeking statements on generational conflict, attitudes toward women, possible calls to revolution, deification of new heroes, and so forth. Naturally, there were those concerned that listening too often to Dylan might cause the listener to abandon his moral standards.

Much concern was being expressed over the various sorts of damage over-Dylanization might cause through purely thematic means, little over the implications of his implied poetics. For instance, one did not hear anybody worrying that Dylan might deform a generation of young people by convincing them that inaccessible poetry was the only authentic mode of expression and making them distrustful of all poets who wrote in an open, clear style, nor that an adolescent who listened to Dylan might be forever stunted in his ability to appreciate or produce tightly structured literary works, leading to a future society in which all poetic forms except the ramble would atrophy away.

Perhaps the only question to be raised concerned with the implied poetics of Dylan's work was the matter of whether, in fact, Dylan ought to be called a poet. Since no very good definition of the word *poet* could be produced, it was another one of those answerless literary debates along the lines of whether literature can ever change society, whether innovative poets are worthier than those who rework traditional forms to make them fresh, and whether there can be a literary work without ideas.

Such questions are no less vigorously debated for being answerless. The major arguments against giving Dylan the status of poet seemed to be that he reelaborated the same to-hell-with-you material too often and that many of his Rimbaud-evoking songs used mere obscurity to give an impression of something profound going on, while the images in the poems were really thrown together quite arbitrarily, without regard for the total rhetoric of the song.

Certainly a tiny stock of themes has never prevented non-singing poets from being classified as such. The charge of incoherence and randomness makes more sense, for some Dylan texts are remarkably loose and fragmented, failing to satisfy because they give the listener no clue as to how he is to fit the barrage of images into some coherent system. However, most of Dylans's songs make an approximate sort of sense. The poetic *I* usually takes such a markedly emotional stance toward his subject, whether one of contempt, despair, or longing, as to provide evidence of what is supposed to be going on.

The arguments against Dylan-as-poet seem to be trying to disqualify him by applying to his work standards not used in cases where the poet refrains from singing his texts. This double standard suggests that what really bothers these objectors to Dylan-as-poet is that he violates the distinction between poetry and song. Many poets fail to make their signs sufficiently clear or to impart to their works a unified feel, but Dylan was a poet of modern times spreading his unsimplified work with a song.

One interesting aspect of the acceptance of lyrics that are complex is the retrospective attitude of those who comment on the lyrics they grew up with, lyrics not merely simple of elaboration but downright simple-minded. One common contention is that the near-inanity was purposeful serving an important function in terms of the rhetoric of the song. As an instance of this rhetoric-of-banality explanation, we have Neil Sedaka reminiscing in the pages of *Rolling Stone* about the genesis of one of the more spectacularly mindless songs penned, "Oh, Carol." Sedaka remembers that his lyricist submitted his work with the preface, "I'm embarrassed, it's terrible." Sedaka, though, who understood something about how a song lyric works its persuasion on the listener, said, "This is perfect, it's just what I want: a simple, ordinary layman thing that will appeal to all the Carols."

A slight variant of this proposed explanation holds that the Cro-Magnon character of some lyrics had to do with the cultural function of rock, that is, its alternative to an overintellectualized, too analytical way of regarding the world, the one being urged upon young people by schools and parents. This being the case, productive metaphors or memorable turns of phrase in the lyrics would spoil the alternative by causing the reader to think, or to perceive things in a new way, as poetic use of language is meant to do. The proponents of this point of view are many and tend to speak of rock monuments of antithought using terms such as "straight from the gut" or "raw energy" or "pure refreshing raunch."

One might well wonder whether the current reworking of no-brains rock into such satirical forms as the musical *Grease* and the group Sha Na Na could not be due partly to acute embarrassment over having spent large amounts of one's adolescent time and funds on a music which now sounds amazingly like nothing. By playing the same music in a sophisticatedly burlesque spirit, one can make it seem to have been a manifestation of the aesthetics-of-excess rather than the not-too-deserving object of straightforward admiration. Of course, whether or not such rewriting of cultural history is actually taking place, and whether those who attend *Grease* are really atoning for their past sins of taste, must remain a matter for speculation.

We can say, though, that while very simple lyrics may always be written, a change has taken place in many listeners' attitude toward song lyrics. The words to many of the songs played on what are vaguely called "progressive rock stations" are written with a complexity one could not have thought possible a few years ago. Nor is it possible to explain away the change by such ad-hoc explanations as that the complexity is a sort of smoke screen to avoid censorship, or that every one of the listeners is so stoned that even lyrics of the sort that rhyme *arms* with *charms* and *heart* with *torn apart* would be inaccessible to them. Censors are not apt to care about progressive stations, and even a sober pedantic listener can tell that the language pouring out of his radio is full of literary devices, often quite well employed. The long-standing distinction between the easy language of songs and the demanding language of poetry is today no longer such a valid one.

James A. Winn

SOURCE: "The Beatles as Artists: A Meditation for December Ninth," in *Michigan Quarterly Review,* Vol. XXIII, No. 1, Winter, 1984, pp. 1-20.

[*In the following essay, Winn traces the developing complexity of the Beatles' music, arguing that their withdrawal from the concert scene to focus on making albums allowed them to more fully realize their collaborative potential.*]

The stark white graphics on the television screen were terrible in both their symmetry and their finality: John Lennon: 1940-1980. If you had thought of him as permanently twenty-five, the knowledge that Lennon had reached age forty became a part of the larger, more horrifying news that he was dead. For even in separation and disarray, the Beatles served several generations as symbols on which to hang fantasies, aspirations, and not-yet-formed identities. And as they came to realize, first from the physically dangerous way their young fans pelted them with jelly beans and grabbed at their clothing, then from the grinding daily impossibility of achieving privacy, their status as symbols was a heavy burden indeed. Typically, it was John who found a way of expressing their plight, with a metaphor many found scandalous; in a song complaining about the way the press hounded him on his honeymoon ("The Ballad of John and Yoko," 1969), he predicted with wry and eerie accuracy the final bloody cost of his notoriety:

> Christ! You know it ain't easy,
> you know how hard it can be.
> The way things are going
> they're going to crucify me.

Predictably, the first eulogies in the press concentrated on the public aspects of Lennon's career: the mass hysteria called Beatlemania, the admissions of drug use, the flirtation with Eastern religions, the naive but touching billboard campaign for world peace. But I shall be arguing here that the lasting accomplishment of Lennon and his mates, their emergence as self-consciously artistic makers of songs, was itself a response to and attempted escape

from the burdens of public notoriety. The Beatles gave their last public concert on 29 August 1966; in that same month, they issued the ironically-titled *Revolver,* an album that signalled a new introspection and a greater willingness to test and tease the hearer. Freed from the exhausting and demeaning business of touring, they were able to sustain their growing complexity and creativity for four highly productive years, during which they produced *Sergeant Pepper's Lonely Hearts Club Band* (1967), *Magical Mystery Tour* (1967), the double album called *The Beatles* (1968), *Abbey Road* (1969), and *Let It Be* (1970)—albums that expanded and apparently exhausted the possibilities of the rock song.

This fruitful withdrawal from public performance necessarily followed at least a decade of frequent performance; indeed, in the early years of the group's development, the Beatles sought every opportunity to perform, presumably because they craved money, success, and notoriety—not because they wished to make an artistic statement. John's wacky and deliberately inaccurate account of their early history, written in 1961, dismisses the motives for their trip to Hamburg as purely monetary: "And then a man with a beard cut off said—will you go to Germany and play mighty rock for the peasants for money? And we said we would play mighty anything for money." One thinks of Dr. Johnson's equally proud and practical statements: "Sir, I could write a preface upon a broomstick" or (even closer) "No man but a blockhead ever wrote, except for money." In both cases, the claim to be motivated by money is at once a declaration of professional pride and a rejection of more Romantic notions of the reasons for creativity. By declaring that one plays concerts or writes prefaces for money, one emphasizes the work involved and casts doubt on the notion that the making of music or literature is a mysterious, metaphysical, quasi-religious calling. By 1968, when "interpretations" of Beatles lyrics were a constant topic of journalism and party conversation, John would debunk the idea of his work as "art" in an even more savage way: "It's nice when people like it, but when they start 'appreciating' it, getting great deep things out of it, making a thing of it, then it's a lot of shit. It proves what we've always thought about most sorts of so-called art. It's all a lot of shit. It is depressing to realize we were right in what we always thought, all those years ago. Beethoven is a con, just like we are now. He was just knocking out a bit of work, that was all." For the young Beatles, playing concerts was basically "knocking out a bit of work," and getting paid meant being able to keep playing, avoiding the duller jobs as deliverymen and factory workers they had briefly held as teenagers. Thus money, as a way to escape the grim Liverpool life of their parents, was a motive they could acknowledge; the notion of making "so-called art," by contrast, was a ludicrous idea they actively rejected.

Fame fell somewhere in between. According to George Harrison, "we used to send up the idea of getting to the top. When things were a real drag and nothing happening, we used to go through this routine: John would shout, 'Where are we going, fellas?' We'd shout back, 'To the Top, Johnny!' Then he would shout, 'What Top? 'To the Toppermost of the Poppermost, Johnny!' " But was this routine a "send-up," a completely ironic gesture of disdain, or was it a therapeutic way of pretending, as record company after record company turned them down, that getting to the top didn't matter, and thus ultimately a ritual of morale-boosting? If, as I suspect, the young Beatles desperately wanted to achieve fame, but had a concurrent need to pretend to disdain it, would it not be possible to extend that argument to cover their attitude toward "so-called art" as well? To be sure, they did not want to be thought of as pale aesthetes; John's remarks about Beethoven make that clear enough. But it was the same John Lennon who described his song "Because" (1969) as "the Moonlight Sonata backwards," and the introduction to that song does strongly suggest the harmonic motion of Beethoven's piece. So despite John's warnings against commentary couched in artistic language, and despite what must always have been their own powerful ambivalence about their status as "artists," the Beatles' tireless work at the making and recording of songs after their withdrawal from public performance was ultimately motivated by a quite subtle and impressive aesthetic sense, and by a driving need to create that they shared with many poets and composers. As John himself once said, "I can't retire. I've got these bloody songs to write."

This remark suggests not only a need to write songs but a sense of that writing as work; like the early story of the morale-boosting routine, it underscores the Beatles' determination and persistence, qualities that would serve them well when their musical ideas became so complex as to require hours of over-dubbing and mixing. Even George Martin, the producer whose technical expertise had so much to do with the excellence of the later albums, has spoken admiringly of the Beatles' patient perfectionism, their capacity for hard work. The Beatles themselves, while sometimes disparaging their group as "an average band," were nonetheless careful to give themselves credit for putting out effort. Speaking of the pressure under which he and John often produced the last few songs to fill out an album, Paul McCartney once referred to such songs, written by "pure slog," as "not necessarily worse than ones done out of imagination," indeed "often better," and John extended this principle to a definition of "talent" as "believing you can do something." This notion of talent as confidence and effort, a curiously overlooked consequence of the Beatles' working-class origins, freed them from the crippling Romantic notion of "originality" as "inspiration." Without knowing it, the Beatles were recovering a philosophy of art frequently encountered in the Renaissance and the eighteenth century, the simpler idea of the artist as artisan. Paul used to write proudly at the top of each of the hundreds of unrecorded songs they wrote as teenagers, "Another Original by Lennon and McCartney," but the songs were actually highly derivative, drawing on Elvis Presley, Chuck Berry, and the English music hall, among other sources. By turning out these imitative exercises, and by striving in their singing for flawless imitations of Elvis or Little Richard, the Beatles were putting themselves through an apprenticeship of the kind thought normal for poets and composers before the triumph of Romanticism: one thinks of Shakespeare's Plautine plays, or of Pope's derivative *Pastorals*, or of Beethoven's early exercises in a style overtly dependent on Haydn and Mozart. For these artists as for the Beatles, creation was hard work, and apprenticeship involved the mastering of idioms learned from earlier artists. At the level of vocal style, those imitated idioms remained with the Beatles as *personae*: as late as *Abbey Road* Paul was using his "Little Richard" voice for "Oh Darling," and his "Elvis" voice for the barrel-house bridge of "You Never Give Me Your Money" ("Out of college, money spent . . .").

> The Beatles' tireless work at the making and recording of songs after their withdrawal from public performance was ultimately motivated by a quite subtle and impressive aesthetic sense, and by a driving need to create that they shared with many poets and composers. As John himself once said, "I can't retire. I've got these bloody songs to write."
>
> —*James A. Winn*

Beyond providing a poet or composer with a sense of what style *is* or a *persona* he may later employ with ironic effect, imitation may also be a way of developing the habit of making; having written their hundreds of teenage "originals," John and Paul were ready to flex those muscles in more personal ways when their chance came. In their very first English recording, made in November 1962, they display, at least in embryo, a distinct idiom as composers and singers, though their lyrics remain shamelessly conventional. They knew that the path "to the Toppermost of the Poppermost" would lead through the recording studios, and that their material for records would have to be different or arresting in some way besides the sheer volume on which they had relied in Hamburg. They also had the good fortune to begin recording at a moment when seeming new or different was not terribly difficult; American and English popular music were both in a period of stagnation. After a great burst of energy in the middle 1950s, largely the result of Elvis Presley's popularizing of a previously black "rhythm and blues" idiom, American "Top 40" hits had settled into a predictable pattern: chord changes were restricted to primary triads (usually I-VI-IV-V, in that order); guitar playing was almost always a mindless banging out of those chords, with very little linear interest; vocal harmony rarely involved anything more complex than the smooth thirds of the Everly Brothers; lyrics, rhythms, and melodies were equally dull. Only the Beach Boys, still at a very early stage, promised any development beyond this pattern. In England, where the top group was Cliff Richard and the Shadows, the situation was no better, indeed, as the antiseptic primness of that group's style suggested, probably worse.

The Beatles' first single "Love Me Do" and "PS I Love You" was palpably different. Their teenage fans, when referring to the "new sound" they heard in these songs, were probably responding first of all to the strong two-part singing of John and Paul, the most immediately obvious of a number of principles of contrast that would make their maturer work so musically interesting. Paul, a natural tenor with unusually clear, well-produced high notes, sounded quite unlike John, a natural baritone singing with obvious but expressive strain when reaching for his high notes. (Later, the Beatles would find uses for John's low range: he sings a low G in "I'm a Loser" and a low A in "Happiness is a Warm Gun.") The frequent open fifths between the voices in "Love Me Do" emphasize this difference in vocal quality; unlike the Everly Brothers and others who sought an anonymously smooth blend, the Beatles had to be heard as individuals working together. Even in "Love Me Do," first composed in their skiffle-group days, John and Paul constantly vary the vocal texture: they sing separately, in unison, in octaves, in fifths, in thirds, and even in contrary motion. This variety of texture, together with George's tight, witty guitar work and John's bluesy harmonica, gives a basically primitive song enough musical content to sustain our interest.

The desire for variety was a compositional principle, not merely a matter of performance. Remembering how they decided to proceed after their highly successful second single ("Please Please Me"), Paul says: "we decided we must do something different for the next song. We'd put on one funny hat, so we took it off and looked for another one to put on." Other groups were content to grind out follow-up songs in the mold of the last hit, but the Beatles had an almost obsessive need to "change hats"; it came to characterize their approach to composition, instrumental texture, electronic production, and form (both the form of individual songs and the larger forms they learned to construct on whole album sides). Groups with immediately identifiable but unchanging "sounds" (the Supremes, for example) had little difficulty producing individual hits, but their albums, which made the similarities between those hits painfully obvious, seemed pointless. The Beatles, with their rhetorical, hat-changing theory of style, were ideally suited to the album format. The strong contrasts between John and Paul, which extended well beyond mere vocal quality, helped them achieve continual variety. Paul began as a facile composer of melodies and bass lines, John as a writer of clever nonsense words, but even as teenagers theirs was no simple collaboration between tune man and word man. By their own account, John began writing tunes to keep up with Paul, and Paul would eventually be encouraged to improve his lyrics by his contact with John. By not rigorously dividing the tasks, one taking responsibility for words, the other for tunes, as other song-writing teams had done, they gained a much richer and more complex kind of collaboration. As they worked together, each constantly adding to, improving, and developing what the other had done, they achieved not one composite style but a kaleidoscopic series of styles. John even thought of the composing process, verbal and musical, as a matter of linking up "bits"-the more different the "bits," the better, as in "I am the Walrus" or "Happiness is a Warm Gun."

Another kind of variety important to the Beatles' later work, its rich harmonic language, is hardly apparent in "Love Me Do," which uses only three chords. But following the principle of contrast, the other side, "PS I Love You," employs augmented dominants and a deceptive cadence on the flatted sixth. Remembering their earliest days together, John once remarked that he and Paul took George into the group "because he knew more chords, a lot more than we knew. So we got a lot from him. Every time we learned a new chord, we'd write a song around it." This reminiscence provides another valuable glimpse into the Beatles' apprenticeship; their willingness to write songs *around* each new chord would prove more important than the chords themselves, which were complex only by comparison with the dull triads of American groups. By writing songs around chords, not merely using chords as ornamental flourishes, the Beatles gained a new principle of variety. Some of the earliest analytical pieces on their music noticed the frequency of major chords built on the flat sixth and the flat third; my point is that phrases moving through such harmonies may be effectively contrasted with phrases moving through more conventional "changes," as in "It Won't Be Long Now" (November 1963), a song in C major which juxtaposes a refrain moving through A minor against a verse moving through A-flat major. The Beatles were learning to use chord changes not only for variety but for wit, and even as expressive devices. "If I Fell" (August 1964), perhaps the most beautiful of the early songs, gains some of its tenderness by beginning in E-flat minor, with an uncertain and unsettled series of harmonies, while the speaker asks, "If I fell in love with you, would you promise to be true, and help me understand?" With his assertion that "love is more than just holding hands," the song finds D major, its true key; the modulation underscores the text, an early example of something the Beatles did continually in their mature period.

During the three years between their first single and the album called *Rubber Soul* (December 1965), despite a hectic schedule of tours and appearances, the Beatles managed to make steady progress as composers and musicians. They relied less and less on the conventional 32-bar AABA form in which pop songs had most often been written in previous decades, increasingly inventing new, less symmetrical forms; "Another Girl" (August 1965), in which a shortened chorus used as an introduction enjambs into the verse, provides one striking example. They also escaped the rock convention of the "fade out" ending; the endings of "A Hard Day's Night", "And I Love Her," and "We Can Work it Out," each of which restates some harmonic or rhythmic motif of the song in a fresh and conclusive way, justify Leonard Bernstein's famous remark that the Beatles were "the greatest composers of codas since Beethoven." But as they improved and developed, they naturally began to seek effects in the studio which they could not reproduce in performance: the string quartet accompaniment to Paul's "Yesterday," for example, or the technically difficult piano solo George Martin plays on "In My Life." As George Harrison later put it, "we were held back in our development by having to go onstage all the time and do it, with the same old guitars, drums, and bass."

"Having to go onstage and do it" held the Beatles' development back in ways less obvious and more important than mere instrumentation. The chaotic conditions under which they performed made them understandably reluctant to try complex rhythms: a concert in a stadium, where the performers often had trouble hearing each other, was hardly the place to experiment with tricky rhythms, nor would such rhythms have been appreciated by fans who expected such concerts to provide a heavy "beat" as an aid to ritual hypnosis. Significantly, the first Beatles song involving a change of meter, John's "She Said She Said," in which 4/4 slides into 3/4 in the third bar of the bridge, was first recorded on *Revolver,* at the point of the withdrawal from public concerts. Once that breakthrough had occurred, effective metrical changes were frequent: the energetic 5/4 bars in "Good Morning, Good Morning" account for some of that song's electricity, while the stumbling alternation of 4/4 and 3/4 in "All You Need Is Love" keeps the hearer off balance. Such innovations, while certainly less complex than the rhythms of modern serious music or those of the Indian music that came to fascinate George Harrison, were previously unheard of in rock and roll, in which one unbreakable rule had been regular dance rhythm. ("It's got a good beat, Murray. You could dance to it. I'd give it about 85.") And by breaking free of that rule, the Beatles gained not only a new kind of variety, but the ability to use regular rhythm ironically, again as a *persona.* In John's "Happiness is a Warm Gun," for example, the words of the title are sung to a slow, mindlessly regular 4/4 beat, while the harmonies move through the I-VI-IV-V triadic pattern of the early 1960s, but that obviously parodic section is preceded by an irregularly accented section in triple time ("Mother Superior, jump the gun"), in which the cross-rhythms suggest African drumming, not American Bandstand. The juxtaposition enriches both segments, and the implication is that the kind of listener who would require that all music have a beat "you could dance to" is the kind likely to respond to the American hunting magazine ad from which John lifted the title. "Mother Superior" is John's wife Yoko Ono, the Oriental who "jumps the gun" by running traffic signals, so of course her music is irregular, non-Western, and vigorous.

This kind of rhythmic complexity, especially when rendered mimetic by a careful matching to words, requires a listener of a far different kind than the listener addressed by "She Loves You." If the early songs were designed to be heard over a public address system, the later songs were produced to be heard through headphones. Despite the melodic and harmonic and formal progress the Beatles were making during their lucrative years as the "Fab Four," the conditions under which they performed virtually arrested their development as lyricists. John could hardly have projected the punning ambiguities of his later style when singing over the din of thousands of prepubescent girls who had come to hear such unambiguous messages as "I wanna hold your hand." But as the recording studio rather than the public stage became their arena, the Beatles' approach to lyrics began to change. An honest appraisal will have to admit that "Drive My Car," "Norwegian Wood," and "Nowhere Man," all first recorded on the British version of *Rubber Soul,* are the first Beatles songs that can claim to have interesting lyrics; the contrast

between these witty, fully shaped lyrics and those of the vapid early love songs is instructive.

In the early songs, the first-person speaker is usually a teenage lover: most often he talks to his girl ("Please please me oh yeh, like I please you"); sometimes he talks about her ("Well, she was just seventeen, And you know what I mean"); if the complains about her ("Well I gave you everything I had, But you left me sitting on my own"), it is only as part of a plea for reconciliation ("I beg you on my bended knees"). The situations dramatized by the songs were simple plots into which a teenage girl could project herself, casting her favorite Beatle as the devoted lover; this ploy was probably as important a cause of Beatlemania as Brian Epstein's aggressive press-agentry. But these songs merely set up situations; they never resolve them, leaving what happens *after* the speaker delivers his message to our imagination. Some of the songs on the album *Help!* (August 1965) have a little more bite: now the speaker responds to mistreatment with more resentment ("For I have got another girl, another girl who will love me to the end") and even addresses another male with a threat ("You're going to lose that girl"). But these situations were still simple; the fourteen-year-old girl apparently assumed as the listener needed only to cast herself as the "other girl" or the mistreated girl whose boyfriend would soon be replaced by a Beatle.

The more complicated songs on *Rubber Soul* make this kind of identification impossible by completing their stories, and by creating characters with whom no teenager would readily identify. In "Drive My Car," for example, we meet a girl who is so confident that she is going to be

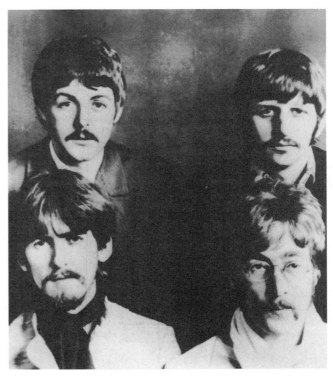

The Beatles circa 1970.

"famous, a star of the screen" that she offers the speaker a job as her chauffeur:

> "Baby, you can drive my car,
> Yes I'm gonna be a star.
> Baby, you can drive my car,
> and maybe I'll love you."

The speaker is attracted but wary:

> I told that girl that my prospects were good,
> She said, "Baby, It's understood.
> Working for peanuts is all very fine,
> But I can show you a better time."
> "Baby, you can drive my car, . . ." (etc.)

So the speaker takes the bait, only to discover that a crucial element is missing:

> I told that girl I could start right away,
> She said, "Baby I've got something to say.
> I got no car and it's breaking my heart,
> But I've found a driver, that's a start."
> "Baby, you can drive my car, . . ." (etc.)

Unlike the early songs, this one does not seem designed to arouse sympathy or affection, nor is it simply a complaint, like "Day Tripper." Both the girl, with her delusions of Hollywood, and the speaker, whose good "prospects" yield to a willingness to "start right away," are satirized, and "Drive My Car" marks the first time in the Beatles' development that a speaker is an object of satire. Indeed, he sounds like the kind of marginally employed Liverpool character the Beatles themselves might have been had they not become "stars of the screen," and the girl sounds suspiciously like someone eager to reach "the Toppermost of the Poppermost." By declaring that she wants to be famous, she is able (for one brief moment) to enjoy one of the fruits of fame, an amorous chauffeur. If talent is "believing you can do something," she has it. She cannot create a car out of thin air, but the Beatles do it for her in the exuberant "Beep Beep" refrain that ends the song. If the song satirizes the longings for fame and comfort of both its characters, it does so from the vantage point of people already ambivalent about fame, though doubtless enjoying its comforts. And it cannot be heard in the way audiences presumably heard the early love songs. No teenage girl would identify with the girl in the song, whose fantasies are exposed as illusory; no teenage boy would identify with the speaker, who is foolish enough to believe her. Nor does the song encourage adulation of its makers as sex objects. If we admire them, we must now admire them as we admire the writers of stories, for the amusing shape they have given their little tale and perhaps for the wry and indirect way it dramatizes something about their own lives, in this case their bemusement about their status as "stars."

"Norwegian Wood," another story about a failed encounter with a woman, features a series of absurdities and ambiguities. In the very first line ("I once had a girl, or should I say, she once had me"), a cliché is redefined in a way that makes it ambiguous: in which of its many senses, we wonder, is the word "had" being used? Like the girl in "Drive My Car" this one is associated with a physical object, apparently real this time, but never defined: "She showed me her room, isn't it good Norwegian wood." If we think that the Norwegian wood is her expensive modern furniture, we soon learn otherwise:

> She asked me to stay and she told me to sit anywhere,
> So I looked around and I noticed there wasn't a chair.

We never learn just what the wood is (panelling?), nor do we learn why, after the speaker has "sat on a rug, biding my time, drinking her wine," the girl apparently rejects him:

> She told me she worked in the morning and started to laugh,
> I told her I didn't and crawled off to sleep in the bath.

Most mysterious of all, we are left to puzzle about what really happens the next morning, when our hero wakes up, finds himself alone, and lights a fire, adding the inevitable refrain, "Isn't it good, Norwegian wood." Perhaps he burns her precious wood in the fireplace; perhaps he merely has a smoke. But the song itself is the real act of arson; its hint of destructiveness at the end dramatizes the resentment a working-class youth (say, a singer from Liverpool) might feel after an awkward social failure in an upperclass *milieu*. Still, just as in "Drive My Car," both figures are satirized; if we sympathize with the speaker, we surely also chuckle as he crawls off to sleep in the bath, and John's ability to include himself in the satire saves the song from being merely destructive. Perhaps it is even another song about the limits of fame, if we may credit John's claim that its story is autobiographical; perhaps he learned from the real encounter here turned into fiction that his fame and money were still insufficient to gain him entry into the upper-class world, the world here symbolized by a woman more interested in wood than in sex.

Similar class or political concerns do figure in the lyrics of the Beatles' maturity (John's "Revolution" and George's "Taxman" and "Piggies" come immediately to mind), but social commentary is finally less important than the basic theme of failed communication established in "Norwegian Wood." As in many later songs, the withholding of information and uncertainty of reference allow "Norwegian Wood" to enact its theme: our confusion about the meaning of the refrain makes us like the speaker who must also wonder why the girl keeps talking about wood. "Nowhere Man," the third striking lyric on *Rubber Soul*, develops this theme of isolation without recourse to a story; here John invents a mythic figure, significantly described in the third person before being compared to both listener and speaker:

> He's a real Nowhere Man,
> Sitting in his Nowhere Land,
> Making all his nowhere plans for nobody.
> Doesn't have a point of view,
> Knows not where he's going to,
> Isn't he a bit like you and me?

After describing Nowhere Man in that verse, the speaker addresses him directly in the bridge:

> Nowhere Man, please listen,

You don't know what you're missing,
Nowhere Man, the world is at your command.

Then the alternation of description and address is recapitulated in even briefer compass:

He's as blind as he can be,
Just sees what he wants to see,
Nowhere Man, can you see me at all?

By talking *about* Nowhere Man and then immediately talking *to* him, John gives the song's point of view a rich confusion. How can we project ourselves into this song? "Please listen, / You don't know what you're missing" sounds like a message to us about the growing complexity of Beatles music, but if we accept that identification of ourselves as Nowhere Man, the song is accusing us of blindness. John's account of the making of the song suggests an alternate possibility: "I was just sitting, trying to think of a song, and I thought of myself sitting there, doing nothing and getting nowhere. . . . Nothing would come. I was cheesed off and went for a lie down, having given up. Then I thought of myself as Nowhere Man— sitting in his nowhere land." But if John is Nowhere Man, then he is talking to himself in this song. By having it both ways ("Isn't he a bit like you *and* me"), the song ultimately shows us how uncertainty about identity and point of view leads to failed communication.

The complexity of these lyrics suggests a more intimate relationship between singer and hearer, and musically these songs are ill-suited to public performance: "Norwegian Wood" employs a sitar and quiet acoustic guitars, while "Nowhere Man" begins with four-part *a capella* singing (a chancy procedure in concert for singers used to instruments—especially Ringo). Musically and lyrically, these are "studio" songs, relying on us to listen carefully and repeatedly to their subtle effects; they are harbingers of the more sweeping changes coming on *Revolver*. On the one single issued between the two albums ("Paperback Writer," June 1966), the Beatles to be musing about the meaning of those changes; Paul was the main composer, though the lyrics confirm John's remark that he "helped out." It is hard to escape the conclusion that beneath its satire, this song concerns the new relationship in which the Beatles were beginning to engage the public. This time the story takes the form of a letter:

Dear Sir or Madam will you read my book?
It took me years to write, will you take a look?
Based on a novel by a man named Lear
And I need a job, so I want to be a paperback
    writer, paperback writer.

Here we have another satirized speaker, again in part a projection of John, whose own books (*In His Own Write* and *A Spaniard in the Works*) are indeed heavily influenced by the nonsense verse of Edward Lear. But the circles of self-consciousness are just beginning to spin; now the writer summarizes his plot:

It's the dirty story of a dirty man,
And his clinging wife doesn't understand.
His son is working for the Daily Mail;
It's a steady job, but he wants to be a paperback
    writer, paperback writer.

Formally, this is a comic use of refrain, a trick as old as the medieval French *rondeau*, enforced by the high seventh chord on the second "paperback writer." Considered as narrative, the song constitutes a tiny example of the Quaker Oats box effect, since the characters in the proffered manuscript are little versions of its maker. But since that maker, the author of the manuscript and the letter, is in turn a version of John, what we finally have here is another consideration of the complex relationship between fame and communication. "Dear Sir or Madam will you read my book" is in many ways the same plea as "Nowhere Man, please listen," but the speaker's need for fame, his hope to be a "paperback writer" (or a "star of the screen" or a Beatle) makes him all too eager to alter his art to gain popularity and money. In the last verse, he is quick to assure the editor that he can write to order: "I can make it longer if you like the style, / I can change it 'round, and I want to be a paperback writer." The main reason why he urges acceptance of his manuscript is its sales potential: "It could make a million for you overnight."

Properly understood, the paperback writer is an even more complex *persona* than the Nowhere Man; he captures the Beatles' ambivalence about fame and communication at the very moment when they made their brave decision to withdraw from that public ritual of fame, the rock concert, a ritual they had come to see as an inferior form of communication—sexual, perhaps political, certainly dramatic, but not finally musical. Leaving the hot, physical communication of such concerts to The Rolling Stones and The Who, they deliberately chose the cooler, more writerly, ultimately more musical medium of the long-playing album, and from *Revolver* on, they made the goal of their work the production of albums: not performances or even individual songs, but whole, structured artifacts with cunning musical and lyrical relations between their parts. Conceived on this larger scale, the later albums demand of the hearer the kind of repeated, serious, analytical attention we normally reserve for high art. Like high art they are impossible to paraphrase: even the published music, roughly accurate as to melodies and chord changes, is hopelessly inadequate as a transcription of *Sergeant Pepper* or *Abbey Road*. The album itself is the text, the finished product, the authority.

The songs on these later albums return to the theme of isolation, questioning whether meaningful communication can ever be achieved, but the albums themselves offer the best answer to that repeated question: they achieve a kind of communication not previously even attempted in popular music, a kind best understood by those fortunate enough to have been part of a successful musical ensemble. Nobody understands how a string quartet achieves perfect attacks and well-tuned chords, but everyone agrees that much of what is involved cannot be discussed verbally. The Beatles in 1966 had already experienced a decade of such privileged musical communication, and their ensemble in the studio years became even tighter. The film *Let it Be,* which preserves some moments from their last recording sessions, offers tantalizing glimpses of this musical communication even though the cohesiveness of the group is already suffering from the strains that would lead to their breakup. Still, we see Paul and Ringo communicating entirely with their eyes as they work out a coherent pattern for bass and drums, John adjusting the tempo of one of Paul's tunes, George working out guitar lines that reveal new features of melodies by the others. And in the case of John and Paul, musical communication was not merely a matter of tight performing ensemble; it extended to composition as well. One example of this uncanny rapport will have to suffice, John's account of the way a tune originally conceived by Paul alone ("Woke up, fell out of bed, dragged a comb across my head"), turned out to be exactly what was needed for the bridge of John's "A Day in the Life." Increasingly aware of the special qualities of this rapport, its superiority as communication to small talk, newspaper interviews, *and concerts,* the Beatles became unable to go through the motions of writing teenage love songs and performing them on stage. That decision doubtless lost them that portion of their audience for whom they were only sex objects or symbols of youthful rebellion, but it gained them the continuing respect of musicians of all kinds.

As John explained in 1968, "We talk in code to each other as Beatles. We always did that, when we had so many strangers round us on tours. We never really communicated with other people. . . . Talking is the slowest form of communicating anyway. Music is much better. We're communicating to the outside world through our music." Indeed they were, and the careful listener to the later albums is not part of a mass audience, but a fortunate eavesdropper, allowed to witness the Beatles' own private kind of communication, and trusted to respond to it; that, I take it, is one meaning of the lines on *Sergeant Pepper* that say "You're such a lovely audience, We'd like to take you home with us." I have been arguing that collaboration was the crucial factor for the Beatles from the beginning, that by finding ways to bring their disparate voices and contrasting musical personalities together, they achieved a richer and more satisfying art than other groups. My point here is that their abandoning of the concert stage enriched their collaboration and extended it, that their communication with the listener, now more intimate and complex, became more like their communication with each other, and that the primary mode of communication, in both cases, was music.

Without knowing it, the Beatles were recovering a philosophy of art frequently encountered in the Renaissance and the eighteenth century, the simpler idea of the artist as artisan.

—*James A. Winn*

Once we understand this fact, we can abandon the hopeless process of trying to understand the lyrics of John's most complex later songs as if they had exact, referential meaning. Some commentators imagine that it is sufficient to explain such songs as "Tomorrow Never Know," "Lucy in the Sky with Diamonds," "I Am the Walrus," "Strawberry Fields," "Glass Onion," and "Happiness is a Warm Gun," by making the obvious point that they seem connected to drug experiences. But even if drugs were a part of the genesis of some of the imagery in these songs, they cannot account for the way that imagery communicates to its hearers. A more serious approach might consider the ways these lyrics achieve the goal of French Symbolist poetry, the way they attain what Pater called "the condition of music." For even if the opaque and nonsensical phrases in these songs originally had some private meaning for the Beatles, we often cannot recover that original reference, so that a phrase like "a soap impression of his wife which he ate and donated to the National Trust" must communicate to us in the way that music *always* communicates to us: not as a series of sounds with precise, lexical meaning, but as a series of sounds rich with suggestion, pregnant with possibilities, resistant to paraphrase. Of the many ways poets have tried to attain "the condition of music," nonsense verse, which prefers rhyming to syntax, sound to logic, is one of the closest approaches. To be sure, part of the fun of nonsense—in Lear, Ionesco, or Lennon—comes from the way it frustrates our instinctive urge to make sense of it; our example is amusing because carving one's wife in soap is absurd, eating the soap carving is more absurd, and donating something one has already eaten is impossible. But pure sound plays a vital role as well; the internal chime of *"ate* and *donated"* produces what W. K. Wimsatt, in his seminal essay on rhyme, called "an alogical pattern of implication." Because rhyming and punning depend on accidental rather than grammatical resemblances between sounds, they produce kinds of meaning which are purely contextual, unique to the phrase, poem, or song in which they occur. And *all* musical meaning is like that: the note G means nothing by itself, but in a given context, it may be a tonic, a leading tone, or (most like a pun) the pivot note for a modulation. The prevalence of punning on the later Beatle albums is another indication of the dominance there of musical kinds of meaning.

In these great albums, all the strengths we noticed in the Beatles' early work reach fulfillment. George's guitar improvisations move well beyond "riffing": his solo on John's "Good Morning, Good Morning" is the most musically convincing use of distortion ever achieved on the electric guitar, and his conversational "fills" between the phrases of Paul's "She Came in Through the Bathroom Window" contribute wonderfully to that song's oddball comedy. The singing, both solo and background, improves much over that on the early albums, in part because each of the singers develops several distinct vocal styles. These include the *personae* already mentioned, but also softer kinds of singing not possible in concert, for example Paul's folk-like warbling on "Blackbird" or John's mournful chant in "Julia," a song for his dead mother. Rhythmic and harmonic ideas, increasingly sophisticated on the small scale, begin to function on the large scale as well: on side two of *Abbey Road,* the songs actually have a continuous sequence of key relations like a Schubert song cycle; they are also related by repeating chord sequences used motivically and by proportional rhythmic schemes, most obviously in the closely connected sequence from "Mean Mr. Mustard to The End." And in ways too subtle and various to list here, all the late albums develop connections between musical and verbal structure.

As any musician knows, the compromising of egos necessary to produce musical ensemble has its costs, and it seems reasonable to infer that when creation, not merely performance, is the goal, the costs are even higher. The talents and egos involved in the Beatles were strong, and sad as it was to witness those final quarrels over the spoils of fame—money, managers, corporations, copyrights— the real wonder is that the inevitable breakup did not occur earlier. Nor was there ever any real hope of a reunion, once the four members had gone their separate and musically disappointing ways. Yet the slightest rumor of some occasion on which they might meet was sufficient for a decade to send a thrill through many of us; the hope that they might somehow regroup, like the hope of the religious for a Second Coming, was a sustaining myth to be cherished in difficult times. As far as popular music is concerned, these are difficult times; in quite different ways, the two dominant styles are both radical rejections of the Beatles' kind of musical communication. Punk, which features crudely revolutionary lyrics, deliberately incompetent playing, and performers selected for their bizarre appearance alone, reduces rock to theatre, virtually eliminating music. Disco, which employs monotonously thick chords purged of expressive value, complex total attack rhythms laid on top of a deadly 4/4 thud, and performers selected for their slick anonymity, reduces rock to Muzak, eliminating any principle of contrast or expression. Faced with that kind of choice, many of us took comfort in the remote hope for a Beatles reunion, and drew sustenance from replaying our Beatle albums. John's death three years ago deprived us of that unrealistic hope; its anniversary may serve to remind us again of the sustenance.

Elizabeth Jane Wall Hinds

SOURCE: "The Devil Sings the Blues: Heavy Metal, Gothic *Fiction* and 'Postmodern' Discourse," in *Journal of Popular Culture*, Vol. 26, No. 3, Winter, 1992, pp. 151-64.

[*In the following essay, Hinds delineates the shared formal, thematic, and historic features of Gothic fiction and heavy-metal music, viewing both as subgenres—a term that Hinds takes care to redefine—that subvert their parent forms, the novel and rock and roll, respectively, and use images of the occult to critique mainstream culture.*]

> Maybe it's the time of year,
> And then maybe it's the time of man.
> —Crosby, Stills, Nash and Young,
> "Woodstock"

It is a long way from the 1764 appearance of Horace Walpole's *Castle of Otranto* to the 1968 *Led Zeppelin I*, but the monstrous subgenre behavior of the latter, one of the first unabashedly Heavy Metal albums, surprisingly resembles the former, both formally and historically. The first in a series of albums that came to define Heavy Metal music, this LP did to what had by then become mainstream Rock

what Walpole, and later, M. G. Lewis and Mary Shelley, had done to the mainstream novel. *Zeppelin I* retained the outward form of its parent—standard LP format, largely with newly-written material, but also with one cover version ("You Shook Me"), the four-man band with bass and electric guitars, drums and vocals and the general outline of the Rock lyric—and proceeded to rearrange those basic elements into a genre with an altogether more brash, raunchy and musically subversive arrangement.

As I will illustrate momentarily, the appearance of Gothic fiction in the late eighteenth century and that of Heavy Metal in the late twentieth follows the same historical path as their two parent-forms, namely the novel and Rock music, both of which served subversive purposes at the time of their birth. While both parent-genres followed the same trajectory from radicalism to mainstream culture as do many new genres, their offspring share more than just the historical movement of subversion-to-hegemonic form. The histories of both subgenres are peculiar in their purposeful deformity and evocation of the Satanic: both can be described as a monstrous Gothic Other whose family resemblance to their respective parent was inescapable, but which was, like an unwashed and slightly retarded younger brother, an Other whose distortions of the parent-form became repulsive to the very audience who had supported its entry into the world.

By concentrating on these two species of subgenre, what I aim to discover is three-fold. First, I will describe the nature of the two species Gothic fiction and Heavy Metal. By "nature," however, I do not mean to abstract a principle of operation separate from its cultural context, or what is better called its historical position, but rather to discover this "nature" in that very historical position itself. Thus, the epigraph to this paper. The second, or ulterior, motive is to come to an understanding of "subgenre" as both a term and a concept—what it is we mean when we say "subgenre" rather than "movement"—thereby reclaiming the value of those generic (i.e., aesthetic) categories that have been lost to the forward rush of New-Historical and ideological criticism. It is by redefining "subgenre," a manageable if somewhat reductive category, as taking its characteristics from the flux of epistemic history that I hope to achieve this recuperation. My third and final goal is to register a critique of the very historicist—indeed Marxist—theorizing gesture that makes this kind of study possible in the first place. Through this final critique, in hopes of opening a new space for understanding, I will imitate the defining feature of the subgenres under discussion in their habit of biting the hands that feed them.

Nineteen sixties Rock music, very like the novel in the mid-eighteenth century, was for a short time a radical, subversive form. No one would argue against the novel's being, by definition, a "new" and popular form, appealing to the sensibilities of an undereducated mass audience and frequently claiming as its own the values of this bourgeois crowd. The 1960s Rock audience was just such a crowd— one who liked the sounds music made, felt its instrumental and lyrical power, but who lacked the resources to educate itself formally. Partly due to its youthful energy and partly due to its position in history, the 1960s Rock band found itself speaking the language of rebellion: instrumentally, it found the sound of Big Bands and Bing Crosby too easy on the ear, too mushy; its lyrics found the crooning of euphemistic love songs and the nonsense verse of 1950s "bubblegum" pop too arid and politically unaware.

This group of musicians—foreseen in Buddy Holly and Elvis Presley—found its leading voices in The Beatles, The Who, The Rolling Stones—those bands who insisted that a handful of people could make a loud and joyful enough noise to forge a Revolution in sound. The music became louder, it became more sexually suggestive, and, most importantly, it began to express the News of the World in lyrics about the pleasures and punishments of the drug culture (The Byrds' "Eight Miles High") and, especially, in lyrics about the Vietnam War (John Lennon and Paul McCartney's "Give Peace a Chance"). Indeed, no one would question the formation of Rock & Roll in the 1960s as a radical casting off of previous popular music standards.

By the late 1960s, however, a hegemonic force had taken hold of Rock music—the same force, spurred by a species of international capitalist ideals brought about by the very nature of "the popular," meaning "that which sells," that had very quickly drawn the novel into its maw in the later eighteenth century. Completely unawares, these two "radical" forms suddenly found themselves co-opted into the mainstream, produced and bought in outrageous numbers, consumed quickly and rehearsed widely. The sign of the novel's sudden acceptance—indeed, an even bourgeois status—came in the lighting bolt of parody, in Sterne's *Tristram Shandy*. Rock was less parodied than simply engulfed and accepted: witness the appearance in 1967 and 1970 respectively of "Eleanor Rigby" and "Hey Jude" in Muzak. Not much later, the lyrics of both began appearing in anthologies used for Freshman English courses.

The power of international capitalism to embrace and celebrate that which is initially subversive had taken hold, in their respective eras, of both the novel and of Rock music, incorporating both genres into its mass marketing strategies, thereby recreating the form itself vis-a-vis the marketplace. It is at this point—or rather the two points of the late eighteenth and late twentieth centuries—of absolute assimilation that the subgenres of Gothic fiction and Heavy Metal were born. The Gothic novel was undoubtedly a relation of the parent in its prose, highly-storied form, the "well-made" novel of Richardson and Fielding. But where the novel had revealed a closely-knit formal design—a beginning, middle and end centered about a causally-connected universe of motivation and action—the Gothic novel was generally episodic in structure, often with much-maligned "flaws" consisting in unmotivated (usually evil) actions and strands of plot that tend to appear and disappear without explanation. Where the novel had espoused restraint, the Gothic novel demonstrated uninhibited libido, even outright perversion with incest, rape and sado-masochism of all varieties. And finally, where the novel had espoused the singularly righteous in moral vision, detailing the rewards of a good heart and virtuous action within the social sphere, the Gothic novel, al-

though conservative like its parent, took the low road, demonstrating in too-close detail the rewards and punishments of the carnally evil, the best full-blown example of which was Maturin's *Melmoth the Wanderer*, organized over a chronology of three hundred years, detailing the desperate attempts of Melmoth who, having sold his soul to the devil for an extended life, attempts to prolong his term on earth by converting others in a series of disconnected episodes ending in Melmoth's eventual failure: in the end, he is "called home" to Satan and must return by way of falling through a craggy abyss, wasting away by starvation for three days and finally being torn to shreds by demons.

Early Heavy Metal music concentrated more intensively on the reward end of the carnal spectrum, but in its totality bespoke the same message of perversion as did the Gothic Novel. Instrumentally, this Heavy Metal style—a name anachronistically applied, I should add—twisted the basic Rock arrangement into what one might call an episodic format. Where the standard Rock single was approximately three minutes long, contained three or sometimes four verses alternating with a two-to-four-line chorus and faded out with repetitions of the chorus, *Led Zeppelin I* contained a range from three to seven and a half minutes (the latter with "Baby, I'm Gonna Leave You") and a very irregular pattern of repetition for the chorus. Further, while the Heavy Metal form retains the electric guitar emphasis and solos of mainstream Rock, these solos became famous for irregularity and a seemingly uncontrolled formlessness; to call on the originators again, "Dazed and Confused"—including the studio version from *Zeppelin I*, but especially the live version of the concert film *The Song Remains the Same*—demonstrates the limits of the guitar solo that changes both rhythm and key and that extends its length to the outrageous—nearly ten minutes. To draw out the analogy, the drum and keyboard solos of early Metal music draw on the "virtuoso" performance style of Rock's Jazz roots to distort and intensify the mainstream Rock concept of the solo. In short, with its irregular placement and number of choruses and verses, its length of solo performances, the intensified role of the bass guitar and lower registers in general, Heavy Metal perverted the well-made, beginning-middle-end structure of the standard into more a series of loosely connected "episodes" than a coherency of "song."

It is in its lyrics, however, that Heavy Metal most systematically subverts its mother form; Robert Pattison accounts for the centrality of these lyrics by writing that they "may be trite, obscene, and idiotic—which is to say, they may be vulgar—but they are certainly not incidental, and the proof of their importance is their consistency." In response to the generally positive—one might say the "feel-good" lyrics of mainstream 1960s Rock—Heavy Metal lyrics focused more particularly on the blatant, the sexual and often, the horrific. Recall some of the most popular of 1960's lyric messages: "Love is all you need" (Beatles, "All You Need is Love") and "I want to hold your hand" (Beatles, "I Want to Hold Your Hand") are both sweetened versions of social and personal closeness. Even the lyrics of the Stones' "Satisfaction" and The Who's "Squeeze Box" euphemistically suggest the sex act, drawing largely on the metaphor and allusion of the previous fifty years of popular music. Subverting the genre, indeed, epitomizing the notion of "subgenre," Heavy Metal made sex, not love. The lyrics here are blatant and often violent. The range of sexual conversation in even the early days of this music moves from the frank—again, the "Dazed and Confused" of *Zeppelin I* repeats, "Sweet little baby, I want you again"—to the outright bluntness of the third Zeppelin album (*Led Zeppelin III*) in "Whole Lotta Love": "Way down inside, woman, you need it. . . ." Coupled with the alternating short bass and guitar notes and Robert Plant's moaning, the sexual message could not be more clear or less softened by any euphemism of romance.

Like many others, Will Straw points out "an expression of violent sexuality" in Heavy Metal, but seeks to gloss over this overt sexual message by hurriedly noting that Heavy Metal's lyrics are often at the same time "explorations of nonromantic and nonerotic themes." It is precisely those "nonromantic and nonerotic themes" which surround the overtly sexual notations that cause Heavy Metal's sexuality to be, or to be received as, "subversive": when "Dazed and Confused" places the line "Sweet little baby, I want you again" in a series of lamentations on the unfaithfulness of women, the juxtaposition is, at the very least, paradoxical. The magnified range of sexual attention in Heavy Metal music should recall the sexual frankness of the Gothic's "School of Horror," of which M.G. Lewis' *The Monk* is only the most notorious example, in which Ambrosio, the monk, rapes and later murders his sister, with the help of Matilda, a young initiate of a Satanic order, who has dressed as a man to enter the monastery and "convert" Ambrosio. The monk's sexual exploits are made all the more "horrific" by placing them in the context of the monastery (appropriately, under the monastery in the labyrinthine dungeon).

More importantly, these subgenres are distinguished by their use of sex as a literal act rather than a metonymic expression of romantic love. If Rock music indeed takes part in what Bram Dijkstra calls an "aesthetic of sensuousness," as one could argue for the novel as well—an aesthetic that glorifies or at least takes as subject and object the physical, everyday activities of dancing, flirting, courting, marrying—then the subgenres of Heavy Metal and Gothic fiction take those barely-disguised and socially sanctioned euphemisms for sex and draw them from the "hidden" background into a surface of literal action. Of the staple Gothic theme of incest, for example, William Patrick Day has pointed out that "it was also an aspect of popular fiction, though the *threat* seems to have been more popular than the *actuality*" (emphasis added). This literal sexuality distinguishes the two subgenres not only from their parent genres, but also from the closely-related subgenres of "hard" Rock and the picaresque novel, both of which went directly for the sensuous throat, as did the Gothic novel and Heavy Metal, and refused the "communalism" implied in mainstream Rock's dance music format (e.g., the Beatles' "She Loves You") and the mainstream novel's insistence on societal values (e.g., Richardson's *Clarissa Harlowe*). These related subgenres *formally* rejected the communal values of the mainstream in much the same way as Heavy Metal and Gothic fiction rejected

the same popular forms, but the message of sexuality in hard Rock and the picaresque remained euphemized: Jethro Tull could produce a number like "Velvet Green," instrumentally and structurally diverse and as evocative of sexuality as any Heavy Metal band, but those evocative lyrics still came from the "lyric" tradition of suggestion ("Won't you have my company? / Yes, take it in your hand"); likewise, Moll Flanders may live and breathe in a loosely episodic universe, peopled by first one husband or lover after another (an important subgenre marker: one cannot always tell the difference), but the sex act itself is kept in the background, even though Moll can thrive, literally, only on sex (Defoe, *Moll Flanders*).

Gothic fiction's and Heavy Metal's making literal the act of sex is, as indicated in the previous plot summary of *The Monk,* frequently of a piece with Satanic subject matter, although the Satanic takes up a life of its own in both subgenres beyond its connection with the sexual. A healthy branch of Metal music is overtly Satanic, beginning popularly with Led Zeppelin's "The Battle of Evermore," from their untitled fourth album, and extending through Blue Oyster Cult's "Don't Fear the Reaper" to the lyrics of present-day Ozzie Osborn, former lead singer for Black Sabbath. The late 1960s was the beginning of outright Satanism in the Rock format, I should say, since the Devil has long been a powerful character in the Blues lyric, another ancestor of both mainstream Rock and Heavy Metal; this diabolical lineage has been noted by almost every critic to write on either the Rock genre or its Heavy Metal subgenre. The Blues lyrics of Leadbelly, Muddy Waters, Skip James, and particularly of Robert Johnson were filled with references to Satan, as in Johnson's line, "Hello, Satan, I believe it's time to go," to such a degree that the Blues became known as "Devil's music." These references continued to thrive in the later Zeppelin and other Heavy Metal lyrics, building up a myth of the Heavy Metal band as necessarily Satanic. The rumor of "backmasking" on "Stairway to Heaven" (*Led Zeppelin,* Untitled) supposedly designed to record the statement, "I worship you, my Satan," backward throughout the song, was no doubt spurred by this overarching myth of the Satanic within the Blues. It is especially interesting that the Satan-hunters felt it necessary to play "Stairway to Heaven" backward in search of the satanic message, when the song preceding it on the album, "The Battle of Evermore," constitutes an openly Satanic epic battle, even played forward.

As Pattison explains, however, the occult underpinnings of the Blues mythology as embraced by Heavy Metal bore only a marginal relationship to "reality"; in effect, occult references play on the already-established mythology in order to forge a sense of the subversive more than through any "real" belief in Satan or occult practices. Pattison argues that the players of both Rock and Heavy Metal are quite aware that their occult is a myth. To put it differently, the occult serves merely as a sign-system within which Satanic references signify, in one sense, only "subversion." What would be the point of an admittedly empty myth, then? To fly in the face of established—mass cultural—mythologies, just as Gothic fiction, particularly in its "school of horror" phase, attempted to supply a shock element to carve out an identity in contradistinction to, not simply as one variation upon, mainstream culture. As Peter Wicke notes, subcultures within "highly developed capitalism" may express "distance through excess." The "horror" of excess, regarding both genres, is best expressed in a news item retailed by Pattison as indicative of actual mass cultural response to the "cult" of Heavy Metal:

> In 1984, the *New York Daily News* ran an Associated Press story under the headline, "Satan-Rock Girl Murdered Mom": "A teenage girl who a prosecutor said was involved with her boyfriend in Satanism and heavy-metal rock music has been convicted of murdering her mother, former chairman of a group dedicated to stopping violence in the home." To make matters worse, her boyfriend "had orange hair."

The orange hair is the give-away: that the Associated Press found the boyfriend's hair color relevant speaks to consumer culture's deep fear of the subculture as it takes the subculture's bait. To some extent, this bait merely enforces "difference." It is in this respect that the two sub-popular forms under discussion represent "subgenre" *par excellence,* and here that they become more than just examples of generic behavior. The subgenre differs in kind from a "movement," such as Imagism in the early twentieth century, which differs from its parent genre, Modernism, only in degree. A movement lifts out a select number of the parent genre's characteristics, to magnify and elaborate those few characteristics. Alastair Fowler's definition of subgenre, in fact, more closely approximates what I see as the behavior of a movement: "such groups have a relatively simple logical relation [to the parent genre]: their features are more or less disjunct subsets of the sets of features characterizing kinds . . . external forms and all." The subgenre, I believe, while it is a "disjunct subset," is labelled "sub-" in the vernacular not without reason. It positively revolts against many of the parent form's "external forms," and in a sort of adolescent rage, pits itself against the very universe its parent inhabits, retaining only the family resemblance. Gothic fiction and Heavy metal epitomize this subgeneric behavior because they manifest the "sub-" in several conceptions: subversive, substandard, subliminal and, if one takes the parent genres' form as the "wellmade" standard, substandard. These two "Satanic" offspring go to great lengths to define and illustrate "difference," and further, a difference "beneath," hidden under the socially acceptable.

This difference, however, does not merely indicate the rebelliousness of youth (although it is that—remember that Lewis was eighteen when he wrote *The Monk*), nor does it merely signify "subversion," but more subtly implies a critique of the mainstream culture it exists within, a critique manifested in the very Satanism which appears to be a mythology emptied of its value. If the subculture, expressed through the subgenres of Heavy Metal and Gothic fiction, rebels through excess in a kind of parody of the mass movements surrounding it, its rebellion is of a deeply conservative nature, one which rejects the ideology that can take part so willingly in mass production and consumption. The now-commodified genres are ridiculed and rejected by their subgenres for the commodification itself,

for their own emptiness of value, while the subgenres Gothic fiction and Heavy Metal attempt to reinsert absolute value into the apparently value-less free-play of commodity consumption.

In effect, both Gothic fiction and Heavy Metal represent a return of the repressed—a once-again, newly repressed freedom of form and sexuality—emerging in the wake of supposedly revolutionary genres whose radicalism had become hegemonic manifestations of the larger culture and who, as a result, had lost their power to move.

—*Elizabeth Jane Wall Hinds*

Absolute value, in this case, is not positive or "religious," yet it does pretend to worship a deity, thereby subscribing to the concept of transcendence. This mythology reinscribes an essential value outside of, or prior to, the alternating currents of supply and demand which equate value with capital and makes valuable only that which sells, in what Dana Polan terms "a spectacle of superficiality." The absolute value asserted by these subgenres, then, can only be spiritual, and then only in the Emersonian sense, in which the nonmaterial is placed in the position of power. The devil positively causes destruction in the Gothic novel; and the devil is the source of energy in "The Battle of Evermore," as is Blake's Satan in *The Marriage of Heaven and Hell.* To be sure, this Satan does destroy—usually individual lives in the Gothic novel, sometimes entire civilizations in Heavy Metal lyrics—but its power is nevertheless spiritual, asserting itself against the Hallmark-card "spiritualism" of commodity culture, the one that pays lip-service to a God who likes everyone equally and wants "only the best" for everyone.

Through this "alternate" spirituality, the Satanic impulse bears out the remarkable ability of popular audiences to make meaning of those products presented as empty form, little more than advertising, whether the ad is for bourgeois moral virtues or for Reeboks. As Paul Willis writes,

> Though the whole commodity form provides powerful implications for the manner of its consumption, it by no means enforces them. Commodities can be taken out of context, claimed in a particular way, developed and repossessed to express something deeply and thereby to change somewhat the very feelings which are their product. And all this can happen under the very nose of the dominant class—and with their products.

To witness this active reinscription of the commodified into an alternate universe of spiritual, albeit retrograde, power, is to return some modicum of power to the otherwise passive receiver of popular genres: the young female of the late eighteenth century, reading novels in place of being educated, or the young male or female sitting in front of MTV.

So how far can we push the analogy between Gothic fiction of the eighteenth century and the Heavy Metal beginning in the late 1960s? Historically, the movements are entirely of a piece: both arose on the heels of new and hugely popular forms of cheap entertainment intended for the amusement of the masses. And as we have seen, both subgenres of those more popular, more widespread forms took shape by intensifying the focus of the parent-genres, by perverting the structure of the parent-genres through appeals to a lower order of sensibility and by making literal what was euphemized in the parent-genres. In effect, both Gothic fiction and Heavy Metal represent a return of the repressed—a once-again, newly repressed freedom of form and sexuality—emerging in the wake of supposedly revolutionary genres whose radicalism had become hegemonic manifestations of the larger culture and who, as a result, had lost their power to move.

Naturally, both Gothic fiction and Heavy Metal music succumbed to the very influences they initially set out to subvert. Naturally, that is, because both subgenres belong to already co-opted discourses, those parent-genres which exist, or existed in the past, only by virtue of participation in commercial culture. By definition, those co-opted discourses can be defined only in terms of their production/consumption matrix, what Mary Poovey describes, discussing Rock music, as the mutual dependence of the product with its advertisement. Fredric Jameson describes Rock music and Gothic fiction alike, in their popular natures, likewise as products of "late capitalism"; as "products," they may only produce subgenres that must finally grow into products as well, in order to survive in a consumer culture. Gothic fiction and Heavy Metal both became instant successes, so much so that as early as 1803 Jane Austen was to publish *Northanger Abbey,* the first widely-known parody of the Gothic form. Heavy Metal has likewise been parodied—most successfully in the 1984 Rob Reiner film *This Is Spinal Tap*—but has, more importantly, been imitated extensively and without variation, possibly more than any other Rock genre. As a result, popular Heavy Metal productions can be nearly indistinguishable from each other. At the same time, some of Heavy Metal's subversive impulse has cooled, resulting in the shortened form and euphemistic lyrics of its parent twenty years ago. A staple of the form has become, in fact, the love ballad, painfully sentimental and often as painfully self-referential, as with Bon Jovi's "Wanted, Dead or Alive," which chronicles the life of the suffering Heavy Metal band on the road. With its quickness to imitate its own form, Heavy Metal, like Gothic fiction, as quickly has ceased to be a subversive, energized genre, and has instead become both a subject of parody and a product of ravenous consumer appetite.

While Jameson's description of this process sheds light on both the nature of the subgenre and the nature of consumerism, it is in the weakness of his (and others'—I only take Jameson as a leading voice of ideological criticism) label "postmodernism" that we may discover the power of the subgenre as an activity. Jameson aptly describes the

"new" of any genre as "ugly, dissonant, bohemian, sexually shocking" to the prevailing bourgeois culture, noting simply that that newness, in becoming co-opted, ceases to shock and opens a space for a yet-newer genre to come along and make its noise. However, he goes on, the postmodern newness is of a different order; "it is not just another word for the description of a particular style." Jameson insists, in fact, that the postmodern is indeed what it sounds like: "a periodizing concept" which describes such a high degree of integration among production, product and consumption that it can take place only in the historical era of late capitalism. Which returns us to the question of Gothic fiction. If what I have argued is correct—that both Gothic fiction upon its first arrival and Heavy Metal Music are by definition subgeneric *because* they assert the transcendent spiritual against a prevailing commodification, and that they both succumbed to weakened stylization in capitulating to consumer demands—then what Jameson describes as "postmodern" cannot be a periodizing concept, rather, must be "the description of a particular style," since the first Gothic fiction arrived, not in a period of late capitalism, but during the boom years of emergent Western capitalism. The Gothic fiction Jameson refers to, in fact, is a "paraliterature" in his terminology, an "airport paperback category."

Jameson's Gothic fiction, it turns out, is not the historical Gothic fiction of this essay, but is instead a genre uprooted from its "periodized" moorings. Jameson's "airport Gothic" is the already co-opted product, already made imitative and already long past its prime; existing in the same culture as Heavy Metal music, this Gothic may indeed be a postmodern product, historically speaking. But the postmodern itself, pastiche in style, effacing of boundaries, particularly the boundaries of high-and mass-culture, and not least of all existing outside the categories of "art" and "taste"—this postmodernism, which Jameson among others insists results in a value-less culture of late capitalism, is precisely what I have described as "mainstream" culture against which the subgenre revolts. In other words, what Jameson has described as a late twentieth-century phenomenon was already emergent with capitalism itself, born with what Foucault has identified as a great epistemic upheaval in the late eighteenth century.

There are, of course, distinguishing features of postmodernism, in particular the species of "hyperspace" Jameson identifies in the postmodern "texts" of architecture and novel; I do not wish, therefore, to disempower the term altogether. I have attempted, instead, to re-historicize the discussion of commodity culture: to identify the *emergence* of two subgenres I see as absolutely dependent upon the economic conditions within which they have prevailed, and thereby to describe the nature of "subgenre" itself, as it exists and existed historically, rather than elide historical necessity with the theoretizing gaze that would telescope all manner of texts, both genre and subgenre, into the space of the postmodern, in spite of their varying historical "ages." What the Satanic subgenres do have in common, historically speaking, is their appearance during respective ages of cultural shift, at times of deep change which bring about a dual sense of belatedness and dread, an understanding that an "age" has passed and the new

Jimmy Page and Robert Plant of Led Zeppelin.

one is none other than chaos itself. As Raymond Williams argues in *The Country and the City,* there have been many ages of such shift, each of which views the just-passed age in its newly historicized or narrative form as unified in ideology and "whole" in the perception of its inhabitants. It matters little whether this deep change is "real," as we have been taught by Foucault to believe of the late eighteenth century, or perceived but untested, as we speculate about the late twentieth century. What matters is that the emergent subgenre, attempting to assert a "nostalgic" value, responds to what is perceived as chaos—the necessary chaos of the ongoing—by thrusting at it a spiritual power of destructive force. But rather than privilege our own age by calling this phenomenon postmodern, it might better be served under the label "the Henry Adams effect," for it was Adams who best described the vertigo of experience in an as-yet-unstoried present. At the Great Exposition of 1900, "his historical neck broken by the sudden irruption of forces totally new," Adams sounds like a guest of "postmodernism," come to remind us of history:

> armed with instruments amounting to new senses of indefinite power and accuracy, while they chased force into hiding-places where Nature herself had never known it to be, making analyses that contradicted being, and syntheses that endangered the elements. . . . In 1900 they were plainly forced back on faith in a unity unproved and an order they had themselves disproved. They had reduced their universe to a series of relations to themselves.

Neil Nehring

SOURCE: "The Shifting Relations of Literature and Popular Music in Postwar England," in *Discourse,* Vol. 12, No. 1, Fall-Winter, 1989-90, pp. 78-103.

[*In the following essay, Nehring relates the transformation of literary texts by subculture music groups in postwar England—specifically, the Rolling Stones' appropriation of Anthony Burgess's* A Clockwork Orange *and the Sex Pistols' resurrection of Graham Greene's* Brighton Rock—*to the avant-garde tradition in aesthetic theory, also discussing Colin MacInnes's documentation of the London music scene of the 1950s in his novel* Absolute Beginners.]

Peter Bürger's *Theory of the Avant-Garde,* looking back to Walter Benjamin and Bertolt Brecht, as well as Dada and Surrealism, describes the true purpose of the avant-garde as the eradication of "art as an institution." That institutional status resulted from specialization, in both the actual "productive and distributive apparatus" and the purveyance by artists, critics, and scholars of ideas about art in the abstract—particularly concerning its autonomy from social life. The avant-garde sought, by reintegrating art and social experience, to overthrow specialization; autonomy, both real and imagined, was merely the obverse of the alienation in bourgeois society that art purported to resist. Thus the concept of the "avant-garde" should not, as in popular parlance, refer to mere aesthetic innovation, especially not to the modernist effort to establish art's absolute autonomy from everyday life. The avant-gardist seeks just the opposite: the volatilizing "sublation," or indissoluble interpeneration, of art and the everyday. According to Bürger, this sublation involves, realistically, some mutual activity on the part of artistic producers and recipients. Bürger is fatalistic about the contemporary possibility of an avant-garde praxis, believing that commercial appropriations by mass culture have already eliminated the distinction between art and everyday life. The sharp dichotomy he draws between hermetic modernism and the avant-garde attack on the institution of art, however, is polemical well beyond refuting their equation in scholarship. Bürger's tendentiousness suggests advocacy of a potential avant-garde praxis, however dour his views of a present ruled by the familiar Frankfurt School monolith, the "culture industry," may be.

The subject of this essay—literature, popular music, and youth subcultures in postwar England—affords a strong example of just the avant-garde praxis Bürger champions but cannot detect (except in a spurious postmodern "neo-avantgarde"). The confluence of these cultural forms, moreover, restores not only the original dialectic of the avant-garde and mass culture—which Andreas Huyssen points out has subsequently been elided by scholarship—but also that of the avant-garde and anarchism, or antiauthoritarianism. During the period of the work of Colin MacInnes, Anthony Burgess, the Rolling Stones, and the Sex Pistols, 1958-78, subcultural groups arrived at a conscious understanding of the anarchistic possibilities in appropriating and recasting "high" art. Literature played a peripheral role, but one nonetheless highly suggestive for future avant-gardes, in the disruption and exposure of the power of the mass media to delimit "common sense." In their use of literature, moreover, youth subcultures indirectly undermined "cultural capital," in Pierre Bourdieu's terms, the elite academic fiat exercised in aesthetic value judgments on mass culture. Postwar English culture provided Raymond Williams with more than sufficient reason to assert, in *Marxism and Literature,* that "no dominant culture ever in reality includes or exhausts all human practice, human energy, or human intention," as embodied in "emergent," oppositional cultures.

The increasingly sophisticated use of literature in youth subcultures which formed around rock and roll music—specifically the mods and punks—confirms that oppositional cultural practice in everyday life has been and continues to be eminently realizable under late capitalism. The role of literature in English subcultural ensembles, however, has not been developed much in the "cultural studies" work on subcultural sociology associated with the University of Birmingham. But the literary connection serves all the more to confirm Dick Hebdige's linkage, almost a decade ago, of subcultural style and the avantgarde tradition, in *Subculture: The Meaning of Style.* Angela McRobbie has cited Hebdige's book as a solitary instance of a *positive* postmodernism, which "brings together art, literature, music, style, dress, and even attitude." That attitude is one of contumacy, or, more generally, negation, in the refusal of a static culture of consensus. The increasing sophistication of the forms of negation in youth subcultures over the postwar period, as a diachronic trajectory, presents an absolute reversal in the relations of "high" and "mass" culture, or literature and rock and roll music, including the subcultures formed around the music. If literature initially incorporates music and subcultures, the latter, ultimately, give literature a use-value either unintended, as in Burgess's case, or lost to scholarly obscurantism, as in Graham Greene's. Each synchronic stage in the presentation of this reversal between high and mass culture, accordingly, will itself move from literature, through music, to youth subcultures.

Benjamin had one great objective in mind when he argued, in the mid-thirties, for the "melting down" of hoary dichotomies like high and mass culture: the elimination of the distinction between artist (or performer) and audience. The point is to make every man and woman not necessarily an artist, but a critical thinker or "expert," at least, a person equipped to act on his or her world. Passing the tactics of Dada and Surrealism through the medium of Brecht, Benjamin sharpens the theory of montage, the technique that melts down cultural levels like "high" and "low." Montage, in the commonly understood sense, involves the juxtaposition of dissimilar cultural artifacts, a disruption of their conventional social (or antisocial) contexts. Unlike the products of specialized, alienated aesthetic practice (like modernism), with their pretense to a "closed, albeit 'complex' unity" or "organic whole," the *fragments* in montage, torn out of their original cultural context, challenge the "recipient to make [them] an integrated part of his or her reality." As an "interruption" of familiar experience, montage generates a shock—Benjamin's "shock-effect," or Brecht's "alienation-effect"—that provokes a potentially critical response from an audience, a heightened presence of mind, in Benjamin's

terms. Ideally, an audience forced to reevaluate its habits in receiving aesthetic texts might also begin to question its reception of ideas and images beyond the particular cultural event.

"The Author as Producer," the high point of Benjamin's essays derived from Brecht's work, provides the seminal definition of these radical, genuinely *avant-garde* aims. The essay specifies the dual understanding of montage that has come to be known as the Benjamin-Brecht position. In somewhat the traditional sense of montage, Benjamin argues that literary forms must be "melted down" with new technologies in mass culture, by directly employing innovations the latter make possible. But he pushes the understanding of montage beyond the provocative amalgamation of diverse forms, in insisting that an individual text—whether filmic, literary, musical, or theatrical—must strive in its *own* form to generate interruption. Shock, in other words, can result not just from linkage with other forms, but in learning from and emulating their formal possibilities. The author-as-*producer* understands his or her work in "the context of living social relations," specifically "literary production relations" and their constraints, and will look to other means of cultural production and reproduction for sources of "technical innovation." Emergent culture, says Raymond Williams, "depends crucially on finding new forms or adaptations of form." (The reference to "adaptations" suggests precisely the commonality of avant-garde montage and youth subcultures.) Benjamin and Brecht were not promoting yet another modernist formalism; Benjamin simply recognizes that revolutionary content presented in a familiar form, and hence easily appropriated by mainstream culture, is futile. The only truly radical aim is the "functional transformation" of the relevant cultural production apparatus—quite sensibly, "within the limits of the possible."

Such functional transformation has a very specific implication: the form of a text innervates the content in the same sense that the text prompts the recipient (Brecht's "expert") to make use of it, when provoked to engage it in further social activity, now as a producer in his or her own right. This dual melting down—of form and content, reception and production—occurs in the first instance, for example, *within* Graham Greene's *Brighton Rock;* in the second instance in the Sex Pistols' appropriation of the novel. First, the attitude of negation, the essential response (in socially engaged, not autonomous form) to reified social life, suffuses Greene's work; his novel's references to "vitriol" thus designate simultaneously both form, or style, and content alike. Second, as the novel's employment by the Sex Pistols illustrates, that vitriol has resonated through further *productive* use of the novel, in a sense provoking or enabling the subsequent relation to social practice. The *formal* practice of montage, then, whether the "interruption" created by Greene's own style or the subsequent appropriation of his text, is "a stimulus to change one's conduct of life," to "search for *meaning*" [Burger]. The audience's own reception and use of a variety of cultural artifacts and texts, finally, would be tantamount to the avant-garde work's employment or emulation of the techniques it finds at hand.

288

Terry Eagleton, in *Walter Benjamin, or Towards a Revolutionary Criticism,* defines a "revolutionary literary criticism" in terms that reflect, naturally, the work of Benjamin. But what might be noted in the following is the presence of the language of Raymond Williams in the invocation of "cultural practices" and "social activity." In the unstated influence of Williams, along with the explicit debt to Benjamin, Eagleton's tenets suggest the meeting ground of cultural studies and the tradition of the avant-garde. A revolutionary literary criticism, he says,

> would dismantle the ruling concepts of "literature," reinserting "literary" texts into the whole field of cultural practices. It would strive to relate such "cultural" practices to other forms of social activity, and to transform the cultural apparatuses themselves. . . . It would deconstruct the received hierarchies of "literature" and transvaluate received judgments and assumptions; engage with the language . . . of literary texts . . . and mobilize such texts . . . in a struggle to transform . . . a wider political context.

This program not only summarizes both "The Author as Producer" and the project of cultural studies, but also, moreover, suits quite well the subcultural appropriations of literature in postwar England.

The contemporary torchbearer of the avant-garde tradition in aesthetic theory has been the field of cultural studies, which emerged from the Centre for Contemporary Cultural Studies at the University of Birmingham in the mid-seventies, under the tutelage of Stuart Hall. As opposed to traditional elitist, text-bound scholarship, cultural studies recognizes the simple fact that audiences make their own, sometimes quite subversive meanings (though more often just the opposite) out of music, television, and commodities in general. This humane realization reflects very specifically the "culturalist" legacy of Williams (along with E.P. Thompson and Richard Hoggart). At the center of Williams's work, Hall has pointed out, is an emphasis on volatile, coexistent "dominant, residual and emergent [or oppositional] cultural practices." And in this domain of meaning-formation and expression, Williams argues, literature and art (including the definition of what these terms presumably exclude) cannot be separated from other social practices—a view corresponding with that of the avant-garde. The humanism of the culturalist approach, Hall says, lies in its materialism, an *"experiential pull"* emphasizing creative, "sensuous human praxis, the activity through which men and women make history."

Hall has been, like Williams, an ardent proponent of Gramsci's theory of hegemony because it emphasizes concrete, continual processes of struggle, rather than theorizing in the abstract about totalitarian cultural and political discourse—a pessimism characteristic of most academic theories of postmodernism, which Hall excoriates. Richard Johnson, the current director of the Centre, specifies that cultural consumption in everyday life is also "a production process, in which the [original] product becomes a material for fresh labour" by its audience: "The text-as-produced is a different object from the text-as-read." (This

point will be most evident in the deviant uses of *A Clockwork Orange.*) Thus Johnson insists that critical approaches concerned primarily with texts and their producers only highlight "the separation between specialist critics and ordinary readers," listeners, or viewers. A current example of the cultural studies approach is the work of Iain Chambers, who asserts that "Change and transformation can no longer be considered as something to be injected into the 'false' world from elsewhere, [but as] a question of inflection, emphasis and direction inside the continuing construction of everyday experience and the conditions we inherit." Meaghan Morris notes, however, the tendency of recent work in cultural studies to celebrate simple pluralism, merely the existence of complex contradictions in mass culture. She strenuously emphasizes that "unambivalently discontented, or *aggressive*" subjects, instead, should be the primary concern. It is important to note that a *feminist* critic makes this point about aggression, just as it is McRobbie who cites the importance of (what one would assume is a similar) "attitude" in subcultural style: though the issues of "aggressive" subcultural resistance and gender—including the failings of English cultural studies on this account—require another study altogether, the almost exclusively male voices of the subjects that follow here should be understood to be *universally* suggestive for subordinate groups engaged in avant-garde praxis. The argument of cultural studies in every case, in its properly radical form, is much like that in "The Author as Producer": the artist, critic, or teacher should aim to transform the cultural apparatuses with which he or she lives and works, not simply to supply them.

Especially now that cultural studies has become an academic growth industry in the United States, it is vital to preserve its emphasis on transforming cultural production and reception by linking it with a longer revolutionary aesthetic tradition. The central concern of Hebdige's *Subculture: The Meaning of Style,* for example, is precisely the avant-gardist elimination of the distance between audience and performance in youth subcultures formed around rock and roll music. In punk, as Hebdige and many others have pointed out, the audience's creative involvement in forming the style frequently led its members into making the music itself. The impetus to eradicate barriers to performance in punk, just as Benjamin would have it, was *style,* the formal embodiment of Refusal as shock-effect, or "noise" (visual more than aural, in Hebdige's reading). Though punk still exercises a considerable influence on a new generation of rebels struggling to find a requisite form of expression, and its impact is still felt in many ways in music itself, punk is commonly regretted as a momentary success. Hebdige nonetheless champions that moment, "the fact of transformation" of various cultural apparatuses, akin to that promoted by Benjamin. Punk expressed "a fundamental tension between those in power and those condemned to subordinate positions," and thus merits recovery as a suggestive model for future efforts at Refusal, not consignment to the dustbin of futile postmodern cultural resistance. Hence McRobbie wrote more recently, with regard to the spate of scholarship on the postmodern period, that "So far only Dick Hebdige . . . has broken out of [the] reproduction of the old divide between high culture and the pop arts"; she notes that Hebdige has since disavowed "the more playful elements of *Subculture*," in reaction against postmodern commercial celebration of an "*excess of style.*" Simon Frith points out that "*Subculture* has, after all, long been essential reading for ad agencies, too," and describes the head of MTV waving a copy of the book and claiming to be a "subcultural force." Hebdige, however, continues to believe in "the living textures of popular culture" as a means to "*effectively* contest . . . authority," eschewing "purely theoretical analysis." Without work in cultural studies like Hebdige's, finally, the subversive transformation of literary texts in postwar England, in subcultural ensembles composed of a variety of expressive forms and commodities, would be difficult if not impossible to apprehend, let alone appreciate.

Benjamin's point about the significance of formal innovation is important, more specifically, because the melting down of literature and popular music in postwar England is not simply a matter of acting on similarities in content. Swinging London did not appropriate Anthony Burgess's *A Clockwork Orange,* nor did the punk bohemians resurrect Greene's *Brighton Rock,* simply because both novels concern teenage hoodlums. In each case, instead, the avant-gardists in question acted on deep affinities in *style* (or form), finding, in literary language, an amplification of the musical voices around which the subcultures formed. Colin MacInnes, however, in *Absolute Beginners,* mocked the working-class voice of the Teddy Boys, the first, relatively inarticulate subcultural style in the postwar period, who were unequipped to respond to such calumny. Thus his attempt to document the rock and roll scene founders in puerility precisely because of his concerted effort to de-class youth culture, in accordance with the hegemonic dominance in the 1950s of the ideology of affluence, and its myths of classlessness and consensus. Burgess actively despised the youth culture he perceived in the so-called castrato-rock of the late fifties and early sixties, and has since excoriated all youth culture. But the Rolling Stones, in the mid-sixties the focal point of the mod subculture—and also part of the rock and roll renaissance based on the bohemianism of English art colleges—gave Burgess's novel a resonance that entirely subverted its intentions. Greene's appropriation by the former art-school radicals behind the Sex Pistols represents the most sophisticated, theoretically informed act of montage here: a neglected avant-garde classic was recovered from the margins of the literary academy, and restored to its rightful pride of place among works of rebellion.

Absolute Beginners is a literary landmark not for any avant-garde impulse, but simply for MacInnes's unique, exuberant interest in the popular music scene. The novel does embody some central features and problems of postmodernist literature, especially in its professed attempt at "documentary" fiction. David Lodge identifies in postmodern writing a short-circuiting of clear relations between the text and the world, in a tendency to intermingle fact and fiction; MacInnes not only documents the London music scene through characters allegorizing different tendencies in music and fashion, but also centers the novel on the Nottingham riots of 1958, which occurred as he was writing. Lodge also refers to postmodernism as a liter-

ature of "excess," and MacInnes's enthusiasm, reflected in his attempt at teen argot (not much more evident than a quasi-Holden Caulfied tone), does sometimes verge on hysteria. His ideal of a classless youth culture, an abdication of social and historical meaning characteristic of much postmodernist writing, can apparently be advanced only through sheer shrillness. And what replaces social class as the significant factor in teenage culture, for MacInnes, is the essence of postmodern cultural experience generally—consumerism. Given this quietism, he naturally found a wide audience, pretty much defining the teenager for England.

MacInnes applauds the fashion in Italian clothing (vaguely predating the mod subculture) that appeared as the Ted subculture waned, neurotically citing its cleanliness—and classlessness—in his essays (collected in *England, Half English*), and conferring it on the novel's narrator. The Teddy Boys, economically empowered by the postwar increase in employment and wages, had come up with an amalgam of Edwardian-revival fashion, the long drape-jacket, and the attire of the Western Gambler in Hollywood films, including satin lapels, shocking colors, and bootlace ties. Relatively unintentionally, the Teds subverted the former's designs on an upper-class clientele, while more deliberately employing the latter, symbolic of the outsider. The Teds preferred American rock and roll—Elvis Presley, Jerry Lee Lewis, Eddie Cochran, and Buddy Holly—a harder music than anything available in England. In these early incarnations, the American music was very much a working-class form, even more so when passed through the traditional English awareness of "Us and Them." MacInnes—who wrote admiringly on Tommy Steele, the first ersatz Presley in England—always took the standard tack of F.R. Leavis, widespread among members of the literary elite in the 1950s, that "Americanization" is an unmixed evil. But, worst of all to MacInnes, the Teds asserted the continuing existence of the working class, despite the new "affluence" summed up in Harold Macmillan's famous line, "You've never had it so good." MacInnes singles out the speech of Ed the Ted for phonetic rendering, to emphasize the moronism of anyone bearing traces of the traditional working-class: " 'Yer'll be earing frm me agen, an ver lads.' "

While the Teds were defined less by their own lights than by sensationalist news media, they do merit some credit for refusing (or ignoring, at least) the hegemonic notion that the significance of social class was disappearing. Their sense of territoriality, in particular, traditional in delinquent "street corner" gangs, either resisted or at least contradicted the perceived break-up of working-class neighborhoods by new tower-block housing. The myth of affluence, on the other hand, is evident not only in MacInnes's work, but also in that of the Angry Young Men (though none were as convinced of "affluence" as MacInnes), especially John Wain's *Hurry on Down* and John Osborne's *Look Back in Anger,* both virtually nostalgic for the certainties of the old class system. The Teds, in contrast, hardly had their "springs of action" unbent by mass culture, hardly experienced the "sensation without commitment" cited by Hoggart (the founder of Birmingham's Centre for Contemporary Cultural Studies) in his nostalgic study of working-class culture, *The Uses of Literacy.* Hoggart has actuality entirely reversed, in describing the "spiritual dry-rot" of the "Juke-Box Boys," living "in a myth-world compounded of a few simple elements which they take to be those of American life." As subsequent cultural studies work has shown, it was precisely the use of American film and music, and their very distance, that enabled the Teds to express at least an imaginary, symbolic resistance to the drabness of their working lives. Rioting in movie theaters while Bill Haley played "Rock around the Clock" in the film *Blackboard Jungle,* they would seem to have escaped the suasion of "You've never had it so good." The Teds' dogged grasp on traditional working-classness, however, did include a large dollop of racism, and they deserve some degree of execration for their participation in the '58 race riots. To MacInnes's own credit, he recognized that the mass media had a great deal to do with enflaming racism—one of the novel's strengths is his dark satire on editorialists fueling the outbreak, and then blithely finding scapegoats elsewhere.

MacInnes, however, never links that scapegoating to the Teds; buying into the general panic over the Ted "folk devil," his novel insists on its insipid thesis that a utopian, classless teenage culture was imminent. The worst moments in the novel, in this respect, occur when the narrator ignores as irrelevant blather his father's memories of the Depression. MacInnes renders that historical memory quite compellingly, but only to signal all the more its anachronistic pathos: " 'You've simply no idea what the pre-war period was like,' " the father says. " 'Poverty, unemployment, fascism and disaster and, worst of all, no chance, no opportunity.' " The narrator's response is " 'hard cheese.' " Contemporary social realities fare no better, even though MacInnes offers acute portrayals of London slums: "huge houses too tall for their width cut up into twenty flatlets, and front facades that it never pays anyone to paint, and broken milk bottles *everywhere* scattering the cracked asphalt roads like snow . . . and a strange number of male urinals tucked away such as you find nowhere else in London, . . . and diarrhoea-coloured street lighting—man, I tell you, you've only got to be there for a minute to know there's something radically wrong." He even describes the evident line between the "blue murder" in the Napoli slums, during the race riots, and the peace and calm of the middle-class world of "What's my line? and England's green and pleasant land." Despite, however, the existence of continuing economic misery, MacInnes seems grotesquely compelled to deny the existence of social inequity: "my Lord, how horrible this country is, how dreary, how lifeless, how blind and busy over *trifles,*" he writes, in a revealingly empty conclusion to his own contrast of "glamour people" and "peasant masses." Finally, not surprisingly, MacInnes delivers a laughable dismissal of Marxism, suggesting that it lives "*outside*" history," loftily unresponsible for dealing with events like the Nottingham riots, unlike the narrator (and MacInnes himself, who apparently thought at the time that he had single-handedly averted further trouble by stuffing leaflets in mailboxes). The dismissal of Marxism is practically compelled by the ahistoricism of his views on class relations; the novel's riot is broken up by a utopian combination of spirited young aristocrats, hip de-

classed teenagers, and adventurous television personalities.

The biases in MacInnes's musical taste, and in his attribution of tastes to others, correspond quite directly with his apolitical quietism. The novel's Marxist, Ron Todd, due to his anachronistic preoccupation with folk cultures and class authenticity, favors black rhythm'n'blues—which would in actuality provide the musical basis of British rock and roll in the sixties. MacInnes is not unjustified, however, in announcing the death of rock and roll in *Absolute Beginners;* the novel opens on the subject of an actual singer, Laurie London, only fourteen years old, whose puerile gospel hit "He's Got the Whole World in His Hands" was one of the low points in the period of "castrato-rock." That period, lasting until the emergence of the Beatles and Rolling Stones in 1962-63, was dominated by conservative producers who carefully controlled and marketed an ersatz youth music. In the belief that packaging is everything, they gave eminently safe performers Dickensian names like Wilde, Furey, Faith, Eager, Storm, Quickly, and so forth. Each element of a song like Marty Wilde's "Bad Boy," from the soothing, barely projected vocal to the lazy, sliding, country-and-western guitar, devotes itself to the essential formal quality, languor. The lyrical content makes the whole aim abundantly apparent: Wilde begs to differ with parents and members of the public-at-large who might find him threatening: "If only they knew how I love you / They'd say a bad boy / Could be a good boy / Who's just in love."

But MacInnes's own musical advocacy hardly has a very different end in mind. He champions jazz, his taste very much in the vein of the American Beat writers (Ginsberg, Kerouac, Mailer) and their "White Negro" affectation; *City of Spades,* the first novel in MacInnes's London trilogy, evidences his patronizing, sometimes lascivious views on race. In *Absolute Beginners,* jazz is, to him, above all else properly classless. Not only is it untainted by social origin (in his view, as if race could be left behind)—"no one, not a soul, cares what your class is" in a jazz club—but, moreover, it evokes a properly soothing euphony. His fictional versions of Count Basie and Ella Fitzgerald, Czar Tudie and Maria Bethlehem, give a concert that leads the narrator to gush "you'd really be astonished how these fans will all sit and *listen.*" If the salient quality of jazz and its audience is, in other words, *passivity,* one wonders why Laurie London is objectionable. While MacInnes makes astute points about the manufacture and promotion of musical pabulum by the culture industry, and the possibility of songs written on English, not mid-Atlantic subjects (a proposition not realized fully until the punk movement), his paternalistic, quietistic attitude towards the youth-culture audience betrays the limited extent of his own rebelliousness: he could shock simply by writing about popular music in the first place.

MacInnes bitterly resented, and not without some reason, the fact that Burgess's *A Clockwork Orange,* published in 1962, was made into a highly successful film. (Julien Temple's recent film of *Absolute Beginners,* his first project after making *The Great Rock Rock'n'Roll Swindle* for the Sex Pistols, appeared nine years after MacInnes's death in

1976.) Burgess has essentially acknowledged the influence of MacInnes's attempt at a teenage argot, which Burgess realizes more successfully by not even attempting authenticity, instead creating his "nadsat-talk" out of derivations from Russian. Burgess also profited from the strong example of Alan Sillitoe's young, anarchistic narrator in *The Loneliness of the Long-Distance Runner,* published, like *Absolute Beginners,* in 1959. MacInnes might instead have resented that his own well-intended parody of the pop music scene becomes, in Burgess's Tory hands, entirely contemptuous satire of its subject. The descriptions of the music, performers, and audience emphasize only one quality, their "yarbleless"-ness, or castration—an accurate enough characterization, though only barely preceding the revival of rock and roll in Liverpool and London. The "MELODIA disk-bootik" in *A Clockwork Orange* features "eunuchs" like "Johnny Burnaway" and "Lay Quiet Awhile with Ed and Id Molotov," the latter typifying the russification of nadsat-culture and England altogether, to Burgess the logical end of the social-welfare state and the cultural levelling visited by a more pervasive mass culture. In this cultural elitism, in particular, Burgess stands at the endpoint of the "Angry Decade": the earlier Angry Young Men were in fact more preoccupied with mass culture and its pacifying, homogenizing effect (as perceived from Leavis's standpoint), than with class. And, finally, though MacInnes presents some addled contradictions on the subject of history, all in the service of describing the new youth culture, Burgess very deliberately dramatizes an entirely ahistorical thesis, in which his youthful subject is a mere pawn, an excrescence.

Alex's affinity for music, Beethoven in particular, serves a pedantic Tory thesis on the cyclical nature of society and history, one far more abstract than any concern with youth subculture. The behavioral conditioning ("Ludovico's Technique") undergone by Alex, which removes his capacity not only for evil but also for moral choice altogether, inadvertently makes Beethoven's symphonies unbearable to him. Thus, Burgess intends us to see, excess, soulless social planning destroys the individual, leaving the mechanical (the clockwork) while eradicating the natural and organic (the orange). To the psychotherapists, the Ninth Symphony is only " 'a useful emotional heightener,' " rather than a "glimpse of heaven," as Alex, but more accurately Burgess (in a number of his works) puts it. According to Burgess's historical schema, elaborated in *The Wanting Seed* and *1985* in particular, Alex lives in a period known as Pelphase, one of three continually, cyclically revolving historical phases. The others are Gusphase and Interphase, the latter the period of transition between the two dominant views of the world Burgess reads off the Pelagian heresy. Briefly put, Pelagius believed man had a free will, and thus could achieve salvation through his own efforts; St. Augustine insisted on the inherent depravity of mortal man, and the mystery of divine grace. Thus Pelphase occurs when a society tries to engineer, to any great degree, social cooperation and community, or even simply to *help* its subjects. This argument is obviously intellectual window-dressing for attacking social democracy; Burgess appears in retrospect a mundane Conservative, *A Clockwork Orange* a satire on contemporary England—especially its youth culture—rather than an exercise in futurism. The ideal of Gusphase would more than likely be laissez-faire capitalism, as opposed to the social-welfare state—let alone the vaguely socialist, apparently Soviet-dominated society in the novel. And in general, as with all cyclical theories of history, social activity is implicitly futile.

Understandably, then, Alex only apparently participates in a youth subculture, but in the final analysis seems quite solitary from it. He is clearly distinguished by his love of classical music, use of Elizabethan speech (" 'Come, gloopy bastard as thou art' "), and theological meditations—"the not-self cannot have the bad, meaning they of the government . . . cannot allow the bad because they cannot allow the self "—all of which render him quite superior to nadsat-culture. The nadsat-talk, which at times has as powerful a sputum as the "poetry of the body" Burgess found in Sillitoe—"tolchock some old veck in an alley and viddy him swim in his blood"—is mere contrivance, a style disjunct from the novel's content. Burgess has recently, in fact, disavowed not only the novel, but specifically—and even more disingenuously—its style as well, as a mere "curtain . . . to muffle the raw response we expect from pornography." His novel is now distasteful to him because of its reputation as a quasi-anarchist text; his sympathies never lay with his "thuggish young protagonist," whom he compels to "grow up" to recognize "that human energy is better expended on creation than destruction." In this last choice of phrase, Burgess is clearly the polar opposite of the likes of Benjamin and Greene, who in the essay "The Destructive Character" (1931) and in the short story "The Destructors" (1954), respectively, both revived the great thesis of the anarchist Michael Bakunin: "the urge to *destruction* is also a *creative* urge." Benjamin understands this destructiveness as that of avant-garde montage—see the concept of *détournement* developed below—while Greene allegorically links destruction directly to subcultural youth groups. This "destructive" form of creativity lies precisely in the appropriation of *A Clockwork Orange* into the mod movement, which gave the visceral style in the novel—a mere "curtain" to Burgess—a life he apparently never intended, and would never have conceded a youth subculture could create. In *1985,* published in 1978 during the heyday of punk, Burgess describes youth cultures in terms redolent of an anachronistic obsession with the sixties counterculture (very much as Allan Bloom has more recently), concluding that they offer only a "bland sense of alienation . . . with no need of stressing alienation through aggression." Like Hoggart's analysis of the passivity of the Teddy Boys, Burgess's elitist blindness leads him to a conclusion diametrically opposed to reality.

The paradoxical transmission of *A Clockwork Orange* as some sort of document of rebellion, which it most certainly is not, clearly has nothing to do with Burgess. Its reputation has come about in part because of the notoriety of Stanley Kubrick's film, which has continued to show up, in various forms, in subcultural youth styles in Great Britain. Burgess disavows it to some extent, seemingly unable to stomach his own subject given any kind of flesh (which explains in part his minimizing of the novel's style as a "curtain"), though the film is quite faithful to the novel. To a lesser extent, the novel's reputation wasn't hurt by the excision (until recently) of the last chapter in the American edition, which has Alex settled down in front of the television. Burgess, at any rate, has certainly traded considerably on his reputation as, in his words, "the god-father of punk." The persisting misconstruction of *A Clockwork Orange,* however, might be partially attributed to its appropriation and subversion by Swinging London, a moment of something like montage.

What happened to the novel now appears a first vague step towards the "revolutionary" use of literature defined by Eagleton: the reinsertion of a literary text into the whole field of cultural practices, with relation to other forms of social activity. For despite the art-school background of some of the principal figures in Swinging London's music scene—and the art colleges continued to be the source of bohemianism and/or avant-gardism in English rock and roll, their influence peaking with punk—the melting down of literature, music, and everyday life appears to have been relatively spontaneous and untheorized. The appropriators of *A Clockwork Orange* were the Rolling Stones of 1964-65, the high point of the mod subculture. Returning to writing from the sixties on the Stones reveals that Mick Jagger's mock-Cockney accent, and their generally slovenly appearance and behavior, by pop music standards, had distinct *working class* connotations, as odd as that role seems in light of their subsequent career. The most pronounced class overtones, however, occurred in their skein of misogynist songs, taken in England as expression of a class revenge of sorts. The entirety of "Play with Fire" concerns class:

> Your mother she's an heiress,
> Owns a block in St. John's Wood,
> And your father'd be there with her,
> If he only could.
> Your old man took her diamonds,
> And tiaras by the score.
> Now she gets her kicks in Stepney,
> Not in Knightsbridge anymore.

At the same time, guitarist Keith Richards said in the seventies, the Stones went through a *Clockwork Orange* phase in their private and public behavior. Rock writer Nik Cohn likewise testifies that producer-manager Andrew Loog Oldham made the group "read *Clockwork Orange* . . . and soon they began to live out its style. They broke up restaurants [and] went out of their way to slag off everyone and everything." Pictures of the group demolishing baby carriages may have Edward Bond's notorious play *Saved* (1965) in mind as well—or Bond, perhaps, had the Stones in mind as models for his degraded working-class youths. The clearest, most widely known indication of the Stones' *Clockwork Orange* period is to be found in Oldham's liner notes, on *The Rolling Stones Now!,* which mimic the *Clockwork* style quite well, and with as much or more malchick threat: "It is the summer of the night London's eyes be tight shut all but . . . six hip malchicks who prance the street. . . . This is THE STONES new disc within. Cast deep in your pockets for loot to buy this disc of groovies and fancy words. If you don't have bread, see that blind man knock him on the head, steal his wallet and low and behold you have the loot, if you put it in the boot, good, another [record] sold!"

Considering the conspicuousness of this use of Burgess, and the centrality of the Rolling Stones in the mod subculture (as recorded by George Melly in *Revolt into Style*), it seems fair to assume that the mods were well aware of the novel.

Burgess himself repeats, in lectures, the legend that he sold the Stones the film rights to *A Clockwork Orange* for $1000 during the famous period of rapid output in which he mistakenly believed he was terminally ill. They supposedly made a quarter-million dollars on the resale of the film rights to Kubrick. Since Oldham admitted in the late seventies to having made up the whole story, this particular matter serves very well to amplify Burgess's indifference to the subject of youth cultures (except as a means for self-promotion) and to history generally. Another damaging error of the same ilk occurs when he misremembers, in *1985,* writing *A Clockwork Orange* for the unimpeachable purpose of counteracting talk of drugging or otherwise conditioning mods and rockers. But those subcultural groups only appeared in the popular press two years after he published the novel; in fact, these suggestions occurred in the fifties, concerning the Teds. The mistake suggests just how little interest Burgess had in the issue at the time as it pertained to youth culture—for him, there was simply a philosophical point to be made.

The mod subculture, like the Rolling Stones, represented an indirectly coded workingclassness in its feverish consumption of high-fashion Italian suits, Chelsea boots, motor-scooters, and amphetamines. The calculated subversiveness of mod style—exceedingly well-groomed but only all the more threatening—lies in the contradiction the mods expressed, allegorically, in their very persons (the essence of subcultural style). Their attitude, a deliberately incomprehensible air, emulated that of black West Indians, just as the Rolling Stones passed black r'n'b through the English awareness of "Us and Them." (The Teddy Boys pre-existed the influx of West Indian immigrants, and thus experienced them as an alien presence.) Like the detailed, brilliant but opaque appearance of a West Indian type like the rude boy (or rudie), mod style was a highly visible but still "private code." The opulence of the mods was in fact an inversion of sharp dress, pushing neatness to the point of absurdity, as Hebdige has pointed out. Their finery belied their actual social status: their money came from dead-end employment in service jobs, such as clerical work. (The Teds expressed, with less sophistication, essentially the same contradiction between work and leisure, the contradiction Hoggart couldn't see, discerning a concomitant oppression in both realms.) The mods, in addition, specifically emulated the appearance of the new, up-scale gangster that appeared with the liberalizing gaming laws of the sixties. That further caricature of traditional capitalism provided the outsider image every working-class youth subculture has sought. The mods, in their vanity and arrogance, celebrated the fact that no one controlled them, opposing traditional frugality with conspicuous consumption, but with an implicit, traditional working-class awareness of domination and control in labor. *A Clockwork Orange* obviously suits very well the noon-day (and weekend) underground described by Tom Wolfe in *The Pump House Gang.* But the Rolling

Stones and the mod subculture brought the novel's ethos of "ultraviolence" to life—the film *Quadrophenia* depicts the nighttime pack-hunting for trouble, and seaside battles with the rockers in 1964—with a purpose and capability Burgess would never allow a youth culture.

Besides the music itself, and its intrusion of an angry working-class voice—better described as an anarchistic, antiauthoritarian tone—into the dominant communications media, punk's noise included the whole ensemble of clothing and other objects that comprised its visual style.

—Neil Nehring

While the appropriation of *A Clockwork Orange* entirely recast a work antipathetic to any youth culture or subculture, not to mention progressive aesthetics and politics, the use of Greene's *Brighton Rock* (1938) in the milieu of punk rock amounts to a revival of a genuinely avant-garde text submerged by the literary canon. Though the punks rejected the Rolling Stones as "boring old farts" (fair enough by the mid-seventies), the Sex Pistols' career of outrage certainly paralleled, and intensified, that of the early Rolling Stones, right down to appropriations from literature. The Sex Pistols' entourage, reflecting, perhaps, the widespread perception of the onset of a new Depression in the mid-seventies, appropriately rediscovered the vitriolic social resentment of Greene's novel, published during the Great Depression. The rage of Greene's character Pinkie Brown suits punk very well: "An awful resentment stirred in him—why shouldn't he have had his chance like all the rest, seen his glimpse of heaven if it was only a crack between the Brighton walls."

Besides the music itself, and its intrusion of an angry working-class voice—better described as an anarchistic, antiauthoritarian tone—into the dominant communications media, punk's noise, as Hebdige suggests, included the whole ensemble of clothing and other objects that comprised its visual style. The subversion of a variety of commodities, like safety-pins stuck through the nose, was its own form of disturbance and disruption of the dominant culture—"noise," but ultimately coherent. Hebdige, following John Clarke, describes the punk ensemble as the most sophisticated example of *bricolage* in the postwar period, in its relocation of a wide range of objects and activities into a new discourse, from plastic trashbags and leather and bondage clothing to homemade "fanzines" and violent anti-dancing like the pogo. More deliberately than preceding subcultures, the punks engaged, in essence, in an avant-gardist reassembly of cultural "fragments" into montage. The coherence of that ensemble lies in a parody of the dominant social discourse in the mid-seventies, the "rhetoric of crisis" that accompanied economic collapse; punk encouraged and satirized mass-media images of de-

praved youth. Punk thus affords the clearest sense of the significance of youth subcultures in postwar England: their function has been not just to resist or disrupt the hegemonic framing of social discourse, the delimiting of the "natural" and "common sense," but also—with increasing sophistication—to *expose* the cultural processes through which the consciousness-forming apparatus sets that agenda, by inviting its manipulation of wrath and hysteria.

Another critical voice, that of Dave Laing, complemented Hebdige's work on punk by closely analyzing style in the musical texts themselves. The ideal of cultural studies, as expressed in Richard Johnson's essay, should be this sort of confluence between analyses of audiences and of texts (even if it occurs across different studies). In somewhat parallel fashion, "The Author as Producer" emphasizes first the "living social relations" invoked by the literal practice of montage, as in the misappropriation and juxtaposition of artifacts on which Hebdige concentrates. Benjamin's further suggestion is that *interruption* might also be generated by the individual text or performance itself, especially through the stylistic possibilities opened up by new cultural technologies. Laing points out that punk rock, as music, restored an awareness that the basic technology involved in making phonograph records did not at all require lavish recording studios, and the backing of vast sums from multinational corporations. Virtually any small recording studio could become the home of an independent record label, and some (such as Rough Trade) flourished, relatively speaking. Nor is any special musical ability essential to rock and roll; punk gave the lie in particular to the "opulence and grandeur" of art-rock, and its asocial, plutocratic "aesthetic of artistic excellence."

Laing's analysis of the amplified working-class *voice* in punk rock, however, provides the exemplary instance of Benjamin's full sense of interruption. Laing uses, in fact, the concept of the "shock-effect," found in Benjamin's famous essay on mechanically reproduced art, to describe a disruption of "bourgeois hegemony" in the cultural sphere by an alternative way of speaking. The voice of Johnny Rotten of the Sex Pistols, or Joe Strummer of the Clash, represented "within a public communications medium a form of expression which previously was merely the object of media reproach ('obscene' chants at football matches, etc.)." By interrupting the "tone of voice [of] Standard English and its musical-vocal equivalents," punk assailed passive, uncritical responses to music. Thus through forms "undigested by the leisure apparatus," punk sought to generate Benjamin's " 'orientation of the expert,' " which might lead the audience to make active connections between [the music and] other areas of social practice." The less documented part of the ensemble that made up punk style is literature. The bohemians and former art-school radicals behind the Sex Pistols, the profane focal point of English punk in 1976-77, understood that literary language, as well, can set up a noise that refuses authority. Thus Fred and Judy Vermorel used *Brighton Rock* in a biographical montage called *The Sex Pistols: The Inside Story.*

The aesthetic theory under which the organization overseen by the group's manager Malcolm McLaren operated, as did the manager of The Clash, Bernard Rhodes, and the group Gang of Four, came from a trans-European but predominantly French group, the Situationist International. The Situationists, who emerged in the mid-fifties, aspired to correct, through direct anarchist action, the failed Surrealist intent to make people face their real desires and act on them. (The Surrealists were condemned for their devotion to psychic automatism, too haphazard a method.) They cited Brecht at the outset, interestingly enough, as the only artist remotely approaching their ambitions. The seminal Situationist text is Guy Debord's *Society of the Spectacle*, relatively well-known in academia for its critique of an image-dominated, passivity-inducing culture, but virtually never cited as a revolutionary document with its own theory of directly political montage, or *détournement*. This omission reflects the book's real threat: published in 1967, read by college students and young workers, it played a significant role in the May Revolution of 1968, during which Situationist slogans decorated the walls of Paris. In legend, at least, McLaren was present for those events, even an acquaintance of student leader Daniel Cohn-Bendit; in any case, he seems to have acquired some sense for the potency of a meeting of bohemia and working-class youth. The Situationists dissolved in the collapse of the May revolt, but their influence persisted in England throughout the seventies (see Howard Brenton's play *Magnificence*). The cover of the Sex Pistols' single "Holidays in the Sun," for example, features two typical works of *détournement* done by McLaren's cohort Jamie Reed, which earlier appeared in Christopher Grey's English anthology *Leaving the 20th Century*. One is an advertisement supplied with banal captions ("nice young lady"), the other an insertion of the song's lyrics, clichés from European economic and political discourse, in the balloons of a saccharin cartoon-advertisement for a Belgian travel agency.

The practice of *détournement*, roughly translatable as diversion, combines texts of all sorts, from contemporary mass media and political theory to institutionalized art, with the intention of a directly radicalizing effect. The purpose is not mere appropriation and reassembly of extant artifacts and texts in a "new coherence," but a *jolt*, a *profane* interruption of "everyday experience and expectation in such a way that people are forced to confront the familiar from an altered perspective." The distinction from montage lies in the definiteness of Situationist aims: in general, the generation of shock should create a "situation" by exposing and/or exploding the spectacle, or orderly cultural consumption. Rather than defamiliarizing the everyday on the model of its subconscious rearrangement in dreams, as in Surrealism, *détournement* contests a society "organized as appearance" precisely in that same field: "What mattered was the puncturing of appearance—speech and action against the spectacle." Thus *détournement* amounts to a "revolution of consumption," says Edward Ball. "The premise: politics is in part the problem of the use or reading of objects." Hence Debord may critique the spectacle, but never rules out the potential use-value of mass-culture artifacts and texts. The specific distinction of *détournement* from montage, in fact, lies in its emphasis on undermining cultural hierarchies in order to bring into play *both* traditional forms and mass culture.

The *détournement* of *Brighton Rock*, accordingly, serves first to illuminate the Sex Pistols' creation of situation, their assault on spectacle by playing to the hilt the role of degraded modern youth; second, as an act of literary recovery. Greene's bitter, throwaway lines of verse—"a dim desire for annihilation stretched in him: the vast superiority of *vacancy*"—clarify, in the Vermorels' book, a song like "Pretty Vacant." Just as Greene is scarcely a simple nihilist, but addresses instead a symptom of social deprivation, the song proves not nihilism, as nearly everyone takes it, but rather a parody of spectacular images of depraved youth. "Pretty Vacant," in fact, directly addresses the spectacle: "I don't believe illusions / When too much isn't real / So stop your cheap comment / 'Cause we know that we feel." The point of the collective effort behind the Sex Pistols' brief career was to expose the essential fraud of everyday life, by fomenting outrage and mercilessly exploiting the resulting media hysteria. Provocation would cause the general manipulations of the spectacle to appear, the entire array of images that comprises a specious, reified ideology of passive consumption. Cursing on television (the appearance of the Sex Pistols on Bill Grundy's chat-show, a national scandal in 1976, making their reputation in one minute), widely reported indecencies of all sorts, themes of anarchy as self-rule, and the unprecedented musical voice of working-class rage—all invited the mass audience to consider the impact of the entertainment and information apparatuses. That most people failed to get the joke was evident; after the release of the scabrous "God Save the Queen" (in 1977, the Queen's Silver Jubilee year) and a torrent of media reproach, Johnny Rotten and other members of McLaren's organization were viciously attacked more than once by ostensible patriots. But, as Benjamin says, one does what one can within the limits of the possible (hopefully without suffering physical assault as a result). If punk was a momentary and limited success, it nonetheless remains an exemplary model, the point of the sort of recovery practiced by cultural studies. Punk can instruct, to use Richard Johnson's terms, *both* "text-based studies," addressed to "avant-garde practitioners, critics, and teachers," and "research into lived cultures . . . upholding the ways of life of subordinated social groups."

By recovering *Brighton Rock*, McLaren's group of English Situationists realized precisely the effect of the more specific facet of *détournement*, its assault on cultural hierarchy, a "subversion of past critical conclusions which were frozen into respectable truths, namely transformed into lies." The resurrection of the novel reminds us that Greene, in the 1930s, wrote intensely angry, anarchistic prose; he was in fact an avant-garde artist with a keen interest in everyday life, especially that of society's victims, and its culture, especially popular music. *Brighton Rock* contains a complex allegory interwoven between theological, social, and cultural planes, at each level redeeming profane, degraded subjects. Catholicism becomes a subcultural, oppositional emblem linked with a working-class misery; the crime that victimization by poverty breeds appears as legitimate social revenge ("nobody could say he hadn't done right to get away . . . to commit any crime"); and popular music, finally, solely and persistently evokes what articulation of anger Pinkie can manage. Greene's use of popular song, even more extensive than in the work of other thirties writers like W.H. Auden and Louis Mac-Niece, can certainly be considered a species of montage, not only melting down the antinomy of high and mass culture, but doing so with clearly aggressive, discontented results. The protopunk Pinkie feels the "catgut" of stringed instruments "vibrating in his heart," as a suitably violent song of Greene's own creation—"The gangsters gunning / Talk of our love"—conveys a desperate conclusion: "life held the vitriol bottle and warned him: I'll spoil your looks. It spoke to him in the music." The song's connotation seems not dissimilar to the Sex Pistols' widely popular chorus "No future for you" in "God Save the Queen." Greene's great metaphor for both the style and content of his novel, that bottle of vitriol, certainly represents a common ground with the punks. The "lie" about Greene, fostered by quietistic scholarship (with the notable exception of Bernard Bergonzi), holds him as a minor novelist generally, his thirties fiction his lesser work, and Catholicism his chief thematic concern. Instead, Greene's own acute awareness of boredom and resentment leads him to a vision of the punk future: Rose, Pinkie's child-bride, imagines their "child . . . and that child would have a child . . . it was like raising an army of friends for Pinkie. If They damned him and her, They'd have to deal with them, too." If Greene's prescience here only arguably foreshadows the subsequent history of youth subcultures, one might look to the anarchist short story of 1954, "The Destructors," very likely inspired by the Teddy Boys, to find an allegory quite directly suited to the entire postwar period.

The English Situationist recovery of *Brighton Rock* fully realizes Eagleton's description of a revolutionary literary criticism, not only in its reinsertion of the novel into the whole field of cultural practices and social activities, but in its correcting of received judgments and, above all, in its deconstruction of received hierarchies. If there is anyone who still questions whether ostensibly distinct levels of high and popular culture might be legitimately melted down—and it is certainly still possible to have execration heaped on one's head for suggesting it—the relations of literature and rock music in postwar England must surely lay objection to rest. The reversal in these relations between 1958 and 1978 indicates a thoroughgoing embroilment of the different forms: initially those in the literary world condescend to evaluate music and its social significance; ultimately, in remarkably short order, music teaches the former about *their* enterprise, both its past and its possibilities.

Richard Shusterman

SOURCE: "The Fine Art of Rap," in *New Literary History,* Vol. 22, No. 3, Summer, 1991, pp. 613-32.

[*In the following essay, Shusterman praises rap music as a postmodern form of high art that challenges such modernist aesthetic conventions as originality, autonomy, integrity, rationalization, and secularization.*]

> . . . rapt Poesy,
> And arts, though unimagined, yet to be.
> —Shelley, *Prometheus Unbound*

In the view of both the culturally elite and the so-called general public, rap music lurks in the underworld of aesthetic respectability. Though it is today's "fastest growing genre of popular music" [Jon Pareles, *New York Times,* January 14, 1990], its claim to artistic status has been drowned under a flood of abusive critique. Rap has not only suffered moral and aesthetic condemnations but also organized censorship, blacklists, arrests, and the police-enforced stopping of concerts. Moreover, on a different level of cultural combat, we find attempts to dilute and undermine rap's ethnic and political content by encouraging and exploiting its most bland, "sanitized," and commercialized forms. None of this should be surprising. For rap's cultural roots and prime following belong to the black underclass of American society; and its militant black pride and thematizing of the ghetto experience represent a threatening siren to that society's complacent status quo. The threat is of course far more audible and urgent for the middle-brow public who not only interact more closely and competitively with the poor black population, but who rely on (and thus compete for) the same mass-media channels of cultural transmission, and who have a greater need to assert their sociocultural (and ultimately political) superiority over black America.

Armed with such powerful political motives for opposing rap, one can readily find aesthetic reasons which seem to discredit it as a legitimate art form. Rap songs are not even sung, only spoken or chanted. They typically employ neither live musicians nor original music; the sound track is instead composed from various cuts (or "samples") of records already made and often well known. Finally, the lyrics seem to be crude and simple-minded, the diction substandard, the rhymes raucous, repetitive, and frequently raunchy. Yet, as my title suggests, these same lyrics insistently claim and extol rap's status as poetry and fine art.

In this paper I wish to examine more closely the aesthetics of rap or "hip hop" (as the cognoscenti often call it). Since I enjoy this music, I have a personal stake in defending its aesthetic legitimacy. But the cultural issues are much wider and the aesthetic stakes much higher. For rap, I believe, is a postmodern popular art which challenges some of our most deeply entrenched aesthetic conventions, conventions which are common not only to modernism as an artistic style and ideology but to the philosophical doctrine of modernity and its differentiation of cultural spheres. By considering rap in the context of postmodern aesthetics, I hope not only to provide academic aestheticians with a better understanding of this much maligned but little studied genre of popular art. I also hope to enhance our understanding of postmodernism through the concrete analysis of one of its unique cultural forms.

Postmodernism is a vexingly complex and contested phenomenon, whose aesthetic consequently resists clear and unchallengeable definition. Nonetheless, certain themes and stylistic features are widely recognized as characteristically postmodern, which is not to say that they cannot also be found to varying degrees in some modernist art.

These characteristics include: recycling appropriation rather than unique originative creation, the eclectic mixing of styles, the enthusiastic embracing of the new technology and mass culture, the challenging of modernist notions of aesthetic autonomy and artistic purity, and an emphasis on the localized and temporal rather than the putatively universal and eternal. Whether or not we wish to call these features postmodern, rap not only saliently exemplifies them, but often consciously highlights and thematizes them. Thus, even if we reject the whole category of postmodernism, these features are essential for understanding rap.

APPROPRIATIVE SAMPLING

Artistic appropriation is the historical source of hip-hop music and still remains the core of its technique and a central feature of its aesthetic form and message. The music derives from selecting and combining parts of prerecorded songs to produce a "new" soundtrack. This soundtrack, produced by the DJ on a multiple turntable, constitutes the musical background for the rap lyrics. These in turn are frequently devoted both to praising the DJ's inimitable virtuosity in sampling and synthesizing the appropriated music, and to boasting of the lyrical and rhyming power of the rapper (called the MC). While the rapper's vaunting self-praise often highlights his sexual desirability, commercial success, and property assets, these signs of status are all presented as secondary to and derivative from his verbal power.

Some whites may find it difficult to imagine that verbal virtuosity is greatly appreciated in the black urban ghetto. But sociological study reveals it is very highly valued there; while anthropological research shows that asserting superior social status through verbal prowess is a deeply entrenched black tradition which goes back to the griots in West Africa and which has long been sustained in the New World through such conventionalized verbal contests or games as "signifying" or "the dozens." Failure to recognize the traditional tropes, stylistic conventions, and constraint-produced complexities of Afro-American English (such as semantic inversion and indirection, feigned simplicity, and covert parody—all originally designed to conceal the real meaning from hostile white listeners) has induced the false belief that all rap lyrics are superficial and monotonous, if not altogether moronic. But informed and sympathetic close reading will reveal in many rap songs not only the cleverly potent vernacular expression of keen insights but also forms of linguistic subtlety and multiple levels of meaning whose polysemic complexity, ambiguity, and intertextuality can sometimes rival that of high art's so-called "open work."

Like its stylized aggressively boasting language, so rap's other most salient feature—its dominant funky beat—can be traced back to African roots, to jungle rhythms which were taken up by rock and disco and then reappropriated by the rap DJs—musical cannibals of the urban jungle. But for all its African heritage, hip hop was born in the disco era of the mid-seventies in the grim ghettos of New York, first the Bronx, and then Harlem and Brooklyn. As it appropriated disco sounds and techniques, it undermined and transformed them, much as jazz (an earlier black art of appropriation) had done with the melodies of popular songs. But in contrast to jazz, hip hop did not take mere melodies or musical phrases, that is, abstract musical patterns exemplifiable in different performances and thus bearing the ontological status of "type entities." Instead it lifted concrete sound-events, prerecorded token performances of such musical patterns. Thus, unlike jazz, its borrowing and trans-figuration did not require skill in playing musical instruments but only in manipulating recording equipment. DJs in ordinary disco clubs had developed the technique of cutting and blending one record into the next, matching tempos to make a smooth transition without violently disrupting the flow of dancing. Dissatisfied with the tame sound of disco and commercial pop, self-styled DJs in the Bronx reapplied this technique of cutting to concentrate and augment those parts of the records which could provide for better dancing. For them

> the important part of the record was the break—the part of a tune in which the drums took over. It could be the explosive Tito Puente style of Latin timbales to be heard on Jimmy Castor records; the loose funk drumming of countless '60s soul records by legends like James Brown or Dyke and the Blazers; even the foursquare bass-drum-and-snare intros adored by heavy metal and hard rockers like Thin Lizzy and the Rolling Stones. That was when the dancers flew and DJ's began cutting between the same few bars on the two turntables, extending the break into an instrumental [David Toop, *The Rap Attack: African Jive to New York Hip Hop;* hereafter cited as *RA*].

In short, hip hop began explicitly as dance music to be appreciated through movement, not mere listening. It was originally designed only for live performance (at dances held in homes, schools, community centers and parks), where one could admire the dexterity of the DJ and the personality and improvisational skills of the rapper. It was not intended for a mass audience, and for several years remained confined to the New York City area and outside the mass media network. Though rap was often taped informally on cassette and then reproduced and circulated by its growing body of fans and bootleggers, it was only in 1979 that rap had its first radio broadcast and released its first records. These two singles, "Rapper's Delight" and "King Tim III (Personality Jock)," which were made by groups outside the core rap community but which had connections with the record industry, provoked competitive resentment in the rap world and the incentive and example to get out of the underground and on to disc and radio. However, even when the groups moved from the street to the studio where they could use live music, the DJ's role of appropriation was not generally abandoned and continued to be thematized in rap lyrics as central to the art.

From the basic technique of cutting between sampled records, hip hop developed three other formal devices which contribute significantly to its sound and aesthetic: "scratch mixing," "punch phrasing," and simple scratching. The first is simply overlaying or mixing certain sounds from one record to those of another already playing. Punch phrasing is a refinement of such mixing, where the

DJ moves the needle back and forth over a specific phrase of chords or drum slaps of a record so as to add a powerful percussive effect to the sound of the other record playing all the while on the other turntable. The third device is a wilder and more rapid back and forth scratching of the record, too fast for the recorded music to be recognized but productive of a dramatic scratching sound which has its own intense musical quality and crazed beat.

These devices of cutting, mixing, and scratching give rap a variety of forms of appropriation, which seem as versatilely applicable and imaginative as those of high art—as those, say, exemplified by Duchamp's mustache on the Mona Lisa, Rauschenberg's erasure of a De Koonig canvas, and Andy Warhol's multiple re-representations of prepackaged commercial images. Rap also displays a variety of appropriated content. Not only does it sample from a wide range of popular songs, it feeds on classical music, TV theme songs, advertising jingles, and the electronic music of arcade games. It even appropriates nonmusical content, such as media news reports and fragments of speeches by Malcolm X and Martin Luther King.

Though some DJs took pride in appropriating from very unlikely and arcane sources and sometimes tried to conceal (for fear of competition) the exact records they were sampling, there was never any attempt to conceal the fact that they were working from prerecorded sounds rather than composing their own original music. On the contrary, they openly celebrated their method of sampling. What is the aesthetic significance of this proud art of appropriation?

First, it challenges the traditional ideal of originality and uniqueness that has long enslaved our conception of art. Romanticism and its cult of genius likened the artist to a divine creator and advocated that his works be altogether new and express his singular personality. Modernism with its commitment to artistic progress and the avantgarde reinforced the dogma that radical novelty was the essence of art. Though artists have always borrowed from each other's works, the fact was generally ignored or implicitly denied through the ideology of originality, which posed a sharp distinction between original creation and derivative borrowing. Postmodern art like rap undermines this dichotomy by creatively deploying and thematizing its appropriation to show that borrowing and creation are not at all incompatible. It further suggests that the apparently original work of art is itself always a product of unacknowledged borrowings, the unique and novel text always a tissue of echoes and fragments of earlier texts.

Originality thus loses its absolute originary status and is reconceived to include the transfiguring reappropriation and recycling of the old. In this postmodern picture there are no ultimate, untouchable originals, only appropriations of appropriations and simulacra of simulacra; so creative energy can be liberated to play with familiar creations without fear that it thereby denies itself the opportunity to be truly creative by not producing a totally original work. Rap songs simultaneously celebrate their originality and their borrowing. And as the dichotomy of creation/appropriation is challenged, so is the deep division between creative artist and appropriative audience; transfigurative appreciation can take the form of art.

CUTTING AND TEMPORALITY

Rap's sampling style also challenges the work of art's traditional ideal of unity and integrity. Since Aristotle, aestheticians have often viewed the work as an organic whole so perfectly unified that any tampering with its parts would damage the whole. Moreover, the ideologies of romanticism and art for art's sake have reinforced our habit of treating artworks as transcendent and virtually sacred ends in themselves, whose integrity we should respect and never violate. In contrast to the aesthetic of organic unity, rap's cutting and sampling reflects the "schizophrenic fragmentation" and "collage effect" characteristic of the postmodern aesthetic [Fredric Jameson, *New Left Review,* Vol. 146, 1984, hereafter cited as *NLR*]. In contrast to an aesthetic of devotional worship of a fixed untouchable work, hip hop offers the pleasures of deconstructive art— the thrilling beauty of dismembering (and rapping over) old works to create new ones, dismantling the prepackaged and wearily familiar into something stimulatingly different.

The DJ's sampling and the MC's rap also highlight the fact that the apparent unity of the original artwork is often an artificially constructed one, at least in contemporary popular music where the production process is frequently quite fragmented: an instrumental track recorded in Memphis, combined with a back-up vocal from New York, and a lead voice from Los Angeles. Rap simply continues this process of layered artistic composition by deconstructing and differently reassembling prepackaged musical products and then superimposing the MC's added layer of lyrics so as to produce a new work. But rap does this without the pretense that its own work is inviolable, that the artistic process is ever final, that there is ever a product which should be so fetishized that it could never be submitted to appropriative transfiguration. Instead, rap's sampling implies that an artwork's integrity as object should never outweigh the possibilities for continuing creation through use of that object. Its aesthetic thus suggests the Deweyan message that art is more essentially process than finished product, a welcome message in our culture whose tendency to reify and commodify all artistic expression is so strong that rap itself is victimized by this tendency while defiantly protesting it.

In defying the fetishized integrity of artworks, rap also challenges traditional notions of their monumentality, universality, and permanence. No longer are admired works conceived in Eliotic fashion as "an ideal order" of "monuments" timelessly existing and yet preserved through time by tradition. In contrast to the standard view that "a poem is forever," rap highlights the artwork's temporality and likely impermanence: not only by appropriative deconstructions but by explicitly thematizing its own temporality in its lyrics. For example, several songs by BDP include lines like "Fresh for '88, you suckers" or "Fresh for '89, you suckers." Such declarations of date imply a consequent admission of datedness; what is fresh for '88 is apparently stale by '89, and so superseded by a new freshness of '89 vintage. But, by rap's postmodern aesthetic, the ephemeral freshness of artistic creations does not render them aesthetically unworthy; no more than the ephemeral freshness of cream renders its sweet taste unreal. For the view that aesthetic value can only be real if it passes the test of time is simply an entrenched but unjustified presumption, ultimately deriving from the pervasive philosophical bias toward equating reality with the permanent and unchanging.

The devices of cutting, mixing, and scratching give rap a variety of forms of appropriation, which seem as versatilely applicable and imaginative as those of high art—as those, say, exemplified by Duchamp's mustache on the Mona Lisa, Rauschenberg's erasure of a De Koonig canvas, and Andy Warhol's multiple re-representations of prepackaged commercial images.

—*Richard Shusterman*

By refusing to treat art works as eternal monuments for permanent hands-off devotion, by reworking works to make them work better, rap also questions their assumed universality—the dogma that good art should be able to please all people and all ages by focusing only on universal human themes. Hip hop does treat universal themes like injustice and oppression, but it is proudly localized as "ghetto music," thematizing its commitment to the black urban ghetto and its culture. While it typically avoids excluding white society (and white artists), rap focuses on features of ghetto life that whites and middle-class blacks would rather ignore: pimping, prostitution, and drug addiction, as well as rampant venereal disease, street killings, and oppressive harassment by white policemen. Most rappers define their local allegiances in quite specific terms, often not simply by city but by neighborhood, like Compton, Harlem, Brooklyn, or the Bronx. Even when rap goes international, it remains proudly local; we find in French rap, for example, the same targeting of specific neighborhoods and concentration on local problems.

Though localization is a salient characteristic of the postmodern breakdown of modernism's international style, rap's strong local sense is probably more the product of its origins in neighborhood conflict and competition. As Toop notes, hip hop helped transform violent rivalries between local gangs into musical-verbal contests between rapping crews (*RA*). By now it is difficult to point to sharp stylistic differences between the music of the different locales, though more Los Angeles rappers seem less concerned with black militancy and white oppression than their brothers in New York. Of course, local differences are hard to maintain once the music begins circulating through the mass-media system and is subjected to its commercializing pressures. For such reasons, rap lyrics often complain about its commercial expansion just as they celebrate it.

TECHNOLOGY AND MASS-MEDIA CULTURE

Rap's complex attitude toward mass circulation and commercialization reflects another central feature of postmodernism: its fascinated and overwhelming absorption of contemporary technology, particularly that of the mass media. While the commercial products of this technology seem so simple and fruitful to use, both the actual complexities of technological production and its intricate relations to the sustaining socioeconomic system are, for the consumer public, frighteningly unfathomable and unmanageable. Mesmerized by the powers technology provides us, we postmoderns are also vaguely disturbed by the great power it has over us, as the all-pervasive but increasingly incomprehensible medium of our lives. But fascination with its awesome power can afford us the further (perhaps illusory) thrill that in effectively employing technology, we prove ourselves its master. Such thrills are characteristic of what Jameson dubs the "hallucinatory exhilaration" of the "postmodern or technological sublime" (*NLR*).

Hip hop powerfully displays this syndrome, enthusiastically embracing and masterfully appropriating mass-media technology, but still remaining unhappily oppressed and appropriated by that same technological system and its sustaining society. Rap was born of commercial mass-media technology: records and turntables, amplifiers and mixers. Its technological character allowed its artists to create music they could not otherwise make, either because they could not afford the musical instruments required or because they lacked the musical training to play them (*RA*). Technology constituted its DJs as artists rather than consumers or mere executant technicians. "Run DMC first said a deejay could be a band / Stand on its own feet, get you out your seat," exclaims a rap by Public Enemy. But without commercial mass-media technology, the DJ band would have had nothing to stand on.

The creative virtuosity with which rap artists have appropriated new technology is indeed astounding and exhilarating, and it is often acclaimed in rap lyrics. By acrobatically juggling the cutting and changing of many records on multiple turntables, skillful DJs showed their physical as well as artistic mastery of commercial music and its technology. From the initial disco equipment, rap artists have gone on to adopt more (and more advanced) technologies: electronic drums, synthesizers, sounds from calculators and touchtone phones, and sometimes computers which scan entire ranges of possible sounds and then can replicate and synthesize the desired ones.

Mass-media technology has also been crucial to rap's impressively growing popularity. As a product of black culture, an essentially oral rather than written culture, rap needs to be heard and felt immediately, through its energetically moving sound, in order to be properly appreciated. No notational score could transmit its crazy collage of music, and even the lyrics cannot be adequately conveyed in mere written form, divorced from their expressive rhythm, intonation, and surging stress and flow. Only mass-media technology allows for the wide dissemination and preservation of such oral performance events. Both through radio and television broadcasting and through the recording media of records, tapes, and compact discs, rap has been able to reach out beyond its original ghetto audience and thus give its music and message a real hearing, even in white America and Europe. Only through the mass media could hip hop become a very audible voice in our popular culture, one which middle America would like to suppress since it often stridently expresses the frustrating oppression of ghetto life and the proud and pressing desire for social resistance and change. Without such systems rap could not have achieved its "penetration to the core of the nation" (Ice-T) or its opportunity to "teach the bourgeois" (Public Enemy). Similarly, only through the mass media could hip hop have achieved artistic fame and fortune, its commercial success enabling renewed artistic investment and serving as an undeniable source of black cultural pride.

Rap not only relies on mass-media techniques and technologies, it derives much of its content and imagery from mass culture. Television shows, sports personalities, arcade games, and familiar name-brand commercial products (for example, Adidas sneakers) are frequently referred to in the lyrics, and their musical themes or jingles are sometimes sampled; a whole series of rap records was based on the Smurf cartoons. Such items of mass-media culture help provide the common cultural background necessary for artistic creation and communication in a society where the tradition of high culture is largely unknown or unappealing, if not also oppressively alien and exclusionary.

But for all its acknowledged gifts, the mass media is not a trusted and unambiguous ally. It is simultaneously the focus of deep suspicion and angry critique. Rappers inveigh against its false and superficial fare, its commercially standardized and sanitized but unreal and mindless content. "False media, we don't need it, do we? It's fake," urge Public Enemy, who also lament (in "She Watch Channel Zero") how standard television shows undermine the intelligence, responsibilities, and cultural roots of black women. Rappers are constantly attacking the radio for refusing to broadcast their more politically potent or sexually explicit raps, and instead filling the air with tame "commercial pap" (BDP). "Radio suckers never play me," complain Public Enemy, a line which gets sampled and punch phrased by Ice-T in an eponymous rap condemning the radio and the FCC for a censorship which denies both freedom of expression and the hard realities of life so as to insure the continuous media fare of "nothin but commercial junk." Scorning the option of a "sell-out," Ice-T raises (and answers) the crucial "media question" troubling all progressive rap: "Can the radio handle the truth? Nope." But he also asserts the reassurance that even with a radio ban he can reach and make millions through the medium of tapes, suggesting that the media provides its own ways of subverting attempts at regulatory control: "They're makin' radio wack, people have to escape / But even if I'm banned, I'll sell a million tapes."

Finally, apart from their false, superficial content and repressive censorship, the media are linked to a global commercial system and society which callously exploits and oppresses hip hop's primary audience. Recognizing that those who govern and speak for the dominating technological-commercial complex are indifferent to the enduring woes of the black underclass ("Here is a land that never gave a damn about a brother like me . . . but the suckers had authority"), rappers protest how our capitalist society exploits the disenfranchised blacks both to preserve its sociopolitical stability (through their service in the military and police) and to increase its profits by increasing their demand for unnecessary consumer goods. One very prominent theme of hip hop is how the advertised ideal of conspicuous consumption—luxury cars, clothes, and high-tech appliances—lures many ghetto youth to a life of crime, a life which promises the quick attainment of such commodities but typically ends in death, jail, or destitution, thus reinforcing the ghetto cycle of poverty and despair.

It is one of the postmodern paradoxes of hip hop that rappers extol their own achievement of consumerist luxury while simultaneously condemning its uncritical idealization and quest as misguided and dangerous for their audience in the ghetto community to which they ardently avow their solidarity and allegiance. In the same way, self-declared "underground" rappers at once denigrate commercialism as an artistic and political sell-out, but nonetheless glorify their own commercial success, often even regarding it as indicative of their artistic power. Such contradictions are perhaps expressive of the postmodern fragmentation of the self into inconsistent personae, but they may be equally expressive of more fundamental contradictions in the sociocultural fields of ghetto life and so-called noncommercial art. Certainly there is a very deep connection in Afro-American culture between independent expression and economic achievement, which would impel even noncommercial rappers to tout their commercial success and property. For, as Houston Baker so well demonstrates, Afro-American artists must always, consciously or unconsciously, come to terms with the history of slavery and commercial exploitation which forms the ground of black experience and expression. As slaves were converted from independent humans to property, their way to regain independence was to achieve sufficient property of their own so as to buy their manumission (as in the traditional liberation narrative of Frederick Douglass). Having long been denied a voice because they were property, Afro-Americans could reasonably conclude "that *only* property enables expression." For underground rappers, then, commercial success and its luxury trappings may function essentially as signs of an economic independence which enables free artistic and political expression, and which is conversely also enabled by such expression. A major dimension of this celebrated economic independence is its independence from crime.

ECLECTICISM, HISTORY, AND AUTONOMY

I have already mentioned the wide-ranging eclecticism of rap's appropriative sampling, which extends even to nonmusical sources. Its plundering and mixing of past sources has no respect for period, genre, and style distinctions; it cannibalizes and combines what it wants with no concern to preserve the formal integrity, aesthetic intention, or historical context of the records it plunders, absorbing and transforming everything it cuts and takes into its funky collage.

Rap historian David Toop gives a sense of this wild eclecticism: "Bambaataa mixed up calypso, European and Japanese electronic music, Beethoven's Fifth Symphony and rock groups like Mountain; Kool DJ Here spun the Doobie Brothers back to back with the Isley Brothers; Grandmaster Flash overlayed speech records and sound effects with The Last Poets; Symphonic B Boys Mixx cut up classical music on five turntables" (*RA*).

Perhaps more than any other contemporary art form, rap not only exemplifies but proudly thematizes the eclectic pastiche and cannibalization of past styles that is central to the postmodern. Some, like Jameson, regret this "random cannibalization of all the styles of the past" (*NLR*) and its unprincipled "play of random stylistic allusion" (*NLR*) for its disintegration and derealization of a coherent and real past, one which might otherwise be retrieved to help us better understand our problematic present and guide us toward a more liberated future. For Jameson, postmodernism's eclectic "historicism effaces history" (*NLR*). Instead of "real history" and "genuine historicity" (*NLR*), the organic reconstruction of "some putative real world" (*NLR*), we are supplied with nostalgia, a jumble of stereotypical images from an imagined past. We are thus confined to the prisonhouse of ideological representations, "condemned to seek History by way of our own pop images and simulacra of that history, which itself remains forever out of reach" (*NLR*) and hence unavailable as a source for political critique and liberation.

But the whole idea of real history, the one true account of a fully determinate past whose structure, content, and meaning are fixed and unrevisable, is itself a repressive ideological construction and a vestige of absolute realism which cannot compel much conviction in our age of postfoundationalist philosophy. Neither the past nor the present is ever purely given or reported; they are always selectively represented and shaped by discursive structures reflecting dominant interests and values, which are often simply those of the politically dominant. In being historicized, history is not so much lost but pluralized and openly politicized, instead of having its implicit political agenda concealed under the guise of neutral objectivity where it cannot be challenged or even recognized as political. History, objectively and univocally conceived, is a metaphysical naturalization of *his*-story, the story of "The Man"—the term black culture uses to denote not only the police but the dominating, oppressive white male society which controls and polices the institutions of cultural legitimacy, including the writing and teaching of history. A fascinating feature of much underground rap is its acute recognition of the politics of culture; its challenge of the univocal claims of white history and education; and its attempt to provide alternative black historical narratives which can stimulate black pride and foster emancipatory impulses. Such alternative narratives extend from biblical history to the history of hip hop itself, which is thus con-

stituted and valorized as a phenomenon worthy of historical testimony and documentation.

If rap's free-wheeling eclectic cannibalism violates high modernist conventions of aesthetic purity and integrity, its belligerent insistence on the deeply political dimension of culture challenges one of the most fundamental artistic conventions of modernity: aesthetic autonomy. Modernity, according to Weber and others, was bound up with the project of occidental rationalization, secularization, and differentiation which disenchanted the traditional religious worldview and carved up its organic domain into three separate and autonomous spheres of secular culture: science, art, and morality, each governed by its own inner logic of theoretical, aesthetic, or moral-practical judgment. This tripartite division was of course powerfully reflected and reinforced by Kant's critical analysis of human thinking in terms of pure reason, practical reason, and aesthetic judgment.

In this division of cultural spheres, art was distinguished from science as not being concerned with the formulation or dissemination of knowledge, since its aesthetic judgment was essentially nonconceptual and subjective. It was also sharply differentiated from the practical activity of the realm of ethics and politics, which involved real interests and appetitive will (as well as conceptual thinking). Instead, art was consigned to a disinterested, imaginative realm which Schiller later described as the realm of play and semblance. As the aesthetic was distinguished from the more rational realms of knowledge and action, it was also firmly differentiated from the more sensate and appetitive gratifications of embodied human nature—aesthetic pleasure residing, rather, in distanced, disinterested contemplation of formal properties.

Hip hop's genre of "knowledge rap" (or "message rap") is dedicated to the defiant violation of this compartmentalized, trivializing, and eviscerating view of art and the aesthetic. Such rappers repeatedly insist that their role as artists and poets is inseparable from their role as insightful inquirers into reality and teachers of truth, particularly those aspects of reality and truth which get neglected or distorted by establishment history books and contemporary media coverage. KRS-One of BDP claims to be not only "a teacher and artist, startin' new concepts at their hardest," but a philosopher (indeed, according to the jacket notes on the *Ghetto Music* album, a "metaphysician") and also a scientist ("I don't drop science, I teach it. Correct?"). In contrast to the media's political whitewash, stereotypes, and empty escapist entertainment, he proudly claims:

> I'm tryin' not to escape, but hit the problem
>   head on
> By bringing out the truth in a song.
> . . .
> It's simple; BDP will teach reality
> No beatin' around the bush, straight up; just like
>   the beat is free.
> So now you know a poet's job is never done.
> But I'm never overworked, cause I'm number
>   one.

Of course, the realities and truths which hip hop reveals

are not the transcendental eternal verities of traditional philosophy, but rather the mutable but coercive facts and patterns of the material, sociohistorical world. Yet this emphasis on the temporally changing and malleable nature of the real (reflected in rap's frequent time tags and its popular idiom of "knowing what time it is") constitutes a respectably tenable metaphysical position associated with American pragmatism. Though few may know it, rap philosophers are really "down with" Dewey, not merely in metaphysics but in a noncompartmentalized aesthetics which highlights social function, process, and embodied experience.

For knowledge rap not only insists on uniting the aesthetic and the cognitive, but equally stresses that practical functionality can form part of artistic meaning and value. Many rap songs are explicitly devoted to raising black political consciousness, pride, and revolutionary impulses; some make the powerful point that aesthetic judgments, and particularly the question of what counts as art, involve political issues of legitimation and social struggle in which rap is engaged as progressive praxis and which it advances by its very self-assertion as art. Other raps function as street-smart moral fables, offering cautionary narratives and practical advice on problems of crime, drugs, and sexual hygiene (for example, Ice-T's "Drama" and "High Rollers," Kool Moe Dee's "Monster Crack" and "Go See the Doctor," BDP's "Stop the Violence" and "Jimmy"). Finally, we should note that rap has been used effectively to teach writing and reading skills and black history in the ghetto classroom.

Since postmodernism dissolves the relative autonomy of the artistic sphere crucial to the differentiating project of modernity and equally crucial to the high modernist aesthetic which refused contamination by the impurities of practical life, politics, and the common vulgarities of mass culture, Jameson suggests that its disintegration of traditional modernist boundaries could provide the redemptive option of "a new radical cultural politics" (*NLR*), a postmodern aesthetic which "foregrounds the cognitive and pedagogical dimensions of political art and culture" (*NLR*). Jameson regards this new cultural form as still "hypothetical" (*NLR*), but I submit that it can be found in rap, whose artists explicitly aim and succeed at teaching and political activism, just as they seek to undermine the socially oppressive dichotomy between legitimate (that is, high) art and popular entertainment by simultaneously asserting the popular and the artistic status of hip hop.

Like most culture critics, Jameson is worried about the potential of postmodernist art to provide effective social criticism and political protest, because of its "abolition of critical distance" (*NLR*). Having undermined the fortress of artistic autonomy and enthusiastically appropriated the content of workaday and commercial living, postmodern art seems to lack the "minimal aesthetic distance" (*NLR*) necessary for art to stand "outside the massive Being of capital" (*NLR*) and thus represent an alternative to (and hence critique of) what Adorno called "the ungodly reality." Though anyone tuned in to the sound of Public Enemy, BDP, or Ice-T can hardly doubt the authenticity and power of their oppositional energy, the charge that all

contemporary "forms of cultural resistance are secretly disarmed and reabsorbed by a system of which they themselves might be considered a part" (*NLR*) might well be directed at rap. For while it condemns media stereotypes, violence, and the quest for luxurious living, rap just as often exploits or glorifies them to make its points. While denouncing commercialism and the capitalist system, rap's lyrics are simultaneously celebrating its commercial success and business histories; some songs, for example, describe and justify the rapper's change of record company for commercial reasons.

Hip hop surely does not lie wholly outside what Jameson, in a questionable organicistic presumption, regards as the "global and totalizing space of the new world system" (*NLR*) of multinational capitalism, as if the congeries of contingent events and chaotic processes which help make up what we call the world could ever be fully totalized in one space or system. But granting for the moment that there is this all-embracing system, why should rap's profitable connection with some of its features void the power of its social critique? Do we need to be fully outside something in order to criticize it effectively? Does not the postmodern and post-structuralist decentering critique of definitive, ontologically grounded boundaries put the whole notion of being "fully outside" seriously into question?

With this challenging of a clear inside/outside dichotomy we should similarly ask, Why does proper aesthetic response traditionally require distanced contemplation by a putatively transcendent and coolly disinterested subject? This assumption of the necessity of distance is yet another manifestation of the modernist convention of artistic purity and autonomy which hip hop repudiates. Indeed, rather than an aesthetic of distanced, disengaged, formalist judgment, rappers urge an aesthetic of deeply embodied participatory involvement, with content as well as form. They want to be appreciated primarily through energetic and impassioned dance, not through immobile contemplation and dispassionate study. Queen Latifah, for example, insistently commands her listeners, "I order you to dance for me." For, as Ice-T explains, the rapper "won't be happy till the dancers are wet" with sweat, "out of control" and wildly "possessed" by the beat, as indeed the captivating rapper should himself be possessed so as to rock his audience with his God-given gift to rhyme. This aesthetic of divine yet bodily possession is strikingly similar to Plato's account of poetry and its appreciation as a chain of divine madness extending from the Muse through the artists and performers to the audience, a seizure which for all its divinity was criticized as regrettably irrational and inferior to true knowledge. More importantly, the spiritual ecstasy of divine bodily possession should remind us of Vodun and the metaphysics of African religion to which the aesthetics of Afro-American music has indeed been traced.

What could be further from modernity's project of rationalization and secularization, what more inimical to modernism's rationalized, disembodied, and formalized aesthetic? No wonder the established modernist aesthetic is so hostile to rap and to rock music in general. If there is a viable space between the modern rationalized aesthetic and an altogether irrational one whose rabid Dionysian excess must vitiate its cognitive, didactic, and political claims, this is the space for a postmodern aesthetic. I think the fine art of rap inhabits that space, and I hope it will continue to thrive there.

JAZZ AND POETRY

Charles Fair

SOURCE: "Poetry and Jazz," in *Chicago Review,* Vol. 29, No. 1, Summer, 1977, pp. 22-9.

[*In the following essay, Fair compares trends in the development of jazz and poetry from the 1920s onward.*]

Even though they didn't mix very well when jazz was played as background music for poetry in the clubs and coffee houses of the later 1950's, the two arts have a good deal in common. Perhaps because of their emotional intensity, both seem to work best in short forms. And their force and directness owe much (but not everything) to technical virtuosity.

Some apparently simple poems (such as Nazim Hikmet's "Oh Living") or relatively unadorned jazz solos (such as Sidney Bechet's "Blue Horizon") can be extremely moving. But these are not to be confused with *really* simple poets or musicians, who, like Leadbelly or Bunk Johnson, are effective through a combination of raw talent, drive and sincerity. Both Hikmet and Bechet were highly accomplished artists who could be technically dazzling when they wanted to. They had the range, the resources, that made them artists in the full sense, as opposed to balladeers or to players like Bunk Johnson who, if not anonymous, remain at least period-pieces—curiosities for the collector.

One difference between modern poetry and jazz is that jazz has evolved with much greater rapidity. There is far more resemblance, in technique and to some extent in theme, between the poetry of Whitman and the *vers libre* written today than, say, between Louis Armstrong's Hot Five recordings (made on the old *Okeh* label) and the kind of music that Bird and Diz and Milt Jackson were playing only twenty years later. The leap from Jelly Roll Morton to Art Tatum, or to such later players as Phineas Newborn or Bill Evans, is, you might say, one of centuries. No other art that I can think of has matured with such speed.

Bop, which had sprung up in New York (notably at Minton's) during the "jump" and big band era of the early 40's, began turning into Modern (or Progressive) Jazz almost immediately. By about 1955, Modern Jazz itself had split into the cool (Miles Davis, Chet Baker-Gerry Mulligan), super-cool (Lenny Tristano, Jimmy Giuffre, West Coast), hard bop (Art Blakey, Blue Mitchell, Horace Silver), and concerthall-university-circuit schools (Modern Jazz Quartet, Paul Desmond and Dave Brubeck). In addition to these, there was the short-lived gospel movement (Silver, Bobby Timmons, *Sister Sadie*), the earlier trend toward no-beat-no-set-bassline jazz (Tristano's Intuition), and, somewhat later, the free-form experiments of Ornette Coleman.

What characterized jazz, from the days of Bird and Diz on, was the inventiveness of its "head-arrangements" and its brilliant solo-work. Overnight, its harmony became immensely complex; and with the new system of "changes," there was a corresponding increase in the intricacy of basslines—a development that led to the bass itself becoming a major solo instrument. Unlike modern "serious" music *à la* Debussy, Ravel and Delius, jazz in that period remained mostly "horizontal," in that all chords reflected an underlying and audible bassline, against which solo lineplayers (horns, guitar, single-note piano) worked contrapuntally. When bassmen themselves soloed, it was with the original bassline in mind, a line continually suggested by the chords dropped in as backing by the guitarist or pianoman.

To play this new music, everybody had to know what he was doing. So, besides a line of great bassmen (Oscar Pettiford, Charles Mingus, Ray Brown, Paul Chambers, Scott LeFaro, "Lefty" Gomez) and piano-players (Bud Powell, Al Haig, Hank Jones, Wynton Kelly, Red Garland), we had a whole generation of hornmen of absolutely stunning ability—trumpets like Fats Navarro and Clifford Brown and Red Rodney, trombonists like Kai Winding and J. J. Johnson, altoists and tenor players too numerous to mention, even a few flutists (Frank Wess, Sam "The Man" Most), and performers on archaic woodwinds (Roland Kirk). Drumming ceased to be the thump-thumping it had been in the old days (and has become since, with the stiff ofay cadences of rock). Drummers such as Kenny Clarke, Max Roach and Art Blakey listened, played *to* the music, composed. Starting with Charlie Christian, back in the swing era, electric guitar turned into an important solo instrument, an oddly large percentage of the later guitarists being white (Jim Hall, Jimmy Raney, Barney Kessel, Tal Farlowe, Herb Ellis, Johnny Smith. Black players included Wes Montgomery, Kenny Burrell and Bola Sete).

A good many of these instrumentalists were what are called "school" musicians—men trained at the Manhattan School of Music or Juilliard who could read "charts" and often double on piano or other instruments. Even the vocalists of the period tended to be virtuosi. Ella Fitzgerald, though she started with Chick Webb, only really came into her own during and after the Bop era. Sarah Vaughan, who could be over-lush or at times plain awful, nevertheless had a beautiful voice and great flexibility. Betty Carter and King Pleasure brought in wholly new ideas of vocal soloing. (Jackie and Roy were more down-the-line post-Bop singers, but very polished and musicianly.) Lamvert-Hendricks-Ross got a unique sound, as did Nina Simone in her more down-home way. (No one remembers Bobby Dorough, but he was good too.)

What most of these musicians had in common most of the time was reality; that is, they seemed to believe in and enjoy and keenly feel what they did, and their technique was a means to that end. They played with intelligence, skill and passion, sometimes with a wild originality, and you can't ask more of an art than that. Short as it was, it was an apogee, that era. There were a few players who consistently sounded empty and overdecorated, as there had been in the swing period. One thinks of Teddy Wilson, back then, and of Ahmad Jamal on records, or some Tristano, later, but the Lisztians were few. On the whole, jazz up into the 1960's very successfully resisted being corrupted by its own phenomenal skills. What has happened to it since is another matter.

Before getting into that, let me briefly look back over what was happening in modern poetry in the fifty years between 1920 and 1970. The '20's opened with Pound and Eliot already established, and the literary tone of the period set. To use Cyril Connolly's terminology, the style of both poets was Mandarin with Dandyish overtones. Eliot in particular (see the first of his *Collected Essays*) strongly believed in tradition—the principle that we grow out of, and in so doing alter, our own past.

The best poets, in his view, were those who—other things, such as talent, being equal—had the clearest understanding of what they were descended from. Only in that way, he believed, could they truly come to themselves, however different those selves might be from their predecessors'. And true to his own principle, Eliot, though a traditionalist, was different, both in the forms he used and in the peculiar bleakness of his language, from the line of English and American poets that went before him.

In the 1930's, the *genre* represented by Auden, Isherwood, and Spender continued to be a modernism-mindful-of-the-past, as was the work of Frost (more conservatively) or MacLeish. Stevens expressly owed much to the Imagists. The present state of our poetry was anticipated by poets such as Marianne Moore and William Carlos Williams, whose loose verse-forms, descended from Whitman, have since become almost standard. Although some poets, some of the time, use the older stricter forms (Robert Lowell, W. S. Merwin) the main trend now appears to be towards a low-keyed colloquial language, an absence of rhyme, assonance or consistent meter, and an avoidance, generally, of what are considered "effects."

At first glance, this might seem to mean that since the mid '60's poetry and jazz had gone in different directions, and begun reflecting quite different states of mind in the respective performers and their public (if one can speak of poetry, today, as having a public). For whereas poetry has technically simplified itself, New Wave jazz sounds even more complex than its predecessors. Herbie Hancock, Miles Davis and Chick Corea are all innovators who paid their dues (as Picasso did) by mastering the older styles first; and like Auden and Thomas in poetry, they are highly sophisticated.

I have the impression, possibly mistaken, that the Iowa Workshop alumni and other young poets publishing in the mid-70's have not paid their dues and might be unable, if called upon, to write more than just passably in traditional forms. Few of them have the fire, or for that matter, the sophistication of their common ancestor, Whitman. Such sophistication as they do have is confined, one feels, to a knowingness about their own time and especially them-

selves. There is little evidence, in their work, of that historical sense which Eliot thought "nearly indispensable to anyone who would continue to be a poet beyond his twenty-fifth year."

That sense, he continues, "involves a perception, not only of the pastness of the past, but of its presence; the historical sense compels a man to write not merely with his own generation in his bones, but with a feeling that the whole of the literature of Europe from Homer, and within it the whole of the literature of his own country, has a simultaneous existence and composes a simultaneous order . . . What happens when a new work of art is created is something that happens simultaneously to all the works of art which proceeded it."

We are, by our own definition, a very "now" people—very tuned in to what's going on, even half a world away, very mobile. We have largely ceased to be parochial in the literal place-bound way our ancestors were, and are parochial in time instead. Our absorption with things here and now amounts to a death-by-neglect of the imagination. For the past is never visible, except indirectly, through an act of imagining. It cannot be read as we read a newspaper because the elements in most news stories are familiar to us, whereas (as Trevelyan once remarked) the past, as it recedes, very soon becomes a lost world whose documents and other traces grow steadily more difficult to interpret.

To have historical sense—to establish a perspective not over miles or decades but over continents and centuries—is consequently a feat of imaginative comprehension far beyond anything required of us by the world of our own time. It is also one whose power to illumine men's minds, to stir them to wonder and deepen their sense of the present, poets have always understood. The fact that Shakespeare, nearly the first and certainly the greatest dramatic poet in English, wrote historical plays, is not I think accidental; nor was the fact that those plays appealed deeply to the awakening imaginations of men in that day. Because they sensed they were going somewhere, they felt a need to know where they had been: or more to the point, *who* they had been.

> Whereas poetry has technically simplified itself, New Wave jazz sounds even more complex than its predecessors. Herbie Hancock, Miles Davis and Chick Corea are all innovators who paid their dues (as Picasso did) by mastering the older styles first; and like Auden and Thomas in poetry, they are highly sophisticated.
>
> —*Charles Fair*

It is just those feelings that we seem to lack—a lack that our poets and jazzmen only too faithfully reflect. We look toward the future with something like horror and at the same time are arrogantly indifferent to the past as though, not being "modern," it had no continuity with our world, no message for us, no "relevance." Even for poets who do not share it, this attitude is a trap. For in what terms are they to address their audience? What is left them? For those who do share this attitude, it is simply fatal, condemning them to a kind of small-talk which, however human and real, is not quite poetry—not something that "happens simultaneously to all the works of art that preceded it."

Indeed our poetry shows signs of becoming what jazz has often (incorrectly) been called—a folk-art. A characteristic of folk-arts, one that may explain their current charm for us, is that they are timeless. Just as the tribe has legends but no real history, tribal arts do not truly evolve, they just *are,* changing, if at all, in the same gradual way the landscape does.

If you listen closely to New Wave jazz, you will hear, I think, the same kind of internal slowdown, as though the evolution of jazz which was so rapid between 1920 and 1966, had since gone into arrest, a vacuum of avant-gardism. The difference is that while poets have backed off and made formlessness—nonvirtuousity—their medium, jazz musicians have stuck with their pride in technique and turned technique itself into a monstrosity.

But even that doesn't alter the basic truth; because under the endless solos, the cascades of thirty-second notes and formal curlicues, what one hears is not more of a bass-line than before, but usually less—sometimes a line of no more than three notes, on which skimpy foundation the piano-man will lay chords so densely voiced, so ambiguous, that the listener may be deceived. But only for a while, because the ear, even more than the eye, is a truthful witness and what it says is that nothing is happening. The solos are not lines, really going someplace, but figures—tonal embellishments that, like jigsaw Gothic, convey nothing and led nowhere.

The final effect is one of monotony, emotional blankness. At times, listening to this strange music, I feel it is all the same piece—just as I have been struck, reading contemporary poets, by how interchangeable their styles and ideas seem.

Here is a poem.

Poem

A country is the things it wants to see,
Kaduna's tin roofs glinting in the afternoon—
So the legend goes.
My eye returns to my double,
An ageless big white horse . . .
Poor measured neurotic man,
Animals are more instinctive virtuosi.
I look at the wide summer,
And a loud noise coming from a barn;
Across the street from the Dyckman house, on
    Broadway,
A Slovak woman sells hot dogs.
So what, life is hard, bitter and sad?
I can't make it my business.
The doorbell rings and I stand
Determined not to answer . . .

Many would agree it contains the things we have come to expect in our poetry, including alienation, a reference to animals as more all-of-piece (and therefore happier) than we are, another to a city not of antiquity and "storied" but of modern Nigeria, with tin roofs; and finally some touches of dooryard realism (the noise from the barn; the Slovak woman and her hot dogs), leading to the bleak last lines.

In fact six poets wrote this one. I assembled it in just under fifteen minutes by lifting their lines, almost at random, from back issues of the *American Poetry Review.* Of course one could do the same with traditional poets, but imagine how much more difficult it would be. If one were to tailor together excerpts, say, from Browning, Swinburne, Blake, Gerard Manley Hopkins and Thomas Hood, the seams would almost certainly show. The last time, in English literature, one could have gotten away with this kind of thing was in the age of the Heroic Couplet, when poetry had degenerated, pro tem, into a mixture of epigrams and formal rhetoric. The reason it is so easy to do now is similar—because poetry is at a pause, because the processes which fifty or a hundred years ago led to the intense individuality of poets themselves, have temporarily gone into reverse. The sameness of much New Wave jazz, not to mention the musical anonymity, the lack of ability to improvise, one finds in most rock players, reflect the same inner condition. All those "egos," but where are the real people?

For whatever reason—because we are too present-bound, because the media have helped to homogenize us, because our mobility rubs us smooth, creating a kind of Mass-think enabling anyone to talk comfortably with anyone else—we are what we read in our arts, a people on the whole without "vital singularity" (as Gertrude Stein said of us long ago). A country is indeed "the things it wants to see," but this may not be one of them. It will perhaps fall to poets who have not yet written or jazz musicians still learning their instruments, to start changing all that.

At first, of course, we will hate them, and some, like Cézanne, will be failures in their own lifetimes. But it is exactly the easiness of avant-gardism just now that should make us suspicious of it. When banks begin buying contemporary paintings and Miles is right up there with the rock stars, when the Iowa Workshop turns out poets the way the Harvard Business School turns out MBA's, it may not be a sign that we have entered a creative Golden Age. It may simply mean that the "experimental" has become so standardized it is a branch of fashion, no more demanding, really, than the latest styles in clothes. This is the impression one has today—that painting is super-chic wall-paper, that poetry is monotonously of the moment, that New Wave Jazz rattles on and on, like Muzak for the In-crowd. It's time for something we'll all hate.

Christopher Logue and Charles Fox

SOURCE: "Jazz and Poetry," in *The Twentieth Century,* Vol. 166, No. 990, August, 1959, pp. 84-94.

[*In the following two-part essay, the author of the first section, Christopher Logue, calls for more innovations in the field of poetry in terms of style, experimentation with which brought about the technique of reading poetry against a background of jazz music; the author of the second section, Charles Fox, identifies three separate traditions in the jazz-and-poetry movement.*]

I

When a great political man retires he must provide for the future. Nothing can beatify his gifts like disturbed conditions drowning incompetent successors. Then the suffering public can remember his rule as golden, and, forgetting that his final acts are the origin of their present woe, vilify the successors he chose for the vain incompetent fools they are. Nor is anyone better placed to assure the drawing of comparisons favourable to himself than the grandee, who, after accepting the careless public's glory, persuades them, and his own loyal supporters, to promote leaders distinguished by that folly his political genius has recognized but managed to conceal. As his first gift to the world was the excrement of his body, so his ultimate creation is to grant his electorate the democratic opportunity to reveal how much they have learnt from his guidance, and to save themselves from national disaster by the quick, final, and jubilant ousting of his faithful colleagues.

Considering the ambitions of government, such measures are reasonable and their achievement by design, virtuous; but the succession and judgement of poetry, particularly the free or romantic poetry composed in Western countries, is not so democratically governed. Its obligations are individual and didactic. Poetical disaster is not to be understood in terms of dying or dithering among serious old writers; it derives from profound, natural causes, like ignorance, torpor, and self-satisfaction among young writers. Votes cannot correct this situation, and, in any case, the populace is indifferent. They have other fish to fry. The work of professional literary critics generally supports inferior modern poetry, for the stale ranks of criticism are thronged with failure poets.

As lack of revolution or constant reform indicates political decadence, so avoidance of experiment and the morbid popularity of exhausted verse forms, show poetic reaction. Politically, if the decadence is aggressive, it leads to counter-revolution, fascism, etc.; the poetic equivalent to this aggression is open hostility towards experiment, with the support of critical systems whose values are drawn from dead literary products as collateral. This, with rare exceptions, is the position of English poetry now. And although the relationship of contemporary politics to contemporary poetics must be recognized if the decadence of the latter is to be grasped, it gives only a general clue about the factors encouraging to decadence. Understanding this relationship will not enable us to create alternatives and increase tradition. To turn a new face to heaven without denying one's ancestors is not a critical function.

It would be foolish to lay the 150-year death of sophisticated English poetry that followed Chaucer at the doors of medieval or Tudor politicians. But the ugly blunderings of Messrs Hawes, Lydgate, and Occleve, represent more than traditional literary obedience vitalizing, for a little while, the naturally untalented. If they did not develop Chaucer's literary inventions it was not because they mis-

understood his technical genius, but because their own slavish attitudes towards social and political authority made them exclude current historical experience. To-day, when it is timely to reject the genteel bellyaching of Messrs Larkin, Amis, and Conquest, we must recognize that the literary disaster they represent could last for many decades, and lies in their general attitude towards moral and political commitment, and their particular attitude to experiment with form, rather than in any gap occasioned by the dotage of Pound and Eliot, the cutting off of Auden and Spender, and the silence of Barker and Graham.

The work of Messrs Larkin & Co., together with their even weaker associates, is characterized by the exclusion of impersonal subject matter, the combination of trivial, subjective impressions with refined techniques, and an academic devotion to Caroline and Georgian poetry. They promoted themselves by means of a group name and radio anthologies. They flourished during the post-war decadence; indeed it may be said that their seedy and niggling views corresponded nicely to the timid political administration of the early fifties. They were, and are still, defended by the critical doctrines of the university teacher Doctor Leavis, but not by that master himself, whose imagination, however spare, requires works of greater significance than theirs to excite its innate puritanism. They are to be distinguished from their predecessors by the unique inferiority of their collective output. Lacking the originality of talent to assimilate the literary discoveries and inventions

Jack Kerouac.

made during the first third of their century, they have not found in themselves the humility to imitate those superior writings. To them, and to their critical supporters, experiment has been anathema. Cleverly, they associated the word with amateur pretentiousness. In fact, any serious experiment that took place during their ascendency, though its practical result was failure, was worth more than all their 'stabilizing'.

Critical appreciations of their position like the above are amusing, but except as exercises in justified abuse, not very useful. To check the disaster they have originated, experiment is necessary, allied to the constant defence of experiment. What is more, any experiment that is made must not start from the position established by their wretched works, but from the necessity to write poetry adequate to the times and conditions in which we live.

For me, experiment in poetry means two things. First, recognition of those factors which must form its subject-matter if the work is to have relevance and meaning for present living experience. This implies a basic change in content. For example: three-quarters of English poetry to-day is written by those who live in, and consumed by those who read in, urban or semi-industrial surroundings; yet, if you idle through one of our innumerable anthologies (Larkin & Co. have something of a corner in anthologies), listing the descriptive contents relative to each poet at the time of writing, you would think they were written by people inhabiting a small sunlit fun-fair set in the middle of a thousand-acre bramble patch. Such poems have no more relevance to our lives than a picture of packaged bacon does to a pig in a slaughterhouse.

A change of subject matter results in technical changes, for stylistic properties are derivative of content. The two are (how many times have we been told?) inseparable; therefore a writer's duty to both is equal. His judgements are unavoidably social as well as aesthetic. Alter your way of writing and you discover that those who imagine poetry to be special, private, and exclusive, no longer enjoy your work. They have to be abandoned and experiments to make a new audience undertaken. This is not so difficult as it sounds. Many people who read poetry, do not read recent poetry; they omit to say this out of humility and politeness. This second class of experiment involves use and communication; it was with this aspect in mind we developed a technique of presenting jazz and poetry together. The field has scarcely been opened. There is room for small operas, song cycles, dramatic stories, a hundred different things. I do not believe that recorded poetry will replace the book—a popular fantasy nowadays; on the other hand, public readings that reassert the traditional association of words and music, increase the sale of books enormously.

Lastly, experiment involving public performance raises problems of audition and visuality. For example: lyrical poems read by one person, about one person, quickly bore an audience no matter how good the poems are. If attention is to be gained and retained, didactic, satirical, and narrative poems are essential. In this way the obligations of public experiment influence the more solitary act of writing. The two aspects cannot be separated; experiment

is total or non-existent. Methods of reading must also develop. The big, fruity enunciation (Thomas school) and the gritty lisping (You-must-accept-me-as-I-am school) are both destitute.

We have made a modest and worthwhile start. Let's see what happens.

II

Gutenberg had a good idea with printing, but it ran away from him and ruined it for the poets! Put the clam on the voice.

(LAWRENCE FERLINGHETTI)

It is very important to get poetry out of the hands of the professors and out of the hands of the squares. If we can get poetry out into the life of the country it can be creative. Homer, or the guy who recited Beowulf, was show business. We simply want to make poetry a part of show business.

(KENNETH REXROTH)

These two quotations sum up pretty accurately the intentions of those San Francisco poets who, during the spring of 1957, began reading their work in public to a background of jazz. Their aim was not only to reintroduce the old bardic relationship between poet and audience, it was also to increase the size of that audience. The idea quickly caught on in San Francisco, a city swarming with beatniks, and soon regular sessions were taking place, either in espresso bars or at The Cellar, a downstairs club which had once been a Chinese restaurant and now became headquarters for the jazz-and-poetry movement. Outside California, however, the response was cooler. Some of the better-known San Francisco writers, among them Kenneth Rexroth and Jack Kerouac, made forays to New York, but apart from Rexroth appearing for a fortnight at the Five Spot, and some Sunday afternoon readings by Langston Hughes at the Village Vanguard, jazz-and-poetry met with only limited success on the East Coast. Some gramophone records were made, a poet or two appeared on TV screens, but otherwise the movement in the United States retreated back to California.

'A good thing too'—that might easily be the reaction of many British men-of-letters, anxious to frustrate such an apparently obscene mingling of the artistic and the vulgar from defiling these shores. Yet that reaction would be stupid, unfair not only to jazz—which should no longer need defending among intelligent people—but also to the possibilities which lie in the blending of poetry with jazz. Most of the San Francisco experiments, alas, scarcely lived up to Rexroth's vision of poetry as 'a part of show business'; indeed, to judge from recordings, Rexroth's own manner of reading (at times he sounds like an Old Testament prophet in mufti) cannot have helped things to go with a swing. And now the trouble is that other attempts at fusing poetry with jazz are likely to be written off without a fair hearing as further outcroppings of the 'Beat' generation. In fact, however, at least three separate traditions can be discovered in jazz-and-poetry to-day: that of the San Francisco movement, the Negro tradition found in the work of Langston Hughes, and what can loosely be described as a European approach.

To attribute a tradition to something quite so temporary as the San Francisco jazz-and-poetry movement might be called misleading. But if there is no precedent for its method of putting poetry and jazz together, there certainly seems to be for the poems and the way they are declaimed. A mixture of Walt Whitman, the Old Testament and the doom-heavy rhetoric of primitive gospellers—this impregnates the style. Only too often Kenneth Rexroth or Allen Ginsberg boom away in denunciatory fervour, their voices edged with hysteria, and while, at its best, this can result in Ginsberg giving a genuinely impassioned, almost frightening reading of 'Howl', at the other extreme one gets such a performance as Rexroth's reading of 'Thou Shalt Not Kill,' a poem in memory of Dylan Thomas:

> He is dead.
> The little spellbinder of Cader Idris.
> He is dead.
> The sparrow of Cardiff.
> He is dead.
> The canary of Swansea.
> Who killed him?
> Who killed the bright-headed bird?
> You did, you son of a bitch.

If a muted trumpet did not echo the cadences, if the final phrase was not quite so forthright, one might swear that Rexroth, finger outstretched, was standing by the lecturn in some Little Bethel, perhaps lamenting the passing of Lloyd George. But if the poets' readings are remarkable for their aggressiveness, exactly the opposite is true of the music. The rôle played by jazz in the recordings of San Francisco poets is a remarkably passive one. Chords may be sustained, a trumpet or saxophone whimper here and there, but the approach is basically negative. In the case of Rexroth's 'Thou Shalt Not Kill,' for example, the accompanying group deliberately used no prearranged chord pattern, key or rhythmic structure. So relentless a quest for spontaneity must be self-defeating. Occasionally there is an exception, as in the case of Lawrence Ferlinghetti's 'Autobiograph' (Ferlinghetti, incidentally, is far less vehement than his associates), where the poet reads between four-bar snatches of jazz improvised on the chords of 'I Got Rhythm.' In nearly every recording, however, the music has been used only to invoke a mood; it has no identity of its own.

One feels, in fact, that the main function of the San Francisco movement has been to reflect a particular rather than a universal set of attitudes, to express the cultural climate of certain people in a certain part of the United States a dozen years after Hiroshima. Yet it is always risky to condemn too glibly those species of art most indigenous to a nation. And where Allen Ginsberg or Lawrence Ferlinghetti are concerned, it may be their Americanism which disconcerts us, just as most Continentals cannot hear what we hear in Elgar or Vaughan Williams. Both Ginsberg and Ferlinghetti, it seems worth noting, are keen admirers of William Carlos Williams, an American poet of undisputed stature and yet a writer who remains practically unknown in this country, except among a very small circle. Yet Williams's work is no more difficult or complex than that of

Wallace Stevens, Marianne Moore or Richard Wilbur, all of whom are cheerfully accepted here. By what can only be called a happy chance, one of the few genuinely successful fusions of poetry and jazz on the West Coast occurred when Hoagy Carmichael read Williams's 'Tract' above a very simple but effective blues played by a trio consisting of guitar, bass and drums. The brilliance here springs almost exclusively from the reading, a remarkably fine one, and the expressive use Carmichael makes of his birch-bark voice, although the poetry is undoubtedly heightened by the way the lines are splayed across the music's slow, metronomic tread.

On only one West Coast recording, however, do poetry and jazz meet on anything like equal terms. That is in Ferlinghetti's 'Dog,' read by Bob Dorough, a young jazz pianist and arranger who also scored the music. 'Dog' belongs to the school of William Carlos Williams, half-playful, half-ironic, very American in its use of the vernacular. The music underlines the narrative, but instead of being subsidiary it moves honestly, obeying its own logic; the performance, in fact, possesses such identity that if a trumpet or tenor saxophone replaced Dorough's voice the music would still have merit in its own right. Dorough also makes effective use of devices peculiar to jazz: the 'break' for instance, where the music stops for two bars (or perhaps four, punctuated by a chord) and where the words that fill this gap take on a special impact, or the way in which a string of comparisons is spoken above a series of descending harmonies or a set of stopchords. There is, in fact, genuine interplay between words and music, a relationship which allows the poetry and the jazz each to enjoy a life of its own, while together they create a third entity.

But before Rexroth, Ferlinghetti and Patchen started their experiments in San Francisco; before Mike Canterino, the owner of the Half Note Club in Greenwich Village, hung up a notice in his window: 'Poets Wanted', and auditioned the applicants ('Anything a bit off colour', said Canterino, 'I cut out. After all, I run a family place.'); long before any of these events took place, jazz had been doing very well on its own, fitting words and music together in a pattern that has been traditional to it for almost half a century. That pattern is the blues, basically the secular folk-song of the American Negro, normally sung in three-line stanzas over twelve bars of music. And it is that tradition, together with the allied tradition of Negro gospel-song, that informs Langston Hughes's poetry, not only the technique of his reading but the actual content and structure of his poems. Hughes, of course, is a Negro, so it is perfectly natural that this should have happened, as well as that he should draw similes and metaphors from the repertoire of Negro blues and folk-singers. When he reads some of his poems against an improvised jazz background, in fact, the effect is not all that different—formally, at any rate—from the semi-recitative blues-shouting of singers like Joe Turner or Jimmy Rushing.

For the European poet, too, a tradition already exists, a way of setting poetry against music that started with the choruses in Greek drama (even if the details of that technique are lost to us) and which embraces such elegant forms as the Provençal ballads. The words, it seems, stayed well on top until the time of the Renaissance. But with the exploration of harmony and counterpoint, with music assuming an artistic status of its own, poetry began to slip into second place. The decline in operatic libretti between the sixteenth and nineteenth centuries provides a clear illustration of this; so does a comparison of the songs of Campion or Dowland with those of the Victorian or Edwardian decades. Yet the idea of setting poetry against music has continued to nag some poets. W. B. Yeats, for instance, chose to ignore his tone-deafness and tried many times to use music behind his poems; unfortunately he rarely ventured beyond employing a psaltery or a harp. Then there was *Façade,* a work which Dame Edith Sitwell claims to be the earliest example of jazz-and-poetry in action, but where the poems were read above Sir William Walton's ingenious pastiches and parodies of popular dance music (not jazz) of the 1920s. In other contexts one could cite Brecht's use of *sprechtesang,* the Ramuz-Schoenberg *Pierrot Lunaire* and Stravinsky's *Histoire du Soldat.*

Red Bird Dancing on Ivory, broadcast in the B B C's Third Programme, and *Fazzetry,* performed at the Royal Court Theatre, set out to continue this tradition. In each case the poetry was written by Christopher Logue and the music—modern jazz of a fairly eclectic kind—composed by Tony Kinsey and Bill Le Sage. Jazz was used because it seemed the obvious music for the job, malleable in form and mood, metrically regular and possessing vigour and an identity of its own. In this country, as in most of Northern Europe, it has filled the gap left by the death of our native folk-music; certainly no idiom of our time is so international, so capable of adaptation. Before starting work on *Red Bird Dancing on Ivory,* all of us connected with the actual putting together of words and music listened to the American records, but only Bob Dorough's performance of 'Dog' turned out to be of much practical help. That recording, however, was taken as a starting-point for the British experiment. There were, it seemed three alternatives: (*a*) to use the words inside the music, going along with the rhythm, cushioned by the melody; (*b*) to deploy words *against* music, counterpointing it rhythmically, running across the structure of the tune; (*c*) to place words and music in ironic contrast. While it would have been interesting to make some use of the last technique, irony seemed out of place in this particular sequence of love poems. Most of the time, therefore, the readings alternated between techniques (*a*) and (*b*), often using both approaches within the same poem. It was necessary, also, for Christopher Logue to resist making any 'orchestral' use of his voice, to avoid getting over-musical or grandiloquent in his reading; instead he was to aim at projecting a cool, sinewy line, almost a companion to the sounds made by the trumpet and trombone.

With the exception of two poems, one virtually a duet between Logue and the trombonist, Ken Wray, all the music (except for individual solos) was scored. So closely did Le Sage and Kinsey work with Logue, in fact, that even the natural pace of his speech was taken into account, to prevent the reading sounding forced or hurried. The reason for concentrating upon arranged rather than improvised

jazz was simply because planning seems necessary if the meaning of a poem is to be underlined and given impetus. With an improvised jazz backing such effects remain a matter of fortuity, the product of happy accidents. Much more successful results come from carefully fitting the poem inside the music and the music around the poem, even when it is an oblique relationship rather than a direct one that is being sought. In 'Wings Whirr by Moon and Midnight,' for instance, the reading draws its poise from the fact that the stanzas never plump down exactly within the eight- or sixteen-bar patterns of the music; they stretch across them, only coinciding at certain points, but because of that giving those passages much greater dramatic emphasis. Similarly, in 'Can You Trap Shadows Like This,' not only is the 'break' used rather effectively, followed by descending harmonies, but the images of headlong flight—'hands out', 'drum', 'stones', 'trees', 'deep holes'— are all pointed up by accents on the drums, a pattern which had to be co-ordinated beforehand.

I think it is fair to claim that *Red Bird Dancing on Ivory* has made more ambitious use of the jazz-and-poetry medium than anything previously attempted. And since that broadcast some aspects of the technique have been developed in further programmes at the Royal Court Theatre, notably by the use of longer narrative poems and poems carrying a heavier residue of meaning. The treatment here was a little more sober, the story-line being allowed to develop without too much distraction and with more use being made of recurring themes. But it would be a great mistake to think that everything possible has now been tried. On the contrary, it will be interesting to see just how many different kinds of poetry can be employed within this medium and whether the extended form can be developed to exploit dialogue, to make, in its own way, a kind of chamber-opera. As far as this country is concerned, further programmes will certainly be attempted (there are already plans for Christopher Logue and the Tony Kinsey Quintet to work together again on both sound radio and TV in the autumn), and these should provide the opportunities for following up some of those fresh approaches.

Al Young, Larry Kart, and Michael S. Harper

SOURCE: "Jazz and Letters: A Colloquy," in *Tri-Quarterly* 68, No. 68, Winter, 1987, pp. 118-58.

[*In the following essay, which was originally presented as a panel discussion among Young, Kart, and Harper at the annual meeting of the Associated Writing Programs in Chicago, Young, Kart, and Harper—all writers with a great interest in jazz—comment on the interrelationship among the arts, especially focusing on how jazz has shaped their creative process, the style and content of their works, their self-identity, and their response to other art forms.*]

YOUNG: My father was a professional jazz musician in the 1930's, back in the days when the tuba held down the rhythm section, along with the drums in the jazz aggregations. It wasn't until a man named Jimmy Blanton came along with the Duke Ellington orchestra that the string bass, the acoustical string bass, became the bottomizing element in swing and jazz music. I grew up in a household where records abounded. In fact, my mother used to get very upset with my father, who worked as an auto mechanic, because when he got his paycheck, he would stop by the record shop and pick up a bunch of records before he ever got to the house.

So I grew up with all these records and later played tuba and baritone horn myself and trumpet in junior high and high-school bands and took music as just a very natural part of life. Because I had been interested in writing from the age of six, the two always went together for me. I never made those distinctions between the arts that a lot of people make, despite the differences in practical approaches to various media. As a teenager I would go to the Detroit Institute of Arts to look at paintings and sculpture, visual and plastic arts. I always carried that same idea about all art with me into that experience. I would look at paintings as a form of music, poetry and literature. I would learn an awful lot of things from the painters when I'd go to museums, and bring it back into my writing, and project those things into the music that I'd listen to. And I think I was very fortunate to grow up in the late forties and during the fifties when there was sort of a ferment in American culture that eventually rose from subterranean level to become a very evident public factor in shaping, I'd say, even the art that we find around today in all media. In the 1950's, when I was at the University of Michigan, the phenomenon of poetry and jazz became very bankable, as they would say out in Hollywood. And you had people like Kenneth Rexroth, Kenneth Patchen and others. Langston Hughes even got into the act, although Langston had been doing the poetry-and-jazz thing way back in the thirties. But they were making national tours with jazz bands and making records and everybody would go and experience this synthesis, myself included.

That was also the period, you have to remember, when abstract expressionism was king. Jackson Pollock and Franz Kline and all these people were holding court and, if you can recall the New York poetry scene at that time—"San Francisco East"—as somebody called it once, you would note that the painters were actually running the show. All the other artists, the musicians and the poets, all looked to the painters, circa 1954-55, for cues as to how to proceed. So that if you talked with somebody like Robert Creeley or LeRoi Jones (as he's calling himself again) they would tell you that they checked out the painters first, before they went on and wrote their poems. And if you look at, say, the poetry of Frank O'Hara, who was very powerful in those days and held a position at the Museum of Modern Art, you'll see that it was very jazz-conscious and very painterly-conscious, and it was a very exciting period when all of these people's ideas were flowing together.

I was a kid then and I was paying attention to this in a very intense way, as you can only do when you're about fifteen, sixteen years old. You're much more serious then than at thirty-five or forty because, like Jan Carew was saying yesterday, those are the days when you can sit up in the treehouse and go through five or six books in a day, or certainly in a week, and really think about them and absorb them. Well, I was doing all that. I was absorbing everything at once. Now the writer who emerged on the scene nationally

and internationally and turned everybody around—and I find people in English Departments still don't understand how this happened—was Jack Kerouac.

Jack Kerouac came out with *On the Road* in 1957. There had been excerpts from it in *New Directions* as early as 1956. There was a lot of noise about the Beat Generation and Kenneth Rexroth was writing all these long manifestos and there was a very exciting groundswell taking place. Everybody I knew in Ann Arbor, Michigan, was reading *On the Road*. Copies were dogeared, and people didn't want to lend you a copy because they were afraid they wouldn't get it back or it would come back with beer stains on it and jelly and bacon grease and all that. And it wasn't so much that the writing was "good," whatever that was supposed to be, but it represented an alternative to what we'd been getting. I think that one of the things that the Beat Generation did was to take art out from under glass. I had been brought up in grade schools and middle schools and high schools where we were taught that art was something that was unapproachable. It really didn't have much to do with your life. It was something you had to learn in order to become a more expanded person, acquire good taste and all that. And one of the things that the Beat Generation did was to restore poetry and literature to the people. The people went out and attended poetry readings. Dylan Thomas had come through town—there were a lot of factors in this—had come through in two or three national tours and given people the idea that you could actually get up and read this stuff aloud and people would respond to it, instead of sitting around underlining it late at night in dormitory rooms. So that all of that excitement seemed to coalesce in the pages of *On the Road*.

Now, I don't know how many of you are familiar with Mr. Kerouac's techniques of writing. But he published a very influential manifesto of his own in the pages of *Evergreen Review* in 1958, which is called "The Essentials of Spontaneous Prose," in which he attempts to articulate the way in which he himself worked. He proposed, for example, that you not think about what you're going to say, just picture in your mind what your objective is going to be on the page. And then just blow. That kind of thing, like a jazz musician. You've got to remember that he, as much as anybody else, was under the influence of things like abstract expressionism. I mean those canvases that Jackson Pollock achieved by getting up on a scaffolding and just taking the paint and just—to the uninformed eye or to the people who didn't know the vocabulary of modern art and all that, it would look as if—like if my Uncle Billy saw it, he'd say, "That man is just splashing paint on the canvas. You call that paintin'? I can do that!"

But there was a very elaborate, articulated esthetic that accompanied it that said that process to the abstract expressionist was more important than product. Those painters themselves were highly influenced by jazz. If you went down to the—what's the name of that place they used to hang out? Tenth Street—aren't there any old-timers around here?

VOICE: The Cedar Bar.

YOUNG: Cedar Bar. If you went to the Cedar Bar, they

> **I think that one of the things that the Beat Generation did was to take art out from under glass. I had been brought up in grade schools and middle schools and high schools where we were taught that art was something that was unapproachable. It really didn't have much to do with your life.**
>
> *—Al Young*

were all talking about Charlie Parker and Miles Davis and whatever was going on in the jazz world at that time and they were trying to recapture the spirit of jazz, the spontaneous spirit of jazz in their work. When the Zen Buddhists turned up during that period, because people like D. T. Suzuki and Alan Watts were also publishing in the pages of *Evergreen Review,* they brought that spirit of Zen spontaneity which enhanced this whole idea that art was supposed to be something that came from the spirit, that for all too long, certainly in the West, it had been dominated by what somebody in those days called the "form freaks," people who were more involved with product and form than they were with content and spirit. Now as a kid I got the idea that still persists with me, that when we look at any painting or piece of writing or listen to any piece of music, what we are actually doing is searching for the human spirit. There's a spirit that accompanies a piece of art that we're usually not aware of except perhaps in a subliminal way. But if it isn't there, it can be the most clever work, it can be perhaps a masterpiece formally and all that, but if it does not have that spirit, if it doesn't swing, as they used to say in antique jazz parlance—what was it that Duke wrote?—"It don't mean a thing if it ain't got that swing." So I got the idea that it was better to sacrifice form if necessary for content.

I was also reading people like William Saroyan, who would sit down and knock out three and four stories in a day and publish all of them. As a kid, you admire this kind of stuff. You think that this is the way it should be. That it should be fun above all else. And jazz always represented this for me, as I think it did for the majority of Americans who were looking beyond everyday, quotidian American values for some meaning to life. I think that jazz mythology has always affected American intellectuals and artists when they were looking for a way out of what Artaud once called "the bourgeoisification" of everything in life. You see these guys who lead odd lives, quite often they have odious habits, personal habits. They stayed up all night, died young. They bared their souls and gave us some pleasure and some insights into a way of life that can be very interesting.

When you look at jazz itself, you see some interesting divisions historically. The early jazz musicians, for example—this is very rough—the early jazz musicians of the New Orleans school, if you want to call them that, the Dixieland people, were heavy drinkers. You go into, even now,

a Dixieland bar, it's very difficult to be depressed because they're stomping that stuff out, and they're drinking that juice, and *rum ta da ta da da dum,* and it engenders a kind of spiritedness that, I don't know, may be artificial, but it's kind of a happy music, happily oriented music. This persisted on over into swing, which was a dance music, and people forget that during the thirties and early forties certainly—I'd say from the mid-twenties up until World War II—jazz was the popular music of the United States because people didn't say, "Oh, I like jazz," they just liked Benny Goodman, they liked Count Basie—they danced to this music, it was a *social* music.

It wasn't until the advent of World War II and the postwar years that musicians tended to switch from alcohol into heavy pharmaceuticals, and became very introspective. Among Afro-American musicians you had this intense awareness of themselves as artists and they took themselves very seriously. Those of you who followed mythologized jazz history would get the stripped-down idea that jazz was invented in one night in Minton's up in Harlem when Thelonious Monk and Dizzy Gillespie and Charlie Parker decided to come up with a music that white musicians couldn't steal because they wouldn't be able to play it.

Much is made of that, but of course that's very distorted. You talk to people who were around and you see that this music evolved over a long period of time. But the jazz spirit has always been solidly grounded in technical ability and in the spirit to soar. In a book called *The Interpretation of Music,* Thurston Dart, who's a musical historian, points out that in western European music prior to the middle-to-late nineteenth century, room was always left for the soloist to express himself or herself. Composers would leave whole sections open for a gifted soloist to come out and improvise, and that was regarded as the apex of a musical performance—somebody not reading the notes, just standing up there playing from the heart. That went out of western European music when inexpensive ways of reproducing musical scores were arrived at—so that what Mr. Dart calls "the tyranny of the composer" set in. Every note, every speck, every sound, every silence was written down on the page. And the drummer Max Roach, who's a professor of jazz these days at the University of Massachusetts, has said, "I wouldn't be in a classical orchestra for anything, because that's like working at the post office. Go there and sort that mail, you get no chance to do anything on your own."

People always gravitate towards where the spirit is. And when jazz in the late fifties and early sixties got to taking itself so seriously, sealed itself off by being available only in clubs where a lot of the young people couldn't get in because they didn't have money or they weren't of drinking age, whatever, then of course rock drew them over. They always go where that beat is and where there's the freedom to say something on your own. Sure, learn your instrument, be firmly grounded in what's gone on before, but have an opportunity to contribute something of your own.

How does this function in writing? It functions for me in a very interesting way. Whenever I sit down to write these days, I always begin by free writing. That is to say, a typical morning for me is to get up and to record remnants of dreams, if there's anything that's taken place in my dream-life. I sit there and I just put some paper in the typewriter and I pay no attention to what's being written, whether it's good, bad or whatever. I have no idea how long it's going to run, and I just start going! And I put all these things in a notebook, and that notebook has become one of the most interesting books in my library, because all this writing hasn't been consciously done, but over the years you've been writing for so long it's hard for you to really write anything bad at a certain point, the same way that it's very difficult for an improvising musician to play anything bad. You might catch a musician on a night when she or he is not so inspired, but their professional level is such that they can be proficient even when they're not feeling well. It's rather like those old Zen painters, who used to look at a tree for fifteen years and meditate upon it and in thirty seconds they'd sit and with pen and ink and just go *brrrrrrr* and get the whole spirit of that tree. I think this is attractive to people the world over. It's no wonder that jazz has been called the music of the twentieth century. We're probably less aware of that in this country than people would be in a lot of—abroad. Whenever I travel abroad, I'm always amazed at how aware people are of American music.

In conclusion, I thought I would read something from a series of books that I've been doing, something very short. There are two volumes of this that have been published so far, and there's one more coming out next year. They're called *Musical Memoirs*. The first volume was called *Bodies & Soul*. The second volume was called *Kinds of Blue*. And the third will be called *Things Ain't What They Used to Be,* which is an old Mercer Ellington title. What I tried to do in these books was to take a piece of music and conjure in prose in one form or another what the music meant to me. It's a difficult thing to do because even though music is powerfully evocative, sometimes it's so private, the experience that it evokes can be so private, that it's difficult to communicate this to anyone else. And so the problem here—and you need a problem when you play jazz—people aren't just up there blowin'. They know the chords, they know sixteen different versions on record of what everybody else has done to this and they know it's going to count if they can do something that's original, that hasn't been stated before. That's the problem for me. How can I say this so that everybody will understand what I'm talking about and at the same time make it, keep it meaningful? And I experiment each time I write one of these things. Probably the most experimental I've been, and with this one I really let go. It's a form that I'm inventing as I go along, so to speak. And so each time I sit down to do it, I say, "Wait a minute, you know, I've already done that. Do I want to do that all over again? Let's try something new." So I depend a lot on intuition. In the sixties, later sixties, Herbie Hancock, a very different Herbie Hancock, wrote something called "Maiden Voyage," which was one of those milestones in contemporary American music—in fact, one critic says that everything that's been produced since "Maiden Voyage", every original sounds like "Maiden Voyage." And I was so taken with this that even though Herbie Hancock came out with it in 1969, I used it as a metaphor for an actual maiden voyage,

my first ocean trip that I took in 1963 when I sailed from Brooklyn Harbor to the Azores and to Portugal on an off-season freighter. And this is how that piece begins. I'll just read a page of it and get out of here. But I tried to—the music was playing in the background as I was writing, and it sort of fired my thoughts as I went along:

"Maiden Voyage/Herbie Hancock, 1969"

Shhh. Listen. Can you hear it? Listen, listen. Shhh. It's like a soft whispery splashing sound. Symbolic. Cymbalic. It's a cymbal tap. The sound of wood barely touching a cymbal. The drummer's poised and ready to slip up on it and the moment Herbie Hancock drops his fingers to the keyboards. Reeeal pianissimo. To sound that lovely dark chord and four bass notes in tricky off-accent time. We'll be on our way. It's still astonishing, isn't it? What is time? I'm laying this down, you're picking it up. Everything happens at the same time. Ask any quantum physicist the kind of dancing that goes on inside atoms, if you get my drift. This time we'll be drifting over and across the Atlantic, sailing away from the Brooklyn pier like an easygoing recreational blimp in an amazing, if not exactly good, year. It just happens to be the very year they shot Medgar Evers in the back, the year they bombed that church in Birmingham and killed those little girls, the Russians put a woman in space, the year they marched 20,000 strong on Washington, D.C. and Martin Luther King and other black leaders met with the President, the year Defense Secretary McNamara and Diem started taking over the headlines, the year they were singing, "Ain't gonna let nobody / turn me round, / turn me round, / turn me round. / Ain't gonna let nobody / turn me round / in Selma, Alabama." The Governor was shouting, "Segregation forever." It was the year they shot Kennedy down like a dog in Dallas and when they started beating those little white kids, especially the girls, beating them with those billy clubs the way they've always done colored people, you knew the American century was coming home to roost. Shhh. Herbie's just mashed down on the go-forward pedal. George Coleman is sounding the ship whistle. The waves are churning all around us and if you look closely, you'll see me, a little brown speck of a speck in eternity, standing on the deck of a freighter pushing off from the Brooklyn pier. It's the twenty-eighth of August, sunny and hot. Standing on the deck waving at the workers on a ship from India docked next to ours, I'm growing a little bit sad and joyous at the same time as I picture myself atop the timeless ocean pondering the vastness of my animal-wrapped soul and vision which I know I must cleanse of false learning before I can go the infinite way of Atlantics and Pacifics, Indian Oceans and Bering Seas. I stand there watching the Statue of Liberty grow greener and tinier in the fog beginning to roll in now. "Roll with the boat," I'm remembering hearing somebody say. "Roll with the boat, don't fight it and that way you won't get seasick." We'll rolling along right now with the beat, which isn't easy to pin down and measure, and all the ghosts outside our porthole ears seem to be portholed ears carrying on in Portuguese. Timelessness, meanwhile, is enfolding me and washing me clean on this maiden voyage. Who am I? What am I doing? Where are we going?

KART: That's a tough solo to follow. I'd like to begin by bouncing off one of the first points you made, which was how you came to the music and, in effect, how Americans manage to decide that something that has the label "art" is theirs. My circumstances were a little different, but I think the process was similar, similar enough that I think there's a general principle involved here. Music was a little bit around me as I grew up, but not jazz. Because the music around me and the literature around me were clearly, at least as I felt, not mine, I was looking without being aware of it, for some way to find something that had the qualities that I knew art had, so that I could say, "This is mine." And it hit me in about adolescence. I think it hits a lot of people in adolescence, and that's another interesting point. Jazz is a music that includes the world. And not until you're an adolescent do you begin to think of yourself as a being moving through a society. Before that, it's the family, or you don't even know that there are other people. But when it hit me, I was about age twelve, which is thirty-one years ago. I think it was maybe a recording by Jackie McLean. I'd heard some jazz before that, but something about Jackie McLean, who's a wonderful alto saxophonist, spoke directly to me, and when that happened, it was like a covenant had been made, a bond that he wasn't of course a direct participant in, but I thought I had made a bond, and thirty-one further years have convinced me that it was for real. The process of making that bond and coming into contact with all the music I readily identified as jazz, all the qualities that it had, enabled me to come into contact with, and make mine, or believe that I could make mine, all kinds of other art. And I think that's one of the basic problems that any young American, black or white, has. How do you deal with this culture which, when you're born into it, seems more or less alien to you, and how to say, "Yeah, I have a role to play in here"? Maybe as a responder only, maybe as a fulltime participant, either with a horn or with a pen. I'm convinced that the notion of covenant is crucial to it, and I was reading something last night about Moses in Egypt, which was where the covenant was first formed, and then was renewed when the Ten Commandments came down. This guy explained, very interestingly I thought, that the word "exodus" in Hebrew has the meaning of liberation *and* covenant and that because of the story of the exodus from Egypt, the idea of liberation takes precedence. But they're one thing. The point I'm trying to make is that, in one way or another, and I think it can be fairly specific a lot of times, jazz is a music of liberation, spiritual liberation. There's a wonderful book that Sidney Bechet wrote, his autobiography. *Treat It Gentle.* And there's no doubt on his part—I can't remember exactly how he puts it. I didn't think to bring that with me.

YOUNG: He says at the beginning of that book that things were—you had this tension in New Orleans between the blacks, the Creoles and the whites, and it was a fixed race, and he said about some other musician they were talking about, "You know, if we developed this music right, it'll be something that'll slip in on these people."

KART: Do you remember the part where he says that the music arose after an actual physical liberation, the Emancipation Proclamation and all that followed in its wake,

but that the music had the role, whether or not the people who made it and the people who were on the receiving end were conscious of it, of teaching the people what to do with the freedom they now had, that they didn't have before. I think that strain in the music has been prominent all the way through, and it can be felt, since a certain kind of liberation is what we're all striving for. It can be felt down through the whole history of it. And I knew that when I listened to Jackie McLean and lots of other people and responded to them the way I did, that I was using that music in an attempt to define myself.

Another point, to switch horses a bit, about the literal connection between jazz and specific writers. You demonstrated how vital the connection is between the music and your writing, and it runs all through Michael Harper's work. But I remember once listening to Charles Olson read on a TV program. I'd always been fascinated by what I thought his rhythms were, as I read them on the page. When I heard him read them live, or live on TV, I said, "He sounds just like Sonny Rollins." He swung in just the same way. It was frightening. And then something later, I ran across this collection of letters that Robert Creeley and Charles Olson exchanged. Creeley, who was very much involved in jazz in Boston in the late forties, was trying to sell Olson on listening to the people that Creeley was interested in. In this one letter he quotes what became one of Creeley's most important poems: "Le Fou," which is, I believe, the breath. I guess I'll try to read it:

"Le Fou"

for Charles

who plots, then, the lines
talking, taking, always the beat from
the breath
        (moving slowly at first
the breath
          which is slow—

I mean, graces come slowly,
it is that way.

So slowly (they are waving
we are moving
        away from   (the trees
             the usual (go by
which is slower than this, is
           (we are moving!
goodbye

And then in the letter Creeley has in parentheses added in pencil, "Thank you, Charles Parker. Et tu, Thelonious Bach." It was so natural. I mean, you get the lists of the guys he's trying to tell Olson to listen to. It's Bud Powell, it's Dizzy Gillespie, it's Al Haig, it's Monk—I mean, it was natural to them. They knew it.

A third point that intrigues me is that the connection between jazz and literature might be that jazz has more or less spontaneously developed in the course of its life musical parallels to preexisting literary forms. I've always thought of the typical good jazz solo as being more or less a lyric poem. It's a way of stating and elaborating your personal identity, as they say in show business, "in one." You're up there, you are you. You don't have a costume on, you're not playing a role. If it's going to be any good, it's your story. I mean, it's almost a truism of jazz that when somebody gets up there and plays well, the reaction of a fan who responds in kind is, "He's a good storyteller." The literal storytelling, the personal lyrical storytelling, just goes without saying.

There's also a sense that orchestral jazz particularly is dramatic. A typical Duke Ellington piece, like "Harlem Airshaft" or "Sepia Panorama," is a play. And the soloists function both as people who are expressing themselves and as actors who have specific roles to play. Ellington casts them in those roles because he knows who they are and what they have to say and he gives them this framework. He says, "O.K., Johnny Hodges, I know what you can do and you're going to be—oh let's say, the lover—in this play. And Cootie Williams or Tricky Sam Nanton, you're going to be maybe the sarcastic commenter on it. And then Ben Webster, you're going to be another kind of romantic lover, maybe one who's a little rougher than Johnny Hodges—maybe it's the male and female principle going on there." But a definite dramatic context, one that includes the lyrical element.

Then there's a way in which over the course of his career the accomplished jazz musician is either compiling an historical account or writing a novel, because there's no doubt that jazz takes place in a specific society in a specific chunk of historical time and it is about, to some extent, being a person in that world over that period of time. John Coltrane would be a perfect example, or Dexter Gordon. Any great player, their music changes over the years, and it changes because of inner musical impulses and psychological impulses, but it's also an accumulated body of knowledge about what it means to have been that person over that period of time. And I think that's not a bad definition of what a novel is. Another way to look at it is that it's autobiographical. But the interesting thing to me—and Kerouac comes in here—is that as jazz musicians have, without necessarily thinking about it, made those literary-musical forms their own, put their own spin on them, they also have affected certain kinds of literary artists. There are techniques about the way jazz musicians state things, state the self, the way they incorporate their history in what they're doing, in response to which various writers have shrewdly or innocently said, "I can use that." I mean, you just did.

YOUNG: Old tunes, man.

KART: In Kerouac's case, I think there's a lot of doubt about how honestly such things were done. I admire his work sometimes, but did he know enough about the materials to use them as high-handedly as he did sometimes; was he a tourist? I think that's one of the problems the music poses to anybody who either writes about it or just comes to it for pleasure or personal enlightenment. Are you part of it, or are you a tourist? Because being a tourist with it doesn't feel good. And it doesn't feel good if you suspect you are a tourist; and if you are one and don't know it, then you're making a big mistake. I wrote a piece about Kerouac and jazz that I brought along, thinking I was going to quote from it, and I guess I am. But I don't know now if I can find a chunk of it that will work.

Kerouac tried to do it in two ways. One, he consciously said, "I'm going to try to imitate in my prose and in my verse"—and I think it worked better in his prose than in his verse—what he felt to be the core structure of a jazz solo. "I'm going to get up there and improvise." What was the name of that essay again?

YOUNG: "The Essentials of Spontaneous Prose."

KART: I think there's a fair amount of evidence that he rarely, if ever, followed those principles, that what really counts is just the work on the page. Does it feel, does it have the joy of spontaneity? Whether he actually labored over it or not. I think he did a lot of laboring over things. Which is fine, as long as it works.

> **There are techniques about the way jazz musicians state things, state the self, the way they incorporate their history in what they're doing, in response to which various writers have shrewdly or innocently said, "I can use that."**
>
> **—Larry Kart**

And the other thing was that a lot of the furniture of his life was jazz. Some of it got a little creepy, for my tastes. I'll quote some things, if I can find them, that will make anybody's hair curl. Let's see. Here's a line from *Visions of Cody*: "I am the blood brother of a Negro Hero." Or he refers elsewhere to "good oldfashioned oldtime jitterbugs that really used to lose themselves unashamed in jazz halls." And he also refers to "wishing I could exchange worlds with the happy"—oh man—"the happy, true-hearted, ecstatic Negroes of America." I mean, you just go, "Wait a minute, Jack." Although you could say in some of these cases, that's a narrative voice, maybe that narrator is supposed to be a little bit of a fool at that point in the book. But a lot of times that doesn't work. He was going all the way with it.

YOUNG: But he's speaking—if I could intrude on your time. . . . Black readers were always aware of that tendency in Kerouac, but it was no different than when I would go with white friends at college to see a Marx Brothers movie and you'd have a sequence where Harpo would go down into Niggertown and everybody'd be dancing and singing and he'd be playing the harp and all that. And my friends would say, "Are you embarrassed?" And I said, "No, I'm not embarrassed, because I know who's making this movie."

KART: It's a good point, because I guess the person, or kind of person, who would be most embarrassed by that would be somebody in my shoes. But also in the back of my mind I'd be thinking, when he's doing something like that, what would his contact with the music be, compared with someone like Al Cohn or Zoot Sims or Bunny Berigan or whatever? Measure it that way. I mean, there's something, there's a strength in the one kind of contact and something presumptuous or weak in the other.

YOUNG: Remember—I haven't talked about this—he was in the hipster tradition, the tradition of the white hipster, which attempted in large degree to turn middle-class white America on its head. If his folks didn't like it, then he liked it, you know.

KART: I'll end with that passage from my piece on Kerouac and jazz, which begins with a quote from his *Book of Dreams*: "I wish [tenor saxophonist] Allen [Eager] would play louder and more distinct, but I recognize his greatness and his prophetic humility of volume, his 'quietness.' " (Eager, by the way, was an excellent white disciple of Lester Young, and his music and his example obviously meant a great deal to Kerouac.)

Then, after the quote, I go on to say [reading]:

> Listening to Allen Eager or Brew Moore, one knows what Kerouac meant, a meditative, inward-turning linear impulse that combines compulsive swing with an underlying resignation—as though at the end of each phrase the shape of the line drooped into a melancholy "Ah, me," which would border on passivity if it weren't for the need to move on, to keep the line going.

> Of course there are other precedents for this, which Kerouac must have had in mind, notably Whitman's long line and Wolfe's garrulous flow. And I wouldn't insist that Kerouac's prose was shaped more by his jazz contemporaries than by his literary forebears. But that isn't the point. For all his moments of softness and romantic overreaching—his "holy flowers . . . floating in the dawn of Jazz America" and "great tenormen shooting junk by broken windows and staring at their horns"—Kerouac's desire to be part of what he called the "jazz century" led to a prose that at its best was jazzlike from the inside out, whether jazz was in the foreground [as in much of *Visions of Cody*] or nowhere to be seen [as in *Big Sur*]. And perhaps none of this could have come without the softness and the romanticism, the sheer boyishness of Kerouac's vision.

> "These are men!" wrote William Carlos Williams of Bunk Johnson's band, and he certainly was right, as he would have been if he had said that of Louis Armstrong or Coleman Hawkins, Benny Carter or Thelonious Monk. But there *is* something boyish in the music of Allen Eager and Brew Moore and in the music of Bix Beiderbecke and Frank Teschmacher for that matter—a sense of loss in the act of achievement, the pathos of being doubly outside, that is an essential part of their grace. When he was on his game, Jack Kerouac knew that too.

HARPER: I have been internalizing this dialogue between these two gentlemen, and I'm going to try and respond. I come out of a very strange background culturally, and I think that's very important in the way in which we define ourselves as Americans. The whole question of self-definition is the American problem, and the way in which you locate yourself in this very strange terrain is a question, of course, of voice. And I've had some considerable

difficulty communicating with my peers on many levels, mostly at the level of assumption. So I'm going to be rather tedious for a moment and go through a few principles of my own way of approaching this self-definition process.

Everybody begins with a notion of autobiography that sometimes expresses itself as sensibility, sometimes in terms of the construction of what I call "work," which is to say the way in which one gets inducted into the culture. Oftentimes this happens by accident, sometimes it happens by geography—the notion of black people in particular being forced to migrate because of all kinds of economic concerns. And something which doesn't get talked about very much but which I'm going to bring up, and that is the notion of terror. Black people in this country have been under a continuous assault, and the response to that assault has a great deal to do with the vibrancy, not to mention the rigor, of the artistic expression.

I'm reminded of a review which I recently wrote for the *New York Times* of Count Basie's autobiography, as told to Albert Murray. A man called me up on the phone and I said, "Well, send it to me," and he did. I looked at it and I wrote this review. And then I saw the review in the *New York Times* on Sunday, and I was amazed at what they'd done to it. They had cut out all of the illustrations of how the tradition gets extended through people, through circumstances and events, particularly events having to do with economics and war, and the kind of continuity which was necessary to understand something about Count Basie's minimalism, his refusal to overplay, and the way in which he developed his "charts," particularly after he got some exposure on the radio. I'm a little bit tired—and I don't want to start throwing stones here—but I'm a little bit tired of people assuming that John Hammond discovered Count Basie. The question is, who did John Hammond bring Count Basie to? And the answer is, to the job market of New York City, publishing and the control of the markets which brought that music to a wider audience. Now this is typical American technological commercialism. But Count Basie was already somebody in his various communities, and the Blue Devils band was wonderful.

I began my review by talking about an incident which took place and seemed to be of no significance. Basie is in Tulsa in 1925 and he's got "a head," which is to say he's drunk himself into sleep. He's a young man and he hears this music, which he assumes can only be Louis Armstrong, the quality of the playing being such. And he wakes up and he says, "I gotta find out who that guy is that's playing. You know, it's gotta be an album. Somebody in here's playing a record." And he wakes up and stumbles downstairs and he runs into some people who are advertising on the back of a wagon and it is the nucleus of the Blue Devils band, including Hot Lips Page, and a number of other people. This is Basie's introduction into the standard of what he has to live with, in terms of artistic excellence. And the narrative begins with this little episode and then it goes back to a kind of chronology, that is, in Albert Murray's handling of the story of Count Basie.

Now it's important that we understand something about the Tulsa riot, because I thought I was just making a kind of aside, but a woman from the *Philadelphia Inquirer* called me on the telephone and said, "By the way, what are your sources to the Tulsa riot?" And I said, "Well, why are you asking me these questions?" And she said, "I'm just interested, because you said it was the first instance of aerial bombardment on any community in the modern world." And I said, "Yeah, well, that's true." She says, "Well, I'd like to know about your sources." So I said, "Well, you know, one of the sources is the *New York Times*," and I gave her the date. I got the sense that she was trying to solve political problems, because those of us who know anything about Philadelphia and MOVE, for example, know that that community was decimated by a certain kind of technological temper tantrum which burned down a whole city block and ruined a neighborhood, a community. And that attitude, I think, is as American as apple pie.

I want to take you back to Tulsa for a minute because it is there that the beginning of the story of Count Basie is framed. Tulsa was a place which had a very burgeoning middle class. The black community was right next to the train station and the community was full of entrepreneurs. The white community was very angry about this because it seemed to be that with the discovery of oil, black people just had too much. They had too much of a frontier enterprising spirit, and they'd gone out to Oklahoma and carved out, among other things, a way of existing with the Indians. And you could oftentimes go into all-black communities or all-Indian communities very much as you do in Narragansett in Rhode Island now. But when the Indians get together—they have a big powwow—and they all look like bloods. I mean, you'd be looking around saying, "These all look like brothers!" And they call themselves Indians, and they are Indians. And so the amount of interchange at the cultural level, not to mention the bloodline level, is long and extensive. The reason why I tell you this is because Basie came to have a standard of playing simply because he ran into some musicians who taught some things that he could have never believed were being done. So the first question I would ask is, Who taught these people how to play like that? I'm talking about the Ben Websters and so on. Somebody taught them, and the people who taught them were people who were invisible—the people who came out of communities and believed in discipline, who knew something about the arts, who knew something about expression and who knew something about living, how one had to make a life. And the communities out of which these people came were black communities, they weren't white communities—and it was kind of a surprise to John Hammond, among other people, that this kind of music had been in existence for a long time.

Now all you have to do is get the albums and listen to the Blue Devils band and you'll know what I'm talking about. That became the nucleus of Counts Basie's band. I tell you that because it seems to me that we have this ongoing dialogue—I think that Ellison said it best in an essay where he corrected Irving Howe for approaching his particular novel (that is, *Invisible Man*) in the wrong way. He said that he was in "a continuous antagonistic cooperation" with Mr. Howe and others. I think that that is a good expression for our use here—"antagonistic cooperation,"

Bessie Smith circa 1923.

which is the willingness to disagree about the way in which we see what we call reality.

Which brings to me to some compositional questions. I as an academic—I characterize myself as an academic because I've spent too many years in American universities explaining—oftentimes to people who don't deserve the kinds of explanations—the complexities of what it is to live one's life, and saying that one does not live one's life exclusively out of books and that one has to have some experience and background. This is a visceral question and has to do with one's attitude about all kinds of things. It has to do with my attitude about composition when I was too stupid to know any better. Which is to say that when I was taken through my paces in courses, literature courses, I was critiquing my teachers at the same time that they were evaluating me.

I'll give you a couple of examples. I remember when we were studying O'Neill. I had seen, because I was a kid who would go to the library and just read randomly, that, for example, in the undergraduate school that I went to, the novels of Richard Wright had never been taken out of the library. Never. No one had to read the books. No one had read *Native Son*. Nobody had read *Black Power*. Nobody had taken these books out. So I was the first one to do this. I mean, the books were there, but one had to read them. I tell you this because when we got to talking about *All God's Chillun Got Wings*, one of O'Neill's plays, we found Eliot had done a review of it. I wa amazed at the way in which Eliot could be so much "on time" when he was talking about Dante, when he was talking about tradition and the individual talent. But the minute he started talking about brothers, his whole expertise, his formal training, just went to hell. I asked myself, How come? What happened all of a sudden with T. S. Eliot? At that time, Eliot was the high priest. He's still that, but there are some other voices now. But at that time everybody was hung up on the New Criticism and so on. I just listened to these white folks and let them say anything they wanted to tell me and I did what they asked, which included writing villanelles and sestinas and Petrarchan sonnets and Shakespearean sonnets and Miltonic sonnets. And they always assumed that you were doing this by accident, you were kind of stealing this. What they didn't know is, they didn't know anything about my life.

I left school and went to the post office. I heard this riff about the post office and I ran into many young men and women who were advanced people, who had gotten an academic degree, who knew more about Melville and Shakespeare, not to mention the Russians! Now, take Gaines. Mr. Ernest Gaines writes about his rural community of Louisiana, has used the framing devices he has learned from other people who have studied peasant communities, like those Russians, so that he could exalt his own and give the speech rhythms, the modes of discussion, the communal interests and values, a kind of relief which hasn't been seen before. People just think that Gaines is somebody who's got a good ear, walking around with a tape recorder, you know. I mean, this is madness. At that same time, there are people walking around with their biases, their attitudes. I was taking a course from Christopher Isherwood, who would come to class sometimes and not say anything, he would just walk in and say, "We're going to have my colleague read to us." And I would look over—I was the only black person in the class—I'd say, "Damn, that looks like Auden." He would read for about forty-five minutes and then he'd stop and say, "Well, are there any questions?" and I'd raise my hand and say, "Well, I wonder if you'd read the memorial poem for W. B. Yeats?" And he'd recite that, and then I'd ask him to read other things. And when we'd walk out of the class, the girl who sat next to me would say, "How did you know that that was Auden?" And I'd say, "Well, I'd seen his picture on the cover of a poetry book, you know." She thought it was kind of magical that anybody black knew anything about anything else.

And she always used to talk to me about Langston Hughes. "Well, are you going to be the next Langston Hughes?" I don't want to be mean now, but I'm kind of reminiscing now, and it's interesting to know about how people develop. She used to drive a bread truck to school and she'd pull this damn bread truck up, and you know, it had a lot of charisma. She'd get out of this bread truck—it didn't say "Wonder Bread," but it said something like that on the side—and she'd come into these seminars, and she assumed that I was a black person and that the best way to get in touch with me was to talk about black people. Well, I didn't share with her my great love for Langston Hughes. I grew up in a household where Langston Hughes's poems were framed and were on the steps going

down into the basement which, as you know, is the real solid part of the house.

All right. So that gives you some sense of the kind of antagonistic cooperation that goes on in this long dialogue in this country, which begins even before the Declaration of Independence, over the American tongue and who's going to control it. The American tongue is something which I think is extraordinarily important and we owe musicians a great debt because musicians were always at the frontier of what we call "parlance," the way in which they express themselves to other people. And by the time the hipsters, the Kerouacs and others, caught on to what black musicians had been talking about, black musicians had gone on to other things. The language was revivified and revitalized as the result of these particular men and women living their lives at literally the margin of destruction from one time to another.

I tell you that because I think we have to have a respect for the historiography of this culture and the lack of memory. There are terrific losses in America that are taking place. And many people don't even know they're there, because nobody took the time to write them down. Or much of the memory is in black periodicals. I'm talking about things like the *Chicago Defender* or the *Pittsburgh Courier* or whatever. And who reads them? I mean, where are the archives on these newspapers? There aren't many, but there are a few. And out of that memory and out of that loss comes a kind of ritual content, which is to say the framing of the experience and the presentation of the experience, which I've spent some time dealing with.

Now I've been asked to tell a few tales. I'm glad to do that, but I want to say a few things first about the interrelationship of the arts. I would speak to you about Romare Bearden, for example, who, in the process of putting together a theory of collage, can manage to give a social context, a social feel and an artistic expression simultaneously. This is something which he learned as a result of studying the technical innovations of collage and modern painting. But his heart and soul lives in the black community and the black community has never been looked upon as a resource for art at the level of cosmetics, of decorating appeal—which is to say black figures which hang on the walls of people's homes. Richard Yard told me a wonderful story one day. He said, "You know, Michael, people love my paintings, but they don't want them hanging on their walls. Too many black faces in there." And I thought he was making a little joke.

Then later on we came to do a little project together, and he had done something on the Savoy Ballroom, making these figures which are about four feet tall in the attitudes of dance as one would run into them playing in front of Chick Webb's band in 1938. This looks like a dance hall of some sort, and in its better days it probably was. If you went to the other end of it, you could just imagine these dancers spread out in various ways, and they were painted in the attitudes of dance. And the musicians up on the bandstand were responding to the dancers—you could imagine Lester Young, for example, who was getting his energy from watching somebody do the Lindy. This is important cultural iconography, and I tried to capture it in an essay.

Now Sterling Brown wrote a poem called "Cabaret 1927, Chicago." It was about the era of Prohibition and it was probably Fletcher Henderson's band playing to a segregated audience. In it, Sterling Brown, in the manipulation of voice, criticizes the lyrics of Irving Berlin, and he has as a backdrop the lyrics of Bessie Smith singing about the Mississippi Flood of 1927, with James P. Johnson on piano. It was James Baldwin who talked about taking that record to a small village in Switzerland so that he could write *Go Tell It on the Mountain*. Now I think that we owe Bessie Smith and James P. Johnson a debt, and the way in which I pay it back is just to say what happened. And maybe to say in either one of their idioms, maybe both combined, that the business of making a poem is a complicated matter.

I ran into Hayden Carruth recently and he was just sitting in the audience and I was there to give a concert with two musicians, a man who plays cello named Abdul Wadud [Ron DeVaughn]—some of you who follow contemporary music might know him—and the other Julius Hemphill, who plays with the World Saxophone Quarter. We were playing to a small library in Scranton, Pennsylvania, which is a depressed area, and we got up and we put together this program in two parts. It was a wonderful evening and it was right next to a church and the acoustics were terrific and we were glad to see one another and to talk about all kinds of things, old times, and there's Hayden Carruth sitting in the back. So he comes up to me at the break, and he says, "You know, Michael, you ought to write a book on jazz." And I said, "Well, there's some people that are writing books on jazz." And I mentioned Al Young's name, because I've known him for years, and other people. And he says, "No, your stories are just as important as their stories."

He says, "If you don't write them, they'll never be down. The poems are fine."

He says, "But nobody's going to read the poems."

He says, "You and I know that."

He says, "Poets only read one another's work."

He says, "And by the way, I liked your book."

He says, "I always do this when I go to people to find out whether they got any heart. I read the last poem in the book, turn to the last page."

He says, "In your recent book, *Peace on Earth* [Which is a takeoff on Coltrane's great song, 'Peace on Earth'], I read that poem and I knew I wanted to read the whole book."

Hayden Carruth knows a good deal about jazz and has written about it wonderfully. He's a fine poet, and he's also an eccentric. He knows that you carry the legacy and the resonance of your experience with you no matter where you are. Certainly musicians do this, and this is why they're all my heroes. I can't imagine a greater tribute than a person who is tired coming into a town and getting up on a bandstand and singing about "love, oh careless love, oh aggravatin' love." And making those particular people who are either on the dance floor or in the audience transformed. That's the hardest work I know, and for people who do it day after day is just beyond me. And so I think we owe them a tribute.

Now, I'm trying to write a poem for the ear as well as for the eye. The New Criticism and postmodernism has forced us away from the ear in large part. I don't think that we can get along without our eyes, but we still need aural quality of poetry. And I remember when Etheridge Knight was talking the other night, when he was talking about his belief that no matter what, as long as he could say a poem to somebody that somebody could hear it, that was pre-technological and pre-textual in the written sense. That that aural quality was very important. And for him to stand up on the bandstand and sing gives me some idea of what it means to be terrorized in a real sense and at the same time to not be totally inarticulate.

Which brings me to a few of my notes in conclusion. My education was rather scattered and what I would call in the vernacular "habit" of putting together disparate things to make a kind of collage. That's certainly my education and it continues to be that way. I have to go back to the University of Iowa in about a month, and I have to lie. I have to say to Paul Engle and others that they helped me become the poet that I am. I have to say it helped me to be a student of Philip Roth, who accused me of writing a pornographic novella. This is Philip Roth in 1961 accusing me of writing a pornographic novella! I've got to lie when [Donald] Justice, who's a friend of mine and whom I love and who's a very decent man, told me in private, "You know, Michael, when I write this letter of recommendation I can't say how angry you are." I was considered angry because I would speak up. I would say things to Paul Engle like, "Don't you think it's important that the next time you have a black person come here, maybe from a foreign country like Nigeria, that you better check and find out whether you can get an apartment for him, because he'll be walking around here in Iowa City, maybe being run over by some farmers who are not used to seeing Nigerians walking around downtown?" He thought I was making a kind of accusation. I wasn't making any accusation. I was telling him about the world he lived in but didn't know about at the level of race relations.

So I've got to go back and be nice. Be euphemistic, forget memory. Forget loss and forget ritual.

Now here are my notes:

"Notions of Prosody"

Because one does not deliberately echo European conventions for prosody does not mean that one is not aware of them. One oftentimes, in a kind of counterpoint, is referencing them.

Notions of personality. How do you get the attributes of a personality into a poem at the level of phrase or the level of diction or the level of meter even, or rhyme? That's a poetic question. It's an artistic question. The analogies, the logic of vocabulary, the shaping of vocabulary—how do you make these choices so as to elicit the time, the time frame, what I call the "mode of expression"? How do you control that? The whole business of the telling of people's dreams. We in this country have nothing but nightmare to record when we talk about this "antagonistic cooperation" because we are actually at war, even now.

. . . . .

There are other people, this panel and people in the audience and people who've got private record collections and people who don't write in newspapers, who buy records, dance to them and tell their daughters and sons that Coltrane's the greatest musician that ever played. But let me play for you Coleman Hawkins's "Body and Soul." Let me tell you something about how he learned to play "Body and Soul" in that way. After being in Europe all those years, trying to escape racism and trying at the same time to live his imaginative life, he heard Herschel Evans's "Blue and Sentimental" on a recording, and he just said, "I just gotta go home." So he went home, and he was met by musicians, four or five hundred of them, and everybody was saying, "Man, how was Europe?" He said, "Man, where is Herschel?" Herschel had died and nobody could tell Coleman that Herschel was dead. So finally they went to a joint and he found out that Herschel was dead and he went into seclusion for a couple of days and the next thing you know, here comes "Body and Soul."

Now that little riff, that little story, was cut out of the *New York Times* review that I gave. I was furious, because I think that that kind of linkage is important for people who could never hear the musicians play in person. They ought to know that story. It's important to know that when Count Basie was a youngster and went to Cleveland, Basie was on Art Tatum's turf and didn't know it. He walked into the place and started playing and thought he was the baddest dude in the world because he'd been traveling around. He sat down and talked to the waitress and the waitress said to him, "You know, there's a local musician that'll be in here in a little while. Why don't you wait, have a drink and listen to him?" Basie was walking around and talking about "I'm going to cut and blow this cat away." And he was downstairs, he was away, and all of a sudden he hears on the piano somebody he ain't never heard before, named Art Tatum. So he goes up to the waitress and he says, "Who is that guy in there?" She says, "Oh, that's Art Tatum." Basie says to her, "Why didn't somebody tell me I was on his territory? Why do I have to have my hands cut off by that hatchet?" And Tatum later on sat Basie down and said, "Show me a few things. What are you doing here, man?" And Tatum gave him some instruction. These kinds of things were cut out of my review.

Two other things in conclusion. The titles of my books are important. I was accused of being a sentimentalist because of *Dear John, Dear Coltrane*. But I've got that "blue and sentimental" in my background, that music going around in my head. And so the word "sentiment" is not a bad word for me. The other thing is that the titles of songs are also important, and Al Young knows some great songs. "All the Things You Are." You've got to hear Charlie Parker play that before you understand all of the residue that is in the mechanics of just assigning a title to a song. There are reservoirs and resonances.

And the last thing I have to say is that it's an honor to give testimony to people who got me through terrible times. When I was in graduate school at Iowa, the only thing that saved me was a record [album] called *Kind of Blue* [by Miles Davis]. A friend of mine, Lawson Inada, who's a Japanese-American, also had a great collection. We had apartments right next to each other, and the walls were so damn thin that if he turned his record player on first I didn't have to turn mine on. And if I turned mine on first, he'd say, "Man"—I mean, he'd do things like this: I'd meet him at the mailbox and he'd say, "Man, you played *Kind of Blue* forty-eight times this morning, Jack." And I'd say, "Really?" He'd say, "Yeah, let me tell you a story." He says, "You know, I bought *Kind of Blue* and I played it and wore out one side, and this morning you turned over *Kind of Blue* and it's the first time I'd ever heard the other side of *Kind of Blue*. I fell out! A two-sided record!" Nowadays you listen to a record and you find your favorite tunes then you decide you're going to tape and if you don't like all of the thing you take little excerpts from here and there and you put that together and then you play that over and over again. But this was before we could make cassettes. We would just play one side, or we'd play one cut! We'd play that over and over again. We didn't want to be bothered going through the entire side. And he said to me, "Kiss my ass—a two-sided jam!"

That was wonderful to me, because I understood exactly what he meant. He meant he'd been playing *Kind of Blue* on one side for a year and a half, and had no idea that there was this mystery on the other side. And to be given this at four o'clock in the morning or whatever time it was, to actually hear a tune he'd never heard before on a record that he'd been carrying around with him all over the country and hadn't had the nerve to turn over because he didn't want to be disappointed! You know, he didn't want to be let down after listening to side one of *Kind of Blue*.

The fact that Al Young's second memoir in his three collections of memoirs is called *Kinds of Blue* speaks volumes to me because I memorized many, many records to the point that I don't have to play them. I know the tunes. They're running around in my head. So when I sit down in the compositional sense these things impact on me. In the process of making up a kind of commentary or an investigation into any one of a number of poetic subjects, I've got those tunes in my head.

They're blessings to me and they wouldn't be there if those musicians hadn't played.

And many of them are *not* on record. Most people don't understand that musicians weren't concerned about records. Musicians that I know are not buying too many records. They've got eighty references or a hundred or a thousand. They've played "Body and Soul" eight hundred times. But I'm playing just one version on the record. It matters a great deal to me as a non-musician. Doesn't matter much to them.

Process and performance are important. Music for black musicians is almost never entertainment. Almost never entertainment. So for you to approach Armstrong through a film with Bing Crosby in it is a way of not understanding Louis Armstrong. If you want to understand Louis Armstrong, listen to "Potato Head Blues" or "What did I do to be so black and blue?" Or look at Mr. Ralph Ellison's *Invisible Man* and ask yourself why is it that he frames his particular tale around the story of a musician [Louis Armstrong] who was perhaps the greatest innovator in music in the twentieth century. Certainly right up there with Stravinsky and all the others that you might bring to mind in talking about twentieth-century culture.

AUDIENCE MEMBER: A given jazz piece can lose a lot of people real quickly because of the nature of it. People know words, but they don't know tonalities. Is jazz dying?

YOUNG: What you're talking about is life. Life doesn't die. It took the forms that we talked about up here today, but there's always a continuum. Life continues to flow. And I think that what jazz is really about, like I said before, is human spirit and life itself. I remember something that William Carlos Williams said in some of his letters. He said he thought that when society became too staid and static, the artist should throw herself or himself on the side of a little bit of chaos. When it would get too chaotic, he would seesaw a little over on the side of order. And the idea was to keep a balance. I think that people will just naturally always gravitate to whatever is life-giving and life-restoring.

KART: Regarding my saying that jazz is dying. I have some questions, which I could briefly go into, about what I think the future or the present problems of jazz are. I don't think—if I understand what post-modernism is in art—that jazz can be a postmodern art. It's an essentially humanistic art. To the degree that play with the codes, in a distant way, is what a lot of arts are up to these days, jazz can't do that. Let me quote from a piece I wrote recently about this problem:

> It seems logical to assume that jazz is a music that can should be played *con amore,* that is because jazz is this century's most humanistic art, a music whose goal, the discovery and expression of one's personal identity, can be reached only when musicians speak openly and honestly to those who are willing to respond in kind. But the belief that such transactions can take place rests on the faith that individual human beings still care to make that kind of response, a faith that is seldom found in the elaborately coded messages of this century's highbrow art and is even less prevalent in the mass-market products of our popular art. So the jazz musician, whose rebelliousness has ranged from bold cultural pioneering to romantic despair, now finds himself cast in the role of the loneliest rebel of them all, an artist who is unable to speak without evasion or artifice in an age which seems to demand little else.

That, in a nutshell, seems to be the problem that the music in general is facing today. Many of those who can and must still speak in that way, and their names are legion, don't seem to be abroad in a culture that is losing its ability to respond to that kind of speech. There are other people, many of them very well-intentioned, who are beginning to play a music that certainly derives from what I would

think of as being the jazz tradition, but who are speaking behind masks, where before that was known not to be the way it could be done. And I think still is the way it cannot be done.

HARPER: I'm going to go back to what I said earlier about American speech and the American tongue. I have great belief that people as makers are never going to be mechanized in any final sense. And I think that one has to believe in the process of improvisation at every level. And I'm going to give you a couple of example here.

I'm reading from the *Collected Prose of Robert Hayden.* "Not too long ago, he [he the persona—in this case, Hayden as he remembers himself as a youngster] decided to include as part of the design of a new series of poems, words and phrases remembered from childhood and youth. Under the title of *Gumbo Ya Ya*—Creole patois for 'Everybody talks'—he wrote down several pages, hoping of course, to make use of them in poems later on. Here are a few selections:

> 1. God don't like ugly and cares damn little for beauty.
>
> 2. She looks like a picture done fell out the frame.
>
> 3. Goodbye. Sweet potato, plant you now and dig you later.
>
> 4. Every shut-eye ain't sleep and every goodbye ain't gone.
>
> 5. Married? The man ain't born and his mother's dead.
>
> 6. He's a bigger liar than old Tom Culpepper and you know the devil kicked him out of hell nine times before breakfast for lying.
>
> 7. Yez, Lawd, I got me three changes a day—in rags, outa rags, and no damn rags a-tall.
>
> 8. I promised God and nine other men I wouldn't do that again.
>
> 9. Gonna hit you so hard your coattail will fly up like a window shade.
>
> 10. To be a good liar you got to have a good remembrance.

Ain't that the bad one! "To be a good liar you've got to have a good remembrance." Which is to say, you've got to be able to tell stories, you have to be able to tell stories in a true idiom, the true idiom that comes out of life. And that the kind of call-response business, which has been highlighted in black American churches, in dramaturgy, in street plays, in bars, in the kind of hopeless, soporific exchange that goes on at academic conferences—*that* can become distilled by a great poet into something which will be a commentary on our age and our culture. And I think that a phrase will sum that up. You know, musicians are terribly economic. I remember when Stevie Wonder came out with a song called "Up Tight, Out of Sight." You remember when the term was appropriated and everybody took "up tight" to mean "psychologically duressed"? You know? And I remember black folks just saying, "What is wrong with them? Don't they understand?" They'd say, "Well I guess we'll just let them have that. You can have that. Take that and we'll come up with something else."

Yusef Komunyakaa and William Matthews, with Robert Kelly

SOURCE: "Jazz and Poetry: A Conversation," in *The Georgia Review,* Vol. XLVI, No. 4, Winter, 1992, pp. 645-61.

[*In the following conversation, which was conducted publicly in a slightly different form on April 14, 1989, in Macon, Georgia, the poets Komunyakaa and Matthews respond to questions by a moderator, Robert Kelly, explaining how the rhythm and tonality of jazz, as well as its improvisational style and emotional appeal, have influenced their writing.*]

ROBERT KELLY: Jazz has been present in literature at least since the twenties and thirties when James Weldon Johnson and Langston Hughes translated the emotion in the music into their poetry. The Beats used jazz to explore more open forms and to create new rhythms. Recently, Al Young and Michael Harper have written openly of their affection for jazz musicians. And James Baldwin reminds us in "Sonny's Blues" that such music has contributed both form and content to literature when he says that jazz helps us to tell "the tale of how we suffer and how we are delighted and how we may triumph." Why is jazz important to the two of you in your work?

YUSEF KOMUNYAKAA: For me, jazz works primarily as a kind of discovery, as a way for me to discover that emotional mystery behind things. It helps me to get to a place I thought I had forgotten. What I mean by that is a closer spiritual connection to the land and the place I came from. For me, the poem doesn't have to have an overt jazz theme as such in order to have a relationship to jazz. But it should embrace the whole improvisational spirit of jazz.

Historically, the African American has had to survive by his or her sheer nerve and wit, and it often seems as if we have been forced to create everything out of nothing. Music kept us closer to the essence of ourselves. Thus, there is little wonder that the drum was outlawed in certain slave-owning locales. The drum was a threat because it articulated cultural unity and communication. But we of course began to clap our hands and stomp our feet to maintain that connection to who we are. Music is serious business in the African-American community because it is so intricately interwoven with our identity. Most of us don't have to strain to see those graceful, swaying shadows of contemporary America in cahoots with the night in Congo Square—committing an act of sabotage merely by dancing to keep forbidden gods alive.

This is almost Hegelian. We refused to become only an antithesis—lost and incomplete. So music was the main thread that linked us to the future, was a process of reclaiming ourselves. Being in motion—improvisation, becoming—this was the root of our creativity, our accentuation of the positive even when the negative pervaded. Our music became an argument with the odds, a nonverbal articulation of our pathos. In this sense, even the blues dirge

is an affirmation—the theft of possibility, words made flesh. Music has always been the bridge to what Houston Baker calls "the journey back," this needful voyage back to the source, the spawning bed of our cultural existence.

WILLIAM MATTHEWS: Yusef's comments seem to me very astute, and I endorse them almost entirely. But I'd like to make one variation on his comment about connection to land and place. There are many Americans, including me, for whom jazz and the best poetry are ways to describe their relationship to rootlessness.

I live in New York City, perhaps our ultimate haven for homeless people. I mean not only those poor souls sleeping on sewer grates and in subway stations, but also the many people who uprooted themselves to come to New York. Some came to work on Wall Street as arbitragers and grow fat, but I'm not thinking of them. I'm thinking of people like my sister, who came to New York because she's a dancer and could most fully pursue that passion in the city, or of a gay friend who left a small town in Oklahoma because he had no emotional or social home there. To find an emotional home, they had to leave a geographical home. This is a very American theme. That's why so much of the blues and jazz—and of American poetry—is full of place names, geography, travel. These songs and poems are set on planes and boats and trains. Perhaps they offer the other side of Whitman's great empathetic ideal that if you can make a home wherever you go, no place is really more a home than any other.

Yusef has stressed the emotional sources of jazz and poetry, and that raises a perplexing question. If the ultimate sources for poetry and jazz are the life of the emotions, the extreme difficulty of describing that life, and the great spiritual cost of *not* trying to describe it, then poetry and jazz are rooted at the very center of what it's like to be human. They ought to be of wide interest, therefore, and yet both poetry and jazz find themselves existing in tenuous relation to a comparatively small audience. Their vitality is honored in largely sanctuarial settings—colleges, art institutes, community centers, and so on. Outside the sanctuaries, the situation reminds me of Yogi Berra's comment about baseball fans not coming out to the stadium: "If they want to stay away in droves, you can't stop them."

The contrast between the centrality of the enterprise and the size of the audience is not something we should necessarily feel guilty about, as if we had ourselves caused it. But there is a danger that despite deep and powerful emotional bases, poetry and jazz can turn into museum arts, losing the nourishment that more direct access to an audience can provide. We couldn't—and shouldn't—have asked John Coltrane to back off and play a lot of four-four stuff in order to enlarge his audience. The artist's job is not to solve the problem—but the problem exists.

KOMUNYAKAA: What I meant by discovery, or rediscovery, is that jazz can link us to surprises in content. I wanted to write a poem that dealt with childhood, so I put on Louis Armstrong. What I'm going to do is just read you "Venus's Flytraps," and see if it has anything to do with jazz and syncopated rhythms:

> I am five,

Wading out into deep
Sunny grass,
Unmindful of snakes
& yellowjackets, out
To the yellow flowers
Quivering in sluggish heat.
Don't mess with me
'Cause I have my Lone Ranger
Six-shooter. I can hurt
You with questions
Like silver bullets.
The tall flowers in my dreams are
Big as the First State Bank,
& they eat all the people
Except the ones I love.
They have women's names,
With mouths like where
Babies come from. I am five.
I'll dance for you
If you close your eyes. No
Peeping through your fingers.
I don't supposed to be
This close to the tracks.
One afternoon I saw
What a train did to a cow.
Sometimes I stand so close
I can see the eyes
Of men hiding in boxcars.
Sometimes they wave
& holler for me to get back. I laugh
When trains make the dogs
Howl. Their ears hurt.
I also know bees
Can't live without flowers.
I wonder why Daddy
Calls Mama honey.
All the bees in the world
Live in little white houses
Except the ones in these flowers.
All sticky & sweet inside.
I wonder what death tastes like.
Sometimes I toss the butterflies
Back into the air.
I wish I knew why
The music in my head
Makes me scared.
But I know things
I don't supposed to know.
I could start walking
& never stop.
These yellow flowers
Go on forever.
Almost to Detroit.
Almost to the sea.
My mama says I'm a mistake.
That I made her a bad girl.
My playhouse is underneath
Our house, & I hear people
Telling each other secrets.

Essentially, what I was hearing were the secrets coming out of Louis Armstrong's trumpet, and I tried to relate to those and let the music take me back to that time when I was five years old—to those memories. The music becomes a place in which to recapture, to reexperience, certain things.

> **In the early 1970's, when I was listening to Miles, Coltrane, Elvin Jones, and a lot of other progressive players, I didn't know they were influencing my poetry. I just loved the sound. The music helped me free up my mind for more vivid extrusions. Jazz was just a part of my life, a continuous score to the images inside my head.**
>
> **—*Yusef Komunyakaa***

As a black American poet, however, I don't want to be stereotyped into a convenient slot—merely a jazz poet. I write about whatever captures my imagination. Anything that touches me significantly: philosophy, psychology, nature, cultural concerns, folklore, world history, sex, science, from the gut-level to the arcane, whatever. Yes, for me, jazz moves underneath many of these topics. It is often a necessary balm. We now refer to jazz as America's classical music. Unfortunately, until recently, many middle-class African Americans saw jazz as the devil's music that evolved from the whorehouses of Storyville. It wasn't sacred. Second-class citizens can be awfully puritanical, and this is especially true when they're striving for acceptance by the dominant culture.

Look at the Harlem Renaissance—the cultural straitjacket—the whole movement defined by European standards, except Langston Hughes, Helene Johnson, and Zora Neale Hurston. In fact, only Hughes whole-heartedly embraces jazz and blues as major influences. Most of these poets, including Claude McKay, Anne Spencer, and Countee Cullen, gravitated toward British Romantics such as Keats and Wordsworth. Many found more interest in New England transcendentalism than in the folk tradition of blues and jazz. Or, they connected to the flight motifs of the spirituals that had informed early black poetry. The two voices that are associated with the postrenaissance period of the 1950's are Sterling Brown and Frank Marshall Davis—both wrote jazz-and-blues-influenced poems. Gwendolyn Brooks also has a few. But the real synthesis of jazz and poetry happened in the 1960's and 1970's with Larry Neal and Amiri Baraka—the two jazz/blues philosophers. And we get someone like Jayne Cortez whose whole body of work is tied completely to jazz.

In the early 1970's, when I was listening to Miles, Coltrane, Elvin Jones, and a lot of other progressive players, I didn't know they were influencing my poetry. I just loved the sound. The music helped me free up my mind for more vivid extrusions. Jazz was just a part of my life, a continuous score to the images inside my head. It helped to expand my creative universe. It taught me I could do anything in a poem—more so than what Villon or Ginsberg taught me. The music took me back to the importance of irony, to how the dynamics of insinuation work, particularly in African-American poetry. Jazz is tonal insinuation, and it showed me how to make writing fun.

KELLY: William, can you speak to the point about the "recaptured past"? Some of your poems refer to Ben Webster, Bud Powell, and other jazz figures from the thirties and forties. Why is that period important for you?

MATTHEWS: Actually the period of jazz I love most is the one that took place in my teens and twenties, when I made my personal discovery of it. I think this may be true for many jazz buffs. Orwell said—I think it was Orwell—"What is patriotism but the love of the food one ate in one's childhood?" Essential jazz for me was Thelonious Monk, the Miles Davis quintet with Coltrane and Red Garland, and the Mingus workshop bands with Danny Richmond on drums. I must have logged a hundred hours listening to those Mingus groups in a little bar called The Showplace, long defunct now, on West 4th Street. I went to school in Massachusetts and Connecticut, and I would come down to New York on weekends to sit in various jazz bars and sip slow beers and spend my small money to rent a place so I could listen to the music.

But I learned that to listen to Mingus more alertly, I needed to know a lot more about Ellington. I started working backwards in order to learn where the musicians I loved had come from, almost in the way that at a certain age people get interested in their parent's youth and their grandparents' lives. The evidence of this is all over the poems—my interest in Webster and Lester Young and the history of the saxophone as a solo instrument. This was all music I was driven to because, I realize now, I was knocked out by a Sonny Rollins solo I heard when I was seventeen. The presence of older musicians in my poems reflects this sort of personal archaeological exploration: those earlier figures are important in the poems, but the crucial years for me were the ones I spent as a weird white be-bop groupie hanging around the Village and trying to figure out what I was listening to and why I loved it so much. The music I heard then helped me to forge an introduction to my emotional life and not to be terrified of it, and my love and gratitude for that help are undying. Also, of course, it's a very great body of music.

KELLY: Yusef, growing up in Louisiana you must have heard about and listened to Louis Armstrong early on, and you've written a poem about Charlie Mingus. What other kind of jazz is important to you?

KOMUNYAKAA: I suppose the whole spectrum of jazz would be important. When I think of be-bop—well, listening to be-bop released me from that whole lineal connection to everything. I could skip around. I could improvise with words and sound—not necessarily to imitate what the musicians were actually doing, but to discover, again, a direction I could take. I think sound is very important—rhythm—a new kind of meter that can approximate our contemporary landscape. And also, you have to realize that there is a kind of internal and psychological landscape that one gets to. This is not necessarily thought out, but is something that is achieved improvisationally.

MATTHEWS: I think it would be wrong not to talk about—though it's very difficult to talk about—the fact that

rhythm is crucial in poetry and rhythm is crucial in jazz. It's not possible to make exact correlations between the two kinds of rhythm, but the complex and beautiful rhythmic patterns of the best jazz allow variation a larger role than is usual in poetry, and the lure of this can be powerful to a young poet.

When I was a student, for example, I might go to sleep with whole passages from Dryden running through my head. They were very beautiful passages, though not in the rhythm of the talk in my classes or the chatter of the guys in the gym I played ball with or the banter of the folks I worked with for beer money while I was in college. I knew all kinds of people who didn't even know who Dryden was, but who were every bit as interesting. Their rhythms, too, were in my head when I lay down to sleep. If it weren't for something I learned listening to jazz, the gap between the two kinds of English would have seemed vast to me, but it didn't because jazz gave me permission to begin composing a poetic language based on the rhythms of the speaking voice: the voice rationalizing to itself, jiving other people, trying to seduce a comparative stranger, explaining why a paper is not ready on time, doing puns and jokes and imitations—in sum, doing the real emotional business of daily life, full of weird quirks and odd lilts. To pay attention to everything I wanted to hear, I needed as many useful models as I could get my hands on, and jazz helped me at least as much as Dryden.

As a kid I spoke a rather special dialect, the patois of the well-educated, bookish kid in the culture. It's the American equivalent, perhaps, of the dialect BBC announcers speak in England. There are a limited number of occasions in life where it's really the dialect that's spoken; in that sense it's just slightly more of a *lingua franca* than Esperanto. I came to want to be able to speak more like my countrymen and countrywomen; there's no reason to order a cheese danish at the corner deli in the words of Samuel Johnson. So, for me, linguistic improvisation meant not staying trapped in the dialect of my upbringing and education, meant moving out and experiencing as a ventriloquist the lives of my fellow citizens. That's what it means to be American, I thought.

I could listen to the weirdest music before I could read Whitman. When I first heard Yusef Lateef or Eric Dolphy, let's say, I had no idea what they were up to, but I knew I was interested by it. That experience taught me to trust my intuition and ignorance, something I couldn't do as easily in front of a text. In a way, I learned to read Whitman by listening to Don Cherry play his pocket trumpet.

KOMUNYAKAA: Jazz also worked for *me* as a way of reestablishing a kind of trust. A trust in what I had known earlier. For some reason, I think it directed me back to my need to say something.

What do I mean by that? Whatever it is, maybe I'm trying to say it in these words, in a poem called "Blue Light Lounge Sutra for the Performance Poets at Harold Park Hotel":

> the need gotta be
> so deep words can't
> answer simple questions

all night long notes
stumble off the tongue
& color the air indigo
so deep fragments of gut
& flesh cling to the song
you gotta get into it
so deep salt crystallizes on eyelashes
the need gotta be
so deep you can vomit up ghosts
& not feel broken
till you are no more
than a half ounce of gold
in painful brightness
you gotta get into it
blow that saxophone
so deep all the sex & dope in this world
can't erase your need
to howl against the sky
the need gotta be
so deep you can't
just wiggle your hips
& rise up out of it
chaos in the cosmos
modern man in the pepperpot
you gotta get hooked
into every hungry groove
so deep the bomb locked
in rust opens like a fist
into it into it so deep
rhythm is pre-memory
the need gotta be basic
animal need to see
& know the terror
we are made of honey
cause if you wanna dance
this boogie be ready
to let the devil use your head
for a drum

Risk: essentially, that's what I'm talking about. You have to have that need to take risks, and they come to us in varied patterns and intensities. McKay's protest sonnet "If We Must Die" took a risk in content. Why else was it read into the *Congressional Record* by Senator Henry Cabot Lodge? But McKay took few risks structurally. Poetry has always been associated with the elite, the leisure class, with "high" culture of Europe, and the African-American poet of the 1920's was still in almost the same dilemma as Phillis Wheatley when her work was defined by Thomas Jefferson as beneath a critical response. That is, well into this century the black poet was still aspiring to acceptance by whites, still binding for the wand of approval and recognition as a mere human being.

Consequently, few black poets were willing to admit the influence of jazz because it was defined as "low" culture; it had been created by the descendants of Africa. Only during the 1960's did we begin to rediscover that which was ours, redefining ourselves with Africa as an emotional backdrop. Young black poets began to accept Langston Hughes and Frank Horne and those white poets associated with modernism—an American tongue and ear. Indeed, jazz shaped the Beat aesthetic, but that movement seemed a privilege only whites could afford. Blacks, fighting for inclusion, didn't have to ostracize themselves voluntarily. Of course, this was a cultural paradox. To many the Beat Movement was nothing more than the latest min-

strel show in town with the new Jim Crows and Zip Coons, another social club that admitted hardly any women or blacks. Yet they said that Charlie Parker was their Buddha.

The whole thing seemed like a love-hate complex magnified. Only the spirit of improvisation held it together like a jam session. This was the element of excitement—the same kind of energy that we poets often try to capture in our jazz-related poems—what we see in the work of Michael Harper, Jay Wright, and many others.

KELLY: I think I see how, to both of you, jazz is crucial for freeing you from having to listen to voices in just one way and for allowing you to appreciate different rhythms of speech and language. Jonathan Holden has written about how contemporary poets borrow from more familiar kinds of discourse (e.g., letters, confessions, patterned conversations) to inform poetry. Do the formal elements in jazz composition (the improvisational component of a piece, predictable chord changes, refrain, contrapuntal harmony) work themselves into the structure of your poems?

MATTHEWS: I think what Holden is talking about has to do with occasions for speech. If you abandon the sonnet and other inherited stanza forms, why not work with rhetorical forms—the letter, the anecdote, etc.? As Mingus once said, "Can't improvise on nothing, man; you gotta improvise on something." Holden, in a way, is talking about getting started.

What I'd like to talk about is not only the discovery of the occasion for how a poem might begin, but the discovery of the whole process of a poem, a way of thinking and feeling at the same time, as if it were all one activity—and it is. Writing is a way of being in the world as if the famous mind/body problem didn't exist. And it doesn't. It's only a poor invention of philosophy, one of those road signs rational intelligence puts up to mark the farthest its powers can carry it. To confuse that road sign with the limits of human intelligence is to shrink the word "intelligence" to a mere synonym for "rationality."

Jazz and poetry are about what it feels like to be whole.

KOMUNYAKAA: Often we hear about the emotional thread holding poems together. But, as in jazz, we also have to think about a *tonal* thread holding the poem together, whereby we are able to make leaps not necessarily through logic, but through feeling.

KELLY: Yusef, which poem of yours is it that has the refrain, "hard love, it's hard love"?

KOMUNYAKAA: That's "Copacetic Mingus." It has an epigraph from the man himself—"Mingus One, Two and Three. / Which is the image you want the world to see?"—and then I carry it on this way:

Heartstring. Blessed wood
& every moment the thing's made of:
ball of fatback
licked by fingers of fire.
Hard love, it's hard love.
Running big hands down
the upright's wide hips,

rocking his moon-eyed mistress
with gold in her teeth.
Art & life bleed
into each other
as he works the bow.
But tonight we're both a long ways
from the Mile High City,
1973. Here in New Orleans
years below sea level,
I listen to *Pithecanthropus
erectus:* Up & down, under
& over, every which way—
thump, thump, dada—ah, yes.
Wood heavy with tenderness,
Mingus fingers the loom
gone on Segovia,
dogging the raw strings
unwaxed with rosin.
Hyperbolic bass line. Oh, no!
Hard love, it's hard love.

KELLY: The poem itself seems to be an instrument, one expressing your feeling about Mingus.

KOMUNYAKAA: I think so. It's the whole thing of putting words together to create tension within the context of the poem. What I'm talking about, I think, has to do with language itself, though subject matter creates a poem's tone, also. In writing the Vietnam poems for my collection *Dien Cai Dau,* I questioned if I could stay close to the jazz motif, and it was very difficult. I don't think those poems were influenced by jazz as much as the ones in *I Apologize for the Eyes in My Head* or *Copacetic.* However, I know that there is at least one poem informed by jazz in the Vietnam book, "You and I Are Disappearing," which has a rhythm that came out of listening to Thelonious Monk. Monk would give you enough space to fit your heart into: repetition with slight variations, playing with pauses and silences, an unspoken call-and-response. Monk knew how to be his own Amen Corner. He had listened closely to those gospel singers he'd accompanied as a teenager; his sound is one that always takes me back home to the foundation of my creative impulse. I love his jagged tonality, how he was able to leave a piece unresolved—a door left ajar that invited you in as a participant. I try to write poems like that.

KELLY: What you just said about "heart" returns me to "Copacetic Mingus" and in particular its lines "Art & life bleed / into each other." They say much about the melding of poetry and jazz.

MATTHEWS: The art/life problem is rather like the mind/body problem. At our best we like them bleeding into one another, and we like to oppose the ease with which we can set up borders between them. Of course, music draws from the history of music, and in that way music is "about" music. In a similar way all art is partially about art. Any music resembles any other music more than it resembles an insurance policy, let's say. Thus, while one of jazz's functions is to be in benign and loving opposition to less improvisational forms of music, it has more in common with them than it does with silence, and perhaps even more than it does with speech. But finally, jazz is not separable from life. Jazz is what life would

sound like if the only expressive form it could find were jazz.

KOMUNYAKAA: John Cage composed pieces that used silence as music, and many of the Black Mountain poets were aware of silence on the page, how the white space contributes to the poem's rhythm. Olson and Creeley come to mind. Perhaps this is what first drew Baraka to them. I can definitely see that influence in *The Dead Lecturer,* but I'm sure that his attraction to jazz was always there. His whole demeanor seems to be informed by jazz, and he also knows the sophisticated nuance of silence in poetry. The jazz-influenced poet is quite aware of silence. Not just how it's broken up or accented on the page, but many times silence as an implied element.

MATTHEWS: The spaces between words are a form of structured silence.

The silence that's terrifying is the one that just goes. . . .

That's the one that is the enemy of love and joy. It's a whole other matter.

KELLY: When you talk about improvisation, I think of the be-bop period and how a lot of improvisational pieces were convoluted re-creations of standard melodies, redefinitions of jazz by a new generation of musicians. To the casual listener, these pieces sounded completely original, but they were built on familiar tunes. When you improvise in a poem, what gives it shape other than your improvisation?

KOMUNYAKAA: I mentioned the whole thing about tonal thread. Many times, if you notice, in the jazz-related poem there's a refrain. Sometimes I will use a refrain during composition—something that I return to—but I'll go back later and remove it. Essentially, the refrain keeps me going—moving on with the same tone pretty much throughout the poem.

MATTHEWS: I've already referred to learnable structures that help you save yourself from getting lost in improvising—Mingus saying, "Can't improvise on nothing, man; you gotta improvise on something." About half the be-bop classics are based on the chord changes of "I Got Rhythm." There are "fake books," so called, that give musicians the changes to numerous songs. There's even a fake book called *The Real Book.* As to improvisation *ex nihilo,* it just doesn't happen.

An interesting question is, "What in the writing of a poem provides something similar?" There are certain devices—repetition, diminuendo and crescendo—that can be described in musical terms. But, naturally, something happens in the course of a poem that doesn't happen in a piece of music. Words have conventional meaning, and so something's being proposed—to the reader at least, and in many poems to an implied listener, some second character of the poem beside the one we usually call "the speaker." Is it believable or not? Interesting or not? There are issues of persuasion and consent raised by any given poem that I believe are important sources of improvisation in the writing of poetry.

Here's a piece of mine with some jazz subject matter. As

While one of jazz's functions is to be in benign and loving opposition to less improvisational forms of music, it has more in common with them than it does with silence, and perhaps even more than it does with speech. But finally, jazz is not separable from life. Jazz is what life would sound like if the only expressive form it could find were jazz.

—William Matthews

Yusef said so wisely at the beginning, it's a sense of procedure rather than subject matter that is the deep link between jazz and poetry. I happen to write frequently about jazz because I write about what I love, but it's the procedural link that interests me most.

This is a poem called "The Accompanist." It's spoken by an old guy who made a career as an accompanist to a famous singer, and who has been asked what it was like to be around her. He also knows a few things to say to people who may be interested in what the skills of a good accompanist are. I had no particular singer or accompanist in mind. The poem's written to discourage identification.

The poem may well be about erotic life, and how hard it is to maintain in erotic life that equilibrium between the parties we rather grandly call "equality." But I choose to quote the poem here partly because it lives, if it does, by raising some of the issues of persuasion and consent and credibility I was just talking about.

Of course, there's an important difference between the kind of improvisation in poetry I was mentioning and improvising on the bandstand. At home, if I get lost, there's always the friendly wastebasket, and then I can make another try at it. Get lost on the bandstand, and you have a bunch of half-drunk people pointing and laughing from the audience—or at least that's how it could feel.

"The Accompanist"

Don't play too much, don't play
too loud, don't play the melody.
You have to anticipate her
and to subdue yourself.
She used to give me her smoky
eye when I got boisterous,
so I learned to play on tip-
toe and to play the better half
of what I might. I don't like
to complain, though I notice
that I get around to it somehow.
We made a living and good music,
both, night after night; the blue
curlicues of smoke rubbing their
staling and wispy backs
against the ceilings, the flat
drinks and scarce taxis, the jazz life
we bitch about the way Army pals
complain about the food and then

re-up. Some people like to say
with smut in their voices how playing
the way we did at our best is partly
sexual. OK, I could tell them
a tale or two, and I've heard
the records Lester cut with Lady Day
and all that rap, and it's partly
sexual but it's mostly practice
and music. As for partly sexual,
I'll take wholly sexual any day,
but that's a duet and we're talking
accompaniment. Remember "Reckless
Blues"? Bessie Smith sings out "Daddy"
and Louis Armstrong plays back "Daddy"
as clear through his horn as if he'd
spoken it. But it's her daddy and her
story. When you play it you become
your part in it, one of her beautiful
troubles, and then, however much music
can do this, part of her consolation,
the way pain and joy eat off each other's
plates, but mostly you play to drunks,
to the night, to the way you judge
and pardon yourself, to all that goes
not unsung, but unrecorded.

KELLY: "When you play it, you become a part in it." Improvisation is participating in something that is already ongoing?

MATTHEWS: Contributing or giving something that is already ongoing, to be sure. Also, for me, the almost theatrical or dramatic meaning of your "part" in it, your role in it. This refers to what I said earlier about experiencing the lives of your countrymen and countrywomen.

There are two responses that people can make to pieces of writing they like. One is "I can really relate to that because my grandmother died, too." But that's not really what reading and writing are about. All our grandmothers are going to die. What that person means is "I looked into your book and lo, it was a mirror, and in it I saw myself." The connection that I love, both as reader and writer, is the other one: "I would never have thought or felt such a thing without this text." It takes you outside your narrowest self. You're other, larger, different and more strange than you knew. So in that way "your part in it" is to be somebody a little different from yourself, to play *that* role and know what it's like.

KELLY: Which means creating the voices.

KOMUNYAKAA: Those are the extended possibilities. I mentioned the Vietnam poems, and the one informed by Thelonious Monk. If you listen to Monk, you hear all of his repetition constantly, and I tried to capture that repetition, that "other role" Bill noted, in the very short space of "You and I Are Disappearing":

The cry I bring down from the hills
belongs to a girl still burning
inside my head. At daybreak
        she burns like a piece of paper.
She burns like foxfire
in a thigh-shaped valley.
A skirt of flames
dances around her
at dusk.

We stand with our hands
hanging at our sides,
while she burns
       like a sack of dry ice.
She burns like oil on water.
She burns like a cattail torch
dipped in gasoline.
She glows like the fat tip
of a banker's cigar,
       silent as quicksilver.
A tiger under a rainbow
   at nightfall.
She burns like a shot glass of vodka.
She burns like a field of poppies
at the edge of a rain forest.
She rises like dragonsmoke
   to my nostrils.
She burns like a burning bush
driven by a godawful wind.

The poem pretty much ended itself when Thelonious ended the record. What I'm saying is that there is a kind of accidental closure, a kind of completion that happens that you cannot plot. Jazz helps you to discover this, too.

MATTHEWS: You may have taken on certain formal housekeeping duties—a twelve or thirty-two bar structure, let's say—and knowing that can help you discover accidental closure, but only a little. You've still got to find your way from the middle to the end, even if you have a notion when the end's coming up. So far as you can manage it, a good place to stop is when you've said what you can find to say—as I will stop right now.

KOMUNYAKAA: I'd like to believe that jazz could parallel the act of demanding a spiritual and cultural freedom, that it can connect us to who we are as well as to others. And I hope it keeps me connected to what I have to do as a poet. I love surprises. As I listen to Dolphy or Dexter, I think their music works like a refrain underneath my life keeping it all together and in focus. If I'm having a writer's block, a couple of days of Coltrane or Miles does the trick. It seems that all my muses are tangled up in music, that they are hip enough to connect me to Soyinka or Robbe-Grillet. I don't have to torture my imagination to put Miles side by side with Sartre in a poolroom. Anything is possible; this is what jazz had taught me about life. My creative universe is always in a flux. Active. Anything and everything inform my work. It is my nature to embrace whatever is out there, and jazz has been the one thing that gives some symmetry to my poetry, gives it shape and tonal equilibrium. This is something that I only realized recently, and I don't want to be overly conscious of it. I like the implied freedom jazz brings to my work; a soloist can go to hell or heaven and back, bending a tune into an extended possibility, and bringing it all around together as if his life depended on it.

For some, jazz-influenced poetry might appear as a threat to the canon. This isn't new. Jazz has always been somewhat of a threat, and not only in America or England. Look at the stir it created in 1938 at that "Entartete Musik" exhibition in Dusseldorf, Germany, with Ernst Krenek's *Jonny spielt auf.* But it has also survived the cultural critics and the accountant's calculator at the record

companies. I feel blessed that something pulled jazz and poetry together inside me.

FURTHER READING

Bibliography

Breton, Marcela. "An Annotated Bibliography of Selected Jazz Short Stories." *African American Review* 26, No. 2 (Summer 1992): 299-306.
    A bibliography of short jazz fiction, listing works published between 1926 and 1989. Breton supplies a brief plot summary for each of the fifty-one stories included.

Modern Language Association. *A Bibliography on the Relations of Literature and the Other Arts, 1952-1967.* Modern Language Association, Discussion Groups, General Topic 9. New York: AMS Press, 1968, 37 p.
    A bibliography divided into two subject headings, music and literature and visual arts and literature, listing commentary published between 1952 and 1967.

Criticism

Cluck, Nancy Anne. *Literature and Music: Essays on Form.* Provo, Utah: Brigham Young University Press, 1981, 258 p.
    A collection of essays focusing on how the popular musical forms of the eighteenth century were incorporated into nineteenth- and twentieth-century literary texts. The book includes essays on the relationship between musical and literary structure, essays on theme and variation form in poetry, and essays on the sonata form in poetry, the novel, and short fiction.

Davenport, Doris. "Music in Poetry: if you can't feel it/you can't fake it." *Mid-American Review* X, No. 2 (1990): 57-64.
    Autobiographical essay in which Davenport places herself in the tradition of black poets who work with music and comments on the requirements, rewards, and frustrations of poetry performance.

Dickson, L. L. " 'Keep It in the Head': Elements in Modern Black American Poetry." *MELUS* 10, No. 1 (Spring 1983): 29-37.
    Demonstrates how jazz music has influenced the rhythm and imagery of contemporary African-American poetry.

Dixon, Wheeler Winston. "Urban Black American Music in the Late 1980s: The 'Word' as Cultural Signifier." *The Midwest Quarterly* XXX, No. 2 (Winter 1989): 229-41.
    Discusses the lyrical concerns of a number of rap artists, including Run DMC, Schooly D, Salt-N-Pepa, and Public Enemy.

Eliot, T. S. "The Music of Poetry." In *On Poetry and Poets,* pp. 17-33. New York: Farrar, Strauss and Cudahy, 1957.
    Argues that the musical qualities of poetry result from the poet's use of the everyday language of conversation.

Fioretos, Aris. "Nothing: Reading Paul Celan's 'Engführung.' " *Comparative Literature Studies* 27, No. 2 (1990): 158-68.
    Speculates on the significance of the asterisks that are marked between stanzas in Paul Celan's poem "Eng-

führung," which means "stretto" in English, a musical device used in the composition of fugues.

Fox, Thomas C. "Oobliadooh or EIKENNGETTNOSET-TISFEKSCHIN: Music, Language, and Opposition in GDR Literature." *The Germanic Review* LXI, No. 3 (Summer 1986): 109-16.
> Analyzes four East German literary texts from the 1960s and 1970s in which jazz and rock and roll music function metaphorically and structurally to signify opposition to socialist politics.

Frye, Northrop, ed. *Sound and Poetry.* English Institute Essays, 1956. New York: Columbia University Press, 1957, 156 p.
> Six essays on the relationship between poetry and music written from the scholarly perspectives of musical composition, musicological criticism, musicological history, rhetoric, rhetorical analysis, and linguistics. The collection also includes an introduction by Frye in which he discusses how music has influenced the sound and rhythm of poetry.

Grayson, David. "The Libretto of Debussy's *Pélleas et Mélisande.*" *Music & Letters* 66, No. 1 (January 1985): 34-50.
> Documents Claude Debussy's nine-year struggle to transform Maurice Maeterlinck's play *Pélleas et Mélisande* into a libretto.

Hertz, David Michael. *The Tuning of the Word: The Musico-Literary Poetics of the Symbolist Movement.* Carbondale: Southern Illinois University Press, 1987, 241 p.
> Studies the Symbolist aesthetic in terms of the historical development of nineteenth-century music and demonstrates the influence of Symbolism on various art forms, including the lyric poem, the song, the cycle of poems, the song cycle, the tone poem, the lyric play, and the opera.

Lees, Heath. "Watt: Music, Tuning, and Tonality." In *The Beckett Studies Reader,* edited by S. E. Gontarski, pp. 167-85. Gainesville: University Press of Florida, 1993.
> An examination of the imagery of tuning and untuning in Samuel Beckett's novel *Watt.*

Lenhart, Charmenz S. *Musical Influence on American Poetry.* Athens: University of Georgia Press, 1956, 337 p.
> Studies the influence of music on America's best-known lyric poets from the seventeenth, eighteenth, and nineteenth centuries, with separate chapters devoted to Edgar Allan Poe, Walt Whitman, and Sidney Lanier.

Mallarmé, Stéphane. "Music and Literature." In *Mallarmé: Selected Prose Poems, Essays, & Letters,* translated by Bradford Cook, pp. 43-56. Baltimore: Johns Hopkins Press, 1956.
> Discusses the then-current state of poetry writing and attributes transcendental qualities to music and literature. Mallarmé's essay was originally delivered as a lecture, first at Oxford University on March 1, 1894, and then at Cambridge University on March 3, 1894.

Matlaw, Ralph E. "Scriabin and Russian Symbolism." *Comparative Literature* 31, No. 1 (Winter 1979): 1-23.
> Underscores the "crucial importance" of Aleksandr Scriabin (1872-1915), a renowned Russian composer and pianist, to the culture of his era, focusing on how his aesthetic theories influenced Russian symbolist drama.

McDonald, Christie. "Unsettling the Score: Poetry and Music." *The Russian Review* LXXVII, No. 3 (May 1986): 254-63.
> An analysis of Stéphane Mallarmé's ideas on the relationship between poetry and music based on Mallarmé's prose writings.

McGlathery, James, ed. *Music and German Literature: Their Relationship since the Middle Ages.* Columbia, S.C.: Camden House, 1992, 352 p.
> A volume of essays on the connection between music and German literature, which the editor claims is the most comprehensive work on the subject. The collection is arranged chronologically, with sections devoted to the Middle Ages, the Baroque era, the Enlightenment, and the nineteenth and twentieth centuries.

Morley, Hilda. "Music and Poetry." *Mid-American Review* X, No. 2 (1990): 65-8.
> Compares the processes of creating music and poetry, noting that while both poetry and music are created out of the material of sound, the poet's tools are limited to the sounds of everyday language.

Noske, Frits. "Sound and Sentiment: The Function of Music in the Gothic Novel." *Music & Letters* 62, No. 2 (April 1981): 162-75.
> Explores how sonorous devices function thematically, structurally, and imagistically in Gothic fiction, concentrating on the novels of Ann Radcliffe, Matthew Lewis, Charles Robert Maturin, and Charlotte Dacre.

O'Connor, Honor. "Sounds and Voices: Aspects of Contemporary Irish Music and Poetry." In *Proceedings of the Ninth International Congress of the International Association for the Study of Anglo-Irish Literature,* Vol. II, pp. 211-17, edited by Birgit Bramsbäck and Martin Croghan. Uppsala, Sweden: Uppsala University, 1988.
> Praises the poems *The Week-End of Dermot and Grace,* by Eugene Watters, *The Rough Field,* by John Montague, and *Cromwell,* by Brendan Kennelly for their innovation—which O'Connor finds lacking in most contemporary Irish poetry—revealing how their structures are more analogous to music than to traditional poetry forms.

Roos, Michael E. "The Walrus and the Deacon: John Lennon's Debt to Lewis Carroll." *Journal of Popular Culture* 18, No. 1 (Summer 1984): 19-29.
> Documents the pervasive influence of Lewis Carroll's *Alice* books on John Lennon's songs from 1966-67. Roos groups the Carroll-inspired songs from these years into four categories: those with a looking-glass motif, those with the theme of childhood reminiscence or escape, those with a dream motif, and those that are based almost entirely on imagery from the *Alice* books, namely, "Lucy in the Sky with Diamonds" and "I Am the Walrus."

Scher, Steven Paul. *Verbal Music in German Literature.* New Haven, Conn.: Yale University Press, 1968, 181 p.
> Studies passages in German literary works in which music is presented in words, focusing on the writings of Wilhelm Wackenroder, Ludwig Tieck, E. T. A. Hoffmann, Heinrich Heine, and Thomas Mann.

Stanley, Patricia Haas. "Verbal Music in Theory and Practice." *The Germanic Review* LII, No. 3 (May 1977): 217-25.
> A structural and stylistic analysis of Wolfgang

Hildesheimer's literary simulation of a toccata in his novel *Tynset.*

Storr, Sherman. "Poetry and Music: The Artful Twins." *Et cetera* 43, No. 4 (Winter 1986): 337-48.

Compares various lines of verse with portions of musical scores to illustrate how poetry and music often parallel one another in terms of mood and technique.

Thomas, Lorenzo. " 'Communicating by Horns': Jazz and Redemption in the Poetry of the Beats and the Black Arts Movement." *African American Review* 26, No. 2 (Summer 1992): 291-98.

Finds that the poets associated with the Beat Generation and the Black Arts movement were inspired by the re-bellious spirit of jazz music and in their writings elevated the jazz musician to the status of a spiritual leader of social and political protest.

Weiner, Marc A. "Urwaldmusik and the Borders of German Identity: Jazz in Literature of the Weimar Republic." *The German Quarterly* 64, No. 4 (Fall 1991): 475-87.

Argues that the writers of the Weimar era used the subject of jazz music to signify various social, political, and cultural concerns of postwar German society.

Yeats, W. B. "Speaking to the Psaltery." In *Essays and Introductions,* pp. 13-27. New York: Macmillan Co., 1961.

Expresses his enthusiasm for the art of reciting poetry to musical notes played on string instruments.

Vorticism

INTRODUCTION

Vorticism was an English avant-garde movement which encompassed both the visual and literary arts. Founded in 1912 by the writer and painter Wyndham Lewis, Vorticism was related to Futurism and Cubism in painting and to Imagism in literature. Chiefly, the movement extolled the virtues of the machine. Its visual art was sharp-edged and angular; its literature is frequently described as turbulent and noisy. In 1914 Lewis and writer Ezra Pound (who coined the term Vorticism) established *Blast,* a magazine dedicated to promoting the new movement. However, the periodical—like Vorticism itself—was shortlived and lasted only two issues. Although several young artists and writers joined the movement, including David Bomberg, Henri Gaudier-Brzeska, T. E. Hulme, and Pound, Vorticism did not endure as a distinct literary and artistic school after the first World War.

WYNDHAM LEWIS AND VORTICISM

William C. Wees

SOURCE: "Wyndham Lewis and Vorticism," in *Blast 3,* edited by Seamus Cooney, and others, Black Sparrow Press, 1984, pp. 47-50.

[*In the following essay, Wees documents Lewis's activities as the founding figure of the Vorticist movement.*]

In 1914 Wyndham Lewis devoted much of his time to what he described as his "undeniable political activity." In the space of half a year Lewis directed London's new Rebel Art Centre, led a widely reported campaign against the Italian Futurists, and edited and made most of the major contributions to BLAST, *Review of the Great English Vortex.* These activities attracted attention—exactly the purpose of art politics—and won for Lewis a reputation as, in the words of the *Daily News* (7 April 1914), "the extremely able leader of the Cubist movement in England."

Lewis's sly self-caricature in *Blasting and Bombardiering* describes "Mr. W.L., Leader of the 'Great London Vortex,'" who discovered in himself the "romantic figure [who] must always emerge to captain the 'group.'" In accordance with his role, he never passed up a chance to explain in articles, interviews and manifestos, "why life had to be changed, and how." "'Kill John Bull with Art!' I shouted. And John and Mrs. Bull leapt for joy, in a cynical convulsion. For they felt as safe as houses. So did I." Exciting and inconsequential—Lewis's role as leader seemed little more than that, when measured strictly in political terms. Nevertheless, without the urge to captain a group, Lewis might not have produced the public pronouncements that were, certainly, propaganda for himself and his group. The pronouncements were critical and aesthetic documents as well, and they emerged from a concerted effort to find new art forms appropriate to the new times.

BLAST was the major document. It was the Vorticist group's statement, not Lewis's alone. In fact, it was one of the fruits of a four-year transformation of the English art world that had begun with Roger Fry's "Manet and the Post-Impressionists" exhibition in November 1910.

In 1910, as the art critic Frank Rutter said at the time, "Art in Paris had entered upon a stage practically unknown to us in Britain." Two years later, however, at Fry's "Second Post-Impressionist Exhibition" there was an "English Group" including some English artists as "advanced" as any in Paris. December 1913 saw a large exhibition of "Post-Impressionists, Cubists and Others" at Brighton, with a separate "Cubist Room" for eight of the exhibiting artists. Most of those eight joined Wyndham Lewis at the Rebel Art Centre when it opened in April 1914.

Intended as a crafts workshop, atelier, gallery and lecture hall, the Rebel Art Centre in reality was little more than a meeting place for some of the English Cubists, who were soon calling themselves Vorticists. This group included Edward Wadsworth, Frederick Etchells, Cuthbert Hamilton, Lawrence Atkinson, William Roberts, Jessie Dismorr, Helen Saunders, Henri Gaudier-Brzeska, Wyndham Lewis and Ezra Pound. It was Pound who first applied the label "Vortex" to their particular phase of English Cubism, and in July 1914, BLAST appeared, defining and illustrating Vorticism as a movement in its own right.

"We worked separately, we found an underlying agreement, we decided to stand together," Pound said of the group. "To stand together" was a political way of talking, and characteristic of a time when "avant-garde" had not lost all of its military connotations, when "revolutionary" or "anarchical" art was still regarded as a political threat to the Establishment, when "militant" was as readily applied to artists as to suffragettes, when artists joined "conspiracies" and "putsches," had "headquarters" and issued "manifestos." The format and predominant tone of BLAST derived from that state of the arts in England, and the way Pound, Lewis and others talked about Vorticism was strongly shaped by it.

The Vorticists' "underlying agreement" revealed itself in the strikingly similar phrases they used to convey their sense of intense artistic expression: "a mental-emotive impulse" (Lewis), "an intellectual and emotional complex" (Pound), "a vast intellectual emotion" (Gaudier-Brzeska). It appeared in the images with which they characterized art they admired: "sharpness and rigidity" (Gaudier), "hard light, clear edges" (Pound), "rigid reflections of stone and steel" (Lewis). It expressed itself most powerfully in the visual and literary styles of the movement, and in the theory and criticism included in BLAST.

The essence of the Vorticists' visual style lay in the kind of solutions those artists found to the problem of formally unifying abstract, geometrical shapes. The most forceful solutions came from Lewis, who had been working on the problem since 1911 or 1912. Lewis brought to his work an Expressionist fascination with strange, stark pictures with powerful psychological overtones; a Futurist desire to shatter his subjects into interpenetrating fragments locked together by dynamic "force-lines"; a Cubist refusal to make more than minimal reference to anything outside the picture's own formal, abstract framework. Perhaps the first fully successful synthesizing of these predilections appeared in his *Timon of Athens* drawings of 1912. There Lewis integrated mask-like faces, stylized limbs, truncated bodies, arcs, lines and wedges, to produce abstract designs with representational details. By the end of 1913, some of Lewis's work eschewed representational elements entirely.

In the "Cubist Room" at Brighton and in subsequent exhibitions of 1914 and 1915, he showed a number of totally abstract pictures. Interlocking lines, arcs, triangles, rectangles and other geometric forms drawn with mechanical precision and painted with flat, lowkeyed hues (when colour appeared at all) had become characteristic of all the Vorticists' work by the time they exhibited together at the "Vorticists' Exhibition" in June 1915. But only Lewis seemed fully capable of conveying what the *Athenaeum* (19 June 1915) called "systems of interacting movement" and the "clash of opposing forces." In Lewis's work, the meeting and interpenetrating of abstract, geometric elements reshaped and energized the spaces they defined, so that the whole design and all of its parts, seemed forever locked in conflict, or in a highly aggressive embrace. Combat, dance and courtship had often served as subject matter for Lewis's pre-Vorticist pictures, and they continued to be reference points or analogies for the brutal and delicate, passionate and coolly precise relationship implicit in his abstract, Vorticist work.

> **The Vorticists intended to build—or rebuild—as well as destroy, and they regarded England as the proper site for their constructive efforts. "The Modern World is due almost entirely to Anglo-Saxon genius—its appearance and its spirit," they announced in their manifesto.**
>
> **— *William C. Wees***

Similar preoccupations were at work when Lewis tried to produce a literary counterpart to the Vorticist visual style. The diction and layout of BLAST's manifesto grew out of Lewis's efforts to bring literature up to the front ranks of the "visual revolution." Gaudier-Brzeska's "Vortex" essay in BLAST 1, and Pound's "Dogmatic Statement on the Game and Play of Chess (Theme for a Series of Pictures)" in BLAST 2, were also contributions to that effort, but the *pièce de résistance* of literary Vorticism was Lewis's *Enemy of the Stars* in the first issue of BLAST.

In that violent closet drama, character, setting and action emerge in glimpses and fragments. A characteristic passage presents a fight (strongly suggestive of the combat relationships in Lewis's visual art) between Argol and his disciple Hanp:

> Flushes on silk epiderm and fierce card-play of fists between them: emptying of "hand" on soft flesh-table.
> Arms of grey windmills, grinding anger on stone of the new heart.
> Messages from one to another, dropped down anywhere when nobody is looking, reaching brain by telegraph: most desolating and alarming messages possible.
> The attacker rushed in drunk with blows. They rolled, swift jagged rut, into one corner of shed: large insect scuttling roughly to hiding. Stopped astonished. (BLAST 1)

The action and language are violent, but individual moments of action are strangely isolated and static. Events are broken down and reconstructed like the interrelated fragments in Vorticist pictures.

No single work, except BLAST itself, fully expressed the whole set of attitudes that constituted Vorticist doctrine. With its pinkish-purple cover crossed diagonally by the single word "BLAST" in three-and-one-quarter-inch-high black letters, its 160 nearly folio-sized pages of unusually heavy paper, its thick, blocky print, some of which was larger than newspaper headlines, its manifesto of "blasts" and "blesses," and its generally aggressive tone, BLAST 1 seemed exceedingly brash and in bad taste. Its sense of humour ("great barbarous weapon," as the manifesto called it) mixed with a tone of righteous indignation, gave BLAST the mien of a modern barbarian bent upon destroying an old, weak, decadent civilization. In the spirit of Nietzsche's declaration. "This universe is a monster of energy without beginning or end, a fixed and brazen quality of energy," BLAST set about establishing a new, virile civilization based on hardness, violence, and the worship of energy. "Will Energy some day reach Earth like violent civilization, smashing or hardening all?" Lewis asked in *Enemy of the Stars.* BLAST was meant to be a harbinger of that Energy pursuing its self-appointed mission of, in Lewis's words, "blowing away dead ideas and worn-out notions."

The Vorticists intended to build—or rebuild—as well as destroy, and they regarded England as the proper site for their constructive efforts. "The Modern World is due almost entirely to Anglo-Saxon genius—its appearance and its spirit," they announced in their manifesto. "Machinery, trains, steam-ships, all that distinguishes externally our time, came far more from here than anywhere else." English artists should be the best equipped to bring "the forms of machinery" into modern art, for the English "are the inventors of this bareness and hardness, and should be the great enemies of Romance." By this line of argument the Vorticists accomplished two things at once. They emphasized the Englishness (and hence, uniqueness) of their movement, and they linked their movement—whether they intended to or not—with T. E. Hulme's crusade against softness, empathy, and other expressions of the "Romantic" point of view.

The Vorticists exceeded Hulme, however, in their invocation of a great, primitive "Art instinct" that used machinery for its models of "bareness and hardness." "Vorticism accepted the machine world," Lewis said later. "It sought out machine-forms." In fact, in BLAST 2 Lewis insisted that all modern artists should strive to express "something of the fatality, grandeur and efficiency of a machine." The perfect Vorticist machine was the dynamo, whose work goes on out of sight, beneath a hard, implacable exterior. Internally dynamic and energy-producing, externally calm—that was the impression aimed for in Vorticist art, and evoked by the image of the Vortex appearing several times in the pages of BLAST 1: a solid cone whirling on an unshakeable axis, a symbol of primordial energy harnessed by the intellect and by art.

The broadest implications of the Vortex led to the division of all art into two categories essentially parallel to Hulme's "abstract" or "Classical" (of which the Vorticists approved) and "empathetic" or "Romantic" (of which they did not). Anything clearcut, hard, rigid, and uncompromising gained the Vorticists' approval; conversely, blurred lines, softness, flexibility, and compromise were rejected and ridiculed. Speed, mass education, democracy, and all forms of sentimentality were attacked because they, too, seemed to blur lines of distinction and break down rigid demarcations.

Of all the Vorticists, Lewis was the most uncompromising. He praised the "disciplined, blunt, thick and brutal" designs he found in a display of German woodcuts, and he referred admiringly to the "savage" artist who prefers to "reduce his Great Art down to the simple black human bullet," rather than risk "dissolv[ing] in vagueness of space." Lewis prescribed a "course of egoistic hardening" for artists to save them from the diluting effects of a social life where men "overlap" and "intersect" and where "promiscuity is normal." "The Vorticist does not suck up to Life," Lewis proclaimed. The Vorticist uses "Life" for his "brothel," so that he can keep himself "pure for non-life, that is Art."

Lewis's "Vortex" was a whirling, arrogant monster of energy: "Our Vortex is fed up with your dispersals, reasonable chicken-men. Our Vortex is proud of its polished sides. Our Vortex will not hear of anything but its disastrous polished dance," Lewis wrote in BLAST 1. This Vortex symbolized the "Art instinct" that expressed itself in a few, distinct cultures. England, with its "iron Jungle [of] the great modern city," was one of those cultures, and Vorticist art, with its "rigid reflections of stone and steel," fulfilled the vigorous demands of the Vortex.

Lewis might have continued to think and work along these lines had war not broken out in August 1914. At first, he regarded the war as simply another expression of the Vortex, and, in itself, unlikely to change his own theory and practice of Vorticism. He wrote in BLAST 2, "All art that matters is already so far ahead that it is beyond the sphere of these disturbances." With equal confidence he promised that BLAST would accompany England into a post-war world of an even "more ardent gaiety." But no more issues of BLAST appeared, and while some of the Vorticists continued to work in the pre-war Vorticist style, Lewis rejected that style when he produced his war paintings and drawings, and he never returned to it. "The geometrics which had interested me so exclusively before, I now felt were bleak and empty," he said. "They wanted *filling*." He had even deserted the Vorticist literary style by the time he published BLAST 2 in 1915 and *Tarr* in 1916. After writing *Enemy of the Stars* he concluded that "words and syntax were not susceptible of transformation into abstract terms, to which process the visual arts lent themselves quite readily."

Some Vorticist ideas continued to be central to Lewis's concerns, but the Vorticist visual and literary styles were not. He just as decisively rejected his "leader" role after a brief regrouping with some of the pre-war Vorticists and a few other artists for the "Group X" exhibition in the spring of 1920. There was, in fact, no longer a movement for Lewis to lead.

"In the early stages of this movement," Lewis once wrote of Vorticism, "we undoubtedly did sacrifice ourselves as painters to the necessity to reform *de fond en comble* the world in which a picture must exist. . . . In the heat of this pioneer action we were even inclined to forget *the picture* altogether in favour of *the frame*. . . ." Though unfair, perhaps, to Vorticist art, Lewis's emphasis on the social commitment of Vorticism is proper. No matter how advanced an art movement may seem to be, no matter how new its art forms, it can make no serious claim to relevance unless it is bound, at some irrevocable point, to society. If it be truly avant-garde, the movement's reference points will be images of the future society embedded in the present one. The avant-garde movement will not so much lead the society, as show that society the direction it is going. Lewis believed that Vorticism had produced images of "a new civilization." The problem was to teach people how to see them. "It was more than just picture-making," he said; "one was manufacturing fresh eyes for people, and fresh souls to go with the eyes"—which is to be political in the profoundest sense of that term.

Wyndham Lewis

SOURCE: "Mr. W. L. as Leader of the *Great London Vortex*" and "Some Specimen Pages of *Blast* No. 1 (June 20, 1914)," in *Blasting and Bombardiering*, 1937. Reprinted by Calder and Boyars, 1967, pp. 32-45.

[*In the following excerpt, Lewis discusses his involvement in the Vorticist movement and his editorship of* Blast.]

At some time during the six months that preceded the declaration of war, very suddenly, from a position of relative obscurity, I became extremely well-known. Roughly this coincided with the publication of *Blast*. I can remember no specific morning upon which I woke and found that this had happened. But by August 1914 no newspaper was complete without news about 'vorticism' and its arch-exponent Mr. Lewis.

As *chef de bande* of the Vorticists I cut a figure in London not unlike that of Degrelle to-day in Brussels. There were no politics then. There was no Rexist Party or suchlike. Instead there was the 'Vorticist Group'. I might have been at the head of a social revolution, instead of merely being the prophet of a new fashion in art.

Really all this organized disturbance was Art behaving as if it were Politics. But I swear I did not know it. It may in fact have been politics. I see that now. Indeed it must have been. But I was unaware of the fact: I believed that this was the way artists were always received; a somewhat tumultuous reception, perhaps, but after all why not? I mistook the agitation in the audience for the sign of an awakening of the emotions of artistic sensibility. And then I assumed too that artists always formed militant groups. I supposed they had to do this, seeing how 'bourgeois' all Publics were—or all Publics of which I had any experience. And I concluded that as a matter of course some romantic figure must always emerge, to captain the 'group'. Like myself! How otherwise could a 'group' get about, and above all *talk*. For it had to have a mouthpiece didn't it? I was so little of a communist that it never occurred to me that left to itself a group might express itself *in chorus*. The 'leadership' principle, you will observe, was in my bones.

Meanwhile the excitement was intense. *Putsches* took place every month or so. Marinetti for instance. You may have heard of him! It was he who put Mussolini up to Fascism. Mussolini admits it. They ran neck and neck for a bit, but Mussolini was the better politician. Well, Marinetti brought off a Futurist *Putsch* about this time.

It started in Bond Street. I counter-putsched. I assembled in Greek Street a determined band of miscellaneous anti-futurists. Mr. Epstein was there; Gaudier Brzeska, T. E. Hulme, Edward Wadsworth and a cousin of his called Wallace, who was very muscular and forcible, according to my eminent colleague, and he rolled up very silent and grim. There were about ten of us. After a hearty meal we shuffled bellicosely round to the Doré Gallery.

Marinetti had entrenched himself upon a high lecture platform, and he put down a tremendous barrage in French as we entered. Gaudier went into action at once. He was very good at the *parlez-vous,* in fact he was a Frenchman. He was sniping him without intermission, standing up in his place in the audience all the while. The remainder of our party maintained a confused uproar.

The Italian intruder was worsted. There was another occasion (before he declared war on us, and especially on me) when Mr. C. R. W. Nevinson—always a dark horse—assisted him. The founder of Fascism had been at Adrianople, when there was a siege. He wanted to imitate the noise of bombardment. It was a poetic declamation, which must be packed to the muzzle with what he called 'la rage balkanique'. So Mr. Nevinson concealed himself somewhere in the hall, and at a signal from Marinetti belaboured a gigantic drum.

But it was a matter for astonishment what Marinetti could do with his unaided voice. He certainly made an extraordinary amount of noise. A day of attack upon the Western Front, with all the 'heavies' hammering together, right back to the horizon, was nothing to it. My equanimity when first subjected to the sounds of mass-bombardment in Flanders was possibly due to my marinettian preparation—it seemed 'all quiet' to me in fact, by comparison.

When I first was present at a lecture of his I accompanied him afterwards in a taxicab to the Café Royal. 'Il faut une force de poumon épouvantable pour faire ca!' He explained to me, wiping the perspiration off his neck, and striking himself upon the chest-wall.

Marinetti was a rich man. It was said that his father owned a lot of Alexandria and other ports in the Eastern Mediterranean. I do not know whether this was true. But he certainly had at his disposal very considerable funds.

'You are a futurist, Lewis!' he shouted at me one day, as we were passing into a lavabo together, where he wanted to wash after a lecture where he had drenched himself in sweat.

'No,' I said.

'Why don't you announce that you are a futurist!' he asked me squarely.

'Because I am not one,' I answered, just as pointblank and to the point.

'Yes. But what's it matter!' said he with great impatience.

'It's most important,' I replied rather coldly.

'Not at all!' said he. 'Futurism is good. It is all right.'

'Not too bad,' said I. 'It has its points. But you Wops insist too much on the Machine. You're always on about these driving-belts, you are always exploding about internal combustion. We've had machines here in England for a donkey's years. They're no novelty to *us*.'

'You have never understood your machines! You have never known the *ivresse* of travelling at a kilometre a minute. Have you ever travelled at a kilometre a minute?'

'Never.' I shook my head energetically. 'Never. I loathe anything that goes too quickly. If it goes too quickly, it is not there.'

'It is not there!' he thundered for this had touched him on the raw. 'It is *only* when it goes quickly that it *is* there!'

'That is nonsense,' I said. 'I cannot see a thing that is going too quickly.'

'See it—see it! Why should you want to *see*?' he exclaimed. 'But you *do* see it. You see it multiplied a thousand times. You see a thousand things instead of one thing.'

I shrugged my shoulders—this was not the first time I had had this argument.

'That's just what I don't want to see. I am not a futurist,' I said. 'I prefer *one* thing.'

'There is no such thing as *one* thing.'

'There is if I wish to have it so. And I wish to have it so.'

'You are a monist!' he said at this, with a contemptuous glance, curling his lip.

'All right. I am not a futurist anyway. *Je hais le mouvement qui déplace les lignes.*'

At this quotation he broke into a hundred angry pieces.

'And you "never weep"—I know, I know. *Ah zut alors!* What a thing to be an Englishman!'

This was the sort of thing that was going on the whole time. And at last this man attempted a *Putsch* against the 'great London Vortex'. He denounced me in letters to the Press, as the major obstacle to the advance of Futurism in England. And this was perfectly true. I 'stood in its path', as Sir Austen Chamberlain would have said.

Then Mr. C. R. W. Nevinson attempted a *Putsch*. He selected a sheet of 'Rebel Art Centre' notepaper. The 'Rebel Art Centre' in Great Ormond Street, founded by Miss Lechmere and myself, was the seat of the 'Great London Vortex'. Upon this notepaper Mr. C. R. W. Nevinson expressed Futurist opinions; he too, I think, went over into the Press, and I had to repudiate him as an interloper and a heretic.

I have said enough to show that the months immediately preceding the declaration of war were full of sound and fury, and that all the artists and men of letters had gone into action before the bank-clerks were clapped into khaki and despatched to the land of Flanders Poppies to do their bit. Life was one big bloodless brawl, prior to the Great Bloodletting.

There was the next thing to barricades; there was everything short of Committees of Public Safety. Gaudier was spoiling for a fight. He threatened at Ford's to sock Bomberg on the jaw, and when I asked him why, he explained that he had an imperfect control over his temper, and he must not be found with Bomberg, for the manner adopted by that gentleman was of a sort that put him beside himself. I had therefore to keep them apart. On the other hand I seized Hulme by the throat; but he transfixed me upon the railings of Soho Square. I never see the summer house in its centre without remembering how I saw it upside down. Mr Epstein and David Bomberg kissed, to seal a truce, beneath the former's 'Rockdrill' or similar fine piece of dynamic statuary. This was in the salons of the Goupil. And Mr. T. S. Eliot (that was just after the War, but no matter) challenged Mr. St. John Hutchinson to a duel, upon the sands at Calais. But the latter gentleman, now so eminent a K.C., replied that he was 'too afraid'. So he got the best of *that* encounter, as one would expect when a K.C. clashes with a poet.

The Press in 1914 had no Cinema, no Radio, and no Politics: so the painter could really become a 'star'. There was nothing against it. Anybody could become one, who did anything funny. And Vorticism was replete with humour, of course; it was acclaimed the best joke ever. Pictures, I mean oil-paintings, were 'news'. Exhibitions were reviewed in column after column. And no illustrated paper worth its salt but carried a photograph of some picture of mine or of my 'school', as I have said, or one of myself, smiling insinuatingly from its pages. To the photograph would be attached some scrap of usually quite misleading gossip; or there would be an article from my pen, explaining why life had to be changed, and how. 'Kill John Bull with Art!' I shouted. And John and Mrs. Bull leapt for joy, in a cynical convulsion. For they felt as safe as houses. So did I.

. . . . .

It has occurred to me that since *Blast* was the centre of this disturbance, it might not be amiss to reproduce a few specimen pages. With a page-area of 12 inches by 9½, this publication was of a bright puce colour. In general appearance it was not unlike a telephone book. It contained manifestoes, poems, plays, stories, and outbursts of one sort and another. I will not reproduce the major Manifesto (of the 'Great London Vortex') signed by R. Aldington, Aubuthnot, L. Atkinson, Gaudier Brzeska, J. Dismor, C. Hamilton, E. Pound, W. Roberts, H. Sanders, E. Wadsworth, Wyndham Lewis. That would be too long. Instead I will select a few random pages from the 'Blasts and Blesses'.

These manifestoes require, I suppose, in order to be popularly consumed, and at this distance of time, some explanation. Take the first *Blast*, 'Blast Humour'. That is straightforward enough. The Englishman has what he calls a 'sense of humour'. He says that the German, the Frenchman, and most foreigners do not possess this attribute, and suffer accordingly. For what does the 'sense of humour' mean but an ability to belittle everything—to make light of everything? Not only does the Englishman not 'make a mountain out of a molehill'; he is able *to make a molehill out of a mountain*. That is an invaluable magic to possess. The most enormous hobgoblin becomes a pigmy on the spot. Or such is the ideal of this destructive 'humorous' standpoint, which has played such a great part in anglosaxon life—just as its opposite, 'quixotry', has played a great part in Spanish life.

This manifesto was written (by myself) immediately before the War. And of course 'the sense of humour' played a very great part in the War. 'Old Bill' was the real hero of the World War, on the English side, much more than any V.C. A V.C. is after all a fellow who does something heroic; almost unenglish. It is taking things a bit too seriously to get the V.C. The really popular fellow is the humorous Ole Bill à la Bairnsfather. And it was really 'Ole Bill' who won the war—with all that that expression 'won the war' implies.

Against the tyranny of the 'sense of humour', I, in true anglo-saxon fashion, humorously rebelled. That is all that 'Blast Humour' means. I still regard 'humour' as an exceedingly dangerous drug. I still regard it as, more often than not, an ignoble specific. In a word, I still 'blast' humour. (But then we come to the 'Blesses', and since there are two sides to every argument, you find me *blessing* what

I had a moment before *blasted*. And example of English 'fairness'!)

Take my next *Blast*—namely, 'Blast years 1837 to 1900'. The triumph of the commercial mind in England, Victorian 'liberalism', the establishment of such apparently indestructible institutions as the English comic paper *Punch*, the Royal Academy, and so on—such things did not appeal to me, they appeal to me even less to-day, and I am glad to say more and more Englishmen share my antipathy. Boehm was, of course, the sculptor responsible for the worst of the bourgeois statuary which, prior to the war-sculptors, like Jagger, was the principle eyesore encountered by the foreign visitor to our 'capital of empire'. The 'eunuchs and stylists' referred to in this second manifesto would be the Paterists and Wildeites: and lastly the 'diabolics' of Swinburne are given a parting kick. For in 1914 there was still a bad hang-over from the puerile literary debauchery of that great Victorian who reacted against the 'non-conformist conscience'; who was 'naughty' before the 'Naughty Nineties' capped his sodawater wildness with a real live Oscar.

The third of these manifestoes (all of my composition) is 'Bless the Hairdresser'. That will be a little more difficult to understand. This might equally well have been headed 'Blast Fluffiness'. It exalts formality, and order, at the expense of the disorderly and the unkempt. It is merely a humorous way of stating the classic standpoint, as against the romantic. Need I say that I am in complete agreement, here, with Mr. W. L. of 1914?

As to 'Bless England', that requires no explanation. Our 'Island home'! And 'Bless all Ports' is just a further outburst of benediction—more 'Island home' stuff. That winds up the specimen pages of the manifestoes from *Blast*. However, here they are, as far as possible produced in facsimile, though you lose the scale of the 12 in. high *Blast* page.

> BLAST HUMOUR—
> Quack ENGLISH drug for stupidity and sleepiness.
> Arch enemy of REAL, conventionalizing like
>   gunshot, freezing supple
>   Real in ferocious chemistry
>   of Laughter.
>
> BLAST SPORT—
> HUMOUR'S FIRST COUSIN AND ACCOMPLICE.
>   impossibility for Englishman to be grave
>   and keep his end up
>   psychologically.
>   impossible for him to use Humour
>   as well and be *persistently*
>   grave.
>   Alas! necessity for the big doll's show
>   in front of mouth.
>   Visitation of Heaven on
>   English Miss.
>   gums, canines of FIXED GRIN
>   Death's Head symbol of Anti-Life.
> CURSE those who will hang over this
>   Manifesto with SILLY CANINES exposed.
>
> BLAST—
> years 1837 to 1900

> CURSE Abysmal inexcusable middle-class
> (also Aristocracy and Proletariat).
>
> BLAST—
>   Pasty shadow cast by gigantic BOEHM
> (imagined at introduction of BOURGEOIS
>   VICTORIAN VISTAS).
> WRING THE NECK OF all sick inventions
>   born in that progressive white wake.
> BLAST their weeping whiskers—hirsute
>   RHETORIC OF EUNUCH and STYLIST—
>   SENTIMENTAL HYGIENICS
>   ROUSSEAUISMS (wild nature cranks)
>   DIABOLICS—
>   —raptures and roses of
>   the erotic bookshelves
>   culminating in
>   PURGATORY OF
>   PUTNEY

> BLESS the HAIRDRESSER.
> He attacks Mother Nature for a small fee.
> Hourly he ploughs heads for sixpence,
> Scours chins and lips for threepence.
> He makes systematic mercenary war on this
> WILDERNESS.————————————
> He trims aimless and retrograde growths
> into CLEAN ARCHED SHAPES AND AN-
>   GULAR PLOTS.

> BLESS this HESSIAN (or SILESIAN) EXPERT
> correcting the grotesque anachronisms of our
> physique.

> BLESS ENGLISH HUMOUR
> It is the great barbarous weapon of
> the genius among races.
> The wild MOUNTAIN RAILWAY from IDEA to
>   IDEA, in the ancient Fair of LIFE.
> BLESS SWIFT for his solemn bleak
> wisdom of laughter.
> SHAKESPEARE for his bitter NORTHERN
>   Rhetoric of Humour.
> BLESS ALL ENGLISH EYES
>   that grow crows-feet with their
>   FANCY and ENERGY.

> BLESS this hysterical WALL build round
>   the EGO.
> BLESS the solitude of LAUGHTER.
> BLESS the Separating, ungregarious
>   BRITISH GRIN.

> BLESS ENGLAND—
> FOR ITS SHPS
>   which switchback on BLUE, GREEN and RED
>   SEAS all round the PINK EARTH-BALL BIG
>   BETS ON EACH.
>   BLESS ALL SEAFARERS—
> THEY exchange not one LAND for another, but
> one ELEMENT for ANOTHER. THE MORE against
> the LESS ABSTRACT.

> BLESS the vast planetary abstraction of the
> OCEAN.

> BLESS the Arabs of the ATLANTIC.

This Island Must be Contrasted With the Bleak
Waves.

―――――――――

BLESS ALL PORTS—
PORTS, RESTLESS MACHINES of scooped out ba-
sins
   heavy insect dredgers
   monotonous cranes
   stations
   lighthouses. blazing
      through the frosty
      starlight, cutting the
      storm like a cake
   beaks of infant boats,
      side by side,
   heavy chaos of
      wharves,
   steep walls of
      factories
   womanly town
BLESS these MACHINES that work the little
boats across clean liquid space in beelines.
BLESS the great PORTS
   HULL
   LIVERPOOL
   LONDON
   NEWCASTLE-ON-TYNE
   BRISTOL
   GLASGOW
BLESS ENGLAND, industrial island machine,
pyramidal workshop, its apex at Shetland, dis-
charging itself on the sea.
BLESS cold
   magnanimous
   delicate
   gauche
   fanciful
   stupid
          ENGLISHMEN.

Wyndham Lewis

SOURCE: "Long Live the Vortex!" in *Wyndham Lewis
on Art: Collected Writings, 1913-1956,* Funk & Wagnalls,
1969, pp. 25-6.

[*The following piece appeared as the opening manifesto to
the first issue of* Blast.]

Long live the great art vortex sprung up in the centre of
this town!

We stand for the Reality of the Present—not for the sentimental Future, or the sacripant Past.

We want to leave Nature and Men alone.

We do not want to make people wear Futurist Patches, or
fuss men to take to pink and sky-blue trousers.

We are not their wives or tailors.

The only way Humanity can help artists is to remain independent and work unconsciously.

WE NEED THE UNCONSCIOUSNESS OF HUMANITY—their
stupidity, animalism and dreams.

We believe in no perfectibility except our own.

Intrinsic beauty is in the Interpreter and Seer, not in the
object or content.

We do not want to change the appearance of the world,
because we are not Naturalists, Impressionists or Futurists (the latest form of Impressionism), and do not depend
on the appearance of the world for our art.

WE ONLY WANT THE WORLD TO LIVE, and to feel its
crude energy flowing through us.

It may be said that great artists in England are always revolutionary, just as in France any really fine artist had a
strong traditional vein.

Blast sets out to be an avenue for all those vivid and violent
ideas that could reach the Public in no other way.

Blast will be popular, essentially. It will not appeal to any
particular class, but to the fundamental and popular instincts in every class and description of people, TO THE IN-
DIVIDUAL. The moment a man feels or realizes himself as
an artist, he ceases to belong to any milieu or time. *Blast*
is created for this timeless, fundamental Artist that exists
in everybody.

The Man in the Street and the Gentleman are equally ignored.

Popular art does not mean the art of the poor people, as
it is usually supposed to. It means the art of the individuals.

Education (art education and general education) tends to
destroy the creative instinct. Therefore it is in times when
education has been nonexistent that art chiefly flourished.

But it is nothing to do with 'the People'.

It is a mere accident that that is the most favourable time
for the individual to appear.

To make the rich of the community shed their education
skin, to destroy politeness, standardization and academic,
that is civilized, vision, is the task we have set ourselves.

We want to make in England not a popular art, not a revival of lost folk art, or a romantic fostering of such unactual conditions, but to make individuals, wherever found.

We will convert the King if possible.

A VORTICIST KING! WHY NOT?

DO YOU THINK LLOYD GEORGE HAS THE VORTEX IN
HIM?

MAY WE HOPE FOR ART FROM LADY MOND?

We are against the glorification of 'the People', as we are
against snobbery. It is not necessary to be an outcast bohemian, to be unkempt or poor, any more than it is necessary
to be rich or handsome, to be an artist. Art is nothing to
do with the coat you wear. A top-hat can well hold the Sis-
tine. A cheap cap could hide the image of Kephren.

AUTOMOBILISM (Marinetteism) bores us. We don't want
to go about making a hullo-bulloo about motor cars, any
more than about knives and forks, elephants or gas-pipes.

Elephants are VERY BIG. Motor cars go quickly.

Wilde gushed twenty years ago about the beauty of machinery.

Gissing, in his romantic delight with modern lodging houses, was futurist in this sense.

The futurist is a sensational and sentimental mixture of the aesthete of 1890 and the realist of 1870.

The 'Poor' are detestable animals! They are only picturesque and amusing for the sentimentalist or the romantic! The 'Rich' are bores without a single exception, *en tant que riches!*

We want those simple and great people found everywhere.

Blast presents an art of Individuals.

Wyndham Lewis and others

SOURCE: "Manifesto," in *Wyndham Lewis on Art: Collected Writings, 1913-1956,* Funk & Wagnalls, 1969, pp. 27-31

[*The following piece was the second manifesto published in the first issue of* Blast *and appeared above the signature of Lewis, Pound, and other members of the Vorticist movement.*]

I

1 Beyond Action and Reaction we would establish ourselves.

2 We start from opposite statements of a chosen world. Set up violent structure of adolescent clearness between two extremes.

3 We discharge ourselves on both sides.

4 We fight first on one side, then on the other, but always for the SAME cause, which is neither side or both sides and ours.

5 Mercenaries were always the best troops.

6 We are Primitive Mercenaries in the Modern World.

7 Our *Cause* is NO-MAN'S.

8 We set Humour at Humour's throat. Stir up Civil War among peaceful apes.

9 We only want Humour if it has fought like Tragedy.

10 We only want Tragedy if it can clench its side-muscles like hands on its belly, and bring to the surface a laugh like a bomb.

II

1 We hear from America and the Continent all sorts of disagreeable things about England: 'the unmusical, anti-artistic, unphilosophic country'.

2 We quite agree.

3 Luxury, sport, the famous English 'Humour', the thrilling ascendancy and *idée fixe* of Class, producing the most intense snobbery in the World; heavy stagnant pools of Saxon blood, incapable of anything but the song of a frog,

in home-counties: these phenomena give England a peculiar distinction, in the wrong sense, among the nations.

4 This is why England produces such good artists from time to time.

5 This is also the reason why a movement towards art and imagination could burst up here, from this lump of compressed life, with more force than anywhere else.

6 To believe that it is necessary for or conducive to art, to 'improve' life, for instance—make architecture, dress, ornament, in 'better taste', is absurd.

7 The Art-instinct is permanently primitive.

8 In a chaos of imperfection, discord, etc., it finds the same stimulus as in Nature.

9 The artist of the modern movement is a savage (in no sense an 'advanced', perfected, democratic, Futurist individual of Mr Marinetti's limited imagination): this enormous, jangling, journalistic, fairy desert of modern life serves him as Nature did more technically primitive man.

10 As the steppes and the rigours of the Russian winter, when the peasant has to lie for weeks in his hut, produce that extraordinary acuity of feeling and intelligence we associate with the Slav; so England is just now the most favourable country for the appearance of a great art.

III

1 We have made it quite clear that there is nothing Chauvinistic or picturesquely patriotic about our contentions.

2 But there is violent boredom with that feeble Europeanism, abasement of the miserable 'intellectual' before anything coming from Paris, Cosmopolitan sentimentality, which prevails in so many quarters.

3 Just as we believe that an Art must be organic with its Time, So we insist that what is actual and vital for the South, is ineffectual and unactual in the North.

4 Fairies have disappeared from Ireland (despite foolish attempts to revive them) and the bull-ring languishes in Spain.

5 But mysticism on the one hand, gladiatorial instincts, blood and asceticism on the other, will be always actual, and springs of Creation for these two peoples.

6 The English Character is based on the Sea.

7 The particular qualities and characteristics that the sea always engenders in men are those that are, among the many diagnostics of our race, the most fundamentally English.

8 That unexpected universality as well, found in the completest English artists, is due to this.

IV

1 We assert that the art for these climates, then, must be a northern flower.

2 And we have implied what we believe should be the specific nature of the art destined to grow up in this country,

and models of whose flue decorate the pages of this magazine.

3 It is not a question of the characterless material climate around us. Were that so the complication of the Jungle, dramatic Tropic growth, the vastness of American trees, would not be for us.

4 But our industries, and the Will that determined, face to face with its needs, the direction of the modern world, has reared up steel trees where the green ones were lacking; has exploded in useful growths, and found wilder intricacies than those of Nature.

V

1 We bring clearly forward the following points, before further defining the character of this necessary native art.

2 At the freest and most vigorous period of ENGLAND's history, her literature, then chief Art, was in many ways identical with that of France.

3 Chaucer was very much cousin of Villon as an artist.

4 Shakespeare and Montaigne formed one literature.

5 But Shakespeare reflected in his imagination a mysticism, madness and delicacy peculiar to the North, and brought equal quantities of Comic and Tragic together.

6 Humour is a phenomenon caused by sudden pouring of culture into Barbary.

7 It is intelligence electrified by flood of Naivety.

8 It is Chaos invading Concept and bursting it like nitrogen.

9 It is the Individual masquerading as Humanity like a child in clothes too big for him.

10 Tragic Humour is the birthright of the North.

11 Any great Northern Art will partake of this insidious and volcanic chaos.

12 No great ENGLISH Art need be ashamed to share some glory with France, tomorrow it may be with Germany, where the Elizabethans did before it.

13 But it will never be French, any more than Shakespeare was, the most catholic and subtle Englishman.

VI

1 The Modern World is due almost entirely to Anglo-Saxon genius—its appearance and its spirit.

2 Machinery, trains, steam-ships, all that distinguishes externally our time, came far more from here than anywhere else.

3 In dress, manners, mechanical inventions, LIFE, that is, ENGLAND, has influenced Europe in the same way that France has in Art.

4 But busy with this LIFE-EFFORT, she has been the last to become conscious of the Art that is an organism of this new Order and Will of Man.

5 Machinery is the greatest Earth-medium: incidentally it

sweeps away the doctrines of a narrow and pedantic Realism at one stroke.

6 By mechanical inventiveness, too, just as Englishmen have spread themselves all over the Earth, they have brought all the hemispheres about them in their original island.

7 It cannot be said that the complication of the Jungle, dramatic tropic growths, the vastness of American trees, is not for us.

8 For, in the forms of machinery, Factories, new and vaster buildings, bridges and works, we have all that, naturally, around us.

VII

1 Once this consciousness towards the new possibilities of expression in present life has come, however, it will be more the legitimate property of Englishmen than of any other people in Europe.

2 It should also, as it is by origin theirs, inspire them more forcibly and directly.

3 They are the inventors of this bareness and hardness, and should be the great enemies of Romance.

4 The Romance peoples will always be, at bottom, its defenders.

5 The Latins are at present, for instance, in their 'discovery' of sport, their Futuristic gush over machines, aeroplanes, etc., the most romantic and sentimental 'moderns' to be found.

6 It is only the second-rate people in France or Italy who are thorough revolutionaries.

7 In England, on the other hand, there is no vulgarity in revolt.

8 Or, rather, there is no revolt, it is the normal state.

9 So often rebels of the North and the South are diametrically opposed species.

10 The nearest thing in England to a great traditional French artist, is a great revolutionary English one.

Signatures for Manifesto

R. Aldington Arbuthnot L. Atkinson Gaudier Brzeska

J. Dismorr C. Hamilton E. Pound W. Roberts

H. Sanders E. Wadsworth Wyndham Lewis.

CHARACTERISTICS AND PRINCIPLES OF VORTICISM

Reed Way Dasenbrock

SOURCE: "Vorticism among the Isms," in *Blast 3*, edited by Seamus Cooney and others, Black Sparrow Press, 1984, pp. 40-6.

[In the following essay, Dasenbrock considers Vorticism in in the context of other literary and artistic movements of the period.]

Though BLAST is principally thought of today as the magazine of Vorticism, it was planned and announced before the birth of Vorticism, and, indeed, most of the first issue was laid out before the Vorticist manifestos which open and close that issue were conceived. Pound wrote to Joyce on April 1, 1914, that "Lewis is starting a new Futurist, Cubist, Imagiste Quarterly," and the advertisement for BLAST which appeared in *The Egoist* on April 15, 1914, announced it as a "Discussion of Cubism, Futurism, Imagisme and all Vital Forms of Modern Art." The most telling evidence that BLAST preceded Vorticism is in BLAST itself. In one of Lewis's notes, "The Melodrama of Modernity," he is willing, despite the critique of Futurism in the same article, to accept the label Futurist for his own art. He does say, however, that "we may hope before long to find a new word."

Only some time in May or June of 1914 did Pound and Lewis come up with that new word, Vorticism, which would describe their art in contradistinction to the other *isms* of modern art, Cubism, Futurism, Imagism, and Expressionism. The launching of their own movement caused a decided change in their attitude towards those *isms*. As late as April, Cubism and Futurism were vital forms of modern art, but in the first issue of BLAST, dated July 2, 1914, they were the objects of extended and hostile critiques.

This abrupt volte-face raises some doubts about these critiques: were they a sincere expression of the Vorticists' differences with Cubism and Futurism, which can be seen in their art as well as their propaganda? Or were these polemics merely worked up quickly so that Vorticism would seem to have an original position? Lewis had been willing to accept the label English Cubist at the "Exhibition of the Camden Town Group and Others" held in Brighton six months before. Then he had accepted the label Futurist in "The Melodrama of Modernity." Can one therefore truly distinguish Vorticism from the other *isms* which were springing up at such a rate all over Europe in this period? Was Vorticism original, and if so what was original about it?

Pound, though he named Vorticism, never distinguished it sharply from its fellow art movements on the Continent. In "Vortex Pound" he referred to "Picasso, Kandinski, father and mother, classicism and romanticism of the movement" (BLAST 1), and in the September 1914 article, "Vorticism," Pound identified Vorticism with Continental art more sweepingly and tendentiously: "now you have vorticism, which is, roughly speaking, expressionism, neo-cubism, and imagism gathered together in one camp and futurism in the other." Pound would not have been unaware of the differences among these movements he has tied together, but here as always he stressed the continuity in the movement of the avant-garde more than the discontinuities. In other words, Pound was less interested in

showing Vorticism's originality than in denying its isolation.

But Lewis drew sharp distinctions between the Vorticists and everyone else, and it is to the writings of Lewis that we must turn to find Vorticism defined. The process of definition is essentially negative: one learns what Vorticism is by learning what it is not, by learning what Lewis found lacking in the 1914 avantgarde. But a genuine and fascinating position is worked out, one reflected in Vorticist art, which shows that the distinction between Vorticism and the Continental art movements is not a paper one. Though one can see Lewis scrambling to find and define the individuality of his hastily assembled group, the evidence of BLAST shows that he did succeed. The heart of the Vorticist position, put simply, is that Vorticism accepted Futurism's critique of Cubism, but criticized Futurism in turn from a standpoint indebted to Cubism. Following these two vectors one arrives at Vorticism.

The Futurist painters on the occasion of their first Paris exhibition in February 1912 declared themselves to be "absolutely opposed" to Cubist painting. They objected primarily to what they considered the lack of energy or dynamism of Cubist painting. According to the catalogue to this exhibition (which also went to London), the Cubists

> are furiously determined to depict the immobility, the frozenness and all the static aspects of nature. They worship the traditionalism of Poussin, of Ingres, of Corot, ageing and petrifying their art with a passéist obstinance that remains, for us, absolutely incomprehensible.

In opposition to this "static art," the Futurists painted objects in motion. Among their favorite subjects were trains, automobiles, and people engaged in physical activity or in demonstrations or riots. They associated static art with a concern with the past largely because they associated their own dynamic art with a concern with the modern. They painted modern urban and industrial subjects, not simply because these lent themselves to the dynamic treatment the Futurists advocated, but also because in their view art had a responsibility to respond to and incorporate these new forces which were transforming society. From this perspective, they attacked the subject matter of Cubist painting. To work in the traditional genres of individual portraiture, landscape, or still life, no matter how revolutionary one's treatment of those genres might be, was to be, as far as the Futurists were concerned (in one of their favorite phrases), "fatally academic."

Lewis's view of Cubism is very similar. Cubist art for Lewis was static and heavy, and its subject matter was embarrassingly trivial:

> HOWEVER MUSICAL OR VEGETARIAN A MAN MAY BE, HIS LIFE IS NOT SPENT EXCLUSIVELY AMONGST APPLES AND MANDOLINES. Therefore there is something to be explained when he foregathers, in his paintings, exclusively with these two objects. (BLAST 2)

But to accept the Futurist critique of Cubism is not to accept Futurism: Lewis criticized Futurism more fiercely than Cubism. This countercritique was not indebted explicitly to Cubism, as the Cubists never responded to the Futurist attack on them. (Cubism was not an organized movement in the way Futurism and Vorticism were, and only the lesser Cubists, Gleizes and Metzinger, formulated principles of Cubism in writing.) But there is an implicit debt to Cubism in Lewis's critique, as the faults he saw in Futurism he sought to guard against in his own art through borrowing from Cubism.

First, Lewis criticized Futurism as the latest form of Impressionism. Its art was too formless and blurred. In trying to be dynamic the Futurists succeeded merely in being fluid and imprecise. Their aim was to be faithful to the sensations they received in the presence of the subject they painted, and they went so far as to claim "that painting and sensation are two inseparable words." For Lewis those two words must be separate, and he would claim the support of Cubism and Cézanne for his contention that the artist must organize and form his material. He should dominate his subject matter; the Futurists were dominated by theirs.

Second, Lewis considered that the fuss that the Futurists made about their subject matter was quite ridiculous. He accepted that subject matter—the modern mechanistic environment—but did not want to treat it with their sentimentality and romance. The Futurists gushed about machines, according to Lewis, only because mechanization was new to Italy. His contrasting ideal was to treat the Futurists' subject matter with the objectivity and analytic perspective of Cubism. The Futurists were right, according to Lewis, in trying to get away from apples and mandolins, but wrong in replacing the coldness and hardness of Cubism with, in his words, sentimental Latin romance.

The human figure was depicted as a machine in Vorticist art, as well as a pattern or rhythmic form, particularly in Lewis's drawings of the period around 1914 and in Jacob Epstein's *Rock Drill*. This mechanization of the human figure was part of the (pessimistic) response of these artists to the modern world: their art was portraying the dehumanization they saw around them.

— *Reed Way Dasenbrock*

The program of Vorticism was therefore to combine (what Lewis saw as) the strengths of these two movements. The subject matter of the Vorticists was modern, but they did not identify with that subject matter in the manner of Futurism. The Vorticists did not paint the mechanistic world they lived in because they found it better or more beautiful than the past. Nowhere in Vorticism can one find the inanities of Futurist propaganda, the urging of the destruction and transformation of Venice into an industrial port, the

claim that a speeding automobile is more beautiful than the *Victory of Samothrace,* or the reference to the art of the past as a great joke. In fact, Lewis argued in "The Exploitation of Vulgarity" in BLAST 1 that a pessimistic attitude towards the modern world dominates modern art and that it was precisely the vulgarity, ugliness and insanity of the modern world which offered art a great opportunity.

This fits in with his idea that England is "just now the most favourable country for the appearance of a great art" (BLAST 1). The English have by and large created "this bareness and hardness" of the modern world, and, as familiarity with mechanization breeds detachment if not contempt, it should be easier for them to adopt a cold and unromantic attitude towards the machine. The great art, Lewis obviously hoped, would be Vorticism, which would be distinguished for its detached attitude towards its modern subject matter. As he put it in "Our Vortex":

> In a Vorticist Universe we don't get excited at what we have invented. . . .
> We hunt machines, they are our favourite game.
> We invent them and then hunt them down.
> This is a great Vorticist age, a great still age of artists. (BLAST 1)

Nothing separated the Vorticists more sharply from the Futurists than this ideal of "a great still age." Yet it seems an odd ideal for them to hold. The paintings of the Cubists are much more obviously still, which is what sparked the Futurist critique of the "static forms" of Cubism. Vorticism sought to reconcile these static forms with Futurist dynamism through painting dynamic forms, such as the vortex, which is in constant motion but has a stable form and a still center. The art in this view is not still; the Vorticist artist is, as he occupies that still center and, looking out with detachment at the chaos whirling around him, he sees that it is really formed, by and around his still point.

This dynamic formism represented by the vortex was central to Vorticist art. Abstract dynamic forms like the vortex were more prominent in the Vorticist polemics than in its painting, but concrete equivalents, human activities which are dynamic yet formed or patterned, are found everywhere in Vorticist art. The subject of the dance, taken up by David Bomberg, William Roberts, Gaudier-Brzeska, and Lewis, in Richard Cork's words, "ran like a connecting thread through the convoluted imagery of Vorticist art." David Bomberg's two great Vorticist canvases, *In the Hold* and *The Mud Bath,* portray human activity in rhythmic motion, the first, laborers handling cargo in the hold of a ship and the second, men in a bath, which is expressed on the canvas as a pattern of interlocking geometric forms.

The human figure was depicted as a machine in Vorticist art, as well as a pattern or rhythmic form, particularly in Lewis's drawings of the period around 1914 and in Jacob Epstein's *Rock Drill.* This mechanization of the human figure was part of the (pessimistic) response of these artists to the modern world: their art was portraying the dehumanization they saw around them. But this response was articulated through the style of dynamic formism. These figures are dynamic and in motion, usually engaged in combat or in physical labor. But the non-naturalistic way in which these figures are portrayed stylizes them, making them seem like machines or robots. The rounded contours of the human figure have been replaced by crisp, harsh diagonal lines, representing their movement in a formed geometric manner.

Probably the central Vorticist subject and certainly Lewis's central subject in this period was the city. In contrast to the cityscapes of Futurism which are characteristically warm and dynamic, filled with chaotic masses of people, Lewis's cityscapes reveal his Vorticist preoccupation with finding the order of that chaos. These paintings are cold and still, depicting bleak and austere shapes which suggest buildings. Yet a kind of dynamism is present: the planes and the colors of the forms are manipulated to generate a sense of motion. The thrusting diagonal lines and extreme color contrasts in the painting *Workshop,* for instance, create a sense of dynamism appropriate to the modern city.

This concern with dynamic forms was thus both an important Vorticist subject and an important part of the style of Vorticist art. Other paintings of the period, Marcel Duchamp's *Nude Descending a Staircase* (1912), Kasimir Malevich's *Knife Grinder* (1912), and Francis Picabia's series of paintings of dancers of 1912-13, tried to reconcile form and motion in ways parallel to Vorticism. But these are isolated works: no other movement tried to effect a synthesis of Cubist form and Futurist movement, and this synthesis unifies many of the disparate subjects of Vorticist art.

But subject matter itself was coming under attack in the years just before World War I. Cubism and Futurism were not the only art movements to which a fledgling art movement in 1914 felt compelled to respond. Both (by and large) retained an element of representation in their paintings, whereas other painters and movements were renouncing representation between 1910 and 1914. The chronology of this development is both complex and confused, but Kandinsky in Munich seems to have been the first to paint non-representational works around 1910. He was closely followed in 1911 by a Czech painter who worked in Paris, Kupka, in 1912 by the Orphist Delaunay, the Futurist Balla, and the Russian Rayonist Larionov, and in 1913 by Léger, Severini, and Malevich.

Most discussions of Vorticism have situated it in this movement towards total abstraction which swept over Europe just before the War. Richard Cork, in the major study of Vorticism revealingly titled *Vorticism and Abstract Art in the First Machine Age,* frankly confesses that Vorticism interests him primarily as "an indigenously English form of abstraction." Elsewhere, Anthony d'Offay has claimed that "certainly our interest in the [Vorticist] movement today must be centered on the degree of abstraction it achieved." D'Offay's claim is easily countered: my interest in Vorticism has nothing to do with the degree of abstraction it achieved. But, more to the point, abstraction was not an important goal of Vorticism. The Vorticists did do some totally abstract works, largely drawings and preparatory sketches, but they returned to a subject

in their major works, because, I think, they agreed with the Futurists that art must respond to the society surrounding it. They willingly retained subject matter in their art because only with a subject could their art have the kind of significance they intended.

Lewis drew a clear distinction between abstraction and the aesthetic of Vorticism. His "A Review of Contemporary Art" in BLAST 2 discussed three groups of artists in detail, Cubism and Futurism (in ways already discussed) and Expressionism, by which he said that he meant the work of Kandinsky. His discussion of Kandinsky focused on the question of representation and abstraction, and in typically Vorticist fashion he arrived at his own doctrine about representation by attacking Kandinsky's. Lewis himself called attention to his discussion:

> In dealing with Kandinsky's doctrine, and tabulating differences, you come to the most important feature of this new synthesis I propose. (BLAST 2)

Lewis focused his discussion on Kandinsky because he considered him "the only PURELY abstract painter in Europe" (BLAST 2). BLAST 1 contained excerpts from and comments by Edward Wadsworth on Kandinsky's book *Concerning the Spiritual in Art.* Moreover, Kandinsky exhibited in London at the Allied Artists' Association in 1909, 1910, 1913, and 1914, where in 1913 and 1914 Lewis, Epstein, Gaudier-Brzeska, and other Vorticists showed. The works Kandinsky showed in 1913 and 1914 included some of his most advanced paintings (*Improvisations No. 29* and *No. 30*), so Lewis's critique was based on first-hand knowledge of Kandinsky's "abstract" work.

However, these paintings no longer seem abstract to us; *Improvisation No. 30,* in particular, is famous because it contains two cannons in the lower right which, according to Kandinsky, made their way into the work unconsciously. Though Lewis discusses Kandinsky's work as if it were totally abstract, the presence of such veiled or unconscious imagery in these paintings actually supports his argument, which is that representation is unavoidable. To "attempt to avoid all representative element is an equal absurdity." It is absurd because

> If you do not use shapes and colours characteristic of your environment, you will only use some others characteristic more or less of somebody else's environment, and certainly no better. (BLAST 2)

The artist works with shapes and forms, and it is impossible, whether or not it is desirable, to avoid using shapes which suggest objects in the material world. He repeats this over and again: "everything is representation, in one sense, even in the most 'abstract' painting" (BLAST 2).

Lewis did not, however, advocate a naturalistic representation of the material world. He called imitative realism "an absurd and gloomy waste of time" (BLAST 2). He advocated a synthesis of, or creative interplay between, abstraction and representation:

> We must constantly strive to ENRICH abstraction till it is almost plain life, or rather to get deeply enough immersed in material life to expe-

rience the shaping power amongst its vibrations, and to accentuate and perpetuate these. (BLAST 2)

For Lewis, the key to art is its shaping power or formal organization. But it does not therefore follow that one must try to use forms without representational content, because it is the material world which suggests to the artist the shapes and forms he paints. Vorticist art is therefore not abstract in the sense of non-representational; the only sense in which it is abstract is that the Vorticist artist wants to extract or abstract the meaning or essence of his subject.

Lewis's cityscapes, for example, works such as *New York, The Crowd,* and *Workshop,* are not paintings of any particular location. Certainly to a beholder of 1914 they must have seemed completely abstract, just as Kandinsky's *Improvisations* seemed abstract to Lewis. But the shapes on the canvas ineluctably suggest modern buildings (and, in *The Crowd,* people in and around buildings), and virtually every other aspect of the paintings supports that suggestion. These paintings try to represent the essence of the modern city which for Lewis can be seen in its huge, cold buildings, its seeming dynamism and activity and yet simultaneous deadness and inhumanity. Lewis wanted to express the mood of his urban subject as much as its appearance, but he would have argued that this mood is a function of that subject, not a projection of the artist.

This brief analysis could be extended to the work of the other Vorticists. Their work retained a subject, and they sought to express or represent the essence of that subject, using formal means inherited from Cubism and Futurism, and like those movements never renouncing the subject. This might not have been the *synthesis* of abstraction and r resentation Lewis desired; it might have been only an uneasy balancing act between them, but this balancing act, in my view, is central to Vorticism. Vorticism has no great importance in the development of abstraction: at least five separate groups on the continent were ahead of it and other movements pursued abstraction with more dedication and rigor. Its originality lies in that, among those who arrived at total abstraction (as it did sporadically), it was the first movement to turn back, retaining subject matter and developing a theory of representation concerned not with illusionistic representation but with schematic or diagrammatic representation.

Pound in his September 1914 essay, "Vorticism," is more explicit than Lewis about his Vorticist attitude towards subject matter. The center of his discussion is an elaborate analogy borrowed from mathematics. (I do not answer for Pound's mathematics.) After saying that Vorticism is "an intensive art," he says that mathematical expressions can be ranked according to intensity. Arithmetic contents itself with statements of fact such as $3^2 + 4^2 = 5^2$. This is true about itself, but does not say anything about any other numbers. A more intensive statement is $a^2 + b^2 = c^2$ because this applies to a lot of facts. More intense yet is to say that these equations govern the ratios of the length of the sides of a right-angle triangle. Pound compares this level of intensiveness to art criticism as it involves criticism of form, but not its creation.

The final level of intensity is reached in analytical geometry. A statement that the equation $(x-a)^2 + (y-b)^2 = r^2$ governs the circle is not a statement about a particular circle but "any circle and all circles." This analytical statement is the form or essence of the circle itself. Pound then claims that "the difference between art and analytical geometry is the difference of subject-matter only." Great works of art similarly "cause form to come into being." They do not treat the accidental appearance of their subject, but its analytic form.

Pound's language differs from Lewis's, but there is an underlying agreement between them on the relationship between Vorticist art and its subject matter. This position is distinct from abstraction and is as uniquely Vorticist as the dynamic formism discussed above. Dynamic formism is Vorticism's synthesis of Cubism and Futurism; this theory of analytic intensity is its synthesis of the representationalism of these movements and Kandinsky's expressive abstractions.

To use the word synthesis is, however, to accept Vorticism's valuation of itself. If one looks at Vorticism from the standpoint of Cubism or that of Kandinsky, one is far more likely to say that Vorticism simply missed the point of the movements it sought to criticize. And it must be admitted that Lewis, obstinately bent on defining Vorticism *against* the other isms, could be extremely reductive in his presentation of other movements. His discussion of Picasso's constructions, collages and *papiers-collés* in "Relativism and Picasso's Latest Work" in BLAST 1 is an excellent case in point. These works were exploring an area of profound interest for Lewis and Vorticism, the possibilities of non-illusionistic representation. But Lewis could only see that Picasso was blurring the distinction between art and life which was of such importance for Lewis. For this reason he utterly rejected these works of Picasso's, whereas someone with the same aesthetic stance but a greater interest in finding allies could have easily found things to praise in these seminal works.

This does not deny the originality of Vorticism; instead, it explains what impelled that originality. Lewis was never comfortable sharing any common ground with anyone, fearful that this would compromise his integrity. This is, one must note, a very curious frame of mind for the leader of a movement, and there was a movement of sympathy towards and identification with other art (and artists) foreign to Lewis running through Vorticism, found, for example, in Pound's criticism and in the Vorticist sculptors' primitivism. But Lewis's attitude dominated just as Lewis dominated Vorticism, which makes it ironic that Richard Cork and others should value and study Vorticism for the extent to which it anticipated and led to the purely abstract art that followed. Yet it is understandable that Cork would try to increase the visibility of Vorticism by ascribing to it an important role in the development of abstraction. For what did it lead to? Why should we study it today?

Lewis put out only two issues of BLAST. Vorticist art was exhibited in one group show in London and one in New York and then ceased to be produced. Gaudier-Brzeska died in the war. Epstein returned to a traditional style of portraiture. Most of the others retreated in style and were forgotten. Lewis turned primarily to figure painting which led to a series of masterful portraits in the 1920s and 1930s which are in my opinion Lewis's greatest paintings. These are also his influential works, for they helped to perpetuate a tradition of English figure painting which blossomed after 1945 in the work of such London-based artists as Michael Ayrton, Francis Bacon, David Hockney, R. B. Kitaj, and Frank Auerbach. Lewis welcomed what he saw of these painters, the work of Ayrton and Bacon, and arguably both his work and that of David Bomberg had an influence on them. But these figure paintings are quite removed from the concerns of Vorticism. Vorticism in art, we must conclude, was largely still-born, a promising movement killed by the war, that more imposing blast of 1914.

But what is lost in Cork's (or any) art historical view of Vorticism is that it was not just a movement in painting and sculpture but a program for all the arts. As Pound put it, "we wished a designation that would be equally applicable to a certain basis for all the arts. Obviously you cannot have 'cubist' poetry or 'imagist' painting." That this was not just Pound's personal notion is shown by Lewis's inclusion of literature, including his own play *Enemy of the Stars,* in BLAST. Lewis conceived of this play as the literary equivalent to his own painting, his attempt to show writers the way to a truly modern literature.

Vorticism was not the isolated and abortive movement it might seem to be to an art historian, for its impact and influence was primarily on Modernist literature, not on the visual arts. Its detached modernism and willingness to use past styles showed Pound how to reconcile his "passéism" and his modernism. This reconciliation leads directly to the Modernist "mythic method" and the creative relationship the major Modernists had with past works of art. Moreover, the dynamic formism Vorticism advocated and represented became a formal pattern underlying central works of Modernist literature. Finally, Lewis's attack on narrative conventions in *Enemy of the Stars* prefigures later, more successful attacks by Eliot, Pound and Joyce.

I obviously cannot show all of this in detail, so I must let one representative moment suffice. Yeats's *A Vision,* in brief, is the delineation of a system of geometric patterns, predominantly gyres or vortices. At times Yeats claims that in the dynamic interaction of these gyres the essence of human history and personality is represented. But in his introduction to *A Vision,* "A Packet for Ezra Pound," Yeats displays a rather different attitude towards the content of *A Vision:*

> Some will ask whether I believe in the actual existence of my circuits of sun and moon. . . . To such a question I can but answer that if sometimes, overwhelmed by miracle as all men must be when in the midst of it, I have taken such periods literally, my reason has soon recovered; and now that the system stands out in my imagination I regard them as stylistic arrangements of experience comparable to the cubes in the drawing of Wyndham Lewis and to the ovoids in the sculpture of Brancusi.

A Vision, then, is a system of geometric but dynamic forms which Yeats conceives of as comparable to the forms of Vorticist and other Modernist art, and which function as the kind of intensive analytics Pound prescribed as the Vorticist ideal. Modernist literature is full of these diagrams and of concrete images which represent them—axles embedded in mud, roses in steel dust, Chinese ideograms—which try to represent essential patterns as dynamic forms in a way parallel to and indebted to the forms of Vorticist art. The Vorticist program or ideal to a large extent becomes the ideal of Modernist literature in English.

Lewis moves away from this concern with representing forms like vortices in his painting, but, in a key passage in his 1922 "Essay on the Objective of Plastic Art in Our Time," the image of the vortex reappears in his thinking about art in a new and striking way. He quotes from what he calls "Schopenhauer's eloquent and resounding words" about art in *The World as Will and Idea:*

> While science, following the unresting and inconstant stream of the fourfold forms of reason and consequent, with each end attained sees further, and can never reach a final goal nor attain full satisfaction, any more than by running we can reach the place where the clouds touch the horizon; art, on the contrary, is everywhere at its goal. For it plucks the object of its contemplation out of the stream of the world's course, and has it isolated before it. . . . It therefore pauses at this particular thing; the course of time stops; the relations vanish for it; only the essential, the Idea, is its object.

Lewis calls this "a splendid description" of what art does. The result is that a "sort of immortality descends upon these objects. It is an immortality, which, in the case of the painting, they have to pay for with death, or at least with its coldness and immobility."

Lewis here redefines the vortex in a manner which suggests the design of his major novels. Art plucks its subject out of life's stream, and analyzes it while it spins to a stop. That passage out of time, from the vitality of life to the deadness of art, is figured forth time and again in Lewis's novels (and his portraits). Groups of characters are isolated and analyzed while their doomed world slowly grinds to a halt. Characteristically, his novels end where they begin (Lady Fredigonde Follett's, Percy Hardcaster's Spanish prison), but with major characters dead and all possible motion blocked. Everything has seized up and the objects of Lewis's scrutiny have attained an immortality which they have paid for with death or its coldness and immobility.

This general pattern, of course, is merely that, and is not rigidly executed in all of Lewis's novels. But the fact that this pattern does shape *The Apes of God, The Revenge for Love,* and *Self Condemned* exemplifies both the impact of Vorticism on literature and the tenacity of a kind of Vorticism in Lewis's work. Vorticism did give rise to the Great English Art envisioned in BLAST, despite its short life and the dispersal of the London Vortex, but that art was not painting, the art for which Lewis was trained, but literature, that which he adopted and in which he ultimately did his greatest work.

Timothy Materer

SOURCE: "The English Vortex: Modern Literature and the *Pattern of Hope*," in *Journal of Modern Literature*, Vol. III, No. 5, July, 1974, pp. 1123-39.

[*In the following essay, Materer provides an overview of Vorticist theories and artistic forms.*]

At the age of 77, Ezra Pound published his final memorial to the Vortex, the association he began with Wyndham Lewis and T. S. Eliot in the crisis year of 1914. "From Canto CXV," one of Pound's *Drafts & Fragments,* laments the disappointed hopes of the group and commemorates its central figure, Wyndham Lewis. The poem opens with an extravagant but moving tribute to Lewis:

> The scientists are in terror and the European
> mind stops Wyndham Lewis chose blindness
> rather than have his mind stop.

A brain tumor blinded Lewis in 1951. He "chose blindness" when he refused to undergo surgery that risked darkening his mental faculties. Lewis continued to paint even while his sight was failing (for example, his second portrait of T. S. Eliot), and total blindness could not stop the writing of his novels and social criticism. In a figurative sense, Lewis' blindness relates him to the writers Pound describes in Canto CXV: "all the resisters blacked out." Lewis when alive was the greatest "resister" in England. "A great energy like that of Lewis," Pound wrote in 1938, "is beyond price in such a suffocated nation. . . ."

Yet the tone of this elegy for Lewis becomes less enthusiastic as Pound reflects on his failure to enlist men like Lewis and Eliot, among others, in his causes:

> When one's friends hate each other How can
> there be peace in the world?
>
> Their asperities diverted me in my green time.

These lines are characteristically overstated. There was no hate among Lewis, Eliot, and Pound at least, even in the 1930s when their relations were most strained. But Pound was deeply frustrated when he failed to convince the two writers to direct their concerted energies at the economic issue. After reading Lewis' *Left Wings over Europe* (1936), Pound pleaded with him to direct his political blasts at the usurers. And he persisted in his vain efforts to educate the man he addressed as "the Vort" on the money issue. Eliot was perhaps more interested in economic issues than Lewis, but Pound believed that Eliot's *Criterion* could have no positive social impact. He concludes bitterly in Canto 102: "But the lot of 'em, Yeats, Possum, Old Wyndham / had no ground to stand on" To understand the depth of Pound's disappointment, the sense that the failure of the Vortex implied the crash of an entire culture, we must examine Pound's "green time" and the "asperities" that so diverted him and raised his hopes.

II

Vorticism primarily represented a visual rather than a verbal revolution. Although Pound invented the term "Vorticism" in 1914, Lewis was using a vortex motif in his drawings as early as 1912. Lewis himself was influenced by the London exhibitions of Italian Futurists in 1912 and 1913, especially by Boccioni's *States of Mind* series, which employs the vortex pattern. In Lewis' *Timon of Athens* illustrations (1912), the geometrical shapes of armored figures struggle in a whirlwind that draws them into its vortex. Although the Vorticists' abstract forms were not invariably bound to the vortex design, it gave them a clearly recognizable trademark.

In literature, however, Vorticism cannot be clearly defined, nor even satisfactorily discriminated from Imagism. In his essay on Vorticism, Pound wrote that "The image is not an idea. It is a radiant node or cluster; it is . . . a VORTEX, from which, and through which, and into which, ideas are constantly rushing." This makes Vorticism seem a more ambitious and dynamic kind of Imagism. By 1913, Pound was exasperated with the Imagist group and the bullying way Amy Lowell had taken it over. The theories he developed in his Imagist phase drew new energy, if not a clearer formulation, from his association with Lewis and with the sculptor Gaudier-Brzeska. He used the term "Vortex" quite subjectively to describe the creative energy the Imagists lacked, as in this description of Lewis' art to John Quinn: "It is not merely knowledge of technique, or skill, it is intelligence and knowledge of life, of the whole of it, beauty, heaven, hell, sarcasm, every kind of whirlwind of force and emotion. Vortex. That is the right word, if I did think of it myself."

Though vague, "Vorticism" was a useful word because it could be applied to more than a single art. Vorticism gave a poet like Pound, a painter like Lewis, and a sculptor like Gaudier-Brzeska the sense that they were working for a common goal. In BLAST, the magazine Lewis founded in June of 1914 to publicize Vorticism, Pound wrote in a section entitled "VORTEX. POUND":

> Every concept, every emotion presents itself to
> the vivid consciousness in some primary form.
> It belongs to the art of this form. If sound, to
> music; if formed words, to literature; the image,
> to poetry; colour in position, to painting; form
> or design in three planes, to sculpture.

Whatever his art, the Vorticist uses "primary form." In Lewis' "Composition in Blue" (1915), the geometric shapes are nonrepresentational and exist only to set off the area of blue watercolor against the black lines and shadings of the composition. In what could be a comment on this severe design, Pound wrote that "Vorticism is art before it has spread itself into flaccidity, into elaboration and secondary application." Similarly, Pound's features are recognizable in Gaudier-Brzeska's "Hieratic Head of Ezra Pound" (1914), but the emphasis falls on the relationship of the curved masses of the hair, the domed forehead and slitted eyes, and the geometrically shaped nose, mouth, and goatee. Could literary Vorticism attempt a similarly abstract treatment of primary form? Pound had little success in doing so until his Cantos were well under way.

Vorticism not only tried to bridge the visual and the verbal arts; it also hoped to humanize the quantitative world of the sciences. In the Vorticism essay, Pound gives us the mathematical formula for the circle, which represents "the circle free of space and time limits": "Great works of art contain this . . . sort of equation. They cause form to come into being. By the 'image' I mean such an equation." At this point in the essay, he redefines the image as the Vortex. This term is ideal because a vortex defines a pattern of energies, as it does in the whirlwind of forces in Lewis' *Timon* drawings; and patterned energies also constitute the physical world. Pound tells us that science reveals "a world of moving energies . . . magnetisms that take form. . . ." The Vorticists hoped to reflect this world in their art. As one critic of Vorticism writes, "Recent advances and popularizations of physics had forced many, like Henry Adams, to quail before the 'new multiverse of forces,' but the Vorticists had no such fears and gladly took on the task of conceptualizing this new world as a world of forms."

Vorticism primarily represented a visual rather than a verbal revolution. Although Pound invented the term "Vorticism" in 1914, Lewis was using a vortex motif in his drawings as early as 1912.

— Timothy Materer

" 'Vorticism,' " Lewis wrote in a 1939 reminiscence, "accepted the machine world: that is the point to stress." When Lewis wrote this, he was opposing Herbert Read's claim that the abstract artist was fleeing from the mechanized world of science into an imaginary world. The Vorticist Manifesto in *BLAST,* on the contrary, asserted that the modern artist must be inspired by "the forms of machinery, Factories, new and vaster buildings, bridges and works." The Vorticists would not deny that the landscapes created by industrialism were generally hideous. But the Vortex would sweep up this ugliness, blast it to pieces, and reassemble it in beautiful, painted forms. In *BLAST,* Lewis writes: "A man could make just as fine an art in discords, and with nothing but 'ugly' trivial and terrible materials, as any classic artist did with only 'beautiful' and pleasant means."

An "art in discords" suggests the finest pieces of verbal art *BLAST* offered, T. S. Eliot's "Preludes" and "Rhapsody on a Windy Night." Eliot was not one of the original Vorticists, and Lewis did not even know him when *BLAST* No. 1 was published. But sometime before the next issue, Lewis walked into Pound's triangular flat in Kensington and met, as he describes it; "the author of *Prufrock*—indeed . . . Prufrock himself: but a Prufrock to whom the mermaids would decidedly have sung. . . ." Eliot was still studying at Oxford then, but he followed the Vorticists' activities in London and tried to break into *BLAST* with appropriately energetic poems. "I have corresponded with Lewis," Eliot wrote to Pound,

"but his Puritanical Principles seem to bar my way to Publicity. I fear that King Bolo and his Big Black Kween will never burst into print." Lewis told Pound that he wished to use Eliot's "excellent bits of scholarly ribaldry . . . but stick to my naif determination to have no 'words ending in -Uck, -Unt, and -Ugger.' "

"Preludes," however, made a positive contribution to the Vorticist cause that "King Bolo," one suspects, could not have. Eliot's poems were the only literary productions in *BLAST* that matched in force and originality the designs of Lewis, the painter Edward Wads-worth, and Gaudier-Brzeska. *BLAST* No. 1 did print a section from Ford Madox Ford's *The Good Soldier* (then entitled *The Saddest Story*). But the novel's prose seems tame next to the Vorticists' proclamations and "Blasts," and its technical innovations could not be appreciated in a brief excerpt. As for Pound, Lewis was right when he commented years later that Pound's "fire-eating propagandist utterances were not accompanied by any very experimental efforts in his particular medium." Pound mixed awkward satire ("Let us deride the smugness of 'The Times' / GUFFAW!") with uninspired attempts to use primary form (as in the two-line poem "L'Art": "Green arsenic spread on an egg-white cloth, / Crushed strawberries! Come let us feast our eyes.")

Eliot's poems, on the other hand, were compressed enough to at least seem inspired by the Vorticist theory of primary form. The modern urban life they reflected was assembled from the poem's "sordid images." Like a work by Gaudier-Brzeska, the poem presents a human figure, but one unlike a conventional representation of a realistic character:

> You had such a vision of the street
> As the street hardly understands;
> Sitting along the bed's edge, where
> You curled the papers from your hair,
> Or clasped the yellow soles of feet
> In the palms of both soiled hands.

The powerful sense of character conveyed by the images of "yellow soles" and "soiled hands" arises from an art, to repeat Pound's phrase, that has not "spread itself into . . . elaboration and secondary application."

But unfortunately Eliot began his association with the Vorticists as the movement was dying. In the second issue of *BLAST,* following a "Vortex" sent from France by Gaudier-Brzeska, appears the black-bordered notice: "MORT POUR LA PATRIE. Henri Gaudier-Brzeska: after months of fighting and two promotions for gallantry." Soon Lewis had also joined the army. As Lewis wrote in his last editorial, "*BLAST* finds itself surrounded by a multitude of other Blasts. . . . [It] will, however, try and brave the wave of blood, for the serious mission it has on the other side of World-War."

The first short-lived phase of the Vortex and the one to follow correspond to what Pound calls the first two phases of "Kulchur": "the nineteen teens, Gaudier, Wyndham L. and I as we were in Blast, and the next phase, the 1920's. The sorting out, the *rappel a l'ordre.*"

III

By dispersing the Vortex, World War I destroyed England's hope for a new Renaissance. This statement may seem extreme, but it represents Pound's and Lewis' opinions. In February of 1915, Pound could still write: "new masses of unexplored arts and facts are pouring into the vortex of London. They cannot help bringing about changes as great as the Renaissance changes." The Vorticists were in effect following Pound's prescription for the making of a Renaissance, as he outlined it in *Patria Mia* (1913). First, dead ideas must be demolished: "A Risorgimento implies a whole volley of liberations; liberations from ideas, from stupidities. . . . " By its very name, *BLAST* promised to do the demolishing, as well as provide two more qualities Pound thought essential to a Renaissance, "enthusiasm and a propaganda." A major target of the Vorticists' blasts was the Victorian age, as in one of the many editorial "Blasts" in Lewis' publication:

BLAST

years 1837 to 1900. . . .

BLAST their weeping whiskers—hirsute
RHETORIC of EUNUCH and STYLIST—
SENTIMENTAL HYGIENICS
ROUSSEAUISMS (wild Nature cranks)
FRATERNIZING WITH MONKEYS

With the remnants of Victorianism cleared away, the arts could lead the way to a remade culture: "This will have its effect not only in the arts," Pound wrote of his Renaissance, "but in life, in politics, and in economics. If I seem to lay undue stress upon the status of the arts, it is only because the arts respond to an intellectual movement more swiftly and more apparently than do institutions." In 1939, Lewis reflected on the intense hopes of the *BLAST* days; he speaks of himself in the third person, as if to disassociate himself from his own "green time":

> He thought the time had come to shatter the visible world to bits, and build it nearer to the heart's desire: and he really was persuaded that this absolute transformation was imminent. . . . The war looked to him like an episode at first—rather proving his contentions than otherwise.

The Vorticists imagined that the war might finish the job of demolishing Victorianism that they had begun. With terrible irony, Gaudier-Brzeska wrote in the "VORTEX" he sent from France just before his death: "THIS WAR IS A GREAT REMEDY."

When Lewis himself went to the front in 1917, he quickly lost any illusions about the "remedial" aspect of the war. Before he was transferred to Lord Beaverbrook's "Canadian War Memorials" project, he saw heavy fighting. (Lewis' friend and colleague T. E. Hulme was killed in a battery less than a quarter of a mile from Lewis' own.) Lewis wrote in 1939 that he understood the war's significance when "he found himself in the mud of Passchend-

aele" and realized that "the community to which he belonged would never be the same again: and that all *surplus vigour* was being bled away and stamped out."

Although his disillusion was intense, much of his vigor, or Vorticist energy, did survive the war. "The thought of the modern and the energy of the cave-man," Eliot wrote in 1918 to describe Lewis' works. Lewis was full of new schemes to rebuild the visual world, but he did not know how to activate them. Plans for a new issue of BLAST fell through. Although the Vorticist painters (including Edward Wadsworth and Frederick Etchells) reassembled as "Group X," they broke up after one exhibition. Pound, Lewis, and Eliot could at least publish together in *The Little Review*, which Pound announced as "a place where the current prose writings of James Joyce, Wyndham Lewis, T. S. Eliot, and myself might appear regularly, promptly, and together. . . . " But the focus of Pound's energies was obviously shifting from England. Even by 1916, he had probably started on what he called his "farewell to London," *Hugh Selwyn Mauberley. Mauberley*, according to Hugh Kenner, is "an elegy for the Vortex." And in section V it is an elegy for men like Gaudier-Brzeska, who died before they could remake a moribund culture:

> There died a myriad,
> And of the best, among them,
> For an old bitch gone in the teeth,
> For a botched civilization. . . .

While Pound was planning to move to Paris, Lewis and Eliot were active in London. They had drawn closer after the War and took a holiday in France together in the summer of 1920, when, as bearers of a present from Ezra Pound (it turned out to be a used pair of brown shoes), they visited Joyce in Paris. In London, they cast around for financial backing for a new magazine. Lewis had interested Sidney Schiff (the author "Stephen Hudson") in financing the project, but he was doubtful because he thought Lewis and Eliot would be the only first-rate contributors to it. Finally, Lewis published his own tiny and inexpensive publication, *The Tyro*, in 1921. Since the paper surveyed the art of painting rather than general cultural trends, *The Tyro* did not meet Eliot's standards. Nevertheless, he loyally contributed three essays and a poem before *The Tyro* folded in 1922.

By 1922, of course, Eliot had begun to dominate London intellectual life as the author of *The Waste Land* and editor of *The Criterion*. Although *The Waste Land* was at first read as an obituary for Western culture, it contains positive elements. First, by the very fact that it was a great poem it bore witness to a degree of vitality in the modern age. Pound felt that it "justified" modern poetry, and after seeing the drafts for it wrote to Eliot, "It is after all a grrrreat litttttterary period." Secondly, although the poem despairs of the present state of culture, it makes us aware of the traditions our culture lacks and implies the need for individual responsibility in attaining them. "Shall I at least set my lands in order?" one of Eliot's protagonists asks. Through the *Criterion*, Eliot intended to recognize his responsibility.

> The Vorticists imagined that the war might finish the job of demolishing Victorianism that they had begun. With terrible irony, Gaudier-Brzeska wrote in the "VORTEX" he sent from France just before his death: "THIS WAR IS A GREAT REMEDY."
>
> — *Timothy Materer*

Unless the three writers published together, there could be no Vortex, which Pound once defined as a "convergence" of the best minds available. Eliot therefore needed Lewis and Pound for *The Criterion*. He told Lewis that he wanted to keep their "association before the public mind," and requested a contribution from him, including a regular art chronicle, in every issue of the quarterly. Eliot also editorialized on Lewis' literary and social criticism-books like *The Art of Being Ruled* (1926) and *Time and Western Man* (1927). In his commentary on the 1926 work, Eliot saw Lewis as representative of the "dispossessed artist," who "may be driven to examining the elements in the situation—political, social, philosophical or religious—which frustrate his labor." In his study of Eliot's intellectual development, John Margolis credits Lewis' example with strengthening Eliot's decision to broaden *The Criterion*'s interest in social issues.

Nevertheless, by 1927 Lewis had lost confidence in Eliot's editing of his quarterly. He felt that Eliot had opened it to the very forces it should be fighting. For example, Eliot published sections from Lewis' great satire of the London art world, *The Apes of God,* and told Lewis that "It is worthwhile running the *Criterion* just to publish these." But at the same time he was also printing works by some of Lewis' prime satiric targets—Sacheverell Sitwell, for example, and Lewis' estranged patron Sidney Schiff. Lewis was doubtlessly over-sensitive. Yet Pound felt much the same as Lewis about Eliot's editing. Pound often urged Lewis to contribute more to *The Criterion,* since it was by default the best outlet in England, and wrote over twenty articles and poems for it himself. But he continually criticized Eliot for his lack of commitment, particularly on economic issues. He closed a complaining letter to the *Criterion* with the reservation, "Far be it from me to deny or affirm or in any way uncriterionisticly to commit myself. . . ." In an economic journal, he wrote that an analysis of many of *The Criterion*'s contributors would result in a libel action.

IV

The Vorticists wanted to build a new world, but they were forced to squander their energy demolishing the old one. Their efforts began to diverge because they did not find a program to unite them. Although they all shared a commitment to order and authority, the events of the 1930s subjected their political ideas to pressures they could not bear.

In *For Launcelot Andrewes,* Eliot praised Lewis because he was "obviously striving courageously toward a positive theory. . . . " Yet Lewis' major theoretical work, *Time and Western Man,* is almost wholly destructive criticism—an attack on what he calls the "time-cult." According to this Bergsonian "cult," all experience is reduced to temporal flux; even one's identity is merely a series of chronological events. Lewis writes, in the most "positive" statement he offers,

> So what we seek to stimulate, and what we give the critical outline of, is a philosophy that will be as much a *spatial-philosophy* as Bergson's is a *time-philosophy*. As much as he enjoys the sight of things 'penetrating' and 'merging' do we enjoy the opposite picture of them standing apart . . . much as he enjoys the 'indistinct,' the 'qualitative,' the misty, sensational and ecstatic, very much more do we value the distinct, the geometric.

Lewis associates the temporal sense with the emotions and a romantic condition of becoming, and the spatial sense with the intellect and a classical state of being. (The reference to "geometric" qualities is related to T. E. Hulme's view of modern classicism.) All experience should be clearly ordered ("with usura is no clear demarcation," Pound writes in Canto XLV). But even though the terms of Lewis' "critical outline" are suggestive, they are no more related to a "positive theory" than Eliot's ambiguous statement (in *For Launcelot Andrewes*) that he considered himself "classicist in literature, royalist in politics, and Anglo-Catholic in religion." Only his Anglo-Catholicism committed Eliot to specific beliefs, but even it did not lead him to support any direct social action—as Pound observed. Reacting to the religious viewpoint of *After Strange Gods* Pound complained that Eliot "implies that we need more religion, but does not specify the nature of that religion; all the implications are such as to lead the readers' minds into a fog."

Pound's own "positive theory," based on Major Douglas' system of Social Credit, was a specific one. And his jagged technique in the Cantos was meant to keep the reader's mind alert: comparing different men and cultures and drawing economic morals that illuminate Douglas' system. Pound invites us to correlate "luminous details": Malatesta's enormous efforts to build the Tempio (Canto IX), John Quinn's story of the "Honest Sailor's" financial success (XII), the hell faced by Gaudier-Brzeska, Hulme, and Lewis in World War I (XVI), and Kublai Kahn's invention of paper money (XVIII). This technique, as several critics have noted, is related to the theories of Vorticism: "The innumerable disparate elements that make up the *Cantos* can be thought of as 'planes in relation' . . . united visually, or spatially, in the same manner as a Lewis painting or a Gaudier carving."

Whatever positive ideas were held by these three artists, the real problem was to put these ideas into action. This was not so much Eliot's concern because he thought that the intellectual should criticize and compare social theories rather than put them into practice. But Pound and Lewis tried to take more direct action, with disastrous results for their careers.

"The great protector of the arts," Pound wrote in 1913, "is as rare as the great artist, or more so." Pound was always watchful for such a patron and found one in John Quinn. He wrote to Quinn, "If there were more like you, we should get on with our renaissance." In Mussolini, Pound believed that he had found not only a man sensitive to the arts (as in Canto 41), but also one capable of reforming a usurious economic system. The artist's duty was to recognize such a leader when he appeared. By presenting figures like Malatesta and Thomas Jefferson in the *Cantos*, Pound supposedly prepares us to recognize the promising qualities in Mussolini. Pound accepted the weakest indications that Mussolini would reform Italy's economics. Behind his desire to believe that the dictator would do so is his conviction that only authoritarian rule could distribute economic goods fairly: "In a hidebound Italy, fascism meant at the start DIRECT action. . . . " He thus convinced himself that "the Duce will stand not with despots and the lovers of power but with the lovers of ORDER."

Lewis also felt that only authoritarian control could change an economic system. In 1931, he wrote a book that was sympathetic toward German National Socialism, a book that he almost immediately regretted, *Hitler*. Lewis was careful to point out that he was an "exponent," not an "advocate," of Hitler's programs. But he was clearly sympathetic to Hitler's economic views (rejecting, however, their anti-Semitic aspect) and at one point cited Eliot on Social Credit to explain the German position on the war debts imposed at Versailles. Like Pound, Lewis believed the simplistic theory that wars are caused by the manipulation of financiers: "the Versailles Treaty Makers must have known that the more 'nations' you make (or break the world up into) . . . the more pickings for the Outsider.

All three men approached these issues as, to use Eliot's phrase for Lewis, "dispossessed artists." As artists, they would all probably have agreed with Lewis' justification of a strong, central authority: "to get some sort of peace to enable us to work, we should naturally seek the most powerful and stable authority that can be devised." Best of all, however, would be the kind of authority that would give the artist some direct influence on society (Pound thought that Mussolini would make this possible in Italy). The work that best reveals the fundamental reason for this fascination with authoritarian government takes us back to the conclusion of the first Vorticist phase: Lewis' pamphlet of 1919, *The Caliph's Design, Architects! Where is your Vortex?*

This brilliant and exuberant critique of the arts begins with a "parable." Lewis imagines a Caliph rising one morning, sketching out some strange designs, and then summoning his chief engineer and architect. He tells them that he is dissatisfied with his city, "so I have done a design of a new city, or rather of a typical street in a new city. It is a little vorticist bagatelle. . . . " The Caliph's men are amused and puzzled, then terrified as they learn that they have only a few hours "to invent the forms and conditions that would make it possible to realize my design," or else "your heads will fall. . . . " Under these conditions, the job gets done. The plans appear on schedule,

"And within a month a strange street transfigured the heart of that cultivated city."

"A VORTICIST KING! WHY NOT?" *BLAST* inquired. An enlightened monarch, by transforming a city's architecture, could ennoble its citizens' lives and make them happier with their lot, as Lewis argues in *The Caliph's Design*. He further developed this argument in *The Tyro*:

> A man might be unacquainted with the very existence of a certain movement in art, and yet his life could be modified directly if the street he walked down took a certain shape. . . . Its forms and colours would have a tonic or a debilitating effect on him. . . . The painting, sculpture and general design of today, such as can be included in the movement we support, aims at nothing short of a physical reconstructing . . . of the visible part of the world.

In admiring the above passage, Stephen Spender finds that it reflects one of the great characteristics of modern art: "The invention through art of a *pattern of hope*, influencing society." Lewis and the Vorticists believed, to use Spender's words, "that modern art might transform the contemporary environment, and hence, by pacifying and ennobling its inhabitants, revolutionize the world. . . . " We should not forget the idealism of these early hopes. But unfortunately the Vorticist Caliph was an artist's dream, the fascist dictator a political reality.

V

The English Vortex reveals not the development of a social or intellectual program, but rather what Spender calls a "pattern of hope." Modern literature was not born in despair after World War I, but before the War, with the hope of transfiguring every aspect of life through a new Renaissance. By the middle Thirties this hope was no longer viable. Pound alone kept pushing for a revival of the Vortex, even suggesting a new issue of *BLAST* to Lewis in 1936. His support of Lewis continued, as Lewis learned to his distress after the War, when Pound went on Fascist radio in Italy during World War II.

Pound's fate during and after the War is well-known. Lewis' fate was not so severe, but harsh nonetheless. His unpopular political writings of the Thirties, especially the Hitler book, put his entire literary career under a cloud; and a series of illnesses left him deeply in debt. His skill as a painter was as fine as ever, and he received valuable publicity when the Royal Academy refused to exhibit his magnificent 1938 portrait of T. S. Eliot—which led Augustus John to resign from the Academy in protest. But the pre-War market for paintings was barren for even the best of artists, and in 1939 Lewis and his wife left for America, where he was promised some commissions. He planned on a short stay, but the War stranded him in Canada with no way of obtaining money to return. His lonely, poverty-stricken years in Toronto became the subject of his greatest novel, *Self Condemned* (1954).

Lewis' novel is representative of the kind of introspection all three writers underwent as a result of the War. The spirit of both *Self Condemned* and *The Pisan Cantos* is reflected in the following great lines from Eliot's "Little Gidding," in which he lists the "gifts reserved for age":

> the conscious impotence of rage
> At human folly, and the laceration
> Of laughter at what ceases to amuse.
> And last, the rending pain of re-enactment
> Of all that you have done, and been; the shame
> Of motives late revealed, and the awareness
> Of things ill done and done to others' harm. . . .

Although the theme of *Self Condemned* is in these lines, it is nowhere stated with this precision and confidence. Sometimes it is hard to tell whether Lewis is justifying or condemning his protagonist. But the greatness of the novel lies in what Eliot called its tone of "almost unbearable spiritual agony."

Lewis' protagonist in *Self Condemned,* René Harding, resigns his chair of history shortly before World War II breaks out because he thinks that his subject as it is presently taught encourages a war psychosis. He claims that historians dignify the war-makers and systematically ignore the economic causes of war. Although he is heartened that "the student masses have begun to regard the world . . . with a cold eye," he feels that he can no longer compromise himself and leaves for Canada. Once there, however, poverty and intellectual isolation transform his rebelliousness and hope into despair. He now believes that the brief periods of civilization man has known will always be the exceptions and animal brutality and greed the rule. Western civilization is dying, he believes: "He estimated that we were perhaps rather more than half-way across that in geological terms, infinitely brief era of 'enlightenment'." This passage echoes the conclusion of one of Lewis' favorite books of the post-World War I period, Julien Benda's *La Trahison des Clercs.* But in this post-World War II novel such ideas are put in a new and harsher light. In Harding's character, they lead to a contempt for the masses who are producing what he considers a new dark ages. Two years before he published *Self Condemned,* Lewis admitted in *The Art of Being Ruled* that "intolerance regarding the backward, slothful, obstructive majority—'homo stultus'—is present." This intolerance, in an extreme form, corrupts René Harding. One senses the book's "spiritual agony" as Lewis traces this corruption in his autobiographical hero. As Harding loses his idealism and writes historical studies that despair of human progress, he ironically becomes a famous author; but he "no longer even believed in his theories of a new approach to History . . . for him it had all frozen into a freak anti-historical wax-works, of which he was the Keeper, containing many libellous wax-works of famous kings and queens. He carried on mechanically with what the bright, rushing, idealistic mind of another man had begun."

By the novel's end, his misanthropy has turned him into a "glacial shell of a man."

"Yuss. my beamish buckO!" Pound wrote after reading *Self Condemned,* "this IZ some book," and he added in a later letter from St. Elizabeth's, "Shd / get yu the Nob-

ble." Pound had plenty of disciples around him at the asylum, but he wasn't deceived by their mere youthful energy. He continued to write to Lewis about his long-standing wish to revive the spirit of the Vortex: "WORTEXXX, gorrdammit, some convergence." He told Lewis, "Have told re / vortex, dominant cell in somatic devilupment. . . . " *The Pisan Cantos* show that even his thoughts about England had mellowed. In Canto LXXX, he recalls his first meeting with Lewis at the Vienna Café, and in Canto LXXVIII he asserts that Lewis and Gaudier-Brzeska are still vital influences:

> in whom are the voices, keeping hand on the reins
> Gaudier's word not blacked out,
>   nor old Hulme's, nor Wyndham's. . . .

As for himself, Pound reveals the kind of remorse Lewis expresses in *Self Condemned.* Pound writes, though not consistently, of a man self-condemned, "that had been a hard man in some ways":

> J'ai eu pitié des autres
> probablement pas assez, and at moments that suited
>   my own convenience. . . .

One finds a similar confession in one of Lewis' war-time letters from Canada. He admits that his politcal writings were too concerned with achieving the best conditions for the "tribe" of the artist: "I now see that I thought if anything too much about our tribe . . . not enough about 'le genre humain' of the revolutionary song."

But Pound kept driving at his social credit theory. Lewis' description of his "rock-drill action . . . he blasts away tirelessly, prodding and coaxing" delighted Pound, and he used Lewis' term for his *Section: Rock-Drill De Los Cantares* (1955). His ambitions still were high in the 1959 *Thrones,* which he described as "an attempt to move out from egoism and to establish some definition of an order possible or at any rate conceivable on earth." They declined only when he was in his eighties. In *Drafts & Fragments* (1969), he admits his failures, but in lines of poetry that are themselves a triumph:

> I have brought the great ball of crystal;
>   who can lift it?
> Can you enter the great acorn of light?
>   But the beauty is not the madness
>   Tho' my errors and wrecks lie about me.

His weariness marks the elegy for Lewis of Canto CXV, with which we began this survey of the Vortex. The "asperities" of his "green time" no longer amuse, and Lewis' time / space categories, or any system that tries to order human experience, now seem meaningless: "Time, space, / neither life nor death is the answer." Pound had the grandest designs for the new culture the Vorticists hoped to build, and he was consequently more painfully disillusioned than Lewis and certainly more than Eliot.

But whatever the practical failures and the errors of judgment, the "pattern of hope" lives in their works. The ordered society that would foster great art was never to be. As Lewis wrote of the "men of 1914," "We are the first men of a Future that has not materialized. We belong to a 'great age' that has not 'come off.' " They have left us instead "some definition of an order possible or at any rate conceivable on earth," as Pound himself suggests in his memorial for Lewis:

> A blown husk that is finished
> but the light sings eternal. . . .

John J. Tucker

SOURCE: "Pound, Vorticism and the New Esthetic," in *Mosaic: A Journal of the Interdisciplinary Study of Literature,* Vol. XVI, No. 4, Fall, 1983, pp. 83-96.

[*In the following essay, Tucker studies Pound's contribution to Vorticism as well as its influence on his work.*]

Groups set the tone for artistic London in the second decade of the century. The shifting alliances and aggressive posturings of the politicians became fashionable among artists, who attacked one another with a fine and contemporary disregard for their shared interests. The young Ezra Pound, appalled by the other war that first threatened and then engulfed his Europe, busied himself on the home front, stirring things up when he found them too quiet, encouraging the creative belligerence on which groups thrive.

Imagism and Vorticism were the groups to which Pound most enthusiastically committed his energies at this time. Of the two, Imagism has evoked the greater scholarly interest, in part, perhaps, because Eliot once described it as "the starting-point of modern poetry," but also because its essentially literary character has made its program more attractive and more accessible to students of literature. Furthermore, the Vorticists were rather too successful in gaining the antipathy of the artistic establishment of London, and this antipathy turned quickly from tonic hostility to a condescending disparagement which persisted for decades. As late as 1959, *A Dictionary of Art and Artists* could write off Vorticism as "a variety of CUBISM, exclusive to England, invented by Wyndham Lewis." Only recently, thanks to the efforts of a number of scholars, has this moment in the modernist revolt begun to receive the careful consideration it deserves.

With the revaluation of Vorticism has come a more careful examination of Pound's contribution to the movement and of its influence on his poetry. An early and sympathetic investigation of these questions by Herbert Schneidau concludes on a telling note of regret: "In summing up the effect of Vorticism on Pound's career it is hard to avoid the conclusion that Pound the Vorticist, a declared enemy to the public will, was the father of the man standing in the public dock charged with treason." A later study invites us to take a more positive view, arguing that the term Vortex should be extended to encompass the "artistic crosscurrents" set in motion in 1914 which for forty years interenergized the works of Pound, Eliot and Lewis. The more recent analysis of Ian Bell turns our attention in the opposite direction, to the origins of Pound's Vortex. "In the notion of the 'vortex'," Bell contends, Pound discovered "ancient cosmology, in the form of pre-Socratic atomism, elucidated and made new by nineteenth-century

field-theory physics." Just how alive the poet was to the intricacies of this intellectual matrix must remain in doubt, yet one cannot deny its general relevance to the poetic of juxtapositions he was working out at the time.

My own concern is similarly with Pound's development as a poet, but I would argue that studies of its Vorticist phase should continue to focus on his immersion in literature's sister arts. For, if the extent of Pound's interest in music, painting and sculpture has often been remarked, the actual relevance of his extra-literary investigation to the formulation of his new poetic remains unclear. Insufficient attention has been paid, I feel, to his search for the techniques by which the new discoveries of one art might be adapted to the needs of another.

Pound's London years, during which the bulk of his criticism was written, were years of conscious self-modernization, and nothing stamped this process more indelibly than the Vortex. Pound, I would argue, invented Imagism as a device to draw attention to his friends, but he was quick to realize that he had created an unexpectedly useful propagandistic device, and he was happy, given the mood of the moment, to exploit it. His participation in Vorticism, in contrast, was more calculated. He allied himself with the "Blast group" in order to confront the developments that were taking place in the other arts and their implications for poetry. He believed, in his words, that "the spirit of a decade strikes properly upon all of the arts" and all the arts must concert their efforts if this spirit is to be advanced.

Throughout his life Pound remained convinced that, as he had put it already in *The Spirit of Romance,* "true poetry is in much closer relation to the best of music, of painting, and of sculpture, than to any part of literature which is not true poetry." His task in 1913-14 was to discover the *best* of music, of painting and of sculpture, which meant, with the appropriate avant-garde inflection, the most modern, the most Vorticist. But he needed also to identify the nature of this "closer relation" between the arts and this required, paradoxically, a clearer understanding of the differences between them. Thus, looking back to this time in *Guide to Kulchur,* he recalls: "My generation found criticism of the arts cluttered with work of men who persistently defined the works of one art in terms of another. For a decade or so we tried to get the arts sorted out." His difficulty was to determine which are the valid connections between the arts and which the necessary distinctions between them.

Although the Vorticist articles exhibit some of the impatience with linear exposition that was to become the hallmark of his criticism, the investigation they chronicle was by no means unsystematic. Carefully considered, these articles reveal that he was preoccupied during this period by a group of problems all connected to the interrelationship of the arts. Since the new poetic toward which he was moving involved precisely an increased emphasis on the musical and visual dimensions of language, it was essential that he understand the "common speech"—and the phrase is his own—through which the effects of one art might properly be transferred to another.

But before we return to this more complex question, which is indeed the ultimate concern of this study, it will be necessary to take up briefly the first of Pound's problems, the broad distinction between the new art and the old. His attitude on this basic issue reveals traces of his earlier medieval studies but also owes something to the preoccupations of his associates. In the earliest of the articles in which his growing interest in the plastic arts is displayed, "The New Sculpture," he describes a meeting of the Quest Society at which he, Hulme and Wyndham Lewis spoke. As his contribution Pound evidently argued for a division he had outlined in previous essays, that between "symptomatic" and "donative" artists or between periods that are "phantastikon-centred" or "germinal." Concerning a speech which can only have been his own he remarks: "A third speaker got himself disliked by saying that one might regard the body either as a sensitized receiver of sensations, or as an instrument for carrying out the decrees of the will (or expressioning [*sic*] the soul, or whatever you choose to term it). These two views are opposed and produce two totally opposed theories of aesthetic." Having in his earier poetry played the sensitized receiver, Pound the Vorticist took up the cause of the will.

Hulme's address, included in the posthumous *Speculations* as "Modern Art and Its Philosophy," pursues a roughly similar theme in its application of Wilhelm Worringer's thesis, *Abstraktion und Einfühlung* to the contemporary avant-garde world of London. According to Worringer's theory, the works of individual artists and, more broadly, the character of particular cultures can be divided into two fundamentally different types: those which stress the empathy of the artist with the material world and the viewer with the work of art, on the one hand, and those which show the artist in conflict with the world producing works of art which resist the viewer's emotional involvement, on the other. Substituting for "empathetic" and "abstract" the terms "vital" and "geometrical," Hulme reworks Worringer's disinterested art history in programmatic form. Vital art is for him not an equally valid, but an inferior alternative, especially in the increasing debilitation it has undergone since the Renaissance.

Although Pound came to be irritated with the respect later accorded Hulme, he seems at the time to have welcomed this complementary approach. Of Hulme's presentation he remarks approvingly: "Mr. Hulme was quite right in saying that the difference between the new art and the old was not a difference in degree but a difference in kind; a difference in intention". The new art, to combine the terms of Hulme and Pound, must strive toward abstraction and it must do so by responding not to sensations but to the decrees of the will. Here surely one can find the simplest definition of Vorticism. The Vortex symbolizes the willed focusing of creative energy that produces pattern instead of reproducing it.

But how, in the absence of any mimetic imperative, is one to evaluate the seriousness or success of Vorticist art? How can the emphasis on the creative will at the expense of external constraints—with the artistic indiscipline and self-indulgence this would seem to sanction—be reconciled with Pound's vision of the artist as a committed, skillful professional? These questions are never far from his mind. The Vorticist articles discover him searching for an answer in his idea of the integrity of the medium. The doctrine of the so-called primary pigment distills the gnomic essence of this idea.

THE PRIMARY PIGMENT

The vorticist relies on this alone; on the primary pigment of his art, nothing else.

Every conception, every emotion presents itself to the vivid consciousness in some primary form.

He proceeds with emphatic iteration to develop the notion of primary form.

EVERY CONCEPT, EVERY EMOTION PRESENTS ITSELF TO THE VIVID CONSCIOUSNESS IN SOME PRIMARY FORM. IT BELONGS TO THE ART OF THIS FORM. IF SOUND, TO MUSIC: IF FORMED WORDS, TO LITERATURE: THE IMAGE, TO POETRY: FORM, TO DESIGN: COLOUR IN POSITION, TO PAINTING: FORM OR DESIGN IN THREE PLANES, TO SCULPTURE: MOVEMENT TO THE DANCE OR TO THE RHYTHM OF MUSIC OR OF VERSES.

The revolutionary consequences of this doctrine may not, at first sight, be apparent. In fact, the statement may seem scarcely more than a truism tricked out in the extravagant typography characteristic of *Blast*. But there is a shift here in the new attention to the constraints and the capacities inherent in the medium. When we examine Pound's discussion of the details of this doctrine, we become aware that its orientation is revolutionary, for the medium is no longer conceived of as a barrier that the artist must overcome, and overcome in such a way as to hide any struggle that may have taken place. The integrity of the medium must be preserved if the artist's will is to be seen interacting with something outside itself.

To work out the revolutionary consequences of the doctrine of the primary pigment, one must take up in turn Pound's comments on the visual arts and on music. Consider his remarks on painting, for example. Whistler, a favorite hero of Pound's because he "proved once and for all . . . that being born an American does not eternally damn a man or prevent him from the ultimate and highest achievement in the arts" and because he chose to pursue his artistic career in Europe, is the great prototype. He discerns a cultural breakthrough in Whistler's remark, quoted imperfectly from memory, "The picture is interesting not because it is Trotty Veg, but because it is an arrangement in colour." For, as Pound goes on to say, "The minute you have admitted that, you let in the jungle, you let in nature and truth and abundance and cubism and Kandinsky, and the lot of us." Actually Whistler said something rather different when he dismissed the advice of those who would have him substitute the title "Trotty Veck" for "Harmony in Grey and Gold": "I should hold it a vulgar and meretricious trick to excite people about Trotty Veck when, if they really care for pictorial art at all, they would know that the picture should have its own merit, and never depend upon dramatic, or legendary, or local interest." Pound has converted a refusal to underline the narrative dimension of a painting into a rejection of the representational imperative. Yet this alteration, although it may cause us to suspect the poet's concern for accuracy, does not invalidate his point: "The vorticist can represent or not as he likes. He *depends*—depends for his artistic effect—upon the arrangement of spaces and line, on the primary media of his art. A resemblance to natural forms is of no consequence one way or the other."

Interestingly enough, although Trotty "Veg" lets in Cubism and Kandinsky, Cubists and Expressionists failed, from the Vorticist point of view, to combine the essential features of the new art. The abstraction of Cubism, for instance, is the discovery of the geometrical sub-structure of natural objects or the assumption of multiple points of view, not the imposition of the creating will. In Lewis' words, "Picasso through the whole of his 'Cubist' period has always had for starting-point in his creations, however abstract, his studio-table with two apples and a mandoline, the portrait of a poet of his acquaintance, or what not. His starting-point is identical with that of Cézanne or Manet." And the Futurists simply submitted modern or moving objects to a similar, if less profound, dissection. The Expressionists, on the other hand, approach the Vorticists in resisting the role of sensitized receivers of sensations. Yet, with the exception of Kandinsky, whom Lewis in the essay just quoted dismissed as "at the best, wandering and slack", they eschewed the thoroughgoing abstraction of the Vorticists. Their preference for distortion and rejection of the conventionally beautiful depends on the existence of the naturalistic tradition whose assumptions they subvert.

But however interested Pound is in painting, sculpture is the art to which his mind most frequently returns and which provides him with the most illuminating exempla of what it means for an artist to respect his medium. Thus a characteristic remark in *Gaudier-Brzeska*: "The key word of vorticist art was objectivity in the sense that we insisted that the value of a piece of sculpture was dependent on its shape". The opening statements of Gaudier-Brzeska's "Vortex" recur time and again in his writing: "Sculptural feeling is the appreciation of masses in relation. Sculptural ability is the defining of these masses by planes". The interest of a sculpture must reside in the interaction of its masses and planes.

Sculpture that strives for empathetic or, in Hulme's dichotomy, *vital* qualities denies its own reality and becomes for Pound the caressable. Although Greek sculpture is usually considered the ideal, it suffers in Pound's opinion from this desire to achieve the caressable: "The weakness of the caressable work of art, of the work of art which depends upon the caressability of the subject, is, incidentally, that its stimulativeness diminishes as it becomes more familiar. The work which depends upon an arrangement of forms becomes more interesting with familiarity in proportion as its forms are well organized". His own experience confirmed this: "I had, for a long time, a most hideous Brzeska statue where the morning light came on it as it woke me, and because of this shifting light plane after plane, outline after expressive outline was given me day after day, emphasized, taken apart from the rest".

The sculptor's basic art of respect for the integrity of his medium consists in his choice of tools. He must not employ any power-enhancing technology, for this would alter his relationship with the stone or metal and introduce an element of dishonesty into his work, which will inevitably weaken the forms that he creates. The existence of an alternative technology yields one benefit, however, for it is only when some means of circumventing this massive resistance appears that one realizes the full value of respecting it. And it is partly for this reason, I imagine, that *"We have again arrived at an age when men can consider a statue as a statue. The hard stone is not the live coney. Its beauty cannot be the same beauty"*. This is the lesson of Gaudier-Brzeska's work: "He had given us a very definite appreciation of stone as stone; he had taught us to feel that the beauty of sculpture is inseparable from its material and that it inheres in the material."

The preservation of the integrity of the material, as opposed to "that combination of patience and trickery which can make marble chains with free links and spin out bronze until it copies the feathers on a general's hat", is vital to the projection of the drama of artistic creativity, the artist's will wrestling with reality. And it is here, I would suggest, that the human or narrative dimension of abstract art resides, in the record it preserves of the struggle involved in its creation. "Our respect is not for the subject-matter, but for the creative power of the artist". The most heroic image of the creative power of the artist is that of the sculptor: "The sculptor must add to the power of imagining form-combination the physical energy required to cut this into the unyielding medium. He must have vividness of perception, he must have this untiringness, he must, beyond that, be able to retain his main idea unwaveringly during the time (weeks or months) of the carving". Doubtless Pound admired in the sculptor just those qualities by which he himself was distinguished, the untiringness and ability to retain his main idea unwaveringly during the years of "carving" the *Cantos*.

During the time of his most intense Vorticist activity, Pound searched in vain to find the composer who would bring forth the new music, for England lacked avant-garde musical artists and he was ignorant or distrustful of their continental counterparts. Looking back some ten years later, he remarks: "The Vorticist Manifestos of 1913-14 left a blank space for music; there was in contemporary music, at that date, nothing corresponding to the work of Wyndham Lewis, Pablo Picasso or Gaudier-Brzeska. Strawinsky arrived as a comfort, but one could not say definitely that his composition was the new music." To supply the perceived want of adequate Vorticist models from his own time, Pound turned to the music of the seventeenth and eighteenth centuries, since in his view the nineteenth century had betrayed the true inheritance as much in music as in the other arts. And for all that it failed to materialize on schedule, a Vorticist music was as urgently needed as Vorticist painting, sculpture or verse.

Music prior to the nineteenth century is characterized for Pound by its "horizontal" construction. That is to say it depends chiefly on musical forms that exist in time: melody and rhythm. Nineteenth-century music is "vertical," dependent on chords and chordal progressions in which rhythmic vitality is sacrificed for the sake of momentary harmonic nuances. The organization of the earlier music, "pattern music" as Pound likes to call it, springs from an internal, abstract, musical logic. It is, in other words, music written to its primary pigment. The second kind of music is written for the kind of emotional response that the composer desires. And, as he explains,

> It is like a drug; you must have more drug, and more noise each time, or this effect, this impression which works from the outside, in from the nerves and sensorium upon the self—is no use, its effect is constantly weaker and weaker. I do not mean that Bach is not emotional, but the early music starts with the mystery of pattern; if you like, with the vortex of pattern; with something which is, first of all, music, and which is capable of being, after that, many things. What I call emotional, or impressionist music, starts with being emotion or impression and then becomes only approximately music. It is, that is to say, something in terms of something else.

Emotional music, in other words, suffers the same attenuation of effect noted in connection with caressable sculpture, and for the same reason, because it fails to respect the integrity of the medium.

Of course, the opposition drawn up here is no discovery of Pound's. It is the substance of the musical struggle that dominated the second half of the nineteenth century, that between Wagner and Brahms, or, more bitterly, between their proponents. It is scarcely conceivable that Pound can have been unaware of this debate, however much his thoughts are advanced as personal discoveries; one imagines rather that he found in it a substantiation for his own reading of the general deterioration of the arts in the preceding period, and of the analogous changes required to correct it.

Pound did not discover anyone undertaking the necessary corrections until he met George Antheil in 1923 and produced in *Antheil and the Treatise on Harmony* the completion of his Vorticist propaganda. His choice of Antheil to bear the Vorticist banner into the musical arena, like his earlier failure to recognize the revolutionary import of musical modernists such as Stravinsky and Schoenberg, must remain something of a puzzle, considering his usual cultural acuity. Even Antheil, as his autobiography makes clear, felt a certain supercilious bemusement: "In the 1923 that I speak of, Ezra still hovered there in artistic space, apparently fighting for me but in reality fighting for himself. He seemed like nothing so much as a ridiculous Don Quixote standing there, shouting all over the battlefield from which the opposing armies had not only long ago gone home, but upon which even the monuments of victory were decaying."

But the ungracious recollections of the self-declared Bad Boy of Music bespeak the callow prodigy of twenty-two that he was at the time—not one of Pound's more successful talent-spotting ventures.

Despite its tardy appearance and its imperfections, the study of Vorticist music did allow Pound to round out his esthetic. The core of *Antheil and the Treatise on Harmony*

is contained in an apothegmatic statement calculated to match Gaudier-Brzeska's statements on sculpture, or his own on the primary pigment: "A SOUND OF ANY PITCH or ANY COMBINATION OF SUCH SOUNDS, MAY BE FOLLOWED BY A SOUND OF ANY OTHER PITCH, OR ANY COMBINATION OF SUCH SOUNDS, providing the time interval between them is properly gauged; and this is true for ANY SERIES OF SOUNDS, CHORDS OR ARPEGGIOS".

The difference between this principle and that followed by the impressionist musicians whom he abhorred resides, to exaggerate very slightly, only in the rider attached to the opening proposition: "providing the time interval between them is properly gauged." The chromaticism of the impressionists justified its departure from the classic rules of harmony by the claim that melodic and harmonic liberties could not be faulted providing, as it were, the emotional effect was properly gauged. The difference, however, is a crucial one, for it represents an attempt on Pound's part to reinstate a purely musical logic in conformity with his demands for the primary pigment but without a return to the traditional harmonic system.

That he should have chosen to emphasize the temporal element reflects his own intense concern for rhythm, understandable enough in a poet, reinforced by Antheil's "time-space" theory. It is perhaps not the most helpful way of describing the needed change, but such pronunciamentos disdain lengthy explanations to achieve the desired impact. The program defined is revolutionary for the very reasons that Lewis' painting and Gaudier-Brzeska's sculpture are, because it respects the integrity of the medium and dismisses the "false" constraints of convention.

If this survey has succeeded in capturing the energy and novelty of Pound's inquiry into painting, sculpture and music, the theoretical and historical interest of his analysis should, I trust, be apparent. Perhaps less obvious, however, will be the relevance of such an inquiry to his search for a new poetic. What, to return to the question with which we began, did the poet learn through his association with the Vorticist artists and his search for a Vorticist music? As it happens, he himself raised the same question in *Gaudier-Brzeska*: "Roughly: What have they done for me these vorticist artists?" And he offers the following provisional answer:

> They have awakened my sense of form, or they "have given me a new sense of form," or what you will. . . .
>
> These new men have made me see form, have made me more conscious of the appearance of the sky where it juts down between houses, of the bright pattern of sunlight which the bath water throws up on the ceiling, of the Great "V's" of light that dart through the chinks over the curtain rings, all these are new chords, new keys of design.

As an example of a poem built around these "new chords, new keys of design," "The Game of Chess," which appeared in *Blast* I, might come to mind. Consider its opening and closing lines:

Red knights, brown bishops, bright queens,
Striking the board, falling in strong "L's of
    colour.
Reaching and striking in angles,
    holding lines in one colour. . . .
"Y" pawns, cleaving, embanking!
Whirl! Centripetal! Mate! King down in the
    vortex,
Clash leaping of bands, straight strips of hard
    colour,
Block lights working in. Escapes. Renewal of
    contest.

A pleasant enough poem, to be sure, but it is hardly the breakthrough for which we had been hoping. This is not mature Pound but an experiment in communicating a new sense of visual form without a really new poetic form. Still, it is to be observed that the use of a new subject matter does mark a choice with its own consequences. Although the poem lacks the elliptical density of Pound's mature work, it stakes out new territory for poetry.

"The Game of Chess" allows us to see how Pound has developed from the earlier schools which anticipated and influenced his concern for, respectively, visual and musical values in poetry, namely the Pre-Raphaelites and the Symbolists. The Pre-Raphaelites had, as we know, devoted themselves to extraordinarily pictorial verse when they were not engaged in creating paintings of, conversely, extreme literalness. Their paintings are both avowedly mimetic in technique and narrative in organization and their poetry is visual in the extreme. It was natural that Pound's early efforts to achieve visual richness in his poetry should have led him into Pre-Raphaelite imitations. But his recognition, in the doctrine of the primary pigment, that one thing ought not to be said in terms of another, brought him soon enough to reject this model.

Similarly the Symbolists were notably aural poets whose chief aim was *"reprendre à la Musique, leur bien."* This notion, of course, accords well with Pound's own notion of his art: "Poetry is a composition of words set to music. Most other definitions of it are indefensible, or metaphysical. The proportion or quality of the music may, and does, vary; but poetry withers and 'dries out' when it leaves music, or, at least an imagined music, too far behind it".

But the music from which the Symbolists wished to take back their own was of a kind that Pound despised: specifically, Wagnerian or post-Wagnerian music. Music, in brief, in which the impressionist, emotional or narrative qualities predominate. In contrast, Pound, although he admits the suggestive power of music, is opposed to its use to create a receptive mood in the audience. The idea of working backward from the desired emotional effect is no more appropriate to the musical dimension of poetry than it is to music itself.

Pound's ability, in other words, to redefine what the new poetry should be trying to do depended to a large extent on his increasing understanding of what the new painting, sculpture and music were or should be trying to do. But the achievement of the new poetry required a greater capacity to assimilate the developments in related arts into his writing. The well-known tripartite division of poetry into *phanopoeia, melopoeia* and *logopoeia,* which reaches its complete articulation in the later *How to Read,* is intended to facilitate this assimilation. *Phanopoeia,* "a casting of images upon the visual imagination," is the dimension of poetry which overlaps with the visual arts. Pound's study of painting and sculpture is part of a larger effort to increase the effectiveness of the phanopoeic element in his poetry. In *melopoeia,* "words are charged, over and above their plain meaning, with some musical property, which directs the bearing or trend of that meaning." The relevance of Pound's work in music, both critical and creative, to this aspect of poetry goes without saying. *Logopoeia,* "the dance of the intellect among words," which might be thought to be the primary pigment of poetry is rather that of prose and therefore of only marginal interest to him.

The transformation of Pound into a modernist poet was not effected overnight. Clearly Wyndham Lewis, though typically ungentle, was not unjust in his assessment of Pound the Vorticist: "his fire-eating propagandist utterances were not accompanied by any very experimental efforts in his particular medium." Lewis might be faulted for his assumption that revolutionary art should try to keep up with its propaganda, but it is an assumption which, with certain modifications, he shared with Pound. Pound, that is, allowed for a certain lag between advances in the theory and changes in the practice of an art when he remarked of criticism that "it tries to forerun composition, to serve as gunsight". The Vorticist phase was preeminently a period of critical forerunning; range-finding shots might be fired but they reached their marks by accident. Thus the poem quoted presents a conventionally mimetic and syntactic treatment of a vaguely Vorticist visual experience. Its procedure is imitative, not analogical. Yet the judgment, ascribed by Lewis to "the more fanatical of the group," that Pound's poetry "was a series of pastiches of old french or old italian poetry, and could lay no claim to participate in the new burst of art in progress," seems not merely dismissive but inaccurate.

It is odd that Lewis, the contemporary and ally, should reveal himself in remarks such as these to have been so insensitive to the evolution through which Pound was passing, for the poet seems never to have lost his respect for the painter and believed always that they were working through the transition together. One finds Pound commenting, for example, "It interests me to find that my surest critic is a contemporary painter who knows my good work from my bad—NOT by a critical process, at least not by a technical process." And he offers his own opinions on painting with a reciprocal assurance. Referring more generally to this phenomenon he draws the natural conclusion: "Certain artists working in different media have managed to understand each other. They know the good and bad in each other's work, which they could not know unless there were a common speech".

The idea of a speech common to the arts, if we regard it as more than simply a nice image, seems to me immensely suggestive. Should such a language exist, it must be possible to isolate its common features. And Pound attempts to do just this. His discovery is not that, in some general way, all the arts are coloristic, emotional, narrative or whatever. His Vorticist investigations brought him rather to the conclusion that arts are alike with respect to their minimal unit of meaning, a unit he might today have called—had he uncharacteristically chosen to follow the fashion of the time—an aestheme. This minimal unit of artistic meaning is created by the conjunction of two minimal units of form—of the primary form, that is, as this was defined by the doctrine of the primary pigment.

Throughout Pound's scattered discussion of it, this fundamental unit appears in many guises. But his favorite image is probably the equation, which occurs in his criticism as early as *The Spirit of Romance*. In this work he comments: "Poetry is a sort of inspired mathematics, which gives us equations, not for abstract figures, triangles, spheres, and the like, but equations for the human emotions". In search of an analogy to explain the four levels of allegory that Dante claims for his *Commedia* he returns to the equation. And "Vorticism" takes up the same image to a somewhat different purpose. In the latter work Pound again presents four different manifestations of the equation $a^2 + b^2 = c^2$. To summarize: *first*, $3^2 + 4^2 = 5^2$ is a simple statement of fact; *second*, $a^2 + b^2 = c^2$ is an abstract expression of an algebraic relation and most like a philosophical proposition; *third*, $a^2 + b^2 = c^2$ describes the ratio of the sides of a right-angled triangle and could be compared to a critical comment; *fourth*, $(x-a)^2 + (y-b)^2 = d^2$, in analytical geometry, generates the infinite series of right-angled triangles whose apexes will describe a circle if the diameter is their common hypotenuse. Because this last equation can be said *"actually to create"* the circle, it is for Pound the important one. It represents not the creative act of the artist but the generation of meaning by the work of art itself.

This is the way in which the Vorticist painting creates meaning, by the relationship between its lines and its blocks of color. And the Vorticist sculpture similarly works through the relation of its masses as defined by the disposition of its planes. In both cases it is the interaction of at least two components that yields the emotional effect. In music, as he was later able to show, the same rule applies. The focus of the pronunciamento quoted above is the sequence of two sounds and the time governing their relation. As he goes on in the same place to argue: "The limits for the practical purposes of music depend solely on our capacity to produce a sound that will last long enough, i.e. remain audible long enough, for the succeeding sound or sounds to catch up, traverse, intersect it." The meaning resides precisely in the catching up, traversing and intersecting.

Poetry also is built up of minimal units of this kind. The well-known "In a Station of the Metro," which consists of one such unit, may stand as a paradigm here, especially since Pound himself presents it as a model for the new poetry:

> The apparition of these faces in the crowd;
> Petals on a wet, black bough.

We might think that the poem comprises two images, but Pound does not. As he remarks of it, "The 'one image poem' is a form of superposition, that is to say, it is one idea set on top of another". To return to his discussion of the fourth kind of equation, that of analytical geometry: "By the 'image' I mean such an equation; not an equation

of mathematics, not something about *a, b,* and *c,* having something to do with form, but about *sea, cliffs, night,* having something to do with mood. The image is not an idea. It is a radiant node or cluster; it is what I can, and must perforce, call a VORTEX". This many-titled vortex, equation, image or gist is also known as the ideogram. The belief that such minimal units of juxtaposition can generate meaning is the basis of the ideogrammic method. The *Cantos* are only the haiku writ large—very large.

Such then is the significance of the Vorticist esthetic. It is an esthetic conceived in opposition to the previously dominant one in its assertion of geometrical as opposed to plastic or empathetic values. In moving against conventions, representational or tonal, it shifts major responsibility to the expression of the artist's will and to the preservation of the integrity of the medium. Individual elements in the esthetic may be enunciated to resolve specific problems raised by each of the arts, but in Pound's words, "What I have said of one vorticist art can be transposed for another vorticist art"—which, for his own purposes, means that all may be transposed for poetry. The discovery that the minimal units of visual art and of music are the same as those of poetry proves to be of crucial importance to Pound, for it allows him to place very heavy demands on the *phanopoeic* and *melopoeic* dimensions of his poetry, even when the syntax and structure of the poetry is broken into fragments.

Pound joined the Vorticists and wrote the Vorticist articles because the natural forces of cultural osmosis or the *Zeitgeist,* which normally ensure roughly contemporary analogical development in the arts, did not answer his urgent needs. He could not begin his endless poem until his poetic had been worked out. As he explains in *"If This Be Treason . . . ":* "Same way for a masterpiece of lit. new pt. of view shd BE either before a man starts his paintin: his recordin contempory Anschauung, contemporary disposition to life, or AFTER he is thru his portrayin." And no poetic, least of all one involving the high levels of *phanopoeia* and *melopoeia* characteristic of Pound's work, can be considered stable if it takes no account of contemporary developments in related arts.

Patricia Rae

SOURCE: "From Mystical Gaze to Pragmatic Game: Representations of Truth in Vorticist Art," in *English Literary History,* Vol. 56, No. 3, Fall, 1989, pp. 689-720.

[In the following essay, Rae examines the art and literature of the Vorticist movement.]

Ezra Pound's proudest contribution to the Vorticist journal *Blast,* and the only poem that he was ever to identify as "pure vorticism," was a "Dogmatic Statement on the Game and Play of Chess." The images in this poem, the brightly colored combatants in a fierce and immediate battle, are nouns transformed into verbs, chesspieces metaphorically identified with the Roman letters that trace their actions. These luminous pawn-Y's, bishop-X's, and knight-L's strike, cleave, and loop one another, breaking and reforming their pattern until an assault on a king renders one army victorious—and the black-and-white design of the empty chessboard, for a moment, definitive. The truce, however, is brief. Harnessed energy leaks, the captured escape, and the vanquished arise from their ashes to propose a "renewing of contest."

Pound subtitled his poem "Theme for a Series of Pictures," and this has led a number of critics to observe that its dynamic images and abrupt rhythms mirror many of those we encounter in Vorticist painting. More intriguing than this, however, is the possibility of reading the chess game as an allegory for the mental processes both of these arts seem to embody and encourage. In the imaginations of many of Pound's contemporaries, including T. E. Hulme and Ernest Fenollosa, the chess or checker game was frequently a metaphor for abstract reasoning. The chesspieces, by their nature representative types, performed a function similar to that of the words or concepts that in such reasoning are substituted for particulars. The rules of the chess game, in which certain counters are capable of certain moves, seemed analogous to the rigorous laws of logic. And the game's object—to reduce variety to simplicity, the different to the same—strikingly resembled the goal of any theoretician. The game of chess, in short, was an apt image for what William James, in a seminal article entitled "The Sentiment of Rationality" (1879), had called the "philosophic passion *par excellence*": the urge to resolve the muddy chaos of phenomena to the clean, geometric grid of abstract theory. In Pound's Vorticist chess game, however, this "theoretic need" does not reign unchecked, but seems to be repeatedly challenged and subverted. The pieces on the grid are not dead counters, enabling the abstract thinker to remain disengaged from the subject of his calculations, but pieces "living in form," their unique vitality an integral part of their identity. The patterns they make, moreover, are inherently unstable, like theories that form and dissolve even as they are made. The "renewing of contest" proposed at the end of the poem lends an ironic edge to Pound's subtitle: the resolution here is no "Dogmatic Statement," but a solution immediately again to be challenged. To borrow once again from James, the passion for abstraction depicted in Pound's poem is counterbalanced by its "sister passion," the "passion for distinguishing": the preference for "incoherence" over order, for the "concrete fulness" of things over any "absolute datum" that subsumes their differences. "A Game of Chess" is a poem about the almost simultaneous operation of two opposite tendencies of mind. As such, I shall argue, it is a model of what I shall call the "tensional" aesthetic of Vorticism.

Historians of the Vorticist movement have struggled to discern consistent and mutual strategies between its verbal and visual manifestations. More often than not, they have concluded that the poets and artists of *Blast* were unified only by the nominal leadership of Wyndham Lewis, and not by any rigorous common philosophy. But there are, indeed, common strategies in the literary branch of Vorticism that Pound called *Imagisme* and the visual art advertised by Lewis as distinctively Vorticist. Although it is often forgotten, Pound explicitly sought a "psychological or philosophical definition" of *Imagiste* poetry, hoping that *Imagisme* would be remembered as a movement about the "creation" of poetry as well as its "criticism."

The same is true of Lewis's specifications for Vorticist art, which seem to stipulate similar principles for the artist's creative process. From the accounts of creative activity that can be pieced together from Pound's and Lewis's early essays and manifestos, furthermore, it is clear that Vorticism belonged to the tradition of expressionist aesthetics, which had originated in the tracts of German Idealism and emerged most recently in the theoretical writings of Post-Impressionist painters such as Whistler and Kandinsky. Its primary aim, as such, was not the imitation of nature but "the search for sincere self-expression." Instead of pursuing mimetic representations, the Vorticist upheld a "musical conception of form," seeking to construct suitable "arrangements," whether in form and color or in language, to express his "complex consciousness." In seeking Vorticism's paradigmatic aesthetic, I proceed on the premise that any expressionist aesthetic entails necessary connections between what the theorist sees as the epistemological status of the insight his artist wishes to express, and the structure of the product he sees as appropriate to that task. There is, I shall propose, an inexorable connection between Pound's and Lewis's conceptions of the cognitive capacities of the artist, on the one hand, and the art their aesthetics produced, on the other—a connection which that dynamic chess game serves to exemplify.

A number of critics have suspected that Pound's attitude to mystical experience had a formative significance for his early aesthetic. When we examine his *Imagisme* as a theory of creative activity in the Idealist tradition, the precise import of his views on mysticism becomes clear. During the four or five years prior to *Blast,* T. E. Hulme had been advertising and defending a new attitude he detected among his contemporaries toward the Idealist, or in his terms "romantic," aesthetic. The "new classical" attitude, as Hulme called it, was suspicious of Idealist aestheticians who represented the artist as a passive medium for some transcendental or mystical truth. The "new classicist," he said, while preserving the intuitive and organic aspects of that aesthetic, was to get rid of all the "metaphysical baggage" that so often accompanied it. He was to eschew all suggestions about the artist's apprehension of entities like the "Soul," the "Infinite" and the "Idea," which in the writings of certain English Romantics and French Symbolists had functioned to aggrandize the artist's vocation. He was to police his own rhetoric, in short, for any tendency to wax excessively optimistic about the artist's cognitive capacities, to "fly away," rhetorically speaking, into the "circumambient gas." Both Pound and Lewis, as we shall see, regarded claims about the mystical nature of a poet's insight with precisely the "new classical" distrust that Hulme described. This led both of them to feel that the particular "arrangements" an artist chose to express his insight should not reflect such mystical assumptions. As a result, the products of the Vorticist aesthetic, from Pound's *Imagiste* poems to Lewis's paintings and Gaudier-Brzeska's sculptures, deliberately defied the formal principles that had characterized the transcendentalist aesthetics of Symbolism, Expressionism, and Cubism.

The work of William James provides a striking model for the strategies at work in a "new classical" aesthetic; indeed, it is curious that his affinity with them has gone largely unnoticed. It is possible to show that James's ideas would have been familiar to Hulme, Pound, and Lewis—if not directly, then through French exponents like Henri Bergson and Jules de Gaultier, or through recent emigrés from Harvard like Robert Frost, T. S. Eliot, and Henry James—but it is not my primary purpose to detail that influence here. My aim, rather, is to demonstrate that the issues at stake for a "new classical" artist with expressionist intentions were very much the same as those facing a psychologist-turned-philosopher in his attempt to determine viable ways of representing "truth." William James's career began, of course, in the field of empirical psychology, and concluded with the formulation and defense of the philosophy of pragmatism. One of his central accomplishments as a psychologist had been the examination and description of those experiences in which a person believes he has apprehended some absolute truth: experiences that had habitually and perhaps erroneously been called "mystical." When he later turned to philosophy, the problem that most intrigued him was how one should represent and wield such insights, when one could have no way of knowing that they were what they seemed. James's project as a philosopher, in other words, was to trace the same inexorable arch as the "new classical" theorists of art: to seek a suitable mode of expression for an insight whose final epistemological status remained uncertain. And the construct he defined in answer to this dilemma, the "pragmatic" truth, had the same tensional structure as the poems and paintings of Vorticism.

The nature of James's work in empirical psychology profoundly influenced his later pragmatic approach to the question of truth. The late nineteenth century saw the emergence of psychology as an empirical science, and James himself was one of its most eloquent and influential proponents. The introductions to *The Principles of Psychology* (1890) and *Psychology: The Briefer Course* (1892) legislate certain principles both for psychological research and for the language in which its results are to be expressed. James contends that the first responsibility of any natural science is a circumscription of its data: in the case of psychology, the field of investigation is to include all *"Thoughts and feelings,"* all "transitory *states of consciousness,"* and along with these the *"Knowledge,* by these states of consciousness, of other things." Like the physical, chemical, and biological sciences before it, furthermore, psychology is to observe certain restrictions in the way it discusses these data. It is to limit itself to the uncritical description of mental phenomena, to accounts of the conditions that undeniably occur in the mind. It is not within its province to engage in "metaphysical" speculation, to inquire into the primary causes or higher significance of the events it describes. This necessitates, James warns, the exorcism of a number of spooks that have traditionally haunted the study of mind. It precludes just what Hulme wished to see excised from discussions of art: all "attempts to *explain* our phenomenally given thoughts as products of deeper-lying entities," whether these entities "be named 'Soul,' 'Transcendental Ego,' 'Ideas,' or 'Elementary Units of Consciousness'." The mind may be the locus for many events so mysterious that one wishes to claim the participation of some external cosmic force, but the psychologist remains satisfied with describing these

events as they happen, and shies away from any transcendentalist claims.

Clearly, this ban on speculation about the relationship of mental phenomena to higher reality is especially important when the psychologist considers the final datum James lists as within his province: the kind of experience in which we feel we possess the *"Knowledge . . .* of other things,"* when we find ourselves in the presence of what seems to be some objective and necessary truth. In the *Briefer Course,* James makes it clear that although the empirical psychologist must study experiences of knowing, he must leave it to "more developed parts of Philosophy to test their ulterior significance and truth." For James, describing states of knowing in terms that scrupulously respected these boundaries was to become something of a preoccupation. He concentrated on describing the *"Sentiment"* we may sometimes have of the "Rationality" of our ideas, the "strong feeling of ease, peace [and] rest" that may accompany them, the *"feeling* of [their] sufficiency"*—the feeling, in other words, that these conceptions are true. But while he describes their seeming character, James refuses to declare himself either a nominalist or a realist, to characterize those apparently sufficient conceptions either as wrongly reified concepts or genuinely transcendental Ideas. A similar suspension of judgment marks James's many attempts to describe apprehensions of supernatural phenomena. He declares himself compelled to accept as "objective" fact the occasional appearance to human minds of apparitions that seem to come from a realm "beyond" them. But—witness his account of the experiences of one "Mrs. Piper"—he is careful not to speculate about their "materiality":

> In the trances of this medium, I cannot resist the conviction that knowledge appears which she has never gained by the ordinary waking use of her eyes and ears and wits. What the source of this knowledge may be I know not, and have not the glimmer of an explanatory suggestion to make; but from admitting the fact of such knowledge I can see no escape.

James's fascination with experiences of knowing culminates in *The Varieties of Religious Experience* (1902), where he catalogues a great variety of moments that he broadly calls "mystical": moments in which people, their wills in abeyance, seem to know certain absolute and ineffable truths. It is part of James's responsibility as a psychologist to note that these experiences are usually characterized by "convincingness," that they are "absolutely authoritative over the individuals to whom they come," yet it is equally incumbent upon him to refrain from declaring whether such revelations are what they seem. In the final analysis, he says, the moment of enchantment might be a "gift of our organism" just as possibly as "a gift of God's grace."

James's application of the methods of empirical psychology to the problem of cognitive experience intrigued and inspired Edmund Husserl, and we may see in James an incipient phenomenology. *Varieties,* as James Edie has recently argued, is justly characterized as the first genuine attempt at a phenomenology of religion. James speaks the language of phenomenology in stipulating that religion means for him "the feelings, acts and experiences of individual men in their solitude, so far as they apprehend themselves to stand in relation to whatever they may consider the divine." His concern for recording only what the mind undeniably experiences adumbrates phenomenology's exclusive interest in the realm of what Husserl calls the "consciousness of" or "appearance of" cognitions. We see in his approach, finally, a version of Husserl's own policy to "bracket," or suspend all judgments about, the status of transcendent objects of knowing. Just as James refuses to judge mystical experiences, so Husserl was to observe that in his phenomenological reduction "cognition is neither *disavowed* nor regarded as in *every* sense doubtful." But for both James and Husserl—as for Pound, whose reflections on mysticism we shall find uncannily similar to theirs—the simple refusal to comment on the truth-value of cognitions does not terminate their inquiries. It remains for both a pressing problem to determine how, in the light of these restricted judgments, a person should regard, represent, and wield these insights. Both recognize that a mere decision to remain equivocal offers no help for living. As Husserl warns, after outlining the terms of phenomenological reduction, "we must take new steps, enter onto new considerations, so that we may gain a firm foothold in the new land and not finally run aground on its shore. For this shore has its rocks, and over it lie clouds of obscurity which threaten us with stormy gales of skepticism."

James's prescriptions for the representation of truth, of which the most mature formulations are in *Pragmatism* (1907), *The Meaning of Truth* (1909), and the posthumous *Essays in Radical Empiricism* (1912), stop short of the extremely rigorous restrictions finally imposed by Husserl. But one point of resemblance is crucial: the stubborn unwillingness of both philosophers to "relapse," as Husserl puts it, into the "absurdities of skepticism." Pragmatism, as James argued strenuously in *The Meaning of Truth*, was *not* skepticism, however much its hostile critics might have considered it to be so. It was not skepticism because, as James had noted as early as "The Sentiment of Rationality" and *Varieties*, the psychological condition of skepticism was both undesirable and impossible to sustain. Indeed, *Varieties* and "Sentiment" recommend a stance of compromise that was to become a prototype for pragmatism: a stance that, while granting final approval to neither skeptical nor dogmatic impulses, was to allow for the operation of both.

James's route from psychology to pragmatism is determined, in part, by his fidelity to the principle of appealing to no higher authority than the stream of experience. It cannot be by their "roots" that we judge the reality of our gods, as he notes in *Varieties,* but only by their "fruits." When he considers how mystical insights are finally to be regarded, he compares the psychological effects of various options. Aware of that intrinsic "convincingness" of mystical insights that might propel the subject towards dogmatism, he holds that such insights have no authority in themselves that would "make it a duty for those who stand outside of them to accept their relations uncritically." But just as he veers towards skepticism, James proposes another attitude to mystical experiences. When they are com-

municated positively, he says, they may have beneficial psychological effects; when they are regarded with hope, that is, they may "open out the possibility of other orders of truth, in which, so far as anything in us vitally responds to them, we may freely continue to have faith." Judging by effects, then, James concludes that the only sensible attitude towards the moment of mystical insight is one of optimism and openmindedness:

> Mystical states indeed wield no authority due simply to their being mystical states. But the higher ones among them point in directions to which the religious sentiments even of nonmystical men incline. They tell of the supremacy of the ideal, of vastness, of union, of safety and of rest. They offer us *hypotheses,* hypotheses which we may voluntarily ignore, but which as thinkers we cannot possibly upset. The supernaturalism and optimism to which they would persuade us may, interpreted in one way or another, be after all the truest of insights into the meaning of this life.

In suggesting that we regard mystical insights as hypotheses, James charts a middle course between dogmatism and skepticism, appeasing our need to invest them with some authority, but not permitting blind faith. A hypothesis, after all, takes the form of a reassuring generalization, but by definition is tested against the empirical world. James strengthens his argument for wielding insights in this way in "The Sentiment of Rationality," where he describes the contrary mental impulses—for authoritative abstractions and for empirical chaos—as equally irresistible. "When weary of the concrete clash and dust and pettiness," he observes, one will undoubtedly seek the comfort of the "immutable natures." But the second tendency ensures that he "will only be a visitor, not a dweller in [that] region." The discovery of any totalizing principle, the *"perfect object for belief,"* will inevitably bring on its heels an urgent need to doubt. "Our mind is so wedded to the process of seeing an other beside every item of its experience," he says, "that when the notion of an absolute datum is presented to it, it goes through its usual procedure and remains pointing at the void beyond, as if in that lay further matter for contemplation." The history of philosophy has shown, in sum, that neither a dogmatic rationalism, with its "barren union of all things," nor a skeptical empiricism, with its discomfiting "uncertainty," is sufficient to endure for any great length of time. The only policy that will prove psychologically satisfying for the majority of men will be one that reconciles the two tendencies, one that effects "a compromise between an abstract monotony and a concrete heterogeneity."

James's empirical researches into noetic experience, then, inform a representation of truth that, like Pound's chess game, is inherently tensional. In his mature description of the pragmatic attitude towards truth, it is a balance between attitudes both "dogmatical" and "skeptical," "rationalistic" and "empiricist," "religious" and "irreligious," "romantic" and "scientific." The construct the pragmatist will call a "truth" is a simplification that is economical and aesthetically appealing, but that also stands up to an immediate testing in and against the "teeming and dramatic richness of the concrete world." If the truth fails to be corroborated by experience, James says, or to lead to beneficial action, it must be summarily dismantled and revised. Like that chess game that concludes in a "Dogmatic Statement," in other words, it is subject immediately to a "renewing of contest." By redefining truth in this way, James's pragmatism furthers Hulme's cause of taking all the hubristic "hocus-pocus" out of cognition. "Truth is no longer the transcendent mystery," James says, "in which so many philosophers have taken pleasure," but dwells on *this side* of the phenomenal barrier. The process of making and unmaking it is a coiling and uncoiling that never ends: "Truths emerge from facts; but they dip forward into facts again and add to them; which facts again create or reveal new truth . . . and so on indefinitely."

Like James's rationale for pragmatism, Pound's route to a tensional aesthetic begins in an attempt to come to terms with mystical experience. As Pound's remarks on the creative experience of the Vorticist or *Imagiste* poet show, he imagines that experience to begin with a moment in which the artist seems to be visited by some truth from beyond himself. They suggest that he condones, in other words, the traditional representation of the poet as *seer*, which had most recently been articulated in the transcendentalist manifestos of French *Symbolisme* and in Yeats's theoretical tracts on the equivalency of art and magic. In a 1910 article on the psychology of the troubadours, published in a forum on psychic experience called *The Quest*, Pound makes an admission similar to the one James made in the face of his psychical researches. It is an "indisputable and very scientific fact," Pound says, that in the normal course of life one may suddenly feel "his immortality upon him," that one may be suddenly struck by a "vision unsought," a "vision gained without machination." These are the moments, in Pound's discourse, when the "gods" appear, and they are moments, like Mrs. Piper's, of absolute conviction. Persephone and Demeter, he says, Laurel and Artemis, "are intelligible, vital, essential . . . to those people to whom they occur"; they are *"for them real."* It is a few years after noting the "delightful psychic experience" of the troubadours that Pound describes the Vorticist poet's moment of inspiration. The creative experience of the *Imagiste*, he says, will begin, like that of any Vorticist artist, with the sudden appearance, to his conscious mind, of his "primary pigment": a vision that will both inform what he articulates and the medium in which he speaks. In the case of the poet, in particular, this vision is the "IMAGE," and its qualities mark it as something descending from a higher, noumenal world. Like any mystical vision, the "Image" is an object of *intuition*, the gift of a moment in which action, will, and intellect are suspended. Like all those experiences James calls "mystical," too, the insight governed by the Image seems to be ineffable; unlike the "FORMED WORDS" that are the primary pigment for the writer of "LITERATURE," Pound says, the Image "is the word beyond formulated language." When one encounters it, moreover, one will feel elevated above the habitual constraints of time and of space, a fact that inspires Pound to compare it to a equation of analytic geometry— such as $(x - a)^2 + (y - b)^2 = r^2$:

It is the circle. It is not a particular circle, it is

any circle and all circles. It is nothing that is not a circle. It is the circle free of space and time limits. It is the universal, existing in perfection, in freedom from space and time.

Described in these quasi-Platonic terms, the Image seems to govern an experience like the one Baudelaire, Mallarmé, and their successors attribute to the *Symboliste* poet, an experience that began, as Swedenborg, Schopenhauer, and Hegel had inspired them to claim, with a glimpse into the "monde d'[I]dées." The *Symbolistes* had frequently invoked the transcendental Idea to account for a process of articulation that was intuitive and exploratory, and that made the poet's mind a locus for truths from beyond himself. Saying that artistic process begins with the apprehension of the Idea enabled them to explain the series of unanticipated utterances flowing from the artist's pen as the idea's endlessly generated particulars: the Idea that "floats before [the artist's] mind," as Schopenhauer phrased it, "resembles a living organism, developing itself and possessed of the power of reproduction, which brings forth what was not put into it." In equating the Image with the equations of analytical geometry, Pound seems to have a comparable purpose in mind, for these are the equations with which, as he recognizes, we are "able actually to *create*." The Image, like the *Symbolistes'* Idea, and unlike the "dead concepts" that initiate the art of allegory, is something that generates in the poet innumerable unforetold particulars: something that guides the poet through a process in which he will continue to discover new ideas, new variations on his original insight. Like the eternal Idea, Pound says, the image is a "VORTEX, from which, and through which, and into which, ideas are constantly rushing."

But if Pound's admissions about the appearance of the gods suggest that he affirms the traditional notions about the divinity of inspiration, if his claims about the poet's apprehension of the Image resemble *Symboliste* claims about art's mystical origins, other aspects of these accounts absolve them of such transcendentalism. As the language of these passages reveals, Pound observes the same limits, in describing those experiences, as those legislated by James for empirical psychology. In his accounts of the noetic experience common to mystic and poet, that is, Pound clearly acknowledges such experience as "scientific fact," but he scrupulously restricts his inquiry to the world as given in consciousness; he does not speculate about the first causes of experiences, about whether or not they *are* what they seem. In the article on "Psychology and Troubadours," Pound's subject is "delightful psychic *experience*"; the mythical gods are "explications of *mood*": the exalted moments occur when an individual *"feels* his immortality upon him." In his catechisms of 1918 and 1921, similarly, a god amounts to "an eternal state of mind"; its status is no different from the "taste of a lemon, or the fragrance of violets, or the aroma of dung-hills, or the feel of a stone or of tree-bark, or any other *direct perception*." And when Pound describes the feeling of transcendence occasioned by the apprehension of the Image, it is no accident that he makes a claim only about the individual's "sense of " that condition, for the Image, however much it might resemble the inspiring Idea of the *Symbolistes*, is in fact an entity firmly situated in that experiential realm approved by empirical psychology.

It has become a commonplace of Pound criticism that his account of the Image, in particular his suggestion that the Image manifests the workings of a subconscious phenomenon called the "complex," owes something to the Freudian psychoanalyst Bernard Hart. What has not been appreciated, however, is the more significant affinity between the Image and a number of like entities described by contemporary empirical-associationist psychologists like Ribot, Paulhan, and Bergson, which had also made their way into the accounts of creative activity formulated by Hulme. In his 1915 essay "Affirmations: As for Imagisme," Pound describes the Image as a "cluster" of percepts and ideas that has been "fused" in the mind by the energetic force of "emotion": an entity that, once given, demands "adequate expression," and inspires an organic process of making. Represented thus, it strongly resembles a construct described by Ribot in his influential *Essai sur l'imagination créatrice* (1900), borrowed by Bergson in a 1902 article "L'Effort intellectuel," and emerging most famously as part of the account of the act of artistic creation that serves as an illustrative analogy for natural creation in Bergson's *L'Evolution créatrice* (1907). This "conception idéale" or "schéma", a cluster of memory-images and ideas associated in the mind because of their "ressemblance à base émotionnelle," enables Ribot and Bergson to describe a process of creation that is organic: both speak of it as a "unité" that presents itself unsought to the consciousness of the artist, and that changes character when translated into the "détails" of words or matter. But crucially for both of them, it does so without necessitating any reference to that metaphysical concept of "un archétype fixe (survivance non déguisée des Idées platoniciennes), illuminant l'inventeur qui le réproduit comme il peut [fixed archetype (an undisguised survival of the Platonic Ideas), illuminating the inventor, who reproduces it as best he can]"; it enables them to describe the intuitive and organic experience described by Schopenhauer without demanding a claim about the poet's contact with a realm beyond time, beyond the phenomenal flux that Bergson called *"la durée."*

Ribot's and Bergson's versions of the intuitive and organic process of creation, a process they knew best as described in the treatises of French *Symbolisme,* make them Promethean demystifiers of creative genius, or more properly, Jamesian equivocators about the status of the passive, intuitive, ineffable, and noetic experience that is creative inspiration. For Ribot, who identifies the creative experience of the *Symboliste* poets and "l'imagination mystique," that equivocation comes in the form of a refusal to speculate about whether the unconscious mind that furnishes the constituents of the developing "unité" is ultimately material or spiritual. For Bergson, who was also to give the name of "image" to the first, inspiring presence in a poet's mind, the affinity with James comes in the form of a refusal to commit himself on the matter of the subjectivity or objectivity of inspiration; in the course of an empathetic correspondence with James, he declares his belief that "il y a l'expérience *pure,* qui n'est ni subjective ni objective [there is *pure* experience, which is neither subjective nor

objective]," and that "j'emploie le mot *image* pour désigner une réalité de ce genre [I employ the word *image* to designate a reality of this sort]."

When Pound feels compelled to comment on the origin of the ineffable Image, he shows just the same kind of hesitation to commit himself. Thinking, very likely, of Yeats's claim that the symbols that present themselves to a poet's consciousness originate in a universal memory, Pound acknowledges at the outset that the cluster of image, emotion, and idea that is the Image may have the effect of suggesting that its constituent image has "an age-old traditional meaning," and further concedes that "this may serve as proof to the professional student of symbology that we have stood in the deathless light, or that we have walked in some particular arbour of his traditional paradisio." But immediately upon suggesting this, he refuses to commit himself further, stressing that such speculation "is not our affair." Pound recognizes, in other words, that the Image may indeed be the vehicle of a "Divine Essence" that Yeats would have it be, but he feels uneasy, as if he has strayed into forbidden territory, when he strays beyond phenomena to first causes. As he was to note in his "Axiomata" about the status of those "gods" that on occasion appear so vital and convincing—in terms that might have been taken directly out of James's records on psychical research—these are equally likely to be either physiological and illusory, or spiritual and genuine, just as possibly "a mirage of the senses" as a genuine "affect from the theos." His view of mystical experience corroborates James's view that our judgments about it must be based not on its "roots," but on its "fruits":

> The consciousness may be aware of the effects of the unknown and of the non-knowable on the consciousness, but this does not affect the proposition that our consciousness is utterly ignorant of the nature of the intimate essence. For instance: a man may be hit by a bullet and not know its composition, not the course of its having been fired, nor its direction, nor that it is a bullet. He may die almost instantly, knowing only the sensation of shock. Thus consciousness may perfectly well register certain results, as sensation, without comprehending their nature. . . . He may even die of a long-considered disease without comprehending its bacillus. . . . Concerning the ultimate nature of the bacillus . . . no knowledge exists; but the consciousness may learn to deal with superficial effects of the bacillus, as with the directing of bullets.

Pound's own policy for describing the mental experience of the Vorticist poet, then, is very much in keeping with the guidelines that James shared with Husserl. His sympathy with the goals of phenomenological reduction may well have been what lay behind his formulation of the first and most famous of *Imagiste* tenets, the resolution to engage in the "Direct treatment of the 'thing,' whether subjective or objective." The Vorticist's inspiration, in his account, is to remain a cognitive experience where the object of cognition is bracketed. It is to be subject to what Husserl called the "principle of all principles": " 'Intuition,' in primordial form . . . is simply to be accepted as it gives itself out to be, though only within the limits in which it then presents itself."

But of what significance is this policy in shaping Pound's prescriptions for Vorticist style? Pound insists that the poet himself observe identical restrictions when expressing his insights to others as Pound has observed when describing them generally. The "serious artist," in his view, is "scientific" in that he is content to confine his expressive efforts to the accurate record of his "state of consciousness." He presents "the image of his desire, of his hate, of his indifference, as precisely that, as precisely the image of his own desire, hate or indifference . . . ." And when it comes to articulating the insight that accompanies the appearance of the Image, even if that insight has all the authority of a mystical revelation, it is his duty simply to "render" it as he has "perceived or conceived it." Pound asks the poet, in other words, to represent his inspiration not as the authoritative insight it has seemed, but simply as the *consciousness* of an insight that it has undeniably been. "As Dante writes of the sunlight coming through the clouds from a hidden source and illuminating part of a field," so the Vorticist poet is to be on the watch for "new vibrations sensible to faculties as yet ill understood . . . neither affirming them to be 'astral' or 'spiritual' nor denying the formula of theosophy."

Like James, Pound makes it clear that the feeling of revelation that inspires the Vorticist poet does not authorize him to express his insight as dogma. The poet, he stresses, must "never consider anything as dogma." "That which the philosopher presents as truth," the *Imagiste* must somehow present "as that which appears as truth to a certain sort of mind under certain conditions." But if he forbids the poet from presenting his insights as gifts from the realm of the absolute, if he denies him the right to a pitch of rhetoric that, in Hulmean terms, flies unchecked into the "circumambient gas," Pound does not condemn him to an incapacitating skepticism. He is just as resistant as are James and Husserl to the prospect of a world in which truths can never be thought anything *other* than idiosyncratic. It was an acquiescence to such limitations—as we shall see more clearly when we consider Lewis's prescriptions for the artist—that had defined the "flaccid" or "spreading" arts of Impressionism and Futurism, and Pound is concerned that Vorticist poetry be more hopeful, more "energized" than these arts. "Imagism," he emphasizes, "is not Impressionism." The difference between Impressionist and *Imagiste* poetry, in his view, will be a deliberate gesture in the latter towards generalization, towards the making of abstract concepts or theories that might just possibly be true in a world wider than his own:

> You may think of man as that toward which perception moves. You may think of him as the TOY of circumstance, as the plastic substance RECEIVING impressions.
>
> OR you may think of him as DIRECTING a certain fluid force against circumstance, as CONCEIVING instead of merely observing and reflecting.

Pound shares James's belief that any man who has experienced a seemingly religious insight has a duty to express

it in a tone that is suitably optimistic. Neither representing what he has apprehended as "propaganda of something called the *one truth*," nor offering "his ignorance [of such truth] as a positive thing," he must chart James's middle course, and offer it "as a sort of working hypothesis." As James imagines the psychologist's findings to be a "provisional body of propositions" about states of mind and their cognitions, which "more developed parts of Philosophy" might one day discover correspond with an absolute truth, so Pound envisions the poet offering up his insights "as the enduring data of philosophy," as propositions that may contribute to that other, deductive quest for metaphysical certainties. Just as James imagines his pragmatic truths being asserted and put to work in the world, so Pound suggests that the poet's insights ought to be recorded in such a way that they may be grasped and tested against experience. The analytical equations, passed on to the reader, become instruments for living. And Pound, like James, refuses to deny the possibility that the insights to which they lead might be "superior points of view, windows through which the mind looks out upon a more extensive and inclusive world":

> Is the formula nothing, or is it cabala and the sign of unintelligible magic? The engineer, understanding and translating to the many, builds for the uninitiated bridges and devices. He speaks their language. For the initiated the signs are a door into eternity and into the boundless either.

There is reason to expect, then, that when Pound comes to discuss the nature of the expressive "arrangement" suitable for the *Imagiste* poet, he will specify an arrangement that is tensional in the same sense as the pragmatic truth. It will be something that aims to satisfy the skeptical, empiricist, irreligious and scientific tendency in its reader, by keeping his eye focused on the phenomenal world. It will leave some opening, however, for that philosophic, dogmatical, religious and romantic part of the consciousness that refuses to concede that the quest for timeless truths is futile. Pound comments that anyone who regards insights as absolute will succumb to a state of "paralysis" or mental "atrophy." He would hardly recommend, therefore, a poetic structure that encouraged such a regard in its reader. Only a construct that encourages the ongoing construction and dismantling of truths—not one that poses as the vehicle of some essential truth—will comply with the restrictions on human inquiry that Pound shares with James. It is in its achievement of such tensionality that the "Image" (which Pound uses in a second sense to designate the poetic arrangement) differs profoundly from the "Symbol."

Pound defines the Image as an "interpretive" or "absolute" metaphor. In distinguishing it thus from what he calls "ornamental" metaphor, he echoes the efforts of champions of the Symbol, from Baudelaire to Yeats, to define a poetic ideal in contradistinction to allegory: an art that will imply a necessary rather than arbitrary relation between itself and what it signifies, and that will somehow reflect in that way the organic rather than mechanical process by which it has come into being. Pound stresses, too, that whatever message the Image conveys, it will do so by "presentation" rather than "description," and so supports the *Symboliste* hostility toward discursiveness. Although these similarities have led a number of critics since Frank Kermode's *Romantic Image* to regard the Image and the Symbol as essentially identical, it is here, in fact, that the similarities end. The constructs that go by the name of Symbol are, to be sure, of many kinds. These structures share, however, the conceived function of *revelation:* they are conduits of "les splendeurs situées dérrière le tombeau [the splendors situated beyond the veil]," pieces of a "pli de sombre dentelle qui retient l'infini [fold of dark lace, which curbs the infinite]," transparent lamps that glow with a "spiritual flame." The *Symboliste* work of art, in the words of André Gide, "est un cristal—paradis partiel ou l'Idée réfleurit en sa pureté supérieure. . . . ou les paroles se font transparentes et révélatrices [is a crystal—a partial paradise where the Idea flowers again in its supreme purity . . . where words become transparent and revelatory]."

Pound imagines the Image, however, as functioning quite differently, in accordance with the more provisional sort of truth he is willing to ascribe to it. If the *Symboliste* puts the reader in the position of a mystic, for whom the natural world dissolves to reveal some absolute truth, the *Imagiste* seeks to restrict his reader's gaze to the stream of the phenomenal, and to bring him instead to the point of departure in the construction of a truth that is manmade and provisional. If a Symbol like Yeats's Rose functions simply to *suggest* things that may be identified with it, the Image is a construct that implies an identity between two concrete images, each of which it identifies explicitly. Pound illustrates with his own "In a Station of the Metro":

> The apparition of these faces in the crowd: Petals, on a wet, black bough.

In this arrangement, as in the precise interpretive metaphor Pound locates in Guido Cavalcanti, "the phrases correspond to definite sensations undergone." The interpretive experience it invites is not one of casting "beyond" the images to search for a metaphor's suppressed tenors, but rather one of pondering the significance of the implied identity between two already clearly identified things.

James observes that the recognition of analogy is the first, delightful step in the effort of the "theoretical need" to simplify the world. In the essay that Pound described as containing "the fundamentals of all aesthetics," Fenollosa notes that the recognition of the "homologies, sympathies, and identities" in nature initiates the construction of all linguistic structures and systems of thought. The beauty of a poetry that works by engaging the reader at that moment when the process of abstraction has just begun, as Pound understood, is that it reminds him that the category he is beginning to see is one that is being created rather than discovered. The ideal condition of English poetry, writes Fenollosa, would be the condition exemplified by the Chinese ideogram: a sign in which the move towards abstraction is arrested at a stage where the particulars remain visible. Bearing "its metaphor on its face," having its "etymology . . . constantly visible," the poem that achieves this will not attempt to hide the fact that it is the product of an attempt to conquer difference, but will bear the evidence of its efforts—like a "blood-stained" battleflag. In doing so, it will not only enable its reader to enjoy recognizing an analogy between concrete things, but will also invite him to critique his impulse to identify those things, to subsume them under a common category. The Metro poem, for example, in implying an identity between the ghost-like faces that emerge in the dark of a subway station and the pink-white petals crowded on a branch in the spring rain, directs the reader towards a generalization about the mutual beauty and fragility of person and blossom. Presently, however, our satisfaction in that thought is disrupted by the uncomfortable equation of the tree-branch and the transit station from which faces and petals seem to spring. Contemplating that identification, we are compelled to object that the affinity between these long, black, thin, backdrops is more than countered by their difference. The faces bear no organic relation to their setting as do the petals to the bough. They do not spring from it, but it from them. The subway station is something the men behind these faces have constructed, something they have built in order to take shelter from that rain the petals accept with complete passivity. And with the refined insight brought by this recognition of difference, we are compelled to seek a new, more exact analogy.

Such an analogy, of course, will elicit its own objections, will be mentally dismantled in favor of one that seems still more fitting, and so the process will continue, perhaps indefinitely. The Image, or interpretive metaphor, in the terms of Paul Ricoeur, represents that "stage in the production of genres where generic kinship has not reached the level of conceptual peace and rest," but engenders instead a very definite state of "tension," as "the movement towards the genus is arrested by the resistance of the difference." By discouraging any propensity on the part of his reader to elevate his insights to the status of absolute truths, by substituting for the vaguely suggestive and talismanic Symbol a tensional, manifestly provisional, postulate of identity, in which, as Fenollosa willed it, "the creative process [remains] visible and at work," the Vorticist poet trips off instead a sidelong quest for temporary insights, momentary satisfactions, incipient categories that dissolve almost as soon as they are conceived. The mind of his reader is to be no still center, gazing into mystical truth, but a whirling Vortex, in which hopeful, centripetal gestures toward truth are as soon undone by a centrifugal motion. The sympathetic reading of the image, Pound's own secularized "symbol," is in his careful words "not necessarily a belief in a permanent world, but it is a belief in that direction."

The affinity between the pragmatic truth and the poetic image extends also to the type of painting and sculpture that Wyndham Lewis called Vorticist. Lewis's clearest prescriptions for Vorticist art are in "A Review of Contemporary Art," in *Blast II*, which stipulates the principles that the Vorticist ought to emulate and to eschew. Addressing the aesthetics of Expressionism, Cubism, Impressionism, and Futurism in turn, Lewis steers a course remarkably similar to those of James and Pound. Like many artists and art-theorists in his time, Lewis identifies the quest for abstraction in visual art with a search for mystical truth. And the most extreme manifestations of this quest arouse in him the same discomfort Hulme, James, and Pound feel at the unchecked flight of the "theoretic need." In the spirit of the "new classicism," Lewis objects strongly to paintings that pose as conduits for the supernatural. Particularly culpable, in his view, is the Expressionist painting of Kandinsky, whom he describes, fairly or unfairly, as "the only PURELY abstract painter in Europe." Kandinsky, of course, had written frequently and eloquently of the artist's capacity for unmediated vision, and had represented his own painting as a medium of revelation. In his *Über das Geistige in der Kunst* (1911), translated and excerpted in the first issue of *Blast,* he makes an appeal for an art that will capture the *"eternal truth"* of the spirit world being explored by Madame Blavatsky and her Theosophical Society. Lewis, predictably, objects to what he sees as Kandinsky's attempt to render spiritual truths at the expense of all references to the empirical world, and calls for the exorcism of the supernatural from aesthetics:

> Kandinsky, docile to the intuitive fluctuations of his soul, and anxious to render his hand and mind elastic and receptive, follows this unreal entity into its cloud-world, out of the material and solid universe.

> He allows the Bach-like will that resides in each good artist to be made war on by the slovenly and wandering Spirit. He allows the rigid chambers of his Brain to become a mystic house haunted by an automatic and puerile Spook, that leaves a delicate trail like a snail.

> The Blavatskyish soul in another Spook that needs laying, if it gets a vogue, just as Michael Angelo does.

If, as James says, "the absence of definite sensible images" is the *"sine qua non* of a contemplation of the divine higher truths," we might interpret Lewis's anxiety in the face of Kandinsky's painting as dismay at its failure to acknowledge its own arbitrariness. Like Pound a few months earlier, he seems to detect in Kandinsky's effort to be "passive and medium-like" an unwillingness to concede a role to his own "Will and consciousness": an effort to represent as eternal truth what Kandinsky's own idiosyncratic mind has played a role in designing.

Lewis experiences a similar discomfort in confronting the theoretic tendency in the increasingly abstract art of Cubism. The Cubist painters aim, in the analytical phase of their art, to refine away from objects all the accidental details of light and perspective that grant due recognition to the arbitrary vantage point of the painter. In the words of a champion Cubist art like Maurice Raynal, who compared the Cubist achievement to that of Mallarmé, the Cubist painting will, when this goal is completely realized, "offer a guarantee of certainty in itself; that is to say of absolutely pure truth . . . and so make the Beautiful . . . into a 'sensible manifestation of the Idea.' " But as James might have predicted, when faced with the "absolute datum" of a Cubist painting, once there is virtually no "otherness" left to annoy his philosophic need, Lewis is gripped by a longing for the very particulars that have

been sacrificed. Just as he laments the way Kandinsky's "ethereal, lyrical and cloud-like" paintings forego the power and definition of representative forms, he regrets that the Cubist quest for absolute truth results in paintings that are "static and representative, not swarming, exploding, or burgeoning with life . . . . " It is unfortunate, he says, when "the Plastic is impoverished for the Idea," for then "we get out of direct contact with these intuitive waves of power, that only play on the rich surfaces where life is crowded and abundant." With an equivocation reminiscent of Pound and James, Lewis concludes that although the artist may "believe in the existence of the supernatural," and think he has access to it, he should regard it "as redundant," as "nothing to do" with the *"life"* that is properly the object of art. He encourages the Vorticist artist, that is, as Hulme and Pound had encouraged their poets and James and Husserl their philosophers, to refrain from dedicating himself to recovering transcendental reality and to rest content with recording phenomenal experience. In 1939, protesting Herbert Read's representation of all modern abstract art as a kind of "spiritual refuge" from phenomenal chaos, Lewis objected that Vorticism had *not* been "a clinging to a lifebelt, or to a spur, or something satisfactory and solid, in the midst of a raging perpetual flux. . . . " "Its artists," he continued, in language reminiscent of Hulme, did not " 'fly' " unchecked into the reassuring transcendency of "geometric expression."

But if Lewis discourages the Vorticist painter from rendering what he conceives as transcendental realities, he does not condemn him to an uncomprehended phenomenal chaos. If he recoils from the dogmatism of Kandinsky's Expressionism or Picasso's Cubism, he does not wholeheartedly embrace the skepticism implicit in Impressionism and Futurism. The Impressionists had worked from the premise that the highest from of truth accessible to an individual mind is, in Jules Laforgue's words, the "response of a unique sensibility to a moment." Their ideology was relativist, pluralist, and democratic; they confined the individual eye to its idiosyneratic impression, and respected all honestly rendered impressions equally. As Laforgue summarized it,

> Each man is, according to his moment in time, his racial milieu and social situation, his moment of individual evolution, a kind of keyboard on which the exterior world plays in a certain way. My own keyboard is perpetually changing, and there is no other like it. All keyboards are legitimate.

The Impressionist was obliged to preserve every accident, every irregularity, in the fleeting picture present to his eye. For Monet and Renoir, to reduce any part of the shimmering panorama of sense-data to the skeletal lines of some mental concept would have been too coercive an interpretation. But for Lewis, such programmatic passivity, however much it satisfies painting's obligation to life, is not an acceptable alternative to pure abstraction. If the Cubist speaks too categorically, Lewis laments, the Impressionist and his Futurist successors are so tentative as not to speak at all, their "democratic [states] of mind" nothing but "cowardice or muddleheadedness." In their dedication to the "inherently unselective registering of impressions," they are engaged in an "absurd and gloomy waste of time." They forfeit the possibility of discerning and articulating any *meaning* in the phenomenal chaos, and remain completely "subjugated" to Nature. In other words, Lewis corroborates James's findings and balks at an art that denies all abstraction. His "theoretic need" makes him object that the involuntary, or "mechanically reactive" craftsmen of Impressionism and Futurism "do not sufficiently dominate the contents of their pictures." Just as Pound refuses to allow the Vorticist to remain a "Toy of Circumstance," Lewis insists that the Vorticist artist must both attend closely to life, and seek its sense, or pattern:

> You must be able to organize the cups, saucers and people, or their abstract plastic equivalent, as naturally as Nature, only with the added personal logic of Art, that gives the grouping significance.

> The Vorticist is not the Slave of Commotion, but it's [sic] Master.

Lewis's Vorticist, then, will neither penetrate the phenomenal veil, nor revel contentedly in its teeming chaos. "The finest Art," Lewis maintains, "is not pure Abstraction, nor is it unorganized life." And the constructs that preserve this balance are, once again, inherently tensional, compromising between abstract monotony and concrete heterogeneity. Lewis repeatedly stresses that Vorticist paintings and sculptures grant free rein to neither the philosophic tendency nor its opposite, but allow each to be *checked* by the operation of the other. "We must constantly strive to ENRICH abstraction," he says, "till it is almost plain life, or rather to get deeply enough immersed in material life to experience the shaping power amongst its vibrations." Like the poem that invites us to analogize between two images, a process countered by the phenomenal particulars preserved by the images themselves, the Vorticist painting or sculpture "must catch the clearness and the logic *in the midst of contradictions:* not settle down and snooze on an acquired, easily possessed and mastered, satisfying shape." The arrangements of Vorticist painters and sculptors, in other words, must not express their insights as divine revelations, but as human constructions, not as absolute truths, but as provisional gestures, subject to dissolution at the very instant of conception. "Finite and god-like lines," Lewis says, "are not for us, but, rather, a powerful but remote suggestion of finality, or an elementary organization of a dark insect swarming, like the passing of a cloud's shadow or the path of a wind."

Lewis's vision of a tensional art, so closely akin to Pound's, is borne out in the sculptures and paintings produced by members of the Vorticist circle, which included Lewis himself, William Roberts, Helen Saunders, Frederick Etchells, David Bomberg, and Edward Wadsworth. Most of the works reproduced in the issues of *Blast,* or exhibited under the Vorticist banner, maintain the tense balance he advocates between the urge to abstraction and the impulse to recognize the fleeting particulars of the phenomenal flux. If the geometric forms of Malevich or Mondrian most closely emulate the condition of the eternal Idea, and if the blurred figures-in-motion of Italian Futurism in some sense carry the contrary ideal of the Impressionists to its logical conclusion, the work of the Vorticist brings these extremes into tense coexistence. Lewis represents his ideal at one point in *Blast* as that of a "LIVING plastic geometry," or, later, as the "burying [of] EUCLID deep in the living flesh," and this ideal is operative in a number of Vorticist works, most particularly Gaudier-Brzeska's magnificent sculpture, "Red Stone Dancer" (1913). In this figure, as Pound was to note in his book on the sculptor, the "mathematical bareness" of a triangle and circle, embedded in the face and breast, is "fully incarnate, made flesh, full of vitality and of energy" by the motion of limbs flowing in and out of them. If the viewer's eye gravitates to one of the unsullied abstractions, as if to what James called an "absolute datum," the sculpture invites it almost simultaneously to point beyond or on either side of them, to see the "other" of the dancer's motion-in-time. The whole body of the dancer, furthermore, whirling energetically into curves that then inspire to the purity and universality of the straight line, threatens to surrender, but never fully concedes, its idiosyncracies to an entirely uniform abstraction. Its head and upper body thus approximate the shape of a "spherical triangle"—what Pound called the "central life-form" in the work of Lewis as well as Gaudier-Brzeska.

The Vorticist *corpus* contains many such figures, aspiring to transcend their vitality and become universal: Lewis's paintings "Centauress" (1912) and "Enemy of the Stars" (1913), along with William Roberts's "Religion" (1913-14), not only embody but seem to narrate such an aspiration, and Bomberg's "Mud Bath" (1914) seems by its title to allude explicitly to the cindery world from which its highly abstract yet still just recognizably human figures spring. There are several works, too, in which landscapes hover midway between the abstract and the representative, the necessary and the accidental, the eternal and the temporal. In Etchell's "Dieppe" (1913), for example, the shape of houses, chimneys, and bridges, though refined of many of their accidental characteristics, retain the energy of a busy port by appearing to whirl about the picture's center. The palpable tension captured here, between the tendencies to move out of and into life, is mirrored in Etchell's later and less figurative "Progression" (1914-15), where the forces of abstraction and chaos battle it out in a degenerating grid. In that painting, as in other Vorticist works such as Bomberg's "Jiu-Jitsu" (1913), where the phenomenal flux is not longer represented by recognizable figurative allusions, the stasis of the squares is characteristically disrupted by the instability of irregular triangles or rhomboids and trapezoids. Another intriguing example of the warring impulses at work is Wadsworth's "Slack Bottom" (1914), where the illusion is of a chessboard whose perfect regularity will not hold, but sags at its center. The latter is reminiscent of the vision of theory-making found in Hulme's notebooks and essays: a world where abstract theories resemble chessboards, perched precariously atop the "cinder-heap" of the phenomenal world, momentarily ordering it, but then quickly collapsing back into it, waiting to be manufactured anew. "Slack Bottom" bring us back, too, to Pound's poetic chessboard, with its reminder that no abstract resolution is final, that every black-and-white solution reasoning may bring is subject immediately to a new, and once again colorful, battle.

The expressive arrangements of the Vorticist poet and artist, then, are similar both in genesis and constitution to the representations of truth James envisions for pragmatism. They reflect the conviction of their "new classical" theorists that it is hubristic to claim the capacity to grasp transcendental truths. They are also informed, however, by the recognition that moments in which such a condition seems to be accomplished are an undeniable part of our experience, and that it would be foolish to deny ourselves the hope that they inspire. James and Pound, in particular, are caught between their discomfort with dogmatism and their inability to adopt an attitude of thoroughgoing skepticism toward intuitions that seem, to them, to be more affirmed than denied by the stream of experience. To be chronically distrustful of our quasi-mystical moments, as James points out to a friend who has challenged him to give up his faith, and as Pound would no doubt have replied to anyone who wished to deny the poet his passion to articulate the Image, would be to assert "a dogmatic disbelief in any extant consciousness higher than that of the . . . human mind, and this in the teeth of the extraordinary vivacity of man's psychological commerce with something ideal that *feels as if it* were also actual." The pragmatic truth, the poetic Image, and the Vorticist painting, accordingly, are energetic assertions that, while not claiming to be windows on eternity, do not extinguish all hope of celestial fire either. They respond to our religious needs, our philosophic passions, by providing hypotheses, intriguing analogues, hints of a universal geometry. At the same time, however, they very deliberately preserve the context in which these insights arise, assaulting our peripheral vision with reminders of the phenomenal life that would be sacrificed to the pattern. The truths they posit seem inherently unstable, liable to revert to chaos at every moment, as our passion for distinguishing reasserts itself and focuses on the details that resist assimilation. By holding each of the two tendencies in check, these constructs fulfill their intended function of expressing not the simple fact of truth attained, but the complex *feeling of* attaining it, not the dead relic of a truth said-and-done, but the electricity of the *consciousness of* a truth coming-into-being. The truths of pragmatism and the poems and paintings of Vorticism actively pursue the condition Heidegger, the immediate heir of Husserl's phenomenology, was to envision for art: they are designed to be the fields for the "fighting of the battle in which the unconcealedness of beings . . . or truth, is won," the *loci* for truth's "*becoming and happening.*" And in offering their audiences simultaneously both the light of unconcealedness and the dark of concealment, both the theoretical objects to inspire belief and the phenomenal evidence to elicit doubt, they invite them to take their place at the table where the chess game of truth-making is played. Their challenge is perpetual, and, if James's understanding of our restless psychic life is right, it is irresistible.

LEWIS AND POUND

W. K. Rose

SOURCE: "Ezra Pound and Wyndham Lewis: The Crucial Years," in *The Southern Review,* Louisiana State University, Vol. 4, Winter, 1968, pp. 72-89.

[*In the following essay, Rose examines the careers and friendship of Lewis and Pound from 1910 to 1920.*]

Of Ezra Pound's many and celebrated literary associations, that with Wyndham Lewis has the unique interest of showing the poet in close contact with the pictorial arts. It is special too in that Lewis, unlike Yeats or Eliot, saw a revolution in the arts as a public battle and shared the poet's zest for skirmishing. Viewed less narrowly, this relationship engages one's attention as would any other involving two dynamic human beings, both of them gifted artists and important influences in the cultural history of their epoch. For all of one's reservations about the "dangers of literary biography," of which Noel Stock warns in his book on Pound, I do not see how some observation of this pair *as a pair* can help but add to our understanding of their works, and of their epoch.

The epoch was, neatly, a decade, 1910-1920. Looking back, one can see it clearly—in London and New York at least—as the seed-time of the new art. What we now think of as "modern poetry," "modern art" came to fruition in the ferment of those years. They are also, not irrelevantly, I believe, the crucial years of the friendship of Lewis and Pound. After Pound left London for the Continent at the end of 1920, he saw Lewis only sporadically and there were long gaps in their correspondence. They did not meet at all during the last eighteen years of Lewis's life. Thus it was during this decade that any catalysing action took place or patterns were set, and that a bond was cemented that was to survive the storms of more than half a century.

The wonder is that these two egoists—both so intransigent, so aggressive and irascible, each exhibitionistic in his own way, one (Lewis) preternaturally suspicious, the other compulsively managerial—could become friends at all. Yet each young man was bound to recognize in the other unusual intellectual energy and artistic creativity, as well as a deep-seated iconoclasm and the iconoclast's rough humor. Moreover, when they met in London, they had already partaken for a time of the same atmosphere there—a disparate concoction of British Museum scholarship, Nietzsche, Bergson, and ninetyish aestheticism, with infusions of French neoclassicism and *symbolisme.* And there were less obvious points of contact. Both, for example, had inhaled enough French air—Lewis through his long apprenticeship in the studios of the Left Bank, Pound through his studies of Romance in college and university—for it to have a permanent effect on their thinking and taste. It was France that fixed them in their respect for intellectual clarity and in their preference for surfaces. Even less discernible so early on, I believe, was a common tendency to fragment, to think and create in segments. If each has produced sizeable coherent works, both have proved themselves by nature impatient, disinclined to organic structures.

The origins of these manifestations can, I think, be traced in the earlier histories of the two. Pound and Lewis (though Lewis did not reveal the fact to Pound for several years) both stemmed from American pioneer stock. Each had forebears who were entrepreneurs in the state of New York; Lewis's father died in Philadelphia, where Ezra was raised. Lewis was born in the Bay of Fundy of an American father and English mother, and he was brought up in and around London. Pound was born in Idaho, son of a Wisconsin father and a New York mother. That uprootedness was a factor in these backgrounds, though more so in Lewis's, would be clear even if Pound had not stressed it in his pieces in *The New Age*—"Through Alien Eyes," January-February 1913, and "The Revolt of Intelligence, V," January 8, 1920. He wrote in the latter: "I was . . . brought up in a district or city with which my forbears had no connection and I am therefore accustomed to being alien in one place or other."

To be sure, Pound had a more settled childhood than did Lewis, whose father defected early. But each was an only child, and each seems to have taken advantage of the fact in his educational career. Lewis was an indifferent student, frequently shifting schools, finally leaving Rugby for the Slade and the Slade for the Continent. Pound managed to go as far as an M.A., though he too moved about and, like Lewis, made an effort only when he was interested. Once finished with their educations, both young men left home for good and, for a few years anyway, changed addresses frequently. Such beginnings do not often end in membership in the establishment, literary or otherwise. Nor will they find fulfillment in works of art that exhibit conventional learning or conventional forms.

Paradoxically, we can discern in these same histories sources of stability and of capacity for feeling. For both boys grew up in environments where intimacy and affection flourished—Ezra with his parents, Percy Wyndham with his mother, grandmother, and a loyal servant. Each experienced the rich moral tone, the sentimentality, and the earnest, if limited, literacy that characterized middle-class households on both sides of the Atlantic in the eighties and nineties. As they matured, they would have something to sustain them.

Whether Pound and Lewis met in 1909 or 1910, whether through Lawrence Binyon or Ford Madox Ford, is not clear. The more likely date seems to be 1909, for it was then that Ford (then Hueffer) became editor of *The English Review* ("the event of 1909-1910," Pound said) and launched the two writers on the literary scene. Lewis's story "The Pole" appeared in the May number and Pound's "Sestina: Altaforte" in June. Lewis was twenty-six and Pound twenty-three. Both had already established themselves as young men of promise—Pound with three small volumes of verse, Lewis with the exhibition of some striking apprentice pictures. Yet it was not what they had done so much as what they *were* that caused their elders among the intelligentsia to notice them. Attractive, arrogant, manifestly gifted, individual outside and in, they were Ford's favorites among *"les jeunes."*

He describes them at the time, and allowing for exaggeration, we can trust him. Pound, a "Rufous Terror, with an immense physical vigour and the restless itch of a devil, pursuing the Irritating-Beautiful—in the disguise of a cattle-hand across the Atlantic. . . . "

> would approach with the step of a dancer, making passes with a cane at an imaginary opponent. He would wear trousers made of green billiard cloth, a pink coat, an immense sombrero, a flaming beard cut to a point, a single large blue earring. . . . his Philadelphia accent was still comprehensible if disconcerting . . . he was astonishingly meagre and agile. He threw himself alarmingly into frail chairs, devoured enormous quantities of your pastry, fixed his pince-nez firmly on his nose, drew out a manuscript from his pocket, threw his head back, closed his eyes to the point of invisibility and looking down his nose would chuckle like Mephistopheles and read to you a translation from Arnaut Daniel.

(Thus to Revisit and Return to Yesterday)

According to Violet Hunt, "He would wear my Connemara cloak or the editor's old Rossetti coat—any old covering—with serenity." Edgar Jepson recalls his "discussing his theories in an earnest whisper after the manner of Ford," and Lewis told the present writer that Ezra was, when they met, a ludicrous mixture of Yankee and Ford. No wonder D. H. Lawrence, down from the Midlands, found him "young, callow, swashbuckling . . . very affected and silly."

Lewis, Ford writes, recalling his first vision of him,

> was extraordinary in appearance. . . . He was very dark in the shadows of the stair case. He wore an immense steeple-crowned hat. Long black locks fell from it. His coat was one of those Russian looking coats that have no revers. He had also an ample black cape. . . . He said not a word. . . . I have never known anyone else whose silence was a positive rather than a negative quality.

(Return to Yesterday)

According to Douglas Jerrold, "he was dark, saturnine and gloomy." In 1935 Douglas Goldring, Ford's young secretary at the Review, recalled the two together:

> Both of them . . . in clothes, hairdressing and manner, made no secret of their calling. Pound contrived to look "every inch a poet," while I have never seen anyone so obviously a "genius," as Wyndham Lewis. . . .

(Odd Man Out)

There follows the dubious tale of Lewis's first appearance at the *English Review* office. He is supposed to have marched unannounced to the flat above, found Ford in his bath, proclaimed himself a genius, and extracted from inside his coat a manuscript which he proceeded to read. This was "The Pole" and Ford accepted it on the spot. "If it didn't happen it ought to have," Goldring concludes. According to Lewis, he did "unexpectedly mount the stairs" but "silently left a bundle of manuscript."

One is not surprised to learn that the two "jeunes" approached one another nervously. Pound evokes the scene in Canto 80:

> And also near the museum they served it mit
> Schlag
> in those days (pre 1914)
> the loss of that café
> meant the end of a B.M. era
> (British Museum era)
> Mr Lewis had been to Spain
> Mr Binyon's young prodigies
> pronounced the word: Penthesilea
>
> . . . . .
>
> So it is to Mr Binyon that I owe, initially,
> Mr Lewis, Mr P. Wyndham Lewis. His bull-dog,
> me,
> as it were against old Sturge M's bull-
> dog. . . .

The café was the Vienna, a favorite rendezvous of the British Museum set in which Binyon and Lewis's mentor Sturge Moore were leading figures.

In Lewis's version nothing came of these Vienna encounters, and it was Ford who finally brought the young bulldogs together. ". . . It was with a complete passivity on my side, tinctured with a certain mild surliness, that acquaintance with Ezra Pound was gradually effected," he writes in *Blasting and Bombardiering.* He ascribes his reluctance in part at least to Pound's being so evidently an outsider—"the perfect fish out of water." For one thing, his linguistic pretensions were mistrusted by the more scholarly English. For another, his lack of European reticence put one off: ". . . he just wanted to impress. . . . Pound socially was a little too much like the 'singing cowboy.' . . . He had rushed with all the raw solemnity of the classic Middle West into a sophisticated post-Nineties society. . . ." ("Ezra Pound," *An Examination of Ezra Pound* [edited by Peter Russell].)

Lewis may of course have been jealous of another rising star. He says that the Vienna group had it that the newcomer was a Jew, so that he "was mildly surprised to see an unmistakable 'nordic blonde,' with fierce blue eyes and a reddishly hirsute jaw," to hear this "cowboy songster" uttering the "staccato of the States." On the second occasion at the Vienna there was speculation as to the whereabouts of a missing prostitute. Pound, still a stranger to Lewis, gestured to him and said, "with a great archness, and regarding me with mischievous good will": "This young man could probably tell you!" Lewis ignored him. When under Ford's auspices they did at last converse, Lewis felt as if he were boarding a "bombastic galleon." Once there, he "discovered beneath its skull and crossbones, intertwined with *fleur de lys* and spattered with preposterous oddities, a heart of gold."

During the ensuing ten years Pound and Lewis were never out of touch for long, and each rose to a position of eminence, indeed dominance, among *"les jeunes."* The world in which they moved has been much chronicled, most recently by Patricia Hutchins in *Ezra Pound's Kensington.* A few of its key names and places conjure up the *mis-enscène:* the Vienna, Stulik's Eiffel Tower restaurant,

Mme. Strindberg's Cabaret Theatre Club (both these last with décor by Wyndham Lewis), Hulme in Frith Street, Ford on Camden Hill, Yeats at Woburn Buildings, May Sinclair and Mrs. Shakespear (Pound's mother-in-law) and Lady Cunard, Marinetti, Monro's Poetry Bookshop, the Rebel Art Center, Gaudier-Brzeska, Epstein, Miss Weaver and *The Egoist,* Orage and *The New Age,* Eliot. London has rarely known so much excitement in the arts. One of the era's distinguishing features was the way it mixed elements—not just the foreign and the native, but the literary establishment and *"les jeunes,"* the socialite and the Bohemian. In 1913, asking Lewis to bring Marinetti and the English Futurist Nevinson to a South Lodge evening, Ford could say that there were "generally some of the swell and wealthy, together with literary gents and picture buyers and people who help on MOVEMENTS." He also counseled sympathy for the maddening Mme. Strindberg: "She is trying to build up a palace of all the Arts with three oyster shells and stale patchouli and sawdust and creme and vers libre and champagne corks . . . which, is what . . . we are all of us trying to do in one field or the other." Even the holocaust of 1914 could not, for a time, halt their activity, though it decimated their numbers.

Lewis and Pound did not assuredly move in unison through the decade. Despite his success in *The English Review,* Lewis persisted in thinking of himself as firstly a painter; Pound's dealings in poetry were far from the center of his interests. Nor would their mercurial temperaments have permitted an unrelenting intimacy. They were frequently together, but most of the time each had companions closer to him than the other. In the years between 1913 and 1918, nevertheless, they enjoyed a kinship of feeling and a solidarity of aim that was unusual in both their lives. If Pound was the aggressor in the relationship, that was a matter of his more outgoing temperament. Lewis clearly liked him, and respected him. Eustace Mullins, whose book on Pound was written under the master's aegis, says flatly, "His closest friend during the Vorticist period was Wyndham Lewis."

Certainly there was in those days no one who came in for more of his promotional zeal. Lewis could well say later, "Ezra . . . has been of the most amazing use to other people." *"The Egoist,"* he writes, "was Miss Weaver's paper, but at the period of which I speak you would rather have supposed it belonged to Ezra Pound." When Margaret Anderson asked him to become European editor of *The Little Review,* Pound replied, early in 1917: ". . . I want a place where I and T. S. Eliot can appear once a month . . . and where Joyce can appear when he likes, and where Wyndham Lewis can appear if he comes back from the war." Of the writing that he did not himself publish in BLAST, almost the whole of Lewis's output from 1914 to 1918 appeared in *The Egoist* and *The Little Review.* At the same time this ubiquitous agent engaged in a campaign for Lewis's pictures, notably with the American collector John Quinn. "Lewis has got Blake scotched to a finish," he wrote Quinn in 1916. Quinn bought; he also arranged for a Vorticist exhibition in New York, another of Pound's projects.

In his capacity as editor and critic, Pound puffed Lewis steadily and extravagantly in every forum at his disposal—" 'Tarr' is the most vigorous and volcanic English novel of our time." For years he was planning an illustrated book on Lewis. He arranged for the publication of *Tarr* by Miss Weaver and by Alfred Knopf. He proposed a "Lewis number" to *The Little Review* and elsewhere. When in 1914 he projected a "College of Arts," Lewis was, according to the Preliminary Announcement, to head the Atelier of Painting. On the social scene he seems to have been just as assiduous. Ford's friend Stella Bowen tells us that "Joyce and Lewis were Ezra's two gods, before whom we were bidden to bend the knees most deeply." But then, as Lewis wrote later, "there was nothing social for him that did not have a bearing on the business of writing. If it had not it would be dull."

The names of Pound and Lewis are coupled most often in reference to Vorticism. Contemplating all that has been written of this shortlived, not very productive movement, one is tempted to quote Lewis in one of his latest letters: "Vorticism. This name is an invention of Ezra Pound. . . . What does this word mean? I do not know."

— W. K. Rose

In *Rude Assignment* Lewis credits Pound with presenting him to Eliot, Gaudier, and Aldington. There were dozens of other introductions, many of them less welcome. The one to Eliot in 1914 or 1915 he remembered with pleasure. It occurred, he writes in "Early London Environment," in Pound's triangular sitting room. Pound "lay flung back in typical posture of aggressive ease." "He blinked and winked with contemplative conceit and contentment, chewing a sugared and wonderfully shrunken pear. . . ." He squinted " 'granpa'-wise over the rims of his glasses . . . as good as saying to me in the Amos and Andy patter of his choice: 'You ole uncle Ezz is wise to wot youse thinkin. . . .' " Lewis could not even quarrel without Pound's intervention; writing to Quinn in 1915, Ezra said that he was "working for a reconciliation" between his friend and Epstein.

To a man of Lewis's independent spirit and sensitiveness, all this attention was bound to irritate as much as it gratified. Nor was he alone in being annoyed. J. B. Yeats wrote to Quinn: "Ezra Pound is a hairshirt of a friend to be worn near the skin." And Epstein in his autobiography recalls a day in 1913 when Pound brought Gaudier to his studio to see the *Rock Drill:* as Pound began to expatiate on the work, Gaudier turned to him and snapped, "Shut up, you understand nothing!" Ezra must often have been aware that he was overstepping. For example, he wrote to Lewis, around 1917, "I have constantly to approach you in the paternal admonitory, cautionary, epicenish bloodguttily

INartistic angle." So Lewis was quite right when, thirty years later, he told a correspondent that this " 'scolding old hen' . . . once wrote that certain people (meaning Eliot and myself) looked upon him as a 'bon vieux papa bourgeois': This was absurd, for it was he who insisted on looking upon himself in this way. . . . "

Lewis's reminiscences of Pound abound in references, often rancorous, to this feature of their relations. Indeed, it seems to have been the main cause of later troubles in the friendship. There is even good reason to believe that Ezra's managerial propensities lay behind Lewis's famous attack on him in *Time and Western Man.* There were genuine conflicts of ideas as as well, conflicts that became more noticeable as time went on—chief among them Pound's infatuation with the past vs. Lewis's impatience with it. What I would emphasize is that Lewis experienced Pound's interference as more than simply a nuisance. Egoist that he was, he felt particularly sharply the kind of nullification that is involved in such behavior.

> When he writes about living people of his acquaintance . . . he never seems to have *seen* the individual at all. . . . there is no direct contact between Ezra and an individual person or thing. People are seen by him only as types.
>
> (*Time and Western Man*)

During the years when they were young and often together, when Ezra's genuine bonhomie could be felt, one could usually joke away one's irritation. After 1920 Lewis was more apt to take a negative view.

The names of Pound and Lewis are coupled most often in reference to Vorticism. Contemplating all that has been written of this shortlived, not very productive movement, one is tempted to quote Lewis in one of his latest letters: "Vorticism. This name is an invention of Ezra Pound. . . . What does this word mean? I do not know." Earlier he had called Vorticist activities "publicist experiments—inseparable from things done just for the day, and regarded as of no more consequence than handbills, and possibly rockets and squibs." An exaggeration no doubt, but not wider of the mark, I think, than some recent scholarly disquisitions on "the Vorticist aesthetic" that miss the fun and haphazardness of the original. Even Pound, writing in 1914, Vorticism's big year, defined it to Harriet Monroe simply as "the generic term now used on all branches of the new art, sculpture, painting, poetry." And decades later he recalled that as Amy was ruining Imagism, "it was opportune to get another lable [*sic*] for vitality in the arts." One need not underestimate the impact of the activity or its importance as a symptom of change in order to caution against the "reconstruction" of systems that never were.

As a chapter in the history of Pound and Lewis, Vorticism marks a high point in the rapprochement of plastic and literary art, and thus in the proximity of these two artists. In *Time and Western Man* Lewis noisily denied this, declaring that "Pound supplied the Chinese Crackers and a trayful of mild jokes . . . also much ingenious support in the . . . press," but his verse was insufficiently experimental, "a series of pastiches of old french or italian poetry. . . . Its novelty consisted largely in the distance it went *back*, not forward. . . . " A look at *BLAST*, "Review of the Great English Vortex," gives him the lie. Lewis's other statements over the years to the effect that Pound had nothing to do with Vorticism—"Vorticism . . . was what I, personally, did, and said, at a certain period"—must also be qualified in view of the facts.

Yet there is a good deal of truth in these assertions about Pound's role in the movement, or the role that has been repeatedly assigned to him. Lewis did, as he wrote in 1949, have "the not very original idea of founding an art paper, to advertise and popularize a movement in the visual arts which I had initiated." Nor has Ezra ever disputed that fact. Lewis "*made* vorticism," he has written. Even if he hadn't said it, there is the evidence of a letter to Joyce, written early in 1914: "Lewis is starting a new Futurist, Cubist, Imagiste Quarterly . . . it is mostly a painters' magazine with me to do the poems." And of another, from St. Elizabeth's asking "Old Vort" just a few months before his death: ". . . do you remember yr/first cheery invitation, to provide you with 'something nasty for *BLAST*'."

What Pound has claimed—rightly, I think—is that (1) before Lewis got things going, he was having some parallel thoughts about the arts, and (2) that he became the movement's chief theorist. Thus, reviewing an exhibition of the new art in March 1914, he could honestly say he found it hard to speak of the paintings because they were "perhaps so close to one's poetic habit of creation." In his article on Vorticism in the *Fortnightly Review*, he expatiated, asserting that "the work of the vorticists and the 'feelings of the inner need' existed before the general noise about vorticism," that the artists in various media came *separately* to their underlying agreement. He made it clear too that it was "vorticist poetry" with which he was "most intimately connected. If, though, one regards Vorticism as "purely a painters' affair," as Lewis had at the beginning anyway, then it *was* largely what he, Lewis, did and said.

The historical facts, at least, are reasonably simple. Lewis, a painter who was also a writer, wanted to start a movement and a review. During the early phase (1913) he enlisted several friends, mostly visual artists, in the project. Pound, a poet with a passion for Lewis's drawings and Gaudier's sculptures, was one of these friends. Once he had come in, some kind of literary-visual amalgam was assured. The presence of Hulme, a philosopher *cum* art-critic (he later withdrew), and Gaudier, a sculptor-writer, strengthened the dual aspect. As Ford wrote, ". . . for a moment in the just-before-the-war days, the Fine, the Plastic and the Literary Arts touched hands with an unusual intimacy and what is called oneness of purpose." In his *Egoist* review of the Goupil exhibition, Pound emphasized, as he always did, the distinctiveness of the arts and thereby disqualified himself as a serious art critic. At the same time he found his appreciation of the new sculpture and painting worth communicating. Was not his one "surest critic . . . a contemporary painter who knows my good work from my bad—NOT by a critical process, at least not by a technical process"? "It indicates," he continued, "a 'life' or a sameness somewhere that we are both

trying with our imperfect means to get at." He was still marvelling at the phenomenon forty years later, when he wrote to Lewis: "I dunno whether you note convergence (from two quite distinct angles) on agreement of 1913 or whenever. At any rate there was a convergence not merely a connexion." Certainly he had done more than anyone to enunciate and elaborate the themes of the conjunction.

I have suggested the folly of trying to reduce Vorticism to a coherent aesthetic, as one might perhaps do with Pre-Raphaelitism. The dispersion, even possible contradiction, of its ideas would seem to result as much from the different casts of mind of Pound and Lewis as from the effort to speak in the same breath of two media. As a programmist Lewis is at once the more adventurous and the more worldly of the two. On the one hand, he wanted to hack out some area in the visual arts wherein his movement would be distinct from impressionism, cubism, and futurism. On the other, that he was feeling his way towards some mystique of energy and form is clear from his drawings and paintings of the period and from writings like the BLAST manifestoes and the play *Enemy of the Stars*. "You think of a whirlpool," he said to Violet Hunt. "At the heart of the whirlpool is a great silent place where all the energy is concentrated. And there, at the point of concentration, is the Vorticist."

Pound's approach was more aesthetic and more passive. He is much occupied with defining the relations of the arts in this new scheme and speaks of "forms about one as a source of 'form-motifs.' " Whereas Lewis's chief aim is to use the imagination to make new forms, Pound seems more concerned to apprehend and organize those that have become available to him. "Vorticism, especially that part of vorticism having to do with form—to wit, vorticist painting and sculpture—has brought me a new series of apperceptions." By the time he had become the movement's leading propagandist, however, Pound could sound Lewis's note interchangeably with his own. "Vorticism is the use of, or the belief in the use of, THE PRIMARY PIGMENT," he announced in his *New Age* "Affirmation" of January, 1915, and went on to declare that "an organization of forms is a confluence of forces." His "Vorticism means that one is interested in the creative faculty as opposed to the mimetic" simply generalizes Lewis's artist "in his studio . . . imagining form" and able to "transmit the substance and logic of his invention to another man." Confronted with one of Lewis's vorticist designs, or rather with the task of selling some to Quinn, Ezra could even approximate the thunder of Wyndham's self-styled Lewis gun: "beauty, heaven, hell, sarcasm, every kind of whirlwind of force and emotion. Vortex."

In a later "Affirmation" Pound took it upon himself to assign, in a rather impressionistic fashion, roles to his favorite rebels. Lewis he credits with "a great faculty of design, synthesis of modern art movements, the sense of emotion in abstract design. . . . A sense of dynamics." His own contribution he sees as purely literary—"an active sense . . . of the need for a uniform criticism of excellence based on world poetry. . . . The quantitative analysis in literature. . . . The Image." Elsewhere he said of Vorticism "that Lewis supplied the volcanic force, Brzeska the animal energy, and perhaps that I had contributed a certain Confucian calm and reserve." If so, it was a Vorticist sort of calm, the stillness at the eye of the hurricane. For having christened the movement, he plunged into its activities with his usual *élan*. He signed all the manifestoes, wrote his own Vortex and poems for *BLAST No. 1*, and sold copies of the "puce monster" from his flat in Holland Place Chambers. Of course he publicized wherever he could, and when Lewis opened the Rebel Art Center in Great Ormond Street in the spring of 1914, he became an habitué. Miss Kate Lechmere, who sponsored the center, recalls an occasion when, to Lewis's annoyance, he put up a sign there reading "End of Christian Era." A month before Lewis's death, Pound reminded him of a day when two Russians came to the center and went away saying, "But you are individualists." That summer of 1914 he wrote to Joyce: "We have been having Vorticist and Imagist dinners, haciendo politicos etc. God save all poor sailors from la vie litteraire."

Douglas Goldring describes a tea party to inaugurate *BLAST* at Lewis's studio in Fitzroy Street:

> Lewis and Ezra Pound presided over it jointly, the guests were the oddest collection of *rapins* in black hats, girls from the Slade, poets and journalists. We solemnly compiled lists of persons who should be blasted and of others who should be blessed. I have often wondered what Pound and Lewis, who occasionally exchanged meaning glances, really thought of their disciples.
>
> *(Odd Man Out)*

There was another occasion at Kensington Town Hall, when Hulme and Lewis were to speak. Neither man being effective on a platform, it looked like being a fiasco when Pound stood up in his poet's garb and "halo of fiery hair." He talked wittily and recited his verse, to the delight it seems of almost everyone. "It's rather a joke hearing poetry read by an American," Lewis muttered to Miss Lechmere. Even more colorful, though less trustworthy, is Ford's anecdote about a walk down Holland Street with Ezra talking "incessantly on one side of me in his incomprehensible Philadelphian which was already ageing," while Lewis, on the other side, "dark, a little less hirsute but more and more like a conspirator went on and on in a vitriolic murmur": *"Tu sais, tu es foûtu! Foûtu! Finished!*. . . Your generation has gone. . . . I . . . I . . . I . . . The Vortex. Blast all the rest."

From the middle of 1915 to the middle of 1918 the two saw less of one another, Lewis first suffering a long illness and then going into the army. The separation and, undoubtedly the stress of the times, brought an unaccustomed ease to the friendship. The tone of their correspondence, with Lewis in training camp or at the front, is one of affectionate camaraderie. Lewis recounts the inanities and vicissitudes of military life; Pound, now completely in charge of his friend's creative output, reports on his progress with Quinn, Miss Weaver, et al. He contemplates a new number of *BLAST*; he offers medical advice! He works to get the Bombardier a commission; he worries over his safety—"I wish you would get a decent and convenient wound. Say the left buttock." Lewis, by now convinced that Ezra was a friend to be trusted, asked him to be his executor.

This was the time of the "Imaginary Letters," with the questionable exception of *BLAST No. 1*, the only instance of literary collaboration between them. Writing as William Bland Burn, Lewis began the series, evidently with no idea of its being a joint venture. Pound published these first three letters in *The Little Review* (May-July, 1917). Then in August he wrote to Lewis: "Mr. Villerant [Burn's friend in Lewis's first letters] . . . has written some letters . . . to keep their 'reader' in mind of the existence of the Burn family. The literary rape and adultery is most underhanded and scandalous." Lewis seems not to have minded; he contributed two more letters the following year, and Pound concluded the series in November, 1918. The letters themselves are informal essays that move casually among the interests of the authors: the artist's relation to his public, Russian literature, poetry, etc. Reading them *en bloc* one is struck by the independence of the two correspondents. Villerant addresses himself to Burn's wife and takes cues from Burn, but develops his ideas without regard to Burn's. In *his* later contributions Burn ignores even Villerant's existence. As Pound wrote to Lewis, Villerant would perhaps "provide Burn with Aunt Sally's. He is not controversing with Burn but discussing matters other, and of interest to his effete and over civilized organism."

The war ended and Lewis having survived the flu epidemic, the two were once more together in London, living near one another in Kensington. Herbert Read, a callow but observant young soldier, saw them there in the fall of 1918. Lewis he regarded as "the ringleader of 'les jeunes.'" Ezra he found "very nice after all. As you would *not* expect he speaks in a quiet soft voice and though affected in appearance ['his side whiskers, dainty beard, Byronic collar and hugh square blue buttons seem rather absurd'] is delightfully normal in manner. . . . He is certainly a sincere artist and no fool." Lewis "is not half so ferocious as you might imagine," though "rather brusque"; perhaps not so loveable as the Pounds, but "very energetic, quite normal in appearance and a good talker." At the end of October, Read had decided that "Lewis and Eliot are by far the most *important* figures. *They have strength.* . . . Pound is a curious mixture. He makes his undoubted talent less effective by his personal expression of it. He does not allow his brains frank egress."

A few months later Ben Hecht reported comically on the pair, still very much *à deux*, to a New York art magazine called *Playboy!* In "Ben Hecht on Lit'ry London"— "written to Henry Blackman Sell of the Chicago Daily News"—he tells of a conversation in Pound's Triangular room, furnished with "two purple and three orange cushions, a clavichord made by Dolmetsch and a dining table fourteen feet long and one foot wide." He mentions Pound's "earrings and his lapis lazuli overcoat buttons," his red hair, and the embarrassing fact that "he is a doting monogamist." Of Lewis he says only that he "has black hair." But Hecht is too lively to paraphrase.

Previous to the conversation proper, Mr. Lewis

had just received word that his father had died in the states. T. S. Elliot [*sic*], the poet, had also just received a cablegram announcing the death of his father. This caused Mr. Elliot to absent himself, Mr. Lewis apologizing for his seeming callousness with the fact that he had not seen his parent for some twenty years, allowed the death of his father as a strange coincidence, it coming simultaneously with the death of Mr. Elliot's father, and remained behind to assist at the merry prattle. . . .

MR. LEWIS—Do you think, Hecht, I could make any money by lecturing in America?

MR. POUND—Nonsense, Lewis. You'd be a dismal sort of failure. Unless you went in your soldier suit and—

MR. LEWIS—I would like to deliver some lectures on painting and make enough money to live on for several years. Do you think it's possible, Hecht?

MR. POUND—Absolutely no. I am the sort of person who could make a fortune at the trick. You see, I am deliciously disliked in the states and would therefore attract a crowd. If I could get a good manager to advertise me and spread broadcast the information that I will appear in blue earrings and that I own the only overcoat that has four lapis lazuli buttons I would really be an astounding success.

MR. LEWIS—If I could clean up enough cash in a year it would be just the thing I want.

MR. POUND—Hecht will tell you that you've no chance. You remember the time you spoke at Hume's [*sic*] lecture? The audience left to a man right in the midst of your eloquence. You're utterly incoherent, Lewis, as a talker, and your intelligence unfits you absolutely as a lecturer. . . . By the way, Hecht, what sort of man is Knopf?

MR. LEWIS—Is Margaret Anderson light or dark?

MR. POUND—I could bring my Dolmetsch clavichord along and deliver the lectures sitting down, or, in fact, from a recumbent position.

We have, unfortunately, only photographs and Iris Barry's description of the painting Lewis did of Pound in 1919; but the several drawings that survive from this time make a strong impression, both of the sitter and of the artist. Vorticism was of course dead; in his reminiscence of 1949, Lewis recalls that "by the time of *Pavannes*" his old friend had "grown into a sort of prickly, aloof, rebel mandarin."

The effects on each man of their association during these crucial years should be discernible in this brief history. Some have ascribed significant direct influences. Lewis, for example, made his sole excursion into abstract painting during the time of his closest contact with Pound, though Geoffrey Wagner sees Hulme as the chief influence in this. And a very great deal has been made in recent years of the impact of Vorticism on Pound's poetry. Many critics, going as far back as Jean de Bosschère in 1917,

have noticed a change to harder outlines and more contemporary interests after *Ripostes*. It has been argued that the scheme of *The Cantos* is Vorticist, and Donald Davie's recent book on Pound is subtitled "Poet as Sculptor." Yet Noel Stock, in *Poet in Exile*, informs us that "Pound himself was under the impression—in later years at any rate—that he first learned to appreciate these qualities while studying Martial and Catullus in the U.S."

The principals seem to have thought, in retrospect, mainly about their differences. Pound did, as we have seen, attest to Vorticist influence. In 1916 he wrote: "They have given me a new sense of form . . . new chords, new keys of design." And he has persisted in taking this line, disclaiming in his *Paris Review* interview of 1962, for example, any influence of Gaudier or Lewis on his writing, at the same time acknowledging that "Vorticism from my angle was a renewal of the sense of construction . . . an attempt to revive the sense of form." Most of his statements have nevertheless been uttered as disclaimers. In 1929 he wrote to a friend: "How the hell many points of agreement do you suppose there were between Joyce, Wyndham Lewis, Eliot and yours truly in 1917; or between Gaudier and Lewis in 1913 . . . ?" And in 1951 he rather plaintively asked a mutual friend "WHEN, at what date IF ever W.L. ever started thinking about ANY thing I said to him?? Unlikely before 1920, as he was then so headed wrong." And while Lewis allows in *Blasting and Bombardiering* that Pound "did succeed in giving a handful of disparate and unassimiliable people the appearance of a *Bewegung*," he too asserts that "four people more dissimilar in every respect . . . it would be difficult to find."

They protest too much. Clearly there were shared ideas—notably their beliefs in the aristocracy of art and mind, in the poverty of bourgeois values, and in the beauty of external arrangements, beliefs that paved the way for authoritarian politics. More important, I think, something of the tone and temper of one "*jeune*" rubbed off on the other, often reinforcing what was already there. The result in later life was visible in certain affinities of style, of renegade stance. One might go so far as to claim that each was the more his own man because he had been for a time *almost* the other's.

William C. Wees

SOURCE: "Ezra Pound as a Vorticist," in *Wisconsin Studies in Contemporary Literature*, Vol. VI, No. 1, Winter-Spring, 1965, pp. 56-72.

[*In the following essay, Wees analyzes Pound's role in the development of Vorticism.*]

Vorticism stands at the center of Ezra Pound's twelve-year stay in London (1908-1920), and it represents his fullest commitment to the attitudes, the activities, and the art of London's avant-garde artists. Although this commitment came during the crucial years in Pound's development as a poet and polemicist, it has yet to be fully described, and its consequences evaluated. In the following pages, then, I will examine, first, the reasons for Pound's desertion of Imagism for Vorticism; second, Pound's contribution to the formation of the Vorticist group and the publication of the Vorticists' magazine, *Blast;* third, the nature of Vorticism, itself, as it is revealed in *Blast;* fourth, Pound's personal efforts to promote and perpetuate the Vorticist movement after the publication of *Blast;* and fifth, the effect Vorticism had on Pound's theory and practice of poetry.

To keep the proper perspective on Pound's place in the Vorticist movement, we should remember that Vorticism was part of a much larger movement that was revolutionizing Western art and letters. As Pound's fellow-Vorticist, Wyndham Lewis, said, "We were not the only people with something to be proud about at that time. Europe was full of titanic stirrings and snortings—a new art coming to flower to celebrate or to announce a 'new age.' " But, Vorticism was the only movement in pre-war England to fully and enthusiastically catch the spirit of the "new age," and at that time Pound was fully and enthusiastically a Vorticist.

He had become a Vorticist while still an Imagist, though he did not "officially" break with Imagism until midsummer 1914, when he was confronted by Amy Lowell's plan to use a "democratized committee" to select poems for an Imagist anthology. Pound was certain that a committee could not uphold the high standards he believed Imagism represented: "Imagism stands, or I should like it to stand, for hard, light, clear edges," he told Amy Lowell. He could not force his standards on the group, and since he had no money to back an anthology of his own, he could only withdraw from the whole scheme, which meant withdrawing from Imagism. Pound said later that Imagism had been simply "a point on the curve of my development. . . . I moved on." By midsummer 1914 he had moved on to Vorticism; indeed, he had begun the move almost simultaneously with the publication of *Des Imagistes* in February 1914.

By that time his own standards were changing in accord with his changing poetic ambitions. He began to break the cool, decorous serenity of the Image and its "hard light, clear edges," by developing a new, more violent mode of expression. This new violence was apparent in his prose as well as his poetry. "To the present condition of things," Pound wrote in the *Egoist* in February 1914, "we have nothing to say but 'merde'. . . ." In June he announced, "We will sweep out the past century as surely as Attila swept across Europe," and in the same article: "Damn the man in the street, once and for all, damn the man in the street who is only in the street because he hasn't intelligence enough to be let in anywhere else. . . ." This new tone of belligerence and verbal violence also appeared in Pound's view of the artist. Instead of the craftsman of language, the careful observer who transforms what he sees into precise Images, the artist is a "savage" who "must live by craft and violence. His gods are violent gods."

This violence becomes part of a new Poundian persona—a combined enfant terrible and moral satirist—through which Pound speaks in such poems as "Salutation the Second," which concludes,

> Ruffle the skirts of prudes
>   speak of their knees and ankles.
> But, above all, go to practical people—

> go! jangle their door-bells!
> Say that you do no work
>   and that you will live forever, . . .

and "Pax Saturni," in which Pound sneers,

> Call this a time of peace,
> Speak well of amateur harlots,
> Speak well of distinguished procurers,
> Speak well of employers of women . . .

and "Commission," in which Pound reveals his satirical purpose by commanding his "songs" to "go like a blight upon the dullness of the world." All three poems appeared in a group called "Contemporania," which Pound published in *Poetry* (Chicago) on April 1, 1914. In October of the same year, Pound wrote to Alice Corbin Henderson, Harriet Monroe's close friend and associate on Poetry, "I wonder if *Poetry* really dares to devote a number to my new work. There'll be a *howl*. They won't like it. It's absolutely the *last* obsequies of the Victorian period. . . . It's not futurism and it's not postimpressionism, but it's work contemporary with those schools and to my mind the most significant that I have yet brought off." It was not Imagism, either, but presumably the sort of work that appeared in *Blast:* such poems as "Fratres Minores" (which even *Blast* did not dare to print without blacking out three of its lines) and the snarling, Juvenalian "Salutation the Third," which begins, "Let us deride the smugness of 'The Times':/ GUFFAW!" and goes on to attack conservative literary critics in the lines,

> You slut-bellied obstructionist,
>   You sworn foe to free speech and good let-
> ters,
> You fungus, you continuous gangrene,

and concludes,

> HERE is the taste of my BOOT,
>   CARESS it, lick off the BLACKING.

The dry, hard, Imagist decorum is gone; a totally new tone, sometimes angry and moralizing, sometimes satirical, but certainly more declamatory, more "rhetorical" than Imagist doctrine allowed, has taken over.

Pound's rejection of Amy Lowell's "democratized committee" and his development of a more violent poetic expression were less important in his turn to Vorticism than was his involvement in the activities of the avant-garde painters and sculptors of London. Here Pound discovered a reforming fervor equal to his own and new artistic forms that were far more revolutionary in painting and sculpture than Imagism was in poetry. This group, generally labeled "English Cubists" at the time, included Wyndham Lewis, Henri Gaudier-Brzeska, Jacob Epstein, Edward Wadsworth, C. R. W. Nevinson, Frederick Etchells, Jessie Etchells, Cuthbert Hamilton, William Roberts, David Bomberg, Helen Saunders and Jessie Dismorr. All of these artists were part of what Sir John Rothenstein calls "the international Cubist movement," but the work of Gaudier-Brzeska and Lewis particularly attracted Pound's attention.

In fact, Pound's admiration for Gaudier-Brzeska and Lewis was virtually unbounded. "Have just bought two statuettes from the coming sculptor, Gaudier-Brzeska," Pound wrote to William Carlos Williams in December 1913. "I like him very much," he added. After Gaudier went to the front with the French army, Pound wrote in the *New Age,* "And if the accursed Germans succeed in damaging Gaudier-Brzeska they will have done more harm to art than they have by the destruction of Rheims Cathedral. . . ." Gaudier was killed at St. Vaast on June 15, 1915, and in "Canto XVI" Pound memorialized his friend's death:

> And Henri Gaudier went to it
>   and they killed him,
> And killed a good deal of sculpture. . . .

Gaudier's white marble "hieratic head" of Pound, which Pound has with him at Brunnenburg today, is a monument to their friendship. Although Pound's enthusiasm for Lewis' work was not as spontaneous as it had been for Gaudier's, it eventually became greater. In June 1914 he told the *Egoist*'s readers that Lewis was "the most articulate voice" of the new age, and by March 1916 he was writing to John Quinn, "The vitality, the fullness of the man! . . . Lewis has got Blake scotched to a finish. He's got so much more in him than Gaudier. . . . It is not merely knowledge of technique, or skill, it is intelligence and knowledge of life. . . ."

Both Lewis and Gaudier had moved from a romantic-realist style in their earlier work to a predominately geometrical-abstract style in their work produced around 1914. Gaudier, as R. H. Wilenski has pointed out, had gone even further than Brancusi in the "geometricization" of sculptural forms, and Lewis was creating completely abstract designs based on complex relationships between light and dark shafts or bands combined with sharp-edged, geometrical blocks. An admiration of sharp, geometrical forms appears in the writings as well as the art of both men. Speaking of himself and a few other modern sculptors, Gaudier wrote in *Blast* No. 1, "We have crystallized the sphere into the cube . . . ", and elsewhere he praised "sharpness and rigidity" in art. Lewis, writing about the work of a group of "English Cubists," including himself, said, "The work of this group of artists for the most part underlines the geometrical bases and structures of life. . . . All revolutionary painting today has in common the rigid reflections of steel and stone in the spirit of the artist. . . . " In common with most of the advanced artists of the day, Lewis and Gaudier concentrated on abstract relationships of line, color, planes, and masses, and set aside any extended consideration of "subject" or "meaning" in art. Their theorizing as well as their actual work made a strong impression on Pound and, as we shall see, helped lead him out of the narrow limits of Imagism to the much broader, all-inclusive aesthetic of Vorticism.

Pound's friendship with Gaudier and Lewis, and his interest in their work, was only one way he became involved in the London art world. He also frequented the galleries and exhibitions; he was a friend of Jacob Epstein and a great admirer of his sculpture, some of which was called "Vorticist" at the time; he attended T. E. Hulme's Tuesday evening salon, where talk of the new painting and sculpture often dominated the conversation, and where

Hulme expounded many of the ideas on art he later printed in his *New Age* articles; he was a mainstay of the café-salon bohemia of London, and joined in its endless discussions of Cubism, Futurism, Expressionism, and the leading experimental artists of England and the Continent; he supported Lewis' Rebel Art Centre, the short-lived headquarters of the "English Cubists," where he gave a lecture on Vorticism; and he signed an anti-Futurist pronouncement circulated by Lewis and the Rebel Art Centre group. It is not surprising, then, to find Pound proclaiming in "Et Faim Sallir Le Loup Des Boys" in *Blast* No. 2,

> Say I believe in Lewis, spit out [sic] the later
>   Rodin,
> Say that Epstein can carve in stone,
> That Brzeska can use the chisel,
> Or Wadsworth paint. . . .

Pound makes no mention, one notices, of H. D. or Aldington; his new allegiances clearly show that he had "moved on" from Imagism. If any doubts remained, his involvement in *Blast* dispelled them.

II

When Wyndham Lewis and C. R. W. Nevinson originally conceived of *Blast* late in 1913, they intended it to be merely a magazine for promoting the new Cubist art in England. As the planning continued, however, and the date for releasing the first issue was set back from April to June 18 to June 20 to July 2, the magazine took on a special character of its own. After some feuding with Nevinson, who had given his allegiance to F. T. Marinetti and Futurism, Lewis became sole editor, though he received assistance from Edward Wadsworth and Pound (who sent out advertisements for *Blast* and provided Lewis with a long list of potential subscribers). Lewis decided to repudiate Cubism, as well as Futurism, and to establish a new movement for himself and his fellow English artists. Joined by Pound, he held a meeting that brought London's avant-garde bohemians into the planning of *Blast*. Douglas Goldring has preserved that meeting for posterity:

> The ceremony took the form of a tea party in a studio which Wyndham Lewis then occupied in Fitzroy Street. Lewis and Pound presided over it jointly, and the guests were the oddest collection of *rapins* in black hats, girls from the Slade, poets and journalists. We solemnly compiled lists of persons who should be blasted and of others who should be blessed. I have often wondered what Pound and Lewis thought of their disciples. I know what I thought of them! The proceedings terminated with a quarrel between Lewis and C. R. W. Nevinson, I fancy on the subject of Futurism.

What Pound's and Lewis' movement still lacked was a focus, or, at least, a device to distinguish it from Futurism, Cubism, and other contemporary *isms*. Here Pound made his most important contribution to the new movement and its magazine by hitting upon a symbol—the Vortex.

Pound had first used the term Vortex in a letter to William Carlos Williams in December 1913 to describe the general literary-art scene of London, but he soon applied it to the particular kind of art that Gaudier-Brzeska, Lewis and the "cubists" of the Rebel Art Centre were creating. In this more restricted context, the Vortex takes on special meanings. "You think of a whirlpool," Lewis explained to Violet Hunt. "At the heart of the whirlpool is a great silent place where all the energy is concentrated. And there at the point of concentration is The Vorticist." Pound, describing the special quality of Lewis' drawing to John Quinn, wrote, "It is every kind of whirlwind of force and emotion. Vortex. That is the right word, if I did find it myself." To the readers of the *Fortnightly Review* Pound explained that even the Image is "a VORTEX, from which, and through which, and into which, ideas are constantly rushing. In decency one can only call it a VORTEX."

The magic of a word! Once "Vortex" had been hit upon, the vague impulses of the movement could be defined in terms of a whirlpool, a whirlwind, a Vortex that unites rushing force and stillness to create a perpetually self-renewing expression of energy. Now Pound and Gaudier could write artistic pronouncements under the same title, "Vortex"; Lewis could make the mise en scène of his closet drama, *The Enemy of the Stars,* a Vortex, and give a focus to the magazine's manifesto. Now *Blast,* which in an advertisement in the *Egoist* of April 1, 1914, promised rather vaguely a "Discussion of Cubism, Futurism, Imagisme and All Vital Forms of Modern Art," could become "The Review of the Great English Vortex," and out of the London world of avant-garde art could appear a new ism, Vorticism.

With a brilliant heliotrope cover and the single word, *Blast,* in huge block letters slashing diagonally across the front and back covers, the Vorticists' magazine was intended, first of all, to make the new movement noticed. "The large type and the flaring cover are merely bright plumage," said Pound. "They are the gay petals which lure." They lured the reader to a long, loud Vorticist manifesto, to Lewis' *The Enemy of the Stars* and "Vortices and Notes," to Pound's poetry and "Vortex" essay and to another "Vortex" essay by Gaudier-Brzeska, to stories by Rebecca West and Ford Madox Ford, a review of Kandinsky's *Ueber das Geistige in der Kunst* by Wadsworth, and twenty-three half-tone reproductions of art works, all of which (except for two by Spencer Gore) could be called Vorticist. Although Lewis, who wanted to make the magazine "a battering ram that was all of one metal," felt that some of the contents were "soft and highly impure," the magazine was sufficiently unified to indicate what the Vorticists were getting at.

Drawing primarily upon the manifesto, *The Enemy of the Stars,* "Vortices and Notes," and the essays of Pound and Gaudier, one can make a fairly accurate summary of the Vorticists' position. The Vorticists consistently attack mildness, softness, compromise, nature, the nineteenth century, education, democracy, curves, soft lines, mingling colors, and what, in general, they call "Romanticism." In contrast, they admire harshness, extremes, violence, the present, machinery, and rigid, sharp, metallic forms that prevent things from moving, changing place, blending and equalizing. This doctrine is emphasized in the Vorticists' writing by innumerable images of violence,

rigidity and geometrical precision. For instance, there is the violent imagery of the manifesto's proclamation: "We only want tragedy if it can clench its side-muscles like hands on it's [sic] belly, and bring to the surface a laugh like a bomb", and the description of the characters in *The Enemy of the Stars:* "Enormous youngsters, bursting everywhere through heavy tight clothes, laboured in by dull explosive muscles. . . ." The rigid, geometrical quality of Vorticism appears in the manifesto's "blessing" of lighthouses "blazing through the frosty starlight, cutting the storm like a cake", and of the hairdresser, who "trims aimless and retrograde growths into CLEAN ARCHED SHAPES and ANGULAR PLOTS".

To reinforce their ideas and images, the Vorticists use visual effects created by special typography and layout. Most notable for its manipulation of typography is the first part of the Vorticist manifesto, where a kind of *prose libre* appears in patterns of large, heavy type carefully arranged on the large pages. In effect, the words create abstract Vorticist designs with lines and blocks of black on planes of white. Complementing the pictorial typography and increasing the visual impact of the magazine are the reproductions of Vorticist art work by Lewis, Gaudier-Brzeska, Wadsworth, Roberts, Etchells, Hamilton and Epstein. In almost every case, the designs are composed of sharply defined, geometrical patterns, and with their conflicting forms locked together by intersecting lines and planes, they suggest a frozen, Vorticist violence. *Blast* expresses visually, in its typography, layout and illustrations, the same attitudes it presents in words. With its garish color, over-sized type, and pugnacious tone, *Blast* is, in itself, a Vorticist work of art, perhaps the most successful of all Vorticist works of art.

The reception of *Blast* varied from easy, Philistine dismissal in such places as the London *Morning Post,* the New York *Times,* and Stephen Philip's *Poetry Review,* to serious, but puzzled admiration in *Poetry,* the *Little Review,* and the *Egoist.* Pound proclaimed in the second issue of *Blast:*

> OYEZ   OYEZ   OYEZ
> Throughout the length and breadth of England
> and through three continents *Blast* has been RE-
> VILED
> by all save the intelligent.
>   WHY?
> Because *Blast* alone has dared to show modernity
> its face in an honest glass.

Certainly *Blast* was widely discussed, and the Vorticists had some fleeting fame. But with the coming of war, real blasting drowned out the Vorticists, who, nevertheless, tried for a while to keep their movement alive. In March 1915, they appeared together in the London Group exhibition at the Goupil Gallery, and in June they presented their own "First Vorticist Exhibition" at the Doré Gallery. In July they issued a second *Blast,* a "War Number," thinner and tamer than the first *Blast.* Pound's contribution was limited to several poems and a brief commentary entitled "Chronicles." By this time Gaudier-Brzeska had been killed in action; Lewis was finishing his novel, *Tarr,* and preparing to go into the army. Only Pound tried to keep Vorticism going.

He kept Vorticism before the public in a series of articles: a discussion of Edward Wadsworth in the *Egoist* of August 15, 1914; an elaboration of his Rebel Art Centre talk on Vorticism for the *Fortnightly Review* of September 1, 1914; an explanation of Vorticism for the *New Age* of January 14, 1915; and a discussion of Gaudier-Brzeska in the same magazine of February 4, 1915. Pound's most important contribution to publicizing Vorticism, however, was his *Gaudier-Brzeska: A Memoir,* published in 1916 by John Lane, which brought together photographs of Gaudier's sculpture, reproductions of his drawings, and reprints of his published writings along with some of his letters written from the front and Pound's somewhat rambling text, composed of previously published essays and some new comments on Gaudier and art in general. After he had finished the Gaudier book, Pound wrote to John Quinn, "I have certainly GOT to do a Lewis book to match the Brzeska. Or perhaps a 'Vorticists' (being nine-tenths Lewis . . .)." As late as January 1917, Pound was still writing to Quinn about the projected book on Lewis, but it never appeared.

Besides acting as promoter of Vorticism, Pound became guardian of a good many Vorticist art works. After Gaudier's death, he fell heir to the "debris of Gaudier's studio," which included sculpture, sketches, paintings and pastels; before Lewis joined the Royal Artillery in March 1916, he turned over to Pound some forty-five of his drawings (with their prices indicated) and a large body of manuscript material. Pound sold several of Lewis' and Gaudier's works to John Quinn, whose interest in the Vorticists was due solely to Pound's efforts.

Continuing his work in behalf of the Vorticists, Pound got together a collection of Vorticist works, and with £ 65 from John Quinn to cover costs, he shipped it to New York in March 1916. In August he remarked in a letter to Iris Barry, "I have just rec'd four large cheques for vorticist pictures sold in America . . . and shall have to turn them over to the artists!!!!!!!!!!" A Vorticist exhibition, including work by Lewis, Gaudier, Wadsworth, Etchells, and Roberts, was held at the Penguin Club in New York during the winter of 1916-1917. At about the same time, Pound worked with the American photographer, Alvin Langdon Coburn, to create "vortographs" by means of the "vortescope," a camera-attachment designed to allow the photographer to make "any arrangement of purely abstract forms. The present machine happens to be rectilinear," Pound explained to John Quinn, "but I can make one that will do any sort of curve, quite easily." The vortographs, Pound thought, were "perhaps as interesting as Wadsworth's woodcuts, perhaps not quite as interesting." Their main value was to "upset the muckers who are already crowing about the death of vorticism."

"The Death of Vorticism" was the title of an article Pound wrote for the *Little Review* early in 1919. He had become a regular contributor to Margaret Anderson's magazine as a covert means of continuing to promote Vorticism. "My corner of the paper is *Blast,*" he wrote to Edgar Jepson, "but *Blast* covered with ice. . . . " In his article on

Vorticism, Pound argued that the movement was not dead, and for proof he pointed to a memorial exhibition of Gaudier's work, which had been held at the Leicester Gallery in May and June 1918; to the war paintings of Lewis and Roberts, both of whom had been made official war artists; and to the assignment of a "vorticist lieutenant" (Edward Wadsworth) to be in charge of naval camouflage. But Gaudier was dead; the war paintings of Lewis and Roberts were not done in the Vorticist manner, and naval camouflage is not a very stable basis for a flourishing art movement. Only a renewed effort by Lewis and his fellow Vorticist painters could have revived Vorticism, but that effort was not forthcoming.

When Wyndham Lewis returned to London after the war, he saw more clearly than Pound that the war had usurped Vorticism's *raison d'etre* by bringing into life what the Vorticists had represented in art and theory: the violence, the blasting, the destruction of the "old world." After a half-hearted attempt to publish a third *Blast* (without even including Pound), Lewis published *The Caliph's Design. Architects! Where is Your Vortex?* in 1919, which weakly echoed some of the ideas in *Blast,* but had none of the pre-war flare and noisy rebelliousness. He then joined with a group of painters, including Etchells, Roberts, Wadsworth and Jessie Dismorr from the old Vorticist group, to form "Group X," which disintegrated after one exhibition at the Mansard Gallery in March and April 1920. Vorticism had dwindled to an "X"—the eviscerated remains of an exhausted Vortex.

Pound's *Little Review* article was his last attempt to resuscitate Vorticism. In 1919 he made a trip to Paris and wrote in the summer issue of Frank Rutter's *Art and Letters,* ". . . I am out of the whirlpool, and have had a few weeks' rest from all sort of aesthetic percussions. . . . " This can be taken as Pound's farewell to the "whirlpool" of the Vortex and the "aesthetic percussions" of *Blast.* In 1920 he returned to Venice, whence he had come to London in 1908. Symbolically, he was starting over again, and this time he rejected London for Paris, and group movements for individual development.

Because Pound had been involved in the Vorticist movement from its inception, and was its only supporter during the war years, some of his contemporaries and later commentators have thought of Pound as the leading Vorticist. May Sinclair called him the "sponsor for Vorticism"; Margaret Anderson, ignoring Lewis' position as *Blast*'s editor, wrote that Pound "issued the first number of *Blast*"; Richard Aldington said that Pound, in 1914, "was busy patenting a new movement, Vorticism"; Malcolm Cowley said Pound "assembled the Vorticists"; and more recently Eustace Mullins has called Vorticism the "Poundian successor" to Imagism. Pound, however, stated plainly in a letter to Reedy's *Mirror* in 1916, "I am not the 'head of the Vorticist movement.' " The pleasure of being a Vorticist, he said, was "to find oneself at last *inter pares,*" and with some irony, he went on, "as an active and informal association it might be said that Lewis supplied the volcanic force, Brzeska the animal energy, and perhaps that I had contributed a certain Confucian calm and reserve." Obviously, Pound contributed more time, energy, and enthusiasm than that comment indicates, but what is more important, finally, is what Vorticism contributed to Pound.

III

"Roughly: What have they done for me these vorticist artists?" Pound asked rhetorically in his memoir of Gaudier-Brzeska, and answered, "They have awakened my sense of form, or they 'have given me a new sense of form,' or what you will. . . . These new men have made me see form, have made me more conscious of the appearance of the sky where it juts down between houses, of the bright pattern of sunlight which the bath water throws up on the ceiling, of the great 'V's' of light that dart through the chinks over the curtain rings, all these are new chords, new keys of design." Elsewhere Pound said that most people do not really look at things, but that he had "on occasion seen more than was meant for me, or even, in the case of Gaudier's sculpture and Wyndham Lewis' drawings back in 1911 to 1914 more than some others did." To see more or to see in a different way was what Pound gained as a Vorticist, and this new way of seeing or new sense of form came to him through the visual arts.

Pound's one clearly Vorticist work, the poem "Dogmatic Statement on the Game and Play of Chess (Theme for a Series of Pictures)" in *Blast* No. 2, "shows the effect of modern abstract art," Pound has said. The poem, like a Vorticist painting, is an abstract composition based on line, color, and pattern; it also presents a Vortex of violent energy held under control by the rigid regularity of the chess board. The chessmen hit the board "in strong 'L's' of colour":

> Reaching and striking in angles,
>   holding lines in one colour.
> The board is alive with light. . . .

The moves of the chessmen "break and reform the pattern," working toward a climax:

> Whirl, centripetal, mate, King down in the vortex:
> Clash, leaping bands, straight strips of hard colour,
> Blocked lights working in, escapes, renewing of
>   contes[t.]

The abstract patterns of line and color with interstices of light and space, and the in-turning, self-perpetuating energy at the end (the contest is renewed), make this an interesting Vorticist poem-picture. Pound did not, however, develop these techniques into a full body of Vorticist poetry, but, as we shall see, the "new sense of form" that the Vorticists gave him and that this poem illustrates, did become an important part of Pound's poetics.

The point to be stressed is that the "new form" Pound discovered in his fellow Vorticists' work was visual form. Pound called it "planes in relation" and to illustrate it he wrote,

> The pine-tree in mist upon the far hill
> looks like a fragment of Japanese armour.
> The beauty of this pine-tree in the mist

is not caused by its resemblance to the plates of the armour.

> The armour, if it be beautiful at all, is not beautiful because of its resemblance to the pine in the mist.

> In either case the beauty, in so far as it is beauty of form, is the result of "planes in relation."

> The tree and the armour are beautiful because their diverse planes overlie in a certain manner.

Through his strong sense of visual form, Pound could even bring Imagism onto a common ground with Vorticism. Imagism, Pound argued in his *Fortnightly* article on Vorticism, is poetry "where painting or sculpture seems as if it were 'just coming over into speech,' " and in so far as a poem is Imagist, it "falls in with the new pictures and the new sculpture."

In turning to the visual arts and visual form for his aesthetic touchstones, Pound was simply following out the logical consequences of his earlier, Imagist doctrine, which, as Joseph Frank has shown, rested upon a spatial rather than a temporal concept of poetry. Such a concept encouraged Pound to find in the spatial (i.e., visual) arts his basic sense of form. He was also responding to a general tendency of the times, which Margaret Anderson described by adapting Pater's famous dictum to the new conditions: "All the arts were striving to approach the condition of painting." Certainly Vorticism fits this description with its emphasis on the visual in the typography of the Vorticist manifesto, in *The Enemy of the Stars,* which, Lewis said, was written to show how the "visual revolution" could be incorporated into writing prose, and in Pound's "Game and Play of Chess." By looking at Vorticist sculpture and painting, Pound was able to develop a sense of visual form that his own inclinations and the tendency of the times were urging him towards.

He did not, however, construct a comprehensive aesthetic based on visual or spatial form, even to the extent that Wyndham Lewis did in *Time and Western Man,* nor did he explore the possibilities of the visual use of words in poetry as did Apollinaire in his "calligrammes" or the Futurists in their "parole in libertà" poems. Instead, Pound applied his new feeling for visual form to the study of the Chinese written character. His beginning work on Fenollosa's manuscripts coincided with his transition from Imagism to Vorticism, and both involved understanding things in a new, visual way. The "pictorial elements" of a single Chinese character come from the arrangement of the radicals, which are extremely simplified abstract pictures of natural forms. A series of characters, said Fenollosa, is like "a continuous moving picture," and poetry composed in characters "speaks at once with the vividness of painting, and with the mobility of sounds." It is exactly this emphasis on the visual basis of communication that Pound also felt in the Vorticists' abstract art.

In the *Cantos,* Chinese characters serve as abstract illustrations for the written text, and one of Pound's favorite characters, chung ("middle" or "axis" or "pivot"), is, in effect, the equivalent of the Vortex, not only in meaning, but pictorially as well. The effect of visual form on the

Cantos is not limited to the presence of Chinese characters, however. The innumerable disparate elements that make up the *Cantos* can be thought of as "planes in relation," as "diverse planes" that, like fragments of Japanese armor, "overlie in a certain manner," and are united visually, or spatially, in the same manner as a Lewis painting or a Gaudier carving. To the extent that Vorticism was responsible for this concept of form in Pound's work, it had a profound impact on all his later poetry.

Vorticism came at the crucial point in Pound's development as a poet. "The difference in style between a poem by Pound written in 1907 and one written in 1917," Peter Russell points out, "is the easiest thing in the world to spot, but if one compares a Canto written in 1920 with one written in 1945, a gap of 25 years, it is not possible to observe any change in style." Another critic calls Pound's poetry of 1913-1915 the "breakthrough in modern poetry." To what extent Pound's change in style and the consequent "breakthrough" would have occurred had there been no Vorticist movement, one cannot say. But the fact that Pound not only left Imagism to join Vorticism, but also worked hard to keep the Vorticist movement alive after its initial burst of glory in *Blast* No. 1, indicates that in Vorticism he felt the kind of inspiration he needed at that time. In the Vorticists' art he found not only a new way of seeing things, but, as the Cantos have proven, a new way of saying things, as well.

William C. Lipke and Bernard W. Rozran

SOURCE: "Ezra Pound and Vorticism: A Polite Blast," in *Wisconsin Studies in Contemporary Literature,* Vol. VII, No. 2, Summer, 1966, pp. 201-10.

[*In the following essay, Lipke and Rozran criticize William Wees's definition of Vorticism.*]

I

In *Who's Who* (London) for the years 1915 through 1918, Ezra Pound contributed the following entry: "EZRA POUND, M.A. vorticist . . . Recreations: fencing, tennis, searching the Times for evidences of almost incredible stupidity." William C. Wees, in an article entitled "Ezra Pound as a Vorticist," described Pound's brief career as a vorticist, his influence on the movement, and its influence on him. Mr. Wees's presentation of the facts of Pound's participation in the vorticist movement is welcome, but Pound's affiliation with vorticism might be clarified if vorticism itself were more clearly understood. As Mr. Wees indicates, vorticism was primarily a movement in the visual arts. The following remarks are aimed not at disputing Mr. Wees's interpretation of the facts of the movement, but at suggesting a more precise meaning of vorticism.

What are the characteristics of vorticism as a visual style? If we examine Mr. Wees's article we have little to go on. He cites, for instance, the first issue of the vorticist magazine *Blast* and notes that all of the illustrations "(except for two by Spencer Gore) could be called Vorticist." We are not told *why* they are "Vorticist," or on what basis we can call *any* work of art "Vorticist." Further, Mr. Wees

presents some suggestions when he refers to Pound's poem "Dogmatic Statement" as being *like* a vorticist painting which "is an abstract composition based on line, color, and pattern." This description could apply to the work of Kandinsky or Picasso—in fact to most of the paintings created between 1907 and 1915 by the avant-garde.

While it is true that Pound coined the term in late 1913, the works executed by the vorticist artist prior to this date can be seen as a logical development of the non-representational vorticist style *labeled* by Pound. T. E. Hulme, writing on "Modern Art" in the *New Age* in 1914, attempted to unravel the complex styles practiced by the more avant-garde English artists since 1905. All of these works were, according to Hulme, part of the "modern movement." This "modern movement" in English painting was characterized by three stylistic phases: post-impressionism, analytical cubism (which Hulme considered the basis of the abstract phase of vorticism), and finally, a "new constructive geometric art" which he found best typified in the work of David Bomberg and Jacob Epstein. This last phase of the "modern movement" was distinct from vorticism, Hulme claimed, because it was more original and less derivative than the vorticist work.

What was the "history" of vorticism and what were the styles within the developing movement? The cubist and futurist inspired experiments of a group of English painters and sculptors executed between 1911 and 1920 are part of a larger and more comprehensive view of the vorticist movement. Three stylistic phases can be distinguished in the decade of vorticism, and all of them can be seen in the illustrations to the first issue of *Blast*. The first phase could be called "primitive cubism." Much of the stimulus of the first phase derives from certain drawings of the cubists and futurists. There are certain works of Picasso and Herbin where emphasis upon the hard-edged line tends to create planes of form rather than a more naturalistic delineation of the object's contour line. This phase is, nevertheless, representational and is inspired primarily by the rediscovery of "primitive sculpture." A related source for this first phase can be found in the vorticists' admiration of Jacob Epstein's growing collection of primitive sculpture. The second phase of vorticism, the style to which I think Hulme was referring when he used the term "analytical cubism," is in fact a rather naïve interpretation of what the vorticists *thought* analytical cubism intended to present. Its characteristics are the stick figures applied to the surface of the canvas, figures which are reminiscent of certain paintings of Picabia and Severini executed between 1910 and 1912. Hulme claimed that this vorticist style was distinguishable from its source ("analytical cubism") in that the English artists made use of mechanical forms. While the first phase, "primitive cubism," dates from as early as 1909 and continues to 1914, the second phase of the vorticist style exists between 1912 and 1915. It appears in some of the war drawings and paintings of the vorticists and reappears after the war. The third phase was essentially less derivative and was non-representational. Growing in part out of the 1913 experiments done at Roger Fry's Omega Workshops, it was the logical termination of experimenting with the previous two phases. This style became fully developed in 1914 and 1915 and reappeared in late 1919 and 1920. It is distinct from other work done in England or on the continent at the time. Angular lines expanding sequentially rather than logically are its characteristics. The scheme is usually worked around an unconventional "unbalanced" composition based on the contrast between open volumes and tightly enclosed spaces. This phase of vorticism is thus distinct from futurism in its repudiation of the painterly technique, its insistence upon the non-figurative motif, and its avoidance of the principle of simultaneous vision.

These stylistic considerations indicate the inaccuracy of some of Mr. Wees's examples of visual vorticism. He claims that "*Blast* is in itself, a Vorticist work of art, perhaps the most successful of all Vorticist works of art," because of its "garish color, over-sized type, and pugnacious tone." Similarly, it is difficult to conceive of the vorticist manifesto which appeared in the first issue of *Blast* as suggesting any of the stylistic phases of vorticism which we have outlined. The manifesto, according to Mr. Wees is "a kind of *prose libre* . . . in patterns of large, heavy type carefully arranged on the large pages. In effect, the words create abstract Vorticist designs with lines and blocks of black on planes of white." IT IS DIFFICULT TO IMAGINE ANY SENTENCE AS AN EXAMPLE OF THE VORTICIST STYLE, or any visual style in painting. Such an interpretation may be tempting, but it hardly does justice to vorticist artists or to the styles they had created.

Since he has not accurately identified visual vorticism, it is surprising that Mr. Wees should be prepared to claim that "Vorticism was the only movement in pre-war England to fully and enthusiastically catch the spirit of the 'new age.'" Hulme and his "constructive-geometricists," Fry and his Omega Workshops, "The British Fauves," and others also enthusiastically caught the spirit and figure very importantly in this decade of British art. It is an oversimplification to state that Ezra Pound was the only person who kept vorticism alive during the war. While he was one of the key figures who helped to sell much of the vorticists' work to the American patron John Quinn, the stimulus for pushing the work of William Roberts, Edward Wadsworth, Jessica Dismorr, and Helen Saunders came from Wyndham Lewis. It was Lewis, not Pound, who had the idea of staging the vorticist show at the Penguin Club in New York, for Pound originally intended Quinn to give a large show of Lewis's works. Horace Brodzky, secretary of the Penguin Club at that time and an earlier pre-war friend of the vorticists, also was instrumental in persuading Quinn to stage a vorticist exhibition.

What then was Pound's contribution to vorticism as a movement in the visual arts? Clearly, Mr. Wees is correct in asserting the importance of the label "vorticism" which was Pound's coinage. But it is certain that the style existed, that the "vortex" was already being depicted *before* the name was attached to "le mouvement." Pound's contribution of the label and his concommitant insistence upon the value of non-representational painting may have helped to push the vorticist artists from the more representational derivative experiments to the non-representational stage of vorticism. One must not forget, however, that the aesthetic theories of Kandinsky, Worringer, and Hulme also

figured as sources for the non-representational phase of vorticism. Perhaps Pound's greatest achievement in the history of vorticism as a visual movement was the conversion of the successful photographer, Alvin Langdon Coburn, to this abstract third phase of vorticism. For while vorticism as a movement in the visual arts has yet to be appreciated, Coburn's vortographs have long been recognized by historians of photography as the first abstract photographs preceding the dadaist photographic experiments of Christian Schad, Man Ray, and Moholy-Nagy. But what did vorticism do for Pound, and can we speak of a "vorticist poetry"?

II

To manipulate a poet's development by progressing him from "ism" to "ism" neglects a simple truth: the source for establishing this development in his poems. The biographical history of Ezra Pound's London years prior to World War I includes his affiliation with the Poet's Club, as well as afternoons with Ford Madox Hueffer and evenings with Yeats, and such influences may be looked to legitimately as the birthplace of the changes in tone, subject matter, word choice, metrics, and visual arrangement of phrases and lines—all facets that emerged in those poems Pound classified as experiments "in building the new art of metrics and of words." To examine carefully the occurrence and contents of these "experiment" poems within the corpus of Pound's poems published after *Ripostes* will focus a critical aspect on evidence from which to justifiably conclude that the poet had (or had not) "moved on."

In the case of early Pound the above approach is essential, for otherwise demonstrable distinctions between "Imagist" and "Vorticist" are blurred or ignored, with the result that a useful descriptive "rubric" is made into an inappropriate label. Whereas Pound's "Imagist" phase has been told and retold, and articles on his "Vorticism" begin to proliferate, the comments to follow intend rather to provoke some questions as to the accuracy of certain boundaries, the validity of existing special categories.

In August 1912, Pound accepted Harriet Monroe's request that he assume the duties of "foreign correspondent" for *Poetry: A Magazine of Verse*. In subsequent contributions to *Poetry* there is a tone of irreverence, sharp and caustic, and in "Salutation" and "Salutation the Second," Pound modulates neither word choice nor meters for the delicate or decorous of the Chicago audience; instead he proclaims his intent to "rejuvenate things." It is language of bombast, of insult; the brazen, haughty tones of sarcasm later to explode on the pages of *Blast*—forceful, vivid language, devoid of rhyme or set meter; *vers libre* close to an everyday speech, into which comes the occasional vulgarity, the occasional pornographic allusion.

These few selections from "Contemporania" have the multitude of characteristics all too frequently delegated only to Pound's later "Vorticist" phase. In fact, this voice of the polemical satirist is clearly one aspect of 1912-1913 poems which, at the same time, contain many examples of the "dry, hard Imagist decorum." Even more surprising, Pound was involved in still another direction, which will be dealt with later on.

Mr. Wees contends that by February 1914 with the publication of *Des Imagistes,* Ezra Pound had "moved on to Vorticism, . . . and its 'hard light, clear edges,' by developing a new, more violent mode of expression." Several comments by Mr. Wees do aid one to construct the Pound milieu, especially after the formal announcement of Vorticism. Unfortunately for the strength of Mr. Wees's presentation, he cites certain poems as evidence of "violence that become part of a new Poundian personae—a combined enfant terrible and moral satirist." Namely: "Salutation the Second" and "Pax Saturni." These two poems were not published in *Poetry* "on April 1, 1914," as Mr. Wees contends, but one year earlier. How then can we accept Mr. Wees's assumption that the contents of these two poems, along with "Commission," indicate that "by midsummer 1914 he [Pound] had moved on to Vorticism"? Surely the mistake in dating would be insignificant, except for an essential point that in the spring of 1913 Pound is claimed by the numerous recorders of "Imagism" as its staunch supporter, having printed in the March 1913 issue of *Poetry* his oft-quoted "A Few Don'ts by an Imagist." In fact, several of the other poems in "Contemporania" (e.g. "The Garret") indicate Pound's continued experimenting with clearly Imagist potentialities. Since those separate harsher qualities claimed by Wees to delineate Pound's "new" Vorticist phase are actually poems undisputedly Imagist, is one to assume that by spring of 1913 Pound was both Imagist and Vorticist? The question becomes ludicrous when one recalls that the first proclamation of "A Great English Vortex" in *Blast* No. 1 did not announce "Vorticism" until June 1914. That "Salutation the Third" in *Blast* No. 1 repeats this "Juvenalian snarling," only enforces this writer's contention that Pound's "Vorticism" consists of other factors. First, "Salutation the Third" originally was intended as a part of the earlier "Contemporania" series of April 1913, thereby contradicting Mr. Wees's point that this poem illustrates "a totally new tone, . . . more declamatory . . . [the] development of a more violent poetic expression." Pound's polemical declamations are, then, one aspect of his early poems; but if Vorticism is to represent some "new" aspect, one must look elsewhere. In fact, one needs to look again at "Contemporania," for in that selection the last poem indicates a form of experiment excitingly original and more visually operative: "In a Station of the Metro"—the two-line "hokku" familiar to the casual reader and to the Pound devotee. And yet how curious that its printed *form*—the word arrangement—as it appears in *Poetry* for April 1913 has nowhere been repeated. Especially when the directions for spacing are in a letter to Harriet Monroe: "In the METRO hokku, I was careful, I think to indicate spaces between the rhythmic units, and I want them observed." The spacings were observed and the poem appears:

IN A STATION OF THE METRO

> The apparition   of these faces   in the crowd:
> Petals   on a wet, black   bough.

How interesting to consider these "spaces between rhythmic units" and to recall the third "rule" of the Imagistes: "3. As regards rhythm, to compose in sequence of the musical phrase, not in the sequence of a metronome." "Metro" was not a single instance of experimenting with this emphasis on the visual arrangement of phrases and lines. One section of "The Garret" presents an "image" as clear, hard, and precise as any by Hulme or H. D., but which is constructed visually as well:

> Dawn enters with little feet
>   like a gilded Pavlova.

Pound's explanation for the visual emphasis indicates his concern for precise effect: "I'm deluded enough to think there is a rhythmic system in the d————— stuff, and I believe I was careful to type it as I wanted it written, i.e. as to line ends and breaking and capitals. Certainly I want the line you give, written just as it is."

A special consideration for rhythm accomplished by selective spacing between words and phrases: precisely the aspect of a unity possible between musical harmony and the harmony of design; the possibility of a visual design in a poem to complement the avant-garde geometric school of English "Cubists." Here was an experiment in the "paradigms of form," for in "METRO" the superposition technique of hokku presents in its one, unified image "an intellectual and emotional complex in an instant of time." Second, "METRO" reflects Pound's interest in the intriguing arrangements of colors and mass in Japanese prints, and the use of just these elements in paintings by a fellow expatriate, James McNeill Whistler. This ever-present awareness and appreciation for dynamic intensities in painting and sculpture of the avant-garde began to be recorded, as in "Les Millwins," by mid 1913:

> The mauve and greenish souls of the
>   little Millwins
> Were seen lying along the upper seats
> Like so many unused boas
>
> ————————
>
> With arms exalted, with Fore-arms
> Crossed in the great futuristic X's,
>   the art students
> Exalted.

The bright vibrance of Fauve colors, as well as suggestion for a pictorial composition in diagonals, this section of the poem sketches a design that thematically foreshadows the later "Dogmatic Statement on the Games and Play of Chess (Theme for a Series of Pictures)" in *Blast* No. 2 (1915), with its "strong L's of colour" which "break and reform the pattern." Why not believe the analysis by Pound himself? The Game of Chess poem shows the effect of modern abstract art, but Vorticism from my angle was a renewal of the sense of construction . . . was an attempt to revive the sense of form.

Pound's enthusiastic response to the geometric sculpture of Henri Gaudier-Brzeska and Jacob Epstein, and to the designs of Wyndham Lewis and Edward Wadsworth—this fact along with his translations from the Fenollosa manuscripts add to the rare richness of his imagination's sources towards the end of 1913.

A magnificent variety of techniques and subject matters, of tones, meters and verse theories were continually exercised, criticized, modulated, even fused, as Pound sought by experiments in verse to "teach the American poet that poetry is an *art,* an art with a technique, with media, an art that must be in constant flux, a constant change of manner, if it is to live." In the multiplicity of his interests, capabilities, affiliations, preferences and compositions, one finds a man dedicated to his craft; if this multiplicity is to be separated into neat distinctions, then facts must be accurate and the view clear before attaching to Ezra Pound some " 'appropriate' ism."

III

Perhaps the influence of vorticism on Pound should be sought not in the poet's style but in his attitude. Babette Deutsch noted in 1917 that Pound was "a modern of moderns, whose credo it is that a study of comparative literature of so many epochs and races is essential to that keen critical faculty which is part of the artist's equipment." Pound is a vorticist, Miss Deutsch claimed, "from whom and through whom and into whom ideas are constantly rushing." Just as Gaudier-Brzeska's "Vortex" was written to show that the sculptor now stood at the center of artistic endeavors of the last two thousand years, and his work paraphrased that of Rodin, Archipenko, Archaic Greek, and Pre-Columbian sculpture; so Ezra Pound's vorticism can be seen in his *approach* to poetry, in his drawing upon the Chinese, the work of Guido Cavalcanti, the ballads of Provence, and the classical Noh drama. Like Gaudier, Pound preferred a paraphrase rather than a literal translation of his sources. It was an attitude which Pound cultivated at this time to give his work a greater "adaptability of metre to mood," as T. S. Eliot phrased it. Vorticism as a visual movement was sustained through the efforts of the poet, but Pound's own vorticism is as elusive to define as Rilke's "impressionism." For as Wellek and Warren have noted:

> Only when we have evolved a successful system of terms for the analysis of literary works of art can we delimit literary periods, not as metaphysical entities dominated by a "time spirit." Having established such outlines of strictly literary evolution, we then can ask the question whether this evolution is, in some way, similar to the similarly established evolution of the other arts. The answer will be, as we can see, not a flat "yes" or "no." It will take the form of an intricate pattern of coincidence and divergences rather than parallel lines.

William C. Wees

SOURCE: "Pound's Vorticism: Some New Evidence and Further Comments," in *Wisconsin Studies in Contemporary Literature,* Vol. VII, No. 2, Summer, 1966, pp. 211-16.

[*In the following essay, Wees debates Lipke and Rozran's critique of his definition of Vorticism.*]

As late as 1956 Ezra Pound was still trying to make people understand what Vorticism was. In a letter dated November 13, 1956, written to the English artist Gladys Hynes, Pound wrote:

> W[yndham] L[ewis] certainly made vorticism.
> To him alone we owe the existence of BLAST.

It is true that he started by wanting a forum for the several ACTIVE varieties of CONTEMPORARY art/ cub/ expressionist/ post-imp etc.

BUT in conversation with E. P. there emerged the idea of defining what WE wanted/ & having a name for it.

Ultimately Gaudier for sculpture, E. P. for poetry, and W. L., the main mover, set down their personal requirements.

I dont know that the ten signers of the manifesto did more than add signatures to oblige.

I cannot recall that [William] Roberts or anyone else contributed to the ideology.

Bobbie [Roberts] was regarded as a whim of W. L.'s. Only verbal manifestation recorded in the oral tradition is that Yakob [Epstein] tried to overawe him Bobbie with question:

"Well, Bobbie, how's vorticism?"

and Mr. Roberts replied: "It's buddin'."

Apart from Gaudier's two "Vortices," all the stimulating criticism of specifically the visual arts came from W. L.

chiefly stating what he found wanting in the continental schools. An individualist and national movement.

As what H. D. termed the "Hippopoetess," Miss Lowell was trying to break down the definition of Imagism by omitting the most vital proposition in the original definition, it was opportune to get another label for vitality in the arts.

BUT W. L. was certainly in charge of the visual arts with Gaudier partly dissenting and partly hunting for something we were agreed on.

I would like to draw upon this brief, general characterization of Vorticism in commenting on what seem to be basically different assumptions underlying the essay written by William C. Lipke and Bernard W. Rozran and the essay they choose to blast politely.

By emphasizing the first person plural—"defining what WE wanted"—Pound touches upon one of the basic assumptions in my first essay: that Vorticism was a group movement. It seemed to me that Vorticism should be approached in the spirit of Pound's definition of a "school" and an "art movement": "A school exists when two or three young men agree, more or less, to call certain things good. . . ." "The term 'art movement' usually refers to something immobile. It refers to a point or an intersection or a declaration of conclusions arrived at." I assumed, in other words, that Vorticism was the group effort of several young artists, that it represented a "point" or "intersection" of the sort Pound describes, and that *Blast* was its "declaration of conclusions arrived at," as well as an illustration of just what sort of art—both literary and visual—those conclusions led to. Lipke and Rozran, on the other hand, think of Vorticism as simply a "visual style."

Furthermore, when Pound points out that although Vorticism began as a "forum" for painting, it eventually became a meeting point for sculpture, painting, and poetry, he is confirming another assumption underlying my first essay: that Vorticism was a movement for the literary, as well as the visual and plastic arts. Pound wrote in his memoir of Gaudier-Brzeska, "We wished a designation that would be equally applicable to a certain basis for all the arts. Obviously you cannot have 'cubist' poetry or 'imagist' painting." Presumably Pound believed you *could* have Vorticist poetry and Vorticist painting. He remarked in his *Fortnightly* article Vorticism, "What I have said for one Vorticist art can be transposed for another Vorticist art." Wyndham Lewis agreed that Vorticism "affected equally the images which issued from its visual inspiration, and likewise the rather less evident literary sources of its ebullience." I assumed, then, that Vorticism and *Blast* reflected an attempt to establish, in Pound's phrase, "the common ground of the arts." Lipke and Rozran do not seem to be willing to grant this point: hence their refusal to entertain the notion that typography, page layout, prose diction, painting, sculpture, and poetry can be talked about in the same terms.

By assuming that Vorticism was a *movement* that sought out "the common ground of the arts," I was able to argue that Pound contributed certain things to the movement and gained certain things from it. But Lipke and Rozran call into question any meaningful relationship between Pound and Vorticism. Pound did not paint, and so could not express the Vorticist "visual style," and it is extremely doubtful that he "helped to push" the Vorticist painters "to the non-representational stage of vorticism." If anything, it was the other way around: the Vorticist art of Lewis, Wadsworth, and the others helped Pound develop his sense of abstract form. Since Pound did not contribute to Vorticist "visual style" either as artist or theorist, then by the logic of Lipke's and Rozran's argument, Pound was not a Vorticist.

In fact, only by shifting from the visual arts to poetry can Lipke and Rozran find a way of discussing Pound at any length. But this very shift emphasizes a division between the visual arts and Pound's literary interests, while it seemed to me that Pound was drawn to Vorticism for the very reason that it helped him draw upon the visual arts to develop his own poetic theory and practice.

Since I assumed that one could describe the nature of Vorticism in fairly specific terms, I was able to talk in fairly specific terms about the place Vorticism held in Pound's attitudes, activities, and poetic development at the time. Lipke and Rozran, on the other hand, say, "Pound's vorticism can be seen in his *approach* to poetry, in his drawing upon the Chinese, the work of Guido Cavalcanti, the ballads of Provence, and the classical Noh drama." If this is true, then the term "Vorticism" stands for virtually everything Pound was interested in at the time, and consequently it can no longer be used to describe one facet of Pound's many-faceted career in London.

Because our assumptions and conclusions are so far apart—even contradictory in places—I see little point in attempting a point-by-point rebuttal. However, there are a few divergences of fact and opinion that call for brief comment.

1. Lipke and Rozran are wrong when they say that my essay offers no "basis" for calling a work of art "Vorticist." A summary of the Vorticists' general doctrine appears [in Wees's essay, excerpted above] and a specific characterization of the Vorticist style of art appears [in Wees's essay above]: "designs . . . composed of sharply defined geometrical patterns . . . conflicting forms locked together by intersecting lines and planes [suggesting] a frozen, Vorticist violence." Lipke and Rozran may, if they wish, designate three styles produced over a ten year period as "Vorticist," but they do not prove that theirs is a better way of defining Vorticist style—it is simply a different way. As a matter of fact, it even differs from the way Lipke, himself, in an earlier essay in the *Arts Review* defined Vorticism. In that essay Lipke said, "Vorticism can be defined as an attitude of English literary and visual artists based in part on a subtle blend of futurist cant about machinery, Pound's belief in the efficacy of the 'primary pigment,' and Kandinsky's philosophy of aesthetics." As for Vorticist "visual style": only the work of the "second phase," says Lipke, exhibits what can be "properly called 'Vorticist style'. . . . " In the light of these comments by Lipke, one is not likely to feel that Lipke's and Rozran's present definition of Vorticism is definitive.

2. I do not claim, as Lipke and Rozran seem to think, that Pound's Imagist and Vorticist phases were mutually exclusive and followed in absolute chronological order. In fact, my whole argument about Pound's shift from Imagism to Vorticism is distorted in Lipke's and Rozran's essay, as anyone who looks back at . . . my first essay will see. For instance, in the sentence, "Mr. Wees contends that by February 1914 with the publication of *Des Imagistes,* Ezra Pound had 'moved on to Vorticism,' . . . and its 'hard light, clear edges,' by developing a new, more violent mode of expression," Lipke and Rozran make four mistakes. (1) I said Pound had begun to move on to Vorticism, not had moved on, by February 1914. (2) I said Pound had begun to move "almost simultaneously with the publication of *Des Imagistes,*" which means not "as exhibited by" *Des Imagistes* (as Lipke's and Rozran's use of the word "with" would imply), but "at the time of." (3) The phrase "hard light, clear edges" is applied by me, as it was by Pound, to Imagism, not Vorticism—and it is used to make exactly the same point Pound makes in his passage on Amy Lowell in the letter to Gladys Hynes. (4) I do not argue that Pound's "developing a new, more violent mode of expression" made him a Vorticist, but that it was one of the indications of a frame of mind that would only get its full expression in the iconoclasm of *Blast.*

3. "Salutation the Second" and "Pax Saturni" were indeed published in 1913, not 1914, and I am glad someone spotted a typographical error that slipped past me in both typescript and proofs. However, my argument is not damaged, since my point was to show that *before* Vorticism came on the scene, Pound had begun to write outside the Imagist mode, and that one reason he became a Vorticist was to have a different, non-Imagist context for his non-Imagist poetry.

4. And finally, one minor point of fact: Pound was not as instrumental in producing vortographs as his letter to

John Quinn had led me—and Lipke and Rozran—to believe. According to Alvin Langdon Coburn, with whom I talked last summer, the original idea for making abstract photographs and the actual means of producing them (photographing reflected images in mirrors joined at varying angles) came from Coburn. Pound simply encouraged Coburn to work on abstract photographs and suggested he call them "vortographs." Pound, in fact, did not rate vortographs very high. "Vortography stands below the other vorticist arts," he wrote in a preface to the catalogue for Coburn's exhibition of vortographs in 1917, "in that it is an art of the eye, not of the eye and hand together." Damning with faint praise, Pound wrote of one of the vortographs, "It is an excellent arrangement of shapes and more interesting than most of the works of Picabia or of the bad imitators of Lewis."

If there is more to be said on the subject of Pound and Vorticism, I think it lies in the direction suggested by the following quotations from Pound's later writing: "If I am introducing anybody to Kulchur, let 'em take the two phases, the nineteen teens, Gaudier, Wyndham L. and I as we were in Blast, and the next phase, the 1920's." "And that [Vorticist] manifesto was the best we could then do toward assertin what has now become known to the world, or at least to the European continent as the crisis OF the system." *Blast* was a "harbinger," a sign that "SOMETHING was going on, . . . the end of the materialist Era/the end of that particularly dirty Anschauung." Perhaps this is not Vorticism as it was, but as Pound wished it had been. Perhaps it is sheer coincidence that one of Pound's favorite Chinese characters in the later cantos, *chung* ("middle," "axis," "pivot,"), bears a strong resemblance, both pictorially and intellectually—one might say "culturally"—to the Vortex. . . .

At least, there can be no doubt that for Pound Vorticism has become an aesthetic not limited to art, an artistic frame of reference on which to build the economics, politics, and general view of "kulchur" we find in the later essays and cantos. Until the consequences of that frame of reference have been fully explored, we will not have exhausted the subject of Ezra Pound as a Vorticist.

VORTICIST WRITING

Ezra Pound

SOURCE: "Vorticism," in *Fortnightly Review,* Vol. XCVI, July-December, 1914, pp. 461-71.

[*In the following excerpt, Pound explains Vorticist poetry.*]

"It is no more ridiculous that a person should receive or convey an emotion by means of an arrangement of shapes, or planes, or colours, than that they should receive or convey such emotion by an arrangement of musical notes."

I suppose this proposition is self-evident. Whistler said as much, some years ago, and Pater proclaimed that "All arts approach the conditions of music."

Whenever I say this I am greeted with a storm of "Yes, but. . . . " "But why isn't this art futurism?" "Why isn't?" "Why don't?" and above all: "What, in Heaven's name, has it got to do with your Imagiste poetry?"

Let me explain at leisure, and in nice, orderly, old-fashioned prose.

We are all futurists to the extent of believing with Guillaume Appollonaire that "On ne peut pas porter *partout* avec soi le cadavre de son père." But "futurism," when it gets into art, is, for the most part, a descendant of impressionism. It is a sort of accelerated impressionism.

There is another artistic descent *viâ* Picasso and Kandinsky; *viâ* cubism and expressionism. One does not complain of neoimpression or of accelerated impressionism and "simultaneity," but one is not wholly satisfied by them. One has perhaps other needs.

It is very difficult to make generalities about three arts at once. I shall be, perhaps, more lucid if I give, briefly, the history of the vorticist art with which I am most intimately connected, that is to say, vorticist poetry. Vorticism has been announced as including such and such painting and sculpture and "Imagisme" in verse. I shall explain "Imagisme," and then proceed to show its inner relation to certain modern paintings and sculpture.

Imagisme, in so far as it has been known at all, has been known chiefly as a stylistic movement, as a movement of criticism rather than of creation. This is natural, for, despite all possible celerity of publication, the public is always, and of necessity, some years behind the artists' actual thought. Nearly anyone is ready to accept "Imagisme" as a department of poetry, just as one accepts "lyricism" as a department of poetry.

There is a sort of poetry where music, sheer melody, seems as if it were just bursting into speech.

There is another sort of poetry where painting or sculpture seems as if it were "just coming over into speech."

The first sort of poetry has long been called "lyric." One is accustomed to distinguish easily between "lyric" and "epic" and "didactic." One is capable of finding the "lyric" passages in a drama or in a long poem not otherwise "lyric." This division is in the grammars and school books, and one has been brought up to it.

The other sort of poetry is as old as the lyric and as honourable, but, until recently, no one had named it. Ibycus and Liu Ch'e presented the "Image." Dante is a great poet by reason of this faculty, and Milton is a wind-bag because of his lack of it. The "image" is the furthest possible remove from rhetoric. Rhetoric is the art of dressing up some unimportant matter so as to fool the audience for the time being. So much for the general category. Even Aristotle distinguishes between rhetoric, "which is persuasion," and the analytical examination of truth. As a "critical" movement, the "Imagisme" of 1912 to '14 set out "to bring poetry up to the level of prose." No one is so quixotic as to believe that contemporary poetry holds any such position. . . . Stendhal formulated the need in his *De L'Amour:*—

"La poésie avec ses comparaisons obligées, sa mythologie que ne croit pas le poète, sa dignité de style à la Louis XIV, et tout l'attirail de ses ornements appelé poétique, est bien au dessous de la prose dès qu'il s'agit de donner une idée claire et précise des mouvements du cœur, or dans ce genre on n'émeut que par la clarté."

Flaubert and De Maupassant lifted prose to the rank of a finer art, and one has no patience with contemporary poets who escape from all the difficulties of the infinitely difficult art of good prose by pouring themselves into loose verses.

The tenets of the Imagiste faith were published in March, 1913, as follows:—

I. Direct treatment of the "thing," whether subjective or objective.

II. To use absolutely no word that does not contribute to the presentation.

III. As regarding rhythm: to compose in sequence of the musical phrase, not in sequence of the metronome.

There followed a series of about forty cautions to beginners, which need not concern us here.

The arts have indeed "some sort of common bond, some interrecognition." Yet certain emotions or subjects find their most appropriate expression in some one particular art. The work of art which is most "worth while" is the work which would need a hundred works of any other kind of art to explain it. A fine statue is the core of a hundred poems. A fine poem is a score of symphonies. There is music which would need a hundred paintings to express it. There is no synonym for the *Victory of Samothrace* or for Mr. Epstein's flemites. There is no painting of Villon's *Frères Humains*. Such works are what we call works of the "first intensity."

A given subject or emotion belongs to that artist, or to that sort of artist who must know it most intimately and most intensely before he can render it adequately in his art. A painter must know much more about a sunset than a writer, if he is to put it on canvas. But when the poet speaks of "Dawn in russet mantle clad," he presents something which the painter cannot present.

I said in the preface to my *Guido Cavalcanti* that I believed in an absolute rhythm. I believe that every emotion and every phase of emotion has some toneless phrase, some rhythm-phrase to express it.

(This belief leads to *vers libre* and to experiments in quantitative verse.)

To hold a like belief in a sort of permanent metaphor is, as I understand it, "symbolism" in its profounder sense. It is not necessarily a belief in a permanent world, but it is a belief in that direction.

Imagisme is not symbolism. The symbolists dealt in "association," that is, in a sort of allusion, almost of allegory. They degraded the symbol to the status of a word. They made it a form of metronomy. One can be grossly "symbolic," for example, by using the term "cross" to mean "trial." The symbolist's *symbols* have a fixed value, like numbers in arithmetic, like 1, 2, and 7. The imagiste's images have a variable significance, like the signs *a, b,* and *x* in algebra.

Moreover, one does not want to be called a symbolist, because symbolism has usually been associated with mushy technique.

On the other hand, Imagisme is not Impressionism, though one borrows, or could borrow, much from the impressionist method of presentation. But this is only negative definition. If I am to give a psychological or philosophical definition "from the inside," I can only do so autobiographically. The precise statement of such a matter must be based on one's own experience.

In the "search for oneself," in the search for "sincere self-expression," one gropes, one finds some seeming verity. One says "I am" this, that, or the other, and with the words scarcely uttered one ceases to be that thing.

I began this search for the real in a book called *Personæ,* casting off, as it were, complete masks of the self in each poem.

I continued in long series of translations, which were but more elaborate masks.

Secondly, I made poems like "The Return," which is an objective reality and has a complicated sort of significance, like Mr. Epstein's "Sun God," or Mr. Brzeska's "Boy with a Coney." Thirdly, I have written "Heather," which represents a state of consciousness, or "implies," or "implicates" it.

A Russian correspondent, after having called it a symbolist poem, and having been convinced that it was not symbolism, said slowly: "I see, you wish to give people new eyes, not to make them see some new particular thing."

These two latter sorts of poems are impersonal, and that fact brings us back to what I said about absolute metaphor. They are Imagisme, and in so far as they are Imagisme, they fall in with the new pictures and the new sculpture.

Whistler said somewhere in the *Gentle Art*: "The picture is interesting not because it is Trotty Veg, but because it is an arrangement in colour." The minute you have admitted that, you let in the jungle, you let in nature and truth and abundance and cubism and Kandinsky, and the lot of us. Whistler and Kandinsky and some cubists were set to getting extraneous matter out of their art; they were ousting literary values. The Flaubertians talk a good deal about "constatation." "The 'nineties" saw a movement against rhetoric. I think all these things move together, though they do not, of course, move in step.

The painters realise that what matters is form and colour. Musicians long ago learned that programme music was not the ultimate music. Almost anyone can realise that to use a symbol *with an ascribed or intended meaning* is, usually, to produce very bad art. We all remember crowns, and crosses, and rainbows, and what not in atrociously mumbled colour.

The Image is the poet's pigment. The painter should use his colour because he sees it or feels it. I don't much care whether he is representative or non-representative. He should *depend*, of course, on the creative, not upon the mimetic or representational part in his work. It is the same in writing poems, the author must use his *image* because he sees it or feels it, *not* because he thinks he can use it to back up some creed or some system of ethics or economics.

An *image*, in our sense, is real because we know it directly. If it have an age-old traditional meaning this may serve as proof to the professional student of symbology that we have stood in the deathless light, or that we have walked in some particular arbour of his traditional paradiso, but that is not our affair. It is our affair to render the image as we have perceived or conceived it.

Browning's "Sordello" is one of the finest *masks* ever presented. Dante's "Paradiso" is the most wonderful *image*. By that I do not mean that it is a perseveringly imagistic performance. The permanent part is Imagisme, the rest, the discourses with the calendar of saints and the discussions about the nature of the moon, are philology. The form of sphere above sphere, the varying reaches of light, the minutiœ of pearls upon foreheads, all these are parts of the Image. The image is the poet's pigment; with that in mind you can go ahead and apply Kandinsky, you can transpose his chapter on the language of form and colour and apply it to the writing of verse. As I cannot rely on your having read Kandinsky's *Ueber das Geistige in der Kunst,* I must go on with my autobiography.

Three years ago in Paris I got out of a "metro" train at La Concorde, and saw suddenly a beautiful face, and then another and another, and then a beautiful child's face, and then another beautiful woman, and I tried all that day to find words for what this had meant to me, and I could not find any words that seemed to me worthy, or as lovely as that sudden emotion. And that evening, as I went home along the Rue Raynouard, I was still trying, and I found, suddenly, the expression. I do not mean that I found words, but there came an equation . . . not in speech, but in little splotches of colour. It was just that—a "pattern," or hardly a pattern, if by "pattern" you mean something with a "repeat" in it. But it was a word, the beginning, for me, of a language in colour. I do not mean that I was unfamiliar with the kindergarten stories about colours being like tones in music. I think that sort of thing is nonsense. If you try to make notes permanently correspond with particular colours, it is like tying narrow meanings to symbols.

That evening, in the Rue Raynouard, I realised quite vividly that if I were a painter, or if I had, often, *that kind* of emotion, or even if I had the energy to get paints and brushes and keep at it, I might found a new school of painting, of "non-representative" painting, a painting that would speak only by arrangements in colour.

And so, when I came to read Kandinsky's chapter on the language of form and colour, I found little that was new to me. I only felt that someone else understood what I understood, and had written it out very clearly. It seems quite natural to me that an artist should have just as much pleasure in an arrangement of planes or in a pattern of figures, as in painting portraits of fine ladies, or in portraying the Mother of God as the symbolists bid us.

When I find people ridiculing the new arts, or making fun of the clumsy odd terms that we use in trying to talk of them amongst ourselves; when they laugh at our talking about the "ice-block quality" in Picasso, I think it is only because they do not know what thought is like, and that they are familiar only with argument and gibe and opinion. That is to say, they can only enjoy what they have been brought up to consider enjoyable, or what some essayist has talked about in mellifluous phrases. They think only "the shells of thought," as De Gourmont calls them; the thoughts that have been already thought out by others.

Any mind that is worth calling a mind must have needs beyond the existing categories of language, just as a painter must have pigments or shades more numerous than the existing names of the colours.

Perhaps this is enough to explain the words in my "Vortex":—

> "Every concept, every emotion, presents itself to
> the vivid consciousness in some primary form.
> It belongs to the art of this form."

That is to say, my experience in Paris should have gone into paint. If instead of colour I had perceived sound or planes in relation, I should have expressed it in music or in sculpture. Colour was, in that instance, the "primary pigment"; I mean that it was the first adequate equation that came into consciousness. The Vorticist uses the "primary pigment." Vorticism is art before it has spread itself into flaccidity, into elaboration and secondary applications.

What I have said of one vorticist art can be transposed for another vorticist art. But let me go on then with my own branch of vorticism, about which I can probably speak with greater clarity. All poetic language is the language of exploration. Since the beginning of bad writing, writers have used images as ornaments. The point of Imagisme is that it does not use images *as ornaments*. The image is itself the speech. The image is the word beyond formulated language.

In the 'eighties there were symbolists opposed to impressionists, now you have vorticism, which is, roughly speaking, expressionism, neo-cubism, and imagism gathered together in one camp and futurism in the other.

— *Ezra Pound*

I once saw a small child go to an electric light switch and say, "Mamma, can I *open* the light?" She was using the age-old language of exploration, the language of art. It was a sort of metaphor, but she was not using it as ornamentation.

One is tired of ornamentations, they are all a trick, and any sharp person can learn them.

The Japanese have had the sense of exploration. They have understood the beauty of this sort of knowing. A Chinaman said long ago that if a man can't say what he has to say in twelve lines he had better keep quiet. The Japanese have evolved the still shorter form of the *hokku*.

> "The fallen blossom flies back to its branch:
>   A butterfly."

That is the substance of a very well-known *hokku*. Victor Plarr tells me that once, when he was walking over snow with a Japanese naval officer, they came to a place where a cat had crossed the path, and the officer said, "Stop, I am making a poem." Which poem was, roughly, as follows:—

> "The footsteps of the cat upon the snow:
>   (are like) plum-blossoms."

The words "are like" would not occur in the original, but I add them for clarity.

The "one image poem" is a form of super-position, that is to say it is one idea set on top of another. I found it useful in getting out of the impasse in which I had been left by my metro emotion. I wrote a thirty-line poem, and destroyed it because it was what we call work "of second intensity." Six months later I made a poem half that length; a year later I made the following *hokku*-like sentence:—

> "The apparition of these faces in the crowd:
>   Petals, on a wet, black bough."

I dare say it is meaningless unless one has drifted into a certain vein of thought. In a poem of this sort one is trying to record the precise instant when a thing outward and objective transforms itself, or darts into a thing inward and subjective.

This particular sort of consciousness has not been identified with impressionist art. I think it is worthy of attention.

The logical end of impressionist art is the cinematograph. The state of mind of the impressionist tends to become cinematographical. Or, to put it another way, the cinematograph does away with the need of a lot of impressionist art.

There are two opposed ways of thinking of a man; firstly, you may think of him as that toward which perception moves, as the toy of circumstance, as the plastic substance *receiving* impressions; secondly, you may think of him as directing a certain fluid force against circumstance, as *conceiving* instead of merely reflecting and observing. One does not claim that one way is better than the other, one notes a diversity of the temperament. The two camps always exist. In the 'eighties there were symbolists opposed to impressionists, now you have vorticism, which is, roughly speaking, expressionism, neo-cubism, and imagism gathered together in one camp and futurism in the other. Futurism is descended from impressionism. It is, in so far as it is an art movement, a kind of accelerated impressionism. It is a spreading, or surface art, as opposed to vorticism, which is intensive.

The vorticist has not this curious tic for destroying past glories. I have no doubt that Italy needed Mr. Marinetti, but he did not set on the egg that hatched me, and as I am wholly opposed to his æsthetic principles I see no reason why I, and various men who agree with me, should be expected to call ourselves futurists. We do not desire to evade comparison with the past. We prefer that the comparison be made by some intelligent person whose idea of "the tradition" is not limited by the conventional taste of four or five centuries and one continent.

Vorticism is an intensive art. I mean by this, that one is concerned with the relative intensity, or relative significance, of different sorts of expression. One desires the most intense, for certain forms of expression *are* "more intense" than others. They are more dynamic. I do not mean they are more emphatic, or that they are yelled louder. I can explain my meaning best by mathematics.

There are four different intensities of mathematical expression known to the ordinarily intelligent undergraduate, namely: the arithmetical, the algebraic, the geometrical, and that of analytical geometry.

For instance, you can write

$$3 \times 3 + 4 \times 4 = 5 \times 5, \text{ or, differently, } 3^2 + 4^2 = 5^2.$$

That is merely conversation or "ordinary common sense." It is a simple statement of one fact, and does not implicate any other.

Secondly, it is true that

$$3^2 + 4^2 = 5^2, \qquad 6^2 + 8^2 = 10^2, \qquad 9^2 + 12^2 = 15^2,$$
$$39^2 + 52^2 = 65^2.$$

These are all separate facts, one may wish to mention their underlying similarity; it is a bore to speak about each one in turn. One expresses their "algebraic relation" as

$$a^2 + b^2 = c^2.$$

That is the language of philosophy. IT MAKES NO PICTURE. This kind of statement applies to a lot of facts, but it does not grip hold of Heaven.

Thirdly, when one studies Euclid one finds that the relation of $a^2 + b^2 = c^2$ applies to the ratio between the squares on the two sides of a right-angled triangle and the square on the hypotenuse. One still writes it $a^2 + b^2 = c^2$, but one has begun to talk about form. Another property or quality of life has crept into one's matter. Until then one had dealt only with numbers. But even this statement does not *create* form. The picture is given you in the proposition about the square on the hypotenuse of the right-angled triangle being equal to the sum of the squares on the two other sides. Statements in plane or descriptive geometry are like talk about art. They are a criticism of the form. The form is not created by them.

Fourthly, we come to Descartian or "analytical geometry." Space is conceived as separated by two or by three axes (depending on whether one is treating form in one or more planes). One refers points to these axes by a series of coefficients. Given the idiom, one is able *actually to create.*

Thus, we learn that the equation $(x - a)^2 + (y - b)^2 = r^2$ governs the circle. It is the circle. It is not a particular circle, it is any circle and all circles. It is nothing that is not a circle. It is the circle free of space and time limits. It is the universal, existing in perfection, in freedom from space and time. Mathematics is dull as ditchwater until one reaches analytics. But in analytics we come upon a new way of dealing with form. It is in this way that art handles life. The difference between art and analytical geometry is the difference of subject-matter only. Art is more interesting in proportion as life and the human consciousness are more complex and more interesting than forms and numbers.

This statement does not interfere in the least with "spontaneity" and "intuition," or with their function in art. I passed my last *exam.* in mathematics on sheer intuition. I saw where the line *had* to go, as clearly as I ever saw an image, or felt *caelestem intus vigorem.*

The statements of "analytics" are "lords" over fact. They are the thrones and dominations that rule over form and recurrence. And in like manner are great works of art lords over fact, over race-long recurrent moods, and over to-morrow.

Great works of art contain this fourth sort of equation. They cause form to come into being. By the "image" I mean such an equation; not an equation of mathematics, not something about *a, b,* and *c,* having something to do with form, but about *sea, cliffs, night,* having something to do with mood.

The image is not an idea. It is a radiant node or cluster; it is what I can, and must perforce, call a VORTEX, from which, and through which, and into which, ideas are constantly rushing.

In decency one can only call it a VORTEX. And from this necessity came the name "vorticism." *Nomina sunt consequentia rerum,* and never was that statement of Aquinas more true than in the case of the vorticist movement.

It is as true for the painting and the sculpture as it is for the poetry. Mr. Wadsworth and Mr. Lewis are not using words, they are using shape and colour. Mr. Brzeska and Mr. Epstein are using "planes in relation," they are dealing with a relation of planes different from the sort of relation of planes dealt with in geometry, hence what is called "the need of organic forms in sculpture."

I trust I have made clear what I mean by an "intensive art." The vorticist movement is not a movement of mystification, though I dare say many people "of good will" have been considerably bewildered.

The organisation of forms is a much more energetic and creative action than the copying or imitating of light on a haystack.

There is undoubtedly a language of form and colour. It is not a symbolical or allegorical language depending on certain meanings having been ascribed, in books, to certain signs and colours.

Certain artists working in different media have managed to understand each other. They know the good and bad in each other's work, which they could not know unless there were a common speech.

As for the excellence of certain contemporary artists, all I can do is to stand up for my own beliefs. I believe that Mr. Wyndham Lewis is a very great master of design; that he has brought into our art new units of design and new manners of organisation. I think that his series "Timon" is a great work. I think he is the most articulate expression of my own decade. If you ask me what his "Timon" means, I can reply by asking you what the old play means. For me his designs are a creation on the same *motif.* That *motif* is the fury of intelligence baffled and shut in by circumjacent stupidity. It is an emotional *motif.* Mr. Lewis's painting is nearly always emotional.

Mr. Wadsworth's work gives me pleasure, sometimes like the pleasure I have received from Chinese and Japanese prints and painting; for example, I derive such pleasure from Mr. Wadsworth's "Khaki." Sometimes his work gives me a pleasure which I can only compare to the pleasure I have in music, in music as it was in Mozart's time. If an outsider wishes swiftly to understand this new work, he can do worse than approach it in the spirit wherein he approaches music.

"Lewis is Bach." No, it is incorrect to say that "Lewis is Bach," but our feeling is that certain works of Picasso and certain works of Lewis have in them something which is to painting what certain qualities of Bach are to music. Music was vorticist in the Bach-Mozart period, before it went off into romance and sentiment and description. A new vorticist music would come from a new computation of the mathematics of harmony, not from a mimetic representation of dead cats in a fog-horn, alias noise-tuners.

Mr. Epstein is too well known to need presentation in this article. Mr. Brzeska's sculpture is so generally recognised in all camps that one does not need to bring in a brief concerning it. Mr. Brzeska has defined sculptural feeling as "the appreciation of masses in relation," and sculptural ability as "the defining of these masses by planes." There comes a time when one is more deeply moved by that form of intelligence which can present "masses in relation" than by that combination of patience and trickery which can make marble chains with free links and spin out bronze until it copies the feathers on a general's hat. Mr. Etchells still remains more or less of a mystery. He is on his travels, whence he has sent back a few excellent drawings. It cannot be made too clear that the work of the vorticists and the "feeling of inner need" existed before the general noise about vorticism. We worked separately, we found an underlying agreement, we decided to stand together.

Jo Anna Isaak

SOURCE: "The Revolution of a Poetics," in *Modernism: Challenges and Perspectives,* Monique Chefdor, Ricardo Quinones, and Albert Wachtel, eds., University of Illinois Press, 1986, pp. 159-79.

[*In the following essay, Isaak compares the Vorticist movement to Russian Futurism.*]

"What strikes me as beautiful, what I should like to do," Flaubert wrote, "is a book without external attachments, which would hold itself together by itself through the internal force of its style." Flaubert's dream of an order of art independent of the referential, the representational, was actualized within certain developments of abstractionism in the early 1900s—when art took to analyzing its own ontology. The movements that follow Flaubert's imperative, creating not art contingent upon empirical experience but art as process and mode of perceptual and formal experience, have one characteristic in common—their strategies of abstraction evolved out of a complex nexus of linguistic and plastic media. It is as though what Roman Jakobson refers to as the "bared medium" could only be realized by investigating the devices of *other* media. In particular, strikingly similar traits can be observed among the group of English vorticists associated with Ezra Pound, Wyndham Lewis, and the manifesto *Blast* (1914) and the group of Russian futurists, an alliance of writers and painters who displayed a comparable urge to write manifestos which would function as "A Slap in the Face to Public Taste" (1912). In the *Blast* manifesto, Pound attempted to delineate what he called the "ancestry" of vorticism by quoting Pater's famous phrase on the etiology of abstraction in art: "all arts approach the condition of music." In the same chapter of *The Renaissance* Pater goes on to make two other much more explicit statements. The first is that "art is always striving to become a matter of pure perception, to get rid of its responsibilities to its *subject*." In the second, abstraction in one medium is seen to be capable of suggesting a means of aesthetic autonomy in another. Pater notes that "in its special mode of handling its given material, each art may be observed to pass into the condition of some other art, by what German critics term an *Anders-streben*—a partial alienation from its own limitations, through which the arts are able, not indeed to supply the place of each other, but reciprocally to lend each other new forces."

The notion of the autonomy of the artistic material was developed by the Russian futurists into a fully articulated aesthetic. Kasimir Malevich's assertion that the object of painting was the expression of its own "body as such" ("The idea is to combine the variety and multiplicity of lines, space, surface, color and texture into one body as such") had its direct linguistic counterpart in Velemir Khlebnikov's and Aleksei Kruchenykh's insistence on the idea of the "word as such," the self-sufficient word, free of its referent. Just as all the other arts consist in the shaping of self-validating material, so too does poetry: its "material" is words, and thus poetry is characterized as obeying immanent laws and its semantic function reduced to a minimum. "Before us there was no art of the word," Kruchenykh wrote in *The Three,* and he asserted the autonomous value of the "autotelic word." The raw material of literature was to be allowed to stand by itself, no longer chained in slavery to meaning, philosophy, psychology, or reason: "The word is broader than its meaning. Each letter, each sound has its relevance. . . . Why not repudiate meaning and write with word-ideas that are freely creat-

ed? We do not need intermediaries—symbols, thought, *we give our own new truth and we do not serve as the reflections of some sun.*" And Benedikt Livshits wrote that now poetry was "free from the sad necessity of expressing the logical connection of ideas." In 1911 Pound had launched a comparable attack against the burden of reference imposed upon poetry, complaining that for over two hundred years poetry in English "had been merely the vehicle . . . the ox-cart and post-chaise for transmitting thoughts poetic or otherwise."

The assertion of the right to an autonomous or autotelic aesthetic praxis should not be understood as synonymous with the solipsistic principle of "art for art's sake," but rather should be accompanied by the following qualification of Jakobson's:

> Of late criticism thinks it fashionable to stress the uncertainty of what is called the formalist science of literature. It seems that this school does not understand the relations between art and social life, it seems that it promotes *l'art pour l'art* and proceeds in the wake of Kantian aesthetics. The critics who make these objections are, in their radicalism, so consistent and so precipitate that they forget the existence of the third dimension, they see everything in the same plane. Neither Tynyanov, nor Mukarovsky, nor Shklovsky, nor I have preached that art is sufficient unto itself; on the contrary, we show that art is part of the social edifice, a component correlating with the others, a variable component, since the sphere of art and its relationship with other sectors of the social structure ceaselessly changes dialectically. *What we stress is not a separation of art, but the autonomy of the aesthetic function.*
>
> I have already said that the content of the notion of poetry was unstable and varied over time, but the poetic function, poeticalness, as the formalists stressed, is an element *sui generis,* an element that cannot be mechanically reduced to other elements. This element must be laid bare and its independence stressed, as the technical devices of cubist paintings, for example, are laid bare and independent. . . .
>
> But how is poeticalness manifested? In that the word is felt as a word and not as a mere substitute for the named object or as an explosion of emotion. In that words and their syntax, their signification, their external and internal form are not indifferent indices of reality, but have their own weight and their own value.

As the manifesto titles suggest, (*Blast, A Slap in the Face to Public Taste*) it is as a reaction against the pluralism of bourgeois taste that these artists posit their stylistic dissent. The enthusiasm and exaltation with which they announce this stylistic dissent indicates that the formal revolution—the redical shifts in modes of aesthetic production, theoretical positions, and treatment of perceptual and linguistic conventions—is the pretext for hurling a Promethean challenge, repudiating their determinate role in producing representations of the ideological world. According to Malraux, modern artists ventured into the field of abstractionism with the intention of escaping the hegemony and homogeneity of that "museum without walls" in which they had found themselves since photographic reproduction provided the technology of pluralism—the immediate assimilation and dissemination of the work of art. Although I do not agree with Malraux's teleology of abstract art, what is important to our discussion here is his observation of the intention of abstractionism as reaction against the dominance of now easily reproduced "high art"—traditional academic culture providing a fictitious, but authoritative, universality and continuity with the past—and against mass culture, which is wholly divorced from any culture created by the people, but which is "art" produced and packaged for the masses. Edmund Wilson has given these two types the contrasting names "classics" and "commercials."

The most famous apostle of the creed of the "classics" is T. S. Eliot, who, in appropriating mythified cultural fragments to shore against his ruin, attempted to appropriate the work of Ezra Pound and James Joyce and to marshal them under the retrospective utopian banner of new literary classicism. "It is simply a way of controlling, of ordering, of giving a shape and a significance to the immense panorama of futility and anarchy which is contemporary history," Eliot writes in *"Ulysses,* Order, and Myth." This is perhaps the most candid revelation of the true compensatory impulse behind the eclectic historicist's static notion of history, which enables him to create a false synthesis of cultural fragments and endow them with notions of grandeur, nobility, universality, authority—all the old verities no longer to be found in the modern world, but which, we are asked to believe, obtained in the past. The mythic method, Eliot claims, is a step toward "making the modern world possible for art." In the *Slap in the Face* manifesto this mode of artistic production, along with Pushkin, Dostoevsky, Tolstoy, et al., is the first to be thrown overboard from the "Ship of Modernity," a reaction analogous to Pound's assertion that you needn't read Shakespeare, you could find out all you needed to know about him from "boring circumjacent conversation." "Better mendacities than the classics in paraphrase."

The greatest ad-man of the "commercials" is F. T. Marinetti, who, in his zeal for "the new," heroically and hysterically attempted to acculturate the entire avant-garde to the modes of production and theoretical positions of commodity capitalism in order to develop devices that would facilitate the swift communication of propaganda for that throughly modern merry-go-round—reification. This is borne out in Marinetti's adulation of all forms of capitalist technology and in his attempts to convert the whole Italian futurist movement into propagandists for Mussolini's fascism.

The ostensibly dissimilar artistic or pseudo-artistic production practices of mass culture and high art converge on the level of the common cult of the cliché. For Pound, whose *Make It New* poetics is shared by the Russian futurists, who used the same slogan, Marinetti's futurism was "only an accelerated sort of impressionism," implying that it is only a new form of mimeticism. but as Jakobson maintains, "Poetry is renewed from within, by specifically linguistic means," and he treats poetic language through-

out his essay on "Modern Russian Poetry" (1919) as a kind of metalanguage. Like Pound, who asserted that "a work of art has in it no idea which is separable from the form," Jakobson, too, denies the distinct existence of subject matter or "content." Analyses of innovations based upon external or social causation are therefore erroneous. Both Pound and Jakobson fault Marinetti for the way he directs poetry to the task of recording new facts in the material world: rapid transit, speeding motor cars, locomotives, airplanes, and so on. "But this is a reform in the field of reportage, not in poetic language," Jakobson observes, and contrasts Marinetti's new mimeticism with Kruchenykh's assertion that "it is not new subject matter that defines genuine innovation. Once there is new form, it follows that there is new content; form thus conditions content. Our creative shaping of speech throws everything into a new light."

Thus Marinetti's futurism and Eliot's neoclassicism—the symbolic modes of concrete anticipation and the allegorical modes of internalized cultural retrospection—are understood to be comparable devices of stultification that reinforce and reinvent the cultural power structure. They are the aesthetic manifestations of the psychic mechanisms of anticipation and melancholy. At the origin of the allegorical is an enforced and incapacitating melancholy, the result of prohibition and repression; at the origin of the valorization of reactionary power and of reification is the continual generation and denial of expectations. When Pound, in an interview in Mayakovsky's magazine, *The Archer,* dissociates himself from Italian futurism he does so in a way that specifically addresses these ideologically induced psychic states and the manner in which they thwart the development of any genuinely innovative artistic activity capable of critical negativity.

> We are "vorticists." . . . Everything that has been created by nature and culture is for us a general chaos which we pierce with our vortex. We do not deny the past—we don't remember it. It is distant and thus sentimental. For the artist and the poet it is a means to divert the instinct of melancholy which hinders pure art. But the future is just as distant as the past, and thus also sentimental. It is a diversion of optimism which is just as pernicious in art as melancholy. The past and the future are two brothels created by nature. Art is periods of flight from these brothels, periods of sanctity. We are not futurists: the past and the future merge for us in their sentimental remoteness, in their projections onto an obscured and impotent perception. Art lives only by means of the present—but only that present which is not subject to nature, which does not suck up to life, limiting itself to perceptions of the existent, but rather creates from itself a new, living abstraction . . . our task is to "dehumanize" the contemporary world; the established forms of the human body and all that is "mere life" have now lost their former significance. One must create new abstractions, bring together new masses, bring out of oneself a new reality.

Concomitant with this insistence on the new and the present, so central to both Russian futurism and English vorticism, is their interest in primitive and folk art. Russian neoprimitivism was to have considerable influence on the inception of abstract art in England. Although ostensibly it arose in Russia out of nationalist sentiments and the need for a viable indigenous art form in opposition to the invasions of Western culture, it was precisely this aspect of Russian art that found the most favorable reception in the West—in fact, it was what the West demanded. Diaghilev's first ballet performed in the West was criticized in the French press for its lack of national atmosphere: "The French desired a folk-lore element, expected a special, almost exotic flavour in the performances. In short, they wanted what they, as Frenchmen, understood to be 'du vrai Russe.'" It was in response to this demand that Diaghilev launched *L'Oiseau de Feu* (1910)—a colorful although unconvincing pastiche of various Russian fairy and folk tales. Nevertheless, it was what the West called for, and by 1911 the influence of the Ballets Russes had spread far beyond the confines of the London and Paris elite. How great this influence was may be judged by the following extract from "Painters and the *Ballets-Russes*" by André Varnod: "In any case, it was a perfect enthusiasm which, sweeping away the artistic, literary and social worlds, reached the man in the street, the wide public, the gown-shops and stores. The fashion in everything was *Ballets-Russes*. There was not a middle-class home without its green and orange cushions on a black carpet." In 1913 Diaghilev very shrewdly enlisted the talents of Goncharova, and in spite of Larionov's declaration of 1913 that "we are against the West, vulgarizing our Oriental forms and rendering everything valueless," by 1914 Goncharova had burst upon Paris and London as the creator of the decor of the *Coq d'Or*—and Larionov too had begun to work for Diaghilev.

The appropriation by the West of ancient Russian art cannot, of course, be attributed wholly to Diaghilev's cultural transportations. T. E. Hulme's complaint about the way in which "elements taken from the extremely intense and serious Byzantine art are used in an entirely meaningless and pointless way" was a response to the Byzantine-style screens, rugs, inlaid tables, and paintings that proliferated in the wake of the Bloomsbury group's visit to Constantinople in 1911. Fry's enthusiasm for the art he saw while on this trip may have resulted in his decision to include the work of Russian artists in his Second Post-Impressionist Exhibition (1912). Here the works of Nikolai Roerich, Mikalojus Ciurlianis, Nataliya Goncharova, Mikhail Larionov, and other Russian artists of what the catalog referred to as the "New Byzantine Group" were exhibited together with the works of Vanessa Bell, Frederick Etchells, Duncan Grant, Cuthbert Hamilton, Wyndham Lewis, and Edward Wadsworth.

In spite of Hulme's justifiable compliant, the English artists' "adaptations" of Byzantine art forms enabled them to familiarize themselves with the use of nonrepresentational design. Roger Fry spoke of the "incredible phenomenon" of Goncharova and Larionov's stage decor, pointing out that now artists could go to the theater "to see experiments in the art of visual design—still more, experiments which indicate new possibilities in the art of picture-making." The early abstract compositions of Bom-

berg in particular were inspired by Diaghilev's ballets. And certainly a great number of the works produced at the Omega Workshop, plans for which began immediately after the Second Post-Impressionist Exhibition, show the influence of Russian folk art and crafts. These connections explain in part the precociousness of the development of abstract art in England. For example, Wyndham Lewis's *Portrait of an Englishwoman* in *The Archer* (1915), which was reproduced in *The Archer* (1915), is markedly similar to Malevich's later suprematist paintings, for example *Dynamischer Suprematismus;* and David Bomberg's *The Dancer* (1914) can be compared to Rodchencko's compass drawings of 1915. Examples such as these illustrate how similar influences can lead to morphologically comparable effects.

The adaptation of Russian neoprimitivist art in England has very different ideological implications from the same activity in Russia. This phenomenon was diagnosed in the twenties by Russian productivist artist and theoretician Boris Arvatov, who writes in *Art and Production:*

> While the total technology of capitalist society is constructed on the highest and latest achievement and represents a technique of mass production (industry, radio, transport, newspapers, scientific laboratories, etc.), bourgeois art in principle has remained on the level of crafts and therefore has been pushed out of the collective social practice of mankind into isolation, into the realm of pure aesthetics. . . . The individual, lonely master, that is the only type of artist in capitalist society, the type of specialist in "pure art" who works outside of the immediately utilitarian practice because this practice is based on machine technology. From here originates the illusion of art's purposelessness and autonomy, from here its whole bourgeois fetishistic nature.

Arvatov's analysis could apply to industrial England, but in post-czarist Russia the development from neoprimitivism to abstract art to constructivist and productivist practices follows a very different trajectory.

In part, this can be explained by analyzing the reasons for the Russian avant-garde's renewed interest in primitive and religious art—particularly orthodox icon painting. Malevich's enigmatic announcement that *The Black Square* (1914-15) was "the icon of our times" was followed by his statements in *The Non-Objective World* that "art no longer cares to serve the state and religion. . . . It wants to have nothing further to do with the object as such and believes that it can exist in and for itself." The paradox of Malevich's position is resolved through a consideration of the semiotic function of the ancient icon itself. The controversy between the iconoclasts and iconodules, of fundamental significance for Orthodox Christianity, may, to a great extent, be seen as a controversy concerning precisely the semiotic character of the icon— the central point of which was the attitude toward the sign. In spite of the icon's extremely formalized but nevertheless figurative form it was originally understood to be nonrepresentational, in that its "referent" was regarded as ineffable—the face of Christ could never be known. Malevich's *Black Square* lays bare the absent referent as the source of the nonreferentiality of the icon and calls into question the whole problematic of any sign's relationship to the phenomenal world. In so doing Malevich exposes the idealism of the theological debate, its assumption of what Derrida calls the "transcendental signified," "which supposedly does not in itself, in its essence, refer back to any signifier but goes beyond the chain of signs, and itself no longer functions as a signifier." Rosalind Coward and John Ellis's discussion of Derrida's critique of the sign is useful here:

> In this way, the distinction or equilibrium of the notions "signified" and "signifier" in the sign allows the metaphysical belief of a reserve or an origin of meaning which will always be anterior and exterior to the continuous productivity of signification. . . .
>
> [Thus Derrida asserts] that a philosophy of language based on such a notion of the sign is "profoundly theological." "Sign and deity have the same place and same time of birth." The pyramid (referent—signified—signifier) ends by resolving itself into the hypostasis of a signified which always culminates in god: "the epoch of the sign is essentially theological."

Malevich conflates the signifier and signified, not as is customarily the case to let the concept present itself in a supposedly unmediated manner, but rather to reverse the process and foreground the signifier, thereby circumventing the idealist problematic that supposes the preexistence of meaning. When Malevich speaks of the primitive tendency in modern art, he does so in terms appropriate to his own use of the icon and makes it clear that the modern adaptation of primitive art is not an atavistic activity, but rather what he calls a "decomposition": "It is the attempt to escape from the objective identity of the image to direct creation and to break away from idealism and pretense." Primitivism, as it was to be employed by the Russian avant-garde, was one of the major strategies for facilitating the creation of the autonomous, autotelic work of art, a work of art relieved of its semantic or representational function, precisely because meaning with an *a priori* existence had been repudiated; signification was now understood to be dependent upon the passage of signifiers themselves.

The repudiation of the transcendental signified appears as the Promethean declaration of *Victory Over the Sun* (1913)—the theatrical collaboration of Kruchenykh (text), Malevich (costumes and set designs), Matyushin (music), and Khlebnikov (prologue). It is extremely significant that Malveich claimed that suprematism originated while he was working on the sets for *Victory Over the Sun*. It has been suggested that Malevich's sketch for the backdrop for the first act may be part of the sun against the dark universe, especially since the diagonal line is actually curved and may be the horizon line of the sun. Also, parts of the sun appear on the cover for the libretto. If this reading is valid then the *Black Square* may be read as the total obliteration of the sun, the climactic event of *Victory Over the Sun*.

Victory Over the Sun is remarkably similar in title, theme, structure, charactery, stage design, and linguistic innovation to Wyndham Lewis's play *Enemy of the Stars,* written

less than a year after *Victory Over the Sun* and Mayakovsky's play *Vladimir Mayakovsky, a Tragedy* had caused a riot at the Luna Park Theatre in St. Petersburg. Lewis may have learned of the plays from Marinetti, who visited Russia a couple of weeks after they were performed. In his memoirs Livshits details the debate Kulbin had with Marinetti concerning the importance of *zaum* or trans-rational language, which Kruchenykh had just developed in *Victory Over the Sun*. What account Marinetti gave of all this when he returned to England a few months later, and whether he brought with him the illustrated text of *Victory Over the Sun* published while he was in St. Petersburg is not known. But it is clear that the innovations of the Russian futurists would be a subject of considerable interest to the English vorticists.

Lewis wrote *Enemy of the Stars* because, as he said, his "literary contemporaries [were] not keeping pace with the visual revolution," yet he did not adopt Marinetti's theories and practices nor his typographic experiments, but instead utilized a great many devices comparable to those employed by the Russian futurists. Mayakovsky's canvas cubes and "slightly slanted" sets may have been the inspiration for Lewis's stage arrangements, in which "overturned cases and other impediments have been covered, throughout arena, with old sail canvas." In the second scene the "audience looks down into scene, as though it were a hut rolled half on its back, door upwards, characters giddily mounting in its opening." A picture of the setting for *Victory Over the Sun* shows an unmatched drop and wings hung upside down; in the sixth scene there is the unusual stage direction that the fat man "peeps inside the watch: the tower the sky the street are upside down—as in a mirror." The colors of the setting in both *Victory Over the Sun* and *Enemy of the Stars* are stark, unmodulated contrasts—predominantly black and white. In the second scene of *Victory Over the Sun* there is the addition of "green walls and floor" for the set of scene 2, on which Malevich had written "green until the funeral"; and in Lewis's play there are "the Red Walls of the Universe . . . till the execution is over."

The artificial light from the spotlights used in *Victory Over the Sun* played an important part in creating its dramatic effects. Malevich had at his disposal a modern console-controlled lighting system that had just been installed in the Luna Park Theatre. Livshits describes how the "tentacles of the spotlights" cut up the bodies of the actors into geometric sections: the figures "broken up by the blades of light . . . alternately lose arms, legs, heads," presumably because the colored spotlights absorbed similar colors in the costumes. These blades of light, which light up what Livshits called "a night of creation for the world" sound remarkably close to the bizarre, tremendously forceful and threatening lighting which pierces the night in *Enemy of the Stars*. "A white, crude volume of brutal light blazes over" the characters, crushing them. The stars, "machines of prey," shine "madly in the archaic blank wilderness of the universe."

The characters are grotesque abstractions of people, their bodies no more resistant to the powerful restructuration than is the rest of the environment. In Mayakovsky's play there is a man without an ear and one without a head; in *Victory Over the Sun* the fat man complains that his head lags two steps behind his body; in *Enemy of the Stars* a disembodied boot appears regularly to kick the protagonist, Arghol. Characters who are not parts of people wear masks and move like animations of monumental statues or distorted half-machine, half-human figures. Arghol "walks like wary shifting of bodies in distant equipoise." In one variation he is described as a "creature of two-dimensions, clumsily cut out in cardboard by coarse scissor-work," a description appropriate to Malevich's costumes, which were made of cardboard and resembled armor. The one illustration Lewis gives of the Enemy of the Stars could be a somewhat modified side-view of Malevich's Futurecountry Strong Man. These are the protagonists of the plays.

The vision of the future, so unformed in the vorticists, was extremely clear to the Russian futurists. They saw themselves as harbingers of a political revolution.

— *Jo Anna Isaak*

The Futurecountry Strong Man, like Lewis's Enemy, is engaged in a Promethean struggle. Man against the sun is the paradigm of the poet's desire to overthrow the agency of meaning—the prohibitionary seat of representation, "the sun of cheap appearances" as Matyushin calls it, or an "immense bleak electric advertisement of God" as Lewis calls it. "We pulled the sun out by its fresh roots / they were fatty permeated with arithmetic," the victors sign. *Victory Over the Sun* is a restructuration of an entire cosmology—language users, not space, time, or causality, determine the order of the universe. "Lookers painted by an artist, will create a change in the look of nature," the prologue promises. Once the victory over the sun has been accomplished the Elocutionist announces: "How extraordinary life is without a past . . . what a joy: liberated from the weight of the earth's gravitation we whimsically arrange our belongings as if a rich kingdom were moving."

The language and structure of both plays is closely akin to that of the carnival. As Julia Kristeva points out:

> Carnivalesque structure is like the residue of a cosmogony that ignored substance, causality, or identity. . . . Figures germane to carnivalesque language, including repetition, "inconsequent" statements (which are nonetheless "connected" within an infinite context), and nonexclusive opposition, which function as empty sets or disjunctive additions, produce a more flagrant dialogism than any other discourse. Disputing the laws of language . . . the carnival challenges God, authority, and social law; insofar as it is dialogical, it is rebellious. . . .
>
> The scene of the carnival . . . is . . . both stage and life, game and dream, discourse and specta-

cle. By the same token, it is proffered as the only space in which language escapes linearity (law) to live as drama in three dimensions. At a deeper level . . . *drama becomes located in language.* On the omnified stage of carnival, language parodies and relativizes itself, repudiating its role in representation.

It is exactly at this level—the drama located in language—that the two plays bifurcate. In *Victory Over the Sun* phonetic and semantic deformations and new meaning generated by them achieve what Jakobson describes as the "significant potential" of neologism, that is, its potential for abstraction. *Victory Over the Sun* is the creation of the non-objective world. The old order of time, space, casuality no longer obtains. Characters travel freely from the tenth to the thirty-fifth centuries of the future or "leave sideways into the 16th century in quotation marks." The final song of the play is pure transrational poetry—*zaum:*

```
luh    luh    luh
Kruuh      Kruuh
         Hee
         Hoomtuh
Krruh      duh      tuh      rruh
     Krruh                   vwubra
     doo             doo
ra luh
     Kuh   buh   ee
          zhub
zeeda
          deeda
```

This is the complete song, as meaningless in English (or rather transliterated, as here) as in Russian.

In Lewis's play, language remains incapable of detaching itself from representation. Even though at times the materiality of language is foregrounded and we are conscious only of what Lewis was later to call "the finely sculptured surface of sheer words," these "sheer words" are not long at liberty—their referents soon overtake them. Lewis's protagonist is posited in opposition to exactly the same forces as Kruchenykh's Futurecountry Strong Man. His play can be read as an allegorical enactment of Worringer's theory of the two oppositional wills to art—abstraction (Arghol) and empathy (Hanp). Arghol is the abstract artist engaged in "the dehumanization of art," but as Lewis makes clear in the beginning he is a "foredoomed Prometheus." He is beaten regularly by the "will of the universe manifested with directness and persistence," and is beset by Hanp, to whom Arghol says, "You are the world, brother, with its family objections to me." Hanp is organic nature with its demands for empathy. In both plays "nature is not an origin, but a run-down trope." In *Victory Over the Sun,* "the violets groan / Under the firm heel" of the Strong Man:

> The flower world doesn't exist anymore
> Sky cover yourself with rot . . .
> Every birth of autumn days
> And blemished fruit of summer
> Not about those, the newest bard
> Will sing.

In *Victory Over the Sun* the victory over cosmic order and the destruction of nature is the abolition of conventions of representation. In *Enemy of the Stars,* however, there is no victory. Arghol is "imprisoned in a messed socket of existence," and his only mode of extricating himself is through language: "Arghol's voice had no modulations of argument. Weak now, it handled words numbly, like tired compositor. His body was quite strong again and vivacious. Words acted on it as rain on a plant. It got a stormy neat brilliance in this soft shower. One flame balanced giddily erect, while another larger one swerved and sang with speech coldly before it." Arghol's decisive struggle takes place in the dream scene. It is within the dream, whose characteristic is, as Kristeva points out, carnivalesque discourse, that language could attain its " 'potential infinity' (to use David Hilbert's term), where prohibitions (representation, 'monologism') and their transgression (dream, body, 'dialogism') coexist." In the dream Arghol fails to transgress the prohibitions, to enact the revolution that would transform him and his environment. He remains Arghol (fixed identity) and others recognize him as such in spite of his attempts to "obliterate or turn into deliberate refuse, accumulations of self." "He was simply Arghol. . . . He repeated his name—like sinister word invented to launch a new Soap, in gigantic advertisement—toilet—necessity, he, to scrub the soul." Nor is he able to rid himself of reality for long. He wakes up to find Hanp has followed him—"Always à deux!" In the end it is Hanp (the world) who kills Arghol, to the "relief of grateful universe." "The night was suddenly absurdly peaceful." The execution is over, the universe satisfied.

Enemy of the Stars is Lewis's most daringly experimental approach to language, "a piece of writing worthy of the hand of the abstractist innovator." "If anything extended could be done with it," Hugh Kenner observed, "this early style would be one of the most impressive inventions in the history of English literature." At the same time, the dramatic action located in the language marks Lewis's retreat from the linguistic revolution. "Words and syntax," he decided, "were not susceptible of transformation into abstract terms, to which process the visual arts lent themselves quite readily." This was the first step in Lewis's withdrawal from the abstractionist experiment. His second would come when he decided that "abstract terms" no longer seemed worth exploring in the visual arts either. The war which he had first complained of as having "stopped Art dead" he later praised for having saved him from what he called the "abstractist cul-de-sac."

Many years later, when Lewis looked back on the period just after the *Blast* publication, he expressed a sense of missed opportunity, a recognition that there was some further potential, some next step to the aesthetic revolution which he had failed to actualize—which, in fact, he had failed to see: "I might have been at the head of a social revolution, instead of merely being the prophet of a new fashion in art. Really all this organized disturbance was Art behaving as if it were Politics. But I swear I did not know it. It may in fact have been politics. I see that now. Indeed, it must have been. But I was unaware of the fact." His fellow vorticists were even more reactionary: "The immediate need of the art of today," Christopher Nevinson announced in 1919, is for "a reactionary, to lead art back to

the academic traditions of the Old Masters and save contemporary art from abstraction."

The vision of the future, so unformed in the vorticists, was extremely clear to the Russian futurists. They saw themselves as harbingers of a political revolution. The subsequent evolution from Malevich's suprematism to the constructivist practices of artists such as Rodchenko and Lissitsky, and their explicit politicization during the productivist period, confirms their vision of themselves: their work was intricately bound into and supportive of the social revolution in the Soviet Union. As Malevich asserted, the overthrow of bourgeois taste, "smashing the old tables of aesthetic values[,] was the first step in smashing the bourgeois order."

Richard Sheppard

SOURCE: "Expressionism and Vorticism: An Analytical Comparison," in *Facets of European Modernism: Essays in Honour of James McFarlane,* edited by Janet Garton, University of East Anglia, 1985, pp. 149-74.

[*In the following essay, Sheppard examines the similarities and differences between Vorticism and German Expressionism.*]

Writing in mid-1914, Ezra Pound indicated that he saw an affinity between Vorticism and Expressionism when he said: "A good vorticist painting is more likely to be mistaken for a good expressionist painting than for the work of Mr Collier", and C.R.W. Nevinson, the English Futurist closely associated with the Vorticist circle, did the same when he referred, in a lecture of 12 June 1914, to "the Expressionists, such as Kandinsky, Wyndham-Lewis [sic], Wadsworth, etc., or Vorticists as I believe the latter now like to be called . . .". Sixty years later, the art historian Richard Cork, in his monumental and exhaustive study, pointed out that the "urgency and harshness" of Vorticism were "akin to the excoriating art of the Expressionists", and in an essay entitled "Vorticism: Expressionism English style", the literary critic Ulrich Weisstein extended the comparison, drawing attention to typographical similarities, the importance of abstraction and primitivism for both movements, and the concern of both movements to explore "the instincts and emotions which play around the dark core of life".

GERMANY AND THE VORTICISTS

Much data legitimizes such comparisons. Even though French art and literature and Italian Futurism made a more dramatic and intensive impact on the Vorticists (belying Weisstein's description of Vorticism as "that Anglo-Saxon offshoot of Expressionism") and even though the Vorticists rarely used the term "Expressionism"—a fact which is not surprising given the same reluctance on the part of the German avant garde during the pre-war years—it is clear, in retrospect, that the English movement owed a certain amount to Germany and its German counterpart.

Several of the Vorticist circle had spent time in Germany. Lewis was in Munich in early 1906 and wrote at least one letter home from the Café Stephanie in the Amalienstrasse, the venue of the Munich artistic *bohéme*; Edward Wadsworth's knowledge of German dated from 1906 when he too studied in Munich; Gaudier-Brzeska had also been there in 1909; Pound visited Giessen and Freiburg in Summer 1911; and T.E. Hulme was in Berlin for nine months—probably November 1912 to July 1913—and visited Marburg at least once during that period where he heard a lecture by Hermann Cohen, the foremost Neo-Kantian philosopher ("Erkenntniskritiker") of the time.

From such contacts, their reading of philosophers such as Nietzsche, Schopenhauer, Weininger and Stirner (who is referred to in Lewis's "Enemy of the Stars" as Stirnir, the author of *Einige und Sein Eigenkeit* [!]) and various personal experiences, the Vorticists formed a double attitude towards Germany: on the one hand a profound antipathy to official, Wilhelmine Germany, and on the other, an ambivalent receptivity towards the German avant garde who were alienated from that system and of whom, for Pound at least, Heine was a worthy predecessor. The former attitude—a more violent version of which marks Expressionism—is evident throughout the Vorticist period and becomes more pronounced after August 1914. In "Enemy of the Stars", for example, Lewis referred to Berlin as the place of heavy, pestilential, oppressive materiality, and *Tarr* not only abounds in anti-German sentiment (see especially the Preface to the first edition), but has two of its main characters—Otto Kreisler and Bertha Lunken—stand respectively for German "melodramatic nihilism" and "the kind of Germanic culture encountered in Hauptmann and Sudermann". Pound openly confessed to being "not particularly fond of Germans" and often attacked German *Kultur, Bildung* and *Wissenschaft* as a more insidious example of the inhuman tyranny of German militarism. Indeed, in February 1917 he even went so far as to blame "the hell of contemporary Europe" on "the lack of representative Government in Germany, and . . . the non-existence of decent prose in the German language". And even Hulme, the least anti-German of the Vorticist circle, devoted a considerable amount of space in his essays in *The New Age* (TNA) and the *Cambridge Magazine* of 1915 and 1916 to attacking the German "objective-organic view of the state", according to which the state is a "metabiological, spiritual organism . . . in which the individual forms a part".

At the same time, Lewis, in the "Editorial" to [*Blast* No. 2 (B2)] also recognized an "unofficial Germany" which "has done more for the movement that this paper was founded to propagate, and for all branches of contemporary activity in Science and Art, than any other country". Had Lewis wanted to acknowledge the Vorticists' debt more precisely, he might well have singled out the painter and theoretician Wassily Kandinsky (referred to by Pound as the "mother" of Vorticism) and the theoretician of abstraction Wilhelm Worringer. The Vorticists would have known Kandinsky's visual work from several sources: he had exhibited twelve engravings and two paintings at the Allied Artists' Association (AAA) salon in 1909; three paintings (including *Improvisation 6* (1909) and *Komposition 1* (1910)) at the 1910 AAA salon; six woodcuts with an album and text at the 1911 AAA salon; three paintings (*Improvisation 29* (1912), *Landschaft mit*

zwei Pappeln (1912) and *Improvisation 30 (Kanonen)* (1913)) at the 1913 salon; three paintings (*Kleines Bild mit Gelb* (1914), *Studie für Improvisation 7* (1910) and *Bild 1914*)) at the 1914 AAA salon, and *Sonntag* (c. 1904-05) and *Zwei Vögel* (1907) at the exhibition of German woodcuts in the Twenty-One Gallery in Spring 1914. At least one of the Vorticists, Wadsworth, was intimately acquainted with Kandinsky's treatise on abstraction, *Über das Geistige in der Kunst* (which had appeared at Christmas 1911), since he published seventeen translated extracts from it in B1, sixteen of which came from the first half of the chapter "Formen- und Farbensprache". As Cork maintains, Kandinsky was primarily important to several of the Vorticist circle because he helped them towards abstraction. Correspondingly, five of the fourteen passages omitted by Wadsworth from "Formen- und Farbensprache" either allow or advocate the use in painting of empirical objects and Wadsworth's development away from the "speeded-up Impressionism" of Futurism evident in his pictures *Radiation, March* and *Scherzo* (1913-14) may well have been connected with his study of Kandinsky's theory. Similarly, although Hulme did not rate Kandinsky's work very highly, he approved of his abstractionism in principle; Nevinson, in "Vital English Art", an article which implicitly used abstraction as the touchstone of modernity, called Kandinsky's three paintings at the 1914 AAA salon "three of the finest modern pictures I have ever seen"; and Lewis (who, according to Weisstein, "never sympathized with Kandinsky's art") not only praised him in an interview as "the chief apostle of absolute abstraction in painting in Europe today" but also, five years later, in *The Caliph's Design,* that "little vorticist bagatelle", called him "the most advanced artist in Europe . . . according to the above criterion of 'modernness' [i.e. abstraction]".

There were, however, two other motives behind Vorticist interest in Kandinsky. Wadsworth's choice of extracts from "Formen- und Farbensprache" indicates that he was drawn to Kandinsky's theories of the mystical origins of the innerer Klang, the inner resonance of a work of art, as do his remarks accompanying his translations concerning "cosmic organisation" and "the deeper and more spiritual standpoint of the soul." And Pound, that "ardent Kandinskyan," having read Kandinsky's "chapter on the language of form and colour," found that it confirmed his ideas on the writing of verse. For Pound, Kandinsky's notion of the "innere Notwendigkeit" which generated a work of art corresponded exactly to his own thinking about "the creative power of the artist"—that unconscious psychic drive which produced the completely appropriate image. In other words, Kandinsky's work contributed to the formulation of both sides of the Vorticist aesthetic—the advocacy of hard-edged, abstract form and the concern with primal energy.

From mid-1909 until he went to Berlin in late 1912, Hulme had been an enthusiastic Bergsonian. He translated his *Introduction à la métaphysique* (which appeared in 1913) and commended him for liberating men from anthropomorphism, the absolute hold of logical reason and a mechanical and deterministic view of the universe. He also expressed his gratitude to him for giving him back a concept of "soul" and a "spiritual view of the world." Hulme's experience of Berlin, the overheated world of its avant garde (described in "German Chronicle") and, most particularly, his discovery of Worringer through reading Paul Ernst's essay "Kunst und Religion" changed all that. Hulme's letter to Marsh indicates that when he first went to Berlin, he knew only of "Einfuhlungsästhetik" which, deriving from the work of Riegl, Lipps and Volkelt, assumed a harmonious relationship between man, the world and art-objects and legitimized a representational art which allowed the beholder to feel himself into the object and at home in the world. Worringer's work, however, (which Hulme, stimulated by Ernst's essay, seems to have got to know only in 1913 since it is not mentioned in the letter to Marsh as featuring in his conversations on aesthetics with Rupert Brooke in late 1912) criticized the Lippsian aesthetic for its anthropo- and ethnocentrism and proposed a different kind of aesthetic—that of "Abstraktion"—as a way of explaining non-representational, non-Western and pre-Renaissance art. According to Worringer such art derived from a drastic sense of not being at home in the world, of being exposed to chthonic, daemonic powers, and represented man's attempt to defend himself against engulfment by means of stable, abstract forms. Worringer's revolutionary notion of "Abstraktion", encountered in the over-heated atmosphere of avant-garde Berlin, had four effects on Hulme. First, it connected with and intensified his sense, already well-developed by his reading of Bergson, that the world was in flux; second, it developed his sense that this flux was chaotic and destructive rather than harmonious and spiritual; third, it made him more open to abstract art; and fourth, it gave him the sense that the era which had produced and was legitimized by "Einfuhlungsästhetik"—the liberal humanist epoch—was coming to an end. The shifts in Hulme's outlook are immediately evident in his publications after his return to England in mid- to late 1913. In "Mr Epstein and the Critics," Hulme, for the first time, announced the end of the post-Renaissance era and declared Epstein's abstract sculpture appropriate to the new age. In "Modern Art I. The Grafton Group," "Modern Art and its Philosophy" and "Modern Art II," Hulme announced the same break-up of the Renaissance humanist attitude, acknowledged his debt to Worringer and proposed an austere, constructive, geometric art. And in "A Lecture on Modern Poetry" delivered in early 1914, he summarized Worringer's views on abstraction and argued that the modern age, being one of impermanence, required a new verse which "resembles sculpture rather than music", which "appeals to the eye rather than to the ear", and which "has to mould images, a kind of spiritual clay, into definite shapes." Thereafter, all Hulme's aesthetic and philosophical writings involved a critique of humanism: Worringer's art-historical distinction had become a polemical weapon.

Although Hulme did not consider himself a Vorticist and was at loggerheads with Lewis, his ideas had an undeniable effect upon the group. First, his insistence on hard, geometric art almost certainly reinforced that tendency to abstraction which was so prevalent among the Vorticists by early 1914; second, his thinking must have strengthened that interest in "primitive" art which was also present by the same date; and third, he must have begun to transmit the conviction—which is, to the best of my knowledge, never foregrounded in the title or substance of any work by any member of the Vorticist group before 1914—that the history of the West was about to undergo a drastic change of direction. The effect of Hulme's reception of Worringer is most evident in the case of Pound. Hulme's demand for hard-edged art was, of course, nothing new to Pound (who had known Hulme since 1909 and who, in his Imagist theorizing of 1912-13, had made just such demands himself). Nevertheless, Pound's essay "The New Sculpture" clearly indicates that he, as a direct result of hearing Hulme's lecture of 22 January 1914, was becoming aware of the cultural-historical implications of those demands. Thus, when Pound wrote that "Mr Hulme was quite right in saying that the difference between the new art and the old was not a difference in degree but a difference in kind, a difference in intention," he implied that he too was beginning to sense the passing of an era, and accordingly, the same essay went on to demand a neo-primitivism in art (which, for Pound, was to be found in the work of Epstein and Gaudier-Brzeska). Whereas Futurism had made the Vorticist group more aware of the technologization of the world, but presented this process—reassuringly—as part of a positive, upward movement of history, Hulme's version of Worringer implied that a much more fundamental upheaval was in store for the modern world from which men would need to seek refuge in works of austere, hardedged geometricity, not works which celebrated the flux of modern life.

Had war not broken out, the Vorticists would probably have become even more familiar with and positive about German Expressionism. The Twenty-One Gallery show of modern German art included twelve paintings by Moriz Melzer, two early woodcuts by Kandinsky (see above); one unidentifiable woodcut by Ernst Ludwig Kirchner, either a woodcut from Die Kleine Passion (1913) or Grosse Kreuzigung (1912) by Wilhelm Morgner, two woodcuts, two water-colours and a drawing by Max Pechstein; and the woodcuts Ruhende Pferde (1911-12), Trinkendes Pferd (1912), Tierlegende (1912), Tiger (1912) and Schöpfungsgeschichte (1914) by Franz Marc; and Lewis, in the Foreword to its Catalogue, praised the exhibits for their disciplined, brutal austerity (i.e. their approximation to a major aspect of the Vorticist aesthetic). Furthermore, in "German Chronicle", Hulme drew his readers' attention to such Expressionist magazines as Pan, Die weissen Blätter, Der Sturm, Der lose Vogel and Die Aktion; reported on a visit to Kurt Hiller's Cabaret GNU on 24 May 1913 at which items by Ernst Blass, Paul Boldt, Arthur Drey, Alfred Wolfenstein and Hiller himself were read out; reviewed Hiller's Der Kondor (1912), the first and controversial anthology of Expressionist poetry, with particular reference to individual poems by Blass, Else Lasker-Schüler, Georg Heym, Drey and René Schickele; mentioned Werfel's anthologies Der Weltfreund (1911) and Wir sind (1913), Max Brod's anthology Tagebuch in Versen (1910), Shickele's anthology Weiss und Rot (1910), Herbert Grossberger's anthology Exhibitionen (1913) and Alfred Lichtenstein's anthology Dämmerung (1913); and indicated that he had had at least one extensive conversation with Hiller's close friend, the psychiatrist Arthur

Kronfeld. Overall, Hulme's article—which must have been the first ever to point English-speaking readers towards Expressionist poetry—gives the impression that things are happening in Berlin which, even if not entirely comprehensible to the Englishman, are new, intelligent, aggressive and worth watching. If the Vorticists failed to follow Hulme's pointers, it was probably more because the War cut off their access to the sources than because there was a quality in Expressionist poetry which made it inherently alien to the Vorticists. Had the Vorticists known that combination of formal discipline and apocalyptic violence which marks much of the poetry of, say, Jakob van Hoddis, Heym or Georg Trakl, they would have had no difficulty in assimilating this mode of writing to their own ambiguous aesthetic.

THE PROBLEMS OF A COMPARATIVE STUDY

Although Vorticist receptivity towards the German avant garde encourages one to take the initial comparative thoughts further, such an undertaking involves two methodological hazards. First, there is the danger that it will degenerate into a nominalistic exercise in which the critic attempts to define an abstracted concept (i.e. Vorticism or Expressionism) either by drawing up a list of doctrines and surface stylistic traits or by narrowing down the concept to one "essential feature". Where the former approach bedevils much of the copious secondary literature on Expressionism, the latter makes itself felt in the much less numerous discussions of Vorticism. Inevitably, both approaches produce artificial questions (such as those which ask how far individuals are representatives of movements); readings of texts, be they literary or visual, which sacrifice complexity to conformity with abstract definition; and the neglect of historical data. It has to be remembered that "Expressionism" was a label imposed by outsiders and accepted by practitioners (if at all) only relatively late, and that the label "Vorticism" was invented by Pound for the Rebel Art Centre group only a few weeks before the appearance of *Blast 1* on 15 July 1914 more as a publicistic slogan than, as was the case with the term "Futurism", the summation of a set of doctrines subscribed to by a closely-knit group. Second, there is the danger—which Weisstein did not entirely avoid—of presenting the two movements as static and self-contained. The two labels apply to phenomena which were both dynamic and diverse. Even Vorticism, which, unlike Expressionism, was small, geographically concentrated and relatively short-lived, underwent a change after the outbreak of war, and there was considerable stylistic diversity not only between but also within the work of the individuals who constituted the two movements.

If then, the two movements are to be compared, it is first necessary to get beyond the reassuring sense of static unity which comes from a reductionist use of their labels, and then to overcome the scepticism about such a comparative project which inevitably arises when the internal diversity, previously concealed by those labels, is recognized. It then becomes possible to identify and compare the problematics which informed the two movements, and, by locating them in the cultural situations from which they arose, to compare the texts which were created as the diverse and

even (self-) contradictory responses to those problematics. By concentrating on the subliminal interplay between problematic and response, such an approach views the resultant texts not as autotelic aesthetic objects but as signifiers of the diverse possibilities generated by that interplay. Concomitantly therefore, the same approach, inasmuch as it concentrates on "libidinal apparatus" rather than surface style, views the two movements not as phases in a linear history of art or literature, but as aspects of that cultural brisure from which European Modernism as a whole arose.

At the same time as they presented a "creative personality" in print or on canvas, or made statements about "creativity" in their essays and manifestos, both Expressionists and Vorticists implicitly posed four linked questions: Is the irrational power of creativity spiritual/intellectual or natural/animal? Is that power only apparently creative and in reality destructive? Is it related to cosmic forces? And are those forces, assuming that they exist, ultimately patterned or destructive?

— Richard Sheppard

Methodological hazards notwithstanding, the Expressionists and Vorticists shared a very similar problematic. As Lewis said, reviewing the "-isms" of the pre-war years: "In every case the structural and philosophic rudiments of life were sought out. On all hands a return to first principles was witnessed." Basic to that search was the rejection of the norms of bourgeois humanism and of classical or representational art Gottfried Benn's Morgue poems one of which begins: "Die Krone der Schöpfung, der Mensch, das Schwein / geht doch mit anderen Tieren um"; Rob Cairn's statement in Lewis's "The French Poodle" that "Man is losing his significance" Alfred Döblin's "Ermordung einer Butterblume" which shows the impotence of human arrogance in the face of Nature; Carl Einstein's fantastic novel *Bebuquin* (1906-09) which is one long inversion of anthropomorphic thinking; Pound's censure of the humanist artist and polemic against the Renaissance the rejection of the anthropocentrism of the Marburg *Erkenntniskritiker* Hermann Cohen which is common to both Hulme and the early Expressionist Neuer Club the scepticism vis-à-vis the capacities of human reason which characterizes Hulme's writings on Bergson and the irrationalist half of the Neuer Club; Hulme's writings from the months after his return from Germany (see above); Kandinsky's mystical view of art; the Vorticists' machine forms; Marc's paintings and woodcuts which placed animals at the centre of Creation; Gaudier-Brzeska's primitivism and rejection, in his letter of 24 October 1912, of "a badly understood tradition which has always taught blind adoration of the Greeks and Romans"—all, in their various ways, aim, like much of Lewis's major prose fiction from the Vorticist decade, at the subversion of "the humanistic paradigm, the received idea of a pre-existing human nature and the illusions of an autonomous, centred 'self' or formal identity."

Conversely, both Vorticists and Expressionists sought, through their artefacts, to envisage a new kind of being—and here, echoes of *Zarathustra* are audible—in whom the repressed powers of creativity—that "lost reality and . . . lost intensity" as Pound puts it—are released; who thereby stands out from the masses and who, precisely because he is not the rationally ordered, harmoniously centred self of bourgeois humanism, is capable of living adequately amid the tumultuous, many-layered violence of the modern world. And it was exactly this connection between art and life that Lewis was making when he said, in retrospect, that the "novel alphabet of shapes and colours" created by Vorticism, Cubism and Expressionism "presupposed" (i.e. was the expression of) a "new human ethos".

At the same time as they presented a "creative personality" in print or on canvas, or made statements about "creativity" in their essays and manifestos, both Expressionists and Vorticists implicitly posed four linked questions: Is the irrational power of creativity spiritual/intellectual or natural/animal? Is that power only apparently creative and in reality destructive? Is it related to cosmic forces? And are those forces, assuming that they exist, ultimately patterned or destructive?

Not surprisingly, the possible answers to such questions are bewilderingly diverse. Not only is there no consensus about the answers within either movement, but individual artists will present a "creative personality" only simultaneously to deconstruct that presentation, or, in several texts from roughly the same period, offer answers to such questions which stand in stark contradiction to one another. In Expressionist literature, Walter Hasenclever's play *Der Sohn* (1913), Reinhard Sorge's play *Der Bettler* (1911), Georg Kaiser's play *Von Morgens bis Mitternachts* (1912) and Hanns Johst's play *Der Einsame* (1917) provide good examples of the former phenomenon. In all four, a hero is presented whose creativity is, at the outset, repressed by a real father, or, in the case of Kaiser's and Johst's plays, patriarchal authority (the bank and small-town philistinism). And in all four, the heroes seek to release that creativity by a desperate revolt. However, after what seems like initial success (episodes when all four heroes experience a moment of intense, unfettered release of their creative potential), the plays, with varying degrees of self-consciousness, deconstruct the ethos of creative vitalism. *Der Sohn* shows that ethos leading the son into the hands of politically suspect, right-wing anarchists; exposes it, in the scene with the prostitute, as nothing more than a dressed-up form of adolescent self-dramatization; and, in the final act, shows it bringing the son to the brink of murder (which is avoided only because the father has a convenient heart-attack when the son is about to pull the trigger). In *Der Bettler,* the same ethos leads the central character to a double murder, and in the other two plays, it brings about the death or ruin of several secondary char-

acters and a state of totally disillusioned, emotional exhaustion in the two central characters (a conclusion which is avoided in the dizzily spiralling *Der Bettler* only because the action stops before its full implications can be realized). In all four cases, the forces of creativity are shown to be closely related with forces of destruction. One can see the same debate in the inner contradictions of the visual, literary and theoretical work of Kandinsky 1908-14, the various strands of the poetry of Jakob van Hoddis and the prose and poetry of Heym. Although critics have often imposed a unity on Heym's work, it actually points in several directions. Where his early poems and dramas (1908-10) point to the conclusion that the irrational powers driving human nature are basically bestial, destructive and linked with a hostile Fate, some of his stories and poems from 1911 involve a sense that behind the dark stratum of human experience, there lies a spiritual power which points beyond itself to a force in the cosmos that is basically good. In none of the cases cited is it a question of simple "development": various alternatives are juxtaposed—probably without the artist's awareness—and the reader is invited to consider and choose.

The abstract debate within Expressionism about the nature of creativity revolved around that untranslatable word *Geist*. For Kandinsky, imbued as he was with theosophical ideas, *Geist* was the creative, metaphysical power behind the cosmos ("das Ewig-Objektive") which also worked in the human personality ("das Zeitlich-Subjektive") to produce art. In contrast, Kurt Hiller, who disliked Kandinsky's mysticism, regarded *Geist* as something purely human, designating a rational/moral faculty of perception, decision and will. Consequently, in 1918, he engaged in a violent, public polemic with his former friend Fritz Koffka over precisely this issue. Whereas Koffka described *Geist* in a religious fashion as "die grosse Liebe, die von ausserhalb her die Welt umfangt", Hiller equated the same concept with "Ratio" and described it as that which imposes morally-directed, human control on the irrational, animal parts of the personality and the chaos of Nature. A third position—one which was particularly characteristic of early Expressionism—was most clearly taken by Ludwig Rubiner who, in the immensely influential essay "Der Dichter greift in die Politik," described *Geist* as the power of "Intensität", the "Wille zur Katastrophe" which produced "Feuersbrünste, Explosionen, Absprünge von hohen Türmen, Licht, Umsichschlagen, Amokschreien." Where, for Kandinsky, *Geist* was spiritual and creative, for the pre-war Rubiner it was chthonic and essentially destructive (even if it did provide the experience of "eine ewige Sättigung in einem einzigen Moment"); where, for Hiller, Geist was a purely human faculty, for the Rubiner of the pre-war years it was linked with the violent forces of untamed Nature.

The same debate went on among the Vorticists and is particularly evident in Lewis's early prose and drama. Here, shifting perspectives within and on the narratives, ironically detached modes of narration and impeccably Vorticist statements in the mouths of characters whose point of view is suspect or flawed combine to show that Lewis was experimenting with psychological and metaphysical attitudes rather than maintaining one dogmatically—a statement which applies to his work both during the narrowly Vorticist period and the decade 1909-20 as a whole. For example, it is clear that Lewis meant at first to celebrate the pre-modern characters of his early short stories (1909-11) as "primitive creatures, immersed in life, as much as birds, or big, obsessed, sun-drunk insects." However, these stories became progressively darker over the two years until, in the last of them, "Brobdingnag," Lewis shows how easy it is for happy, primitive "naturalness" to tip over into murder and insanity, and the story (which, significantly perhaps, was Lewis's last piece of prose fiction to be published for three years) ends: "I felt, in quitting Kermanec, that the shadow of doom had fallen upon this roof ". Possibly as a result of this conclusion, Arghol, the central figure of "Enemy of the Stars," is the complete antithesis of the early "primitives". In Arghol, Lewis has created a being whose creative principle is not an earthy vitality, but a cold, white, brutal, intellectual will. Arghol has set himself against the threat posed by chaotic Nature and deliberately expunged the (associated) female side of his personality. At first, it seems that Lewis is unambiguously celebrating this monster (who is so akin to the typically Vorticist man-machine), but the values that he stands for are called into question when Hanp, his "half-disciple" in whom there is still a "deep female strain," murders him out of resentment at his massively male authority—whereupon the "relief of a grateful universe" becomes audible. "Enemy of the Stars" is as much a critique as a celebration of Arghol (and, by implication, the notion of creativity as hard-edged, monumental will): the play shows the self-destructiveness of Arghol's way of life even while setting it up as an ideal.

If Lewis's early stories and Vorticist play provided the two poles of the problematic, his prose fiction of the first two war years complicated it. *Tarr,* written during the Vorticist period and before the Great War had made its impact, is, to some extent, a restatement of what Lewis had already said. Otto Kreisler, "the place of archaic regression" is a more extreme version of Lewis's early primitives, whose self-destructiveness forms its own critique. And Tarr himself, whose very actions are heavy and machine-like, who finds the flesh and the female repugnant and who preaches a view of creativity based on the ascetic intellect and will, is similar in type to Arghol. And as with Arghol, Lewis offers an implicit critique of what Tarr stands for: despite his repugnance, he has an affair with Bertha, a heavily fleshly, Romantic German Maiden; he comes across as an "emotionally shallow" and "boorish young man"; he hardly ever seems to produce any art of note despite his claim to be an artist; his name, Sorbert [Sorbet] Tarr, with its implications of black stickiness and melting sweetness, fits ill with the icy clarity he professes and makes him more than slightly comic; and in the second half of the novel, he succumbs to the sensuality of Anastasya who completely overturns all the ideals he had earlier professed. Lewis, even while putting ideas into Tarr's mouth, deconstructs them through his presentation of the total character. Consequently, within the context of Vorticism, *Tarr* can be read as a critique of the two extreme notions of creativity with which that movement is associated. On the one hand, Tarr is frequently depicted, in the first part of the novel, as an amalgam of machine-parts, a hard-

shelled, mechanical automaton whose actions are not governed by a personal pronoun. As such, he is reminiscent of the inhuman beings to be found in Lewis's pictures of the same period and the change he undergoes through the agency of Anastasya clearly implies the unacceptability of that ideal of personality. On the other hand, Kreisler's name derives from the German word for a spinning-top, "Kreisel", an image which relates directly to the notion of the Vortex as that is depicted in *Blast*—"stable and self-contained, yet suggesting whirling concentrations of energy . . . spinning in space on an unshakeable axis." Clearly, the fact that Kreisler destroys himself indicates that Lewis had reservations about the Vorticist ideal of energy as well. Nevertheless, having shown the limitations of both hard-edged form and unconstrained energy, *Tarr* explores a third possibility in Anastasya (whose name comes from the Greek word for "resurrection"). In her, the extremes of intellect and energy—Apollo and Dionysos—have been fused into a being who is whole, balanced and self-possessed without anarchy or egotism. Although Lewis offers no label for the creative drive which impels her and makes her so special, it is very different from the angular violence hymned in the pages of Blast and points beyond the "conflictual organization" of the rest of the novel and, indeed, of the Vorticist movement as a whole.

The same debate about the nature of creativity is continued and made more complex elsewhere. "The French Poodle" is not certain whether men are driven by a power which is the same as or different from that which drives animals, whether the spontaneity of animal nature is higher or lower than that of the creative force behind human nature, and whether war is a product of the vital forces of Nature, the animal powers in man or a perverse destructiveness that is peculiar to man. "A Young soldier" is uncertain whether to admire or condemn the vital urges in a young soldier glimpsed in the Tube, depicting him as a Nietzschean blond beast, "a born warrior, meant to kill other men as much as a woman is meant to bear children". Similar ambiguities are evident in the two narratives which involve Cantleman, another of Lewis's personae. In "The War-Crowds 1914" (part of an unpublished book written in July-August 1914, some of which appeared as a variant entitled "The Crowd Master"). Cantleman is presented as yet another, lesser Arghol who, despite his cerebral detachment, permits himself to experience the "female" enthusiasm which drives the crowds in Trafalgar Square at the outbreak of war. This does nothing for him, however, and confirmed in his previous beliefs, he rejects the female even more emphatically for the superior, male, intellectual detachment of "the stone Nelson" on his column. In "Cantleman's Spring-Mate", however, written three years later, this version of the creative personality is deconstructed. After a vision of lush, natural fecundity (a passage which, in its sensuality and freedom from narrative irony, is unlike anything else in Lewis's early prose and in which the procreative urges in man are derived unequivocally from the powers of Nature), the previously aloof Cantleman makes a country girl pregnant. So far, as Materer says, this is a straightforward case of "ironic defeat", but then, to complicate matters, Lewis links the sexual drive with the War, concluding: "And when [Cantleman] beat a German's brains out, it was with the same impartial malignity that he had displayed in the English night with his Springmate": clearly, in terms of this story, to succumb to Dionysos is as dangerous as to ignore him. In none of these shorter pieces, however, is there a figure like Anastasya: their multiple ambiguities are presented and the reader is left to puzzle further.

A similar process is implicit in the three visual styles of the illustrations of *Blast*. Moving as they do between representationalism and abstraction; balance and imbalance; violently and less obtrusively imposed form, they are at one level visual attempts to get beyond anthropomorphism and, at another, visual responses to the question of how far rigid form needs to be imposed on natural energy. The same problematic underlies Gaudier-Brzeska's diverse sculptures of 1914. On the one hand, hard-edged Vorticist works like *Bird Swallowing a Fish* and *Toy* imply the necessity of subjecting chaotically violent Nature to humanly imposed form, but on the other hand, vitalistic works like *Stags* and *Birds Erect* imply that Nature, which may seem chaotic to the conventional eye, has its own inherent principle of organic form which the artist must learn to perceive and reproduce. The same applies to Ford Madox Hueffer's "The Saddest Story" (a chapter from his novel *The Good Soldier*) and Rebecca West's "Indissoluble Matrimony" in *Blast 1*. Neither Hueffer nor West were Vorticists in the reductionist or doctrinal sense, but Lewis must have perceived that both pieces bore on the problematic which exercised his circle. The former piece is a relatively straightforward investigation of the nature and effect of the passional, sexual energies on the excessively civilized, humanized world of polite society, but the latter piece is much more complex. Here, an enfeebled, excessively cerebral petit-bourgeois is seized by the violence of Nature (personified by his "over-sexed", quarter-negro wife). As a result of swimming at night in the "Devil's Cauldron", they both turn into completely primitive beings who nearly murder each other. Clearly, "Indissoluble Matrimony" is both an implicit critique of the male who has done violence to the female in himself (and on whom, therefore, the female inevitably takes revenge), and a statement about the close relationship between the creative, sexual urge and the destructiveness of inhuman Nature. Like Lewis in his war-time stories, West shuns a simple resolution, leaving the reader to find his own way between a series of polar suggestions about the nature of creativity which are both antithetical and complementary.

The Vorticists' theoretical statements on the same subject are similarly complex. To take one detailed example only: throughout the years 1909-1918, Pound veered between an immanentist view of creativity which locates the source of that power in human nature or a human tradition, and a more mystical neo-Platonism. And in the more strictly defined Vorticist period, he veered between a view of creativity as an ordered, spiritual, pythagorean power (hence the mathematical imagery in "Vorticism [1]") and a violent, cathonic, barbarian power (cf "The New Sculpture"). Nor will one find Pound making any consistent statements about Nature during this period. Sometimes, like Lewis in "A Review of Contemporary Art," he writes as though Nature were inherently patterned, commends Chinese geomancers for their intuitive sense of that pat-

terning and counsels the modern artist to seek it out and reproduce it abstractly in his work. Sometimes, however, he writes as though Nature were pure chaos and implies that the artist's task is to impose form upon that chaos. Pound is typical of the movement as a whole: like the Expressionists—and this is the major similarity between the two movements—the Vorticists were collectively agreed that a lost principle of creativity must be recovered, but differed widely over the nature of that power and the proper relationship between it and humankind. Accordingly, while the Vorticists' machine aesthetic of hard-edged forms is characteristic of many of their explicitly programmatic statements and foregrounded in many of their artworks, it is not the whole picture but simply one product of a more fundamental debate, the innermost terms of which have to be discovered at a much more subliminal level.

THE CULTURAL-HISTORICAL SITUATIONS OF VORTICISM AND EXPRESSIONISM

The above debate did not go on in abstraction. Rather, the terms in which it was conducted were closely bound up with the cultural-historical situations of the two movements. These differed in three important ways. To begin with, most Expressionists were born (in the 1870s and 1880s) into a society which was largely agrarian and semi-feudal; grew up in a society which was changing its nature at an unprecedented rate; and achieved maturity in a society which was centered on large, industrialized cities. In contrast, the Vorticists were active in a society where the same process had been going on gradually, over the best part of a century, so that industry and machines seemed an accepted, "natural" part of the landscape rather than anything drastically new. As Lewis claimed to have told Marinetti: "We've had machines here in England for a donkey's years. They're no novelty to us." Second, by 1914, the very nature of the emergent social and economic order in Germany stood in clear contradiction to the highly authoritarian, rigidly stratified institutions by which it had been uneasily, not to say forcibly, contained. In contrast, Liberal England did not suffer from the same sense of inner contradiction even if, in reality, that contradiction was there. Having come about more slowly, industrialization had been assimilated with greater ease, and the English ruling class, more adaptable than its German counterpart, had, to a markedly greater extent than in Germany, succeeded in taking the new monied classes into itself: despite the Feinians and Suffragettes, English society seemed to be in a state of harmonious evolution, not inner contradiction. Third, partly because of the rate of social change and partly because of the brevity of its existence as a nation, Wilhelmine Germany was haunted by a sense of historical impermanence, the paradoxical symptom of which was the exaggerated monumentality of so many of its institutions. English institutions, however, had never seemed so unselfconsciously secure, supported as they were by centuries of unbroken tradition and the wealth of a still submissive Empire.

As a result, the basic experience of the Vorticists differed from that of the Expressionists in several important respects. To begin with, the early Expressionists suffered from a threefold sense of oppression. At one and the same time, they felt cut off from a living past, oppressed by the huge weight of static, authoritarian institutions above their heads, and threatened by the violence which they perceived in the mushrooming cities. This threefold sense explains why so much of their most typical poetry consists in a collage of simultaneous impressions rather than a diachronic narrative; why the father (who, in their imaginations, was a hypostatized amalgam of the old authority of semi-feudal Prussia and the new authority of the successful capitalist) was such a major problem in their writings; why so many of their paintings and poems evince such a powerful sense of apocalyptic violence and why, in order to find roots, so many of them identified so readily with mythicized worlds, which were geographically or historically as far removed from the present as possible. In contrast, the Vorticists evinced a strong sense of standing within a well-grounded social continuum which had become stodgy and sterile rather than static and oppressive and whose modern manifestation—the mechine age—was exciting rather than threatening. The whole of Pound's critical and poetic work during the Vorticist years (i.e. until he lost faith in England and moved to Paris) was rooted in a confidence that English social institutions, although in a bad way, could be revitalized by the power of art. Accordingly, for Pound, the Vorticists were the radical inheritors of a tradition which was basically good but temporarily sterile and it was in this spirit that he proclaimed: "The futurists are evidently ignorant of tradition . . . We [the Vorticists] do not desire to cut ourselves off from the past" and: "The vorticist has not this curious tic for destroying past glories." Similarly, as late as *Blast 2* (July 1915), Lewis could not envisage England losing her Empire which, in his view, was the "one thing that would have deeply changed her" and could confidently assert that "life after the War will be the same brilliant life as it was before the War." Accordingly, it is significant that of the Vorticist circle, only Hulme, *primarily as a result of his exposure to Berlin,* lost this sense of social continuity to any marked degree during the Vorticist period itself. Where his articles on Bergson from late 1911 proclaim the continuity of history, its "fixity and sameness," his post-Berlin articles imply that the present has somehow become detached from the past until, in late 1915, he could write quite explicitly: "One of the main achievements of the Nineteenth Century was the elaboration and universal application of the principle of continuity. The destruction of this conception is . . . an urgent necessity of the present."

In contrast, the early Expressionists had an ambiguous relationship with their society: although oppressed by and alienated from it, they were also, as good Bürgersöhne, dependent on and eager for recognition by it. And it was precisely this ambiguity which generated the violence of their social attitudes such as is to be found in Sorge's *Der Bettler* or Hasenclever's *Der Sohn.* This signified on the one hand a desire to smash the source of oppression, and, on the other, a resentment against a patriarchal society for failing to give them proper recognition. The Vorticist circle, however, had a much less polarized relationship with literary and artistic London and certainly did not feel so oppressed by English social institutions. Indeed, some of them even

gained the entrée for a while to the highest social circles. Lady Cunard wanted them to design little presents for the rich and influential guests attending a dinner in honour of George Moore, asked Lewis and Nevinson to lunch, invited Lewis to share her box at Covent Garden and expressed her admiration for one of Cuthbert Hamilton's pictures. Lady Muriel Paget wanted the group around Lewis to design *avant-garde tableaux vivants* for a Picture Ball at the Albert Hall and Nevinson recalled being invited to dine by Lady Lavery and Lady Constance Hatch. In late 1913, Lady Drogheda commissioned Lewis to decorate her dining-room and he later recorded that, after the publication of *Blast 1,* coronetted envelopes showered into his letter-box and that, at one of Lady Ottoline Morrell's gatherings, he met the then Prime Minister, Mr Asquith, whom he was able to reassure about the a-political nature of Vorticism! Even though the less socially acceptable members of the Vorticist circle—Epstein the American Jew, Pound the professional Bohemian, Bomberg the East End Jew and Gaudier-Brzeska the wild Frenchman—may well have disapproved of such contacts, none of them seems to have known that acute sense of social alienation which characterized German Expressionism. Conversely, one cannot imagine the German counterpart of English polite society extending the same kind of invitation to, say, Kurt Hiller, Emil Nolde, Herwarth Walden or Ludwig Meidner!

In consequence, where a prophetic or revolutionary stance came naturally to the Expressionists, the Vorticists, for all their apparent radicalism, rarely used the word "revolution". Affectionate if violent rebels, they existed much more within the given social institutions and did not feel the need to smash them because they did not feel trapped by them to anything like the same extent. Thus, in *Blast 1,* England is blasted and blessed (a series of texts for which there is no parallel in German Expressionist magazines), its institutions are attacked and enjoyed. Where the Expressionists looked for an apocalypse that would sweep everything away and initiate a society which was qualitatively different—an attitude encapsulated in Rubiner's "Der Dichter greift in die Politik"—the Vorticists, while accusing English society of being dead, had a much greater faith in its ability to resurrect itself without violent upheaval. Lewis wrote, for instance: "Optimism is very permissible. England appears to be recovering" and advocated a modification (not a revolutionizing) of the national temperament. Pound liked London, describing it on 18 March 1914 as "the only sane place for anyone to live if they've any pretence to letters" and until he went to Paris, continually expressed his faith in "the power of tradition, of centuries of race consciousness, of agreement, of association" to renew the arts and society. Right in the middle of the Vorticist period, Pound even described what was happening in present-day England as a "renaissance, or awakening" (i.e. of what was dormant in the tradition) not as a cataclysmic irruption of powers from outside into that tradition. And *Blast,* its radical clangour notwithstanding, presented England optimistically, as a "lump of compressed life," and the machine age as the continuation rather than the antithesis of an older social tradition, in which the vitality that had moved past epochs was still active. Although the Vorticists felt that violent movement was occurring beneath the placid surface of English society, they also felt, with the exception of Hulme after his return from Berlin, that that movement was taking English society in the same direction in which it had been moving before the sterility of the late Victorian epoch had intervened. In contrast, the Expressionists had an acute sense that violent forces were about to blow their society apart. As Heym remarked to Friedrich Schulze-Maizier in early 1910 as they walked home at night through the streets of Berlin: "Nun schauen Sie sich das einmal an. Wie gehetzt, wie hohl, wie gottverlassen! Das *kann* nicht bleiben, das muss zugrundegehen. Irgend etwas Ungeheures muss kommen, ein grosser Krieg, eine Revolution oder sonst etwas. Aber nur nicht so weiter!" Accordingly, when Pound came, on 15 November 1918, to describe the events of the Vorticist years, he remarked: "As for the 'revolution', we have had one here during the war, *quite orderly* [my italics], in the extension of the franchise. Nobody much minds there being several more." The double irony is evident: not only has a revolution not taken place, but Pound is actually more than a little pleased that this should have been so. There was a tacit collusion between English society and its aesthetic radicals: on the one hand, the Vorticists hurled ideas around that were revolutionary and subversive to a certain degree only while finding support from the stability of the very institutions they purported to be assailing, and on the other hand, established society took those ideas into itself from on high, proving, in the process, its liberalism and their harmlessness. What Lewis said of himself could apply to Vorticism as a whole: "Kill John Bull' I shouted. And John and Mrs Bull leapt for joy, in a cynical convulsion. For they felt as safe as houses. So did I"—an ambivalence which is also present in the contrast between the stable, realist setting of *Tarr* and the expressionistoid antics of its central figures. In Germany, however, there was not the same collusion: early Expressionism may have been as socially harmless as Vorticism, but its representatives were never so lionized by the social establishment and genuinely wanted violent social change which, as Korte has put it, was to be the "Inbegriff und Synthese aller Sehnsüchte des entfremdeten, den perhorreszierten Zwängen des Wilhelminismus ausgelieferten Subjekts nach Vitalität, exzeptionellen Erlebnissen, Erfüllung, Verwirklichung und Identität."

Because of their differing cultural experiences, Nietzsche was far less important for the Vorticists than for the Expressionists. Whereas, on the whole, the Expressionists received Nietzsche positively, being particularly drawn by his apocalyptic cultural criticism and its counterpart, his ecstatic vitalism, the Vorticists, rooted in an apparently reliable tradition, had less need of this. Although some of them were, for various reasons, drawn to Nietzsche before 1910, their comments became guarded or ambiguous from 1910 to 1913 and hostile from 1914 onwards. Thus, in "Redondillas, or something of that Sort" (c.1910-11), Pound said that he believed in "some parts of Nietzsche" but suspected him "of being the one modern christian"; Hulme, writing in mid-to-late 1913, associated Nietzsche with a linguistic experimentation with which he was not altogether happy; Pound, writing in Autumn 1913, used the word "Nietzschean" pejoratively; in *Blast 1*, Lewis associated Nietzsche with Marinetti's "war-talk, sententious

elevation and much besides"; on Lewis's own admission, Nietzsche was "another and more immediate source of infection" for the ironically distanced *Tarr* in general and the negatively presented Kreisler in particular; in *Blast 2*, Lewis connected Nietzsche with ecstatic war-fever and the absurd Beresin of "The War Baby" (c.1916) is a caricature of the Nietzschean aristocrat. Precisely because the Vorticists were not haunted by a sense of imminent apocalypse, they could flirt selectively with aspects of Nietzsche's thought without, as so many Expressionists did, having to take his Dionysiac vision of chaos and rebirth seriously as a vitalist gospel of salvation. Thus, when they came to link that vision with Prussianism and the War, they could distance themselves from it with relative ease, as an unfortunate aberration which, as Pound said, was "all very well in conversation"—but not, by implication, in practice.

Given the above situation, Vorticist works differ from Expressionist ones in several major respects. First and foremost, the Dionysiac values—orgiastic sexuality, social apocalypse, natural violence and pan-demonism—are much more prominent in the German movement. In contrast, such elements are either totally absent from works by Vorticists, or present in a muted form, or controlled by strictly imposed form, or subject to a process of humanization. For example, most of Pound's poems from the Vorticist years do not foreground the demonic even when they deal with potentially demonic subjects, and this is true even of those he published in the two *Blasts*. The (deleted) sexual reference of "Fratres Minores" and the "Goddam" of "Ancient Music" are innocuous compared with the sexuality and obscenity to be found, say, in the poems of Hugo Ball, Lichtenstein and Benn; the satire of "The Social Order" is mild compared with the Germans' vitriolic attacks on the *Bürger;* and "Et faim sallir le loup des boys" may be contemptuous of family life, but unlike Trakl's "Im Osten" (1914), in which wild wolves burst through the city gates, it contains, despite its title, no ravenous wolves! Apart from Pound's brief flirtation with primitivism in Spring 1914, it is the same with his criticism. Joyce is praised for not "ploughing the underworld for horror" and "presenting a macabre subjectivity" and Pound's version of the god Pan evoked a "bewildering and pervasive music moving from precision to precision within itself"— not the "panic terror" which afflicted so many of the German *avant garde*. Analogously, although Eliot's poems depict the surreal, empty surfaces of the modern city, they do not conjure up its demonic night-side as do the poems of Heym, van Hoddis and Lichtenstein.

The Vorticists' sense of the controllability of violence is particularly evident in their paintings, woodcuts and sculptures. Where, in the visual Expressionist work, a violent and anarchic background often appears to be about to burst through the lines which roughly and barely contain it, Vorticist visual works, with their thick geometric lines, transmit a much more secure sense that such violence can be contained. The same sense informs Pound's most Vorticist poem, "Dogmatic Statement on the Game and Play of Chess"; Lewis's *Tarr,* the potential explosiveness of whose main characters is checked by the firm realism of its city setting and the easy, detached irony of the narrator, and Hulme's vision of flux, which, after his return from Germany, was accompanied by a growing advocacy of rigid artistic, ethical and religious form. Even Hulme's translation of Sorel's *Réflexions sur la violence* (1916) commends not undirected, but carefully disciplined violence, used for precisely defined ends. Indeed, it was their attachment to form which led the Vorticists to bless the Hairdresser for making "systematic mercenary war" on the "wildness" of Mother Nature!

The Vorticists' tendency to humanize what is potentially demonic becomes more evident after 1914. In *Blast 2,* it is to be found in Hueffer's poem "The Old Houses of Flanders" which offers a vision of genteel decay, not violent collapse; Jessie Dismorr's "London Notes" which, despite its Cubist surface, is, apart from the last line, actually a very naturalized picture of London; and Helen Sanders's "A Vision of Mud" which, beginning as a terrifying vision of engulfment, loses its threat when we hear, at the end, that its subject is a health resort. Similarly, the "religious attitude" behind Hulme's theology of 1915-16, far from being akin to Rudolf Otto's sense of the numinous or Karl Barth's sense of demonic *krisis,* has been reduced to a much more manageable intellectual belief in original sin; and Part I of Lewis's "A Soldier of Humour" evokes elemental and primitive powers only for these to be naturalized into a farce and rendered harmless in Part II.

By the same token, there is no equivalent in Vorticist works for the sense of imminent apocalypse to be found in Kandinsky's pre-1914 paintings and woodcuts, van Hoddis's "Weltende" (1910) or Heym's "Der Krieg" (1911)—and a comparison of Pound's "Meditatio" (c.1914) with Benn's "Der Arzt II" (1912) makes it quite clear that the Vorticists did not share the Expressionists' extreme sense of the animal in man. Consequently, when the Vorticists confronted Expressionist works, it was precisely such elements that they overlooked or played down. Kandinsky's paintings were appreciated for their abstraction rather than their sense of apocalyptic disorder; Lewis, appraising the woodcuts in the Twenty-One Gallery, saw "man and objects subject to him" and thick, blunt, brutal discipline—not the elemental suffering of Morgner's passion scenses, or the dormant animalism of Marc's *Ruhendes Pferd, Trinkendes Pferd* and *Tierlegende,* or the apocalyptic creativity of Marc's *Schöpfungsgeschichte.* Hulme remarked briefly on the "ferocity" of the Expressionist poetry that he heard in the Cabaret GNU, only then to concentrate his account of it on its hard, cerebral and formal qualities. Only rarely do the Vorticists allow the dark, chaotic underworld of Nature and the Unconscious into the foreground of their work—one finds it in the natural violence of "Enemy of the Stars", the description of the Restaurant Lejeune in Part II, Chapter 5 of *Tarr,* the presentation of primal Nature in "Indissoluble Matrimony" and "Cantleman's Spring-Mate", Pound's single glimpse of the horrors of London's lower depths and Hulme's more developed sense of the chaos in Nature after his return from Berlin. However, such texts (which approach Expressionism in their intensity) are rare, not typical, and accordingly, the extremism of Vorticism is, to a certain extent, deceptive. Pound wrote of *Blast:* "The

large type and the flaring cover are merely bright plumage. They are the gay petals which lure"; and Lewis said in April 1919: "When you leap on to a new continent for the first time you are compelled to make a slight din to frighten away any savages that may be lurking in the neighbourhood". The apocalyptic din of a world tearing itself apart which is to be heard among the Expressionists becomes, within Vorticism, a deliberately induced noise aimed at a world experienced as basically stable: the Vorticist knows of Dionysos and even approaches him, but only appears to let him get the upper hand.

Consequently, where early Expressionist works stress the unreality of the present, being situated in the vacant instant before things blow apart, Vorticism affirms the reality and plenitude of the present; where Expressionist works are torn by extremes, Vorticist works move much more confidently between those extremes; where the "Ich" of the Expressionist artist is continually attracted by mindless ecstasy or threatened by destructive violence, the Vorticist ego is confidently affirmed as the creator of form; where the "Reihungsstil" of early Expressionist poetry is the product of a desperate attempt to hold together an assemblage of fragments which is in danger of being exploded, the Poundian haiku is as centred, and therefore as secure as the circle-creating formula of analytical geometry with which Pound compared it. Correspondingly, where Expressionist art involves a sense that objects are illusory, mere aspects of flux and hence in constant danger of breaking apart, the Vorticists have a much greater, though by no means unambiguous sense of the reality of objects. Thus, although the objects in their works are packed with or surrounded by energy, it is a propellant, not a destructive energy. The same attitude is visible in their theoretical work. Although Hulme could, in late 1911, agree with the proposition that "reality is a continuum" and "cannot be cut up into discrete objects," by 1915, his essay "Cinders" is based on the idea that the fundament of reality is not energy but hard, individualized objects. Similarly, although Pound's imagination was, throughout the Vorticist period, engaged by Ernest Fenollosa's *The Chinese Written Character as a Medium for Poetry,* with its basic notion that reality is flux, his own theoretical pronouncements, especially during his Imagist period, assumed the objectivity of things. And Lewis's statements on the same subject, consonant with his ambivalent statements on abstraction, veered between a sense of the object as having an irreducibly concrete structure and a sense of the object as a temporary constellation of energy.

Correspondingly, the Vorticists' attitude to language is much more conservative than the Expressionists'. Only the early Hulme—interestingly enough under Nietzsche's influence—shows any marked sense that language is a system of arbitrary conventions which cannot do justice to reality. By 1915, however, even he is writing as though there were a necessary connection between words and things. For the rest, the Vorticists' attitude to language is summarized in the quotation from Aquinas which Pound used in "Vorticism [1]": "Nomina sunt consequentia rerum," and if they have any doubts in that proposition, they are evinced only obliquely, in the emphaticness with which Pound, for example, despite his familiarity with

Fenollosa, consistently demands "the welding of word and thing." Consequently, Vorticism never produced experimental poetry of the order, say, of Kandinsky's *Klänge* or Stramm's *Sturm* publications—indeed, Hulme was actually a little disturbed by and even disapproving of the relatively unadventurous "moderne Dichtkunst" which he heard in GNU. And despite Fenollosa's view that poetry, as an ideogram of a universe in flux, should be based on active verbs, Vorticist poetry is, on the whole, firmly noun-centred. In contrast, Expressionist poetry, deriving from a greater sense of instability, is marked by an inner conflict between superficially stable nouns and dynamic verbs. Thus, although Vorticist writing involves a robust sense of play, it does not have that irony towards language itself which one can find in the cynical rhymes, mixed registers and discordant use of classical form of early Expressionist poetry. For the Vorticists, ironic humour was a means of keeping primal violence within the control of language: for the Expressionists, irony was a more complex phenomenon—a means of dealing both with primal violence and with the fragility of that ultimate means of control. Because of their belief in the consonance of objects and language, grounded as it was in a more stable social experience, the Vorticists were that much farther away from the experience of "panic terror" which lies at the heart of continental Modernism.

The above distinctions explain the Vorticists' and Expressionists' differing attitudes to the machine and the city. The early Expressionists—like Heym, van Hoddis, Kirchner and Schmidt-Rottluff—saw the machine-city as a profoundly ambiguous irruption: although, on the surface, it seemed to be the quintessentially human context, in which rational control was most perfectly exercized and the range of human possibilities extended, beneath that surface they perceived a demonic, violent night-side, coextensive with chaotic Nature and populated by semi- if not inhuman beings. The machine was an aspect of this ambivalence: apparently a monument to the human ability to systematize and control, but in reality a monster which, like the Golem of Paul Wegener's two films (1914 and 1920), was out of control and destroying its creator. For a while, the late Expressionists—like the Activists and the architectural theoretician Bruno Taut—played with the utopian hope of restructuring this environment so that the machine could become the servant of man, but the German Revolution of 1918-20 demolished these exaggerated hopes with the result that after 1921, more than a few Expressionists turned their back on machine civilization or died by their own hand. Because Vorticism began from a much less drastic sense of cultural crisis, was not so intensely aware of the connection between Dionysos and the city and displayed greater confidence in man's ability to control, its representatives were able initially, to affirm machine civilisation to the extent that its artifacts could be transformed into "beautiful, painted forms." At the same time, they were also conscious of industrial civilization's "capacity for emotional brutality," and with time, this consciousness came to outweigh any impulse to celebrate the machine-city. Thus, Eliot's poems in *Blast 2* present it as a "Waste Land"; Lewis's paintings *Workshop* and *The Crowd* (1914-15) depict, more clearly than ever before, the city as a dehumanizing prison; the history of

Epstein's *Rock Drill* (1914-16) shows a clear movement away from "involvement with a mechanical culture" to "an indictment of a world that was rapidly becoming tyrannized by the machine"; and Pound, once he had awoken to the reality of machine civilization—and of the Vorticists, he, living in the rarified atmosphere of literary London was slowest to do so—rejected it decisively in *Hugh Selwyn Mauberley* (1920) for an idealized past. This shift did not, however, involve those inflated visions of a machine utopia which marked late Expressionism, and, because there was no revolution in England in 1918 onto which to project such fantasies, the possibilities for disillusion were not so great either.

Behind both developments lay the War, and, as with the machine-city, the Expressionists' attitude to the War underwent a dramatic change. Having, in their prewar writings, either prophesied its coming with a fascinated dread, or yearned for it in a romanticized form as a release from the tedium and repression of Wilhelmine society; more than a few, as Korte has shown, succumbed to the "Ideen von 1914" and greeted the War ecstatically, as soon as it broke out, as a means of spiritual and national renewal. Its reality was, however, shattering. Lotz, for example, who on 8 August 1914 had written an ecstatic letter to his wife, praising the sense of mystical unity he was experiencing in the army, wrote, on 21 August, after his experience of battle: ". . . in diesen Tagen ist mir der Krieg ein Greuel geworden". Other Expressionists—like Oskar Kokoschka, Klabund, Paul Zech, Hugo Ball, Franz Marc, Rudolf Leonhard and Ludwig Rubiner, not to mention Friedrich, the hero of Ernst Toller's play *Die Wandlung* (1917-18)—experienced similar reversals. The powers of ecstatic unreason to which pre-war Expressionism had been particularly drawn turned, on the battle-field, when coupled with the technology of the machine-city, into horrific violence and it is probably true to say that by about mid-1915, almost no Expressionists were pro-war. Consequently, from that date, one finds the Expressionists trying, like Franz Marc in "Das geheime Europa" and "Im Fegefeuer des Krieges", to deal with the War by seeing it as a "Leidensweg", a purgatorial experience out of which a spiritually purified society would inevitably emerge. The Vorticists, in contrast, took longer to awaken to the reality of war and longer still to oppose it—indeed, of the Vorticist circle, only Nevinson (ironically enough, the self-styled Futurist) had turned against the War by Christmas 1914. Pound rarely mentioned it in his letters, wrote only one or two war poems (one of which was a paraphrase of Hulme's war diary (*Early Poems*)), and, when, from about Spring 1915, the War began to get into his consciousness and essays, it was supported as a crusade against German *Kultur*. Gaudier-Brzeska (killed on 5 June 1915) positively enjoyed battle, calling it a "GREAT REMEDY" in the belief that it would complete the work the Vorticists had begun. Lewis's initial attitude, on his own admission, was "unsatisfactory" and "complex", being a mixture of moral crusading, intellectual curiosity and sheer romanticism from which a fascination for violence cannot be excluded; and when, after Passchendaele (Summer 1917), he turned against the War, he did so from an aesthetic feeling that it was "stupid" and a "nonsense" rather than from moral or political conviction. And despite the privations of the trenches in early 1915 and his anger at the generals after the Dardanelles fiasco (Autumn/Winter 1915), Hulme too saw the War as a moral crusade against Prussianism and remained consistently prowar until his death on 28 September 1917—even if, by early 1916, he was "unable to name any great *positive* 'good' " for which he was fighting. As with the Dionysiac powers in general, the Vorticists managed to shield themselves from the War in a way that the Expressionists could not. If not physically, the Vorticists were, because of their protected cultural situation, less exposed psychically to its violence—which meant that they were less prone to ecstatic enthusiasm when it broke out, less overwhelmed by black disillusion and traumatic shock when its comforting justifications began to crumble, and less in need of millenarian interpretations when they had to find meaning in its continuation.

As a result of this distance and their growing antipathy to the machine civilization which seemed to have generated the War, Vorticist art and theory after about mid-1916 changed in two significant ways. On the one hand, the theory increasingly deemphasized energy and gave greater weight to form and design, and on the other hand, the art moved back from extreme abstraction and a fascination with the vitalist-primitive to more representational and recognizably human modes. Hence the humanism of Epstein's bronze *The Tin Hat* (1916), Pound's growing attraction to the humaneness of Chinese culture and advocacy of "clear, unexaggerated, realistic literature." Hence, too, the civilized world of Pound's *Homage to Sextus Propertius* (1919) where love is a game, not a destructive passion, the formalism of Lewis's *The Caliph's Design* (1919), the relative realism of Lewis's "Guns" show (February 1919) and the move back to realism which marks the work of Bomberg, Etchells, Nevinson and Wadsworth around the end of the War. Having set out from a complex problematic and experimented with extreme notions of art and the creative personality, the Vorticists' experience of the War drove them back to a more moderate position which, despite their initially anti-humanist stance, one might describe as a "chastened, modernized humanism". In contrast, the Expressionists' experience of war and machine civilization, deriving from a more drastic sense of cultural crisis and even more extreme notions of art and the creative personality, led them, after 1915, to yet another extreme. Where the Vorticists could fall back on a sense of tradition, the Expressionists felt flung by the War into a a void where any sense of meaning or order had to be created *ex nihilo*. Thus, late Expressionist art and literature are marked by a strident, even hysterical resolve to resituate the "Neuer Mensch", purged of his violence and immoralism, in the centre of Creation, and, by utilizing his potential for "Menschlichkeit" and "Gemeinschaft", found a utopia in which his *Geist,* now understood predominantly as ethical potential, could be exercized to the full. Such inflated, utopian hopes came to nothing after the failure of the German Revolution, and the subsequent disillusion is recorded in works like Toller's *Masse Mensch* (1920) and Kaiser's two *Gas* plays (1917-18). Faced with an even more apocalyptically perceived problematic than were the Vorticists, and having committed themselves, with an intensity and single-mindedness from which the Vorticists drew back, to even more extreme resolutions,

the Expressionists' situation was, when these failed, that much more desperate than that of their English counterparts. Consequently, one finds no suicides among the Vorticists and nothing so extreme as the Gnostic Catholicism to which Hugo Ball committed himself in 1920. None of the Vorticists became, as did Johannes R. Becher, a leading ideologue of an authoritarian Marxist state; Lewis, fascist though he was for a while, never matched Hanns Johst's achievement in becoming an SS Brigadier General; and Pound's espousal of Mussolini's Italy as a modern version of the corporate, mediaeval state had more to do with literary fantasies than existential desperation.

Inasmuch as both movements are aspects of European Modernism, the preceding discussion involves four assumptions about that broader phenomenon: first, Modernism was not a uniform phenomenon throughout Europe; second, Modernism was a problematic to which there were several inter-related aspects and levels; third, any given individual or group of individuals could perceive that problematic in a more or less complex way and experience it in a more or less intense way; and fourth, there were various ways in which that problematic might be resolved. While it is true that Modernism was "a break with the traditions of the past", that "break" was a much more cataclysmic experience for the German than for the English *avant garde* and provoked a "response" which was both more "conservative" than Eliot's and more "radical" even than D.H. Lawrence's. Accordingly, a comparison of Expressionism and Vorticism inevitably reminds one of the un-Englishness of Modernism: several of the major "English" Modernists—Conrad, Pound, Eliot, Joyce, Yeats, Gaudier-Brzeska and Epstein—were not English at all; Lawrence detested England and lived outside it as much as he could; and the major formative experiences behind the work of Hulme and Lewis were as continental as they were English. That massive sense of institutional stability and historical continuity generated a feeling, not unknown today, that *anomie* begins at Calais, and created a cultural context which tempered the radicalism and experimentation which characterized continental Modernism. Given which, it is not surprising that England should have produced a Modernist movement which combined a will to explore with a fundamental and durable sense of security, but it is surprising that England should have produced a version of Modernism at all.

David Graver

SOURCE: "Vorticist Performance and Aesthetic Turbulence in *Enemy of the Stars,*" in *PMLA,* Vol. 107, No. 3, May, 1992, pp. 482-96.

[In the following essay, Graver provides an analysis of Lewis's play Enemy of the Stars.]

Lewis and Ezra Pound coined the concept "vorticism" to identify the artistic trend that includes *Enemy of the Stars,* but the existing studies of this movement do not go very far in explaining the play's complexities. Hugh Kenner and Timothy Materer study the notion of the Vortex in detail, but neither examines closely the formal affinities between *Enemy of the Stars* and the avant-garde movement sweeping around it. William Wees, in contrast, claims that Lewis's play is "the *pièce de résistance* of literary Vorticism" and notes some important affinities the play has with Lewis's paintings and theoretical writings, but Wees is reluctant to examine its intricacies in their own right. . . . Other studies of the play make valuable observations, but none has been able to explain thoroughly the metamorphic logic and lines of force that inform the whole.

Since this play is the major literary text to appear at the founding of vorticism, it is natural to look in it for the practical application of Lewis's theoretical pronouncements. We should, however, be wary of forcing on the play a concept of vorticism developed from a backward gaze across the lifework of Lewis, Pound, and others. When Lewis wrote *Enemy of the Stars* his notion of vorticism was not as refined or fixed as the concept delineated by Kenner and Materer. His first vorticist proclamations were, in fact, the last pieces he wrote for the initial issue of *Blast*. Taken as a whole, Lewis's work in *Blast* does not suggest that "a Vortex is a circulation with a still center: a system of energies drawing in whatever comes near," nor does it imply "that a culture's most vital ideas would be gathered in the Vortex and brought to a still point of clarity." Lewis does say, "The Vorticist is at his maximum point of energy when stillest," but in the same manifesto he claims that "[o]ur Vortex desires the immobile rythm [sic] of its swiftness," and in another he declares:

> 2. We start from opposite statements of a chosen world. Set up violent structure of adolescent clearness between two extremes. . . .

> 4. We fight first on one side, then on the other, but always for the SAME cause, which is neither side or both sides and ours.

Clearly, in *Blast* Lewis is more interested in provocative paradoxes than in a coherent aesthetic program. The studies by Kenner and Materer make the mistake of assuming that vorticism is one coherent concept. Wees notes that Lewis and Pound interpreted vorticism differently: "For Lewis, the Vortex was a whirling, arrogant, polished monster of energy; for Pound, it was a stable, strong source of creative energy."

The notion of a central point of stability essential to Materer's and Kenner's concept of the vortex certainly finds no formal corollary in *Enemy of the Stars*. Lewis's play is too volatile and agitated a fluid to form one well-focused vortex. My reading shows that the still point around which the world turns is (in a phrase of the protagonist Arghol) "[a]lways a deux." The terms under which the play lives are always threatened and displaced by rival terms. Lewis pits the cool prestige of modernism against the heated rebellion of the avant-garde, the appeal of the image against the appeal of the word, allegory against realism, and narrative against drama. Nothing is left unchallenged by a nemesis, not even the autonomy of the work itself. The play's vortex spins, but it does not converge.

This paper charts the wandering course of *Enemy of the Stars*'s eccentric vortex. The broad array of aesthetic forms and thematic focuses through which the play pro-

ceeds create a number of distinct discursive or representational realms, ranging from an avant-garde critique of the social apparatus and of the ideological assumptions of high culture through an allegorical meditation on the foundations of human consciousness and action to a wheelwright's yard on the Russian steppes, where Arghol and Hanp enact a clownish agon that anticipates both the physical humor and the metaphysical desolation of Beckett's plays.

Understanding the heady mixture of aesthetic modes turning on one another in this work fosters an appreciation of more than the play. *Enemy of the Stars* is a pointed example of the nonprogrammatic avant-garde of the early twentieth century. More than just innovative and inventive, it deploys forms and themes that assail conventional notions of art, but the play does not rationalize its attack by appealing to an explicit aesthetic or social program as does, say, Italian futurism or Berlin Dada. The notions of vorticism developed by Materer and Kenner apply better to later works by Lewis in which his aesthetic interests reach a discursive stability. In *Enemy of the Stars* he is not so much defending an aesthetic position as playing with the idea of aesthetic positioning. If, as Wees suggests, *Enemy of the Stars* is the pièce de résistance of vorticism, the play epitomizes a performative rather than a programmatic version of the movement—a vorticism that dances and spins through a variety of aesthetic and meta-aesthetic worlds instead of attempting to make a particular aesthetic statement. In the rich concept of performance we can see some of the complexities involved in an avant-garde art that forsakes both a conventional aesthetic existence and a dissident life supported by manifestos. *Enemy of the Stars* shows how a predominantly literary text can manipulate its constructive principles to move into the fluid world of performance.

SHIFTING AESTHETIC BOUNDARIES

The play begins with a conventional assertion of literary autonomy: a title page with inch-and-a-half-high letters sets it off from the preceding material in *Blast* and encourages the reader to expect unity and coherence in a literary representation of some sort. The second page, however, begins to trouble the reader's expectations by announcing a "synopsis in programme." As one reads further it becomes clear that *Enemy of the Stars* is not conceived as the text of a play that might be performed but as a performance in itself. The readers find themselves in a theater of printed words, confronted with a confusing spectacle and unfortunately lacking the "programme" that might aid in explaining the events before them.

The confusion is increased by the references to "you and me" made in the advertisement and elaborated on elsewhere:

> "Yet you and me: why not from the English metropolis?"—Listen: it is our honeymoon. We go abroad for the first scene of our drama. Such a strange thing as our coming together requires a strange place for initial stages of our intimate ceremonious acquaintance.

The familiar tone here suggests that the writer is speaking

directly to his readers and, hence, implies that the drama concerns the act of reading, the drawing together of author and audience. The circle of aesthetic autonomy moves beyond the play to enclose the authorial voice and the eyes that draw it from the page. With one turn of the page, however, the familiar tone is gone, and the readers and author have been replaced by "the cream of Posterity, assembled in silent banks," and by the spectacle they gaze on: "a gladiator [Arghol] who has come to fight a ghost, Humanity—the great Sport of Future Mankind." Here the circle of aesthetic autonomy expands to include the meta-aesthetic, social conditions of art, making the ideology of high culture part of the artwork itself.

After posterity "sinks into the hypnotic trance of Art" the play's autonomous field of aesthetic display and the universe inhabited by "you and me" contract to the scene occupied by Arghol and Hanp, but the representation remains unstable. Dramatic action is usually anchored to a protagonist and an antagonist with fixed forms of existence, but here the polymorphous characters erode the significance of the action with their ambiguous proliferation of meanings. Even with only Arghol and Hanp on the stage, the action vacillates between the realistic, allegorical, ritualistic, mechanical, oneiric, parodic, and hallucinatory. The aesthetic autonomy of the play remains unstable both because of its dubious beginnings and because of the ambiguous, shifting ground on which it finally appears to settle.

The shifting claims on autonomy made in the early pages are complicated by the general ambiguity in the relation between a dramatic literary text and the possibilities of its staged performance. The dramatic form itself usually implies the question, Does this text stand on its own as a literary work or is it merely the outline of a theatrical work that exists in its entirety only in performance? The extravagant stage directions and elaborate prologue material in *Enemy of the Stars* decide the question of the text's status: the play is a closet drama meant only to be read. Closet dramas have a long history in European literature; they have been written by authors such as Hroswitha, Goethe, and Ibsen, but Lewis's play stands out in this genre through its resistance to the possibility of a theatrical staging.

Since closet dramas usually stage themselves before the mind's eye when read, transferring their mise-en-scènes to the boards of a theater rarely presents insurmountable obstacles. Lewis's play resists such a transfer because it is not simply staged in the mind's visual field and it does not unfold solely in the act of reading. The work's shifting circle of autonomy and the visual delights that the layout and graphic art offer independent from any act of reading create a performance impossible to contain on the reader's mental stage. To perform this play in a physical theater would require suppressing the performance that is already taking place on the pages of *Blast*.

Despite being distant from conventional closet drama, the performance in *Blast* still necessarily involves the act of reading. This imperative gives the performance an intimacy and insidiousness missing from physical theater. At the theater audience and spectacle each have a significant de-

gree of autonomy. The audience can ignore the spectacle, and the spectacle can proceed without the audience's attention. (The separation is significant enough for Artaud to wish to overcome it and for Brecht to wish to refine it.) But for the performance of *Enemy of the Stars* to proceed, the reader's mind must take it in. Once there, however, it asserts its performative autonomy, drawing attention to the distance between reader and text and to the ideological rituals involved in "[s]uch a strange thing as [their] coming together."

NARRATIVE DRAMA

In addition to having a multivalent representational significance and manipulating the intimacy of reading, the play is disturbingly duplicitous in its representational mode, for Lewis couches the text almost entirely in narrative prose. Indeed, the only approximations of dramatic dialogue are a few episodes of extended direct-discourse quotation. This play is, hence, a drama by virtue not of its form but solely of its subject matter, its thematic focus. Lewis uses the narrative form to explore areas of dramatic representation that are usually beyond the reach of conventional dramatic mimesis. We have already noted the attention he draws to publicity, posterity, and the box office. The extravagant description of impossible scenery— for example, "ponderous arabesques of red cloud, whose lines did not stop at door's frame, but pressed on into shadows within the hut, in tyrannous continuity"— highlights the psychological, rather than physical, importance of objects and milieu. The narrative also imparts a physical presence to the characters and events that they do not usually enjoy in the dramatic text. Rather than remain the disembodied voices of dialogue, the characters are transformed into "enormous youngsters, bursting everywhere through heavy tight clothes. . . . " This vivid physicality continues throughout the play: "Arghol lay silent, his hands a thick shell fitting back of head, his face grey vegetable cave"; Hanp "sprang from the bridge clumsily, too unhappy for instinctive science, and sank like lead, his heart a sagging weight of stagnant hatred."

The narrative in this play, besides commenting on the world of dramatic representation, becomes a creature of that world. One generally associates with narrative a marked freedom, the ability to move quickly and effortlessly from subject to subject, from one time and place to another, but in *Enemy of the Stars* this freedom is stripped away. While able to explore the dark, secretive recesses of dramatic representation—exemplified by the institutional apparatus surrounding the spectacle or by the interior surfaces of the characters' bodies—the narrative of this play is tied inextricably to the place and time of the representation. The words are no longer the instruments used by a narrative voice to manipulate a scene of action in which it is not immediately implicated but are transformed into elements of the scene in which the action occurs. The words take on a solidity and presentness unusual for narrative. They become part of the play's spectacle and part of the milieu in which the characters move and act. Note, for instance, the furious verbal setting created during the fight between Arghol and Hanp:

Arms of grey windmills, grinding anger on stone
of the new heart.

Messages from one to another, dropped down
anywhere when nobody is looking, reaching
brain by telegraph: most desolating and alarming messages possible.

The attacker rushed in drunk with blows. They
rolled, swift jagged rut, into one corner of shed:
large insect scuttling roughly to hiding.

When Materer complains that "[t]he action of the *Enemy
of the Stars* . . . is not powerful enough to shine through
the thick layers of static images," he misunderstands the
formal logic of the play. Action clogged with static images
is the natural outcome of forcing narrative into the mimetic confines of drama. Wees has a better grasp of the aesthetic rationale of the piece and notes that while the narrative vignettes do not propel forward the overarching action, they are not in themselves unmoving: "The action
and language are violent, but individual moments of action are strangely isolated and static. Events are broken
down and reconstructed like the interrelated fragments of
Vorticist pictures." If, as Wees suggests, a montage effect
of fragmentation and reassembly is the central point of
vorticism, then *Enemy of the Stars,* with its iconoclastic
aesthetic, surpasses this movement. The collision of drama
and narrative orchestrated in the play breaks up representational space as thoroughly as do the shifted and distorted surfaces in Lewis's visual art, but *Enemy of the Stars*
lacks a unifying universe of discourse equivalent to the
picture plane in which to reconstruct itself. This point becomes clearer as I continue my analysis.

The static, fragmenting weight of the words is formally
emphasized and compensated for by the use of numerous
episodes. The narrative concentration on the here and now
in each verbal vignette would prevent the action from
moving ahead without the abrupt changes of narrative
scene afforded by the episodic structure. The thin theme
of the central action connects the episodes but does not acquire enough prominence to push the action forward from
one scene to the next. Consequently, each episode stands
virtually on its own as a narrative performance. Each
creates a unique representational scene. All the scenes are
actually just different ways of observing the same central
agon, but the differences in perspective are so extreme that
the unity of the object observed is often not obvious. One
episode scans the audience awaiting the show, another
plunges into the dream of the sleeping Arghol, another
moves through the nerve endings of the battered Hanp.
Here are two examples of the bewildering shifts in perspective and in mode of observation that rise above the
representational unity of the story: "Two hundred miles
to north the Arctic circle swept. Sinister tramps, its winds
came wandering down the high road, fatigued and chill,
doors shut against them"; "A strong flood of thought
passed up to his fatigued head, and at once dazed him."

Although the narrative scene moves in and out of the
characters, it remains fundamentally dramatic in the
terms it deploys. The world of this work, whether located
in the characters' heads or in their pasts, is made up entirely of objects and actions. Thoughts leap and strike; a soul

is an ocean town. The narrative voice manipulates and distorts the properties of this world with anarchic abandon
but with no real freedom. Shifting the attributes of things
about compulsively but unable to break away from the
universe of discourse prescribed by drama, the writing
traces a tightly closed world in which desires for freedom
turn to vandalism.

Lewis's narrative delineation of drama gives his play both
an immediacy and a distance unusual for the form. Narrative brings the action closer to the reader than do the dramatic conventions of the playscript—a narrative gives the
scene directly to the reader while a playscript asks the
reader to picture the scene on a stage. Nevertheless, while
presenting the action immediately to the mind, narrative
withholds it from the eye: the reader hears the narrative
voice describing the events but lacks the premise that they
are observable. In this play the physical impossibilities,
volatile transformations, and polymorphous personifica-
tions that the scene undergoes emphasize its unobserva-
bility, while the concrete dramatic terms in which the narrative is couched invade the reader's ear with disturbingly
visual imagery.

Lewis's dramatic concretion of narrative causes the representational existence of the work to vibrate giddily before
the reader, while the narrative delineation of the drama
sweeps the scene around and within the reader. Just as the
narrative freedom *within* the scene violates the boundaries
between objects and can turn characters inside out, the
narrative presentation *of* the scene violates the space of
readers, at times incorporating them in the scene, at others
forcing them to be distant spectators.

WORD VERSUS IMAGE

While trapping his narrative in the cumbersome concretion of the dramatic here and now, Lewis also sinks both
narrative and drama within the physical presence of the
printed page, using the visual appeal of the illustrations
that intrude on the text and of the layout to fuse representation with the presentation of the book. Just as the tension between narrative and drama is not resolved, the
printed page does not unequivocally dominate the literary
representation but sets up a competing center of activity
and a competing mode of aesthetic existence within the
artwork.

The bold layout of the text's first three pages, particularly
of the advertisement, encourages an appreciation of the
text as visual image, but the images conjured verbally in
the advertisement disrupt the visual enticements of advertising by inviting the viewer to a world beyond sight
("some bleak circus . . . packed with posterity . . . silent,
like the dead, and more pathetic . . . very well acted by you
and me"). The rupture in the play's text caused by the six
following pages of pictures is repeated in the way these abstract arrangements of swirling, colliding tonal planes relate to their provocatively denotative titles (*Plan of War,
Timon of Athens, Portrait of an Englishwoman,* etc.). The
pictures are incongruous both with their titles and with
the play's text.

Lewis never allows the viewer or reader a comfortably secure approach to the artwork. The striking graphic design

used in the advertisement encourages the artwork's recipient to view this page as much as read it, while the titling of the pictures and their intrusion on the literary text prompt an attempt to read them as much as simply view them. Thus, reading and seeing vie with each other for possession of the artwork. Breaches of the boundary between word and image are, of course, fairly common in the history of Western art, but Lewis does more than contribute another example. He so confounds the territories of word and image that a unique and inhospitable aesthetic realm arises in the disputed space. Because the play refuses to be entirely literary or entirely visual or even to demark which of its aspects are visual and which literary, it remains independent of the logic that constitutes particular art forms. *Enemy of the Stars* establishes itself in an aesthetic sphere of its own making that floats eerily above the usual categories of artworks.

Even the pictures resist formal, thematic, or stylistic coherence. The styles vary from the distorted, tense protodeco of *Decoration for the Countess of Drogheda's House* and *The Enemy of the Stars* through the broad, blocklike structures of *Portrait of an Englishwoman* and *Plan of War* to the tumbling fragments of *Timon of Athens* and *Slow Attack*. Some of the images suppress perspectival depth while others exploit it. The themes include a stylized but recognizably human figure, in *The Enemy of the Stars;* architectural abstractions, in *Portrait of an Englishwoman* and *Timon of Athens;* and forthrightly nonrepresentational studies of motion and force, in *Plan of War* and *Slow Attack*. The discursive rationale that each image claims for itself ranges from *Slow Attack's* avant-garde celebration of energy and movement similar to futurism to the parodic assault on the social and aesthetic conventions of portraiture in *Portrait of an Englishwoman,* from the reverential submission to social hierarchy and the marketplace of high culture implicit in *Decoration for the Countess of Drogheda's House* to the textual illustration provided by *The Enemy of the Stars*.

The heteroclite visual imagery introduces the deepest irregularities in the work's claim on unity, but as the play proper opens step by step through seven introductory pages, the work gradually returns to the signifying field of literature. Space does not permit a detailed examination of the subsidence of the visual and the growth of the verbal over these pages, but a few highlights will give a sense of the process.

Page 60 describes the stage arrangements, with remarks on the two scenes to come in the play and on the position of the "audience." Three fonts, underscoring, and boxing are used. Page 61 presents the opening of the play: Arghol's entrance and the audience's shift of attention to the spectacle. Three fonts and the setting of some paragraphs all in capitals make the printed text contract and expand as "THE ACTION OPENS":

> Posterity slowly sinks into the hypnotic trance of Art, and the Arena is transformed into the necessary scene.
>
> THE RED WALLS OF THE UNIVERSE NOW SHUT THEM IN, WITH THIS CONDEMNED PROTAGONIST.

> THEY BREATHE THE CLOSE ATMOSPHERE OF TERROR AND NECESSITY TILL THE EXECUTION IS OVER, THE RED WALLS RECEDE, THE UNIVERSE SATISFIED.
>
> THE BOX OFFICE RECEIPTS HAVE BEEN ENORMOUS.

Page 62, entitled "The Yard," establishes the representational scene of the action (as distinct from the stage arrangements described on page 60): "The Earth has burst, a granite flower, and disclosed the scene."

From here on the narrative is blind to the audience, the box office, and the rest of the extra-representational apparatus of drama. The typography also becomes subdued, with fewer titles and no capitalized paragraphs.

The central dramatic event of the play, the confrontation between Arghol and Hanp, begins on page 65. The visual aspect of the remainder of the text submits entirely to the conventions of narrative literature and becomes as insignificant as *Blast's* large, distinctive format will allow. Henceforth, major section divisions are marked simply by roman numerals at the tops of pages, and minor divisions and breaks are made with dashes between paragraphs.

In passing from the pictures, where the eye dominates, to page 65, where the reading faculty prevails, Lewis makes calculated use of page breaks, layout, and titles to impart a tactile quality as well as a specular one to the activity of his readers. Not only their eyes and reading faculty but their hands and arms are involved in constructing the scene of the drama as they turn the pages to reveal character descriptions, stage arrangements, the creation of aesthetic autonomy, the conjuring of the mimetic scene, an initiating act of violence, the universe that encloses the scene, and, finally, the beginning of the central dramatic event. These pages induce a performative vignette in their own right as the motion of the reader's arm in turning them seems to wave away the visual impact of the unruly typography while summoning up the dramatic setting.

ACTION VERSUS ALLEGORY

The central agon in *Enemy of the Stars* comes as close as modern drama usually can to constituting a dramatic action as that concept is defined by Aristotle and Hegel. This action begins with Hanp's growing animosity toward Arghol and with Arghol's self-destructive indifference to the threats that surround him. The terms of the dramatic conflict are established in the dialogue, then theatrically manifested in a physical battle between the protagonists. At the end of the struggle Arghol has beaten Hanp unconscious and fallen asleep. Here the mechanisms of action retreat from the physical scene to the separate mental worlds to the two characters (Arghol dreams and Hanp meditates murder), but the consequences of their interior monologues carry the central action to its denouement in the communal dramatic scene: Hanp kills the sleeping Arghol and then drowns himself in the canal that flanks the field of their battle.

The dramatic action in this play does not indicate Lewis's capitulation to a conventional aesthetic of representation but rather forms another facet of an aesthetic built on conflicting conventions of representation. While subduing the conflict between reading and seeing, Lewis continues the one between narrative and drama and opens up another, between mimesis and metaphysics. He pits the clear, persuasive line of the action against a metaphysical allegory that threatens to dissolve the foundations of the drama, while the drama, in turn, attempts to sensualize the metaphysics into the inconsequential pleasures of a mental game. This confrontation leads to an entwinement of allegory and representation that makes the ontic character of the space in which the play unfolds perplexingly ambiguous.

Although Roman Ingarden speaks of the "ontic character" of "represented objects" and how it is altered by their presence in "represented space," I think it makes better philosophical sense to speak of the ontic character of the space in which objects exist. After all, does an object not take up space or at least find itself within a particular universe of discourse? From my point of view, an object is "real" if it exists in real space, "oneiric" if it exists in a dream, "ideal" if it inhabits a universe of carefully defined ideas, and so on. Focusing on the ontic character of a space as a whole is also useful for grouping objects and events—for example, real people and their real actions.

Literary space presents a special problem because it can mimic the ontic character of other kinds of space. Indeed, Maurice Blanchot considers literary space the most dangerous and deceptive kind of all, always ambiguous and shifting (*L'espace*). Nevertheless, I think we can generally speak of the ontic character of a given literary space (i.e., the space in which objects in a specific literary work exist) as being, or at least claiming to be, primarily either representational or allegorical. Blanchot disputes the possibility of making this distinction, but he discriminates between writing that (dishonestly or naively) tries to make it and writing that exploits the impossibility of doing so, exemplified for him by Kafka and Mallarmé, among others. *Enemy of the Stars* also sabotages the separation between allegory and representation to create ontological disturbances within literary space.

To understand how Lewis overlays and confounds inimical ontic characteristics, we should first examine in some detail the metaphysical allegory that he pits against mimesis. In an appendix to the second version of *Enemy of the Stars* Lewis states that his play "is intended to show the human mind in its traditional role of the enemy of life, as an oddity outside the machine." The mind he equates with the intellect and the principle of "not-self," which is characterized by its strict rationality and ability to understand and identify with others and the world in general. The not-self turns out to be very unhuman in its rarity. The enemy of the mind is life, the machinelike existence of the universe, which is driven by egoism. Whereas the intellect is interested in truth and is willing to sacrifice itself to it, the ego is interested only in power, in the sphere of its own influence. The egoistic self sees the passive intellectualization of the not-self as a mortal threat and attempts to crush the opponent. *Enemy of the Stars* charts this destruction.

In Lewis's allegory of self and not-self Arghol represents the self-effacing mind. The ego, which is in alliance with the forces of life and nature, is represented by Hanp. The powers of the self turn out to be no match for the powers of the not-self when Arghol defeats Hanp in hand-to-hand combat, but Arghol becomes vulnerable when he is overcome by his own dreams, and Hanp dispatches him. That Hanp also kills himself signifies, presumably, that life means nothing without mind, that the intellect of the not-self gives form and direction to the self.

This is the allegorical reading to which the bare outlines of the characters and action are susceptible. Actually reading the allegory in the text is complex and difficult, however. The allegory is deflected by the elaborate subjectivities of the characters, these subjectivities are overwhelmed by the imagistic undulations of the scene, and then the scene is in turn swallowed up by the machinelike logic of the allegory. At times the struggle between allegory and mimesis is made part of the central dramatic conflict. Arghol champions the rigorous intellectual logic of the allegory, and Hanp stands for the casual, vitalistic play of mimesis. As the struggle between the two develops, however, their positions are adulterated. Arghol descends to the mimetic world of combative psyches, and Hanp asserts the allegorical primacy of certain metaphysical ideas. Arghol's victory contributes to the allegorical argument for his superiority but also weakens his allegorical consistency, as Hanp bitterly notes:

> Sullen indignation at Arghol ACTING, he who had not the right to act. Violence in him was indecent. . . .
>
> He gave men one image with one hand, and at same time a second, its antidote with the other.

At this point both Arghol and Hanp are highly conscious of their allegorical significances, and one expects Arghol's death to proceed (in the allegorical space established) like a ritual sacrifice, but Lewis allows mimesis to wrest control of the action just when the allegory is about to bring a closure: Hanp decides to murder Arghol on a whim rather than in defense of his own allegorical position.

> Tip him over into cauldron in which he persistently gazed: see what happened!
>
> This sleepy desire leapt on to young man's mind, after a hundred other thoughts—clown in the circus, springing on horses back, when the elegant riders have hopped, with obsequious dignity down gangway.

This clownish thought trots in to disrupt the classical structure of the dramatic action as well as the allegorical consistency. Hanp's resolution to murder Arghol defies in its offhandedness the central importance Aristotle attaches to decision making in dramatic mimesis. Hanp is more a desultory clown than a dramatic agent, and in failing to live up to the demands of Aristotelian drama, he also fails to give the play a firm superstructure on which to hang its allegory. In *casually* tipping Arghol into the cauldron of death, he also tips the drama into the volitionless bog of naturalism, degrading the action to an event. By this point, however, the agitation produced by the interplay of allegory and mimesis prevents the play from sinking into a naturalist representation as Hanp sinks in the canal. The ending only raises the volatility of the work by adding a third factor, modern naturalist representation, to the agon already established between classical dramatic mimesis and allegorical symbolism. This struggle counterpoints the confrontation that Arghol and Hanp pursue throughout *Enemy of the Stars* and continues to rage even as the characters meet their ends.

DISPLACEMENTS OF PERFORMANCE

The aspects of *Enemy of the Stars* we have examined thus far all emphasize conflict and disintegration. These elements decisively distance this play from the constructive principles of the organic artwork and from the discursive consistency of the programmatic avant-gardes, but Lewis checks the dissolution with three forms of cohesion: (1) a demonstration of aesthetic construction, (2) the continuity of the dramatic event, and (3) the performative display of the work as a whole.

The first two sources of cohesion do not encompass the whole play but, rather, run a relay race through it: after the dramatic situation solidifies following the chaotic interplay of word and image in the opening pages of the text, the struggle between Arghol and Hanp sustains cohesion to the end. The play as a whole coalesces only in its performative display, but this unity exists solely in the continuous discord of its elements.

By the phrase "performative display" I intend all the potential ontological ambiguities of performance and theater. An object exhibited on the stage is always at least two things, itself and what it represents. Thus, the world of the real and the world of the represented overlap during a theatrical performance. Lewis exploits this overlapping and multiplies it. In place of the theater's usual tension between presentation and representation, Lewis develops tensions between narrative and drama, word and image, allegory and mimesis, reading and the page.

In addition, because Lewis performs his version of theatrical display within a printed text rather than on the boards of a stage, the constancy of place common to most theater evaporates. Lewis's play is set simultaneously or in alternation within *Blast;* within the institution of art (the realm of "trance" and of box office receipts); within a narrative voice; within the act of reading; between "you" and "me," self and not-self, personality and humanity; before posterity; and in a wheelwright's yard on the Russian steppes. The constant fluctuations in the narrative focus, allegorical portent, and dominant imagery prevent the ground in the wheelwright's yard from becoming any firmer than the other more or less ontologically distinct spaces that are developed in the text. The primarily textual existence of the play also denies it the grounding of a physical presence. The page layout early in the play pleads for the primacy of physical presence, but Lewis is careful to undercut this source of stability as decisively as he does every other.

The closest physical corollary to the performative display of this text would be a multi-ring circus. The text's aesthetic performances take place in a number of distinct ontological rings. Sometimes these performances follow one another; sometimes they overlap; sometimes they proceed simultaneously. Indeed, the groundlessness of Lewis's theatrical display is achieved not by dissolving the particularities of place but by multiplying them, by setting the drama in a bewildering array of conceptually disparate milieus. Unlike the multi-ring circus, however, the particularities of place in *Enemy of the Stars* are extremely volatile.

Fredric Jameson identifies hypallage as the central trope of Lewis's narrative style. Jameson suggests that Lewis creates, in his novels and short stories, "a world in which the old-fashioned substances, like marbles in a box, have been rattled so furiously together that their 'properties' come loose and stick to the wrong places." In *Enemy of the Stars,* where the narrative voice must make its way among other modes of aesthetic construction, hypallage transcends the status of a central trope to become a metaphysical principle. The various ontological spheres of the work (reality, literary and aesthetic representation, allegory, meta-aesthetic commentary) constantly rattle against one another and exchange properties, producing hybrid spheres of existence that develop out of and dissolve into one another.

The ontological turbulence of this artwork is so great that neither montage nor collage, constructive principles often used in avant-garde art, can contain it. The work eschews montage by refusing to subordinate the heterogeneity of its constituent elements to a central purpose in the way that, say, Brecht does in his drama. Because the visual imagery, narrative voice, and allegory are allowed lives of their own, we might be tempted to liken the construction of *Enemy of the Stars* to that of a collage, whose heterogeneous elements disrupt its unity with persistent gestures to their independence. But if Lewis is using collage, to what is he gluing the components? Avant-garde playwrights such as Raymond Roussel and Roger Vitrac take the dramatic form as a baseboard, but Lewis attenuates and dilutes this form with other elements so thoroughly that it cannot offer any significant cohesion. Jameson's metaphor for hypallage proves apt for describing the unifying principle of *Enemy of the Stars.* Lewis's title and the theatrical gesture with which the play is presented on the pages of *Blast* serve as a kind of box within which the elements of the artwork rattle against and intermingle with one another.

Enemy of the Stars is exemplary of one extreme in the early-twentieth-century avant-garde. It borrows an iconoclastic flippancy from manifesto-inspired movements such as futurism (with which Lewis was very familiar) but then ironically manages to enhance its commitment to aesthetic anarchy by refusing to adhere to a particular antiaesthetic program. Instead of protesting against the conventional concept of art, as Peter Bürger suggests the most radical avant-gardes do, Lewis creates a performance with elements of such a protest. Instead of dismissing the active-passive relation between artwork and audience, he infuses it with disturbing shifts in perspective and significance. The vortex of this avant-garde aesthetic cannot converge because each source of stability is confronted with a nemesis, each image is undercut by its antidote. An aesthetic of performance eliminates the stability of the artwork.

Given the primarily textual nature of *Enemy of the Stars,* what is implied in calling it a performance? Since most theories of performance focus their attention on the human performing agent and many locate the essence of performance in the felt experience of engaging in it (what Victor Turner calls "flow"), it may seem perverse to suggest that a text can perform. Nevertheless, I think the ontic character of performance, when examined closely, can tell a great deal about the ontic character of Lewis's play. A performance is not a statement, although it may contain or make a statement, nor is it simply a signal, although it may emit signals of various kinds. A performance is an action. Theories on the subject suggest that performance can take place in a wide variety of contexts, ranging from the narrowly aesthetic to the more broadly cultural, from the psychospiritual interior of the individual to the wide stage of international politics (Schechner). I would like to suggest that the following elements are required to make an action a performance in any arena: an agent engaged in an activity who is aware that it is observed by an audience (real or imagined) and who acts in a formalized setting in space and time that separates the performance from other objects and activities.

Literary texts cannot normally be considered performances for a number of reasons. First, the reader is not always constituted as an audience. The text often excludes the reader from its represented world in a way that even the most naturalistic theatrical performance does not. Even when readers are brought into the text through direct or implied address, they tend to remain individual and isolated in space and time both from the text and from one another. Thus, even if a literary text acknowledges and manipulates how it is received, the reception still lacks the collective, spatial and temporal focus of the audience-performance nexus. Reading is not constituted as a group activity and is not tied physically or conceptually to the place of the text.

The second major difference between the two forms is that texts do not generally occupy particular settings in the way performances do. The text floats free of all outside circumstances. Of course, the contexts in which a literary work is created and canonized and read certainly influence the text and its meaning, but the places and times of such contexts are matters of the text's performance in particular cultural milieus rather than evidence of the text's being a performance in itself. We should distinguish between a literary text and its involvement in specific cultural activities in the same way that we should distinguish between a performance and its involvement in the culture that surrounds it. If we grant that both text and performance can be considered, at least provisionally, in themselves, we see that they are quite different. Taken autonomously, the text is a disembodied series of gestures and movements within a particular space.

Finally, although the literary text may contain voices that in some sense perform, it does not normally constitute itself as a performing agent. The text is more analogous to the site of a performance than to the performance itself.

Thus, the major difference between literature and performance is that literature creates the parameters of its aesthetic space and performance fills an aesthetic space with its activity.

I hope my reading of *Enemy of the Stars* demonstrates some of the ways in which the play crosses the boundaries between literature and performance. First, it turns its readers into an audience by means of the various theatrical motifs introduced at the text's entrance—the "synopsis in programme" and "[p]osterity, assembled in silent banks," for example. Publication in *Blast* focuses the text's place and occasion and drew initial readers together in the collectivity of the subscribers. The text receives a formalized setting within the rather spectacularly laid-out pages of the large, pink-covered periodical. As I note, the play makes much of setting and shifting other boundaries within which it performs. Finally, the text constitutes itself as a performing agent by its self-conscious display of itself on the page and before posterity and by its impressive dexterity in juggling modes of being rather than simply narrative voices. Working within multiple aesthetic frames allows the text to make itself seem an activity rather than a constituting entity. Even when it is establishing the context for the agon of Arghol and Hanp, the text's act of creation becomes a performative gesture tied to a physical here and now by the turning of the pages.

The emphasis on setting, gesture, and audience in *Enemy of the Stars* links the play's subversive, vertiginous qualities less to Blanchot's literary space (where the sirens call one to the absence of the imaginary) than to a performative space (filled with activity rather than absence). The literary qualities of the text infiltrate the performance, however, robbing the agent of the comfortably fixed existence of standard performers. The text overlays and shifts the ontological terms within which it performs, creating a performative space as deceptive as any literary one. Instead of converging on the still point of the performer, the aesthetic turbulence of *Enemy of the Stars* remains constant, fueled by the play's literary existence.

Scott Klein

SOURCE: "The Experiment of Vorticist Drama: Wyndham Lewis and *Enemy of the Stars,*" in *Twentieth Century Literature,* Vol. 37, No. 2, Summer, 1991, pp. 225-39.

[*In the following essay, Klein explores the narrative motifs that dominate Vorticist drama.*]

Wyndham Lewis was the only writer and painter in England during the early part of the twentieth century who was consistently engaged by the continental avant-garde. His movement, vorticism, spearheaded by the 1914 magazine *Blast,* brought the radicalism of futurism and cubism into British painting and the theoretical concerns of continental manifestos into English writing, proclaiming both the importance of the individual and the artist's freedom from Romantic and Victorian thought. *Blast* also contains an attempt at vorticist drama, *Enemy of the Stars.* This prose experiment, comparable in its extravagant unperformability to works by the Russian futurists and Artaud, occupies a crucial position in Lewis's work. The centerpiece of *Blast,* it attempts to demonstrate that language can be abstracted from representation as earlier experimentation had done with the visual arts. Yet in contrast to its continental fellows its dramatic form is a matter of Lewis's assertion rather than actable form. Its scenes are entirely composed of narrative prose, which makes liberal use of the block capitals typical of *Blast's* manifestos; the text is undivided into autonomous speaking parts. Passages of abstract description alternate with more conventional dialogue that is nonetheless presented novelistically, spoken passages placed between quotation marks rather than cued as speeches by particular actors. *Enemy of the Stars,* in short, is fully presented in readerly form, and is a play only insofar as Lewis declared it to be so.

Attention to *Enemy of the Stars* has tended to diminish the theoretical problems raised by its overt assumption of a form it only problematically occupies, scanting the issues of its narrative in favor of analyzing the audacity of its style. Yet the relationship between the narrative of *Enemy of the Stars* and its style illuminates a paradigmatic crux in Lewis's work. The concerns of his nascent modernism are theoretically and practically incompatible with its chosen genre, and that incompatibility is a key contradiction of the vorticist aesthetic, particularly in its presentation of the individual artist as self-reliant creator of new forms. *Enemy of the Stars* narrates the artistic struggle of mind against nature as a parable of the vorticist movement's own contradictory attitude toward tradition and creation. This mode is made clearer when the play is positioned first within vorticism itself and then within the tradition of Romantic "closet" drama, the philosophic form that *Enemy of the Stars* both repudiates and obliquely follows.

To explore the modernism of the play one must look first at the manifestos of *Blast.* Vorticism was based upon graphic models and the ascendancy in Europe of artistic abstraction. It also rejected the turn to the past as both political and aesthetic gesture. According to Lewis England was built upon "Dickens' sentimental ghoul-like gloating over the death of little Nell." Even more than the historically defined products of the Victorian age *Blast* objects to Romanticism, which Lewis understands not so much as a period as a philosophical approach that led to, and included, the sentimentality of the Victorians. Although *Blast* criticizes Keats directly, Lewis, with T. E. Hulme, associated "romantic" art more generally with habits of thought unrelated to particular historical conditions. For Lewis Romanticism meant temporality, and he therefore rejected his contemporary futurism as "romantic" for fetishizing time, while he lauded "classicism," which emphasized hard-edged form, or space. That English artists should be the "great enemies of Romance" is *Blast's* rallying cry, for romance is the "fostering of unfactual conditions" whether that fostering be the excessive valuation of time or the sentimentalizing of mass culture. Lewis indeed conflates the futurist movement with the excesses of Victorian decadence and realism: "Wilde gushed twenty years ago about the beauty of machinery," Lewis writes, "Gissing, in his romantic delight with modern housing was futurist in this sense."

Against this nineteenth-century model of retrogressive ex-

cess Lewis proposes the revolutionary classicist, the independent self devoted to the aesthetic exploration of space. This spatiality depended upon the shaping power of the artist, whom Lewis envisioned as a self independent from the world, producing "vortices" of self-enclosed geometries. Art was imperfect when it dealt too much with the unformed materials of nature, and threatened the integrity of the self. The true artist or vorticist, unlike the Romantic, stands aloof from the seductions and divisions of the external. He creates forms that reaffirm, rather than threaten, his individuality and independence. Yet while the artist stands in opposition to the world, he is himself the product of oppositions. In *Blast* Lewis describes the vorticist's ability to create and hold oppositions within the self, containing and therefore achieving a "harmonious and sane duality," as a function of a will to artistic power. In the paradoxical language typical of avant-grade movements of the period, he emerges as the generator and container of doubleness:

> 1. Beyond action and reaction we would establish ourselves.
>
> 2. We start from opposite statements of a chosen world. Set up violent structures of adolescent clearness between two extremes.
>
> 3. We discharge ourselves on both sides.
>
> 4. We fight first for one side, then on the other, but always for the SAME cause, which is neither side or both sides and ours.

In this passage the vorticist is above all an omnipotent selfhood. "Beyond Action and Reaction we would establish ourselves" expresses his transcendental goal, which is Nietzsche's good and evil translated into the painter's dialectic of physical law. Similarly Nietzschean are Lewis's implicit implicit claims for the vorticist's ability to control his environment. Although the "would" of "we would establish ourselves" suggests intention rather than ability, Lewis unambiguously grants his artist the power to break free of the boundaries that confine realist painters—the artist starts from a "chosen" world rather than the received phenomena of the external. He erects "violent structures" of signification rather than working within the parameters typically available to the artist.

> *Enemy of the Stars* **narrates the artistic struggle of mind against nature as a parable of the vorticist movement's own contradictory attitude toward tradition and creation.**
>
> **— *Scott Klein***

"We establish ourselves" therefore roots the vorticist in the closed system of self-nomination. The artist is empowered by his own consciousness rather than by the surfaces of the world, by his sheer ability, as Lewis writes, to break free from origin, to "invent [him]self properly." Lewis's vocabulary further suggests his oppositional independence. "We discharge ourselves on both sides," adapts the language of both battle and purgation. The vorticist artist is a "Primitive Mercenary," that is, one who is free of allegiance, and is therefore able to turn against, rather than surrender to, the external world. The sole containing force for his own energies, Lewis's ideal artist is an unpredicated model of the powerful self. Able to hold dualities in balance as part of his overarching coherence, he stands free of the external—both the inanimate world and the world of other people.

This emphasis on the creative individual's singularity and paradoxical doubleness finds its detailed expression in *Enemy of the Stars.* As independence from the other (which includes the past and mass culture) is Lewis's first requirement of creation, it is suitably, therefore, the concern of the narrative. Arghol, the protagonist, is an intellectual who "has come to fight a ghost, Humanity." He represents the possibility of the self's independence, a "statue-mirage of Liberty in the great desert" of human affairs. He stands against nature even as he uses it for his obscure and metaphorical purposes. He is the "enemy of the stars" of the title, who stands alone as a "MAGNET OF SUBTLE, VAST, SELFISH THINGS" and attempts to give some shape to the "archaic blank wilderness of the universe." Lewis stresses that Arghol is discontinuous with the world around him in his descriptions of the landscape—"The canal ran in one direction, his blood weakly, in the opposite." Arghol rejects the world of desire in order to achieve a transcendent distance from it.

Like the vorticist, he wants to "leave violently slow monotonous life" in order to enter the void that is the merging of paradoxical opposites, to "take header into the boiling starry cold." He hopes to achieve this transcendence through solitude. If he keeps the "fire of friction unspent in solitariness," he explains to Hanp, he will "reach the stars." Hanp, on the other hand, epitomizes the "BLACK BOURGEOIS ASPIRATIONS" that threaten to undermine Arghol's "BLATANT VIRTUOSITY OF SELF"; he is an indistinct form who merges with all around him. Arghol castigates him in the same metaphoric terms with which Lewis dismisses the Romantic artist—"You cling to any object," he says, "dig your nails in earth, not to drop into it." Arghol sees in Hanp only a general portrait of homogeneous mankind, an "anonymous form of the vastness of humanity" that he must counteract with his theories of selfhood. He asserts that the self represents the opposite of Hanp's mass mediocrity. "Between Personality and Mankind it is always a question of dog and cat," Arghol states, "they are diametrically opposed species." He therefore rejects all that is not the self as repulsive to the purity of the individual, blaming the other for its gradual destruction—"The process and condition of life, without exception, is a grotesque degradation and 'soillure' of the original solitude of the soul. There is no help for it. . . . Anything but yourself is dirt. Anybody that is."

In living out this startlingly egoistic and misanthropic philosophy, moreover, Arghol rejects all action, even in self-protection. When Hanp suggests that he avenge himself against the uncle who appears regularly to beat him, for instance, Arghol declines, for any contact with the other, however defensive, can only tarnish the self. Arghol considers himself to be a superior force, "too superb ever to lift a finger when harmed," he argues, and cannot lower himself by responding to the world. In rejecting the kinetic impulses of life, moreover, he believes he can ultimately transcend mortality. He trusts that the metaphysical weight of his adopted symbols can prevent his dissolution. His intellectual activities are a form of exercise to ward off destruction, the production of an art that can transcend time. "The stone of the stars will do for my seal and emblem," he says, "I practice with it, monotonously 'putting,' that I may hit Death when he comes."

Yet as the play progresses it becomes clear that Arghol, unlike the ideal artist of Lewis's manifestos, cannot protect himself from the world through his trust in self and symbols. When Hanp attacks Arghol after being contemptuously dismissed as a parasite, Arghol has no choice but to fight back in Hanp's sphere of "life," "break[ing] vows and spoil[ing] continuity of instinctual behavior." He becomes an extension of the world rather than its opposite. He becomes a "soft, blunt paw of Nature" and loses his distinctiveness, falling into Hanp's condition of integration with the surrounding real as "part of the responsive landscape." This grudging acceptance of nature seals Arghol's downfall. Infuriated by his inconsistency and in "sullen indignation at Arghol ACTING, he who had not the right to act," Hanp turns against him a second time and murders him as he sleeps.

Arghol's defense against Hanp therefore foreshadows his own destruction. Hanp cannot resolve the contradictions between Arghol's transcendent theories and worldly actions without obliterating their source. Arghol's death is Hanp's dramatic proof that despite his opposition to nature Arghol is still "imprisoned in a messed socket of existence." Yet although Hanp is the direct agent of his death, Arghol's downfall results logically from his programmatic rejection of the other. This is implicit in the dream that Arghol has before his death. He remembers himself as a student in the city who, furious with the confinement of his room, rejects the book that lies "stalely open" before him, *Einege und Sein Eigenkeit* by the German philosopher Max Stirner. Disgusted with the book as yet another of the tarnishing influences of the external world, Arghol flings it from his window. He calls it "one of the seven arrows in my martyr mind," and dismisses it both because it is a drain of the authenticity of the self and because its otherness is a perverse call to external experience—"These books are all parasites . . . eternal prostitute." A dream figure appears at the door to return the book, however, a "young man he had known in the town" who changes first into Hanp and then into a "self-possessed" and "free" image, "Stirner as he imagined him." The figure ignores Arghol's repeated attempts to eject him, and, as Stirner, provokes Arghol into a repetition of his recent struggle with Hanp—"A scrap ensued, physical experiences of recent fight recurring."

Although Arghol succeeds in banishing the dream figure from his room, his rejection of Stirner is puzzling. As Tom

Kinnimont has noted, Stirner's ideas are substantially those of Arghol, and, insofar as Arghol is a figure of Lewis, of Lewis himself. *Der Einzige und Sein Eigentum* asserts the truth of the self, and attempts to establish its independence from society's falsehoods and the limitations of the real by declaring that the self is all-sufficient, its own master and owner. For Stirner, as for Arghol, the self is an ultimate good that can be achieved only by egoistically conserving one's power. "My *own* I am at all times and under all circumstances," he writes, "if I do not throw myself away on others." Stirner emphasizes that man needs to cast off the bonds of the external world, rejecting desire and the societal constructs that limit his autonomy. "I am my *own* only when I am mastered by myself," he writes, "instead of being mastered by sensuality, or by anything else . . . what is of use to me . . . my selfishness pursues." The similarity of Stirner's formulations to those of Arghol is obvious. Yet *Der Einzige* also provides the actions of *Enemy of the Stars* with their underlying metaphor. Stirner describes man as a slave who must endure the torments of a mastering reality in order to assert his natural power:

> The fetters of reality cut the sharpest welts in my flesh every moment. But *my own* I remain. Given up as a serf to a master, I think only of myself and my own advantage; his blows strike me indeed, I am not *free* from them; but I endure them only for *my benefit,* perhaps in order to deceive him and make him secure by the semblance of patience, or, again, not to draw worse upon myself by subordination. But, as I keep my eye on myself and my selfishness, I take by the forelock the first good opportunity to trample the slave holder into the dust.

This is also the response to the self's limitations represented in the play by Arghol's rejection of action and Hanp's revenge. Arghol refuses to fight against his uncle, the "master" of the play for Stirner's reasons. He will not condescend to act because his uncle is of use to him—"He loads my plate" Arghol explains. Moreover, like Stirner's self, Arghol obscurely intends to use the energy of the attacks to liberate himself from mastery, "as prisoner his bowl or sheet for escape: not as means of idle humiliation." Yet Arghol is also a master, to Hanp, and he abuses his disciple as severely as he is himself maltreated by his uncle. Hanp's revenge is therefore also a response to the play's avowal of the self's power. He endures Arghol's abuse, like Stirner's selfhood, for his own benefit, eagerly accepting it because it is the only way he can find out about the city, which desire has placed him "under Arghol's touch." Only when Arghol dismisses him completely does he take the occasion of Arghol's sleep to "trample him into the dust." Both Arghol and Hanp therefore act according to Stirner's ideas of the self. Arghol explicitly presents the theoretical side of philosophical egoism, while Hanp embodies the destructive action of that theory. "I serve my freedom with regard to the world in the degree that I make the world my own," Stirner concludes; both Arghol, who claims to dominate the stars, and Hanp, who murders his master, are versions of the self that seeks its freedom through the egoistic domination of its environment.

Arghol's rejection of Stirner exposes the defective contradictions in his own thought. If he rejects the other simply because it is not the self, then Arghol blinds himself to the possibility that the object of his scorn, in this case Stirner, may be an equal who shares his ideas and therefore his power. When he rejects Stirner on the automatic grounds of his externality, therefore, Arghol unwittingly rejects his own selfhood. The dream figure, who initially appears as "a young man he had known in the town, but now saw for the first time, seemingly" can be read as a figure of Arghol's division. As an aspect of the self he "had known in town" the figure offers him the literal opportunity to see himself for the first time. He gives Arghol the chance to reintegrate his personality by reaccepting the book that he has rejected, implicitly offering him the awareness that his self is also, in a sense, other. Their fight demonstrates, however, that Arghol refuses to recognize the contradictions implicit in the cult of selfhood. By throwing Stirner's book from the window he both adheres to his philosophy of selfhood and transgresses it. By refusing to reaccept it he completes his destruction. Arghol emerges from the fight with only a partial understanding of his endangered self. He tears up his books, and in a paradoxical effort to reclaim his identity he wanders through the streets of the city denying himself to those he meets—"I am not Arghol," he claims, "This man has been masquerading as me."

Yet although Arghol believes he can control the logic of his self with his paradoxes, his avowals only underscore his actual loss of control. Lewis has described him earlier in the play as "a large open book, full of truth and insults." When he destroys all of his books the reader understands that he has completed metaphorically the eradication of the self that began with his rejection of Stirner. When he returns to the wheelwright's yard at the play's beginning, then, he has already been defeated. In rejecting the other he has already rejected himself.

Enemy of the Stars is therefore a narrative about failure. Arghol's theories foreshadow his destruction, for he can no more overcome the material world than he can be consistent with himself. His fall, as Lewis warns the reader in the play's first line, is part of an "IMMENSE COLLAPSE OF CHRONIC PHILOSOPHY," not simply of temporal philosophy but of continuous and excessive thought *Enemy of the Stars* therefore occupies a problematic position within *Blast*. Where the manifestos insist that the autonomous self is the basis of the artist's power, the play both rejects the efficacy of that philosophy and exposes the vorticist self as a divisive delusion. Arghol's theories serve only to divide him from himself, and he and Hanp can only be united in their mutual obliteration. The play's content is therefore opposed to that of the manifestos.

In the play opposites are irreconcilable, for they result only in destruction. In the manifestos, on the other hand, the balance of oppositions leads to a higher creativity. *Enemy of the Stars* therefore presents the reader of *Blast* with a fundamental paradox. If the manifestos' version of opposition is authentic, then the play's apparent contradiction of that truth is not a real contradiction. It can be read as one of the "opposite statements of a chosen world" that the artist erects as part of his power, an extreme whose denial makes the self stronger. Yet the struggle between apparent opposites has quite different results within the play. The intellectual is unable to balance himself against his negation, and the powerlessness of his rhetoric leads to his destruction. *Enemy of the Stars* therefore threatens to invalidate the very principles upon which the manifestos are erected even while formally fulfilling them.

The paradox is underlined by Lewis's presentation of his failed hero as a quintessential practitioner of the manifestos' doctrines. Like Lewis's ideal artist he tries to use a studied inactivity to escape from the "action and reaction" of common life. His approach to the world is familiarly figurative and double. According to Hanp, Arghol's logic is mysterious, his association of opposites inscrutable—like the vorticist "He gave men one image with one hand, and at the same time a second, its antidote with the other." Moreover, the play takes place in a "wheelwright's yard," a setting where whirling products, metaphorical verions of the vortex, are created. Like the vorticist, moreover—or at least the vorticist author of "Enemy of the Stars"—Arghol is a metaphorical playwright, creating from the materials of nature that he attempts to rule and elude—"The stars are his cast." Arghol's struggles are therefore implicitly the struggles of his author, an identification made explicit in Lewis's introduction to the play. In the "advertisement" that precedes it Lewis writes that *Enemy of the Stars* is a version of the conflict between an artist and his audience. He informs the reader that the play is "VERY WELL ACTED BY YOU AND ME." (One notes already the element of agon with the unsympathetic readership in *Blast* at large, where Lewis lambastes his own scoffing readers: "CURSE those who will hang over this Manifesto with SILLY CANINES exposed.") Lewis therefore appears to implicate himself in his own fictional designs. Just as Arghol falls prey to self-contradiction by dismissing the text of himself as his opposite, Lewis seems to negate himself by creating a text whose content suggests his own necessary failure.

The play's narrative of division and failure, however, can be read as a reflection of its problematic position within both Lewis's artistic canon and the tradition of "readerly" drama. Lewis wrote *Enemy of the Stars* with the goal of inventing a vorticist prose, and it stands out strikingly from the other prose offerings in *Blast,* stylistically conservative efforts by Ford Madox Ford and Rebecca West. He hoped to create a language that would be analogous to his painterly abstractions, revivifying literature with nonrepresentational techniques borrowed from other forms of modernism. "My literary contemporaries I looked upon as too bookish and not keeping pace with the visual revolution," he later explained. "A kind of play, *The Enemy of the Stars . . .* was my attempt to show them the way." Yet the relative conservatism of the resulting abstraction of language is striking next to the visual experimentation of the canvases that Lewis reproduced in *Blast* under the play's rubric. Here, for instance, is an example of description from the middle of the play: "Throats iron eternities, drinking heavy radiance, limbs towers of blatant light, the stars poised immensely distant, with their metal sides, pantheistic machines."

Lewis here distorts expected structure and connotation, much as he rejected expected shapes in his canvases. He places short phrases in apposition without consistent grammatical markers, juxtaposes nouns illogically, and uses verbs to shape disjunct fragments within the sentence rather than to relate them to one another. Yet the sentence's grammar can be easily normalized. If one places the word "are" between "throats" and "iron," "limbs" and "towers," "stars" and "poised," the apparent idiosyncrasy of the sentence's structure is recontained as "proper" English. It depends upon the elision, rather than the subversion, of traditional perceptual markers, and its syntax can still be perceived through its apparent discontinuities. The abstraction of its content is similarly limited. A phrase such as "throats iron eternities" depends entirely upon juxtaposition for its abstract effect. The words invoke three distinct images, whose proximity creates an aggregate nonrepresentational image. Yet even if the phrase as a whole has no direct corollary in the world, and is therefore abstract, its components remain indivisibly referential. The words "throat" "iron" and "eternities" always invoke real objects or concepts separate yet pragmatically connected to the words themselves, even when they are juxtaposed in otherwise extravagant contexts. Lewis himself condemned juxtaposition for artistic effect in his later criticisms of surrealism. Its interest was psychological rather than pictorial, he wrote, for it arranged "the same old units of the same old stock-in-trade" in novel patterns but added nothing to the vocabulary of representation. By Lewis's own stringent criteria, therefore, abstraction and language are intrinsically incompatible. Words, more than visual symbols, are inseparable from their logical systems and fixed referents. Sentences cannot be radically distorted without obliterating their structural sense, while the words themselves can never be separated entirely from the signified.

Lewis would later admit the hopelessness of the experiment. The writing of *Tarr,* he explains in *Rude Assignment,* made him see "that words and syntax were not susceptible of transformation into abstract terms." Later in *Men without Art* he states the more general disbelief "that anything in the literary field can be done that will correspond with what has been called 'abstract design'." The form as well as the content of *Enemy of the Stars* already suggest its contradictions with his ideal art. By designating his prose experiment a "play" Lewis emphasized the work's visual origin; it is intended to be "seen" rather than read, "acted by you and me" rather than confined to the page. By presenting it as drama Lewis draws particular attention to those aspects of *Enemy of the Stars* that coexist uneasily with vorticist ideals. As narrative it necessarily unfolds over time; its linearity emphasizes and replicates the temporal nature of the signs with which it is constructed. As drama, moreover, it necessarily places action in its foreground. Its visual and narrative interest must be propelled by the same kinetic surrender to desire that the manifestos associate with fragmentation. Arghol is condemned as much by the logic of the dramatic form as his ideas. He cannot avoid nature or mortality, for the language in which he is described cannot transcend a synchrony or the necessary presentation of action. His failure of transcendence within the play mirrors Lewis's self-created failure of form. As author Lewis cannot escape the demands of the word and its related structures of syntax and narrative. His use of narrative language is therefore a capitulation to the temporal desire and explicit representation that vorticism elsewhere rejects. Like Arghol's unwilling acceptance of nature Lewis's use of the signs of language intrinsically contradicts his claims to power.

The very unperformability of *Enemy of the Stars* is therefore a part of the aesthetic implication of its narrative. In order to reject action and desire one must erect a language that can remain only theoretical. *Enemy of the Stars* therefore operates within *Blast* both as a reminder of the paradoxes of the transcendental aspects of the vorticist position, and of its own paradox: as modernist drama, it is rooted in a self-contradictory vision of representation inimical to its own expressed intentions. It can be enacted only as an act of cognition by reader and author, and the tale it tells is of the author's dissolution.

As drama, moreover, it marks a problematic historical return of the nineteenth-century models against which vorticism has implicitly defined itself. Arghol's murder by Hanp is an example of the Gothic archetype of the doppelgänger, in which a divided and unacknowledged part of the self returns to wreak destruction upon the agent of its own repression. This narrative motif of German Romanticism persists in Lewis's work despite the thematic denial of Romanticism as a historical category, a pattern similarly visible in the persistence of E. T. A. Hoffman and Dostoyevski in *Tarr*. But these terms suggest the more curious generic affiliations of *Enemy of the Stars* as a programmatically unperformable "play." For it is surprisingly closer in generic intent to the verse drama of the English Romantics, in which an essentially non-narrative form is pressed into narrative service, than to the theatrical pieces of its contemporary European avant-garde.

This is particularly true of its dramatic motifs. In his study of English poetic drama from Wordsworth to Beddoes, Alan Richardson has abstracted the narrative features that bind together prominent representatives of the genre. The plays deal with the history of an individual protagonist's consciousness; they hinge upon highly rhetorical confrontations between the protagonist and his opposite, who represents an aspect of the divided consciousness of the hero. The hero is seduced into transgression by his daimon and lapses into repetition of that transgression, having become dependent upon his Other, as Hegel's master and slave come to depend dialectically upon one another. Finally, the divisions within the protagonist revealed, he becomes destructive, either toward others (cynically replaying his own seduction into transgression with another) or toward himself.

The pattern of *Manfred* and works that resemble it is also that of *Enemy of the Stars*. Arghol is seduced into action by Hanp in an atmosphere of intense rhetorical opposition (here including the stylistic opposition of non-narrative vorticist prose against the demands of action), which betrays Arghol into his own repetitions. The dream of struggle repeats Hanp's attack, as Hanp's attack is itself a repetition of the attack of Arghol's uncle. Arghol's dependence on his uncle—"he loads my plate"—is itself a Hege-

lian reduplication of Hanp's dependence upon Arghol, as the importance of Stirner's work here, formatively influenced by Hegel, grudgingly suggests. And Arghol recognizes overtly that Hanp is a part of himself—"Why do I speak to you? . . . ," he says, "It's not to you but myself. . . . You are an unclean little beast, crept gloomily out of my ego." The narrative of Hanp's murder of Arghol is therefore, as Richardson notes of *Manfred*, "less a celebration of isolated subjectivity than a critique of the false assumptions behind psychic autonomy." The unitary protagonist is revealed to be divided, and his transgressions against his self destroy him.

To reclaim *Enemy of the Stars* as what Byron called "mental theatre" is not simply to note that it fits into a preexistent pattern of motif and form, but to insist upon a family resemblance between nominally diverse works that deal with similar themes of rebellion and individuality, including such works as Arnold's "Empedocles on Etna," and work through their themes with analogous styles and narratives. Like the Romantics, Lewis was attempting to forge a style that was by definition private, to construct a personal language. Yet this essentially lyric impulse (for Lewis the creation of a style rather than a narrative form) is in conflict with the necessity of the artist's public pronouncement of that style. The verse or readerly drama is caught between the realms of the non-narrative and the public realm of narrative, and is produced as the problematic product of that dialectic. The divisions between ideal and actual, private and public, are enacted in Lewis and in the plays that share his representational concerns, by the work's characters, who are themselves rent by self-destructive yet potentially transcendental division. And this may in turn be seen as part of the legacy of the English theater itself, which traces its heritage not from the interplay of individuality and society implied by the structure of chorus and individual performer of the Greeks, but from the dialogic dramas of Seneca. In Seneca, unlike Aeschylus and Sophocles, the philosopher/author, like Lewis, divides issues of thought into characters that reify, through the logic of the dramatic form, the spectacle of mutilation rather than cultural affirmation.

Vorticism and *Enemy of the Stars* do not merely recapitulate the forms and genres of the Romanticism that *Blast* claims implicitly to reject, nor the tradition of philosophic drama since Seneca. Yet the avant-garde reappropriation of outmoded forms, the philosopher/poet's divided voice enacted through warring opposites, the tragedy of consciousness and self ending in destruction, all suggest continuity rather than break between the avant-garde practices of the early nineteenth and the early twentieth centuries. Nor are other precedents absent in the vorticist experiment. From Arnold, indeed, Lewis may have gained the insight, as he expresses elsewhere in the manifestos, that "pessimism [is] the triumphant note in modern art."

From Shakespeare Lewis learned tragic irony, the sense, as he says in *The Lion and the Fox*, that Shakespeare's characters are caught in "a *real* action; whereas they come from, and naturally inhabit, an ideal world." But the shadowing of the genre of the unperformable play suggests most powerfully the persistence of the myth of the Promethean creative impulse within the avant-garde, and reveals, by utilizing a form that contains its own critique, that its author, like its hero, can be led into the tragic transgression enacted by style and form. In *Enemy of the Stars* Lewis therefore reveals the "fostering of unactual conditions," his own definition of Romanticism, rife within his own avant-garde. The play, by insisting upon its own programmatic unperformability, exposes the degree to which the stylistic experimentation of vorticism is its own unperformable act, containing within itself the failure of its own transcendence—of language, self, and narrative genre.

VORTICIST PAINTING

Ezra Pound

SOURCE: "Affirmations," in *The New Age,* Vol. XVI, No. 11, January, 14, 1915, pp. 277-8.

[*In the following essay, Pound explains the forms and techniques of Vorticist painting.*]

There is perhaps no more authentic sign of the senility of a certain generation of publicists (now, thank heaven, gradually fading from the world) than their abject terror in the face of motive ideas. An age may be said to be decadent, or a generation may be said to be in a state of prone senility, when its creative minds are dead and when its survivors maintain a mental dignity—to wit, the dignity or stationariness of a corpse in its cerements. Excess or even absinthe is not the sure sign of decadence. If a man is capable of creative, or even of mobile, thought he will not go in terror of other men so endowed. He will not call for an inquisition or even a persecution of other men who happen to think something which he has not yet thought, or of which he may not yet have happened to hear.

The public divides itself into sections according to temper and alertness; it may think with living London, or with moribund London, or with Chicago, or Boston, or even with New Zealand; and behind all these there are possibly people who think on a level with Dublin, antiquarians, of course, and students of the previous age. For example, Sir Hugh Lane tried to give Dublin a collection of pictures, Degas, Corot and Manet, and they called him a charlatan and cried out for real pictures "like the lovely paintings which we see reproduced in our city art shops." I have even seen a paper from Belfast which brands J. M. Synge as a "decadent." Is such a country fit for Home Rule? I ask as the merest outsider having not the slightest interest in the question. I have met here in London two men still believing in Watts, and I suppose anything is possible—any form of atavism that you may be willing to name.

I suppose any new development or even any change in any art has to be pushed down the public throat with a ramrod. The public has always squealed. A public which has gushed over the sentimentalities of Rodin adorns Epstein's work with black butterflies, à cause de pudeur. The wickedest and most dashing publisher of "the nineties," of the

"vicious, disreputable nineties," demands that our antiseptic works be submitted to ladylike censorship. And the papers in Trieste rejoice that futurism is a thing of the past, that a new god is come to deliver them. Such is the state of the world at the beginning of A.D. 1915.

The political world is confronted with a great war, a species of insanity. The art world is confronted with a species of quiet and sober sanity called Vorticism, which I am for the third or fourth time called upon to define, quietly, lucidly, with precision.

Vorticism is the use of, or the belief in the use of, THE PRIMARY PIGMENT, straight through all of the arts.

If you are a cubist, or an expressionist, or an imagist, you may believe in one thing for painting and a very different thing for poetry. You may talk about volumes, or about colour that "moves in," or about a certain form of verse, without having a correlated æsthetic which carries you through all of the arts. Vorticism means that one is interested in the creative faculty as opposed to the mimetic. We believe that it is harder to make than to copy. We believe in maximum efficiency, and we go to a work of art not for tallow candles or cheese, but for something which we cannot get anywhere else. We go to a particular art for something which we cannot get in any other art. If we want form and colour we go to a painting, or we make a painting. If we want form without colour and in two dimensions, we want drawing or etching. If we want form in three dimensions, we want sculpture. If we want an image or a procession of images, we want poetry. If we want pure sound, we want music.

These different desires are not one and the same. They are divers desires and they demand divers sorts of satisfaction. The more intense the individual life, the more vivid are the divers desires of that life. The more alive and vital the mind, the less will it be content with dilutations; with diluted forms of satisfaction.

I might put it differently. I might say, "I like a man who goes the whole hog." If he wants one sort of, say, "philosophy," he goes to Spinoza. If he wants another sort of "philosophy," he goes to Swedenborg. But nothing under heaven will induce him to have recourse to the messy sort of author who tries to mix up these two incompatible sorts of thought, and who produces only a muddle. Art deals with certitude. There is no "certitude" about a thing which is pretending to be something else.

A painting is an arrangement of colour patches on a canvas, or on some other substance. It is a good or bad painting according as these colour-patches are well or ill arranged. After that it can be whatever it likes. It can represent the Blessed Virgin, or Jack Johnson, or it need not represent at all, it can be. These things are a matter of taste. A man may follow his whim in these matters without the least harm to his art sense, so long as he remembers that it is merely his whim and that it is not a matter of "art criticism" or of "æsthetics." When a man prefers a Blessed Virgin by Watts to a portrait of a nasty pawnbroker by Rembrandt, one ceases to consider him as a person seriously interested in painting. There is nothing very new about that. When a man begins to be more interested in the "arrangement" than in the dead matter arranged, then he begins "to have an eye for" the difference between the good, the bad and the mediocre in Chinese painting. His remarks on Byzantine, and Japanese, and on ultra-modern painting begin to be interesting and intelligible. You do not demand of a mountain or a tree that it shall be like something; you do not demand that "natural beauty" be limited to mean only a few freaks of nature, cliffs looking like faces, etc. The worst symbolist of my acquaintance—that is to say, the most fervent admirer of Watts' pictures—has said to me more than once, quoting Nietzsche most inadvertently, "The artist is part of nature, therefore he never imitates nature." That text serves very well for my side of the case. Is a man capable of admiring a picture on the same terms as he admires a mountain? The picture will never become the mountain. It will never have the mountain's perpetual variety. The photograph will reproduce the mountain's contour with greater exactitude. Let us say that a few people choose to admire the picture on more or less the same terms as those on which they admire the mountain. Then what do I mean by "forms well organised"?

Vorticism is the use of, or the belief in the use of, THE PRIMARY PIGMENT, straight through all of the arts.

— *Ezra Pound*

An organisation of forms expresses a confluence of forces. These forces may be the "love of God," the "life-force," emotions, passions, what you will. For example: if you clap a strong magnet beneath a plateful of iron filings, the energies of the magnet will proceed to organise form. It is only by applying a particular and suitable force that you can bring order and vitality and thence beauty into a plate of iron filings, which are otherwise as "ugly" as anything under heaven. The design in the magnetised iron filings expresses a confluence of energy. It is not "meaningless" or "inexpressive."

There are, of course, various sorts or various sub-divisions of energy. They are all capable of expressing themselves in "an organisation of form." I saw, some months since, the "automatic" paintings of Miss Florence Seth. They were quite charming. They were the best automatic paintings I have seen. "Automatic painting" means paintings done by people who begin to paint without preconception, who believe, or at least assert, that the painting is done without volition on their part, that their hands are guided by "spirits," or by some mysterious agency over which they have little or no control. "Will and consciousness are our vortex." The friend who sent me to see Miss Seth's painting did me a favour, but he was very much in the wrong if he thought my interest was aroused because Miss Seth's painting was vorticist.

Miss Seth's painting was quite beautiful. It was indeed much finer than her earlier mimetic work. It had richness of colour, it had the surety of articulation which one finds in leaves and in viscera. There was in it also an unconscious use of certain well-known symbols, often very beautifully disguised with elaborate detail. Often a symbol appeared only in a fragment, wholly unrecognisable in some pictures, but capable of making itself understood by comparison with other fragments of itself appearing in other pictures. Miss Seth had begun with painting obviously Christian symbols, doves, etc. She had gone on to paint less obvious symbols, of which she had no explanation. She had no theories about the work, save that it was in some way mediumistic. In her work, as in other "automatic" paintings which I have seen, the structure was similar to the structure of leaves and viscera. It was, that is to say, exclusively *organic*. It is not surprising that the human mind in a state of lassitude or passivity should take on again the faculties of the unconscious or sub-human energies or minds of nature; that the momentarily dominant atom of personality should, that is to say, retake the pattern-making faculty which lies in the flower-seed or in the grain or in the animal cell.

This is not vorticism. They say that an infant six weeks old is both aquatic and arboreal, that it can both swim and hang from a small branch by its fist, and that by the age of six months it has lost these faculties. I do not know whether or no this is true. It is a scientist's report, I have never tried it on a six-weeks-old infant. If it is so, we will say that instinct "revives" or that "memory throws back," or something of that sort. The same phrase would apply to the pattern-making instinct revived in somnolents or in mediumistic persons.

Note especially that their paintings have only organic structures, that their forms are the forms already familiar to us in sub-human nature. Their work is interesting as a psychological problem, not as creation. I give it, however, along with my paragraph on iron filings, as an example of energy expressing itself in pattern.

We do not enjoy an arrangement of "forms and colours" because it is a thing isolated in nature. Nothing is isolated in nature. This organisation of form and colour is "expression"; just as a musical arrangement of notes by Mozart is expression. The vorticist is expressing his complex consciousness. He is not like the iron filings, expressing electrical magnetism; not like the automatist, expressing a state of cell-memory, a vegetable or visceral energy. Not, however, that one despises vegetable energy or wishes to adorn the rose or the cyclamen, which are vegetable energies expressed in form. One, as a human being, cannot pretend fully to express oneself unless one express instinct and intellect together. The softness and the ultimate failure of interest in automatic painting are caused by a complete lack of conscious intellect. Where does this bring us? It brings us to this: Vorticism is a legitimate expression of life.

My personal conviction is as follows: Time was when I began to be interested in "the beauties of nature." According to impressionism I began to see the colour of shadows, etc. It was very interesting. I noted refinements in colour. It was very interesting. Time was when I began to make something of light and shade. I began to see that if you were representing a man's face you would represent the side on which light shone by very different paint from that whereby you would express the side which rested in shadow. All these things were, and are, interesting. One is more alive for having these swift-passing, departmentalised interests in the flow of life about one. It is by swift apperceptions of this sort that one differentiates oneself from the brute world. To be civilised is to have swift apperception of the complicated life of today; it is to have a subtle and instantaneous perception of it, such as savages and wild animals have of the necessities and dangers of the forest. It is to be no less alive or vital than the savage. It is a different kind of aliveness.

And vorticism, especially that part of vorticism having to do with form—to wit, vorticist painting and sculpture—has brought me a new series of apperceptions. It has not brought them solely to me. I have my new and swift perceptions of forms, of possible form-motifs; I have a double or treble or tenfold set of stimulæ in going from my home to Piccadilly. What was a dull row of houses is become a magazine of forms. There are new ways of seeing them. There are ways of seeing the shape of the sky as it juts down between the houses. The tangle of telegraph wires is conceivable not merely as a repetition of lines; one sees the shapes defined by the different braches of wire. The lumber yards, the sidings of railways cease to be dreary.

The muscial conception of form, that is to say the understanding that you can use form as a musician uses sound, that you can select motives of form from the forms before you, that you can recombine and recolour them and "organise" them into new form—this conception, this state of mental activity, brings with it a great joy and refreshment. I do not wish to convert anyone. I simply say that a certain sort of pleasure is available to anyone who wants it. It is one of the simple pleasures of those who have no money to spend on joy-rides and on suppers at the Ritz.

This "musical conception of form" is more than post-impressionism. Manet took impressions of colour. They say Cezanne began taking "impressions of form." That is not the same thing as conceiving the forms about one as a source of "form-motifs," which motifs one can use later at one's pleasure in more highly developed compositions.

It is possible that this search for form-motif will lead us to some synthesis of western life comparable to the synthesis of oriental life which we find in Chinese and Japanese painting. This lies with the future. Perhaps there is some adumbration of it in Mr. Wadsworth's "Harbour of Flushing."

At any rate I have put down some of my reasons for believing in the vorticist painters and sculptors. I have at least in part explained why I believe in Mr. Wyndham Lewis; why I think him a more significant artist than Kandinsky (admitting that I have not yet seen enough of Kandinsky's work to use a verb stronger than "think"); why I think that Mr. Lewis' work will contain certain elements not to be found in Picasso, whom I regard as a great

artist, but who has not yet expressed all that we mean by vorticism.

Note that I am not trying to destroy anyone's enjoyment of the Quattrocento, nor of the Victory of Samothrace, nor of any work of art which is approximately the best of its kind. I state that there is a new gamut of artistic enjoyments and satisfactions; that vorticist painting is not meaningless; and that anyone who cares to may enjoy it.

C. H. Collins Baker

SOURCE: "Dry Bones," in *The Saturday Review*, Vol. CXIX, No. 3099, March 20, 1915, pp. 304-5.

[*In the following excerpt, Baker presents a negative perspective on Vorticist art.*]

In having degenerated so suddenly into such a bore, the Vorticists, or whatever they used to call themselves, have been a little unlucky. I am inclined to think their reputation as amusing creatures and puzzle painters might, in normal conditions, have carried them through another season (provided that a rival group had not been yet more amusing). But Life decreed that something serious should come to the rescue of a costive world, whose ennui was barely mitigated by all sorts of ingenuity and elaborate bright notions. So in August, to our horror, we were tipped right into things that really mattered. And now, when we have opportunity to look again at those old ingenious notions, our nerves still tingling with the impact of reality, we simply wonder what on earth was up with us that we should ever have been entertained by them.

Generally speaking, the trouble with the Vortex school is that its members are either dull or dishonest. Some are both. Being dull needs no definition, but being artistically dishonest should perhaps be explained. Mr. Kramer's "Earth" at the Goupil Gallery is just poor fun; anyone could devise its clownish antics. On the other hand, Mr. Nevinson's "Arrival at Dunkirk", Mr. Ginner's "Leeds Roofs", and Mr. Wadsworth's "Blackpool" are academic "fakes", more dishonest than the typical popular Royal Academician's sentimental anecdotes. That is to say, they deliberately falsify their impression of life for the sake of a convention. Instead of setting down some genuine impression, almost unconsciously received, Mr. Nevinson, when he arrived at Dunkirk, was preoccupied in translating his impressions into the jargon of his school. I suspect he went about with a note-book collecting little bits of local colour and, as perhaps he phrased it to himself, of "significance". Then he turned to and cast his carefully amassed notes into the form prescribed by his system of emotion expression—a blue stripe signifying this, a yellow cube that, and an arc and diamond pattern the other. The culminating bright idea was to print "Transatlantic", left, centre, in large capitals. As if a man's emotions or sensations come to him in Roman letters! I have no doubt that Mr. Nevinson received sensations and emotions when he got to France. And I am as sure as he that his painting renders not their spontaneity, but his deliberate perversion of the actuality into a conventional ideal. That is why his picture bores us; at the moment we have no use for elaborate ingenuity.

In much the same fictitious and intellectual way Mr. Wadsworth's sensations on visiting Blackpool were worked up. I have never been there; all that I derive from his arrangement is an impression of blue and white, yellow and french-mustard strips. Mr. Wadsworth doubtless went to Blackpool and felt that it was something or other. Perhaps it was noisy and gave him a headache; he consulted his dictionary of emotion phrases and found that a brass band should be expressed by a yellow stripe, a crowd of trippers by a yellow octagon. And so he worked it out, at the last perhaps really persuading himself that the crowd and the glare and the pierrots gave him blue and white emotions. So, too, at length academicians become convinced that artists' models, attired in picturesque raiment hired from the costumiers, are real life.

I am not sure, without looking up the literature on the subject, whether Mr. Ginner is a Vorticist or something else. Whatever he is, his "Leeds Roofs" is a deliberate falsification, reasoned out by rule. There can be no doubt that if he has had any training or experience, or if he is naturally perceptive, his picture does not try to express what he received from Nature, but something that he considers an improvement. For if, for example, he saw the chimneys on the left like this, he would not have seen those on the right, which are against a different background, identically. His uncoached and intuitive perception would have received a new, a unique impression from each separate chimney. But he, working by some intellectual rule, substitutes a formula for spontaneous feeling. That is why his painting seems so tame and unadventurous compared with life. All these painters only prove once more what has been proved a hundred times. Their attempts to discover a system that will prove superior to Nature is the old common plan tried by all the schools, from before that of the Carracci down to that of Leighton. But no good has come of schools that work by recipes. The only art that matters long is that which happens, as it were, unreasonedly; that is unrepeatable and for ever on the wing. Genuine perception has passed almost before it is consciously noted. A sketch owes its superior quality, that can never be reproduced in a finished picture, just to that: it comes as near as a painter can go to expressing transient perception, almost unconsciously made. It is those passive, unaware impressions that record the truly living and therefore deeply interesting things. Receiving them a man is in touch with something greater than his intellect; editing them according to an intellectual system he is working within his little scope.

On the whole, and always excepting people who cannot help taking seriously irrelevant trivialities (such as the Derby and the new fashion in skirts), we have for the time been sobered and braced by contact with enormous forces. Hence it seems silly nonsense, I dare say—all these solemn painters exercising their tidy little intellectual artifices and bothering about their diagrams of emotional significance. It is a hard fate to find that no one really cares a pin whether you sensations are vermilion spots or canary-yellow stripes. It is disheartening that your brightest ideas for being novel should seem as new and as effectual as the old horse 'bus one sees in Bond Street.

John Cournos

SOURCE: "The Death of Vorticism," in *The Little Review,* Vol. VI, No. 2, June, 1919, pp. 46-8.

[*In the following essay, Cournos outlines the effects of World War I on Vorticist art.*]

—"Where there is no wit, there is insolence." As an example of this truth we have Mr. Ezra Pound. If final proof were wanting that Vorticism is dead, we have him writing about it. We know Mr. Pound's predilection for the dead. The dead, having the misfortune to die before Mr. Pound, cannot defend themselves. And all the while he has been digging his own literary grave.

When a man persistently denies life, life will end by completely denying him. There is Mr. Pound, for whom the five years' destructive war have left no dead, no ruins. Can he have been so dead that the great war should have passed by and over him and left him contemplating the year 1919 with the same eyes that he contemplated the early part of 1914? Does he think that by "blasting" he can reerect the fallen walls of his Vorticistic Jericho?

If art were merely an intellectual formula (as Mr. Pound would have us believe) this phenomenon would be understandable. But art also has its relation to the time, and is bound up irrevocably with the social processes of the moment, whether the individual instance be one of action or reaction. This is true of nations as well as of individuals. After 1870 the French produced a great art, the Germans almost ceased producing. Great wars usually kill something, and give birth to something. I already have pointed out in articles written about two years ago why the war was bound to kill the sister arts of Vorticism and Futurism. I will restate the case briefly. In the first place, because they were primarily prewar arts, i.e., arts created in the social cul-de-sac preceding the war. They were moreover war-like in theory and in expression, prophetic of war if you like. You have Mr. Lewis wanting to "laugh like a bomb" (which sounded very nice before the air-raids), his pictures, "Plan of War," etc.; and you have Marinetti's "glory of war" and "contempt of women", etc. Having been translated into life, being after all no more than an integral part of the social processes which produced on the one hand Prussianism (the Vortex that failed), on the other, Bolshevism (which is all for scatteredness and dispersion), Vorticism (an off-shoot of Cubism) and Futurism have lost their raison d'etre. There is no liking war when you have seen it, there is no liking Bolshevism when you have seen it. It was still early in the war that the Russian Futurist Mayakovsky, with an intellectual honesty, which I commend to Mr. Pound, in referring to the prewar art as "diabolic intuition, incarnated in the stormy today," declared that Futurism was dead because it had become fully realized in life. Again, the Russian Futurists, after Bolshevism had come into power, subscribed as a body to the new regime, proclaiming that it had realized their doctrines. This at any rate is honest, if uncouth.

I would like to correct Mr. Pound on certain small details.

He proudly asserts that the government has had to apply

to the Vorticist for a successful camouflage. That is quite natural. Vorticism is preeminently a camouflage art.

Again, Mr. Pound asserts that the government "after trying all kinds of war painters . . . with lamentable or at any rate negligible results . . . has taken on Mr. Lewis . . . and is now getting its finest pictures." Then Mr. Pound tells us that "Mr. Roberts, the youngest member of the *Blast* group, is also doing work for the government, and 'giving satisfaction'." What Mr. Pound does not tell us is that both Mr. Lewis and Mr. Roberts, as far as their work for the government is concerned, have compromised with their art. In their pictures, painted for the Canadian War Museum and exhibited recently at the Royal Academy, they have returned to realistic representation to such a degree that "the elderly" have indeed every justification for comparing their work to Lucca Signorelli.

It is quite true that "Vorticism has not yet had its funeral." The poor dear has died on the battlefield and no one even knows where its decayed remains are. If there is to be a funeral it shall have to be over an effigy, which Mr. Pound is very busy putting together.

Wylie Sypher

SOURCE: "A Mechanical Operation of the Spirit," in *The Sewanee Review,* Vol. LXXXV, No. 3, Summer, 1977, pp. 512-19.

[*In the following essay, Sypher discusses the artists associated with Vorticism.*]

Well under way is a revival of interest in the era of World War I, and not only as the first machine age. Witness the many books on the Great War, on Bloomsbury, on Wyndham Lewis as critic, novelist, and apostle of Vorticist art. Richard Cork's two monumental folio volumes [*Vorticism and Abstract Art in the First Machine Age.* Vol. 1: *Origins and Development.* 322 pages; Vol. 2: *Synthesis and Decline*], lavishly illustrated and exhaustively documented, at last record the full story of Vorticism, that brief, sometimes comic, episode in art and criticism intensely focused in London between 1913 and the early days of the war. Born amid the furor roused by Marinetti's Futurist obsession with the machine and Wyndham Lewis's revolt against Impressionism, Cubism, and the very Futurism to which he was indebted, Vorticism "was a measure of the vitality of London's artistic life during these hectic prewar months, when so many new and intoxicating ideas were being passed around from poet to painter, philosopher to sculptor." Lewis and Hulme furnished the theory of abstraction that rejected mimetic art in favor of forces symbolized by mechanical power—the Vortex of an exploding technology.

The Vorticist doctrine was stimulated by Hulme, fostered by Pound in his discontent with his own Imagist program, and finally given spasmodic form by Lewis, that tyrant of the Rebel group. While painting his iconoclastic "Composition" in 1913, Lewis began promoting Vorticism and was able by July 1914 to give British art a shock treatment by publishing the first issue of *Blast.* Loosely and independently associated with Lewis were artists like David Bomberg, Henri Gaudier-Brzeska, Jacob Epstein, and transient figures like Wadsworth, Etchells, Nevinson, Atkinson, along with a few women—Jessica Dismoor, Helen Saunders, and Dorothy Shakespear. All of them at times rivaled Lewis in creating an abstract art refusing the conservatism of the Slade School, the New English Art Club, Roger Fry, Clive Bell, and the Bloomsburies. *Blast* no. 2 appeared in July 1915; there was no *Blast* no. 3, for the Vortex was breaking up under the impact of war. Gaudier and Hulme were killed, and Lewis of necessity turned to fiction. By 1920 the remaining Rebels were absorbed into the naturalistic painting of the Group X exhibition, and even Lewis admitted that Vorticism was done. Cork has told it all in his epical, definitive account.

Affected by Futurism as Lewis may have been, his Vorticist theory is not really Futurist, since the benchmark of Vorticist art is hardedge abstraction. The true Vortex is an abstraction of fractured geometry with rigid angularity and faceting of design, often into dazzling effects. Lewis says: "I considered the world of machinery as real to us, or more so, as nature's forms." The Futurists were also intoxicated by the machine, but their art was a wave-motion pulsing in time, like Boccioni's rippling bronze striding male figure. The Futurists *felt* the machine from within; Lewis regards its dynamism from outside, critically. The Vorticism abstraction is a spatial arrest with a jackhammer, sawtooth, cerebral fragmenting alien to the Futurist subjective rhythms. The retinal splintering of Vorticism was used by Wadsworth in camouflaging ships. Cork calls it "frozen jazz." While not found in Lewis's painting or prose, the throbbing Futurist tempo reappears in Epstein and Gaudier, who modulated Lewis's savage geometry.

As the most unruly Vorticist, Lewis was given to "satire for its own sake." He was essentially a caricaturist—a caricaturist of the novel, of Cubism, and, in his effort to disburden painting of all reference to nature, of abstraction itself whenever he had trouble in deleting the object. As Cork says, Lewis hovered "on the border-line between two alternative conventions." So his form-without-object is a brittle parody of the purist abstractions that followed. Lewis was facing the dilemma phrased by Kandinsky: What should replace the missing object? Kandinsky was wise enough to see that his own abstractions were "a thundering collision of different worlds." Or, as Picasso said, a painting is a sum of destructions—destructions of things which always leave their indelible marks. So also Wallace Stevens would agree that "the real is only the base; but it is the base." Stevens called a poem a countergeography erected over against the geography where we live. The girl in "So-and-So Reclining on Her Couch"

> . . . floats in the contention, the flux,
> Between the thing as idea and
> The idea as thing.

The Cubists had already erected their counter-geography with great assurance, with poise and calm, even with a placidity inhabiting their reorganization of objects. But Lewis urged that "we must disinculpate ourselves of Picasso at once" because Picasso always started with his studio table, two apples, and a mandolin.

Had they followed Lewis, the Vorticists should have

reached the suicide of representation achieved in Malevich's White, or Ad Reinhardt's Black, a total absence, a zero degree of painting. But things do leave their traces in Lewis's shattered geometry even if he saw himself as "an artist in destruction" and remarked that "any idea should be regarded as 'sentimental' that is not taken to its ultimate conclusion." Especially his early painting belies his frenzy to sabotage the object. And Lewis ends by painting some highly attentive portraits.

It is easy to understand why Lewis, like the Futurists, should have been obsessed with the machine. Sensing an apocalypse of power, he asked: "Will Energy some day reach Earth like violent civilisation, smashing or hardening all?" Yet it is equally easy to understand why Lewis so loudly scorned Futurism, which he called mere automobilism because it sentimentalized machinery. He told Marinetti: "You Wops insist too much on the Machine." Lewis admired not the machine itself (its obvious "speed" or acceleration in time) but rather what in *Blast* he calls "the energy of a mind." As rebel against time Lewis was fond of quoting Baudelaire's line *"Je hais le mouvement qui déplace les lignes."* Lewis's geometry is violent but static.

His rage for order was not Stevens's, and Lewis's fracturings were a bleak Fauvism of *conceived* movement diagrammed into a cruel mechanistic classicism. Hulme noted that Lewis's "only interest in the human body was in a few abstract mechanical relations perceived in it." Lewis has no Great God Pan to worship orgiastically like Lawrence. His painting is, like his prose, a seismic faulting, a disruption with overtones of schizophrenia, a shattering of actuality. As gadfly sent to torment the academy, Fry's Omega Workshops, and all political creeds, Lewis says, "I am the pure revolutionary." His early painting "Timon of Athens," inspired by that bitter Shakespearean play, shows in its diagonal attack how Lewis wanted to represent *"ideas, that's the great thing."*

As the most unruly Vorticist, Lewis was given to "satire for its own sake." He was essentially a caricaturist—a caricaturist of the novel, of Cubism, and, in his effort to disburden painting of all reference to nature, of abstraction itself whenever he had trouble in deleting the object.

— Wylie Sypher

Concurrently, however, Lewis was arguing that "the moment the Plastic is impoverished for the Idea, we get out of direct contact with these intuitive waves of power, that only play on the rich surfaces where life is crowded and abundant." His unresolved impasse was how to incorporate "as much of the material poetry of Nature as the plastic vessel will stand." (One recalls Ruskin's perplexity about how many details from nature a painter can allow.)

Lewis offers a programmed version of Cubist abstraction: the painting congealed into Idea. When Lewis dismantles the object, the Cubist harmony becomes discord, thus parodying Cubism. In fact Lewis, who accepted "the geometric bases and structure of life," had no right to accuse Virginia Woolf of an inability to digest experience without intellectualizing it.

In this ambiguity Lewis was not alone, for Pound too was confused by his ideas. Pound's Imagist program demanded that a poem present a picture; he urged "Go in fear of abstractions." But like Lewis Pound was attracted to Hulme's quest for the hard dry design. Hulme predicted that the trend toward abstraction would end "not so much in the simple geometrical forms found in archaic art, but in the more complicated ones associated in our minds with the idea of machinery."

Pound defined Lewis's art as "a Vortex, from which, and through which, and into which, ideas are constantly rushing." He saw in Lewis "the fury of intelligence" positing "an arrangement of shapes, or planes, or colours" like an atonal musical composition. (Ruskin had already said that a painting is an "arrangement of colours and lines analogous to the composition of music.")

Behind Pound and Hulme and Lewis was Wilhelm Worringer, whose *Abstraction and Empathy* (1908) was also a revolt against the mimetic. Worringer spoke of the Will to Form releasing art from representation to a crystalline transcendence. Worringer's pure geometry, however, was an art of redemption "creating a world beyond appearance, an absolute, in which it may rest from the agony of the relative." This is the hieratic art of Yeats's Byzantium, not the Vortex of agonized geometry. As Lewis noted, Vorticism is affiliated with the chill art of Paolo Uccello, whom Berenson termed a scientist strayed into painting to study the tension of forces among objects. Lewis grimly observed that "the puritanical potentialities of science have never been forecast." In his geometry gone mad Lewis gives us the art of Swift's Laputa. His statement is prophetic: Lewis once noted that "all living art is the history of the future." In Lewis the machine is already a menacing wild body.

The Wild Body is the symbolic title of some of Lewis's stories about the human comedy. Like Hulme, he sensed the energy in the machine, yet he saw the mechanical as absurd. As satirist Lewis endorsed Bergson's view that comedy arises whenever the human being becomes automated into *l'homme machine*. Lewis explains: "The root of the comic is to be sought in the sensations resulting from the observations of a *thing* behaving like a person. But from that point of view all men are necessarily comic: for they are all *things*, or physical bodies, behaving as *persons*. . . . There is nothing that is animal (and we as bodies are animals) that is not absurd. This sense of the absurdity, or, if you like, the madness of our life, is at the root of every true philosophy." In *Tarr* Lewis confirms that "anything living, quick and changing is bad art." The lines of a statue are its soul: "It has no inside." Of his novel *The Apes of God* Lewis claims: "No book has ever been written that has paid more attention to the *outside* of people," their "shells or pelts." He approves Pound's view of sex as comedy: "The twitching of two abdominal muscles/Cannot be a lasting Nirvana." So Lewis invents his own caricature of man in the figure of the Tyro, a mechanical "bobbin" who grins with a commotion of the face like a fabrication of dentistry that mocks by laying bare the teeth—with "a screaming voice underneath."

This disabused image of man reveals the *saeva indignatio* of Jonathan Swift, who also looked on human behavior from outside and regarded it as a mechanical operation of the spirit. For Swift emotion is a "fanatick strain," a reductio ad absurdum of flesh and blood.

As master of satire for its own sake Lewis referred to himself as a condottière. He describes "the nature of my own humour, making a drama of mock violence of every social relationship." "Why always *violence?*" he asks. "It is reminiscent of war." Lewis, whom Etchells called "a tremendous bully," quarreled with all: with Tonks, Sickert, Fry, the Sitwells ("God's own Peterpaniest family"). Everyone drew a salvo: Hemingway as "dumb ox," Faulkner as "a moralist with a corncob," Gertrude Stein with her "gargantuan mental stutter" as "a Monument sitting upon patience," and Eliot making "a virtue of developing himself into an incarnate Echo, as it were." Offended by T. E. Hulme's praise of Epstein, Lewis set out one evening wanting to kill Hulme, who "dragged Lewis downstairs and out into Soho Square, where he hung him up" on a railing. Lewis was at odds with Herbert Read ("I am sorry, for I like the beggar"), and he told F. M. Ford: "What people want is me, not you. They want to see me. A Vortex. To liven them up . . . I . . . I . . . I."

Pound spoke of Lewis as "restless, turbulent, intelligent. A man with this kind of intelligence is bound always to be crashing and opposing and breaking." Lewis called himself the Enemy. After a breakfast, he says, of some raw meat, blood oranges, a stick of ginger, and a shot of vodka, he springs to the telephone to have a row with anyone whose number he first sees and to abuse him for five minutes. Replying to one of Lewis's insulting letters, Pound writes: "There are some matters in which you really do behave like, and *some* (some not all) lines in this letter of yours in which you really do write like, a God damn fool," signing himself "Candidly and cordially yours E. P."

Such violence reappears in Lewis's *Blast* prose with its explosive typography (perhaps suggested by Marinetti's and Apollinaire's manifestoes). The telegraphy of the paintings is repeated in his Vorticist narratives: "The bookworm shoulders rolled above the ravishing toy-girl, like impending seas above a pygmy skiff: in hooligan hardiness he clutched the little skull, he had the sensation of great knees sticking out, giant toe-tendons clutching the rough work-man's footwear: many flattering indications of a probable event were distinctly signalled" (*Apes of God*). Yet Eliot termed Lewis "the greatest prose master of style of my generation." It is arguable that Lewis, whose range of interests yielded over forty books, is more important as critic than as painter. His epigrams are searching. In writing of our inhumane modern architecture, for instance, he remarks that "a box is always a box, however high."

Cork's encyclopedic survey of Vorticism abundantly proves that Lewis's affiliates—notably Bomberg, Gaudier, and Epstein—by their very resistance to Lewis's autocracy achieved in painting and sculpture what Lewis did not, except in a few works like his fragile "Composition in Blue."

Bomberg's painting "In the Hold" thoroughly revises Cubist analysis into kaleidoscopic line and color in a tension of grid and figuration. The carefully refined glitter of "Ju-Jitsu," dismembering the human figure, is a cinematic montage and a premonition of the Op Art of Vasarely and Bridget Riley. In this planar conflict of the dynamic and the rigid Bomberg translates the Cubist enigma into flickering mosaic. Then Bomberg's severe geometry of color in "The Mud Bath" foreshadows the Hourloupe algebra of Dubuffet; and the "scaffolding" in "The Dancer" is qualified by Kandinsky-like curvilinear washes. Cork justly classifies Bomberg's art as "a worthy English counterpart to the many experiments being conducted on the Continent."

With his incorrigible independence Gaudier, working in small scale, warped stone into a new topology that Ruskin would have called zooplastic. His "Red Stone Dancer" recovers the abandoned modeling of authentic primitive statuary, its surging rhythm and tactility. Gaudier's syntax of mass and surface was derived, perhaps, from Rodin, but was cleansed of all romantic anxiety and agitation—a truly classic and substantial Fauvism of both flesh and mind. The dense volumes of "Stags" and "Birds Erect" look backward toward Michelangelo and forward to Henry Moore. Cork speaks of the "organic warmth which belongs to Gaudier alone."

The curious union of primitive and mechanical occurs in Epstein's sculpture. His early versions of "Marble Venus" are indebted to African images and have the vitality of a totem pole; then, about 1913, he created his studies for "Rock Drill," in which he originally intended to incorporate an actual pneumatic drill to symbolize the phallus. The final variant of the figure deleted this mechanism, which would have made the work a primary venture in kinetic art. But Epstein soon moved away from Vorticism to conventional portrait busts.

The most sensitive Vorticism was for a while expressed in a fringe cluster of minor painters like Frederick Etchells, Edward Wadsworth, Lawrence Atkinson, and the women Vorticists tolerated by the male-chauvinist Lewis group: Jessica Dismoor, Helen Saunders, and Pound's wife, Dorothy Shakespear. Some of the most transparent abstractions were painted by these women, whose main task, we are told, was to serve tea to the rebels. Wadsworth alone remained faithful to the Vorticist geometry, which found practical use in his camouflage of wartime vessels, again anticipating Op Art.

What Cork terms the death of Vorticism came in 1917-1918 when the Canadian War Memorial Fund invited many rebels to submit paintings to illustrate episodes of combat—with the proviso that these paintings be representational. Even Bomberg complied, against his will. Meanwhile Lewis, looking back on the war, discovered that his Vorticism remained "a programme, rather than an accomplished fact." As Cork says, the very aggressiveness of Vorticism "carried within itself a kind of death-wish." Cork considers this retreat a defeat. In a sense, yes; but history repeats itself, and a return to representational painting is recurring today in the reaction against the wilder experimental versions of abstract and conceptual art. The retreat from militant Vorticism was evidence of a humanizing that occurred during the slaughter of trench warfare. Violence in art and violence in history were different.

The turn from any theory of violence is apparent in Lewis's novel *The Revenge for Love* and in his autobiographical *Rude Assignment*. In a rather noble reversal upon himself Lewis admits in his notes for the retrospective Vorticist exhibition of 1949 that "in the year or two prior to World War I, I attempted totally to eliminate from my work all reference to nature"—but the war, he said, cut off all that went before. "The geometrics which had interested me so exclusively before, I now felt were bleak and empty. They wanted *filling*." He insisted, "This is not retraction: it is contradiction." By 1934 Lewis realized that Vorticism was an architecture providing a frame but forgetting the picture. He could be speaking of his own painting "The Crowd" (1914-1915), with its subjection of mechanical human figures to an imprisoning structural grid. In a note for the retrospective exhibition of his work in 1956 Lewis adds: "Finally, I am sure that, in one form or another, Nature supplies us with all we need." Lewis has willingly left Laputa.

The Vorticists have been called British Fauves. But the British temperament is so prudential that it hardly allowed for the Wild Beasts loosed across the channel. Lewis remained a moralist. *Blast* may have owed something to Apollinaire, but even Lewis was never in key with Dada. The Vorticists simply wanted to defeat the academy and the tradition that Marinetti called the pretty-pretty, the sickly Pre-Raphaelite medievalism, and all morris dances. Vorticism did jar British art from arts-and-crafts (Omega) mannerisms and from Bloomsbury. It was harbinger of the very violence that destroyed it. To that extent it did belong to the First Machine Age.

Vorticism was never a coherent movement, though it did move through distinguishable phases: from the Slade through the Omega Workshops and the Marinetti-Futurist agitation to the Rebel Art Center and a campaign attending the programs of Hulme, Pound with his Imagism, and at last Lewis with his blasting and bombardiering. Lewis was not one to stress what his Vortex owed to Futurism, to Art Nouveau, to Kandinsky, Kupka, Delaunay, and the whole post-impressionist Cubist vision. But no matter, for Vorticism was a needed, though inconclusive and sometimes crackbrained, revision of English aesthetics. Lewis may have exploited logic, but there is substance in his maxim, phrased by Zagreus in *The Apes of God*, that "the world created by Art—Fiction, Drama, Poetry, etc.—must be sufficiently removed from the real world so that no character from the one could under any circumstances enter the other (the situation imagined by Pirandello), without the anomaly being apparent at once." As we read these two indispensable volumes by Cork, we realize that Lewis is our modern John Ruskin (more

"heavily armored") in his enormous scope of interest, in his claim to have been painter, novelist, philosopher, editor, lecturer, and journalist, and in his lifelong contradictory, irritating, dogmatic provocations.

William Lipke

SOURCE: "Futurism and the Development of Vorticism," in *Studio International,* Vol. 173, No. 888, April, 1967, pp. 173-5, 177.

[*In the following essay, Lipke documents the impact of Italian Futurism on Vorticist painting.*]

The events which marked the Futurist 'invasion' of English soil from 1911 through the summer of 1914 are as intriguing as they are complex, forming part of the history of the Vorticist movement, culminating in the final yet half-hearted repudiation of Futurism by the British *avant-garde.*

I

As early as 1911, Marinetti had come to lecture before the Lyceum Club. His delivery was well-timed and to the point. 'Don't you believe fervently,' he exclaimed, 'that the Puritans saved England, and that Chastity is the most important virtue?' Then, launching into his protest *viva voce,* Marinetti chided his audience for praising Ruskin, who 'with his hate of the machine, of gas, and electricity, is responsible for the odious cult of the past.'

It was not until March 1912 that the Futurist painters came to England. Fresh from the initial Futurist exhibition in Paris (February 5-24), their works filled London's Sackville Gallery. The works were not well received, and Boccioni, who attended the London opening, somewhat bitterly recorded five days after the opening: 'London, beautiful, monstrous, elegant, well-fed, well-dressed but with brains as heavy as steaks. . . . When I think of all the socialist, cooperativist, positivist, hygienist imbecility that pretends to judge Italian things through the obsession of what is English, I feel nauseated.'

A little more than a year later, in April 1913, the Futurists made another attempt at converting the British painters and critics to the philosophy of *ambiente.* This time it was a single-handed assault by Gino Severini, who showed some thirty-four works, with accompanying remarks in the exhibition catalogue, at the Marlborough Gallery. Within the month, the first appreciative criticism of Futurism by the British critics was published. 'It is essential to realize,' wrote Horace B. Samuel, 'that [Futurist paintings] constitute an integral part of a living scheme which . . . has yet serious claims to be considered as a substantial movement, artistic, literary, economic, sociological, and above all, human. . . . It is in essence a concentrated manifestation of the whole vital impulse of the twentieth century.'

The literati of London were quick to follow in Samuel's praise of Futurism. The September 1913 issue of Harold Monro's *Poetry and Drama* was devoted entirely to Futurism, and Monro confidently wrote: 'we claim ourselves, also, to be futurist.' Frank Rutter included the work of

Severini in the October 1913 *Post-Impressionist and Futurist Exhibit: From Pissarro to Severini*. In November 1913 Marinetti returned to give five lectures in London, and some five months later (April 1914) organized the important Doré Gallery's Futurist exhibit which included seventy-nine Futurist works. When the Doré exhibit closed, the remaining Futurist activity in London included a lecture by Marinetti on May 6, 1914 at the Vorticists' Rebel Art Centre, a 'Futurist Declamation' by Marinetti on June 4 at the Doré Gallery, a June 12 lecture on 'Vital English Art' by Marinetti and the English 'futurist' C. R. W. Nevinson, and a June 15 demonstration ('Inventors and Constructors of NOISE-Tuners') by Marinetti, Russolo and Piatti at the Albert Hall.

Outside of Paris and Milan, the London art world appeared at this point to be most responsive to the Futurist declamations and exhibitions. It has been pointed out how certain critics and poets embraced Futurism, however vague their comprehension of the aesthetic principles spelled out by the Italians. But what was the reaction of the Vorticist painters to the Italian intrusion upon the London art world?

II

There was, to be sure, no love lost between the leader of the Vorticist movement (Wyndham Lewis) and the director of the Italian Futurist Movement. 'Lewis,' Douglas Goldring recalled later, 'who from the first regarded Marinetti with deep suspicion, used to say that the lavish funds which he [Marinetti] had at his disposal were derived from a chain of deluxe brothels in Egypt, controlled by Marinetti *père*.'

If Lewis was harsh in word, he did not in practice seem to repudiate Futurism or the title 'Futurist'. In January 1914 Nevinson and Lewis went to locate a publisher. Nevinson records that 'Lewis was at that time anxious to produce a paper somewhat on the lines of the Futurist Manifesto. He asked me to help him and I went so far as to suggest the title, which was *Blast*.' They carried with them a note from Nevinson's father, H. W. Nevinson, the celebrated journalist. 'Let me introduce to you,' he wrote, 'my son Richard and his friend Wyndham Lewis, both revolutionary artists of Futurist fame, who want to consult you about bringing out an artistic magazine they have in mind.' And in March 1914, the '*Blast* Group' sponsored a lecture by Marinetti at the Doré Gallery to raise funds for the new Cubist Art Centre. Marinetti also lectured at the Rebel Art Centre on 8 May 1914, evidently without incident. At this time, Nevinson was still attached to the Centre and the Vorticist Group. Within a month, however, Nevinson had joined forces with Marinetti, issued a manifesto, and declared himself to be an 'English Futurist', splitting the relations between the Vorticists and the Futurists wide open.

Less than a month after the closing of the Second Post-Impressionist show, C. R. W. Nevinson had exhibited a work entitled *The City Rises* at the January 1913 Friday Club exhibition. *The City Rises* was also the title of a composition exhibited by Boccioni at the 1912 Sackville show. Was it simply coincidence? Nevinson's work has since

been lost, but we know from other work executed by Nevinson in late 1912 and early 1913 that he was obviously referring to the Boccioni prototype; *The Arrival* and *Gare St Lazare* both employ the simultaneous vision and word-lettering in the canvas.

Frank Rutter corroborates Nevinson's early attachment to Futurism when he notes that 'Nevinson's *Gare St Lazare,* shown at the Allied Artists in 1913, was the first English Futurist picture.' The 1912 Futurist exhibition thus provoked response among the English *avant-garde* and was, in fact, championed by Rutter; for in his October 1913 *Post-Impressionism and Futurism* exhibit, Rutter reproduced Nevinson's *Gare St Lazare* on the invitation card and stated in the catalogue introduction that ' "Cubism" and "Futurism" have already stirred English artists [as] is shown by the contribution of Mr Wyndham Lewis, Mr Wadsworth, Mr Nevinson, and others.'

In November 1913, Nevinson, Frederick Etchells, Cuthbert Hamilton, Edward Wadsworth, and Lewis organized a dinner at the Florence Restaurant in London to honour Signor Marinetti. Nevinson claimed that it was at this dinner that his friendship with Lewis started to falter because Nevinson 'gave a speech in French after the dinner, and Marinetti took to him.' That Lewis and the Vorticists were interested in what Marinetti had to say is obvious by their willingness to entertain *il maestro*, but that friendliness was terminated by the defection of Nevinson. Surely, the break with Futurism was a direct result of Nevinson's leaving the Rebel Art Centre and siding with Marinetti.

On June 12, 1914, Marinetti and Nevinson lectured on 'Vital English Art', having printed excerpts from their manifesto in the June 7 issue of the *Observer*. Claiming they were against 'the worship of tradition . . . the commercial acquiescence of English artists, the effeminacy of their art, and their complete absorption towards a purely decorative sense,' Marinetti and his new 'Futurist' chided the 'sham revolutionaries of the New English Art Club, who, having destroyed the prestige of the Royal Academy, now show themselves grossly hostile to the later movements of the advance guard.'

The Vorticists replied: 'There are certain artists in England who do not belong to the Royal Academy nor to any passéist groups, and who do not on their account agree with the futurism of Sign. Marinetti . . .' When *Blast* appeared on June 20, the Manifesto of Vorticism claimed that Futurism was 'the latest form of Impressionism . . . equated with Automobilism.' Although Lewis admitted that Severini and Balla were 'good painters', he concluded that Futurism was 'a picturesque, superficial and romantic rebellion of young Milanese painters against the academies which surrounded them.' 'In any case,' Ezra Pound wrote to H. L. Mencken in 1915, 'you might keep in mind that Vorticism is not Futurism, most emphatically NOT.'

III

Contrary to Sir John Rothenstein's thesis (that 'Vorticism had little in common with Futurism, [that] the English Movement rejected the principal tenets of the Italian'), Futurism, especially the Futurist activities in London between 1910 and 1914, played a considerable role in forming part of the visual vocabulary of Vorticism, contributed to its aesthetic theory, and provided an attitude, both literary and philosophic, for the English movement. Both movements—declamatory, decidedly 'anti', and proselytizing in attitude—are distinguishable from Cubism in these respects.

While Pound claimed that he had invented the term 'Vorticism', many of the Vorticist ideas and the notion of 'The Vortex' as a theme in visual arts come from Futurism.

— *William Lipke*

It has been noted that the most immediate and obvious influence of the Futurist 'vision' on English painting was to be found in the work of C. R. W. Nevinson who, until 1914, was closely associated with Vorticism. To a large degree, Nevinson was the most successful manipulator of Futurist devices, employing the simultaneous images already pointed out in his *Gare St Lazare* and *Arrival*. But he was also skilful in capturing the dynamism and movement emphasized by the Italians and most graphically practised in Balla's *Dynamism of a Dog on Leash: Leash in Motion* (1912) and *Rhythm of the Violinist* (1912). Here, as in Nevinson's *On the Way to the Trenches* (1914), illustrated in *Blast,* the forms are worked gradually across the two dimensional surface; there is no attempt to show three dimensional simultaneity, but rather to employ techniques from the cinema to show animation of form. It was this type of Futurist device which Nevinson most satisfactorily used in his finest 'Futurist' works, the war paintings of 1914-17. His success in subsequent exhibitions of this type of Futurism earned him enormous popularity, but by the early 1920s he had abandoned the style, and his reputation receded accordingly. But there were other contemporary British artists who were influenced by Futurism during the 1910-14 period.

The late 1912 and early 1913 experiments in interior design developed at Roger Fry's Omega Workshops in London show an awareness of the Futurist principles of vision. The Omega Workshops included by early 1913 almost the entire group of artists at one time affiliated with Vorticism: Lewis, Etchells, Gaudier-Brzeska, Grant, Adeney, Roberts, Nevinson, Dismorr, Wadsworth, Bomberg, and others. For a short but productive period, until Lewis and his coterie withdrew from the Workshops in the autumn of 1913, the Bloomsburies and the Vorticists worked side by side, producing very obviously futurist-cubist influenced furnishings. Such works as the decorations for the Cadena Café are almost copies of Severini's 1913 abstract experiments in light. The fabric designs, designed and titled by Fry, such as *Margery* and *Amenophis,* are directly influenced by Severini's *Ballerina* of 1913, using the same overlapping cone-shaped devices.

As for the influence on Vorticist painting, there is a striking parallel between Lewis's 1912 *Kermesse* and Severini's 1912 *Dancer,* exhibited at the 1912 Sackville show, both composing large arc-shaped forms in a simple tri-partite division on the canvas. It is primarily in Lewis's 1912 *Timon* series, exhibited as was the *Kermesse* in Fry's Second Post-Impressionist exhibition, that Lewis's 'futurism' is most evident. The mass of figures drawn into the centre of the composition, and the single curvilinear treatment of individual forms apparently are derived from Carra's *The Funeral of the Anarchist Galli* and Boccioni's *States of the Mind: Those Who Stay,* both exhibited in the March 1912 Sackville Gallery show. When the Vorticists turned to the non-representational phase (*circa* 1913-15 and 1919-20), there are only vague suggestions, if any, of Futurism. It is probable, however, that Balla's *Vortex of an Automobile* and his seven works entitled *Vortex* (all of 1913 and illustrated in *Archivi del Futurismo,* nos. 65, 107-12) are sources, both thematically and technically, for the non-representational phase of Vorticism.

While Pound claimed that he had invented the term 'Vorticism', many of the Vorticist ideas and the notion of 'The Vortex' as a theme in visual arts come from Futurism. For the term was not used before late 1913, and there are many examples to show that the Vorticists were using the 'vortex' as an organizing motif in their work as early as 1912. Such a unique notion could only be the result of the impression made by the Futurist exhibition of 1912 and Severini's one-man show of 1913 upon the English *avant-garde*.

The then emerging Vorticist aesthetic was the least altered by Futurism. There was no attempt by the Vorticists to use an elaborate colour theory, nor was there a programme for any one kind of subject matter. The Vorticists rejected the philosophy of *ambiente* as they rejected the Crocean and Bergsonian belief in the supremacy of intuition; both philosophers received a 'blast' in the first issue of *Blast*. There was no adherence to 'dynamic sensation' or 'Impressionistic primitivism'; and this will in part help to explain why in early 1913 Lewis was already being called 'Cubist'.

The Vortex or Vorticism was an attitude as well as a visual configuration. The visual form of Vorticism, the belief in the centripetal movement of each object, might well have come from Futurism, as I have attempted to show. Similarly, there is a parallel between the Vorticist attitude toward the world and the anti-traditional thinking of the Futurists. The Vorticist, unlike the Futurist, stands at the *still* centre of civilization 'directed to reverting to *ancient canons* of taste, and by rigid propaganda, scavenging away the refuse that has accumulated for the last century or so.' [Italics mine.] If the first part of Lewis's remark is not suited to the philosophy of Futurism, the last section is in keeping with the violent hatred of the past fostered by Futurism. The irreverent point of view voiced by Pound, Lewis, and Gaudier-Brzeska owes a great deal to Futurist propaganda techniques, and the 'Vortices' written by Gaudier-Brzeska, Lewis, and Pound are coined in the hyperboles of Futurism just as the layout of *Blast* is based on that of the Futurists' magazine *Lacerba*.

Although Futurist philosophy, style, and techniques of appealing to or attacking the public all influenced the Vorticists, the British movement was much more than 'English Futurism'. The Italian movement became for Vorticism what Cubism had been for the development of Futurism.

FURTHER READING

Cooney, Seamus. *Blast 3*. Santa Barbara, Calif.: Black Sparrow Press, 1984, 356 p.

Collection of new and reprinted essays discussing various aspects of Vorticism and focusing on the works of Lewis and Pound.

"The Death of Vorticism." *The Little Review* V, Nos. 10-11 (February-March 1919): 45-51.

Contends that Vorticism did not "die" but became an accepted part of England's artistic life.

"Vorticism and the Politics of Art." *The Times Literary Supplement* (22 November 1957): 700.

Review of William Roberts's book *The Resurrection of Vorticism and the Apotheosis of Wyndham Lewis,* finding that Roberts has legitimate grievances with how Lewis and Sir John Rothenstein present his role in the Vorticist movement.

Wees, William C. "England's *Avant-Garde:* The Futurist-Vorticist Phase." *Western Humanities Review* XXI, No. 2 (Spring 1967): 117-28.

Describes the differences and similarities between the Futurist and Vorticist art movements.

———. *Vorticism and the English Avant-Garde.* Toronto: University of Toronto Press, 1972, 273 p.

A study of Vorticism's place in the English artistic milieu of the pre-World War I period.

Zinnes, Harriet. "Nature and Design: 'Burying Euclid Deep in the Living Flesh'." In *Ezra Pound: The Legacy of Kulchur,* edited by Marcel Smith and William A. Ulmer, pp. 51-66. Tuscaloosa and London: University of Alabama Press, 1988.

Recounts the influence of sculptor Henri Gaudier-Brzeska on Vorticism and Ezra Pound.

Twentieth-Century
Literary Criticism

Cumulative Indexes
Volumes 1-62

How to Use This Index

The main references

list all author entries in the following Gale Literary Criticism series:

BLC = *Black Literature Criticism*
CLC = *Contemporary Literary Criticism*
CLR = *Children's Literature Review*
CMLC = *Classical and Medieval Literature Criticism*
DA = *DISCovering Authors*
DC = *Drama Criticism*
HLC = *Hispanic Literature Criticism*
LC = *Literature Criticism from 1400 to 1800*
NCLC = *Nineteenth-Century Literature Criticism*
PC = *Poetry Criticism*
SSC = *Short Story Criticism*
TCLC = *Twentieth-Century Literary Criticism*
WLC = *World Literature Criticism, 1500 to the Present*

The cross-references

list all author entries in the following Gale biographical and literary sources:

AAYA = *Authors & Artists for Young Adults*
AITN = *Authors in the News*
BEST = *Bestsellers*
BW = *Black Writers*
CA = *Contemporary Authors*
CAAS = *Contemporary Authors Autobiography Series*
CABS = *Contemporary Authors Bibliographical Series*
CANR = *Contemporary Authors New Revision Series*
CAP = *Contemporary Authors Permanent Series*
CDALB = *Concise Dictionary of American Literary Biography*
CDBLB = *Concise Dictionary of British Literary Biography*
DLB = *Dictionary of Literary Biography*
DLBD = *Dictionary of Literary Biography Documentary Series*
DLBY = *Dictionary of Literary Biography Yearbook*
HW = *Hispanic Writers*
JRDA = *Junior DISCovering Authors*
MAICYA = *Major Authors and Illustrators for Children and Young Adults*
MTCW = *Major 20th-Century Writers*
NNAL = *Native North American Literature*
SAAS = *Something about the Author Autobiography Series*
SATA = *Something about the Author*
YABC = *Yesterday's Authors of Books for Children*

Literary Criticism Series
Cumulative Author Index

Alcott, Amos Bronson 1799-1888 . . **NCLC 1**
See also DLB 1

Alcott, Louisa May
1832-1888 . . . . **NCLC 6; DA; DAB;**
DAC; WLC
See also CDALB 1865-1917; CLR 1, 38;
DAM MST, NOV; DLB 1, 42, 79; JRDA;
MAICYA; YABC 1

Aldanov, M. A.
See Aldanov, Mark (Alexandrovich)

Aldanov, Mark (Alexandrovich)
1886(?)-1957 . . . . **TCLC 23**
See also CA 118

Aldington, Richard 1892-1962 . . . . . . **CLC 49**
See also CA 85-88; CANR 45; DLB 20, 36,
100, 149

Aldiss, Brian W(ilson)
1925- . . . . **CLC 5, 14, 40**
See also CA 5-8R; CAAS 2; CANR 5, 28;
DAM NOV; DLB 14; MTCW; SATA 34

Alegria, Claribel 1924- . . . . **CLC 75**
See also CA 131; CAAS 15; DAM MULT;
DLB 145; HW

Alegria, Fernando 1918- . . . . **CLC 57**
See also CA 9-12R; CANR 5, 32; HW

Aleichem, Sholom . . . . **TCLC 1, 35**
See also Rabinovitch, Sholem

Aleixandre, Vicente 1898-1984 . . . **CLC 9, 36**
See also CA 85-88; 114; CANR 26;
DAM POET; DLB 108; HW; MTCW

Alepoudelis, Odysseus
See Elytis, Odysseus

Aleshkovsky, Joseph 1929-
See Aleshkovsky, Yuz
See also CA 121; 128

Aleshkovsky, Yuz . . . . **CLC 44**
See also Aleshkovsky, Joseph

Alexander, Lloyd (Chudley) 1924- . . **CLC 35**
See also AAYA 1; CA 1-4R; CANR 1, 24,
38; CLR 1, 5; DLB 52; JRDA; MAICYA;
MTCW; SAAS 19; SATA 3, 49, 81

Alfau, Felipe 1902- . . . . **CLC 66**
See also CA 137

Alger, Horatio, Jr. 1832-1899 . . . . . **NCLC 8**
See also DLB 42; SATA 16

Algren, Nelson 1909-1981 . . . . **CLC 4, 10, 33**
See also CA 13-16R; 103; CANR 20;
CDALB 1941-1968; DLB 9; DLBY 81,
82; MTCW

Ali, Ahmed 1910- . . . . **CLC 69**
See also CA 25-28R; CANR 15, 34

Alighieri, Dante 1265-1321 . . . . **CMLC 3**

Allan, John B.
See Westlake, Donald E(dwin)

Allen, Edward 1948- . . . . **CLC 59**

Allen, Paula Gunn 1939- . . . . **CLC 84**
See also CA 112; 143; DAM MULT;
NNAL

Allen, Roland
See Ayckbourn, Alan

Allen, Sarah A.
See Hopkins, Pauline Elizabeth

Allen, Woody 1935- . . . . **CLC 16, 52**
See also AAYA 10; CA 33-36R; CANR 27,
38; DAM POP; DLB 44; MTCW

Allende, Isabel 1942- . . . . **CLC 39, 57; HLC**
See also CA 125; 130; DAM MULT, NOV;
DLB 145; HW; INT 130; MTCW

Alleyn, Ellen
See Rossetti, Christina (Georgina)

Allingham, Margery (Louise)
1904-1966 . . . . **CLC 19**
See also CA 5-8R; 25-28R; CANR 4;
DLB 77; MTCW

Allingham, William 1824-1889 . . . **NCLC 25**
See also DLB 35

Allison, Dorothy E. 1949- . . . . **CLC 78**
See also CA 140

Allston, Washington 1779-1843 . . . . **NCLC 2**
See also DLB 1

Almedingen, E. M. . . . . **CLC 12**
See also Almedingen, Martha Edith von
See also SATA 3

Almedingen, Martha Edith von 1898-1971
See Almedingen, E. M.
See also CA 1-4R; CANR 1

Almqvist, Carl Jonas Love
1793-1866 . . . . **NCLC 42**

Alonso, Damaso 1898-1990 . . . . **CLC 14**
See also CA 110; 131; 130; DLB 108; HW

Alov
See Gogol, Nikolai (Vasilyevich)

Alta 1942- . . . . **CLC 19**
See also CA 57-60

Alter, Robert B(ernard) 1935- . . . . . . **CLC 34**
See also CA 49-52; CANR 1, 47

Alther, Lisa 1944- . . . . **CLC 7, 41**
See also CA 65-68; CANR 12, 30; MTCW

Altman, Robert 1925- . . . . **CLC 16**
See also CA 73-76; CANR 43

Alvarez, A(lfred) 1929- . . . . **CLC 5, 13**
See also CA 1-4R; CANR 3, 33; DLB 14,
40

Alvarez, Alejandro Rodriguez 1903-1965
See Casona, Alejandro
See also CA 131; 93-96; HW

Alvaro, Corrado 1896-1956 . . . . **TCLC 60**

Amado, Jorge 1912- . . . . . . **CLC 13, 40; HLC**
See also CA 77-80; CANR 35;
DAM MULT, NOV; DLB 113; MTCW

Ambler, Eric 1909- . . . . **CLC 4, 6, 9**
See also CA 9-12R; CANR 7, 38; DLB 77;
MTCW

Amichai, Yehuda 1924- . . . . . . **CLC 9, 22, 57**
See also CA 85-88; CANR 46; MTCW

Amiel, Henri Frederic 1821-1881 . . **NCLC 4**

Amis, Kingsley (William)
1922- . . . . . . **CLC 1, 2, 3, 5, 8, 13, 40, 44;**
DA; DAB; DAC
See also AITN 2; CA 9-12R; CANR 8, 28;
CDBLB 1945-1960; DAM MST, NOV;
DLB 15, 27, 100, 139; INT CANR-8;
MTCW

Amis, Martin (Louis)
1949- . . . . **CLC 4, 9, 38, 62**
See also BEST 90:3; CA 65-68; CANR 8,
27; DLB 14; INT CANR-27

Ammons, A(rchie) R(andolph)
1926- . . . . **CLC 2, 3, 5, 8, 9, 25, 57**
See also AITN 1; CA 9-12R; CANR 6, 36;
DAM POET; DLB 5; MTCW

Amo, Tauraatua i
See Adams, Henry (Brooks)

Anand, Mulk Raj 1905- . . . . **CLC 23**
See also CA 65-68; CANR 32; DAM NOV;
MTCW

Anatol
See Schnitzler, Arthur

Anaya, Rudolfo A(lfonso)
1937- . . . . **CLC 23; HLC**
See also CA 45-48; CAAS 4; CANR 1, 32;
DAM MULT, NOV; DLB 82; HW 1;
MTCW

Andersen, Hans Christian
1805-1875 . . . . **NCLC 7; DA; DAB;**
DAC; SSC 6; WLC
See also CLR 6; DAM MST, POP;
MAICYA; YABC 1

Anderson, C. Farley
See Mencken, H(enry) L(ouis); Nathan,
George Jean

Anderson, Jessica (Margaret) Queale
. . . . **CLC 37**
See also CA 9-12R; CANR 4

Anderson, Jon (Victor) 1940- . . . . **CLC 9**
See also CA 25-28R; CANR 20;
DAM POET

Anderson, Lindsay (Gordon)
1923-1994 . . . . **CLC 20**
See also CA 125; 128; 146

Anderson, Maxwell 1888-1959 . . . . . **TCLC 2**
See also CA 105; DAM DRAM; DLB 7

Anderson, Poul (William) 1926- . . . . **CLC 15**
See also AAYA 5; CA 1-4R; CAAS 2;
CANR 2, 15, 34; DLB 8; INT CANR-15;
MTCW; SATA-Brief 39

Anderson, Robert (Woodruff)
1917- . . . . **CLC 23**
See also AITN 1; CA 21-24R; CANR 32;
DAM DRAM; DLB 7

Anderson, Sherwood
1876-1941 . . . . **TCLC 1, 10, 24; DA;**
DAB; DAC; SSC 1; WLC
See also CA 104; 121; CDALB 1917-1929;
DAM MST, NOV; DLB 4, 9, 86;
DLBD 1; MTCW

Andouard
See Giraudoux, (Hippolyte) Jean

Andrade, Carlos Drummond de . . . . . . **CLC 18**
See also Drummond de Andrade, Carlos

Andrade, Mario de 1893-1945 . . . . . **TCLC 43**

Andreae, Johann V. 1586-1654 . . . . . . **LC 32**

Andreas-Salome, Lou 1861-1937 . . . **TCLC 56**
See also DLB 66

Andrewes, Lancelot 1555-1626 . . . . **LC 5**
See also DLB 151

Andrews, Cicily Fairfield
See West, Rebecca

Andrews, Elton V.
See Pohl, Frederik

Andreyev, Leonid (Nikolaevich)
1871-1919 .... TCLC 3
See also CA 104

Andric, Ivo 1892-1975 .... CLC 8
See also CA 81-84; 57-60; CANR 43;
DLB 147; MTCW

Angelique, Pierre
See Bataille, Georges

Angell, Roger 1920- .... CLC 26
See also CA 57-60; CANR 13, 44

Angelou, Maya
1928- .... CLC 12, 35, 64, 77; BLC; DA;
DAB; DAC
See also AAYA 7; BW 2; CA 65-68;
CANR 19, 42; DAM MST, MULT,
POET, POP; DLB 38; MTCW; SATA 49

Annensky, Innokenty Fyodorovich
1856-1909 .... TCLC 14
See also CA 110

Anon, Charles Robert
See Pessoa, Fernando (Antonio Nogueira)

Anouilh, Jean (Marie Lucien Pierre)
1910-1987 ...... CLC 1, 3, 8, 13, 40, 50
See also CA 17-20R; 123; CANR 32;
DAM DRAM; MTCW

Anthony, Florence
See Ai

Anthony, John
See Ciardi, John (Anthony)

Anthony, Peter
See Shaffer, Anthony (Joshua); Shaffer,
Peter (Levin)

Anthony, Piers 1934- .... CLC 35
See also AAYA 11; CA 21-24R; CANR 28;
DAM POP; DLB 8; MTCW; SATA 84

Antoine, Marc
See Proust, (Valentin-Louis-George-Eugene-)
Marcel

Antoninus, Brother
See Everson, William (Oliver)

Antonioni, Michelangelo 1912- ..... CLC 20
See also CA 73-76; CANR 45

Antschel, Paul 1920-1970
See Celan, Paul
See also CA 85-88; CANR 33; MTCW

Anwar, Chairil 1922-1949 .... TCLC 22
See also CA 121

Apollinaire, Guillaume .. TCLC 3, 8, 51; PC 7
See also Kostrowitzki, Wilhelm Apollinaris
de
See also DAM POET

Appelfeld, Aharon 1932- .... CLC 23, 47
See also CA 112; 133

Apple, Max (Isaac) 1941- .... CLC 9, 33
See also CA 81-84; CANR 19; DLB 130

Appleman, Philip (Dean) 1926- ..... CLC 51
See also CA 13-16R; CAAS 18; CANR 6,
29

Appleton, Lawrence
See Lovecraft, H(oward) P(hillips)

Apteryx
See Eliot, T(homas) S(tearns)

Apuleius, (Lucius Madaurensis)
125(?)-175(?) .... CMLC 1

Aquin, Hubert 1929-1977 .... CLC 15
See also CA 105; DLB 53

Aragon, Louis 1897-1982 .... CLC 3, 22
See also CA 69-72; 108; CANR 28;
DAM NOV, POET; DLB 72; MTCW

Arany, Janos 1817-1882 .... NCLC 34

Arbuthnot, John 1667-1735 .... LC 1
See also DLB 101

Archer, Herbert Winslow
See Mencken, H(enry) L(ouis)

Archer, Jeffrey (Howard) 1940- .... CLC 28
See also AAYA 16; BEST 89:3; CA 77-80;
CANR 22; DAM POP; INT CANR-22

Archer, Jules 1915- .... CLC 12
See also CA 9-12R; CANR 6; SAAS 5;
SATA 4, 85

Archer, Lee
See Ellison, Harlan (Jay)

Arden, John 1930- .... CLC 6, 13, 15
See also CA 13-16R; CAAS 4; CANR 31;
DAM DRAM; DLB 13; MTCW

Arenas, Reinaldo
1943-1990 .... CLC 41; HLC
See also CA 124; 128; 133; DAM MULT;
DLB 145; HW

Arendt, Hannah 1906-1975 .... CLC 66
See also CA 17-20R; 61-64; CANR 26;
MTCW

Aretino, Pietro 1492-1556 .... LC 12

Arghezi, Tudor .... CLC 80
See also Theodorescu, Ion N.

Arguedas, Jose Maria
1911-1969 .... CLC 10, 18
See also CA 89-92; DLB 113; HW

Argueta, Manlio 1936- .... CLC 31
See also CA 131; DLB 145; HW

Ariosto, Ludovico 1474-1533 .... LC 6

Aristides
See Epstein, Joseph

Aristophanes
450B.C.-385B.C. .... CMLC 4; DA;
DAB; DAC; DC 2
See also DAM DRAM, MST

Arlt, Roberto (Godofredo Christophersen)
1900-1942 .... TCLC 29; HLC
See also CA 123; 131; DAM MULT; HW

Armah, Ayi Kwei 1939- .... CLC 5, 33; BLC
See also BW 1; CA 61-64; CANR 21;
DAM MULT, POET; DLB 117; MTCW

Armatrading, Joan 1950- .... CLC 17
See also CA 114

Arnette, Robert
See Silverberg, Robert

Arnim, Achim von (Ludwig Joachim von
Arnim) 1781-1831 .... NCLC 5
See also DLB 90

Arnim, Bettina von 1785-1859 .... NCLC 38
See also DLB 90

Arnold, Matthew
1822-1888 ..... NCLC 6, 29; DA; DAB;
DAC; PC 5; WLC
See also CDBLB 1832-1890; DAM MST,
POET; DLB 32, 57

Arnold, Thomas 1795-1842 ...... NCLC 18
See also DLB 55

Arnow, Harriette (Louisa) Simpson
1908-1986 .... CLC 2, 7, 18
See also CA 9-12R; 118; CANR 14; DLB 6;
MTCW; SATA 42; SATA-Obit 47

Arp, Hans
See Arp, Jean

Arp, Jean 1887-1966. .... CLC 5
See also CA 81-84; 25-28R; CANR 42

Arrabal
See Arrabal, Fernando

Arrabal, Fernando 1932- ... CLC 2, 9, 18, 58
See also CA 9-12R; CANR 15

Arrick, Fran. .... CLC 30
See also Gaberman, Judie Angell

Artaud, Antonin (Marie Joseph)
1896-1948 .... TCLC 3, 36
See also CA 104; 149; DAM DRAM

Arthur, Ruth M(abel) 1905-1979.... CLC 12
See also CA 9-12R; 85-88; CANR 4;
SATA 7, 26

Artsybashev, Mikhail (Petrovich)
1878-1927 .... TCLC 31

Arundel, Honor (Morfydd)
1919-1973 .... CLC 17
See also CA 21-22; 41-44R; CAP 2;
CLR 35; SATA 4; SATA-Obit 24

Asch, Sholem 1880-1957 .... TCLC 3
See also CA 105

Ash, Shalom
See Asch, Sholem

Ashbery, John (Lawrence)
1927- ...... CLC 2, 3, 4, 6, 9, 13, 15, 25,
41, 77
See also CA 5-8R; CANR 9, 37;
DAM POET; DLB 5; DLBY 81;
INT CANR-9; MTCW

Ashdown, Clifford
See Freeman, R(ichard) Austin

Ashe, Gordon
See Creasey, John

Ashton-Warner, Sylvia (Constance)
1908-1984 .... CLC 19
See also CA 69-72; 112; CANR 29; MTCW

Asimov, Isaac
1920-1992 ...... CLC 1, 3, 9, 19, 26, 76
See also AAYA 13; BEST 90:2; CA 1-4R;
137; CANR 2, 19, 36; CLR 12;
DAM POP; DLB 8; DLBY 92;
INT CANR-19; JRDA; MAICYA;
MTCW; SATA 1, 26, 74

Astley, Thea (Beatrice May)
1925- .... CLC 41
See also CA 65-68; CANR 11, 43

Aston, James
See White, T(erence) H(anbury)

Asturias, Miguel Angel
1899-1974 . . . . CLC 3, 8, 13; HLC
See also CA 25-28; 49-52; CANR 32;
CAP 2; DAM MULT, NOV; DLB 113;
HW; MTCW

Atares, Carlos Saura
See Saura (Atares), Carlos

Atheling, William
See Pound, Ezra (Weston Loomis)

Atheling, William, Jr.
See Blish, James (Benjamin)

Atherton, Gertrude (Franklin Horn)
1857-1948 . . . . TCLC 2
See also CA 104; DLB 9, 78

Atherton, Lucius
See Masters, Edgar Lee

Atkins, Jack
See Harris, Mark

Atticus
See Fleming, Ian (Lancaster)

Atwood, Margaret (Eleanor)
1939- . . . . . CLC 2, 3, 4, 8, 13, 15, 25, 44,
84; DA; DAB; DAC; PC 8; SSC 2; WLC
See also AAYA 12; BEST 89:2; CA 49-52;
CANR 3, 24, 33; DAM MST, NOV,
POET; DLB 53; INT CANR-24; MTCW;
SATA 50

Aubigny, Pierre d'
See Mencken, H(enry) L(ouis)

Aubin, Penelope 1685-1731(?) . . . . LC 9
See also DLB 39

Auchincloss, Louis (Stanton)
1917- . . . . CLC 4, 6, 9, 18, 45
See also CA 1-4R; CANR 6, 29;
DAM NOV; DLB 2; DLBY 80;
INT CANR-29; MTCW

Auden, W(ystan) H(ugh)
1907-1973 . . . . . CLC 1, 2, 3, 4, 6, 9, 11,
14, 43; DA; DAB; DAC; PC 1; WLC
See also CA 9-12R; 45-48; CANR 5;
CDBLB 1914-1945; DAM DRAM, MST,
POET; DLB 10, 20; MTCW

Audiberti, Jacques 1900-1965 . . . . . . CLC 38
See also CA 25-28R; DAM DRAM

Audubon, John James
1785-1851 . . . . NCLC 47

Auel, Jean M(arie) 1936- . . . . CLC 31
See also AAYA 7; BEST 90:4; CA 103;
CANR 21; DAM POP; INT CANR-21

Auerbach, Erich 1892-1957 . . . . TCLC 43
See also CA 118

Augier, Emile 1820-1889 . . . . NCLC 31

August, John
See De Voto, Bernard (Augustine)

Augustine, St. 354-430 . . . . . . CMLC 6; DAB

Aurelius
See Bourne, Randolph S(illiman)

Austen, Jane
1775-1817 . . . . . NCLC 1, 13, 19, 33, 51;
DA; DAB; DAC; WLC
See also CDBLB 1789-1832; DAM MST,
NOV; DLB 116

Auster, Paul 1947- . . . . CLC 47
See also CA 69-72; CANR 23

Austin, Frank
See Faust, Frederick (Schiller)

Austin, Mary (Hunter)
1868-1934 . . . . TCLC 25
See also CA 109; DLB 9, 78

Autran Dourado, Waldomiro
See Dourado, (Waldomiro Freitas) Autran

Averroes 1126-1198 . . . . CMLC 7
See also DLB 115

Avicenna 980-1037 . . . . CMLC 16
See also DLB 115

Avison, Margaret 1918- . . . . CLC 2, 4; DAC
See also CA 17-20R; DAM POET; DLB 53;
MTCW

Axton, David
See Koontz, Dean R(ay)

Ayckbourn, Alan
1939- . . . . CLC 5, 8, 18, 33, 74; DAB
See also CA 21-24R; CANR 31;
DAM DRAM; DLB 13; MTCW

Aydy, Catherine
See Tennant, Emma (Christina)

Ayme, Marcel (Andre) 1902-1967 . . . CLC 11
See also CA 89-92; CLR 25; DLB 72

Ayrton, Michael 1921-1975 . . . . CLC 7
See also CA 5-8R; 61-64; CANR 9, 21

Azorin . . . . CLC 11
See also Martinez Ruiz, Jose

Azuela, Mariano
1873-1952 . . . . TCLC 3; HLC
See also CA 104; 131; DAM MULT; HW;
MTCW

Baastad, Babbis Friis
See Friis-Baastad, Babbis Ellinor

Bab
See Gilbert, W(illiam) S(chwenck)

Babbis, Eleanor
See Friis-Baastad, Babbis Ellinor

Babel, Isaak (Emmanuilovich)
1894-1941(?) . . . . . . TCLC 2, 13; SSC 16
See also CA 104

Babits, Mihaly 1883-1941 . . . . TCLC 14
See also CA 114

Babur 1483-1530 . . . . LC 18

Bacchelli, Riccardo 1891-1985 . . . . . CLC 19
See also CA 29-32R; 117

Bach, Richard (David) 1936- . . . . CLC 14
See also AITN 1; BEST 89:2; CA 9-12R;
CANR 18; DAM NOV, POP; MTCW;
SATA 13

Bachman, Richard
See King, Stephen (Edwin)

Bachmann, Ingeborg 1926-1973 . . . . . CLC 69
See also CA 93-96; 45-48; DLB 85

Bacon, Francis 1561-1626 . . . . LC 18, 32
See also CDBLB Before 1660; DLB 151

Bacon, Roger 1214(?)-1292 . . . . . . CMLC 14
See also DLB 115

Bacovia, George . . . . TCLC 24
See also Vasiliu, Gheorghe

Badanes, Jerome 1937- . . . . CLC 59

Bagehot, Walter 1826-1877 . . . . . . NCLC 10
See also DLB 55

Bagnold, Enid 1889-1981 . . . . CLC 25
See also CA 5-8R; 103; CANR 5, 40;
DAM DRAM; DLB 13, 160; MAICYA;
SATA 1, 25

Bagritsky, Eduard 1895-1934 . . . . . TCLC 60

Bagrjana, Elisaveta
See Belcheva, Elisaveta

Bagryana, Elisaveta . . . . CLC 10
See also Belcheva, Elisaveta
See also DLB 147

Bailey, Paul 1937- . . . . CLC 45
See also CA 21-24R; CANR 16; DLB 14

Baillie, Joanna 1762-1851 . . . . NCLC 2
See also DLB 93

Bainbridge, Beryl (Margaret)
1933- . . . . CLC 4, 5, 8, 10, 14, 18, 22, 62
See also CA 21-24R; CANR 24;
DAM NOV; DLB 14; MTCW

Baker, Elliott 1922- . . . . CLC 8
See also CA 45-48; CANR 2

Baker, Nicholson 1957- . . . . CLC 61
See also CA 135; DAM POP

Baker, Ray Stannard 1870-1946 . . . TCLC 47
See also CA 118

Baker, Russell (Wayne) 1925- . . . . . . CLC 31
See also BEST 89:4; CA 57-60; CANR 11,
41; MTCW

Bakhtin, M.
See Bakhtin, Mikhail Mikhailovich

Bakhtin, M. M.
See Bakhtin, Mikhail Mikhailovich

Bakhtin, Mikhail
See Bakhtin, Mikhail Mikhailovich

Bakhtin, Mikhail Mikhailovich
1895-1975 . . . . CLC 83
See also CA 128; 113

Bakshi, Ralph 1938(?)- . . . . CLC 26
See also CA 112; 138

Bakunin, Mikhail (Alexandrovich)
1814-1876 . . . . NCLC 25

Baldwin, James (Arthur)
1924-1987 . . . . . . CLC 1, 2, 3, 4, 5, 8, 13,
15, 17, 42, 50, 67, 90; BLC; DA; DAB;
DAC; DC 1; SSC 10; WLC
See also AAYA 4; BW 1; CA 1-4R; 124;
CABS 1; CANR 3, 24;
CDALB 1941-1968; DAM MST, MULT,
NOV, POP; DLB 2, 7, 33; DLBY 87;
MTCW; SATA 9; SATA-Obit 54

Ballard, J(ames) G(raham)
1930- . . . . CLC 3, 6, 14, 36; SSC 1
See also AAYA 3; CA 5-8R; CANR 15, 39;
DAM NOV, POP; DLB 14; MTCW

Balmont, Konstantin (Dmitriyevich)
1867-1943 . . . . TCLC 11
See also CA 109

Balzac, Honore de
1799-1850 . . . . NCLC 5, 35, 53; DA;
DAB; DAC; SSC 5; WLC
See also DAM MST, NOV; DLB 119

Bambara, Toni Cade
1939- . . . . . CLC 19, 88; BLC; DA; DAC
See also AAYA 5; BW 2; CA 29-32R;
CANR 24, 49; DAM MST, MULT;
DLB 38; MTCW

Bamdad, A.
    See Shamlu, Ahmad

Banat, D. R.
    See Bradbury, Ray (Douglas)

Bancroft, Laura
    See Baum, L(yman) Frank

Banim, John 1798-1842 . . . . **NCLC 13**
    See also DLB 116, 158, 159

Banim, Michael 1796-1874 . . . . . . **NCLC 13**
    See also DLB 158, 159

Banks, Iain
    See Banks, Iain M(enzies)

Banks, Iain M(enzies) 1954- . . . . **CLC 34**
    See also CA 123; 128; INT 128

Banks, Lynne Reid . . . . **CLC 23**
    See also Reid Banks, Lynne
    See also AAYA 6

Banks, Russell 1940- . . . . **CLC 37, 72**
    See also CA 65-68; CAAS 15; CANR 19;
    DLB 130

Banville, John 1945- . . . . **CLC 46**
    See also CA 117; 128; DLB 14; INT 128

Banville, Theodore (Faullain) de
    1832-1891 . . . . **NCLC 9**

Baraka, Amiri
    1934- . . . . **CLC 1, 2, 3, 5, 10, 14, 33;**
                BLC; DA; DAC; DC 6; PC 4
    See also Jones, LeRoi
    See also BW 2; CA 21-24R; CABS 3;
    CANR 27, 38; CDALB 1941-1968;
    DAM MST, MULT, POET, POP;
    DLB 5, 7, 16, 38; DLBD 8; MTCW

Barbauld, Anna Laetitia
    1743-1825 . . . . **NCLC 50**
    See also DLB 107, 109, 142, 158

Barbellion, W. N. P. . . . . **TCLC 24**
    See also Cummings, Bruce F(rederick)

Barbera, Jack (Vincent) 1945- . . . . . . **CLC 44**
    See also CA 110; CANR 45

Barbey d'Aurevilly, Jules Amedee
    1808-1889 . . . . **NCLC 1; SSC 17**
    See also DLB 119

Barbusse, Henri 1873-1935 . . . . **TCLC 5**
    See also CA 105; DLB 65

Barclay, Bill
    See Moorcock, Michael (John)

Barclay, William Ewert
    See Moorcock, Michael (John)

Barea, Arturo 1897-1957 . . . . **TCLC 14**
    See also CA 111

Barfoot, Joan 1946- . . . . **CLC 18**
    See also CA 105

Baring, Maurice 1874-1945 . . . . **TCLC 8**
    See also CA 105; DLB 34

Barker, Clive 1952- . . . . **CLC 52**
    See also AAYA 10; BEST 90:3; CA 121;
    129; DAM POP; INT 129; MTCW

Barker, George Granville
    1913-1991 . . . . **CLC 8, 48**
    See also CA 9-12R; 135; CANR 7, 38;
    DAM POET; DLB 20; MTCW

Barker, Harley Granville
    See Granville-Barker, Harley
    See also DLB 10

Barker, Howard 1946- . . . . **CLC 37**
    See also CA 102; DLB 13

Barker, Pat(ricia) 1943- . . . . **CLC 32**
    See also CA 117; 122; CANR 50; INT 122

Barlow, Joel 1754-1812 . . . . **NCLC 23**
    See also DLB 37

Barnard, Mary (Ethel) 1909- . . . . **CLC 48**
    See also CA 21-22; CAP 2

Barnes, Djuna
    1892-1982 . . . **CLC 3, 4, 8, 11, 29; SSC 3**
    See also CA 9-12R; 107; CANR 16; DLB 4,
    9, 45; MTCW

Barnes, Julian 1946- . . . . **CLC 42; DAB**
    See also CA 102; CANR 19; DLBY 93

Barnes, Peter 1931- . . . . **CLC 5, 56**
    See also CA 65-68; CAAS 12; CANR 33,
    34; DLB 13; MTCW

Baroja (y Nessi), Pio
    1872-1956 . . . . **TCLC 8; HLC**
    See also CA 104

Baron, David
    See Pinter, Harold

Baron Corvo
    See Rolfe, Frederick (William Serafino
    Austin Lewis Mary)

Barondess, Sue K(aufman)
    1926-1977 . . . . **CLC 8**
    See also Kaufman, Sue
    See also CA 1-4R; 69-72; CANR 1

Baron de Teive
    See Pessoa, Fernando (Antonio Nogueira)

Barres, Maurice 1862-1923 . . . . **TCLC 47**
    See also DLB 123

Barreto, Afonso Henrique de Lima
    See Lima Barreto, Afonso Henrique de

Barrett, (Roger) Syd 1946- . . . . **CLC 35**

Barrett, William (Christopher)
    1913-1992 . . . . **CLC 27**
    See also CA 13-16R; 139; CANR 11;
    INT CANR-11

Barrie, J(ames) M(atthew)
    1860-1937 . . . . **TCLC 2; DAB**
    See also CA 104; 136; CDBLB 1890-1914;
    CLR 16; DAM DRAM; DLB 10, 141,
    156; MAICYA; YABC 1

Barrington, Michael
    See Moorcock, Michael (John)

Barrol, Grady
    See Bograd, Larry

Barry, Mike
    See Malzberg, Barry N(athaniel)

Barry, Philip 1896-1949 . . . . **TCLC 11**
    See also CA 109; DLB 7

Bart, Andre Schwarz
    See Schwarz-Bart, Andre

Barth, John (Simmons)
    1930- . . . . . . **CLC 1, 2, 3, 5, 7, 9, 10, 14,**
                27, 51, 89; SSC 10
    See also AITN 1, 2; CA 1-4R; CABS 1;
    CANR 5, 23, 49; DAM NOV; DLB 2;
    MTCW

Barthelme, Donald
    1931-1989 . . . . . . **CLC 1, 2, 3, 5, 6, 8, 13,**
                23, 46, 59; SSC 2
    See also CA 21-24R; 129; CANR 20;
    DAM NOV; DLB 2; DLBY 80, 89;
    MTCW; SATA 7; SATA-Obit 62

Barthelme, Frederick 1943- . . . . **CLC 36**
    See also CA 114; 122; DLBY 85; INT 122

Barthes, Roland (Gerard)
    1915-1980 . . . . **CLC 24, 83**
    See also CA 130; 97-100; MTCW

Barzun, Jacques (Martin) 1907- . . . . **CLC 51**
    See also CA 61-64; CANR 22

Bashevis, Isaac
    See Singer, Isaac Bashevis

Bashkirtseff, Marie 1859-1884 . . . **NCLC 27**

Basho
    See Matsuo Basho

Bass, Kingsley B., Jr.
    See Bullins, Ed

Bass, Rick 1958- . . . . **CLC 79**
    See also CA 126

Bassani, Giorgio 1916- . . . . **CLC 9**
    See also CA 65-68; CANR 33; DLB 128;
    MTCW

Bastos, Augusto (Antonio) Roa
    See Roa Bastos, Augusto (Antonio)

Bataille, Georges 1897-1962 . . . . **CLC 29**
    See also CA 101; 89-92

Bates, H(erbert) E(rnest)
    1905-1974 . . . . . . **CLC 46; DAB; SSC 10**
    See also CA 93-96; 45-48; CANR 34;
    DAM POP; MTCW

Bauchart
    See Camus, Albert

Baudelaire, Charles
    1821-1867 . . . . . **NCLC 6, 29; DA; DAB;**
                DAC; PC 1; SSC 18; WLC
    See also DAM MST, POET

Baudrillard, Jean 1929- . . . . **CLC 60**

Baum, L(yman) Frank 1856-1919 . . . **TCLC 7**
    See also CA 108; 133; CLR 15; DLB 22;
    JRDA; MAICYA; MTCW; SATA 18

Baum, Louis F.
    See Baum, L(yman) Frank

Baumbach, Jonathan 1933- . . . . **CLC 6, 23**
    See also CA 13-16R; CAAS 5; CANR 12;
    DLBY 80; INT CANR-12; MTCW

Bausch, Richard (Carl) 1945- . . . . . . **CLC 51**
    See also CA 101; CAAS 14; CANR 43;
    DLB 130

Baxter, Charles 1947- . . . . **CLC 45, 78**
    See also CA 57-60; CANR 40; DAM POP;
    DLB 130

Baxter, George Owen
    See Faust, Frederick (Schiller)

Baxter, James K(eir) 1926-1972 . . . . **CLC 14**
    See also CA 77-80

Baxter, John
    See Hunt, E(verette) Howard, (Jr.)

Bayer, Sylvia
    See Glassco, John

Baynton, Barbara 1857-1929 . . . . . . **TCLC 57**

Beagle, Peter S(oyer) 1939- . . . . CLC 7
See also CA 9-12R; CANR 4; DLBY 80;
INT CANR-4; SATA 60

Bean, Normal
See Burroughs, Edgar Rice

Beard, Charles A(ustin)
1874-1948 . . . . TCLC 15
See also CA 115; DLB 17; SATA 18

Beardsley, Aubrey 1872-1898 . . . . . NCLC 6

Beattie, Ann
1947- . . . . CLC 8, 13, 18, 40, 63; SSC 11
See also BEST 90:2; CA 81-84; DAM NOV,
POP; DLBY 82; MTCW

Beattie, James 1735-1803 . . . . NCLC 25
See also DLB 109

Beauchamp, Kathleen Mansfield 1888-1923
See Mansfield, Katherine
See also CA 104; 134; DA; DAC;
DAM MST

Beaumarchais, Pierre-Augustin Caron de
1732-1799 . . . . DC 4
See also DAM DRAM

Beaumont, Francis 1584(?)-1616 . . . . . . DC 6
See also CDBLB Before 1660; DLB 58, 121

Beauvoir, Simone (Lucie Ernestine Marie
Bertrand) de
1908-1986 . . . . CLC 1, 2, 4, 8, 14, 31, 44,
50, 71; DA; DAB; DAC; WLC
See also CA 9-12R; 118; CANR 28;
DAM MST, NOV; DLB 72; DLBY 86;
MTCW

Becker, Jurek 1937- . . . . CLC 7, 19
See also CA 85-88; DLB 75

Becker, Walter 1950- . . . . CLC 26

Beckett, Samuel (Barclay)
1906-1989 . . . . . . CLC 1, 2, 3, 4, 6, 9, 10,
11, 14, 18, 29, 57, 59, 83; DA; DAB;
DAC; SSC 16; WLC
See also CA 5-8R; 130; CANR 33;
CDBLB 1945-1960; DAM DRAM, MST,
NOV; DLB 13, 15; DLBY 90; MTCW

Beckford, William 1760-1844 . . . . NCLC 16
See also DLB 39

Beckman, Gunnel 1910- . . . . CLC 26
See also CA 33-36R; CANR 15; CLR 25;
MAICYA; SAAS 9; SATA 6

Becque, Henri 1837-1899 . . . . NCLC 3

Beddoes, Thomas Lovell
1803-1849 . . . . NCLC 3
See also DLB 96

Bedford, Donald F.
See Fearing, Kenneth (Flexner)

Beecher, Catharine Esther
1800-1878 . . . . NCLC 30
See also DLB 1

Beecher, John 1904-1980 . . . . CLC 6
See also AITN 1; CA 5-8R; 105; CANR 8

Beer, Johann 1655-1700 . . . . LC 5

Beer, Patricia 1924- . . . . CLC 58
See also CA 61-64; CANR 13, 46; DLB 40

Beerbohm, Henry Maximilian
1872-1956 . . . . TCLC 1, 24
See also CA 104; DLB 34, 100

Beerbohm, Max
See Beerbohm, Henry Maximilian

Beer-Hofmann, Richard
1866-1945 . . . . TCLC 60
See also DLB 81

Begiebing, Robert J(ohn) 1946- . . . . . CLC 70
See also CA 122; CANR 40

Behan, Brendan
1923-1964 . . . . CLC 1, 8, 11, 15, 79
See also CA 73-76; CANR 33;
CDBLB 1945-1960; DAM DRAM;
DLB 13; MTCW

Behn, Aphra
1640(?)-1689 . . . . . . LC 1, 30; DA; DAB;
DAC; DC 4; PC 13; WLC
See also DAM DRAM, MST, NOV, POET;
DLB 39, 80, 131

Behrman, S(amuel) N(athaniel)
1893-1973 . . . . CLC 40
See also CA 13-16; 45-48; CAP 1; DLB 7,
44

Belasco, David 1853-1931 . . . . TCLC 3
See also CA 104; DLB 7

Belcheva, Elisaveta 1893- . . . . CLC 10
See also Bagryana, Elisaveta

Beldone, Phil "Cheech"
See Ellison, Harlan (Jay)

Beleno
See Azuela, Mariano

Belinski, Vissarion Grigoryevich
1811-1848 . . . . NCLC 5

Belitt, Ben 1911- . . . . CLC 22
See also CA 13-16R; CAAS 4; CANR 7;
DLB 5

Bell, James Madison
1826-1902 . . . . TCLC 43; BLC
See also BW 1; CA 122; 124; DAM MULT;
DLB 50

Bell, Madison (Smartt) 1957- . . . . . . CLC 41
See also CA 111; CANR 28

Bell, Marvin (Hartley) 1937- . . . . . CLC 8, 31
See also CA 21-24R; CAAS 14;
DAM POET; DLB 5; MTCW

Bell, W. L. D.
See Mencken, H(enry) L(ouis)

Bellamy, Atwood C.
See Mencken, H(enry) L(ouis)

Bellamy, Edward 1850-1898 . . . . . . NCLC 4
See also DLB 12

Bellin, Edward J.
See Kuttner, Henry

Belloc, (Joseph) Hilaire (Pierre)
1870-1953 . . . . TCLC 7, 18
See also CA 106; DAM POET; DLB 19,
100, 141; YABC 1

Belloc, Joseph Peter Rene Hilaire
See Belloc, (Joseph) Hilaire (Pierre)

Belloc, Joseph Pierre Hilaire
See Belloc, (Joseph) Hilaire (Pierre)

Belloc, M. A.
See Lowndes, Marie Adelaide (Belloc)

Bellow, Saul
1915- . . . . . . CLC 1, 2, 3, 6, 8, 10, 13, 15,
25, 33, 34, 63, 79; DA; DAB; DAC;
SSC 14; WLC
See also AITN 2; BEST 89:3; CA 5-8R;
CABS 1; CANR 29; CDALB 1941-1968;
DAM MST, NOV, POP; DLB 2, 28;
DLBD 3; DLBY 82; MTCW

Belser, Reimond Karel Maria de
See Ruyslinck, Ward

Bely, Andrey . . . . TCLC 7; PC 11
See also Bugayev, Boris Nikolayevich

Benary, Margot
See Benary-Isbert, Margot

Benary-Isbert, Margot 1889-1979 . . . CLC 12
See also CA 5-8R; 89-92; CANR 4;
CLR 12; MAICYA; SATA 2;
SATA-Obit 21

Benavente (y Martinez), Jacinto
1866-1954 . . . . TCLC 3
See also CA 106; 131; DAM DRAM,
MULT; HW; MTCW

Benchley, Peter (Bradford)
1940- . . . . CLC 4, 8
See also AAYA 14; AITN 2; CA 17-20R;
CANR 12, 35; DAM NOV, POP;
MTCW; SATA 3

Benchley, Robert (Charles)
1889-1945 . . . . TCLC 1, 55
See also CA 105; DLB 11

Benda, Julien 1867-1956 . . . . TCLC 60
See also CA 120

Benedict, Ruth 1887-1948 . . . . TCLC 60

Benedikt, Michael 1935- . . . . CLC 4, 14
See also CA 13-16R; CANR 7; DLB 5

Benet, Juan 1927- . . . . CLC 28
See also CA 143

Benet, Stephen Vincent
1898-1943 . . . . TCLC 7; SSC 10
See also CA 104; DAM POET; DLB 4, 48,
102; YABC 1

Benet, William Rose 1886-1950 . . . TCLC 28
See also CA 118; DAM POET; DLB 45

Benford, Gregory (Albert) 1941- . . . . CLC 52
See also CA 69-72; CANR 12, 24, 49;
DLBY 82

Bengtsson, Frans (Gunnar)
1894-1954 . . . . TCLC 48

Benjamin, David
See Slavitt, David R(ytman)

Benjamin, Lois
See Gould, Lois

Benjamin, Walter 1892-1940 . . . . . . TCLC 39

Benn, Gottfried 1886-1956 . . . . TCLC 3
See also CA 106; DLB 56

Bennett, Alan 1934- . . . . . CLC 45, 77; DAB
See also CA 103; CANR 35; DAM MST;
MTCW

Bennett, (Enoch) Arnold
1867-1931 . . . . TCLC 5, 20
See also CA 106; CDBLB 1890-1914;
DLB 10, 34, 98, 135

Bennett, Elizabeth
See Mitchell, Margaret (Munnerlyn)

Bennett, George Harold 1930-
See Bennett, Hal
See also BW 1; CA 97-100

Bennett, Hal . . . . **CLC 5**
See also Bennett, George Harold
See also DLB 33

Bennett, Jay 1912- . . . . **CLC 35**
See also AAYA 10; CA 69-72; CANR 11,
42; JRDA; SAAS 4; SATA 41;
SATA-Brief 27

Bennett, Louise (Simone)
1919- . . . . **CLC 28; BLC**
See also BW 2; DAM MULT; DLB 117

Benson, E(dward) F(rederic)
1867-1940 . . . . **TCLC 27**
See also CA 114; DLB 135, 153

Benson, Jackson J. 1930- . . . . **CLC 34**
See also CA 25-28R; DLB 111

Benson, Sally 1900-1972 . . . . **CLC 17**
See also CA 19-20; 37-40R; CAP 1;
SATA 1, 35; SATA-Obit 27

Benson, Stella 1892-1933 . . . . **TCLC 17**
See also CA 117; DLB 36

Bentham, Jeremy 1748-1832 . . . . . **NCLC 38**
See also DLB 107, 158

Bentley, E(dmund) C(lerihew)
1875-1956 . . . . **TCLC 12**
See also CA 108; DLB 70

Bentley, Eric (Russell) 1916- . . . . **CLC 24**
See also CA 5-8R; CANR 6; INT CANR-6

Beranger, Pierre Jean de
1780-1857 . . . . **NCLC 34**

Berendt, John (Lawrence) 1939- . . . . **CLC 86**
See also CA 146

Berger, Colonel
See Malraux, (Georges-)Andre

Berger, John (Peter) 1926- . . . . . . **CLC 2, 19**
See also CA 81-84; DLB 14

Berger, Melvin H. 1927- . . . . **CLC 12**
See also CA 5-8R; CANR 4; CLR 32;
SAAS 2; SATA 5

Berger, Thomas (Louis)
1924- . . . . **CLC 3, 5, 8, 11, 18, 38**
See also CA 1-4R; CANR 5, 28;
DAM NOV; DLB 2; DLBY 80;
INT CANR-28; MTCW

Bergman, (Ernst) Ingmar
1918- . . . . **CLC 16, 72**
See also CA 81-84; CANR 33

Bergson, Henri 1859-1941 . . . . **TCLC 32**

Bergstein, Eleanor 1938- . . . . **CLC 4**
See also CA 53-56; CANR 5

Berkoff, Steven 1937- . . . . **CLC 56**
See also CA 104

Bermant, Chaim (Icyk) 1929- . . . . . . **CLC 40**
See also CA 57-60; CANR 6, 31

Bern, Victoria
See Fisher, M(ary) F(rances) K(ennedy)

Bernanos, (Paul Louis) Georges
1888-1948 . . . . **TCLC 3**
See also CA 104; 130; DLB 72

Bernard, April 1956- . . . . **CLC 59**
See also CA 131

Berne, Victoria
See Fisher, M(ary) F(rances) K(ennedy)

Bernhard, Thomas
1931-1989 . . . . **CLC 3, 32, 61**
See also CA 85-88; 127; CANR 32;
DLB 85, 124; MTCW

Berriault, Gina 1926- . . . . **CLC 54**
See also CA 116; 129; DLB 130

Berrigan, Daniel 1921- . . . . **CLC 4**
See also CA 33-36R; CAAS 1; CANR 11,
43; DLB 5

Berrigan, Edmund Joseph Michael, Jr.
1934-1983
See Berrigan, Ted
See also CA 61-64; 110; CANR 14

Berrigan, Ted . . . . **CLC 37**
See also Berrigan, Edmund Joseph Michael,
Jr.
See also DLB 5

Berry, Charles Edward Anderson 1931-
See Berry, Chuck
See also CA 115

Berry, Chuck . . . . **CLC 17**
See also Berry, Charles Edward Anderson

Berry, Jonas
See Ashbery, John (Lawrence)

Berry, Wendell (Erdman)
1934- . . . . **CLC 4, 6, 8, 27, 46**
See also AITN 1; CA 73-76; CANR 50;
DAM POET; DLB 5, 6

Berryman, John
1914-1972 . . . . . . **CLC 1, 2, 3, 4, 6, 8, 10,
13, 25, 62**
See also CA 13-16; 33-36R; CABS 2;
CANR 35; CAP 1; CDALB 1941-1968;
DAM POET; DLB 48; MTCW

Bertolucci, Bernardo 1940- . . . . **CLC 16**
See also CA 106

Bertrand, Aloysius 1807-1841 . . . . **NCLC 31**

Bertran de Born c. 1140-1215 . . . . . **CMLC 5**

Besant, Annie (Wood) 1847-1933 . . . **TCLC 9**
See also CA 105

Bessie, Alvah 1904-1985 . . . . **CLC 23**
See also CA 5-8R; 116; CANR 2; DLB 26

Bethlen, T. D.
See Silverberg, Robert

Beti, Mongo . . . . **CLC 27; BLC**
See also Biyidi, Alexandre
See also DAM MULT

Betjeman, John
1906-1984 . . . **CLC 2, 6, 10, 34, 43; DAB**
See also CA 9-12R; 112; CANR 33;
CDBLB 1945-1960; DAM MST, POET;
DLB 20; DLBY 84; MTCW

Bettelheim, Bruno 1903-1990 . . . . . . **CLC 79**
See also CA 81-84; 131; CANR 23; MTCW

Betti, Ugo 1892-1953 . . . . **TCLC 5**
See also CA 104

Betts, Doris (Waugh) 1932- . . . . **CLC 3, 6, 28**
See also CA 13-16R; CANR 9; DLBY 82;
INT CANR-9

Bevan, Alistair
See Roberts, Keith (John Kingston)

Bialik, Chaim Nachman
1873-1934 . . . . **TCLC 25**

Bickerstaff, Isaac
See Swift, Jonathan

Bidart, Frank 1939- . . . . **CLC 33**
See also CA 140

Bienek, Horst 1930- . . . . **CLC 7, 11**
See also CA 73-76; DLB 75

Bierce, Ambrose (Gwinett)
1842-1914(?) . . . . **TCLC 1, 7, 44; DA;
DAC; SSC 9; WLC**
See also CA 104; 139; CDALB 1865-1917;
DAM MST; DLB 11, 12, 23, 71, 74

Billings, Josh
See Shaw, Henry Wheeler

Billington, (Lady) Rachel (Mary)
1942- . . . . **CLC 43**
See also AITN 2; CA 33-36R; CANR 44

Binyon, T(imothy) J(ohn) 1936- . . . . **CLC 34**
See also CA 111; CANR 28

Bioy Casares, Adolfo
1914- . . . **CLC 4, 8, 13, 88; HLC; SSC 17**
See also CA 29-32R; CANR 19, 43;
DAM MULT; DLB 113; HW; MTCW

Bird, Cordwainer
See Ellison, Harlan (Jay)

Bird, Robert Montgomery
1806-1854 . . . . **NCLC 1**

Birney, (Alfred) Earle
1904- . . . . **CLC 1, 4, 6, 11; DAC**
See also CA 1-4R; CANR 5, 20;
DAM MST, POET; DLB 88; MTCW

Bishop, Elizabeth
1911-1979 . . . . . . **CLC 1, 4, 9, 13, 15, 32;
DA; DAC; PC 3**
See also CA 5-8R; 89-92; CABS 2;
CANR 26; CDALB 1968-1988;
DAM MST, POET; DLB 5; MTCW;
SATA-Obit 24

Bishop, John 1935- . . . . **CLC 10**
See also CA 105

Bissett, Bill 1939- . . . . **CLC 18; PC 14**
See also CA 69-72; CAAS 19; CANR 15;
DLB 53; MTCW

Bitov, Andrei (Georgievich) 1937- . . . **CLC 57**
See also CA 142

Biyidi, Alexandre 1932-
See Beti, Mongo
See also BW 1; CA 114; 124; MTCW

Bjarme, Brynjolf
See Ibsen, Henrik (Johan)

Bjornson, Bjornstjerne (Martinius)
1832-1910 . . . . **TCLC 7, 37**
See also CA 104

Black, Robert
See Holdstock, Robert P.

Blackburn, Paul 1926-1971 . . . . . . **CLC 9, 43**
See also CA 81-84; 33-36R; CANR 34;
DLB 16; DLBY 81

Black Elk 1863-1950 . . . . **TCLC 33**
See also CA 144; DAM MULT; NNAL

Black Hobart
See Sanders, (James) Ed(ward)

Blacklin, Malcolm
See Chambers, Aidan

Blackmore, R(ichard) D(oddridge)
1825-1900 . . . . TCLC 27
See also CA 120; DLB 18

Blackmur, R(ichard) P(almer)
1904-1965 . . . . CLC 2, 24
See also CA 11-12; 25-28R; CAP 1; DLB 63

Black Tarantula, The
See Acker, Kathy

Blackwood, Algernon (Henry)
1869-1951 . . . . TCLC 5
See also CA 105; DLB 153, 156

Blackwood, Caroline 1931- . . . . CLC 6, 9
See also CA 85-88; CANR 32; DLB 14;
MTCW

Blade, Alexander
See Hamilton, Edmond; Silverberg, Robert

Blaga, Lucian 1895-1961 . . . . CLC 75

Blair, Eric (Arthur) 1903-1950
See Orwell, George
See also CA 104; 132; DA; DAB; DAC;
DAM MST, NOV; MTCW; SATA 29

Blais, Marie-Claire
1939- . . . . CLC 2, 4, 6, 13, 22; DAC
See also CA 21-24R; CAAS 4; CANR 38;
DAM MST; DLB 53; MTCW

Blaise, Clark 1940- . . . . CLC 29
See also AITN 2; CA 53-56; CAAS 3;
CANR 5; DLB 53

Blake, Nicholas
See Day Lewis, C(ecil)
See also DLB 77

Blake, William
1757-1827 . . . . NCLC 13, 37; DA; DAB;
DAC; PC 12; WLC
See also CDBLB 1789-1832; DAM MST,
POET; DLB 93; MAICYA; SATA 30

Blake, William J(ames) 1894-1969 . . . PC 12
See also CA 5-8R; 25-28R

Blasco Ibanez, Vicente
1867-1928 . . . . TCLC 12
See also CA 110; 131; DAM NOV; HW;
MTCW

Blatty, William Peter 1928- . . . . CLC 2
See also CA 5-8R; CANR 9; DAM POP

Bleeck, Oliver
See Thomas, Ross (Elmore)

Blessing, Lee 1949- . . . . CLC 54

Blish, James (Benjamin)
1921-1975 . . . . CLC 14
See also CA 1-4R; 57-60; CANR 3; DLB 8;
MTCW; SATA 66

Bliss, Reginald
See Wells, H(erbert) G(eorge)

Blixen, Karen (Christentze Dinesen)
1885-1962
See Dinesen, Isak
See also CA 25-28; CANR 22, 50; CAP 2;
MTCW; SATA 44

Bloch, Robert (Albert) 1917-1994 . . . CLC 33
See also CA 5-8R; 146; CAAS 20; CANR 5;
DLB 44; INT CANR-5; SATA 12;
SATA-Obit 82

Blok, Alexander (Alexandrovich)
1880-1921 . . . . TCLC 5
See also CA 104

Blom, Jan
See Breytenbach, Breyten

Bloom, Harold 1930- . . . . CLC 24
See also CA 13-16R; CANR 39; DLB 67

Bloomfield, Aurelius
See Bourne, Randolph S(illiman)

Blount, Roy (Alton), Jr. 1941- . . . . . CLC 38
See also CA 53-56; CANR 10, 28;
INT CANR-28; MTCW

Bloy, Leon 1846-1917 . . . . TCLC 22
See also CA 121; DLB 123

Blume, Judy (Sussman) 1938- . . . CLC 12, 30
See also AAYA 3; CA 29-32R; CANR 13,
37; CLR 2, 15; DAM NOV, POP;
DLB 52; JRDA; MAICYA; MTCW;
SATA 2, 31, 79

Blunden, Edmund (Charles)
1896-1974 . . . . CLC 2, 56
See also CA 17-18; 45-48; CAP 2; DLB 20,
100, 155; MTCW

Bly, Robert (Elwood)
1926- . . . . CLC 1, 2, 5, 10, 15, 38
See also CA 5-8R; CANR 41; DAM POET;
DLB 5; MTCW

Boas, Franz 1858-1942 . . . . TCLC 56
See also CA 115

Bobette
See Simenon, Georges (Jacques Christian)

Boccaccio, Giovanni
1313-1375 . . . . CMLC 13; SSC 10

Bochco, Steven 1943- . . . . CLC 35
See also AAYA 11; CA 124; 138

Bodenheim, Maxwell 1892-1954 . . . TCLC 44
See also CA 110; DLB 9, 45

Bodker, Cecil 1927- . . . . CLC 21
See also CA 73-76; CANR 13, 44; CLR 23;
MAICYA; SATA 14

Boell, Heinrich (Theodor)
1917-1985 . . . . CLC 2, 3, 6, 9, 11, 15, 27,
32, 72; DA; DAB; DAC; WLC
See also CA 21-24R; 116; CANR 24;
DAM MST, NOV; DLB 69; DLBY 85;
MTCW

Boerne, Alfred
See Doeblin, Alfred

Boethius 480(?)-524(?) . . . . CMLC 15
See also DLB 115

Bogan, Louise
1897-1970 . . . . . . CLC 4, 39, 46; PC 12
See also CA 73-76; 25-28R; CANR 33;
DAM POET; DLB 45; MTCW

Bogarde, Dirk . . . . CLC 19
See also Van Den Bogarde, Derek Jules
Gaspard Ulric Niven
See also DLB 14

Bogosian, Eric 1953- . . . . CLC 45
See also CA 138

Bograd, Larry 1953- . . . . CLC 35
See also CA 93-96; SAAS 21; SATA 33

Boiardo, Matteo Maria 1441-1494 . . . . LC 6

Boileau-Despreaux, Nicolas
1636-1711 . . . . LC 3

Boland, Eavan (Aisling) 1944- . . . CLC 40, 67
See also CA 143; DAM POET; DLB 40

Bolt, Lee
See Faust, Frederick (Schiller)

Bolt, Robert (Oxton) 1924-1995 . . . . CLC 14
See also CA 17-20R; 147; CANR 35;
DAM DRAM; DLB 13; MTCW

Bombet, Louis-Alexandre-Cesar
See Stendhal

Bomkauf
See Kaufman, Bob (Garnell)

Bonaventura . . . . NCLC 35
See also DLB 90

Bond, Edward 1934- . . . . CLC 4, 6, 13, 23
See also CA 25-28R; CANR 38;
DAM DRAM; DLB 13; MTCW

Bonham, Frank 1914-1989 . . . . CLC 12
See also AAYA 1; CA 9-12R; CANR 4, 36;
JRDA; MAICYA; SAAS 3; SATA 1, 49;
SATA-Obit 62

Bonnefoy, Yves 1923- . . . . CLC 9, 15, 58
See also CA 85-88; CANR 33; DAM MST,
POET; MTCW

Bontemps, Arna(ud Wendell)
1902-1973 . . . . CLC 1, 18; BLC
See also BW 1; CA 1-4R; 41-44R; CANR 4,
35; CLR 6; DAM MULT, NOV, POET;
DLB 48, 51; JRDA; MAICYA; MTCW;
SATA 2, 44; SATA-Obit 24

Booth, Martin 1944- . . . . CLC 13
See also CA 93-96; CAAS 2

Booth, Philip 1925- . . . . CLC 23
See also CA 5-8R; CANR 5; DLBY 82

Booth, Wayne C(layson) 1921- . . . . . CLC 24
See also CA 1-4R; CAAS 5; CANR 3, 43;
DLB 67

Borchert, Wolfgang 1921-1947 . . . . . TCLC 5
See also CA 104; DLB 69, 124

Borel, Petrus 1809-1859 . . . . NCLC 41

Borges, Jorge Luis
1899-1986 . . . CLC 1, 2, 3, 4, 6, 8, 9, 10,
13, 19, 44, 48, 83; DA; DAB; DAC;
HLC; SSC 4; WLC
See also CA 21-24R; CANR 19, 33;
DAM MST, MULT; DLB 113; DLBY 86;
HW; MTCW

Borowski, Tadeusz 1922-1951 . . . . . . TCLC 9
See also CA 106

Borrow, George (Henry)
1803-1881 . . . . NCLC 9
See also DLB 21, 55

Bosman, Herman Charles
1905-1951 . . . . TCLC 49

Bosschere, Jean de 1878(?)-1953 . . . TCLC 19
See also CA 115

Boswell, James
1740-1795 . . . . . . LC 4; DA; DAB; DAC;
WLC
See also CDBLB 1660-1789; DAM MST;
DLB 104, 142

Bottoms, David 1949- . . . . CLC 53
See also CA 105; CANR 22; DLB 120;
DLBY 83

Boucicault, Dion 1820-1890 . . . . . . NCLC 41

Boucolon, Maryse 1937-
See Conde, Maryse
See also CA 110; CANR 30

Bourget, Paul (Charles Joseph)
1852-1935 . . . . **TCLC 12**
See also CA 107; DLB 123

Bourjaily, Vance (Nye) 1922- . . . . **CLC 8, 62**
See also CA 1-4R; CAAS 1; CANR 2;
DLB 2, 143

Bourne, Randolph S(illiman)
1886-1918 . . . . **TCLC 16**
See also CA 117; DLB 63

Bova, Ben(jamin William) 1932- . . . . **CLC 45**
See also AAYA 16; CA 5-8R; CAAS 18;
CANR 11; CLR 3; DLBY 81;
INT CANR-11; MAICYA; MTCW;
SATA 6, 68

Bowen, Elizabeth (Dorothea Cole)
1899-1973 . . . . . . **CLC 1, 3, 6, 11, 15, 22;**
SSC 3
See also CA 17-18; 41-44R; CANR 35;
CAP 2; CDBLB 1945-1960; DAM NOV;
DLB 15; MTCW

Bowering, George 1935- . . . . **CLC 15, 47**
See also CA 21-24R; CAAS 16; CANR 10;
DLB 53

Bowering, Marilyn R(uthe) 1949- . . . **CLC 32**
See also CA 101; CANR 49

Bowers, Edgar 1924- . . . . **CLC 9**
See also CA 5-8R; CANR 24; DLB 5

Bowie, David . . . . **CLC 17**
See also Jones, David Robert

Bowles, Jane (Sydney)
1917-1973 . . . . **CLC 3, 68**
See also CA 19-20; 41-44R; CAP 2

Bowles, Paul (Frederick)
1910- . . . . **CLC 1, 2, 19, 53; SSC 3**
See also CA 1-4R; CAAS 1; CANR 1, 19,
50; DLB 5, 6; MTCW

Box, Edgar
See Vidal, Gore

Boyd, Nancy
See Millay, Edna St. Vincent

Boyd, William 1952- . . . . **CLC 28, 53, 70**
See also CA 114; 120

Boyle, Kay
1902-1992 . . . . . **CLC 1, 5, 19, 58; SSC 5**
See also CA 13-16R; 140; CAAS 1;
CANR 29; DLB 4, 9, 48, 86; DLBY 93;
MTCW

Boyle, Mark
See Kienzle, William X(avier)

Boyle, Patrick 1905-1982 . . . . **CLC 19**
See also CA 127

Boyle, T. C. 1948-
See Boyle, T(homas) Coraghessan

Boyle, T(homas) Coraghessan
1948- . . . . **CLC 36, 55, 90; SSC 16**
See also BEST 90:4; CA 120; CANR 44;
DAM POP; DLBY 86

Boz
See Dickens, Charles (John Huffam)

Brackenridge, Hugh Henry
1748-1816 . . . . **NCLC 7**
See also DLB 11, 37

Bradbury, Edward P.
See Moorcock, Michael (John)

Bradbury, Malcolm (Stanley)
1932- . . . . **CLC 32, 61**
See also CA 1-4R; CANR 1, 33;
DAM NOV; DLB 14; MTCW

Bradbury, Ray (Douglas)
1920- . . . . **CLC 1, 3, 10, 15, 42; DA;**
DAB; DAC; WLC
See also AAYA 15; AITN 1, 2; CA 1-4R;
CANR 2, 30; CDALB 1968-1988;
DAM MST, NOV, POP; DLB 2, 8;
INT CANR-30; MTCW; SATA 11, 64

Bradford, Gamaliel 1863-1932 . . . . . **TCLC 36**
See also DLB 17

Bradley, David (Henry, Jr.)
1950- . . . . **CLC 23; BLC**
See also BW 1; CA 104; CANR 26;
DAM MULT; DLB 33

Bradley, John Ed(mund, Jr.)
1958- . . . . **CLC 55**
See also CA 139

Bradley, Marion Zimmer 1930- . . . . . **CLC 30**
See also AAYA 9; CA 57-60; CAAS 10;
CANR 7, 31; DAM POP; DLB 8;
MTCW

Bradstreet, Anne
1612(?)-1672 . . . . . . **LC 4, 30; DA; DAC;**
PC 10
See also CDALB 1640-1865; DAM MST,
POET; DLB 24

Brady, Joan 1939- . . . . **CLC 86**
See also CA 141

Bragg, Melvyn 1939- . . . . **CLC 10**
See also BEST 89:3; CA 57-60; CANR 10,
48; DLB 14

Braine, John (Gerard)
1922-1986 . . . . **CLC 1, 3, 41**
See also CA 1-4R; 120; CANR 1, 33;
CDBLB 1945-1960; DLB 15; DLBY 86;
MTCW

Brammer, William 1930(?)-1978 . . . . **CLC 31**
See also CA 77-80

Brancati, Vitaliano 1907-1954 . . . . . **TCLC 12**
See also CA 109

Brancato, Robin F(idler) 1936- . . . . . **CLC 35**
See also AAYA 9; CA 69-72; CANR 11,
45; CLR 32; JRDA; SAAS 9; SATA 23

Brand, Max
See Faust, Frederick (Schiller)

Brand, Millen 1906-1980 . . . . **CLC 7**
See also CA 21-24R; 97-100

Branden, Barbara . . . . **CLC 44**
See also CA 148

Brandes, Georg (Morris Cohen)
1842-1927 . . . . **TCLC 10**
See also CA 105

Brandys, Kazimierz 1916- . . . . **CLC 62**

Branley, Franklyn M(ansfield)
1915- . . . . **CLC 21**
See also CA 33-36R; CANR 14, 39;
CLR 13; MAICYA; SAAS 16; SATA 4,
68

Brathwaite, Edward Kamau 1930- . . . **CLC 11**
See also BW 2; CA 25-28R; CANR 11, 26,
47; DLB 125

Brautigan, Richard (Gary)
1935-1984 . . . . **CLC 1, 3, 5, 9, 12, 34, 42**
See also CA 53-56; 113; CANR 34;
DAM NOV; DLB 2, 5; DLBY 80, 84;
MTCW; SATA 56

Braverman, Kate 1950- . . . . **CLC 67**
See also CA 89-92

Brecht, Bertolt
1898-1956 . . . . . . **TCLC 1, 6, 13, 35; DA;**
DAB; DAC; DC 3; WLC
See also CA 104; 133; DAM DRAM, MST;
DLB 56, 124; MTCW

Brecht, Eugen Berthold Friedrich
See Brecht, Bertolt

Bremer, Fredrika 1801-1865 . . . . . **NCLC 11**

Brennan, Christopher John
1870-1932 . . . . **TCLC 17**
See also CA 117

Brennan, Maeve 1917- . . . . **CLC 5**
See also CA 81-84

Brentano, Clemens (Maria)
1778-1842 . . . . **NCLC 1**
See also DLB 90

Brent of Bin Bin
See Franklin, (Stella Maraia Sarah) Miles

Brenton, Howard 1942- . . . . **CLC 31**
See also CA 69-72; CANR 33; DLB 13;
MTCW

Breslin, James 1930-
See Breslin, Jimmy
See also CA 73-76; CANR 31; DAM NOV;
MTCW

Breslin, Jimmy . . . . **CLC 4, 43**
See also Breslin, James
See also AITN 1

Bresson, Robert 1901- . . . . **CLC 16**
See also CA 110; CANR 49

Breton, Andre 1896-1966 . . . **CLC 2, 9, 15, 54**
See also CA 19-20; 25-28R; CANR 40;
CAP 2; DLB 65; MTCW

Breytenbach, Breyten 1939(?)- . . **CLC 23, 37**
See also CA 113; 129; DAM POET

Bridgers, Sue Ellen 1942- . . . . **CLC 26**
See also AAYA 8; CA 65-68; CANR 11,
36; CLR 18; DLB 52; JRDA; MAICYA;
SAAS 1; SATA 22

Bridges, Robert (Seymour)
1844-1930 . . . . **TCLC 1**
See also CA 104; CDBLB 1890-1914;
DAM POET; DLB 19, 98

Bridie, James . . . . **TCLC 3**
See also Mavor, Osborne Henry
See also DLB 10

Brin, David 1950- . . . . **CLC 34**
See also CA 102; CANR 24;
INT CANR-24; SATA 65

Brink, Andre (Philippus)
1935- . . . . **CLC 18, 36**
See also CA 104; CANR 39; INT 103;
MTCW

Brinsmead, H(esba) F(ay) 1922- . . . . **CLC 21**
See also CA 21-24R; CANR 10; MAICYA;
SAAS 5; SATA 18, 78

Buck, Pearl S(ydenstricker)
 1892-1973 .... **CLC 7, 11, 18; DA; DAB; DAC**
 See also AITN 1; CA 1-4R; 41-44R;
 CANR 1, 34; DAM MST, NOV; DLB 9,
 102; MTCW; SATA 1, 25

Buckler, Ernest 1908-1984.... **CLC 13; DAC**
 See also CA 11-12; 114; CAP 1;
 DAM MST; DLB 68; SATA 47

Buckley, Vincent (Thomas)
 1925-1988 .... **CLC 57**
 See also CA 101

Buckley, William F(rank), Jr.
 1925- .... **CLC 7, 18, 37**
 See also AITN 1; CA 1-4R; CANR 1, 24;
 DAM POP; DLB 137; DLBY 80;
 INT CANR-24; MTCW

Buechner, (Carl) Frederick
 1926- .... **CLC 2, 4, 6, 9**
 See also CA 13-16R; CANR 11, 39;
 DAM NOV; DLBY 80; INT CANR-11;
 MTCW

Buell, John (Edward) 1927-........ **CLC 10**
 See also CA 1-4R; DLB 53

Buero Vallejo, Antonio 1916- ... **CLC 15, 46**
 See also CA 106; CANR 24, 49; HW;
 MTCW

Bufalino, Gesualdo 1920(?)-........ **CLC 74**

Bugayev, Boris Nikolayevich 1880-1934
 See Bely, Andrey
 See also CA 104

Bukowski, Charles
 1920-1994 .... **CLC 2, 5, 9, 41, 82**
 See also CA 17-20R; 144; CANR 40;
 DAM NOV, POET; DLB 5, 130; MTCW

Bulgakov, Mikhail (Afanas'evich)
 1891-1940 .... **TCLC 2, 16; SSC 18**
 See also CA 105; DAM DRAM, NOV

Bulgya, Alexander Alexandrovich
 1901-1956 .... **TCLC 53**
 See also Fadeyev, Alexander
 See also CA 117

Bullins, Ed 1935- .. **CLC 1, 5, 7; BLC; DC 6**
 See also BW 2; CA 49-52; CAAS 16;
 CANR 24, 46; DAM DRAM, MULT;
 DLB 7, 38; MTCW

Bulwer-Lytton, Edward (George Earle Lytton)
 1803-1873 .... **NCLC 1, 45**
 See also DLB 21

Bunin, Ivan Alexeyevich
 1870-1953 .... **TCLC 6; SSC 5**
 See also CA 104

Bunting, Basil 1900-1985.... **CLC 10, 39, 47**
 See also CA 53-56; 115; CANR 7;
 DAM POET; DLB 20

Bunuel, Luis 1900-1983 .. **CLC 16, 80; HLC**
 See also CA 101; 110; CANR 32;
 DAM MULT; HW

Bunyan, John
 1628-1688 ...... **LC 4; DA; DAB; DAC; WLC**
 See also CDBLB 1660-1789; DAM MST;
 DLB 39

Burckhardt, Jacob (Christoph)
 1818-1897 .... **NCLC 49**

Burford, Eleanor
 See Hibbert, Eleanor Alice Burford

Burgess, Anthony
 . **CLC 1, 2, 4, 5, 8, 10, 13, 15, 22, 40, 62, 81; DAB**
 See also Wilson, John (Anthony) Burgess
 See also AITN 1; CDBLB 1960 to Present;
 DLB 14

Burke, Edmund
 1729(?)-1797 .... **LC 7; DA; DAB; DAC; WLC**
 See also DAM MST; DLB 104

Burke, Kenneth (Duva)
 1897-1993 .... **CLC 2, 24**
 See also CA 5-8R; 143; CANR 39; DLB 45,
 63; MTCW

Burke, Leda
 See Garnett, David

Burke, Ralph
 See Silverberg, Robert

Burney, Fanny 1752-1840 .... **NCLC 12**
 See also DLB 39

Burns, Robert 1759-1796............ **PC 6**
 See also CDBLB 1789-1832; DA; DAB;
 DAC; DAM MST, POET; DLB 109;
 WLC

Burns, Tex
 See L'Amour, Louis (Dearborn)

Burnshaw, Stanley 1906-..... **CLC 3, 13, 44**
 See also CA 9-12R; DLB 48

Burr, Anne 1937- .... **CLC 6**
 See also CA 25-28R

Burroughs, Edgar Rice
 1875-1950 .... **TCLC 2, 32**
 See also AAYA 11; CA 104; 132;
 DAM NOV; DLB 8; MTCW; SATA 41

Burroughs, William S(eward)
 1914- .... **CLC 1, 2, 5, 15, 22, 42, 75;
 DA; DAB; DAC; WLC**
 See also AITN 2; CA 9-12R; CANR 20;
 DAM MST, NOV, POP; DLB 2, 8, 16,
 152; DLBY 81; MTCW

Burton, Richard F. 1821-1890.... **NCLC 42**
 See also DLB 55

Busch, Frederick 1941- ... **CLC 7, 10, 18, 47**
 See also CA 33-36R; CAAS 1; CANR 45;
 DLB 6

Bush, Ronald 1946- .... **CLC 34**
 See also CA 136

Bustos, F(rancisco)
 See Borges, Jorge Luis

Bustos Domecq, H(onorio)
 See Bioy Casares, Adolfo; Borges, Jorge
 Luis

Butler, Octavia E(stelle) 1947- ..... **CLC 38**
 See also BW 2; CA 73-76; CANR 12, 24,
 38; DAM MULT, POP; DLB 33;
 MTCW; SATA 84

Butler, Robert Olen (Jr.) 1945-..... **CLC 81**
 See also CA 112; DAM POP; INT 112

Butler, Samuel 1612-1680 .... **LC 16**
 See also DLB 101, 126

Butler, Samuel
 1835-1902 ...... **TCLC 1, 33; DA; DAB;
 DAC; WLC**
 See also CA 143; CDBLB 1890-1914;
 DAM MST, NOV; DLB 18, 57

Butler, Walter C.
 See Faust, Frederick (Schiller)

Butor, Michel (Marie Francois)
 1926- .... **CLC 1, 3, 8, 11, 15**
 See also CA 9-12R; CANR 33; DLB 83;
 MTCW

Buzo, Alexander (John) 1944-...... **CLC 61**
 See also CA 97-100; CANR 17, 39

Buzzati, Dino 1906-1972 .... **CLC 36**
 See also CA 33-36R

Byars, Betsy (Cromer) 1928-....... **CLC 35**
 See also CA 33-36R; CANR 18, 36; CLR 1,
 16; DLB 52; INT CANR-18; JRDA;
 MAICYA; MTCW; SAAS 1; SATA 4,
 46, 80

Byatt, A(ntonia) S(usan Drabble)
 1936-................. **CLC 19, 65**
 See also CA 13-16R; CANR 13, 33, 50;
 DAM NOV, POP; DLB 14; MTCW

Byrne, David 1952-............... **CLC 26**
 See also CA 127

Byrne, John Keyes 1926-
 See Leonard, Hugh
 See also CA 102; INT 102

Byron, George Gordon (Noel)
 1788-1824 ..... **NCLC 2, 12; DA; DAB;
 DAC; WLC**
 See also CDBLB 1789-1832; DAM MST,
 POET; DLB 96, 110

C. 3. 3.
 See Wilde, Oscar (Fingal O'Flahertie Wills)

Caballero, Fernan 1796-1877..... **NCLC 10**

Cabell, James Branch 1879-1958 ... **TCLC 6**
 See also CA 105; DLB 9, 78

Cable, George Washington
 1844-1925 .... **TCLC 4; SSC 4**
 See also CA 104; DLB 12, 74; DLBD 13

Cabral de Melo Neto, Joao 1920-... **CLC 76**
 See also DAM MULT

Cabrera Infante, G(uillermo)
 1929-............ **CLC 5, 25, 45; HLC**
 See also CA 85-88; CANR 29;
 DAM MULT; DLB 113; HW; MTCW

Cade, Toni
 See Bambara, Toni Cade

Cadmus and Harmonia
 See Buchan, John

Caedmon fl. 658-680............. **CMLC 7**
 See also DLB 146

Caeiro, Alberto
 See Pessoa, Fernando (Antonio Nogueira)

Cage, John (Milton, Jr.) 1912- ..... **CLC 41**
 See also CA 13-16R; CANR 9;
 INT CANR-9

Cain, G.
 See Cabrera Infante, G(uillermo)

Cain, Guillermo
 See Cabrera Infante, G(uillermo)

Cary, (Arthur) Joyce (Lunel)
1888-1957 . . . . **TCLC 1, 29**
See also CA 104; CDBLB 1914-1945;
DLB 15, 100

Casanova de Seingalt, Giovanni Jacopo
1725-1798 . . . . **LC 13**

Casares, Adolfo Bioy
See Bioy Casares, Adolfo

Casely-Hayford, J(oseph) E(phraim)
1866-1930 . . . . **TCLC 24; BLC**
See also BW 2; CA 123; DAM MULT

Casey, John (Dudley) 1939- . . . . **CLC 59**
See also BEST 90:2; CA 69-72; CANR 23

Casey, Michael 1947- . . . . **CLC 2**
See also CA 65-68; DLB 5

Casey, Patrick
See Thurman, Wallace (Henry)

Casey, Warren (Peter) 1935-1988 . . . **CLC 12**
See also CA 101; 127; INT 101

Casona, Alejandro . . . . **CLC 49**
See also Alvarez, Alejandro Rodriguez

Cassavetes, John 1929-1989 . . . . **CLC 20**
See also CA 85-88; 127

Cassill, R(onald) V(erlin) 1919- . . . **CLC 4, 23**
See also CA 9-12R; CAAS 1; CANR 7, 45;
DLB 6

Cassirer, Ernst 1874-1945 . . . . **TCLC 61**

Cassity, (Allen) Turner 1929- . . . . **CLC 6, 42**
See also CA 17-20R; CAAS 8; CANR 11;
DLB 105

Castaneda, Carlos 1931(?)- . . . . **CLC 12**
See also CA 25-28R; CANR 32; HW;
MTCW

Castedo, Elena 1937- . . . . **CLC 65**
See also CA 132

Castedo-Ellerman, Elena
See Castedo, Elena

Castellanos, Rosario
1925-1974 . . . . **CLC 66; HLC**
See also CA 131; 53-56; DAM MULT;
DLB 113; HW

Castelvetro, Lodovico 1505-1571 . . . . . **LC 12**

Castiglione, Baldassare 1478-1529 . . . **LC 12**

Castle, Robert
See Hamilton, Edmond

Castro, Guillen de 1569-1631 . . . . **LC 19**

Castro, Rosalia de 1837-1885 . . . . . **NCLC 3**
See also DAM MULT

Cather, Willa
See Cather, Willa Sibert

Cather, Willa Sibert
1873-1947 . . . . **TCLC 1, 11, 31; DA;
DAB; DAC; SSC 2; WLC**
See also CA 104; 128; CDALB 1865-1917;
DAM MST, NOV; DLB 9, 54, 78;
DLBD 1; MTCW; SATA 30

Catton, (Charles) Bruce
1899-1978 . . . . **CLC 35**
See also AITN 1; CA 5-8R; 81-84;
CANR 7; DLB 17; SATA 2;
SATA-Obit 24

Cauldwell, Frank
See King, Francis (Henry)

Caunitz, William J. 1933- . . . . **CLC 34**
See also BEST 89:3; CA 125; 130; INT 130

Causley, Charles (Stanley) 1917- . . . . . **CLC 7**
See also CA 9-12R; CANR 5, 35; CLR 30;
DLB 27; MTCW; SATA 3, 66

Caute, David 1936- . . . . **CLC 29**
See also CA 1-4R; CAAS 4; CANR 1, 33;
DAM NOV; DLB 14

Cavafy, C(onstantine) P(eter)
1863-1933 . . . . **TCLC 2, 7**
See also Kavafis, Konstantinos Petrou
See also CA 148; DAM POET

Cavallo, Evelyn
See Spark, Muriel (Sarah)

Cavanna, Betty . . . . **CLC 12**
See also Harrison, Elizabeth Cavanna
See also JRDA; MAICYA; SAAS 4;
SATA 1, 30

Cavendish, Margaret Lucas
1623-1673 . . . . **LC 30**
See also DLB 131

Caxton, William 1421(?)-1491(?) . . . . . **LC 17**

Cayrol, Jean 1911- . . . . **CLC 11**
See also CA 89-92; DLB 83

Cela, Camilo Jose
1916- . . . . **CLC 4, 13, 59; HLC**
See also BEST 90:2; CA 21-24R; CAAS 10;
CANR 21, 32; DAM MULT; DLBY 89;
HW; MTCW

Celan, Paul . . . . . . **CLC 10, 19, 53, 82; PC 10**
See also Antschel, Paul
See also DLB 69

Celine, Louis-Ferdinand
. . . . **CLC 1, 3, 4, 7, 9, 15, 47**
See also Destouches, Louis-Ferdinand
See also DLB 72

Cellini, Benvenuto 1500-1571 . . . . **LC 7**

Cendrars, Blaise . . . . **CLC 18**
See also Sauser-Hall, Frederic

Cernuda (y Bidon), Luis
1902-1963 . . . . **CLC 54**
See also CA 131; 89-92; DAM POET;
DLB 134; HW

Cervantes (Saavedra), Miguel de
1547-1616 . . . . **LC 6, 23; DA; DAB;
DAC; SSC 12; WLC**
See also DAM MST, NOV

Cesaire, Aime (Fernand)
1913- . . . . **CLC 19, 32; BLC**
See also BW 2; CA 65-68; CANR 24, 43;
DAM MULT, POET; MTCW

Chabon, Michael 1965(?)- . . . . **CLC 55**
See also CA 139

Chabrol, Claude 1930- . . . . **CLC 16**
See also CA 110

Challans, Mary 1905-1983
See Renault, Mary
See also CA 81-84; 111; SATA 23;
SATA-Obit 36

Challis, George
See Faust, Frederick (Schiller)

Chambers, Aidan 1934- . . . . **CLC 35**
See also CA 25-28R; CANR 12, 31; JRDA;
MAICYA; SAAS 12; SATA 1, 69

Chambers, James 1948-
See Cliff, Jimmy
See also CA 124

Chambers, Jessie
See Lawrence, D(avid) H(erbert Richards)

Chambers, Robert W. 1865-1933 . . . **TCLC 41**

Chandler, Raymond (Thornton)
1888-1959 . . . . **TCLC 1, 7**
See also CA 104; 129; CDALB 1929-1941;
DLBD 6; MTCW

Chang, Jung 1952- . . . . **CLC 71**
See also CA 142

Channing, William Ellery
1780-1842 . . . . **NCLC 17**
See also DLB 1, 59

Chaplin, Charles Spencer
1889-1977 . . . . **CLC 16**
See also Chaplin, Charlie
See also CA 81-84; 73-76

Chaplin, Charlie
See Chaplin, Charles Spencer
See also DLB 44

Chapman, George 1559(?)-1634 . . . . . . **LC 22**
See also DAM DRAM; DLB 62, 121

Chapman, Graham 1941-1989 . . . . . . **CLC 21**
See also Monty Python
See also CA 116; 129; CANR 35

Chapman, John Jay 1862-1933 . . . . . **TCLC 7**
See also CA 104

Chapman, Walker
See Silverberg, Robert

Chappell, Fred (Davis) 1936- . . . . **CLC 40, 78**
See also CA 5-8R; CAAS 4; CANR 8, 33;
DLB 6, 105

Char, Rene(-Emile)
1907-1988 . . . . **CLC 9, 11, 14, 55**
See also CA 13-16R; 124; CANR 32;
DAM POET; MTCW

Charby, Jay
See Ellison, Harlan (Jay)

Chardin, Pierre Teilhard de
See Teilhard de Chardin, (Marie Joseph)
Pierre

Charles I 1600-1649 . . . . **LC 13**

Charyn, Jerome 1937- . . . . **CLC 5, 8, 18**
See also CA 5-8R; CAAS 1; CANR 7;
DLBY 83; MTCW

Chase, Mary (Coyle) 1907-1981 . . . . . . **DC 1**
See also CA 77-80; 105; SATA 17;
SATA-Obit 29

Chase, Mary Ellen 1887-1973 . . . . **CLC 2**
See also CA 13-16; 41-44R; CAP 1;
SATA 10

Chase, Nicholas
See Hyde, Anthony

Chateaubriand, Francois Rene de
1768-1848 . . . . **NCLC 3**
See also DLB 119

Chatterje, Sarat Chandra 1876-1936(?)
See Chatterji, Saratchandra
See also CA 109

Chatterji, Bankim Chandra
1838-1894 . . . . **NCLC 19**

Conrad, Robert Arnold
See Hart, Moss

Conroy, Pat 1945-............. **CLC 30, 74**
See also AAYA 8; AITN 1; CA 85-88;
CANR 24; DAM NOV, POP; DLB 6;
MTCW

Constant (de Rebecque), (Henri) Benjamin
1767-1830 .... **NCLC 6**
See also DLB 119

Conybeare, Charles Augustus
See Eliot, T(homas) S(tearns)

Cook, Michael 1933- .... **CLC 58**
See also CA 93-96; DLB 53

Cook, Robin 1940- .... **CLC 14**
See also BEST 90:2; CA 108; 111;
CANR 41; DAM POP; INT 111

Cook, Roy
See Silverberg, Robert

Cooke, Elizabeth 1948- .... **CLC 55**
See also CA 129

Cooke, John Esten 1830-1886..... **NCLC 5**
See also DLB 3

Cooke, John Estes
See Baum, L(yman) Frank

Cooke, M. E.
See Creasey, John

Cooke, Margaret
See Creasey, John

Cooney, Ray .... **CLC 62**

Cooper, Douglas 1960- .... **CLC 86**

Cooper, Henry St. John
See Creasey, John

Cooper, J. California.............. **CLC 56**
See also AAYA 12; BW 1; CA 125;
DAM MULT

Cooper, James Fenimore
1789-1851 .... **NCLC 1, 27**
See also CDALB 1640-1865; DLB 3;
SATA 19

Coover, Robert (Lowell)
1932- .. CLC 3, 7, 15, 32, 46, 87; SSC 15
See also CA 45-48; CANR 3, 37;
DAM NOV; DLB 2; DLBY 81; MTCW

Copeland, Stewart (Armstrong)
1952- .... **CLC 26**

Coppard, A(lfred) E(dgar)
1878-1957 .... **TCLC 5; SSC 21**
See also CA 114; YABC 1

Coppee, Francois 1842-1908 ...... **TCLC 25**

Coppola, Francis Ford 1939-....... **CLC 16**
See also CA 77-80; CANR 40; DLB 44

Corbiere, Tristan 1845-1875 ..... **NCLC 43**

Corcoran, Barbara 1911-.......... **CLC 17**
See also AAYA 14; CA 21-24R; CAAS 2;
CANR 11, 28, 48; DLB 52; JRDA;
SAAS 20; SATA 3, 77

Cordelier, Maurice
See Giraudoux, (Hippolyte) Jean

Corelli, Marie 1855-1924........ **TCLC 51**
See also Mackay, Mary
See also DLB 34, 156

Corman, Cid..................... **CLC 9**
See also Corman, Sidney
See also CAAS 2; DLB 5

Corman, Sidney 1924-
See Corman, Cid
See also CA 85-88; CANR 44; DAM POET

Cormier, Robert (Edmund)
1925- ..... CLC 12, 30; DA; DAB; DAC
See also AAYA 3; CA 1-4R; CANR 5, 23;
CDALB 1968-1988; CLR 12; DAM MST,
NOV; DLB 52; INT CANR-23; JRDA;
MAICYA; MTCW; SATA 10, 45, 83

Corn, Alfred (DeWitt III) 1943-.... **CLC 33**
See also CA 104; CANR 44; DLB 120;
DLBY 80

Corneille, Pierre 1606-1684.... **LC 28; DAB**
See also DAM MST

Cornwell, David (John Moore)
1931- .... **CLC 9, 15**
See also le Carre, John
See also CA 5-8R; CANR 13, 33;
DAM POP; MTCW

Corso, (Nunzio) Gregory 1930-... **CLC 1, 11**
See also CA 5-8R; CANR 41; DLB 5, 16;
MTCW

Cortazar, Julio
1914-1984 ...... CLC 2, 3, 5, 10, 13, 15,
33, 34; HLC; SSC 7
See also CA 21-24R; CANR 12, 32;
DAM MULT, NOV; DLB 113; HW;
MTCW

CORTES, HERNAN 1484-1547..... **LC 31**

Corwin, Cecil
See Kornbluth, C(yril) M.

Cosic, Dobrica 1921- .... **CLC 14**
See also CA 122; 138

Costain, Thomas B(ertram)
1885-1965 .... **CLC 30**
See also CA 5-8R; 25-28R; DLB 9

Costantini, Humberto
1924(?)-1987 .... **CLC 49**
See also CA 131; 122; HW

Costello, Elvis 1955-.............. **CLC 21**

Cotter, Joseph Seamon Sr.
1861-1949 .... **TCLC 28; BLC**
See also BW 1; CA 124; DAM MULT;
DLB 50

Couch, Arthur Thomas Quiller
See Quiller-Couch, Arthur Thomas

Coulton, James
See Hansen, Joseph

Couperus, Louis (Marie Anne)
1863-1923 .... **TCLC 15**
See also CA 115

Coupland, Douglas 1961-..... **CLC 85; DAC**
See also CA 142; DAM POP

Court, Wesli
See Turco, Lewis (Putnam)

Courtenay, Bryce 1933-........... **CLC 59**
See also CA 138

Courtney, Robert
See Ellison, Harlan (Jay)

Cousteau, Jacques-Yves 1910-...... **CLC 30**
See also CA 65-68; CANR 15; MTCW;
SATA 38

Coward, Noel (Peirce)
1899-1973 .... **CLC 1, 9, 29, 51**
See also AITN 1; CA 17-18; 41-44R;
CANR 35; CAP 2; CDBLB 1914-1945;
DAM DRAM; DLB 10; MTCW

Cowley, Malcolm 1898-1989 .... **CLC 39**
See also CA 5-8R; 128; CANR 3; DLB 4,
48; DLBY 81, 89; MTCW

Cowper, William 1731-1800....... **NCLC 8**
See also DAM POET; DLB 104, 109

Cox, William Trevor 1928-... **CLC 9, 14, 71**
See also Trevor, William
See also CA 9-12R; CANR 4, 37;
DAM NOV; DLB 14; INT CANR-37;
MTCW

Coyne, P. J.
See Masters, Hilary

Cozzens, James Gould
1903-1978 .... **CLC 1, 4, 11**
See also CA 9-12R; 81-84; CANR 19;
CDALB 1941-1968; DLB 9; DLBD 2;
DLBY 84; MTCW

Crabbe, George 1754-1832....... **NCLC 26**
See also DLB 93

Craig, A. A.
See Anderson, Poul (William)

Craik, Dinah Maria (Mulock)
1826-1887 .... **NCLC 38**
See also DLB 35; MAICYA; SATA 34

Cram, Ralph Adams 1863-1942.... **TCLC 45**

Crane, (Harold) Hart
1899-1932 .... TCLC 2, 5; DA; DAB;
DAC; PC 3; WLC
See also CA 104; 127; CDALB 1917-1929;
DAM MST, POET; DLB 4, 48; MTCW

Crane, R(onald) S(almon)
1886-1967 .... **CLC 27**
See also CA 85-88; DLB 63

Crane, Stephen (Townley)
1871-1900 .... TCLC 11, 17, 32; DA;
DAB; DAC; SSC 7; WLC
See also CA 109; 140; CDALB 1865-1917;
DAM MST, NOV, POET; DLB 12, 54,
78; YABC 2

Crase, Douglas 1944-.............. **CLC 58**
See also CA 106

Crashaw, Richard 1612(?)-1649...... **LC 24**
See also DLB 126

Craven, Margaret
1901-1980 .... **CLC 17; DAC**
See also CA 103

Crawford, F(rancis) Marion
1854-1909 .... **TCLC 10**
See also CA 107; DLB 71

Crawford, Isabella Valancy
1850-1887 .... **NCLC 12**
See also DLB 92

Crayon, Geoffrey
See Irving, Washington

Creasey, John 1908-1973 .... **CLC 11**
See also CA 5-8R; 41-44R; CANR 8;
DLB 77; MTCW

Crebillon, Claude Prosper Jolyot de (fils)
1707-1777 .... **LC 28**

Credo
See Creasey, John

Creeley, Robert (White)
1926- ..... **CLC 1, 2, 4, 8, 11, 15, 36, 78**
See also CA 1-4R; CAAS 10; CANR 23, 43;
DAM POET; DLB 5, 16; MTCW

Crews, Harry (Eugene)
1935- .... **CLC 6, 23, 49**
See also AITN 1; CA 25-28R; CANR 20;
DLB 6, 143; MTCW

Crichton, (John) Michael
1942- .... **CLC 2, 6, 54, 90**
See also AAYA 10; AITN 2; CA 25-28R;
CANR 13, 40; DAM NOV, POP;
DLBY 81; INT CANR-13; JRDA;
MTCW; SATA 9

Crispin, Edmund .... **CLC 22**
See also Montgomery, (Robert) Bruce
See also DLB 87

Cristofer, Michael 1945(?)- .... **CLC 28**
See also CA 110; DAM DRAM; DLB 7

Croce, Benedetto 1866-1952 ...... **TCLC 37**
See also CA 120

Crockett, David 1786-1836 .... **NCLC 8**
See also DLB 3, 11

Crockett, Davy
See Crockett, David

Crofts, Freeman Wills
1879-1957 .... **TCLC 55**
See also CA 115; DLB 77

Croker, John Wilson 1780-1857 .. **NCLC 10**
See also DLB 110

Crommelynck, Fernand 1885-1970 .. **CLC 75**
See also CA 89-92

Cronin, A(rchibald) J(oseph)
1896-1981 .... **CLC 32**
See also CA 1-4R; 102; CANR 5; SATA 47;
SATA-Obit 25

Cross, Amanda
See Heilbrun, Carolyn G(old)

Crothers, Rachel 1878(?)-1958..... **TCLC 19**
See also CA 113; DLB 7

Croves, Hal
See Traven, B.

Crowfield, Christopher
See Stowe, Harriet (Elizabeth) Beecher

Crowley, Aleister.................. **TCLC 7**
See also Crowley, Edward Alexander

Crowley, Edward Alexander 1875-1947
See Crowley, Aleister
See also CA 104

Crowley, John 1942-.............. **CLC 57**
See also CA 61-64; CANR 43; DLBY 82;
SATA 65

Crud
See Crumb, R(obert)

Crumarums
See Crumb, R(obert)

Crumb, R(obert) 1943-............ **CLC 17**
See also CA 106

Crumbum
See Crumb, R(obert)

Crumski
See Crumb, R(obert)

Crum the Bum
See Crumb, R(obert)

Crunk
See Crumb, R(obert)

Crustt
See Crumb, R(obert)

Cryer, Gretchen (Kiger) 1935-...... **CLC 21**
See also CA 114; 123

Csath, Geza 1887-1919 .... **TCLC 13**
See also CA 111

Cudlip, David 1933- .... **CLC 34**

Cullen, Countee
1903-1946 ...... **TCLC 4, 37; BLC; DA;**
DAC
See also BW 1; CA 108; 124;
CDALB 1917-1929; DAM MST, MULT,
POET; DLB 4, 48, 51; MTCW; SATA 18

Cum, R.
See Crumb, R(obert)

Cummings, Bruce F(rederick) 1889-1919
See Barbellion, W. N. P.
See also CA 123

Cummings, E(dward) E(stlin)
1894-1962 ...... **CLC 1, 3, 8, 12, 15, 68;**
DA; DAB; DAC; PC 5; WLC 2
See also CA 73-76; CANR 31;
CDALB 1929-1941; DAM MST, POET;
DLB 4, 48; MTCW

Cunha, Euclides (Rodrigues Pimenta) da
1866-1909 .... **TCLC 24**
See also CA 123

Cunningham, E. V.
See Fast, Howard (Melvin)

Cunningham, J(ames) V(incent)
1911-1985 .... **CLC 3, 31**
See also CA 1-4R; 115; CANR 1; DLB 5

Cunningham, Julia (Woolfolk)
1916- .... **CLC 12**
See also CA 9-12R; CANR 4, 19, 36;
JRDA; MAICYA; SAAS 2; SATA 1, 26

Cunningham, Michael 1952- .... **CLC 34**
See also CA 136

Cunninghame Graham, R(obert) B(ontine)
1852-1936 .... **TCLC 19**
See also Graham, R(obert) B(ontine)
Cunninghame
See also CA 119; DLB 98

Currie, Ellen 19(?)-.............. **CLC 44**

Curtin, Philip
See Lowndes, Marie Adelaide (Belloc)

Curtis, Price
See Ellison, Harlan (Jay)

Cutrate, Joe
See Spiegelman, Art

Czaczkes, Shmuel Yosef
See Agnon, S(hmuel) Y(osef Halevi)

Dabrowska, Maria (Szumska)
1889-1965 .... **CLC 15**
See also CA 106

Dabydeen, David 1955-........... **CLC 34**
See also BW 1; CA 125

Dacey, Philip 1939- .... **CLC 51**
See also CA 37-40R; CAAS 17; CANR 14,
32; DLB 105

Dagerman, Stig (Halvard)
1923-1954 .... **TCLC 17**
See also CA 117

Dahl, Roald
1916-1990 ...... **CLC 1, 6, 18, 79; DAB;**
DAC
See also AAYA 15; CA 1-4R; 133;
CANR 6, 32, 37; CLR 1, 7; DAM MST,
NOV, POP; DLB 139; JRDA; MAICYA;
MTCW; SATA 1, 26, 73; SATA-Obit 65

Dahlberg, Edward 1900-1977... **CLC 1, 7, 14**
See also CA 9-12R; 69-72; CANR 31;
DLB 48; MTCW

Dale, Colin .... **TCLC 18**
See also Lawrence, T(homas) E(dward)

Dale, George E.
See Asimov, Isaac

Daly, Elizabeth 1878-1967........ **CLC 52**
See also CA 23-24; 25-28R; CAP 2

Daly, Maureen 1921-............. **CLC 17**
See also AAYA 5; CANR 37; JRDA;
MAICYA; SAAS 1; SATA 2

Damas, Leon-Gontran 1912-1978 ... **CLC 84**
See also BW 1; CA 125; 73-76

Dana, Richard Henry Sr.
1787-1879 .... **NCLC 53**

Daniel, Samuel 1562(?)-1619........ **LC 24**
See also DLB 62

Daniels, Brett
See Adler, Renata

Dannay, Frederic 1905-1982 .... **CLC 11**
See also Queen, Ellery
See also CA 1-4R; 107; CANR 1, 39;
DAM POP; DLB 137; MTCW

D'Annunzio, Gabriele
1863-1938 .... **TCLC 6, 40**
See also CA 104

d'Antibes, Germain
See Simenon, Georges (Jacques Christian)

Danvers, Dennis 1947-............. **CLC 70**

Danziger, Paula 1944- .... **CLC 21**
See also AAYA 4; CA 112; 115; CANR 37;
CLR 20; JRDA; MAICYA; SATA 36,
63; SATA-Brief 30

Da Ponte, Lorenzo 1749-1838 .... **NCLC 50**

Dario, Ruben 1867-1916 .... **TCLC 4; HLC**
See also CA 131; DAM MULT; HW;
MTCW

Darley, George 1795-1846 .... **NCLC 2**
See also DLB 96

Daryush, Elizabeth 1887-1977.... **CLC 6, 19**
See also CA 49-52; CANR 3; DLB 20

Dashwood, Edmee Elizabeth Monica de la
Pasture 1890-1943
See Delafield, E. M.
See also CA 119

Daudet, (Louis Marie) Alphonse
1840-1897 .... **NCLC 1**
See also DLB 123

Daumal, Rene 1908-1944 .... **TCLC 14**
See also CA 114

Davenport, Guy (Mattison, Jr.)
1927- .... **CLC 6, 14, 38; SSC 16**
See also CA 33-36R; CANR 23; DLB 130

Denby, Edwin (Orr) 1903-1983..... **CLC 48**
See also CA 138; 110

Denis, Julio
See Cortazar, Julio

Denmark, Harrison
See Zelazny, Roger (Joseph)

Dennis, John 1658-1734........... **LC 11**
See also DLB 101

Dennis, Nigel (Forbes) 1912-1989.... **CLC 8**
See also CA 25-28R; 129; DLB 13, 15;
MTCW

De Palma, Brian (Russell) 1940-.... **CLC 20**
See also CA 109

De Quincey, Thomas 1785-1859 ... **NCLC 4**
See also CDBLB 1789-1832; DLB 110; 144

Deren, Eleanora 1908(?)-1961
See Deren, Maya
See also CA 111

Deren, Maya .... **CLC 16**
See also Deren, Eleanora

Derleth, August (William)
1909-1971 .... **CLC 31**
See also CA 1-4R; 29-32R; CANR 4;
DLB 9; SATA 5

Der Nister 1884-1950............ **TCLC 56**

de Routisie, Albert
See Aragon, Louis

Derrida, Jacques 1930-........ **CLC 24, 87**
See also CA 124; 127

Derry Down Derry
See Lear, Edward

Dersonnes, Jacques
See Simenon, Georges (Jacques Christian)

Desai, Anita 1937- ..... **CLC 19, 37; DAB**
See also CA 81-84; CANR 33; DAM NOV;
MTCW; SATA 63

de Saint-Luc, Jean
See Glassco, John

de Saint Roman, Arnaud
See Aragon, Louis

Descartes, Rene 1596-1650 .... **LC 20**

De Sica, Vittorio 1901(?)-1974 ..... **CLC 20**
See also CA 117

Desnos, Robert 1900-1945....... **TCLC 22**
See also CA 121

Destouches, Louis-Ferdinand
1894-1961 .... **CLC 9, 15**
See Celine, Louis-Ferdinand
See also CA 85-88; CANR 28; MTCW

Deutsch, Babette 1895-1982 .... **CLC 18**
See also CA 1-4R; 108; CANR 4; DLB 45;
SATA 1; SATA-Obit 33

Devenant, William 1606-1649 .... **LC 13**

Devkota, Laxmiprasad
1909-1959 .... **TCLC 23**
See also CA 123

De Voto, Bernard (Augustine)
1897-1955 .... **TCLC 29**
See also CA 113; DLB 9

De Vries, Peter
1910-1993 .... **CLC 1, 2, 3, 7, 10, 28, 46**
See also CA 17-20R; 142; CANR 41;
DAM NOV; DLB 6; DLBY 82; MTCW

Dexter, Martin
See Faust, Frederick (Schiller)

Dexter, Pete 1943-............ **CLC 34, 55**
See also BEST 89:2; CA 127; 131;
DAM POP; INT 131; MTCW

Diamano, Silmang
See Senghor, Leopold Sedar

Diamond, Neil 1941- .... **CLC 30**
See also CA 108

Diaz del Castillo, Bernal 1496-1584 .. **LC 31**

di Bassetto, Corno
See Shaw, George Bernard

Dick, Philip K(indred)
1928-1982 .... **CLC 10, 30, 72**
See also CA 49-52; 106; CANR 2, 16;
DAM NOV, POP; DLB 8; MTCW

Dickens, Charles (John Huffam)
1812-1870 ...... **NCLC 3, 8, 18, 26, 37,
50; DA; DAB; DAC; SSC 17; WLC**
See also CDBLB 1832-1890; DAM MST,
NOV; DLB 21, 55, 70, 159; JRDA;
MAICYA; SATA 15

Dickey, James (Lafayette)
1923- .... **CLC 1, 2, 4, 7, 10, 15, 47**
See also AITN 1, 2; CA 9-12R; CABS 2;
CANR 10, 48; CDALB 1968-1988;
DAM NOV, POET, POP; DLB 5;
DLBD 7; DLBY 82, 93; INT CANR-10;
MTCW

Dickey, William 1928-1994 ...... **CLC 3, 28**
See also CA 9-12R; 145; CANR 24; DLB 5

Dickinson, Charles 1951-.......... **CLC 49**
See also CA 128

Dickinson, Emily (Elizabeth)
1830-1886 .... **NCLC 21; DA; DAB;
DAC; PC 1; WLC**
See also CDALB 1865-1917; DAM MST,
POET; DLB 1; SATA 29

Dickinson, Peter (Malcolm)
1927- .... **CLC 12, 35**
See also AAYA 9; CA 41-44R; CANR 31;
CLR 29; DLB 87, 161; JRDA; MAICYA;
SATA 5, 62

Dickson, Carr
See Carr, John Dickson

Dickson, Carter
See Carr, John Dickson

Diderot, Denis 1713-1784 .... **LC 26**

Didion, Joan 1934-..... **CLC 1, 3, 8, 14, 32**
See also AITN 1; CA 5-8R; CANR 14;
CDALB 1968-1988; DAM NOV; DLB 2;
DLBY 81, 86; MTCW

Dietrich, Robert
See Hunt, E(verette) Howard, (Jr.)

Dillard, Annie 1945-............ **CLC 9, 60**
See also AAYA 6; CA 49-52; CANR 3, 43;
DAM NOV; DLBY 80; MTCW;
SATA 10

Dillard, R(ichard) H(enry) W(ilde)
1937- .... **CLC 5**
See also CA 21-24R; CAAS 7; CANR 10;
DLB 5

Dillon, Eilis 1920-1994............ **CLC 17**
See also CA 9-12R; 147; CAAS 3; CANR 4,
38; CLR 26; MAICYA; SATA 2, 74;
SATA-Obit 83

Dimont, Penelope
See Mortimer, Penelope (Ruth)

Dinesen, Isak........... **CLC 10, 29; SSC 7**
See also Blixen, Karen (Christentze
Dinesen)

Ding Ling....................... **CLC 68**
See also Chiang Pin-chin

Disch, Thomas M(ichael) 1940-... **CLC 7, 36**
See also AAYA 17; CA 21-24R; CAAS 4;
CANR 17, 36; CLR 18; DLB 8;
MAICYA; MTCW; SAAS 15; SATA 54

Disch, Tom
See Disch, Thomas M(ichael)

d'Isly, Georges
See Simenon, Georges (Jacques Christian)

Disraeli, Benjamin 1804-1881 .. **NCLC 2, 39**
See also DLB 21, 55

Ditcum, Steve
See Crumb, R(obert)

Dixon, Paige
See Corcoran, Barbara

Dixon, Stephen 1936-..... **CLC 52; SSC 16**
See also CA 89-92; CANR 17, 40; DLB 130

Dobell, Sydney Thompson
1824-1874 .... **NCLC 43**
See also DLB 32

Doblin, Alfred .... **TCLC 13**
See also Doeblin, Alfred

Dobrolyubov, Nikolai Alexandrovich
1836-1861 .... **NCLC 5**

Dobyns, Stephen 1941-............ **CLC 37**
See also CA 45-48; CANR 2, 18

Doctorow, E(dgar) L(aurence)
1931- ...... **CLC 6, 11, 15, 18, 37, 44, 65**
See also AITN 2; BEST 89:3; CA 45-48;
CANR 2, 33; CDALB 1968-1988;
DAM NOV, POP; DLB 2, 28; DLBY 80;
MTCW

Dodgson, Charles Lutwidge 1832-1898
See Carroll, Lewis
See also CLR 2; DA; DAB; DAC;
DAM MST, NOV, POET; MAICYA;
YABC 2

Dodson, Owen (Vincent)
1914-1983 .... **CLC 79; BLC**
See also BW 1; CA 65-68; 110; CANR 24;
DAM MULT; DLB 76

Doeblin, Alfred 1878-1957........ **TCLC 13**
See also Doblin, Alfred
See also CA 110; 141; DLB 66

Doerr, Harriet 1910-............. **CLC 34**
See also CA 117; 122; CANR 47; INT 122

Domecq, H(onorio) Bustos
See Bioy Casares, Adolfo; Borges, Jorge
Luis

Domini, Rey
See Lorde, Audre (Geraldine)

Dominique
See Proust, (Valentin-Louis-George-Eugene-)
Marcel

Don, A
See Stephen, Leslie

Donaldson, Stephen R. 1947-....... **CLC 46**
See also CA 89-92; CANR 13; DAM POP;
INT CANR-13

Dujardin, Edouard (Emile Louis)
1861-1949 .... **TCLC 13**
See also CA 109; DLB 123

Dumas, Alexandre (Davy de la Pailleterie)
1802-1870 ...... **NCLC 11; DA; DAB;**
DAC; WLC
See also DAM MST, NOV; DLB 119;
SATA 18

Dumas, Alexandre
1824-1895 .... **NCLC 9; DC 1**

Dumas, Claudine
See Malzberg, Barry N(athaniel)

Dumas, Henry L. 1934-1968 ..... **CLC 6, 62**
See also BW 1; CA 85-88; DLB 41

du Maurier, Daphne
1907-1989 .... **CLC 6, 11, 59; DAB;**
DAC; SSC 18
See also CA 5-8R; 128; CANR 6;
DAM MST, POP; MTCW; SATA 27;
SATA-Obit 60

Dunbar, Paul Laurence
1872-1906 ...... **TCLC 2, 12; BLC; DA;**
DAC; PC 5; SSC 8; WLC
See also BW 1; CA 104; 124;
CDALB 1865-1917; DAM MST, MULT,
POET; DLB 50, 54, 78; SATA 34

Dunbar, William 1460(?)-1530(?) .... **LC 20**
See also DLB 132, 146

Duncan, Lois 1934- .... **CLC 26**
See also AAYA 4; CA 1-4R; CANR 2, 23,
36; CLR 29; JRDA; MAICYA; SAAS 2;
SATA 1, 36, 75

Duncan, Robert (Edward)
1919-1988 .... **CLC 1, 2, 4, 7, 15, 41, 55;**
PC 2
See also CA 9-12R; 124; CANR 28;
DAM POET; DLB 5, 16; MTCW

Duncan, Sara Jeannette
1861-1922 .... **TCLC 60**
See also DLB 92

Dunlap, William 1766-1839 .... **NCLC 2**
See also DLB 30, 37, 59

Dunn, Douglas (Eaglesham)
1942- .... **CLC 6, 40**
See also CA 45-48; CANR 2, 33; DLB 40;
MTCW

Dunn, Katherine (Karen) 1945- ..... **CLC 71**
See also CA 33-36R

Dunn, Stephen 1939- .... **CLC 36**
See also CA 33-36R; CANR 12, 48;
DLB 105

Dunne, Finley Peter 1867-1936 .... **TCLC 28**
See also CA 108; DLB 11, 23

Dunne, John Gregory 1932- .... **CLC 28**
See also CA 25-28R; CANR 14, 50;
DLBY 80

Dunsany, Edward John Moreton Drax
Plunkett 1878-1957
See Dunsany, Lord
See also CA 104; 148; DLB 10

Dunsany, Lord .... **TCLC 2, 59**
See also Dunsany, Edward John Moreton
Drax Plunkett
See also DLB 77, 153, 156

du Perry, Jean
See Simenon, Georges (Jacques Christian)

Durang, Christopher (Ferdinand)
1949- .... **CLC 27, 38**
See also CA 105; CANR 50

Duras, Marguerite
1914- ..... **CLC 3, 6, 11, 20, 34, 40, 68**
See also CA 25-28R; CANR 50; DLB 83;
MTCW

Durban, (Rosa) Pam 1947- .... **CLC 39**
See also CA 123

Durcan, Paul 1944- .... **CLC 43, 70**
See also CA 134; DAM POET

Durkheim, Emile 1858-1917 ...... **TCLC 55**

Durrell, Lawrence (George)
1912-1990 .... **CLC 1, 4, 6, 8, 13, 27, 41**
See also CA 9-12R; 132; CANR 40;
CDBLB 1945-1960; DAM NOV; DLB 15,
27; DLBY 90; MTCW

Durrenmatt, Friedrich
See Duerrenmatt, Friedrich

Dutt, Toru 1856-1877 .... **NCLC 29**

Dwight, Timothy 1752-1817 ..... **NCLC 13**
See also DLB 37

Dworkin, Andrea 1946- .... **CLC 43**
See also CA 77-80; CAAS 21; CANR 16,
39; INT CNAR-16; MTCW

Dwyer, Deanna
See Koontz, Dean R(ay)

Dwyer, K. R.
See Koontz, Dean R(ay)

Dylan, Bob 1941- ...... **CLC 3, 4, 6, 12, 77**
See also CA 41-44R; DLB 16

Eagleton, Terence (Francis) 1943-
See Eagleton, Terry
See also CA 57-60; CANR 7, 23; MTCW

Eagleton, Terry .... **CLC 63**
See also Eagleton, Terence (Francis)

Early, Jack
See Scoppettone, Sandra

East, Michael
See West, Morris L(anglo)

Eastaway, Edward
See Thomas, (Philip) Edward

Eastlake, William (Derry) 1917- ..... **CLC 8**
See also CA 5-8R; CAAS 1; CANR 5;
DLB 6; INT CANR-5

Eastman, Charles A(lexander)
1858-1939 .... **TCLC 55**
See also DAM MULT; NNAL; YABC 1

Eberhart, Richard (Ghormley)
1904- .... **CLC 3, 11, 19, 56**
See also CA 1-4R; CANR 2;
CDALB 1941-1968; DAM POET;
DLB 48; MTCW

Eberstadt, Fernanda 1960- .... **CLC 39**
See also CA 136

Echegaray (y Eizaguirre), Jose (Maria Waldo)
1832-1916 .... **TCLC 4**
See also CA 104; CANR 32; HW; MTCW

Echeverria, (Jose) Esteban (Antonino)
1805-1851 .... **NCLC 18**

Echo
See Proust, (Valentin-Louis-George-Eugene-)
Marcel

Eckert, Allan W. 1931- .... **CLC 17**
See also CA 13-16R; CANR 14, 45;
INT CANR-14; SAAS 21; SATA 29;
SATA-Brief 27

Eckhart, Meister 1260(?)-1328(?) .. **CMLC 9**
See also DLB 115

Eckmar, F. R.
See de Hartog, Jan

Eco, Umberto 1932- .... **CLC 28, 60**
See also BEST 90:1; CA 77-80; CANR 12,
33; DAM NOV, POP; MTCW

Eddison, E(ric) R(ucker)
1882-1945 .... **TCLC 15**
See also CA 109

Edel, (Joseph) Leon 1907- ...... **CLC 29, 34**
See also CA 1-4R; CANR 1, 22; DLB 103;
INT CANR-22

Eden, Emily 1797-1869 .... **NCLC 10**

Edgar, David 1948- .... **CLC 42**
See also CA 57-60; CANR 12;
DAM DRAM; DLB 13; MTCW

Edgerton, Clyde (Carlyle) 1944- .... **CLC 39**
See also AAYA 17; CA 118; 134; INT 134

Edgeworth, Maria 1768-1849 ... **NCLC 1, 51**
See also DLB 116, 159; SATA 21

Edmonds, Paul
See Kuttner, Henry

Edmonds, Walter D(umaux) 1903- .. **CLC 35**
See also CA 5-8R; CANR 2; DLB 9;
MAICYA; SAAS 4; SATA 1, 27

Edmondson, Wallace
See Ellison, Harlan (Jay)

Edson, Russell .... **CLC 13**
See also CA 33-36R

Edwards, Bronwen Elizabeth
See Rose, Wendy

Edwards, G(erald) B(asil)
1899-1976 .... **CLC 25**
See also CA 110

Edwards, Gus 1939- .... **CLC 43**
See also CA 108; INT 108

Edwards, Jonathan
1703-1758 .... **LC 7; DA; DAC**
See also DAM MST; DLB 24

Efron, Marina Ivanovna Tsvetaeva
See Tsvetaeva (Efron), Marina (Ivanovna)

Ehle, John (Marsden, Jr.) 1925- .... **CLC 27**
See also CA 9-12R

Ehrenbourg, Ilya (Grigoryevich)
See Ehrenburg, Ilya (Grigoryevich)

Ehrenburg, Ilya (Grigoryevich)
1891-1967 .... **CLC 18, 34, 62**
See also CA 102; 25-28R

Ehrenburg, Ilyo (Grigoryevich)
See Ehrenburg, Ilya (Grigoryevich)

Eich, Guenter 1907-1972 .... **CLC 15**
See also CA 111; 93-96; DLB 69, 124

Eichendorff, Joseph Freiherr von
1788-1857 .... **NCLC 8**
See also DLB 90

Eigner, Larry .... **CLC 9**
See also Eigner, Laurence (Joel)
See also DLB 5

Espriella, Don Manuel Alvarez
See Southey, Robert

Espriu, Salvador 1913-1985 . . . . **CLC 9**
See also CA 115; DLB 134

Espronceda, Jose de 1808-1842 . . . **NCLC 39**

Esse, James
See Stephens, James

Esterbrook, Tom
See Hubbard, L(afayette) Ron(ald)

Estleman, Loren D. 1952- . . . . **CLC 48**
See also CA 85-88; CANR 27; DAM NOV,
POP; INT CANR-27; MTCW

Eugenides, Jeffrey 1960(?)- . . . . **CLC 81**
See also CA 144

Euripides c. 485B.C.-406B.C. . . . . **DC 4**
See also DA; DAB; DAC; DAM DRAM,
MST

Evan, Evin
See Faust, Frederick (Schiller)

Evans, Evan
See Faust, Frederick (Schiller)

Evans, Marian
See Eliot, George

Evans, Mary Ann
See Eliot, George

Evarts, Esther
See Benson, Sally

Everett, Percival L. 1956- . . . . **CLC 57**
See also BW 2; CA 129

Everson, R(onald) G(ilmour)
1903- . . . . **CLC 27**
See also CA 17-20R; DLB 88

Everson, William (Oliver)
1912-1994 . . . . **CLC 1, 5, 14**
See also CA 9-12R; 145; CANR 20; DLB 5,
16; MTCW

Evtushenko, Evgenii Aleksandrovich
See Yevtushenko, Yevgeny (Alexandrovich)

Ewart, Gavin (Buchanan)
1916- . . . . **CLC 13, 46**
See also CA 89-92; CANR 17, 46; DLB 40;
MTCW

Ewers, Hanns Heinz 1871-1943 . . . **TCLC 12**
See also CA 109; 149

Ewing, Frederick R.
See Sturgeon, Theodore (Hamilton)

Exley, Frederick (Earl)
1929-1992 . . . . **CLC 6, 11**
See also AITN 2; CA 81-84; 138; DLB 143;
DLBY 81

Eynhardt, Guillermo
See Quiroga, Horacio (Sylvestre)

Ezekiel, Nissim 1924- . . . . **CLC 61**
See also CA 61-64

Ezekiel, Tish O'Dowd 1943- . . . . **CLC 34**
See also CA 129

Fadeyev, A.
See Bulgya, Alexander Alexandrovich

Fadeyev, Alexander . . . . **TCLC 53**
See also Bulgya, Alexander Alexandrovich

Fagen, Donald 1948- . . . . **CLC 26**

Fainzilberg, Ilya Arnoldovich 1897-1937
See Ilf, Ilya
See also CA 120

Fair, Ronald L. 1932- . . . . **CLC 18**
See also BW 1; CA 69-72; CANR 25;
DLB 33

Fairbairns, Zoe (Ann) 1948- . . . . **CLC 32**
See also CA 103; CANR 21

Falco, Gian
See Papini, Giovanni

Falconer, James
See Kirkup, James

Falconer, Kenneth
See Kornbluth, C(yril) M.

Falkland, Samuel
See Heijermans, Herman

Fallaci, Oriana 1930- . . . . **CLC 11**
See also CA 77-80; CANR 15; MTCW

Faludy, George 1913- . . . . **CLC 42**
See also CA 21-24R

Faludy, Gyoergy
See Faludy, George

Fanon, Frantz 1925-1961 . . . . . **CLC 74; BLC**
See also BW 1; CA 116; 89-92;
DAM MULT

Fanshawe, Ann 1625-1680 . . . . **LC 11**

Fante, John (Thomas) 1911-1983 . . . **CLC 60**
See also CA 69-72; 109; CANR 23;
DLB 130; DLBY 83

Farah, Nuruddin 1945- . . . . **CLC 53; BLC**
See also BW 2; CA 106; DAM MULT;
DLB 125

Fargue, Leon-Paul 1876(?)-1947 . . . **TCLC 11**
See also CA 109

Farigoule, Louis
See Romains, Jules

Farina, Richard 1936(?)-1966 . . . . **CLC 9**
See also CA 81-84; 25-28R

Farley, Walter (Lorimer)
1915-1989 . . . . **CLC 17**
See also CA 17-20R; CANR 8, 29; DLB 22;
JRDA; MAICYA; SATA 2, 43

Farmer, Philip Jose 1918- . . . . **CLC 1, 19**
See also CA 1-4R; CANR 4, 35; DLB 8;
MTCW

Farquhar, George 1677-1707 . . . . **LC 21**
See also DAM DRAM; DLB 84

Farrell, J(ames) G(ordon)
1935-1979 . . . . **CLC 6**
See also CA 73-76; 89-92; CANR 36;
DLB 14; MTCW

Farrell, James T(homas)
1904-1979 . . . . **CLC 1, 4, 8, 11, 66**
See also CA 5-8R; 89-92; CANR 9; DLB 4,
9, 86; DLBD 2; MTCW

Farren, Richard J.
See Betjeman, John

Farren, Richard M.
See Betjeman, John

Fassbinder, Rainer Werner
1946-1982 . . . . **CLC 20**
See also CA 93-96; 106; CANR 31

Fast, Howard (Melvin) 1914- . . . . . . **CLC 23**
See also AAYA 16; CA 1-4R; CAAS 18;
CANR 1, 33; DAM NOV; DLB 9;
INT CANR-33; SATA 7

Faulcon, Robert
See Holdstock, Robert P.

Faulkner, William (Cuthbert)
1897-1962 . . . . . **CLC 1, 3, 6, 8, 9, 11, 14,
18, 28, 52, 68; DA; DAB; DAC; SSC 1;
WLC**
See also AAYA 7; CA 81-84; CANR 33;
CDALB 1929-1941; DAM MST, NOV;
DLB 9, 11, 44, 102; DLBD 2; DLBY 86;
MTCW

Fauset, Jessie Redmon
1884(?)-1961 . . . . **CLC 19, 54; BLC**
See also BW 1; CA 109; DAM MULT;
DLB 51

Faust, Frederick (Schiller)
1892-1944(?) . . . . **TCLC 49**
See also CA 108; DAM POP

Faust, Irvin 1924- . . . . **CLC 8**
See also CA 33-36R; CANR 28; DLB 2, 28;
DLBY 80

Fawkes, Guy
See Benchley, Robert (Charles)

Fearing, Kenneth (Flexner)
1902-1961 . . . . **CLC 51**
See also CA 93-96; DLB 9

Fecamps, Elise
See Creasey, John

Federman, Raymond 1928- . . . . . . **CLC 6, 47**
See also CA 17-20R; CAAS 8; CANR 10,
43; DLBY 80

Federspiel, J(uerg) F. 1931- . . . . **CLC 42**
See also CA 146

Feiffer, Jules (Ralph) 1929- . . . . **CLC 2, 8, 64**
See also AAYA 3; CA 17-20R; CANR 30;
DAM DRAM; DLB 7, 44;
INT CANR-30; MTCW; SATA 8, 61

Feige, Hermann Albert Otto Maximilian
See Traven, B.

Feinberg, David B. 1956-1994 . . . . . . **CLC 59**
See also CA 135; 147

Feinstein, Elaine 1930- . . . . **CLC 36**
See also CA 69-72; CAAS 1; CANR 31;
DLB 14, 40; MTCW

Feldman, Irving (Mordecai) 1928- . . . . **CLC 7**
See also CA 1-4R; CANR 1

Fellini, Federico 1920-1993 . . . . . **CLC 16, 85**
See also CA 65-68; 143; CANR 33

Felsen, Henry Gregor 1916- . . . . **CLC 17**
See also CA 1-4R; CANR 1; SAAS 2;
SATA 1

Fenton, James Martin 1949- . . . . **CLC 32**
See also CA 102; DLB 40

Ferber, Edna 1887-1968 . . . . **CLC 18**
See also AITN 1; CA 5-8R; 25-28R; DLB 9,
28, 86; MTCW; SATA 7

Ferguson, Helen
See Kavan, Anna

Ferguson, Samuel 1810-1886 . . . . . **NCLC 33**
See also DLB 32

Fergusson, Robert 1750-1774 . . . . **LC 29**
See also DLB 109

Forster, E(dward) M(organ)
1879-1970 . . . . . **CLC 1, 2, 3, 4, 9, 10, 13, 15, 22, 45, 77; DA; DAB; DAC; WLC**
See also AAYA 2; CA 13-14; 25-28R; CANR 45; CAP 1; CDBLB 1914-1945; DAM MST, NOV; DLB 34, 98; DLBD 10; MTCW; SATA 57

Forster, John 1812-1876 . . . . **NCLC 11**
See also DLB 144

Forsyth, Frederick 1938- . . . . . . **CLC 2, 5, 36**
See also BEST 89:4; CA 85-88; CANR 38; DAM NOV, POP; DLB 87; MTCW

Forten, Charlotte L. . . . . **TCLC 16; BLC**
See also Grimke, Charlotte L(ottie) Forten
See also DLB 50

Foscolo, Ugo 1778-1827 . . . . **NCLC 8**

Fosse, Bob . . . . **CLC 20**
See also Fosse, Robert Louis

Fosse, Robert Louis 1927-1987
See Fosse, Bob
See also CA 110; 123

Foster, Stephen Collins
1826-1864 . . . . **NCLC 26**

Foucault, Michel
1926-1984 . . . . **CLC 31, 34, 69**
See also CA 105; 113; CANR 34; MTCW

Fouque, Friedrich (Heinrich Karl) de la Motte
1777-1843 . . . . **NCLC 2**
See also DLB 90

Fourier, Charles 1772-1837 . . . . . . **NCLC 51**

Fournier, Henri Alban 1886-1914
See Alain-Fournier
See also CA 104

Fournier, Pierre 1916- . . . . **CLC 11**
See also Gascar, Pierre
See also CA 89-92; CANR 16, 40

Fowles, John
1926- . . . . . . **CLC 1, 2, 3, 4, 6, 9, 10, 15, 33, 87; DAB; DAC**
See also CA 5-8R; CANR 25; CDBLB 1960 to Present; DAM MST; DLB 14, 139; MTCW; SATA 22

Fox, Paula 1923- . . . . **CLC 2, 8**
See also AAYA 3; CA 73-76; CANR 20, 36; CLR 1; DLB 52; JRDA; MAICYA; MTCW; SATA 17, 60

Fox, William Price (Jr.) 1926- . . . . . **CLC 22**
See also CA 17-20R; CAAS 19; CANR 11; DLB 2; DLBY 81

Foxe, John 1516(?)-1587 . . . . **LC 14**

Frame, Janet . . . . **CLC 2, 3, 6, 22, 66**
See also Clutha, Janet Paterson Frame

France, Anatole . . . . **TCLC 9**
See also Thibault, Jacques Anatole Francois
See also DLB 123

Francis, Claude 19(?)- . . . . **CLC 50**

Francis, Dick 1920- . . . . **CLC 2, 22, 42**
See also AAYA 5; BEST 89:3; CA 5-8R; CANR 9, 42; CDBLB 1960 to Present; DAM POP; DLB 87; INT CANR-9; MTCW

Francis, Robert (Churchill)
1901-1987 . . . . **CLC 15**
See also CA 1-4R; 123; CANR 1

Frank, Anne(lies Marie)
1929-1945 . . . . **TCLC 17; DA; DAB; DAC; WLC**
See also AAYA 12; CA 113; 133; DAM MST; MTCW; SATA-Brief 42

Frank, Elizabeth 1945- . . . . **CLC 39**
See also CA 121; 126; INT 126

Franklin, Benjamin
See Hasek, Jaroslav (Matej Frantisek)

Franklin, Benjamin
1706-1790 . . . . . **LC 25; DA; DAB; DAC**
See also CDALB 1640-1865; DAM MST; DLB 24, 43, 73

Franklin, (Stella Maraia Sarah) Miles
1879-1954 . . . . **TCLC 7**
See also CA 104

Fraser, (Lady) Antonia (Pakenham)
1932- . . . . **CLC 32**
See also CA 85-88; CANR 44; MTCW; SATA-Brief 32

Fraser, George MacDonald 1925- . . . . **CLC 7**
See also CA 45-48; CANR 2, 48

Fraser, Sylvia 1935- . . . . **CLC 64**
See also CA 45-48; CANR 1, 16

Frayn, Michael 1933- . . . . . . **CLC 3, 7, 31, 47**
See also CA 5-8R; CANR 30; DAM DRAM, NOV; DLB 13, 14; MTCW

Fraze, Candida (Merrill) 1945- . . . . . **CLC 50**
See also CA 126

Frazer, J(ames) G(eorge)
1854-1941 . . . . **TCLC 32**
See also CA 118

Frazer, Robert Caine
See Creasey, John

Frazer, Sir James George
See Frazer, J(ames) G(eorge)

Frazier, Ian 1951- . . . . **CLC 46**
See also CA 130

Frederic, Harold 1856-1898 . . . . . . **NCLC 10**
See also DLB 12, 23; DLBD 13

Frederick, John
See Faust, Frederick (Schiller)

Frederick the Great 1712-1786 . . . . . . **LC 14**

Fredro, Aleksander 1793-1876 . . . . . **NCLC 8**

Freeling, Nicolas 1927- . . . . **CLC 38**
See also CA 49-52; CAAS 12; CANR 1, 17, 50; DLB 87

Freeman, Douglas Southall
1886-1953 . . . . **TCLC 11**
See also CA 109; DLB 17

Freeman, Judith 1946- . . . . **CLC 55**
See also CA 148

Freeman, Mary Eleanor Wilkins
1852-1930 . . . . **TCLC 9; SSC 1**
See also CA 106; DLB 12, 78

Freeman, R(ichard) Austin
1862-1943 . . . . **TCLC 21**
See also CA 113; DLB 70

French, Albert 1943- . . . . **CLC 86**

French, Marilyn 1929- . . . . . . **CLC 10, 18, 60**
See also CA 69-72; CANR 3, 31; DAM DRAM, NOV, POP; INT CANR-31; MTCW

French, Paul
See Asimov, Isaac

Freneau, Philip Morin 1752-1832 . . **NCLC 1**
See also DLB 37, 43

Freud, Sigmund 1856-1939 . . . . **TCLC 52**
See also CA 115; 133; MTCW

Friedan, Betty (Naomi) 1921- . . . . . . **CLC 74**
See also CA 65-68; CANR 18, 45; MTCW

Friedlaender, Saul 1932- . . . . **CLC 90**
See also CA 117; 130

Friedman, B(ernard) H(arper)
1926- . . . . **CLC 7**
See also CA 1-4R; CANR 3, 48

Friedman, Bruce Jay 1930- . . . . **CLC 3, 5, 56**
See also CA 9-12R; CANR 25; DLB 2, 28; INT CANR-25

Friel, Brian 1929- . . . . **CLC 5, 42, 59**
See also CA 21-24R; CANR 33; DLB 13; MTCW

Friis-Baastad, Babbis Ellinor
1921-1970 . . . . **CLC 12**
See also CA 17-20R; 134; SATA 7

Frisch, Max (Rudolf)
1911-1991 . . . . . **CLC 3, 9, 14, 18, 32, 44**
See also CA 85-88; 134; CANR 32; DAM DRAM, NOV; DLB 69, 124; MTCW

Fromentin, Eugene (Samuel Auguste)
1820-1876 . . . . **NCLC 10**
See also DLB 123

Frost, Frederick
See Faust, Frederick (Schiller)

Frost, Robert (Lee)
1874-1963 . . . . **CLC 1, 3, 4, 9, 10, 13, 15, 26, 34, 44; DA; DAB; DAC; PC 1; WLC**
See also CA 89-92; CANR 33; CDALB 1917-1929; DAM MST, POET; DLB 54; DLBD 7; MTCW; SATA 14

Froude, James Anthony
1818-1894 . . . . **NCLC 43**
See also DLB 18, 57, 144

Froy, Herald
See Waterhouse, Keith (Spencer)

Fry, Christopher 1907- . . . . **CLC 2, 10, 14**
See also CA 17-20R; CANR 9, 30; DAM DRAM; DLB 13; MTCW; SATA 66

Frye, (Herman) Northrop
1912-1991 . . . . **CLC 24, 70**
See also CA 5-8R; 133; CANR 8, 37; DLB 67, 68; MTCW

Fuchs, Daniel 1909-1993 . . . . **CLC 8, 22**
See also CA 81-84; 142; CAAS 5; CANR 40; DLB 9, 26, 28; DLBY 93

Fuchs, Daniel 1934- . . . . **CLC 34**
See also CA 37-40R; CANR 14, 48

Fuentes, Carlos
1928- . . . . . . **CLC 3, 8, 10, 13, 22, 41, 60; DA; DAB; DAC; HLC; WLC**
See also AAYA 4; AITN 2; CA 69-72; CANR 10, 32; DAM MST, MULT, NOV; DLB 113; HW; MTCW

Fuentes, Gregorio Lopez y
See Lopez y Fuentes, Gregorio

Fugard, (Harold) Athol
1932- .... **CLC 5, 9, 14, 25, 40, 80; DC 3**
See also AAYA 17; CA 85-88; CANR 32;
DAM DRAM; MTCW

Fugard, Sheila 1932- .... **CLC 48**
See also CA 125

Fuller, Charles (H., Jr.)
1939- .... **CLC 25; BLC; DC 1**
See also BW 2; CA 108; 112;
DAM DRAM, MULT; DLB 38;
INT 112; MTCW

Fuller, John (Leopold) 1937-....... **CLC 62**
See also CA 21-24R; CANR 9, 44; DLB 40

Fuller, Margaret .... **NCLC 5, 50**
See also Ossoli, Sarah Margaret (Fuller
marchesa d')

Fuller, Roy (Broadbent)
1912-1991 .... **CLC 4, 28**
See also CA 5-8R; 135; CAAS 10; DLB 15,
20

Fulton, Alice 1952-.............. **CLC 52**
See also CA 116

Furphy, Joseph 1843-1912....... **TCLC 25**

Fussell, Paul 1924-............... **CLC 74**
See also BEST 90:1; CA 17-20R; CANR 8,
21, 35; INT CANR-21; MTCW

Futabatei, Shimei 1864-1909...... **TCLC 44**

Futrelle, Jacques 1875-1912 ...... **TCLC 19**
See also CA 113

Gaboriau, Emile 1835-1873...... **NCLC 14**

Gadda, Carlo Emilio 1893-1973 .... **CLC 11**
See also CA 89-92

Gaddis, William
1922- ..... **CLC 1, 3, 6, 8, 10, 19, 43, 86**
See also CA 17-20R; CANR 21, 48; DLB 2;
MTCW

Gaines, Ernest J(ames)
1933-........ **CLC 3, 11, 18, 86; BLC**
See also AITN 1; BW 2; CA 9-12R;
CANR 6, 24, 42; CDALB 1968-1988;
DAM MULT; DLB 2, 33, 152; DLBY 80;
MTCW

Gaitskill, Mary 1954-............ **CLC 69**
See also CA 128

Galdos, Benito Perez
See Perez Galdos, Benito

Gale, Zona 1874-1938 .... **TCLC 7**
See also CA 105; DAM DRAM; DLB 9, 78

Galeano, Eduardo (Hughes) 1940-... **CLC 72**
See also CA 29-32R; CANR 13, 32; HW

Galiano, Juan Valera y Alcala
See Valera y Alcala-Galiano, Juan

Gallagher, Tess 1943-.... **CLC 18, 63; PC 9**
See also CA 106; DAM POET; DLB 120

Gallant, Mavis
1922- ...... **CLC 7, 18, 38; DAC; SSC 5**
See also CA 69-72; CANR 29; DAM MST;
DLB 53; MTCW

Gallant, Roy A(rthur) 1924- .... **CLC 17**
See also CA 5-8R; CANR 4, 29; CLR 30;
MAICYA; SATA 4, 68

Gallico, Paul (William) 1897-1976 ... **CLC 2**
See also AITN 1; CA 5-8R; 69-72;
CANR 23; DLB 9; MAICYA; SATA 13

Gallup, Ralph
See Whitemore, Hugh (John)

Galsworthy, John
1867-1933 ...... **TCLC 1, 45; DA; DAB;**
DAC; WLC 2
See also CA 104; 141; CDBLB 1890-1914;
DAM DRAM, MST, NOV; DLB 10, 34,
98

Galt, John 1779-1839............ **NCLC 1**
See also DLB 99, 116, 159

Galvin, James 1951-.............. **CLC 38**
See also CA 108; CANR 26

Gamboa, Federico 1864-1939...... **TCLC 36**

Gandhi, M. K.
See Gandhi, Mohandas Karamchand

Gandhi, Mahatma
See Gandhi, Mohandas Karamchand

Gandhi, Mohandas Karamchand
1869-1948 .... **TCLC 59**
See also CA 121; 132; DAM MULT;
MTCW

Gann, Ernest Kellogg 1910-1991.... **CLC 23**
See also AITN 1; CA 1-4R; 136; CANR 1

Garcia, Cristina 1958- .... **CLC 76**
See also CA 141

Garcia Lorca, Federico
1898-1936 ... **TCLC 1, 7, 49; DA; DAB;**
DAC; DC 2; HLC; PC 3; WLC
See also CA 104; 131; DAM DRAM, MST,
MULT, POET; DLB 108; HW; MTCW

Garcia Marquez, Gabriel (Jose)
1928- .... **CLC 2, 3, 8, 10, 15, 27, 47, 55,**
68; DA; DAB; DAC; HLC; SSC 8; WLC
See also AAYA 3; BEST 89:1, 90:4;
CA 33-36R; CANR 10, 28, 50;
DAM MST, MULT, NOV, POP;
DLB 113; HW; MTCW

Gard, Janice
See Latham, Jean Lee

Gard, Roger Martin du
See Martin du Gard, Roger

Gardam, Jane 1928-.............. **CLC 43**
See also CA 49-52; CANR 2, 18, 33;
CLR 12; DLB 14, 161; MAICYA;
MTCW; SAAS 9; SATA 39, 76;
SATA-Brief 28

Gardner, Herb.................. **CLC 44**

Gardner, John (Champlin), Jr.
1933-1982 ..... **CLC 2, 3, 5, 7, 8, 10, 18,**
28, 34; SSC 7
See also AITN 1; CA 65-68; 107;
CANR 33; DAM NOV, POP; DLB 2;
DLBY 82; MTCW; SATA 40;
SATA-Obit 31

Gardner, John (Edmund) 1926-..... **CLC 30**
See also CA 103; CANR 15; DAM POP;
MTCW

Gardner, Noel
See Kuttner, Henry

Gardons, S. S.
See Snodgrass, W(illiam) D(e Witt)

Garfield, Leon 1921-.............. **CLC 12**
See also AAYA 8; CA 17-20R; CANR 38,
41; CLR 21; DLB 161; JRDA; MAICYA;
SATA 1, 32, 76

Garland, (Hannibal) Hamlin
1860-1940 .... **TCLC 3; SSC 18**
See also CA 104; DLB 12, 71, 78

Garneau, (Hector de) Saint-Denys
1912-1943 .... **TCLC 13**
See also CA 111; DLB 88

Garner, Alan 1934-.......... **CLC 17; DAB**
See also CA 73-76; CANR 15; CLR 20;
DAM POP; DLB 161; MAICYA;
MTCW; SATA 18, 69

Garner, Hugh 1913-1979 .... **CLC 13**
See also CA 69-72; CANR 31; DLB 68

Garnett, David 1892-1981 .... **CLC 3**
See also CA 5-8R; 103; CANR 17; DLB 34

Garos, Stephanie
See Katz, Steve

Garrett, George (Palmer)
1929-.................. **CLC 3, 11, 51**
See also CA 1-4R; CAAS 5; CANR 1, 42;
DLB 2, 5, 130, 152; DLBY 83

Garrick, David 1717-1779 .... **LC 15**
See also DAM DRAM; DLB 84

Garrigue, Jean 1914-1972 .... **CLC 2, 8**
See also CA 5-8R; 37-40R; CANR 20

Garrison, Frederick
See Sinclair, Upton (Beall)

Garth, Will
See Hamilton, Edmond; Kuttner, Henry

Garvey, Marcus (Moziah, Jr.)
1887-1940 .... **TCLC 41; BLC**
See also BW 1; CA 120; 124; DAM MULT

Gary, Romain .... **CLC 25**
See also Kacew, Romain
See also DLB 83

Gascar, Pierre .... **CLC 11**
See also Fournier, Pierre

Gascoyne, David (Emery) 1916- .... **CLC 45**
See also CA 65-68; CANR 10, 28; DLB 20;
MTCW

Gaskell, Elizabeth Cleghorn
1810-1865 .... **NCLC 5; DAB**
See also CDBLB 1832-1890; DAM MST;
DLB 21, 144, 159

Gass, William H(oward)
1924- ... **CLC 1, 2, 8, 11, 15, 39; SSC 12**
See also CA 17-20R; CANR 30; DLB 2;
MTCW

Gasset, Jose Ortega y
See Ortega y Gasset, Jose

Gates, Henry Louis, Jr. 1950-...... **CLC 65**
See also BW 2; CA 109; CANR 25;
DAM MULT; DLB 67

Gautier, Theophile
1811-1872 .... **NCLC 1; SSC 20**
See also DAM POET; DLB 119

Gawsworth, John
See Bates, H(erbert) E(rnest)

Gaye, Marvin (Penze) 1939-1984 ... **CLC 26**
See also CA 112

Gebler, Carlo (Ernest) 1954-....... **CLC 39**
See also CA 119; 133

Gee, Maggie (Mary) 1948-......... **CLC 57**
See also CA 130

Gee, Maurice (Gough) 1931- .... **CLC 29**
See also CA 97-100; SATA 46

Gelbart, Larry (Simon) 1923- ... **CLC 21, 61**
See also CA 73-76; CANR 45

Gelber, Jack 1932- .... **CLC 1, 6, 14, 79**
See also CA 1-4R; CANR 2; DLB 7

Gellhorn, Martha (Ellis) 1908- .. **CLC 14, 60**
See also CA 77-80; CANR 44; DLBY 82

Genet, Jean
1910-1986 ... **CLC 1, 2, 5, 10, 14, 44, 46**
See also CA 13-16R; CANR 18;
DAM DRAM; DLB 72; DLBY 86;
MTCW

Gent, Peter 1942- .... **CLC 29**
See also AITN 1; CA 89-92; DLBY 82

Gentlewoman in New England, A
See Bradstreet, Anne

Gentlewoman in Those Parts, A
See Bradstreet, Anne

George, Jean Craighead 1919-...... **CLC 35**
See also AAYA 8; CA 5-8R; CANR 25;
CLR 1; DLB 52; JRDA; MAICYA;
SATA 2, 68

George, Stefan (Anton)
1868-1933 .... **TCLC 2, 14**
See also CA 104

Georges, Georges Martin
See Simenon, Georges (Jacques Christian)

Gerhardi, William Alexander
See Gerhardie, William Alexander

Gerhardie, William Alexander
1895-1977 .... **CLC 5**
See also CA 25-28R; 73-76; CANR 18;
DLB 36

Gerstler, Amy 1956- .... **CLC 70**
See also CA 146

Gertler, T. .... **CLC 34**
See also CA 116; 121; INT 121

Ghalib 1797-1869 .... **NCLC 39**

Ghelderode, Michel de
1898-1962 .... **CLC 6, 11**
See also CA 85-88; CANR 40;
DAM DRAM

Ghiselin, Brewster 1903- .... **CLC 23**
See also CA 13-16R; CAAS 10; CANR 13

Ghose, Zulfikar 1935-............. **CLC 42**
See also CA 65-68

Ghosh, Amitav 1956- .... **CLC 44**
See also CA 147

Giacosa, Giuseppe 1847-1906 ...... **TCLC 7**
See also CA 104

Gibb, Lee
See Waterhouse, Keith (Spencer)

Gibbon, Lewis Grassic .... **TCLC 4**
See also Mitchell, James Leslie

Gibbons, Kaye 1960- .... **CLC 50, 88**
See also DAM POP

Gibran, Kahlil
1883-1931 .... **TCLC 1, 9; PC 9**
See also CA 104; DAM POET, POP

Gibson, William
1914- .... **CLC 23; DA; DAB; DAC**
See also CA 9-12R; CANR 9, 42;
DAM DRAM, MST; DLB 7; SATA 66

Gibson, William (Ford) 1948- ... **CLC 39, 63**
See also AAYA 12; CA 126; 133;
DAM POP

Gide, Andre (Paul Guillaume)
1869-1951 .... **TCLC 5, 12, 36; DA;
DAB; DAC; SSC 13; WLC**
See also CA 104; 124; DAM MST, NOV;
DLB 65; MTCW

Gifford, Barry (Colby) 1946-....... **CLC 34**
See also CA 65-68; CANR 9, 30, 40

Gilbert, W(illiam) S(chwenck)
1836-1911 .... **TCLC 3**
See also CA 104; DAM DRAM, POET;
SATA 36

Gilbreth, Frank B., Jr. 1911-....... **CLC 17**
See also CA 9-12R; SATA 2

Gilchrist, Ellen 1935-.. **CLC 34, 48; SSC 14**
See also CA 113; 116; CANR 41;
DAM POP; DLB 130; MTCW

Giles, Molly 1942- .... **CLC 39**
See also CA 126

Gill, Patrick
See Creasey, John

Gilliam, Terry (Vance) 1940-....... **CLC 21**
See also Monty Python
See also CA 108; 113; CANR 35; INT 113

Gillian, Jerry
See Gilliam, Terry (Vance)

Gilliatt, Penelope (Ann Douglass)
1932-1993 .... **CLC 2, 10, 13, 53**
See also AITN 2; CA 13-16R; 141;
CANR 49; DLB 14

Gilman, Charlotte (Anna) Perkins (Stetson)
1860-1935 .... **TCLC 9, 37; SSC 13**
See also CA 106

Gilmour, David 1949-............. **CLC 35**
See also CA 138, 147

Gilpin, William 1724-1804....... **NCLC 30**

Gilray, J. D.
See Mencken, H(enry) L(ouis)

Gilroy, Frank D(aniel) 1925-........ **CLC 2**
See also CA 81-84; CANR 32; DLB 7

Ginsberg, Allen
1926- ...... **CLC 1, 2, 3, 4, 6, 13, 36, 69;
DA; DAB; DAC; PC 4; WLC 3**
See also AITN 1; CA 1-4R; CANR 2, 41;
CDALB 1941-1968; DAM MST, POET;
DLB 5, 16; MTCW

Ginzburg, Natalia
1916-1991 .... **CLC 5, 11, 54, 70**
See also CA 85-88; 135; CANR 33; MTCW

Giono, Jean 1895-1970......... **CLC 4, 11**
See also CA 45-48; 29-32R; CANR 2, 35;
DLB 72; MTCW

Giovanni, Nikki
1943- ...... **CLC 2, 4, 19, 64; BLC; DA;
DAB; DAC**
See also AITN 1; BW 2; CA 29-32R;
CAAS 6; CANR 18, 41; CLR 6;
DAM MST, MULT, POET; DLB 5, 41;
INT CANR-18; MAICYA; MTCW;
SATA 24

Giovene, Andrea 1904-............ **CLC 7**
See also CA 85-88

Gippius, Zinaida (Nikolayevna) 1869-1945
See Hippius, Zinaida
See also CA 106

Giraudoux, (Hippolyte) Jean
1882-1944 .... **TCLC 2, 7**
See also CA 104; DAM DRAM; DLB 65

Gironella, Jose Maria 1917- .... **CLC 11**
See also CA 101

Gissing, George (Robert)
1857-1903 .... **TCLC 3, 24, 47**
See also CA 105; DLB 18, 135

Giurlani, Aldo
See Palazzeschi, Aldo

Gladkov, Fyodor (Vasilyevich)
1883-1958 .... **TCLC 27**

Glanville, Brian (Lester) 1931- ...... **CLC 6**
See also CA 5-8R; CAAS 9; CANR 3;
DLB 15, 139; SATA 42

Glasgow, Ellen (Anderson Gholson)
1873(?)-1945 .... **TCLC 2, 7**
See also CA 104; DLB 9, 12

Glaspell, Susan (Keating)
1882(?)-1948 .... **TCLC 55**
See also CA 110; DLB 7, 9, 78; YABC 2

Glassco, John 1909-1981 .... **CLC 9**
See also CA 13-16R; 102; CANR 15;
DLB 68

Glasscock, Amnesia
See Steinbeck, John (Ernst)

Glasser, Ronald J. 1940(?)-........ **CLC 37**

Glassman, Joyce
See Johnson, Joyce

Glendinning, Victoria 1937-........ **CLC 50**
See also CA 120; 127; DLB 155

Glissant, Edouard 1928-........ **CLC 10, 68**
See also DAM MULT

Gloag, Julian 1930- .... **CLC 40**
See also AITN 1; CA 65-68; CANR 10

Glowacki, Aleksander
See Prus, Boleslaw

Glueck, Louise (Elisabeth)
1943- .... **CLC 7, 22, 44, 81**
See also CA 33-36R; CANR 40;
DAM POET; DLB 5

Gobineau, Joseph Arthur (Comte) de
1816-1882 .... **NCLC 17**
See also DLB 123

Godard, Jean-Luc 1930-........... **CLC 20**
See also CA 93-96

Godden, (Margaret) Rumer 1907-... **CLC 53**
See also AAYA 6; CA 5-8R; CANR 4, 27,
36; CLR 20; DLB 161; MAICYA;
SAAS 12; SATA 3, 36

Godoy Alcayaga, Lucila 1889-1957
See Mistral, Gabriela
See also BW 2; CA 104; 131; DAM MULT;
HW; MTCW

Godwin, Gail (Kathleen)
1937- .... **CLC 5, 8, 22, 31, 69**
See also CA 29-32R; CANR 15, 43;
DAM POP; DLB 6; INT CANR-15;
MTCW

Godwin, William 1756-1836...... **NCLC 14**
See also CDBLB 1789-1832; DLB 39, 104,
142, 158

Gray, Amlin 1946- .... **CLC 29**
See also CA 138

Gray, Francine du Plessix 1930-.... **CLC 22**
See also BEST 90:3; CA 61-64; CAAS 2;
CANR 11, 33; DAM NOV;
INT CANR-11; MTCW

Gray, John (Henry) 1866-1934 .... **TCLC 19**
See also CA 119

Gray, Simon (James Holliday)
1936- .... **CLC 9, 14, 36**
See also AITN 1; CA 21-24R; CAAS 3;
CANR 32; DLB 13; MTCW

Gray, Spalding 1941- .... **CLC 49**
See also CA 128; DAM POP

Gray, Thomas
1716-1771 ...... **LC 4; DA; DAB; DAC;**
PC 2; WLC
See also CDBLB 1660-1789; DAM MST;
DLB 109

Grayson, David
See Baker, Ray Stannard

Grayson, Richard (A.) 1951-....... **CLC 38**
See also CA 85-88; CANR 14, 31

Greeley, Andrew M(oran) 1928-.... **CLC 28**
See also CA 5-8R; CAAS 7; CANR 7, 43;
DAM POP; MTCW

Green, Brian
See Card, Orson Scott

Green, Hannah
See Greenberg, Joanne (Goldenberg)

Green, Hannah .... **CLC 3**
See also CA 73-76

Green, Henry .... **CLC 2, 13**
See also Yorke, Henry Vincent
See also DLB 15

Green, Julian (Hartridge) 1900-
See Green, Julien
See also CA 21-24R; CANR 33; DLB 4, 72;
MTCW

Green, Julien .... **CLC 3, 11, 77**
See also Green, Julian (Hartridge)

Green, Paul (Eliot) 1894-1981...... **CLC 25**
See also AITN 1; CA 5-8R; 103; CANR 3;
DAM DRAM; DLB 7, 9; DLBY 81

Greenberg, Ivan 1908-1973
See Rahv, Philip
See also CA 85-88

Greenberg, Joanne (Goldenberg)
1932- .... **CLC 7, 30**
See also AAYA 12; CA 5-8R; CANR 14,
32; SATA 25

Greenberg, Richard 1959(?)-....... **CLC 57**
See also CA 138

Greene, Bette 1934- .... **CLC 30**
See also AAYA 7; CA 53-56; CANR 4;
CLR 2; JRDA; MAICYA; SAAS 16;
SATA 8

Greene, Gael .... **CLC 8**
See also CA 13-16R; CANR 10

Greene, Graham
1904-1991 .... **CLC 1, 3, 6, 9, 14, 18, 27,**
37, 70, 72; DA; DAB; DAC; WLC
See also AITN 2; CA 13-16R; 133;
CANR 35; CDBLB 1945-1960;
DAM MST, NOV; DLB 13, 15, 77, 100;
DLBY 91; MTCW; SATA 20

Greer, Richard
See Silverberg, Robert

Gregor, Arthur 1923-.............. **CLC 9**
See also CA 25-28R; CAAS 10; CANR 11;
SATA 36

Gregor, Lee
See Pohl, Frederik

Gregory, Isabella Augusta (Persse)
1852-1932 .... **TCLC 1**
See also CA 104; DLB 10

Gregory, J. Dennis
See Williams, John A(lfred)

Grendon, Stephen
See Derleth, August (William)

Grenville, Kate 1950-............. **CLC 61**
See also CA 118

Grenville, Pelham
See Wodehouse, P(elham) G(renville)

Greve, Felix Paul (Berthold Friedrich)
1879-1948
See Grove, Frederick Philip
See also CA 104; 141; DAC; DAM MST

Grey, Zane 1872-1939 .... **TCLC 6**
See also CA 104; 132; DAM POP; DLB 9;
MTCW

Grieg, (Johan) Nordahl (Brun)
1902-1943 .... **TCLC 10**
See also CA 107

Grieve, C(hristopher) M(urray)
1892-1978 .... **CLC 11, 19**
See also MacDiarmid, Hugh; Pteleon
See also CA 5-8R; 85-88; CANR 33;
DAM POET; MTCW

Griffin, Gerald 1803-1840 .... **NCLC 7**
See also DLB 159

Griffin, John Howard 1920-1980.... **CLC 68**
See also AITN 1; CA 1-4R; 101; CANR 2

Griffin, Peter 1942- .... **CLC 39**
See also CA 136

Griffiths, Trevor 1935-......... **CLC 13, 52**
See also CA 97-100; CANR 45; DLB 13

Grigson, Geoffrey (Edward Harvey)
1905-1985 .... **CLC 7, 39**
See also CA 25-28R; 118; CANR 20, 33;
DLB 27; MTCW

Grillparzer, Franz 1791-1872...... **NCLC 1**
See also DLB 133

Grimble, Reverend Charles James
See Eliot, T(homas) S(tearns)

Grimke, Charlotte L(ottie) Forten
1837(?)-1914
See Forten, Charlotte L.
See also BW 1; CA 117; 124; DAM MULT,
POET

Grimm, Jacob Ludwig Karl
1785-1863 .... **NCLC 3**
See also DLB 90; MAICYA; SATA 22

Grimm, Wilhelm Karl 1786-1859 .. **NCLC 3**
See also DLB 90; MAICYA; SATA 22

Grimmelshausen, Johann Jakob Christoffel
von 1621-1676 .... **LC 6**

Grindel, Eugene 1895-1952
See Eluard, Paul
See also CA 104

Grisham, John 1955- .... **CLC 84**
See also AAYA 14; CA 138; CANR 47;
DAM POP

Grossman, David 1954- .... **CLC 67**
See also CA 138

Grossman, Vasily (Semenovich)
1905-1964 .... **CLC 41**
See also CA 124; 130; MTCW

Grove, Frederick Philip .... **TCLC 4**
See also Greve, Felix Paul (Berthold
Friedrich)
See also DLB 92

Grubb
See Crumb, R(obert)

Grumbach, Doris (Isaac)
1918- .... **CLC 13, 22, 64**
See also CA 5-8R; CAAS 2; CANR 9, 42;
INT CANR-9

Grundtvig, Nicolai Frederik Severin
1783-1872 .... **NCLC 1**

Grunge
See Crumb, R(obert)

Grunwald, Lisa 1959-............. **CLC 44**
See also CA 120

Guare, John 1938- .... **CLC 8, 14, 29, 67**
See also CA 73-76; CANR 21;
DAM DRAM; DLB 7; MTCW

Gudjonsson, Halldor Kiljan 1902-
See Laxness, Halldor
See also CA 103

Guenter, Erich
See Eich, Guenter

Guest, Barbara 1920-............. **CLC 34**
See also CA 25-28R; CANR 11, 44; DLB 5

Guest, Judith (Ann) 1936-....... **CLC 8, 30**
See also AAYA 7; CA 77-80; CANR 15;
DAM NOV, POP; INT CANR-15;
MTCW

Guevara, Che .... **CLC 87; HLC**
See also Guevara (Serna), Ernesto

Guevara (Serna), Ernesto 1928-1967
See Guevara, Che
See also CA 127; 111; DAM MULT; HW

Guild, Nicholas M. 1944-.......... **CLC 33**
See also CA 93-96

Guillemin, Jacques
See Sartre, Jean-Paul

Guillen, Jorge 1893-1984.......... **CLC 11**
See also CA 89-92; 112; DAM MULT,
POET; DLB 108; HW

Guillen (y Batista), Nicolas (Cristobal)
1902-1989 ..... **CLC 48, 79; BLC; HLC**
See also BW 2; CA 116; 125; 129;
DAM MST, MULT, POET; HW

Guillevic, (Eugene) 1907-.......... **CLC 33**
See also CA 93-96

Guillois
See Desnos, Robert

Guiney, Louise Imogen
1861-1920 .... **TCLC 41**
See also DLB 54

Guiraldes, Ricardo (Guillermo)
1886-1927 .... **TCLC 39**
See also CA 131; HW; MTCW

Gumilev, Nikolai Stephanovich
1886-1921 .... **TCLC 60**

Gunn, Bill .... **CLC 5**
See also Gunn, William Harrison
See also DLB 38

Gunn, Thom(son William)
1929- .... **CLC 3, 6, 18, 32, 81**
See also CA 17-20R; CANR 9, 33;
CDBLB 1960 to Present; DAM POET;
DLB 27; INT CANR-33; MTCW

Gunn, William Harrison 1934(?)-1989
See Gunn, Bill
See also AITN 1; BW 1; CA 13-16R; 128;
CANR 12, 25

Gunnars, Kristjana 1948- .... **CLC 69**
See also CA 113; DLB 60

Gurganus, Allan 1947- .... **CLC 70**
See also BEST 90:1; CA 135; DAM POP

Gurney, A(lbert) R(amsdell), Jr.
1930- .... **CLC 32, 50, 54**
See also CA 77-80; CANR 32;
DAM DRAM

Gurney, Ivor (Bertie) 1890-1937 ... **TCLC 33**

Gurney, Peter
See Gurney, A(lbert) R(amsdell), Jr.

Guro, Elena 1877-1913 .... **TCLC 56**

Gustafson, Ralph (Barker) 1909- ... **CLC 36**
See also CA 21-24R; CANR 8, 45; DLB 88

Gut, Gom
See Simenon, Georges (Jacques Christian)

Guthrie, A(lfred) B(ertram), Jr.
1901-1991 .... **CLC 23**
See also CA 57-60; 134; CANR 24; DLB 6;
SATA 62; SATA-Obit 67

Guthrie, Isobel
See Grieve, C(hristopher) M(urray)

Guthrie, Woodrow Wilson 1912-1967
See Guthrie, Woody
See also CA 113; 93-96

Guthrie, Woody .... **CLC 35**
See also Guthrie, Woodrow Wilson

Guy, Rosa (Cuthbert) 1928- .... **CLC 26**
See also AAYA 4; BW 2; CA 17-20R;
CANR 14, 34; CLR 13; DLB 33; JRDA;
MAICYA; SATA 14, 62

Gwendolyn
See Bennett, (Enoch) Arnold

H. D. .... **CLC 3, 8, 14, 31, 34, 73; PC 5**
See also Doolittle, Hilda

H. de V.
See Buchan, John

Haavikko, Paavo Juhani
1931- .... **CLC 18, 34**
See also CA 106

Habbema, Koos
See Heijermans, Herman

Hacker, Marilyn 1942- .... **CLC 5, 9, 23, 72**
See also CA 77-80; DAM POET; DLB 120

Haggard, H(enry) Rider
1856-1925 .... **TCLC 11**
See also CA 108; 148; DLB 70, 156;
SATA 16

Hagiwara Sakutaro 1886-1942 .... **TCLC 60**

Haig, Fenil
See Ford, Ford Madox

Haig-Brown, Roderick (Langmere)
1908-1976 .... **CLC 21**
See also CA 5-8R; 69-72; CANR 4, 38;
CLR 31; DLB 88; MAICYA; SATA 12

Hailey, Arthur 1920- .... **CLC 5**
See also AITN 2; BEST 90:3; CA 1-4R;
CANR 2, 36; DAM NOV, POP; DLB 88;
DLBY 82; MTCW

Hailey, Elizabeth Forsythe 1938- ... **CLC 40**
See also CA 93-96; CAAS 1; CANR 15, 48;
INT CANR-15

Haines, John (Meade) 1924- .... **CLC 58**
See also CA 17-20R; CANR 13, 34; DLB 5

Hakluyt, Richard 1552-1616 .... **LC 31**

Haldeman, Joe (William) 1943- ..... **CLC 61**
See also CA 53-56; CANR 6; DLB 8;
INT CANR-6

Haley, Alex(ander Murray Palmer)
1921-1992 .... **CLC 8, 12, 76; BLC; DA;**
DAB; DAC
See also BW 2; CA 77-80; 136; DAM MST,
MULT, POP; DLB 38; MTCW

Haliburton, Thomas Chandler
1796-1865 .... **NCLC 15**
See also DLB 11, 99

Hall, Donald (Andrew, Jr.)
1928- .... **CLC 1, 13, 37, 59**
See also CA 5-8R; CAAS 7; CANR 2, 44;
DAM POET; DLB 5; SATA 23

Hall, Frederic Sauser
See Sauser-Hall, Frederic

Hall, James
See Kuttner, Henry

Hall, James Norman 1887-1951 ... **TCLC 23**
See also CA 123; SATA 21

Hall, (Marguerite) Radclyffe
1886(?)-1943 .... **TCLC 12**
See also CA 110

Hall, Rodney 1935- .... **CLC 51**
See also CA 109

Halleck, Fitz-Greene 1790-1867 .. **NCLC 47**
See also DLB 3

Halliday, Michael
See Creasey, John

Halpern, Daniel 1945- .... **CLC 14**
See also CA 33-36R

Hamburger, Michael (Peter Leopold)
1924- .... **CLC 5, 14**
See also CA 5-8R; CAAS 4; CANR 2, 47;
DLB 27

Hamill, Pete 1935- .... **CLC 10**
See also CA 25-28R; CANR 18

Hamilton, Alexander
1755(?)-1804 .... **NCLC 49**
See also DLB 37

Hamilton, Clive
See Lewis, C(live) S(taples)

Hamilton, Edmond 1904-1977 ...... **CLC 1**
See also CA 1-4R; CANR 3; DLB 8

Hamilton, Eugene (Jacob) Lee
See Lee-Hamilton, Eugene (Jacob)

Hamilton, Franklin
See Silverberg, Robert

Hamilton, Gail
See Corcoran, Barbara

Hamilton, Mollie
See Kaye, M(ary) M(argaret)

Hamilton, (Anthony Walter) Patrick
1904-1962 .... **CLC 51**
See also CA 113; DLB 10

Hamilton, Virginia 1936- .... **CLC 26**
See also AAYA 2; BW 2; CA 25-28R;
CANR 20, 37; CLR 1, 11; DAM MULT;
DLB 33, 52; INT CANR-20; JRDA;
MAICYA; MTCW; SATA 4, 56, 79

Hammett, (Samuel) Dashiell
1894-1961 .... **CLC 3, 5, 10, 19, 47;**
SSC 17
See also AITN 1; CA 81-84; CANR 42;
CDALB 1929-1941; DLBD 6; MTCW

Hammon, Jupiter
1711(?)-1800(?) .... **NCLC 5; BLC**
See also DAM MULT, POET; DLB 31, 50

Hammond, Keith
See Kuttner, Henry

Hamner, Earl (Henry), Jr. 1923- ... **CLC 12**
See also AITN 2; CA 73-76; DLB 6

Hampton, Christopher (James)
1946- .... **CLC 4**
See also CA 25-28R; DLB 13; MTCW

Hamsun, Knut .... **TCLC 2, 14, 49**
See also Pedersen, Knut

Handke, Peter 1942- .. **CLC 5, 8, 10, 15, 38**
See also CA 77-80; CANR 33;
DAM DRAM, NOV; DLB 85, 124;
MTCW

Hanley, James 1901-1985 ... **CLC 3, 5, 8, 13**
See also CA 73-76; 117; CANR 36; MTCW

Hannah, Barry 1942- .... **CLC 23, 38, 90**
See also CA 108; 110; CANR 43; DLB 6;
INT 110; MTCW

Hannon, Ezra
See Hunter, Evan

Hansberry, Lorraine (Vivian)
1930-1965 ...... **CLC 17, 62; BLC; DA;**
DAB; DAC; DC 2
See also BW 1; CA 109; 25-28R; CABS 3;
CDALB 1941-1968; DAM DRAM, MST,
MULT; DLB 7, 38; MTCW

Hansen, Joseph 1923- .... **CLC 38**
See also CA 29-32R; CAAS 17; CANR 16,
44; INT CANR-16

Hansen, Martin A. 1909-1955 ..... **TCLC 32**

Hanson, Kenneth O(stlin) 1922- .... **CLC 13**
See also CA 53-56; CANR 7

Hardwick, Elizabeth 1916- .... **CLC 13**
See also CA 5-8R; CANR 3, 32;
DAM NOV; DLB 6; MTCW

Hardy, Thomas
1840-1928 ...... **TCLC 4, 10, 18, 32, 48,
53; DA; DAB; DAC; PC 8; SSC 2; WLC**
See also CA 104; 123; CDBLB 1890-1914;
DAM MST, NOV, POET; DLB 18, 19,
135; MTCW

Hare, David 1947- .... **CLC 29, 58**
See also CA 97-100; CANR 39; DLB 13;
MTCW

Harford, Henry
See Hudson, W(illiam) H(enry)

Hargrave, Leonie
See Disch, Thomas M(ichael)

Harjo, Joy 1951- .... **CLC 83**
See also CA 114; CANR 35; DAM MULT;
DLB 120; NNAL

Harlan, Louis R(udolph) 1922- ..... **CLC 34**
See also CA 21-24R; CANR 25

Harling, Robert 1951(?)- .... **CLC 53**
See also CA 147

Harmon, William (Ruth) 1938- ..... **CLC 38**
See also CA 33-36R; CANR 14, 32, 35;
SATA 65

Harper, F. E. W.
See Harper, Frances Ellen Watkins

Harper, Frances E. W.
See Harper, Frances Ellen Watkins

Harper, Frances E. Watkins
See Harper, Frances Ellen Watkins

Harper, Frances Ellen
See Harper, Frances Ellen Watkins

Harper, Frances Ellen Watkins
1825-1911 .... **TCLC 14; BLC**
See also BW 1; CA 111; 125; DAM MULT,
POET; DLB 50

Harper, Michael S(teven) 1938- .. **CLC 7, 22**
See also BW 1; CA 33-36R; CANR 24;
DLB 41

Harper, Mrs. F. E. W.
See Harper, Frances Ellen Watkins

Harris, Christie (Lucy) Irwin
1907- .... **CLC 12**
See also CA 5-8R; CANR 6; DLB 88;
JRDA; MAICYA; SAAS 10; SATA 6, 74

Harris, Frank 1856(?)-1931 ...... **TCLC 24**
See also CA 109; DLB 156

Harris, George Washington
1814-1869 .... **NCLC 23**
See also DLB 3, 11

Harris, Joel Chandler
1848-1908 .... **TCLC 2; SSC 19**
See also CA 104; 137; DLB 11, 23, 42, 78,
91; MAICYA; YABC 1

Harris, John (Wyndham Parkes Lucas)
Beynon 1903-1969
See Wyndham, John
See also CA 102; 89-92

Harris, MacDonald .... **CLC 9**
See also Heiney, Donald (William)

Harris, Mark 1922- .... **CLC 19**
See also CA 5-8R; CAAS 3; CANR 2;
DLB 2; DLBY 80

Harris, (Theodore) Wilson 1921-.... **CLC 25**
See also BW 2; CA 65-68; CAAS 16;
CANR 11, 27; DLB 117; MTCW

Harrison, Elizabeth Cavanna 1909-
See Cavanna, Betty
See also CA 9-12R; CANR 6, 27

Harrison, Harry (Max) 1925- ...... **CLC 42**
See also CA 1-4R; CANR 5, 21; DLB 8;
SATA 4

Harrison, James (Thomas)
1937- .... **CLC 6, 14, 33, 66; SSC 19**
See also CA 13-16R; CANR 8; DLBY 82;
INT CANR-8

Harrison, Jim
See Harrison, James (Thomas)

Harrison, Kathryn 1961- .... **CLC 70**
See also CA 144

Harrison, Tony 1937- .... **CLC 43**
See also CA 65-68; CANR 44; DLB 40;
MTCW

Harriss, Will(ard Irvin) 1922- ...... **CLC 34**
See also CA 111

Harson, Sley
See Ellison, Harlan (Jay)

Hart, Ellis
See Ellison, Harlan (Jay)

Hart, Josephine 1942(?)- .... **CLC 70**
See also CA 138; DAM POP

Hart, Moss 1904-1961 .... **CLC 66**
See also CA 109; 89-92; DAM DRAM;
DLB 7

Harte, (Francis) Bret(t)
1836(?)-1902 .... **TCLC 1, 25; DA; DAC;
SSC 8; WLC**
See also CA 104; 140; CDALB 1865-1917;
DAM MST; DLB 12, 64, 74, 79;
SATA 26

Hartley, L(eslie) P(oles)
1895-1972 .... **CLC 2, 22**
See also CA 45-48; 37-40R; CANR 33;
DLB 15, 139; MTCW

Hartman, Geoffrey H. 1929- .... **CLC 27**
See also CA 117; 125; DLB 67

Hartmann von Aue
c. 1160-c. 1205 .... **CMLC 15**
See also DLB 138

Hartmann von Aue 1170-1210.... **CMLC 15**

Haruf, Kent 1943- .... **CLC 34**
See also CA 149

Harwood, Ronald 1934- .... **CLC 32**
See also CA 1-4R; CANR 4; DAM DRAM,
MST; DLB 13

Hasek, Jaroslav (Matej Frantisek)
1883-1923 .... **TCLC 4**
See also CA 104; 129; MTCW

Hass, Robert 1941- .... **CLC 18, 39**
See also CA 111; CANR 30, 50; DLB 105

Hastings, Hudson
See Kuttner, Henry

Hastings, Selina .... **CLC 44**

Hatteras, Amelia
See Mencken, H(enry) L(ouis)

Hatteras, Owen .... **TCLC 18**
See also Mencken, H(enry) L(ouis); Nathan,
George Jean

Hauptmann, Gerhart (Johann Robert)
1862-1946 .... **TCLC 4**
See also CA 104; DAM DRAM; DLB 66,
118

Havel, Vaclav
1936- .... **CLC 25, 58, 65; DC 6**
See also CA 104; CANR 36; DAM DRAM;
MTCW

Haviaras, Stratis .... **CLC 33**
See also Chaviaras, Strates

Hawes, Stephen 1475(?)-1523(?) .... **LC 17**

Hawkes, John (Clendennin Burne, Jr.)
1925- ...... **CLC 1, 2, 3, 4, 7, 9, 14, 15,
27, 49**
See also CA 1-4R; CANR 2, 47; DLB 2, 7;
DLBY 80; MTCW

Hawking, S. W.
See Hawking, Stephen W(illiam)

Hawking, Stephen W(illiam)
1942- .... **CLC 63**
See also AAYA 13; BEST 89:1; CA 126;
129; CANR 48

Hawthorne, Julian 1846-1934 ..... **TCLC 25**

Hawthorne, Nathaniel
1804-1864 .... **NCLC 39; DA; DAB;
DAC; SSC 3; WLC**
See also CDALB 1640-1865; DAM MST,
NOV; DLB 1, 74; YABC 2

Haxton, Josephine Ayres 1921-
See Douglas, Ellen
See also CA 115; CANR 41

Hayaseca y Eizaguirre, Jorge
See Echegaray (y Eizaguirre), Jose (Maria
Waldo)

Hayashi Fumiko 1904-1951....... **TCLC 27**

Haycraft, Anna
See Ellis, Alice Thomas
See also CA 122

Hayden, Robert E(arl)
1913-1980 ...... **CLC 5, 9, 14, 37; BLC;
DA; DAC; PC 6**
See also BW 1; CA 69-72; 97-100; CABS 2;
CANR 24; CDALB 1941-1968;
DAM MST, MULT, POET; DLB 5, 76;
MTCW; SATA 19; SATA-Obit 26

Hayford, J(oseph) E(phraim) Casely
See Casely-Hayford, J(oseph) E(phraim)

Hayman, Ronald 1932-............. **CLC 44**
See also CA 25-28R; CANR 18, 50;
DLB 155

Haywood, Eliza (Fowler)
1693(?)-1756 .... **LC 1**

Hazlitt, William 1778-1830 ...... **NCLC 29**
See also DLB 110, 158

Hazzard, Shirley 1931- .... **CLC 18**
See also CA 9-12R; CANR 4; DLBY 82;
MTCW

Head, Bessie 1937-1986... **CLC 25, 67; BLC**
See also BW 2; CA 29-32R; 119; CANR 25;
DAM MULT; DLB 117; MTCW

Headon, (Nicky) Topper 1956(?)- ... **CLC 30**

Heym, Georg (Theodor Franz Arthur)
1887-1912 . . . . **TCLC 9**
See also CA 106

Heym, Stefan 1913- . . . . **CLC 41**
See also CA 9-12R; CANR 4; DLB 69

Heyse, Paul (Johann Ludwig von)
1830-1914 . . . . **TCLC 8**
See also CA 104; DLB 129

Heyward, (Edwin) DuBose
1885-1940 . . . . **TCLC 59**
See also CA 108; DLB 7, 9, 45; SATA 21

Hibbert, Eleanor Alice Burford
1906-1993 . . . . **CLC 7**
See also BEST 90:4; CA 17-20R; 140;
CANR 9, 28; DAM POP; SATA 2;
SATA-Obit 74

Higgins, George V(incent)
1939- . . . . **CLC 4, 7, 10, 18**
See also CA 77-80; CAAS 5; CANR 17;
DLB 2; DLBY 81; INT CANR-17;
MTCW

Higginson, Thomas Wentworth
1823-1911 . . . . **TCLC 36**
See also DLB 1, 64

Highet, Helen
See MacInnes, Helen (Clark)

Highsmith, (Mary) Patricia
1921-1995 . . . . **CLC 2, 4, 14, 42**
See also CA 1-4R; 147; CANR 1, 20, 48;
DAM NOV, POP; MTCW

Highwater, Jamake (Mamake)
1942(?)- . . . . **CLC 12**
See also AAYA 7; CA 65-68; CAAS 7;
CANR 10, 34; CLR 17; DLB 52;
DLBY 85; JRDA; MAICYA; SATA 32,
69; SATA-Brief 30

Higuchi, Ichiyo 1872-1896 . . . . **NCLC 49**

Hijuelos, Oscar 1951- . . . . . . **CLC 65; HLC**
See also BEST 90:1; CA 123; CANR 50;
DAM MULT, POP; DLB 145; HW

Hikmet, Nazim 1902(?)-1963 . . . . . . **CLC 40**
See also CA 141; 93-96

Hildesheimer, Wolfgang
1916-1991 . . . . **CLC 49**
See also CA 101; 135; DLB 69, 124

Hill, Geoffrey (William)
1932- . . . . **CLC 5, 8, 18, 45**
See also CA 81-84; CANR 21;
CDBLB 1960 to Present; DAM POET;
DLB 40; MTCW

Hill, George Roy 1921- . . . . **CLC 26**
See also CA 110; 122

Hill, John
See Koontz, Dean R(ay)

Hill, Susan (Elizabeth)
1942- . . . . **CLC 4; DAB**
See also CA 33-36R; CANR 29;
DAM MST, NOV; DLB 14, 139; MTCW

Hillerman, Tony 1925- . . . . **CLC 62**
See also AAYA 6; BEST 89:1; CA 29-32R;
CANR 21, 42; DAM POP; SATA 6

Hillesum, Etty 1914-1943 . . . . **TCLC 49**
See also CA 137

Hilliard, Noel (Harvey) 1929- . . . . . **CLC 15**
See also CA 9-12R; CANR 7

Hillis, Rick 1956- . . . . **CLC 66**
See also CA 134

Hilton, James 1900-1954 . . . . **TCLC 21**
See also CA 108; DLB 34, 77; SATA 34

Himes, Chester (Bomar)
1909-1984 . . . . **CLC 2, 4, 7, 18, 58; BLC**
See also BW 2; CA 25-28R; 114; CANR 22;
DAM MULT; DLB 2, 76, 143; MTCW

Hinde, Thomas . . . . **CLC 6, 11**
See also Chitty, Thomas Willes

Hindin, Nathan
See Bloch, Robert (Albert)

Hine, (William) Daryl 1936- . . . . **CLC 15**
See also CA 1-4R; CAAS 15; CANR 1, 20;
DLB 60

Hinkson, Katharine Tynan
See Tynan, Katharine

Hinton, S(usan) E(loise)
1950- . . . . **CLC 30; DA; DAB; DAC**
See also AAYA 2; CA 81-84; CANR 32;
CLR 3, 23; DAM MST, NOV; JRDA;
MAICYA; MTCW; SATA 19, 58

Hippius, Zinaida . . . . **TCLC 9**
See also Gippius, Zinaida (Nikolayevna)

Hiraoka, Kimitake 1925-1970
See Mishima, Yukio
See also CA 97-100; 29-32R; DAM DRAM;
MTCW

Hirsch, E(ric) D(onald), Jr. 1928- . . . **CLC 79**
See also CA 25-28R; CANR 27; DLB 67;
INT CANR-27; MTCW

Hirsch, Edward 1950- . . . . **CLC 31, 50**
See also CA 104; CANR 20, 42; DLB 120

Hitchcock, Alfred (Joseph)
1899-1980 . . . . **CLC 16**
See also CA 97-100; SATA 27;
SATA-Obit 24

Hitler, Adolf 1889-1945 . . . . **TCLC 53**
See also CA 117; 147

Hoagland, Edward 1932- . . . . **CLC 28**
See also CA 1-4R; CANR 2, 31; DLB 6;
SATA 51

Hoban, Russell (Conwell) 1925- . . **CLC 7, 25**
See also CA 5-8R; CANR 23, 37; CLR 3;
DAM NOV; DLB 52; MAICYA;
MTCW; SATA 1, 40, 78

Hobbs, Perry
See Blackmur, R(ichard) P(almer)

Hobson, Laura Z(ametkin)
1900-1986 . . . . **CLC 7, 25**
See also CA 17-20R; 118; DLB 28;
SATA 52

Hochhuth, Rolf 1931- . . . . **CLC 4, 11, 18**
See also CA 5-8R; CANR 33;
DAM DRAM; DLB 124; MTCW

Hochman, Sandra 1936- . . . . **CLC 3, 8**
See also CA 5-8R; DLB 5

Hochwaelder, Fritz 1911-1986 . . . . . **CLC 36**
See also CA 29-32R; 120; CANR 42;
DAM DRAM; MTCW

Hochwalder, Fritz
See Hochwaelder, Fritz

Hocking, Mary (Eunice) 1921- . . . . . **CLC 13**
See also CA 101; CANR 18, 40

Hodgins, Jack 1938- . . . . **CLC 23**
See also CA 93-96; DLB 60

Hodgson, William Hope
1877(?)-1918 . . . . **TCLC 13**
See also CA 111; DLB 70, 153, 156

Hoffman, Alice 1952- . . . . **CLC 51**
See also CA 77-80; CANR 34; DAM NOV;
MTCW

Hoffman, Daniel (Gerard)
1923- . . . . **CLC 6, 13, 23**
See also CA 1-4R; CANR 4; DLB 5

Hoffman, Stanley 1944- . . . . **CLC 5**
See also CA 77-80

Hoffman, William M(oses) 1939- . . . **CLC 40**
See also CA 57-60; CANR 11

Hoffmann, E(rnst) T(heodor) A(madeus)
1776-1822 . . . . **NCLC 2; SSC 13**
See also DLB 90; SATA 27

Hofmann, Gert 1931- . . . . **CLC 54**
See also CA 128

Hofmannsthal, Hugo von
1874-1929 . . . . **TCLC 11; DC 4**
See also CA 106; DAM DRAM; DLB 81,
118

Hogan, Linda 1947- . . . . **CLC 73**
See also CA 120; CANR 45; DAM MULT;
NNAL

Hogarth, Charles
See Creasey, John

Hogg, James 1770-1835 . . . . **NCLC 4**
See also DLB 93, 116, 159

Holbach, Paul Henri Thiry Baron
1723-1789 . . . . **LC 14**

Holberg, Ludvig 1684-1754 . . . . **LC 6**

Holden, Ursula 1921- . . . . **CLC 18**
See also CA 101; CAAS 8; CANR 22

Holderlin, (Johann Christian) Friedrich
1770-1843 . . . . **NCLC 16; PC 4**

Holdstock, Robert
See Holdstock, Robert P.

Holdstock, Robert P. 1948- . . . . **CLC 39**
See also CA 131

Holland, Isabelle 1920- . . . . **CLC 21**
See also AAYA 11; CA 21-24R; CANR 10,
25, 47; JRDA; MAICYA; SATA 8, 70

Holland, Marcus
See Caldwell, (Janet Miriam) Taylor
(Holland)

Hollander, John 1929- . . . . . . **CLC 2, 5, 8, 14**
See also CA 1-4R; CANR 1; DLB 5;
SATA 13

Hollander, Paul
See Silverberg, Robert

Holleran, Andrew 1943(?)- . . . . **CLC 38**
See also CA 144

Hollinghurst, Alan 1954- . . . . **CLC 55**
See also CA 114

Hollis, Jim
See Summers, Hollis (Spurgeon, Jr.)

Holmes, John
See Souster, (Holmes) Raymond

Holmes, John Clellon 1926-1988 . . . . **CLC 56**
See also CA 9-12R; 125; CANR 4; DLB 16

Holmes, Oliver Wendell
1809-1894 .... **NCLC 14**
See also CDALB 1640-1865; DLB 1;
SATA 34

Holmes, Raymond
See Souster, (Holmes) Raymond

Holt, Victoria
See Hibbert, Eleanor Alice Burford

Holub, Miroslav 1923- .... **CLC 4**
See also CA 21-24R; CANR 10

Homer
c. 8th cent. B.C.- ..... **CMLC 1, 16; DA;**
DAB; DAC
See also DAM MST, POET

Honig, Edwin 1919- .... **CLC 33**
See also CA 5-8R; CAAS 8; CANR 4, 45;
DLB 5

Hood, Hugh (John Blagdon)
1928- .... **CLC 15, 28**
See also CA 49-52; CAAS 17; CANR 1, 33;
DLB 53

Hood, Thomas 1799-1845 .... **NCLC 16**
See also DLB 96

Hooker, (Peter) Jeremy 1941- ...... **CLC 43**
See also CA 77-80; CANR 22; DLB 40

Hope, A(lec) D(erwent) 1907- .... **CLC 3, 51**
See also CA 21-24R; CANR 33; MTCW

Hope, Brian
See Creasey, John

Hope, Christopher (David Tully)
1944- .... **CLC 52**
See also CA 106; CANR 47; SATA 62

Hopkins, Gerard Manley
1844-1889 .... **NCLC 17; DA; DAB;**
DAC; WLC
See also CDBLB 1890-1914; DAM MST,
POET; DLB 35, 57

Hopkins, John (Richard) 1931- ...... **CLC 4**
See also CA 85-88

Hopkins, Pauline Elizabeth
1859-1930 .... **TCLC 28; BLC**
See also BW 2; CA 141; DAM MULT;
DLB 50

Hopkinson, Francis 1737-1791 ...... **LC 25**
See also DLB 31

Hopley-Woolrich, Cornell George 1903-1968
See Woolrich, Cornell
See also CA 13-14; CAP 1

Horatio
See Proust, (Valentin-Louis-George-Eugene-)
Marcel

Horgan, Paul (George Vincent O'Shaughnessy)
1903-1995 .... **CLC 9, 53**
See also CA 13-16R; 147; CANR 9, 35;
DAM NOV; DLB 102; DLBY 85;
INT CANR-9; MTCW; SATA 13;
SATA-Obit 84

Horn, Peter
See Kuttner, Henry

Hornem, Horace Esq.
See Byron, George Gordon (Noel)

Hornung, E(rnest) W(illiam)
1866-1921 .... **TCLC 59**
See also CA 108; DLB 70

Horovitz, Israel (Arthur) 1939- ..... **CLC 56**
See also CA 33-36R; CANR 46;
DAM DRAM; DLB 7

Horvath, Odon von
See Horvath, Oedoen von
See also DLB 85, 124

Horvath, Oedoen von 1901-1938 ... **TCLC 45**
See also Horvath, Odon von
See also CA 118

Horwitz, Julius 1920-1986 .... **CLC 14**
See also CA 9-12R; 119; CANR 12

Hospital, Janette Turner 1942- ..... **CLC 42**
See also CA 108; CANR 48

Hostos, E. M. de
See Hostos (y Bonilla), Eugenio Maria de

Hostos, Eugenio M. de
See Hostos (y Bonilla), Eugenio Maria de

Hostos, Eugenio Maria
See Hostos (y Bonilla), Eugenio Maria de

Hostos (y Bonilla), Eugenio Maria de
1839-1903 .... **TCLC 24**
See also CA 123; 131; HW

Houdini
See Lovecraft, H(oward) P(hillips)

Hougan, Carolyn 1943- .... **CLC 34**
See also CA 139

Household, Geoffrey (Edward West)
1900-1988 .... **CLC 11**
See also CA 77-80; 126; DLB 87; SATA 14;
SATA-Obit 59

Housman, A(lfred) E(dward)
1859-1936 ...... **TCLC 1, 10; DA; DAB;**
DAC; PC 2
See also CA 104; 125; DAM MST, POET;
DLB 19; MTCW

Housman, Laurence 1865-1959 ..... **TCLC 7**
See also CA 106; DLB 10; SATA 25

Howard, Elizabeth Jane 1923- ... **CLC 7, 29**
See also CA 5-8R; CANR 8

Howard, Maureen 1930- ..... **CLC 5, 14, 46**
See also CA 53-56; CANR 31; DLBY 83;
INT CANR-31; MTCW

Howard, Richard 1929- ...... **CLC 7, 10, 47**
See also AITN 1; CA 85-88; CANR 25;
DLB 5; INT CANR-25

Howard, Robert Ervin 1906-1936 ... **TCLC 8**
See also CA 105

Howard, Warren F.
See Pohl, Frederik

Howe, Fanny 1940- .... **CLC 47**
See also CA 117; SATA-Brief 52

Howe, Irving 1920-1993 .... **CLC 85**
See also CA 9-12R; 141; CANR 21, 50;
DLB 67; MTCW

Howe, Julia Ward 1819-1910 ..... **TCLC 21**
See also CA 117; DLB 1

Howe, Susan 1937- .... **CLC 72**
See also DLB 120

Howe, Tina 1937- .... **CLC 48**
See also CA 109

Howell, James 1594(?)-1666 .... **LC 13**
See also DLB 151

Howells, W. D.
See Howells, William Dean

Howells, William D.
See Howells, William Dean

Howells, William Dean
1837-1920 .... **TCLC 7, 17, 41**
See also CA 104; 134; CDALB 1865-1917;
DLB 12, 64, 74, 79

Howes, Barbara 1914- .... **CLC 15**
See also CA 9-12R; CAAS 3; SATA 5

Hrabal, Bohumil 1914- .... **CLC 13, 67**
See also CA 106; CAAS 12

Hsun, Lu
See Lu Hsun

Hubbard, L(afayette) Ron(ald)
1911-1986 .... **CLC 43**
See also CA 77-80; 118; CANR 22;
DAM POP

Huch, Ricarda (Octavia)
1864-1947 .... **TCLC 13**
See also CA 111; DLB 66

Huddle, David 1942- .... **CLC 49**
See also CA 57-60; CAAS 20; DLB 130

Hudson, Jeffrey
See Crichton, (John) Michael

Hudson, W(illiam) H(enry)
1841-1922 .... **TCLC 29**
See also CA 115; DLB 98, 153; SATA 35

Hueffer, Ford Madox
See Ford, Ford Madox

Hughart, Barry 1934- .... **CLC 39**
See also CA 137

Hughes, Colin
See Creasey, John

Hughes, David (John) 1930- .... **CLC 48**
See also CA 116; 129; DLB 14

Hughes, (James) Langston
1902-1967 ..... **CLC 1, 5, 10, 15, 35, 44;**
BLC; DA; DAB; DAC; DC 3; PC 1;
SSC 6; WLC
See also AAYA 12; BW 1; CA 1-4R;
25-28R; CANR 1, 34; CDALB 1929-1941;
CLR 17; DAM DRAM, MST, MULT,
POET; DLB 4, 7, 48, 51, 86; JRDA;
MAICYA; MTCW; SATA 4, 33

Hughes, Richard (Arthur Warren)
1900-1976 .... **CLC 1, 11**
See also CA 5-8R; 65-68; CANR 4;
DAM NOV; DLB 15, 161; MTCW;
SATA 8; SATA-Obit 25

Hughes, Ted
1930- .... **CLC 2, 4, 9, 14, 37; DAB;**
DAC; PC 7
See also CA 1-4R; CANR 1, 33; CLR 3;
DLB 40, 161; MAICYA; MTCW;
SATA 49; SATA-Brief 27

Hugo, Richard F(ranklin)
1923-1982 .... **CLC 6, 18, 32**
See also CA 49-52; 108; CANR 3;
DAM POET; DLB 5

Hugo, Victor (Marie)
1802-1885 .... **NCLC 3, 10, 21; DA;**
DAB; DAC; WLC
See also DAM DRAM, MST, NOV, POET;
DLB 119; SATA 47

Huidobro, Vicente
See Huidobro Fernandez, Vicente Garcia

Huidobro Fernandez, Vicente Garcia
1893-1948 .... **TCLC 31**
See also CA 131; HW

Hulme, Keri 1947- .... **CLC 39**
See also CA 125; INT 125

Hulme, T(homas) E(rnest)
1883-1917 .... **TCLC 21**
See also CA 117; DLB 19

Hume, David 1711-1776............ **LC 7**
See also DLB 104

Humphrey, William 1924-......... **CLC 45**
See also CA 77-80; DLB 6

Humphreys, Emyr Owen 1919-..... **CLC 47**
See also CA 5-8R; CANR 3, 24; DLB 15

Humphreys, Josephine 1945-.... **CLC 34, 57**
See also CA 121; 127; INT 127

Hungerford, Pixie
See Brinsmead, H(esba) F(ay)

Hunt, E(verette) Howard, (Jr.)
1918- .... **CLC 3**
See also AITN 1; CA 45-48; CANR 2, 47

Hunt, Kyle
See Creasey, John

Hunt, (James Henry) Leigh
1784-1859 .... **NCLC 1**
See also DAM POET

Hunt, Marsha 1946-.............. **CLC 70**
See also BW 2; CA 143

Hunt, Violet 1866-1942 .... **TCLC 53**

Hunter, E. Waldo
See Sturgeon, Theodore (Hamilton)

Hunter, Evan 1926- .... **CLC 11, 31**
See also CA 5-8R; CANR 5, 38;
DAM POP; DLBY 82; INT CANR-5;
MTCW; SATA 25

Hunter, Kristin (Eggleston) 1931-... **CLC 35**
See also AITN 1; BW 1; CA 13-16R;
CANR 13; CLR 3; DLB 33;
INT CANR-13; MAICYA; SAAS 10;
SATA 12

Hunter, Mollie 1922-............. **CLC 21**
See also McIlwraith, Maureen Mollie
Hunter
See also AAYA 13; CANR 37; CLR 25;
DLB 161; JRDA; MAICYA; SAAS 7;
SATA 54

Hunter, Robert (?)-1734............. **LC 7**

Hurston, Zora Neale
1903-1960 .... **CLC 7, 30, 61; BLC; DA;
DAC; SSC 4**
See also AAYA 15; BW 1; CA 85-88;
DAM MST, MULT, NOV; DLB 51, 86;
MTCW

Huston, John (Marcellus)
1906-1987 .... **CLC 20**
See also CA 73-76; 123; CANR 34; DLB 26

Hustvedt, Siri 1955-.............. **CLC 76**
See also CA 137

Hutten, Ulrich von 1488-1523...... **LC 16**

Huxley, Aldous (Leonard)
1894-1963 ..... **CLC 1, 3, 4, 5, 8, 11, 18,
35, 79; DA; DAB; DAC; WLC**
See also AAYA 11; CA 85-88; CANR 44;
CDBLB 1914-1945; DAM MST, NOV;
DLB 36, 100; MTCW; SATA 63

Huysmans, Charles Marie Georges
1848-1907
See Huysmans, Joris-Karl
See also CA 104

Huysmans, Joris-Karl............. **TCLC 7**
See also Huysmans, Charles Marie Georges
See also DLB 123

Hwang, David Henry
1957- .... **CLC 55; DC 4**
See also CA 127; 132; DAM DRAM;
INT 132

Hyde, Anthony 1946-............. **CLC 42**
See also CA 136

Hyde, Margaret O(ldroyd) 1917- ... **CLC 21**
See also CA 1-4R; CANR 1, 36; CLR 23;
JRDA; MAICYA; SAAS 8; SATA 1, 42,
76

Hynes, James 1956(?)-........... **CLC 65**

Ian, Janis 1951- .... **CLC 21**
See also CA 105

Ibanez, Vicente Blasco
See Blasco Ibanez, Vicente

Ibarguengoitia, Jorge 1928-1983.... **CLC 37**
See also CA 124; 113; HW

Ibsen, Henrik (Johan)
1828-1906 .... **TCLC 2, 8, 16, 37, 52;
DA; DAB; DAC; DC 2; WLC**
See also CA 104; 141; DAM DRAM, MST

Ibuse Masuji 1898-1993........... **CLC 22**
See also CA 127; 141

Ichikawa, Kon 1915-............. **CLC 20**
See also CA 121

Idle, Eric 1943-................. **CLC 21**
See also Monty Python
See also CA 116; CANR 35

Ignatow, David 1914-...... **CLC 4, 7, 14, 40**
See also CA 9-12R; CAAS 3; CANR 31;
DLB 5

Ihimaera, Witi 1944- .... **CLC 46**
See also CA 77-80

Ilf, Ilya........................ **TCLC 21**
See also Fainzilberg, Ilya Arnoldovich

Immermann, Karl (Lebrecht)
1796-1840 .... **NCLC 4, 49**
See also DLB 133

Inclan, Ramon (Maria) del Valle
See Valle-Inclan, Ramon (Maria) del

Infante, G(uillermo) Cabrera
See Cabrera Infante, G(uillermo)

Ingalls, Rachel (Holmes) 1940-..... **CLC 42**
See also CA 123; 127

Ingamells, Rex 1913-1955 .... **TCLC 35**

Inge, William Motter
1913-1973 .... **CLC 1, 8, 19**
See also CA 9-12R; CDALB 1941-1968;
DAM DRAM; DLB 7; MTCW

Ingelow, Jean 1820-1897 .... **NCLC 39**
See also DLB 35; SATA 33

Ingram, Willis J.
See Harris, Mark

Innaurato, Albert (F.) 1948(?)- .. **CLC 21, 60**
See also CA 115; 122; INT 122

Innes, Michael
See Stewart, J(ohn) I(nnes) M(ackintosh)

Ionesco, Eugene
1909-1994 .... **CLC 1, 4, 6, 9, 11, 15, 41,
86; DA; DAB; DAC; WLC**
See also CA 9-12R; 144; DAM DRAM,
MST; MTCW; SATA 7; SATA-Obit 79

Iqbal, Muhammad 1873-1938 ..... **TCLC 28**

Ireland, Patrick
See O'Doherty, Brian

Iron, Ralph
See Schreiner, Olive (Emilie Albertina)

Irving, John (Winslow)
1942- .... **CLC 13, 23, 38**
See also AAYA 8; BEST 89:3; CA 25-28R;
CANR 28; DAM NOV, POP; DLB 6;
DLBY 82; MTCW

Irving, Washington
1783-1859 ..... **NCLC 2, 19; DA; DAB;
SSC 2; WLC**
See also CDALB 1640-1865; DAM MST;
DLB 3, 11, 30, 59, 73, 74; YABC 2

Irwin, P. K.
See Page, P(atricia) K(athleen)

Isaacs, Susan 1943- .... **CLC 32**
See also BEST 89:1; CA 89-92; CANR 20,
41; DAM POP; INT CANR-20; MTCW

Isherwood, Christopher (William Bradshaw)
1904-1986 .... **CLC 1, 9, 11, 14, 44**
See also CA 13-16R; 117; CANR 35;
DAM DRAM, NOV; DLB 15; DLBY 86;
MTCW

Ishiguro, Kazuo 1954- ...... **CLC 27, 56, 59**
See also BEST 90:2; CA 120; CANR 49;
DAM NOV; MTCW

Ishikawa Takuboku
1886(?)-1912 .... **TCLC 15; PC 10**
See also CA 113; DAM POET

Iskander, Fazil 1929-............. **CLC 47**
See also CA 102

Ivan IV 1530-1584 .... **LC 17**

Ivanov, Vyacheslav Ivanovich
1866-1949 .... **TCLC 33**
See also CA 122

Ivask, Ivar Vidrik 1927-1992....... **CLC 14**
See also CA 37-40R; 139; CANR 24

Jackson, Daniel
See Wingrove, David (John)

Jackson, Jesse 1908-1983 .... **CLC 12**
See also BW 1; CA 25-28R; 109; CANR 27;
CLR 28; MAICYA; SATA 2, 29;
SATA-Obit 48

Jackson, Laura (Riding) 1901-1991
See Riding, Laura
See also CA 65-68; 135; CANR 28; DLB 48

Jackson, Sam
See Trumbo, Dalton

Jackson, Sara
See Wingrove, David (John)

Jackson, Shirley
1919-1965 .... **CLC 11, 60, 87; DA;
DAC; SSC 9; WLC**
See also AAYA 9; CA 1-4R; 25-28R;
CANR 4; CDALB 1941-1968;
DAM MST; DLB 6; SATA 2

Jacob, (Cyprien-)Max 1876-1944 ... **TCLC 6**
See also CA 104

Johnson, Uwe
1934-1984 . . . . **CLC 5, 10, 15, 40**
See also CA 1-4R; 112; CANR 1, 39;
DLB 75; MTCW

Johnston, George (Benson) 1913- . . . **CLC 51**
See also CA 1-4R; CANR 5, 20; DLB 88

Johnston, Jennifer 1930- . . . . **CLC 7**
See also CA 85-88; DLB 14

Jolley, (Monica) Elizabeth
1923- . . . . **CLC 46; SSC 19**
See also CA 127; CAAS 13

Jones, Arthur Llewellyn 1863-1947
See Machen, Arthur
See also CA 104

Jones, D(ouglas) G(ordon) 1929-. . . . **CLC 10**
See also CA 29-32R; CANR 13; DLB 53

Jones, David (Michael)
1895-1974 . . . . **CLC 2, 4, 7, 13, 42**
See also CA 9-12R; 53-56; CANR 28;
CDBLB 1945-1960; DLB 20, 100; MTCW

Jones, David Robert 1947-
See Bowie, David
See also CA 103

Jones, Diana Wynne 1934- . . . . **CLC 26**
See also AAYA 12; CA 49-52; CANR 4,
26; DLB 161; CLR 23; JRDA; MAICYA;
SAAS 7; SATA 9, 70

Jones, Edward P. 1950- . . . . **CLC 76**
See also BW 2; CA 142

Jones, Gayl 1949-. . . . . **CLC 6, 9; BLC**
See also BW 2; CA 77-80; CANR 27;
DAM MULT; DLB 33; MTCW

Jones, James 1921-1977. . . . **CLC 1, 3, 10, 39**
See also AITN 1, 2; CA 1-4R; 69-72;
CANR 6; DLB 2, 143; MTCW

Jones, John J.
See Lovecraft, H(oward) P(hillips)

Jones, LeRoi . . . . **CLC 1, 2, 3, 5, 10, 14**
See also Baraka, Amiri

Jones, Louis B. . . . . **CLC 65**
See also CA 141

Jones, Madison (Percy, Jr.) 1925- . . . **CLC 4**
See also CA 13-16R; CAAS 11; CANR 7;
DLB 152

Jones, Mervyn 1922- . . . . **CLC 10, 52**
See also CA 45-48; CAAS 5; CANR 1;
MTCW

Jones, Mick 1956(?)- . . . . **CLC 30**

Jones, Nettie (Pearl) 1941- . . . . **CLC 34**
See also BW 2; CA 137; CAAS 20

Jones, Preston 1936-1979 . . . . **CLC 10**
See also CA 73-76; 89-92; DLB 7

Jones, Robert F(rancis) 1934-. . . . . . . **CLC 7**
See also CA 49-52; CANR 2

Jones, Rod 1953- . . . . **CLC 50**
See also CA 128

Jones, Terence Graham Parry
1942- . . . . **CLC 21**
See also Jones, Terry; Monty Python
See also CA 112; 116; CANR 35; INT 116

Jones, Terry
See Jones, Terence Graham Parry
See also SATA 67; SATA-Brief 51

Jones, Thom 1945(?)-. . . . . **CLC 81**

Jong, Erica 1942-. . . . . . **CLC 4, 6, 8, 18, 83**
See also AITN 1; BEST 90:2; CA 73-76;
CANR 26; DAM NOV, POP; DLB 2, 5,
28, 152; INT CANR-26; MTCW

Jonson, Ben(jamin)
1572(?)-1637 . . . . **LC 6; DA; DAB; DAC;
DC 4; WLC**
See also CDBLB Before 1660;
DAM DRAM, MST, POET; DLB 62,
121

Jordan, June 1936-. . . . . **CLC 5, 11, 23**
See also AAYA 2; BW 2; CA 33-36R;
CANR 25; CLR 10; DAM MULT,
POET; DLB 38; MAICYA; MTCW;
SATA 4

Jordan, Pat(rick M.) 1941-. . . . . **CLC 37**
See also CA 33-36R

Jorgensen, Ivar
See Ellison, Harlan (Jay)

Jorgenson, Ivar
See Silverberg, Robert

Josephus, Flavius c. 37-100 . . . . . . **CMLC 13**

Josipovici, Gabriel 1940-. . . . . **CLC 6, 43**
See also CA 37-40R; CAAS 8; CANR 47;
DLB 14

Joubert, Joseph 1754-1824 . . . . **NCLC 9**

Jouve, Pierre Jean 1887-1976. . . . . . **CLC 47**
See also CA 65-68

Joyce, James (Augustine Aloysius)
1882-1941 . . . . **TCLC 3, 8, 16, 35, 52;
DA; DAB; DAC; SSC 3; WLC**
See also CA 104; 126; CDBLB 1914-1945;
DAM MST, NOV, POET; DLB 10, 19,
36; MTCW

Jozsef, Attila 1905-1937. . . . . **TCLC 22**
See also CA 116

Juana Ines de la Cruz 1651(?)-1695 . . . **LC 5**

Judd, Cyril
See Kornbluth, C(yril) M.; Pohl, Frederik

Julian of Norwich 1342(?)-1416(?) . . . . **LC 6**
See also DLB 146

Juniper, Alex
See Hospital, Janette Turner

Just, Ward (Swift) 1935- . . . . **CLC 4, 27**
See also CA 25-28R; CANR 32;
INT CANR-32

Justice, Donald (Rodney) 1925- . . **CLC 6, 19**
See also CA 5-8R; CANR 26; DAM POET;
DLBY 83; INT CANR-26

Juvenal c. 55-c. 127 . . . . **CMLC 8**

Juvenis
See Bourne, Randolph S(illiman)

Kacew, Romain 1914-1980
See Gary, Romain
See also CA 108; 102

Kadare, Ismail 1936- . . . . **CLC 52**

Kadohata, Cynthia. . . . . **CLC 59**
See also CA 140

Kafka, Franz
1883-1924 . . . . **TCLC 2, 6, 13, 29, 47, 53;
DA; DAB; DAC; SSC 5; WLC**
See also CA 105; 126; DAM MST, NOV;
DLB 81; MTCW

Kahanovitsch, Pinkhes
See Der Nister

Kahn, Roger 1927-. . . . . **CLC 30**
See also CA 25-28R; CANR 44; SATA 37

Kain, Saul
See Sassoon, Siegfried (Lorraine)

Kaiser, Georg 1878-1945 . . . . **TCLC 9**
See also CA 106; DLB 124

Kaletski, Alexander 1946-. . . . . **CLC 39**
See also CA 118; 143

Kalidasa fl. c. 400- . . . . **CMLC 9**

Kallman, Chester (Simon)
1921-1975 . . . . **CLC 2**
See also CA 45-48; 53-56; CANR 3

Kaminsky, Melvin 1926-
See Brooks, Mel
See also CA 65-68; CANR 16

Kaminsky, Stuart M(elvin) 1934-. . . **CLC 59**
See also CA 73-76; CANR 29

Kane, Paul
See Simon, Paul

Kane, Wilson
See Bloch, Robert (Albert)

Kanin, Garson 1912-. . . . . **CLC 22**
See also AITN 1; CA 5-8R; CANR 7;
DLB 7

Kaniuk, Yoram 1930-. . . . . **CLC 19**
See also CA 134

Kant, Immanuel 1724-1804 . . . . . . **NCLC 27**
See also DLB 94

Kantor, MacKinlay 1904-1977 . . . . . . **CLC 7**
See also CA 61-64; 73-76; DLB 9, 102

Kaplan, David Michael 1946- . . . . . . **CLC 50**

Kaplan, James 1951- . . . . **CLC 59**
See also CA 135

Karageorge, Michael
See Anderson, Poul (William)

Karamzin, Nikolai Mikhailovich
1766-1826 . . . . **NCLC 3**
See also DLB 150

Karapanou, Margarita 1946-. . . . . . . **CLC 13**
See also CA 101

Karinthy, Frigyes 1887-1938. . . . . . . **TCLC 47**

Karl, Frederick R(obert) 1927-. . . . . . **CLC 34**
See also CA 5-8R; CANR 3, 44

Kastel, Warren
See Silverberg, Robert

Kataev, Evgeny Petrovich 1903-1942
See Petrov, Evgeny
See also CA 120

Kataphusin
See Ruskin, John

Katz, Steve 1935-. . . . . **CLC 47**
See also CA 25-28R; CAAS 14; CANR 12;
DLBY 83

Kauffman, Janet 1945-. . . . . **CLC 42**
See also CA 117; CANR 43; DLBY 86

Kaufman, Bob (Garnell)
1925-1986 . . . . **CLC 49**
See also BW 1; CA 41-44R; 118; CANR 22;
DLB 16, 41

Kaufman, George S. 1889-1961 . . . . . **CLC 38**
See also CA 108; 93-96; DAM DRAM;
DLB 7; INT 108

Kaufman, Sue . . . . **CLC 3, 8**
See also Barondess, Sue K(aufman)

Kavafis, Konstantinos Petrou 1863-1933
See Cavafy, C(onstantine) P(eter)
See also CA 104

Kavan, Anna 1901-1968 . . . . . . **CLC 5, 13, 82**
See also CA 5-8R; CANR 6; MTCW

Kavanagh, Dan
See Barnes, Julian

Kavanagh, Patrick (Joseph)
1904-1967 . . . . **CLC 22**
See also CA 123; 25-28R; DLB 15, 20;
MTCW

Kawabata, Yasunari
1899-1972 . . . . . **CLC 2, 5, 9, 18; SSC 17**
See also CA 93-96; 33-36R; DAM MULT

Kaye, M(ary) M(argaret) 1909- . . . . . **CLC 28**
See also CA 89-92; CANR 24; MTCW;
SATA 62

Kaye, Mollie
See Kaye, M(ary) M(argaret)

Kaye-Smith, Sheila 1887-1956 . . . . . **TCLC 20**
See also CA 118; DLB 36

Kaymor, Patrice Maguilene
See Senghor, Leopold Sedar

Kazan, Elia 1909- . . . . **CLC 6, 16, 63**
See also CA 21-24R; CANR 32

Kazantzakis, Nikos
1883(?)-1957 . . . . **TCLC 2, 5, 33**
See also CA 105; 132; MTCW

Kazin, Alfred 1915- . . . . **CLC 34, 38**
See also CA 1-4R; CAAS 7; CANR 1, 45;
DLB 67

Keane, Mary Nesta (Skrine) 1904-
See Keane, Molly
See also CA 108; 114

Keane, Molly . . . . **CLC 31**
See also Keane, Mary Nesta (Skrine)
See also INT 114

Keates, Jonathan 19(?)- . . . . **CLC 34**

Keaton, Buster 1895-1966 . . . . **CLC 20**

Keats, John
1795-1821 . . . . **NCLC 8; DA; DAB;**
DAC; PC 1; WLC
See also CDBLB 1789-1832; DAM MST,
POET; DLB 96, 110

Keene, Donald 1922- . . . . **CLC 34**
See also CA 1-4R; CANR 5

Keillor, Garrison . . . . **CLC 40**
See also Keillor, Gary (Edward)
See also AAYA 2; BEST 89:3; DLBY 87;
SATA 58

Keillor, Gary (Edward) 1942-
See Keillor, Garrison
See also CA 111; 117; CANR 36;
DAM POP; MTCW

Keith, Michael
See Hubbard, L(afayette) Ron(ald)

Keller, Gottfried 1819-1890 . . . . **NCLC 2**
See also DLB 129

Kellerman, Jonathan 1949- . . . . **CLC 44**
See also BEST 90:1; CA 106; CANR 29;
DAM POP; INT CANR-29

Kelley, William Melvin 1937- . . . . . . **CLC 22**
See also BW 1; CA 77-80; CANR 27;
DLB 33

Kellogg, Marjorie 1922- . . . . **CLC 2**
See also CA 81-84

Kellow, Kathleen
See Hibbert, Eleanor Alice Burford

Kelly, M(ilton) T(erry) 1947- . . . . **CLC 55**
See also CA 97-100; CAAS 22; CANR 19,
43

Kelman, James 1946- . . . . **CLC 58, 86**
See also CA 148

Kemal, Yashar 1923- . . . . **CLC 14, 29**
See also CA 89-92; CANR 44

Kemble, Fanny 1809-1893 . . . . **NCLC 18**
See also DLB 32

Kemelman, Harry 1908- . . . . **CLC 2**
See also AITN 1; CA 9-12R; CANR 6;
DLB 28

Kempe, Margery 1373(?)-1440(?) . . . . . **LC 6**
See also DLB 146

Kempis, Thomas a 1380-1471 . . . . **LC 11**

Kendall, Henry 1839-1882 . . . . **NCLC 12**

Keneally, Thomas (Michael)
1935- . . . . . . **CLC 5, 8, 10, 14, 19, 27, 43**
See also CA 85-88; CANR 10, 50;
DAM NOV; MTCW

Kennedy, Adrienne (Lita)
1931- . . . . **CLC 66; BLC; DC 5**
See also BW 2; CA 103; CAAS 20; CABS 3;
CANR 26; DAM MULT; DLB 38

Kennedy, John Pendleton
1795-1870 . . . . **NCLC 2**
See also DLB 3

Kennedy, Joseph Charles 1929-
See Kennedy, X. J.
See also CA 1-4R; CANR 4, 30, 40;
SATA 14

Kennedy, William 1928- . . . **CLC 6, 28, 34, 53**
See also AAYA 1; CA 85-88; CANR 14,
31; DAM NOV; DLB 143; DLBY 85;
INT CANR-31; MTCW; SATA 57

Kennedy, X. J. . . . . **CLC 8, 42**
See also Kennedy, Joseph Charles
See also CAAS 9; CLR 27; DLB 5

Kenny, Maurice (Francis) 1929- . . . . . **CLC 87**
See also CA 144; CAAS 22; DAM MULT;
NNAL

Kent, Kelvin
See Kuttner, Henry

Kenton, Maxwell
See Southern, Terry

Kenyon, Robert O.
See Kuttner, Henry

Kerouac, Jack . . . . . **CLC 1, 2, 3, 5, 14, 29, 61**
See also Kerouac, Jean-Louis Lebris de
See also CDALB 1941-1968; DLB 2, 16;
DLBD 3

Kerouac, Jean-Louis Lebris de 1922-1969
See Kerouac, Jack
See also AITN 1; CA 5-8R; 25-28R;
CANR 26; DA; DAB; DAC; DAM MST,
NOV, POET, POP; MTCW; WLC

Kerr, Jean 1923- . . . . **CLC 22**
See also CA 5-8R; CANR 7; INT CANR-7

Kerr, M. E. . . . . **CLC 12, 35**
See also Meaker, Marijane (Agnes)
See also AAYA 2; CLR 29; SAAS 1

Kerr, Robert . . . . **CLC 55**

Kerrigan, (Thomas) Anthony
1918- . . . . **CLC 4, 6**
See also CA 49-52; CAAS 11; CANR 4

Kerry, Lois
See Duncan, Lois

Kesey, Ken (Elton)
1935- . . . . . . **CLC 1, 3, 6, 11, 46, 64; DA;**
DAB; DAC; WLC
See also CA 1-4R; CANR 22, 38;
CDALB 1968-1988; DAM MST, NOV,
POP; DLB 2, 16; MTCW; SATA 66

Kesselring, Joseph (Otto)
1902-1967 . . . . **CLC 45**
See also DAM DRAM, MST

Kessler, Jascha (Frederick) 1929- . . . . **CLC 4**
See also CA 17-20R; CANR 8, 48

Kettelkamp, Larry (Dale) 1933- . . . . **CLC 12**
See also CA 29-32R; CANR 16; SAAS 3;
SATA 2

Keyber, Conny
See Fielding, Henry

Keyes, Daniel 1927- . . . . **CLC 80; DA; DAC**
See also CA 17-20R; CANR 10, 26;
DAM MST, NOV; SATA 37

Khanshendel, Chiron
See Rose, Wendy

Khayyam, Omar
1048-1131 . . . . **CMLC 11; PC 8**
See also DAM POET

Kherdian, David 1931- . . . . **CLC 6, 9**
See also CA 21-24R; CAAS 2; CANR 39;
CLR 24; JRDA; MAICYA; SATA 16, 74

Khlebnikov, Velimir . . . . **TCLC 20**
See also Khlebnikov, Viktor Vladimirovich

Khlebnikov, Viktor Vladimirovich 1885-1922
See Khlebnikov, Velimir
See also CA 117

Khodasevich, Vladislav (Felitsianovich)
1886-1939 . . . . **TCLC 15**
See also CA 115

Kielland, Alexander Lange
1849-1906 . . . . **TCLC 5**
See also CA 104

Kiely, Benedict 1919- . . . . **CLC 23, 43**
See also CA 1-4R; CANR 2; DLB 15

Kienzle, William X(avier) 1928- . . . . **CLC 25**
See also CA 93-96; CAAS 1; CANR 9, 31;
DAM POP; INT CANR-31; MTCW

Kierkegaard, Soren 1813-1855 . . . . **NCLC 34**

Killens, John Oliver 1916-1987 . . . . . **CLC 10**
See also BW 2; CA 77-80; 123; CAAS 2;
CANR 26; DLB 33

Killigrew, Anne 1660-1685 . . . . **LC 4**
See also DLB 131

Kim
See Simenon, Georges (Jacques Christian)

Kincaid, Jamaica 1949- . . . **CLC 43, 68; BLC**
See also AAYA 13; BW 2; CA 125;
CANR 47; DAM MULT, NOV;
DLB 157

King, Francis (Henry) 1923- . . . . . **CLC 8, 53**
See also CA 1-4R; CANR 1, 33;
DAM NOV; DLB 15, 139; MTCW

King, Martin Luther, Jr.
1929-1968 . . . . **CLC 83; BLC; DA; DAB;
DAC**
See also BW 2; CA 25-28; CANR 27, 44;
CAP 2; DAM MST, MULT; MTCW;
SATA 14

King, Stephen (Edwin)
1947- . . . . . **CLC 12, 26, 37, 61; SSC 17**
See also AAYA 1, 17; BEST 90:1;
CA 61-64; CANR 1, 30; DAM NOV,
POP; DLB 143; DLBY 80; JRDA;
MTCW; SATA 9, 55

King, Steve
See King, Stephen (Edwin)

King, Thomas 1943- . . . . **CLC 89; DAC**
See also CA 144; DAM MULT; NNAL

Kingman, Lee. **CLC 17**
See also Natti, (Mary) Lee
See also SAAS 3; SATA 1, 67

Kingsley, Charles 1819-1875 . . . . . **NCLC 35**
See also DLB 21, 32; YABC 2

Kingsley, Sidney 1906-1995. . . . . . . **CLC 44**
See also CA 85-88; 147; DLB 7

Kingsolver, Barbara 1955- . . . . . . **CLC 55, 81**
See also AAYA 15; CA 129; 134;
DAM POP; INT 134

Kingston, Maxine (Ting Ting) Hong
1940- . . . . **CLC 12, 19, 58**
See also AAYA 8; CA 69-72; CANR 13,
38; DAM MULT, NOV; DLBY 80;
INT CANR-13; MTCW; SATA 53

Kinnell, Galway
1927- . . . . **CLC 1, 2, 3, 5, 13, 29**
See also CA 9-12R; CANR 10, 34; DLB 5;
DLBY 87; INT CANR-34; MTCW

Kinsella, Thomas 1928- . . . . **CLC 4, 19**
See also CA 17-20R; CANR 15; DLB 27;
MTCW

Kinsella, W(illiam) P(atrick)
1935- . . . . **CLC 27, 43; DAC**
See also AAYA 7; CA 97-100; CAAS 7;
CANR 21, 35; DAM NOV, POP;
INT CANR-21; MTCW

Kipling, (Joseph) Rudyard
1865-1936 . . . . . . **TCLC 8, 17; DA; DAB;
DAC; PC 3; SSC 5; WLC**
See also CA 105; 120; CANR 33;
CDBLB 1890-1914; CLR 39; DAM MST,
POET; DLB 19, 34, 141, 156; MAICYA;
MTCW; YABC 2

Kirkup, James 1918- . . . . **CLC 1**
See also CA 1-4R; CAAS 4; CANR 2;
DLB 27; SATA 12

Kirkwood, James 1930(?)-1989 . . . . . . **CLC 9**
See also AITN 2; CA 1-4R; 128; CANR 6,
40

Kirshner, Sidney
See Kingsley, Sidney

Kis, Danilo 1935-1989 . . . . **CLC 57**
See also CA 109; 118; 129; MTCW

Kivi, Aleksis 1834-1872 . . . . **NCLC 30**

Kizer, Carolyn (Ashley)
1925- . . . . **CLC 15, 39, 80**
See also CA 65-68; CAAS 5; CANR 24;
DAM POET; DLB 5

Klabund 1890-1928. . . . . **TCLC 44**
See also DLB 66

Klappert, Peter 1942- . . . . **CLC 57**
See also CA 33-36R; DLB 5

Klein, A(braham) M(oses)
1909-1972 . . . . **CLC 19; DAB; DAC**
See also CA 101; 37-40R; DAM MST;
DLB 68

Klein, Norma 1938-1989 . . . . **CLC 30**
See also AAYA 2; CA 41-44R; 128;
CANR 15, 37; CLR 2, 19;
INT CANR-15; JRDA; MAICYA;
SAAS 1; SATA 7, 57

Klein, T(heodore) E(ibon) D(onald)
1947- . . . . **CLC 34**
See also CA 119; CANR 44

Kleist, Heinrich von
1777-1811 . . . . **NCLC 2, 37**
See also DAM DRAM; DLB 90

Klima, Ivan 1931- . . . . **CLC 56**
See also CA 25-28R; CANR 17, 50;
DAM NOV

Klimentov, Andrei Platonovich 1899-1951
See Platonov, Andrei
See also CA 108

Klinger, Friedrich Maximilian von
1752-1831 . . . . **NCLC 1**
See also DLB 94

Klopstock, Friedrich Gottlieb
1724-1803 . . . . **NCLC 11**
See also DLB 97

Knebel, Fletcher 1911-1993 . . . . **CLC 14**
See also AITN 1; CA 1-4R; 140; CAAS 3;
CANR 1, 36; SATA 36; SATA-Obit 75

Knickerbocker, Diedrich
See Irving, Washington

Knight, Etheridge
1931-1991 . . . . **CLC 40; BLC; PC 14**
See also BW 1; CA 21-24R; 133; CANR 23;
DAM POET; DLB 41

Knight, Sarah Kemble 1666-1727 . . . . . **LC 7**
See also DLB 24

Knister, Raymond 1899-1932. . . . . . **TCLC 56**
See also DLB 68

Knowles, John
1926- . . . . . . **CLC 1, 4, 10, 26; DA; DAC**
See also AAYA 10; CA 17-20R; CANR 40;
CDALB 1968-1988; DAM MST, NOV;
DLB 6; MTCW; SATA 8

Knox, Calvin M.
See Silverberg, Robert

Knye, Cassandra
See Disch, Thomas M(ichael)

Koch, C(hristopher) J(ohn) 1932- . . . **CLC 42**
See also CA 127

Koch, Christopher
See Koch, C(hristopher) J(ohn)

Koch, Kenneth 1925- . . . . **CLC 5, 8, 44**
See also CA 1-4R; CANR 6, 36;
DAM POET; DLB 5; INT CANR-36;
SATA 65

Kochanowski, Jan 1530-1584. . . . . . . **LC 10**

Kock, Charles Paul de
1794-1871 . . . . **NCLC 16**

Koda Shigeyuki 1867-1947
See Rohan, Koda
See also CA 121

Koestler, Arthur
1905-1983 . . . . **CLC 1, 3, 6, 8, 15, 33**
See also CA 1-4R; 109; CANR 1, 33;
CDBLB 1945-1960; DLBY 83; MTCW

Kogawa, Joy Nozomi 1935- . . . **CLC 78; DAC**
See also CA 101; CANR 19; DAM MST,
MULT

Kohout, Pavel 1928- . . . . **CLC 13**
See also CA 45-48; CANR 3

Koizumi, Yakumo
See Hearn, (Patricio) Lafcadio (Tessima
Carlos)

Kolmar, Gertrud 1894-1943 . . . . **TCLC 40**

Komunyakaa, Yusef 1947- . . . . **CLC 86**
See also CA 147; DLB 120

Konrad, George
See Konrad, Gyoergy

Konrad, Gyoergy 1933- . . . . . . **CLC 4, 10, 73**
See also CA 85-88

Konwicki, Tadeusz 1926- . . . . . **CLC 8, 28, 54**
See also CA 101; CAAS 9; CANR 39;
MTCW

Koontz, Dean R(ay) 1945- . . . . **CLC 78**
See also AAYA 9; BEST 89:3, 90:2;
CA 108; CANR 19, 36; DAM NOV,
POP; MTCW

Kopit, Arthur (Lee) 1937- . . . . **CLC 1, 18, 33**
See also AITN 1; CA 81-84; CABS 3;
DAM DRAM; DLB 7; MTCW

Kops, Bernard 1926- . . . . **CLC 4**
See also CA 5-8R; DLB 13

Kornbluth, C(yril) M. 1923-1958. . . . **TCLC 8**
See also CA 105; DLB 8

Korolenko, V. G.
See Korolenko, Vladimir Galaktionovich

Korolenko, Vladimir
See Korolenko, Vladimir Galaktionovich

Korolenko, Vladimir G.
See Korolenko, Vladimir Galaktionovich

Korolenko, Vladimir Galaktionovich
1853-1921 . . . . **TCLC 22**
See also CA 121

Korzybski, Alfred (Habdank Skarbek)
1879-1950 . . . . **TCLC 61**
See also CA 123

Kosinski, Jerzy (Nikodem)
1933-1991 . . . . **CLC 1, 2, 3, 6, 10, 15, 53,
70**
See also CA 17-20R; 134; CANR 9, 46;
DAM NOV; DLB 2; DLBY 82; MTCW

Kostelanetz, Richard (Cory) 1940- . . . **CLC 28**
See also CA 13-16R; CAAS 8; CANR 38

Lane, Patrick 1939- . . . . CLC 25
See also CA 97-100; DAM POET; DLB 53;
INT 97-100

Lang, Andrew 1844-1912 . . . . TCLC 16
See also CA 114; 137; DLB 98, 141;
MAICYA; SATA 16

Lang, Fritz 1890-1976 . . . . CLC 20
See also CA 77-80; 69-72; CANR 30

Lange, John
See Crichton, (John) Michael

Langer, Elinor 1939- . . . . CLC 34
See also CA 121

Langland, William
1330(?)-1400(?) . . . . . . LC 19; DA; DAB;
DAC
See also DAM MST, POET; DLB 146

Langstaff, Launcelot
See Irving, Washington

Lanier, Sidney 1842-1881 . . . . NCLC 6
See also DAM POET; DLB 64; DLBD 13;
MAICYA; SATA 18

Lanyer, Aemilia 1569-1645 . . . . . . LC 10, 30
See also DLB 121

Lao Tzu . . . . CMLC 7

Lapine, James (Elliot) 1949- . . . . CLC 39
See also CA 123; 130; INT 130

Larbaud, Valery (Nicolas)
1881-1957 . . . . TCLC 9
See also CA 106

Lardner, Ring
See Lardner, Ring(gold) W(ilmer)

Lardner, Ring W., Jr.
See Lardner, Ring(gold) W(ilmer)

Lardner, Ring(gold) W(ilmer)
1885-1933 . . . . TCLC 2, 14
See also CA 104; 131; CDALB 1917-1929;
DLB 11, 25, 86; MTCW

Laredo, Betty
See Codrescu, Andrei

Larkin, Maia
See Wojciechowska, Maia (Teresa)

Larkin, Philip (Arthur)
1922-1985 . . . . CLC 3, 5, 8, 9, 13, 18, 33,
39, 64; DAB
See also CA 5-8R; 117; CANR 24;
CDBLB 1960 to Present; DAM MST,
POET; DLB 27; MTCW

Larra (y Sanchez de Castro), Mariano Jose de
1809-1837 . . . . NCLC 17

Larsen, Eric 1941- . . . . CLC 55
See also CA 132

Larsen, Nella 1891-1964 . . . . . CLC 37; BLC
See also BW 1; CA 125; DAM MULT;
DLB 51

Larson, Charles R(aymond) 1938- . . . CLC 31
See also CA 53-56; CANR 4

Las Casas, Bartolome de 1474-1566 . . LC 31

Lasker-Schueler, Else 1869-1945 . . TCLC 57
See also DLB 66, 124

Latham, Jean Lee 1902- . . . . CLC 12
See also AITN 1; CA 5-8R; CANR 7;
MAICYA; SATA 2, 68

Latham, Mavis
See Clark, Mavis Thorpe

Lathen, Emma . . . . CLC 2
See also Hennissart, Martha; Latsis, Mary
J(ane)

Lathrop, Francis
See Leiber, Fritz (Reuter, Jr.)

Latsis, Mary J(ane)
See Lathen, Emma
See also CA 85-88

Lattimore, Richmond (Alexander)
1906-1984 . . . . CLC 3
See also CA 1-4R; 112; CANR 1

Laughlin, James 1914- . . . . CLC 49
See also CA 21-24R; CAAS 22; CANR 9,
47; DLB 48

Laurence, (Jean) Margaret (Wemyss)
1926-1987 . . . . CLC 3, 6, 13, 50, 62;
DAC; SSC 7
See also CA 5-8R; 121; CANR 33;
DAM MST; DLB 53; MTCW;
SATA-Obit 50

Laurent, Antoine 1952- . . . . CLC 50

Lauscher, Hermann
See Hesse, Hermann

Lautreamont, Comte de
1846-1870 . . . . NCLC 12; SSC 14

Laverty, Donald
See Blish, James (Benjamin)

Lavin, Mary 1912- . . . . . . CLC 4, 18; SSC 4
See also CA 9-12R; CANR 33; DLB 15;
MTCW

Lavond, Paul Dennis
See Kornbluth, C(yril) M.; Pohl, Frederik

Lawler, Raymond Evenor 1922- . . . . CLC 58
See also CA 103

Lawrence, D(avid) H(erbert Richards)
1885-1930 . . . . TCLC 2, 9, 16, 33, 48, 61;
DA; DAB; DAC; SSC 4, 19; WLC
See also CA 104; 121; CDBLB 1914-1945;
DAM MST, NOV, POET; DLB 10, 19,
36, 98; MTCW

Lawrence, T(homas) E(dward)
1888-1935 . . . . TCLC 18
See also Dale, Colin
See also CA 115

Lawrence of Arabia
See Lawrence, T(homas) E(dward)

Lawson, Henry (Archibald Hertzberg)
1867-1922 . . . . TCLC 27; SSC 18
See also CA 120

Lawton, Dennis
See Faust, Frederick (Schiller)

Laxness, Halldor . . . . CLC 25
See also Gudjonsson, Halldor Kiljan

Layamon fl. c. 1200- . . . . CMLC 10
See also DLB 146

Laye, Camara 1928-1980 . . . CLC 4, 38; BLC
See also BW 1; CA 85-88; 97-100;
CANR 25; DAM MULT; MTCW

Layton, Irving (Peter)
1912- . . . . CLC 2, 15; DAC
See also CA 1-4R; CANR 2, 33, 43;
DAM MST, POET; DLB 88; MTCW

Lazarus, Emma 1849-1887 . . . . NCLC 8

Lazarus, Felix
See Cable, George Washington

Lazarus, Henry
See Slavitt, David R(ytman)

Lea, Joan
See Neufeld, John (Arthur)

Leacock, Stephen (Butler)
1869-1944 . . . . TCLC 2; DAC
See also CA 104; 141; DAM MST; DLB 92

Lear, Edward 1812-1888 . . . . NCLC 3
See also CLR 1; DLB 32; MAICYA;
SATA 18

Lear, Norman (Milton) 1922- . . . . . . CLC 12
See also CA 73-76

Leavis, F(rank) R(aymond)
1895-1978 . . . . CLC 24
See also CA 21-24R; 77-80; CANR 44;
MTCW

Leavitt, David 1961- . . . . CLC 34
See also CA 116; 122; CANR 50;
DAM POP; DLB 130; INT 122

Leblanc, Maurice (Marie Emile)
1864-1941 . . . . TCLC 49
See also CA 110

Lebowitz, Fran(ces Ann)
1951(?)- . . . . CLC 11, 36
See also CA 81-84; CANR 14;
INT CANR-14; MTCW

Lebrecht, Peter
See Tieck, (Johann) Ludwig

le Carre, John . . . . CLC 3, 5, 9, 15, 28
See also Cornwell, David (John Moore)
See also BEST 89:4; CDBLB 1960 to
Present; DLB 87

Le Clezio, J(ean) M(arie) G(ustave)
1940- . . . . CLC 31
See also CA 116; 128; DLB 83

Leconte de Lisle, Charles-Marie-Rene
1818-1894 . . . . NCLC 29

Le Coq, Monsieur
See Simenon, Georges (Jacques Christian)

Leduc, Violette 1907-1972 . . . . CLC 22
See also CA 13-14; 33-36R; CAP 1

Ledwidge, Francis 1887(?)-1917 . . . TCLC 23
See also CA 123; DLB 20

Lee, Andrea 1953- . . . . CLC 36; BLC
See also BW 1; CA 125; DAM MULT

Lee, Andrew
See Auchincloss, Louis (Stanton)

Lee, Don L. CLC 2
See also Madhubuti, Haki R.

Lee, George W(ashington)
1894-1976 . . . . CLC 52; BLC
See also BW 1; CA 125; DAM MULT;
DLB 51

Lee, (Nelle) Harper
1926- . . . . CLC 12, 60; DA; DAB; DAC;
WLC
See also AAYA 13; CA 13-16R;
CDALB 1941-1968; DAM MST, NOV;
DLB 6; MTCW; SATA 11

Lee, Helen Elaine 1959(?)- . . . . CLC 86
See also CA 148

Lee, Julian
See Latham, Jean Lee

Lee, Larry
See Lee, Lawrence

Lewis, Matthew Gregory
        1775-1818 . . . . **NCLC 11**
        See also DLB 39, 158

Lewis, (Harry) Sinclair
        1885-1951 . . . . . **TCLC 4, 13, 23, 39; DA;**
                                                DAB; DAC; WLC
        See also CA 104; 133; CDALB 1917-1929;
        DAM MST, NOV; DLB 9, 102; DLBD 1;
        MTCW

Lewis, (Percy) Wyndham
        1884(?)-1957 . . . . **TCLC 2, 9**
        See also CA 104; DLB 15

Lewisohn, Ludwig   1883-1955. . . . . . **TCLC 19**
        See also CA 107; DLB 4, 9, 28, 102

Lezama Lima, Jose   1910-1976 . . . **CLC 4, 10**
        See also CA 77-80; DAM MULT;
        DLB 113; HW

L'Heureux, John (Clarke)   1934-. . . . **CLC 52**
        See also CA 13-16R; CANR 23, 45

Liddell, C. H.
        See Kuttner, Henry

Lie, Jonas (Lauritz Idemil)
        1833-1908(?) . . . . **TCLC 5**
        See also CA 115

Lieber, Joel   1937-1971. . . . . **CLC 6**
        See also CA 73-76; 29-32R

Lieber, Stanley Martin
        See Lee, Stan

Lieberman, Laurence (James)
        1935- . . . . **CLC 4, 36**
        See also CA 17-20R; CANR 8, 36

Lieksman, Anders
        See Haavikko, Paavo Juhani

Li Fei-kan   1904-
        See Pa Chin
        See also CA 105

Lifton, Robert Jay   1926-. . . . . **CLC 67**
        See also CA 17-20R; CANR 27;
        INT CANR-27; SATA 66

Lightfoot, Gordon   1938-. . . . . **CLC 26**
        See also CA 109

Lightman, Alan P.   1948- . . . . **CLC 81**
        See also CA 141

Ligotti, Thomas (Robert)
        1953- . . . . **CLC 44; SSC 16**
        See also CA 123; CANR 49

Li Ho   791-817. . . . . **PC 13**

Liliencron, (Friedrich Adolf Axel) Detlev von
        1844-1909 . . . . **TCLC 18**
        See also CA 117

Lilly, William   1602-1681 . . . . **LC 27**

Lima, Jose Lezama
        See Lezama Lima, Jose

Lima Barreto, Afonso Henrique de
        1881-1922 . . . . **TCLC 23**
        See also CA 117

Limonov, Edward   1944-. . . . . **CLC 67**
        See also CA 137

Lin, Frank
        See Atherton, Gertrude (Franklin Horn)

Lincoln, Abraham   1809-1865. . . . . **NCLC 18**

Lind, Jakov . . . . **CLC 1, 2, 4, 27, 82**
        See also Landwirth, Heinz
        See also CAAS 4

Lindbergh, Anne (Spencer) Morrow
        1906- . . . . **CLC 82**
        See also CA 17-20R; CANR 16;
        DAM NOV; MTCW; SATA 33

Lindsay, David   1878-1945 . . . . **TCLC 15**
        See also CA 113

Lindsay, (Nicholas) Vachel
        1879-1931 . . . **TCLC 17; DA; DAC; WLC**
        See also CA 114; 135; CDALB 1865-1917;
        DAM MST, POET; DLB 54; SATA 40

Linke-Poot
        See Doeblin, Alfred

Linney, Romulus   1930- . . . . **CLC 51**
        See also CA 1-4R; CANR 40, 44

Linton, Eliza Lynn   1822-1898. . . . **NCLC 41**
        See also DLB 18

Li Po   701-763 . . . . **CMLC 2**

Lipsius, Justus   1547-1606 . . . . **LC 16**

Lipsyte, Robert (Michael)
        1938- . . . . **CLC 21; DA; DAC**
        See also AAYA 7; CA 17-20R; CANR 8;
        CLR 23; DAM MST, NOV; JRDA;
        MAICYA; SATA 5, 68

Lish, Gordon (Jay)   1934-. . **CLC 45; SSC 18**
        See also CA 113; 117; DLB 130; INT 117

Lispector, Clarice   1925-1977. . . . . . **CLC 43**
        See also CA 139; 116; DLB 113

Littell, Robert   1935(?)- . . . . **CLC 42**
        See also CA 109; 112

Little, Malcolm   1925-1965
        See Malcolm X
        See also BW 1; CA 125; 111; DA; DAB;
        DAC; DAM MST, MULT; MTCW

Littlewit, Humphrey Gent.
        See Lovecraft, H(oward) P(hillips)

Litwos
        See Sienkiewicz, Henryk (Adam Alexander
        Pius)

Liu E   1857-1909 . . . . **TCLC 15**
        See also CA 115

Lively, Penelope (Margaret)
        1933- . . . . **CLC 32, 50**
        See also CA 41-44R; CANR 29; CLR 7;
        DAM NOV; DLB 14, 161; JRDA;
        MAICYA; MTCW; SATA 7, 60

Livesay, Dorothy (Kathleen)
        1909- . . . . **CLC 4, 15, 79; DAC**
        See also AITN 2; CA 25-28R; CAAS 8;
        CANR 36; DAM MST, POET; DLB 68;
        MTCW

Livy   c. 59B.C.-c. 17 . . . . **CMLC 11**

Lizardi, Jose Joaquin Fernandez de
        1776-1827 . . . . **NCLC 30**

Llewellyn, Richard
        See Llewellyn Lloyd, Richard Dafydd
        Vivian
        See also DLB 15

Llewellyn Lloyd, Richard Dafydd Vivian
        1906-1983 . . . . **CLC 7, 80**
        See also Llewellyn, Richard
        See also CA 53-56; 111; CANR 7;
        SATA 11; SATA-Obit 37

Llosa, (Jorge) Mario (Pedro) Vargas
        See Vargas Llosa, (Jorge) Mario (Pedro)

Lloyd Webber, Andrew   1948-
        See Webber, Andrew Lloyd
        See also AAYA 1; CA 116; 149;
        DAM DRAM; SATA 56

Llull, Ramon   c. 1235-c. 1316. . . . . **CMLC 12**

Locke, Alain (Le Roy)
        1886-1954 . . . . **TCLC 43**
        See also BW 1; CA 106; 124; DLB 51

Locke, John   1632-1704 . . . . **LC 7**
        See also DLB 101

Locke-Elliott, Sumner
        See Elliott, Sumner Locke

Lockhart, John Gibson
        1794-1854 . . . . **NCLC 6**
        See also DLB 110, 116, 144

Lodge, David (John)   1935-. . . . . **CLC 36**
        See also BEST 90:1; CA 17-20R; CANR 19;
        DAM POP; DLB 14; INT CANR-19;
        MTCW

Loennbohm, Armas Eino Leopold   1878-1926
        See Leino, Eino
        See also CA 123

Loewinsohn, Ron(ald William)
        1937- . . . . **CLC 52**
        See also CA 25-28R

Logan, Jake
        See Smith, Martin Cruz

Logan, John (Burton)   1923-1987. . . . . **CLC 5**
        See also CA 77-80; 124; CANR 45; DLB 5

Lo Kuan-chung   1330(?)-1400(?). . . . . **LC 12**

Lombard, Nap
        See Johnson, Pamela Hansford

London, Jack. . **TCLC 9, 15, 39; SSC 4; WLC**
        See also London, John Griffith
        See also AAYA 13; AITN 2;
        CDALB 1865-1917; DLB 8, 12, 78;
        SATA 18

London, John Griffith   1876-1916
        See London, Jack
        See also CA 110; 119; DA; DAB; DAC;
        DAM MST, NOV; JRDA; MAICYA;
        MTCW

Long, Emmett
        See Leonard, Elmore (John, Jr.)

Longbaugh, Harry
        See Goldman, William (W.)

Longfellow, Henry Wadsworth
        1807-1882 . . . . . **NCLC 2, 45; DA; DAB;
                                                                DAC**
        See also CDALB 1640-1865; DAM MST,
        POET; DLB 1, 59; SATA 19

Longley, Michael   1939-. . . . . **CLC 29**
        See also CA 102; DLB 40

Longus   fl. c. 2nd cent. - . . . . **CMLC 7**

Longway, A. Hugh
        See Lang, Andrew

Lonnrot, Elias   1802-1884. . . . . **NCLC 53**

Lopate, Phillip   1943- . . . . **CLC 29**
        See also CA 97-100; DLBY 80; INT 97-100

Lopez Portillo (y Pacheco), Jose
        1920- . . . . **CLC 46**
        See also CA 129; HW

Lopez y Fuentes, Gregorio
1897(?)-1966 . . . . **CLC 32**
See also CA 131; HW

Lorca, Federico Garcia
See Garcia Lorca, Federico

Lord, Bette Bao 1938- . . . . **CLC 23**
See also BEST 90:3; CA 107; CANR 41;
INT 107; SATA 58

Lord Auch
See Bataille, Georges

Lord Byron
See Byron, George Gordon (Noel)

Lorde, Audre (Geraldine)
1934-1992 . . . . **CLC 18, 71; BLC; PC 12**
See also BW 1; CA 25-28R; 142; CANR 16,
26, 46; DAM MULT, POET; DLB 41;
MTCW

Lord Jeffrey
See Jeffrey, Francis

Lorenzo, Heberto Padilla
See Padilla (Lorenzo), Heberto

Loris
See Hofmannsthal, Hugo von

Loti, Pierre . . . . **TCLC 11**
See also Viaud, (Louis Marie) Julien
See also DLB 123

Louie, David Wong 1954- . . . . **CLC 70**
See also CA 139

Louis, Father M.
See Merton, Thomas

Lovecraft, H(oward) P(hillips)
1890-1937 . . . . **TCLC 4, 22; SSC 3**
See also AAYA 14; CA 104; 133;
DAM POP; MTCW

Lovelace, Earl 1935- . . . . **CLC 51**
See also BW 2; CA 77-80; CANR 41;
DLB 125; MTCW

Lovelace, Richard 1618-1657 . . . . **LC 24**
See also DLB 131

Lowell, Amy 1874-1925 . . **TCLC 1, 8; PC 13**
See also CA 104; DAM POET; DLB 54,
140

Lowell, James Russell 1819-1891 . . **NCLC 2**
See also CDALB 1640-1865; DLB 1, 11, 64,
79

Lowell, Robert (Traill Spence, Jr.)
1917-1977 . . . **CLC 1, 2, 3, 4, 5, 8, 9, 11,
15, 37; DA; DAB; DAC; PC 3; WLC**
See also CA 9-12R; 73-76; CABS 2;
CANR 26; DAM MST, NOV; DLB 5;
MTCW

Lowndes, Marie Adelaide (Belloc)
1868-1947 . . . . **TCLC 12**
See also CA 107; DLB 70

Lowry, (Clarence) Malcolm
1909-1957 . . . . **TCLC 6, 40**
See also CA 105; 131; CDBLB 1945-1960;
DLB 15; MTCW

Lowry, Mina Gertrude 1882-1966
See Loy, Mina
See also CA 113

Loxsmith, John
See Brunner, John (Kilian Houston)

Loy, Mina . . . . **CLC 28**
See also Lowry, Mina Gertrude
See also DAM POET; DLB 4, 54

Loyson-Bridet
See Schwob, (Mayer Andre) Marcel

Lucas, Craig 1951- . . . . **CLC 64**
See also CA 137

Lucas, George 1944- . . . . **CLC 16**
See also AAYA 1; CA 77-80; CANR 30;
SATA 56

Lucas, Hans
See Godard, Jean-Luc

Lucas, Victoria
See Plath, Sylvia

Ludlam, Charles 1943-1987 . . . . . **CLC 46, 50**
See also CA 85-88; 122

Ludlum, Robert 1927- . . . . **CLC 22, 43**
See also AAYA 10; BEST 89:1, 90:3;
CA 33-36R; CANR 25, 41; DAM NOV,
POP; DLBY 82; MTCW

Ludwig, Ken . . . . **CLC 60**

Ludwig, Otto 1813-1865 . . . . **NCLC 4**
See also DLB 129

Lugones, Leopoldo 1874-1938 . . . . . **TCLC 15**
See also CA 116; 131; HW

Lu Hsun 1881-1936 . . . . . . **TCLC 3; SSC 20**
See also Shu-Jen, Chou

Lukacs, George . . . . **CLC 24**
See also Lukacs, Gyorgy (Szegeny von)

Lukacs, Gyorgy (Szegeny von) 1885-1971
See Lukacs, George
See also CA 101; 29-32R

Luke, Peter (Ambrose Cyprian)
1919-1995 . . . . **CLC 38**
See also CA 81-84; 147; DLB 13

Lunar, Dennis
See Mungo, Raymond

Lurie, Alison 1926- . . . . **CLC 4, 5, 18, 39**
See also CA 1-4R; CANR 2, 17, 50; DLB 2;
MTCW; SATA 46

Lustig, Arnost 1926- . . . . **CLC 56**
See also AAYA 3; CA 69-72; CANR 47;
SATA 56

Luther, Martin 1483-1546 . . . . **LC 9**

Luzi, Mario 1914- . . . . **CLC 13**
See also CA 61-64; CANR 9; DLB 128

Lynch, B. Suarez
See Bioy Casares, Adolfo; Borges, Jorge
Luis

Lynch, David (K.) 1946- . . . . **CLC 66**
See also CA 124; 129

Lynch, James
See Andreyev, Leonid (Nikolaevich)

Lynch Davis, B.
See Bioy Casares, Adolfo; Borges, Jorge
Luis

Lyndsay, Sir David 1490-1555 . . . . . . **LC 20**

Lynn, Kenneth S(chuyler) 1923- . . . . **CLC 50**
See also CA 1-4R; CANR 3, 27

Lynx
See West, Rebecca

Lyons, Marcus
See Blish, James (Benjamin)

Lyre, Pinchbeck
See Sassoon, Siegfried (Lorraine)

Lytle, Andrew (Nelson) 1902- . . . . . . **CLC 22**
See also CA 9-12R; DLB 6

Lyttelton, George 1709-1773 . . . . **LC 10**

Maas, Peter 1929- . . . . **CLC 29**
See also CA 93-96; INT 93-96

Macaulay, Rose 1881-1958 . . . . . **TCLC 7, 44**
See also CA 104; DLB 36

Macaulay, Thomas Babington
1800-1859 . . . . **NCLC 42**
See also CDBLB 1832-1890; DLB 32, 55

MacBeth, George (Mann)
1932-1992 . . . . **CLC 2, 5, 9**
See also CA 25-28R; 136; DLB 40; MTCW;
SATA 4; SATA-Obit 70

MacCaig, Norman (Alexander)
1910- . . . . **CLC 36; DAB**
See also CA 9-12R; CANR 3, 34;
DAM POET; DLB 27

MacCarthy, (Sir Charles Otto) Desmond
1877-1952 . . . . **TCLC 36**

MacDiarmid, Hugh
. . . . **CLC 2, 4, 11, 19, 63; PC 9**
See also Grieve, C(hristopher) M(urray)
See also CDBLB 1945-1960; DLB 20

MacDonald, Anson
See Heinlein, Robert A(nson)

Macdonald, Cynthia 1928- . . . . . . **CLC 13, 19**
See also CA 49-52; CANR 4, 44; DLB 105

MacDonald, George 1824-1905 . . . . . **TCLC 9**
See also CA 106; 137; DLB 18; MAICYA;
SATA 33

Macdonald, John
See Millar, Kenneth

MacDonald, John D(ann)
1916-1986 . . . . **CLC 3, 27, 44**
See also CA 1-4R; 121; CANR 1, 19;
DAM NOV, POP; DLB 8; DLBY 86;
MTCW

Macdonald, John Ross
See Millar, Kenneth

Macdonald, Ross . . . . . **CLC 1, 2, 3, 14, 34, 41**
See also Millar, Kenneth
See also DLBD 6

MacDougal, John
See Blish, James (Benjamin)

MacEwen, Gwendolyn (Margaret)
1941-1987 . . . . **CLC 13, 55**
See also CA 9-12R; 124; CANR 7, 22;
DLB 53; SATA 50; SATA-Obit 55

Macha, Karel Hynek 1810-1846 . . **NCLC 46**

Machado (y Ruiz), Antonio
1875-1939 . . . . **TCLC 3**
See also CA 104; DLB 108

Machado de Assis, Joaquim Maria
1839-1908 . . . . **TCLC 10; BLC**
See also CA 107

Machen, Arthur . . . . **TCLC 4; SSC 20**
See also Jones, Arthur Llewellyn
See also DLB 36, 156

Machiavelli, Niccolo
1469-1527 . . . . . . **LC 8; DA; DAB; DAC**
See also DAM MST

MacInnes, Colin 1914-1976...... **CLC 4, 23**
See also CA 69-72; 65-68; CANR 21;
DLB 14; MTCW

MacInnes, Helen (Clark)
1907-1985 .... **CLC 27, 39**
See also CA 1-4R; 117; CANR 1, 28;
DAM POP; DLB 87; MTCW; SATA 22;
SATA-Obit 44

Mackay, Mary 1855-1924
See Corelli, Marie
See also CA 118

Mackenzie, Compton (Edward Montague)
1883-1972 .... **CLC 18**
See also CA 21-22; 37-40R; CAP 2;
DLB 34, 100

Mackenzie, Henry 1745-1831 .... **NCLC 41**
See also DLB 39

Mackintosh, Elizabeth 1896(?)-1952
See Tey, Josephine
See also CA 110

MacLaren, James
See Grieve, C(hristopher) M(urray)

Mac Laverty, Bernard 1942-....... **CLC 31**
See also CA 116; 118; CANR 43; INT 118

MacLean, Alistair (Stuart)
1922-1987 .... **CLC 3, 13, 50, 63**
See also CA 57-60; 121; CANR 28;
DAM POP; MTCW; SATA 23;
SATA-Obit 50

Maclean, Norman (Fitzroy)
1902-1990 .... **CLC 78; SSC 13**
See also CA 102; 132; CANR 49;
DAM POP

MacLeish, Archibald
1892-1982 .... **CLC 3, 8, 14, 68**
See also CA 9-12R; 106; CANR 33;
DAM POET; DLB 4, 7, 45; DLBY 82;
MTCW

MacLennan, (John) Hugh
1907-1990 .... **CLC 2, 14; DAC**
See also CA 5-8R; 142; CANR 33;
DAM MST; DLB 68; MTCW

MacLeod, Alistair 1936- ..... **CLC 56; DAC**
See also CA 123; DAM MST; DLB 60

MacNeice, (Frederick) Louis
1907-1963 ...... **CLC 1, 4, 10, 53; DAB**
See also CA 85-88; DAM POET; DLB 10,
20; MTCW

MacNeill, Dand
See Fraser, George MacDonald

Macpherson, James 1736-1796 ...... **LC 29**
See also DLB 109

Macpherson, (Jean) Jay 1931-...... **CLC 14**
See also CA 5-8R; DLB 53

MacShane, Frank 1927-........... **CLC 39**
See also CA 9-12R; CANR 3, 33; DLB 111

Macumber, Mari
See Sandoz, Mari(e Susette)

Madach, Imre 1823-1864 .... **NCLC 19**

Madden, (Jerry) David 1933- .... **CLC 5, 15**
See also CA 1-4R; CAAS 3; CANR 4, 45;
DLB 6; MTCW

Maddern, Al(an)
See Ellison, Harlan (Jay)

Madhubuti, Haki R.
1942- .... **CLC 6, 73; BLC; PC 5**
See also Lee, Don L.
See also BW 2; CA 73-76; CANR 24;
DAM MULT, POET; DLB 5, 41;
DLBD 8

Maepenn, Hugh
See Kuttner, Henry

Maepenn, K. H.
See Kuttner, Henry

Maeterlinck, Maurice 1862-1949 ... **TCLC 3**
See also CA 104; 136; DAM DRAM;
SATA 66

Maginn, William 1794-1842....... **NCLC 8**
See also DLB 110, 159

Mahapatra, Jayanta 1928-......... **CLC 33**
See also CA 73-76; CAAS 9; CANR 15, 33;
DAM MULT

Mahfouz, Naguib (Abdel Aziz Al-Sabilgi)
1911(?)-
See Mahfuz, Najib
See also BEST 89:2; CA 128; DAM NOV;
MTCW

Mahfuz, Najib................. **CLC 52, 55**
See also Mahfouz, Naguib (Abdel Aziz
Al-Sabilgi)
See also DLBY 88

Mahon, Derek 1941-.............. **CLC 27**
See also CA 113; 128; DLB 40

Mailer, Norman
1923-...... **CLC 1, 2, 3, 4, 5, 8, 11, 14,
28, 39, 74; DA; DAB; DAC**
See also AITN 2; CA 9-12R; CABS 1;
CANR 28; CDALB 1968-1988;
DAM MST, NOV, POP; DLB 2, 16, 28;
DLBD 3; DLBY 80, 83; MTCW

Maillet, Antonine 1929-...... **CLC 54; DAC**
See also CA 115; 120; CANR 46; DLB 60;
INT 120

Mais, Roger 1905-1955 .... **TCLC 8**
See also BW 1; CA 105; 124; DLB 125;
MTCW

Maistre, Joseph de 1753-1821 .... **NCLC 37**

Maitland, Sara (Louise) 1950-...... **CLC 49**
See also CA 69-72; CANR 13

Major, Clarence
1936-.............. **CLC 3, 19, 48; BLC**
See also BW 2; CA 21-24R; CAAS 6;
CANR 13, 25; DAM MULT; DLB 33

Major, Kevin (Gerald)
1949-.................. **CLC 26; DAC**
See also AAYA 16; CA 97-100; CANR 21,
38; CLR 11; DLB 60; INT CANR-21;
JRDA; MAICYA; SATA 32, 82

Maki, James
See Ozu, Yasujiro

Malabaila, Damiano
See Levi, Primo

Malamud, Bernard
1914-1986 ...... **CLC 1, 2, 3, 5, 8, 9, 11,
18, 27, 44, 78, 85; DA; DAB; DAC;
SSC 15; WLC**
See also AAYA 16; CA 5-8R; 118; CABS 1;
CANR 28; CDALB 1941-1968;
DAM MST, NOV, POP; DLB 2, 28, 152;
DLBY 80, 86; MTCW

Malaparte, Curzio 1898-1957 ..... **TCLC 52**

Malcolm, Dan
See Silverberg, Robert

Malcolm X................. **CLC 82; BLC**
See also Little, Malcolm

Malherbe, Francois de 1555-1628..... **LC 5**

Mallarme, Stephane
1842-1898 .... **NCLC 4, 41; PC 4**
See also DAM POET

Mallet-Joris, Francoise 1930-...... **CLC 11**
See also CA 65-68; CANR 17; DLB 83

Malley, Ern
See McAuley, James Phillip

Mallowan, Agatha Christie
See Christie, Agatha (Mary Clarissa)

Maloff, Saul 1922-................. **CLC 5**
See also CA 33-36R

Malone, Louis
See MacNeice, (Frederick) Louis

Malone, Michael (Christopher)
1942-...................... **CLC 43**
See also CA 77-80; CANR 14, 32

Malory, (Sir) Thomas
1410(?)-1471(?) ...... **LC 11; DA; DAB;
DAC**
See also CDBLB Before 1660; DAM MST;
DLB 146; SATA 59; SATA-Brief 33

Malouf, (George Joseph) David
1934-..................... **CLC 28, 86**
See also CA 124; CANR 50

Malraux, (Georges-)Andre
1901-1976 ...... **CLC 1, 4, 9, 13, 15, 57**
See also CA 21-22; 69-72; CANR 34;
CAP 2; DAM NOV; DLB 72; MTCW

Malzberg, Barry N(athaniel) 1939-... **CLC 7**
See also CA 61-64; CAAS 4; CANR 16;
DLB 8

Mamet, David (Alan)
1947-....... **CLC 9, 15, 34, 46; DC 4**
See also AAYA 3; CA 81-84; CABS 3;
CANR 15, 41; DAM DRAM; DLB 7;
MTCW

Mamoulian, Rouben (Zachary)
1897-1987 .... **CLC 16**
See also CA 25-28R; 124

Mandelstam, Osip (Emilievich)
1891(?)-1938(?) ...... **TCLC 2, 6; PC 14**
See also CA 104

Mander, (Mary) Jane 1877-1949... **TCLC 31**

Mandiargues, Andre Pieyre de....... **CLC 41**
See also Pieyre de Mandiargues, Andre
See also DLB 83

Mandrake, Ethel Belle
See Thurman, Wallace (Henry)

Mangan, James Clarence
1803-1849 .... **NCLC 27**

Maniere, J.-E.
See Giraudoux, (Hippolyte) Jean

Manley, (Mary) Delariviere
1672(?)-1724 .... **LC 1**
See also DLB 39, 80

Mann, Abel
See Creasey, John

Mann, (Luiz) Heinrich 1871-1950. . . TCLC 9
    See also CA 106; DLB 66

Mann, (Paul) Thomas
        1875-1955 . . . . TCLC 2, 8, 14, 21, 35, 44,
                60; DA; DAB; DAC; SSC 5; WLC
    See also CA 104; 128; DAM MST, NOV;
    DLB 66; MTCW

Manning, David
    See Faust, Frederick (Schiller)

Manning, Frederic 1887(?)-1935 . . . TCLC 25
    See also CA 124

Manning, Olivia 1915-1980 . . . . . CLC 5, 19
    See also CA 5-8R; 101; CANR 29; MTCW

Mano, D. Keith 1942- . . . . CLC 2, 10
    See also CA 25-28R; CAAS 6; CANR 26;
    DLB 6

Mansfield, Katherine
    . . . . . TCLC 2, 8, 39; DAB; SSC 9; WLC
    See also Beauchamp, Kathleen Mansfield

Manso, Peter 1940- . . . . CLC 39
    See also CA 29-32R; CANR 44

Mantecon, Juan Jimenez
    See Jimenez (Mantecon), Juan Ramon

Manton, Peter
    See Creasey, John

Man Without a Spleen, A
    See Chekhov, Anton (Pavlovich)

Manzoni, Alessandro 1785-1873 . . NCLC 29

Mapu, Abraham (ben Jekutiel)
        1808-1867 . . . . NCLC 18

Mara, Sally
    See Queneau, Raymond

Marat, Jean Paul 1743-1793 . . . . LC 10

Marcel, Gabriel Honore
        1889-1973 . . . . CLC 15
    See also CA 102; 45-48; MTCW

Marchbanks, Samuel
    See Davies, (William) Robertson

Marchi, Giacomo
    See Bassani, Giorgio

Margulies, Donald. . . . . CLC 76

Marie de France c. 12th cent. - . . . . CMLC 8

Marie de l'Incarnation 1599-1672 . . . . LC 10

Mariner, Scott
    See Pohl, Frederik

Marinetti, Filippo Tommaso
        1876-1944 . . . . TCLC 10
    See also CA 107; DLB 114

Marivaux, Pierre Carlet de Chamblain de
        1688-1763 . . . . LC 4

Markandaya, Kamala . . . . CLC 8, 38
    See also Taylor, Kamala (Purnaiya)

Markfield, Wallace 1926- . . . . CLC 8
    See also CA 69-72; CAAS 3; DLB 2, 28

Markham, Edwin 1852-1940 . . . . . . TCLC 47
    See also DLB 54

Markham, Robert
    See Amis, Kingsley (William)

Marks, J
    See Highwater, Jamake (Mamake)

Marks-Highwater, J
    See Highwater, Jamake (Mamake)

Markson, David M(errill) 1927- . . . . . CLC 67
    See also CA 49-52; CANR 1

Marley, Bob. CLC 17
    See also Marley, Robert Nesta

Marley, Robert Nesta 1945-1981
    See Marley, Bob
    See also CA 107; 103

Marlowe, Christopher
        1564-1593 . . . . . LC 22; DA; DAB; DAC;
                                     DC 1; WLC
    See also CDBLB Before 1660;
    DAM DRAM, MST; DLB 62

Marmontel, Jean-Francois
        1723-1799 . . . . LC 2

Marquand, John P(hillips)
        1893-1960 . . . . CLC 2, 10
    See also CA 85-88; DLB 9, 102

Marquez, Gabriel (Jose) Garcia
    See Garcia Marquez, Gabriel (Jose)

Marquis, Don(ald Robert Perry)
        1878-1937 . . . . TCLC 7
    See also CA 104; DLB 11, 25

Marric, J. J.
    See Creasey, John

Marrow, Bernard
    See Moore, Brian

Marryat, Frederick 1792-1848 . . . . NCLC 3
    See also DLB 21

Marsden, James
    See Creasey, John

Marsh, (Edith) Ngaio
        1899-1982 . . . . CLC 7, 53
    See also CA 9-12R; CANR 6; DAM POP;
    DLB 77; MTCW

Marshall, Garry 1934- . . . . CLC 17
    See also AAYA 3; CA 111; SATA 60

Marshall, Paule
        1929- . . . . CLC 27, 72; BLC; SSC 3
    See also BW 2; CA 77-80; CANR 25;
    DAM MULT; DLB 157; MTCW

Marsten, Richard
    See Hunter, Evan

Martha, Henry
    See Harris, Mark

Martial c. 40-c. 104 . . . . PC 10

Martin, Ken
    See Hubbard, L(afayette) Ron(ald)

Martin, Richard
    See Creasey, John

Martin, Steve 1945- . . . . CLC 30
    See also CA 97-100; CANR 30; MTCW

Martin, Valerie 1948- . . . . CLC 89
    See also BEST 90:2; CA 85-88; CANR 49

Martin, Violet Florence
        1862-1915 . . . . TCLC 51

Martin, Webber
    See Silverberg, Robert

Martindale, Patrick Victor
    See White, Patrick (Victor Martindale)

Martin du Gard, Roger
        1881-1958 . . . . TCLC 24
    See also CA 118; DLB 65

Martineau, Harriet 1802-1876. . . . NCLC 26
    See also DLB 21, 55, 159; YABC 2

Martines, Julia
    See O'Faolain, Julia

Martinez, Jacinto Benavente y
    See Benavente (y Martinez), Jacinto

Martinez Ruiz, Jose 1873-1967
    See Azorin; Ruiz, Jose Martinez
    See also CA 93-96; HW

Martinez Sierra, Gregorio
        1881-1947 . . . . TCLC 6
    See also CA 115

Martinez Sierra, Maria (de la O'LeJarraga)
        1874-1974 . . . . TCLC 6
    See also CA 115

Martinsen, Martin
    See Follett, Ken(neth Martin)

Martinson, Harry (Edmund)
        1904-1978 . . . . CLC 14
    See also CA 77-80; CANR 34

Marut, Ret
    See Traven, B.

Marut, Robert
    See Traven, B.

Marvell, Andrew
        1621-1678 . . . . . . LC 4; DA; DAB; DAC;
                                     PC 10; WLC
    See also CDBLB 1660-1789; DAM MST,
    POET; DLB 131

Marx, Karl (Heinrich)
        1818-1883 . . . . NCLC 17
    See also DLB 129

Masaoka Shiki. . . . . TCLC 18
    See also Masaoka Tsunenori

Masaoka Tsunenori 1867-1902
    See Masaoka Shiki
    See also CA 117

Masefield, John (Edward)
        1878-1967 . . . . CLC 11, 47
    See also CA 19-20; 25-28R; CANR 33;
    CAP 2; CDBLB 1890-1914; DAM POET;
    DLB 10, 19, 153, 160; MTCW; SATA 19

Maso, Carole 19(?)- . . . . CLC 44

Mason, Bobbie Ann
        1940- . . . . CLC 28, 43, 82; SSC 4
    See also AAYA 5; CA 53-56; CANR 11,
    31; DLBY 87; INT CANR-31; MTCW

Mason, Ernst
    See Pohl, Frederik

Mason, Lee W.
    See Malzberg, Barry N(athaniel)

Mason, Nick 1945- . . . . CLC 35

Mason, Tally
    See Derleth, August (William)

Mass, William
    See Gibson, William

Masters, Edgar Lee
        1868-1950 . . . . . . TCLC 2, 25; DA; DAC;
                                     PC 1
    See also CA 104; 133; CDALB 1865-1917;
    DAM MST, POET; DLB 54; MTCW

Masters, Hilary 1928- . . . . CLC 48
    See also CA 25-28R; CANR 13, 47

Mastrosimone, William 19(?)- . . . . . . CLC 36

Mathe, Albert
    See Camus, Albert

McInerney, Jay 1955- . . . . **CLC 34**
See also CA 116; 123; CANR 45;
DAM POP; INT 123

McIntyre, Vonda N(eel) 1948- . . . . . **CLC 18**
See also CA 81-84; CANR 17, 34; MTCW

McKay, Claude
. . . . **TCLC 7, 41; BLC; DAB; PC 2**
See also McKay, Festus Claudius
See also DLB 4, 45, 51, 117

McKay, Festus Claudius 1889-1948
See McKay, Claude
See also BW 1; CA 104; 124; DA; DAC;
DAM MST, MULT, NOV, POET;
MTCW; WLC

McKuen, Rod 1933- . . . . **CLC 1, 3**
See also AITN 1; CA 41-44R; CANR 40

McLoughlin, R. B.
See Mencken, H(enry) L(ouis)

McLuhan, (Herbert) Marshall
1911-1980 . . . . **CLC 37, 83**
See also CA 9-12R; 102; CANR 12, 34;
DLB 88; INT CANR-12; MTCW

McMillan, Terry (L.) 1951- . . . . . **CLC 50, 61**
See also BW 2; CA 140; DAM MULT,
NOV, POP

McMurtry, Larry (Jeff)
1936- . . . . **CLC 2, 3, 7, 11, 27, 44**
See also AAYA 15; AITN 2; BEST 89:2;
CA 5-8R; CANR 19, 43;
CDALB 1968-1988; DAM NOV, POP;
DLB 2, 143; DLBY 80, 87; MTCW

McNally, T. M. 1961- . . . . **CLC 82**

McNally, Terrence 1939- . . . . . **CLC 4, 7, 41**
See also CA 45-48; CANR 2;
DAM DRAM; DLB 7

McNamer, Deirdre 1950- . . . . **CLC 70**

McNeile, Herman Cyril 1888-1937
See Sapper
See also DLB 77

McNickle, (William) D'Arcy
1904-1977 . . . . **CLC 89**
See also CA 9-12R; 85-88; CANR 5, 45;
DAM MULT; NNAL; SATA-Obit 22

McPhee, John (Angus) 1931- . . . . . . **CLC 36**
See also BEST 90:1; CA 65-68; CANR 20,
46; MTCW

McPherson, James Alan
1943- . . . . **CLC 19, 77**
See also BW 1; CA 25-28R; CAAS 17;
CANR 24; DLB 38; MTCW

McPherson, William (Alexander)
1933- . . . . **CLC 34**
See also CA 69-72; CANR 28;
INT CANR-28

Mead, Margaret 1901-1978 . . . . **CLC 37**
See also AITN 1; CA 1-4R; 81-84;
CANR 4; MTCW; SATA-Obit 20

Meaker, Marijane (Agnes) 1927-
See Kerr, M. E.
See also CA 107; CANR 37; INT 107;
JRDA; MAICYA; MTCW; SATA 20, 61

Medoff, Mark (Howard) 1940- . . . **CLC 6, 23**
See also AITN 1; CA 53-56; CANR 5;
DAM DRAM; DLB 7; INT CANR-5

Medvedev, P. N.
See Bakhtin, Mikhail Mikhailovich

Meged, Aharon
See Megged, Aharon

Meged, Aron
See Megged, Aharon

Megged, Aharon 1920- . . . . **CLC 9**
See also CA 49-52; CAAS 13; CANR 1

Mehta, Ved (Parkash) 1934- . . . . **CLC 37**
See also CA 1-4R; CANR 2, 23; MTCW

Melanter
See Blackmore, R(ichard) D(oddridge)

Melikow, Loris
See Hofmannsthal, Hugo von

Melmoth, Sebastian
See Wilde, Oscar (Fingal O'Flahertie Wills)

Meltzer, Milton 1915- . . . . **CLC 26**
See also AAYA 8; CA 13-16R; CANR 38;
CLR 13; DLB 61; JRDA; MAICYA;
SAAS 1; SATA 1, 50, 80

Melville, Herman
1819-1891 . . . . . **NCLC 3, 12, 29, 45, 49;**
DA; DAB; DAC; SSC 1, 17; WLC
See also CDALB 1640-1865; DAM MST,
NOV; DLB 3, 74; SATA 59

Menander
c. 342B.C.-c. 292B.C. . . . . **CMLC 9; DC 3**
See also DAM DRAM

Mencken, H(enry) L(ouis)
1880-1956 . . . . **TCLC 13**
See also CA 105; 125; CDALB 1917-1929;
DLB 11, 29, 63, 137; MTCW

Mercer, David 1928-1980 . . . . **CLC 5**
See also CA 9-12R; 102; CANR 23;
DAM DRAM; DLB 13; MTCW

Merchant, Paul
See Ellison, Harlan (Jay)

Meredith, George 1828-1909 . . . **TCLC 17, 43**
See also CA 117; CDBLB 1832-1890;
DAM POET; DLB 18, 35, 57, 159

Meredith, William (Morris)
1919- . . . . **CLC 4, 13, 22, 55**
See also CA 9-12R; CAAS 14; CANR 6, 40;
DAM POET; DLB 5

Merezhkovsky, Dmitry Sergeyevich
1865-1941 . . . . **TCLC 29**

Merimee, Prosper
1803-1870 . . . . **NCLC 6; SSC 7**
See also DLB 119

Merkin, Daphne 1954- . . . . **CLC 44**
See also CA 123

Merlin, Arthur
See Blish, James (Benjamin)

Merrill, James (Ingram)
1926-1995 . . . . **CLC 2, 3, 6, 8, 13, 18, 34**
See also CA 13-16R; 147; CANR 10, 49;
DAM POET; DLB 5; DLBY 85;
INT CANR-10; MTCW

Merriman, Alex
See Silverberg, Robert

Merritt, E. B.
See Waddington, Miriam

Merton, Thomas
1915-1968 . . **CLC 1, 3, 11, 34, 83; PC 10**
See also CA 5-8R; 25-28R; CANR 22;
DLB 48; DLBY 81; MTCW

Merwin, W(illiam) S(tanley)
1927- . . . **CLC 1, 2, 3, 5, 8, 13, 18, 45, 88**
See also CA 13-16R; CANR 15;
DAM POET; DLB 5; INT CANR-15;
MTCW

Metcalf, John 1938- . . . . **CLC 37**
See also CA 113; DLB 60

Metcalf, Suzanne
See Baum, L(yman) Frank

Mew, Charlotte (Mary)
1870-1928 . . . . **TCLC 8**
See also CA 105; DLB 19, 135

Mewshaw, Michael 1943- . . . . **CLC 9**
See also CA 53-56; CANR 7, 47; DLBY 80

Meyer, June
See Jordan, June

Meyer, Lynn
See Slavitt, David R(ytman)

Meyer-Meyrink, Gustav 1868-1932
See Meyrink, Gustav
See also CA 117

Meyers, Jeffrey 1939- . . . . **CLC 39**
See also CA 73-76; DLB 111

Meynell, Alice (Christina Gertrude Thompson)
1847-1922 . . . . **TCLC 6**
See also CA 104; DLB 19, 98

Meyrink, Gustav . . . . **TCLC 21**
See also Meyer-Meyrink, Gustav
See also DLB 81

Michaels, Leonard
1933- . . . . **CLC 6, 25; SSC 16**
See also CA 61-64; CANR 21; DLB 130;
MTCW

Michaux, Henri 1899-1984 . . . . . . **CLC 8, 19**
See also CA 85-88; 114

Michelangelo 1475-1564 . . . . **LC 12**

Michelet, Jules 1798-1874 . . . . **NCLC 31**

Michener, James A(lbert)
1907(?)- . . . . **CLC 1, 5, 11, 29, 60**
See also AITN 1; BEST 90:1; CA 5-8R;
CANR 21, 45; DAM NOV, POP; DLB 6;
MTCW

Mickiewicz, Adam 1798-1855 . . . . . **NCLC 3**

Middleton, Christopher 1926- . . . . . . **CLC 13**
See also CA 13-16R; CANR 29; DLB 40

Middleton, Richard (Barham)
1882-1911 . . . . **TCLC 56**
See also DLB 156

Middleton, Stanley 1919- . . . . **CLC 7, 38**
See also CA 25-28R; CANR 21, 46;
DLB 14

Middleton, Thomas 1580-1627 . . . . **DC 5**
See also DAM DRAM, MST; DLB 58

Migueis, Jose Rodrigues 1901- . . . . . **CLC 10**

Mikszath, Kalman 1847-1910 . . . . . **TCLC 31**

Miles, Josephine
1911-1985 . . . . **CLC 1, 2, 14, 34, 39**
See also CA 1-4R; 116; CANR 2;
DAM POET; DLB 48

Militant
See Sandburg, Carl (August)

Mill, John Stuart 1806-1873 . . . . . **NCLC 11**
See also CDBLB 1832-1890; DLB 55

Millar, Kenneth 1915-1983 . . . . **CLC 14**
See also Macdonald, Ross
See also CA 9-12R; 110; CANR 16;
DAM POP; DLB 2; DLBD 6; DLBY 83;
MTCW

Millay, E. Vincent
See Millay, Edna St. Vincent

Millay, Edna St. Vincent
1892-1950 . . . . . . **TCLC 4, 49; DA; DAB;**
DAC; PC 6
See also CA 104; 130; CDALB 1917-1929;
DAM MST, POET; DLB 45; MTCW

Miller, Arthur
1915- . . . . **CLC 1, 2, 6, 10, 15, 26, 47, 78;**
DA; DAB; DAC; DC 1; WLC
See also AAYA 15; AITN 1; CA 1-4R;
CABS 3; CANR 2, 30;
CDALB 1941-1968; DAM DRAM, MST;
DLB 7; MTCW

Miller, Henry (Valentine)
1891-1980 . . . . **CLC 1, 2, 4, 9, 14, 43, 84;**
DA; DAB; DAC; WLC
See also CA 9-12R; 97-100; CANR 33;
CDALB 1929-1941; DAM MST, NOV;
DLB 4, 9; DLBY 80; MTCW

Miller, Jason 1939(?)- . . . . **CLC 2**
See also AITN 1; CA 73-76; DLB 7

Miller, Sue 1943- . . . . **CLC 44**
See also BEST 90:3; CA 139; DAM POP;
DLB 143

Miller, Walter M(ichael, Jr.)
1923- . . . . **CLC 4, 30**
See also CA 85-88; DLB 8

Millett, Kate 1934- . . . . **CLC 67**
See also AITN 1; CA 73-76; CANR 32;
MTCW

Millhauser, Steven 1943- . . . . **CLC 21, 54**
See also CA 110; 111; DLB 2; INT 111

Millin, Sarah Gertrude 1889-1968 . . **CLC 49**
See also CA 102; 93-96

Milne, A(lan) A(lexander)
1882-1956 . . . . **TCLC 6; DAB; DAC**
See also CA 104; 133; CLR 1, 26;
DAM MST; DLB 10, 77, 100, 160;
MAICYA; MTCW; YABC 1

Milner, Ron(ald) 1938- . . . . **CLC 56; BLC**
See also AITN 1; BW 1; CA 73-76;
CANR 24; DAM MULT; DLB 38;
MTCW

Milosz, Czeslaw
1911- . . . **CLC 5, 11, 22, 31, 56, 82; PC 8**
See also CA 81-84; CANR 23; DAM MST,
POET; MTCW

Milton, John
1608-1674 . . . . . . **LC 9; DA; DAB; DAC;**
WLC
See also CDBLB 1660-1789; DAM MST,
POET; DLB 131, 151

Min, Anchee 1957- . . . . **CLC 86**
See also CA 146

Minehaha, Cornelius
See Wedekind, (Benjamin) Frank(lin)

Miner, Valerie 1947- . . . . **CLC 40**
See also CA 97-100

Minimo, Duca
See D'Annunzio, Gabriele

Minot, Susan 1956- . . . . **CLC 44**
See also CA 134

Minus, Ed 1938- . . . . **CLC 39**

Miranda, Javier
See Bioy Casares, Adolfo

Mirbeau, Octave 1848-1917 . . . . . . **TCLC 55**
See also DLB 123

Miro (Ferrer), Gabriel (Francisco Victor)
1879-1930 . . . . **TCLC 5**
See also CA 104

Mishima, Yukio
. . . . **CLC 2, 4, 6, 9, 27; DC 1; SSC 4**
See also Hiraoka, Kimitake

Mistral, Frederic 1830-1914 . . . . . . **TCLC 51**
See also CA 122

Mistral, Gabriela. . . . . **TCLC 2; HLC**
See also Godoy Alcayaga, Lucila

Mistry, Rohinton 1952- . . . . . . **CLC 71; DAC**
See also CA 141

Mitchell, Clyde
See Ellison, Harlan (Jay); Silverberg, Robert

Mitchell, James Leslie 1901-1935
See Gibbon, Lewis Grassic
See also CA 104; DLB 15

Mitchell, Joni 1943- . . . . **CLC 12**
See also CA 112

Mitchell, Margaret (Munnerlyn)
1900-1949 . . . . **TCLC 11**
See also CA 109; 125; DAM NOV, POP;
DLB 9; MTCW

Mitchell, Peggy
See Mitchell, Margaret (Munnerlyn)

Mitchell, S(ilas) Weir 1829-1914 . . **TCLC 36**

Mitchell, W(illiam) O(rmond)
1914- . . . . **CLC 25; DAC**
See also CA 77-80; CANR 15, 43;
DAM MST; DLB 88

Mitford, Mary Russell 1787-1855 . . **NCLC 4**
See also DLB 110, 116

Mitford, Nancy 1904-1973 . . . . **CLC 44**
See also CA 9-12R

Miyamoto, Yuriko 1899-1951 . . . . . **TCLC 37**

Mo, Timothy (Peter) 1950(?)- . . . . . . **CLC 46**
See also CA 117; MTCW

Modarressi, Taghi (M.) 1931- . . . . . . **CLC 44**
See also CA 121; 134; INT 134

Modiano, Patrick (Jean) 1945- . . . . . **CLC 18**
See also CA 85-88; CANR 17, 40; DLB 83

Moerck, Paal
See Roelvaag, O(le) E(dvart)

Mofolo, Thomas (Mokopu)
1875(?)-1948 . . . . **TCLC 22; BLC**
See also CA 121; DAM MULT

Mohr, Nicholasa 1935- . . . . . . **CLC 12; HLC**
See also AAYA 8; CA 49-52; CANR 1, 32;
CLR 22; DAM MULT; DLB 145; HW;
JRDA; SAAS 8; SATA 8

Mojtabai, A(nn) G(race)
1938- . . . . **CLC 5, 9, 15, 29**
See also CA 85-88

Moliere
1622-1673 . . . . . **LC 28; DA; DAB; DAC;**
WLC
See also DAM DRAM, MST

Molin, Charles
See Mayne, William (James Carter)

Molnar, Ferenc 1878-1952 . . . . **TCLC 20**
See also CA 109; DAM DRAM

Momaday, N(avarre) Scott
1934- . . . **CLC 2, 19, 85; DA; DAB; DAC**
See also AAYA 11; CA 25-28R; CANR 14,
34; DAM MST, MULT, NOV, POP;
DLB 143; INT CANR-14; MTCW;
NNAL; SATA 48; SATA-Brief 30

Monette, Paul 1945-1995 . . . . **CLC 82**
See also CA 139; 147

Monroe, Harriet 1860-1936 . . . . **TCLC 12**
See also CA 109; DLB 54, 91

Monroe, Lyle
See Heinlein, Robert A(nson)

Montagu, Elizabeth 1917- . . . . **NCLC 7**
See also CA 9-12R

Montagu, Mary (Pierrepont) Wortley
1689-1762 . . . . **LC 9**
See also DLB 95, 101

Montagu, W. H.
See Coleridge, Samuel Taylor

Montague, John (Patrick)
1929- . . . . **CLC 13, 46**
See also CA 9-12R; CANR 9; DLB 40;
MTCW

Montaigne, Michel (Eyquem) de
1533-1592 . . . . . . **LC 8; DA; DAB; DAC;**
WLC
See also DAM MST

Montale, Eugenio
1896-1981 . . . . **CLC 7, 9, 18; PC 13**
See also CA 17-20R; 104; CANR 30;
DLB 114; MTCW

Montesquieu, Charles-Louis de Secondat
1689-1755 . . . . **LC 7**

Montgomery, (Robert) Bruce 1921-1978
See Crispin, Edmund
See also CA 104

Montgomery, L(ucy) M(aud)
1874-1942 . . . . **TCLC 51; DAC**
See also AAYA 12; CA 108; 137; CLR 8;
DAM MST; DLB 92; JRDA; MAICYA;
YABC 1

Montgomery, Marion H., Jr. 1925- . . **CLC 7**
See also AITN 1; CA 1-4R; CANR 3, 48;
DLB 6

Montgomery, Max
See Davenport, Guy (Mattison, Jr.)

Montherlant, Henry (Milon) de
1896-1972 . . . . **CLC 8, 19**
See also CA 85-88; 37-40R; DAM DRAM;
DLB 72; MTCW

Monty Python
See Chapman, Graham; Cleese, John
(Marwood); Gilliam, Terry (Vance); Idle,
Eric; Jones, Terence Graham Parry; Palin,
Michael (Edward)
See also AAYA 7

Moodie, Susanna (Strickland)
1803-1885 . . . . **NCLC 14**
See also DLB 99

Mooney, Edward 1951-
See Mooney, Ted
See also CA 130

Mooney, Ted . . . . **CLC 25**
 See also Mooney, Edward

Moorcock, Michael (John)
 1939- . . . . **CLC 5, 27, 58**
 See also CA 45-48; CAAS 5; CANR 2, 17,
 38; DLB 14; MTCW

Moore, Brian
 1921- . . . . . . **CLC 1, 3, 5, 7, 8, 19, 32, 90;**
                                                  DAB; DAC
 See also CA 1-4R; CANR 1, 25, 42;
 DAM MST; MTCW

Moore, Edward
 See Muir, Edwin

Moore, George Augustus
 1852-1933 . . . . **TCLC 7; SSC 19**
 See also CA 104; DLB 10, 18, 57, 135

Moore, Lorrie . . . . **CLC 39, 45, 68**
 See also Moore, Marie Lorena

Moore, Marianne (Craig)
 1887-1972 . . . . **CLC 1, 2, 4, 8, 10, 13, 19,**
                                    47; DA; DAB; DAC; PC 4
 See also CA 1-4R; 33-36R; CANR 3;
 CDALB 1929-1941; DAM MST, POET;
 DLB 45; DLBD 7; MTCW; SATA 20

Moore, Marie Lorena   1957-
 See Moore, Lorrie
 See also CA 116; CANR 39

Moore, Thomas   1779-1852. . . . . . . **NCLC 6**
 See also DLB 96, 144

Morand, Paul   1888-1976 . . . . **CLC 41**
 See also CA 69-72; DLB 65

Morante, Elsa   1918-1985 . . . . **CLC 8, 47**
 See also CA 85-88; 117; CANR 35; MTCW

Moravia, Alberto . . . . . . **CLC 2, 7, 11, 27, 46**
 See also Pincherle, Alberto

More, Hannah   1745-1833 . . . . **NCLC 27**
 See also DLB 107, 109, 116, 158

More, Henry   1614-1687. . . . . **LC 9**
 See also DLB 126

More, Sir Thomas   1478-1535 . . . . **LC 10, 32**

Moreas, Jean. . . . . **TCLC 18**
 See also Papadiamantopoulos, Johannes

Morgan, Berry   1919- . . . . **CLC 6**
 See also CA 49-52; DLB 6

Morgan, Claire
 See Highsmith, (Mary) Patricia

Morgan, Edwin (George)   1920- . . . . . **CLC 31**
 See also CA 5-8R; CANR 3, 43; DLB 27

Morgan, (George) Frederick
 1922- . . . . **CLC 23**
 See also CA 17-20R; CANR 21

Morgan, Harriet
 See Mencken, H(enry) L(ouis)

Morgan, Jane
 See Cooper, James Fenimore

Morgan, Janet   1945- . . . . **CLC 39**
 See also CA 65-68

Morgan, Lady   1776(?)-1859. . . . . . **NCLC 29**
 See also DLB 116, 158

Morgan, Robin   1941- . . . . **CLC 2**
 See also CA 69-72; CANR 29; MTCW;
 SATA 80

Morgan, Scott
 See Kuttner, Henry

Morgan, Seth   1949(?)-1990 . . . . **CLC 65**
 See also CA 132

Morgenstern, Christian
 1871-1914 . . . . **TCLC 8**
 See also CA 105

Morgenstern, S.
 See Goldman, William (W.)

Moricz, Zsigmond   1879-1942 . . . . . **TCLC 33**

Morike, Eduard (Friedrich)
 1804-1875 . . . . **NCLC 10**
 See also DLB 133

Mori Ogai . . . . **TCLC 14**
 See also Mori Rintaro

Mori Rintaro   1862-1922
 See Mori Ogai
 See also CA 110

Moritz, Karl Philipp   1756-1793 . . . . . . **LC 2**
 See also DLB 94

Morland, Peter Henry
 See Faust, Frederick (Schiller)

Morren, Theophil
 See Hofmannsthal, Hugo von

Morris, Bill   1952- . . . . **CLC 76**

Morris, Julian
 See West, Morris L(anglo)

Morris, Steveland Judkins   1950(?)-
 See Wonder, Stevie
 See also CA 111

Morris, William   1834-1896 . . . . **NCLC 4**
 See also CDBLB 1832-1890; DLB 18, 35,
 57, 156

Morris, Wright   1910- . . . **CLC 1, 3, 7, 18, 37**
 See also CA 9-12R; CANR 21; DLB 2;
 DLBY 81; MTCW

Morrison, Chloe Anthony Wofford
 See Morrison, Toni

Morrison, James Douglas   1943-1971
 See Morrison, Jim
 See also CA 73-76; CANR 40

Morrison, Jim . . . . **CLC 17**
 See also Morrison, James Douglas

Morrison, Toni
 1931- . . . . **CLC 4, 10, 22, 55, 81, 87;**
                                    BLC; DA; DAB; DAC
 See also AAYA 1; BW 2; CA 29-32R;
 CANR 27, 42; CDALB 1968-1988;
 DAM MST, MULT, NOV, POP; DLB 6,
 33, 143; DLBY 81; MTCW; SATA 57

Morrison, Van   1945- . . . . **CLC 21**
 See also CA 116

Mortimer, John (Clifford)
 1923- . . . . **CLC 28, 43**
 See also CA 13-16R; CANR 21;
 CDBLB 1960 to Present; DAM DRAM,
 POP; DLB 13; INT CANR-21; MTCW

Mortimer, Penelope (Ruth)   1918- . . . . **CLC 5**
 See also CA 57-60; CANR 45

Morton, Anthony
 See Creasey, John

Mosher, Howard Frank   1943- . . . . . . **CLC 62**
 See also CA 139

Mosley, Nicholas   1923- . . . . **CLC 43, 70**
 See also CA 69-72; CANR 41; DLB 14

Moss, Howard
 1922-1987 . . . . **CLC 7, 14, 45, 50**
 See also CA 1-4R; 123; CANR 1, 44;
 DAM POET; DLB 5

Mossgiel, Rab
 See Burns, Robert

Motion, Andrew (Peter)   1952- . . . . . . **CLC 47**
 See also CA 146; DLB 40

Motley, Willard (Francis)
 1909-1965 . . . . **CLC 18**
 See also BW 1; CA 117; 106; DLB 76, 143

Motoori, Norinaga   1730-1801 . . . . **NCLC 45**

Mott, Michael (Charles Alston)
 1930- . . . . **CLC 15, 34**
 See also CA 5-8R; CAAS 7; CANR 7, 29

Moure, Erin   1955- . . . . **CLC 88**
 See also CA 113; DLB 60

Mowat, Farley (McGill)
 1921- . . . . **CLC 26; DAC**
 See also AAYA 1; CA 1-4R; CANR 4, 24,
 42; CLR 20; DAM MST; DLB 68;
 INT CANAR-24; JRDA; MAICYA;
 MTCW; SATA 3, 55

Moyers, Bill   1934- . . . . **CLC 74**
 See also AITN 2; CA 61-64; CANR 31

Mphahlele, Es'kia
 See Mphahlele, Ezekiel
 See also DLB 125

Mphahlele, Ezekiel   1919- . . . . . **CLC 25; BLC**
 See also Mphahlele, Es'kia
 See also BW 2; CA 81-84; CANR 26;
 DAM MULT

Mqhayi, S(amuel) E(dward) K(rune Loliwe)
 1875-1945 . . . . **TCLC 25; BLC**
 See also DAM MULT

Mr. Martin
 See Burroughs, William S(eward)

Mrozek, Slawomir   1930- . . . . **CLC 3, 13**
 See also CA 13-16R; CAAS 10; CANR 29;
 MTCW

Mrs. Belloc-Lowndes
 See Lowndes, Marie Adelaide (Belloc)

Mtwa, Percy   (?)- . . . . **CLC 47**

Mueller, Lisel   1924- . . . . **CLC 13, 51**
 See also CA 93-96; DLB 105

Muir, Edwin   1887-1959 . . . . **TCLC 2**
 See also CA 104; DLB 20, 100

Muir, John   1838-1914 . . . . **TCLC 28**

Mujica Lainez, Manuel
 1910-1984 . . . . **CLC 31**
 See also Lainez, Manuel Mujica
 See also CA 81-84; 112; CANR 32; HW

Mukherjee, Bharati   1940- . . . . **CLC 53**
 See also BEST 89:2; CA 107; CANR 45;
 DAM NOV; DLB 60; MTCW

Muldoon, Paul   1951- . . . . **CLC 32, 72**
 See also CA 113; 129; DAM POET;
 DLB 40; INT 129

Mulisch, Harry   1927- . . . . **CLC 42**
 See also CA 9-12R; CANR 6, 26

Mull, Martin   1943- . . . . **CLC 17**
 See also CA 105

Mulock, Dinah Maria
 See Craik, Dinah Maria (Mulock)

Munford, Robert 1737(?)-1783 .... **LC 5**
See also DLB 31

Mungo, Raymond 1946-.......... **CLC 72**
See also CA 49-52; CANR 2

Munro, Alice
1931- ... **CLC 6, 10, 19, 50; DAC; SSC 3**
See also AITN 2; CA 33-36R; CANR 33;
DAM MST, NOV; DLB 53; MTCW;
SATA 29

Munro, H(ector) H(ugh) 1870-1916
See Saki
See also CA 104; 130; CDBLB 1890-1914;
DA; DAB; DAC; DAM MST, NOV;
DLB 34; MTCW; WLC

Murasaki, Lady................. **CMLC 1**

Murdoch, (Jean) Iris
1919- ...... **CLC 1, 2, 3, 4, 6, 8, 11, 15,
22, 31, 51; DAB; DAC**
See also CA 13-16R; CANR 8, 43;
CDBLB 1960 to Present; DAM MST,
NOV; DLB 14; INT CANR-8; MTCW

Murnau, Friedrich Wilhelm
See Plumpe, Friedrich Wilhelm

Murphy, Richard 1927-.......... **CLC 41**
See also CA 29-32R; DLB 40

Murphy, Sylvia 1937-............. **CLC 34**
See also CA 121

Murphy, Thomas (Bernard) 1935-... **CLC 51**
See also CA 101

Murray, Albert L. 1916- .... **CLC 73**
See also BW 2; CA 49-52; CANR 26;
DLB 38

Murray, Les(lie) A(llan) 1938- ..... **CLC 40**
See also CA 21-24R; CANR 11, 27;
DAM POET

Murry, J. Middleton
See Murry, John Middleton

Murry, John Middleton
1889-1957 .... **TCLC 16**
See also CA 118; DLB 149

Musgrave, Susan 1951- .... **CLC 13, 54**
See also CA 69-72; CANR 45

Musil, Robert (Edler von)
1880-1942 .... **TCLC 12; SSC 18**
See also CA 109; DLB 81, 124

Muske, Carol 1945- .... **CLC 90**
See also Muske-Dukes, Carol (Anne)

Muske-Dukes, Carol (Anne) 1945-
See Muske, Carol
See also CA 65-68; CANR 32

Musset, (Louis Charles) Alfred de
1810-1857 .... **NCLC 7**

My Brother's Brother
See Chekhov, Anton (Pavlovich)

Myers, L. H. 1881-1944......... **TCLC 59**
See also DLB 15

Myers, Walter Dean 1937- ... **CLC 35; BLC**
See also AAYA 4; BW 2; CA 33-36R;
CANR 20, 42; CLR 4, 16, 35;
DAM MULT, NOV; DLB 33;
INT CANR-20; JRDA; MAICYA;
SAAS 2; SATA 41, 71; SATA-Brief 27

Myers, Walter M.
See Myers, Walter Dean

Myles, Symon
See Follett, Ken(neth Martin)

Nabokov, Vladimir (Vladimirovich)
1899-1977 ..... **CLC 1, 2, 3, 6, 8, 11, 15,
23, 44, 46, 64; DA; DAB; DAC; SSC 11;
WLC**
See also CA 5-8R; 69-72; CANR 20;
CDALB 1941-1968; DAM MST, NOV;
DLB 2; DLBD 3; DLBY 80, 91; MTCW

Nagai Kafu..................... **TCLC 51**
See also Nagai Sokichi

Nagai Sokichi 1879-1959
See Nagai Kafu
See also CA 117

Nagy, Laszlo 1925-1978............ **CLC 7**
See also CA 129; 112

Naipaul, Shiva(dhar Srinivasa)
1945-1985 .... **CLC 32, 39**
See also CA 110; 112; 116; CANR 33;
DAM NOV; DLB 157; DLBY 85;
MTCW

Naipaul, V(idiadhar) S(urajprasad)
1932- .... **CLC 4, 7, 9, 13, 18, 37; DAB;
DAC**
See also CA 1-4R; CANR 1, 33;
CDBLB 1960 to Present; DAM MST,
NOV; DLB 125; DLBY 85; MTCW

Nakos, Lilika 1899(?)-............ **CLC 29**

Narayan, R(asipuram) K(rishnaswami)
1906-.................. **CLC 7, 28, 47**
See also CA 81-84; CANR 33; DAM NOV;
MTCW; SATA 62

Nash, (Frediric) Ogden 1902-1971 .. **CLC 23**
See also CA 13-14; 29-32R; CANR 34;
CAP 1; DAM POET; DLB 11;
MAICYA; MTCW; SATA 2, 46

Nathan, Daniel
See Dannay, Frederic

Nathan, George Jean 1882-1958 ... **TCLC 18**
See also Hatteras, Owen
See also CA 114; DLB 137

Natsume, Kinnosuke 1867-1916
See Natsume, Soseki
See also CA 104

Natsume, Soseki .... **TCLC 2, 10**
See also Natsume, Kinnosuke

Natti, (Mary) Lee 1919-
See Kingman, Lee
See also CA 5-8R; CANR 2

Naylor, Gloria
1950- ..... **CLC 28, 52; BLC; DA; DAC**
See also AAYA 6; BW 2; CA 107;
CANR 27; DAM MST, MULT, NOV,
POP; MTCW

Neihardt, John Gneisenau
1881-1973 .... **CLC 32**
See also CA 13-14; CAP 1; DLB 9, 54

Nekrasov, Nikolai Alekseevich
1821-1878 .... **NCLC 11**

Nelligan, Emile 1879-1941....... **TCLC 14**
See also CA 114; DLB 92

Nelson, Willie 1933-.............. **CLC 17**
See also CA 107

Nemerov, Howard (Stanley)
1920-1991 .... **CLC 2, 6, 9, 36**
See also CA 1-4R; 134; CABS 2; CANR 1,
27; DAM POET; DLB 5, 6; DLBY 83;
INT CANR-27; MTCW

Neruda, Pablo
1904-1973 ..... **CLC 1, 2, 5, 7, 9, 28, 62;
DA; DAB; DAC; HLC; PC 4; WLC**
See also CA 19-20; 45-48; CAP 2;
DAM MST, MULT, POET; HW; MTCW

Nerval, Gerard de
1808-1855 ..... **NCLC 1; PC 13; SSC 18**

Nervo, (Jose) Amado (Ruiz de)
1870-1919 .... **TCLC 11**
See also CA 109; 131; HW

Nessi, Pio Baroja y
See Baroja (y Nessi), Pio

Nestroy, Johann 1801-1862...... **NCLC 42**
See also DLB 133

Neufeld, John (Arthur) 1938- ...... **CLC 17**
See also AAYA 11; CA 25-28R; CANR 11,
37; MAICYA; SAAS 3; SATA 6, 81

Neville, Emily Cheney 1919-....... **CLC 12**
See also CA 5-8R; CANR 3, 37; JRDA;
MAICYA; SAAS 2; SATA 1

Newbound, Bernard Slade 1930-
See Slade, Bernard
See also CA 81-84; CANR 49;
DAM DRAM

Newby, P(ercy) H(oward)
1918- .... **CLC 2, 13**
See also CA 5-8R; CANR 32; DAM NOV;
DLB 15; MTCW

Newlove, Donald 1928- .... **CLC 6**
See also CA 29-32R; CANR 25

Newlove, John (Herbert) 1938-..... **CLC 14**
See also CA 21-24R; CANR 9, 25

Newman, Charles 1938-.......... **CLC 2, 8**
See also CA 21-24R

Newman, Edwin (Harold) 1919- .... **CLC 14**
See also AITN 1; CA 69-72; CANR 5

Newman, John Henry
1801-1890 .... **NCLC 38**
See also DLB 18, 32, 55

Newton, Suzanne 1936-........... **CLC 35**
See also CA 41-44R; CANR 14; JRDA;
SATA 5, 77

Nexo, Martin Andersen
1869-1954 .... **TCLC 43**

Nezval, Vitezslav 1900-1958 ...... **TCLC 44**
See also CA 123

Ng, Fae Myenne 1957(?)-.......... **CLC 81**
See also CA 146

Ngema, Mbongeni 1955- .... **CLC 57**
See also BW 2; CA 143

Ngugi, James T(hiong'o)........ **CLC 3, 7, 13**
See also Ngugi wa Thiong'o

Ngugi wa Thiong'o 1938-..... **CLC 36; BLC**
See also Ngugi, James T(hiong'o)
See also BW 2; CA 81-84; CANR 27;
DAM MULT, NOV; DLB 125; MTCW

Nichol, B(arrie) P(hillip)
1944-1988 .... **CLC 18**
See also CA 53-56; DLB 53; SATA 66

Nichols, John (Treadwell) 1940- .... **CLC 38**
See also CA 9-12R; CAAS 2; CANR 6;
DLBY 82

Nichols, Leigh
See Koontz, Dean R(ay)

Nichols, Peter (Richard)
1927- .... **CLC 5, 36, 65**
See also CA 104; CANR 33; DLB 13;
MTCW

Nicolas, F. R. E.
See Freeling, Nicolas

Niedecker, Lorine 1903-1970.... **CLC 10, 42**
See also CA 25-28; CAP 2; DAM POET;
DLB 48

Nietzsche, Friedrich (Wilhelm)
1844-1900 .... **TCLC 10, 18, 55**
See also CA 107; 121; DLB 129

Nievo, Ippolito 1831-1861 .... **NCLC 22**

Nightingale, Anne Redmon 1943-
See Redmon, Anne
See also CA 103

Nik. T. O.
See Annensky, Innokenty Fyodorovich

Nin, Anais
1903-1977 ...... **CLC 1, 4, 8, 11, 14, 60;**
SSC 10
See also AITN 2; CA 13-16R; 69-72;
CANR 22; DAM NOV, POP; DLB 2, 4,
152; MTCW

Nissenson, Hugh 1933- .... **CLC 4, 9**
See also CA 17-20R; CANR 27; DLB 28

Niven, Larry .... **CLC 8**
See also Niven, Laurence Van Cott
See also DLB 8

Niven, Laurence Van Cott 1938-
See Niven, Larry
See also CA 21-24R; CAAS 12; CANR 14,
44; DAM POP; MTCW

Nixon, Agnes Eckhardt 1927- ...... **CLC 21**
See also CA 110

Nizan, Paul 1905-1940 .... **TCLC 40**
See also DLB 72

Nkosi, Lewis 1936- .... **CLC 45; BLC**
See also BW 1; CA 65-68; CANR 27;
DAM MULT; DLB 157

Nodier, (Jean) Charles (Emmanuel)
1780-1844 .... **NCLC 19**
See also DLB 119

Nolan, Christopher 1965- .... **CLC 58**
See also CA 111

Norden, Charles
See Durrell, Lawrence (George)

Nordhoff, Charles (Bernard)
1887-1947 .... **TCLC 23**
See also CA 108; DLB 9; SATA 23

Norfolk, Lawrence 1963- .... **CLC 76**
See also CA 144

Norman, Marsha 1947- .... **CLC 28**
See also CA 105; CABS 3; CANR 41;
DAM DRAM; DLBY 84

Norris, Benjamin Franklin, Jr.
1870-1902 .... **TCLC 24**
See also Norris, Frank
See also CA 110

Norris, Frank
See Norris, Benjamin Franklin, Jr.
See also CDALB 1865-1917; DLB 12, 71

Norris, Leslie 1921- .... **CLC 14**
See also CA 11-12; CANR 14; CAP 1;
DLB 27

North, Andrew
See Norton, Andre

North, Anthony
See Koontz, Dean R(ay)

North, Captain George
See Stevenson, Robert Louis (Balfour)

North, Milou
See Erdrich, Louise

Northrup, B. A.
See Hubbard, L(afayette) Ron(ald)

North Staffs
See Hulme, T(homas) E(rnest)

Norton, Alice Mary
See Norton, Andre
See also MAICYA; SATA 1, 43

Norton, Andre 1912- .... **CLC 12**
See also Norton, Alice Mary
See also AAYA 14; CA 1-4R; CANR 2, 31;
DLB 8, 52; JRDA; MTCW

Norton, Caroline 1808-1877 ...... **NCLC 47**
See also DLB 21, 159

Norway, Nevil Shute 1899-1960
See Shute, Nevil
See also CA 102; 93-96

Norwid, Cyprian Kamil
1821-1883 .... **NCLC 17**

Nosille, Nabrah
See Ellison, Harlan (Jay)

Nossack, Hans Erich 1901-1978 ..... **CLC 6**
See also CA 93-96; 85-88; DLB 69

Nostradamus 1503-1566 .... **LC 27**

Nosu, Chuji
See Ozu, Yasujiro

Notenburg, Eleanora (Genrikhovna) von
See Guro, Elena

Nova, Craig 1945- .... **CLC 7, 31**
See also CA 45-48; CANR 2

Novak, Joseph
See Kosinski, Jerzy (Nikodem)

Novalis 1772-1801 .... **NCLC 13**
See also DLB 90

Nowlan, Alden (Albert)
1933-1983 .... **CLC 15; DAC**
See also CA 9-12R; CANR 5; DAM MST;
DLB 53

Noyes, Alfred 1880-1958 .... **TCLC 7**
See also CA 104; DLB 20

Nunn, Kem 19(?)- .... **CLC 34**

Nye, Robert 1939- .... **CLC 13, 42**
See also CA 33-36R; CANR 29;
DAM NOV; DLB 14; MTCW; SATA 6

Nyro, Laura 1947- .... **CLC 17**

Oates, Joyce Carol
1938- ...... **CLC 1, 2, 3, 6, 9, 11, 15, 19,**
33, 52; DA; DAB; DAC; SSC 6; WLC
See also AAYA 15; AITN 1; BEST 89:2;
CA 5-8R; CANR 25, 45;
CDALB 1968-1988; DAM MST, NOV,
POP; DLB 2, 5, 130; DLBY 81;
INT CANR-25; MTCW

O'Brien, Darcy 1939- .... **CLC 11**
See also CA 21-24R; CANR 8

O'Brien, E. G.
See Clarke, Arthur C(harles)

O'Brien, Edna
1936- ... **CLC 3, 5, 8, 13, 36, 65; SSC 10**
See also CA 1-4R; CANR 6, 41;
CDBLB 1960 to Present; DAM NOV;
DLB 14; MTCW

O'Brien, Fitz-James 1828-1862... **NCLC 21**
See also DLB 74

O'Brien, Flann........ **CLC 1, 4, 5, 7, 10, 47**
See also O Nuallain, Brian

O'Brien, Richard 1942- .... **CLC 17**
See also CA 124

O'Brien, Tim 1946-......... **CLC 7, 19, 40**
See also AAYA 16; CA 85-88; CANR 40;
DAM POP; DLB 152; DLBD 9;
DLBY 80

Obstfelder, Sigbjoern 1866-1900... **TCLC 23**
See also CA 123

O'Casey, Sean
1880-1964 ...... **CLC 1, 5, 9, 11, 15, 88;**
DAB; DAC
See also CA 89-92; CDBLB 1914-1945;
DAM DRAM, MST; DLB 10; MTCW

O'Cathasaigh, Sean
See O'Casey, Sean

Ochs, Phil 1940-1976............. **CLC 17**
See also CA 65-68

O'Connor, Edwin (Greene)
1918-1968 .... **CLC 14**
See also CA 93-96; 25-28R

O'Connor, (Mary) Flannery
1925-1964 .... **CLC 1, 2, 3, 6, 10, 13, 15,**
21, 66; DA; DAB; DAC; SSC 1; WLC
See also AAYA 7; CA 1-4R; CANR 3, 41;
CDALB 1941-1968; DAM MST, NOV;
DLB 2, 152; DLBD 12; DLBY 80;
MTCW

O'Connor, Frank........... **CLC 23; SSC 5**
See also O'Donovan, Michael John

O'Dell, Scott 1898-1989.......... **CLC 30**
See also AAYA 3; CA 61-64; 129;
CANR 12, 30; CLR 1, 16; DLB 52;
JRDA; MAICYA; SATA 12, 60

Odets, Clifford
1906-1963 .... **CLC 2, 28; DC 6**
See also CA 85-88; DAM DRAM; DLB 7,
26; MTCW

O'Doherty, Brian 1934- .... **CLC 76**
See also CA 105

O'Donnell, K. M.
See Malzberg, Barry N(athaniel)

O'Donnell, Lawrence
See Kuttner, Henry

O'Donovan, Michael John
1903-1966 . . . . **CLC 14**
See also O'Connor, Frank
See also CA 93-96

Oe, Kenzaburo
1935- . . . . **CLC 10, 36, 86; SSC 20**
See also CA 97-100; CANR 36, 50;
DAM NOV; DLBY 94; MTCW

O'Faolain, Julia 1932- . . . . **CLC 6, 19, 47**
See also CA 81-84; CAAS 2; CANR 12;
DLB 14; MTCW

O'Faolain, Sean
1900-1991 . . . . **CLC 1, 7, 14, 32, 70;**
SSC 13
See also CA 61-64; 134; CANR 12;
DLB 15; MTCW

O'Flaherty, Liam
1896-1984 . . . . **CLC 5, 34; SSC 6**
See also CA 101; 113; CANR 35; DLB 36;
DLBY 84; MTCW

Ogilvy, Gavin
See Barrie, J(ames) M(atthew)

O'Grady, Standish James
1846-1928 . . . . **TCLC 5**
See also CA 104

O'Grady, Timothy 1951- . . . . **CLC 59**
See also CA 138

O'Hara, Frank
1926-1966 . . . . **CLC 2, 5, 13, 78**
See also CA 9-12R; 25-28R; CANR 33;
DAM POET; DLB 5, 16; MTCW

O'Hara, John (Henry)
1905-1970 . . . . . . **CLC 1, 2, 3, 6, 11, 42;**
SSC 15
See also CA 5-8R; 25-28R; CANR 31;
CDALB 1929-1941; DAM NOV; DLB 9,
86; DLBD 2; MTCW

O Hehir, Diana 1922- . . . . **CLC 41**
See also CA 93-96

Okigbo, Christopher (Ifenayichukwu)
1932-1967 . . . . . **CLC 25, 84; BLC; PC 7**
See also BW 1; CA 77-80; DAM MULT,
POET; DLB 125; MTCW

Okri, Ben 1959- . . . . **CLC 87**
See also BW 2; CA 130; 138; DLB 157;
INT 138

Olds, Sharon 1942- . . . . **CLC 32, 39, 85**
See also CA 101; CANR 18, 41;
DAM POET; DLB 120

Oldstyle, Jonathan
See Irving, Washington

Olesha, Yuri (Karlovich)
1899-1960 . . . . **CLC 8**
See also CA 85-88

Oliphant, Laurence
1829(?)-1888 . . . . **NCLC 47**
See also DLB 18

Oliphant, Margaret (Oliphant Wilson)
1828-1897 . . . . **NCLC 11**
See also DLB 18, 159

Oliver, Mary 1935- . . . . **CLC 19, 34**
See also CA 21-24R; CANR 9, 43; DLB 5

Olivier, Laurence (Kerr)
1907-1989 . . . . **CLC 20**
See also CA 111; 129

Olsen, Tillie
1913- . . . . . **CLC 4, 13; DA; DAB; DAC;**
SSC 11
See also CA 1-4R; CANR 1, 43;
DAM MST; DLB 28; DLBY 80; MTCW

Olson, Charles (John)
1910-1970 . . . . . **CLC 1, 2, 5, 6, 9, 11, 29**
See also CA 13-16; 25-28R; CABS 2;
CANR 35; CAP 1; DAM POET; DLB 5,
16; MTCW

Olson, Toby 1937- . . . . **CLC 28**
See also CA 65-68; CANR 9, 31

Olyesha, Yuri
See Olesha, Yuri (Karlovich)

Ondaatje, (Philip) Michael
1943- . . . **CLC 14, 29, 51, 76; DAB; DAC**
See also CA 77-80; CANR 42; DAM MST;
DLB 60

Oneal, Elizabeth 1934-
See Oneal, Zibby
See also CA 106; CANR 28; MAICYA;
SATA 30, 82

Oneal, Zibby . . . . **CLC 30**
See also Oneal, Elizabeth
See also AAYA 5; CLR 13; JRDA

O'Neill, Eugene (Gladstone)
1888-1953 . . . . . . **TCLC 1, 6, 27, 49; DA;**
DAB; DAC; WLC
See also AITN 1; CA 110; 132;
CDALB 1929-1941; DAM DRAM, MST;
DLB 7; MTCW

Onetti, Juan Carlos 1909-1994 . . . **CLC 7, 10**
See also CA 85-88; 145; CANR 32;
DAM MULT, NOV; DLB 113; HW;
MTCW

O Nuallain, Brian 1911-1966
See O'Brien, Flann
See also CA 21-22; 25-28R; CAP 2

Oppen, George 1908-1984 . . . . **CLC 7, 13, 34**
See also CA 13-16R; 113; CANR 8; DLB 5

Oppenheim, E(dward) Phillips
1866-1946 . . . . **TCLC 45**
See also CA 111; DLB 70

Orlovitz, Gil 1918-1973 . . . . **CLC 22**
See also CA 77-80; 45-48; DLB 2, 5

Orris
See Ingelow, Jean

Ortega y Gasset, Jose
1883-1955 . . . . **TCLC 9; HLC**
See also CA 106; 130; DAM MULT; HW;
MTCW

Ortese, Anna Maria 1914- . . . . **CLC 89**

Ortiz, Simon J(oseph) 1941- . . . . **CLC 45**
See also CA 134; DAM MULT, POET;
DLB 120; NNAL

Orton, Joe . . . . **CLC 4, 13, 43; DC 3**
See also Orton, John Kingsley
See also CDBLB 1960 to Present; DLB 13

Orton, John Kingsley 1933-1967
See Orton, Joe
See also CA 85-88; CANR 35;
DAM DRAM; MTCW

Orwell, George
. . . . . **TCLC 2, 6, 15, 31, 51; DAB; WLC**
See also Blair, Eric (Arthur)
See also CDBLB 1945-1960; DLB 15, 98

Osborne, David
See Silverberg, Robert

Osborne, George
See Silverberg, Robert

Osborne, John (James)
1929-1994 . . . . . **CLC 1, 2, 5, 11, 45; DA;**
DAB; DAC; WLC
See also CA 13-16R; 147; CANR 21;
CDBLB 1945-1960; DAM DRAM, MST;
DLB 13; MTCW

Osborne, Lawrence 1958- . . . . **CLC 50**

Oshima, Nagisa 1932- . . . . **CLC 20**
See also CA 116; 121

Oskison, John Milton
1874-1947 . . . . **TCLC 35**
See also CA 144; DAM MULT; NNAL

Ossoli, Sarah Margaret (Fuller marchesa d')
1810-1850
See Fuller, Margaret
See also SATA 25

Ostrovsky, Alexander
1823-1886 . . . . **NCLC 30**

Otero, Blas de 1916-1979 . . . . **CLC 11**
See also CA 89-92; DLB 134

Otto, Whitney 1955- . . . . **CLC 70**
See also CA 140

Ouida . . . . **TCLC 43**
See also De La Ramee, (Marie) Louise
See also DLB 18, 156

Ousmane, Sembene 1923- . . . . **CLC 66; BLC**
See also BW 1; CA 117; 125; MTCW

Ovid 43B.C.-18(?) . . . . **CMLC 7; PC 2**
See also DAM POET

Owen, Hugh
See Faust, Frederick (Schiller)

Owen, Wilfred (Edward Salter)
1893-1918 . . . . . . **TCLC 5, 27; DA; DAB;**
DAC; WLC
See also CA 104; 141; CDBLB 1914-1945;
DAM MST, POET; DLB 20

Owens, Rochelle 1936- . . . . **CLC 8**
See also CA 17-20R; CAAS 2; CANR 39

Oz, Amos 1939- . . . **CLC 5, 8, 11, 27, 33, 54**
See also CA 53-56; CANR 27, 47;
DAM NOV; MTCW

Ozick, Cynthia
1928- . . . . **CLC 3, 7, 28, 62; SSC 15**
See also BEST 90:1; CA 17-20R; CANR 23;
DAM NOV, POP; DLB 28, 152;
DLBY 82; INT CANR-23; MTCW

Ozu, Yasujiro 1903-1963 . . . . **CLC 16**
See also CA 112

Pacheco, C.
See Pessoa, Fernando (Antonio Nogueira)

Pa Chin . . . . **CLC 18**
See also Li Fei-kan

Pack, Robert 1929- . . . . **CLC 13**
See also CA 1-4R; CANR 3, 44; DLB 5

Padgett, Lewis
See Kuttner, Henry

Padilla (Lorenzo), Heberto 1932- . . . **CLC 38**
See also AITN 1; CA 123; 131; HW

Page, Jimmy 1944- . . . . **CLC 12**

Page, Louise 1955- .... **CLC 40**
See also CA 140

Page, P(atricia) K(athleen)
1916- .... **CLC 7, 18; DAC; PC 12**
See also CA 53-56; CANR 4, 22;
DAM MST; DLB 68; MTCW

Paget, Violet 1856-1935
See Lee, Vernon
See also CA 104

Paget-Lowe, Henry
See Lovecraft, H(oward) P(hillips)

Paglia, Camille (Anna) 1947- .... **CLC 68**
See also CA 140

Paige, Richard
See Koontz, Dean R(ay)

Pakenham, Antonia
See Fraser, (Lady) Antonia (Pakenham)

Palamas, Kostes 1859-1943 .... **TCLC 5**
See also CA 105

Palazzeschi, Aldo 1885-1974 .... **CLC 11**
See also CA 89-92; 53-56; DLB 114

Paley, Grace 1922- .... **CLC 4, 6, 37; SSC 8**
See also CA 25-28R; CANR 13, 46;
DAM POP; DLB 28; INT CANR-13;
MTCW

Palin, Michael (Edward) 1943- ..... **CLC 21**
See also Monty Python
See also CA 107; CANR 35; SATA 67

Palliser, Charles 1947- .... **CLC 65**
See also CA 136

Palma, Ricardo 1833-1919 .... **TCLC 29**

Pancake, Breece Dexter 1952-1979
See Pancake, Breece D'J
See also CA 123; 109

Pancake, Breece D'J .... **CLC 29**
See also Pancake, Breece Dexter
See also DLB 130

Panko, Rudy
See Gogol, Nikolai (Vasilyevich)

Papadiamantis, Alexandros
1851-1911 .... **TCLC 29**

Papadiamantopoulos, Johannes 1856-1910
See Moreas, Jean
See also CA 117

Papini, Giovanni 1881-1956 .... **TCLC 22**
See also CA 121

Paracelsus 1493-1541 .... **LC 14**

Parasol, Peter
See Stevens, Wallace

Parfenie, Maria
See Codrescu, Andrei

Parini, Jay (Lee) 1948- .... **CLC 54**
See also CA 97-100; CAAS 16; CANR 32

Park, Jordan
See Kornbluth, C(yril) M.; Pohl, Frederik

Parker, Bert
See Ellison, Harlan (Jay)

Parker, Dorothy (Rothschild)
1893-1967 .... **CLC 15, 68; SSC 2**
See also CA 19-20; 25-28R; CAP 2;
DAM POET; DLB 11, 45, 86; MTCW

Parker, Robert B(rown) 1932- ...... **CLC 27**
See also BEST 89:4; CA 49-52; CANR 1,
26; DAM NOV, POP; INT CANR-26;
MTCW

Parkin, Frank 1940- .... **CLC 43**
See also CA 147

Parkman, Francis, Jr.
1823-1893 .... **NCLC 12**
See also DLB 1, 30

Parks, Gordon (Alexander Buchanan)
1912- .... **CLC 1, 16; BLC**
See also AITN 2; BW 2; CA 41-44R;
CANR 26; DAM MULT; DLB 33;
SATA 8

Parnell, Thomas 1679-1718 .... **LC 3**
See also DLB 94

Parra, Nicanor 1914- .... **CLC 2; HLC**
See also CA 85-88; CANR 32;
DAM MULT; HW; MTCW

Parrish, Mary Frances
See Fisher, M(ary) F(rances) K(ennedy)

Parson
See Coleridge, Samuel Taylor

Parson Lot
See Kingsley, Charles

Partridge, Anthony
See Oppenheim, E(dward) Phillips

Pascoli, Giovanni 1855-1912 ...... **TCLC 45**

Pasolini, Pier Paolo
1922-1975 .... **CLC 20, 37**
See also CA 93-96; 61-64; DLB 128;
MTCW

Pasquini
See Silone, Ignazio

Pastan, Linda (Olenik) 1932- ...... **CLC 27**
See also CA 61-64; CANR 18, 40;
DAM POET; DLB 5

Pasternak, Boris (Leonidovich)
1890-1960 ...... **CLC 7, 10, 18, 63; DA;
DAB; DAC; PC 6; WLC**
See also CA 127; 116; DAM MST, NOV,
POET; MTCW

Patchen, Kenneth 1911-1972 ... **CLC 1, 2, 18**
See also CA 1-4R; 33-36R; CANR 3, 35;
DAM POET; DLB 16, 48; MTCW

Pater, Walter (Horatio)
1839-1894 .... **NCLC 7**
See also CDBLB 1832-1890; DLB 57, 156

Paterson, A(ndrew) B(arton)
1864-1941 .... **TCLC 32**

Paterson, Katherine (Womeldorf)
1932- .... **CLC 12, 30**
See also AAYA 1; CA 21-24R; CANR 28;
CLR 7; DLB 52; JRDA; MAICYA;
MTCW; SATA 13, 53

Patmore, Coventry Kersey Dighton
1823-1896 .... **NCLC 9**
See also DLB 35, 98

Paton, Alan (Stewart)
1903-1988 ...... **CLC 4, 10, 25, 55; DA;
DAB; DAC; WLC**
See also CA 13-16; 125; CANR 22; CAP 1;
DAM MST, NOV; MTCW; SATA 11;
SATA-Obit 56

Paton Walsh, Gillian 1937-
See Walsh, Jill Paton
See also CANR 38; JRDA; MAICYA;
SAAS 3; SATA 4, 72

Paulding, James Kirke 1778-1860 .. **NCLC 2**
See also DLB 3, 59, 74

Paulin, Thomas Neilson 1949-
See Paulin, Tom
See also CA 123; 128

Paulin, Tom .... **CLC 37**
See also Paulin, Thomas Neilson
See also DLB 40

Paustovsky, Konstantin (Georgievich)
1892-1968 .... **CLC 40**
See also CA 93-96; 25-28R

Pavese, Cesare
1908-1950 ..... **TCLC 3; PC 13; SSC 19**
See also CA 104; DLB 128

Pavic, Milorad 1929- .... **CLC 60**
See also CA 136

Payne, Alan
See Jakes, John (William)

Paz, Gil
See Lugones, Leopoldo

Paz, Octavio
1914- .... **CLC 3, 4, 6, 10, 19, 51, 65;
DA; DAB; DAC; HLC; PC 1; WLC**
See also CA 73-76; CANR 32; DAM MST,
MULT, POET; DLBY 90; HW; MTCW

Peacock, Molly 1947- .... **CLC 60**
See also CA 103; CAAS 21; DLB 120

Peacock, Thomas Love
1785-1866 .... **NCLC 22**
See also DLB 96, 116

Peake, Mervyn 1911-1968 .... **CLC 7, 54**
See also CA 5-8R; 25-28R; CANR 3;
DLB 15, 160; MTCW; SATA 23

Pearce, Philippa .... **CLC 21**
See also Christie, (Ann) Philippa
See also CLR 9; DLB 161; MAICYA;
SATA 1, 67

Pearl, Eric
See Elman, Richard

Pearson, T(homas) R(eid) 1956- .... **CLC 39**
See also CA 120; 130; INT 130

Peck, Dale 1967- .... **CLC 81**
See also CA 146

Peck, John 1941- .... **CLC 3**
See also CA 49-52; CANR 3

Peck, Richard (Wayne) 1934- ...... **CLC 21**
See also AAYA 1; CA 85-88; CANR 19,
38; CLR 15; INT CANR-19; JRDA;
MAICYA; SAAS 2; SATA 18, 55

Peck, Robert Newton
1928- .... **CLC 17; DA; DAC**
See also AAYA 3; CA 81-84; CANR 31;
DAM MST; JRDA; MAICYA; SAAS 1;
SATA 21, 62

Peckinpah, (David) Sam(uel)
1925-1984 .... **CLC 20**
See also CA 109; 114

Pedersen, Knut 1859-1952
See Hamsun, Knut
See also CA 104; 119; MTCW

Peeslake, Gaffer
See Durrell, Lawrence (George)

Peguy, Charles Pierre
1873-1914 . . . . TCLC 10
See also CA 107

Pena, Ramon del Valle y
See Valle-Inclan, Ramon (Maria) del

Pendennis, Arthur Esquir
See Thackeray, William Makepeace

Penn, William 1644-1718. . . . . LC 25
See also DLB 24

Pepys, Samuel
1633-1703 . . . . . LC 11; DA; DAB; DAC;
WLC
See also CDBLB 1660-1789; DAM MST;
DLB 101

Percy, Walker
1916-1990 . . . . CLC 2, 3, 6, 8, 14, 18, 47,
65
See also CA 1-4R; 131; CANR 1, 23;
DAM NOV, POP; DLB 2; DLBY 80, 90;
MTCW

Perec, Georges 1936-1982 . . . . CLC 56
See also CA 141; DLB 83

Pereda (y Sanchez de Porrua), Jose Maria de
1833-1906 . . . . TCLC 16
See also CA 117

Pereda y Porrua, Jose Maria de
See Pereda (y Sanchez de Porrua), Jose
Maria de

Peregoy, George Weems
See Mencken, H(enry) L(ouis)

Perelman, S(idney) J(oseph)
1904-1979 . . . CLC 3, 5, 9, 15, 23, 44, 49
See also AITN 1, 2; CA 73-76; 89-92;
CANR 18; DAM DRAM; DLB 11, 44;
MTCW

Peret, Benjamin 1899-1959 . . . . TCLC 20
See also CA 117

Peretz, Isaac Loeb 1851(?)-1915 . . . TCLC 16
See also CA 109

Peretz, Yitzkhok Leibush
See Peretz, Isaac Loeb

Perez Galdos, Benito 1843-1920 . . . TCLC 27
See also CA 125; HW

Perrault, Charles 1628-1703 . . . . LC 2
See also MAICYA; SATA 25

Perry, Brighton
See Sherwood, Robert E(mmet)

Perse, St.-John . . . . CLC 4, 11, 46
See also Leger, (Marie-Rene Auguste) Alexis
Saint-Leger

Perutz, Leo 1882-1957 . . . . TCLC 60
See also DLB 81

Peseenz, Tulio F.
See Lopez y Fuentes, Gregorio

Pesetsky, Bette 1932- . . . . CLC 28
See also CA 133; DLB 130

Peshkov, Alexei Maximovich 1868-1936
See Gorky, Maxim
See also CA 105; 141; DA; DAC;
DAM DRAM, MST, NOV

Pessoa, Fernando (Antonio Nogueira)
1888-1935 . . . . TCLC 27; HLC
See also CA 125

Peterkin, Julia Mood 1880-1961. . . . CLC 31
See also CA 102; DLB 9

Peters, Joan K. 1945- . . . . CLC 39

Peters, Robert L(ouis) 1924- . . . . CLC 7
See also CA 13-16R; CAAS 8; DLB 105

Petofi, Sandor 1823-1849 . . . . NCLC 21

Petrakis, Harry Mark 1923- . . . . CLC 3
See also CA 9-12R; CANR 4, 30

Petrarch 1304-1374. . . . . PC 8
See also DAM POET

Petrov, Evgeny . . . . TCLC 21
See also Kataev, Evgeny Petrovich

Petry, Ann (Lane) 1908- . . . . . . CLC 1, 7, 18
See also BW 1; CA 5-8R; CAAS 6;
CANR 4, 46; CLR 12; DLB 76; JRDA;
MAICYA; MTCW; SATA 5

Petursson, Halligrimur 1614-1674 . . . . LC 8

Philips, Katherine 1632-1664. . . . . . . LC 30
See also DLB 131

Philipson, Morris H. 1926- . . . . CLC 53
See also CA 1-4R; CANR 4

Phillips, David Graham
1867-1911 . . . . TCLC 44
See also CA 108; DLB 9, 12

Phillips, Jack
See Sandburg, Carl (August)

Phillips, Jayne Anne
1952- . . . . CLC 15, 33; SSC 16
See also CA 101; CANR 24, 50; DLBY 80;
INT CANR-24; MTCW

Phillips, Richard
See Dick, Philip K(indred)

Phillips, Robert (Schaeffer) 1938- . . . CLC 28
See also CA 17-20R; CAAS 13; CANR 8;
DLB 105

Phillips, Ward
See Lovecraft, H(oward) P(hillips)

Piccolo, Lucio 1901-1969. . . . . CLC 13
See also CA 97-100; DLB 114

Pickthall, Marjorie L(owry) C(hristie)
1883-1922 . . . . TCLC 21
See also CA 107; DLB 92

Pico della Mirandola, Giovanni
1463-1494 . . . . LC 15

Piercy, Marge
1936- . . . . CLC 3, 6, 14, 18, 27, 62
See also CA 21-24R; CAAS 1; CANR 13,
43; DLB 120; MTCW

Piers, Robert
See Anthony, Piers

Pieyre de Mandiargues, Andre 1909-1991
See Mandiargues, Andre Pieyre de
See also CA 103; 136; CANR 22

Pilnyak, Boris . . . . TCLC 23
See also Vogau, Boris Andreyevich

Pincherle, Alberto 1907-1990 . . . CLC 11, 18
See also Moravia, Alberto
See also CA 25-28R; 132; CANR 33;
DAM NOV; MTCW

Pinckney, Darryl 1953- . . . . CLC 76
See also BW 2; CA 143

Pindar 518B.C.-446B.C. . . . . CMLC 12

Pineda, Cecile 1942- . . . . CLC 39
See also CA 118

Pinero, Arthur Wing 1855-1934 . . . TCLC 32
See also CA 110; DAM DRAM; DLB 10

Pinero, Miguel (Antonio Gomez)
1946-1988 . . . . CLC 4, 55
See also CA 61-64; 125; CANR 29; HW

Pinget, Robert 1919- . . . . CLC 7, 13, 37
See also CA 85-88; DLB 83

Pink Floyd
See Barrett, (Roger) Syd; Gilmour, David;
Mason, Nick; Waters, Roger; Wright,
Rick

Pinkney, Edward 1802-1828 . . . . . NCLC 31

Pinkwater, Daniel Manus 1941- . . . . CLC 35
See also Pinkwater, Manus
See also AAYA 1; CA 29-32R; CANR 12,
38; CLR 4; JRDA; MAICYA; SAAS 3;
SATA 46, 76

Pinkwater, Manus
See Pinkwater, Daniel Manus
See also SATA 8

Pinsky, Robert 1940- . . . . CLC 9, 19, 38
See also CA 29-32R; CAAS 4;
DAM POET; DLBY 82

Pinta, Harold
See Pinter, Harold

Pinter, Harold
1930- . . . . . CLC 1, 3, 6, 9, 11, 15, 27, 58,
73; DA; DAB; DAC; WLC
See also CA 5-8R; CANR 33; CDBLB 1960
to Present; DAM DRAM, MST; DLB 13;
MTCW

Pirandello, Luigi
1867-1936 . . . . . . TCLC 4, 29; DA; DAB;
DAC; DC 5; WLC
See also CA 104; DAM DRAM, MST

Pirsig, Robert M(aynard)
1928- . . . . CLC 4, 6, 73
See also CA 53-56; CANR 42; DAM POP;
MTCW; SATA 39

Pisarev, Dmitry Ivanovich
1840-1868 . . . . NCLC 25

Pix, Mary (Griffith) 1666-1709 . . . . . . LC 8
See also DLB 80

Pixerecourt, Guilbert de
1773-1844 . . . . NCLC 39

Plaidy, Jean
See Hibbert, Eleanor Alice Burford

Planche, James Robinson
1796-1880 . . . . NCLC 42

Plant, Robert 1948- . . . . CLC 12

Plante, David (Robert)
1940- . . . . CLC 7, 23, 38
See also CA 37-40R; CANR 12, 36;
DAM NOV; DLBY 83; INT CANR-12;
MTCW

Plath, Sylvia
1932-1963 . . . . . CLC 1, 2, 3, 5, 9, 11, 14,
17, 50, 51, 62; DA; DAB; DAC; PC 1;
WLC
See also AAYA 13; CA 19-20; CANR 34;
CAP 2; CDALB 1941-1968; DAM MST,
POET; DLB 5, 6, 152; MTCW

Plato
428(?)B.C.-348(?)B.C. . . . . **CMLC 8; DA; DAB; DAC**
See also DAM MST

Platonov, Andrei . . . . **TCLC 14**
See also Klimentov, Andrei Platonovich

Platt, Kin 1911- . . . . **CLC 26**
See also AAYA 11; CA 17-20R; CANR 11;
JRDA; SAAS 17; SATA 21

Plautus c. 251B.C.-184B.C. . . . . **DC 6**

Plick et Plock
See Simenon, Georges (Jacques Christian)

Plimpton, George (Ames) 1927- . . . . . **CLC 36**
See also AITN 1; CA 21-24R; CANR 32;
MTCW; SATA 10

Plomer, William Charles Franklin
1903-1973 . . . . **CLC 4, 8**
See also CA 21-22; CANR 34; CAP 2;
DLB 20; MTCW; SATA 24

Plowman, Piers
See Kavanagh, Patrick (Joseph)

Plum, J.
See Wodehouse, P(elham) G(renville)

Plumly, Stanley (Ross) 1939- . . . . . . **CLC 33**
See also CA 108; 110; DLB 5; INT 110

Plumpe, Friedrich Wilhelm
1888-1931 . . . . **TCLC 53**
See also CA 112

Poe, Edgar Allan
1809-1849 . . . . . **NCLC 1, 16; DA; DAB;
DAC; PC 1; SSC 1; WLC**
See also AAYA 14; CDALB 1640-1865;
DAM MST, POET; DLB 3, 59, 73, 74;
SATA 23

Poet of Titchfield Street, The
See Pound, Ezra (Weston Loomis)

Pohl, Frederik 1919- . . . . **CLC 18**
See also CA 61-64; CAAS 1; CANR 11, 37;
DLB 8; INT CANR-11; MTCW;
SATA 24

Poirier, Louis 1910-
See Gracq, Julien
See also CA 122; 126

Poitier, Sidney 1927- . . . . **CLC 26**
See also BW 1; CA 117

Polanski, Roman 1933- . . . . **CLC 16**
See also CA 77-80

Poliakoff, Stephen 1952- . . . . **CLC 38**
See also CA 106; DLB 13

Police, The
See Copeland, Stewart (Armstrong);
Summers, Andrew James; Sumner,
Gordon Matthew

Polidori, John William
1795-1821 . . . . **NCLC 51**
See also DLB 116

Pollitt, Katha 1949- . . . . **CLC 28**
See also CA 120; 122; MTCW

Pollock, (Mary) Sharon
1936- . . . . **CLC 50; DAC**
See also CA 141; DAM DRAM, MST;
DLB 60

Polo, Marco 1254-1324 . . . . **CMLC 15**

Polybius c. 200B.C.-c. 118B.C. . . . . **CMLC 17**

Pomerance, Bernard 1940- . . . . **CLC 13**
See also CA 101; CANR 49; DAM DRAM

Ponge, Francis (Jean Gaston Alfred)
1899-1988 . . . . **CLC 6, 18**
See also CA 85-88; 126; CANR 40;
DAM POET

Pontoppidan, Henrik 1857-1943 . . . **TCLC 29**

Poole, Josephine . . . . **CLC 17**
See also Helyar, Jane Penelope Josephine
See also SAAS 2; SATA 5

Popa, Vasko 1922-1991 . . . . **CLC 19**
See also CA 112; 148

Pope, Alexander
1688-1744 . . . . . **LC 3; DA; DAB; DAC;
WLC**
See also CDBLB 1660-1789; DAM MST,
POET; DLB 95, 101

Porter, Connie (Rose) 1959(?)- . . . . . **CLC 70**
See also BW 2; CA 142; SATA 81

Porter, Gene(va Grace) Stratton
1863(?)-1924 . . . . **TCLC 21**
See also CA 112

Porter, Katherine Anne
1890-1980 . . . . . . **CLC 1, 3, 7, 10, 13, 15,
27; DA; DAB; DAC; SSC 4**
See also AITN 2; CA 1-4R; 101; CANR 1;
DAM MST, NOV; DLB 4, 9, 102;
DLBD 12; DLBY 80; MTCW; SATA 39;
SATA-Obit 23

Porter, Peter (Neville Frederick)
1929- . . . . **CLC 5, 13, 33**
See also CA 85-88; DLB 40

Porter, William Sydney 1862-1910
See Henry, O.
See also CA 104; 131; CDALB 1865-1917;
DA; DAB; DAC; DAM MST; DLB 12,
78, 79; MTCW; YABC 2

Portillo (y Pacheco), Jose Lopez
See Lopez Portillo (y Pacheco), Jose

Post, Melville Davisson
1869-1930 . . . . **TCLC 39**
See also CA 110

Potok, Chaim 1929- . . . . **CLC 2, 7, 14, 26**
See also AAYA 15; AITN 1, 2; CA 17-20R;
CANR 19, 35; DAM NOV; DLB 28, 152;
INT CANR-19; MTCW; SATA 33

Potter, Beatrice
See Webb, (Martha) Beatrice (Potter)
See also MAICYA

Potter, Dennis (Christopher George)
1935-1994 . . . . **CLC 58, 86**
See also CA 107; 145; CANR 33; MTCW

Pound, Ezra (Weston Loomis)
1885-1972 . . . . . . **CLC 1, 2, 3, 4, 5, 7, 10,
13, 18, 34, 48, 50; DA; DAB; DAC; PC 4;
WLC**
See also CA 5-8R; 37-40R; CANR 40;
CDALB 1917-1929; DAM MST, POET;
DLB 4, 45, 63; MTCW

Povod, Reinaldo 1959-1994 . . . . **CLC 44**
See also CA 136; 146

Powell, Adam Clayton, Jr.
1908-1972 . . . . **CLC 89; BLC**
See also BW 1; CA 102; 33-36R;
DAM MULT

Powell, Anthony (Dymoke)
1905- . . . . **CLC 1, 3, 7, 9, 10, 31**
See also CA 1-4R; CANR 1, 32;
CDBLB 1945-1960; DLB 15; MTCW

Powell, Dawn 1897-1965 . . . . **CLC 66**
See also CA 5-8R

Powell, Padgett 1952- . . . . **CLC 34**
See also CA 126

Powers, J(ames) F(arl)
1917- . . . . **CLC 1, 4, 8, 57; SSC 4**
See also CA 1-4R; CANR 2; DLB 130;
MTCW

Powers, John J(ames) 1945-
See Powers, John R.
See also CA 69-72

Powers, John R. . . . . **CLC 66**
See also Powers, John J(ames)

Pownall, David 1938- . . . . **CLC 10**
See also CA 89-92; CAAS 18; CANR 49;
DLB 14

Powys, John Cowper
1872-1963 . . . . **CLC 7, 9, 15, 46**
See also CA 85-88; DLB 15; MTCW

Powys, T(heodore) F(rancis)
1875-1953 . . . . **TCLC 9**
See also CA 106; DLB 36

Prager, Emily 1952- . . . . **CLC 56**

Pratt, E(dwin) J(ohn)
1883(?)-1964 . . . . **CLC 19; DAC**
See also CA 141; 93-96; DAM POET;
DLB 92

Premchand . . . . **TCLC 21**
See also Srivastava, Dhanpat Rai

Preussler, Otfried 1923- . . . . **CLC 17**
See also CA 77-80; SATA 24

Prevert, Jacques (Henri Marie)
1900-1977 . . . . **CLC 15**
See also CA 77-80; 69-72; CANR 29;
MTCW; SATA-Obit 30

Prevost, Abbe (Antoine Francois)
1697-1763 . . . . **LC 1**

Price, (Edward) Reynolds
1933- . . . . **CLC 3, 6, 13, 43, 50, 63**
See also CA 1-4R; CANR 1, 37;
DAM NOV; DLB 2; INT CANR-37

Price, Richard 1949- . . . . **CLC 6, 12**
See also CA 49-52; CANR 3; DLBY 81

Prichard, Katharine Susannah
1883-1969 . . . . **CLC 46**
See also CA 11-12; CANR 33; CAP 1;
MTCW; SATA 66

Priestley, J(ohn) B(oynton)
1894-1984 . . . . **CLC 2, 5, 9, 34**
See also CA 9-12R; 113; CANR 33;
CDBLB 1914-1945; DAM DRAM, NOV;
DLB 10, 34, 77, 100, 139; DLBY 84;
MTCW

Prince 1958(?)- . . . . **CLC 35**

Prince, F(rank) T(empleton) 1912- . . **CLC 22**
See also CA 101; CANR 43; DLB 20

Prince Kropotkin
See Kropotkin, Peter (Aleksieevich)

Prior, Matthew 1664-1721 . . . . **LC 4**
See also DLB 95

Pritchard, William H(arrison)
1932- .... **CLC 34**
See also CA 65-68; CANR 23; DLB 111

Pritchett, V(ictor) S(awdon)
1900- ...... **CLC 5, 13, 15, 41; SSC 14**
See also CA 61-64; CANR 31; DAM NOV;
DLB 15, 139; MTCW

Private 19022
See Manning, Frederic

Probst, Mark 1925- .... **CLC 59**
See also CA 130

Prokosch, Frederic 1908-1989.... **CLC 4, 48**
See also CA 73-76; 128; DLB 48

Prophet, The
See Dreiser, Theodore (Herman Albert)

Prose, Francine 1947-............ **CLC 45**
See also CA 109; 112; CANR 46

Proudhon
See Cunha, Euclides (Rodrigues Pimenta) da

Proulx, E. Annie 1935- .... **CLC 81**

**Proust, (Valentin-Louis-George-Eugene-)
Marcel**
1871-1922 .... **TCLC 7, 13, 33; DA;
DAB; DAC; WLC**
See also CA 104; 120; DAM MST, NOV;
DLB 65; MTCW

Prowler, Harley
See Masters, Edgar Lee

Prus, Boleslaw 1845-1912 .... **TCLC 48**

Pryor, Richard (Franklin Lenox Thomas)
1940- .... **CLC 26**
See also CA 122

Przybyszewski, Stanislaw
1868-1927 .... **TCLC 36**
See also DLB 66

Pteleon
See Grieve, C(hristopher) M(urray)
See also DAM POET

Puckett, Lute
See Masters, Edgar Lee

Puig, Manuel
1932-1990 ... **CLC 3, 5, 10, 28, 65; HLC**
See also CA 45-48; CANR 2, 32;
DAM MULT; DLB 113; HW; MTCW

Purdy, Al(fred Wellington)
1918- .... **CLC 3, 6, 14, 50; DAC**
See also CA 81-84; CAAS 17; CANR 42;
DAM MST, POET; DLB 88

Purdy, James (Amos)
1923- .... **CLC 2, 4, 10, 28, 52**
See also CA 33-36R; CAAS 1; CANR 19;
DLB 2; INT CANR-19; MTCW

Pure, Simon
See Swinnerton, Frank Arthur

Pushkin, Alexander (Sergeyevich)
1799-1837 ..... **NCLC 3, 27; DA; DAB;
DAC; PC 10; WLC**
See also DAM DRAM, MST, POET;
SATA 61

P'u Sung-ling 1640-1715 .... **LC 3**

Putnam, Arthur Lee
See Alger, Horatio, Jr.

Puzo, Mario 1920- .... **CLC 1, 2, 6, 36**
See also CA 65-68; CANR 4, 42;
DAM NOV, POP; DLB 6; MTCW

Pym, Barbara (Mary Crampton)
1913-1980 .... **CLC 13, 19, 37**
See also CA 13-14; 97-100; CANR 13, 34;
CAP 1; DLB 14; DLBY 87; MTCW

Pynchon, Thomas (Ruggles, Jr.)
1937- ..... **CLC 2, 3, 6, 9, 11, 18, 33, 62,
72; DA; DAB; DAC; SSC 14; WLC**
See also BEST 90:2; CA 17-20R; CANR 22,
46; DAM MST, NOV, POP; DLB 2;
MTCW

Qian Zhongshu
See Ch'ien Chung-shu

Qroll
See Dagerman, Stig (Halvard)

Quarrington, Paul (Lewis) 1953-.... **CLC 65**
See also CA 129

Quasimodo, Salvatore 1901-1968 ... **CLC 10**
See also CA 13-16; 25-28R; CAP 1;
DLB 114; MTCW

Queen, Ellery .... **CLC 3, 11**
See also Dannay, Frederic; Davidson,
Avram; Lee, Manfred B(ennington);
Sturgeon, Theodore (Hamilton); Vance,
John Holbrook

Queen, Ellery, Jr.
See Dannay, Frederic; Lee, Manfred
B(ennington)

Queneau, Raymond
1903-1976 .... **CLC 2, 5, 10, 42**
See also CA 77-80; 69-72; CANR 32;
DLB 72; MTCW

Quevedo, Francisco de 1580-1645.... **LC 23**

Quiller-Couch, Arthur Thomas
1863-1944 .... **TCLC 53**
See also CA 118; DLB 135, 153

Quin, Ann (Marie) 1936-1973 .... **CLC 6**
See also CA 9-12R; 45-48; DLB 14

Quinn, Martin
See Smith, Martin Cruz

Quinn, Simon
See Smith, Martin Cruz

Quiroga, Horacio (Sylvestre)
1878-1937 .... **TCLC 20; HLC**
See also CA 117; 131; DAM MULT; HW;
MTCW

Quoirez, Francoise 1935-........... **CLC 9**
See also Sagan, Francoise
See also CA 49-52; CANR 6, 39; MTCW

Raabe, Wilhelm 1831-1910 .... **TCLC 45**
See also DLB 129

Rabe, David (William) 1940-... **CLC 4, 8, 33**
See also CA 85-88; CABS 3; DAM DRAM;
DLB 7

Rabelais, Francois
1483-1553 ...... **LC 5; DA; DAB; DAC;
WLC**
See also DAM MST

Rabinovitch, Sholem 1859-1916
See Aleichem, Sholom
See also CA 104

Racine, Jean 1639-1699 .... **LC 28; DAB**
See also DAM MST

Radcliffe, Ann (Ward) 1764-1823 .. **NCLC 6**
See also DLB 39

Radiguet, Raymond 1903-1923 .... **TCLC 29**
See also DLB 65

Radnoti, Miklos 1909-1944 .... **TCLC 16**
See also CA 118

Rado, James 1939-............... **CLC 17**
See also CA 105

Radvanyi, Netty 1900-1983
See Seghers, Anna
See also CA 85-88; 110

Rae, Ben
See Griffiths, Trevor

Raeburn, John (Hay) 1941-........ **CLC 34**
See also CA 57-60

Ragni, Gerome 1942-1991 .... **CLC 17**
See also CA 105; 134

Rahv, Philip 1908-1973 .... **CLC 24**
See also Greenberg, Ivan
See also DLB 137

Raine, Craig 1944- .... **CLC 32**
See also CA 108; CANR 29; DLB 40

Raine, Kathleen (Jessie) 1908- ... **CLC 7, 45**
See also CA 85-88; CANR 46; DLB 20;
MTCW

Rainis, Janis 1865-1929 .... **TCLC 29**

Rakosi, Carl .... **CLC 47**
See also Rawley, Callman
See also CAAS 5

Raleigh, Richard
See Lovecraft, H(oward) P(hillips)

Raleigh, Sir Walter 1554(?)-1618 .... **LC 31**
See also CDBLB Before 1660

Rallentando, H. P.
See Sayers, Dorothy L(eigh)

Ramal, Walter
See de la Mare, Walter (John)

Ramon, Juan
See Jimenez (Mantecon), Juan Ramon

Ramos, Graciliano 1892-1953 ..... **TCLC 32**

Rampersad, Arnold 1941-.......... **CLC 44**
See also BW 2; CA 127; 133; DLB 111;
INT 133

Rampling, Anne
See Rice, Anne

Ramsay, Allan 1684(?)-1758 .... **LC 29**
See also DLB 95

Ramuz, Charles-Ferdinand
1878-1947 .... **TCLC 33**

Rand, Ayn
1905-1982 ...... **CLC 3, 30, 44, 79; DA;
DAC; WLC**
See also AAYA 10; CA 13-16R; 105;
CANR 27; DAM MST, NOV, POP;
MTCW

Randall, Dudley (Felker)
1914- .... **CLC 1; BLC**
See also BW 1; CA 25-28R; CANR 23;
DAM MULT; DLB 41

Randall, Robert
See Silverberg, Robert

Ranger, Ken
See Creasey, John

Ransom, John Crowe
  1888-1974 . . . . **CLC 2, 4, 5, 11, 24**
  See also CA 5-8R; 49-52; CANR 6, 34;
  DAM POET; DLB 45, 63; MTCW

Rao, Raja 1909- . . . . **CLC 25, 56**
  See also CA 73-76; DAM NOV; MTCW

Raphael, Frederic (Michael)
  1931- . . . . **CLC 2, 14**
  See also CA 1-4R; CANR 1; DLB 14

Ratcliffe, James P.
  See Mencken, H(enry) L(ouis)

Rathbone, Julian 1935- . . . . **CLC 41**
  See also CA 101; CANR 34

Rattigan, Terence (Mervyn)
  1911-1977 . . . . **CLC 7**
  See also CA 85-88; 73-76;
  CDBLB 1945-1960; DAM DRAM;
  DLB 13; MTCW

Ratushinskaya, Irina 1954- . . . . **CLC 54**
  See also CA 129

Raven, Simon (Arthur Noel)
  1927- . . . . **CLC 14**
  See also CA 81-84

Rawley, Callman 1903-
  See Rakosi, Carl
  See also CA 21-24R; CANR 12, 32

Rawlings, Marjorie Kinnan
  1896-1953 . . . . **TCLC 4**
  See also CA 104; 137; DLB 9, 22, 102;
  JRDA; MAICYA; YABC 1

Ray, Satyajit 1921-1992 . . . . **CLC 16, 76**
  See also CA 114; 137; DAM MULT

Read, Herbert Edward 1893-1968 . . . . **CLC 4**
  See also CA 85-88; 25-28R; DLB 20, 149

Read, Piers Paul 1941- . . . . . . **CLC 4, 10, 25**
  See also CA 21-24R; CANR 38; DLB 14;
  SATA 21

Reade, Charles 1814-1884 . . . . **NCLC 2**
  See also DLB 21

Reade, Hamish
  See Gray, Simon (James Holliday)

Reading, Peter 1946- . . . . **CLC 47**
  See also CA 103; CANR 46; DLB 40

Reaney, James 1926- . . . . **CLC 13; DAC**
  See also CA 41-44R; CAAS 15; CANR 42;
  DAM MST; DLB 68; SATA 43

Rebreanu, Liviu 1885-1944 . . . . **TCLC 28**

Rechy, John (Francisco)
  1934- . . . . **CLC 1, 7, 14, 18; HLC**
  See also CA 5-8R; CAAS 4; CANR 6, 32;
  DAM MULT; DLB 122; DLBY 82; HW;
  INT CANR-6

Redcam, Tom 1870-1933 . . . . **TCLC 25**

Reddin, Keith . . . . **CLC 67**

Redgrove, Peter (William)
  1932- . . . . **CLC 6, 41**
  See also CA 1-4R; CANR 3, 39; DLB 40

Redmon, Anne . . . . **CLC 22**
  See also Nightingale, Anne Redmon
  See also DLBY 86

Reed, Eliot
  See Ambler, Eric

Reed, Ishmael
  1938- . . . **CLC 2, 3, 5, 6, 13, 32, 60; BLC**
  See also BW 2; CA 21-24R; CANR 25, 48;
  DAM MULT; DLB 2, 5, 33; DLBD 8;
  MTCW

Reed, John (Silas) 1887-1920 . . . . . . **TCLC 9**
  See also CA 106

Reed, Lou . . . . **CLC 21**
  See also Firbank, Louis

Reeve, Clara 1729-1807 . . . . **NCLC 19**
  See also DLB 39

Reich, Wilhelm 1897-1957 . . . . **TCLC 57**

Reid, Christopher (John) 1949- . . . . . **CLC 33**
  See also CA 140; DLB 40

Reid, Desmond
  See Moorcock, Michael (John)

Reid Banks, Lynne 1929-
  See Banks, Lynne Reid
  See also CA 1-4R; CANR 6, 22, 38;
  CLR 24; JRDA; MAICYA; SATA 22, 75

Reilly, William K.
  See Creasey, John

Reiner, Max
  See Caldwell, (Janet Miriam) Taylor
  (Holland)

Reis, Ricardo
  See Pessoa, Fernando (Antonio Nogueira)

Remarque, Erich Maria
  1898-1970 . . . . **CLC 21; DA; DAB; DAC**
  See also CA 77-80; 29-32R; DAM MST,
  NOV; DLB 56; MTCW

Remizov, A.
  See Remizov, Aleksei (Mikhailovich)

Remizov, A. M.
  See Remizov, Aleksei (Mikhailovich)

Remizov, Aleksei (Mikhailovich)
  1877-1957 . . . . **TCLC 27**
  See also CA 125; 133

Renan, Joseph Ernest
  1823-1892 . . . . **NCLC 26**

Renard, Jules 1864-1910 . . . . **TCLC 17**
  See also CA 117

Renault, Mary . . . . **CLC 3, 11, 17**
  See also Challans, Mary
  See also DLBY 83

Rendell, Ruth (Barbara) 1930- . . **CLC 28, 48**
  See also Vine, Barbara
  See also CA 109; CANR 32; DAM POP;
  DLB 87; INT CANR-32; MTCW

Renoir, Jean 1894-1979 . . . . **CLC 20**
  See also CA 129; 85-88

Resnais, Alain 1922- . . . . **CLC 16**

Reverdy, Pierre 1889-1960 . . . . **CLC 53**
  See also CA 97-100; 89-92

Rexroth, Kenneth
  1905-1982 . . . . . . **CLC 1, 2, 6, 11, 22, 49**
  See also CA 5-8R; 107; CANR 14, 34;
  CDALB 1941-1968; DAM POET;
  DLB 16, 48; DLBY 82; INT CANR-14;
  MTCW

Reyes, Alfonso 1889-1959 . . . . **TCLC 33**
  See also CA 131; HW

Reyes y Basoalto, Ricardo Eliecer Neftali
  See Neruda, Pablo

Reymont, Wladyslaw (Stanislaw)
  1868(?)-1925 . . . . **TCLC 5**
  See also CA 104

Reynolds, Jonathan 1942- . . . . **CLC 6, 38**
  See also CA 65-68; CANR 28

Reynolds, Joshua 1723-1792 . . . . **LC 15**
  See also DLB 104

Reynolds, Michael Shane 1937- . . . . **CLC 44**
  See also CA 65-68; CANR 9

Reznikoff, Charles 1894-1976 . . . . **CLC 9**
  See also CA 33-36; 61-64; CAP 2; DLB 28,
  45

Rezzori (d'Arezzo), Gregor von
  1914- . . . . **CLC 25**
  See also CA 122; 136

Rhine, Richard
  See Silverstein, Alvin

Rhodes, Eugene Manlove
  1869-1934 . . . . **TCLC 53**

R'hoone
  See Balzac, Honore de

Rhys, Jean
  1890(?)-1979 . . . . **CLC 2, 4, 6, 14, 19, 51;
  SSC 21**
  See also CA 25-28R; 85-88; CANR 35;
  CDBLB 1945-1960; DAM NOV; DLB 36,
  117; MTCW

Ribeiro, Darcy 1922- . . . . **CLC 34**
  See also CA 33-36R

Ribeiro, Joao Ubaldo (Osorio Pimentel)
  1941- . . . . **CLC 10, 67**
  See also CA 81-84

Ribman, Ronald (Burt) 1932- . . . . **CLC 7**
  See also CA 21-24R; CANR 46

Ricci, Nino 1959- . . . . **CLC 70**
  See also CA 137

Rice, Anne 1941- . . . . **CLC 41**
  See also AAYA 9; BEST 89:2; CA 65-68;
  CANR 12, 36; DAM POP

Rice, Elmer (Leopold)
  1892-1967 . . . . **CLC 7, 49**
  See also CA 21-22; 25-28R; CAP 2;
  DAM DRAM; DLB 4, 7; MTCW

Rice, Tim(othy Miles Bindon)
  1944- . . . . **CLC 21**
  See also CA 103; CANR 46

Rich, Adrienne (Cecile)
  1929- . . . . **CLC 3, 6, 7, 11, 18, 36, 73, 76;
  PC 5**
  See also CA 9-12R; CANR 20;
  DAM POET; DLB 5, 67; MTCW

Rich, Barbara
  See Graves, Robert (von Ranke)

Rich, Robert
  See Trumbo, Dalton

Richard, Keith . . . . **CLC 17**
  See also Richards, Keith

Richards, David Adams
  1950- . . . . **CLC 59; DAC**
  See also CA 93-96; DLB 53

Richards, I(vor) A(rmstrong)
  1893-1979 . . . . **CLC 14, 24**
  See also CA 41-44R; 89-92; CANR 34;
  DLB 27

Richards, Keith 1943-
See Richard, Keith
See also CA 107

Richardson, Anne
See Roiphe, Anne (Richardson)

Richardson, Dorothy Miller
1873-1957 . . . . **TCLC 3**
See also CA 104; DLB 36

Richardson, Ethel Florence (Lindesay)
1870-1946
See Richardson, Henry Handel
See also CA 105

Richardson, Henry Handel . . . . **TCLC 4**
See also Richardson, Ethel Florence
(Lindesay)

Richardson, Samuel
1689-1761 . . . . . . **LC 1; DA; DAB; DAC;**
WLC
See also CDBLB 1660-1789; DAM MST,
NOV; DLB 39

Richler, Mordecai
1931- . . . . **CLC 3, 5, 9, 13, 18, 46, 70;**
DAC
See also AITN 1; CA 65-68; CANR 31;
CLR 17; DAM MST, NOV; DLB 53;
MAICYA; MTCW; SATA 44;
SATA-Brief 27

Richter, Conrad (Michael)
1890-1968 . . . . **CLC 30**
See also CA 5-8R; 25-28R; CANR 23;
DLB 9; MTCW; SATA 3

Ricostranza, Tom
See Ellis, Trey

Riddell, J. H. 1832-1906 . . . . **TCLC 40**

Riding, Laura . . . . **CLC 3, 7**
See also Jackson, Laura (Riding)

Riefenstahl, Berta Helene Amalia 1902-
See Riefenstahl, Leni
See also CA 108

Riefenstahl, Leni . . . . **CLC 16**
See also Riefenstahl, Berta Helene Amalia

Riffe, Ernest
See Bergman, (Ernst) Ingmar

Riggs, (Rolla) Lynn 1899-1954 . . . . **TCLC 56**
See also CA 144; DAM MULT; NNAL

Riley, James Whitcomb
1849-1916 . . . . **TCLC 51**
See also CA 118; 137; DAM POET;
MAICYA; SATA 17

Riley, Tex
See Creasey, John

Rilke, Rainer Maria
1875-1926 . . . . **TCLC 1, 6, 19; PC 2**
See also CA 104; 132; DAM POET;
DLB 81; MTCW

Rimbaud, (Jean Nicolas) Arthur
1854-1891 . . . . . **NCLC 4, 35; DA; DAB;**
DAC; PC 3; WLC
See also DAM MST, POET

Rinehart, Mary Roberts
1876-1958 . . . . **TCLC 52**
See also CA 108

Ringmaster, The
See Mencken, H(enry) L(ouis)

Ringwood, Gwen(dolyn Margaret) Pharis
1910-1984 . . . . **CLC 48**
See also CA 148; 112; DLB 88

Rio, Michel 19(?)- . . . . **CLC 43**

Ritsos, Giannes
See Ritsos, Yannis

Ritsos, Yannis 1909-1990 . . . . . **CLC 6, 13, 31**
See also CA 77-80; 133; CANR 39; MTCW

Ritter, Erika 1948(?)- . . . . **CLC 52**

Rivera, Jose Eustasio 1889-1928 . . . **TCLC 35**
See also HW

Rivers, Conrad Kent 1933-1968 . . . . . . **CLC 1**
See also BW 1; CA 85-88; DLB 41

Rivers, Elfrida
See Bradley, Marion Zimmer

Riverside, John
See Heinlein, Robert A(nson)

Rizal, Jose 1861-1896 . . . . **NCLC 27**

Roa Bastos, Augusto (Antonio)
1917- . . . . **CLC 45; HLC**
See also CA 131; DAM MULT; DLB 113;
HW

Robbe-Grillet, Alain
1922- . . . . . . **CLC 1, 2, 4, 6, 8, 10, 14, 43**
See also CA 9-12R; CANR 33; DLB 83;
MTCW

Robbins, Harold 1916- . . . . **CLC 5**
See also CA 73-76; CANR 26; DAM NOV;
MTCW

Robbins, Thomas Eugene 1936-
See Robbins, Tom
See also CA 81-84; CANR 29; DAM NOV,
POP; MTCW

Robbins, Tom . . . . **CLC 9, 32, 64**
See also Robbins, Thomas Eugene
See also BEST 90:3; DLBY 80

Robbins, Trina 1938- . . . . **CLC 21**
See also CA 128

Roberts, Charles G(eorge) D(ouglas)
1860-1943 . . . . **TCLC 8**
See also CA 105; CLR 33; DLB 92;
SATA-Brief 29

Roberts, Kate 1891-1985 . . . . **CLC 15**
See also CA 107; 116

Roberts, Keith (John Kingston)
1935- . . . . **CLC 14**
See also CA 25-28R; CANR 46

Roberts, Kenneth (Lewis)
1885-1957 . . . . **TCLC 23**
See also CA 109; DLB 9

Roberts, Michele (B.) 1949- . . . . **CLC 48**
See also CA 115

Robertson, Ellis
See Ellison, Harlan (Jay); Silverberg, Robert

Robertson, Thomas William
1829-1871 . . . . **NCLC 35**
See also DAM DRAM

Robinson, Edwin Arlington
1869-1935 . . . . **TCLC 5; DA; DAC; PC 1**
See also CA 104; 133; CDALB 1865-1917;
DAM MST, POET; DLB 54; MTCW

Robinson, Henry Crabb
1775-1867 . . . . **NCLC 15**
See also DLB 107

Robinson, Jill 1936- . . . . **CLC 10**
See also CA 102; INT 102

Robinson, Kim Stanley 1952- . . . . . . **CLC 34**
See also CA 126

Robinson, Lloyd
See Silverberg, Robert

Robinson, Marilynne 1944- . . . . **CLC 25**
See also CA 116

Robinson, Smokey . . . . **CLC 21**
See also Robinson, William, Jr.

Robinson, William, Jr. 1940-
See Robinson, Smokey
See also CA 116

Robison, Mary 1949- . . . . **CLC 42**
See also CA 113; 116; DLB 130; INT 116

Rod, Edouard 1857-1910 . . . . **TCLC 52**

Roddenberry, Eugene Wesley 1921-1991
See Roddenberry, Gene
See also CA 110; 135; CANR 37; SATA 45;
SATA-Obit 69

Roddenberry, Gene . . . . **CLC 17**
See also Roddenberry, Eugene Wesley
See also AAYA 5; SATA-Obit 69

Rodgers, Mary 1931- . . . . **CLC 12**
See also CA 49-52; CANR 8; CLR 20;
INT CANR-8; JRDA; MAICYA;
SATA 8

Rodgers, W(illiam) R(obert)
1909-1969 . . . . **CLC 7**
See also CA 85-88; DLB 20

Rodman, Eric
See Silverberg, Robert

Rodman, Howard 1920(?)-1985 . . . . . **CLC 65**
See also CA 118

Rodman, Maia
See Wojciechowska, Maia (Teresa)

Rodriguez, Claudio 1934- . . . . **CLC 10**
See also DLB 134

Roelvaag, O(le) E(dvart)
1876-1931 . . . . **TCLC 17**
See also CA 117; DLB 9

Roethke, Theodore (Huebner)
1908-1963 . . . . . . **CLC 1, 3, 8, 11, 19, 46**
See also CA 81-84; CABS 2;
CDALB 1941-1968; DAM POET; DLB 5;
MTCW

Rogers, Thomas Hunton 1927- . . . . . **CLC 57**
See also CA 89-92; INT 89-92

Rogers, Will(iam Penn Adair)
1879-1935 . . . . **TCLC 8**
See also CA 105; 144; DAM MULT;
DLB 11; NNAL

Rogin, Gilbert 1929- . . . . **CLC 18**
See also CA 65-68; CANR 15

Rohan, Koda . . . . **TCLC 22**
See also Koda Shigeyuki

Rohmer, Eric . . . . **CLC 16**
See also Scherer, Jean-Marie Maurice

Rohmer, Sax . . . . **TCLC 28**
See also Ward, Arthur Henry Sarsfield
See also DLB 70

Roiphe, Anne (Richardson)
1935- . . . . CLC 3, 9
See also CA 89-92; CANR 45; DLBY 80;
INT 89-92

Rojas, Fernando de   1465-1541 . . . . . LC 23

Rolfe, Frederick (William Serafino Austin
Lewis Mary) 1860-1913. . . . . TCLC 12
See also CA 107; DLB 34, 156

Rolland, Romain   1866-1944. . . . . . TCLC 23
See also CA 118; DLB 65

Rolvaag, O(le) E(dvart)
See Roelvaag, O(le) E(dvart)

Romain Arnaud, Saint
See Aragon, Louis

Romains, Jules   1885-1972 . . . . CLC 7
See also CA 85-88; CANR 34; DLB 65;
MTCW

Romero, Jose Ruben   1890-1952 . . . TCLC 14
See also CA 114; 131; HW

Ronsard, Pierre de
1524-1585 . . . . LC 6; PC 11

Rooke, Leon   1934- . . . . CLC 25, 34
See also CA 25-28R; CANR 23; DAM POP

Roper, William   1498-1578 . . . . LC 10

Roquelaure, A. N.
See Rice, Anne

Rosa, Joao Guimaraes   1908-1967 . . . CLC 23
See also CA 89-92; DLB 113

Rose, Wendy   1948- . . . . CLC 85; PC 13
See also CA 53-56; CANR 5; DAM MULT;
NNAL; SATA 12

Rosen, Richard (Dean)   1949- . . . . CLC 39
See also CA 77-80; INT CANR-30

Rosenberg, Isaac   1890-1918. . . . . . TCLC 12
See also CA 107; DLB 20

Rosenblatt, Joe . . . . CLC 15
See also Rosenblatt, Joseph

Rosenblatt, Joseph   1933-
See Rosenblatt, Joe
See also CA 89-92; INT 89-92

Rosenfeld, Samuel   1896-1963
See Tzara, Tristan
See also CA 89-92

Rosenthal, M(acha) L(ouis)   1917- . . . CLC 28
See also CA 1-4R; CAAS 6; CANR 4;
DLB 5; SATA 59

Ross, Barnaby
See Dannay, Frederic

Ross, Bernard L.
See Follett, Ken(neth Martin)

Ross, J. H.
See Lawrence, T(homas) E(dward)

Ross, Martin
See Martin, Violet Florence
See also DLB 135

Ross, (James) Sinclair
1908- . . . . CLC 13; DAC
See also CA 73-76; DAM MST; DLB 88

Rossetti, Christina (Georgina)
1830-1894 . . . . . NCLC 2, 50; DA; DAB;
DAC; PC 7; WLC
See also DAM MST, POET; DLB 35;
MAICYA; SATA 20

Rossetti, Dante Gabriel
1828-1882 . . . . NCLC 4; DA; DAB;
DAC; WLC
See also CDBLB 1832-1890; DAM MST,
POET; DLB 35

Rossner, Judith (Perelman)
1935- . . . . CLC 6, 9, 29
See also AITN 2; BEST 90:3; CA 17-20R;
CANR 18; DLB 6; INT CANR-18;
MTCW

Rostand, Edmond (Eugene Alexis)
1868-1918 . . . . . . TCLC 6, 37; DA; DAB;
DAC
See also CA 104; 126; DAM DRAM, MST;
MTCW

Roth, Henry   1906- . . . . CLC 2, 6, 11
See also CA 11-12; CANR 38; CAP 1;
DLB 28; MTCW

Roth, Joseph   1894-1939. . . . . TCLC 33
See also DLB 85

Roth, Philip (Milton)
1933- . . . . . . CLC 1, 2, 3, 4, 6, 9, 15, 22,
31, 47, 66, 86; DA; DAB; DAC; WLC
See also BEST 90:3; CA 1-4R; CANR 1, 22,
36; CDALB 1968-1988; DAM MST,
NOV, POP; DLB 2, 28; DLBY 82;
MTCW

Rothenberg, Jerome   1931- . . . . CLC 6, 57
See also CA 45-48; CANR 1; DLB 5

Roumain, Jacques (Jean Baptiste)
1907-1944 . . . . TCLC 19; BLC
See also BW 1; CA 117; 125; DAM MULT

Rourke, Constance (Mayfield)
1885-1941 . . . . TCLC 12
See also CA 107; YABC 1

Rousseau, Jean-Baptiste   1671-1741 . . . LC 9

Rousseau, Jean-Jacques
1712-1778 . . . . . LC 14; DA; DAB; DAC;
WLC
See also DAM MST

Roussel, Raymond   1877-1933 . . . . . TCLC 20
See also CA 117

Rovit, Earl (Herbert)   1927- . . . . CLC 7
See also CA 5-8R; CANR 12

Rowe, Nicholas   1674-1718. . . . . LC 8
See also DLB 84

Rowley, Ames Dorrance
See Lovecraft, H(oward) P(hillips)

Rowson, Susanna Haswell
1762(?)-1824 . . . . NCLC 5
See also DLB 37

Roy, Gabrielle
1909-1983 . . . . . CLC 10, 14; DAB; DAC
See also CA 53-56; 110; CANR 5;
DAM MST; DLB 68; MTCW

Rozewicz, Tadeusz   1921- . . . . CLC 9, 23
See also CA 108; CANR 36; DAM POET;
MTCW

Ruark, Gibbons   1941- . . . . CLC 3
See also CA 33-36R; CANR 14, 31;
DLB 120

Rubens, Bernice (Ruth)   1923- . . . CLC 19, 31
See also CA 25-28R; CANR 33; DLB 14;
MTCW

Rudkin, (James) David   1936- . . . . . . CLC 14
See also CA 89-92; DLB 13

Rudnik, Raphael   1933- . . . . CLC 7
See also CA 29-32R

Ruffian, M.
See Hasek, Jaroslav (Matej Frantisek)

Ruiz, Jose Martinez . . . . CLC 11
See also Martinez Ruiz, Jose

Rukeyser, Muriel
1913-1980 . . . . CLC 6, 10, 15, 27; PC 12
See also CA 5-8R; 93-96; CANR 26;
DAM POET; DLB 48; MTCW;
SATA-Obit 22

Rule, Jane (Vance)   1931- . . . . CLC 27
See also CA 25-28R; CAAS 18; CANR 12;
DLB 60

Rulfo, Juan   1918-1986. . . . . CLC 8, 80; HLC
See also CA 85-88; 118; CANR 26;
DAM MULT; DLB 113; HW; MTCW

Runeberg, Johan   1804-1877. . . . . . NCLC 41

Runyon, (Alfred) Damon
1884(?)-1946 . . . . TCLC 10
See also CA 107; DLB 11, 86

Rush, Norman   1933-. . . . . CLC 44
See also CA 121; 126; INT 126

Rushdie, (Ahmed) Salman
1947- . . . . . . CLC 23, 31, 55; DAB; DAC
See also BEST 89:3; CA 108; 111;
CANR 33; DAM MST, NOV, POP;
INT 111; MTCW

Rushforth, Peter (Scott)   1945- . . . . . CLC 19
See also CA 101

Ruskin, John   1819-1900. . . . . TCLC 20
See also CA 114; 129; CDBLB 1832-1890;
DLB 55; SATA 24

Russ, Joanna   1937-. . . . . CLC 15
See also CA 25-28R; CANR 11, 31; DLB 8;
MTCW

Russell, George William   1867-1935
See A. E.
See also CA 104; CDBLB 1890-1914;
DAM POET

Russell, (Henry) Ken(neth Alfred)
1927- . . . . CLC 16
See also CA 105

Russell, Willy   1947-. . . . . CLC 60

Rutherford, Mark . . . . TCLC 25
See also White, William Hale
See also DLB 18

Ruyslinck, Ward   1929-. . . . . CLC 14
See also Belser, Reimond Karel Maria de

Ryan, Cornelius (John)   1920-1974 . . . CLC 7
See also CA 69-72; 53-56; CANR 38

Ryan, Michael   1946- . . . . CLC 65
See also CA 49-52; DLBY 82

Rybakov, Anatoli (Naumovich)
1911- . . . . CLC 23, 53
See also CA 126; 135; SATA 79

Ryder, Jonathan
See Ludlum, Robert

Ryga, George   1932-1987 . . . . . CLC 14; DAC
See also CA 101; 124; CANR 43;
DAM MST; DLB 60

S. S.
See Sassoon, Siegfried (Lorraine)

Saba, Umberto 1883-1957 . . . . **TCLC 33**
See also CA 144; DLB 114

Sabatini, Rafael 1875-1950 . . . . . . **TCLC 47**

Sabato, Ernesto (R.)
1911- . . . . **CLC 10, 23; HLC**
See also CA 97-100; CANR 32;
DAM MULT; DLB 145; HW; MTCW

Sacastru, Martin
See Bioy Casares, Adolfo

Sacher-Masoch, Leopold von
1836(?)-1895 . . . . **NCLC 31**

Sachs, Marilyn (Stickle) 1927- . . . . . **CLC 35**
See also AAYA 2; CA 17-20R; CANR 13,
47; CLR 2; JRDA; MAICYA; SAAS 2;
SATA 3, 68

Sachs, Nelly 1891-1970 . . . . **CLC 14**
See also CA 17-18; 25-28R; CAP 2

Sackler, Howard (Oliver)
1929-1982 . . . . **CLC 14**
See also CA 61-64; 108; CANR 30; DLB 7

Sacks, Oliver (Wolf) 1933- . . . . **CLC 67**
See also CA 53-56; CANR 28, 50;
INT CANR-28; MTCW

Sade, Donatien Alphonse Francois Comte
1740-1814 . . . . **NCLC 47**

Sadoff, Ira 1945- . . . . **CLC 9**
See also CA 53-56; CANR 5, 21; DLB 120

Saetone
See Camus, Albert

Safire, William 1929- . . . . **CLC 10**
See also CA 17-20R; CANR 31

Sagan, Carl (Edward) 1934- . . . . **CLC 30**
See also AAYA 2; CA 25-28R; CANR 11,
36; MTCW; SATA 58

Sagan, Francoise . . . . **CLC 3, 6, 9, 17, 36**
See also Quoirez, Francoise
See also DLB 83

Sahgal, Nayantara (Pandit) 1927- . . . **CLC 41**
See also CA 9-12R; CANR 11

Saint, H(arry) F. 1941- . . . . **CLC 50**
See also CA 127

St. Aubin de Teran, Lisa 1953-
See Teran, Lisa St. Aubin de
See also CA 118; 126; INT 126

Sainte-Beuve, Charles Augustin
1804-1869 . . . . **NCLC 5**

Saint-Exupery, Antoine (Jean Baptiste Marie
Roger) de
1900-1944 . . . . **TCLC 2, 56; WLC**
See also CA 108; 132; CLR 10; DAM NOV;
DLB 72; MAICYA; MTCW; SATA 20

St. John, David
See Hunt, E(verette) Howard, (Jr.)

Saint-John Perse
See Leger, (Marie-Rene Auguste) Alexis
Saint-Leger

Saintsbury, George (Edward Bateman)
1845-1933 . . . . **TCLC 31**
See also DLB 57, 149

Sait Faik . . . . **TCLC 23**
See also Abasiyanik, Sait Faik

Saki . . . . **TCLC 3; SSC 12**
See also Munro, H(ector) H(ugh)

Sala, George Augustus . . . . **NCLC 46**

Salama, Hannu 1936- . . . . **CLC 18**

Salamanca, J(ack) R(ichard)
1922- . . . . **CLC 4, 15**
See also CA 25-28R

Sale, J. Kirkpatrick
See Sale, Kirkpatrick

Sale, Kirkpatrick 1937- . . . . **CLC 68**
See also CA 13-16R; CANR 10

Salinas, Luis Omar 1937- . . . **CLC 90; HLC**
See also CA 131; DAM MULT; DLB 82;
HW

Salinas (y Serrano), Pedro
1891(?)-1951 . . . . **TCLC 17**
See also CA 117; DLB 134

Salinger, J(erome) D(avid)
1919- . . . . . . **CLC 1, 3, 8, 12, 55, 56; DA;
DAB; DAC; SSC 2; WLC**
See also AAYA 2; CA 5-8R; CANR 39;
CDALB 1941-1968; CLR 18; DAM MST,
NOV, POP; DLB 2, 102; MAICYA;
MTCW; SATA 67

Salisbury, John
See Caute, David

Salter, James 1925- . . . . **CLC 7, 52, 59**
See also CA 73-76; DLB 130

Saltus, Edgar (Everton)
1855-1921 . . . . **TCLC 8**
See also CA 105

Saltykov, Mikhail Evgrafovich
1826-1889 . . . . **NCLC 16**

Samarakis, Antonis 1919- . . . . **CLC 5**
See also CA 25-28R; CAAS 16; CANR 36

Sanchez, Florencio 1875-1910 . . . . . **TCLC 37**
See also HW

Sanchez, Luis Rafael 1936- . . . . **CLC 23**
See also CA 128; DLB 145; HW

Sanchez, Sonia 1934- . . . **CLC 5; BLC; PC 9**
See also BW 2; CA 33-36R; CANR 24, 49;
CLR 18; DAM MULT; DLB 41;
DLBD 8; MAICYA; MTCW; SATA 22

Sand, George
1804-1876 . . . . . **NCLC 2, 42; DA; DAB;
DAC; WLC**
See also DAM MST, NOV; DLB 119

Sandburg, Carl (August)
1878-1967 . . . . **CLC 1, 4, 10, 15, 35; DA;
DAB; DAC; PC 2; WLC**
See also CA 5-8R; 25-28R; CANR 35;
CDALB 1865-1917; DAM MST, POET;
DLB 17, 54; MAICYA; MTCW; SATA 8

Sandburg, Charles
See Sandburg, Carl (August)

Sandburg, Charles A.
See Sandburg, Carl (August)

Sanders, (James) Ed(ward) 1939- . . . **CLC 53**
See also CA 13-16R; CAAS 21; CANR 13,
44; DLB 16

Sanders, Lawrence 1920- . . . . **CLC 41**
See also BEST 89:4; CA 81-84; CANR 33;
DAM POP; MTCW

Sanders, Noah
See Blount, Roy (Alton), Jr.

Sanders, Winston P.
See Anderson, Poul (William)

Sandoz, Mari(e Susette)
1896-1966 . . . . **CLC 28**
See also CA 1-4R; 25-28R; CANR 17;
DLB 9; MTCW; SATA 5

Saner, Reg(inald Anthony) 1931- . . . . **CLC 9**
See also CA 65-68

Sannazaro, Jacopo 1456(?)-1530 . . . . . . **LC 8**

Sansom, William
1912-1976 . . . . **CLC 2, 6; SSC 21**
See also CA 5-8R; 65-68; CANR 42;
DAM NOV; DLB 139; MTCW

Santayana, George 1863-1952 . . . . . **TCLC 40**
See also CA 115; DLB 54, 71; DLBD 13

Santiago, Danny . . . . **CLC 33**
See also James, Daniel (Lewis)
See also DLB 122

Santmyer, Helen Hoover
1895-1986 . . . . **CLC 33**
See also CA 1-4R; 118; CANR 15, 33;
DLBY 84; MTCW

Santos, Bienvenido N(uqui) 1911- . . . **CLC 22**
See also CA 101; CANR 19, 46;
DAM MULT

Sapper . . . . **TCLC 44**
See also McNeile, Herman Cyril

Sappho fl. 6th cent. B.C.- . . . . **CMLC 3; PC 5**
See also DAM POET

Sarduy, Severo 1937-1993 . . . . **CLC 6**
See also CA 89-92; 142; DLB 113; HW

Sargeson, Frank 1903-1982 . . . . **CLC 31**
See also CA 25-28R; 106; CANR 38

Sarmiento, Felix Ruben Garcia
See Dario, Ruben

Saroyan, William
1908-1981 . . . . . **CLC 1, 8, 10, 29, 34, 56;
DA; DAB; DAC; SSC 21; WLC**
See also CA 5-8R; 103; CANR 30;
DAM DRAM, MST, NOV; DLB 7, 9, 86;
DLBY 81; MTCW; SATA 23;
SATA-Obit 24

Sarraute, Nathalie
1900- . . . . **CLC 1, 2, 4, 8, 10, 31, 80**
See also CA 9-12R; CANR 23; DLB 83;
MTCW

Sarton, (Eleanor) May
1912- . . . . **CLC 4, 14, 49**
See also CA 1-4R; CANR 1, 34;
DAM POET; DLB 48; DLBY 81;
INT CANR-34; MTCW; SATA 36

Sartre, Jean-Paul
1905-1980 . . . . **CLC 1, 4, 7, 9, 13, 18, 24,
44, 50, 52; DA; DAB; DAC; DC 3; WLC**
See also CA 9-12R; 97-100; CANR 21;
DAM DRAM, MST, NOV; DLB 72;
MTCW

Sassoon, Siegfried (Lorraine)
1886-1967 . . . . **CLC 36; DAB; PC 12**
See also CA 104; 25-28R; CANR 36;
DAM MST, NOV, POET; DLB 20;
MTCW

Satterfield, Charles
See Pohl, Frederik

Saul, John (W. III) 1942- . . . . **CLC 46**
See also AAYA 10; BEST 90:4; CA 81-84;
CANR 16, 40; DAM NOV, POP

Saunders, Caleb
See Heinlein, Robert A(nson)

Saura (Atares), Carlos 1932- ...... **CLC 20**
See also CA 114; 131; HW

Sauser-Hall, Frederic 1887-1961.... **CLC 18**
See also Cendrars, Blaise
See also CA 102; 93-96; CANR 36; MTCW

Saussure, Ferdinand de
1857-1913 .... **TCLC 49**

Savage, Catharine
See Brosman, Catharine Savage

Savage, Thomas 1915- .... **CLC 40**
See also CA 126; 132; CAAS 15; INT 132

Savan, Glenn 19(?)- .... **CLC 50**

Sayers, Dorothy L(eigh)
1893-1957 .... **TCLC 2, 15**
See also CA 104; 119; CDBLB 1914-1945;
DAM POP; DLB 10, 36, 77, 100; MTCW

Sayers, Valerie 1952- .... **CLC 50**
See also CA 134

Sayles, John (Thomas)
1950- .... **CLC 7, 10, 14**
See also CA 57-60; CANR 41; DLB 44

Scammell, Michael .... **CLC 34**

Scannell, Vernon 1922- .... **CLC 49**
See also CA 5-8R; CANR 8, 24; DLB 27;
SATA 59

Scarlett, Susan
See Streatfeild, (Mary) Noel

Schaeffer, Susan Fromberg
1941- .... **CLC 6, 11, 22**
See also CA 49-52; CANR 18; DLB 28;
MTCW; SATA 22

Schary, Jill
See Robinson, Jill

Schell, Jonathan 1943- .... **CLC 35**
See also CA 73-76; CANR 12

Schelling, Friedrich Wilhelm Joseph von
1775-1854 .... **NCLC 30**
See also DLB 90

Schendel, Arthur van 1874-1946 ... **TCLC 56**

Scherer, Jean-Marie Maurice 1920-
See Rohmer, Eric
See also CA 110

Schevill, James (Erwin) 1920- .... **CLC 7**
See also CA 5-8R; CAAS 12

Schiller, Friedrich 1759-1805 .... **NCLC 39**
See also DAM DRAM; DLB 94

Schisgal, Murray (Joseph) 1926- ..... **CLC 6**
See also CA 21-24R; CANR 48

Schlee, Ann 1934- .... **CLC 35**
See also CA 101; CANR 29; SATA 44;
SATA-Brief 36

Schlegel, August Wilhelm von
1767-1845 .... **NCLC 15**
See also DLB 94

Schlegel, Friedrich 1772-1829 .... **NCLC 45**
See also DLB 90

Schlegel, Johann Elias (von)
1719(?)-1749 .... **LC 5**

Schlesinger, Arthur M(eier), Jr.
1917- .... **CLC 84**
See also AITN 1; CA 1-4R; CANR 1, 28;
DLB 17; INT CANR-28; MTCW;
SATA 61

Schmidt, Arno (Otto) 1914-1979 .... **CLC 56**
See also CA 128; 109; DLB 69

Schmitz, Aron Hector 1861-1928
See Svevo, Italo
See also CA 104; 122; MTCW

Schnackenberg, Gjertrud 1953- ..... **CLC 40**
See also CA 116; DLB 120

Schneider, Leonard Alfred 1925-1966
See Bruce, Lenny
See also CA 89-92

Schnitzler, Arthur
1862-1931 .... **TCLC 4; SSC 15**
See also CA 104; DLB 81, 118

Schopenhauer, Arthur
1788-1860 .... **NCLC 51**
See also DLB 90

Schor, Sandra (M.) 1932(?)-1990 ... **CLC 65**
See also CA 132

Schorer, Mark 1908-1977 .... **CLC 9**
See also CA 5-8R; 73-76; CANR 7;
DLB 103

Schrader, Paul (Joseph) 1946- ...... **CLC 26**
See also CA 37-40R; CANR 41; DLB 44

Schreiner, Olive (Emilie Albertina)
1855-1920 .... **TCLC 9**
See also CA 105; DLB 18, 156

Schulberg, Budd (Wilson)
1914- .... **CLC 7, 48**
See also CA 25-28R; CANR 19; DLB 6, 26,
28; DLBY 81

Schulz, Bruno
1892-1942 .... **TCLC 5, 51; SSC 13**
See also CA 115; 123

Schulz, Charles M(onroe) 1922- .... **CLC 12**
See also CA 9-12R; CANR 6;
INT CANR-6; SATA 10

Schumacher, E(rnst) F(riedrich)
1911-1977 .... **CLC 80**
See also CA 81-84; 73-76; CANR 34

Schuyler, James Marcus
1923-1991 .... **CLC 5, 23**
See also CA 101; 134; DAM POET; DLB 5;
INT 101

Schwartz, Delmore (David)
1913-1966 ... **CLC 2, 4, 10, 45, 87; PC 8**
See also CA 17-18; 25-28R; CANR 35;
CAP 2; DLB 28, 48; MTCW

Schwartz, Ernst
See Ozu, Yasujiro

Schwartz, John Burnham 1965- .... **CLC 59**
See also CA 132

Schwartz, Lynne Sharon 1939- ..... **CLC 31**
See also CA 103; CANR 44

Schwartz, Muriel A.
See Eliot, T(homas) S(tearns)

Schwarz-Bart, Andre 1928- .... **CLC 2, 4**
See also CA 89-92

Schwarz-Bart, Simone 1938- .... **CLC 7**
See also BW 2; CA 97-100

Schwob, (Mayer Andre) Marcel
1867-1905 .... **TCLC 20**
See also CA 117; DLB 123

Sciascia, Leonardo
1921-1989 .... **CLC 8, 9, 41**
See also CA 85-88; 130; CANR 35; MTCW

Scoppettone, Sandra 1936- .... **CLC 26**
See also AAYA 11; CA 5-8R; CANR 41;
SATA 9

Scorsese, Martin 1942- .... **CLC 20, 89**
See also CA 110; 114; CANR 46

Scotland, Jay
See Jakes, John (William)

Scott, Duncan Campbell
1862-1947 .... **TCLC 6; DAC**
See also CA 104; DLB 92

Scott, Evelyn 1893-1963........... **CLC 43**
See also CA 104; 112; DLB 9, 48

Scott, F(rancis) R(eginald)
1899-1985 .... **CLC 22**
See also CA 101; 114; DLB 88; INT 101

Scott, Frank
See Scott, F(rancis) R(eginald)

Scott, Joanna 1960- .... **CLC 50**
See also CA 126

Scott, Paul (Mark) 1920-1978.... **CLC 9, 60**
See also CA 81-84; 77-80; CANR 33;
DLB 14; MTCW

Scott, Walter
1771-1832 .... **NCLC 15; DA; DAB;**
DAC; PC 13; WLC
See also CDBLB 1789-1832; DAM MST,
NOV, POET; DLB 93, 107, 116, 144, 159;
YABC 2

Scribe, (Augustin) Eugene
1791-1861 .... **NCLC 16; DC 5**
See also DAM DRAM

Scrum, R.
See Crumb, R(obert)

Scudery, Madeleine de 1607-1701..... **LC 2**

Scum
See Crumb, R(obert)

Scumbag, Little Bobby
See Crumb, R(obert)

Seabrook, John
See Hubbard, L(afayette) Ron(ald)

Sealy, I. Allan 1951- .... **CLC 55**

Search, Alexander
See Pessoa, Fernando (Antonio Nogueira)

Sebastian, Lee
See Silverberg, Robert

Sebastian Owl
See Thompson, Hunter S(tockton)

Sebestyen, Ouida 1924- .... **CLC 30**
See also AAYA 8; CA 107; CANR 40;
CLR 17; JRDA; MAICYA; SAAS 10;
SATA 39

Secundus, H. Scriblerus
See Fielding, Henry

Sedges, John
See Buck, Pearl S(ydenstricker)

Sedgwick, Catharine Maria
1789-1867 .... **NCLC 19**
See also DLB 1, 74

Singh, Khushwant 1915-.......... **CLC 11**
See also CA 9-12R; CAAS 9; CANR 6

Sinjohn, John
See Galsworthy, John

Sinyavsky, Andrei (Donatevich)
1925-...................... **CLC 8**
See also CA 85-88

Sirin, V.
See Nabokov, Vladimir (Vladimirovich)

Sissman, L(ouis) E(dward)
1928-1976 .... **CLC 9, 18**
See also CA 21-24R; 65-68; CANR 13;
DLB 5

Sisson, C(harles) H(ubert) 1914-..... **CLC 8**
See also CA 1-4R; CAAS 3; CANR 3, 48;
DLB 27

Sitwell, Dame Edith
1887-1964 .... **CLC 2, 9, 67; PC 3**
See also CA 9-12R; CANR 35;
CDBLB 1945-1960; DAM POET;
DLB 20; MTCW

Sjoewall, Maj 1935-.............. **CLC 7**
See also CA 65-68

Sjowall, Maj
See Sjoewall, Maj

Skelton, Robin 1925-............. **CLC 13**
See also AITN 2; CA 5-8R; CAAS 5;
CANR 28; DLB 27, 53

Skolimowski, Jerzy 1938-......... **CLC 20**
See also CA 128

Skram, Amalie (Bertha)
1847-1905 .... **TCLC 25**

Skvorecky, Josef (Vaclav)
1924- .... **CLC 15, 39, 69; DAC**
See also CA 61-64; CAAS 1; CANR 10, 34;
DAM NOV; MTCW

Slade, Bernard................ **CLC 11, 46**
See also Newbound, Bernard Slade
See also CAAS 9; DLB 53

Slaughter, Carolyn 1946-.......... **CLC 56**
See also CA 85-88

Slaughter, Frank G(ill) 1908- ...... **CLC 29**
See also AITN 2; CA 5-8R; CANR 5;
INT CANR-5

Slavitt, David R(ytman) 1935-.... **CLC 5, 14**
See also CA 21-24R; CAAS 3; CANR 41;
DLB 5, 6

Slesinger, Tess 1905-1945 .... **TCLC 10**
See also CA 107; DLB 102

Slessor, Kenneth 1901-1971........ **CLC 14**
See also CA 102; 89-92

Slowacki, Juliusz 1809-1849 ..... **NCLC 15**

Smart, Christopher
1722-1771 .... **LC 3; PC 13**
See also DAM POET; DLB 109

Smart, Elizabeth 1913-1986........ **CLC 54**
See also CA 81-84; 118; DLB 88

Smiley, Jane (Graves) 1949- .... **CLC 53, 76**
See also CA 104; CANR 30, 50;
DAM POP; INT CANR-30

Smith, A(rthur) J(ames) M(arshall)
1902-1980 .... **CLC 15; DAC**
See also CA 1-4R; 102; CANR 4; DLB 88

Smith, Anna Deavere 1950-....... **CLC 86**
See also CA 133

Smith, Betty (Wehner) 1896-1972... **CLC 19**
See also CA 5-8R; 33-36R; DLBY 82;
SATA 6

Smith, Charlotte (Turner)
1749-1806 .... **NCLC 23**
See also DLB 39, 109

Smith, Clark Ashton 1893-1961 .... **CLC 43**
See also CA 143

Smith, Dave................... **CLC 22, 42**
See also Smith, David (Jeddie)
See also CAAS 7; DLB 5

Smith, David (Jeddie) 1942-
See Smith, Dave
See also CA 49-52; CANR 1; DAM POET

Smith, Florence Margaret 1902-1971
See Smith, Stevie
See also CA 17-18; 29-32R; CANR 35;
CAP 2; DAM POET; MTCW

Smith, Iain Crichton 1928- .... **CLC 64**
See also CA 21-24R; DLB 40, 139

Smith, John 1580(?)-1631 .... **LC 9**

Smith, Johnston
See Crane, Stephen (Townley)

Smith, Joseph, Jr. 1805-1844 .... **NCLC 53**

Smith, Lee 1944-.............. **CLC 25, 73**
See also CA 114; 119; CANR 46; DLB 143;
DLBY 83; INT 119

Smith, Martin
See Smith, Martin Cruz

Smith, Martin Cruz 1942-......... **CLC 25**
See also BEST 89:4; CA 85-88; CANR 6,
23, 43; DAM MULT, POP;
INT CANR-23; NNAL

Smith, Mary-Ann Tirone 1944-..... **CLC 39**
See also CA 118; 136

Smith, Patti 1946- .... **CLC 12**
See also CA 93-96

Smith, Pauline (Urmson)
1882-1959 .... **TCLC 25**

Smith, Rosamond
See Oates, Joyce Carol

Smith, Sheila Kaye
See Kaye-Smith, Sheila

Smith, Stevie .... **CLC 3, 8, 25, 44; PC 12**
See also Smith, Florence Margaret
See also DLB 20

Smith, Wilbur (Addison) 1933-..... **CLC 33**
See also CA 13-16R; CANR 7, 46; MTCW

Smith, William Jay 1918- .... **CLC 6**
See also CA 5-8R; CANR 44; DLB 5;
MAICYA; SATA 2, 68

Smith, Woodrow Wilson
See Kuttner, Henry

Smolenskin, Peretz 1842-1885.... **NCLC 30**

Smollett, Tobias (George) 1721-1771 .. **LC 2**
See also CDBLB 1660-1789; DLB 39, 104

Snodgrass, W(illiam) D(e Witt)
1926- .... **CLC 2, 6, 10, 18, 68**
See also CA 1-4R; CANR 6, 36;
DAM POET; DLB 5; MTCW

Snow, C(harles) P(ercy)
1905-1980 .... **CLC 1, 4, 6, 9, 13, 19**
See also CA 5-8R; 101; CANR 28;
CDBLB 1945-1960; DAM NOV; DLB 15,
77; MTCW

Snow, Frances Compton
See Adams, Henry (Brooks)

Snyder, Gary (Sherman)
1930- .... **CLC 1, 2, 5, 9, 32**
See also CA 17-20R; CANR 30;
DAM POET; DLB 5, 16

Snyder, Zilpha Keatley 1927- ...... **CLC 17**
See also AAYA 15; CA 9-12R; CANR 38;
CLR 31; JRDA; MAICYA; SAAS 2;
SATA 1, 28, 75

Soares, Bernardo
See Pessoa, Fernando (Antonio Nogueira)

Sobh, A.
See Shamlu, Ahmad

Sobol, Joshua.................... **CLC 60**

Soderberg, Hjalmar 1869-1941 .... **TCLC 39**

Sodergran, Edith (Irene)
See Soedergran, Edith (Irene)

Soedergran, Edith (Irene)
1892-1923 .... **TCLC 31**

Softly, Edgar
See Lovecraft, H(oward) P(hillips)

Softly, Edward
See Lovecraft, H(oward) P(hillips)

Sokolov, Raymond 1941-........... **CLC 7**
See also CA 85-88

Solo, Jay
See Ellison, Harlan (Jay)

Sologub, Fyodor .... **TCLC 9**
See also Teternikov, Fyodor Kuzmich

Solomons, Ikey Esquir
See Thackeray, William Makepeace

Solomos, Dionysios 1798-1857 ... **NCLC 15**

Solwoska, Mara
See French, Marilyn

Solzhenitsyn, Aleksandr I(sayevich)
1918- ...... **CLC 1, 2, 4, 7, 9, 10, 18, 26,
34, 78; DA; DAB; DAC; WLC**
See also AITN 1; CA 69-72; CANR 40;
DAM MST, NOV; MTCW

Somers, Jane
See Lessing, Doris (May)

Somerville, Edith 1858-1949 ...... **TCLC 51**
See also DLB 135

Somerville & Ross
See Martin, Violet Florence; Somerville,
Edith

Sommer, Scott 1951- .... **CLC 25**
See also CA 106

Sondheim, Stephen (Joshua)
1930-................... **CLC 30, 39**
See also AAYA 11; CA 103; CANR 47;
DAM DRAM

Sontag, Susan 1933-... **CLC 1, 2, 10, 13, 31**
See also CA 17-20R; CANR 25;
DAM POP; DLB 2, 67; MTCW

Sophocles
496(?)B.C.-406(?)B.C. . . . . **CMLC 2; DA; DAB; DAC; DC 1**
See also DAM DRAM, MST

Sordello 1189-1269 . . . . **CMLC 15**

Sorel, Julia
See Drexler, Rosalyn

Sorrentino, Gilbert
1929- . . . . **CLC 3, 7, 14, 22, 40**
See also CA 77-80; CANR 14, 33; DLB 5; DLBY 80; INT CANR-14

Soto, Gary 1952- . . . . **CLC 32, 80; HLC**
See also AAYA 10; CA 119; 125; CANR 50; CLR 38; DAM MULT; DLB 82; HW; INT 125; JRDA; SATA 80

Soupault, Philippe 1897-1990 . . . . . . **CLC 68**
See also CA 116; 147; 131

Souster, (Holmes) Raymond
1921- . . . . **CLC 5, 14; DAC**
See also CA 13-16R; CAAS 14; CANR 13, 29; DAM POET; DLB 88; SATA 63

Southern, Terry 1926- . . . . **CLC 7**
See also CA 1-4R; CANR 1; DLB 2

Southey, Robert 1774-1843 . . . . **NCLC 8**
See also DLB 93, 107, 142; SATA 54

Southworth, Emma Dorothy Eliza Nevitte
1819-1899 . . . . **NCLC 26**

Souza, Ernest
See Scott, Evelyn

Soyinka, Wole
1934- . . . . **CLC 3, 5, 14, 36, 44; BLC; DA; DAB; DAC; DC 2; WLC**
See also BW 2; CA 13-16R; CANR 27, 39; DAM DRAM, MST, MULT; DLB 125; MTCW

Spackman, W(illiam) M(ode)
1905-1990 . . . . **CLC 46**
See also CA 81-84; 132

Spacks, Barry 1931- . . . . **CLC 14**
See also CA 29-32R; CANR 33; DLB 105

Spanidou, Irini 1946- . . . . **CLC 44**

Spark, Muriel (Sarah)
1918- . . . . **CLC 2, 3, 5, 8, 13, 18, 40; DAB; DAC; SSC 10**
See also CA 5-8R; CANR 12, 36; CDBLB 1945-1960; DAM MST, NOV; DLB 15, 139; INT CANR-12; MTCW

Spaulding, Douglas
See Bradbury, Ray (Douglas)

Spaulding, Leonard
See Bradbury, Ray (Douglas)

Spence, J. A. D.
See Eliot, T(homas) S(tearns)

Spencer, Elizabeth 1921- . . . . **CLC 22**
See also CA 13-16R; CANR 32; DLB 6; MTCW; SATA 14

Spencer, Leonard G.
See Silverberg, Robert

Spencer, Scott 1945- . . . . **CLC 30**
See also CA 113; DLBY 86

Spender, Stephen (Harold)
1909- . . . . **CLC 1, 2, 5, 10, 41**
See also CA 9-12R; CANR 31; CDBLB 1945-1960; DAM POET; DLB 20; MTCW

Spengler, Oswald (Arnold Gottfried)
1880-1936 . . . . **TCLC 25**
See also CA 118

Spenser, Edmund
1552(?)-1599 . . . . **LC 5; DA; DAB; DAC; PC 8; WLC**
See also CDBLB Before 1660; DAM MST, POET

Spicer, Jack 1925-1965 . . . . . . **CLC 8, 18, 72**
See also CA 85-88; DAM POET; DLB 5, 16

Spiegelman, Art 1948- . . . . **CLC 76**
See also AAYA 10; CA 125; CANR 41

Spielberg, Peter 1929- . . . . **CLC 6**
See also CA 5-8R; CANR 4, 48; DLBY 81

Spielberg, Steven 1947- . . . . **CLC 20**
See also AAYA 8; CA 77-80; CANR 32; SATA 32

Spillane, Frank Morrison 1918-
See Spillane, Mickey
See also CA 25-28R; CANR 28; MTCW; SATA 66

Spillane, Mickey . . . . **CLC 3, 13**
See also Spillane, Frank Morrison

Spinoza, Benedictus de 1632-1677 . . . . **LC 9**

Spinrad, Norman (Richard) 1940-. . . **CLC 46**
See also CA 37-40R; CAAS 19; CANR 20; DLB 8; INT CANR-20

Spitteler, Carl (Friedrich Georg)
1845-1924 . . . . **TCLC 12**
See also CA 109; DLB 129

Spivack, Kathleen (Romola Drucker)
1938- . . . . **CLC 6**
See also CA 49-52

Spoto, Donald 1941- . . . . **CLC 39**
See also CA 65-68; CANR 11

Springsteen, Bruce (F.) 1949- . . . . . . **CLC 17**
See also CA 111

Spurling, Hilary 1940- . . . . **CLC 34**
See also CA 104; CANR 25

Spyker, John Howland
See Elman, Richard

Squires, (James) Radcliffe
1917-1993 . . . . **CLC 51**
See also CA 1-4R; 140; CANR 6, 21

Srivastava, Dhanpat Rai 1880(?)-1936
See Premchand
See also CA 118

Stacy, Donald
See Pohl, Frederik

Stael, Germaine de
See Stael-Holstein, Anne Louise Germaine Necker Baronn
See also DLB 119

Stael-Holstein, Anne Louise Germaine Necker Baronn 1766-1817 . . . . **NCLC 3**
See also Stael, Germaine de

Stafford, Jean 1915-1979 . . . **CLC 4, 7, 19, 68**
See also CA 1-4R; 85-88; CANR 3; DLB 2; MTCW; SATA-Obit 22

Stafford, William (Edgar)
1914-1993 . . . . **CLC 4, 7, 29**
See also CA 5-8R; 142; CAAS 3; CANR 5, 22; DAM POET; DLB 5; INT CANR-22

Staines, Trevor
See Brunner, John (Kilian Houston)

Stairs, Gordon
See Austin, Mary (Hunter)

Stannard, Martin 1947- . . . . **CLC 44**
See also CA 142; DLB 155

Stanton, Maura 1946- . . . . **CLC 9**
See also CA 89-92; CANR 15; DLB 120

Stanton, Schuyler
See Baum, L(yman) Frank

Stapledon, (William) Olaf
1886-1950 . . . . **TCLC 22**
See also CA 111; DLB 15

Starbuck, George (Edwin) 1931- . . . . **CLC 53**
See also CA 21-24R; CANR 23; DAM POET

Stark, Richard
See Westlake, Donald E(dwin)

Staunton, Schuyler
See Baum, L(yman) Frank

Stead, Christina (Ellen)
1902-1983 . . . . **CLC 2, 5, 8, 32, 80**
See also CA 13-16R; 109; CANR 33, 40; MTCW

Stead, William Thomas
1849-1912 . . . . **TCLC 48**

Steele, Richard 1672-1729 . . . . **LC 18**
See also CDBLB 1660-1789; DLB 84, 101

Steele, Timothy (Reid) 1948- . . . . **CLC 45**
See also CA 93-96; CANR 16, 50; DLB 120

Steffens, (Joseph) Lincoln
1866-1936 . . . . **TCLC 20**
See also CA 117

Stegner, Wallace (Earle)
1909-1993 . . . . **CLC 9, 49, 81**
See also AITN 1; BEST 90:3; CA 1-4R; 141; CAAS 9; CANR 1, 21, 46; DAM NOV; DLB 9; DLBY 93; MTCW

Stein, Gertrude
1874-1946 . . . . . . **TCLC 1, 6, 28, 48; DA; DAB; DAC; WLC**
See also CA 104; 132; CDALB 1917-1929; DAM MST, NOV, POET; DLB 4, 54, 86; MTCW

Steinbeck, John (Ernst)
1902-1968 . . . . . **CLC 1, 5, 9, 13, 21, 34, 45, 75; DA; DAB; DAC; SSC 11; WLC**
See also AAYA 12; CA 1-4R; 25-28R; CANR 1, 35; CDALB 1929-1941; DAM DRAM, MST, NOV; DLB 7, 9; DLBD 2; MTCW; SATA 9

Steinem, Gloria 1934- . . . . **CLC 63**
See also CA 53-56; CANR 28; MTCW

Steiner, George 1929- . . . . **CLC 24**
See also CA 73-76; CANR 31; DAM NOV; DLB 67; MTCW; SATA 62

Steiner, K. Leslie
See Delany, Samuel R(ay, Jr.)

Steiner, Rudolf 1861-1925 . . . . **TCLC 13**
See also CA 107

Stendhal
1783-1842 . . . . **NCLC 23, 46; DA; DAB; DAC; WLC**
See also DAM MST, NOV; DLB 119

Stephen, Leslie 1832-1904 . . . . **TCLC 23**
See also CA 123; DLB 57, 144

Stephen, Sir Leslie
See Stephen, Leslie

Stephen, Virginia
See Woolf, (Adeline) Virginia

Stephens, James 1882(?)-1950...... **TCLC 4**
See also CA 104; DLB 19, 153

Stephens, Reed
See Donaldson, Stephen R.

Steptoe, Lydia
See Barnes, Djuna

Sterchi, Beat 1949-.............. **CLC 65**

Sterling, Brett
See Bradbury, Ray (Douglas); Hamilton, Edmond

Sterling, Bruce 1954-............ **CLC 72**
See also CA 119; CANR 44

Sterling, George 1869-1926....... **TCLC 20**
See also CA 117; DLB 54

Stern, Gerald 1925-.............. **CLC 40**
See also CA 81-84; CANR 28; DLB 105

Stern, Richard (Gustave) 1928-... **CLC 4, 39**
See also CA 1-4R; CANR 1, 25; DLBY 87; INT CANR-25

Sternberg, Josef von 1894-1969..... **CLC 20**
See also CA 81-84

Sterne, Laurence
1713-1768...... **LC 2; DA; DAB; DAC; WLC**
See also CDBLB 1660-1789; DAM MST, NOV; DLB 39

Sternheim, (William Adolf) Carl
1878-1942................... **TCLC 8**
See also CA 105; DLB 56, 118

Stevens, Mark 1951-.............. **CLC 34**
See also CA 122

Stevens, Wallace
1879-1955....... **TCLC 3, 12, 45; DA; DAB; DAC; PC 6; WLC**
See also CA 104; 124; CDALB 1929-1941; DAM MST, POET; DLB 54; MTCW

Stevenson, Anne (Katharine)
1933-.................... **CLC 7, 33**
See also CA 17-20R; CAAS 9; CANR 9, 33; DLB 40; MTCW

Stevenson, Robert Louis (Balfour)
1850-1894..... **NCLC 5, 14; DA; DAB; DAC; SSC 11; WLC**
See also CDBLB 1890-1914; CLR 10, 11; DAM MST, NOV; DLB 18, 57, 141, 156; DLBD 13; JRDA; MAICYA; YABC 2

Stewart, J(ohn) I(nnes) M(ackintosh)
1906-1994.............. **CLC 7, 14, 32**
See also CA 85-88; 147; CAAS 3; CANR 47; MTCW

Stewart, Mary (Florence Elinor)
1916-................. **CLC 7, 35; DAB**
See also CA 1-4R; CANR 1; SATA 12

Stewart, Mary Rainbow
See Stewart, Mary (Florence Elinor)

Stifle, June
See Campbell, Maria

Stifter, Adalbert 1805-1868...... **NCLC 41**
See also DLB 133

Still, James 1906-................ **CLC 49**
See also CA 65-68; CAAS 17; CANR 10, 26; DLB 9; SATA 29

Sting
See Sumner, Gordon Matthew

Stirling, Arthur
See Sinclair, Upton (Beall)

Stitt, Milan 1941-................ **CLC 29**
See also CA 69-72

Stockton, Francis Richard 1834-1902
See Stockton, Frank R.
See also CA 108; 137; MAICYA; SATA 44

Stockton, Frank R................. **TCLC 47**
See also Stockton, Francis Richard
See also DLB 42, 74; DLBD 13; SATA-Brief 32

Stoddard, Charles
See Kuttner, Henry

Stoker, Abraham 1847-1912
See Stoker, Bram
See also CA 105; DA; DAC; DAM MST, NOV; SATA 29

Stoker, Bram.......... **TCLC 8; DAB; WLC**
See also Stoker, Abraham
See also CDBLB 1890-1914; DLB 36, 70

Stolz, Mary (Slattery) 1920-....... **CLC 12**
See also AAYA 8; AITN 1; CA 5-8R; CANR 13, 41; JRDA; MAICYA; SAAS 3; SATA 10, 71

Stone, Irving 1903-1989............ **CLC 7**
See also AITN 1; CA 1-4R; 129; CAAS 3; CANR 1, 23; DAM POP; INT CANR-23; MTCW; SATA 3; SATA-Obit 64

Stone, Oliver 1946-................ **CLC 73**
See also AAYA 15; CA 110

Stone, Robert (Anthony)
1937-.................. **CLC 5, 23, 42**
See also CA 85-88; CANR 23; DLB 152; INT CANR-23; MTCW

Stone, Zachary
See Follett, Ken(neth Martin)

Stoppard, Tom
1937-...... **CLC 1, 3, 4, 5, 8, 15, 29, 34, 63; DA; DAB; DAC; DC 6; WLC**
See also CA 81-84; CANR 39; CDBLB 1960 to Present; DAM DRAM, MST; DLB 13; DLBY 85; MTCW

Storey, David (Malcolm)
1933-.................. **CLC 2, 4, 5, 8**
See also CA 81-84; CANR 36; DAM DRAM; DLB 13, 14; MTCW

Storm, Hyemeyohsts 1935-......... **CLC 3**
See also CA 81-84; CANR 45; DAM MULT; NNAL

Storm, (Hans) Theodor (Woldsen)
1817-1888................. **NCLC 1**

Storni, Alfonsina
1892-1938............. **TCLC 5; HLC**
See also CA 104; 131; DAM MULT; HW

Stout, Rex (Todhunter) 1886-1975 ... **CLC 3**
See also AITN 2; CA 61-64

Stow, (Julian) Randolph 1935- .. **CLC 23, 48**
See also CA 13-16R; CANR 33; MTCW

Stowe, Harriet (Elizabeth) Beecher
1811-1896..... **NCLC 3, 50; DA; DAB; DAC; WLC**
See also CDALB 1865-1917; DAM MST, NOV; DLB 1, 12, 42, 74; JRDA; MAICYA; YABC 1

Strachey, (Giles) Lytton
1880-1932................... **TCLC 12**
See also CA 110; DLB 149; DLBD 10

Strand, Mark 1934-...... **CLC 6, 18, 41, 71**
See also CA 21-24R; CANR 40; DAM POET; DLB 5; SATA 41

Straub, Peter (Francis) 1943-...... **CLC 28**
See also BEST 89:1; CA 85-88; CANR 28; DAM POP; DLBY 84; MTCW

Strauss, Botho 1944-............. **CLC 22**
See also DLB 124

Streatfeild, (Mary) Noel
1895(?)-1986.................. **CLC 21**
See also CA 81-84; 120; CANR 31; CLR 17; DLB 160; MAICYA; SATA 20; SATA-Obit 48

Stribling, T(homas) S(igismund)
1881-1965................... **CLC 23**
See also CA 107; DLB 9

Strindberg, (Johan) August
1849-1912...... **TCLC 1, 8, 21, 47; DA; DAB; DAC; WLC**
See also CA 104; 135; DAM DRAM, MST

Stringer, Arthur 1874-1950....... **TCLC 37**
See also DLB 92

Stringer, David
See Roberts, Keith (John Kingston)

Strugatskii, Arkadii (Natanovich)
1925-1991................... **CLC 27**
See also CA 106; 135

Strugatskii, Boris (Natanovich)
1933-................... **CLC 27**
See also CA 106

Strummer, Joe 1953(?)-........... **CLC 30**

Stuart, Don A.
See Campbell, John W(ood, Jr.)

Stuart, Ian
See MacLean, Alistair (Stuart)

Stuart, Jesse (Hilton)
1906-1984........ **CLC 1, 8, 11, 14, 34**
See also CA 5-8R; 112; CANR 31; DLB 9, 48, 102; DLBY 84; SATA 2; SATA-Obit 36

Sturgeon, Theodore (Hamilton)
1918-1985................. **CLC 22, 39**
See also Queen, Ellery
See also CA 81-84; 116; CANR 32; DLB 8; DLBY 85; MTCW

Sturges, Preston 1898-1959....... **TCLC 48**
See also CA 114; 149; DLB 26

Styron, William
1925-.......... **CLC 1, 3, 5, 11, 15, 60**
See also BEST 90:4; CA 5-8R; CANR 6, 33; CDALB 1968-1988; DAM NOV, POP; DLB 2, 143; DLBY 80; INT CANR-6; MTCW

Suarez Lynch, B.
See Bioy Casares, Adolfo; Borges, Jorge Luis

Taylor, Mildred D. . . . . CLC 21
See also AAYA 10; BW 1; CA 85-88;
CANR 25; CLR 9; DLB 52; JRDA;
MAICYA; SAAS 5; SATA 15, 70

Taylor, Peter (Hillsman)
1917-1994 . . . . . CLC 1, 4, 18, 37, 44, 50,
71; SSC 10
See also CA 13-16R; 147; CANR 9, 50;
DLBY 81, 94; INT CANR-9; MTCW

Taylor, Robert Lewis 1912- . . . . CLC 14
See also CA 1-4R; CANR 3; SATA 10

Tchekhov, Anton
See Chekhov, Anton (Pavlovich)

Teasdale, Sara 1884-1933 . . . . TCLC 4
See also CA 104; DLB 45; SATA 32

Tegner, Esaias 1782-1846 . . . . NCLC 2

Teilhard de Chardin, (Marie Joseph) Pierre
1881-1955 . . . . TCLC 9
See also CA 105

Temple, Ann
See Mortimer, Penelope (Ruth)

Tennant, Emma (Christina)
1937- . . . . CLC 13, 52
See also CA 65-68; CAAS 9; CANR 10, 38;
DLB 14

Tenneshaw, S. M.
See Silverberg, Robert

Tennyson, Alfred
1809-1892 . . . . NCLC 30; DA; DAB;
DAC; PC 6; WLC
See also CDBLB 1832-1890; DAM MST,
POET; DLB 32

Teran, Lisa St. Aubin de . . . . CLC 36
See also St. Aubin de Teran, Lisa

Terence 195(?)B.C.-159B.C. . . . . . . CMLC 14

Teresa de Jesus, St. 1515-1582 . . . . . . LC 18

Terkel, Louis 1912-
See Terkel, Studs
See also CA 57-60; CANR 18, 45; MTCW

Terkel, Studs . . . . CLC 38
See also Terkel, Louis
See also AITN 1

Terry, C. V.
See Slaughter, Frank G(ill)

Terry, Megan 1932- . . . . CLC 19
See also CA 77-80; CABS 3; CANR 43;
DLB 7

Tertz, Abram
See Sinyavsky, Andrei (Donatevich)

Tesich, Steve 1943(?)- . . . . CLC 40, 69
See also CA 105; DLBY 83

Teternikov, Fyodor Kuzmich 1863-1927
See Sologub, Fyodor
See also CA 104

Tevis, Walter 1928-1984 . . . . CLC 42
See also CA 113

Tey, Josephine . . . . TCLC 14
See also Mackintosh, Elizabeth
See also DLB 77

Thackeray, William Makepeace
1811-1863 . . . . NCLC 5, 14, 22, 43; DA;
DAB; DAC; WLC
See also CDBLB 1832-1890; DAM MST,
NOV; DLB 21, 55, 159; SATA 23

Thakura, Ravindranatha
See Tagore, Rabindranath

Tharoor, Shashi 1956- . . . . CLC 70
See also CA 141

Thelwell, Michael Miles 1939- . . . . . CLC 22
See also BW 2; CA 101

Theobald, Lewis, Jr.
See Lovecraft, H(oward) P(hillips)

Theodorescu, Ion N. 1880-1967
See Arghezi, Tudor
See also CA 116

Theriault, Yves 1915-1983 . . . . CLC 79; DAC
See also CA 102; DAM MST; DLB 88

Theroux, Alexander (Louis)
1939- . . . . CLC 2, 25
See also CA 85-88; CANR 20

Theroux, Paul (Edward)
1941- . . . . CLC 5, 8, 11, 15, 28, 46
See also BEST 89:4; CA 33-36R; CANR 20,
45; DAM POP; DLB 2; MTCW;
SATA 44

Thesen, Sharon 1946- . . . . CLC 56

Thevenin, Denis
See Duhamel, Georges

Thibault, Jacques Anatole Francois
1844-1924
See France, Anatole
See also CA 106; 127; DAM NOV; MTCW

Thiele, Colin (Milton) 1920- . . . . CLC 17
See also CA 29-32R; CANR 12, 28;
CLR 27; MAICYA; SAAS 2; SATA 14,
72

Thomas, Audrey (Callahan)
1935- . . . . CLC 7, 13, 37; SSC 20
See also AITN 2; CA 21-24R; CAAS 19;
CANR 36; DLB 60; MTCW

Thomas, D(onald) M(ichael)
1935- . . . . CLC 13, 22, 31
See also CA 61-64; CAAS 11; CANR 17,
45; CDBLB 1960 to Present; DLB 40;
INT CANR-17; MTCW

Thomas, Dylan (Marlais)
1914-1953 . . . TCLC 1, 8, 45; DA; DAB;
DAC; PC 2; SSC 3; WLC
See also CA 104; 120; CDBLB 1945-1960;
DAM DRAM, MST, POET; DLB 13, 20,
139; MTCW; SATA 60

Thomas, (Philip) Edward
1878-1917 . . . . TCLC 10
See also CA 106; DAM POET; DLB 19

Thomas, Joyce Carol 1938- . . . . CLC 35
See also AAYA 12; BW 2; CA 113; 116;
CANR 48; CLR 19; DLB 33; INT 116;
JRDA; MAICYA; MTCW; SAAS 7;
SATA 40, 78

Thomas, Lewis 1913-1993 . . . . CLC 35
See also CA 85-88; 143; CANR 38; MTCW

Thomas, Paul
See Mann, (Paul) Thomas

Thomas, Piri 1928- . . . . CLC 17
See also CA 73-76; HW

Thomas, R(onald) S(tuart)
1913- . . . . CLC 6, 13, 48; DAB
See also CA 89-92; CAAS 4; CANR 30;
CDBLB 1960 to Present; DAM POET;
DLB 27; MTCW

Thomas, Ross (Elmore) 1926- . . . . . . CLC 39
See also CA 33-36R; CANR 22

Thompson, Francis Clegg
See Mencken, H(enry) L(ouis)

Thompson, Francis Joseph
1859-1907 . . . . TCLC 4
See also CA 104; CDBLB 1890-1914;
DLB 19

Thompson, Hunter S(tockton)
1939- . . . . CLC 9, 17, 40
See also BEST 89:1; CA 17-20R; CANR 23,
46; DAM POP; MTCW

Thompson, James Myers
See Thompson, Jim (Myers)

Thompson, Jim (Myers)
1906-1977(?) . . . . CLC 69
See also CA 140

Thompson, Judith . . . . CLC 39

Thomson, James 1700-1748 . . . . . . LC 16, 29
See also DAM POET; DLB 95

Thomson, James 1834-1882 . . . . NCLC 18
See also DAM POET; DLB 35

Thoreau, Henry David
1817-1862 . . . . . NCLC 7, 21; DA; DAB;
DAC; WLC
See also CDALB 1640-1865; DAM MST;
DLB 1

Thornton, Hall
See Silverberg, Robert

Thucydides c. 455B.C.-399B.C. . . . . CMLC 17

Thurber, James (Grover)
1894-1961 . . . . CLC 5, 11, 25; DA; DAB;
DAC; SSC 1
See also CA 73-76; CANR 17, 39;
CDALB 1929-1941; DAM DRAM, MST,
NOV; DLB 4, 11, 22, 102; MAICYA;
MTCW; SATA 13

Thurman, Wallace (Henry)
1902-1934 . . . . TCLC 6; BLC
See also BW 1; CA 104; 124; DAM MULT;
DLB 51

Ticheburn, Cheviot
See Ainsworth, William Harrison

Tieck, (Johann) Ludwig
1773-1853 . . . . NCLC 5, 46
See also DLB 90

Tiger, Derry
See Ellison, Harlan (Jay)

Tilghman, Christopher 1948(?)- . . . . . CLC 65

Tillinghast, Richard (Williford)
1940- . . . . CLC 29
See also CA 29-32R; CANR 26

Timrod, Henry 1828-1867 . . . . NCLC 25
See also DLB 3

Tindall, Gillian 1938- . . . . CLC 7
See also CA 21-24R; CANR 11

Tiptree, James, Jr. . . . . CLC 48, 50
See also Sheldon, Alice Hastings Bradley
See also DLB 8

Titmarsh, Michael Angelo
See Thackeray, William Makepeace

Tocqueville, Alexis (Charles Henri Maurice
Clerel Comte) 1805-1859 . . . . . NCLC 7

Tolkien, J(ohn) R(onald) R(euel)
1892-1973 ...... **CLC 1, 2, 3, 8, 12, 38;
DA; DAB; DAC; WLC**
See also AAYA 10; AITN 1; CA 17-18;
45-48; CANR 36; CAP 2;
CDBLB 1914-1945; DAM MST, NOV,
POP; DLB 15, 160; JRDA; MAICYA;
MTCW; SATA 2, 32; SATA-Obit 24

Toller, Ernst 1893-1939 .... **TCLC 10**
See also CA 107; DLB 124

Tolson, M. B.
See Tolson, Melvin B(eaunorus)

Tolson, Melvin B(eaunorus)
1898(?)-1966 .... **CLC 36; BLC**
See also BW 1; CA 124; 89-92;
DAM MULT, POET; DLB 48, 76

Tolstoi, Aleksei Nikolaevich
See Tolstoy, Alexey Nikolaevich

Tolstoy, Alexey Nikolaevich
1882-1945 .... **TCLC 18**
See also CA 107

Tolstoy, Count Leo
See Tolstoy, Leo (Nikolaevich)

Tolstoy, Leo (Nikolaevich)
1828-1910 ...... **TCLC 4, 11, 17, 28, 44;
DA; DAB; DAC; SSC 9; WLC**
See also CA 104; 123; DAM MST, NOV;
SATA 26

Tomasi di Lampedusa, Giuseppe 1896-1957
See Lampedusa, Giuseppe (Tomasi) di
See also CA 111

Tomlin, Lily .... **CLC 17**
See also Tomlin, Mary Jean

Tomlin, Mary Jean 1939(?)-
See Tomlin, Lily
See also CA 117

Tomlinson, (Alfred) Charles
1927- .... **CLC 2, 4, 6, 13, 45**
See also CA 5-8R; CANR 33; DAM POET;
DLB 40

Tonson, Jacob
See Bennett, (Enoch) Arnold

Toole, John Kennedy
1937-1969 .... **CLC 19, 64**
See also CA 104; DLBY 81

Toomer, Jean
1894-1967 ...... **CLC 1, 4, 13, 22; BLC;
PC 7; SSC 1**
See also BW 1; CA 85-88;
CDALB 1917-1929; DAM MULT;
DLB 45, 51; MTCW

Torley, Luke
See Blish, James (Benjamin)

Tornimparte, Alessandra
See Ginzburg, Natalia

Torre, Raoul della
See Mencken, H(enry) L(ouis)

Torrey, E(dwin) Fuller 1937- .... **CLC 34**
See also CA 119

Torsvan, Ben Traven
See Traven, B.

Torsvan, Benno Traven
See Traven, B.

Torsvan, Berick Traven
See Traven, B.

Torsvan, Berwick Traven
See Traven, B.

Torsvan, Bruno Traven
See Traven, B.

Torsvan, Traven
See Traven, B.

Tournier, Michel (Edouard)
1924- .... **CLC 6, 23, 36**
See also CA 49-52; CANR 3, 36; DLB 83;
MTCW; SATA 23

Tournimparte, Alessandra
See Ginzburg, Natalia

Towers, Ivar
See Kornbluth, C(yril) M.

Towne, Robert (Burton) 1936(?)- .... **CLC 87**
See also CA 108; DLB 44

Townsend, Sue 1946- .. **CLC 61; DAB; DAC**
See also CA 119; 127; INT 127; MTCW;
SATA 55; SATA-Brief 48

Townshend, Peter (Dennis Blandford)
1945- .... **CLC 17, 42**
See also CA 107

Tozzi, Federigo 1883-1920 .... **TCLC 31**

Traill, Catharine Parr
1802-1899 .... **NCLC 31**
See also DLB 99

Trakl, Georg 1887-1914 .... **TCLC 5**
See also CA 104

Transtroemer, Tomas (Goesta)
1931- .... **CLC 52, 65**
See also CA 117; 129; CAAS 17;
DAM POET

Transtromer, Tomas Gosta
See Transtroemer, Tomas (Goesta)

Traven, B. (?)-1969 .... **CLC 8, 11**
See also CA 19-20; 25-28R; CAP 2; DLB 9,
56; MTCW

Treitel, Jonathan 1959- .... **CLC 70**

Tremain, Rose 1943- .... **CLC 42**
See also CA 97-100; CANR 44; DLB 14

Tremblay, Michel 1942- ...... **CLC 29; DAC**
See also CA 116; 128; DAM MST; DLB 60;
MTCW

Trevanian .... **CLC 29**
See also Whitaker, Rod(ney)

Trevor, Glen
See Hilton, James

Trevor, William
1928- ..... **CLC 7, 9, 14, 25, 71; SSC 21**
See also Cox, William Trevor
See also DLB 14, 139

Trifonov, Yuri (Valentinovich)
1925-1981 .... **CLC 45**
See also CA 126; 103; MTCW

Trilling, Lionel 1905-1975 .... **CLC 9, 11, 24**
See also CA 9-12R; 61-64; CANR 10;
DLB 28, 63; INT CANR-10; MTCW

Trimball, W. H.
See Mencken, H(enry) L(ouis)

Tristan
See Gomez de la Serna, Ramon

Tristram
See Housman, A(lfred) E(dward)

Trogdon, William (Lewis) 1939-
See Heat-Moon, William Least
See also CA 115; 119; CANR 47; INT 119

Trollope, Anthony
1815-1882 ..... **NCLC 6, 33; DA; DAB;
DAC; WLC**
See also CDBLB 1832-1890; DAM MST,
NOV; DLB 21, 57, 159; SATA 22

Trollope, Frances 1779-1863 ..... **NCLC 30**
See also DLB 21

Trotsky, Leon 1879-1940 .... **TCLC 22**
See also CA 118

Trotter (Cockburn), Catharine
1679-1749 .... **LC 8**
See also DLB 84

Trout, Kilgore
See Farmer, Philip Jose

Trow, George W. S. 1943- .... **CLC 52**
See also CA 126

Troyat, Henri 1911- .... **CLC 23**
See also CA 45-48; CANR 2, 33; MTCW

Trudeau, G(arretson) B(eekman) 1948-
See Trudeau, Garry B.
See also CA 81-84; CANR 31; SATA 35

Trudeau, Garry B. .... **CLC 12**
See also Trudeau, G(arretson) B(eekman)
See also AAYA 10; AITN 2

Truffaut, Francois 1932-1984 .... **CLC 20**
See also CA 81-84; 113; CANR 34

Trumbo, Dalton 1905-1976 .... **CLC 19**
See also CA 21-24R; 69-72; CANR 10;
DLB 26

Trumbull, John 1750-1831 .... **NCLC 30**
See also DLB 31

Trundlett, Helen B.
See Eliot, T(homas) S(tearns)

Tryon, Thomas 1926-1991 .... **CLC 3, 11**
See also AITN 1; CA 29-32R; 135;
CANR 32; DAM POP; MTCW

Tryon, Tom
See Tryon, Thomas

Ts'ao Hsueh-ch'in 1715(?)-1763 .... **LC 1**

Tsushima, Shuji 1909-1948
See Dazai, Osamu
See also CA 107

Tsvetaeva (Efron), Marina (Ivanovna)
1892-1941 .... **TCLC 7, 35; PC 14**
See also CA 104; 128; MTCW

Tuck, Lily 1938- .... **CLC 70**
See also CA 139

Tu Fu 712-770 .... **PC 9**
See also DAM MULT

Tunis, John R(oberts) 1889-1975 ... **CLC 12**
See also CA 61-64; DLB 22; JRDA;
MAICYA; SATA 37; SATA-Brief 30

Tuohy, Frank .... **CLC 37**
See also Tuohy, John Francis
See also DLB 14, 139

Tuohy, John Francis 1925-
See Tuohy, Frank
See also CA 5-8R; CANR 3, 47

Turco, Lewis (Putnam) 1934- ... **CLC 11, 63**
See also CA 13-16R; CAAS 22; CANR 24;
DLBY 84

Turgenev, Ivan
1818-1883 .... **NCLC 21; DA; DAB; DAC; SSC 7; WLC**
See also DAM MST, NOV

Turgot, Anne-Robert-Jacques
1727-1781 .... **LC 26**

Turner, Frederick 1943-.......... **CLC 48**
See also CA 73-76; CAAS 10; CANR 12, 30; DLB 40

Tutu, Desmond M(pilo)
1931- .... **CLC 80; BLC**
See also BW 1; CA 125; DAM MULT

Tutuola, Amos 1920- ... **CLC 5, 14, 29; BLC**
See also BW 2; CA 9-12R; CANR 27; DAM MULT; DLB 125; MTCW

Twain, Mark
..... **TCLC 6, 12, 19, 36, 48, 59; SSC 6; WLC**
See also Clemens, Samuel Langhorne
See also DLB 11, 12, 23, 64, 74

Tyler, Anne
1941- .... **CLC 7, 11, 18, 28, 44, 59**
See also BEST 89:1; CA 9-12R; CANR 11, 33; DAM NOV, POP; DLB 6, 143; DLBY 82; MTCW; SATA 7

Tyler, Royall 1757-1826.......... **NCLC 3**
See also DLB 37

Tynan, Katharine 1861-1931 .... **TCLC 3**
See also CA 104; DLB 153

Tyutchev, Fyodor 1803-1873 ..... **NCLC 34**

Tzara, Tristan .... **CLC 47**
See also Rosenfeld, Samuel
See also DAM POET

Uhry, Alfred 1936-............. **CLC 55**
See also CA 127; 133; DAM DRAM, POP; INT 133

Ulf, Haerved
See Strindberg, (Johan) August

Ulf, Harved
See Strindberg, (Johan) August

Ulibarri, Sabine R(eyes) 1919- ..... **CLC 83**
See also CA 131; DAM MULT; DLB 82; HW

Unamuno (y Jugo), Miguel de
1864-1936 .... **TCLC 2, 9; HLC; SSC 11**
See also CA 104; 131; DAM MULT, NOV; DLB 108; HW; MTCW

Undercliffe, Errol
See Campbell, (John) Ramsey

Underwood, Miles
See Glassco, John

Undset, Sigrid
1882-1949 .... **TCLC 3; DA; DAB; DAC; WLC**
See also CA 104; 129; DAM MST, NOV; MTCW

Ungaretti, Giuseppe
1888-1970 .... **CLC 7, 11, 15**
See also CA 19-20; 25-28R; CAP 2; DLB 114

Unger, Douglas 1952-............. **CLC 34**
See also CA 130

Unsworth, Barry (Forster) 1930-.... **CLC 76**
See also CA 25-28R; CANR 30

Updike, John (Hoyer)
1932-...... **CLC 1, 2, 3, 5, 7, 9, 13, 15, 23, 34, 43, 70; DA; DAB; DAC; SSC 13; WLC**
See also CA 1-4R; CABS 1; CANR 4, 33; CDALB 1968-1988; DAM MST, NOV, POET, POP; DLB 2, 5, 143; DLBD 3; DLBY 80, 82; MTCW

Upshaw, Margaret Mitchell
See Mitchell, Margaret (Munnerlyn)

Upton, Mark
See Sanders, Lawrence

Urdang, Constance (Henriette)
1922- .... **CLC 47**
See also CA 21-24R; CANR 9, 24

Uriel, Henry
See Faust, Frederick (Schiller)

Uris, Leon (Marcus) 1924-....... **CLC 7, 32**
See also AITN 1, 2; BEST 89:2; CA 1-4R; CANR 1, 40; DAM NOV, POP; MTCW; SATA 49

Urmuz
See Codrescu, Andrei

Urquhart, Jane 1949-........ **CLC 90; DAC**
See also CA 113; CANR 32

Ustinov, Peter (Alexander) 1921-.... **CLC 1**
See also AITN 1; CA 13-16R; CANR 25; DLB 13

Vaculik, Ludvik 1926-............. **CLC 7**
See also CA 53-56

Valdez, Luis (Miguel)
1940- .... **CLC 84; HLC**
See also CA 101; CANR 32; DAM MULT; DLB 122; HW

Valenzuela, Luisa 1938-... **CLC 31; SSC 14**
See also CA 101; CANR 32; DAM MULT; DLB 113; HW

Valera y Alcala-Galiano, Juan
1824-1905 .... **TCLC 10**
See also CA 106

Valery, (Ambroise) Paul (Toussaint Jules)
1871-1945 .... **TCLC 4, 15; PC 9**
See also CA 104; 122; DAM POET; MTCW

Valle-Inclan, Ramon (Maria) del
1866-1936 .... **TCLC 5; HLC**
See also CA 106; DAM MULT; DLB 134

Vallejo, Antonio Buero
See Buero Vallejo, Antonio

Vallejo, Cesar (Abraham)
1892-1938 .... **TCLC 3, 56; HLC**
See also CA 105; DAM MULT; HW

Valle Y Pena, Ramon del
See Valle-Inclan, Ramon (Maria) del

Van Ash, Cay 1918-............. **CLC 34**

Vanbrugh, Sir John 1664-1726 ...... **LC 21**
See also DAM DRAM; DLB 80

Van Campen, Karl
See Campbell, John W(ood, Jr.)

Vance, Gerald
See Silverberg, Robert

Vance, Jack .... **CLC 35**
See also Vance, John Holbrook
See also DLB 8

Vance, John Holbrook 1916-
See Queen, Ellery; Vance, Jack
See also CA 29-32R; CANR 17; MTCW

Van Den Bogarde, Derek Jules Gaspard Ulric Niven 1921-
See Bogarde, Dirk
See also CA 77-80

Vandenburgh, Jane .... **CLC 59**

Vanderhaeghe, Guy 1951- .... **CLC 41**
See also CA 113

van der Post, Laurens (Jan) 1906- ... **CLC 5**
See also CA 5-8R; CANR 35

van de Wetering, Janwillem 1931- .. **CLC 47**
See also CA 49-52; CANR 4

Van Dine, S. S. .... **TCLC 23**
See also Wright, Willard Huntington

Van Doren, Carl (Clinton)
1885-1950 .... **TCLC 18**
See also CA 111

Van Doren, Mark 1894-1972..... **CLC 6, 10**
See also CA 1-4R; 37-40R; CANR 3; DLB 45; MTCW

Van Druten, John (William)
1901-1957 .... **TCLC 2**
See also CA 104; DLB 10

Van Duyn, Mona (Jane)
1921- .... **CLC 3, 7, 63**
See also CA 9-12R; CANR 7, 38; DAM POET; DLB 5

Van Dyne, Edith
See Baum, L(yman) Frank

van Itallie, Jean-Claude 1936-...... **CLC 3**
See also CA 45-48; CAAS 2; CANR 1, 48; DLB 7

van Ostaijen, Paul 1896-1928 ..... **TCLC 33**

Van Peebles, Melvin 1932- ...... **CLC 2, 20**
See also BW 2; CA 85-88; CANR 27; DAM MULT

Vansittart, Peter 1920-............ **CLC 42**
See also CA 1-4R; CANR 3, 49

Van Vechten, Carl 1880-1964 ...... **CLC 33**
See also CA 89-92; DLB 4, 9, 51

Van Vogt, A(lfred) E(lton) 1912-..... **CLC 1**
See also CA 21-24R; CANR 28; DLB 8; SATA 14

Varda, Agnes 1928- .... **CLC 16**
See also CA 116; 122

Vargas Llosa, (Jorge) Mario (Pedro)
1936- .... **CLC 3, 6, 9, 10, 15, 31, 42, 85; DA; DAB; DAC; HLC**
See also CA 73-76; CANR 18, 32, 42; DAM MST, MULT, NOV; DLB 145; HW; MTCW

Vasiliu, Gheorghe 1881-1957
See Bacovia, George
See also CA 123

Vassa, Gustavus
See Equiano, Olaudah

Vassilikos, Vassilis 1933-........ **CLC 4, 8**
See also CA 81-84

Vaughan, Henry 1621-1695........ **LC 27**
See also DLB 131

Vaughn, Stephanie. .... **CLC 62**

Vazov, Ivan (Minchov)
1850-1921 . . . . **TCLC 25**
See also CA 121; DLB 147

Veblen, Thorstein (Bunde)
1857-1929 . . . . **TCLC 31**
See also CA 115

Vega, Lope de 1562-1635 . . . . **LC 23**

Venison, Alfred
See Pound, Ezra (Weston Loomis)

Verdi, Marie de
See Mencken, H(enry) L(ouis)

Verdu, Matilde
See Cela, Camilo Jose

Verga, Giovanni (Carmelo)
1840-1922 . . . . **TCLC 3; SSC 21**
See also CA 104; 123

Vergil
70B.C.-19B.C. . . . . . **CMLC 9; DA; DAB;
DAC; PC 12**
See also DAM MST, POET

Verhaeren, Emile (Adolphe Gustave)
1855-1916 . . . . **TCLC 12**
See also CA 109

Verlaine, Paul (Marie)
1844-1896 . . . . **NCLC 2, 51; PC 2**
See also DAM POET

Verne, Jules (Gabriel)
1828-1905 . . . . **TCLC 6, 52**
See also AAYA 16; CA 110; 131; DLB 123;
JRDA; MAICYA; SATA 21

Very, Jones 1813-1880 . . . . **NCLC 9**
See also DLB 1

Vesaas, Tarjei 1897-1970 . . . . **CLC 48**
See also CA 29-32R

Vialis, Gaston
See Simenon, Georges (Jacques Christian)

Vian, Boris 1920-1959 . . . . **TCLC 9**
See also CA 106; DLB 72

Viaud, (Louis Marie) Julien 1850-1923
See Loti, Pierre
See also CA 107

Vicar, Henry
See Felsen, Henry Gregor

Vicker, Angus
See Felsen, Henry Gregor

Vidal, Gore
1925- . . . . . **CLC 2, 4, 6, 8, 10, 22, 33, 72**
See also AITN 1; BEST 90:2; CA 5-8R;
CANR 13, 45; DAM NOV, POP; DLB 6,
152; INT CANR-13; MTCW

Viereck, Peter (Robert Edwin)
1916- . . . . **CLC 4**
See also CA 1-4R; CANR 1, 47; DLB 5

Vigny, Alfred (Victor) de
1797-1863 . . . . **NCLC 7**
See also DAM POET; DLB 119

Vilakazi, Benedict Wallet
1906-1947 . . . . **TCLC 37**

**Villiers de l'Isle Adam, Jean Marie Mathias
Philippe Auguste Comte**
1838-1889 . . . . **NCLC 3; SSC 14**
See also DLB 123

Villon, Francois 1431-1463(?) . . . . **PC 13**

Vinci, Leonardo da 1452-1519 . . . . **LC 12**

Vine, Barbara . . . . **CLC 50**
See also Rendell, Ruth (Barbara)
See also BEST 90:4

Vinge, Joan D(ennison) 1948- . . . . . . **CLC 30**
See also CA 93-96; SATA 36

Violis, G.
See Simenon, Georges (Jacques Christian)

Visconti, Luchino 1906-1976 . . . . **CLC 16**
See also CA 81-84; 65-68; CANR 39

Vittorini, Elio 1908-1966 . . . . . . **CLC 6, 9, 14**
See also CA 133; 25-28R

Vizinczey, Stephen 1933- . . . . **CLC 40**
See also CA 128; INT 128

Vliet, R(ussell) G(ordon)
1929-1984 . . . . **CLC 22**
See also CA 37-40R; 112; CANR 18

Vogau, Boris Andreyevich 1894-1937(?)
See Pilnyak, Boris
See also CA 123

Vogel, Paula A(nne) 1951- . . . . **CLC 76**
See also CA 108

Voight, Ellen Bryant 1943- . . . . **CLC 54**
See also CA 69-72; CANR 11, 29; DLB 120

Voigt, Cynthia 1942- . . . . **CLC 30**
See also AAYA 3; CA 106; CANR 18, 37,
40; CLR 13; INT CANR-18; JRDA;
MAICYA; SATA 48, 79; SATA-Brief 33

Voinovich, Vladimir (Nikolaevich)
1932- . . . . **CLC 10, 49**
See also CA 81-84; CAAS 12; CANR 33;
MTCW

Vollmann, William T. 1959- . . . . **CLC 89**
See also CA 134; DAM NOV, POP

Voloshinov, V. N.
See Bakhtin, Mikhail Mikhailovich

Voltaire
1694-1778 . . . . . **LC 14; DA; DAB; DAC;
SSC 12; WLC**
See also DAM DRAM, MST

von Daeniken, Erich 1935- . . . . **CLC 30**
See also AITN 1; CA 37-40R; CANR 17,
44

von Daniken, Erich
See von Daeniken, Erich

von Heidenstam, (Carl Gustaf) Verner
See Heidenstam, (Carl Gustaf) Verner von

von Heyse, Paul (Johann Ludwig)
See Heyse, Paul (Johann Ludwig von)

von Hofmannsthal, Hugo
See Hofmannsthal, Hugo von

von Horvath, Odon
See Horvath, Oedoen von

von Horvath, Oedoen
See Horvath, Oedoen von

von Liliencron, (Friedrich Adolf Axel) Detlev
See Liliencron, (Friedrich Adolf Axel)
Detlev von

Vonnegut, Kurt, Jr.
1922- . . . . . . **CLC 1, 2, 3, 4, 5, 8, 12, 22,
40, 60; DA; DAB; DAC; SSC 8; WLC**
See also AAYA 6; AITN 1; BEST 90:4;
CA 1-4R; CANR 1, 25, 49;
CDALB 1968-1988; DAM MST, NOV,
POP; DLB 2, 8, 152; DLBD 3; DLBY 80;
MTCW

Von Rachen, Kurt
See Hubbard, L(afayette) Ron(ald)

von Rezzori (d'Arezzo), Gregor
See Rezzori (d'Arezzo), Gregor von

von Sternberg, Josef
See Sternberg, Josef von

Vorster, Gordon 1924- . . . . **CLC 34**
See also CA 133

Vosce, Trudie
See Ozick, Cynthia

Voznesensky, Andrei (Andreievich)
1933- . . . . **CLC 1, 15, 57**
See also CA 89-92; CANR 37;
DAM POET; MTCW

Waddington, Miriam 1917- . . . . **CLC 28**
See also CA 21-24R; CANR 12, 30;
DLB 68

Wagman, Fredrica 1937- . . . . **CLC 7**
See also CA 97-100; INT 97-100

Wagner, Richard 1813-1883 . . . . **NCLC 9**
See also DLB 129

Wagner-Martin, Linda 1936- . . . . . . **CLC 50**

Wagoner, David (Russell)
1926- . . . . **CLC 3, 5, 15**
See also CA 1-4R; CAAS 3; CANR 2;
DLB 5; SATA 14

Wah, Fred(erick James) 1939- . . . . . . **CLC 44**
See also CA 107; 141; DLB 60

Wahloo, Per 1926-1975 . . . . **CLC 7**
See also CA 61-64

Wahloo, Peter
See Wahloo, Per

Wain, John (Barrington)
1925-1994 . . . . **CLC 2, 11, 15, 46**
See also CA 5-8R; 145; CAAS 4; CANR 23;
CDBLB 1960 to Present; DLB 15, 27,
139, 155; MTCW

Wajda, Andrzej 1926- . . . . **CLC 16**
See also CA 102

Wakefield, Dan 1932- . . . . **CLC 7**
See also CA 21-24R; CAAS 7

Wakoski, Diane
1937- . . . . **CLC 2, 4, 7, 9, 11, 40**
See also CA 13-16R; CAAS 1; CANR 9;
DAM POET; DLB 5; INT CANR-9

Wakoski-Sherbell, Diane
See Wakoski, Diane

Walcott, Derek (Alton)
1930- . . . . **CLC 2, 4, 9, 14, 25, 42, 67, 76;
BLC; DAB; DAC**
See also BW 2; CA 89-92; CANR 26, 47;
DAM MST, MULT, POET; DLB 117;
DLBY 81; MTCW

Waldman, Anne 1945- . . . . **CLC 7**
See also CA 37-40R; CAAS 17; CANR 34;
DLB 16

Waldo, E. Hunter
See Sturgeon, Theodore (Hamilton)

Waldo, Edward Hamilton
See Sturgeon, Theodore (Hamilton)

Walker, Alice (Malsenior)
1944- . . . . **CLC 5, 6, 9, 19, 27, 46, 58;
BLC; DA; DAB; DAC; SSC 5**
See also AAYA 3; BEST 89:4; BW 2;
CA 37-40R; CANR 9, 27, 49;
CDALB 1968-1988; DAM MST, MULT,
NOV, POET, POP; DLB 6, 33, 143;
INT CANR-27; MTCW; SATA 31

Walker, David Harry   1911-1992. . . . **CLC 14**
See also CA 1-4R; 137; CANR 1; SATA 8;
SATA-Obit 71

Walker, Edward Joseph   1934-
See Walker, Ted
See also CA 21-24R; CANR 12, 28

Walker, George F.
1947- . . . . **CLC 44, 61; DAB; DAC**
See also CA 103; CANR 21, 43;
DAM MST; DLB 60

Walker, Joseph A.   1935- . . . . **CLC 19**
See also BW 1; CA 89-92; CANR 26;
DAM DRAM, MST; DLB 38

Walker, Margaret (Abigail)
1915- . . . . **CLC 1, 6; BLC**
See also BW 2; CA 73-76; CANR 26;
DAM MULT; DLB 76, 152; MTCW

Walker, Ted. . . . . **CLC 13**
See also Walker, Edward Joseph
See also DLB 40

Wallace, David Foster   1962- . . . . **CLC 50**
See also CA 132

Wallace, Dexter
See Masters, Edgar Lee

Wallace, (Richard Horatio) Edgar
1875-1932 . . . . **TCLC 57**
See also CA 115; DLB 70

Wallace, Irving   1916-1990 . . . . . . **CLC 7, 13**
See also AITN 1; CA 1-4R; 132; CAAS 1;
CANR 1, 27; DAM NOV, POP;
INT CANR-27; MTCW

Wallant, Edward Lewis
1926-1962 . . . . **CLC 5, 10**
See also CA 1-4R; CANR 22; DLB 2, 28,
143; MTCW

Walley, Byron
See Card, Orson Scott

Walpole, Horace   1717-1797. . . . . **LC 2**
See also DLB 39, 104

Walpole, Hugh (Seymour)
1884-1941 . . . . **TCLC 5**
See also CA 104; DLB 34

Walser, Martin   1927- . . . . **CLC 27**
See also CA 57-60; CANR 8, 46; DLB 75,
124

Walser, Robert
1878-1956 . . . . **TCLC 18; SSC 20**
See also CA 118; DLB 66

Walsh, Jill Paton. . . . . **CLC 35**
See also Paton Walsh, Gillian
See also AAYA 11; CLR 2; DLB 161;
SAAS 3

Walter, Villiam Christian
See Andersen, Hans Christian

Wambaugh, Joseph (Aloysius, Jr.)
1937- . . . . **CLC 3, 18**
See also AITN 1; BEST 89:3; CA 33-36R;
CANR 42; DAM NOV, POP; DLB 6;
DLBY 83; MTCW

Ward, Arthur Henry Sarsfield   1883-1959
See Rohmer, Sax
See also CA 108

Ward, Douglas Turner   1930- . . . . **CLC 19**
See also BW 1; CA 81-84; CANR 27;
DLB 7, 38

Ward, Mary Augusta
See Ward, Mrs. Humphry

Ward, Mrs. Humphry
1851-1920 . . . . **TCLC 55**
See also DLB 18

Ward, Peter
See Faust, Frederick (Schiller)

Warhol, Andy   1928(?)-1987 . . . . **CLC 20**
See also AAYA 12; BEST 89:4; CA 89-92;
121; CANR 34

Warner, Francis (Robert le Plastrier)
1937- . . . . **CLC 14**
See also CA 53-56; CANR 11

Warner, Marina   1946- . . . . **CLC 59**
See also CA 65-68; CANR 21

Warner, Rex (Ernest)   1905-1986. . . . **CLC 45**
See also CA 89-92; 119; DLB 15

Warner, Susan (Bogert)
1819-1885 . . . . **NCLC 31**
See also DLB 3, 42

Warner, Sylvia (Constance) Ashton
See Ashton-Warner, Sylvia (Constance)

Warner, Sylvia Townsend
1893-1978 . . . . **CLC 7, 19**
See also CA 61-64; 77-80; CANR 16;
DLB 34, 139; MTCW

Warren, Mercy Otis   1728-1814. . . **NCLC 13**
See also DLB 31

Warren, Robert Penn
1905-1989 . . . . **CLC 1, 4, 6, 8, 10, 13, 18,
39, 53, 59; DA; DAB; DAC; SSC 4; WLC**
See also AITN 1; CA 13-16R; 129;
CANR 10, 47; CDALB 1968-1988;
DAM MST, NOV, POET; DLB 2, 48,
152; DLBY 80, 89; INT CANR-10;
MTCW; SATA 46; SATA-Obit 63

Warshofsky, Isaac
See Singer, Isaac Bashevis

Warton, Thomas   1728-1790 . . . . **LC 15**
See also DAM POET; DLB 104, 109

Waruk, Kona
See Harris, (Theodore) Wilson

Warung, Price   1855-1911. . . . . **TCLC 45**

Warwick, Jarvis
See Garner, Hugh

Washington, Alex
See Harris, Mark

Washington, Booker T(aliaferro)
1856-1915 . . . . **TCLC 10; BLC**
See also BW 1; CA 114; 125; DAM MULT;
SATA 28

Washington, George   1732-1799 . . . . . . **LC 25**
See also DLB 31

Wassermann, (Karl) Jakob
1873-1934 . . . . **TCLC 6**
See also CA 104; DLB 66

Wasserstein, Wendy
1950- . . . . **CLC 32, 59, 90; DC 4**
See also CA 121; 129; CABS 3;
DAM DRAM; INT 129

Waterhouse, Keith (Spencer)
1929- . . . . **CLC 47**
See also CA 5-8R; CANR 38; DLB 13, 15;
MTCW

Waters, Frank (Joseph)   1902- . . . . . . **CLC 88**
See also CA 5-8R; CAAS 13; CANR 3, 18;
DLBY 86

Waters, Roger   1944-. . . . . **CLC 35**

Watkins, Frances Ellen
See Harper, Frances Ellen Watkins

Watkins, Gerrold
See Malzberg, Barry N(athaniel)

Watkins, Paul   1964-. . . . . **CLC 55**
See also CA 132

Watkins, Vernon Phillips
1906-1967 . . . . **CLC 43**
See also CA 9-10; 25-28R; CAP 1; DLB 20

Watson, Irving S.
See Mencken, H(enry) L(ouis)

Watson, John H.
See Farmer, Philip Jose

Watson, Richard F.
See Silverberg, Robert

Waugh, Auberon (Alexander)   1939- . . **CLC 7**
See also CA 45-48; CANR 6, 22; DLB 14

Waugh, Evelyn (Arthur St. John)
1903-1966 . . . . . . **CLC 1, 3, 8, 13, 19, 27,
44; DA; DAB; DAC; WLC**
See also CA 85-88; 25-28R; CANR 22;
CDBLB 1914-1945; DAM MST, NOV,
POP; DLB 15; MTCW

Waugh, Harriet   1944- . . . . **CLC 6**
See also CA 85-88; CANR 22

Ways, C. R.
See Blount, Roy (Alton), Jr.

Waystaff, Simon
See Swift, Jonathan

Webb, (Martha) Beatrice (Potter)
1858-1943 . . . . **TCLC 22**
See also Potter, Beatrice
See also CA 117

Webb, Charles (Richard)   1939- . . . . . . **CLC 7**
See also CA 25-28R

Webb, James H(enry), Jr.   1946- . . . . **CLC 22**
See also CA 81-84

Webb, Mary (Gladys Meredith)
1881-1927 . . . . **TCLC 24**
See also CA 123; DLB 34

Webb, Mrs. Sidney
See Webb, (Martha) Beatrice (Potter)

Webb, Phyllis   1927-. . . . . **CLC 18**
See also CA 104; CANR 23; DLB 53

Webb, Sidney (James)
1859-1947 . . . . **TCLC 22**
See also CA 117

Webber, Andrew Lloyd. . . . . **CLC 21**
See also Lloyd Webber, Andrew

Weber, Lenora Mattingly
1895-1971 . . . . CLC 12
See also CA 19-20; 29-32R; CAP 1;
SATA 2; SATA-Obit 26

Webster, John   1579(?)-1634(?) . . . . DC 2
See also CDBLB Before 1660; DA; DAB;
DAC; DAM DRAM, MST; DLB 58;
WLC

Webster, Noah   1758-1843 . . . . NCLC 30

Wedekind, (Benjamin) Frank(lin)
1864-1918 . . . . TCLC 7
See also CA 104; DAM DRAM; DLB 118

Weidman, Jerome   1913- . . . . CLC 7
See also AITN 2; CA 1-4R; CANR 1;
DLB 28

Weil, Simone (Adolphine)
1909-1943 . . . . TCLC 23
See also CA 117

Weinstein, Nathan
See West, Nathanael

Weinstein, Nathan von Wallenstein
See West, Nathanael

Weir, Peter (Lindsay)   1944- . . . . CLC 20
See also CA 113; 123

Weiss, Peter (Ulrich)
1916-1982 . . . . CLC 3, 15, 51
See also CA 45-48; 106; CANR 3;
DAM DRAM; DLB 69, 124

Weiss, Theodore (Russell)
1916- . . . . CLC 3, 8, 14
See also CA 9-12R; CAAS 2; CANR 46;
DLB 5

Welch, (Maurice) Denton
1915-1948 . . . . TCLC 22
See also CA 121; 148

Welch, James   1940- . . . . CLC 6, 14, 52
See also CA 85-88; CANR 42;
DAM MULT, POP; NNAL

Weldon, Fay
1933- . . . . CLC 6, 9, 11, 19, 36, 59
See also CA 21-24R; CANR 16, 46;
CDBLB 1960 to Present; DAM POP;
DLB 14; INT CANR-16; MTCW

Wellek, Rene   1903- . . . . CLC 28
See also CA 5-8R; CAAS 7; CANR 8;
DLB 63; INT CANR-8

Weller, Michael   1942- . . . . CLC 10, 53
See also CA 85-88

Weller, Paul   1958- . . . . CLC 26

Wellershoff, Dieter   1925- . . . . CLC 46
See also CA 89-92; CANR 16, 37

Welles, (George) Orson
1915-1985 . . . . CLC 20, 80
See also CA 93-96; 117

Wellman, Mac   1945- . . . . CLC 65

Wellman, Manly Wade   1903-1986 . . CLC 49
See also CA 1-4R; 118; CANR 6, 16, 44;
SATA 6; SATA-Obit 47

Wells, Carolyn   1869(?)-1942 . . . . . . TCLC 35
See also CA 113; DLB 11

Wells, H(erbert) G(eorge)
1866-1946 . . . . TCLC 6, 12, 19; DA;
DAB; DAC; SSC 6; WLC
See also CA 110; 121; CDBLB 1914-1945;
DAM MST, NOV; DLB 34, 70, 156;
MTCW; SATA 20

Wells, Rosemary   1943- . . . . CLC 12
See also AAYA 13; CA 85-88; CANR 48;
CLR 16; MAICYA; SAAS 1; SATA 18,
69

Welty, Eudora
1909- . . . . . . CLC 1, 2, 5, 14, 22, 33; DA;
DAB; DAC; SSC 1; WLC
See also CA 9-12R; CABS 1; CANR 32;
CDALB 1941-1968; DAM MST, NOV;
DLB 2, 102, 143; DLBD 12; DLBY 87;
MTCW

Wen I-to   1899-1946 . . . . TCLC 28

Wentworth, Robert
See Hamilton, Edmond

Werfel, Franz (V.)   1890-1945 . . . . . . TCLC 8
See also CA 104; DLB 81, 124

Wergeland, Henrik Arnold
1808-1845 . . . . NCLC 5

Wersba, Barbara   1932- . . . . CLC 30
See also AAYA 2; CA 29-32R; CANR 16,
38; CLR 3; DLB 52; JRDA; MAICYA;
SAAS 2; SATA 1, 58

Wertmueller, Lina   1928- . . . . CLC 16
See also CA 97-100; CANR 39

Wescott, Glenway   1901-1987 . . . . CLC 13
See also CA 13-16R; 121; CANR 23;
DLB 4, 9, 102

Wesker, Arnold   1932- . . CLC 3, 5, 42; DAB
See also CA 1-4R; CAAS 7; CANR 1, 33;
CDBLB 1960 to Present; DAM DRAM;
DLB 13; MTCW

Wesley, Richard (Errol)   1945- . . . . . . CLC 7
See also BW 1; CA 57-60; CANR 27;
DLB 38

Wessel, Johan Herman   1742-1785 . . . . LC 7

West, Anthony (Panther)
1914-1987 . . . . CLC 50
See also CA 45-48; 124; CANR 3, 19;
DLB 15

West, C. P.
See Wodehouse, P(elham) G(renville)

West, (Mary) Jessamyn
1902-1984 . . . . CLC 7, 17
See also CA 9-12R; 112; CANR 27; DLB 6;
DLBY 84; MTCW; SATA-Obit 37

West, Morris L(anglo)   1916- . . . . . CLC 6, 33
See also CA 5-8R; CANR 24, 49; MTCW

West, Nathanael
1903-1940 . . . . . TCLC 1, 14, 44; SSC 16
See also CA 104; 125; CDALB 1929-1941;
DLB 4, 9, 28; MTCW

West, Owen
See Koontz, Dean R(ay)

West, Paul   1930- . . . . CLC 7, 14
See also CA 13-16R; CAAS 7; CANR 22;
DLB 14; INT CANR-22

West, Rebecca   1892-1983 . . CLC 7, 9, 31, 50
See also CA 5-8R; 109; CANR 19; DLB 36;
DLBY 83; MTCW

Westall, Robert (Atkinson)
1929-1993 . . . . CLC 17
See also AAYA 12; CA 69-72; 141;
CANR 18; CLR 13; JRDA; MAICYA;
SAAS 2; SATA 23, 69; SATA-Obit 75

Westlake, Donald E(dwin)
1933- . . . . CLC 7, 33
See also CA 17-20R; CAAS 13; CANR 16,
44; DAM POP; INT CANR-16

Westmacott, Mary
See Christie, Agatha (Mary Clarissa)

Weston, Allen
See Norton, Andre

Wetcheek, J. L.
See Feuchtwanger, Lion

Wetering, Janwillem van de
See van de Wetering, Janwillem

Wetherell, Elizabeth
See Warner, Susan (Bogert)

Whalen, Philip   1923- . . . . CLC 6, 29
See also CA 9-12R; CANR 5, 39; DLB 16

Wharton, Edith (Newbold Jones)
1862-1937 . . . . . . TCLC 3, 9, 27, 53; DA;
DAB; DAC; SSC 6; WLC
See also CA 104; 132; CDALB 1865-1917;
DAM MST, NOV; DLB 4, 9, 12, 78;
DLBD 13; MTCW

Wharton, James
See Mencken, H(enry) L(ouis)

Wharton, William (a pseudonym)
. . . . CLC 18, 37
See also CA 93-96; DLBY 80; INT 93-96

Wheatley (Peters), Phillis
1754(?)-1784 . . . . LC 3; BLC; DA; DAC;
PC 3; WLC
See also CDALB 1640-1865; DAM MST,
MULT, POET; DLB 31, 50

Wheelock, John Hall   1886-1978 . . . . CLC 14
See also CA 13-16R; 77-80; CANR 14;
DLB 45

White, E(lwyn) B(rooks)
1899-1985 . . . . CLC 10, 34, 39
See also AITN 2; CA 13-16R; 116;
CANR 16, 37; CLR 1, 21; DAM POP;
DLB 11, 22; MAICYA; MTCW;
SATA 2, 29; SATA-Obit 44

White, Edmund (Valentine III)
1940- . . . . CLC 27
See also AAYA 7; CA 45-48; CANR 3, 19,
36; DAM POP; MTCW

White, Patrick (Victor Martindale)
1912-1990 . . CLC 3, 4, 5, 7, 9, 18, 65, 69
See also CA 81-84; 132; CANR 43; MTCW

White, Phyllis Dorothy James   1920-
See James, P. D.
See also CA 21-24R; CANR 17, 43;
DAM POP; MTCW

White, T(erence) H(anbury)
1906-1964 . . . . CLC 30
See also CA 73-76; CANR 37; DLB 160;
JRDA; MAICYA; SATA 12

White, Terence de Vere
1912-1994 . . . . CLC 49
See also CA 49-52; 145; CANR 3

White, Walter F(rancis)
1893-1955 .... TCLC **15**
See also White, Walter
See also BW 1; CA 115; 124; DLB 51

White, William Hale　1831-1913
See Rutherford, Mark
See also CA 121

Whitehead, E(dward) A(nthony)
1933- .... CLC **5**
See also CA 65-68

Whitemore, Hugh (John)　1936- ..... CLC **37**
See also CA 132; INT 132

Whitman, Sarah Helen (Power)
1803-1878 .... NCLC **19**
See also DLB 1

Whitman, Walt(er)
1819-1892 ..... NCLC **4, 31; DA; DAB;
DAC; PC 3; WLC**
See also CDALB 1640-1865; DAM MST,
POET; DLB 3, 64; SATA 20

Whitney, Phyllis A(yame)　1903- .... CLC **42**
See also AITN 2; BEST 90:3; CA 1-4R;
CANR 3, 25, 38; DAM POP; JRDA;
MAICYA; SATA 1, 30

Whittemore, (Edward) Reed (Jr.)
1919- .... CLC **4**
See also CA 9-12R; CAAS 8; CANR 4;
DLB 5

Whittier, John Greenleaf
1807-1892 .... NCLC **8**
See also CDALB 1640-1865; DAM POET;
DLB 1

Whittlebot, Hernia
See Coward, Noel (Peirce)

Wicker, Thomas Grey　1926-
See Wicker, Tom
See also CA 65-68; CANR 21, 46

Wicker, Tom .... CLC **7**
See also Wicker, Thomas Grey

Wideman, John Edgar
1941- .... CLC **5, 34, 36, 67; BLC**
See also BW 2; CA 85-88; CANR 14, 42;
DAM MULT; DLB 33, 143

Wiebe, Rudy (Henry)
1934- .... CLC **6, 11, 14; DAC**
See also CA 37-40R; CANR 42;
DAM MST; DLB 60

Wieland, Christoph Martin
1733-1813 .... NCLC **17**
See also DLB 97

Wiene, Robert　1881-1938 .... TCLC **56**

Wieners, John　1934- .... CLC **7**
See also CA 13-16R; DLB 16

Wiesel, Elie(zer)
1928- ...... CLC **3, 5, 11, 37; DA; DAB;
DAC**
See also AAYA 7; AITN 1; CA 5-8R;
CAAS 4; CANR 8, 40; DAM MST,
NOV; DLB 83; DLBY 87; INT CANR-8;
MTCW; SATA 56

Wiggins, Marianne　1947- .... CLC **57**
See also BEST 89:3; CA 130

Wight, James Alfred　1916-
See Herriot, James
See also CA 77-80; SATA 55;
SATA-Brief 44

Wilbur, Richard (Purdy)
1921- ... CLC **3, 6, 9, 14, 53; DA; DAB;
DAC**
See also CA 1-4R; CABS 2; CANR 2, 29;
DAM MST, POET; DLB 5;
INT CANR-29; MTCW; SATA 9

Wild, Peter　1940- .... CLC **14**
See also CA 37-40R; DLB 5

Wilde, Oscar (Fingal O'Flahertie Wills)
1854(?)-1900 .... TCLC **1, 8, 23, 41; DA;
DAB; DAC; SSC 11; WLC**
See also CA 104; 119; CDBLB 1890-1914;
DAM DRAM, MST, NOV; DLB 10, 19,
34, 57, 141, 156; SATA 24

Wilder, Billy .... CLC **20**
See also Wilder, Samuel
See also DLB 26

Wilder, Samuel　1906-
See Wilder, Billy
See also CA 89-92

Wilder, Thornton (Niven)
1897-1975 ...... CLC **1, 5, 6, 10, 15, 35,
82; DA; DAB; DAC; DC 1; WLC**
See also AITN 2; CA 13-16R; 61-64;
CANR 40; DAM DRAM, MST, NOV;
DLB 4, 7, 9; MTCW

Wilding, Michael　1942- .... CLC **73**
See also CA 104; CANR 24, 49

Wiley, Richard　1944- .... CLC **44**
See also CA 121; 129

Wilhelm, Kate .... CLC **7**
See also Wilhelm, Katie Gertrude
See also CAAS 5; DLB 8; INT CANR-17

Wilhelm, Katie Gertrude　1928-
See Wilhelm, Kate
See also CA 37-40R; CANR 17, 36; MTCW

Wilkins, Mary
See Freeman, Mary Eleanor Wilkins

Willard, Nancy　1936- .... CLC **7, 37**
See also CA 89-92; CANR 10, 39; CLR 5;
DLB 5, 52; MAICYA; MTCW;
SATA 37, 71; SATA-Brief 30

Williams, C(harles) K(enneth)
1936- .... CLC **33, 56**
See also CA 37-40R; DAM POET; DLB 5

Williams, Charles
See Collier, James L(incoln)

Williams, Charles (Walter Stansby)
1886-1945 .... TCLC **1, 11**
See also CA 104; DLB 100, 153

Williams, (George) Emlyn
1905-1987 .... CLC **15**
See also CA 104; 123; CANR 36;
DAM DRAM; DLB 10, 77; MTCW

Williams, Hugo　1942- .... CLC **42**
See also CA 17-20R; CANR 45; DLB 40

Williams, J. Walker
See Wodehouse, P(elham) G(renville)

Williams, John A(lfred)
1925- .... CLC **5, 13; BLC**
See also BW 2; CA 53-56; CAAS 3;
CANR 6, 26; DAM MULT; DLB 2, 33;
INT CANR-6

Williams, Jonathan (Chamberlain)
1929- .... CLC **13**
See also CA 9-12R; CAAS 12; CANR 8;
DLB 5

Williams, Joy　1944- .... CLC **31**
See also CA 41-44R; CANR 22, 48

Williams, Norman　1952- .... CLC **39**
See also CA 118

Williams, Sherley Anne
1944- .... CLC **89; BLC**
See also BW 2; CA 73-76; CANR 25;
DAM MULT, POET; DLB 41;
INT CANR-25; SATA 78

Williams, Shirley
See Williams, Sherley Anne

Williams, Tennessee
1911-1983 ..... CLC **1, 2, 5, 7, 8, 11, 15,
19, 30, 39, 45, 71; DA; DAB; DAC;
DC 4; WLC**
See also AITN 1, 2; CA 5-8R; 108;
CABS 3; CANR 31; CDALB 1941-1968;
DAM DRAM, MST; DLB 7; DLBD 4;
DLBY 83; MTCW

Williams, Thomas (Alonzo)
1926-1990 .... CLC **14**
See also CA 1-4R; 132; CANR 2

Williams, William C.
See Williams, William Carlos

Williams, William Carlos
1883-1963 .... CLC **1, 2, 5, 9, 13, 22, 42,
67; DA; DAB; DAC; PC 7**
See also CA 89-92; CANR 34;
CDALB 1917-1929; DAM MST, POET;
DLB 4, 16, 54, 86; MTCW

Williamson, David (Keith)　1942- .... CLC **56**
See also CA 103; CANR 41

Williamson, Ellen Douglas　1905-1984
See Douglas, Ellen
See also CA 17-20R; 114; CANR 39

Williamson, Jack .... CLC **29**
See also Williamson, John Stewart
See also CAAS 8; DLB 8

Williamson, John Stewart　1908-
See Williamson, Jack
See also CA 17-20R; CANR 23

Willie, Frederick
See Lovecraft, H(oward) P(hillips)

Willingham, Calder (Baynard, Jr.)
1922-1995 .... CLC **5, 51**
See also CA 5-8R; 147; CANR 3; DLB 2,
44; MTCW

Willis, Charles
See Clarke, Arthur C(harles)

Willy
See Colette, (Sidonie-Gabrielle)

Willy, Colette
See Colette, (Sidonie-Gabrielle)

Wilson, A(ndrew) N(orman)　1950- .. CLC **33**
See also CA 112; 122; DLB 14, 155

Wilson, Angus (Frank Johnstone)
1913-1991 .. CLC **2, 3, 5, 25, 34; SSC 21**
See also CA 5-8R; 134; CANR 21; DLB 15,
139, 155; MTCW

Wroth, LadyMary 1587-1653(?) ..... **LC 30**
See also DLB 121

Wu Ch'eng-en 1500(?)-1582(?)........ **LC 7**

Wu Ching-tzu 1701-1754 .... **LC 2**

Wurlitzer, Rudolph 1938(?)- ... **CLC 2, 4, 15**
See also CA 85-88

Wycherley, William 1641-1715.... **LC 8, 21**
See also CDBLB 1660-1789; DAM DRAM;
DLB 80

Wylie, Elinor (Morton Hoyt)
1885-1928 .... **TCLC 8**
See also CA 105; DLB 9, 45

Wylie, Philip (Gordon) 1902-1971... **CLC 43**
See also CA 21-22; 33-36R; CAP 2; DLB 9

Wyndham, John.................. **CLC 19**
See also Harris, John (Wyndham Parkes
Lucas) Beynon

Wyss, Johann David Von
1743-1818 .... **NCLC 10**
See also JRDA; MAICYA; SATA 29;
SATA-Brief 27

Xenophon
c. 430B.C.-c. 354B.C........ **CMLC 17**

Yakumo Koizumi
See Hearn, (Patricio) Lafcadio (Tessima
Carlos)

Yanez, Jose Donoso
See Donoso (Yanez), Jose

Yanovsky, Basile S.
See Yanovsky, V(assily) S(emenovich)

Yanovsky, V(assily) S(emenovich)
1906-1989 .... **CLC 2, 18**
See also CA 97-100; 129

Yates, Richard 1926-1992 ..... **CLC 7, 8, 23**
See also CA 5-8R; 139; CANR 10, 43;
DLB 2; DLBY 81, 92; INT CANR-10

Yeats, W. B.
See Yeats, William Butler

Yeats, William Butler
1865-1939 ..... **TCLC 1, 11, 18, 31; DA;**
DAB; DAC; WLC
See also CA 104; 127; CANR 45;
CDBLB 1890-1914; DAM DRAM, MST,
POET; DLB 10, 19, 98, 156; MTCW

Yehoshua, A(braham) B.
1936- .... **CLC 13, 31**
See also CA 33-36R; CANR 43

Yep, Laurence Michael 1948- ...... **CLC 35**
See also AAYA 5; CA 49-52; CANR 1, 46;
CLR 3, 17; DLB 52; JRDA; MAICYA;
SATA 7, 69

Yerby, Frank G(arvin)
1916-1991 .... **CLC 1, 7, 22; BLC**
See also BW 1; CA 9-12R; 136; CANR 16;
DAM MULT; DLB 76; INT CANR-16;
MTCW

Yesenin, Sergei Alexandrovich
See Esenin, Sergei (Alexandrovich)

Yevtushenko, Yevgeny (Alexandrovich)
1933- .... **CLC 1, 3, 13, 26, 51**
See also CA 81-84; CANR 33;
DAM POET; MTCW

Yezierska, Anzia 1885(?)-1970 ..... **CLC 46**
See also CA 126; 89-92; DLB 28; MTCW

Yglesias, Helen 1915-........... **CLC 7, 22**
See also CA 37-40R; CAAS 20; CANR 15;
INT CANR-15; MTCW

Yokomitsu Riichi 1898-1947 ...... **TCLC 47**

Yonge, Charlotte (Mary)
1823-1901 .... **TCLC 48**
See also CA 109; DLB 18; SATA 17

York, Jeremy
See Creasey, John

York, Simon
See Heinlein, Robert A(nson)

Yorke, Henry Vincent 1905-1974 ... **CLC 13**
See also Green, Henry
See also CA 85-88; 49-52

Yosano Akiko 1878-1942.. **TCLC 59; PC 11**

Yoshimoto, Banana................ **CLC 84**
See also Yoshimoto, Mahoko

Yoshimoto, Mahoko 1964-
See Yoshimoto, Banana
See also CA 144

Young, Al(bert James)
1939- .... **CLC 19; BLC**
See also BW 2; CA 29-32R; CANR 26;
DAM MULT; DLB 33

Young, Andrew (John) 1885-1971.... **CLC 5**
See also CA 5-8R; CANR 7, 29

Young, Collier
See Bloch, Robert (Albert)

Young, Edward 1683-1765.......... **LC 3**
See also DLB 95

Young, Marguerite 1909-........ **CLC 82**
See also CA 13-16; CAP 1

Young, Neil 1945-................ **CLC 17**
See also CA 110

Yourcenar, Marguerite
1903-1987........ **CLC 19, 38, 50, 87**
See also CA 69-72; CANR 23; DAM NOV;
DLB 72; DLBY 88; MTCW

Yurick, Sol 1925-................. **CLC 6**
See also CA 13-16R; CANR 25

Zabolotskii, Nikolai Alekseevich
1903-1958 .... **TCLC 52**
See also CA 116

Zamiatin, Yevgenii
See Zamyatin, Evgeny Ivanovich

Zamora, Bernice (B. Ortiz)
1938- .... **CLC 89; HLC**
See also DAM MULT; DLB 82; HW

Zamyatin, Evgeny Ivanovich
1884-1937 .... **TCLC 8, 37**
See also CA 105

Zangwill, Israel 1864-1926........ **TCLC 16**
See also CA 109; DLB 10, 135

Zappa, Francis Vincent, Jr. 1940-1993
See Zappa, Frank
See also CA 108; 143

Zappa, Frank.................... **CLC 17**
See also Zappa, Francis Vincent, Jr.

Zaturenska, Marya 1902-1982.... **CLC 6, 11**
See also CA 13-16R; 105; CANR 22

Zelazny, Roger (Joseph)
1937-1995 .... **CLC 21**
See also AAYA 7; CA 21-24R; 148;
CANR 26; DLB 8; MTCW; SATA 57;
SATA-Brief 39

Zhdanov, Andrei A(lexandrovich)
1896-1948 .... **TCLC 18**
See also CA 117

Zhukovsky, Vasily 1783-1852.... **NCLC 35**

Ziegenhagen, Eric................. **CLC 55**

Zimmer, Jill Schary
See Robinson, Jill

Zimmerman, Robert
See Dylan, Bob

Zindel, Paul
1936- ..... **CLC 6, 26; DA; DAB; DAC;**
DC 5
See also AAYA 2; CA 73-76; CANR 31;
CLR 3; DAM DRAM, MST, NOV;
DLB 7, 52; JRDA; MAICYA; MTCW;
SATA 16, 58

Zinov'Ev, A. A.
See Zinoviev, Alexander (Aleksandrovich)

Zinoviev, Alexander (Aleksandrovich)
1922- .... **CLC 19**
See also CA 116; 133; CAAS 10

Zoilus
See Lovecraft, H(oward) P(hillips)

Zola, Emile (Edouard Charles Antoine)
1840-1902 ...... **TCLC 1, 6, 21, 41; DA;**
DAB; DAC; WLC
See also CA 104; 138; DAM MST, NOV;
DLB 123

Zoline, Pamela 1941-............. **CLC 62**

Zorrilla y Moral, Jose 1817-1893.. **NCLC 6**

Zoshchenko, Mikhail (Mikhailovich)
1895-1958 .... **TCLC 15; SSC 15**
See also CA 115

Zuckmayer, Carl 1896-1977........ **CLC 18**
See also CA 69-72; DLB 56, 124

Zuk, Georges
See Skelton, Robin

Zukofsky, Louis
1904-1978 .... **CLC 1, 2, 4, 7, 11, 18;**
PC 11
See also CA 9-12R; 77-80; CANR 39;
DAM POET; DLB 5; MTCW

Zweig, Paul 1935-1984........ **CLC 34, 42**
See also CA 85-88; 113

Zweig, Stefan 1881-1942 .... **TCLC 17**
See also CA 112; DLB 81, 118

Literary Criticism Series
Cumulative Topic Index

This index lists all topic entries in Gale's *Classical and Medieval Literature Criticism, Contemporary Literary Criticism, Literature Criticism from 1400 to 1800, Nineteenth-Century Literature Criticism,* and *Twentieth-Century Literary Criticism.*

Topic Index

Topic Index

TCLC Cumulative Nationality Index

ISBN 0-8103-9307-7